A History of Russian Literature

A HISTORY OF
RUSSIAN
LITERATURE

ANDREW KAHN
MARK LIPOVETSKY
IRINA REYFMAN
STEPHANIE SANDLER

OXFORD
UNIVERSITY PRESS

OXFORD
UNIVERSITY PRESS

Great Clarendon Street, Oxford, OX2 6DP,
United Kingdom

Oxford University Press is a department of the University of Oxford.
It furthers the University's objective of excellence in research, scholarship,
and education by publishing worldwide. Oxford is a registered trade mark of
Oxford University Press in the UK and in certain other countries

First Edition published in 2018

Impression: 1

Published in the United States of America by Oxford University Press
198 Madison Avenue, New York, NY 10016, United States of America

British Library Cataloguing in Publication Data
Data available

Library of Congress Control Number: 2017909825

ISBN 978–0–19–966394–1

Printed and bound by
CPI Group (UK) Ltd, Croydon, CR0 4YY

Contents

Part II The Seventeenth Century

Part III The Eighteenth Century

Part V The Twentieth and Twenty-First Centuries

Note on the Text

THE following transliteration conventions and abbreviations have been adopted in the *History of Russian Literature*.

We use a modified Library of Congress system of transliteration in the text, adopting y in names to match the ending -*ii*. We use the standard spelling of first and last names adopted in the West: Alexander Pushkin, Alexander Herzen, Alexander Nevsky, Leo Tolstoy, Maxim Gorky, Vladimir Mayakovsky, Osip Mandelstam, Lydia Ginzburg, Lydia Chukovskaya, Natalia Baranskaya, Natalia Gorbanevskaya, Tatyana Tolstaya, Liudmila Petrushevskaya, Ludmila Ulitskaya. We also spell Sofia, Natalia, and Dunia, rather than Sofiia, Nataliia, and Duniia. Other modifications include: Asya, Ilya, Yakov, Yulian, Yuri, Tatiana, and Olga. We omit soft signs from the ends of both first and family names, such as Igor, Gogol, Dal. The soft sign is retained mid-word to indicate underlying phoneme or palatalization, for example, Murav 'ev (and not Muravyev), L 'vov (and not Lvov). The soft sign is also retained at the end of place names. German surnames that have not been Russified include Benckendorff, Küchelbecker, and the characters Stoltz and Sachs.

When citing Russian sources in the bibliography and notes, we use the Library of Congress system without diacritics.

Dates

In Parts I and II, the year of composition is given for all works unless otherwise noted. In Part III, the date given for poems is usually the publication date, as is the case for prose works and works of theater (for which a performance date is provided). In Parts IV and V, dates reflect the date of first publication except for most poems, where date of composition is given. Exceptions are noted.

Translations

Unless otherwise attributed, all translations are our own. Prose quotations at length are given only in English with no block quotation in Russian. For poetry, we provide original Russian block quotations in Cyrillic for substantial extracts (usually more than three lines). Otherwise, when we quote a phrase in the body of the text, English translation comes first followed by transliteration in parentheses.

List of Abbreviations

In the notes and Guides to Further Reading the following will be used:

BLDR	*Biblioteka literatury Drevnei Rusi*
NLO	*Novoe literaturnoe obozrenie*
PLDR	*Pamiatniki literatury Drevnei Rusi*
SEER	*Slavonic and East European Review*
SEEJ	*Slavic and East European Journal*
TODRL	*Trudy otdela drevnerusskoi literatury*

List of Figures

List of Plates

Acknowledgments

OUR work on this *History* has been helped by many colleagues in and beyond the field of Russian literature. Several generously read and extensively commented on portions of the draft manuscript, sometimes very large portions: Catherine Ciepiela, Nicholas Cronk, Evgeny Dobrenko, Caryl Emerson, Ann Jefferson, Ilya Kukulin, Olga Maiorova, Jennifer Nuttall, Cathy Popkin, Kelsey Rubin-Detlev, William Mills Todd III, Alexandra Vukovich, Justin Weir, and Wes Williams. We are grateful for their deep engagement with our ideas as well as their corrections, additions, and emendations, and we extend the same thanks to our anonymous readers, who offered scrupulous readings and suggestions for improvement on the final draft. We also thank the following individuals for much valued help of different kinds: Natalia Ashimbaeva, Jennifer Baines, Nadezhda Bourova, Tatiana Goriaeva, Catriona Kelly, Irina Koshchienko, Ilja Kukuj, Henrike Lähnemann, Peter McDonald, Deborah A. Martinsen, Martin McLaughlin, Nikita Okhotin, Florentina Viktorovna-Panchenko, Lynn E. Patyk, Stanley Rabinowitz, Ritchie Robertson, Gisèle Sapiro, Fiona Stafford, Jonathan Stone, Natalia Strizhkova, and Boris Tikhomirov.

For generous financial and other research support, the authors would like to acknowledge the British Academy (Conference Grant); the Arts and Sciences Fund of Excellence and Eugene Kayden Research Fund at the University of Colorado-Boulder; the Publication Committee of the Harriman Institute at Columbia University; the FAS Tenured Faculty Publication Fund, Harvard University; the John Fell Fund, the University of Oxford; the Fellows' Research Fund, St Edmund Hall, Oxford; the Humanities Division, University of Oxford; and CEELBAS, University College London. Librarians at several institutions have offered generous help during our work. We would like to thank Nick Hearne and Elena Franklin of the Taylor Institution Library, Oxford; Amanda Saville, The Queen's College, Oxford; the staff at Houghton Library, Harvard University; Tanya Chebotarev, Curator, Bakhmeteff Archive, Columbia University; the Amherst Center for Russian Culture.

In preparing the manuscript, we have been aided by Alison Oliver, Gillian Pink, Rebecca du Plessis, and Philip Redko; and by Emily Kanner, Jenya Mironova, Sara Powell, Alex Tullock, and Sarah Vitali, who fact-checked the draft manuscript.

We owe special gratitude to our editors at Oxford University Press. Jacqueline Norton has been a stalwart source of expert advice and deft encouragement from the conception of this project and over its long gestation. Eleanor Collins has offered good-humored, astute guidance. We thank Ela Kotkowska for her copyediting and work on translations of poetry. For advice about the reproduction and rights to images included here, we are grateful to Deborah Protheroe, and we thank our picture researcher Sophie Basilevitch, Penny Trumble, Viki Kapur, and Hannah Newport-Watson, Senior Production Editor, for their skillful assistance. Warm thanks to all.

Introduction

The shapes of literary history

Russia possesses one of the richest and most admired literatures of Europe, reaching back to the eleventh century. Our *History of Russian Literature* provides a comprehensive account of Russian writing from its earliest origins in the monastic works of Kiev up to the present day, which is still rife with the creative experiments of post-Soviet literary life. Readers will find here accounts of genres, including heroic lays and spiritual poetry (*dukhovnye stikhi*), the novel, elegy and love poetry; movements such as classicism, Sentimentalism, Romanticism, Realism, modernism, the avant-garde, and postmodernism. And readers will find discussions of the well- and lesser-known writers who have contributed to this influential and vital tradition for each of these periods and genres.

Do twenty-first-century readers still need histories of national literatures now that the obsession with the global has virtually displaced the interest in discrete traditions? In a word, yes. The rise of world literature and the sense of new deracinated global canons taking form before our very eyes do not inherently invalidate national literary history. Global histories might encourage an assumption that the national is by definition static or one-dimensional. The border crossings that dominate globalized literature do seem manifestly more dynamic than any single tradition.[1] Yet those border crossings can help us comprehend Russia's own literary history, which vividly belies the idea of insularity. The map of Russian literature has never been identical with Russia's borders: its centers of creative production occupy territories both within and beyond Russia, and it includes works written in Russian (even if not always in Russia nor necessarily by ethnic Russians). Cold War isolation was never the whole story for a literary tradition and culture that was open to Byzantine and Balkan influences in the medieval period and Ruthenian, Polish, and Latin trends in the seventeenth century. Russian literature continued to be manifestly cosmopolitan and oriented toward Europe (mostly France and Germany) in the eighteenth century; it became one of the great European literatures in the nineteenth century, and then extended across new terrains in phases of diaspora in the modern period, starting with the Romantic exiles of the nineteenth century and several waves of emigration from the 1920s to the 2010s.

The professional modern study of Russian literature in the West has always forged connections between native and foreign. Émigré scholars from Russia and Eastern Europe founded many Slavic departments in the United States and Europe, among them the School of Slavonic Studies, established by the influential critic and popularizer D. S. Mirsky (born Prince Dmitry Petrovich Sviatopolk-Mirsky, 1890–1939), while Roman Jakobson (1896–1982) modernized the Slavic Department at Harvard. In the post-Soviet era, Russian writing is being produced and studied globally, and over the past decades the study of Russian literature as a discipline has reacted to numerous changes, of which the most important might be another infusion of talented scholars educated in Russia. In the 1990s and 2000s, two-way conversations became the norm between Russian scholarship abroad and at home. Perestroika and the dismantling of Marxist-Leninist shibboleths, as well as catch-up with Western critical schools, opened a conduit for dialogue among students of Russian literature. This phenomenon of changing places and exchanging ideas across open borders has coincided with paradigm shifts in the study of literature, that have generally moved it closer to other disciplines, making it more comparative, more historical, and more cultural without undermining a fundamental belief in the traditional tools of philology and poetics.

Each decade has brought notable shifts in how we study and teach literature. The process has become more cumulative as literary scholars have built on the insights of structuralism and semiotics, at their height in the 1960s and 1970s, and of post-structuralism and deconstruction, absorbing lessons of the rediscovery of Bakhtin in the 1970s and 1980s, the rise of feminist scholarship in the 1980s, and cultural history of the 1990s. In the classroom, and among popular readerships, awareness of the depth of Russian literature has certainly changed. Translation, often owing to the efforts of smaller presses, has made available in English and European languages a much wider corpus of writers than what was featured on university syllabuses even a generation ago. Attention to the history of women's writing in the context of both gender studies and cultural history has not only broadened the canon but raised important questions about readership and literary evolution. The collapse of the Soviet Union brought an end to censorship (although the 2010s have seen a rise in concern that some forms of censorship are returning), but the history of censorship in Russia of all periods, and most strikingly during the Soviet period, has never been a story of silence but rather of extraordinary networks of underground literature. Archival research and critical editions, among other benefits of the post-Soviet transformation of fields, have put pressure on old ideas of a canon. Textual editing as a field has been intensively active over the past decades, and the legacies of many writers from the imperial or Soviet periods, some now read for the first time in their entirety, have been redefined.

All histories work with the idea of a canon, and no modern conceptualization of the canon can be aloof from cultural politics. In the 1990s, identity politics led to intense debate about literary canons and national literature.[2] Russian literature was not immune, but it did not experience a violent splintering along cultural and ethnic lines. Geography more than ethnography determined earlier splits. From the 1920s to the 1990s, Russian literary émigré circles disputed the status of Soviet writing, also raising questions as to whether Russians who had "made it" in English, like Nabokov, could genuinely be called Russian. The question of whether Gogol was a Ukrainian-Russian, Russian-Ukrainian, Ukrainian Russian-language writer, or Russian writer, an old question, remains a legitimate debating point and an invitation to abandon entrenched positions. The net effect of the collapse of the Soviet Union was not a spate of culture wars but a massive upsurge in the availability of writing, new and old. Scholars have responded with discussions of canon formation and readership communities within and outside Russia; openness to outside traditions poses productive questions about the relationship of several canons in dialogue with each other.[3]

A second current development is the scale and volume of material now available. In an age of information retrieval, readers can access and verify more facts and read a wider range of works than ever before in all national traditions. The wish to attain perspective on the new and multiple also compels us to recast our understanding of the old and monolithic. This may be why the 2000s have seen a significant revival of literary history repackaged into introductory manuals, handbooks, and companions. The growth of specialist research and its mass availability have altered the challenges of writing a large-scale literary history, creating a productive tension between different demands of objective discourse and subjective narration, comprehensive coverage and deliberate selection.

In thinking about the scale of this *History* we have aimed for historical breadth for a number of reasons. The first is a belief in the intrinsic value of the literary works we discuss. The second comes from a recognition that literature tells a narrative about its own traditions and circumstances of creation that is intertwined with changing views on Russianness. The third is a conviction, based on experience in the undergraduate classroom and graduate seminar, that many works of Russian literature innovate and draw inspiration from a profound sense of rootedness in the nation's history. The history of Russian literature is about authors, forms, and debates, and it also continuously responds to the complex relationship between writing and the state, a dynamic that extends from the medieval period to the present day.

The contexts of Russian literary history

Literary history in Russia became an academic field in the second half of the nineteenth century. Modern literary history has its intellectual origins in philology (and thus in the study of languages; philology is now understood as a combination of literary criticism, history, and linguistics), and philological investigations were augmented in the late nineteenth century by Comtean positivism and a drive toward systemizing and cataloguing.[4] Putting the right facts in the right order was the basic task, requiring no small amount of labor. But literary histories were never just encyclopedias or ordered collections of facts. First- and second-generation nineteenth-century Russian literary histories—and they were many—had agendas.

From the 1850s, Russian literary history as a genre became de facto a form of national narrative open to politicization from both the radical left and the conservative right. At first, the disciplinary boundaries between history and literary history were not clearly drawn. Practitioners of both disciplines did much basic work of retrieval in recovering the nation's documentary heritage, especially from the period before 1800. The creation of a national historical school by Vasily Kliuchevsky (1841–1911) in the 1860s, well after the Russian authorities in the 1830s made "nationality" one official aspect of literature, found a ready and large reading public, much augmented by the expansion of secondary and higher education. This same public was avid for the masterpieces of the Great Russian Novel.[5] Literary histories emulated the model of the national historical school and assumed that national literatures must tell a national story. Not everyone saw things this way, and literary history created its own dynamic of revisionism. For instance, the editor, educator, and literary critic S. A. Vengerov (1855–1920) felt that literature could best be accessed through biography formulated in reference manuals.[6] From 1901 he directed the four-volume *Library of Great Writers* (*Biblioteka velikikh pisatelei*, 1901–1902). Vengerov's method refuses both narrative and continuous institutional history, and is further atomized by its multiple detached biographies (a method that continues to attract adherents). This approach set the backdrop for the work of the Formalists, many of whom had participated in his seminars; subsequently, in the 1910s–20s, they moved away from the biographical approach.

Unlike literary historians influenced by the social science methods of Comte, A. N. Pypin (1833–1904) was an outsider to the academic establishment, an important historian of censorship and freemasonry who was a standard-bearer for philology and regarded literary history as a vast archive. He was unusual and precociously modern in being influenced by social science methods in studying institutional practices and intellectual groups, thereby creating a frame within which he could practice traditional philology by editing and disseminating texts. Yet thanks to his emphasis on political circumstance and his tenet that almost all writers necessarily reacted to the regime, his narrative pays valuable attention to practices of censorship, publishing, and journalism. Pypin anticipated the approaches of the sociology of literature used in a more integrated fashion by V. F. Pereverzev (1882–1968), the French Pushkinist André Meynieux, and—in the United States—by William Mills Todd III.

After the Revolution of 1917, the story of Russian literary history becomes more international. Giants of nineteenth-century literary criticism, such as the English Matthew Arnold and French Hippolyte Taine, had made it the business of the critic to construct literary history as the story of masterpieces identified by the subjective authority of the critic. This is the tradition in which D. S. Mirsky works in *A History of Russian Literature: From the Earliest Times to the Death of Dostoevsky* (that is, up to 1881). In aiming to reconcile his own judgments as a critic with his work to educate an English-language readership, Mirsky helpfully differentiates between literature and other forms of writing. His perception of canonical authors, however, reflects the narrower biases of the literary critic rather than offering the broader account of the literary field open to the historian. Published in 1926, Mirsky's classic book essentially proceeds by moving from one masterpiece to the next. He demonstrates a bias toward modern literature in his evident disdain for writing before Pushkin, apart from certain works and writers that cannot be ignored (such as the *Lay of Igor's Campaign* and Avvakum). Mirsky's history shaped the Russian literary canon for generations of Anglo-American readers. While it was the work of an individual literary critic with a mission to rank major and minor classics, his account long enjoyed its own status outside Russia as the authoritative guide.[7]

Every generation writes its literary histories. This is not only because the story of an ongoing literature is open-ended. Several motivations are usually at work. Hans Ulrich Gumbrecht has seen in scholars' sensitivity to previous conceptualizations and discursive formations a reason to conclude that literary histories may have long shelf lives but over time their conclusions remain subject to revision. Still, he finds literary history a medium for original approach to received ideas as well as a way to restate them, provided authors strike a balance in narrative between research agendas and accessibility.[8] Scholarly innovation has revised our understanding of literature, history, and, very often, the national subject under discussion. In the Russian field, a number of excellent volumes stand out for various reasons. Among single-volume works, Victor Terras's *History of Russian Literature* (1991) and the multi-author Cambridge *History of Russian Literature* edited by Charles Moser (1992) can continue to serve student readers as a first port of call for reliable plot summary and biographies, and for comprehensive, lively accounts of some literary movements and genres, although the march of time means that coverage of the modern ceases in the Soviet period for both volumes. Devised as reference guides, now certainly to be supplemented by many newer works online, these manuals see literary history as a factual record to be used as a frame for further inquiry.

An important next step is found in the range and method of Caryl Emerson's *Cambridge Introduction to Russian Literature* (2008). In strictly period terms, the modern era predominates here, from the second part of the eighteenth century to 2005, very much the span that any undergraduate Russian major would hope to cover. Despite the modest title, the essayistic originality offers many readerships, graduate and professional, searching ideas about the literary traditions and especially the innovations of Russian prose. Although its consecutive coverage begins with the modern, Emerson's book offers a broad historical perspective that ranges across historical periods, including the medieval, indicating a deeper hinterland that stands behind the fine treatments of major authors and their literary heroes. In their stimulating *Russian Literature*, Andrew Wachtel and Ilya Vinitsky (2009) adopt a nodal structure, grouping an eclectic selection of texts chronologically, ordered around themes explored sometimes from their medieval origin to the mid-twentieth century where the account ends. The result is deliberately more synchronic than historical in perspective, often defamiliarizing in productive ways; the volume is highly focused on distilling themes into memorable sets of features that suggest many avenues for further study.

The scope and shape of the *History of Russian Literature*

Inevitably, perhaps, in all literary histories, the story of Russia and the story of Russian literature converge. The present *History* has faith in the heuristic uses of narrative as a way to elucidate the stories a literature tells about itself and its origins. It also employs other methods—biography, close reading, intellectual history—that make it possible to zoom in on the different ways literary history can be processed as life-writing, verbal genius, and the representation of ideas. A literary history that moves forward in time and aims to create a "thick description" can use questions in order to join up writers and works. In providing examples our guiding principle has been to select material that is both of intrinsic value and interest but also most likely to illustrate larger points; we also seek to identify and understand important writers and episodes that do not fit easily into a forward-moving narrative. Some expansiveness of scope and method gives latitude for a literary landscape of diverse contours: not everything adds up, nor must everything be seen from the same perspective.

Literature, however, has produced many answers to representing nationality, state, and people rather than the single answer of *narodnost'* touted in nineteenth-century nationalist accounts. The narrative of literary development we adopt here seeks to raise questions about the nature of Russian literature and its history. Why, and how, have the grand narratives of sacredness and exceptionalism in literature and history been so durable? What has the balance between imitation and innovation been in a literature that obsessively mapped itself on Western literatures? How much and during what periods has translation contributed to trends in Russia's literary culture? What are the consequences of the close relationship between literary theory and literary practice from the eighteenth century to the early twentieth-century Formalists and on to the postmodern movements in the 1990s? Why has poetry enjoyed such cultural prestige? Is it true that literature has acted as a second government in Russia? Have exile and censorship led to particularly innovative types of writing? These are questions that recur across the entire span of our *History*, often because a thematic discourse already exists that writers and readers activate and revise.

In an influential set of articles, Boris Uspensky and Yuri Lotman posited a binary dynamic to Russian culture, suggesting that a "specific feature of Russian culture . . . is a fundamental polarization expressed in the binary nature of its structure." Their overarching concept does not address historical causes; their purpose was to bring out the rules of near-Hegelian shape governing how successive periods establish, accommodate, negate, and then synthesize cyclical cultural trends.[9] Binary thinking has been much criticized, but it has also lingered, in such heuristic pairings as big city and provinces; center and periphery; official and underground; Symbolist and Acmeist; sanctioned and dissident; and Socialist Realist vs. just about anything else. Some of these geographical pairings, like that of center vs. periphery, have long histories in Russian thought, but from about 1900, a noticeably vociferous tone resounded when these apparent differences were trumpeted, particularly those that involved political power. Writers and critics claim that the contexts could no longer be reconciled.

An alternative, as applied here, is to bring out the recurrent stories and national frameworks through which literature responds to social, historical, and political reality, and through these interactions to demonstrate the transformations of literature rather than emphasize perennially repeating elements and structures. The orientation of our *History* is toward explicating the contexts in which multifaceted, modern Russian culture has survived and even thrived. No one piece of this culture makes complete sense without reference to the others, for which reason our *History* draws on examples from different spheres and discursive formations. Literature as a form of cultural and historical memory does not represent a disembodied force that speaks through writers, but rather is the larger body of work to which individual writers make their contribution, often in dialogue.

Our own approach uses a resolutely historical framework, but we move around within time periods to address the fundamental intellectual and cultural questions that define each era. We make use of historical overview and close reading in order to bring out disruption and innovation. Our *History of Russian Literature* works as a continuous essay in five main parts. We begin with Kievan Rus' in the eleventh century and end in the time in which we are ourselves writing, the 2010s. The book thus overall follows the narrative mode of the traditional literary history, but varies that chronological structure in a number of ways, including a willingness to zigzag repeatedly across decades as our thematic topic changes within each main part. Our coverage aims to strike a balance between extensive overview and in-depth thematic discussion. We also strive to balance conceptualization and close analysis of writing and writers. To achieve this dual focus, chapters include two types of paratextual material. In instances where trans-historical questions are prominent, or where the history of a particular phenomenon requires treatment in connected ways, we pull out from strict chronological sequence in order to foreground a given problem or theory across the decades. Case studies provide individual mini-essays detailing the importance of texts, figures, and notions. These discussions stand outside our narrative, but aim to bridge the distance between the perspective of the narrative and the experience of literature up-close. Case studies offer essays on individual authors, such as Avvakum, Nikolai Gogol, Leo and Sofia Tolstoy, Isaac Babel, Elena Guro, Anna Akhmatova, and Joseph Brodsky, while topical case studies include hagiography, travel literature, versification, cultural spaces, *War and Peace*, and show trials. The case studies can be read as independent essays, but they also reflect what is going on in the narrative and aim to enrich narrative contextualization with specific examples. Keywords, formatted in text boxes, are much shorter and serve a reference function by giving brief definitions of important terms, literary and historical, some of which (such as "classicism," "baroque," and "Romanticism") recur throughout the *History*. Keywords aim to introduce students to these terms and also to clarify our own usage of them.

The use of keywords reminds us that the history of literature could be written as a story of *-isms*. It is a besetting but sometimes unavoidable pitfall of literary history as a genre that it often attempts to fit material into standard analytical categories. One way to avoid reductive description is to remain alert to the constant revisionism to which literature subjects these terms. Sometimes, different definitions of aesthetic terms can operate within a single period, often in contradiction. What appears settled from the perspective of hindsight looks unsettled and active in real time. Eighteenth-century classicism, a term coined by art historians retrospectively in the nineteenth century, routinely denotes a fixed set of rules, when in fact the reality was more muddled. Few writers in the eighteenth century, at least in Russia, used the term "classical" in defining the rules of good taste, the ultimate value of literature in the period. Similarly, while the Age of Realism is commonly invoked to describe the goal of fidelity to experience toward which the Great Russian Novel was seen to strive, we find that realism is a moving target. The grotesque modernism of the 1920s–30s, an interlude before the enforced mimetic codes of Socialist Realism, survived well past its seeming demise to reemerge in the late Soviet and post-Soviet eras; its vivid new forms would then infuse critical tastes which in turn led to reevaluations of earlier Soviet work. When it comes to aesthetic modes and trends or even the shape of genres, a continuous feedback loop marks experimentation. This is true of all forms of poetry, but it may be most conspicuous in the novel because of its scope, centrality, and popularity with readerships. The genre of the novel also represents a particularly striking case of openness because of its formal complexity, and because its close relation to social reality stimulated writers to develop and diversify character prototypes that actually turn out to be surprisingly flexible.

Our *History*'s five chronological parts by design unfold in diachronic histories; they may be read individually but are presented as inseparable across the span of a national literature. The reader will not find a traditional gallery of miniature monographs on the most famous Russian writers, but rather multiple contexts in which writers, major and minor, created the traditions of Russian literature. We see the history of the institutions of literature as inseparable from an account of texts and authors. Our foregrounding of institutional structures, broadly conceived, is perhaps unusual. For much of the twentieth century, political alignment rather than institutional development served as the framework for conceptualizing Russian literary history. It was a fixture of a Western liberal narrative, and a standard pedagogical line as well, that literature served as an "unofficial government." But we see the literary field as a more flexible, capacious, and subtle discourse to organize the variables that contribute to the production of literature. While our approach does not give undue emphasis to any single aspect of sociology of literature, or any single school, whether that of Bourdieu or Jameson, we consistently wish to draw attention to the processes in which the authors and readers as creators and consumers can be inscribed. From the monastic centers onward we trace the development of writing into popular, court, and secular literature. Beginning with the second half of the seventeenth century, we analyze the role of different groups, coteries, salons, and schools, and their concomitant conflicts and ideologies. Changing ideas about the meaning of authorship, the language of literature, and readerships are discussed as part of this process. In the nineteenth century, the question of readerships leads to the important role of literary journalism and criticism, particularly in Russia's thick journals. The formation and disintegration of the canon, critical debates, and the influence of translations come increasingly within our purview with the shift from ecclesiastical writing to a secular modern print culture.

One legacy of the nineteenth century in the succeeding hundred years is the intermittent return to old questions. How to define art, a major topic of debate for the generation of the 1860s, galvanizes writers and groups in the late 1920s and 1930s. In the twentieth century, the theory of literature (Formalism, Bakhtin, Moscow–Tartu school of semiotics) becomes an additional factor because it both sums up ongoing processes in the history of literature and influences creative practices. In the 2000s, as Part V explains, energy for progress and self-expression is shunted into the new approaches pioneered by modernism circa 1900–20 and the postmodernism of the 1990s and 2000s. Furthermore, the internet provides novel ways of disseminating and reading literature; it creates vast archives of recorded events and provides forums in which writers and readers can interact.

Throughout its course, this *History* follows literary processes as they worked in respective periods and places, whether in monasteries, at court, in publishing houses, in the literary marketplace, or the Writers' Union. Yet at the same time there is an equal commitment to the idea of writers' agency in responding to tradition and reacting to larger forces such as church and state that compel them to find modes of survival in a stifling regime. The picture also encompasses alternative institutions and movements, such as émigré literature and the underground writing of the 1960s through the 1980s. The still ongoing wholesale reform of literature as a social institution that began with Perestroika and the fall of the Soviet Union is the concluding part of our story.

Attention to secondary and minor writers and works constitutes a further constant throughout our *History*. In the 1920s, the Russian Formalists, and especially Yuri Tynianov, revised approaches to writing literary history by emphasizing the codependence of major and minor writers during their own creative period. The Formalists rightly argued for the value of considering lesser talents and not just the greatest names always in the spotlight, and also underscored the importance of non-canonical genres (such as the literary anecdote). Comprehensiveness for its own sake, endorsed by the positivist model, is no longer the goal (in fact, it must be a vanishing point in the age of information). In real time, as perceived by contemporaries, the development of literature does not unfold as a set of stepping-stones from one giant to the next (although the story can be told that way). For this reason, and with increasing attention to literary criticism as an important institution of literature from the nineteenth century, the *History* from Part III onward devotes attention to journals, their book-reviewing culture, and fluctuations in reputation (Pushkin and Gogol's images are a case in point). Consideration of random and dead-end experiments, the authors and works that do not fit a system, also mark the terrain as we map it.

This book also treats the historical development of poetry and the poetics of Russian literature from oral folklore to medieval writing to postmodernism. From the seventeenth century (Part II), the practice of writing poetry experiences unstoppable growth. Overall, Parts III–V acknowledge the continued energy and staying power of poetry and do not follow the decline model often used in accounts of the nineteenth century as a changeover between ages of prose and poetry. Poetry remains an essential creative force, abundantly read and learned, and the cumulative appreciation of the poetic traditions feeds into literary prose, drama, and the academic criticism that generate a complex relationship between theory and practice. Unlike other histories, this book maintains its focus on the evolution of poetry in which we see not only a laboratory of artistic forms but also a part of the literary field in which new models of subjectivity arise and are tested alongside the poetics of prose. For this reason, we offer discussions of poetic styles and movements, essays on a number of important individual poets, and close readings of poems by Osip Mandelstam, Elena Shvarts, and Dmitry Prigov, examples chosen as models of types of poetic art.

This attention to poetry allows us to follow changing models of subjectivities (which we also consider in other genres). So, in addition to our attention to institutional contexts for literature, we trace in the evolution of literature two interrelated processes: changes in subjectivities and the construction of national narratives, suggesting that it is precisely through these categories that the intense influence of literature on a culture as a whole occurs. There are certain indelible categories of nationhood, literary politics and literary life, forms of selfhood, and forms of expression that run through literature; evolving institutional practices used to organize literature are themselves a part of the story of literature told in poetry, drama, and prose including diaries and essays. Since the eighteenth century, literature more than philosophy has served as a vehicle for exploring subjectivity and selfhood. We follow from sensibility to confessional lyric the various modes of self-exploration, very much pioneered by poets both men and women. How to understand the self is, of course, one of the projects of psychological prose, most famously associated with the nineteenth-century novel, but it first appeared in the so-called "society tale," often authored by women. Russian literature has demonstrated much ingenuity in exploiting intergeneric forms of writing, such as diaries, memoirs, and autobiographies (fictional and documentary), to create new modes of self-exploration. In Russia, individual and certain group identities, such as that of the intelligentsia in the nineteenth century, are formed, projected, and tested through the practices of literature. This fact attests to "literature-centrism" as a stable feature of Russian culture. Questions about the formation and practice of subjectivities through literary movements and forms, whether sensibility, psychological realism, autobiography, or anything else, also open up other issues about the representation of gender, class, ethnicity, and regional differentiation, impinging on the creation of the heroes, heroines, and antiheroes who define for a culture its ethical horizons at a specific moment.

From the medieval period to the late twentieth century, literature has furnished the discursive models in which historical memory and collective identity have found expression. Catastrophic narratives and nineteenth-century versions of stories of empire and collapse persist throughout the history of Russian literature. This is the case whether we are talking about the *Lay of Igor's Campaign* or stories about the Gulag, narratives of center and periphery, Russia and abroad. An absolutist narrative about the ruler and state naturally dominates the span from the medieval period well into the eighteenth century. In subsequent periods, this discourse yields to new narratives that remain powerful to this day—the narratives about Enlightenment and progress driven by the intelligentsia. The tight and complex connections binding the history of literary institutions, the evolution of poetic forms, and the production of subjectivities and national narratives obviate any need to see literature as a disembodied force that speaks through writers. In our approach, literature emerges as a sphere in which the agency of its historical participants is most conspicuous.

Tradition seems to imply monolithic lists of classics, but in fact literary histories of Russia have long turned to models of influence and dialogue, at least with reference to individual writers and their affiliations, to suggest that tradition remains a generative principle. Continuities of theme and preoccupation demonstrate the dynamic revisionism that surfaces as a creative principle in Russian literary culture. We thus adapt our historical approach to suit the material and argument, drawing on the methods of the sociology of literature, Formalism and cultural semiotics (especially for the twentieth century), and history. Consider, for example, the literary dimension of historical and political disruptions and geographical displacement. These events have created an enhanced platform from which to ask questions about the meaning of dislocation and deterritorialization over a longer period. This is a phenomenon that arguably starts in the medieval period. Just as our *History* aims to bridge thematically some dauntingly long chronological time spans, so we have attempted to bring together forms of literary discourse that have often been kept separate—and that have imagined themselves as resolutely distinct. We move rather freely between émigré and Soviet literature on many topics, for example. Yet we do not propose to conceive of Russian and Soviet literatures as one literature in a single language or as two separate entities. Rather, in taking them together, we remain aware with our reader that questions of boundaries and perspective are continually important and subject to different responses that cannot be explained by a unified theory.

We address major continuities and discontinuities in the history of Russian literature across all periods, and in particular bring out transhistorical features that contribute to the notion of a national literature. The volume's chronological range has the merit of identifying from the early modern period onward a vital set of national stereotypes and popular folklore. The earlier periods generate material about boundaries, space, Holy Russia, and the charismatic tsar that remains culturally relevant to later writers. But the approach aims to remain sensitive to the particular historical contours of writing in Russia. For this reason, the balance of coverage is roughly equal among the chronological parts. There is no aim to decenter the nineteenth century at the core of the modern canon but rather to see that canon in the larger context of its connections (and disconnections) to past and future, and to explore rich areas that also do what Russian literature of the nineteenth century seems to do particularly well—to represent individual and collective, self and nation, fate and history, and to strike a balance between old and new forms.

Part I

The Medieval Period

Introduction:
Defining the medieval

O F all periods a literary history can cover, the medieval and early modern most visibly challenge assumptions about a "literary" tradition. The institutions of the medieval world, essentially monastic, are not those of the literary field out of which the individual talents and movements of a modern literature emerge. And the use of a medieval language (Old Church Slavonic and Church Slavonic) raises the question of the degree to which works are either "Russian" or "literature." Furthermore, even basic aspects of periodization and terminology create uncertainty. Establishing end points of opening and closure is less problematic than trying to demarcate subdivisions that are not political dates. The type of precise discriminations that can be used to delineate the chronology of aesthetic movements (such as the Silver Age within modernism) proves useless for medieval Russian. Textual production, while influenced by dynastic politics and sensitive to events like invasion, tracked the rhythms of the Christian calendar and the history of the monastery itself rather than the history of writing. In a manuscript culture, signposts such as publication dates are largely unavailable. The proliferation of copies and multiple redactions of texts also mean that the dates of origin can be open-ended. Why, then, should a *History of Russian Literature* include the medieval period? Partly the answer lies in the intrinsic quality of the writing. The richness of medieval Russian literature can be—and has been—overlooked. Yet within the span of a literary history, a different and modern understanding of literature prevails, and it is diachronic and developmental rather than synchronic and static.

Some boundary-work would be helpful in establishing qualitatively what separates literature from a much larger body of non-literary writing. Medieval studies typically employ a much broader, philological definition of literature that conflates all forms of writing in ways that look almost senseless from the perspective of a modern canon. When conceived within the larger framework of a single-volume history, the selection of medieval literary texts should bear some relation to forms and purposes of writing that have a place in the longer history of the literature. Identifying the literary criteria—in practice, this means aspects of rhetoric, message, and form (mostly narrative)—allows us to focus on works that are essential within a medieval and modern canon, historically important yet also recognizable as works that are not of solely documentary or linguistic interest. Properly motivated, the differentiation of medieval literary texts from other forms of writing creates opportunities to argue for the appreciation of earlier forms of writing on various grounds while also remaining historically sensitive.

Continuity and the place of the medieval in the national tradition and its cultural imagination provide a second explanation of the selective coverage undertaken in Part I. Over the course of six hundred years, writing will be the essential medium through which political leaders and clergy react to aspects of faith, commemorate local and national politics, formulate interconnected ideals of Church and state, and articulate in words (alongside the rich tradition of icon painting) a theory of absolute rule that combines Christian charisma and political authority. Early medieval Russian writing consistently reflects not only its own historical context but also an awareness of the ideologies underlying that creation that recur, *mutatis mutandis*, in later centuries. Scribes, the main knowledge-workers of the medieval period, implicitly and sometimes explicitly used writing to shape and respond to the relationship between the institutions of religious and political power. For all the highly specific conditions of readership and authorship that determined content, significant medieval literary works offer responses to universal questions of identity, belief, and life and death that are equivalent to (and even look forward to) modern responses.

Cultural continuity is also a factor. From the discovery of a medieval epic, the *Lay of Igor's Campaign*, in the 1790s, to the rise of a national historical school in the 1860s, and the production of literary histories from the 1870s onward, the Russian intellectual and literary establishment has eagerly claimed the medieval period as a part of Russian literature. When nineteenth-century writers and historians over a long period formulated an idea of the Russian nation, giving literature an important status in its cultural distinctiveness, a vision of the medieval was seen as an organic part of the story. The reflex of bearing witness that seems so typical of the modern Russian writer, no doubt reinforced in the nineteenth century by Slavophile ideas of collective identity—the concept of *sobornost'* on which a discussion follows in Part II—appeared to extend organically out of the sense of responsibility and truth ascribed to the role of the (albeit usually anonymous) scribe and chronicler. In the medieval period, sacred metanarratives developed which positioned the saints, churchmen, and chroniclers as engaged in the definition and protection of the lands of Rus′ understood as Orthodox space even before its political definition as a nation became more focused from the sixteenth century.

Yet that argument should not blind us to discontinuities and differences. The tendency in literary histories has been to lump together everything written before the early eighteenth century into a single container called "ancient" (*drevniaia*) or "Old Russian" (*drevnerusskaia*), with an emphasis on the Russianness of the literature as a single continuum from origins to the present day: old and new are just forms of one type of Russianness whose differences can be papered over or accommodated within larger frameworks such as national identity and Orthodoxy.[1] In this *History of Russian Literature*, we prefer the term "medieval" because it lacks those connotations, and because the label better aligns Rus′ with the current norms in Western medieval historiography (where debate on terms continues).[2]

When it comes to coverage and treatment, the reader may wish to bear in mind that the story of medieval Russian writing is closely intertwined with both the history of Orthodoxy in medieval Russia and forms of political leadership. Many of the works discussed here can stand on their own as works of literary art, but arguably most benefit from some contextualization in their ecclesiastical and political circumstances.

The political and social history of medieval Russia is often divided into three discrete periods punctuated by changes in political and power structures leading to the domination of Moscow and the emergence of autocracy under a tsar beginning in the sixteenth century. While Part I aims broadly to follow this chronology, the thematic organization means that the treatment of some earlier material will be deferred for the sake of a more continuous and coherent analysis within a thematic discussion.

The earliest is the Kievan period from the tenth to the early thirteenth century; in other words, from the formation of the principalities of Rus′ to the waves of Tatar invasion beginning in the 1220s. Rus′ is the name applied to the terrain of the Eastern Slavs, often called Kievan or early Rus′. The Eastern Slavs were tribal groups that initially settled in the territory of Kievan Rus′ between the Western Bug, the Dniepr, and the Black Sea and around Novgorod and in the Tver′ region (in contradistinction to the Southern Slavs in Bulgaria, Croatia, Bosnia, and Serbia and the Western Slavs in Poland and the Holy Roman Empire).[3] The period when the land was organized according to competing principalities in which the Grand Prince of Kiev was preeminent has generally been known as the appanage period, although newer approaches stress the independence of principalities from one another in a region devoid of an overarching political mechanism for centralization (as appanage presupposes).[4] Inheritance of power or the princely seat was collateral rather than vertical, from father to son, and this led to situations in which younger males, often nephews who had not inherited from ruling fathers, contested the authority of the reigning prince. Obedience to the clan was an ideal more often honored in the breach than in the observance. Princelings vied for power against the authority of the Grand Prince, trying to usurp or succeed him. Internecine strife, now thought to have been sparked by an abundance of land opportunities rather than scarcity as earlier historical research held, was a norm as junior members of a clan tested the traditional authority of the eldest male.

Such strife exacerbated fragmentation. It is within this context and under the aegis of the Tatar occupation (continually weakened until the sixteenth century) that, in a second phase, political influence shifted north with long-term consequences for the ensuing consolidation of the principalities under Moscow and the emergence of a political system under the tsar. The tendency toward subdivision and the creation of new principalities continued in northeastern Russia well into the fourteenth century. But it also opened up opportunities for the princes of Moscow (or Muscovy) eventually to annex and consolidate less well-established entities, fueling their determination to assume the throne of the neighboring city-state of Vladimir, also known as Suzdalia, on the Kliazma River. In the thirteenth century, the heads of the church or metropolitans followed from Kiev to Vladimir and then to Moscow. By the early fourteenth century—the date of 1328 is often given—the princes of Moscow had acquired the territories associated with the throne of Prince Vladimir, in due course becoming preeminent by subduing rival princes.[5]

While nineteenth-century Russian historiography tended to depict the subordination of the princes of Rus′ and the Grand Prince of Vladimir to Tatar dominion (known as the Golden Horde) as an extended era of devastation and cultural paralysis, modern accounts are more revisionist and suggest a highly active revival of monastic culture and traditional practices of writing; and that these principalities and ecclesiastical centers, especially in Moscow, remained open to new trends in writing, scribal practice, and iconography from monasteries in the much broader Orthodox world of the Balkans, Bulgaria, and Greece.[6]

The third phase covers the consolidation of Muscovy's political control over northeast Russia as it subordinated neighboring towns, sacked the independent city of Novgorod in the northwest, and moved in the southeast against the Crimean Khanate. The reign of Ivan III (r. 1462–1505) consolidated the unification of the separate city-states into a single state ruled from Moscow. Ivan III's aim was to dismantle conclusively the old appanage principalities, subordinating rivals to the Grand Prince and consolidating alliances. As Ivan III, and then Vasily III (r. 1505–33), expanded their realm westward into the Chernigov and Smolensk lands, there seemed to be a real prospect that Muscovy could reunite the principalities of Kievan Rus′. After his annexation of Novgorod in 1478, an ancient city proud of its republican heritage, Ivan III regularly used the title "sovereign of all Rus′," which implied a territorial claim to the southwest lands (contested by the Lithuanian monarch Casimir IV).

With the fall of Constantinople in 1453, Moscow as the seat of the church positioned itself as a last bastion of Eastern Orthodoxy against Islam in the east and Catholicism in the west. The Grand Prince of Vladimir and Moscow acquired further luster by proximity to the country's spiritual authority. He enlarged the central administrative machine; court life was radically reformed and etiquette introduced to enhance the dignity of the Grand Prince. It was under Ivan III that the Grand Prince of Moscow became an "autocrat." These changes, while mainly to be studied for their political and ecclesiastical history, have a resonance in literary works that communicated an awareness of the period and views on identity.

Institutions and contexts: Writing and authorship, 1100–1400

T HE start of a written literary tradition in Kievan Rus´ rests on the acceptance of Christianity, and the complex acculturation in Kiev of the monastic traditions of Byzantium and the scriptoria of Mount Athos and other scribal centers. The exact date of the conversion of the Rus´ has been a matter of polemic.[1] The consensus is for 988 or 989. It is possible that a small group of Christians kept the faith and attracted converts even earlier in the tenth century. No traces remain of this first putative phase of ecclesiastical organization which, to quote the historian Dimitri Obolensky, "seems to have been submerged, later in the century, by a wave of paganism which swept away the pro-Christian rulers of Kiev and replaced them by a rival group of Scandinavians from North Russia."[2]

Prince Vladimir's baptism of the Kievans in the Dnieper River is recorded by Byzantine and Kievan annalists as occurring in the spring of 988. Twelfth-century Kievan sources made a point of demonstrating that the Kievans made a positive choice not to join the Latins.[3] The *Primary Chronicle* (*Povest' vremennykh let*, c.1115), the most important annalistic work of the Kievan period, tells how the ruler sent an embassy to the religious capitals of the Mediterranean basin. The legend relates that the beauty of St. Sophia in Constantinople moved them to choose Orthodox Christianity. In actuality, realpolitik through military alliance and dynastic relations motivated religious realignments. The superpower in the Black Sea region was Byzantium, or the Eastern Roman Empire, created when the Emperor Diocletian divided the Roman Empire during the Tetrarchy in the late third century to facilitate control over its vast territory.[4] When Vladimir (or Volodimer) engaged in battle with Swedish warriors and Novgorodians and conquered Kiev in 980, he bolstered the pagan cult. According to the *Primary Chronicle*, Vladimir's conversion in 988 occurred at the end of a difficult campaign in which he was an ally to the Byzantine emperors Basil II (r. 976–1025) and his brother Constantine VIII Porphorygenitus (r. 1025–28) as they quelled rebellions in the region.[5] In the final political negotiations in 987, the Kievan leader Vladimir negotiated for a military alliance with the Byzantines in return for military assistance and dynastic marriage to Anna the sister of the Byzantine Emperor at the time of the conversion. In marrying a Porphyrogenite (meaning "born in the purple" with reference to the birthing room of the Great Palace rather than filiation), Vladimir may have wished to acquire the cultural and social prestige of association with the Byzantine court and Church. It is unclear whether Vladimir initially wished to align the culture of his court with that of Byzantium; and whether, like the Bulgarians at the end of the ninth century, he attempted to impose Greek learning on his followers and make Greek the language of the liturgy.[6] Some sources may have exaggerated the extent of his youthful debauchery and paganism as a way of underscoring the profoundness of the conversion.[7] The monk Nestor, the author-copyist of a redaction of the *Primary Chronicle*, presents Vladimir before his conversion as a just man, kind to the poor, the orphaned, and widows—but also a Hellene, that is, a pagan, and goes as far as comparing him with St. Placidus, a celebrated convert.

A new cultural landscape took shape in which types of writing practiced elsewhere across the medieval world, like the saint's life, the sermon, and the chronicle tale, appeared in Kievan Rus' following the act of conversion and the establishment of monasteries in the eleventh and twelfth centuries. How to assess the legacy of Byzantium in Kievan Rus', and whether one should speak of cultural independence or dependence, remains actively debated in scholarship. Until the 1980s a powerful scholarly consensus argued that by joining the larger world of the Byzantine Commonwealth the Kievans gained access to a Christian heritage that was already at least seven centuries old. The question of the autonomy or derivativeness of early Rus' has generated an enormous amount of research on all areas of cultural practice, including writing, the law, religions, building, and dogma. Debates remain open-ended in the scholarship on whether substantial contacts with Byzantine culture should be the dominant element in a description of how the Eastern Slavs positioned themselves; or whether indigenous or exogenous traditions substantially shaped cultural practice.

In any discussion, much depends on the disciplinary point of view and evidence adduced—archaeological, literary, and philological or military and historical. Guided by research on trade, diplomatic, and ecclesiastical relations, and also architectural developments, the more Byzantinocentric historians have seen the polities of southern Russia as outward looking, oriented toward Constantinople and through it toward the West. This is the conclusion of Obolensky, who situates Kievan Rus' from the eleventh century within the Byzantine Commonwealth, his term for the sphere of religious and cultural influence that extended to autonomous kingdoms outward from Byzantium even beyond its imperial boundaries.[8] In his account, Kiev entered into a primarily political alliance with Constantinople, in which cultural praxis abetted political alliance and spiritual confraternity.

For other historians working from within Slavic rather than Byzantine studies, the boundaries are to be drawn around the network of Orthodox monasteries situated in northern Greece, Macedonia, and the Balkans. This description is less Byzantinocentric and sees the adoption of Christian types of writing as emanating from the monastic workshops founded by the pupils of Sts. Cyril and Methodius after their Moravian mission to bring Christianity (and a written language fit for translating the Scriptures) to the Slavs in the ninth century. In the aftermath of the Cyrillo-Methodian mission, newly established scribal, literary, and linguistic practices adopted from Byzantine monasteries developed to suit the customs and vernaculars of local populations, including Kievan Rus'. Riccardo Picchio has termed this model of cultural orientation Slavia Orthodoxa. The concept draws attention to cultural cross-border continuities and affinities created by the spread of learning from monasteries that mediated between Byzantine learning and local scribal practices, a state that Picchio finds valid until the fifteenth century.[9] For historians of medieval literature and language such as Picchio and A. P. Vlasto, the Kievans, like the Serbians and Moravians, became part of this less Byzantine dependent world. Research in the areas of dynastic marriage and political history, imperial rituals, economic relations and the law, have lent support to this more pluralist description of the cultural interfaces of southern Rus', shifting away from a binary description of Rus' as Byzantine or non-Byzantine, Eastern or Western. Christian Raffensperger has taken the argument yet a step further in arguing for early Rus' as part of Europe rather than as an extension of Byzantium.[10]

The extant legacy of Kievan writing is sparse and fragmentary. The presence of Byzantine learning in East Slavic written culture was sporadic. The Kievans might have regarded themselves as new Israelites but they did not regard themselves as "moderns" vis-à-vis ancients: the precise reason for their pride lay in the highly conscious transition from the pagan to the sacred within which a highly qualified and tangential relationship to Byzantium has been inscribed.[11] In the assimilation of literary models from the larger Orthodox world, much of the literary culture of Eastern Rome's traditions of translation, exegesis, and classical rhetoric was filtered out. Was this meant to be a systematic repudiation of a pagan legacy by any teachers and monks working in the thinly Christianized principalities of Rus'? Whether the modest presence of classical antiquity was the result of high selectivity or the accident of transmission remains a matter for conjecture. It may be that the record offers so little information on Greek learning because its presence was ephemeral. Within source studies of medieval Russian—that is the branch of scholarship dedicated to identifying how intellectual property was transmitted, borrowed, and refashioned—the cumulative effect has been a twofold recognition of the welter of origins (Anglo-Saxon, Frankish, Bulgarian, and Byzantine); and acknowledgment of the mismatch between Byzantium and a fledgling Kievan Rus' not yet equipped to secure its take up.

In parallel, there has been a shift within literary study away from the assumption that the Kievans had a stable literary system toward greater recognition of the inconsistency of textual praxis. This derives partly from an adjusted picture of the reception of Byzantine learning as highly incomplete, limited, among other factors, by a modest talent pool of teachers and scribes and the thin spread of literacy, and also to a degree shaped by local tendencies that curtailed knowledge of the classics and emphasized the catechism. Viktor Zhivov may be uniquely forceful, but he is not alone in concluding that the "culture of Kievan Rus' did not repeat and did not transplant contemporary Byzantine culture, but assimilated isolated aspects and even within this legacy exercised its own fundamental emphasis."[12]

A new language for a new people: Old Church Slavonic

Writing served the administrative purposes of the Kievan principality after Christianity was adopted as the religion of the ruling dynasty. Conversion to Christianity brought a new literary language and script, and with it a conduit to an already rich set of sources of liturgy, history, homily, and saintly biography. Christian writings were disseminated through the monastic foundations and workshops (to be seen as distinct from the scriptorium of Latin monasticism) established in the ninth and tenth centuries in the Balkans, especially in Bulgaria, that eventually served as a source for churchmen in Kiev.

The Cyrillo-Methodian mission denotes the activities of the evangelical monks, starting with the brothers Constantine and Methodius, who in the ninth century offered ecclesiastical assistance in Moravia. Through the translation of Scripture and liturgy they worked to offset the Frankish influence of the Catholic Church. Disciples in subsequent generations continued their work, and transformed the cultural outlook of lands around the Black Sea region and into central Europe. The pupils of Cyril and Methodius taught in the flourishing monasteries of Bulgaria at Ohrid and Preslav during the reign of Tsar Symeon (r. 893–927), who supported the Byzantine strategy of keeping the Balkans within the Eastern fold and offset the influence of the Franks. Tsar Symeon's collection of books was not just a luxury to be used as a symbol of power and prestige. His library contributed to an ambitious program of translation undertaken by monks in Ohrid with his support, perhaps a model for rulers of Rus' like Iaroslav Vladimirovich (d. 1054, known as "Iaroslav the Wise"), who wished to be known for his love of books and support of cultural advancement.

These monastic workshops made an important contribution to the copying culture of Kievan Rus'. The churchmen of Kiev undertook the daunting task of setting the foundations for the Christian religion in Rus' and establishing Old Church Slavonic culture there as had already happened in Bulgaria approximately a century earlier. This aligned Rus' with the seminal achievements of the Cyrillo-Methodian reforms. Constantine (later St. Cyril, 826/827–69) and his older brother Methodius (815–85) were born to a highly placed official in the city of Thessalonica. Methodius, who served as a functionary in the administration of the Slavs, took monastic vows, joining his learned religious brother. Both brothers moved to Constantinople to complete their studies (including philosophy and rhetoric), and were sent to the Khazar court on the Lower Volga in 860 on a diplomatic mission. While at Chersonesus in Crimea, Constantine was said to have discovered the relic of St. Clement, the second bishop of Rome, and composed a sermon in which he also talked about learning the Hebrew language and scriptures (the Khazars had adopted Judaism). Three years later, after their return to Constantinople, as related in the *Life of Methodius*, the two Thessalonians embarked on a Frankish mission to the Slavs at the behest of emissaries from Moravia and with the agreement of the Byzantine Emperor Michael III. Their mission had a linguistic element, since the two brothers had devised a new alphabet, later called Glagolitic, for transcribing the sounds of the Macedonian dialect thought to have been used near Thessalonica. This literary language is known as Old Church Slavonic, and from sometime in the tenth century the Cyrillic alphabet was used concurrently with Glagolitic letters, and then overtook it. This rendering of the literary language was used for translating liturgical texts (mainly the liturgical offices and the liturgy of St. John Chrysostom), as well as excerpts from the Gospels.[13] (Inflected with the regional usages and spellings of the Kievan vernacular, a close but distinctive version of the literary language is known as Old Eastern Slavic or Old Russian).[14]

The brothers were the subjects of two biographies. *The Life of Constantine*, a work written in Old Church Slavonic (between his death in 869 and 875), and the *Life of Methodius* give no details of their itinerary or of dates. Little is known about the historical channels through which the Cyrillo-Methodian heritage reached Rus' from Moravia. Although some original writings by the immediate pupils of Sts. Cyril and Methodius have been identified, their energies in the Balkans were principally devoted to translations from Greek: excerpts from both Testaments, followed by the full translation of the Gospels, liturgical books, sayings of the monks, and codes of ecclesiastical and secular law. After Methodius' death in 885, his disciples were expelled from Moravia and scattered. According to the *Life of St. Clement of Ohrid*, at least three disciples were sent to Tsar Boris in Pliska, and from there Boris sent Clement to the newly conquered region of Macedonia to the religious center on the northern shore of Lake Ohrid. These monasteries and royal foundations became bastions of Christianization. The largest manuscript written in Old Church Slavonic, the Codex Suprasiliensis, is a Bulgarian collection of saints' lives and homilies written in the Cyrillic alphabet (as opposed to Glagolitic).

Ecclesiastical book culture had made tentative inroads to Kiev even before the storied conversion of Prince Vladimir as early as the tenth century, following the success of Cyril and Methodius's mission in Moravia. For Kievan Rus', the conversion to Christianity marked the substantive beginning of a written culture and ecclesiastical practice. Because the historical record remains scant (although the archaeological record contains much evidence of early church building),[15] a description of the precise mechanisms of cultural transfer has been hard to achieve independent of the retrospective accounts provided in Kievan Rus' through its main foundational narrative, the *Primary Chronicle*. The *Primary Chronicle* in the entry for 1037 tells us that Iaroslav the Wise "assembled many scribes and had them translate from Greek into the Slavonic language. And they wrote many books."[16] But the historian is tantalizingly brief, specifying neither the nationality nor the origin of Iaroslav's translators. Questions continue to be asked about how many were Greek, how many Russian, how many Bulgarian, and how many Moravian. Nor is it certain which translations were executed in the reign of

Iaroslav, between 1010 and 1054. Were most made in Bulgaria and then copied in Rus'? From the scanty literary remains of the twelfth century and the inscriptions found on mosaics in St. Sophia it appears that Greek was at least initially the only written language.[17] What was the initial importance of the Greek language in early Russian (or Rusian) culture? In an account dated to 988, the *Primary Chronicle* relates that, after the Eastern Slavs had been baptized, Vladimir "went round to assemble the children of noble families, and arranged for them to be instructed in book-learning."[18] Some church historians maintained that Vladimir initially wished to align the culture of his court with that of Byzantium, and, like the Bulgarians at the end of the ninth century, attempted to impose Greek learning on his followers and make it the language of the liturgy. A new script was a necessary condition behind the cultural convergence with the monastic learning and religious practices of Byzantium. Two schools of conjecture have emerged on who gets the credit for translation, one giving pride of place to the contributions of outsiders to Rus', the other crediting the development of a home-grown literary and ecclesiastical culture. One view is that the Kievan elite was effectively bilingual in Greek and Slavonic. Simon Franklin in his authoritative analysis concludes that the evidence for Greek learning is highly sporadic and mainly numismatic and epigraphic, but Ihor Ševčenko credits the Kievans for their mastery of Greek and active role in disseminating new practices.[19]

The weight of evidence suggests that the cultural uses and functions of Greek remained highly circumscribed. In the early decades after Christianization, Greek was the literary language of certain members of the church hierarchy and the monks who visited Mt. Athos and other Byzantine monasteries. The written evidence identifies only one translator working in Kievan Rus'. He is Feodosy (Slavonic for Theodore) the Greek who confesses that he is not really skilled enough to "translate from the Greek language." He does not self-identify as Greek, and might have been a Bulgarian or even Kievan. In the mid- to late eleventh century, inscriptions on coins and mosaics fluctuate inconsistently between Greek and Slavonic. It is possible that educated Byzantine Greeks produced them or that the monks from Rus' educated on Athos reproduced fossilized formulae.

The safest general formulation, therefore, would be to say that, as a literary medium, the Old Church Slavonic language, and then Church Slavonic (a local version of the written language produced through contact with other Slavonic vernacular languages such as Bulgarian Church Slavonic), was formed by two generations of Byzantine and Slavic missionaries in the second half of the ninth and early tenth centuries; this language was a tool with which to translate from the Greek and thus spread the word of God, namely, the New Testament, in Russian Slavonic. There is no explicit evidence, however, to show that Byzantine missionaries in Russia deliberately promoted the Slavonic vernacular as a means of evangelizing the country.

Monastic writing: Translation, open boundaries, and selectivity

Over the entire medieval period from the eleventh century until the gradual modernization of the seventeenth century, the geographic reach of monasteries will extend across the land from Kiev in the south to Arkhangelsk in the north and throughout the regions of the northwest. A first phase of cultural and textual flourishing occurred early in the medieval period with the selective reception of Byzantine culture in Kiev through the monastic establishments of Bulgaria that had been proselytized in the ninth century by Slav-speaking religious advisors to Tsar Boris I (d. 907), the Bulgarian emperor who was Christian convert and protector to Cyril and Methodius. Medieval literature from early Kievan Rus' to Muscovite Rus' is coextensive with writing practices of the monasteries.

Monks worked as scribes. Their tasks were those of the copyist rather than the exegete. A small community of émigré monks from Byzantium, if such a band of teachers had established themselves in Kiev, would have found an insurmountable task in adapting the vast legacy of early medieval Christian philosophy, thought, and literary criticism. The writing that survives, both translations of Scripture and Byzantine ecclesiastical and legal codes, was produced in the Kiev Monastery of the Caves. Located outside the complex of princely palaces, it housed the authors whose writings constitute the main literary legacy of the period before 1240. Later texts retrospectively assert that in the eleventh century the monk Antony founded the Monastery of the Caves, also crediting the learned preacher Ilarion as a joint founder.

An overview of literature must begin with the fundamental realization that, unlike their Western and even Byzantine counterparts, few if any of the Russian brethren knew Greek and knew it well. Emphasis fell on continuity of faith and some monastic practices rather than on asserting the cultural privilege and priority of a new hermeneutical tradition with aims to supersede Byzantium. Whatever the separate political negotiations over the ecclesiastical authority of the new Kievan metropolitan, acculturation was selective.

Byzantine literary culture existed in relation to its pagan and antique past. By contrast, for Kiev, the function of Byzantium was not primarily to lay a path to the ancient world but to serve as a conduit to the selective appropriation of a Christian textual tradition and liturgical canons of prayer and preaching.[20] It is impossible for an intellectual system that has its roots among one nation to be transferred in its entirety to another in the absence of a comparable institutional framework. The mission of Cyril and Methodius was originally to preach Christianity to the Moravians and to evangelize. Their eventual legacy was to open the world of the Christian Scriptures, translated into a literary version of the vernacular tongue as part of the acceptance of a new religion. The new context severely limited potential for a new theological iteration of Christian dogma.[21] No significant tradition of ecclesiastical hermeneutics arises in medieval Russia until the sixteenth century. Given their limited means and numbers, Kievan clergy were not in a position to supplement or replace an entire tradition of Byzantine patristic learning. If there were few people in Kiev capable of generating exegetical learning and vernacular translations, we can only imagine that the intended audience would have been as limited if not even smaller. The repertory of modes of writing remains largely fixed until the fifteenth century when new ambitions for rhetoric and abstract conceptualization of metaphysical ideas in language would enjoy a brief flowering.[22]

Francis J. Thomson noted, "Cyril and Methodius created a literary language fully capable of expressing the most profound and abstract philosophical and religious ideas and of being the medium for works of great poetic beauty; but the tragic fate of Bulgaria prevented Slavia orthodoxa from assimilating more than a part of the Byzantine cultural tradition after the fall of Byzantium."[23]

The development of a written language adequate for the purpose of translating the holy texts of the new faith, above all the Gospels, plays an important role in the establishment of a sense of cultural identity (although a complete Slavonic codex of the Bible, the Gennady Bible, was not to be produced until 1499 when commissioned in Novgorod by the Archbishop Gennady [d. 1505]).[24] The literary remains of the period predating the foundation of monasteries are lamentably small, comprising very few original manuscripts (about 170) from the eleventh century (Bulgarian texts have vanished altogether).[25] Two major goals were the correct and faithful translation of the holy books and the establishment of monastic rule conducted according to Christian precepts.[26] Later texts exaggerate the amount of translation that took place in these early stages; the corpus remains a matter for scholarly reconstruction.[27] In the first instance, translation was the sanctioned way to establish Christianity through the presence of its seminal texts: the Bible most of all, and the liturgy required for private meditation as well as church services. Through monasteries in Bulgaria and the Balkans, some cultural transfer from Byzantium to the larger Orthodox community occurred. Examples of Byzantine eloquence (such as the writings of John Chrysostom) were brought together in collections like the *Prologue*, an ecclesiastical anthology that circulated among the Slavs in three versions from the thirteenth to fifteenth centuries containing short versions of saints' lives, including military saints, arranged according to the ecclesiastical calendar (and based on the Byzantine *synaxarion*, a collection of brief commemorations of saints).[28] Whereas Cyril and Methodius were also steeped in classical learning, familiar with Homer and Plato, Kievan bookishness largely ignored poetry and philosophical learning. More typical is the work of John Exarch, a Bulgar of noble origin, author of learned sermons and eulogies written in praise of Tsar Symeon. He lived in Preslav, the capital of the First Bulgarian Empire for nearly a century from 893 and the center from which the scriptorial innovation associated with the introduction of the Cyrillic alphabet, that is, the literary script of Old Church Slavonic, was probably developed and spread to other regions of Bulgaria and beyond. The style of quoting extensively in Old Church Slavonic adopted in Preslav and Ohrid by writers like John Exarch may have influenced native Kievan preachers of the twelfth century.[29] Dogmatic learning, therefore, was packaged in works like his anthology *Six Days*, or *Hexameron* (*Shestodnev*), which combined the biblical account of the Creation with excerpts from scientific and philosophical works. Copied in several different redactions, of which the earliest extant manuscripts date from the thirteenth and fifteenth centuries, the selections include John of Damascus's *On the Orthodox Faith*, a Byzantine set of patristic homilies on Genesis, and numerous prayers. Before the thirteenth century, Kievans also acquired a translation of the *Physiologus* (*Fiziolog*), a bestiary that originated in the second century AD and survived in medieval translations into Latin, Armenian, Syriac, Coptic, Ethiopic, and Georgian, treated living creatures, mainly real ones but also the imaginary phoenix, siren, and centaur, and a few plants. Each account, often in poetic terms, listed the properties of the creature and followed with a symbolic description in the vein of Christian allegory. For instance, the *Physiologus* says that when pelicans are born they begin to peck their parents until the latter kill them. After mourning their children for three days, the mother pierces her rib and her blood drips onto the young bringing them to life. The behavior of the pelican symbolizes the fate of mankind, which fell into sin, but was saved by Christ's blood. It is impossible to know for certain whether this twelfth-century translation into Old Church Slavonic reflects a positive interest in sophisticated forms of allegory.

While our account cannot dilate on the Biblical translations, it would be remiss not to note certain important landmarks. The oldest of the manuscripts copied in Russia dates from after the death of Iaroslav and is known as the Ostromir Gospel or Lectionary (*Ostromirovo Evangelie*), named after a Kievan who served as an emissary to Novgorod. It is one of the most beautiful of all Slavonic manuscripts, richly illuminated with miniatures of the Evangelists (as the image of Mark in Plate 1 shows).

Letter-forms changed gradually by the twelfth century into the semi-uncial (*polu-ustav*), a more fluid letter-form. Manuscripts such as the Ostromir Lectionary and the Mstislav Lectionary, commissioned in 1117 by the eponymous prince of Novgorod and later restored in 1551 at the behest of Ivan IV (or the Terrible; r. 1547–84), a tsar renowned for his piety at the time, contain readings designed for the feast days of the church calendar. These are not complete Gospels but examples of the Byzantine type of Aprakos Gospels or Acts of the Apostles in which weekly readings integrate passages from the New Testament. The *Life* of the monk Constantine, later St. Cyril, cites his work as translator, but there has been tremendous debate and uncertainty about which versions of the Gospels and Psalms he used in translating into the Slavic script he had devised. The Old Testament survives only in the form of excerpts compiled in the *paroemia*, the readings designated for religious holidays.

But the extensive translation of patristic landmarks did not represent a primary goal for the earliest generation of church figures of Kievan Rus' whose priority concerned ritual, icon veneration, and liturgy rather than church law. Seemingly little attention was paid to Biblical exegesis and hermeneutics, staples of the Western medieval schools. The sub-tradition of Biblical and patristic commentary could be folded into autonomous works that demonstrated the self-generating nature of Kievan writing as a new tradition. Sermons written by learned preachers engage in vulgarizing theological arguments. Yet as a rule scribes did not much engage in the explication of classical authors and Biblical scholarship after Byzantine models never much caught on.

Literacy was largely confined to the cultural elite and most especially clerical persons who used devotional, historical, Biblical, and other ecclesiastical texts written in Church Slavonic (rarely Latin and Greek before the seventeenth century when Ukrainian book-learning makes inroads into Muscovite ecclesiastical training). Before the growth of the centralized state with its concomitant administration in the fifteenth century, there is little evidence for the practice of the literary arts outside the Church and upper echelons of the state occupied with the internal matters of law and order. It stands to reason that at least some princes, beginning with Iaroslav in the twelfth century, were able to read and write, although no evidence survives to suggest regional magnates and princelings outside the upper reaches in major principalities like Kiev, Vladimir, and then Moscow, were either readers or writers. Magnates expected scribes in local monasteries to record their activities, conquests, and even to catalogue wealth. No evidence suggests they read beyond the requirements of practical literacy (*delovaia pis'mennost'*). But while a law code existed, court cases convened, and justice was dispensed, there were no lawyers or legal materials requiring expert provincial administrative classes.[30] (The evidence of the Novgorod birch-bark papyri from the fourteenth century, fragments of documents including personal letters, shows that the use of writing could be diverse, and that literacy was more widely spread than had been supposed, including among women.)

The limits of the literary system: Rhetoric, compilation, and genre

Great is the benefit of book-learning; for through books we are instructed and inducted into the path of repentance; for from the words of books we attain wisdom and continence. For the words of books are rivers that water the whole earth; they are wellsprings of wisdom: the depth of books is unfathomable.[31]

So reads a eulogy of books in the *Primary Chronicle*, and the admiration of their powers of edification sounds wondrous here. How did medieval writers or scribes conceive the task of engaging and persuading? Did they follow models or invent when not translating? Is there literature without a concept of genre?

A revisionist account that scales back the dependence of Kievan Rus' on Byzantium has implications for how we talk about genre as a model of authorial intention and apply it as a method of formal description. With the learning at their disposal, and within the copying traditions that arose locally, scribes made formal decisions about expressivity that are hard to explain by reference to a system of genres that may have existed only skeletally, if at all. In the 1950s and 1960s, Soviet medieval studies, led by the highly eminent Dmitry Likhachev (1906–99), regularly applied the idea of a genre system. The approach found influential support in a much-cited article by Dmitrij Tschiževskij.[32] Historically, the application of genre criticism to medieval Russian texts dominated in textbooks: classification by function was a productive and clear-cut way to credit scribes with artistic intention and also elevate their authorial role.

The open textual tradition allowed copyists to exercise judgment in adding and editing materials, sometimes extensively.

Skepticism about the validity of genre has grown since the 1970s in Western medieval studies. American and German scholars, in particular, expressed doubt that formal imperatives motivated and shaped composition, a tenable position given how few works seem to consistently conform to a pattern.[33] Genre no longer attracts much support although it is hard to dispense with it entirely as a convenient category.[34] Behind this reconsideration stands the essential fact that Russian medieval writers produced no treatises on poetics and no theory of art, and left virtually no trace of an analytical vocabulary on the methods of literary writing. Early texts, in particular, present problems of classification because of their mixed purposes and style. What was the intention? What was the result of accidental arrangement? The strong role of compilation and translation meant that larger anthologies arranged by calendar or subject matter, rather than genre, served as repositories of prayers, local histories, saints' lives, homilies, hymnographic writings, and so on, without separate division into anthology by subgenre. And many of the texts translated into the written language of the Orthodox Slavs belonged to the "classical" canon of the Christian Church, a model that was not generative of new works requiring authorial initiative.

The question about the fit between modern genre categories and medieval uses of writing matters in this instance because subgenres such as the tale, biography, and adventure story, come bundled in chronicle-writing that often purports to be drily factual. A new emphasis on the communicative function of the work has been more productive as a critical tool than the older style of genre-criticism. This method interprets the meaning of literary writing partly with reference to its inherent structure and use of devices, partly with reference to its function in the community and social context. This type of contextualization (sometimes known as *Sitz im Leben*, that is, "situation in life") allows us, on the basis of the text and its structures, to ask who wrote, why they wrote, and who heard or read them.[35] Outside the hugely complex and very detailed work of source criticism that remains a pillar of medieval scholarship for specialists (and very much alive within the Russian academic establishment), this approach has gained adherents because it can recuperate works of literature to a tradition and broader readership, while also remaining historically sensitive.[36] Revisionist scholarly work on this period by Norman Ingham, Gail Lenhoff, and Renate Lachmann challenged the view that medieval Slavdom thought in terms of genre as defined by a "meta" system of rules (either in writing or painting).[37] A dichotomy between the purely functional (as non-literary) and the purely imaginative (as with a modern definition of literature) is too restrictive, and not only because all writing (*pis'mennost'*) even within a bureaucratic and institutional context has forms and conventions that filter viewpoint and shape an authorial voice.

Arguably, the absence of works of commentary mattered more for the production of literature than for theology. Medieval Rus' produced nothing like St. Augustine's influential account of the ancient theory of rhetorical persuasion (set out in *De doctrina christiana*), in which he reformulated Ciceronian norms of eloquence as a means of persuasion through pleasing and satisfaction with precise prescriptions on the manner and material of speeches, and much information on the grand, middle, and plain styles, all illustrated with examples from the Church Fathers. In that light, it would be hard to maintain for medieval Russia that there was a specific moment when literary form could provide the basis of classification of works. Rather, insofar as classification mattered at all, the function of works determined the style of composition loosely understood. This feature of Russian medieval book culture lasted well into the early modern period, that is, up to the seventeenth century. Medieval Russian writers were not interested in establishing theoretical distinctions between writing and knowledge, rhetoric and poetics. Their concern was to maintain traditional subject matters of writing first established in the twelfth century. One result was the creation of a narrative idiom adequate to the literal events and also sufficient for the purpose of speaking figuratively and eloquently when occasions required more formal rhetoric.

An absence of fixed genre rules is not a fatal impediment to the effective (and intuitive) use of literary means of communication, and especially rhetoric. Andrei Robinson, unlike Dmitry Likhachev, for instance, emphasizes both the international character of writing between the eleventh and thirteenth centuries, and the role of typology by which he means emulation of approved models.[38] Tradition and training rather than theory or handbooks conditioned writers to follow norms they had assimilated practically through listening and reading. Despite the professed admiration for book-learning as great and deep, there is no evidence to suggest that on Kievan soil grammarians and theologians elaborated a theory of affective intention comparable to Renaissance and Humanist hermeneutics. In Rus´, writers seem to have acquired an understanding of style based on imitation of their reading. Although there were no medieval Russian treatises on poetics or rhetoric that discussed the role of the reader, a functional definition of literature is not necessarily determined by contemporaneous theory. Scribes demonstrated an appreciation of affect by absorbing lessons from foreign works, sometimes silently and sometimes overtly; furthermore, there are texts involving authorial narrators, some who use the first person without naming themselves, who clearly have a sense of style and rhetorical purpose; third, there are important writers who behave like authors, exceptions who prove the rule.

Court settings as well as religious ceremony, as can be inferred from sermons and narrative works, created opportunities for learning the art of eloquence as a pragmatic skill in addressing worshippers and different cohorts of auditors. One of the striking features that genuinely sets off literary works from writing more broadly is the quality of voice that rhetorical artistry produces, implying a clear sense that writing requires devices, thought, and a persona in order to teach, persuade, and, above all, to stir emotions. The liturgical and paraliturgical genres of the Byzantine Church that were transmitted to the Slavs, many in translations imported from Bulgaria, then picked up by copyists in Kievan Rus´, must have created a sense of individual and congregation, voice and listener.[39] Awareness of authorial voice, even when anonymous, was one legacy of a Christian context marked by liturgy, prayer, and ceremony to writers engaged in non-liturgical composition.

Eloquence was unquestionably one skill channeled through Byzantine models even without the adoption of formal rhetorical systems. A small number of sermons, epistles, prayers, and eulogies—markedly rhetorical pieces—now stand as canonical works of medieval literature because they combine artistry and message in a way that qualifies them as lasting examples of literature. These modes were practiced nearly continuously from the time of Kievan Rus´ to the Petrine period, from the great eleventh-century preacher Ilarion to Gavriil Buzhinsky (1680–1731) and Feofan Prokopovich (1681–1736), architects of Peter's political ideology, accomplished practitioners of the sermon, and, in Prokopovich's case, the author of one of the few theories of literature, his Latin *De arte rhetorica* (1706).

Where theoretical knowledge was lacking, eloquence could be accessed through copying and reading, and some literature was available. Among the most important of the eleventh-century manuscripts are the two *Izborniki* (literally "selections") of Sviatoslav Iaroslavich of 1073 and 1076.[40] The first *Izbornik* is a copy commissioned by Prince Iziaslav before he was dethroned in 1073 of a selection of Greek texts translated originally for Tsar Symeon of Bulgaria. It is an exceptional manuscript book with beautiful illuminations that include a portrait of Sviatoslav and his family. An edificatory compilation rather than a manual, it contains some rare instruction on rhetoric, drawn from Byzantine sources, with illustrations from pagan literature. The second *Izbornik* is a smaller book also descending from Bulgarian models and compiled by the signatory "the sinner Ioann." He identifies himself as the selector and compiler of excerpts from works supposedly drawn from the library of Iaroslav the Wise. The aim is to put the reader on the "path to salvations" (*put' spaseniia*) and to instruct on points of liturgy and church ritual, also identifying, as Prince Vladimir Monomakh would enunciate in the twelfth century, the wisdom of a humble "meekness" (*smirenie*) as a defining virtue of Orthodoxy.

These compilations will be the first in a long line of manuscript anthologies that are a feature of writing in medieval Russia. They may also be noteworthy as a sample of the wisdom literature a literate prince might have read and suggest an appreciation of the arts of eloquence. One of the most famous of Russian compilations of patristic writings is the *Zlatostrui* (*The Golden Stream*, c.893–927), a collection of sermons attributed to St. John Chrysostom (349–407), first translated in the tenth century for Tsar Symeon I of Bulgaria, who presided over a cultural golden age in Preslav in the 890s. Another type of compilation, with a more specialized purpose, was the so-called *Paleia* from the Greek word *palaios*, meaning "ancient."[41] In its basic outline the *Paleia* contained canonical texts and Apocrypha treating the history of the Jewish people, and served as a complement to Old Testament texts collected in the *paremeiniki*.

Larger codices, or bound manuscript books, also existed, bringing together a wider range of works. Among the early collections that may have helped to establish the model of the anthology as a useful convoy for miscellaneous works of writing, and to promote a culture of eloquence, was *The Bee* (*Pchela*). Probably compiled in the tenth or eleventh centuries, this florilegium, which appeared in Slavonic translation not later than the thirteenth century, contained numerous Christian apothegms as well as thematic discussions of virtue, vice, pious behavior, illustrated Christian moralistic writings amplified by quotations from the Psalter and Gospels, sayings, stories, and anecdotes, some from classical ancient sources. It also contained numerous precepts on political duty and social structure, cognate with the theme of the clan and brotherly love that will be treated in narrative and moralistic literature in medieval Russia. This florilegium associates good behavior with eloquence and uses eloquence to foster good behavior. Copied and adapted in multiple versions until the eighteenth century, its Slavonic version served as a prototype for similar types of cento-works produced by a writer like Nikolai Kurganov in his *Pis'movnik* (*Miscellany*, 1769) at a moment when moralistic literature cast as Christian precept, especially for children, enjoyed a great vogue.[42]

The terms for chronicle and chronicle-writing (*letopis'*, *letopisanie*) cover a vast body of material that stretches from Kievan Rus' into the early seventeenth century. A chronicle is a record of events, an annalistic narrative numbered, in the Byzantine tradition, from the creation of the world, that is 5508 years before the birth of Christ; each year began on 1 September. Their use of sources and institutional origins make chronicles a very complex and fragmented type of history-writing that achieve their form through recensions or variant versions compiled from source texts, moments of compilation, and then editing (or redactions). A chronicle can exist as a single identifiable work but will often be disseminated in multiple copies differentiated by variations that can be meaningful, depending on the practice and viewpoint of the scribes.

Chronicles, sometimes capacious works, as was the case with the *Litsevoi svod* (known in English as the *Illustrated Chronicle*) compiled 1568–76 for Ivan IV, might be bundled in even larger manuscript collections, called a *svod*. The name and description of a chronicle has traditionally been a function of the monastic provenance, ownership, or geographic region from which the manuscript comes. Local chronicles concentrate on their own terrain, but their perspective, shaped by the sources available, need not be parochial. From the fifteenth century, chronicles written in Pskov extended their purview to happenings in the wider region, aware of their importance for the city's own independence. Among the facts reported in chronicles, most space was given over to political, church, and dynastic events as well as military affairs; sometimes natural and man-made disasters are reported. The tradition is accretive, and narratives may be comprehensive or more selective in episode and detail. They often extend existing chronicle versions. Most take a sequential view of the past up to the present, and might be prefaced by summaries of source materials or other introductions taken wholesale from a source.

Chronicle-writing reminds us not to overvalue genre description in relation to scribal practices. While linearity defines structure, the genre is not merely factual: it could be augmented through interpolation of stories, hagiographies, prayers, legends, and rhetorical expostulations. If the chronicle creates a frame ordering events in time, the story is the connected events, with both beginning and ending. Narratives tend to be short, certainly shorter than the few pure historical works that survive like the sixteenth-century *History of Kazan'* (*Istoriia o Kazanskom tsarstve*, sometimes known as the *Kazanskaia Istoriia*, 1564–66) or Prince Kurbsky's *History of the Grand Prince of Moscow Concerning Deeds Heard from Reliable Men and Seen with our own Eyes* (*Istoriia kniazia velikogo Moskovskogo o delekh, iazhe slyshakhom u dostovernykh muzhei i iazhe videkhom ochima nashima*, composed after 1564), and involve no self-questioning about genre or scrutiny about inclusion and exclusion of material. The political history of princely clans, and the often-conflicted relations between ecclesiastical and political leaders, constitute plot lines in chronicles; digressions into local custom and saints' lives overflow the annalistic form. Plot lines often come with an embedded point of view representing the interests voiced anonymously through the scribe of one princely or ecclesiastical faction.

The corpus of *letopisi* is vast, and the relationship between archetypes and copies was densely reticulated.[43] Chronicle scholarship is often source scholarship fixated on textual boundaries, linguistic features, and other practices such as dating.[44] Most chronicle scholarship, therefore, draws on a variety of methodologies such as codicology and redaction criticism in order to reconstruct a putative original (or archetype) and establish the order and provenance of material added later. In Russian philology, pioneering textual studies were undertaken by Aleksei Shakhmatov (1864–1920), whose complex reconstruction of the stages of composition of the *Primary Chronicle* was a major historico-literary accomplishment, foundational in understanding scribal production of eleventh and twelfth century Kiev.[45] Shakhmatov, in effect, established a highly productive branch of medieval scholarship in Russia that has transformed the study of Rus'. While the oldest manuscripts of Russian chronicles date to the late thirteenth and early fourteenth centuries, reconstructions place the origins of chronicle-writing considerably earlier in the reign of Grand Prince Iaroslav (*c.*978–1054) around 1039 with the composition of what has been called the "most ancient compilation" (*drevneishii svod*) commissioned for the scriptorium in the Cathedral of St. Sophia.

The oldest extant Russian chronicle, the *Primary Chronicle* or *Povest' vremennykh let* (*Tale of Bygone Years*), has an abbreviated title taken from a heading affixed long after its first stage of composition: "These are the tales of the storied years from which arrived the Russian land that began to rule first in Kiev and whence came the Russian land." The *Primary Chronicle*, completed by Nestor around 1115, was copied in his lifetime for other princely houses, giving rise to new versions that independently incorporated local material. Two important scribal redactions of the *Primary Chronicle* were subsequently produced. Each contains significant new material as well as minute adjustments: the *Laurentian Chronicle* (*Lavrent'ski spisok*), a copy dating to 1377 traced back to a 1305 copy containing fundamental changes, and the *Hypatian Chronicle* (*Ipat'evskii spisok*), dating to the beginning of the fifteenth century. How these versions evolved can be explained through the reconstruction of the intermediary sources on which the scribes drew. Such analysis is of a complexity to defeat summary. Yet in the present context it remains useful to note that the history of this important work illustrates a process fundamental to textual production in the medieval period: that is, how a codex (or in Russian *svod*) came into being by gathering up separate works that sometimes originate in a single monastery or had different provenances and levels of authority. At each stage in its ongoing history, monks copied and added new writing, sometimes signing as if the *Primary Chronicle* were their own (hence the hegumen or monastic official Silvester takes credit for writing or copying in an entry dates to 1118). One important variation between the two later versions of the *Primary Chronicle* is that they have different chronological end points.[46]

These facts are worthy of note because they demonstrate a percipient awareness by rulers of the symbiosis between writing and power, and the dependence of rulers on the skills of the learned Christian brethren. Compilation occurred in ecclesiastical and political circumstances that saw the authorities of Church and state using writing to settle present uncertainties, such as a civil war between related princes. The inference that compilation was only mechanical should be resisted. Within the limits imposed by copying and imitation, interpolation and revision remained the best way to introduce new information and sometimes to put old material to the service of a different viewpoint. Readers of Alexander Pushkin's play *Boris Godunov* (1825) will recognize in the character Pimen a memorable portrait of a monk, a scribe of conscience, and a witness to history. The single-author model breaks down conclusively in relation to chronicle-writing. Few chronicles empower the scribe with any personal voice, and most contain countless witnesses whose emotional interjections and moralizing conclusions punctuate episodes that have been transferred rather than invented; they are often action-packed with tragedy or the drama of battle. Both distance and immediacy let characters speak for themselves. Not only did the scribes retrospectively elaborate on texts and thereby produce new redactions, they also combined earlier historical accounts in new compositional schemes so as to create compilations of potentially different import.[47] There was no standard blueprint according to which the copyist had to arrange his material, thus keeping open the possibility of fresh combinations of texts and not just citations with new emphases.

The medieval period saw the widespread use of narrative forms such as epic, poetic prose, legends, stories, and fairy tales; and chronicles can contain them all. In recounting events that are said to have occurred, narrative genres apply different standards of historicity. Chronicle-writing professes to be grounded in fact, while tales, often based on oral legends, make plausibility the standard of verisimilitude, and fairy tales make free use of the magical and extraordinary. Yet history-writing as a discipline and science did not exist. And while fiction was not recognized as a separate category, much narrative writing exhibits an approach to events that we would now describe as fictional. Storytelling may aim to educate, entertain, and persuade, and the boundary between historiography and invention remains fluid for the entire period. If chronicles occupy a space between literature and writing of a documentary kind it is because they accommodate varied material selected mainly with reference to relevance to the topic or location of the scribe.[48] Between the historical and the fictive there is little room, and no sense of the fictive that has to be defended (as can be found in Philip Sidney's *Defense of Poesy*, 1595, which argues for the value of fiction as moral instruction and delight). Nor is there any deep moral objection to pure narrative or sense of anxiety about storytelling.

The scribe retains control of a kind by streamlining multiple perspectives into a single point of view. But the medieval Russian scribal system accepted interpolation and insertion into new texts as a way of adding shades of significance. Given the increasing politicization of writing in the medieval period, it is open to conjecture that this gesture is implicitly aimed at limiting knowledge rather than opening up a narrative to questioning. It was routine for copyists to incorporate extensive source material (for instance, an account of the creation of the world or a tale of dynastic foundation) and extend their narrative to cover recent events. To make a chronicle was to be a compiler: to collect, carefully arrange, and in some cases, extend and amplify source materials (including lists and geographic information) and identified authorities.

For instance, the thirteenth-century *Uspensky Anthology* (*Uspenskii sbornik*), brings together in one manuscript book saints' lives of Byzantine origin, a life of St. Methodius of Moravian origin, a eulogy of his brother St. Cyril, and three important literary works: the *Tale of Boris and Gleb* (*Skazanie o Borise i Glebe*), the *Tale of Miracles* (*Skazanie o chudesakh*), and the monk Nestor's *Life of St. Feodosy* (*Zhitie Feodosiia Pecherskogo*). Modern scholarship has found in textology a method to reconstruct how chronicles were put together and also, importantly, to trace implied allegiances and shifting loyalties. Copyists could alter the balance between positive and negative evaluation of the princes by suppressing positive attributes, curtailing praise, or by switching between positive and damning adjectives for their actions, all intended perhaps to please a patron, for the sake of good relations between the monastery and local branch of the dynasty, pride and prejudice, or other motivations that remain conjecture.[49] Textual analysis, mapped onto a tree showing the origin and destination of passages from a prototype disseminated out to new compilations, help historians produce hypotheses and sometimes reach conclusions about what lay behind new versions of known identified episodes. Considerable knowledge about the internal politics of principalities and the use of narrative in determining a message has been gleaned from painstaking collation of variants. Scrutiny of the *Sofia Second Chronicle* (*Sofiiskaia Vtoraia Letopis'*, 16th c.), for example, has exposed a gap between passages favorable to the interests of the Church in Pskov that draw on late fifteenth-century material, and correspondingly critical writing about the princely dynasty clearly at variance with princely chronicles that were more flattering.[50]

For historians of medieval Russia, the chronicles are important primarily as factual sources on events, religious attitudes including discussion of confessional choices, and the attitudes of the ruling house since chronicles were intended to reflect the views of the ruler and sometimes the Church. In writing his *History of the Russian State* (*Istoriia gosudarstva rossiiskogo*), a masterpiece of the nineteenth century that immediately changed the literary landscape after its final volumes were published in 1824, Nikolai Karamzin immersed himself in the close study of the chronicles, building into his narrative a massive documentary apparatus of chronicles that he treated as primary sources, and it is partly owing to his extensive quotations that it has been possible to produce a hypothetical reconstruction of one lost source, the *Troistkaia Chronicle*.[51] Literary portraits of secular as well as religious leaders work with a limited set of features, and while they can fossilize into stereotypes, variation can be subtle but significant, and often only discernible to the student of comparative manuscripts willing to collate descriptive vocabulary as it migrates with the characterization of princes to different pieces of writing. For students of literature, source criticism and the reconstruction of an archetype (through manuscript copies arranged as a tree or stemma) can inform an understanding of the function of literature in its context by revealing how the editing of texts, sometimes through original interpolation, sometimes through collation of different sources, could produce new meanings within circumstances—and these circumstances might relate to a doctrinal dispute or the legitimization of dynastic claims regarding a contested seat of power or imperial ideology.[52] Such findings about provenance and revision can help to illuminate how the manipulation of textual material became particularly important when the production of chronicles became centralized in the Kremlin and communicated aspects of Muscovite political ideology, especially from the fifteenth century.[53]

Overall, the growth of writing and its use to convey pride and aspiration, even within a thinly populated region, gives the impression that writing was invested with great cultural significance. From the mythic moment of Iaroslav, the lover of book-learning and wisdom, writing attracted a symbolic status as a marker of cultural value. This new dispensation elevated the present as subject matter deserving commemoration not only for practical or functional purposes. This is a point of literary anthropology and the formation of cultural capital that can help to explain how writing became a privileged technology. Yet the growth of a literate and literary culture was narrow because the lack of universities, the delay of printing until almost a century after Gutenberg, the scattered network of monasteries distant from northern Russia, and entrenched scribal practice slowed the transformations that would only begin in the seventeenth century.

The meaning of readership

In Old Church Slavonic, the word *knigy* means "letters," in both the narrow and larger sense of characters and writings; the *knizhnik* is the literate bookman or man of letters, and his chief interest is the books of Scripture. Because Christianity supplied the purpose of a literary culture, it also motivated the forms of storytelling, including the telling of lives as well as narration of events, that lend themselves to forms of emotional statement requiring rhetoric.

The question "How many readers were there at that time?" is a rhetorical one for book historians. Even the question of what these readers read can only be partially answered. When the distinguished Russian medievalist Yakov Lur'e asks, "What did medieval Russians read?," it is hard not to hear a note of doubt that they read at all. Some examples give an indication of what reading entailed, at least for clergy. For instance, a thirteenth-century *Life of Avraam of Smolensk (Zhitie Avraamiia Smolenskogo)* provides rare information by listing the books he read: mainly the writings of St. John Chrysostom (347–407 AD), the Archbishop of Constantinople famed for his homilies and command of rhetoric; and the lives of the founding monks of the Kiev Monastery of the Caves (also known as the Kiev Pechersk Lavra).[54] Efrosin, a monk of the Kirillo-Belozersky Monastery, founded in 1397 in the Vologda region, was one of the most active scribes of his time. He produced six volumes of compilation for personal use in his own cell. In the extant copy of one anthology of prayers, he recorded the date on which he completed copying each section, making a total of four years of labor. His reading consisted of hagiographic works, excerpted from the *Prologue*, the homilies, Biblical texts, prayers and monastic rules, pilgrimage accounts, and polemical works on canon law. He also knew writings about nature by Dionysius the Areopagite (a figure much quoted in the fifteenth century) and *The Mirror (Dioptra)*, a poem by the Byzantine writer Philip Monotropos on the nature of the body and soul, which was translated into Church Slavonic in Bulgaria, attracting learned commentary, before numerous Russian copies made in the fifteenth century began to serve as a source of extracts and commentary. (Although an abstruse work, Dmitry Bulanin regards it as one of the most informative reflections for the period on human existence.) There is little suggestion, however, that much, if any, writing was designed for lay readers. And even from the sixteenth century, when a typographic press existed in Moscow, the Church (through its administrative office, the Holy Synod) strictly superintended the dissemination of printed matter until the 1720s.

We cannot hear lost voices. But we can note the signals of epideictic rhetoric attuned to delivery before a congregation or fashioned for an implied reader kept in mind. In an essay about enclosed spaces in medieval England, Lynn Staley comments on the conceptual (and therefore "placeless") space of a church.[55] By contrast, the Russian tradition defines its own territorial integrity by locating the church, which can never be placeless and must always be a jurisdiction containing spiritual energy. Reading and listening to works read aloud according to the monastic rule was the intellectual activity of the monastery that educated monks in the emulation of Christian values and a Christian life. It is clear that reading aloud carried an expectation of emotional response. The *Instruction to my Brothers (Pouchenie k bratii*, 1055) by the Novgorod preacher Luka Zhidiata (d. 1060) interlaces points of dogma with practical admonitions on good behavior, an object lesson in human edification.[56] Texts we discuss here by the monk Nestor (d. 1116), Grand Prince Vladimir Vsevolodovich of Kiev, usually referred to as Vladimir Monomakh (1053–1125), and the preachers Metropolitan Ilarion (d. 1054) and St. Kirill of Turov (1130–82), use introductory passages that address a reader and listener, asserting the importance and content of the reading. As Kirill tells his listener, "Having heard by listening, you will rejoice" ("Slukhom slishav, radueshisia..."),[57] an expression close to the traditional scribal hope that "my words will henceforth be in your heart and in your soul."[58] Copyists might even take the liberty of repeating their introductory appeal later in the text: a late-twelfth-century copy of Nestor's *Life of St. Feodosy* repeats the prefatory passage at the end, instead of the conclusion used in other versions. The introductions or prefaces of some liturgical works, even when entirely translated rather than composed originally, also use rhetoric to establish an element of reader-response.[59]

It is to be expected that gifted preachers were practiced in forms of address. They stepped outside the anonymous role of the scribe and chronicler, and excelled in translating their erudition into messages to be understood by auditors as well as by readers. Extant works from the twelfth to the fourteenth centuries demonstrate that preachers like Ilarion, Kirill of Turov, and Klim (Kliment) Smoliatich (d. 1164), exhibit their polish and also their skill in quoting patristic exegeses. Metropolitan Ilarion was a highly accomplished writer, steeped in scripture, and also adept at a sophisticated form of Biblical criticism known as typology that uses exegetical comparison to establish parallelism between the old and new faiths.

Who outside the monastic world used or read written works? Demographic evidence for the entire medieval period suggests a thinly populated country with few urban centers and low rates of literacy. The written evidence about schools, curricula, and use of writing remains scant. When the *Primary Chronicle* praises Iaroslav for his love of books—not for nothing was he known as Iaroslav the Wise—it is because he reads the discourses of the prophets and the Gospels, Acts and Epistles, and the lives of the Holy Fathers. This basic list of reading matter remains virtually unchanged from the eleventh century to the Tatar conquest in the thirteenth. Copies of books originally owned by monasteries and absorbed into the library of the Moscow Printing Office rarely have any marginalia before the seventeenth century. The context for literature was more virtual than real until monastic centers spread from the late fourteenth century and expanded scribal networks. The proliferation of writing reflects internal demand and the growth of educated monastic labor. Monks found value in producing Christian works. This may also suggest that the written word had cultural prestige and a certain mystique that was of reciprocal benefit to both the princes and the Church.

Location was also a factor. Many works were composed and recited in the purpose-built churches that rulers hastened to erect and sometimes decorate expensively with mosaics and frescoes. Within the walls of a monastery, services followed the monastic office and a church calendar that eventually became populated by the celebration of domestic saints (and more strictly regulated from 1551 during the reign of Ivan IV. Newly translated and written texts would have been of immediate use for liturgical purposes. The Orthodox Office, or liturgical service, is composed above all of readings from the Old Testament, the Psalms, readings from the prophetic and historical books, and from all the books of the New Testament. Afterwards come the litanies, or special prayers of supplication, other prayers, and finally sacred chants; there are also sermons. During the sermon, or the readings of saints' lives, and during the chanting, the worshippers remained standing. Out of the depths of darkness there mysteriously flickered the faces of saints, the Virgin from the wall paintings or mosaics. Surrounded by these images and symbols, the crowd of men and women with heads covered out of respect, crossed themselves numerous times and pressed forward toward the main focal point of the church, the Iconostasis.

Monks were both readers and listeners depending on the offices and occasion. Illiterate worshippers flocked to monasteries to attend services and hear tales of holy figures who later in Russian culture would be revered as the righteous (*pravedniki*).[60] For shorter accounts similar to Western breviaries, monastic readers could also turn to the *Prologue* and its lections organized according to the fixed feasts of the church calendar.[61] Copies of the *Prologue* contained the lives of Byzantine church individuals, to which new stories about later Kievan saints (Feodosy, Boris and Gleb, and Prince Mstislav), together with homilies and proverbs, were added. Daily readings of this shorter type, sometimes only a paragraph in length, reinforced the images of saints depicted in icons and frescoes. These readings contained translated excerpts from saints' lives that were read out to monks during their mealtimes.

Kievan clergy used their new written language for a small audience of the elite comprised of warriors and traders as well as the newly formed clergy. In practice, the literary function of language did not exist separately from religious and political ideology. As Simon Franklin observes, "princely power and ecclesiastical authority complemented each other."[62] The disciplinary context in which a new grammar and rhetoric for the Slavic vernacular arose was entirely ecclesiastical, offering no exposure to the European medieval systems of learning and critique out of which other vernacular traditions of scholastic commentary, translation, and writing developed. From inception—and therefore not as a result of the Turkic invasions of the thirteenth century—the uses of writing in East Slavic lands had a narrower theological purpose and well-demarcated ideological bias. None of that meant artlessness, however.

Within this dual elite literary audience, the two groups of readers shared a single body of reading. Princes who wished to be thought pious and learned relied on monks to supply prayer books and chronicles (sometimes finely illuminated). The church exercised strict oversight of the production of prayer books including primers containing the religious offices made up of psalms and prayers. On two occasions—in the 1540 to 1550s and in the early 1650s—the "correction of the books" constituted a major cultural episode as tsar and patriarch, the head of the Russian Orthodox Church, collaborated to eradicate evidence of corruption, whether copyist errors in the reproduction of prayers or vestigial aspects of the Greek rite.[63] Outside the royal domain, most magnates relied on a chosen monastery for places of prayer rather than building their own chapels or engaging in the expensive purchase of books for their private performance of liturgical office. Textual production surged in Moscow from the fifteenth century; and in the sixteenth century a printing press run by Ivan Fedorov (*c.*1520–83) inaugurated print culture. The idea of being literate as its own good, however, would not gain any traction even among the power elite until the late seventeenth century.

Scribal culture and the author function

The copying culture of medieval Russia (i) is essentially accretive and iterative, until the sixteenth century when the emergence of Moscow as a super city-state smoothed out local stories; (ii) distributed material impersonally to scribes whose collective activity and voice impersonate the authority of the institution, normally a monastery. Few writers represented themselves, although sometimes individuals signed in their own name usually in polemical works and epistles about dogmatic disputes, such as the monk Savva who wrote in the second half of the fifteenth century.[64] Scribes generally professed no authority and achieved faceless anonymity. No life of an author can be found in medieval Russian texts before the seventeenth century. Scribes exerted their power over the meaning of a text through editing rather than by making overt commentary, and by collating and merging versions within larger collections. In an area in which translation and copying are dominant, the author function yields to these scribal ideals.[65] Crucially, copyists do not announce the editorial strategies contained in texts such as lengthening, shortening, reordering, and interpolation that infiltrate an authoritative view. Intentionality and initiative show through the selection and addition of new texts.

The category of "author" is problematic in a world that largely assigns agency to institutions and presents works that are compilatory and anonymous. Scribal practice and manual copying, a technique rather than an art, dominated the production of texts, in consequence militating against an idea of authorship, channeling the notion of writing into a much narrower and monolithic set of practices. By definition, intentionality remains latent or disabled. And because authorial intention is neither transparent nor ambivalent, the impersonality of writing produced as a system seems calculated to eliminate the potential for irony, contradiction, and viewpoint. In Western Europe, clergy and Humanist scholars dedicated their learning and skill to the explication of the Christian literature, while the scribes of medieval Russia did not assume an exegetical purpose.

Within works, monks as a rule do not use a word for author, but instead use the verbs meaning "to write" and "to copy out." In the *Primary Chronicle*, the word *pisets* (writer, copyist) occurs only once. The medieval term signifies not just a writer but also an authority, whereas the modern Russian *pisatel'* has no such immediate connotation and is not an accolade indicating intrinsic worth.[66] A. J. Minns has noted that in England and France in the thirteenth century, a series of terms came to be employed in theological commentaries that differentiated the literary activity characteristic of an *auctor* from the activities of the scribe (*scriptor*), compiler (*compilator*), and commentator (*commentator*).[67] No such job descriptions appear relevant in the Russian context where, until the fifteenth and sixteenth centuries and the growth of a centralized bureaucracy, most if not all scribes would have been monks and clergy. While Nestor's *Life of Feodosy* contains much personal statement, the first-person speaker represents his own activity not as creation but as an act of direct mimesis in which language reflects the inner and outer reality of events and their spiritual significance. Trust in the action of writing obviates reflection, as there would be in Western medieval thought, on language as a problematic and unstable medium. In the *Galitsko-Volynskaya Chronicle*, composed originally in the thirteenth and fourteenth centuries, authorship must have been multiple and multigenerational. But at moments of emotional tension, the scribe is typical because he speaks in the first-person plural and injects pathos in a tour de force of synonyms to express continual strife: "Let us begin to tell of the endless battles, and the great hardships, and frequent wars, and the great number of squabbles, and recurring rebellions, that from the youth of the two princes never gave them rest."[68]

Few scribes will ever draw attention to themselves and comment critically on their own practice, the sort of self-consciousness that can be taken for granted as a mark of modern literature. However, the scribe is not always a neutral vessel whose intentionality remains in check. Despite the primacy of copying, many works aim to convey feeling and have a claim to being read as literature because they show an impressive mastery of expression well beyond the utilitarian communication of a message. While scribes view themselves as custodians of a textual tradition, they also assume responsibility as witnesses to local traditions, news, events, and stories that provoke an interest.

What medieval bookmen thought about their methods for organizing manuscripts, old and new, remains impossible to judge. In referring to their compositions as either "writing" or "copying," scribes of medieval Russia do not rationalize their own practice, but submit naively to follow an implicit acceptance of the influences of previous models for arranging accounts of actions. No tension exists between individual and tradition because works tend to make the achievement of others their subject matter with little attention to the state of vernacular writing as a discursive field.

The anonymous effect of the open copying tradition heavily compromised any opportunity to speak individually. In taking over the works of other scribes, the copyist of a new chronicle or new entries also appropriated standard narrative structures and techniques. The power of the compiler lay in the way that he could hide the manipulation of antecedent texts. Compilers make an unspoken virtue out of the competent consolidation of versions into a near-exact copy or a new version in which new material and possibly new values override textual loyalty as a default mode. Local traditions can powerfully intrude on the handling of material that originates elsewhere.[69] Compilation and copying alleviated the risk of speaking in an individual voice. But not to have mastered correct practice would in itself have been a grave lapse.

Readers of literature inclined to accept the author function that scribes fulfill, and to recognize that the systematic implementation of a genre system is not here a pre-condition of literary writing, can find compensation for modern expectations in the rhetorical and storytelling values carried forward in texts from the eleventh to the seventeenth centuries in works that sustain visions of a land and people (if not yet nation and individuals). It is a mark of the power of writing that within the world of court and monastery users understood that the value of notions about land and people, and religious identity, could not be fully realized until written down. And it is a mark of the power of works that can be called literature that increasingly authors find a voice in which to do so—sometimes the voice has an unemotional quality, sometimes it becomes highly personal as is the case with saints' lives and the autobiographical writing of some rulers. Stories in medieval texts erect a scaffolding from which to display the interdependence of Church and state, ethnic/territorial identity and holiness—and for that reason to serve ideas that become absorbed into nineteenth-century thought and beyond as an ideal of Russia distinct from major secular trends in the modern literature.[70]

Literary identity: Collective writing and singularity

A. J. Minnis, in an important study of the medieval theory of authorship in England and France, has commented that to be "authentic" a saying or a piece of writing had to be the genuine production of a named *auctor*.[71] By contrast, medieval Russia does not discount works of unknown authorship as inferior and intrinsically unreliable: the prestige of a monastery or the princely house from which the works emanated could be sufficient seal of approval. Numerous medieval works have an abiding claim to being literature because of their skill in fusing content and style. The presence of an authorial name does not automatically confer more personality.

Modern discussions of literature take it for granted that voice is the distinctive attribute of the writer and the mark of uniqueness and value. The term "literature" implies the use of language and style to affective ends exceeding a mere informational purpose. To do so requires rhetorical skills. Certain assumptions about an implied reader and reader competence follow: namely, that within each text there is a model reader who exists as both a theoretical ideal within the text and actual historical reader. For these reasons, the question of how appropriate this model of literature is for medieval writing represents a particular challenge in the case of Russia. Where is the voice in the works that have a greater claim to being called literature by virtue of their use of eloquence and personal appeal? While the historical reader has been lost, where is the implied reader to whom these writers appeal?

In practice, writing by definition emphasized the functional rather than imaginative or subjective. Yet there are also many occasions when characters consider their own life story and intentions in relation to their institution and to Christianity. Motivated by the need to bear witness, they capture the effects of their motivation rather than their own subjectivity and self-portraiture. From the start, monasticism was both a culture of self-abjection and emulation of archetypes in order to learn the cenobitic rule by following hagiographical models of conduct. Local pride and the idea of scribal activity as a form of bearing witness seem to inform a more prevalent wish to leave a trace. When composing saints' lives, hagiographers, as a matter of credibility rather than subjectivity, corroborate their endeavor with reference to divine inspiration and proceed with untroubled confidence that their task is to produce a literal record of what they have witnessed. As human authors, they do not express the view that they speak an allegorical language conveying divine intention and theories about causality or assume that because of the divine authorship of the Bible the Holy Spirit moves through its new translators (issues much discussed by medieval theologians such as St. Thomas Aquinas). The human author of the text is the scribal community as a collective, and their authority comes from a confidence in the cenobitic rule of the monastery and respect for the elder. Given the political and administrative appetite for writing, this adherence to literalism looks expected, but it also helps to explain the prominent role of chronicle-writing and narrative exposition.

It is not surprising, then, that the voices that remain compelling are those of the saints, hagiographers, and the Christian homiletics at which mostly Kievan authors excelled. To have "intrinsic worth," a literary work had to conform, in one way or another, to Christian truth. The personal voice was persistently filtered through and interwoven with quotation. There is a tacit understanding among twelfth-century writers, such as Metropolitan Ilarion, that Vladimir's conversion and subsequent actions on behalf of Christianity saw in writing a means of validation, a point that also holds for hagiographers who stake their authenticity as authors on their eyewitness knowledge of pious acts. Many texts remain anonymous works and still use the first-person as a way to represent a collective perspective. Prose narratives such as the "Lay of the Destruction of the Russian Land" ("Slovo o pogibeli russkoi zemli") and the *Tales of the Battle of Kulikovo* (*Povesti o Kulikovskoi bitve*), a narrative cycle on a late-fourteenth-century counteroffensive to Tatar control, make gripping reading because the narrator adopts the tone of an eyewitness experiencing the battle, and makes good use of viewpoint technique. Also memorable are the anonymous but deeply poignant voices in folk genres, collected much later and seen as preserving layers of an authentic culture.

Nonetheless, some authorial names do appear, and writers can touch on circumstances of biography and personal motivation that are more than formulaic (the posture of bearing eyewitness is typical of the writer of saints' lives). Some of the most anthologized writers of medieval Russian are not anonymous. For both the twelfth-century ruler Vladimir Monomakh in his *Instruction* (*Pouchenie Vladimira Monomakha*) and the seventeenth-century religious dissenter (that is, schismatic) Avvakum in his *Life* (*Zhitie protopopa Avvakuma*, 1682), the authority of their names matters indelibly in the impact of confessional statement.[72] The writing of the *Primary Chronicle* serves as a model for a text like Monomakh's *Instruction*, empowered by the sense of historical time conferred on individual deeds by the act of recording them. Similarly, there is a qualitative difference between the performances of Nestor as author of two important saints' lives (both discussed at greater length below). In the *Lection on Boris and Gleb* (*Chtenie o zhitii i pogublenii blazhennykh strastoterptsev Borisa i Gleba*), a narrative work about the martyrdom of two eleventh-century princes who are venerated as saints, and whose cult and image (a typical icon can be seen in Plate 2), originally local in origin, would eventually be adopted more widely across principalities and then by Muscovite Rus', Nestor is author but not an eyewitness, and his synthesis of prior materials creates distance on historical events for the purpose of extracting a religious and personal message.

By contrast, in his *Life of Feodosy*, as is often the case with hagiography, Nestor injects urgency and conviction by adducing details of his personal relationship with the saint, and while some hagiography relies on legend and second-hand anecdote to satisfy the eyewitness function, part of the freshness and enthusiasm of his work lies in the sense that he is experiencing the miracle of Christianity embodied by this man first-hand and for the first time on Kievan soil. The spectrum is not always one of stark contrast. While devoid of self-description,

Ilarion's *Sermon on Law and Grace* (*Slovo o zakone i blagodati*), grounded in the vernacular translations of the time, serves as a reference point and precedent for later statements on the cultural authority of the Church and writing. That sense of authority emanates in the first instance from the conspicuous display of learning that Ilarion makes.

And while learning and repetition could militate against the personal voice, reliance on models afforded access to instant eloquence. How many of Ilarion's listeners would have heard the citations from the Old and New Testaments for the first time as divine utterances rather than learned citation?[73] Preaching was the act of mediating the divine Word through varieties of human interpretation. The equivalent to civic oratory, it required persuasion to instruct the converted and newly saved based on the intelligent selection of Biblical material. In medieval Russia, the oratorical office found in scripture a commentary on contemporary history used to awaken feeling to an unfolding story that promised the cultural advancement of Rus' on a par with Byzantium, and then Rome and Jerusalem.[74] To "spread the word," even to a small elite of Rus' who were probably already convinced, required all the great sermonists from the eleventh to fourteenth centuries to explain the meaning of Christianity to their land.

Most texts do not take literary aspiration as their stated goal. But some works express autobiographical curiosity. An awareness of the boundaries of the Orthodox world shaped one's sense of identity. Travel writing, for instance, contains instances of a singular voice and authorial identity. Each traveler is both a universal man as a Christian and unique as a viewer of new sights. Writing as a means to attesting a Christian life and belief puts a high value on the idea of being a witness to a saint's qualities or indeed one's own. Such manifestation of belief seems sufficient to vouchsafe credibility in giving an impression of individual experience.

CASE STUDY *The Voyage of Afanasy Nikitin*: Self and other

Questions about money and faith, descriptions of man-made marvels, and an adaptable religious identity feature in the account the merchant Afanasy Nikitin produced of the commercial journey he undertook from Tver' starting in 1466 and ending around 1474–75 (the approximate dates have been worked out by historians on the basis of references to fixed religious holidays in the Christian calendar). The *Journey Across Three Seas* (*Khozhdenie za Tri Moria Afanasia Nikitina*) survives in two versions: a copy made in the early sixteenth century and a slightly later, more detailed version from which some references to Islam may have been expurgated. His original aim was to trade in the markets of the Caucasian principality of Sirvan. Pirates, setbacks, and opportunities diverted him to the distant sultanates, Muslim and Hindu, of medieval India, and he extended his route through Chapakur, Sari, Amol, Rei, Kashan, Yezd, Lar, Bender, Hormuz, and finally Muscat and India. Nineteenth-century discussions of Afanasy, reflecting the values of their own imperial age, portrayed him as a remarkable traveler gifted with unusual stamina and vision. More recent accounts pull back from this Victorian portraiture, and identify a financial rather than exploratory incentive as the key to his journey. Arguments about his financial affairs are purely conjectural, and we cannot know for sure whether his ambit encompassed the emporia east of Hormuz out of opportunistic profiteering or because the pressure of debt increased the risks he had to take. Arguably, the truth lies somewhere in between. On the one hand, at least initially, a need to sell goods and make a profit impels him to "follow the money" and pursue his trade expedition beyond his initial plan to work in the area of the lower Volga. He moves further and further from Tver', almost on a market-by-market basis until he has covered a great distance. On the other hand, the very impulse to record his experiences in writing, and the tenacity and unfaltering curiosity he manifests in a work that has more unity than random travel-notes, make him an uncommon sort of merchant.

By the Petrine period, the generic tag *khozhdenie* could denote a travelogue written in connection with secular (such as diplomatic and commercial) or religious purposes (such as pilgrimage), organized chronologically or topically, or written up as travel notes, and recounted with an emphasis on convincing the reader of the reality of the actual journey through sufficient attention to documentary details of time and place.[75] At an earlier period, the *khozhdenie* referred primarily to religious pilgrimages to the Holy Land or monastic destinations, and while an account featured details of actual itineraries, the primary purpose was to give a record attesting the visitation of religious sites, the worshipper's veneration of relics and the strength of a Christian faith that sustained the voyager through sometimes perilous mishaps. From the early days of monastic Christianity in Kiev, monks undertook pilgrimage to the Holy Land, of which the *Paterikon of the Kiev Cave Monastery* gives more than one example. For instance, Nestor notes that it was a journey to Mt. Athos that inspired the monk Antony to find a worthy site for his own Monastery of the Caves in Kiev. The oldest of the Russian pilgrimage narratives is the *Journey of the Abbot Daniil (Khozhdenie igumena Daniila)*. This twelfth-century work describes the journey from Constantinople to Palestine, then newly conquered by the Crusaders. During the two years of his journey Daniil "experienced all the holy sites," a source of pride. Nikitin's journey was never religious in purpose, at least not by the usual terms of pilgrim narratives. All manners of experience attract his attention, engaging a methodical and more than routine interest. He lavishes detail on the experience of the religious festivals and rituals ("the Hindus worship to the east as do the Rus; they raise both hands high, place them on their temples and lie prostrate on the ground and stretch out when they bow down"), dietary customs ("The Hindus eat no type of meat, neither beef nor lamb nor poultry nor fish nor pork despite having a great many pigs") and the attitudes to nudity of these denominations:

> And here is the land of India, and people go about naked, and their heads uncovered, bare-chested, and hair plaited into a single braid. They go about this way when pregnant, and children are born year in year out, and what a lot of children there are. And the men and women both are completely naked; indeed, they are all black. Wherever I go loads of people follow me—they are amazed by a white man. The local prince wears a cloth on his head and another one over his loins, while the local nobles (boyars) place the cloth over their shoulder and over their loins. But the princely servitors, and those of the nobles, wear their loin-cloth turned inside out; they have a shield and sword in their hands while some carry spears, others daggers and yet others sabers and some have bows and arrows. All are naked, all are barefoot, very strong and they do not shave their heads. Their women go about with uncovered heads, bare breasts, and little boys and girls go about until the age of seven with their sex uncovered.[76]

But the journey across three oceans—the Black Sea into Transcaucasia, the Caspian Sea after a stay in Baku, the Indian Ocean after his residence in Persia—also turned into an account of three confessions. This is because Afanasy was an Orthodox Christian who attempted to keep track of time according to the feasts of the church calendar. Yet as he experienced his life among Muslim traders in Persia and India he became acculturated to the practices of Islam, while his interaction with Hindus at a further point in the trip provoked his curiosity about their customs and beliefs.

Nikitin's own behavior fluctuates between adherence to the customs of the Orthodox Christian, who accentuates his Russianness at the beginning of the account, and an increasing propensity to adapt to the ways of Islam. As he moves episodically through his tale he uses quotation to dramatize his encounters with local rulers who speak for themselves. Phrases of Christian supplication ("Lord, my God") trip off his tongue, but increasingly we wonder which deity he has in mind. By the time he marks his sixth Easter on the road, his prayers mix Turkic, Persian, and Arabic phonetically spelled out in Cyrillic. The epithet *greshnyi*, meaning "sinner" or "mortal" attaches to his name five times; initially it is formulaic, but as his itinerary extends in time and space the word intimates his fear that he is losing touch with his Orthodox roots. While there is a clear logic in Boris Uspensky's argument that Nikitin's diminished Christian faith inverts the usual spiritual journey of the pilgrimage tale, a different conclusion would be to observe the degree to which Nikitin proves adaptable to and respectful of other faiths.[77] In May 1470, upon returning to Bidar from the Hindu trade fair at Shriparvati, his perplexed feelings about his loosening memory of the Christian calendar come to a head, and he appears to be in mourning for his religion: "I have forgotten all of the Christian faith." This pattern of partial Orthodox traditionalism and partly unconscious relinquishing of identity cannot tell us definitively whether Nikitin converted to Islam, but it might be read as more than tactical adjustment and temporary concealment that he adopted in order to protect his financial interests. At one time scholarly argument entertained the likelihood that Nikitin had become a convert to Islam, and had even gone as far as undergoing ritual circumcision. Recent views, however, stop short of a conversion narrative and cast his behavior as a combination of sympathy for other faiths with a habit of protective mimicry that would have facilitated the commercial transactions that were ultimately his prime purpose.

Who was Nikitin's readership? Fellow merchants, clergymen, and local scribes, all would be Orthodox Christians, and presumably more at ease with Nikitin's tales of foreign cultures if on returning home and to the fold he made clear his repentance about his partial observance of Muslim obligations, including the confession of faith that "there is no God but Allah, and Mohammed is the apostle of God." Whether he writes for himself or to be read by others, the act of narrating his own story has a penitential and therapeutic aspect. He blames himself for drifting toward Islam. Caught between an imperfect observance of Islam and his precarious sense of Christian identity, he responds to the proselytizing of one Melik, who urges him to get off the fence and choose one religion. The spontaneous nature of his outbursts, rendered in a form of Arabic that he has picked up, suggests that the process of going native has been more profound than just a tactical maneuver. At these moments he moves from being a traveler to being an immigrant. Nikitin expresses his feelings through an interior monologue meant to capture the hard reflection the dilemma causes him ("I thought long and hard about it" ["Az zhe vo mnogya v pomyshlenia padokh"]). Yet his interiorized speech blends Orthodox prayer and foreign expressions, suggesting that conversion is less a matter of religious confession and rather one part of a process of assimilation of the idioms and behavioral norms of another culture.[78] The historians Gail Lenhoff and Janet Martin are persuasive in drawing the conclusion that "he came to embrace Islam in more than token fashion," but the narrative captures how ambivalence, denial, and unconscious conformity characterize the process.[79]

Historians have argued that Nikitin's purpose in extending his journey leg-by-leg was in response to trading conditions in local markets and out of a profit motive. This seems undeniable. Yet to speak solely of purpose would be to ignore the multifaceted quality of Nikitin's writing and his outlook, and to undersell a literary personality marked by drive and curiosity and considerable descriptive gifts. It is, in fact, arguable that the further Nikitin journeys from home the more his commercial purposes recede. Instead, questions of identity and religion in relation to peoples, who collectively embody an Other, occupy the foreground of his story. Nikitin often shifts from a past tense (imperfective or aorist) in setting up a narrative frame to the present. Throughout he maintains the sense that the narrative proceeds in real time as a lived drama; and because the narrative breaks off and is open-ended we might be left with a feeling that the more retrospective moments when Nikitin takes stock of what's befallen him capture a cumulative, ongoing sense of change in a character that has near novelistic roundedness and potential for further development.

Lenhoff and Martin convincingly argue that Nikitin moves with those around him: a Lenten fast blurs in his mind with Ramadan, a prayer for safety that he would have uttered to himself in Slavonic comes out in a transcription of Arabic as a concession to his fellow travelers; a Christian among the Muslims of Persia, he becomes a non-Indian Muslim among the Hindus whose dislike of Christianity he might rightly have feared. Afanasy uses writing as a form of self-analysis, holding up his behavior to his scrutiny. Awareness of his outsider status accompanies increasing evidence of his conformity to local norms. Compliance with local custom might proceed from defensive need. Alternatively, the changes may reflect a genuine blurring of the boundaries of his faith transmuted into a more complex version of monotheism. The process has a spontaneous, unstudied quality that adds psychological complexity to the anthropological distance he tries to maintain in describing practices that look exotic to him. Nikitin's experience of the East coincides roughly with the late Renaissance and the discoveries of West and East that comprise a cultural theme in Italian and French writing. Like a long line of travelers from Herodotus (whose *Histories* he cannot possibly have read in his native Tver´) to the merchant explorers of his age, like Columbus, Nikitin tells a story not only of the conditions of real trade, important as that strand is in his narrative, but also focuses on the shock of discovery and effect of the marvelous. Nikitin's log of observations regularly quantifies effects. Descriptions employ rounded numbers on an epic scale. At a great annual market in Hindustan he sees "twenty thousand horses," while local lords have anywhere from twenty to two hundred thousand soldiers at their command. These "boyars" travel in the greatest splendor with huge retinues of "ten thousand riders," "two hundred elephants, all in gilded trappings," a "hundred trumpet players," and "fifty thousand followers on foot."

As a chronicle of adjustments the *Journey* is open to different readings. Might we see it as a record of a pragmatic instinct for survival? Or might we read it as an account, nonjudgmental, and open-minded, of the multicultural and multiethnic nature of life, economic relations, and culture two centuries after the Tatar invasion, under the Golden Horde, and before the extension of Muscovite rule in the sixteenth century? Rather than reading the outbursts of anxiety about his faith as "religious-lyrical digressions," a known approach, we might do better to see them as in character and part of his metaphorical journey to a less well defined and more personal condition of belief.

Afanasy Nikitin's *Journey* is a story, rather than an essay about questions of cultural identity, which would require more self-consciousness than he displays and a degree of subjectivity well beyond the psychology typically captured in writing of the period. Yet for a writer of his time he displays an uncommon skill in using the first person to transcribe his impressions, his linguistic habits, and to render his states of mind. Those literary qualities are yoked to some implicit assumptions he holds about his own identity. He does not see the entire world as an orderly place governed by the disciplines and rules of his native land. In fact, his awareness of boundaries and the shape of countries bears out Valerie

Kivelson's analysis of how the early modern Russian person conceived of space and location. Positioning is relative rather than absolute, depending on the measurable distances that can be plotted on a journey rather than a map.[80] The spiritual realm of Russia is coterminous with the tsar or prince's dominion but also part of a larger world. The index of Russianness, as used in the *Journey*, is adherence to Orthodoxy, and Russia is the land in which God preserves the Orthodox faith rather than a geographic identity. Otherwise, individuals are labeled according to their city-state, Moscow or Tver′. While it would be anachronistic to speak of Nikitin's outlook as an example of cultural relativism, if we do not see his adjustments merely as cynical ploys that help him fit in, we can surmise that his experience as a merchant has sensitized him to different cultural beliefs and stimulated his interest. Unlike other texts, especially written closer to the events of 1237 (when the Tatars invaded) and then 1380 (when the Golden Horde suffered a defeat at Kulikovo), the *Journey* does not use the standard pejorative binary opposition between Russians as Christians and aliens as "accursed" (*okaiannyi* or *pogany*).[81] It is possible that Nikitin's flexibility owes something to the status of Orthodoxy as a belief system characterized by custom and practice rather than a dogma professed in universities or theological colleges. Nikitin does not struggle with difference as an intellectual matter. His confusion and muddled blend of languages, and of ritual custom, are part and parcel of the persona of the traveler, practical and also aware.

Travelers within Russia, whether in folkloric literature or on religious accounts, underscore the marvels of their own land. Travelers leaving Russia might have thought of their land locally and more largely as a realm governed by Christian faith practiced in its monasteries and churches—and not necessarily a realm apart but rather as a member of the larger Christian world. Early in the twelfth century, the hegumen Daniil, a monk at the Kiev Monastery of the Caves recorded details of his sixteen-month return journey to Constantinople and then on to the Holy Land with a stop at Ephesus. His *Life and Journey of Daniila, hegumen of the Russian Land* (*Zhitie i khozhenie Daniila, Rus′skyia zemli igumena*, c.1107) is full of stories, mainly apocryphal, that he heard in Jericho, Bethlehem, Galilei, and Tiberius. Local information and very detailed attention to the distances he travels add a sense of reality to high points in his spiritual journey as when he is blessed by the Latin monks on Mt. Tabor, while also showing piety by remembering the princes, magnates, and "all Christians" of Rus′ during his prayers. His work was much copied, surviving in more than a hundred copies.[82]

Archbishop Antony of Novgorod recorded his trip to Constantinople in 1200 in a *Pilgrims′ Book* (*Kniga Palomnik*). Because he visited between the Third and Fourth Crusades, Antony was still fortunate to see antiquities and miraculous objects that were plundered later. An accomplished narrator with a tendency to digression, he describes at length the use of relics (drawing attention to the church of Boris and Gleb, the martyred princes whose burial is depicted in Figure 1.01) as well as architectural wonders like the Byzantine basilica Hagia Sophia. In the fourteenth century, Stefan of Novgorod, probably a lay person of some distinction and learning, also traveled to Constantinople in order "to revere the holy places and kiss the bodies of saints."

His account (*The Journey of Stefan of Novgorod, Khozhdenie Stefana Novgorodtsa*, 1348–49), at times physically precise about topography and the location of objects and monuments, conveys a certain fervor and love of detail that communicate the personal impact of the visit: he comments, for instance, that the water in the baptismal font in Hagia Sophia, sourced from the Jordan River, "he finds of unparalleled sweetness"; counts the number of marble columns in the ambulatory (thirty-five), and confesses to a sense of awe ("On the holy Divine Wisdom

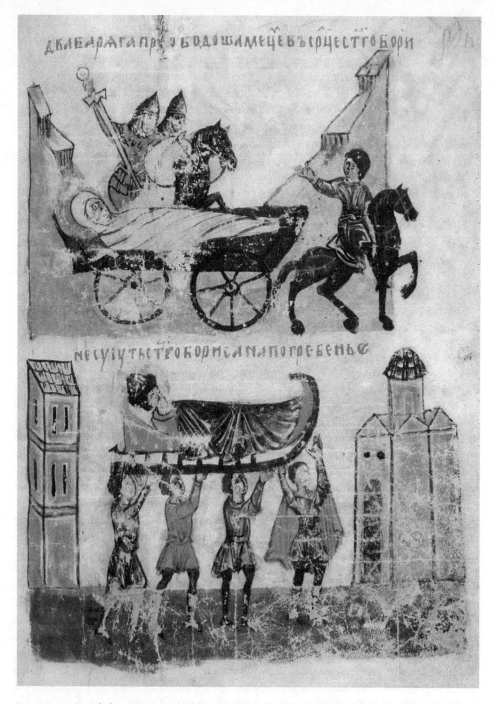

Figure 1.01. Sts. Vladimir, Boris, and Gleb with the *Lives of Boris and Gleb*, first half of 16th c.

the mind does not have the strength to say everything and to enumerate...") and religious admiration for the humility of the saints ("O the great miracle of the saints! We do not have their way of life!").[83]

Kievan travelers to Constantinople and the Holy Land were well aware of the legendary stories about icons that miraculously turned up in these places. Most likely commissioned by the prince himself, the "Tale of the Miracles of the Vladimir Icon of the Virgin" ("Skazanie o chudesakh Vladimirskoi ikony Bogoroditsy") treats the then popular theme of the veneration of icons. The protagonist compares the icon and the love of the Virgin to the sun which warms all the lands of the earth, extending its rays even to new lands and distant peoples, and then tells the story of how Prince Andrei, rather than transporting the icon from his principality to his new city, prayed that it would serve the people of Vladimir, the happy eventuality of a tale which charts the icon's difficult itinerary up the Dnieper River to Rostov.

Despite the determining role of sources, certain works stand out as literature in a modern sense because their use of the first-person is extensive, grounded in an account of experience and having the authentic ring of personal composition (rather than the "I" manufactured by copyists). In chronicle-writing the required technique calls for the mechanical rearrangement of episodes and material in order to alter perspective. In hagiography, homily, and travelers' tales, the immediacy of viewpoint necessary to impart religious faith and respect requires an ability to create a voice and authorial persona. Several prominent works drawn from the period convey how readily authors vent their feeling, for themselves or for their ruler or for their city-state, as a way of crystallizing drama and message. The opening invocation of Ilarion in his *Sermon on Law and Grace*, for example, locates the speaker in a complex relationship to his own time as a Kievan, to Byzantium as an Orthodox Kievan, to Christianity as an evangelist. His display of erudition and quotation from the Bible newly translated into Church Slavonic was powerful proof of religious conviction because it inscribed the history of the dynasty and land within a sacred frame. Ilarion achieves a singular level of literary accomplishment because his speech folds an official message into the language of personal commitment and vision. His rhetoric and image system universalize personal urgency for the benefit of the congregation and later readers (perhaps one reason why the *Sermon* was appreciated later in the medieval period).

When the narrator of the *Lay of Igor's Campaign* apostrophizes the land (in terms borrowed from hymnography), the emotion seems heartfelt and direct. In letters he exchanged with Prince Andrei Kurbsky (1528–83) a noble defector between 1564 and 1579, Ivan the Terrible (1530–84) excoriates Prince Kurbsky in the first person. The style is performative, immediate, and, because of autobiographical information that Ivan adduces, unmistakably personal in content and tone. We are far from the anonymity of much medieval writing. A century later, the Archpriest Avvakum (1620–82) will write the story of his own martyrdom and make much use of personal invective in order to personalize the antagonism of his relationship with Tsar Aleksei Mikhailovich as a cosmic drama of faith and heresy.

It is from within this unity of writing and belief, literature and history, that writers set out their critique of the moral and political disorder that results from human failures attributed more often to sin than the political system itself.

2

Holy Rus´:
Landmarks in medieval literature

FROM the eleventh century, writers began to tell the story of their own and their land's piety within the ambit of court and Church. This chapter discusses the different types of discourse—sermons, saints' lives, forms of autobiography and prayer—that fore-ground the experience of religion as a matter of identity. In the most memorable cases, writers evince a literary quality by successfully creating a voice that speaks to an addressee and reader. Inherent in statements of emotion and self-definition are conviction and hope that writing can demonstrate a prescience about spiritual redemption for the self and a larger community to be set against the myopia of wrongheaded contemporaries. While each writer historicizes his moment, each also aspires to see his life in a wider context of a transcendent Christian narrative and to convey a message about belonging.

The purpose of writing, when it is not purely functional, is to connect the sacred and a vision of the land of Rus´ as a distinctive domain (if not yet a nation state) defined by its spiritual culture and Orthodox Christian practices. This chapter pays attention to this idea of distinctiveness as it develops through some of the most important and lasting works of the period. In the literary landmarks treated here, writers explicitly aim, sometimes through didactic rhetoric, sometimes through storytelling, to capture the experience of the local, the exotic, the miraculous, and the routine as manifestations of Holy Rus´. A foundational narrative of the conversion of Kievan Rus´, revived again in the fifteenth century at a turning point toward Tsardom, makes out of literature a world within which mutually confirming discourses attest the definition of the self in religious more than experiential terms.

Founding stories: *The Primary Chronicle*

Throughout the medieval period, narrative originates in the local. Scribes, monks, and other writers recorded events they witnessed, or copied out and collated accounts that had been handed down; local legends could also provide new material. The coexistence of Christian self-definition and pagan belief, largely glossed over by Ilarion as a transformative myth, per-vades writing until the thirteenth century when rousing antagonism against the invader as Other and unorthodox is heavily accented in historical tales. The tension that erupts in times of historical stress revives a memory of origins. According to the *Primary Chronicle*, Vladimir returned to Kiev and set about creating the cultic center for the rapidly if sparsely Christianizing settlements in the middle Dnieper region. Vladimir began by destroying the various idols, including local weather and agricultural gods Perun and Volos, and the passage Nestor devotes to describing this more than a century after the fact shows him projecting Vladimir's character according to terms used in *Deuteronomy* 7: 5. He corralled the Slavs and Viking dwellers of the forest zone and settled them in new forts in order to protect Kiev from raiders and to secure trade relations. Novgorod was made an Episcopal see, and churches were built in Smolensk and Polotsk, actions that firmly ensconced the new faith (while also strengthening his own dynastic line). Throughout the profusion of detail, names, dates, and locations, or legends, folktales, and mythic plots, an important connecting thread and literary component in the *Primary Chronicle* is the conviction that Holy Rus' is its own civilization, sometimes threatened, sometimes graced, sometimes historical, and sometimes magical, protected by a sovereign and the Orthodox Church.

An important, often overarching theme in different forms of writing, including the sermon, eulogy, and chronicle, is the baptism of Rus' and its adoption of Christianity as a historic moment that elevated Rus' and then Moscow as the valid successors to the status, culture, and sanctity of the Eastern Empire of Rome, a new Jerusalem and seat of spiritual enlightenment. The monks of Kievan Rus' became themselves engaged in producing an explanatory narrative in proto-versions of a chronicle account that would become the basis for a cornerstone of historical study of early Rus', the *Primary Chronicle*.[1]

For the writers of the twelfth century, the use of Church Slavonic, a written language rooted in the Old Russian vernacular, signified a new historical moment. Linguistic presence legitimated the claim that Christianity has been transmitted to Rus' with the purpose of spiritual and cultural enlightenment. The chroniclers gave retrospective importance to the conversion of Princess Olga (r. 945–c.963) whose journey has been analyzed by historians as an attempt to gain status in striking a better trade deal with the Byzantines: her conversion was part of a very public political maneuver. Yet among legends about the dissemination of Christianity her private conversion in 945 or 957 AD stands out because she associated herself sacramentally with the rulers of Byzantium.[2] The chronicler qualifies the impact of her initiative through a metaphor: "Like the moon in the night, she shone amidst the pagans, she was like a pearl lost in the gloom." Byzantine sources record that by 967 the Rus' had accepted a bishop from Byzantium and that Constantinople delegated an archbishop to Kiev in 974. Dmitry Likhachev, the eminent medieval scholar, hypothesized that a now-missing chronicle on Kievan Christianity recording Princess Olga's conversion in the tenth century was probably written in the mid-eleventh century in the Kiev Monastery of the Caves.

It is unclear when systematic chronicle writing in Kiev began; it may date to the second half of the eleventh century. The *Primary Chronicle* relates in chronological order the establishment of the founding of Rus', the origins of the ruling dynasty from Viking traders and warriors, their values and their conversion to Christianity, their works, founding of churches, defense of the realm, and ultimately their consolidation of power in the interests of their faith and people.[3] As the story is told, and in the manner of Byzantine chronography, there is an opening account of the creation of the world. Initially, much attention goes to the description of the rivers that delimit the territory inhabited by the Greek and Varangian traders who travel down the Dnieper from the Black Sea (called by its Greek name "Pontus"). The geographic overview also looks outward by noting that "from Rus' one can sail along the Volga to the Bulgars... and down the Duina to the Varangians and from the Varangians to Rome, and from Rome all the way to the tribe of Ham," anticipating precisely the itinerary and worldview of a later traveler like Afanasy Nikitin.

While the spotlight remains firmly on Rus', the narrative situates the newly Christianized country within a friendly international context stretching from the Byzantine Imperium across to France through central Europe all the way to Scandinavia. Ruled by families of princes who are shown to have shed blood against foreign invaders and for their belief, guided by active monasteries and their scribal and missionary practices, straddling Byzantium on the East and the Carolingian lands in the West, the world of Rus´ appears part of a shared cultural heritage that is broadly Christian and in the case of this new empire distinctly Orthodox.

Despite its multiple authorship and omnibus nature, its unity of style and tone of great conviction make the *Primary Chronicle* gripping reading. A perfect example of the complexities of the open-text tradition described above, it accommodates within the progressive historical framework numerous modes, such as hagiographic episodes, battle scenes, prayers, proverbs, and sermon-like asides. Complex language and psychology, hallmarks of modern literature, do not inform the chroniclers' project. But the work is not just a dry recital of facts and dates. The opening excursus on the rivers of southern Russia anticipates the importance that a nineteenth-century historian such as Vasily Kliuchevsky (1841–1911) will give to geography as a factor in the creation of the state. As in the manner of Herodotus, the father of history whose work influenced the Byzantine chroniclers, the *Primary Chronicle* dwells on the transition from the pagan to the Christian as a matter of belief systems, ritual practices, and institutions. Many paragraphs treat changes in burial procedures, for instance, and there are conscious attempts throughout to use detail that is realistic and memorable, a principle of storytelling that dramatizes the eyewitness account and combines distance and closeness. Its aesthetic of distanced perspective on the remote and recent past creates a sense of profound trust in the unfolding of events that does not want for drama. Conviction stems from the writers' sense of history-in-the-making that deserves to be told because events confirm the wisdom of rulers and monks in the service to the clan, people and, above all, religion. The manner of observation is undemonstrative and seemingly objective. Viewpoint will be not so much a matter of how a story is told as what has been included and excluded.

Didacticism is implicit rather than outspoken, but nobody can doubt that episodes are chosen in order to place events within a Christian framework. After all, the writers are monks, and history remained an art of storytelling with only the loosest sense of cause and effect and scarcely an analytical function outside the mundane. The fact that bad rulers come to bad ends or cause discord scarcely requires great moralizing. By contrast, rulers and monks who preach cooperation and abet Christian acts are inevitably labeled "very wise" (*premudryi*), the meaning of which praise is exemplified by an extended discussion of King Solomon. While there are no grand recapitulations, the editorial voice can be relied on to convey quiet enthusiasm when things go well and to reward the good and condemn antagonists.

In narratives contained within the annalistic framework of a chronicle, storytelling tended to be forward-moving and linear. The organization of manuscript sections satisfied an intrinsic recognition that at a minimum tales must have a beginning and end. Sections can begin with a date and then in several hundred words related in the aorist (past) tense deliver an account of an event that has a beginning, middle, and outcome, often followed by a short moralizing coda to make the point. The organization of narrative according to discrete units such as chapters or smaller segments also lent suitability to the material for teaching purposes. It was axiomatic that while writing should be orderly, it was also susceptible to expansion for the sake of dramatic effect. Between the structural positions of a beginning and an ending, sometimes newly demarcated by a copyist who interpolates material, the episodic nature of many narratives made it easy to add new content.

The introduction of episodes for the most part follows a set formula, giving date, followed by a main verb and subject ("In the year 6606 [1098]. There came Vladimir, and David and Oleg to meet Sviatopolk, they met at Gorodets and made peace").[4] Yet the writers often employ more diverse means both structurally and rhetorically and display consistent sensitivity to the shaping of episodes for dramatic effect. Some variation occurs through an expository aside, for example, "let us return to what we were saying earlier."

The writers of the *Primary Chronicle* know how to use surprise and ironic twists. Episodes are sometimes composed as dramas of discovery, as in accounts of miracles in which the impact of the miracle is focalized through the tale of a non-believer, as we see in the narrative of the transfer and reburial of the relics of Boris and Gleb. Disinclined to credit them as Christian martyrs, the local metropolitan shows contempt at the burial site only to be overwhelmed by a demonstration of their relics' divine power. Closure shows greater variety than openings: vignettes can add with the conclusion of the action or an additional comment or a longer reflection. We find an example of the last type immediately after the events told under the year 1098 in which peace is concluded and the character of Vladimir Monomakh is discussed more generally. Having made peace between his sons, the ruler earns the praise of the chronicler:

> Vladimir was full of love: he bore love for the metropolitans, the bishops and the priests; most especially did he love the monastic rank and file, and he fed and sustained those who approached him as does a mother her children. When he saw anyone misbehaving or in some shameful situation, he did not condemn them, but behaved towards all with love and calmed them down.[5]

The point of the chronicle's moral evaluation is to stir emotion and corroborate the veracity of the narrative.[6] For instance, in writing about the Monastery of the Caves, the chronicler wishes to commemorate the tenderness of a future saint, dwelling on a story of how the young Feodosy washed and dressed the infirm founder Antony. The story takes both of these future saints out of the realm of the holy into the human roles of elder and caring adept. Yet the divine remains present, says the narrator, repeatedly commenting on the saint's spiritual drive as a capacity "to pacify the soul through all manner of restraint and to mortify the flesh through work and devotion." Or consider the victory of the Polovtsians, a Turkic tribe of the steppe, over Prince Iziaslav. Praised in the *Primary Chronicle* as a founder of monasteries, he was killed, as the entry for 1078 notes, on the third day of October:

> [T]hey took his body and transported it by ship...and the entire city of Kiev came out to greet him; putting his body on a sled, they took it and priests, monks accompanied it with the singing of songs into the city. But the singing was inaudible because of the great lamentation and the cries, for the whole city of Kiev wept for him.[7]

Another didactic and narrative technique employed in the *Primary Chronicle* is the use of Biblical parallels. Interpolated tales from the Old Testament suggest analogies between the past and the present (a comparison that Ilarion will develop extensively). For instance, in the dramatic account of how the Israelites departed to the Promised Land, the writer identifies a parallel between the Kievans and the Israelites as new peoples. The chronicler closes his account by underscoring a belief in history as storytelling to suit a divine purpose. This message articulates for the first time one of the major narrative themes of the period: namely, the endorsement of rulers who serve the interests of Rus' rather than their own ambitions by promoting their clan (*rod*), supporting the monastery, and showing commitment to their faith. The *Primary Chronicle* also establishes a second tenet of the contemporary value system by identifying divine retribution as a form of justice. This assumption about religious redress becomes an automatic reflex, occasionally expressed in a set of binary oppositions pitting the Russian and Christian against the heathen who tends to be external and diabolical (as the narrator says "men unstable in their beliefs were seduced by devils, as used to happen in previous times").[8] Even so, the *Primary Chronicle* is not relentlessly normative in touting the values of a newly converted population. While it condemns the Polovtsian practice of polygamy, and forms of incestuous coupling among other peoples as examples of one among a variety of forms of uncleanliness (*nechistota*), it acknowledges that the people "adhere to the law of their fathers."

Local practices give evidence that the assimilation of Christianity has been gradual and that personal belief rather than dogma instilled an affinity with the saints. An important story of the transfer in 1115 of the relics of saints Boris and Gleb, grandsons of Vladimir slain by a disloyal brother, provides a more official perspective on the dissemination of religion by naming key personages, describing ritual practices, recording charitable acts and prayers delivered, and noting how processions worked. The connection between national destiny and religion becomes the subject of extensive treatment by Metropolitan Ilarion. His sermon, later quoted in fifteenth-century Muscovite texts as an exemplar of Christian vision, can be read as much as a showcase for the art of rhetoric as for its fusion of ideology and history.

CASE STUDY **The *bylina* and Russia's magical kingdom**

Liturgical writing, monastic scribal culture, and historiographical narrative cast Russia as a Christian realm and inheritor of the theology and literary traditions of Byzantium. Outside this domain of learned culture there also existed other forms of literary expression that reveal another dimension to national identity. With all its wealth of artistry, the medieval Russian literary heritage is almost wholly concerned with the lives of saints and pious men, with devotional legends, prayers, sermons, ecclesiastical discourses, and chronicles in a monastic vein. From the eighteenth century, when Mikhail Chulkov (1743–92) anthologized popular songs, to the researches into the *byliny* undertaken in the 1920s, the recovery of an "authentic" oral culture emanating from the Russian laity has comprised an important strand of literary and cultural studies. Although the idea of using the written word for secular poetry was thoroughly alien to the early Russian tradition, medieval texts do feature popular storytelling and bear the influence of folklore.

The most ambitious and extensive of popular narrative forms is the *bylina*, or heroic lay.[9] A style of oral and, arguably popular, origin and transmission, this mode is classified as one of a number of folkloric genres, including the fairy tale (*skazka*) and lyrical song (*liricheskaia pesnia*), that began to attract anthologists' interest largely from the eighteenth century.[10] Genre labels are unquestionably retrospective and anachronistic although useful for the modern reader. The term *bylina* is a scholarly invention of the 1830s, taken by the amateur ethnographer and folklorist Ivan Sakharov from the reference in the first line of the *Lay of Igor's Campaign* to the "heroic tales of another time" ("byliny sego vremeni"). Among the singers of these historical songs, the texts were known as *stariny*. The first transcriptions of these works are no earlier than the seventeenth century, made by the Englishman Richard James during a commercial trip to Russia in 1619–20. From the eighteenth century we have the anthology of seventy *byliny* compiled by Kirsha Danilov, about whom little is known apart from the fact that he worked for one of the Demidov family who had mining interests in the Ural region.[11] Transcriptions of the *bylina* from a wide geographic range covering virtually all of Great Russia have been preserved, but it is only in northern Russia, the areas of Arkhangelsk, Olonetsk, the Onega region, and parts of Siberia that the active transmission of *byliny* continued into the twentieth century. Substantial documentation and editions of these *byliny* were made by Soviet folklorists in the 1920s and 1930s who interviewed and recorded the performances of numerous bards (*skaziteli*) most of whom were peasants.

In the 1860s, a school of analysts intent on preserving the fairy-tale basis of the *bylina* argued that a fundamental mythological basis had been overlaid by a historical stratum and thus given it a more contemporary veneer. At the end of the nineteenth century this approach gave way to the view of a historical school that argued that the form developed independently, and that features normally associated with the fairy tale represented later contamination rather than a genetic link. In his classic *The Historical Roots of the Magical Fairy Tale* (*Istoricheskie korni volshebnoi skazki*, 1946), Vladimir Propp had initially maintained that the *bylina* evolved from fairy tales. He and Boris Putilov backtracked on this theory in later editions because they discerned no genetic relationship between the fairy tale and heroic legend. They argued for the independent development of the *bylina* and the fairy tale from a common mythological source. Others, like the Formalist critic Viktor Zhirmunsky (1891–1971), agreed with this conclusion but argued that historical material in the *byliny* implied a more recent origin.[12]

Where the heroic tradition ceases, many of the usual formulas and sometimes even entire plots are taken over from the epic song by the fairy tale. For instance, Vladimir, the favorite sovereign of the Russian heroic songs, eventually takes his place in the fairy-tale tradition. In his retinue we find the leading Russian valiant knight (*bogatyr*, from the Persian *bagadur* "athlete"), Ilya Muromets, a peasant's son, as well as another popular hero, Alesha, son of a priest; his historical prototype, Aleksandr Popovich, was mentioned in the *Primary Chronicle* under the year 1223 as being among the knights killed by the Tatars. The epic tradition ascribes to Alesha the victory over the dragon Tugarin, a poetic reflection of the Polovtsian chief Tugor-Kan, and the fairy tale recounts this story.

As a matter of convention it has been customary to classify works according to the principalities in which they occur: Kiev and Novgorod, hiving off the mythological *byliny* into separate groups. The *byliny* grouped as a Kievan cycle revolves around Vladimir, Grand Prince of Kiev who is a composite figure rather than a single ruler. He never functions as a hero, but serves to trigger the action. The works in this cycle sing of heroes such as Ilya Muromets, Dobryna Nikitch, and Alesha Popovich, who protect Russia against invaders, monsters, robbers, and brigands; these would include the *byliny* with a more overt historical context that recount fictive victories against the Tatars, for example, "Ilya Muromets and Kalin-tsar'" and "Vasily Ignat'evich and Batyga," all undatable. By contrast, the Novgorod *byliny* pursue commercial adventure and social strife between clans, more overtly making use of fairy-tale motifs combined with a sometimes frank depiction of merchant guilds.

Formally, the typical structure of the *bylina* is in three basic parts: an introduction, a narrative portion, and sometimes an epilogue. Some *byliny* also have introductory verses (*zachin*). Most introductions of the Kievan *byliny* describe a feast at Grand Prince Vladimir's palace where the heroes boast, and one is given a task to fulfill. Propp observed that in the *skazka* the imposed task never involves a fight with a dragon. This is not necessarily true of the *bylina*. Both genres exhibit an essential pattern: the inactive king imposes tasks upon the hero, and the hero carries them out with a donor's assistance. The linkage between difficult tasks and the struggle with a dragon (as depicted in the iconic image of St. George in Plate 3) is understandable in the *bylina* epos. As a rule, the lay aims for the heroic, and victory over a dragon satisfies this plot requirement.

As in fairy tales, the plot structure has a wish-fulfillment element in pursuing a hero who must prove his worth through the performance of tasks. In the *bylina* the narrative follows the accomplishment normally of a single task, whereas, in the fairy tale, the hero faces three trials before he can succeed. Historical personal and place names are present throughout the *byliny*, but these works tend to feature fairy-tale, rather than historical, names. And while historians of popular culture and social historians have in the past mined the heroic tales for details of the mentality and cultural and religious practices of the medieval world, the fact is that toponyms, distances, and time frames are sometimes invented, unstable, and often approximate, and can change between variants of a single plot. For instance, one of the most celebrated epic tales is *Ilya and the Robber Nightingale* (*Ilya i Solovei Razboinik*) which currently exists in nearly fifty variants, all of which are very close but vary on points of topography, small factual details, or stylistic finish. In many versions, the adventure of the hero (or *bogatyr*) ensues after he has freed a city from a heathen attacker, but the name of the besieged city varies: Chernigov, Cherniagin, Sebezh, Smoliagin, and others. Similarly, in all versions the hero enters the city and is greeted as a conqueror, but the identity of those receiving him changes: sometimes judges, sometimes warriors; sometimes he accepts hospitality, but most often refuses and simply demands to know the way to Kiev. In all versions, the function of this moment is to cue an account of the Robber Nightingale. Here again descriptions of the Nightingale vary. Some versions concentrate the warnings about the dangers awaiting along the path in a monologue, while others distribute them as signs perceived throughout the journey. Those signs themselves can fluctuate: for instance, a warning whistle might be sounded two or three times. Sometimes the earth rumbles under the might of the Nightingale, rivers roil, forests creak; sometimes the Nightingale sits on a single oak branch, sometimes straddles three; sometimes his weapon is a whip made of a serpent; while the news of Ilya's victory may be either believed or received with skepticism by Prince Vladimir and his retinue. Only in about twenty variants, all attested in late sources from the seventeenth to the twentieth centuries, does the miraculous acquisition of a weapon occur. The hero does not need a supernatural source of power; the fact that he is an epic hero is justification enough. In other cases, the amazed and overjoyed residents open the gates and triumphantly march out to greet Ilya, asking him who he is, and offering him gifts: keys to the city are brought to him on a golden platter and he is asked to remain as governor or prince and "to rule as tsar, to assume the saddle, to drink and eat his fill, and to scatter alms." Initial confrontations between the hero and the adversary employ the typical fairy-tale theme: man versus dragon. However, in the *skazka*, the hero always kills the dragon rather than risk another confrontation. The *bylina* epic hero may let his opponent live. Unlike his fairy-tale counterpart, the warrior hero is sufficiently sure of himself to be generous with the adversary.

Despite the variation in detail, whether through omission or new elaboration, the plot outline, major tropes, and use of the quest motif remain fixed in storylines. The variations seem to reflect either the accidents of memory, as new recitalists and bards picked up tales, or choices made about how to enhance the dramatic effect of a recitation for a local audience. Characters, too, are unchanging no matter the circumstances. In producing effects of enjoyment and astonishment, the *bylina* does not recognize complex, human reactions. The heroes are remarkably goal-oriented and dauntingly worthy; their entire nature, their literary DNA programs them to pursue the quest, and their course of action is determined by the conventions of the genre with little room for chance interruptions. Enemies tend to be gross—in *Dobryna and the Dragon* (*Dobrynia i zmeia*) the evil creature is "as large as a cloud"—and heroes becomingly modest, chaste, and comely.[13]

Both in the heroic lay and the fairy tale, heroes can be born miraculously or naturally; the former are predictably brave, invincible heroes who require no donors while the latter are helpless without an external source of magic. In the fairy tale, the hero encounters a donor who bestows on him the gift of a magical weapon once he is away from home; whereas in the heroic lay, the donor meets the hero in his own house. Unlike the miraculously born hero, the *bylina* protagonist often obtains an agent from the donor, which he utilizes to his advantage. Every male fairy-tale hero must have an external source of prowess, be it a gift or a miraculous birth; whereas the epic hero does not need such a source. The origin of his epic strength is his epic status. The fairy tale denies altogether the value of human prowess. In the case of *Dobrynia*, the whip his mother gives the eponymous hero is not miraculous; the cap of invisibility (like the German fairy-tale *Tarnhelm*) is faulty. Despite the resemblance to the miraculously born fairy-tale hero, the protagonist of this epic also resembles a naturally born hero by triumphing through his own skill.

A clash on the way to the quest is another essential component in testing the hero's mettle. More often than not the triumph is surprisingly easy and a surefire proof of the virtue and superior quality of the *bogatyr*. When the battle lasts longer, as in the case of Dobrynia who requires three days to vanquish the dragon, it only serves to magnify the epic ordeals. And when his strength proves to be unequal to the challenge, the *bogatyr* can also call on his native cunning to outsmart the foe. We see an example of the value of cleverness in the example of the wise virgin exemplified by Fevronia, the heroine of a sixteenth-century tale by Ermolai Erazm of Murom. Fevronia, who both asks and answers riddles, serves as a wonder-working healer to the local prince and eventually earns renown as his royal consort.

The structure of the *bylina* subordinates most functions to the syntax of a plot that puts the hero through his paces in the fulfillment of the quest function. Secondary characters, such as the donor of a wonder-working weapon, make only cameo appearances as they facilitate progress to the next episode. In certain cases, such as *Ilya Muromets* and *Ilya and the Robber Nightingale*, all traces of the fairy-tale pattern of hero, donor, and magical agent have vanished. Instead, the hero performs ceremonial actions before engaging the adversary. Given the tendency toward fixed plots and characterization, the variety, entertainment, and pace of these tales lies in their visual brilliance, rhythmic energy, and manipulation of formulaic phrases within stylized conventions. For instance, depictions of nature in the *bylina* fall into a pattern of stock images, including: (i) description of a garden, where the character or characters of a song are found; (ii) description of a meadow where the characters are located; (iii) description of a tree under which the characters are found (this last description is further complicated by images of: a grave; a well near which the character is found; or a horse); they might also substitute (iv) the motif of the "bird in the tree" for a house. In all these cases the descriptions maintain a principle of contraction in which the visual field zooms in rapidly on the locus. There is a comparable patterning and visual dynamic in the representation of the dwelling place, which follows a progressively organized description of a bower, yard, cabin, room, or tent, or a table set for a feast. On occasion, the speaker might home in on a woman in the bower and describe embroidery, an image of intricacy that might be thought to be self-referential. Such contraction formulas omit links in the progressive series of descriptive detail.

All types of *bylina* make use of dialogue, although it has been argued that the action-driven heroic *bylina* minimizes verbal exchanges. Direct speech often serves to initiate new lines of action, while dialogue precedes a hostile encounter. Less frequently, as in the Sea King's speech early in the Novgorodian tale "Sadko," speech summarizes events before they unfold. The folklorist Margarita Gabel has argued that, unlike in the fairy tale, in the *bylina* dialogue contributes more to the ordering of the narration because it focuses on the reactions of the listeners within the tale to the events that have already become known to the reader.[14] Dialogue can be anticipatory and make use of prophetic speech (such as the bones that speak in the heroic narrative of *Vasily Buslaev*). The repetition of stories or themes in the form of a narrative recapitulation using direct speech (often to bring a new participant up to date) constituted structural echoes that probably served as mnemonic devices but also provided a cumulative, layered texture. Students of folkloric works have produced detailed taxonomies of features such as dialogue; the presence of symmetry in speeches, including antithetical parallelisms; and the use of formulas or commonplaces, such as stock epithets and phrases that are used to describe a banquet table, battlefield slaughter, or precious objects. Stock epithets prove to be detachable from the storylines and can migrate across all plots. Words in combination with their stock epithets usually lose their specific meaning and acquire an indefinite quality. Thus, for instance, the adjective "deep," when modifying "river," does not denote actual physical dimension, but rather conveys the idea of a river in general, or is simply part of the emotional lexicon of the work. Yet despite that general tendency, a phrase containing a stock epithet may be sometimes disassociated from its concrete meaning to such an extent that it assumes the character of a symbol. For instance, one recurrent motif is that of a black raven that is all-knowing and reveals crucial information to the characters. Another is the "thick shrub" connoting the place of death of people who have met a violent end. Generally the meaning of the portent is not explained in the text, but becomes apparent from the narration.

Other forms of expression that descend to the medieval period, such as bardic narrative, oral tales, folklore, and fairy tales, combine the bookish and the popular, the written and the oral, the pagan and the Christian, and cast Russia as a magical realm. It is necessarily the case that this body of storytelling, while oral in provenance and presumably ancient, survives only in subsequent written versions. Modern researchers in ethnography and folklore studies have tried to recover authentic versions from the contamination that inevitably accrues through copying and transcription and even from recordings.

The sermon: Ilarion and the chosen people of Kiev

Early Kievan bookmen were amazed by their own newness, dazzled and triumphant at the very fact that the inhabitants of Rus´, through conversion and the acceptance of book-learning, has emerged into sacred history. In his *Parable of the Body and the Soul* (*Kirila mnikha pritcha o chelovechstei dushi i o telesi*), written in the mid-1160s, the preacher Kirill of Turov (d. 1182) says that reading divine books keeps one away from thoughts of glory (*slava*). This is also one of the main themes of the *Sermon on Law and Grace* by Metropolitan Ilarion. Metropolitan Ilarion was born in Rus´; he remains an outstanding intellectual figure of his time. Evidence concerning his life is scant; he appears to have begun his career as a priest in Berestovo outside Kiev where he served at the Church of the Holy Apostles, named after a great church in Constantinople, the traditional burial place of emperors. Simon Franklin suggests that Iaroslav's patronage of the Church of the Holy Apostles was certainly a feature of his program of architectural and cultural emulation.[15] The *Primary Chronicle* noted that Prince Iaroslav extended patronage to bookmen, scribes, and clergy. We cannot say whether Ilarion was one who benefited directly, but he lends his eloquence in paying tribute to Iaroslav's cultural ambitions and Christian piety. Steeped in both the Old and New Testaments, Ilarion must have acquired a considerable knowledge of the Byzantine homiletic and exegetical tradition.

The sermon was written and delivered before he became a metropolitan; internal evidence allows scholars to fix a date before 1051, but the references to the construction of St. Sophia make it difficult to establish the precise occasion for which the sermon was produced.[16] Ilarion refers to Kiev as the "city of the most glorious Holy Mother of God, a speedy helper of Christians." The comparison of the city with the Virgin as speedy helper occurs elsewhere, including the liturgy of the Intercession of the Veil of the Mother of God (*Pokrov*, that is, the Feast of the Mother of God). However, Ilarion is not specific about the venue where the sermon was read, with possibilities ranging from St. Sophia, owing to the majesty of the theme; the Church of the Annunciation, because of the echoes of the gospel story of the Annunciation; the Church of the Tithe, where Vladimir was buried, since Ilarion seems to have it before him; or to the Church of the Holy Apostles. Similarly, it is impossible to pinpoint the exact sources of Ilarion's work since they come mediated through a series of exegetical traditions, and parallels can be drawn between the imagery he uses and those found in numerous patristic writings.[17]

The *Sermon on Law and Grace* shows breathtaking aspiration in formulating the religious ideology of Kiev. The aim of the sermon is to explain, and pay tribute to, the status of newly converted Rus′ in sacred and temporal history, and to celebrate the achievement of Vladimir. This first vision of succession will be re-elaborated in the much more ambitious form of a concept of *translatio imperii* in the sixteenth century, namely when, following the fall of the Roman and Eastern Empires, theorists positioned Russia as the Third Rome and the seat of Christendom.[18] The splendor of the sermon's form and message are inseparable and make it a consummate literary work. Its meaning lies in a sophisticated deployment of analogy, extended through allusion and repetition, and a vivid use of apostrophe.

The central method, and idea, of the *Sermon on Law and Grace* is the juxtaposition between the faith of the Old Testament with that of the New Testament, while the organizing structure of the *Sermon* is the binary opposition between the new and the old. Ilarion's achievement was to translate conceptually the past and present of Rus′ into the terms and structures of the Christian hermeneutics of typology. He also successfully translated into highly correct and expressive Old Church Slavonic many quotations from the Septuagint, the Greek version of the Old Testament, and from the Gospels, including passages from the Psalms, the Book of Isaiah, and the Gospel of St. John. His sermon erects a verbal monument equivalent to the architectural aggrandizement of Kiev undertaken by Grand Prince Iaroslav.[19] Ilarion, like Iaroslav, is an heir to and cultural representative of Vladimir, whose conversion to Christianity he lauds. Ilarion proves himself to be a master of a full panoply of prosodic, syntactic, and verbal techniques. He uses syntactic and sound structures with an eye for symmetry and pattern so that paragraphs, sentences, and phrases echo with anaphoric repetitions and rhetorical questions, doublets and triplets of word and clauses, agglomerations of balanced antitheses, and assonance and alliteration. He also makes ample use of similes and epideictic tropes, seeming to point to the congregation before him and to the physical space where he stands, in order to heighten the sense of the present as a timeless moment in the history of Christianity and a historical moment in the development of Rus′.[20]

The argument of Ilarion's lengthy sermon unfolds in three stages: theoretical, historical, and personal in a final encomium. In the first stage, Ilarion explicates the course of sacred history as expressed in the progression from Law to Grace, or from bondage to freedom, from the Old Testament to the New, from Judaism to Christianity. To illustrate his point, he adduces the story of Hagar and Ishmael, and reads the tale literally as an account of the origins of different religions. He then rereads it in the manner of a scholar as a prefiguration of the New Testament account of the different paths taken by Judaism and Christianity. This typology-based exegesis is a classic form of early Biblical criticism and Christian theology, and a rare example of commentary in Kievan Rus′.[21] But Ilarion is concerned not just with demonstrating the static fulfillment of a prophecy but also with its presence in history. On this view, Vladimir's acceptance of Christianity is not an arbitrary decision made in a restricted location at a restricted time; rather it is an integral and essential part of the divine plan for mankind. Ilarion presents Vladimir's decision as unprecedented—and inexplicable except through divine Grace. According to Ilarion the future Christianity of Rus′ is latent in the Old Testament story of Hagar and Sarah. The relative belateness of the actual conversion, however, is not a sign of inferiority. Historians have detected clear parallels between the praise of Iaroslav in the *Sermon* and other monastic texts that treat the personal role of the sovereign in restoring harmony to the state and to stabilizing its governance, and they underscore the moral and intellectual qualities displayed by Iaroslav in his reign as the deeds of a philosophical, wise ruler—precisely the image crafted by Metropolitan Ilarion as he addressed Vladimir's sarcophagus in the encomium that closes the sermon.[22]

The use of epideictic rhetoric makes the visual field seem real and visceral within the sermon itself. Clearly, Ilarion sees his work as a monument equivalent in words to the deeds it extols, and—the medium being worthy of the message—he regards the effect of his own style as a powerful proof of the success of Vladimir's mission. Ilarion's eulogy reflects Vladimir's legitimate status as a ruler in the Kievan hierarchy, but also elevates his mission to that of the Apostles and places Rus´ at the same level as the first Christians.[23] Vladimir's accomplishments live on through the works of the current Grand Prince Iaroslav.

Having summarized the Christian credo based on the precepts of the fifth-century Council of Nicaea, Ilarion turns to the destiny of the people of Rus´. In his eyes, when the Kievans adopted Christianity they became equals of all Christian peoples, including the Greeks. He regarded the Russian Church as having the same dignity, status, and rights as the Byzantine Church. The *Sermon* may have an element of wishful thinking in investing the efforts of a newly established Church and its few members with the ability to sacralize the power of the prince of Kiev (thereby strengthening the links between churchmen and the ruling house) through the canonization of Vladimir, whose lasting achievement as founder of the dynasty is the conversion of the Kievans. Ilarion is the spokesman of this ideal who hails Vladimir as a "new Constantine."

The encomium admits surprise at how unexpected Vladimir's conversion was since, unlike other emperors, he was born a pagan. What allowed him to find the true, righteous path was his reason and intelligence, and it was in these qualities that divine Grace found its instrument. His personal conversion was in effect inseparable from that of his subjects, and it was achieved by a combination of intelligence and ultimately through his authority. The climactic description of the conversion confers on Vladimir the spiritual distinction typically associated with saints: from the question of Vladimir's distinguished birth to his performance of miracles; his belief in Christ as something miraculous; his piety and charity; his likeness to the Roman Emperor Constantine the Great as a fellow builder of churches; and his miracle works achieved through his successor, Iaroslav. In the final address, Ilarion plays on the theme of the Annunciation: as the archangel said to the Virgin, "Rejoice, for joy is given you," so it could be said to the city of Kiev.

In celebrating Iaroslav's foundation of the Cathedral of St. Sophia, Ilarion affirms that the ruler has only undertaken an enterprise that had already been foretold, more or less, in the story of Solomon who completes the Temple in Jerusalem started by King David. Ilarion moves beyond typology into history, concerned not just with the use of prefiguration of the New Testament in the Old. The New Testament shows the meaning of history, but it is not the end of history. Just as history is prefigured in time, so it is fulfilled in time. Just as Isaac superseded Ishmael, and Grace superseded Law, so, in time, the Christianity of the gentiles superseded Judaism; and so, toward the end of time, Rus´ also becomes Christian and supersedes the Byzantine faith. Thus Vladimir's initiative to bring Christianity to Rus´ was not an arbitrary act of a local, late-tenth-century ruler; instead, Ilarion casts it as a vital moment in sacred history and as a part of the providential plan for mankind. Whereas the writers of the *Primary Chronicle* also give credit to the Church, monks, and scribes for the consolidation of the conversion, Ilarion mobilizes his learning to pay tribute to the dynasty and a single ruler whose newfound piety and baptism make him nearly divine, even while an everyman in the eyes of Ilarion's parishioners. The Grand Prince and his family found themselves not only at the center of the ecclesiastical institution but in the midst of its sacramental life. Until the late fourteenth century, there will not be in the Russian lands a more spectacular demonstration of the role of eloquence in the establishment of the piety of the ruling house than the Encomium to Vladimir. It was, however, not long before narratives of Christian teleology gave way to meditations on the hazards of actual history and defeat through disunity.

Because the pedagogical history of early Rus′ remains largely lost, there is no basis on which to make generalizations about homiletic practices on the whole. Yet Ilarion is not the only master of eloquence. The legacy of works attributed to Kirill of Turov a century later suggests that a high level of oratory could be attained by a local preacher. Scant biographical information comes from an account of his life written in the thirteenth century that has survived only in fragmentary form. It dates his life as a monk to around 1169, noting that he corresponded with the Grand Prince of Vladimir, Prince Andrei Bogoliubsky, from 1157, and died in 1182. Kirill of Turov served a parish near Kiev and flourished approximately in the 1160s. His literary remains comprise three works of Biblical exegesis (including the "Tale of the White Cowl and Monasticism" ["Povest′ o belom klobuke"], much copied in the thirteenth century), a number of prayers, and nine sermons written for feast days. He also wrote many parables based on Biblical subjects; these allegories are devoted to the cause of promoting monastic asceticism and, like Ilarion, Kirill employs typology to identify those elements in the Old Testament that appear to prefigure the religion of the New Testament. His claim to renown rests with the nine masterpieces of homily composed for various dates in the church calendar.[24] Medieval compilers anthologized Kirill's sermons alongside classic texts from late antiquity, a proof that he was regarded as no less a master than the Church Fathers and other Byzantine authorities, such as Gregory the Theologian, a fourth-century writer, and Theophylact of Bulgaria, the Bishop of Ohrid, a great commentator on early Christian texts.[25]

The Russian medievalist Igor Eremin divides Kirill of Turov's sermons into two groups: first, works composed originally for the twelve main feast days of the Orthodox calendar, and second, those written for the Sunday service beginning with Easter.[26] Both groups of works were written with the worshipper in mind, to be delivered in front of a congregation during a service, and each sermon addressed an aspect of the holiday on which it would be given, explaining its significance and origin. It is this sense of immediacy that lends Kirill's rhetoric an unusual liveliness and energy, for, as he says more than once, his goal is to adorn the holiday, to "praise, hymn, aggrandize and adorn in words" the service. A sermon by Kirill of Turov resembles a series of scenes, or thematically linked word-pictures, often using typological comparison, rather than a continuously unfolding story.[27] His sermons seem to be organized into interconnected units, or what Eremin called "rhetorical tirades," treating discrete points of the argument, rather than flowing as a seamless whole. A tirade is an elaboration of a sub-theme, usually with the use of a recurring construction or phrase. There is no logical end for each tirade, and the transitions can appear abrupt. For Kirill, artful variation is a way of exhausting a theme and giving it the emotional impact he seeks.[28] A relentless logic of argument is a prominent feature of his style.[29] As commentaries on Biblical texts, Kirill's works deploy the art of persuasion to demonstrate the cohesiveness of his own argument and the coherence of the inner meaning. His sermons aim to bring events to his listeners, by reliving them in the cycles of the liturgical year. The rhetorical key to Kirill's sermons, the trope that he learned from his readings of Byzantine literature, is that of amplification. It is never enough merely to announce a theme; rather, he delights in synonymy, parallel syntactic constructions and carefully maintained symmetries, as in the prominent use of anaphora, as well as repetition through morphological rhyme and consistency, creating an elaborate syntax that will be imitated during the literary revival from the late fourteenth century, when Kievan writing is remembered and quoted.[30]

Kirill is the most explicitly intellectual of writers. He has a distinct worldview and strives to create a sense of the cosmos in his work. References to the mind are frequent as he contemplates the world as a miracle of creation, referring to existence as a miracle and mystery. And because one is unable to understand fully the miracle of creation, he finds all the more reason to exhort himself and his fellow monks to "praise and sing and glorify the Lord."[31] By virtue of the voice and style, all rhetoric, of which the homily is a particular type, aims to affect the listener, to move, to outrage, to stir, to spellbind, or to humble through the application of sophisticated stylistic devices and arguments. This is literary writing in a way that chronicle-writing is not. The aim of a sermon is to create in the celebrant a sense of universal unity in joy and collective involvement.

The prayer: Daniil Zatochnik

Hagiography and stories of monks are highly productive forms of life-writing which, like chronicles, can capture self-expression that seems lived and spontaneous rather than scripted by the conventions of institutional devotion. Authors can also detach themselves from matters of ideology and from ecclesiastical institutions. No awareness of inner psychology or goal of self-knowledge operates here—the Rus´ were not, after all, readers of St. Augustine in the twelfth century any more than Russians read Montaigne in the sixteenth—but writers do follow a very human impulse to "narrativize" the story of their emotions. Prayer created instances of voice, and serves as a particularly clear example of how writing can conjure authorial identity. The worshipper is both a universal man and a unique individual. Prayers, usually brief and lacking formal or rhetorical complexity, occur infrequently in medieval Russian writing outside the more formal hymnography used in the liturgy. The petition of Daniil Zatochnik stands out as a rare example because the writer is unusually expansive and also unusually explicit about the nature of his appeal to both his prince and to the Lord.

Little is certain about the authorship (one writer or two?) of a work profusely copied in two similar versions differentiated by title as the "Speech" ("Slovo") and the "Prayer" ("Molenie," c.1213–26) ascribed to Daniil Zatochnik.[32] The troubled speaker, who describes himself as young, regrets the better life that he has lost through a series of misfortunes. In highly rhythmic language, he petitions "his prince Iaroslav Vsevolodovich" for personal help.[33] He rouses the prince to action through verbal enthusiasm: "Let us trumpet the reason of our mind like a gilt horn / And let us start to beat the silver organs in the weavings of our wise words." Initial vanity about his powers of eloquence suggests that he feels that the privilege of writing to a prince and being heard is his by entitlement. The directness of expression, a sense of humor, a gift for aphorism, and a sense of literary style evident in the well-formed phrases and apposite use of erudite quotation and parable, mark both texts (which differ largely in respect of title and one interpolated section).

The precise cause of Daniil's downfall is more touched on than explained, but like a Slavonic Timon of Athens or Job, he notes that he has been cast away from the princely table and now "wanders poor and scorned." Eloquence matters a great deal because, he says, that while everyone heeds the rich man, the poor man will be, he says, despised. Repeatedly, Daniil apostrophizes his addressee ("O Prince") whose "friendly love" he seeks, and while he fears the prince's scorn, he places his trust in a ruler who will perhaps regard him the way a mother does her child. He makes remarkable use of the device of personification by casting the prince's imagined responses in sections of dialogue saturated with bookish metaphors and Biblical allusions.[34] The author's heart is a "face without eyes," and his reason like "an owl atop ruins." The poverty that assails him is "like the Black Sea of a pharaoh," but even as he writes, the shame he feels at his confession impels him to flee writing "just as the slave Hagar fled her mistress Sarah." And while he musters his eloquence like the "reed of a bookman-scribe," proud of his "quickness of tongue," he feels shame and fears that, "like the cursed fig tree" (mentioned in the Gospels of Mark and Matthew), his work will be fruitless. There is a painful directness to his appeal at its most trenchant and exposed ("Save me from this destitution") that makes this among the most personal and vivid monologues in the entire medieval period and a high point of literary artistry in terms of emotional effect. Daniil manages to capture the plight of an individual who has the qualities of an everyman, directing his eloquence toward the divine as attainable. That sense of religion as its own reality, accessible through scripture, expressed through worship, and practiced in ritual, is also the purpose of hagiography, the most extensive type of life-writing used from Kievan Rus´ well until the early modern period.

Hagiography as life-writing

A sacred realm requires saints and ethical teaching, and this section examines storytelling that suited the talents and vision of local scribes and their monastic and political masters. Saints were omnipresent in the medieval and early modern world. Works about the monastic life in Old Church Slavonic, translated in the Slavic lands outside Kiev in the 900s, included collections of tales from the lives of monks and hermits, known as the *Lives of the Desert Fathers* (*Apopthegmata Patrum*), and another collection of tales known as *Roman Paterik* (after Pope Gregory the Great, its compiler), translated into Greek and then into Old Church Slavonic by John of Rila. From the eleventh century to the end of the medieval period in the seventeenth century, one constant in Russian political culture is the association of the power of the ruler with the defense of Orthodoxy. Given the low levels of literacy among the lay population, including the political elite, very few people would have been able to read the works produced in centers of copying. But from a functional point of view, it is clear that writing provided abundant material to be read aloud and heard in monasteries, churches, chapels, and at burial sites often within a setting, whether in St. Sophia in Kiev or in the Church of the Assumption in the Kremlin of the fifteenth century, richly decorated by icons and frescoes as visual equivalents of sacred texts. And from a symbolic point of view, the writing was a means to recording, copying, and commemorating local people as saints; or to rendering significant events as turning points in the history of a ruling house or in the promotion of Christianity. These uses reflected a sense of mission. Writing brought the "good news" of the status of Holy Rus´ by confirming that since the conversion of Prince Vladimir the land had acquired its own saints, pious preachers, and Christian rulers.

The transition from the pagan culture of the Varangian princes of early Kiev to the acceptance and promotion of Christianity was an essential condition for the rise of a written culture from the tenth century. Pagan practices undoubtedly continued, and references to the pagan gods in saints' lives, chronicles, and other texts suggest that Orthodoxy was the faith of an urban, ruling elite well before it found complete acceptance at a popular level.[35] In the apocryphal story known as *The Virgin's Journey through Hell* (*Khozhdenie Bogoroditsy po mukam*), Church Slavonic versions of which proliferated from the eleventh century, the Virgin intercedes on behalf of sinners who profess to praying to pagan gods. (*The Virgin's Journey through Hell*, copied well into the eighteenth century and first published in full by A. N. Pypin in 1856, is an example of a medieval text that entered into the popular imagination: Dostoevsky's hero Ivan Karamazov mentions it in an argument about godlessness.)[36] Early versions of the lives of saints such as Boris and Gleb pay some attention to topography, since the location of the princely cult in a parish was clearly of crucial importance. Later hagiographic narratives, such as the *Life of St. Stephan of Perm* in the fourteenth century and the work of the Archpriest Avvakum in the seventeenth, often turn out to be attempts at mapping sacred space. For a missionary and church founder, just as for an evangelical dissenter, no place could be more spiritually charged than the site of the church or the place of martyrdom.

The veneration of the saints became an important feature in writing from the twelfth century onward. Ideology in itself could not secure the future of Christianity. The agency of living worshippers was required to transform the hope and aspiration of the leadership into the institution that the cult of the saints became. How reading and writing contributed to the inculcation of new religious belief is unclear. Yet from the start, political power and writing were closely intertwined with the spread of Christianity. Hagiography as a form of sacred life-writing treats the biographies of famous priests, patriarchs, monks, and founders of monasteries who have been recognized by the Church at the local level (at least before the sixteenth century). The saint's life (the Slavonic word *zhitie* is a cognate of the Greek *bios* and Latin *vita*) combines biographical narrative and Christian narrative as exemplified in the tales, parables, and miracles of the New Testament.

The origins of Kievan hagiography have been the subject of some speculation. Byzantine theology transmitted the Christian aesthetic of the imitation of Christ from the early Church Fathers, and elaborated it further.[37] It is unclear whether the Kievans directly followed the examples of Byzantine hagiography in Greek or whether they read Bulgarian versions or gradually worked out a version of hagiography based on their knowledge of Byzantine biography and Christian dogma. Monks knew some of the more significant Byzantine *vitae* also in Slavonic translation.[38] Written no earlier than the twelfth century and built on translations of Greek texts about fourth-century saints, the founding narratives of Kievan Christianity back-dated stories of their own devotion and the interests of a clerical elite to an earlier period about which little hard information now remains.

This monastic ideal, set out in the influential long and short rules of Basil the Great (c.329–79), taught the emulation of Christ as an archetype of piety and virtue whom the monks strove to emulate. The role of spiritual biography was both to commemorate the devotional qualities of the heroes and to circulate information about their achievements in order to attract more recruits to the monasteries. Just as icons preserved the visual memory of the saints of the past, so hagiography was a form of literary icon, or a verbal picture of its subject. And just as the icon provided a summary of the attributes of the saint, hagiography also aspired to portray in words the salient points of the subject's vocation in relation to accepted norms of spiritual behavior.

Hagiography historicizes its subject by flattering the local culture that fostered the saint but also dehistoricizes it by putting the saint in direct line with the values of the evangelists, early Christian martyrs, and even Jesus himself (and in the Orthodox tradition saints were almost always male).[39] In this way scribes created a parallelism between their own narratives and the Gospels, between their own protagonists and Christ. The product of this operation was the Christian saint, the new hero, whose individual life story was transformed into a *mimesis Christou* (imitation of Christ) and a revelation of the other, supra-historical reality that became manifest in history through the mystery of the Incarnation.

For this reason, there is often considerable difficulty when we read saints' lives in disentangling any kind of historical reality from the idealized spiritual portrait, and the essentially didactic nature of the genre must be borne in mind. The commonplaces of hagiography must be regarded as a supplementary rhetorical repository from which the individual hagiographers selected their phrases, combining them into continuous accounts of their saints' childhood, adolescence, ascetic achievements, death, and glorification according to the norms of the genre.

And because references in the *vitae* to a historical reality outside the text so often turn out to be conventional, it is difficult to infer conclusions about the hagiographer's personality and the genesis of the *vita* on the strength of the text alone. The key idea is that Christ represents "the model of the Christian" and that his perfect imitator will be the ethical holy man who lives according to his precepts; or the martyr who follows him in his suffering and reproduces his passion in himself. In telling the story of a pious man, the hagiographer works toward the elevation of his subject in conformity with the divine prototype of Christ. In the *Life of Antony* (*Zhitie Antoniia*, c.1234), Antony's sanctification takes the form of a gradual approximation to the divine. His *Life* describes a journey that ascends from an earthly present to a higher state, on the threshold between life and death, joining a larger, divine whole. Through imitation of the Christological archetype, achieved largely by reading and absorbing the example of the *zhitie*, the monks in theory internalized the features of the model, in turn becoming worthy of imitation as images of that divine ideal (much like the theory of icon painting which perpetuates a stable portrait of the Apostles). It was traditional to compose the lives of the pious, particularly in monastic communities, soon after their death or within several generations, as in the case of the Kievan priest Nestor's *Life of Feodosy*. The tradition stretched back to a fourth-century work of late antiquity, the *Life of St. Antony*, founder of Egyptian monasticism, one important model for hagiography in the monastic workshops of the Slavic lands. The Bulgarian hermit John of Rila (later St. John, 876–946) recommended in his *Testament* (*Zavet*, 941) the *Life of St. Antony* as the archetype for the anchoritic life, and stressed the ascetic style of monasticism, the importance of eschewing wealth, while praising manual labor as a value and showing no hostility toward cenobitic monasticism.[40]

Medieval Russian foundation accounts of monasteries rarely dwell on the physical settings or draw attention to the distance between the outside world and the cloister (unlike later works, such as Tolstoy's story "Father Sergii," a story of an aristocrat who adopts the ways of hermetic monasticism). Epifanyi Premudry, writing in the first quarter of the fifteenth century about St. Stephan of Perm's missionary work, notes how Stephan, accompanied by a young novice, "walked round many places in the forest" and when they had "found a place of emptiness in the groves where there was water," built a cell, and "chopped down trees" for a "small church."[41] Extensive lives of saints like Stephan of Perm or the earlier Feodosy disregard nature, garden, trees, or even village architecture, suggesting that while pilgrims abroad were expected to recount the exotic, the gaze of monks at home was directed inward. Here the emphasis was on individual tranquility in which each monk developed his own relationship with God and fought with his own spiritual strength against the onslaughts of demons.[42] The lives of such figures were often retold in anthologies in which isolated hermits are the heroes. Whereas St. Antony and his disciples led the lives of anchorites, the hagiographer Cyril of Scythopolis immortalized Palestinian monks who organized their lives between the communal ways of the monastery and the contemplative solitude of their cells. The monk Nestor, the most important of the Kievan hagiographers, used St. Cyril's works as exemplars for his *Life of St. Feodosy* in promoting a communal ideal of monastic life instead of the solitary retreat of the hermetic tradition.

Saintly models were to be found among monks and holy brethren (while martyrdom is much less prominent than among the early Christians of late antiquity).[43] The aim of the biographer was to recount to the world (*povedat' miru* is the formula), the life, and the deeds of the hallowed figure and preserve his name. Hagiography, as a form of sacred life-writing, combines biographical narrative and Christian narrative as exemplified in the tales, parables, and miracles of the New Testament. Generic flexibility remains a key principle in the blend of biographical narrative and scripted martyrdom or elevation. Novella-like stories, dialogues, letters, encomia, miracle tales, and visions, are strung together on a simple additive principle or integrated into higher, more complex structures. Typically, the composition of the *vita* often follows a fixed biographical pattern adopted from the Byzantine template, through the main events of the saint's life; its aim is teleological, showing in each chapter a stage on the way to holiness. The *zhitie* moves through (i) the prenatal, the family background, and provenance; (ii) birth; (iii) childhood and education, during which time the saint is usually modest and precociously pious; (iv) awakening spirituality, when the youth becomes disinclined to play games or do the usual juvenile things, while the youthful saint's relationship with his family will be strained; (v) early manhood, when he discovers his vocation, goes out into the world to perform charitable acts and missionary work; (vi) longevity and the manner of his death. Despite the developmental structure, character often seems fixed in the womb (as in the *Discourse on the Life and Teaching of our Blessed Father of St. Stephan, the Bishop of Perm* [*Slovo o zhitii i uchenii sviatogo ottsa nashego Stephana, byvshego v Permi episkopa*]). A saint's life can be framed by a foreword (*prooimion*) and an afterword (*epilogos*), sometimes followed by a section containing either an account of the saint's life and spiritual accomplishments or a eulogy.

Characterization is one important criterion in the genre. Hagiographical heroes fall into three main types: the Apostles, who were the first witnesses to the Christian faith; the martyrs, or "blood witnesses," who suffered death for Christ's sake; and the confessors, revered for their quest for individual perfection and for their "bloodless martyrdom." Hagiographical texts may be classified in a similar way: a martyr story (Latin *passio*; *athlesis* or *maturion* in Greek; *strast'* or *muchenie* in Slavonic) focuses on the arrest, interrogation, and death of the hero. The central part of a martyr story is a dialogue between the hero and his antagonist, the pagan interrogator. While there are fewer martyrs for the faith than founders of churches and pious clergy in medieval Russian literature, some memorable examples exist. One notable martyr is St. Leontius of Rostov whose *vita* (*Zhitie Leontiia Rostovskogo*) generated many copies (well over two hundred) throughout the period; each of the versions added further examples of miracles performed at the site of the tomb. A bishop of Rostov, Leontius was an eleventh-century missionary who left Kiev to evangelize in the area of Rostov and was killed. An original short legend composed in the twelfth century was titled the "Discovery of the Glorious Body of our Saint and Father Leontius, the Bishop of Rostov" ("Obretenie chestnogo telesi sviatogo ottsa nashego Leont'ia, episkopa Rostovskogo"). This piece (included in a synaxary) generated more elaborate versions that dramatize the discovery of his relics as the miracle that marked the building of the Church of the Assumption in Rostov in the 1160s. These works also associate a local ruler, Prince Andrei Bogoliubsky (*c.*1111–74), with him faithfully.[44]

The New Testament provided another narrative model in the stories of the Apostles that deal with their acts and journeys. These accounts acquired a paradigmatic significance for the subsequent literature about the lives of the confessors of the true faith. They represent the struggle of the holy heroes to gain eternal bliss through a pious existence, in contrast to the sanctification of the martyrs in the blood-baptism of death. As experienced in life, miracles indicate divine presence and participation among the living. Posthumous miracles can confirm the apotheosis of a saint and encourage deification. Miracle tales were essential to the didactic function of the work, also giving proof of local cultic practices. They could be added to virtually any biographical material, whether a single episode such as a story of martyrdom or a fuller life, and could sometimes be longer than the basic biographical core. No fixed formula determined the size of these parts in relation to one another. The eulogy of the saint (in Byzantine hagiography, sometimes a separate piece of rhetoric called the *enkomion*), might also feature miracle tales. These disparate parts did not necessarily dovetail seamlessly, but that did not vitiate the purpose of a work that attested belief in the righteousness and ongoing presence of a saint. In the early Kievan period, the editorial titles of works reveal the synthetic nature of their composition: examples of formulaic headings such as "lection and passion and eulogy" (skazanie i strast' i pokhvala) or "martyrdom and saint's life" (muchenie i zhitie) can be found in a compilation like the Muscovite Uspensky Sbornik. The zhitie and the concluding encomium differ in the emphasis and choice of protagonists' exploits. Chronology structures the biography. In an encomium, a form that can also stand on its own, the exploits of the protagonist are not arranged chronologically, but according to the various forms of virtue they represent.

Sometimes the entire conclusion of a zhitie is written in the form of a laudation, and such epilogues will recount numerous miracles, attesting to the presence of the saint among the worshippers. One exception that proves the rule to the pattern, for instance, would be the fifteenth-century life (in two stylistically disparate versions) of the monk Mikhail of Klopsk ("Zhitie Mikhaila Klopskogo," c.1453), which does away with biographical narrative and focuses on posthumous miracles of a local Novgorod saint (perhaps not without political undertones, since it was written after the conquest of Novgorod by Moscow and the dissolution of its monastic lands).[45]

In practice, hagiographers adapted the style of writing to the institutional context, the development of a local cult of worship, and their own literary competence. Scribes identified where in a larger svod or annalistic and liturgical convoy to position text about a holy man. Saints lives could stand on their own as separate items pegged to the church calendar or be part of a larger set of stories relating to a specific location associated with the saint or related to a theme treated in adjacent material within the manuscript book or codex.[46] The literary forms of telling the saints' stories varied from a summary to a gigantic documentary (as in the Story of the Life and Teaching of St. Stephan of Perm). The function, or the educational and liturgical purpose, influenced formal choices. The life, deeds, and miracles of a saint could be presented in a highly stylized, concise, and formulaic manner for the liturgical service (sluzhba) or reading (chtenie) by incorporating modes familiar from other subgenres, like sermons and chronicles. Biographical material could also be presented in a more elaborate and detailed form such as a short narrative (skazanie), a eulogy (pokhvala), or a separate passion account (passio strast'), or more modestly a prayer (molitva). Scribes could then incorporate these shorter forms, which had been copied separately into monastic compilations, into new larger works.[47] Often, types such as the pokhvala or molitva could be incorporated into oratorical compositions, for example, the section in the Sermon on Law and Grace in praise of Vladimir Sviatoslavich. The compositions of a hagiographic text could also depend on the type of literary collections it might enter. Lives were included in collections such as the Prologue, menologies, and the paterik. The Prologue and synaxary are collections of short hagiographic compositions arranged according to the calendar of saints. Menologies (or Slavonic mineia) were religious anthologies read on the feast day of each saint and arranged chronologically. Early Russian hagiography imported to Kiev the Byzantine model of the paterica, or lives of the fathers (Slavonic pateriki) (from the Greek paterikon, plural paterica). A paterik is a type of anthology made up of novella-like stories. Some of the best and most popular examples of medieval Russian hagiography are in the Paterikon of the Kiev Cave Monastery (Kievo-Pecherskii Paterik), which provides examples of monks who lived as hermits (whereas Nestor's Life of St. Feodosy, with its repeated addresses to "brethren," often mentions the monastery as the heart of Christian communal life).

While ecclesiastical function could be a determinant of form, there have been fruitful attempts to see an emotional authenticity within the stylized immanent features of the genre.

A distinctive feature of Dmitry Likhachev's method is his concentration on the emotive impact of the *vita* as a demonstration of the author's attitude toward his subject as an act of tribute to a figure whose deeds reverberate in current monastic life (and beyond). In this respect, Likhachev differs from scholars like Varvara Adrianova-Perets, who is primarily interested in tracing a historical course of events in the texts, or Nikolai Trubetzkoy, who lays particular emphasis on the hagiographer's didactic intention.[48] Ultimately, this tension between the historical and the moral approaches may lie in an antinomy between two systems that was identified by Igor Eremin: on the one hand, the factuality of official records which is in itself devoid of poetical meaning; and, on the other hand, a system of literary conventions that permit a "constant transformation of reality" on the model of a given set of ideals.

Saints' lives played a role in creating and sustaining the institution of the monastery, and while not all saints may have led entirely virtuous lives, monastic founders well into the seventeenth century were suitable subjects of life-writing because of the institutions they established. While martyrs for the faith would continue to be regarded as saints, and memorialized by hagiographers, within the Russian Orthodox tradition monks predominate, revered for their devotion to a new life in the spirit. Religious devotion thus often meant not the abandonment of human relationships, such as family feeling or friendship, or the discarding of claims to leadership in society, but recasting them in a different, spiritually orientated context.

Saints alive

Hagiographic collections

Common themes in saints' lives include the struggle of the monks to focus single-mindedly on ritual devotion; the tensions between the political practices of local princes and the monastic rules; and the temptations of monks who fall prey to the fantasy of imagination from a love of reading and stray from the monastic ideal. Time and again, hermits and holy fools (such as Isaac the Cave-Dweller, the priest Simon, the monk Polycarp, and the *hegumen* Akindin) will see their faith tempted; will be put through trials of the flesh and emerge triumphant:[49] Stories tend to be laconic, visual, and highly emotive. The perpetuation of the monastic ideal serves as an underlying purpose of collections in which the pious seem to live in both the real world and an endless Christian continuum that extends to the beginnings of Christianity. The overall effect is to reinforce the message, also prominent in other works like the *bylina*, that the land of Rus´ is a sacred space in which the newfound adherents of Christianity express the will of providence. This is a message that will echo through masterworks of medieval literature from Ilarion's panegyric to Ivan the Terrible in the mid-sixteenth century.

Translated *pateriki* incorporated versions of the *Spiritual Meadow* of John Moschos, the *Lausiac History* of Palladios of Galatia (the *Egyptian Paterik*), the *Sayings of the Fathers* (*Azbuchno-Ierusalimskij Paterik*), and the *Sinai Paterik*, a seventh-century collection that may have been an influence on Russian hagiography in the Kievan period (as attested by surviving fourteenth-century Bulgarian recensions). It was a mark of confidence in both the establishment of Christianity independent from Byzantium and their mastery of storytelling that the monks of Kievan Rus´, and later of the northern monasteries, devoted their energies to authoring original anthologies that documented the independent existence of early Kievan spirituality and monastic life. Patterned on Byzantine collections, such as the *Sinai Paterik* (produced at a scriptorium on Mt. Sinai), the *Paterikon of the Kiev Cave Monastery* was for Russia a seminal collection. It absorbed sets of tales about a generation of monks who lived as hermits before the establishment and confirmation of the cenobitic order by the Byzantine spiritual leaders,

Antony and Theodosius, in the eleventh century.[50] Early Kievan writers, whether Byzantine émigrés or natives of the region, showed great skill and inflected their early portraits with local color, detail, and character, merging a patristic ideal with a sense of individual merit. Research suggests that while initial compilations arranged individual tales and lives in chronological order, over time, the absorption of different layers of material, including new content such as sayings and teachings, favored accumulation over chronology in the shaping of the monk's portrait. Material was grouped and reordered around an outstanding clergyman. Different versions of a life could also include smaller forms, like short lections, prayers, and sermons, which were available to copyists who could transfer material verbatim or sometimes modify the source (even within traditions of copying certain rules of openness allowed for variation and innovation).

Unlike a saint's life or *zhitie*, which follows a single subject from cradle to grave, *paterik* stories tend to illustrate one aspect of character and concentrate on a single side of life. Episodes can be arranged as cycles around a figure or a theme such as the dangers of temptation and ways of combatting it. Local legends, gossip, and unverified stories (many of which were apparently collected by the monk Simeon [d. 1226] whose versions were incorporated into early versions) shape the character portrayals, a combination of diverse materials for which the modern term "intergeneric" seems suitable, since texts are confected out of biography, historical anecdote, memoir, and invention. Often, different tales are adduced to illustrate a single theme. For instance, episodes in one of the earliest of translated *pateriki*, the *Sinai Paterik*, depict a world in which the forces of good and evil are constantly struggling for people's souls and in which the righteous are not merely pious, but pious to the point of exaltation.

The *Paterikon of the Kiev Cave Monastery* and the *Paterik of the Volokolamsk Monastery* (*Volokolamskii Paterik*), two of the most important and most widely copied collections, contain significant cycles of tales about the choices of single individuals to become monks and pursue the cenobitic life.[51] Implicitly, this choice looks like a repudiation of the desert monasticism that continued to attract acolytes who preferred isolation to community. The *Paterikon of the Kiev Cave Monastery* is the most extensive original cycle of tales on the early monastic life of Rus'. Within the monastery, here as elsewhere, successive monks working as editors shaped episodes by grouping material thematically around prominent figures. The earliest versions of more than two hundred extant manuscript copies of the *Paterikon of the Kiev Cave Monastery* descend from the fifteenth century: Arseny, the Bishop of Tver' undertook the compilation of the first version in 1406. This version was the first to include the *Life of Feodosy* as well as the surviving part of a correspondence between the disgruntled monk Polycarp and his spiritual mentor, Simon, the Bishop of Suzdal'. That correspondence, concerned with disputes about monastic life, also contained micro-*vitae*, accounts of monks' lives. The Arsenev copy (named after Arseny) is thought to have reorganized and significantly edited a prototype dating to the Kievan period. It appeared at a juncture in monastic life when nostalgia for Kiev as a golden age of monastic culture started to become a feature of Muscovite worldview.

As the editor of a second edition of the *Paterikon of the Kiev Cave Monastery*, the mission of the monk Kassian (*fl.* fifteenth century) was to amplify the record of the acts of individuals at that institution. To this end, he showed a marked preference for translated stories about the Desert Fathers, the original hermits of the fourth century, as models. When Kassian looked back to Kiev, he conceived the acts of their Kievan successors in the context of institutional history of the monastery itself whose founding, activity, and survival depended on pious workers and evangelists, starting with Feodosy. One innovation of the second edition was to arrange the constituent lives in chronological order. Many later accretions include stories about the baptism of Princess Olga and Prince Vladimir, and the life of Andrei the Holy Fool.

In preparing his new edition in the summer of 1460, Kassian used multiple sources, including saints' lives, short biographies, and excerpts from historical chronicles at the Kiev Monastery of the Caves. An even fuller version followed in 1462, and it is this edition that served as the base text for all later major redactions in a process that continued well into the seventeenth century of editing and amplifying the selection of stories. In addition to formal changes relating to headings and framing devices, the versions differ through addition and subtraction.[52] Additions included a story about the transfer of the relics of St. Feodosy, a tale about the foundation of the Kiev Monastery of the Caves, and a significant tale on Prince Iziaslav's interest in, and rejection of, the Latins (and therefore papal influence), added at a time when concerns about heresy had rocked the patriarchal establishment.

The effect of Kassian's edition was to create an emphatic narrative about the continuity of the history of early Russian spirituality and monasticism. Undoubtedly, the production of a fresh new version had the purpose of enhancing the position of a monastery that had survived since the earlier period whose only rival for distinction was now the Trinity-Sergiev Monastery. This redaction (and a further third version) was eventually incorporated into larger *minei* collections, including the *Great Menology* (*Velikie Chet´i Minei*) assembled in Moscow starting in the mid-sixteenth century. All the later scribes involved in these huge compilations shared the goal of forging into a single theocratic unity and history the work of monasteries and offices of state, tracing the origins of Moscow back to the baptism of Olga and Vladimir: students of the different versions have argued that if anything Kassian increased later stories at the expense of the earliest layer in order to remind one of Kiev as a point of origin. His copy was produced at a time of acute rivalry between the princes of Tver´ and Moscow who vied for preeminence, and the Kievan legacy had meaning as a legitimating factor.[53] A professed peacemaker, Kassian's goal was not to give local princes ammunition for their own claims, but rather to keep Kievan spirituality in the limelight. A love of local legend plays its part, for Kassian includes a story about the foundation of the monastery of St. Antony and St. Feodosy at Tver´ by Prince Andrei Bogoliubsky and the dedication of the Church of the Assumption of the Virgin.

The *Paterik of Volokolamsk*, another major collection, is named for its editor Iosif Volotsky (sometimes known as Joseph of Volokolamsk) of the Volokolamsk Monastery (1439/40–1515). Located north of Moscow, the monastery was one of the most important spiritual centers in the fifteenth and sixteenth centuries. *The Paterik of Volokolamsk* was compiled during the sixteenth century, at a moment of ferocious debates between religious and political authorities on the question of church landownership and wealth. The Grand Prince of Muscovy had acquired more power and with it a need to secure the loyalty of servitors by redistributing wealth and land, possibly at the expense of the Church. Within this collection, "The Tales of Father Pafnuty" ("Povesti ottsa Pafnutiia", c.1447), assembled in support of the Possessors (*Stiazhateli*), justified Joseph's theory of a strong Church that used its material wealth to guard against heresy.

Tales of holy men feature traditional tropes such as dreams, miracles, glimpses of the afterlife—in which saints on their ascent to heaven sometimes meet a Grand Prince deprived of posthumous elevation—as well as heroic feats composed in a folkloric style. Eventually in the late sixteenth century the *Life of the Reverence Joseph of Volotsky* (*Zhitie prepodobnogo Iosifa Volotskogo*) in short and then long versions was incorporated in later editions of this particular *paterik*. The compiler used tales of piety and foundation of monasteries as polemical tools to refute "Non-Possessors" (*Nestiazhateli*) as enemies of monasticism and monastic wealth.

The greatest compilation of saints' lives, in scale and complexity, is the *Great Menology*. With the support of Tsar Ivan IV, the Church sought to impose order on unstandardized liturgical practices and church calendars that had arisen locally in parishes across a vast, if thinly populated, territory. Under the initiatives of the great reformer Metropolitan Makary, the One-Hundred Chapter Council of 1551 (*Stoglavyi Sobor*) brought together the Estates of the Russian Empire and issued a set of regulations concerning the church calendar, the celebration of saints' days, the procedure for identifying saints and confirming their approved list, and aspects of the liturgy.[54] The work on the *Great Menology*, begun twenty years earlier, in the 1530s, in the city of Novgorod, was given considerable priority. The brainchild of Metropolitan Makary, this compilation of both original and translated ecclesiastical works was intended as a vast, encyclopedic in scale, collection of medieval Russian writings.[55] Individual *pateriki* were recopied and included alongside a tremendous range of sermons, Biblical works, the Psalter, and much more. No complete version of a single copy has yet appeared in a modern print edition. As a work of Muscovite organization, its very scale and structure as an accumulation seemed to reflect the ideology of a city that had become a super-state by absorbing surrounding principalities. Each of the *minei* represented a month in the liturgical year, and each *svod*, or codex, contained twelve *minei*. The texts arranged under the monthly rubric according to the liturgical calendar assembled a complete range of the approved and reedited texts to be used. The enormous labor of collecting materials from across a vast, loosely connected network of monasteries, and then copying this wealth of texts, fell to scribes in a number of monasteries. It has been estimated that the textual production took twenty-five years, and since correction and copying had to be done by hand, this led to some local variation and alteration in the three main copies (called the *Sofiisky spisok*, the *Uspensky spisok*, and the "*Tsarsky*" *spisok*) as assembled in Novgorod and Moscow, the last two copies having been commissioned for Tsar Ivan IV.

Founders and Holy Fathers: The example of St. Feodosy

The stories of the *pateriki*, while often quite brief, cast the lives of more ordinary monastic brethren according to the rituals of their community and the tropes of Christian salvation. On a different scale are lives devoted to figures of singular importance through their foundational acts. Nestor's *Life of Feodosy of Pechera* is the first masterpiece of medieval Russian writing. Nearly 20,000 words in length, it is the longest and most elaborate *zhitie* to survive from the Kievan period (although much shorter than the *Primary Chronicle*). Composed by the prolific monk Nestor, one of the earliest authors to speak about himself and his religious values, the text likely dates to the 1080s (there has been much conjecture on dating with reference to internal events). This saint's life lays down a factual and spiritual record of a leading clergyman known to the author who bears witness to his spiritual dedication and personal history.[56]

One tradition of Byzantine monasticism was hermetic. Monasteries organized as caves (the Slavonic *lavra*) consisted of separate cells as dwellings for the hermits. These monks lived in isolation throughout the week and only came together for the weekly liturgy, to collect food and materials for handiwork, and on great festivals. Mountains and other desolate spots were the setting for the most extreme form of asceticism that Byzantine monasticism could offer.

Some churchmen doubted whether solitary wrestling with the temptations of the flesh and the demons was likely to succeed. For them, the ideal of spiritual life was embodied in the *koinobion*, a community where imposed obedience, the denial of personal property, and the subordination of the individual will to that of the group could lead to positive deindividuation that helped avoid the risk of taking any pride in extreme forms of individual asceticism. In addition, the hegumen, as both shepherd and spiritual father of his flock, would, it was thought, ensure the ascetic development of all the monks and their adherence to orthodox practices.

Feodosy took his name from Theodore the Studite (759–825), the hegumen of the Monastery of St. John the Baptist at Stoudios in Constantinople, an opponent of iconoclasm whose monastic rule restored the teachings of the Fathers, emphasized the cenobitic or communal, fully regulated ways of daily life, and valued asceticism. The Byzantine *Rule of the Fathers*, in Theodore's view, rather than imparting knowledge of God through contemplation, aimed to realize the old ideals of primitive monasticism, where the monastery was a Christian village of an essentially practical type. Manual labor rather than meditation was the order of the day, for work was seen as a measurement of spiritual fervor to which every monk should aspire. The hegumen, in addition to being in general charge of the affairs of the monastery, was particularly concerned with the spiritual guidance of the monks, and, every day, as the spiritual father to the community, heard private revelations of every member's thoughts, concerns, and confessions.

Nestor's portrait of Feodosy closely follows the stricter Byzantine model of hagiography in exploring the inner life and motivation of a pious monk whose elevation is the result of his devotion to the communal life of the monastery—the very monastery in which Nestor himself lived and served—and whose life represents an ideal worthy of emulation because of piety rather than martyrdom.[57] By opening with a traditional prayer for divine aid that will make him worthy of his authorial task, Nestor identifies himself as the author of an account of the lives of Boris and Gleb, but now asserts his authority to write this new life as a member of the very monastery in which the brothers served and which commemorates the older monk's death.[58] That sense of occasion and personal commitment shapes Nestor's rhetoric as he bids his brethren, the fellow monks who may have listened to a recital of the whole *Life*, or excerpts, to "heed with total concentration" a "discourse that will be full of use to them."[59]

The portrait of the singular figure of Feodosy unfolds episodically. The principle of narrative follows the New Testament example of assembling anecdotes about the holy nature of the protagonist in a loosely progressive sequence. Scenes are well constructed and the moral is clear and self-contained (thereby facilitating the work of other copyists collecting extracts to be included in liturgical works such as prayers and sermons). Cumulatively, it is also a portrait of the cenobitic practice of monastic organization he helped to establish at the Kiev Monastery of the Caves, lovingly exploring his actions as an educator, builder of churches (and therefore to some degree a missionary) as well as his courage in defending the sometimes deposed Grand Prince of Kiev, Prince Iziaslav Iaroslavich (*c.*1024–78) after his exile by his ambitious brother Prince Sviatoslav. That relationship is the subject of an epistle by Feodosy. The letter is one of a handful of his attributed writings to have survived (in copies from the fifteenth century), and it includes short spiritual lessons on subjects like "spiritual usefulness" against the sin of sloth; fasting, charity, love, and "resignation" (*smirenie*); the ability to accept one's fate and the divine will, which is seen specifically as a feature of Eastern Orthodox thought. It is this latter trait, repeatedly praised in Feodosy's writing alongside obedience to the monastic order (*poslushanie*), that was the source of his vocation and his outstanding devotion. The voice and character that emerge from his own writings prove compatible with the hero of Nestor's narrative.

The author Nestor modeled his work after the exemplary Byzantine hagiographies of saints Antony, Euthymius the Great (377–473), a Palestine abbot, and Sabbas the Sanctified (439–532), a Cappadocian monk in Palestine who led an exemplary eremitical life. By adopting the biographical framework of the stages of saintly life, such as childhood, education, and spiritual discovery, Nestor masterfully combines standard scene construction with original and memorable details, including the saint's first interview in the caves with the blessed Antony, and repeated examples of Feodosy's ability to win over troubled souls to prayer and of his devotion to the cult of the Virgin Mary.[60] Nestor foregrounds unique, rather than generic, traits of the saint, including the highly volatile character of his adolescent relationship with his spiritual but overbearing mother, and the stages of his dawning spirituality which led Feodosy from the parental home on a pilgrimage to Kiev where he took the tonsure and, with two other

fathers, Nikon the Great and Antony, co-founded the Kiev Monastery of the Caves. Pithy dialogue woven into the narrator's third-person account, everyday details such as diet (largely
bread and water), elegantly cited Biblical verses, historical information on the various churches
founded by Feodosy, and a straightforward manner of storytelling are all devices Nestor uses
to create a vivid historical and biographical canvas that foregrounds his faith.

In monasteries, degrees of obedience differentiated between the practice of monastic and
hermetic concepts of religious life. The spiritual benefits of monastic life could not fully be
achieved if the cenobitic style were not strictly followed. For hermits, by contrast, the acme of
spiritual achievement was seen to lie in solitary life outside the monastery. Kievan hermits,
such as Isaac the Cave Dweller, envisaged a state in which the individual could reach communion with God; the strict cenobites, by comparison, believed that the subordination of the
individual will was the path to the truly ascetic life. The influence of the depiction of Russian
spirituality and the monastic ideals of asceticism and renunciation of worldly life on modern
literature can be seen in classics such as Tolstoy's story, "Father Sergius" ("Otets Sergei,"
published in 1911) and Part One of Dostoevsky's *Brothers Karamazov* (1879) with its remarkable
portrait of Father Zosima.

Miracles, always essential as evidence of sainthood, appear to be almost common occurrences, woven into the pattern of daily life.[61] Consider a dramatic episode from *Life of Feodosy
of Pechera* in which brigands attack monks while at prayer in the chapel. Facing certain disaster, the parishioners are amazed when the church and congregation rise into the air from the
spot, saving the assembled and dispersing the terrified attackers. More mundanely, Nestor also
gives credit to Feodosy for the growth of the monastery and the brotherhood in what is perhaps the most important miracle attested by witnesses: the appearance of a column of fire
and smoke points Feodosy to the site on which he should build a new church, a miracle the
news of which spread by word of mouth according to Nestor.

The *Life* devotes some attention to the relationship between rulers and monks and the
absolution the former sought at the hands of the latter, as well as surveying the activities of
other Christians in principalities close to Kiev, painting a picture of how essential these activities
were to the establishment of Christianity in Rus'. A prolonged deathbed scene (always an
important moment in the affirmation of faith) shows Feodosy surrounded by monks who
have gathered round as he teaches them his final lessons on the salvation of the soul and the
meaning of their Christian fraternity. Once they have scattered, a single monk peers through
a chink in the door at the lone figure and watches him utter his final devotions. Acts of piety,
including repeated tussles with the devil (an important motif in the separate lives included
in the *Paterikon of the Kiev Cave Monastery*), the performance of miracles, and the popular
legend that helped to secure Feodosy's reputation in his lifetime all figure in a text that aims to
secure it in perpetuity, starting with the burial of his relics in the monastery in 1108 as recorded
in the *Primary Chronicle*. Nestor's *Life* clearly enjoyed the appreciation of other scribes since
copies multiplied in the fourteenth and fifteenth centuries ushering the next great age of
hagiographical composition.

Miracle workers, the Virgin, and holy fools

The subset of official female saints is minuscule and restricted to the deeds of aristocratic
women. The twelfth-century *Life of Euphrosinia of Polotsk* (*Zhitie Evfrosinii Polotskoi*)
appeared in several redactions and many copies throughout the period. (She is not to be
confused with another Euphrosinia who helped to found a monastery in Suzdal' and was
canonized in the sixteenth century when copies of her *Life*, written by the monk Grigory, an
accomplished practitioner of word-weaving, circulated.) Euphrosinia was the granddaugh-
ter of Prince Vseslav Briachislavicha, and her hagiography attests to the precocious piety of

a princess who, aged twelve, became a nun and founded two monasteries in Polotsk. As recorded, her life conforms to the tradition of granting sainthood to those whose achievements included founding monastic institutions. However, according to the *Life*—which ends with an encomium, albeit without miracles—before making pilgrimage to Jerusalem where she died, she earned sanctification by acquiring for her city an icon of the Virgin Mother of Ephesus, attributed to St. Luke, the Evangelist credited with the invention of icon-painting.

The *Life of Euphrosinia of Polotsk* is a rare instance of an early life of a woman saint. The institutional predominance of the Virgin Mary stood in the way of devotion to other female figures; and because there were relatively few translations of female saints' lives, the archetype would not have been readily available. The Virgin Mary, known as the Theotokos in Greek terminology or as the Bogoroditsa in a direct Slavonic translation (both meaning the "Mother of God"), was central to Byzantine spirituality as one of its most important figures of spirituality. The Bogoroditsa is the subject of important liturgical hymns, such as the Akathistos Hymn, sung at the Feast of the Annunciation (March 25) and during Lent. Of the five basic iconographic types created to represent the holy actions of the Virgin, the most important ones, borrowed from Byzantine prayers and iconography included the Virgin as a symbol of mercy (*elousa* in Greek, *umilenie* in Slavonic) and the Virgin as the Mother of Christ. Certain postures and gestures developed into "types" that lent names to sanctuaries and engendered poetic epithets. Thus an icon of the Virgin was meant to represent her image and, at the same time, was the replica of a famous original icon. Most images of the Virgin stress her role as Christ's Mother, showing her standing and holding her son. In the Eastern Church, including the territories of Kievan and Muscovite Rus´, the Virgin Hodegetria (named after a monastery in Constantinople) is a compassionate force, often represented in icons (as in a famous icon of Smolensk, painted by the great painter Dionysius in 1482, in which she is shown bending over to touch her cheek to the cheek of her child, who reciprocates this affection by placing his arm around her neck). The Virgin Mary was widely venerated for her powers of benign intercession in moments of crisis and more generally as the mediator between suffering mankind and Christ, and as the protector of Constantinople and Russian cities: such was the power ascribed to the Vladimir Virgin, an icon painted in Byzantium, which first appeared in Kiev before it was transferred to the city of Vladimir after the Tatar invasions of the thirteenth century.

Narrative artistic representations of Christ's Mother focus on her conception and childhood, or her eternal sleep (the Greek *koimesis* and Slavonic *uspenie*). The beginnings of the Marian cult in Russia date to the fourteenth century, adopting these practices and beliefs virtually intact.[62] That century also saw the circulation of numerous copies of the life of another Mary, so-called Maria of Egypt (*Zhitie Marii Egipetskoi*), which narrates the story of a prostitute from Alexandria who discovered faith, repented, and as a penitent took solitary retreat in the desert of the Jordan valley. Her story was anthologized, and medieval prayers composed to be read out on her name-day reveal a clear association between her and the Virgin Mother ("Maiden, Queen, Mother of God"). A translation of the Byzantine *Life of the Virgin*, a work of the 1100s, provided worshippers with an account of all the major periods of her life, including the Virgin birth and her ascension and *koimesis*. Excerpts from this translation also made their way into separate prayers.

Worshippers turned to the Virgin Mother in veneration, whereas holy fools—or fools for Christ—lived outside institutions and often suffered persecution as freaks. "Holy foolery" (*iurodstvo*) refers to the special codes of behavior adopted by the "holy fool" (*iurodivyi*), almost always a male figure, widely attested in Russian religious discourse, literature, and iconography from the medieval period to the present day. Self-abasement, signs of insanity, unruliness, and shocking unconventionality can mask the commitment of the holy fool to spiritual enlightenment in accordance with Christian, and specifically Orthodox, teaching. The paradoxical union of feigned insanity or stupidity and spiritual insight protects the pious intent and ascetic ideal of the *iurodivyi* by deflecting worldly praise and eliminating the risk of establishment corruption. His vocation is not to enjoy worldly praise, but rather by acting the fool to challenge received norms and earthly power structures. Foolery is to be associated with the wisdom of folly rather than mere silliness or foolishness, and sanctity (*blazhenstvo*) often goes hand in hand with blasphemy.

Although widely attested in Byzantine religious and literary culture from the sixth century, South Slavic portrayals of holy fools remain sporadic and inconsistent, hard to verify as tales of actual personages.[63] The earliest among the handful of portraits deemed to be authentic— including Nikolai Kachanov ("The Cabbage"), Fedor of Novgorod, and Ioann of Ustiug— is Isaac the Cave Dweller, whose eleventh-century antics are among the most colorful. The *Paterikon of the Kiev Cave Monastery* recounts how, as a crotchety monk dissatisfied with communal life, Isaac made mischief (*urodstovo tvoriti*), eventually turning to the life of a solitary hermit before rejoining his religious brethren. In the twelfth century, a translation was produced of the Byzantine *Life of Andrew the Fool*, possibly a model for the East Slavic articulation of its own version of the holy fool. The establishment of the feast of the Intercession of the Veil of the Mother of God in the twelfth century had a close connection to the cult of this saint who is depicted in a Suzdal' icon of the fourteenth century, his flowing beard and tattered dress modeled on Elijah the Prophet. The Russian figure of the holy fool begins to appear regularly in local hagiographic and historical texts in the sixteenth century.

In its full Russian guise, "holy foolery" adopts the traditional paradox of antisocial piety but adds a function that will remain crucial to the cultural associations the term evokes. Depictions of *iurodvsto* will continually pit the wise fool against the authorities, thus shaping the type of a fearless sage who confronts an unjust ruler in the name of religious truth. For example, the full version of Isidor of Tverdislav's *vita* began to circulate in multiple copies in the early sixteenth century, to be subsequently incorporated into Metropolitan Makary's *Great Menology* and thus implicitly recognized as a faithful account of a model life. The blessed Isidor inhabits a recognizable urban Moscow, visits the Grand Prince's quarters, and "wanders for Christ's sake" like a "fool" (*iurod*). When he is beaten, the writer praises him for his endurance. The *vita* may have been the textual authority needed to demonstrate that Isidor was not merely "playing the fool," but was in fact the real thing—holy and subversive, respected and disrespectful, humble but outspoken. Other virtues are exemplified in *The Life of Ioann the Hairy the Merciful* (*Zhitie Blazhennego Ioanna Vlasatogo*), who haunted church porches, relying on widows and priests to satisfy his basic material needs, but was venerated because he prayed in Greek day and night, and posthumously performed miracles that confirmed his standing. Other holy fools in the sixteenth century would adhere to this behavioral model, occasionally also showing prophetic powers and skills as miracle workers, as in the case of Mikhail of Klopsk, who is alleged in some versions to have predicted the rise of Metropolitan Iona.

Traditional holy foolery as a combination of social justice, Orthodox piety, and personal eccentricity must reach an apogee with Nikola of Pskov, who is recorded by a German adventurer in Muscovy, Heinrich Staden, as standing up to Ivan the Terrible after the tsar allegedly caused the slaughter of thousands of churchmen and residents in Pskov.[64] The historical evidence suggests that Nikola, a wealthy peasant who might have had a brave streak, was nothing like a holy fool. According to Georgy Fedotov, a distinguished early historian of Russian spirituality, subsequent chronicles provide a rare demonstration of how writers manipulated his image and aligned it with the prototype. For instance, the version given in the *First Pskov Chronicle* has Ivan the Terrible beseeching Nikola for his blessing. Nikola relented only on the condition that Ivan would agree to cease the bloodshed. Later versions elaborate a more extensive scene, and attribute subversive predictions to Nikola, now transformed into a beggar. When Ivan continued attacking the city and ordered the bell removed from the Troitsa Church, "that very day the tsar's best horse fell, as the saint had foretold; and they reported this to the tsar, who was afraid and quickly fled the city."[65]

CASE STUDY The holy fool in the modern tradition

Medieval *iurodstvo* continues to resonate as an influential paradigm that privileges the use of paradox, comical didacticism, and self-denigration. Like Nikola, other holy fools engage in the same condemnation of tsars as "man eaters." Rumors of ever more frequent miracles at the grave of the *iurodivyi* Vasily the Blessed accompanied the accession of Fedor in 1584. Giles Fletcher, an English merchant and envoy of Queen Elizabeth I, comments extensively on holy fools as an exotic feature of the Muscovite landscape, describing them as figures that "go naked" and "inveigh against the state, and government, especially against the Godunovs." Pushkin, in his play *Boris Godunov*, and Modest Musorgsky, in his opera of the same title, expand on this aspect of holy foolery by creating a cameo part for a fictional Holy Fool. Nikolka, as he is named in the story, goes around begging (the alms go into his tin hat), speaking in riddles, and tormenting Tsar Boris with allusions to his supposed murder of the tsarevich. Yet he is the one person who can speak the truth to the tsar.

This more outspoken role began to concern Church authorities as they tried to halt the decline of the monasteries and stave widespread unrest sparked in the Time of Troubles. Before becoming a Schismatic, the priest Avvakum had in fact campaigned as a religious hardliner against popular religion, opposing popular carnivalesque rituals and the entertainments of the *skomorokhi*, or wandering minstrels. He nonetheless speaks with reverence about his spiritual brother Fedor the Fool, who fearlessly confronts Tsar Aleksei. While Fedor "plays the fool all day," Avvakum notes approvingly that he "prays tearfully all night." The publication of Avvakum's *Life* in the 1850s, when Slavophile interest in Russian history ran high, provided yet another example of a holy fool. A worthy predecessor to the nineteenth-century classic prose writers Mikhail Saltykov-Schedrin, Nikolai Leskov, Ivan Turgenev, and Leo Tolstoy, Avvakum characterized vagabonds and beggars as holy fools who embodied native wisdom. Through their stoicism or passive acceptance, they taught how to accept life as it is and how to do good and combat evil. While the Russian paradigm of holy foolery continues to be important in modern literary culture, the characterization of idiocy as a valuable type of marginality moves away from the original Pauline and Orthodox Christian codes. Its Christian roots are not immediately severed, and Dostoevsky's strong debt to the New Testament informs some of his most complex characters such as Sonia in *Crime and Punishment*, Prince Myshkin in *The Idiot*, and Alesha Karamazov. Like the classic *iurod*, these characters suffer from social exclusion and weakness to which they respond with grace and intellectual humility (or *kenosis*); however, only Myshkin attains the combination of idiocy and wisdom that conforms to the original Orthodox model. Myshkin's case is a particularly good example of the gradual process of adaptation that shows the appropriation of folly to a broader set of messages beyond Christian values. Dostoevsky arguably modernized the type by investing all his powers of psychological characterization and grasp of cultural politics into figures like Prince Myshkin, who is caught between Russian Orthodoxy and Western secularity, prophetic insight and pathology. Harriet Murav argues that the writer's own behavior and public persona represented a form of artistic holy foolery.[66] Furthermore, Myshkin seems to descend genetically from both the traditional holy fool and heroes like Hamlet and Don Quixote, both supremely naive yet deeply insightful, innocent and questing, worldly and flawed. The association of his epilepsy with wisdom, and his own religiousness, make him a good approximation of the traditional fool in Christ. Yet he is also a representative of the gentry, and remains worlds apart from the seemingly more authentic folk figures like Grisha of Tolstoy's *Childhood* or the hero of Gleb Uspensky's "Paramon the Holy Fool" ("Paromon-iurodivyi," 1877), both bearers of the meekness, poverty, and sheer bodily filth straight out of the pages of the world of Avvakum or the earlier saints.[67]

By the nineteenth century, the recognition of non-conformity as a necessary vantage for wise evaluation of society becomes a fixture of cultural commentary and increasingly allied to folly as well as holy foolery. Hence the officially designated "madness" of the philosopher Petr Chaadaev (1794–1856) or the irony of Chatsky, the hero of *Woe from Wit*, serve as examples of worldly characters whose intelligence and jaundiced view on their times marginalize them rather than condemning them as outcasts. Dignified and genteel, they display none of the irascibility or self-abasement of Pauline fools. And when the critic Razumnik Ivanov-Razumnik (1878–1946) called his contemporary Vasily Rozanov (1856–1919) "the holy fool of Russian literature," he used the term proverbially to characterize this essayist's love of paradox and provocation. Types of foolishness and idiocy (*odurenie*) multiply in response to the realities of Soviet life. The tradition of using a fool to underscore the lunacy of certain norms adapts the figure of the folkloric popular fool Ivan Durak—see, for instance, Andrei Sinyavsky's seminal book *Ivan Durak: The Essays on Russian Folk Faith* (*Ivan Durak: ocherk russkoi narodnoi very*, 1991). In his pseudo-folktale "Blessedness and damnation" ("Blazhenstvo i okaianstvo"), Yuri Mamleev created a true descendant of the type in the hero Ivashko, whose prophetic utterances about the founding of St. Petersburg are (strangely) quotations from Pushkin's *The Bronze Horseman*. Elsewhere, manifestations of idiocy are more behavioral than religious, and it is understandable why writers in the context of an atheist state downplayed or eschewed Christian elements of the figure. The argument has been made that Zoshchenko and Platonov integrated elements of humor as well as pathos in their respective approaches to heroes as transitional or marginal figures. Late and dissident Soviet writers such as Venedikt Erofeev (1938–90), Dmitry Galkovsky (b. 1960) (an admirer of both Rozanov and Dostoevsky), and Yuz Aleshkovsky (b. 1929) have produced some memorable non-conformist literary cousins whose folly shares traits of the traditional type endowed with subversive idiocy (*durachestvo*). The recourse to holy foolery has also served writers as a way to tap into visions (and supposed values) of a prerevolutionary past. The heroine of Solzhenitsyn's much-admired novella "Matriona's Home" ("Matrionin dvor," 1959), the selfless victim of a grasping family finds mute consolation in religious devotion and work, traditional signs of *smirenie*. Yuz Aleshkovsky's eponymous hero in *Nikolai Nikolaevich* uses buffoonery to attack the stultification and false piety of Soviet ideology. Yet because his outrageous volubility also exudes pathos, his character descends from the fool-in-Christ model. This phenomenon of updating the prototype continues in Russian culture today, whether in literature (in the writing of Yury Buida (b. 1954), Asar Eppel (1935–2012), Vladimir Makanin (b. 1937), Vladimir Sharov (b. 1952)) or on screen, as in the popular TV version of Dostoevsky's *The Idiot* (dir. Vladimir Bortko, 2003) and Pavel Lungin's *The Island* (2006).[68]

While the fool-like heroes of these fictions derive directly from the traditional figure of the fool, the postmodern fashion for types of foolery may owe some inspiration to the prominent place in literary scholarship that eminent critics such as Bakhtin, Lotman, Likhachev, and A. M. Panchenko accorded the fool as a specifically Russian phenomenon in fiction and in national culture. One modern fool who survives not from the medieval period but rather from the period of the Enlightenment (the age of rational religion), is Ksenia of Petersburg (canonized in 1988), an eighteenth-century figure who, after the death of her husband, assumed his identity and lived as a male. She is the subject of a popular play by Vadim Levanov (2007). In an eponymous poem about Ksenia, Elena Shvarts (1948–2010) venerates a figure who has entered "someone else's memory, someone else's dreams." Evgeny Vodolazkin (b. 1964) adapted the idiom and the tropes of medieval chronicle and hagiographic writing in his novel *Laurus (Lavr)*, winner of the 2013 Big Book Prize. His account of a fifteenth-century healer, also selflessly devoted to others, sports a rich cast of characters, including two holy fools Foma and Karp. While they add color and a note of historical authenticity, in this vision of indigenous rituals and community they are important also because, as the narrator says, the "holy fool always tells the truth." Cast in the mold of the classic *iurodivyi*, these works' social marginal and ambivalent characters, whose antics are fueled by drink and lunacy, mask social critique as comedy. All corroborate the survival the marginal invoked positively as a counter-cultural and specifically Russian hero.

Ilarion redux: The fifteenth-century elaboration of hagiography

From the nineteenth century, medieval Russia in the popular imagination has been virtually synonymous with waves of Mongol or Tatar invasions that began in the early thirteenth century. Despite the gravity of the situation, which led to the permanent eclipsing of Kievan Rus´ and to the retrenchment of principalities northward toward the principality of Vladimir, the Mongol invasion did not obliterate the heritage of Kievan Rus´. While the political clout of southwestern Rus´ atrophied as power shifted to the northeast (principalities in that region fragmented in turn), coexistence with the Golden Horde, the Russian name for the Kipchak khanate, involved much compromise.[69] Thirteenth-century works of narrative represent the year 1237 as the date of the most severe in a series of incursions ever experienced by the Eastern Slavs. Tales, a poetic lay, and chronicles vent hostility to the marauding tribes that invade from the area of the Black Sea over the steppe.[70]

None of these tribal peoples attempted to integrate Rus´ into their territories; even the Mongols, who had achieved some form of conquest and annexation, never attempted to overhaul the Rus´ regime of governance. Current historical research suggests that, far from the fragmentation and chaos emphasized in some accounts,[71] the reality was one of cooperation among the different princes to advance the interests of the wider region long before centralization and the emergence of national identity associated with the growth of Moscow. From the 1340s to the 1440s, over 150 new monasteries sprang up throughout the Russian territory, generally in isolated and remote places. Subsistence, however, was insufficient to guarantee intellectual renewal in Russia and across the Balkans, where the regional powers faced pressures from the Golden Horde and the Ottomans. In the fourteenth century, the weakened and impoverished Byzantine government, faced with financial crises and the Turkish menace, could afford no more than sporadic interest in the Eastern Slavs, and contacts were limited. A. I. Sobolevsky, an influential scholar of thirteenth- and fourteenth-century literature, described the poor state of "Old Russian" letters in that period.[72] He pointed to the distortions and mistakes that plagued text production as a result of the carelessness of scribes and the lack of any set rules for copying of manuscripts. Following the recapture of the Byzantine Empire from the Latin rule in 1261 and the period of restoration that followed, combined with the weakening of the Khanate in the late fourteenth century, the Southern Slavs turned once again toward Byzantium. The many Serbian translators and copyists at work in Hilandar and in other Athonite monasteries furthered the reputation of Serbian literary activity within the Orthodox Slavic community.[73] When Byzantium collapsed in the fifteenth century, the repercussions of the loss of this original source of prestige resonated all the way to Moscow (which had superseded Kiev).

The fall of the Eastern Empire raised the question of how to protect Orthodoxy from the corruption that was deemed to have undermined Byzantium. At various points in the sixteenth and seventeenth centuries, the Church conducted an examination of scribal practices and a "correction of books" in order to purge ecclesiastical writing and scripture of errors.[74] The question of how changes to the literature and language occurred has been much debated. Patriarch Euthymius of Trnovo's (fl. 1375) linguistic reforms aimed to establish a pan-Orthodox ecclesiastical Slavonic literary language in the Balkan and Russian lands, and in so doing eradicate local spelling and dialectical practices and other inaccuracies that had infiltrated religious books. To that end, standardized practice aimed at exactitude and literalness in translations from the Greek and strove to establish a distinct orthographic form for each meaning of a given word. Keen to restore the purity of the Slavonic vernacular used by the followers of Cyril and Methodius, the reformers sought to prevent the encroachments of the specifically "Bulgarian," "Serbian," or "Russian" elements into the literary language.

The changes to scribal practice at the level of spelling, morphology, and word usage were undergirded by ideas about language adopted in the late fourteenth century by a movement known as Hesychasm (from the Greek word *hesuxia*, meaning "quiet"). Based on the Neo-Platonic teachings of Gregory of Sinai and the theoretical elaborations of Gregory Palamas (1296–1359), the Hesychastic system entailed a gradual progression from the practice of monastic virtues and the rejection of all earthly preoccupations to the attainment of divine contemplation. The achievement of a mystical union with the Godhead was aided by certain physical exercises and by the continual repetition of a specific prayer. Hesychast monasteries trained Serbian, Bulgarian, as well as Greek monks who disseminated these ideas more widely. Like Mt. Athos, the Hesychast monastic centers founded in Bulgaria, at Paroria, Kilifarevo, and Veliko Trnovo, became educational and cultural training centers, and homes to important ecclesiastical scholars like Grigory Camblack, Metropolitan Kiprian, Nicodemus of Tismana, and the Bulgarian monk and grammarian Constantin Kostenecki (fl. 1380, d. after 1431), some of whom made it to Moscow. These new centers of Christian learning were supported and subsidized by the last two Bulgarian rulers, Tsar Ivan Alexander (r. 1331–71) and his son Tsar Ivan Shishman (r. 1371–95). After the Ottoman occupation of the Bulgarian monastic center at Veliko Trnovo, the Serbian lands no longer proved propitious for such intellectual activity and some proponents moved to Russia.

Followers of Hesychasm believed that the Church Slavonic books needed to be purged of heretical corruptions.[75] Old texts, especially translations, underwent re-examination and correction on the basis of comparison with the Greek originals, and new translations of a variety of Greek literary and religious works appeared. Along with writing practices, history, too, was subject to revision. Some new writing expressed veneration and nostalgia for the glorious past of Kievan Rus', to which Moscow (often referred to as the principality of Vladimir-Suzdal') was the direct heir, starting with warding off the Golden Horde by Moscow and Vladimir, and the subsequent subordination of neighboring principalities. The chronicles portray the consolidation of Rus' as necessary to the preservation of Orthodoxy against internal discord and further invasions.

Scholars have wrestled with the once-fashionable idea of a cultural and intellectual movement spearheaded by mass migration that followed the reorientation of Slavic Orthodox cultural activity to Moscow from the South Slavic lands (usually referred to as the Second South

Slavic Influence). Former assumptions about migration on a large scale, extrapolated from the reform of orthography and standardization of linguistic elements, have now been discounted.[76] Henrik Birnbaum affirmed a new consensus that, while the influx fell short of a movement, at least some South Slavic scribes did migrate to Russia and assumed influential positions. Clerics from all Orthodox Slavdom, operating in monasteries located primarily on Mt. Athos and in other Balkan monasteries, collectively reformed Church Slavonic orthography, and through the efforts of prominent individuals these ideas influenced a number of productive scribes and church figures in Moscow.

The most influential figures include the clergymen Kiprian (1330–1406), either a Bulgarian or Serb, and Grigory Camblak (1365–1419/20, appointed Metropolitan in 1406), and the Serbian Pakhomy Logofet (d. 1484), the author and editor of numerous saints' lives in fifteenth-century Russia.[77] After a period on Mt. Athos, Kiprian was sent to Lithuania and Russia on a diplomatic mission. He was eventually consecrated as Metropolitan of Kiev, succeeding Metropolitan Aleksei in Moscow in 1381.[78] Kiprian brought a large collection of works by Serbian writers into Russia. Among the liturgical texts, he may have translated a *Book of Prayers* (*Trebnik*), which prescribed the rites for administering the sacraments, and the Psalter, both of which manuscripts are now lost. He planned a compilation of an all-Russian chronicle, gleaned from local annals, that would separate ecclesiastical and princely chronicle-writing. Although this project was not realized during his lifetime, it gives an indication of his ambition for Moscow as a theological center.

In 1381, Kiprian composed in Church Slavonic his most important work, a hagiography of Metropolitan Peter (1308–26). It is a text of some literary sophistication, since it revises an earlier, anonymous biography of the saint and combines elegance with a highly personal viewpoint. *The Life of St. Peter, Metropolitan of Kiev and All Russia* (*Zhitie sviatitelia Petra, Mitropolita Kieva i vseia Rossii*) has been read as strongly autobiographical because it draws parallels between the vicissitudes endured by both clergymen. A tale of the triumph of the Metropolitan of Kiev, a virtuous clergyman, over his spiteful rivals, it glorifies individual dedication to harmonious relations between the Metropolitan and the Muscovite ruler.[79] In 1325, Metropolitan Peter demonstrated his support for Ivan I, who battled his way to the throne in a series of wars with the princes of Tver´. Peter moved from Kiev to Moscow and designated the Church of the Dormition, newly built of stone, as his future burial place.[80]

Like Peter, Kiprian backed the princes of Muscovy. *The Life of Peter* in effect warns against attempts to drive a wedge between the emerging ecclesiastical–political establishment and the tsar, and repeatedly praises the principality of Moscow and "the elevated throne of the glorious metropolitanate of Russia." Kiprian was guided by a lofty conception of the role the Church could play in the construction of a national self-image. He believed that God entrusted the clergy with the sacred obligation to preserve an uncorrupted Orthodox tradition.

Whatever the truth about the migration of monks from the Balkans, there is no denying the fact that a few monastic centers in the Russian lands proved to be powerhouses of a revitalized Orthodox culture under the aegis of the Muscovite princes. The religious life of the Muscovite state acquired fresh inspiration through a revitalized monastic movement. Hagiography was the default mode in which to certify the vitality of Orthodoxy. Outstanding spiritual leaders like Sergii of Radonezh (d. 1392, seen in a seventeenth-century icon in Plate 4) revitalized older ideals of spirituality and monastic practice.[81]

The late fourteenth and early fifteenth centuries witnessed organized attempts in monastic workshops throughout the Balkans and Muscovy to establish a more standard Church Slavonic language. Against this background, new textual practices like the correction of books, based on a memory of a halcyon period of monastic growth and intended to restore a pristine version of Orthodoxy, conferred a prestige and antiquity internal to Holy Rus´ as its own civilization. The Trinity-Sergiev Monastery, which St. Sergii of Radonezh founded around 1342, was the location of a number of Hesychast-inspired personalities.[82] The canonization of Sergii in 1448/49, following the discovery of his relics in the 1420s, inspired a new wave of writing and editing: in the 1430s and 1440s Pakhomy rewrote Epifany's *Life*, his third version dated to around 1442, in which he increased the number of miracles associated with the spiritual leader. The liturgical and philological activity of Metropolitan Kiprian, the embodiment in Russia of the Euthymian tradition and practice, reflected yet another aspect of the renewed Russian religious and cultural life. It became foundational not only for the realization of new linguistic and liturgical reforms, but also for the elaboration of a new rhetorical style, characteristic of the hagiographic production of this community. The morphological and lexical changes enabled the Eastern Slavs to emerge from the fifteenth century with an enhanced stylistic inventory and a new literary canon. Word-weaving (*pletenie sloves*) was a new hagiographic technique which first developed on South Slavic soil under Byzantine influence; it was based on a careful consideration of the word and its prosodic and philological properties.

KEYWORD **Word-weaving**

This nostalgia for the old linguistic unity associated with the epoch of Cyril and Methodius coincided with the spread of a spiritual movement known as Hesychasm, which, following the neo-Platonic tradition, strove to access spiritual elevation through the written word and the emotional expressiveness of language, creating verbal icons for the godhead. One means of achieving this was the technique of "word-weaving" (*pletenie sloves*) utilized in ecclesiastical works. "Word-weaving" is based on the phonological, etymological, and semantic properties of words, and favors striking prosodic effects and tautology as well as neologism. Epifany Premudry, author of *The Life of St. Stephan of Perm*, is its most illustrious medieval practitioner. Syntax is periodic and extended, and the use of metaphor is widespread. In the modern period, Aleksei Remizov (1877–1957) was famed for his pseudo-medieval works that revived "word-weaving" as an authentic Russian style.

This new stylistic preoccupation with the word entailed an analytic approach toward the various lexical features, including phonology (alliteration, assonance), etymology, subtleties of semantics (tautological combinations), neologisms, word comparisons, and calques. The concept of orthography, as interpreted by Hesychast ideology, implied not only the problem of how to spell correctly but also that of how to write correctly in the broader sense of the spiritual message. According to the Hesychastic attitude toward language, the essence of a word was contained in the word itself. By accurately preserving the Word of God in the texts, the purity of Orthodoxy would also be preserved. The Hesychast identification of the word with its essence lay at the base of the Euthymian linguistic reforms and maximized the striving for "emotional expressiveness." This style expressed the conviction that any hagiographic work had to convey an element of the saint's own essence. Accordingly, the saint's life had to be written in an appropriate vocabulary, capable of inspiring the same reverence as the saint himself.

There is more than nostalgia involved in the practices of copying and elaboration of new forms of writing, such as *pletenie sloves*, that claim to be grounded in the models of a Rus' that might have seemed remote. Scribal activity attested to the continual repositioning of Kievan writings against later vernacular productions. Recalling the fame of Kiev of a bygone era also reminded fellow scribes and readers of the glory that can be lost through the loss of continuity. From the vantage point of fifteenth-century Moscow, the legacy of Kiev looked both venerable and foundational: in the history of successions, Kiev was to Moscow as Jerusalem was to Athens and Athens to Rome. A new ornate and elevated style achieved a philological sophistication by producing original coinages, phraseology, neologisms, and archaisms. Rhythm, cadence, and emotionality shaped writing in ways not seen since the twelfth century. From the late fourteenth century, these changes reflected Moscow's absolutist ecclesiology as well as the state's ambitions for hegemonic intellectual dominance.

The tradition of the unabridged *zhitie* reaches an apogee of emotional conviction and rhetorical splendor in the fifteenth century, remaining a staple until the seventeenth century. The most notable writer of the post-Kievan period is Epifany Premudry (also known in English as Epiphanius the Wise, *fl.* 1420), a monk at the Trinity-Sergiev Monastery, follower (and biographer) of St. Sergii, and the author of two outstanding saints' lives of the fifteenth century. References in his writings suggest that he traveled to Constantinople and Jerusalem; otherwise little is known about him apart from the information he imparts.[83] In contrast to Kiprian's more political *The Life of Peter* and the "Eulogy of Metropolitan Peter" ("Pokhval'noe slovo za mitropolit Petr"), the work of Epifany Premudry manifests a conscious awareness that great figures can stand out in the crowd only if masterful portraits bring their belief and deeds to life through language that stirs the reader's or the listener's imagination.

Epifany Premudry's subjects were so important in the history of clerical institutions and the Orthodox state that his seminal writings were much copied and excerpted, edited and revised, expanded, and sometimes completely rewritten. Establishing a definitive edition of his original work has remained an elusive task, and a particularly complex one in the case of the *Life of St. Sergii of Radonezh* (*Zhitie prepodobnogo Sergiia*). This is because the manuscript tradition remained active over nearly two centuries, if not longer, and because Epifany Premudry's work has survived only in copies reprised as part of later texts rather than as separate works. Both of these facts illustrate how, in a copying culture, the dissemination of works can perpetuate authorial stature without guaranteeing attribution of authorship. Based mainly on sixteenth-century versions, textual editors have been able to reconstruct the version of the *Life of St. Sergii*, which then served as a prototype for many later renditions.

The consensus is that Epifany Premudry almost certainly produced a first version nearly thirty years after Sergii's death around 1417/18, and based his text on the materials he mentions collecting over a twenty-year period, including eyewitness accounts, legends, and other biographical writings that circulated among scribes. That so much writing and storytelling should have accumulated around the figure of Sergii is noteworthy since it made a national figure out of the monastery's founding spiritual leader. In the historical context, his powerful presence long after his lifetime is not surprising because the Trinity-Sergiev Monastery was "at the vortex of the Muscovite dynastic conflict" as factions appropriated the monastery's authority in pressing their claims.[84] In addition to supporting figures, such as Epifany Premudry and the great icon painter Andrei Rublev (the 1360s–*c.*1428), the monastery was a highly active educational center that would send out numerous founders of new churches and monasteries.

Epifany Premudry lavished his eloquence to create an ideal spiritual figure commensurate with Kiprian's earlier vision of Moscow as a center of Orthodoxy from the Balkans to the Urals. An evidently learned monk at the Trinity-Sergiev Monastery, an institution whose leaders supported the authority of the Muscovite princes and the notion of an Orthodox realm, Epifany Premudry demonstrated a mastery of rhetoric. In the five-part introduction to his masterpiece, the *Discourse on the Life and Teaching of Our Father St. Stephan of Perm* (*Slovo o zhitii i uchenii ottsa nashego Stefana Permskogo*), Epiphany Premudry injects a personal tone into his hagiographical work. As a younger contemporary of both his subjects, Sts. Stephan and Sergii, Epifany Premudry personally witnessed their activity. He sets out his theory of hagiography as a spiritual act of "writing on the tablets of the heart" ("na chuvstvennykh khartiiakh"). He makes a show of rejecting eloquence as "pagan," and claims to eschew its practice because wisdom comes, he asserts, from the contemplation of God and not from human craft. Piety and attentiveness to God allow the hagiographer to "write on the tablets of the heart," a tradition that goes back to St. Paul ("Forasmuch as ye are manifestly declared to be the epistle of Christ ministered by us, written not with ink, but with the Spirit of the living God; not in tablets of stone, but in fleshy tablets of the heart," 2 *Corinthians* 3:3). Together with this aspiration comes an exaggerated profession of ignorance that exceeds the modesty topos. Although his learning and skill will be evident in the quality of the writing, he nonetheless belittles himself for being "ignorant of verbal art," speaks of his "poor mind" and "crooked reasoning" and, above all, rejects the rhetorical "weavings and eloquence of Plato and Aristotle's orations." What Epifany as a Christian writer seeks from the Holy Spirit is, echoing Pauline language, a gift of mind and spirit that will afford him a gift adequate to do justice to his subject:

> I ask for the gift: that He send me his grace to my aid, that He grant me a firm intellective and wide ranging; that He stir my mind which is burdened with despondency and roughness of the flesh, that He purify my heart which is wounded by many wounds of spiritual defaults and bodily passions, so that I might be able to write and praise the good Stephan.

Riccardo Picchio observed that because Epifany Premudry confessed at the outset that he did not possess the ability "to write what is invisible on the tablets of intelligence and heart," and therefore all he could do was to operate on human senses, it was inevitable that his "poetics of prayer" became bound up with a continuous, humble search for glimpses of the divine that can be achieved through "word-weaving."[85] In fact, after Epifany disparaged word-weaving in the introduction he proceeded to a skillful application of all the stylistic devices that both he and contemporary scholars would define as *pletenie sloves*.

Pletenie sloves does not make an impact through logical argumentation. Beneath the stylistic intricacies and eloquence of the new style lay the mystical-linguistic theory of the word harking back to its origins in Bulgaria and its association with Hesychasm and the teachings of Bishop Euthymius.[86] Elaborate rhetorical techniques used in composing Serbian princely lives reflected the Euthymian approach to expressive language as a neo-Platonic vehicle for, and a medium of, Orthodox theology. Rhetoric was thought to give the hagiographer access to a "divine language" that would afford a silent, or apophatic, contemplation of God.[87] In the Hesychast conception, the combination, first, of various vowel and consonant sounds and then of different verbal units into syntactic chains, might induce in the reader and the listener a moment of revelation achieved through a mental effort to conceive the relation between complex signifiers and the supernal signifieds. In its very complex use of morphology, sound patterning, syntactic subordination, and metaphor, *pletenie sloves* presented a complete contrast to the standard paratactic syntax.

The trope of the eyewitness is familiar in hagiography. Occasionally, the writer might refer to known miracles rather than claim to have encountered the holy man directly. Like his predecessor Nestor, Epifany Premudry tempers pride with modesty, portraying himself as a "poor and unworthy modest monk," a "monk scribe" motivated by love. His imposing *Discourse on the Life and Teaching of our Father Stephan of Perm*, most likely dating to the 1390s, records the biography and pious acts of Stephan (c.1330–96), a missionary who, around 1379, abandoned his position of a priest in Rostov and set out to educate and convert the pagan populations of northern Russia. He translated Slavonic liturgical texts as well as the Greek Bible into the vernacular of the Perm region. For his labors, the Metropolitan of Moscow promoted him to the head of the Permian Diocese. Stephan was canonized for his missionary activities only in 1549, as part of Metropolitan Makary's program of systematizing the recognition of saints; his relics, however, have been lost. Published for the first time in 1862, the *Discourse on the Life of Stephan* has a complex textual history; most reprints and excerpts are drawn from the edition published in 1897 to mark the 500th anniversary of the death of St. Stephan of Perm.

Despite the absence of a proper modern scholarly edition, the *Discourse on the Life of Stephan of Perm* has been recognized as a landmark of Russian hagiographical writing, remarkable for its personal tone, eloquence, as well as its display of learning and erudition. The text is enriched by hundreds of excerpts from the Old and New Testaments, which are sometimes spliced together to form one cascading quotation—an evidence of the erudition of the author capable of weaving them into an original composition. The author takes pains to establish an analogy between his accomplishments, as an evangelist among pagans, and those of St. Cyril, placing St. Cyril in a direct line of the Cyrillo-Methodian inheritance, and describing him as a New Philosopher in respect of his learning and commitment.[88] As he shows Stephan earning acclaim, above all, for his work among the heathen, the writer dwells on the saint's intellectual qualities, praising his industry, the care with which he worked as a scribe and copyist, and, above all, the fact that he "was learned in the love of wisdom, that is, philosophy and had studied the Greek language and Greek books and constantly read them." Epifany Premudry omits the early chapters of birth and upbringing that were sometimes standard, zooming in on Stephan's pity for the tribes benighted by the absence of faith, which led him to hear his apostolic call and ask his bishop, Gerasim, to release him for missionary work. Stephan's conversation with Gerasim directly ushers in the narrative, which recounts the saint's journey, his labors, and his dedication of a new church to the Virgin Mary. A determined missionary, Stephan even confronts an angry mob of idolaters whose pagan statues he sets out to destroy. The narrative tells of him winning allies through the "meekness with which he preaches the word of the Lord" before giving a dramatic account of the moment when he destroys the pagan statues.

Epifany Premudry's use of an early form of oral history is evidenced by the vivid narrative of Stephan's dramatic contest against a determined enemy, a Permian magician or shaman, in which the saint not only triumphs but also shows mercy. An evocative chapter on sorcerers demonstrates that "reason," by which the writer means intelligence and true faith combined, is the most potent weapon of all. Such examples of Christian virtue serve as a transition to an overview of Stephan of Perm's good works, the impact of his teachings on many new converts and pupils, and the application of his learning to achieve divine enlightenment, in the spirit of the early Apostles, rather than for its own sake. A highly stylized deathbed scene is devoid of human physicality, painting an abstract, icon-like portrait removed in time and place and focused on eternity. The *Life* ends with Epifany Premudry's observation that princes, noblemen, as well as the entire church hierarchy and local population, attended Stephan's burial and interment. This observation suggests that by their attendance at ceremonies the clergy and monastic leaders wished to signal a common interest between Church and state, consistent with the claim made in passing that Stephan enjoyed the support of Grand Prince Vasily I, the son of Dmitry Donskoi, and Kiprian, whose strong advocacy of the role of the Church in Muscovite governance constitutes an implicit lesson of contemporary chronicle-writing and hagiography.

Epifany's achievement remained productive well beyond the fifteenth century. Versions of both the original and secondary archetypes for the *Life of St. Sergii of Radonezh* were included in the *Great Menology* (Figure 1.02 represents Tsar Ivan IV's veneration of the saint), extensively re-edited yet again at the Trinity-Sergiev Monastery in the seventeenth century, and published with other materials at the express request of Tsar Aleksei Mikhailovich. The most usable and

FIGURE 1.02. Tsar Ivan the Terrible arrives on pilgrimage at the Holy Trinity Monastery of St. Sergii, miniature from an illuminated manuscript chronicle, 16th c.

the most reprinted version of the text is largely the labor of sixteenth-century editors consistent with the approach to narration and portraiture used in the earlier *Life of St. Stephan of Perm*. While a saint's biography could be available in separate copies, the more usual method of dissemination would have been an open-ended *svod*, or compilation. A prayer serves as a bridge between the earlier text and the *Life of St. Sergii*, inserted on separate pages or written subsequently in a codex. This prayer originates with Epifany Premudry who, although unnamed, identifies himself as a familiar of the holy man and laments the lack of a thorough hagiography within two years of the saint's death.

The complex textual history of the *Life of St. Sergii* illustrates how hagiography could subordinate forms of medieval and ecclesiastical life-writing to create an enduring narrative of the saint's continued relevance to the ideals of the Church and political authorities.[89] In addition to his rewritings of the *Life of St. Sergii*, Pakhomy also composed a prayer (*kanon*) as well as a service to be used on the saint's day. Trained at the Monastery of Mt. Athos, Pakhomy appeared on the Russian scene in the 1440s in Novgorod where he was involved in editing saints' lives (he is thought to have composed a total of eleven himself), before moving to the Trinity-Sergiev Monastery. His activities at a number of important monasteries in Muscovy, including the Kirillo-Belozersky Monastery founded by Metropolitan Kirill (commemorated by him as a saint in the *Life of Kirill*), suggest a highly peripatetic existence and much demand for his skills, which is corroborated by a royal rescript commissioning from him prayers and other writings to be used in the rededication of the Uspensky Cathedral in the Kremlin. His mastery of the more elaborate panegyric of Serbian hagiography[90] made him a match for Epifany's style, fully up to the challenge of amplifying the praises of Sergii through erudite quotation and elaborate figures of speech. The effect was to remove Sergii from the fluctuations of history (any local references to his origins in Rostov were abandoned) and insert him into the world of pure spirit, as befitting a saint.

Biography provides the central narrative axis of Epifany's *Life of St. Sergii*. Headings demarcate individual chapters and serve as milestones in the stages in the saint's growth. A miracle attends his very birth: the writer alleges that during a service Sergii responded to the liturgy by crying out from his mother's womb in unison with the prayer, a sure sign to his mother Mary and other parishioners of his special status. Numerous other miracles, as well as more circumstantial details such as his baptism, will elicit comments from the author who underscores their significance and continually reaffirms Sergii's sanctity. And while the writer will engage in the trope of *recusatio*, and ask, "why should I speak in long speeches and exhaust the hearing of listeners?," his magisterial commentary will continue to accompany the opening sequences of the biographical chapters. Spiritual precociousness naturally leads to Sergii's taking of the tonsure at a young age. The numerous chapters that follow at length characterize his learning, piety, and traits of character and bearing, such as modesty (while others regard him as a prophet he declines to become Metropolitan) and threadbare clothing, thereby setting the stage for further miracles, all of which correspond to New Testament modes of saintly presence (such as resurrection of the dead through prayer and exorcism of devils) and his devotion to the cenobitic ideal adopted by the monasteries founded by the saint and his brethren.

Such spiritual authority comes into its own in another of Epifany's celebrated works, the *Discourse on the Life and Death of Dmitry Donskoi* (*Slovo o zhitii i o prestavlenii velikogo kniazia Dmitria Ivanovicha, Tsaria Ruskogo*). It extols the role of the prince as supported by the monastery in repelling the Tatars as led by Mamai in 1380. In the sweeping final eulogy (over 4,000 words long) that follows the death scene, Epifany Premudry amplifies his word-weaving to compose a verbal tapestry of tropes, cadenced phrases, puns and etymological wordplay, extensive metaphors and similes, neologisms, and compound epithets.[91]

The sun is praised for its beauty and greatness, and for its movement, and speed, and force, and the strength that it commands since it illuminates the entire earth from one end to the other equally, without depriving anyone of warmth. Thus was Dmitry triumphant and good in character, great in his greatness, decisive in virtuous deeds before he went to his rest; and in his might he circles round like the sun, emitting rays and warming all whom his rays attained—such a one was he. With no hesitations shall I say about him that through the entire world was his fame transported and to the ends of the earth was his magnificence. To whom shall I liken this great prince, this Russian tsar? Come, dear ones, worshippers of the holy, for words of praise to praise the ruler of the earth as befits him! Shall I call you an angel? But in life you assumed the flesh of an angel. Shall I call you a man? But you achieved deeds beyond human nature. Shall I call you primordial? But he who accepted the Testament from the Lord violated it while you kept the commandments accepted in holy baptism and preserved them in their purity...Shall I liken you to a new Noah?

Imagery and language here derive from hymnography and a rich liturgical tradition. Despite the use of oral legends and eyewitness accounts, the style immobilizes the life of the saint into an act of prayer and piety, more static than dynamic.

3

Local narratives

Unhappy families: The trauma of invasion

From Kievan Rus' to the Mongol conquest, literary works of the fourteenth to the fifteenth centuries addressed the vulnerability of boundaries, urging princes to keep their ritualized promises and join forces against invaders. Writings that dramatize the plight of Rus' look back to an admonitory tradition represented by Vladimir Monomakh (1053–1125), unusual as a ruler-author who predicted in his famous *Instruction* that political instability would make Rus' vulnerable to exogenous shocks and catastrophes, unless some forms of stable cooperation were established. Under the pressure of impending crisis, writers like Monomakh deplored factionalism. Yet it is arguable that the sudden appearance of the Mongols, rather than some internal disaster, propelled Rus' into a period of decline. The theme of fragmentation had its advantages as a basis for a new vision of a centralized state. The narratives that emerged in the fourteenth century about the rise of Muscovy and recovering prosperity and economic expansion, exploited the contrast between centralization as a force for promoting national interests and the appanage system resulting in fragmentation and disaster.

Local chronicles attest to a shared awareness of place, dynastic power-base, and common interests among the Eastern Slavs, giving them a foundation for something like a proto-national identity. In the principality of Galicia-Volhynia, the chronicler praises clergy for trying to intervene and pacify warring factions, as clan members descended from Prince Igor' Sviatoslavich, the hero of the *Lay of Igor's Campaign*, vie for preeminence and leave one another vulnerable to attack.[1] Amid formulaic expressions of grief, chronicle accounts risk glossing over the fact that some princes broke ranks and abetted the invaders to satisfy personal ambition.

Hierarchies of obedience and clan loyalty are a recurrent theme, beginning with an eleventh-century story in which the machinations of the sons of Grand Prince Vladimir end in fratricide. Three accounts are devoted to the *c*.1015 murders of Princes Boris and Gleb, Vladimir's younger sons and half-brothers of Iaroslav. The first of these accounts is a hypothetical prototype of the story that was included in the Laurentian and Hypatian versions of the *Primary Chronicle* and in the Novgorod Chronicle. A chronicle episode "On the murder of the Boris" may have been the basis for the later, more extensive *Tale* (*Skazanie*), written somewhere between 1015 and 1037, and which was expanded, most likely post-1073, to include accounts of miracles. Nearly two hundred copies of this tale, first attested in the *Uspensky Sbornik* of the late twelfth century, are known.[2] The *Tale* is sometimes used as evidence of popular religion on the supposition that its author would have been recording local legends.[3] The third account is Nestor's *Lection on the Life and Wrongful Death of the Blessed Martyrs Boris and Gleb*.

Part chronicle, part lament, the *Tale* may be the work of several independent authors whose disparate source material was arranged into a drama of martyrdom, perhaps with an ulterior political motive.[4] Whatever the hypothesis about authorship and the dating of the individual sections, the *Tale* is subdivided into three parts, starting with a brief genealogy of the Kievan ruling family and a condemnation of Prince Sviatopolk as an assassin. Throughout the story, Sviatopolk is named as the villainous brother who aspired to the throne and to satisfy his hunger for power, murdered his two younger brothers, Boris and Gleb. The *Primary Chronicle*, by contrast, noted that the two martyred brothers had a stronger claim to the throne based on their pedigree, because their mother was a Byzantine princess, whereas Sviatopolk's mother is said to have been no more than a "local woman."[5]

In the body of the work, the *Tale* recounts Sviatopolk's machinations and the savage murders. Although this is clearly meant to be a martyrdom narrative, and Boris and Gleb show a touching meekness (*smirenie*) in accepting their fate as divinely ordained, the writer produces no other religious evidence to justify their short lives with reference to Christian faith. By way of compensation, the final third of the work relates miracles performed at their grave after the brother's relics have been moved from the nearby town of Vyshegorod to a site that had once served as a pagan temple for Vladimir and had been reconsecrated. This third section reads like a supplement intended to corroborate and validate, in ecclesiastical terms, a cult of the brothers that may have originated in popular belief and gained authority as a founding myth of the ruling house.

By the time we reach the early twelfth century, that is a hundred years after the early Riurikid dynasty, the monk Nestor has distanced his reading of the story from the historical events and, with his *Lection*, produced a narrative fit for performance on the saints' feast day. Written in the Kiev Monastery of the Caves a century after the events, Nestor's work is much closer than the *Tale* to the sequential form and the emotional tone of a hagiography. Nestor strives to adapt the historical material to the generic shape of a saint's life, injecting pathos into the plight of the doomed princes, and successfully obscuring the background history of political assassination behind an edifying story of Christian devotion. The work expresses a clear sympathy with the ruling dynasty descended from Vladimir; and while the *Lection* strains to turn political murders into a case for Christian sanctification, it finds a basis for this view in an ideal of loyalty, seen as a Christian virtue contrasted with the strife that marred the Biblical ideal of the Garden of Eden.

The opening sections of the *Lection on the Holy Martyrs Boris and Gleb* review the story of Vladimir's conversion and the history of the clan (*rod*), as well as the history of pagan Rus'. The genealogic sub-plot serves as a vehicle for exploring the tensions inherent in the paradigm of royal succession, underscoring the relative positions of Boris and Gleb, two minor princes whose filial piety cost them their lives at the hands of their scheming half-brother.[6] The brothers' own good conduct as the rulers of Kiev's satellite cities, and their respect for the horizontal power relations between sons and nephews that made the appanage system workable, could not protect them against Sviatopolk, cast as a Cain intent on destroying his two Abel-like rivals. By incorporating different sources, including oral accounts of events beyond living memory, the *Lection* represents a sea change in the quality of narrative. The writer uses the tragedy of the two princes to corroborate their saintly qualities, including meekness in the face of death as an expression of loyalty toward their elder brother. Character portrayals seem to draw on the iconographic tradition, and the depicted figures are stylized as brave, reserved, and impersonal, their place in history determined by divine will.

Is this fact or fiction? Cyril Mango noted pithily that "Byzantine hagiography is full of fictions," and there is little reason to assume that Slavonic lives took fewer liberties.[7] Based on the discrepancies among the various accounts of Boris and Gleb, historians have speculated that the tale whitewashes the true role of Prince Iaroslav, no longer alive by the time of composition. Conjecture focuses on the possibility that Iaroslav, cast as a virtuous and loving brother in the *Lection*, schemed so that his half-brother Sviatopolk took the fall for his own misdeeds. Whatever the reality, the textual lives of Boris and Gelb, and especially Nestor's well-crafted, readable narrative, established the topos of the internecine strife between power-hungry brothers. Filtered through the hagiographic conventions, at which Nestor was expert, the literary image of the brothers who sacrificed their lives for the sake of the *rod*, or the ruling dynasty, sent a powerful message.

Nestor's version of Boris and Gleb's martyrdom invests the brothers with a religiosity that is ahead of its time and almost certainly exaggerated in the historical context. Their legend offers Nestor a way to pay tribute to an ideal in which good Christian conduct and brotherly love evoke a vision of the Kievan state: Prince Iaroslav, who vanquished the usurper Sviatopolk and reburied his martyred brothers Boris and Gleb, here stands for the continuity and stability of the dynasty thanks to his moral distinction and piety. While in other accounts Iaroslav is praised for his many Christian acts, his love of books, and patronage of monasteries, Nestor, as did Ilarion, reflects Iaroslav's canny affiliation of the cult of the martyred brothers with the interests of the ruling house. Boris and Gleb's iconography tracks their textual image, too. Since at least the fourteenth century, icons had established a visual portrait of the brothers that emphasized their youth. In image after image, they stand foursquare before the viewer: young, regal warriors, one bearded, the other clean-shaven, their gaze timeless. A second iconographic tradition depicts them on horseback, their eyes fixed firmly on the worshipper. They are represented more as valiant warriors, figures which will be invoked in fourteenth-century texts.

It would be a mistake to attribute a forensic historical function to any storytelling forms of the period. The role of medieval writing was often to remind the readers, whether monks or princes, to emulate the Christian ideal of piety and meekness. Tragic accounts might be thought of as models that need to be avoided, cautionary tales to others. Should this be called propaganda? It is reasonable to suppose that the affirmation of the dynasty and of the Christian faith through a legitimizing story would have done no harm to the position of the monastery: the perceived value of writing would have added luster to the Church. Later accounts even turn Prince Vladimir, whose early life was supposedly marked by pagan practice and wanton behavior, into an exception that proves the rule. If there is a new message, it lies in the sense that the fortunes of the ruling house have been positive for the religious institutions that foster writing, already seen as the vital medium of cultural memory. As examples of good and evil, and of the imitation of Christ through martyrdom, Boris and Gleb's lives provided a lesson to the holy brethren of the monastery. But the texts about their death do more than demonstrate Christian meekness. From the start, their story was fashioned as an imaginative demonstration of the necessity of subservience to the larger interests of a corporate body whether it be a dynasty or a monastic community, and as a pragmatic example of the Orthodox virtue of humility (*smirenie*). Once outsiders intrude on the world of Kievan Rus', the themes of historical disaster and disunity intersect. The tragedy of princely hubris is counterbalanced by the valorization of princely martyrdom.[8]

The Lay of Igor's Campaign *and the princely image*

The twelfth century saw the establishment of churches dedicated to Sts. Boris and Gleb in Chernigov, Polotsk, Kideksh (near Suzdal'), and the city-state of Novgorod (often called Novgorod the Great). Unsurprisingly, literary characterization of the princes, both negative and positive, will gradually come to appraise the moral worth of rulers in relation to an ideal of family loyalty and the interests of the city-state. The veneration of older princes, including

Vladimir, became a feature of local worship and writing. The best princes will emerge as warrior-saints, religious and military in equal measure. The princely image will become consolidated as a type from the fourteenth century to the reign of Ivan IV in the sixteenth century consistent with the consolidation of power under the Grand Prince of Vladimir and Moscow. Over time the development of an ideal of a Christian warrior prince becomes a more explicit image of leadership by fusing political leadership and charismatic religious identity.

There is no better example of the theme of the hapless prince than the sole surviving specimen of bardic literature from the period, the *Lay of Igor's Campaign*. The work tells of an unsuccessful campaign against the Polovtsians (sometimes referred to as Cumans), led by Prince Igor Sviatoslavich of Novgorod-Severs in 1185. The prince ignored the advice of his elders and engaged in battle against the Polovtsian horde invading across the steppe. The vividness of the account, now famed for its nature imagery, stunning metaphor, and avian and astrological symbolism, convinced the early readers that the author-cum-narrator must have been an eyewitness to the events.

The text, which has been alternatingly formatted as prose and as rhythmic units comparable to lines of verse, employs oral techniques familiar from the Scandinavian saga, as well as drawing on Byzantine chronicles and local history, and at points seems quite bookish. At barely two hundred lines, this "lay" (the word *slovo* designates a narrative discourse or sermon) is clearly not on the scale of a Homeric or even Byzantine epic. Yet the term "epic" has stuck to the *Lay* as a work that conveys the grandeur of an event, and, although the battle was a local conflict, the writer seems to speak for the nation: he refers to the Russian "land" as a unity rather than a collection of peoples. He enhances the impression of ethnic (over political) unity by representing the conflict as between the Christian Kievans and the nomadic people of the steppe. Igor's defeat brought a costly but critical lesson in disunity generated by the appanage system. The term "epic" is also appropriate due to the pathos the narrator injects into this story. While the actual battle may have been no more than a skirmish, into a relatively compact form the writer packs a wealth of language, psychological and socio-historical insights into religion, leadership, and national identity; in other words, it is an epic by virtue of its scale and vision.

Throughout the story, a self-reflexive and highly emotive narrator injects judgmental commentary on the nature of the disaster:

> This has all happened because the two brave sons of Sviatoslav, Igor and Vsevolod, had aroused the treachery (of the Polovtsians), which their father (Sviatoslav Vsevolodovich) the great Kievan menacing in his wrath would have put to rest: he stopped (the Polovtsians) with his strong forces and sharp swords; entered the Polovtsian land (in his earlier campaign), trod through the hills and ravines, muddied the rivers and lakes, dried out streams and swamps, and tore the very pagan khan Kobiak out of the creek from his great steel troops—and Kobiak fell in the city of Kiev in the palace.

Over the course of four days—the timeframe is marked by an ominous eclipse, reminiscent of the battle of Jericho—the narrator tracks the two opposing forces headed for a collision. When the battle erupts, the emphasis is placed on the suffering of the land. It is as if the author could not bring himself to confront the occasion and surrendered to a lyrical meditation, contemplating the history and the present moment, expressing anxiety about the fate of one or another of his heroes, and bitterly deploring the historical fate of the principalities of Rus'. Other rhetorical and poetic features, such as pathetic fallacy, nature symbolism, apostrophe, and vivid metaphor add stunning effects to an account of a single battle that laments the vulnerability of the cities of Rus'. The narrator unhesitatingly evokes older pagan gods within a Christian framework; critics have cited a vast array of sources, including Kievan chronicles,

Byzantine hymnography, and Scandinavian bardic practices that add texture to the narrative and depth to the explicit message.[9]

The narrator of the *Lay of Igor's Campaign* acknowledges that the goal of many campaigns against the Polovtsians was not defense, but rather vengeance for what he throughout calls "injury" (*obida*). In a highly emotional language, he deplores how vengeance drives leaders to pursue reckless aims for personal glory. Vanity and self-interest jeopardize the welfare of their people and their city for the sake of short-term military success. The speaker makes a point of juxtaposing fame as a reward for just deeds (*slava*) and honor as self-promotion (*chest'*). Self-interest and disregard for the collective good precipitate a series of disasters, which the writer casts in terms of a tension between fathers and sons.[10] We are often reminded that Igor is one of the grandsons of Prince Oleg of Chernigov, a friend of Vladimir Monomakh who entered into an alliance with the Polovtsians and invaded Rus' after being forced out of the city of Vladimir by an uncle. His own family woes stand in contrast to the advantages his enemies had through a united front. The writer is also well versed in Polovtsian history and cites with authority the fact that Khan Sharukan, the Polovtsian leader defeated by the Russian princes in 1106, was the grandfather of Khan Konchak who defeated Prince Igor in 1185.

Arguably, the real subject of this dramatic tale is an unhappy family history rather than the battle. The outcomes of both stories, already foreshadowed by omens such as the solar eclipse, occasion lyric outbursts of reproach rather than a suspenseful plot. As the narrator ponders the sad, historical fate of the land of Rus', he distinguishes between true courage and the mere vanity of the princes. A mastery of family genealogies is not essential to follow the logic of the author's thoughts as they turn from the case of Igor to the entire clan, wondering whether the real cost of warmongering is the bad example it sets for the next generations. There is a moralistic element to the analysis of the allure of fame. The first figure to be evaluated is Igor's brother, Prince Vsevolod, also known as Bui Tur (meaning "wild auroch"). The author describes Vsevolod's victory and his bravery, for in the heat of the battle Vsevolod does not notice the wound he sustains. Although Vsevolod might initially strike one as an exemplar of selflessness, the author shifts from praise to disapproval. Vsevolod, he charges, had forgotten to ask the Grand Prince, Sviatoslav of Kiev, for his permission to serve under Igor. The impulse to fight and to achieve glory had led him to forget all that he possessed—the wealth of his estate and his principality. He had also forgotten about the interests of his father's seat in Chernigov, subjecting it to the danger of retaliation from the Polovtsy, a fierce nomadic tribe of the steppe. Finally, Vsevolod had neglected the plight of his wife. This last detail is not unimportant: warfare and the male world in the *Lay of Igor's Campaign* are often juxtaposed with scenes from everyday life, be it harvests or feasts. The contrast between the domestic ritual with the costs of recklessness (even more than heroism) constitutes a poignant axis of interpretation, and the poem culminates in the lament of Igor's wife, Iaroslavna.

In mid-action, the bard shifts the perspective to Sviatoslav just as we surmise that the battle has been lost, loosely linking temporally and geographically distant settings. Transported in his mind to Sviatoslav's side in Kiev, in the very heart of Rus', the author observes all the dire repercussions of Igor's defeat: darkness covers the sky; the Eastern tribes rejoice in their victory; and Goth women jingle their Russian gold. The coup of the writer's imagination lies in the creation of a dream language that condenses much of the poem's symbolism and action. The dream roughly marks the midpoint of the *Lay of Igor's Campaign*, when Sviatoslav learns of the defeat of Igor and Vsevolod. Sviatoslav sees his own home with its golden turrets, but there is no prince—a sign that some unhappiness is about to fall on the princely abode. The dream uses poetic language to foreground the message of the narrative and capture the meaning of loss. The complete passage, loaded with the images of funerary ritual, repeatedly mentions

FIGURE 1.03. *The Battle of Suzdal and Novgorod*, School of Novgorod, second half of the 15th c.

the crepuscular darkness that surrounds the prince in this symbolic, both central and elevated, location. Sviatoslav sees himself laid out on a bier where his body is being dressed:

And Sviatoslav saw a troubling dream in Kiev on the hills. "On this night, from the evening they dressed me—he said—in a black funerary cover on a cedar bed; they scooped for me blue wine mixed with grief; they showered me, using the empty quivers of the pagan foreigners, with pearl upon my chest and were tender to me. Already there are boards without a support in my golden-turreted palace. All night from the evening the grey crows cawed (foretelling misfortune) at the Plesen´ka (near Kiev)."

The entire dream is constructed out of a series of inversions that travesty the real world of the *Tale*, starting with a mise-en-scène in which the living Sviatoslav sees his own burial, and where spring is a season of death rather than rebirth. Details of sinister transformations are precise and surreal: instead of arrows, tears-cum-pearls drop from the enemy quivers; the wine turns blue; the *terem* or abode of aristocratic women turns into a battlefield; the marital bed is changed into a funerary sled; and at the moment of the departure of the prince's soul he sees a nameless figure caress him while the roof is lifted. The inverted dream language is harbinger of Igor's unheroic fate and brilliantly conveys the anxiety of a fellow ruler.[11]

Whereas a chronicle entry relates that the captive Igor was quickly ransomed, the literary work prolongs his distress to the very final lines when his ransom at last brings freedom, restoration, and near-resurrection. Meanwhile, Igor's wife Iaroslavna and her household grieve together, the land itself seen to yearn for an earlier age when princes were less mettlesome. Although the narrative hints that the Polovtsians continue to plot against the younger princes—there is talk of "ensnaring the eaglets"—Igor manages to return, the sun rises, and young people sing. Upon his return, Igor heads directly to the shrine of the Virgin in order to render his thanks; the story, however, breaks off rather abruptly, with no explicit moral or closing remarks about the security of the Russian lands. There is a clear sense that, even while this story ends, fraternal discord will continue to run its course (sometimes depicted in illustrations such as Figure 1.03).

CASE STUDY **National identity, medievalism, and the discovery of the *Lay of Igor's Campaign***

The discovery of the *Lay of Igor's Campaign* in the 1790s could not have been better timed, coming as it did when interest in the Russian national past, its history, and culture, was gaining momentum. The question of what it meant to have a distinctive national culture became a central theoretical issue in aesthetics and historiography in the late eighteenth century. Models of literary development and progress imply views on national identity. An idea of the past, sometimes embodied in a seminal text, can represent a means of legitimation and a way of benchmarking continuity and innovation against an external standard. Even by European standards, the practice of secular literature in Russian literature looked well established by the end of the reign of Catherine the Great. Self-questioning about the depths of Russia's Europeanization had been an undercurrent in the cultural discourse since the 1770s. By the 1790s, such figures as the writer (and later historian) Nikolai Karamzin, the architect Nikolai L´vov, the painters Fedor Rokotov and Vladimir Borovikovsky, the poet Gavrila Derzhavin, and the novelist and collector Mikhail Chulkov had actively drawn on native subjects in an effort to discover, or create, an authentic Russian cultural past. This new emphasis on Russian sources—thematic, linguistic, stylistic, decorative—reflected a concern about the "native," which in itself marked the degree to which Russian and European trends were now synchronized, since an emphasis on the local and "original" marked the long transition into Romanticism across Europe. Historiography as a discipline was in its fledgling stages in the late eighteenth century. Nonetheless, the value invested in the *Lay of Igor's Campaign*, as evidence of a lost literary tradition accompanied the rise of antiquarianism as a path to rediscovering the country's past, visible in the efforts of semi-professional historians, including German scholars at the Academy of Sciences in St. Petersburg (namely, K. F. Müller and Academician Schlözer), to recover the past by collecting and publishing primary sources such as local legends. Within this context, it is no wonder that the discovery of a single medieval manuscript in 1792 containing an ancient tale of the twelfth century caused a stir, and seemingly put a small circle of readers in touch with the lost world of Russia's cultural origins in the Kievan principality before the Tatar invasions of 1223, the Battle of the Kalka River, and 1237, the year when Batu Khan demanded submission of the princes of Rus´.

Nikolai Karamzin announced the discovery of the text in the Hamburg journal the *Spectateur du Nord* in 1797, describing it as a "fragment of an epic." The mystery of the manuscript's recovery, and its subsequent loss, are worthy of Gothic thrillers so popular in the period. Karamzin noted briefly that Aleksei Musin-Pushkin, a celebrated antiquarian whose collection had attracted the patronage of Catherine II, had discovered the manuscript. Over the course of several years, the editors, who were amateurs in the fields of paleography and textual criticism, attempted to prepare this uniquely challenging text for publication. The archivist and historian Konstantin Kalaidovich questioned the secretive Musin-Pushkin about the provenance of the manuscript of this "incomparable song." Musin-Pushkin claimed that the sole copy of this text was appended to a medieval chronicle, probably dating to the early fifteenth-century. Archimandrite Ioel of the Spaso-Iaroslav Monastery, which had fallen into desuetude, is alleged to have sold it in 1795 to Musin-Pushkin who found the irregular spelling, the lack of punctuation, and the irregular word breaks an impediment to accurate transcription. A flawed manuscript presented a problem not only with respect to authentication but also to establishing an authoritative text. In 1800, Musin-Pushkin published his transcription alongside a translation into modern Russian under the direction of two other connoisseurs, Aleksei Malinovsky and Nikolai Bantysh-Kamensky.

The original manuscript perished in the 1812 Moscow fire. All that remained was the *editio princeps* plus the translation and the philological notes, and a not very accurate copy of the manuscript that had been presented in 1795 to Catherine the Great, herself the author of historical works. The loss of any medieval archival material in the destruction of Moscow in 1812 would have been devastating, but the disappearance of this particular manuscript fueled curiosity about its authenticity and authorship. What was it that Musin-Pushkin found? Was the manuscript a flawed fifteenth-century copy of an original twelfth-century text? Was it an original fifteenth-century work rather than a contemporary text describing twelfth-century events? Editors have attempted to differentiate historic linguistic features from later scribal corruptions and errors made by the first editors who worked deductively.

What was at stake was evidence of an original literary heritage that was both erudite and cosmopolitan and authentically Kievan. It was a standard view that a national epic represented a degree of civilization. While only Greece had Homer, and only Italy had Virgil, other cultural elites measured national standing with reference to imitation and translation of these epic poets. Yet uniqueness bred doubt: cases like James Macpherson's invention of Ossian in the 1760s and Thomas Chatterton's medieval forgeries had raised suspicions about genius coming from unlikely places. Why was it that a text of such importance was preserved in only one copy, and in a copy that had itself perished? How could something so valuable have been overlooked for so long? For some readers, the archaic and sometimes impenetrable language was not just surprising in its detail, but generally a mark of authenticity. Why, for that matter, was there not a single allusion to this work in the six centuries preceding its reappearance? The story of attempts to locate other copies and the production of forgeries would provide enough material for a separate book. From 1810 to 1840, the *Lay of Igor's Campaign* seems to have led a double life. On the one hand, it enjoyed considerable esteem, providing Alexander Pushkin, for example, with the subject of an article, and prompting a number of translations and imitations including a distinguished version by Vasily Zhukovsky, memorable for its enhanced Romantic tone. Russian Ossianism, for instance, had enjoyed a long vogue from the 1790s to the 1810s when Karamzin published posthumously Mikhail Murav'ev's Ossianic tale "Oskol'd" (reprinted in 1819). For a readership that was not yet familiar with historical linguistics, and that viewed the past through the Ossianic mist, the very contemporary feel of the *Lay of Igor's Campaign*, such as its use of pathetic fallacy, were decisive literary proofs of its authenticity. But as the Ossianic cloud of mysticism and romance had lifted and as historical linguistics had developed, the work became the subject of more scientific scrutiny. The situation changed radically in 1852 with the discovery of a verifiable medieval work on a similar scale and subject, evidence which was taken to confirm the authenticity of the *Lay of Igor's Campaign*. The *Zadonshchina*, which depicts Prince Dmitry Donskoi's victory over the Tatars in the famous Battle of Kulikovo, dates no later than to the early fifteenth century. While it never quotes the *Lay of Igor's Campaign* extensively, numerous borrowings, in the form of images, the structure of historical scenes, rare phrases, and adjective–noun collocations, found only in the other text, all together strongly suggested a genetic relation between the two works. Given the consensus that the *Lay of Igor's Campaign* is of superior quality—and that the superior work must, accordingly, be older— the existence of a second, lesser epic chock full of allusions suggested either a common source or direct descent from the medieval masterpiece.

For the next half century, the assumption that the *Lay of Igor's Campaign* was a genuine Kievan text exercised considerable influence on medieval Russian scholarship and on the study of the mythology and religious beliefs of the Kievans. Yet skeptics were waiting in the wings. In the early twentieth century, the French scholar Louis Leger advanced the hypothesis that the *Igor Tale* had not inspired the *Zadonshchina*, but rather that it was the other way round: a now-lost manuscript of the *Zadonshchina* served as a model for a late eighteenth-century forger. The idea was forgotten until Leger's distinguished compatriot André Mazon revived the hypothesis in 1940.[12] First, Mazon addressed the problem of the numerous linguistic anomalies in the text. Whereas earlier scholars blamed these anomalies on the original publishers, Mazon treated them as a sure sign of an ambitious forger whose system of images was not medieval in origin, but showed telltale signs of pre-Romanticism and Polish influence. Until the appearance of the *Zadonshchina*, it seemed completely out of the question that anyone would have a basis for imitation; now it was necessary to admit the possibility that an ingenious forger had made a good use of an authentic medieval epic. What was at stake then was the entire scholarly structure erected around the unquestioned authenticity of the document.

In 1948, Roman Jakobson, who headed a team of émigré researchers in New York, produced a systematic refutation of Mazon's critique, arguing in favor of the originality of the vocabulary and the images that Mazon had discredited.[13] By adducing numerous parallel passages from folklore and Byzantine literature, Jakobson made a powerful case for the authenticity of the *Lay of Igor's Campaign*. Importantly, he acknowledged the complexity and the sophistication of the work, and recognized its genuine poetic achievements as a decisive refutation of the view that medieval literature suffered from impoverished imagination and language. Jakobson was not to have the last word. In the 1960s, the distinguished Soviet medievalist Aleksandr Zimin sided with Mazon (causing something of a national scandal) by accepting that while the *Zadonshchina* in its long and short versions was authentic, it did not corroborate the authenticity of the *Lay of Igor's Campaign*. He argued that if anything the *Zadonshchina* had served an eighteenth-century forger of the latter as a source. In response, Jakobson and the American linguist Dean Worth produced their own proto-version of the *Zadonshchina*, which was closer to the Jakobsonian reconstruction of the *Lay of Igor's Campaign*.[14]

The debate over the *Lay of Igor's Campaign* is a debate about the precise nature of medieval Russian culture and its European connections. It is therefore not at all surprising that over the next fifty years a vast bibliography had accrued precisely on this question. Both sides have been known to resort to arguments from silence and circular reasoning. The strategy of the doubters is founded on an oversimplified presentation of the language, the poetics, and the culture of early Rus´ which could hardly accommodate the *Lay of Igor's Campaign*. The defenders of the work's authenticity continue to explain away the aberrations by referring to a tangled textual history; it must be admitted, however, that, in the absence of any manuscript evidence, the researcher is free to construct almost any theoretically satisfying model.

While the controversy revives now and again, the debate seems to have ended in favor of authenticity. The extrinsic story of discovery, recovery, scholarly debate, and reception constitute a set of episodes in cultural history, spanning from the Enlightenment to Soviet Russia (authenticity was hotly debated again in the 1950s and 1960s), and demonstrate the degree to which the status of a text and the changing assumptions made about literature and literary periods intersect. The debate also demonstrates the degree to which questions of national importance can be invested in a literary work. The simple fact of the work's existence has completely overturned the received wisdom that monasteries, essentially the sole centers of literacy, had produced writings (*pis´mennost´*) but no literature. The work's abiding literary interest lies in its remarkable—and for Russia unprecedented—combination of oral and written techniques. These were taken by some eighteenth-century scholars as evidence of a popular native genius endowed with considerable erudition, and later on as evidence of Kievan Rus´ embodying a continuity of what the historian Dimitri Obolensky called the Byzantine Commonwealth. In the twentieth century, D. S. Mirsky, the literary historian and a brilliant critic of contemporary poetry, believed that the text was a genuine medieval work, and observed that its use of visual techniques seemed remarkably modernist.[15] The work has been much admired and imitated by modern Russian poets, including Marina Tsvetaeva and Nikolai Zabolotsky, masters of verse narrative.[16]

Narratives of invasion

Warnings of impending disaster reverberate through the writing of the twelfth century, most eloquently in the *Instruction* of Monomakh and in the *Lay of Igor's Campaign*, also informing less famous prose accounts that ponder the theme of causation and blame. Political treachery was seen not only as inherent in the appanage system but almost as a family curse. The vanity of ambition (rather than honor or *chest´*) that drove princes to forget their loyalty to the clan (*rod*) serves as an important moralizing topos until the end of the fourteenth century. The topos persisted because it continued to reflect (and may have exaggerated and outlived) the nature of power in the appanage city-states. A self-contained and fragmentary entry in the Novgorod

Chronicle, known as "The Tale of the Crime of the Princes of Riazan'" ("Rasskaz o prestuplenii Riazanskikh kniazei") gives a perspective on fratricidal seizures of power, and the theme comes to a head in other prose accounts written in Riazan'.

Riazan' was a principality in the orbit of the city of Vladimir, and was eventually annexed by Moscow during its inexorable rise in the fifteenth century.[17] Written sometime in the second third of the thirteenth century, the "Tale of the Crime of the Princes of Riazan'," perhaps based on an oral legend, demonizes the descendants of Oleg Sviatoslavich (through his brother), whose treachery features in the *Lay of Igor's Campaign*. The younger princes Gleb Vladimirovich and his brother Konstantin, "inspired by the devil," plot to overthrow the ruling Prince Ingvar and his retinue ("If we kill them, we'll seize all the power"). They set a trap and invite Ingvar to a feast in order to slaughter him and his followers. The fragment omits the fact, noted elsewhere, that Ingvar escaped. "The Tale of the Crime of the Princes of Riazan'" condemns the princes in terms that deliberately echo the admonitions of Vladimir Monomakh. And like the *Lay of Igor's Campaign*, it treats these betrayals and defeats as a matter of shared calamity as well as personal anguish.

The sense of catastrophe engulfing Rus' persisted for another two centuries, turning the focus onto new martyrs in family sagas, invasions, and finally the emergence of a princely ideal. Along the way, writers continued to pay tribute to figures acting as aggressors and victims in the political cut and thrust. Prince Yuri Dolgoruky of Suzdal' became Grand Prince of Kiev by deposing his brother, distributed towns to his sons, and sent Prince Andrei Bogoliubsky to Vyshegorod. On succeeding his father, Andrei established connections between the important medieval centers of Vladimir, Suzdal', and Riazan', well before Moscow began its consolidation of the north.[18] The *Life of Andrei Bogoliubsky* (*Zhitie Andreia Bogoliubskogo*), copies of which began to circulate in the seventeenth century, omits negative facets of his career mentioned in the twelfth-century *Laurentian Chronicle*, such as his power-hungry raids against his brother and the rivalry that existed between father and son (noted by a more contemporaneous chronicle), insisting instead on his obedience to a higher authority and suggesting that he moved northward out of a sense of duty and in order to secure the spiritual legacy of Kiev already menaced by enemies.[19] On his journey north, he took with him the Byzantine icon of the Virgin (famed as "Our Lady of Vladimir"); the author of the *Life* casts the journey as a pilgrimage and the beginning of Andrei's reign as the fulfillment of a divine ordinance.

The tone of narrative in chronicles can seem dry and objective, but the selection of content and manipulation of sources was a way to convey viewpoint and adjust the reputations of dynasties and rulers. By tracing the provenance and revisions to episodes about individual rulers and city-states, historians have established that chronicles were prone to adopt the bias of the ruling house, their account acquiring the status of a near official record of how things came to be. Bogoliubsky is one example of a princely reputation burnished by chroniclers despite a checkered historical record. Although he rebuffed the Polovtsians in the south, Bogoliubsky engaged in continual warfare against brothers and cousins in neighboring towns and challenged a cousin for the seat of Kiev (a fact that will be noted by Nikolai Karamzin in his pioneering *History of the Russian State*, 1811–24).[20]

Another work, called the "Tale of the Murder of Andrei Bogoliubsky," ("Povest' ob ubienii Andreia Bogoliubskogo") contained in a 1175 chronicle, takes an affirmative view about his efforts to centralize power in Vladimir, depicting him as a sufferer on par with Boris and Gleb who, like them, prays for forgiveness just before being murdered and expresses willingness to die to protect the city. Princely virtue is also directly proportional to the lavishness of church decoration. Searching for superlatives, the writer of the "Tale of the Murder of Andrei Bogoliubsky" equates Bogoliubsky's accomplishment with the splendors of a church interior, omitting to mention his treacherous acts of political discord: the "magnificent pearls," the "altar of gold and silver," "the abundance of gold vessels and silver lamps," "precious stone carvings" and "gilt cupolas" represent splendor worthy of King Solomon and celebrate Andrei's reputation as a founder of monasteries.[21] Andrei's speeches cited by the writer contain echoes of Monomakh's self-abasement as a "poor and sinful slave," while comparisons of him to the sun draw on hymnographic images also found in the *Lay of Igor's Campaign*.

The chronicles record numerous martyred princes from the twelfth century.[22] Among the most dramatic narratives are the stories of two princes, Fedor and Mikhail, who lose their lives to invaders when they refuse to worship pagan deities. In the end, a blazing fire engulfs their tormentors and illuminates the place of their martyrdom for their fellow Christians. Even more dramatic is the story of a Moravian servitor to a Russian prince, which is told in the "Lay of Merkury of Smolensk" ("Slovo o Merkurii Smolenskom") as included in the *Great Menology*. Inspired by the Virgin, to whom he prays all night on the eve of the battle against Batu in 1239, Merkury heroically slaughters the enemies in droves until one of the Tatar soldiers decapitates him, just as the Virgin had predicted. Merkury picks up his own head and returns to Smolensk, where the Virgin appears to him and makes his corpse whole again.[23]

Pathos reaches new heights in accounts of the successive waves of Tatar or Mongol invasions dating to the mid-thirteenth century. The triggering event was a 1222 or 1223 battle on the River Kalka near the Sea of Azov in southern Rus'. The Tatars continued their incursions into northeastern Russia in 1237, conquering major cities like Riazan', Vladimir, and Suzdal', culminating in the sack of Kiev in 1240. Kiev was leveled and its population exterminated. The wars reshaped the map of Rus', with Vladimir, northeast of Moscow, replacing Kiev as the dominant principality.

The occupation of the southern steppe deprived the Rus' for over two centuries of much of their best land. Scribes reacted with particular bitterness to the invasion possibly because it isolated monasteries from centers of learning in Byzantium and the Balkans. Another century would elapse before, in the latter half of the fourteenth and first half of the fifteenth centuries, Moscow had emerged under the descendants of Ivan I or Ivan Kalita (Ivan the Money-Bag, 1288–c.1341), the first of the Daniilovich clan to hold the title of Grand Prince of Vladimir and Moscow, as a unifying force in northeastern Russia. Narratives nonetheless focus more on catastrophe as pervasive, depicting scenes of devastation, brave resistance, female mourning, and submission.

The debacle created opportunity for the advancement of tenacious princely lines. The descendants of the Vladimir princes from Kievan Rus', the Vsevolodichi, established their dominance over the region from the mid-thirteenth century. Their scion Alexander Nevsky (1221–63) became the prince of Vladimir in 1252 with the approval of the Golden Horde whose cooperation he sought. Local legends favorable to him helped to establish the literary image of the prince as a pious defender.

Monastic culture survived the historical disruptions of the mid-thirteenth century when the repeated waves of invading Turkic tribes and the Tatar Empire drove the population to resettle toward the north. Monastic foundations in small principalities like Vladimir, Suzdal', and eventually in Riazan', and in larger centers such as Pskov and Novgorod perpetuated the practices acquired in Kiev. Copying rather than innovation was the mainstay of writing. Yet continuity and stability permitted clergy, whatever the continued maneuverings of their princes, to respond to the invasion as an unprecedented trauma. The short prose work "The Discourse on the Destruction of the Land of Rus'," ("Slovo o pogibeli russkoi zemli") opens with an apostrophe to a land of paradise undermined by disunity and made vulnerable to incursions, most damagingly the Tatar invasion:

O, brilliant light and beautifully adorned land of Rus'! You are famed thanks to your many beauties: you have renown thanks to many lakes, local rivers and springs, mountains, lovely hills, tall oaks, fertile fields, amazing animals, varied birds, endless great cities, pious churches and eminent princes, honorable courtiers, many nobles. You have all this in abundance, Russian land, o Orthodox Christian faith![24]

The questions of how to secure the territory of the Orthodox Rus' and how to rekindle the glory days of Kiev, animates writings which revisit stories of catastrophe and revival.[25]

Mid-thirteenth- and fourteenth-century annals project a uniformly gloomy mood. Tales embedded within larger narratives balance grief with examples of valor. The "Tale of the Destruction of Riazan' by Batu" ("Povest' o razorenii Riazani Batyem") is one of a cycle of tales about a wonder-working saint and his icon collected in the *First Novgorod Chronicle*.[26] Largely a work of pure historical chronicle-writing, the "Tale of the Destruction of Riazan' by Batu" exercises its principal historical function by listing the names of warriors and places.[27] The text, however, reaches the heights of eloquence in describing the grief of the bereaved Eupraksia, the widow of Prince Fedor. A concluding miracle tale about the suicide of Eupraksia and her burial alongside her son and husband celebrates and enhances the worship of the wonder-working icon of St. Nicholas, the object of a local cult.[28] This tribute to the icon, along with the accompanying list of priests who attended to its care, is derived from other sources. Its inclusion at the end of the cycle of tales about the history of Riazan' is an example of how scribal editing alters the function of the materials that went into the new composition, injecting pathos into a dry annalistic narrative and giving historical depth to the underlying religion.

The most important works about the fourteenth century date to the early and mid-fifteenth century and position it as a turning point. Combining historicity and fiction to a new degree, these works serve the interests of current rulers by glorifying their remote ancestors. The open system of literary production makes it possible to elaborate out of a nucleus of historical writing more extensive portraits of rulers and extended narrative sequences. By the fifteenth century, the availability of more sophisticated devices, such as word-weaving and a more ornamental style imitating Serbian princely lives, enhanced the drama of historical action and the role of the ruler.[29] The stark contrast between the "lawless heretic invader" and the Orthodox defenders of the faith, evident from as early as the *Lay of Igor's Campaign*, surfaces repeatedly not only in new redactions of old texts but also in newer works, such as the "Tale of Stephan Batory's Invasion of the City of Pskov" ("Povest' o prikhozhenii Stefana Batoriia na grad Pskov," 1581).[30]

The literary picture may well differ from the reality. Modern historians no longer paint the period as one of uniform devastation and grimness. In addition to the financial burdens imposed on the Russian princes, there is evidence of collaboration and of the assimilation of various Mongol customs, suggesting that, in political terms, there were elements of controlled autonomy and little interference in religious practices. However, the image of the savage Tatar will remain a powerful topos, haunting even much later writing. One particularly striking example comes in the seventeenth-century "Legend of Kitezh." Later celebrated as the inspiration for Rimsky-Korsakov's opera *The Legend of the Invisible City of Kitezh and the Maiden Fevronia (Skazanie o nevidimom grade Kitezhe i deve Fevronii*, 1905), the tale lauds the stalwart bravery of the grandsons of Prince Vladimir of Kiev and the Vsevolodovich family line, whose descendant Prince Georgy Vsevolodovich is a paragon of piety. A builder of churches in the small towns surrounding Moscow, who also encouraged Prince Andrei Bogoliubsky to dedicate an imposing shrine to the Virgin Mary, Prince Georgy founded Greater and Smaller Kitezh. In 1239, the Tatar invader Batu laid waste to the towns and devastated their churches.

The legend ends by announcing that the two cities will remain invisible until the Second Coming of Christ, when the Kitezh monasteries will be rebuilt, ushering an era of utopian flourishing.

Catastrophic narratives: Defending Holy Russia

Writing helped further dynastic ambitions and legitimate family lines. Whether biographical, historical, or ecclesiastical, the ideal of a just ruler and, increasingly, of a Christian warrior, persisted diachronically in works of prose and poetry (such as the verse narrative *Zadonshchina*). The "Miracle of St. George over the Dragon" ("Chudo Georgiia o zmie") was a version of a widespread legend of the Christian protector of cities found in icon-painting, fairy tales, and folklore, and first attested in Eastern Slavic versions in the thirteenth century. Historical figures, however, provided the more lasting vehicles for the elaboration of the idea of a Christian warrior.

Over the next 150 years, or until the rule of Ivan III (1462–1505), internal rivalries among princes led to collaboration and collusion with the Tatars, as cousins and uncles vied for power in a system that favored succession of the eldest male. The open-ended model of composition made it possible to update the narratives retrospectively in order to substantiate the ambitions of later generations by creating a foundational figure and dynastic myth. Perhaps there is no better example of this phenomenon than a cycle of tales and a biography of Dmitry Donskoi, the Grand Prince of Moscow, whose victory over the forces of Mamai, the then Khan of the Golden Horde, in the Battle of Kulikovo in 1380 was seen (exaggeratedly) as a fatal blow to the Tatar hegemony.

With the gradual fragmentation of the Golden Horde and its definitive break up in the 1420s, and against the backdrop of political unrest in northeastern Russia, the Daniilovichi princes outmaneuvered their dynastic rivals and consolidated their legitimacy as rulers of the principality of Muscovy. The Golden Horde conferred on Prince Dmitry Ivanovich the writ (*gramota*) for the grand principality of Vladimir in 1362, bolstering his clan's status and his accession as ruler in 1389 (he had already ruled as prince of Novgorod and maintained an alliance with the principality of Suzdal'). Dmitry further proved adept at forging alliances and recruiting troops. Other local city-states, such as Galich, Beloozero, and Uglich, were annexed by Moscow, while Dmitry proclaimed himself the ruler of Vladimir, Pereiaslavl', Kostroma, and Iur'ev, cities which he bequeathed as part of his princely patrimony to Vasily I.

Through its chronicle-writing and storytelling, Muscovite Rus' produced texts about dynastic legitimation. In the fifteenth century, a revival of interest in Kiev accorded the city a hallowed place in the cultural memory: Ilarion's eulogy was remembered and quoted, and the *Primary Chronicle* inspired contemporary annalists.[31] With this revival came a newfound awareness of the Kievan ruler as a model for the Grand Prince of Vladimir and Moscow that subsequently shaped the representations of the tsar as a charismatic ruler and Christian fighter.[32] An account of unification is constructed through texts that serve as a counter-narrative to the tradition of blaming the princes for weakening Kievan Rus'. The logic of domestic politics of the Muscovite period was, rather than attribute the decline of Rus' to the Tatar invasion, to look back to the fragmentation of the appanage period as an inherent weakness. The reality was, of course, far more complex. In 1390, Metropolitan Kiprian commissioned an important new chronicle, based on a 1305 redaction written in Vladimir at the request of Grand Prince Mikhail Iaroslavich. Kiprian's commission was completed only in 1408; its best copy is known as the *Trinity Chronicle*. The authors of this chronicle give proof of their loyalty to the Grand Prince, Vasily I (d. 1425), but they do not refrain from passing judgment on other principalities and sometimes on Muscovy itself. In an entry of 1376, as he describes the Muscovites' defeat by the Tatars on the banks of the River Piana, the chronicler notes in a rare joke that the losing side was *p'iany* (drunk).

In the northeast, the establishment of Moscow's hegemony also generated a considerable body of historiography composed at court, including a 1453 compilation, which contained an account—possibly autobiographical—of Vasily II's blinding in 1446. A tone of partisanship for Muscovy and enmity for her rivals gradually becomes the norm. Chronicle-writing comes increasingly within the purview of Moscow authorities. However, in certain important monasteries (for instance, in the cities of Kirillo-Belozersk and Rostov), scribes continued writing and sometimes voiced criticism aimed at Moscow. It was in the early sixteenth century that the ideologizing of *letopisanie* took a new turn. Over the course of the late fifteenth to mid-sixteenth centuries, the final unification of Muscovy under Vasily III, the acceptance of the ideology of Iosif Volotsky and the Possessors, founded on the belief in the absolutism of the Orthodox ruler, would be reflected in revisionist history of what was increasingly conceptualized as "Russia."

We now turn to literary works that dramatize the joining of forces against common enemies. These works also represent a sea change in the narrative technique. After 1389, following two centuries of infighting that continued even under the Tatar dominion, it was clear that Moscow had taken the lead and the city-state's power kept growing even as the rule of the Golden Horde continued to disintegrate. The Grand Prince of Moscow had come to be regarded as a model ruler-manager and a peacemaker, the restorer of civil order and the leader of the Russian people in its struggle against foreign enemies. At the same time, Moscow was seen as the instrument of success against the heathen, or the "devourers of raw flesh," as the Mongols were called. In reality, however, Prince Dmitry Ivanovich (d. 1389), confirmed as Grand Prince of Vladimir, had resumed his role of a loyal agent of the khan, but the arrangement was unsustainable. In 1382, the Tatar warlord Tokhtamysh invaded Muscovy with the help of Oleg of Riazan', moving on to Moscow abandoned by Donskoi's retreating forces. The people of the city turned to the Lithuanian prince, Ostei, to lead the defense of the city. The Tatars killed him and destroyed large parts of Moscow before retreating and sacking Riazan'. Dmitry was restored, and in 1386 he compelled the Novgorodians to pay their tribute to the Golden Horde. Affairs had already come to a head in 1380 in the Battle of Kulikovo, which inspired a narrative cycle now referred to as the *Tales of the Battle of Kulikovo* (*Povesti o Kulikovskoi bitve*).

These stories build up a legend of Kulikovo as a turning point in the re-establishment of the sovereignty of northern Rus' over the Tatars. They include a verse narrative, *Zadonshchina*, and a cycle of tales, the most notable of which are the *Narrative of the Battle of Mamai* (*Skazanie o Mamaevom Poboishche*), the *Tale of the Invasion of Tokhtamysh* (*Povest' o nashestvii Tokhtamysha*), both titled after the Tatar warlords, and a life of Dmitry Donskoi (as discussed below). The *Narrative of the Battle of Mamai* exists in many copies and six different redactions from the fifteenth and sixteenth centuries, and it describes events from the viewpoint of the leaders and the Church.[33] Composed in phrasal units of equal length (*isocola*) of rhythmic force and vivid expression, *Zadonshchina* celebrates the heroic rivalries between the victorious princes. There is a considerable overlap in expressions between *Zadonshchina* and the *Lay of Igor's Campaign*, and borrowings have been used to substantiate arguments authenticating the *Lay* as a genuine medieval work. The title *Zadonshchina* amalgamates three parts of speech: the prefix *za-* meaning "beyond," the nominal root *don*, signifying the Don River, and the suffix *-shchina* meaning "relating to." Events rapidly succeed one another as the poem unfolds: the enemy approaches from beyond the River Don, and the eye of the narrator has a camera-like ability of zooming in and panning out. It is no wonder that that Aleksandr Blok, one of the great modernist poets, imitated *Zadonshchina* in his shorter poem "On the Field of Kulikovo" ("Na pole Kulikovom," 1908), written after the catastrophic destruction of the Russian navy by the Japanese in 1905. *Zadonshchina* provides a vivid description of the mustering of forces:

Already the falcons, the gyrfalcons, and
the goshawks from Belozersk swiftly cross the River Don.
And they strike against flocks of geese and swans.
They are Russian sons, who strike against the great Tatar army,
And who, with their steel lances, clash against Tatar armors,
Whose tempered swords sunder Tatar helmets,
On the prairie of Kulikovo,
At the small river, Nepriadva.

The earth became black from horse hooves.
The field became strewn with Tatar bones.
Much blood was spilled upon the field.
Strong regiments came together and clashed,
And they trampled the hills and the meadows.
The calm waters of rivers and lakes became stirred up.
The Div bird called out in the Russian land,
Calling all lands to listen.
And the glory of the Russian princes resounded,
From the roar of battle to the Iron Gates
To Rome . . .
O great land of Russia,
You have defeated Mamai on the plain of Kulikovo.[34]

Here, as in the *Lay of Igor's Campaign*, the opposing sides are both associated with avian imagery; pathetic fallacy creates an eerie atmosphere; while the panoramic perspective creates an effect of scale. Highly attentive to the silence that falls over the natural world as destruction spreads, the speaker combines historical narrative (revenge), human tragedy (bloodshed), and his own dismay. Perhaps the most important claim made in the *Zadonshchina* is that the "Russian sons" are fighting together.

Tales of destruction and woe provided plot lines for epic works such as the *Lay of Igor's Campaign* and *Zadonshchina*. With a verbal and figurative agility uncommon in medieval Russian writing, these quasi-poetic bardic tales interweave clusters of dense metaphors and a striking use of pathetic fallacy to convey the dramatic story of battle, portraying both defeats and victories, and elevating the depicted events to the status of symbols. Both narratives foreground the perils of pursuing individual glory and honor at the expense of national solidarity.[35] One notable feature of these works is how they characterize the work of mourning undertaken by women, usually princesses lamenting their fallen husbands, who express the grief of the city in the traditional forms of keening.

The set of three prose works about Kulikovo is roughly contemporary with *Zadonshchina*. Drawing on chronicle accounts of the events, the cycle of tales shows evidence of newly developed narrative skills. As relatively long works—the *Narrative of the Battle of Mamai* contains over 10,000 words—they have the requisite breadth to create momentum and suspense; to structure themes according to sub-plots; to focus on individual heroes and their choices; to manipulate the readers' emotions and stir their imagination. The narrative serves as a vehicle for a vision of a post-Tatar settlement in which Moscow is seen to dominate its fellow polities. Causality remains, at least superficially, a matter of divine sanction and reward. It is unsurprising to hear the characters invoke "our sins" as the reason heathen enemies menace Moscow—a reasoning familiar from the early medieval period. Writings now pay much more attention to various types of motivation—motivation that remains mixed since the historical problem of rivalries cannot be put entirely aside. For example, in the *Tale of the Invasion of Tokhtamysh* the writer exposes Prince Oleg of Riazan' for self-interested collusion with the enemy and con-demns his "swinishness to Christians" ("na pakost' Khristianam").

The *Tale of the Invasion of Tokhtamysh*, probably contemporaneous with the events described, pays close attention to the topography of Moscow. It describes a "stone city" rising tall with its numerous churches, which would become a topos through the duration of the imperial period. The wealth of the Church appears in vast stores of mead and wine (eventu-ally ransacked by a population driven terrified before the invasion). The old motif of sacrilege as the scourge of invasion gains a material dimension. When invading Suzdal' in a preliminary move, the invaders grabbed hold of

> the holy crosses, the wonder-working icons adorned in gold and silver and pearl and mother of pearl and precious stones; snatched textiles woven with gold and framed in pearl; broke off the frames from the holy icons, stamping on some, picked up the holy, gilt-plated and silver, expensive vessels used in church ceremonies, and stole the expensive vestments of the priests; and also made off with innumerable books preserved in the church, many of which they destroyed.[36]

The *Tale of the Invasion of Tokhtamysh* vividly depicts turmoil and destruction by cataloguing calamity and fatalities as they happen in the present tense. Whereas the *Narrative* focuses on regal figures, the *Tale* seems to adopt a more popular viewpoint by emphasizing the sacrifice made by the people of Moscow during the serious incursions leading up to the main battle. The nature of the people of Moscow, their patriotic ardor, the city's dense throngs, their restiveness and rebellious nature will be aspects taken up by historical narratives in the seventeenth century.

Formally, these narratives make a more complex use of a variety of modes than earlier tales and chronicles did. Monologues, exchanges, interpolated documents, prayers, and panoramic descriptions combine to create variety, involvement, and a sense of historical importance, far exceeding earlier brevity thanks to the amplification of traditional expostulations and epithets and by building on physical detail. The scribes who worked on the compilation of the *Tale of the Invasion of Tokhtamysh* drew liberally on *Zadonshchina* for allusions and expressive figures of speech, while also borrowing historical and Biblical comparisons to convey a sense of scale. In fact, there are scarcely any battle scenes, and for long stretches the writer favors stasis over momentum (although in the last third of the work, chaos and panic ensue when Dmitry is reported missing in action).

Two new devices mark out changes in the narrative style. First, there is a greater use of complex invented speeches to reveal intentions, strategies, and reasons, subordinating the creation of suspense and action to capturing motivation and mood.[37] Character is built up through accumulation of monologues and aggrandizement of each heroic figure. Second, the narrator stirs up drama by using stock phrases such as "the fateful hour approached" ("i den' groznyi priblizilsia") and, most especially by narrowing the timeframe the closer the narrative moves to its climax: from months to weeks to days, until, in the final section, the narrator compresses the details of eight hours of fighting. Like chronicles, the *Tale of the Invasion of Tokhtamysh* uses the conventional device of the list, enumerating the troops (unrealistic and epic) and the names of princes who have perished. Yet perhaps its most powerful moment as a narrative of catastrophe is the evocation of silence and ruin in the aftermath of the invasion:

> For until that time, and previously, Moscow was the greatest of the cities, a marvelous city, a populous city, in which there were many people and many masters, and many types of wealth. In the flash of an eye its image changed when it was captured and plundered and burned. There was nothing left to view for there was only earth and dust and ruin and ash and many death corpses lay around, and holy churches were destroyed as though orphaned, as though widowed. Like a

mother weeping for its children, the church weeps for the children of the church and even more for all who have died. O children of the church, o murdered martyrs who suffered a violent death…And the churches remain, stripped for their majesty and beauty. Where is their former beauty?…Woe is me! Terrifying to hear, even more terrifying to behold!…No bells toll and no one summons the population by ringing the signal, no one hastens to their groan; no voices in song are heard from the churches, no Hosannas or words of praise are heard; there is no poetry in the churches or thanks. In truth the life of man is in vain and in vain is human vanity. Such was the end of siege of Moscow.[38]

The protagonists are the Tatar leader Mamai, something of a stock villain ("an unquenchable serpent who breathes malice") who wishes to achieve a definitive victory by "killing the princes"; Prince Oleg of Riazan´ whose stupidity leads him to collaborate with the enemy; and numerous other princes cast in a more favorable light when they come to the aid of Dmitry Donskoi whose behavior in the *Narrative* from the very outset establishes him as a Christian warrior leader. The *Narrative of the Battle of Mamai* amplifies the basic biographical plot of the warrior prince with extensive descriptions of battle scenes and with a moral portrait:

> For his Highness, the Grand Prince Dmitry Ivanovich, a peaceful man and the model of wise restraint (*smirenomudriia*), wished to enjoy life in heaven, expecting from the Lord future eternal blessings, and was unaware that his close friends were plotting a dastardly plot against him. For about such things the prophet had said: "Do not do evil unto your neighbor, do not stir up, do not dig a ditch for your enemy, but rely on the Lord since it is the Lord God who gives and takes life."[39]

When the compilation of these works began, dating to less than twenty years after the battle, their prose and poetry bolstered Dmitry's legacy. A literary ideal of military prowess and piety, Church and state allied, was well ahead of the political reality. Writing that emanated from the ruling house and monasteries strengthened the image of groups coalescing under a Grand Prince of the Daniilovich line whose support of the Orthodox Church was reciprocated. But dynastic succession remained vexed. Dmitry's successor, his son, Vasily I rebuffed enemies, but his successor Vasily II (r. 1425–62) oversaw a period of intense intra-dynastic warfare, further complicated by the disintegration of the Golden Horde into smaller khanates that sided with rival princes mounting challenges to the Grand Prince. Intra-dynastic warfare lasted from 1425 until Vasily II had emerged as the ruler of Muscovy and the Grand Prince, and had asserted his position as the strongest ruler in the region. Scarred by political competition, he mandated that succession thereafter be vertical and son succeed father. Defeated in battle and taken prisoner by the Kazan´ Khanate in 1439, Vasily II lost control of Moscow to his brother Dmitry Shemyaka who had Vasily blinded (hence Vasily's nickname as "the Blind"). Against the backdrop of the fall of Constantinople (which led bishop Jonah, the Metropolitan, to declare the de facto independence of the Russian Orthodox Church from the Patriarch of Constantinople), Vasily stabilized his authority finally in the 1450s (extracting revenge on his brother by having him poisoned) and mandated that succession thereafter be vertical and son succeed father (an arrangement writers traced back to Donskoi for legitimation). A dynastic principle enshrined in the overarching narrative of centralization was taken forward by Vasily II's successor, Ivan III (known as "the Great" or *Velikii*).

While, in the Kulikovo cycle, the image of the prince is more military than monastic, the *Narrative* assigns a significant part to the Church and the critical support of the Metropolitan of Moscow. The Metropolitan's role in the events is to conduct magnificent religious ceremonies and to hold a wonder-working icon at the head of processions. A growing symbiosis between the Church and the state forms the background of much medieval writing. Behind the façade of cooperation cultivated in the works of the Kulikovo cycle, which circulated and were edited from the first quarter of the fifteenth century, lay dynastic politics and tactical relationships between political and ecclesiastical leaders. Church history during this period had also been unsettled, and, in 1378, after a stormy relationship with Dmitry, Kiprian worked with Vasily I to unify the metropolitanate of Kiev and entire Rus´. This effort was carried on in the 1450s by Vasily II, who relied on the Church to enhance his claims to rule by casting it as a matter of divine favor, propping up his military prowess with a spiritual claim to legitimacy.[40] Kiprian resumed his tenure as Metropolitan in 1390 after the death of Dmitry Donskoi, and was approved by Tsar Vasily I (r. 1412–25). Under Kiprian and his successor, Photius, the head of the Russian Orthodox Church continued to reside in Moscow and retain close contact with the ruler. This was symbolically significant because Kiprian worked to revitalize the Eastern Orthodox community by emphasizing Eastern Orthodox countries' shared loyalty to Constantinople, a view reflected in a celebrated letter written by the Patriarch of Constantinople to Vasily I of Moscow in 1393.[41] The document criticized the Grand Prince for forbidding the Metropolitan to commemorate the Byzantine emperor in the liturgy and, as a corrective, reiterated with particular force that the Eastern Orthodox lands ultimately belong to a universal Christian polity ruled by the emperor. In the end, Kiprian apparently succeeded in bringing the Russian Church to recognize the emperor's symbolic leadership of the whole Orthodox community, a position that became redundant with the fall of Constantinople in 1453. While the status of the metropolitanate and the right to the title, whether determined by the tsar or the Church, would be challenged in the second half of the fifteenth century, in the longer term, the changes established the position of Moscow as the cultural and religious center of a unified Orthodox community, the heir to Kiev. This unity of purpose informed historical writings, such as the *Trinity Chronicle* (itself based on the foundational *Primary Chronicle*), and other texts that painted a picture of ecclesiastical and political unity.

The texts of the Kulikovo cycle project an ideal of synergy between the Church and the state, which in reality was a work in progress. While clerical figures are mainly absent from the *Tale of the Invasion of Tokhtamysh*, in the *Narrative*, Donskoi himself shares the spotlight with the monk St. Sergii. This is not surprising since the work emanates from Sergii's monastery. Sergii intervenes virtually at each and every turn in the action, either by sending a message lending his authority to military actions or by advising the Grand Prince in person. Dmitry is depicted throughout as loyal, patriotic, and pious, virtues that place him beyond reproach and that in the end lead him to victory. Sergii's advice is critical in persuading Dmitry to act. Sergii appears to be highly hesitant. Initially he preaches a message of resignation (*smirenie*) and even appeasement, before recognizing the fault of the fractious princes and giving his blessing to a campaign that will pit Russian against Russian, demanding clear evidence from Dmitry that he has tried to make peace with Oleg and other defectors. Pious and fair-minded, Dmitry initially refuses to believe that fellow princes may be scheming against him. In preparing him for battle, Sergii "gave him instead of perishable weaponry something imperishable—a Christian cross sewn onto a cowl and ordered him to put this on instead of golden helmets." No image can better convey the intention of the writer to portray the Grand Prince as a warrior of the righteous.

Whatever the historical reality behind the gestures and gifts, symbols of the Church's solidarity with the ruler, the *Narrative* is concerned with projecting lasting images rather than exploring the root causes of the events. The Virgin of the Intercession, whose icon galvanizes Dmitry into prayer, presides over all his actions. Other signs of piety attend his military preparation, including prayers at the Cathedral of Archangel Michael in the Kremlin, a site that will grow as the royal burial site and the repository of the iconography of royal power. The authors of the *Narrative* have a grasp of the totemic power of objects and the political authority conveyed by images. Each text is careful to note how rumor spreads as confidence builds and ebbs. This power of superstition is especially true of the impact of religion on the psychology of the armed forces. Sensitive to omens, the enemy is spooked when the Church throws its authority behind the Grand Prince. The Grand Prince of Kiev as historical figure also casts a long shadow over Dmitry's ambitions. Donskoi quotes Vladimir in a speech about the value of the unity of the Russian lands, and has a dream-vision of Boris and Gleb and their sacrifice which inspires his own sense of mission. It is out of the crucible of perennial opposition, not to fellow princes but to the non-Orthodox enemy, that an image of a national leader gradually develops.

From Grand Prince to Tsar, 1200–1565: Elevation through charisma

In literature about the position of the territories of Rus´, a corollary of the dismay over disunity, aggravated by vulnerability to larger powers in the region, whether the Byzantine empire, the Mongols, or the Ottomans, is the nearly formulaic endorsement of the need for a strong ruler capable of unifying the different interests. Over the period 1462–1533, from the accession of Ivan III, who nurtured and realized a vision of a centralized state governed by an absolute ruler through the years of Vasily III (r. 1503–33), to the beginning of the reign of Ivan IV, the city-state of Moscow expanded its territory by subordinating and absorbing republics such as Novgorod in 1478 and Pskov in 1510, and numerous other principalities. The principality of Moscow evolved from a confederation of territories where it had influence, although not supreme reign, to a position of dominance and a new model of governance, headed by a strong monarch, supported by a bureaucratic administrative structure and a council of advisors. Moscow's military expansion and territorial growth projected power, facilitated growth in trade, influence, and the machinery of state. Following the fall of Constantinople in 1453, literature aimed at dynastic legitimation began to incorporate some elements of the Byzantine models. Over time, as Donald Ostrowski has pointed out, a sense of "manifest destiny" accompanied the centralizing measures, and texts written under the aegis of the state and the Church articulated a message that was both prospective, in asserting Muscovite hegemony, and retrospective, in recasting history as a providential tale of Moscow's inevitable rise.[42]

On occasion, the outlook of a literary work and the interests of the ruling house were demonstrably aligned. This can be seen in the interventions of the narrator in the *Lay of Igor's Campaign* or in the chronicles of sixteenth-century Moscow, such as the *Russian Chronograph* (or *Chronograph of 1512*). Compiled in several versions over the sixteenth and seventeenth centuries, each of which can be studied for its specific ideological nuances, its original version is now thought to date back to 1512. The first 208 chapters set out the history of the world based on Biblical stories and ancient accounts of the deeds of Alexander the Great, extending ahead to the lives of Serbian princes. It is the first work produced on the Russian soil that aims to integrate the country into the history of the world. It emphatically promulgates the idea of a nation-state defined by opposition to the Latins and the Turks.[43]

Genealogies of princely lines record the names of myriad figures who are mostly unknowable. The most impressive of these records, and indicative of how biographies could be used to consolidate political clout, was the *Book of Royal Degrees* (*Stepennaia kniga*, c.1560), initiated and advanced by Metropolitans Kiprian and Makary. Its project was to extract and order according to family genealogy information about the princely clans (as relating to the Grand Prince) from the mass of chronicle mentions.[44] When narratives singled out figures for the mention and magnification of their deeds, the ulterior purpose was to accommodate a local ruling house wishing to consolidate their authority through the claims of lineage. Valorous deeds that originate in earlier periods were therefore worth copying and revising in a new framework in order to confirm the current dominance of Moscow as providential. By the sixteenth century that emphasis contributed to an overdetermined assumption about the growth of Moscow. As Moscow transformed from a city-state to a super-state, dismantling the appanage system, the acts of copying and editing stories, and ultimately storytelling, were essential to shaping a ruler who could double as a military leader and a Christian apostle, and ultimately rise above the fray as a timeless tsar. In a number of important cases, the writing is notable for its quality as much as for its instrumental purpose.

While scribes continued to uphold local traditions, Moscow began promoting a more comprehensive "Russian" approach. The name "Russia" (*Rossiia*) began to supplant "Rus'" during Ivan III's reign, reflecting the sense of a greater Russia beyond the Muscovite principality (regardless of Ivan's failure to extend his empire westward during the Livonian wars). In 1472, the marriage of Ivan III to the Byzantine Princess Zoe Palaeologus added luster to the position of Moscow and its rulers, and spurred attempts to affiliate the Muscovite tsars with the Byzantine empire as heirs to Rome and ultimately the Emperor Augustus (although the influence of Mongolian ideas in the Muscovite ideology of kingship was a factor).[45] Historical writing such as genealogical reconstructions of the legend of Vladimir Monomakh and stories like the "Tales of the Babylonian Kingdom" ("Skazaniia o Vavilonskom Tsarstve") or the "Epistle of Spiridon-Savva on the Crown of Monomakh" ("Poslanie Spiridona-Savvy o Monamakhovom ventse"), legitimated Muscovite claims.[46] The distinctiveness of Russian Orthodoxy and the status of the Church as independent from Byzantium also required legitimation. *Translatio imperii* was a flattering concept that might have been open to question after two centuries in which the Church dealt with doctrinal rows, heretical movements and their suppression, a proliferation of local saints canonized by regional churches, and debates over the wealth of monasteries, manifested in the conflict between two groups known as the "Possessors" (*stiazhateli* or *iosifliane*, from their leader, Iosif Volotsky) and the "Non-Possessors" (led by the monk and ascetic Nil of Sorsk).

At the end of the fifteenth century, in the wake of the fall of Constantinople, different accounts arose of how spiritual authority was inherited. Evoking the Kievan ideal of the Russians as the new Israelites, certain Church figures articulated a version of this analogy. Writing during the reign of Ivan III, and citing the *Life of Prince Dmitry Ivanovich* as evidence of the tsar's spiritual pedigree, Metropolitan Zosima cast the tsar, the protector of the faith, as a New Constantine, and Moscow, both the city and the territory, as a New Jerusalem.[47] In three theological epistles (whose dating is problematic), the monk Filofei, active during the reign of Vasily III, gave expression to the theory of Moscow as a Third Rome, an idea that achieved long-term resonance in the Russian cultural imagination. Imbued with an eschatological sense that the attempted rapprochement between the Latin and Eastern Churches at the Council of Florence (1418) had been a betrayal of Orthodoxy and precipitated the downfall of Byzantium, Filofei envisages Muscovite Rus' as a new confessional realm that is messianic, but also a historical equivalent of the Roman kingdom.[48] Sensitivity to the fate of Constantinople and a fear of a domino effect that would lead the Ottoman Empire to topple Eastern Christianity, including Moscow, made the Russian Church and leadership alert to heresy and both cautious and hostile about the world beyond their country's borders.

Fear of heresy was the cause of one of the most notorious episodes of sixteenth-century cultural life, namely, the mission of Maksim Grek (Maximus the Greek, born Michael Trivolis *c.*1475) to Moscow. Born in Greece, educated in northern Italy, and acquainted with great Renaissance figures, such as the Venetian printer Aldus Manutius and the scholars Angelo Poliziano and Marsilio Ficino (instrumental in the Renaissance reinterpretation of classical antiquity), Maksim was invited to Moscow in 1516 at the initiative of Grand Prince Vasily III in order to produce new translations of works into Church Slavonic (he began with the Psalter, possibly because it was a key text in one of the main disputes of the age about a heretical sect known as Judaizers or *zhidovstvuiushchie*) and to correct the liturgy and prayer books.[49] During his working life, spent mainly at the Chudov Monastery in the Kremlin, he was immensely productive in four main areas: theology, secular philosophy, statecraft, and social problems, as well as in producing works of Biblical exegesis and correcting textual errors in translations of Biblical and liturgical works. He was rash at criticizing the isolation of Muscovite life, the exploitation of the peasantry, and the political authoritarianism of the city-state. He recanted his positive impression of Moscow as the genuine Third Rome and expressed his disillusionment with "this meretricious substitute for the East Roman ecumenical idea."[50] Maksim also weighed in on the long-running dispute over monastic wealth, siding with the "Non-Possessors" and befriending the legal scholar Vassian Patrikeev who had antagonized Vasily III and the then Metropolitan Daniel, an association that ultimately undermined Maksim's relationship with the authorities. His ill-timed sincerity led to accusations of heresy, a charge corroborated partly on the basis of errors he made in translations due to his imperfect knowledge of Church Slavonic. These charges were compounded by accusations of treason based on a suspicion of his collusion with the Ottoman Empire against Moscow. The charges led to Maksim's interrogation in 1525 and arrest and imprisonment in 1531. As Dimitri Obolensky says, "the list of charges is long and impressive. It included holding heretical views, practicing sorcery, criticizing the grand prince, having treasonable relations with the Turkish government, claiming that the Russian Church's independence from the patriarchate of Constantinople was illegal, and denouncing the monasteries and the Church for owning land and peasants."[51] In 1531, Maksim was sentenced to twenty years in exile in the Otroch Monastery in Tver'. He failed to win appeal from Vasily III's successor, Ivan IV (with whom he had an audience at the Trinity-Sergiev Monastery according to an account by Prince Kurbsky), and from Metropolitan Makary, and died in Russia in 1556. We dwell on Maksim here not because of a direct impact of his writings on Russian literature, but rather because his story illustrates the obstacles any version of a humanist culture would have encountered. In this new political context the Church acted to consolidate its status as a national body: the promulgation of the Stoglav Council in 1551 issuing an extensive set of ecclesiastical regulations reflected its conception of Muscovite ecclesiastical supremacy.[52]

This is the context in which the "Life of the Prince" as a warrior and a spiritual figure (an ideal illustrated in Plate 5) emerged as a particular type of quasi-hagiographic composition, a mode that defies precise generic classification.[53] History was written by both the winners and the losers, but edited over time by the winners in politic, and eventually in Moscow, with an opportunistic eye to the retrospective legitimation of outcomes that were uncertain as they unfolded. By blending fact and fiction (modern categories not strictly understood or applied in the period), chronicle writers contrived to produce a new type of hero in the figure of the saintly prince. The elaboration of the literary type was cumulative and gradual, very much a function of the compilatory nature of medieval writing.[54] Tributes to princes took no fixed form in the period, and while Igor Eremin argued that the genre of a princely life (as a type of *povest'*) developed out of the need to commemorate deceased princes, writing about princes was not uniformly generic. The degree to which accounts varied because of scribal interpolations and adjustments, suggests that, as in other types of writing, scribes took a functional approach, and conceived their brief very flexibly.[55] A eulogy (*pokhvala*, also used in saints' lives) could be added to a document, a biography, a chronicle episode, or a narrative tale, depending on the scribe's own choice and his loyalty to the ruling dynasty. The copyist of the "Eulogy to the clan of the princes of Riazan'" ("Pokhvala rodu riazanskikh kniazei") managed to fit in an entire branch of the princely line, and obituaries of dead princes inserted in the chronicles include rhetorical flourishes enhancing a standard form of delivery that covers the acts and deeds: heroic deaths generally attracted the most intense tributes.[56]

No single editor or author proved responsible for the organic evolution of "The Life of a Prince" as a template for writing about the Grand Princes of Kiev and Vladimir (and then tsar) in a story that extends from Vladimir Monomakh to Ivan IV. Against the background of centralization and admiration of Kievan Rus´, the clergy invented lineages to trace the Grand Princes of Moscow back to Kiev.[57] We have already seen that one of the best known of these compositions is the Monomakh legend, concerning the transfer of royal regalia from Byzantium to Grand Prince Vladimir Monomakh of Kiev (r. 1113–25), and thence to the Grand Princes of Moscow. This tale probably originated in the early sixteenth century, and became a part of the official ideology at the time of Ivan IV's coronation as tsar. According to the legend, the Grand Princes of Moscow were supposedly crowned with the regalia sent from Byzantium (in fact, the crown was of Tatar origin) by the Byzantine Emperor Constantine Monomachus to Vladimir Monomakh. The stature of the latter was also partly a function of the legacy he left as a writer.[58]

Vladimir Monomakh

Even in Kievan Rus´, confessional utterances were capable of emotional power when a first-person author understood how to put rhetoric to effective use. Alongside the supplicating Daniil Zatochnik and the vivid personality of Afanasy Nikitin we can place Vladimir Monomakh. Among the most anthologized works of the medieval period, prized now as a rare example of the personal voice, is the *Instruction of Vladimir Monomakh* (*Pouchenie Vladimira Monomakha*) made up of advisory admonitions of a moralistic kind addressed to his children and a short autobiography. A work of allusive eloquence (there are references to the Psalms and the famous preacher St. Basil the Great, the Bishop of Caesarea), the *Instruction* has often been thought to be the first Russian autobiography.[59] This assessment may be somewhat exaggerated, since Monomakh's life-writing unfolds according a rhetorical function rather than psychological analysis, and his underlying purpose is to pre-empt strife among his sons caused by an unequal settlement of territorial claims.[60] Likely models would have included the lives of local saints as well as the now-lost "Testament" of Iaroslav the Wise. It has also been suggested that Monomakh may have been influenced by an Anglo-Saxon example (possibly King Alfred's spiritual testament known to Monomakh through his Anglo-Saxon wife, Gytha of Wessex).[61]

A contemporary of Nestor, Monomakh takes stock of the appanage system, which has created rivals out of natural allies among the collateral lines of princes. In the "Testament", the second biographical section, Monomakh relates how, battle-scarred from the campaigns against the Polovtsian raiders in the south of the country, he staunchly promoted the cult of Sts. Boris and Gleb and the idea of a national identity based on shared values. He concludes that fratricidal strife combined with the defense against invaders from the steppe (which is the basis of the plot of the *Lay of Igor's Campaign*) will make Rus´ vulnerable to even greater enemies. Monomakh further expounds on the theme of unity over discord in his "Testament." From the opening lines, he strikes a cord of weary thoughtfulness and piety: "As I sit on my throne, I have thought in my soul and given thanks to God for having preserved me, a sinner." Monomakh argues that war represents divine punishment for transgressions against the Christian values of brotherly love and loyalty to the clan, and, above all, for the sin of pride. Monomakh eloquently elaborates on each point, drawing on a range of quotations from the Bible and the Psalter and offering ethical lessons on the proper conduct of princes that recur like a refrain: "Learn, you man of faith, to be the fulfiller of honor, learn, according to the lesson of the Gospel, the control of your eyes, the restraint of our tongue, a meekness of man, power over the body, the suppression of anger, and to have pure ideas that will encourage you to good words for the sake of the Lord."[62]

Alexander Nevsky

In the thirteenth century, Alexander Nevsky embodied the noble defender of Rus´, the scourge of the Tatars, and a peacemaker among his clan. The gap between a compromised historical reality and the ideal did not trouble the authors and copyists of the *Life of Alexander Nevsky* (*Zhitie Aleksandra Nevskogo*). Indeed, the figure of Alexander Nevsky has enjoyed a remarkable longevity from its thirteenth-century origins through to Sergei Eisenstein's eponymous film of 1938—often read as an allegory of Russia facing the German threat on the brink of the Second World War—to his cult as a nationalist symbol in the early twenty-first century.

The precise role of Alexander Nevsky in repelling the Mongols can never be known entirely. Historians such as John Fennell found evidence that Alexander Nevsky, far from being loyal to the other princes and joining forces against the enemy, colluded with the invaders out of self-interest.[63] Whatever the reality, the *Life of Alexander Nevsky* was instrumental in shaping the legend.[64] The initial version, dating to the 1280s and after his burial, originated in the Rozhdestvensky Monastery in northern Russia. As is true of other works of this type, the genetic model for the production of the *Life of Alexander Nevsky* was compilatory, and experts have tried to identify various sources of the text. Thus the introduction to the *Life of Alexander Nevsky* is plausibly thought, based on lexical evidence, to have been borrowed from now-lost parts of the "Discourse on the Destruction of the Russian Land." Other scholars advanced the hypothesis that the factual framework of the narrative derived from a biography, written by a member of the Prince's retinue.

The history of the redactions of the *Life of Alexander Nevsky* is a perfect example of the open-endedess of the copying tradition: the text was expanded to incorporate new accounts associated with the cult of Alexander Nevsky that formed around his burial place, especially after the Battle of Kulikovo in September 1380, a symbolic (perhaps more than military) turning point in the pushback against the Golden Horde. A total of fifteen editions, the last dating to the late seventeenth century, show how the textual tradition kept pace with the ideology of a growing centralized state. The second version of the text, composed sometime between 1430 and 1450 and incorporating Novgorodian and Muscovite sources, has been identified as the seminal redaction because it shifts perspective from the local to the incipiently Russian: Nevsky now takes the stage as a national figure whose bravery, piety, and loyalty represent the ideal of what the Grand Prince of Vladimir should be (this is clearly a retrospective adjustment, since the position of the Grand Prince evolved significantly after his death). This shift reflects in part Nevsky's status as the founder of a new dynastic line. Two years after the sack of Kiev in 1240, the Khan granted Prince Iaroslav Vsevolodovich of Vladimir the titles of Grand Prince of Kiev and Grand Prince of Vladimir.[65] During the thirteenth, fourteenth, and part of the fifteenth centuries, the city of Vladimir belonged to the members of the strongest ruling dynasty. Alexander Nevsky is the father of Prince Daniil, who changed the face of the post-invasion state and set Moscow on its longer-term trajectory of expansion by uniting the offices of the prince of Vladimir and the prince of Moscow into the position of the Grand Prince.

Princely portrayals continued to circulate long after their period of rule. The *Life of Alexander Nevsky* was subject to further ideological manipulation in the context of the synergy, promoted by the powerful spiritual leader Metropolitan Makary, between the Church and the political authorities in sixteenth-century Moscow. A version of the *Life* was produced for the *Great Menology*, while numerous other copies were incorporated in the chronicles of formerly independent polities that had been absorbed by Moscow, including Suzdal´, Novgorod, and Pskov.[66] Later medieval versions augmented the second half of the *Life* to include accounts of new miracles witnessed at Nevsky's tomb as well as invented episodes extolling his monk-like virtues: chastity, philanthropy, and obedience, which would come to dominate Nevsky's portrait.

The extinction of the Riurikid Muscovite princes in the late sixteenth century eventually led to the foundation of the Romanov dynasty. Around 1630 Tsar Aleksei Mikhailovich and the Patriarch dedicated a chapel in the Kremlin to Alexander Nevsky and instituted a feast day on 23 November. Nevsky's figure took on a new life, inspiring a fresh wave of post-medieval texts written in the eighteenth century, such as a version of the *Life of Alexander Nevsky* composed in 1772 in Vladimir and sent to St. Petersburg, which adds four new miracles.

In its earlier editions, however, the *Life of Alexander Nevsky* offered a historical portrait of a military warrior, paying only secondary tribute to his Christian virtues.[67] The fourteenth-century versions lavished praise on Nevsky's political achievements as a negotiator with the Golden Horde and his military prowess in the battlefield (such as the historically questionable but now famous battle on ice which became the centerpiece of Eisenstein's film). Hints of discord among the princes can be detected beneath the surface of the text as the writer rationalizes the failure of some princes to join forces with Alexander. Others, however, heeded his call, including Pelugy, the elder of a village, about whom little is known otherwise, who has a vision of the Kievan martyrs Boris and Gleb standing shoulder to shoulder, dressed in red (true to popular iconography) on board a ship arising out of the sea. In Pelugy's vision, Boris bids his brother to ask the rowers to make haste so that they can come to the aid of Prince Alexander. The character's point of view aims to bring out the timeless, rather than historical, aspects, and for this reason it shares many parallels with anonymous images of rulers that began to appear in church frescoes.

Like a saint's life, the writer of the *Life of Alexander Nevsky* opens with the standard topos of humility ("I am a wanton sinner, not advanced in thought...") and an affirmation of authenticity ("Much have I heard from my fathers and I myself was a witness to his late years..."[68]). However, in contrast to a hagiographer, the writer does not take a developmental approach, focusing instead on key episodes that illustrate the prince's deeds. Of noble birth, the future Grand Prince has universal rather than individual attributes. His character traits are corroborated not with reference to verifiable facts but to Biblical precedent. "His beauty was unsurpassed, and his voice resounded like a clarion among the people, his face like the face of Joseph whom the King of Egypt made second in charge, his strength was on the order of Samson's strength, and God granted him the wisdom of Solomon, while he had the bravery of the Roman King Vespasian who had conquered all of Judaea."[69]

In this version of the *Life of Alexander Nevsky*, the narrative is propelled forward through the use of internal monologues, as the writer reveals how the characters strategized and acted on their intentions. Prayers for divine intercession accompany nearly every thought and every act, including a splendid scene in which Alexander visits the Church of St. Sophia in Vladimir and falls on his knees in prayer and then proclaims that "The Lord is not in power, but in truth," quotes the Psalms as encouragement, and marches out against the enemy. The style is eloquent, although it has none of the word-weaving and overt rhetorical flourish that characterize a much grander text in this tradition, the *Discourse on the Life and Death of Dmitry Donskoi*.

Unlike chronicle accounts, this sort of life-writing dispenses with dates in favor of abstract descriptions, and secondary actors are known by soubriquets rather than names: the Swedish king, for instance, is "the King of the Roman country of the North," while the Tatar Batu is the "strong king of the Eastern land." The account of the first battle is largely a roll call of the individuals who joined forces to fight alongside Alexander. Thereafter, the narrative lists numerous other skirmishes thanks to which Nevsky's "name become renowned across the lands from the Caspian Sea to Mt. Ararat, from the Baltic Ocean to ancient Rome."[70] Several paragraphs briskly discuss Nevsky's interactions with the "tsar," meaning the Tatar overlord who from the seat of the Golden Horde in Sarai allowed the Russian principalities to continue under their own governance as his tributaries. "In those days," says the writer, "there was great pressure from the pagans, and they oppressed the Christians, forcing them to fight on their side. But Grand Prince Alexander went to the tsar in order to intercede and save his people from this woe."

The *Life* ends with his decision to "take the cowl" and become a monk. His act puts Orthodoxy at the center of a princely life, and the writer ends the work by recounting a posthumous miracle: the hand of the dead saint reaches out from the grave to grasp a religious document from the metropolitan standing on the spot. The composite portrait of the ruler as a historical warrior and spiritual defender of the realm will become an ineluctable combination when writers in the early part of the fifteenth century conceptualized the achievements of Grand Prince Dmitry Donskoi at the Battle of Kulikovo.

Dmitry Donskoi

The culmination in this line of princely literary portraiture is the remarkable *Discourse on the Life and Death of Grand Prince Dmitry Donskoi* in three near equal parts. The sources of the tripartite *Discourse on the Life and Death* includes biographical narrative, drawn from chroniclewriting (similar to the material to be found in the *Mamai* cycle); legal documents; and Hesychast-inspired eulogy or sermon. The resulting compilation is highly purposeful and guided by the desire to promote a new ideology of leadership. It begins with an account of Dmitry's early life, parentage, and his qualities as a family man, further citing virtues associated with monasticism, such as chastity. In the Orthodox ascetic tradition, purity was seen as the first step to the recovery of the lost likeness of God through the victory over the passions. Although not born with a sense of religious mission, Dmitry inherently excels as a spiritual figure.

The eulogy in Part III is characterized by unity and integrity, and its style resembles Epifany Premudry's writings dating between the late 1390s and 1410s.[71] It is unclear whether the author of the *Discourse* (assumed to be Epifany Premudry) is also responsible for unifying the entire text and interpolating an important deathbed scene. Thematic affinities and similarities in characterization establish the Kulikovo cycle, written around 1390, as a clear source for the prose narratives in Part I of the *Discourse*, whereas Parts II and III are more likely to date to later decades. Individual sections may have been composed separately and the definitive compilation assembled as late as the 1430s to 1450s. When the issue of dating is examined from a more functional point of view, the question is why a new, synthetic portrait of the life of the Grand Prince would have been worth producing at mid-century. The answer is that an ideology of kingship has a bearing on the genetic or compilatory history of the work. In accepting a date of composition that reflects the political context of the 1430s and 1440s, Harvey Goldblatt has noted that, "given the possibility of an open textual tradition, there is no justification for assuming that an analysis of an individual textual portion and an assigned dating may be generalized to include the entire text."[72]

The second part of the narrative, seamlessly connected with the first, recounts Dmitry Donskoi's military triumphs, glossing over any difficulties he may have had with other political and church leaders, and burnishing the halo of the victor of Kulikovo. However, politics cannot be kept entirely at a distance. Part II ends with a remarkable deathbed scene, purporting to contain an account of the reading of Dmitry's final testament in nearly documentary terms. It is reasonable to suppose that a later copyist interpolated material from the will of Dmitry Donskoi concerning the succession from the prince to the eldest son. The document clearly intends to disqualify the collateral model of succession, whether prescriptively or retroactively, and favor descendants in the direct line, over brothers or uncles, at a time when the position of the Grand Prince was highly precarious within the power structure.[73] Finely crafted and full of elegiac pathos, the deathbed scene is reminiscent of the apostrophe to Vladimir in Ilarion's *Sermon*. The scene offers a dignified show of family unity, paying tribute to Dmitry's success as the father of the family. The historical and political dimension of this key moment comes to the fore when Dmitry names the next ruler, and thereby solves the problem of succession and rivalry that beset so many other leaders.

Textual scholars view the scene as a mid-fifteenth-century interpolation, added as late as sixty years after the events, when the collateral branches of the family were once again vying for power during the reign of Vasily II.[74] The scene may have been conceived retrospectively as a useful fiction of primogeniture. The final section of the *Discourse on the Life and Passing of Dmitry Ivanovich* represents a milestone in the creation of a kingship myth. This part, attributed with more confidence to Epifany Premudry, makes a seminal contribution to the idea of a theocratic ruler who, as half-prince and half-saint, is spiritually anointed.

Like the "Encomium to Vladimir" in Ilarion's *Sermon on Law and Grace*, quoted in the *Discourse*, the third section is tantamount to a funerary elegy for Dmitry. It achieves a remarkable combination of rhetorical brilliance and iconographic significance by employing a panoply of rhetorical and linguistic devices associated with the poetics of prayer and word-weaving, established in Russia by Metropolitan Kiprian and other learned churchmen educated in Bulgarian and Athonite monasteries. The purpose of texts goes beyond mere storytelling. In the *Discourse*, words are pregnant with metaphysical value invested in their phonetic properties, syntactic arrangement, and the power of connotations in fixing abstract ideas. Epifany Premudry's texts are mystically oriented and directed toward the Orthodox spirituality of monastic life.[75]

The author assures his audience that his panegyric will not be composed in the manner of the stories by "those ancient Hellenic philosophers." Instead, it will be a trustworthy reflection of the life of a saintly prince or princely saint in harmony with the "understanding of the Scripture" ("razum bozhestvennogo pisaniia"). The panegyrist appeals to the Holy Spirit for creative inspiration. The heart, the tongue, and the mind come together to paint a portrait of a leader who is both eternal, owing to his sanctity, and historical, owing to his defense of the Russian territory. The aim of the writer is to convey, but not to explain, the effect of a phenomenon that exists mystically on two planes, that is, in the real physical world and in an ideal intellectual realm. Through a set of anagogical correspondences, the eulogist proposes the terms of comparison for the earthly and the sacred Dmitry. He asks the reader and listener to suppose that feelings are like water; that the mind is like the sun; that heart acts through the tongue; and that the word is like fruit. Once the mind subdues emotions, and the "moisture of the soil is dried by the sun" ("mokrota zemli solntsem podybaet") and becomes one with them ("spriazheniem chiuvstva"), says the encomiast, it "plants a garden in the heart, and the heart bears intelligent fruit into the language of the world" ("v serdtsii sad vkoreniaet, serdtse zhe plod umnyi iazykom miru podavaet").[76]

Through a complex chain of analogies and elaborate imagery, the reader is taken to a second level of abstract comparison. The author holds up his mind as a mirror to the prince's life. He compares the prince's fame to a breeze that sets his own feelings astir to the point where they begin to make noise. The author then finds a new metaphor to describe his feelings, likened to boiling water. Self-consciously, the author considers the implications of the metaphor and builds on it. Just as water when boiled will turn into vapor and then condense when cooled, so it is that our minds, when we contemplate the greatness of the prince in his abstract state, rise like vapor and then fall back again, failing to reach him or the essence of God. Ultimately, in contemplating the image of Dmitry, the eulogist paints a highly abstract image.

His portrait is a verbal icon that subordinates physical traits to the concept of an absolute ideal. By the sheer power of thought, he turns his feelings into a fruit in the heart, fashions in his heart a discourse of praise, and then gives his eulogy to the world. The author quotes the teachings of the Neo-Platonic theorist, Dionysius the Areopagite, who believed that every earthly image should be taken not only literally, but also as a reflection and expression of other planes of existence that could be reached only intellectually. In this sense, the reference to Dionysius offers an interpretative key to the work. Yet ultimately the author reconciles his sense of falling short and his striving to fix an ideal through language with his awareness of its unattainability, admitting that the true Dmitry is as distant and inconceivable to the mind of the writer as God is to Dmitry. Form and content coincide marvelously and take hagiography to new heights in an effort to attain a transcendent contemplation of the ruler as a form of icon beyond the visual image.

As a portrait of the ruler, the eulogy is also a landmark in producing a timeless ideal of kingship, the perfect example of a king's two bodies. As Ernest Kantorowicz argued in his famous work on medieval kingship in England, the medieval king is historical and corporeal as well as the embodiment of a timeless ideal.[77] Sentence after sentence and paragraph after paragraph, the prose moves away from the flesh-and-bones image of the Grand Prince to his transformation into a spiritual entity that can be represented only in metaphor. The blurring of the boundaries between the encomiastic function of the sermon and the tropes of funeral oration, noted as a more general tendency in the period, produces here a unique synthesis: the figure born at the very beginning of the work is here reborn into an angelic, semi-divine spirit shorn of any earthly dimension and open to worship through contemplation. His purified soul cleansed from all passions recovers the image and likeness of the divine archetype.

Beyond its surface pathos, intentionality in a work of this kind lies in the interrelation between political and historical context, on the one hand, and textual production, on the other. Victory at Kulikovo did not immediately end Tatar domination, but it led to the relaxation of external control and symbolically positioned the Grand Prince as the key player in the unification of the lands of Muscovite Rus', a process encouraged by the Tatars. In the years between 1380 and 1462, the victor of Kulikovo and his successors struggled to survive and retain their preeminence in the Russian territory. In the late fourteenth century, Vladimir was, as a grand principality, more of an ideal than a reality. In practice, Dmitry Donskoi ruled the territory around Moscow, Rostov, Iaroslavl, Kostroma, and smaller holdings, such as Galich, Uglich, and Beloozero. The rulers of the remaining east Russian principalities showed increasing independence in their relations with Lithuania and the Golden Horde in the late fourteenth and early fifteenth centuries and often styled themselves "Grand Princes." Novgorod steered its own course by balancing the competing pressures of Moscow and Lithuania. In the early fifteenth century, the republic's oligarchic government achieved stability that lasted until Ivan the Terrible sacked the city in 1570.

The ideological repercussions of Dmitry's victory at Kulikovo were long-lasting, ensuring the Grand Prince's posthumous reputation well into the middle decades of the fifteenth century. Church and state had a common interest in casting Dmitry in the role of their shared standard-bearer. The creation of a symbolic leader required a mutually acceptable narrative pieced together from at-times divergent interests. At the end of the eulogy to Grand Prince Dmitry, Epifany Premudry quotes at length from Ilarion's *Sermon on Law and Grace* as an example of fine writing and, above all, to communicate a belief in the spiritual and political continuity between the epoch of Grand Prince Vladimir and Donskoi.

It is this vision of continuity between Kievan Rus' and an ascendant Moscow that gives unity to the parts of the work, heterogenous in origin but cumulative in the achieved image of a princely ideal built-up from birth to death and then in the afterlife. A Grand Prince who

dies in battle exemplifies military values; however, a Grand Prince who dies peacefully surrounded by his family and designates his son as heir sends a different message. The import of
Dmitry's deathbed wishes, as recorded in documents and literature, were subject to change
depending on the political context, and proved to be vulnerable to inclusion, exclusion, or
revision. Looked at again but in this specific context, Dmitry's testament, as incorporated in
the *Discourse on the Life and Death of Grand Prince Dmitry Ivanovich*, and as adapted from one
version of Donskoi's will in circulation, articulates a view of succession based on primogeniture rather than on the traditional collateral transmission of power. The deathbed scene was
most likely intended to retrospectively vindicate the politics of the 1430s at the expense of the
historical truth; but since the emphasis of the text is on spiritual aptitude and preeminence
rather than on history, it makes a case for Dmitry as a national leader in a post-Mongol period,
and therefore transforms him into a legitimating authority with respect to his descendants and
to the Church, which had stood behind the charismatic figure of the princely saint.

When we read the *Discourse on the Life and Death of Grand Prince Dmitry Ivanovich* with
the historical context in mind, we can see how writers, imbued with a new sense of mission,
powerfully shaped the contents and the style of their work to send a specific message. The
use of rhetoric is more artful, while the use of biography more subtle and abstract than in
annalistic writing. It is a work whose meaning comes into better focus in relation to our
understanding of its "horizon of expectation": the pattern of communication reflects the
structure of the historical world, including its ideology. The converse is also possible when literature assumes a "society-building" function by shaping expectations.

Despite the strong endorsement of a theocratic princely ideal, literary princely portraits do
not promulgate a doctrine of kingship in the abstract. The issue is how an implied reader
understands the historical horizon embedded in the work, since the creation of a timeless
image of the ruler can rarely be separated from its various stages of redaction. Whose interests were served through the creation and dissemination of versions of a text committed to
such a de-historicized ruler? At what point does the corroboration of a royal political ideology
make historical sense? Another way to put the question would be to ask: when did the circumstances induce the creation of a literary work of this kind?

At the surface level, then, the *Discourse on the Life and Death of Grand Prince Dmitry Ivanovich*
marks an important consolidation of earlier trends in princely biographies. Part warrior, part
father, part saint or angel, the Grand Prince combines the earthly and the spiritual in unequal
parts. The *Life of Alexander Nevsky* maintained a similar imbalance between factual material
and conventional elements of praise, whereas the eulogy and lament nearly overshadow the
military narrative. For some, the literary portrait of Donskoi perhaps frustratingly, interrupts
"progress towards historical biography."[78] Arguably, it may be more productive to recognize the
effectiveness with which the portrait was assimilated to a rather different norm of representation
of the ruler. An analogy with icon painting is instructive, because visual and literary portraiture
are equally generalized: in neither medium can the portrait of the ruler be called even remotely
realistic, and most figures are interchangeable at the level of description. Like a figure in an
icon, the tsar is both human and imbued with divinity, a mortal man but also timeless, an
individual but ultimately more a type belonging to a category of interchangeable beings that
pass on the essence or the charisma of the ruler (through grace and divine anointment).[79]

Ivan the Terrible: Tsardom and the absolutist "I"

In the late sixteenth century, more than a hundred and fifty years after Epifany Premudry
flourished, the uses of eloquence will find new applications of self-assertion and diatribe in
the writings of Ivan IV (or "the Terrible", Figure 1.04). In the case of the portrait of Dmitry,
word-weaving was a way to access the eternal and impersonal that was the essence of the

FIGURE 1.04. Anonymous, Parsuna [portrait] of Ivan IV, early 17th c.

divine in the historical. In the case of Ivan, eloquence is yoked to the biography of the historical individual, and used to dramatic effect in order to assert his own theory of absolutism according to which personal charisma vouchsafes the unassailable position of the tsar. European history in the Middle Ages can be told as a story of conflicts between a would-be unifying sovereign and the nobility. In Russia, the successes of Ivan III's reign, skipping a generation, built the foundation for Ivan IV's assertion of a Byzantine conception of the divine right.[80] Having lost his father at a tender age and his mother five years later in 1538, Ivan was bereft of a Grand Princely role-model and had no personal experience of a stable court, which had undoubtedly influenced his view of the "boyar rule" as a detestable form of government. His "First Letter" to Prince Kurbsky makes clear his unwillingness to forgive the boyars for their designs on the throne, especially during his illness in 1553.[81] He decided that his only recourse was to wrest power away from the boyars and reaffirm autocratic monarchical rule, to be achieved through repression. As Maureen Perrie concludes, "he was to spend the rest of his reign constantly inventing and reinventing the role of the Muscovite ruler, and attempting to renegotiate his relationships with the boyars."[82]

With Metropolitan Makary officiating, Ivan was crowned in January 1547. The ceremony was based on the Byzantine model, as was Ivan's idea of absolute rule. Russia did not have its own patriarchate until 1589, and for that reason the patriarch of Constantinople granted only conditional approval of Ivan's coronation as tsar.[83] The word "tsar'," derived from the Latin *Caesar*, was used in the Middle Ages interchangeably with "kniaz'" to mean "prince." From the fifteenth century, it increasingly designated the Grand Prince of Vladimir and then of Moscow.[84] Under Ivan, it became the equivalent of the single absolute ruler, the *samoderzhets*, or autocrat.[85]

In April 1564, Prince Andrei Kurbsky, a once-loyal servitor of Ivan IV as the governor of Iur'ev-Livonskii with responsibility for Livonia, defected to the Polish-Lithuanian Commonwealth. King Sigismund II August granted him asylum. From there Kurbsky wrote to his former master, unleashing a vehement epistolary exchange.[86] A purely historical evalu-ation of the correspondence between Ivan IV and Kurbsky risks missing both participants' breakthrough innovation in fashioning a unique epistolary identity and voice as vehicles for radically different theories of kingship. The paucity of information about the production of the letters increases the uncertainty about Ivan's intentions. Did he dictate the letters to a scribe who transcribed them without reducing a jarring style created by Ivan's mangled syn-tax, sudden shifts in register and use of bathos, incorrect grammar, and profanity (in sharp contrast to his learned use of Biblical quotation)? Whether spontaneous or carefully crafted, the letters, and the "First Letter" in particular, are a remarkable achievement. Earlier Russian rulers did not self-consciously build their own image, but relied on depictions penned by church writers keen on perpetuating the stereotype of the saintly prince.[87] The latter type of king was all spirit and no flesh. In asserting his view of kingship as a matter of personal achievement, Ivan in effect makes his authority a function of his charisma and his towering, "resounding" voice.[88]

There is a strong claim for treating the five letters (two pairs of letters initiated by Kurbsky followed by his closing reply) not only as political commentary but as literary works in their own right. Their content is inseparable from their style. Both writers dramatize their posi-tions, and their rhetorical prowess matches their shrewd understanding of hierarchy. Both writers also conform to the literary norms of the period, opening their letters with Biblical quotations and drawing on tradition to build their arguments. Lastly, both writers give us further insights into modes of writing and forms of eloquence developed at the time.

The medieval English proverb, "Manners makyth man," would make an apposite label for the attitude about style that governs a correspondence in which personal conduct comes in for criticism because both writers agree, if they agree on anything at all, that the personal and the political cannot be separated. Medieval Moscow was not without codes of courtliness and personal standards of decorum.[89] The system of seniority known as *mestnichestvo* carefully prescribed the proximity to the tsar on formal occasions such as banquets, religious proces-sions, and royal visits, on the basis of genealogy and status. Respect was a matter of upholding strictly defined decorum. Conversely, any departure from decorum constituted a form of injury (*obida*) that had legal status. An act of defection, such as the one committed by Kurbsky, in addition to being treason, constituted in Ivan's eyes a grievous personal insult that required commensurate response. While opposing each other on fundamental points of political ideol-ogy and theories of absolutism, each also berated his opponent for the manner of his utter-ance. While readers might have a strong impression that neither Ivan nor Kurbsky actually listened to what the other was saying in terms of content, and that the letters are not to be read as genuine attempts at persuasion, there is no question that each performs for the other. Each equates the merits of their radically contradictory literary styles with the value of their respective arguments on the nature of governance.

Adamant about his unfettered power, Ivan eschews the impersonal style of the anonymous, timeless tsar. Instead, he resorts to a highly personal, vehement, and uncontrolled style, his emotions exploding the syntax as his sentences run on in protracted, meandering paragraphs. The violence of Ivan's diatribe does not preclude learned outbursts. Although the tsar is not the head of the Russian Orthodox Church, and is neither a Metropolitan or a Patriarch, Ivan initially adopts the moral high ground as his opening gambit by quoting Biblical chapter and verse to justify his royal prerogative (his spiritual leadership is also depicted in the grand icon (see Plate 6) showing Tsar Ivan following the Archangel Michael away from conquered

Kazan´), alleging that as a defector to his country and sovereign Kurbsky has "repudiated his only soul." But the pretense of sorrow rather than anger finally cannot restrain Ivan in his "First Letter" and he metes out what seems to be divine punishment. "And should you come to possess the entire world, death will nonetheless snatch you," he argues, reasoning that since Kurbsky is mortal, and since death is inevitable, he might as well have saved his soul by showing obedience to the tsar even at the cost of his life since such obedience might have saved his soul.

Such sophistry, delivered with stirring eloquence and flashes of pathos, does not unduly detain Ivan. "Your writing has been received and carefully read. But since you hide the poison of a serpent under your tongue, and while your letter is cunningly filled with honey and honeycombs of sweetness, its taste is more bitter than wormwood." The accusation of hypoc-risy gives Ivan license to summarize their personal history, an opportunity to vilify Kurbsky ("How can you, you cur, commit such an act of villainy and then write and complain?"). His "First Letter" shifts to an account of his rule and his motivations, on the basis of which he formulates a theory of kingship. Throughout, he makes abundant use of rhetorical questions, apostrophes, and metaphors, as well as Biblical quotations; the resulting combination of savage denunciation and pious learning reminds us that in his own lifetime, and long after, Ivan enjoyed the reputation of being awesome not only for his violence but for his fanatical piety. If his rhetoric runs away with him, it is because as an absolute ruler he can violate canons of style with impunity. If his self-image betrays the faceless ideal of an atemporal and eternal tsar, it is because he wishes to expose kingship as a political struggle and authority as a matter of personal charisma. If he writes badly and sounds ridiculous, it is because the king—but only the king—can engage in a carnivalesque reversal and play the fool.

From the safety of Poland, a country with a parliament of landed aristocrats who elected their own king, Kurbsky from the start strikes a senatorial pose. He cultivates an appropriate style, writing in a Slavonic that is accurate (unlike Ivan, he uses the aorist tense correctly), and his syntax is Latinate and formed in balanced periods. In short, he turns a polished style into a virtue, citing the example of Cicero as a model prose writer. The reference is pointed. While Russia remained closed to Latin humanism, Poland had a strong Renaissance culture in which humanist and neo-Latin learning flourished. Mentioning Cicero is a way for Kurbsky to signal his cultural progressiveness over Ivan's obscurantism. But it is also politically pointed, for Cicero was not only a model letter-writer for the Renaissance; he was also a Roman senator who turned into virtue his belief in the senatorial class as a counterbalance to tyranny, and died in the process. A double role-model, Cicero inspires the posture and tone Kurbsky adopts in the three letters he wrote. An aloof interlocutor, it is no wonder that Kurbsky responds to the savage denunciations of Ivan's massive "First Letter" with insolent restraint and clever compound epithets newly coined in order to needle Ivan about his bombast: "I received your vastly resonant [*shirokoveschatel´noe*] and noisily sounding epistle [*mnogoshumiashee poslanie*], and understood, and truly understood that it is belched forth with poisonous words from an uncontrollable rage of a king that is not only inappropriate for a tsar, however great and acclaimed around the world—but unsuitable even to a simple soldier."[90]

Ivan's "First Letter" is in effect a short treatise that grounds his political theory in precedent, but also justifies his increasingly irascible behavior on the basis of biography and the unhappi-ness of his childhood and fear of persecution. No earlier Russian ruler had left any personal state-ments of this kind. From the time of Dmitry Donskoi, as commemorated by Epifany Premudry, and well through the rule of the great consolidators of Moscow, Vasily III, and Ivan III, no self-portraits in words or true likeness in images remain. The Russian tsar essentially had one eternal body, rather than both the eternal body and the historico-biographical body, as Kantorowicz's influential theory of medieval kingship maintained. In rehearsing how the death of his parents, the guardianship of the boyars, and eruptions of crowd violence all scarred him at an early age, Ivan created a biography for himself, but also left himself vulnerable to Kurbsky's criticisms that he had offended the sacred majesty of his office. And indeed Kurbsky does not shrink from lampooning Ivan for "stories that are in truth like old wives' tales." Moreover, now that he lives in a land inhabited by "people ... who know not only grammar and rhetoric, but also dialectic and philosophy," he finds in Ivan's uncouth style the perfect expression of the tyranny that he abhors.

Center and periphery and the localism of the *Tale of Petr and Fevronia*

Kurbsky's resistance to absolutism took the form of a literary-epistolary petition. We can also see in one of the most famous, and charming, works of medieval Russian literature how prose fiction refracted concerns about kingship. The *Tale of Petr and Fevronia* by the monk Ermolai Erazm (*fl.* first half of 16th c.) is an example of how original literature can be assembled from preconstituted parts. Its basic story uses information provided in local chronicles with which Ermolai integrates local legends, folkloric characterization, and miracle tales as part of its function as hagiography. His tale integrates local legends and folklore in characterization, and then at the end adduces miracle tales. Read simply as fiction, this work can be appreciated for the artfulness of its construction and for the rare representation of a female heroine. But within its purview are the same questions of leadership and Christian ideals that have animated the works discussed above. The Grand Prince is never mentioned, but the shadow of Moscow looms large over the town of Murom described by Ermolai.

For lay figures like Afanasy Nikitin and religious figures like Feodosy the local was also the spiritual, and the perception of boundaries between the Christian and non-Christian characterize their attention to spaces. Consider the story of St. Serapion, a monk trained at the Kiev Monastery of the Caves, who was transferred to Vladimir in the north in 1274, became a bishop, his position being evidence of the growth of the ecclesiastical administration to support the expansion of churches, and died and was buried in Vladimir in 1275. Little else is known about him, but five sermons on the subject of the disaster of the Mongol invasion survive and have been attributed to him.[91] In drawing the closed boundaries of a nation, his writing sees the sanctity of Russia as vulnerable.[92] A similar sense of place emerges in the "Tale of the Miracles of the Vladimir Icon of the Virgin" composed in the twelfth century during the reign of Prince Andrei Bogoliubsky (r.11 57–74), who actively founded churches in the towns within the Vladimir–Suzdal' principality.[93] In the story, Prince Andrei rests the icon on his knees and beseeches the Virgin to favor the "newly enlightened," that is, converted, people.

Born at the end of the reign of Ivan the Great, Ermolai Erazm was concerned both with sacred spaces and the economic space of agriculture (before the formal binding of the peasants to the land a century later in 1648). In the decade following his coronation as tsar, Ivan instituted many reforms, both agrarian and administrative (and for twenty-four years he waged a war against the state of Livonia, that is, Estonia and Latvia, and against the Kingdom of Lithuania).[94] The territories of late Rus' made enormous gains at the expense of the successors of the Golden Horde and the remaining principalities. Moscow's policy toward the Volga khanates had shifted away from its earlier practice of imposing client-rulers on them, and was directed instead toward their direct annexation. The overriding factor in the adoption of a more aggressive policy was undoubtedly the need to counter the danger that Kazan' would become an outpost of the Crimean khanate. Moscow's ideological motives for the conquest reflected her growing national self-awareness and self-confidence, together with her new imperial aspirations, and the desire to launch a crusade against the infidel—ideas originating with the church leaders.

Whereas previous rulers sought the cooperation of lesser princes or boyars, there now emerged the concept of the absolute authority of the Grand Prince, commensurate with the idea of a nation and a state. An important architect of the new theory of absolutism was the soldier Ivan Peresvetov. From an Orthodox Lithuanian petty-noble family, Peresvetov entered Russian service in the late 1530s.[95] Embittered by the confiscation his own estate suffered by the "strong men," he denounced the boyars' misrule during Ivan's minority, and advised the tsar to rule the country terribly (grozno) and crush the magnates. His ideal political system was the Ottoman Empire, which derived its strength from the support of rank-and-file military servicemen and from the general concern of the Turkish authorities to maintain the welfare and military capacity of the armed forces. Peresvetov identified the magnates as the culprits in the failure of the Byzantine Empire. In support of this political ideology, Metropolitan Makary in turn provided a religious argument, calling on the Russians to fight "for the holy churches and our holy Orthodox faith against the godless sons of Hagar."[96] The significance of this campaign is represented symbolically in the great icon of the Church Militant in which Ivan follows the Archangel Michael in leading the Russian troops, in the form of the heavenly host, back from Kazan′ to Moscow.

In the Bible, the Archangel Michael overthrows Satan; in the icon, the imagery borrowed from the Book of Daniel and from Revelation imbued the victory over the Tatars with an apocalyptic significance of the battle between good and evil. It also equated the Muscovites with God's chosen people, Israel (Jerusalem = Moscow in the icon), a typical motif in sixteenth century rhetoric. In Palm Sunday rituals, as the historian Nancy Kollmann has observed, Ivan enacted his relationship with God and demonstrated to the people that he was God's representative on earth and the shepherd of his flock as he rode on an ass into Moscow, symbolically suggesting that during the Second Coming the Orthodox tsar would lead his people to the New Jerusalem and salvation.[97] Similar motifs adorned the Kremlin when parts of it were rebuilt after the fire of 1547. Metropolitan Makary, in one of his letters to the tsar in 1552, called on the Archangel Michael to assist Ivan against the Tatars. The Archangel was long associated with the Muscovite dynasty: the Cathedral of the Archangel Michael in the Kremlin was the burial place of the Grand Princes until the end of the seventeenth century. The cathedral contains the tombs of most of the Muscovite Grand Princes and tsars from Ivan I (r. 1325–41) to Ivan V (r. 1682–96), forty-six in all. An association between Ivan and the Archangel Michael was an important theme of the age. In the first letter to Kurbsky, the tsar referred to Michael as the "champion of Moses, of Joshua the son of Nun and of all Israel ... he was also the protector of Constantine the Great." Michael Flier has also analyzed how in Palm Sunday rituals Ivan's humble behavior allowed the tsar to act out his relationship with God and demonstrated that the tsar "functioned as God's lieutenant on earth and shepherd of his flock."[98] The annual restaging of the procession on Palm Sunday linked the Kazan′ victory not just with Christ's historical entry into Jerusalem, but also with the future Second Coming.

This is the moment when it became politically expedient to see the history of the lands of Kievan Rus′ and Muscovite Rus′ as stages in the growth of Moscow. In the Nikon Chronicle, named after its editor at the Chudov Monastery, extracts from earlier chronicles were regrouped in order to produce a rereading of the entire history of the Eastern Slavs in light of the doctrine of the Third Rome.[99] Massive chronicle-writing—like the Trinity (Troitskaia Letopis′, early 15th c.), destroyed in the Napoleonic invasion of 1812 or the Voskresenskaia Chronicle (sixteenth century)—absorbed local histories just as Moscow itself had swallowed up neighboring principalities in Suzdalia. The scribes arranged their material according to the topics, but the open model of copying led from the sixteenth century to extending the length of the texts. No reader could grasp a whole containing many thousands of folio sheets: the very comprehensive but unworkable size of such recensions puts in question whether any notion at all of the reader operates in such a model of textual production. While works of this scope might unquestionably look commensurate with the power and image Moscow as a country and not just city-state, they also obliterate any notion of individual authorship: through the numerous scribes who penned the pages, history seems to write itself as an anonymous and impersonal force. This in itself may well be a calculated effect. Such manipulation of compilations was intended to stabilize the winners in a game of dynastic politics.

Massive compilations reflected the hegemony of the Muscovite state. This political dominance is the backdrop against which shorter, local accounts continued to be produced (as in Pskov). The monk Ermolai Erazm (d. mid-sixteenth century) is one of the most accomplished writers of the sixteenth century. His *Tale of Petr and Fevronia* interweaves local legend, folkloric plots, hagiographic topoi, and political narrative in portraying the eponymous prince and princess who ruled Murom. By the time of its composition, this small city-state had already been absorbed into the larger neighboring city of Riazan′ and was well within the orbit of nearby Moscow. While its charm lies in the fairy-tale like quality of its plot and characters, because the work emanates from the periphery of the super-state it stands out in the period as unusual in championing the beauty of the small and local, and in celebrating the female. Although the protagonists are stock figures, their language is highly affecting, and Ermolai's use of devices and postures such as doubling, second-guessing, projection, wish fulfillment, and interior monologue implies a rounded view of psychology enhanced by a winning fusion of written and oral styles.

When the story begins, Prince Petr is a loyal servitor of his older brother Prince Pavel. But the devil, who may represent inner drives, such as libido or political ambition, or may be a projection of rivalry between brothers, instigates strife by impersonating Prince Pavel. Petr sees through this ruse, slays his brother's doppelganger by using a gifted weapon. As he dies, the devil turns into a flying serpent, combining the qualities of a fairy-tale dragon with the Biblical seducer of *Genesis*, and sprays Petr with poisonous venom. This leads to the second marital sub-plot in which the desperate retainers, seeking a cure, encounter a peasant girl named Fevronia. Her reputation for miraculous cures precedes her, but she plays hard to get and tests them with riddles. Like the Princess in Snow White, she awaits a noble husband who can satisfy certain conditions. She makes his complete cure conditional on a promise to marry her, and while the Prince initially rejects her proposal on class grounds ("How can a Prince marry the daughter of a woodcutter?") eventually she outsmarts him. Her potion cures and bewitches him, and they marry. The portrait of Fevronia, who when we first meet her is like the maiden in a French fabliau shown spinning cloth surrounded by animals like a dancing rabbit, owes its mixture of charm and sorcery, cleverness and drive, to the folkloric figure of the wise maiden (*mudraia deva*) who manages situations through the use of riddles.

Petr and Fevronia reign together, and, while Fevronia's humble origins cause a rebellion among evil boyars at the court, her cunning and charity prevail, with popular support. Class divisions recur on the death of the royal couple when the boyars and the Church refuse to bury an aristocrat and a commoner together in one grave. Through a miracle, the separate tombs in which their bodies had been laid stand empty, and the couple repose together in their royal sepulcher in the Church of the Virgin in Murom. A final prayer in praise of the Virgin's intercession follows, reflecting the widespread Marian cult firmly established across the Christian world from the thirteenth century (as illustrated in Figure 1.05). The emphasis on their domestic life, and the veneration of the Virgin as an extension of uxorious fidelity, has its own beauty for a modern reader as a representation outside historical time of gender equality and romantic love. But even these aspects, for all their debt to folklore, look motivated by the response of Ermolai to the sumptuary policies of the Muscovite state.

FIGURE 1.05. Madonna and St. Sergius, 15th c.

Domestic regulation was another prong in the assertion of national unity, evidenced in the massive textual productions such as the *Great Menology* and the *Household Manual* (*Domostroi*). The latter text is an extensive manual of household management, attributed to the monk Silvester and dated to the sixteenth century. It covers everything from savoir-faire, such as table manners, to conjugal relations, including the punishment for adultery. Husbands emerge as despots endowed with unfettered power over their family, and most especially over their wife who is supposed to embody an ideal of submission and passivity. This vision of the intimate world, expressed in a series of numbered paragraphs laid out like a law code, admits no gap between the public and private, discouraging any sense of interiority, because the writer regulates and judges behavior on the basis of external models of comportment and compliance.

An age-old fear of sin and mistrust of the body defines the ideological premises of otherwise different works like the *Household Manual* and the essayistic "Discourse on Bad Women" ("Slovo o zlykh zhenakh"). Many copies of the latter circulated from the eleventh century well into the sixteenth. Its initial purpose was, of course, to admonish monks against sins of the flesh. Later versions differ significantly, as advice literature aimed not only at bookmen and monks, but also at a wider audience whose morals are seen to be always vulnerable to sin (a feature that extends into seventeenth-century novellas and morality literature as a source of both Christian teaching and picaresque amorality). The protection of the social order through marriage and hierarchically ordered domesticity dominates gender roles. "What is a wife?," asks the anonymous writer, answering that she is "a trap laid to seduce men into pleasures when she paints her face and large eyes, when she stretches her high cheekbones, sings with her voice, charms with her words, attracts with her clothes, plays with her feet, kills with her deeds." And what is a bad wife? "A poisoned well, cursed arrow, a northern wind, a nasty, famine to the house, a mad bitch, a furious goat."[100] Against this harsh representation of female gender, Ermolai's refashioning of the folkloric wise maiden, her elevation to the position of a ruler, her talent for personal and public happiness, and finally her official canonization and burial in the Church of the Virgin, produce a radically different vision of the feminine. In his writings, and above all in the delightful and highly readable *Tale of Petr and Fevronia*, Ermolai used literature to project different models of governance for the provincial city-state, in contrast to the absolutist discourse propagated from Moscow.

Overall, the narrative displays great artistry in producing a compelling story out of known elements and mythic devices, such as the challenge, riddles, the motif of the search for a bride, and the slaying of a dragon. While Fevronia's folk origins and her miracle cure smack of pagan beliefs, Petr's slaying of the dragon and the couple's later acts of piety attest to their Christian virtue. It is worth considering whether the final miracle was meant to encourage the establishment of the cult or whether it reflected popular feeling and drew on current belief.

Local history, beliefs, and legends constitute the bedrock of the story, and they promote the image of polity in which people and rulers (possibly to the disadvantage of boyars shown as a cabal) get along. The special feature of a dynasty composed of a commoner and aristocrat, while filtered through the fairy-tale motifs, also conveys a political point. Whether it was historically true matters less than the fact that Ermolai does have ideological convictions about power structures and class that might be rooted in a Christian regard for equality and spirituality over wealth. He wrote in an age when the expansion of Moscow looked unstoppable, threatening not only the autonomy of other city-states but also conscription of peasants into a larger army, the gradual binding of the peasantry to the land (leading to the formal creation of serfdom) and the centralization of religious practice. He also set out his views on land reform in a separate technical treatise on land boundaries and arable parcels of land.[101] Metropolitan Makary in Moscow imposed new procedures for regulating canonization, ordering the Church calendar and feasts.[102] In addition, as Maureen Perrie and Andrei Pavlov have noted, the Church began to produce a number of literary works which traced the lineage of the Grand Princes of Moscow back to Kiev, including as we have seen a version of the "Monomakh legend," concerning the transfer of royal regalia from Byzantium to Grand Prince Vladimir Monomakh of Kiev and later to the Grand Princes of Moscow.[103] Retrospective accounts of this type corroborated the legitimacy of the dynastic right to rule the Russian lands, a tenet of the ideology of sixteenth-century Moscow.

Ermolai's story presents the local rather than the national, the uxorious over the patriarchal, and in keeping with other writings such as the *Instruction on Land Measurement to Tsars* (*Blagokhotiashchim tsarem pravitel'nitsa i zemlemerie*), a treatise on social improvement and tax reform in which Ermolai argues for economic justice for the peasantry and the egalitarian over the authoritarian. In the world of the story, good rule and fairness contain an element of self-interest since they reduce social strife. Among the forces militating against a stable economic model, as expounded in his *Instruction*, are the self-interested boyars (referred to as "scroungers" or "parasites"), whose harsh treatment stands in contrast to the Christian ideal of brotherly love a good tsar should feel for the peasantry. There is only a short step between these social positions and the values espoused in the *Tale of Petr and Fevronia*, which allegorizes these aspects of the contemporary world while managing to lift the hero and heroine onto another plane of meaning when it is read as a fairy tale about undying love.

Ermolai's celebration of Fevronia is more than a reflexive appreciation of the Marian cult transferred onto a local peasant girl. Pious and cunning, Fevronia is a model of wifely devotion yet never merely obedient and serves as the real power behind the throne. The characterization breaks with behavioral norms and female stereotypes of the period (the most venerated being that of Bogoroditsa exemplified in Plate 7). Ermolai astutely registered from his perspective as a provincial clergyman the impact of the new super-state on the domestic mores, popular beliefs, and landholding patterns of the local within this national context. Moscow was the spiritual and political capital of a much larger nation created through internal colonization and expansion both south into the Caucasus (Ivan the Terrible conquered Kazan') and eastwards into the Urals. Beyond the normalization of the liturgy and liturgical and ecclesiastical practice, Church reforms created an ideal subject of the state. Writ large at the social level, this entailed piety and a fundamental sense of obedience to the social hierarchies established by *mestnichestvo* according to which aristocrats, boyars, and servitors literally knew their place at the table of the tsar, within ritual processions and in public ceremonies. The individual household was supposed to reflect in microcosm these same ideals of orderliness and devotion from wife and children to the husband whose power was unlimited.

Conclusion

Over its long history and through a large corpus of works, medieval literature consistently reflects not just genuine historical context but the projection of its circumstances of creation and their ideologies. Rulers invested the writing of medieval Russia with a political agenda, twinning the fortunes of the dynasty with the propagation of Christianity. Scribes repeatedly articulate the relationship between the authority of the Church and the princes, often finding equivalence between forms of obedience to the senior prince as head of the clan and the head of the Church or local saints.

Medieval Russian literature has national and individual stories to tell, and it does so through a variety of narrative modes. The Part has brought out the different types of storytelling that flourished across the principalities from the heyday of the Kievan appanage system to the rise of Muscovy from the fifteenth century when national narratives supplanted local histories.

The *Primary Chronicle*, the eleventh-century master narrative of the establishment of the Riurikid dynasty and conversion of Slavs to Christianity, made a virtue of the late advent of "divine grace" to the peoples of Rus'. The grand narrative that accumulates through the eleventh to seventeenth centuries associates the institutions of power (kingship, the Church, writing) with forms of the holy and with Christianity in particular. Stories of individual piety and cultic narratives were one way in which writing helped to define the sacred boundaries of the country within the world. Telling the story of holy men and women was a way of conferring a charismatic status on local rulers who supported monastic foundations; and of demonstrating how certain individuals made a conscientious commitment to a certain ethical ideal of renunciation, conscience, and devotion that could be imitated through good conduct and good works. At the level of the city-state, storytelling focused on narratives of Christianization and heroic resistance to invasion from the steppe or from the east. Narratives that vilified invaders tended to sanctify the Grand Prince or tsar, an unsurprising approach given the origin of most of these texts in ecclesiastical institutions that aimed to forge close relations with powerful rulers.

In response to the disruptions of the Tatar conquest, monastic culture evolved a narrative of national catastrophe and trauma, survival and revival. This story remained a stable and adaptable mode that recurred until the Time of Troubles early in the seventeenth century and the installation of the Romanov dynasty. The image of Kiev as the New Jerusalem was originally established in the eleventh-century sermon of the Metropolitan Ilarion, a tour de force of rhetoric and historical revisionism. That cultural myth became a topos in fifteenth-century writing; it substantiated hopes for a post-Mongol vision of Moscow as a new Rome by quoting the sermon and placing before the eyes and ears of readers a mirage of the greatness that had been. Even in folkloric works, the myth of a country that could be overrun and devastated but disappear and re-emerge gained traction. The sequel to the Tatar invasion was the displacement of power to Vladimir, the transfer of Church authority to its Grand Prince, and the consolidation of secular and Christian authority in the princes of Muscovy. From the fifteenth century the story of the Muscovite juggernaut is told in chronicles. These codices were super-genres, endlessly expansive vehicles for all types of writing that recorded local knowledge, saints' lives with tales of miracles that affirmed the legitimacy of local cults and promoted the status of monasteries and local princes. As they were re-edited, they both perpetuated local legends while elaborating a teleological and providential narrative about the rise of Moscow as a last bastion of Christianity. The metanarratives in prose and poetry that organize the story of the rise of the Russian state and its defense will continue to serve literature during the Time of Troubles in the early seventeenth century as writers tell a story of the trauma of conquest and near disaster with the potential for renewal.

Part II

The Seventeenth Century

Introduction:
The problem of transition and
a new approach

L ITERARY histories of Russia have difficulty with the seventeenth century and tend to treat it as a transitional no-man's land. Should it be integrated into the Middle Ages? Or seen as the precursor to the eighteenth century? In Part II, we argue that the writing produced in the second half of the seventeenth century has a richness of its own, distinct from its medieval origins, and is loosely bound by the political chronology of the beginning of the Time of Troubles in 1603 and the accession of Peter the Great as tsar in 1689. The span of nearly a century deserves to come more into focus as a period in its own right.[1] We find it more helpful and appropriate to apply the term "early modern" as a way of avoiding the teleological and retrospective assumptions that go with seeing sequences in terms of developmental narrative. The idea of an early modern age allows for both the distinctiveness of seventeenth-century innovation and also for the fact that, to a large degree, its relation to the eighteenth century is more dead-end than launch pad for the defining trends of that later time.

Nineteenth-century historians, starting with Nikolai Karamzin in his *History of the Russian State* (*Istoriia gosudarstva Rossiiskogo*, 1818, 1821–24) and continuing into the late part of the century with important figures like A. N. Pypin (1833–1904), determined periodization chiefly according to a political narrative, which stopped with the foundation of the Romanov dynasty. The seventeenth century emerged in these and other influential accounts as the waning of the Middle Ages to be resolved as a prologue to Peter the Great. And to a large degree, the intellectual and institutional character of Russia remained recognizably the same until the mid-seventeenth century. Political bias also encouraged historians from the more radical side of politics (like Pypin) to find in popular culture the missing link to their own high culture. Native forms of storytelling were published as evidence of "democratic satire" and taken as proof of a winning propensity among the peasantry to use oral literature for the purpose of social subversion.[2] At the same time, a nationalist bias made it more difficult to acknowledge the origins in Rus' (and therefore Ukraine) of high culture, much of which, in fact, remained little known and unpublished until editions began to appear in the 1970s. Arguably, the emphasis on folklore, legends, and saints' lives artificially extended the medieval part; in turn, this sense of continuity exaggerated the shock of the new marked by the reign of Peter the Great, starting in 1696.[3]

Periodization is one way in which literary histories conceptualize development. There has been a long-standing trend to valorize the Petrine period as a sharp break with the medieval past, and this has overshadowed the preceding decades. There are, however, substantial drawbacks to the disruption and continuity arguments in both directions. Sustained links of the seventeenth century to the medieval world need to be acknowledged; they lie positively in the consistent practices of scribal writing, book production, and monastic life. Yet significant changes in writing practices and cultural movements certainly distance it from the Middle

Ages as leaning toward the worldly, secular, and personal, an outlook more typical of the early modern period. Despite the impression of surface stability in education, monastic culture, and kingship model, aspects of storytelling, and the number and quality of storytellers change in ways that challenge the implied idea of a steady state embedded in the narrative of continuity. The sources, techniques of writing, the transition to a print culture, and the model of the author, differentiate the seventeenth century substantially from both surrounding epochs.

The seventeenth century, especially the latter half, witnessed a spectacular and innovative literary flourishing with the creation of court culture and the emergence of narrative writing. Possibly for the first time since Kievan Rus´, poetry became a vehicle for personal reflection. Court ceremony and royal patronage inaugurated a tradition of occasional poetry that conferred prestige on the author. Consider the title of Aleksandr M. Panchenko's *Russia on the Eve of the Petrine Reforms*, a fundamental study of a whole raft of poets who remained invisible and unread until Pachenko's extensive archival publications. The poets published by Panchenko (1937–2002), a major cultural historian responsible for discoveries of much primary literature, represent a critical mass of literary activity that deserves to be seen as more than a slow crescendo to the eighteenth century, and as the real starting point of innovation and modernization.[4] Arguably, the title underplays an important cultural episode that was more self-contained than a bridge to the Petrine vision. It announces a portentous expectation for a turning point that actually remains decades away. These achievements risk being overlooked if seen merely as the rump of the medieval; or as a false start to the Enlightenment.

Although "beginning" is one of the most frequent words to be encountered in titles of books and articles on the period, it is perhaps a sign of gradual reconceptualization, building on the foundational work of Panchenko and others, that Lydia Sazonova, the preeminent scholar in seventeenth-century studies, now applies the more gradualist language of "an early New Time."[5] New purposes of writing included moral and social instruction, and entertainment for a small number of lay readers. The introductory essay to the seventeenth-century chapters in the *Histoire de la littérature russe* is a case in point. Its author, Ilya Serman, reiterates a long-held assumption that the period should be regarded as a transition ("vers une littérature ouverte") to a modern literature, positioning the eighteenth century, and Peter the Great's reign, as the true "big bang."[6] This argument rests on two assumptions: first, that the end result of the medieval period was isolation; and, second, that the primary accomplishment of the seventeenth century was to pave the way for the creation of an open literature. The periodization of the *Histoire*, using a model of persistent continuity (atrophy followed by evolution) rather than the more disruptive and inconsistent dynamic identified in this book, divides literary history into distinct eras and finds little other intrinsic value in the seventeenth century. The overall conclusion, however, is problematic, not least because it sets up the medieval world as a straw man of insularity and imagines a relatively smooth transition into Peter's vision of a new modernity.

Leaving aside the question, already treated in Part I, of whether isolation as a term does justice to the medieval period, Parts II and III of the present *History of Russian Literature* will suggest that the claim for continuity between the centuries is open to revision. Discontinuities as much as continuities, and even false continuities, can be observed over long spans (a judgment made solely in terms of literary matters without reference to the obvious backward nature of the seventeenth century in the spheres of science and technology). There is considerable validity to the first claim that the seventeenth century was a time of greater openness to foreign influences although the openness was highly qualified. Perhaps more importantly, the foreign influences that generated new forms of literary culture in the seventeenth century are for the most part not replicated in the eighteenth century when other factors prevail. And the very question of the foreign, whether defined by origin, language, or religious dogma, lacks nuance as a model of influence and intellectual transmission given the extensive crossovers between Jesuit, Orthodox, Ruthenian, and Muscovite figures and cultural practices that blur the boundaries of identity. To the complications of ethnic, linguistic, and institutional identity the greatest poet of the period, Simeon Polotsky, bore witness at the end of his life in 1680. In the verse "Preface to the Respected Reader" ("Predislovie ko blagochestivomu chitateliu") of his poetic collection the *Rifmologion*, Polotsky refers to his own work as polyglot, written, as it was, in his native Belorussian, and in the Slavonic he learned ("I saw there was much use/ in learning pure Slavonic"), to which he adds Muscovite or the Russian vernacular.

Histories that proceed in a linear fashion and look for national genius, political watersheds, or cast their narrative in terms of a single sustained movement, cannot absorb the sideways movements, much less the ebb and flow of a culture riven by contradictions that prove creative but unevenly consequential. It might be argued that the term "early modern" is also an uneasy designation, since Russia lagged in establishing universities and in accepting the scientific method. This is true, but there were important, albeit limited, changes to Russian education, and the category has the merit of acknowledging momentum and tradition.

The best reasons to study the seventeenth century are, first, for the intrinsic quality of the texts, institutions, and arguments, and, second, because it was a period in which the modern notion of authorship began to emerge. Early modern literature captures transitions and tensions that are part of a longer-term national story. The monastery is no longer the sole locus for figures, whose defining activity is writing. The towering personalities and talents of the period are the poet and courtier Simeon Polotsky (1629–80) and the preacher and dissenter clergyman Avvakum Petrovich, known simply as Avvakum (1620–82). Polotsky was a monk, Ruthenian by birth and educated initially by the Jesuits in Kiev and Vilnius before traveling to universities in Western Europe (detailed accounts are lacking). He settled in Moscow in 1664 and can be considered the first modern Russian poet. He was also the first Russian court writer, composing epistles addressed to the tsar and various members of the tsar's family, and producing plays for the newly-established court theater. Avvakum Petrovich, author of sermons and works of dogmatic theology, was one of the Old Believers whose dissent from Nikon's reforms led to schism. The *Life of the Archpriest Avvakum* (*Zhitie protopopa Avvakuma*) found new uses for the traditional messages and forms of hagiography and Scripture, while drawing on the narrative modes that became popular in the seventeenth century.

Both of these writers amply satisfy the demands for the intrinsic quality as well as the authorial stature we might require if the aim were to define a period solely through its greatest figures. From a historical perspective, they emerge out of a broader literary field of lesser, non-canonical writers without whom their own creative genius would have been impossible. When read within their ideological and religious matrix, their works—but of course not their works alone—suggest considerable dynamism in the development of a literary system rather than just the "waiting game" of a transitional period anticipating the Petrine reforms. Notably, we increasingly find scribes, who—more like writers than scribes—begin to align their intentions with popular tastes: some write out of self-awareness and a set of feelings largely unexplored in Russian culture to this date; and others write to acquire fame and prestige that patronage at court can bestow.

Literary and political histories also tend to cast the seventeenth century entirely in terms of conflict ("rebellious," or *buntarskii*), pegging all writing as belonging to one of the warring sides in doctrinal disputes and power plays between the Church and the tsar.[7] According to Panchenko, the entire period falls into sharp splits between the religious and the secular, faith and reason, the medieval, as a permanent transition, and a new culture. These tensions frame Panchenko's view of the seventeenth century as defined by a culture and a series of institutional wars ultimately grounded in an opposition between Western and Orthodox values.

These assertions are perhaps true in the same way that, in Western Europe, the Reformation serves as a framework rather than a system of total control of cultural practice. When the seventeenth century is viewed from within the literary field, it is easy, for instance, to feel sympathy with a scholar of the Anglican Reformation who, when looking at England in the sixteenth century, rues the standard scholarly narrative for maintaining that "the institutional simplifications and centralizations of the sixteenth century provoked correlative simplifications and narrowings in literature."[8] Profound cultural transformations involving religion, writing systems, and reception histories do not play out quickly, neatly, or directly either in England or in Russia. It could be said that in the seventeenth century the monopoly of the Church and monasteries on writing and content began to crack, but this cannot entirely explain new trends in poetry and prose. Monasteries still educated the scribes who applied their skilled labor to new modes of writing. Otherwise much quality writing is non-partisan or dogmatic and conceived for the sake of literary practices of storytelling and self-expression in poetry.

I

Paradise lost:
National narratives

THE idea of discontinuity originates in the primary material itself. Historical accounts, saints' lives, and other modes of storytelling reflect contemporary anxiety as the collapse of the Riurikid dynasty left a power vacuum and invited invasions. At the beginning of the seventeenth century, contemporary writers treated the Time of Troubles from 1598 to the establishment of the Romanov dynasty in 1613 with the enthronement of Tsar Mikhail (r. 1613–45) as a cataclysm and threat.

Social historians have argued that the cultural context of the seventeenth century changed in response to violent social and economic disruptions.[1] The Time of Troubles, as the beginning of the seventeenth century is known, aggravated a growing tendency down the social scale to shun the traditional religious institutions like the monastery and the Church. The increasing centralization of the state during the fifteenth and sixteenth centuries shifted the center of gravity away from the landholding class toward the court and its religious ceremonies. As the gap increased between landholders and serfs, the serf population sought its own explanations for its plight in local cults, miracle cures, and custom. Even as the court became dominant in the life of the boyars, and writing became a technology associated with central government, the now legally enserfed population reacted. The Time of Troubles provoked doubt about Russia's moral compass and direction, and sowed doubts among clergy and ordinary parishioners about the state of Orthodoxy.

Narrative prose extends the focus of medieval writing about the state of the nation and its spiritual condition. Throughout the seventeenth century, monasteries guaranteed the longevity of the saint's life as a staple of Orthodox writing by putting out new copies of existing saints' lives, sometimes in revised versions, and by writing new hagiographies. To expand this genre, clerical writers produced new tales, sometimes based on local accounts of visions and miracles that circulated in manuscript (some stories lent themselves to pictorial versions with captions as found on woodcuts or *lubki*). These works reinforced the value of religion at the personal level of the worshipper and added a new narrative line to the stock of writing about Holy Russia.

Because writing was mainly done by the clergy and the upper echelons of government, it is no wonder that the rough transfer of power, culminating in the story of Boris Godunov and the founding of the Romanov dynasty, galvanized the attention of writers starting in the sixteenth century. By the end of the century, the state of Muscovy had developed a narrative that privileged its links to the Kievan past, valorized its resistance to the Tatars as a national myth (glossing over a more complex history of collusion), and enshrined the idea that following the fall of Constantinople Moscow served Christendom as a Third Rome.

In the seventeenth century, the contribution of monks to literary culture reflects the position of monasteries caught in the historical flux between defensiveness and idealism, collectivism and individual salvation. Attentive to the invasions and insecurities of the seventeenth century, clerical writers, like the medieval chroniclers, dramatized history. Hardships, falling monastic recruitment, and religious malaise brought on by the perception of pervasive sin inspire the use of religious allegory, folkloric style, and verse fable to capture the personal and universal dimension. Catastrophic narratives reflect in traditional terms the causes of crises and individual plights.

Narratives from the Time of Troubles to the Schism (1613–82)

In 1347, the Novgorod bishop Vasily Kalika (*fl.* 1331–42) sent an "Epistle on Paradise" ("Poslanie o rae") to Fedor Dobry (Fedor the Good), a fellow clergyman. This work addressed the theological dispute raging in the town of Tver' about paradise as either a spiritual entity or an earthly realm. Having rebutted views he considered heretical, Vasily affirmed his belief that "spiritual paradise" ("dukhovnyi rai") existed on earth, and he ended with the statement that "paradise, as created for the sake of Adam, has not perished and is in the East." There is little doubt as to its location, identified with the Russian lands, and the story of its loss and eventual recovery represent an important motif in seventeenth-century works.[2]

Paradise lost plays at least as large a part in the stories contemporaries tell of their own time. In addition to the material devastation at the Time of Troubles (*Smuta*), literature of the period recorded its psychological impact. Political and social instability shook the confidence of the ruling class, fighting among rivals and claimants for the throne eroded national unity and emboldened invaders keen to exploit Russian disunity. Famine and popular unrest, aggravated by superstition and rumormongering, made the turn of the century a time ripe for meditation on national destiny. Previously, such reflection depended entirely on the skill of monks working within the copyist tradition. Drawn from among the ranks of the boyars, from the chanceries and from the monasteries, a larger pool of scribes modified the earlier styles of writing, bringing in the "Chancery language," rapidly evolving in Moscow, which was closer to the vernacular and more sensitive than Church Slavonic to recording factual descriptions that also extended the late medieval application of "eloquence" (*dobroslovie*).[3]

Catastrophic narratives that seem to be told in real time balance the present sense of disaster with the sense of a paradisiacal past. There is a pervasive acceptance that history is a form of punishment for collective sins and for the people's acquiescence in the policies of corrupt tsars and boyars. This is the recurrent message of the massive *Chronicle* (*Vremennik*, edited around the 1650s) compiled by the Chancery scribe Ivan Timofeev (1555–1631). Remarkable for its learning, and steeped in a range of Russian literary traditions, including Kievan writing such as the Boris and Gleb cycle and the *Life of St. Feodosy*, this intergeneric work has been described as a "mosaic" containing autobiographical passages, miracle tales, political commentary, and gossip organized chronologically. Timofeev, inspired by Biblical analogies between contemporary Russia and Josephus's *The Jewish War*, explores the sins of his contemporaries and the cure for anomie manifested in the "wordless silence" of the political elite.[4] Similarly, in the prose narrative "Words on Muscovite Days, Tsars and Saints" ("Slovesa dnei i tsarei"), the bookish I. A. Khvorostinin, whose work as a syllabic poet is also noteworthy, begins with a recounting of the Genesis myth of Eden and original sin as the precondition for Christian salvation.[5] Its language and imagery are reminiscent of Ilarion's *Sermon on Law and Grace*, Timofeev's story of how Russia adopted Christianity, and suggests that, because Russia was late to achieve conversion, the turmoil of the early seventeenth century looks almost inevitable:

The land is exhausted by hunger, and many have become impure from famine, and the dead bodies of people, and birds, and beasts, and fish, and everything about which one cannot relate in a tale: they ate the bark of trees, the roots of aquatic plants, indigestible dirt, and the like.[6]

Yet throughout the literature of the period—from allegories praising the halcyon days of monasteries to Avvakum's evocation in the 1680s of the natural wonders of Siberian cornucopia, to the baroque symbolism of the garden in Simeon Polotsky's court poetry—the image of Russia as a land of timeless wonders, full of folkloric magic, persists. The *Chronograph* of 1617, a chronicle summary covering the period from the end of Ivan IV's reign to the end of the Time of Troubles, speaks of Ivan's ill-fated son Tsar Fedor as a "garden of innumerable virtues, watered by divine rivers, a living paradise who preserved blessed gardens." A "New Tale of the Wonderful Russian Kingdom" ("Novaia povest' o preslavnom rossiiskom tsarstve," 1611), composed about the time of the invasion of Smolensk by Sigismund III, takes the form of a letter by the author to any future reader who has remained true to Orthodoxy. The author alternates between thunderous denunciation of the invaders and the comparison of Russia to a stunted tree whose roots have "rotted because it grows in the shade" deprived of the "sun of righteousness" ("v zastenii stoiashchego na nego zhe, mniu, pravednomu solntsu malo siiati"). But once his listeners choose the "right branch to cultivate for the sake of greatness" and, evoking baptismal imagery, water it and consecrate it with the Spirit, and "plant it in a high place," they will "grow the branch and let it flourish in the light of the right faith [Orthodoxy]" ("I rosti bo toi vetvi i tsvesti vo svete blagoveriia"), and the tree will flourish and grow "tall and outstanding."[7] The reward will be a sweet fruit to be given to all, and the roots of the tree will be strong.

This stunning evocation of a paradise achieved through the cultivation of faith, as well as the sense of the country as a scenic place, resonates with, as the historian Valerie Kivelson points out, seventeenth-century discovery of nature description.[8] Nature is largely absent in sixteenth-century works. Scenery, instead, favors desolate landscapes, settings for hermits and miracles or for the flat representation of holy figures and scenes similar to those used in bordering icons against a gold background.[9] Aided by new techniques in cartography, mapmakers turned their attention to the spatial representation of landscapes, including fauna and flora; and writers, bolstered by increasing literacy, showed newfound interest in the physical world. Kivelson has observed that seventeenth-century mapmakers inserted "vivid green trees" into maps marked out with more obviously Christian symbols (like the crucifix to designate churches), evidence of what she calls Christian undertones and linked to a larger Edenic theme in writing and iconography.[10] It is in this context that the writer of the "New Tale," for instance, appropriates this semantic field in his vision of post-catastrophe Russia, while Avvakum combines naturalism with religious symbolism to celebrate the remote Siberia as a world untouched by heresy. And even Khvorostinin expresses tempered optimism that, with the expulsion of the Pretender, the false Dmitry, and the restoration of the churches, the apostolic faith in Moscow will enjoy a revival.

Seventeenth-century narrative prose about the Time of Troubles perpetuates the style of historical writing developed in the medieval chronicles (vividly remembered, as can be seen in Figure 11.01), also featuring set-pieces including speeches and lamentations to capture the trauma of invasion. Of all the works about the Time of Troubles the best known is the *Narration of Avraamy Palitsyn* (*Skazanie Avraamiia Palitsyna*), written most likely in 1620, since the events in his narrative break off at 1619.[11] Born near Rostov probably no later than the 1550s as Averky Palitsyn, in 1588 he suffered disgrace and the confiscation of his property. Forcibly tonsured at the Solovetsky Monastery, he assumed the name Avraamy. It has been conjectured that he backed the wrong side in a boyar intrigue against Boris Godunov. After his exile was

FIGURE 11.01. Battle between the Russian and Tatar troops in 1380, 1640s.

commuted in 1600, Palitsyn lived for a period in the Trinity-Sergiev Monastery, and subsequently occupied a number of administrative posts. In 1608, two years after his ally Prince Shuisky had taken control in Moscow, he returned to the monastery. His managerial role thrust him into historical events when Shuisky, who succeeded the toppled Pretender, faced opposition from the Poles and the Swedes: Palitsyn released the great grain reserves of the monastery in order to help stabilize Shuisky's tenuous grasp on power. Although Palitsyn regarded Shuisky's eventual downfall as justified after he forced the monastery to melt its coinage, Palitsyn remained a visible player, and negotiated with the Polish king for a secure settlement on behalf of the monastery. His account remains silent about his role, although Palitsyn disingenuously portrays himself later on as taking an active role in the emancipation of Moscow from the Poles and as a supporter of Mikhail Romanov. With the repatriation of the Patriarch Filaret, Palitsyn once again suffered punishment, in the form of exile to the Solovki archipelago in the White Sea, where he spent seven years until his death on September 13, 1626.

His account in seventy-seven chapters reveals a sharp observer, a gifted rhetorician of great eloquence and pathos. Diffident or cautious, throughout the work he refers to himself only occasionally and even then only in the third-person as the elder Avraamy. His own involvement in the events does not make him a reliable historical source; in fact, another variant of his work exists in which the first six chapters have been strongly edited, clearly in light of the outcome of the power struggle between the Polish invaders and Russian defenders—although it is debatable whether Palitsyn himself or a well-meaning colleague introduced these differences. Within its annalistic frame, the work encompasses battle scenes, lyrical descriptions of nature, meditative passages, and prayers, embellished sometimes with cadenced prose. His language can be elaborate and bookish in the best tradition of writing in Church Slavonic, but also straightforward as in the battle scenes where a complex periodic style would hinder an action-packed narrative.

Whatever its evidentiary value, Palitsyn's *Narration* is a tour de force with a number of great set pieces showing innovation (including much colloquial language), and also considerable continuity with the late medieval narrative tradition. The heart of the piece is his account of the siege of the Trinity-Sergiev Monastery where Palitsyn had become a monk under duress. In the battle scenes, Palitsyn has clearly borrowed a good deal from earlier military descriptions, specifically the fifteenth-century "Tale of Constantinople" ("Povest' o Tsar'-grade") by Nestor-Iskander, which is the source of a number of formulaic expressions and themes. Palitsyn's account of the opening of the siege similarly speaks about the significance of the monastery and its fortifications, while dwelling on the behavior of the defenders, a recurring topos that culminates in the claim that the monastery was saved in the end not by its walls or its leaders, but by its brethren and the people.

Palitsyn's visions happen on a Biblical scale. As danger approaches, he spies a fiery column above the monastery's chapel, a repetition of the same omen's appearance during an earlier skirmish between the Poles and Russians. He uses frequent metaphors, such as the battle as a deadly feast (also attested in medieval texts), as in the eighth chapter: "A blood-soaked table appeared to all and the cup of the dead was poured for all."[12] His narration of battle scenes owe their style to chronicle-writing and are no less dramatic than the fourteenth and fifteenth-century tales about attacks on Muscovy. He avails himself of extensive descriptions of battle landscapes, departs from stock motifs by enumerating actual participants, and also structures actions in sets of three: the famine lasts three years, there are three assaults on the fortress, the ambassadors of Tsar Mikhail meet with their Polish counterparts three times. The groupings might be intended to recall the folkloric patterning of events in triplets. However, Palitsyn offsets the sense of a stale recycling of conventions by providing an abundance of sharp detail, probably by drawing on local chronicles. He also achieves a more individual voice by stressing his eyewitness involvement in the events. In combination, the two styles make him an uncommonly memorable storyteller who straddles the world of medieval chronicle and the world of more immediate, seventeenth-century storytelling.

In addition to historical narratives, popular and clerical response to the Time of Troubles was expressed mainly in two forms: the ritual lamentation (*plach*) and the vision (*videnie*). Lamentations tangentially incorporated a narrative context for the sake of rhetorical effect, castigating the invader. Texts generally subscribe to the sentiments voiced by the anonymous author of the "Lamentation on the Captivity and Final Destruction of the Muscovite State" ("Plach o plenenii i o konechnom razorenii prevysokago i presvetleishago Moskovskogo gosudarstva," 1610–12), who blames the "Russian people who suffer from no end of infernal wounds" and the tsars who have "taken part in diabolical quarrels, magic and sorcery, and are smitten with pride and evil."[13] Causality formulated in these terms has a medieval precedent, but there is more immediacy in the way stories draw age-old conclusions from vividly felt experiences of loss. Such accounts, of which a further example is the short "On the Causes of the Demise of Kingdoms" ("O prichinakh gibeli tsarstv," around 1600), underscore the clash between native and invader as a fundamentally binary conflict between the devout and the heretical. In this period, however, the opponent is not the erstwhile pagan or Muslim antagonists of medieval texts but rather Catholics. Typical in this regard is the way in which the lamentation creates a sense of present danger through a combination of rumor and fact. Many accounts use documentary materials and written sources to corroborate personal statements of eyewitnesses. Storytelling and history-writing were not separate disciplines or prose forms. The "Lamentation on the Captivity and Final Destruction of the Muscovite State," while literary in tone, draws readily on documentary material. The author refers to safe-conduct passes sent out by Prince Dmitry Pozharsky (1578–1642, a royal servitor and, from the nineteenth century, legendary hero), to clergy and administration guaranteeing safe-conduct during the insurrection against the Polish invaders, dating the text around 1612. In a few places the author also inserts rhyming couplets for added expressivity. In order to reinforce the effect of historical authenticity, scribes often include a date in the title of the manuscript title.

Visions of salvation

Accounts such as those of Palitsyn and Timofeev give the impression of coming close to actual features of Russian life and thought, and reflecting something of religious consciousness. Alongside their documentary aspect, the extensive treatment of religious episodes involving visions, sightings of the victims of the calamity, or other apparently supernatural entities, localizes national experience. Such reports intensify the religious component that plays an important part in the questioning and reflection about Russia's misfortunes that we find in many of these works.

Throughout the seventeenth century, stories and legends juxtapose paradise and dystopian visions of Russia, often focalized through personal devotion and the experience of the current state of the monasteries. Outside chronicle compilations, the previous convoy or destination for many prose works, miracle tales, personal stories, and autobiographical fictions existed separately, allowing for more individual viewpoints and emphasis on the here and now, the local and personal. Writers tried to make sense of what happened on every level—political, military, economic, agricultural, and theological—and poured their anxieties about the state of monasteries, towns, cities, and the nation into different forms of storytelling, such as historical narratives, parables and allegories, and lamentations. Alongside straightforward historical writing that purports to offer a rational analysis of cause and effect and blames poor religious observance for divine retribution, we find visionary narratives that involve an encounter with an otherworldly entity and revelation, sometimes cast in a dream, sometimes in a waking state.

Vision literature (*videniia*), sometimes in the form of a solitary dream, lamentation, or a story, connects the inner world of the teller to the social horizon of an unsettled country.[14] Dreams and visions convey a sense of living in a country buffeted by invasion, uncertain dynastic succession, and increasing challenges to Orthodoxy, and express an anxiety to restore Christian identity and safeguard local community. Visions intensify and personalize the experience of national misfortune as something immediate rather than remote; they also bring consolation and encouragement to preserve everyday religious worship as a source of moral awareness. When it is not a dream, a vision can be a supernatural occurrence (such as Palitsyn's column of fire) or the manifestation of a saint. And saints who arrive in visions can speak, as happens in the early episodes of Avvakum's *Life* set in prison. These visitations bespeak his belief in his own spiritual elevation and confirm the impression that he is one of the elect. Avvakum's visions are, like the rest of his *Life*, of a different order of literary complexity from most storytelling in the period because the episodes have autobiographical depth (they come in the form of memories) and because they also serve as parables, connecting his present with Christian temporality. Works about saints provide a helpful way of tracking continuity and innovation. If writers continued to see Russia as holy, a boom in the creation of saints suggested this was a grassroots phenomenon.

Historians of the Church interested in the function of miracles draw a distinction between miracles of power and miracles of cure. In miracles of power, a visit to a shrine occasions a manifestation of the saint's power that demonstrates the saint's protection over the community. By contrast, a miracle of cure is performed for individuals whose piety and supplication at the shrine earn them an individual favor from the saint. Russian Church historians have argued that there is a shift from miracles of power to miracles of cure in seventeenth-century Russia, and that the growth of miracle cures mirrors a change in the social composition of worshippers. Russian aristocrats were not the beneficiaries of miracles at the shrines, and only a few lesser landholders were cured among a crowd of peasants, soldiers, townsmen, and lesser clergy.[15] There is no doubt that miracle stories provide evidence of social context: the cured were mainly merchants and artisans in the towns and peasants, provincial landholders, soldiers, clergy, and petty officials. Church councils of 1547 and 1551 had sanctioned the spread of miracle cults. The next century saw their increasing multiplication and the concomitant growth of the cult of relics and icons.[16]

We can turn for examples to works that typify how popular religion channeled its values through storytelling. The moving "Tale of Martha and Mary" ("Povest' o Marfe i Marii," c.1638–1651), a strange recasting of the New Testament parable, filters its Christian message of salvation, belief, and revelation, employing folkloric tropes and legends such as the symmetrical use of twins and associated subplots. Formally, the work is closer to a tale (povest') than a saint's life, reminding us that local taste and expectations, rather than a genre system, determined style. Two sisters from Murom get married: Martha weds a poor but noble man from Riazan', while Mary weds a modest but wealthy man from Murom. When the husbands die exactly on the same day and hour, the two sisters have complementary dreams: Martha in her vision receives gold from the hands of an angel who bids her to erect a cross, while Mary receives silver to construct a coffer or an ark. When they awaken, the dreams come true as three passing monks leave the women gold and silver. When the sisters return to Murom, their relations greet them with suspicion. Before they can ascertain whether the precious metals have been stolen, a group of elders in procession arrive from Constantinople bearing a golden cross and a silver casket, which they give to Martha and Mary, who ask about a fitting location for the cross. The elders answer by pointing in the direction of a church in another part of the province, where the women install the cross. From that moment, the cross becomes the destination of pilgrimages and a source of miracle cures.

As is often the case with works of the period, scholarship has largely focused on whether the sources of this tale were written or oral legends, an issue of importance in both the nineteenth century and the Soviet period, when the question of authenticity was linked to tendencies in both post-Romantic culture and Soviet ideology to invest the common folk with special status as guardians of national culture. This question aside, we see a work that distills a widespread belief that the saints are alive and intervene in daily life, performing small and sometimes big miracles. Whether this is high or popular culture is a moot point when we consider how intensely nineteenth-century writers, such as Ivan Turgenev, Nikolai Leskov, and Leo Tolstoy admired and imitated these sorts of plots and religious manifestations in order to portray qualities of spirituality they associated with Russianness.

As early as the *Paterik of the Kievo-Pechersk Monastery*, the boundary lines between legend, biography, and hagiography were porous, allowing for a convergence of mundane storytelling practices and religious discourse. No work better illustrates this openness between the popular and ecclesiastical, oral and written, than the "Tale of Iuliana Osorina" ("Povest' ob Ul'ianii Osor'inoi," alternatively "Zhitie Iulianii Lazarevskoi," 1640s) from Murom, an area known to be rich in spiritual legends and saints' lives. The subject is a noblewoman who was worshipped as a local saint by the time of her death. Composed between 1625 and 1640 by her son, the bookish Kalistrat (known as Druzhina Osorin), and thereafter circulated in many handwritten copies, the work is a biography-cum-hagiography of a figure who, the author claims, "like a star shone most greatly through her miracles and her active virtue."[17] The tale operates on two planes: historical time works through its biographical axis and Christian time through its accounts of miracles and parable-like episodes. Born late in the reign of Ivan the Terrible, Iuliana manifested the precocious ascetic inclinations associated with a saint, although her pedigreed family was not notable for its religious devotion. Unlike other saints, Iuliana continued to lead a worldly life, never entering a convent or renouncing her family or her daily practice. According to the "Tale," her piety lay in her tireless display of love for her fellow man, her family and impoverished strangers alike. It is Christian love for her neighbor that is the hall-mark of her virtue, rather than church-building or martyrdom; yet after her death she became the subject of a cult and her burial place and relics inspired miracle accounts (a pamphlet version of the tale was produced for the use of visitors). As with Avvakum's *Life*, the "Tale of Iuliana" foregrounds the saint's spiritual struggles and search for salvation, while painting a richly detailed portrait of the world populated by believable local figures. Like many hagiog-raphers, the author is a valuable eyewitness to the piety of the saintly figure and uses his prox-imity to recount episodes from daily life. But in this case, he displays an unusual ability to abstract himself from his role as son: when in due course he describes the discovery of her relics and their powers his surprise feels genuine.

The "Life of Eleazar as Written by Himself" ("Zhitie Eleazara napisannoe im samim") describes the founding of the Troitsyn Monastery on the island of Anzer by a monk from Solovki (represented by a contemporary painter in Plate 8) who, his "soul purified from sin," earned the support of Tsar Aleksei Mikhailovich (1629–76). Composed sometime between 1636 and 1656, the work generated a number of other tales about this northern figure, and also attracted the interest of nineteenth-century historians because its autobiographical and more emotional character seemed close to lived reality.

A surviving seventeenth-century copy contains a postscript (*svitok*) supposedly autographed by Eleazar himself attesting to the truthfulness of the visions. The writer interwove real-life episodes about the establishment of his hermitage (*skit*) with hagiographic topoi used as standard corroboration in presenting stories of sanctity (the title *zhitie*, possibly affixed by a later copyist, gives an indication that the work is meant to be read as substantiation of the life of a saint). Most late nineteenth-century writing about this work concerned itself with estab-lishing sources, demonstrating that the author drew on tales written by monastic founders, bridging the experiential and the textual. "The Life of Eleazar" is also a further example of the degree to which writing about figures such as saints and clergy relied on conceptual models of holiness originating in Kievan hagiography. They aim to create a greater "reality effect" through increased reference to locale, some attention to personal motivation, and memorable accounts of miracles.[18] Numerous other texts demonstrate the survival of hagiography in the written culture of the seventeenth century. The "Tale of the Life of Varlaam Keretskii" ("Povest' o zhitii Varlaama") recounts how a husband who murdered his wife then sought expiation by sailing across the White Sea in a boat bearing her corpse. Originally composed in the sixteenth century, the tale in seventeenth-century versions opened up the conclusion by adding legends concerning the main character's travels, maritime adventures, and the daily routines of the fishing communities he visited. As in the "Tale of Iuliana," here the integration of hagiographic and secular modes of biography with a more mimetic attentiveness to description achieves a double and complementary purpose. Daily life invested with a sense of the sacred reflects an assumption of popular religion that the saints dwell among ordinary worshippers. Conversely, the application of a more expansive narrative style dramatizes and enlivens human stories.

The availability of new narrative modes created combinations of subject and technique that upend expectations of traditional themes. In the absence of a strongly regimented genre system the handling of content varied. Consider, for instance, the "Tale of the Tver Youth Monastery" ("Povest' o Tverskom otroche monastyre"), a seventeenth-century work copied in a local chronicle about an event dated to the thirteenth century (that attracted the interest of Karamzin who, writing in the early 1810s, referred to it in his *History of the Russian State*). Monastic foundation tales were normally either self-contained stories, or incorporated into a saint's life or a local chronicle as a episode. In the case of the "Tale of the Tver Youth Monastery," however, the foundational tale becomes the pretext for a romance. The motivation may have been a wish to please the contemporary ruler, Prince Mikhail Iaroslavich, who instituted a service in memory of his late wife whose relics attracted worshippers. It has also been reasonably supposed that the purpose of the tale was retrospectively to create a myth to legitimate the unusual name of the monastery itself. Grigory, a servant of Prince Iaroslav of Tver', is in the service of the prince when he meets a lovely young maiden and falls in love. He receives his master's permission to marry. The Prince fortuitously comes upon the wedding ceremony and happens to enter the church just before the groom. When the maiden sees him, she proclaims "He is my bridegroom," and the Prince falls in love, marries her despite popular discontent, and deprives Grigory of his love. Like Fevronia in "The Tale of Petr and Fevronia," the virtuous "wise" maiden has crossed class boundaries. Forlorn and desperate, Grigory flees to a solitary spot, and pines in the wilderness where he has numerous spiritual visions. The Prince wishes to care for him, but Grigory recounts his experience and persuades the Prince to make amends by building and dedicating a church to the Dormition of the Virgin. The Prince, his wife, and court consecrate in his honor the Youth Monastery (from the word *otrok*), where the youth, formerly known as Grigory, serves as a monk, dies, and is buried. R. P. Dmitrieva, an eminent medievalist, concludes that the copious use of local and historical references reflects the aim of the writer to evoke the spiritual life of the thirteenth century.[19]

Alternatively, we might suppose that the writer wished to represent Christian life as a matter of daily practice and piety, and that the purpose of realistic detail was less archaeological than trans-historical, intending to demonstrate the continued vitality of the Church and the relevance of faith in daily life. In this instance that very relevance seems to be a function of the story's fusion of folk legends about marriage with its universal feelings of love, jealousy, and renunciation, and local history.

"The Spiritually Useful Tale of Nikodimus Tipikaris of Solovetsky Monastery about a Certain Novice" ("Povest' dushepolezna startsa Nikodima Solovetskogo monastyria o nekoem inoke") survives in many manuscript copies from the 1630s.[20] It unites in a single plot a number of motifs and devices that are typical of the period, often appearing separately. Possibly autobiographical in character, the tale relates how a monk, plagued by alcoholism, finds spiritual salvation from his demons after an epiphany in which the Archangel Michael appears to him and extracts a promise to remain pious and sober. When the monk leaves the monastery to visit his mother, he breaks his vow, takes to drink, and suffers hallucinations, but once again finds a cure in religion, this time in a vision of the famous icon of the Virgin of Vladimir. From a literary perspective, the tale contains noteworthy depictions of the hero's encounter with his demons and inner meditations on suffering. While it has a moral lesson to drive home, the tale contains a concentration of local landscape detail that provides a reference point for the attention to such detail Avvakum's *Life* displays in the next generation.

Another example of this style can be found in the contemporary "Tale of Tobacco," ("Povest' o tabake"), a cycle of short tales about the origins of a magical herb that could induce hallucination, and was a powerful weapon in the hands of the devil. (In the 1920s, these and other tales including the "Tale of Petr and Fevronia" were the basis of stylizations by A. M. Remizov, including his legend "What is tobacco" ["Chto est' tabak"].[21]) New consumption practices, such as smoking, elicited associations with the ancient superstitions of doubled faith (*dvoeverie*). Based on popular legends about magical herbs that grow around burial places and threaten the living, in the view of scholars of legends such as V. N. Perets, the cycle uses motifs of graveyard magic, impurity, shame, and condemnation in the afterlife for sacrilege.[22] The later written versions have grafted onto these legends admonitions and cautions against luxury and excess, thereby realigning superstitious practices to ward off evil with more explicitly Christian types of restrained conduct encouraged by the Church.

CASE STUDY   *Dukhovnye stikhi* (poetic songs or spiritual rhymes)

Dukhovnye stikhi, or spiritual poems (hereafter *DS*), are poetic songs or poems with Christian, mostly Orthodox, content; they originated with the advent of Christianity in the lands of Rus', and they have enjoyed enduring popularity. The well-attested doubled faith of the Orthodox peoples who did not easily shed their pagan gods (*dvoeverie*) is also felt in *DS*, where motifs of pagan belief, including worship of natural forces and of Mother Earth, coexist with praise for Jesus Christ and with wonder at a universe ordered by a single, all-powerful divine presence. Although eventually written down both in monasteries and families, and by ethnographers-collectors, *DS* were for centuries transmitted orally, sung by the poor pilgrims (called in the literature *kaleki perekhozhie*, sometimes *kaliki perekhozhie*, that is, "itinerant cripples"). *DS* generated somewhat fewer controversies among ethnographers about whether they were a purely oral form of composition or were contaminated by influences from written sources, since it was obvious that Biblical sources were always a major inspiration.

Unlike other folk genres, like *byliny* or *khorovody*, which did not originate in Biblical or ecclesiastical material, *DS* are distinctive in their proximity to Orthodox thinking and themes, but they are by their very nature not a part of the official Church culture. *DS* depart often from the sanctioned ecclesiastical writings even while staying within familiar scenarios like the expulsion from the Garden of Eden, the Last Judgment, and the trials and tribulations of a saintly life. One important site of performance of *DS* also demonstrates the ambiguous proximity to official Church life: although the creators and performers of *DS*, the *kaleki perekhozhie*, were known to be poor pilgrims and itinerant wanderers, they also performed *DS* at church gates, singing out their verses as the faithful arrived for prayer and celebration. This threshold position is expressive of the social position of the *kaleki perekhozhie*—at the margins of official culture, indeed at its very doorstep since the term *perekhozhii* can mean both "wandering" and "overstepping." The lasting impact of *DS* derives in part from their seeming to be at once outside formal Church control and deeply dependent on the images and traditions of Orthodoxy. Equally important, especially after the seventeenth century, has been the association of *DS* with movements formed in resistance to Orthodoxy, like sectarianism and the Old Belief. The sustained and broader power of *DS* in Russian culture is enhanced by this association with subversion and by the claim to deeper spiritual authority than that of the established Church.

An inherent uncertainty around the term *DS* is also telling. For this very substantial genre, with its long tradition, there is no equivalent term or precise genre in English, which is why we refer to them here as *DS* rather than as the vaguer "spiritual poems"; there are of course in English religious folk songs (and in the US context, spirituals), both of which also enjoy great popularity among the faithful and, particularly for spirituals, seem to bespeak more resonant spiritual and social truths. But these are comparable, not similar traditions. In Russian, the names for *DS* are in fact multiple. They were called simply folksongs (*narodnye pesni*) by one of the first scholars to collect them, the Slavophile

P. V. Kireevsky. Another name for *DS* is *kanty* (from Latin *cantus*—and the Latin derivation shows a Polish influence, felt especially starting in the seventeenth century). Also often heard even earlier is another Russian name, *psal 'my* (from *psal 'ma*, a feminine noun, not to be confused with the masculine noun for psalm, *psalom*). Although less used in the twentieth century, the term *psal 'my* was often recorded by folklorists and is thought to be a folk term. The multiplication of names for *DS* is typical of folk genres—compare the common name for folk epics in Russian, *bylina*, a term almost certainly initiated by scholars and collectors in the nineteenth century, as opposed to the term used by folk performers, *starina*. The accumulation of names for these forms of folk literature should make us aware of the role played by ethnographers and recorders of folk songs in fixing *DS* in writing, and in categorizing them as distinct kinds of artistic creation.

As with other folk genres, the origins of *DS* are disputed. There are attestations as early as the twelfth century, although scholars believe that *DS* began to be sung by wanderers as soon as Christianity was officially introduced to Russia (in the tenth century), if not earlier, in the very earliest Christian communities that sprang up on the lands of Rus´. The actual *DS* began to be attested only later—sparse records have come down from as early as the sixteenth century. Serious transcription and collecting commenced in the eighteenth century and intensified in the nineteenth, as part of the larger trend to record Slavic folk poetry and folktales. Many of these efforts at collecting are associated with broader social and cultural movements like Slavophilism and *Pochvennichestvo*. Petr Kireevsky was one of the first to collect *DS*, but he published only a small fraction of his work. Petr Bessonov brought out a substantial edition of Kireevsky's work, as well as his own six-volume edition of *DS* in the 1860s. Bessonov's work remains foundational. Collecting or recording *DS* was not officially permitted during Soviet rule, although some ethnographers included *DS* in their accounts of folk literature (the scholar Mark Azadovsky, among others); collecting resumed in the post-Soviet period, as has some historiographical investigation of the patterns and implications of collecting across the centuries.

Scholars of Russian poetry have taken some interest in the versification and formal properties of *DS*, although much work remains to be done. *DS* have come down to us in a number of verse forms, including syllabics (another sign of the impact of Polish versification), syllabotonic forms, and in less strictly patterned verse-lines as well. Some use rhyme or anaphora as well as verbal repetition and syntactic parallelism. Length also varies tremendously, and many *DS* exist in both lengthy (several hundred lines) and quite brief versions.

Most *DS* exist in multiple versions, and authorship is largely unknown. The wandering poor who sang *DS* often traveled in groups, and scholars have speculated that the performers may not have been the authors, and perhaps the groups of *kaleki perekhozhie* included both authors and performers who worked together. As with all performed folklore, the singers of *DS* made their individual mark on the verse with every performance, and it is fair to think of wandering singers as central to the creative process, even if they perceived themselves as largely repeating what they had heard from others. (The same is true of the ethnographers and folklore specialists who collected these materials and first wrote them down—for all their efforts to record precisely what they heard, they inevitably misheard or regularized some of what was performed, and perhaps sometimes shaped the performances with their own requests.) But *DS* were also written down by those who created them, particularly in the nineteenth century and later; Old Believers were among those who kept written versions, and they were the first publishers of *DS* (in 1805 and 1825).[23] Monasteries have been found to hold some collections, a phenomenon that was renewed in the early Soviet period, when they became refuges for religious men and women fleeing the anti-religion campaigns. At that time, monasteries became both repositories of written records of *DS* and sites in which the poems could be recited, transmitted, and in some cases created. Elena Buchilina records a striking instance of a poem created in the 1930s by a future Elder, Arseniia, about her sufferings in the labor camps, and recited in the 1960s to another future Elder, Makaria, in Pochaevo Monastery.

The groups of wanderers from the earliest days of Rus´ traveled in pilgrimage, and the oldest recorded observations of *kaleki perekhozhie* are references to people who walk from one holy shrine or church to another; some *DS* also record these practices or otherwise refer to the act of creating the songs themselves. Although all accounts of *DS* feature these wanderers, records also show that *DS* were sung and often cherished in sedentary communities, and played a role in family and holiday rituals. Particularly well-studied in this regard are Old Believer communities as well as a broad cross-section of the Orthodox faithful in the Nizhny Novgorod region and in the Russian Far North. The singing, preservation, and transmission of *DS* flourished in sectarian and especially Old Believer communities, usually in sung versions or, when the melodies were no longer remembered and only written versions remained, as spoken poems.

As transcribed in and after the nineteenth century, *DS* are especially associated with death and with the spiritual journey of mortality. *DS* respond to and describe burial rituals, and thus are recited at funerals; they also give accounts of the soul's departure from the body, or of the fate of a sinning soul. The narrowing of topics over time is partly an effect of lost texts or forgotten melodies within a given community. In the earliest period, the topics of *DS* were broad; extant collections draw on the Old and New Testaments, the Apocrypha, tales of saints, miracle workers, and martyrs, of the righteous and the sinner, and of the end of time and the Last Judgment. Eschatological motifs are particularly common, and are thought to have served an allegorical purpose at historical junctures like the Church Schism, or later collectivization and famine.

A much-loved example of *DS* is the "Depe Book" ("Golubinaia kniga"; "golubinyi" is an archaic or folk form of the word for "deep," hence our translation using a Middle English variant), a lengthy account of the nature of the universe structured as a set of questions and answers. The cosmology in the poem fuses Christian and pagan worldviews, and the hierarchy of knowledge puts the biblical King David alongside the ruler of the lands of Rus´, Prince Vladimir. Both seek to read the book of the universe and of Mother Earth. The book is praised as unknowable and thus a perfect figure for the mysteriously unknowable universe created by God and the gods. The poem ends with the question-and-answer structure transformed into a dispute between truth and falsehood (*pravda* and *krivda*), with the spread of falsehood among mortal humans offered as a final metaphor for the ignorance in which people live and for the fallen state of human life more generally. The state of a sinning soul is the subject of multiple other *DS*, as is the fall from grace in the Garden of Eden, "Adam's Lament" ("Plach Adama"). Other popular *DS* tell of saints' lives, the most cherished of which tells the life of Aleksei (often "Aleksei, Bozhii chelovek"). His chosen path of suffering and self-abasement is typical of many saints' lives, and has an especially stark element of renunciation of domestic comforts and of family, indeed even of their recognition.

The study of *DS* has become part of a broader attempt to understand folk traditions; *DS* are treated by these scholars as documents of popular religion. Some ethnographers and philologists have emphasized the folk tradition and sought to understand what *DS* can tell us about the worldview of the common folk (A. N. Afanas´ev and F. I. Buslaev); conversely, others have studied cultural history and emphasized the origins of the themes and motifs of *DS* in the Greek, Latin, and Hebrew source texts (A. N. Veselovsky, G. P. Fedotov). Fedotov's work from the 1930s has enjoyed particular admiration thanks to a 1991 reissue of his 1935 study. His authority comes from a combined knowledge of cultural history and theology, and struck post-Soviet scholars as a valuable antidote to the insistently atheistic position of Soviet-era ethnographers.

The growth of popular religion provoked a backlash from the clerical hierarchy. In the 1640s, the Printing Office became responsible for vetting stories about miracles that were submitted for publication. In the 1650s, the liturgical reforms of Patriarch Nikon buttressed the policy of the Church to regulate miracle cults as popular behavior spread. The clerical hierarchy aimed to suppress the proliferation of popular tales based on alleged miracles that in their view threatened to cheapen sanctioned worship. Nikon shared the traditionalists' view that saints must possess moral and spiritual values, and wished to curb the unregulated reporting of miracles. Documentary evidence shows the refusal of the Printing Office to publish manuscripts because the secretaries rejected the accounts and argued that the eyewitnesses confused coincidences with miracles (*sluchai, ne v chudo*). It is not surprising therefore that there are fewer miracle narratives in official Church writings, even while their popular appeal continued to grow and miracle stories informed such texts as Avvakum's *Life*. Nonetheless, the effort the Church made to control the circulation of miracle tales at the parish level had no discernible effect on the dissemination of local tales in manuscript copies.

Over the course of the seventeenth century, visions came to play a bigger part in the accounts of saints. Many of these, like the versions of the life of Iuliana Osorina of Murom and Avvakum's *Life*, to name two of the most celebrated, are also anchored in the social reality of the time. Religious legends and vision tales tend to feature a modest social figure who wished to capture the plight of his immediate group, admitted a fault of some kind, personal or collective, expressed penance through prayer or religious deeds, normally fasting and ritual prayer and weeping, and was granted salvation of some kind. Several dozen vision tales dating to the Time of Troubles exist in manuscript from a wide variety of locations, including Nizhny Novgorod, Novgorod, Moscow, Vladimir, and Perm´. Despite this dispersal, there is some geographic concentration of works in monasteries such as the Solovetsk Monastery and the Trinity-Sergiev Monastery, as well as smaller hermitages (*skity*). Vision tales tend to assume that the cause behind the present catastrophes is corruption of Russia's religious borders. The "Tale of a Vision in Novgorod" ("Povest´ o videnii v Novgorode," 1611), more local in its purview and concerns (such as Swedish rather than Polish invaders), reserves its deepest despair for the conviction that the Virgin herself, relied on as a stalwart defender, has abandoned the city to its vices. Visions often encompass miracles, and the seventeenth century is replete with tales of miracles often emanating from distant places.[24]

For example, Hermogen, the author of "The Tale of the Manifestation and Miracles of the Kazan Icon of the Virgin" ("Povest´ o iavlenii i chudesakh Kazanskoi ikony Bogoroditsy," 1594), a priest who became patriarch, encouraged confidence that through the wonder-working power of her icon, ensconced in Kazan´ since 1579, the Virgin will assume her traditional role as intercessor.[25] "Another Vision" ("Inoe videnie," 1607), subsequently incorporated in later chronicle accounts, tells of six guards who, in the early morning, heard sounds of laughter and speech and perceived a flickering light coming from within the Cathedral of the Archangel in Moscow. The "Visions of Euthymius Chakol´sky" ("Videniia Evfimiia Chakol´skogo," 1611–14), a set of records of religious visions that survive in a single copy, are set against the backdrop of the Time of Troubles (though events are hardly alluded to). As recounted in church to a priest who notes down in the third person a first-person account, they are among the most vivid examples of religious fervor and private consolation embraced as a solution to the historical catastrophes "caused" by the decline of religiosity.

Outside monasteries and urban centers, visions served a purpose in pointing the way toward shelter from harm for those under pressure from invaders who were viewed as heretics such as Lithuanians and Poles. The "Miracles of Zosima and Savvaty in the Solovetsk Monastery" ("Chudesa Zosimy i Savvatiia Solovetskikh," c.1625) and other works such as the miracle narratives of followers of St. Stephan of Perm', Gerasim, and Pitirim, dated between the first half of the seventeenth century and 1716, share Avvakum's world, in which the saints are alive and believers perceive sentient proofs of a sacred sphere.

Literature of the Schism (*Raskol*)

The religious turmoil of the second half of the century stimulated expressions of catastrophe that bound the individual to the national. Fear of doctrinal contamination and heresy rather than actual invasion, as seventy years earlier, gripped the minds of Schismatics known as Old Believers. For the tsar and the clergy, life on earth was entirely bound up with the fight against heresy and the maintenance of religious purity. In the 1640s and 1650s, at the beginning of the reign of Aleksei Mikhailovich (r. 1645–76), there arose a movement of purists, the Zealots of Piety, which included their leader, the clergyman Stefan Vonifat'ev (d. 1656), the future Patriarch Nikon (1605–81), the priest Ivan Neronov (1591–1670), the boyar Fedor Rtishchev, and others who wanted to root out corruption in the parish priesthoods, to abolish popular religious festivals, to restore the full recitation of the liturgy, often abbreviated, and the strict observance of feast days of the Orthodox calendar.[26] The Zealots of Piety sought to bring religion closer to the laity and to oppose the influence of laymen who were beginning to argue that morality and virtue could be found outside the Church.[27] Their agitation against popular religion and festivals precipitated a series of decrees by the tsar outlawing a variety of rituals, from the masquerade and erotic games traditional in the Christmas–Epiphany season to boxing at Shrovetide. At the same time the Printing Office increased the number of Russian saints' festivals to a new high of ninety-three in an effort to suppress the proliferation of local saints and make canonization a matter for the government.

As the leader of the Church, Patriarch Nikon felt that Orthodox ritual had to conform to the practices of the Greeks. For members of the Zealots of Piety, however, adherence to the Greek model proved controversial. In their eyes, the fall of Constantinople represented punishment wreaked on the Byzantines for the attempt at rapprochement with the Papacy sealed by the Council of Florence (1438–45). From the fifteenth century Russian Orthodox relations to Eastern and Latin Christendom were colored partly by the idea of the Third Rome—namely, that leadership of the Orthodox world had passed from Rome to Constantinople and, finally, to Moscow. According to this belief, Russia stood as the last bastion of the true Christian faith. The Schism began in reaction to a rescript from Nikon to the priest Neronov, sent in 1653, setting out seemingly small changes on how the sign of the cross was to be made, the number of bows required, and the elimination of contested formulas from the definition of the Holy Spirit. According to Avvakum, "We thought when we met that we could see winter coming; our hearts froze and our legs shook."[28] The Schism mounted a serious challenge to tsar and patriarch, and Nikon's inability to maintain a united front with Tsar Aleksei Mikhailovich ended in his deposition as patriarch in 1666. It would only be a matter of thirty or so years before Peter the Great abolished the Patriarchate altogether and placed the Church under the tsar's direct control.

The religious pessimism that became widespread in the reign of Tsar Aleksei Mikhailovich was sensitive to modest but distinctive elements of the Humanist culture that reached Moscow via centers of learning in the Ukraine. Interest in Latin and Greek learning, scholasticism, syllabic versification, and in the technology of printing as opposed to scribal craft, were equated with modernization, and possibly heresy. Among the most resistant to any changes in dogma and ritual were the Old Believers. Their autobiographical literature began to appear clandestinely in manuscript in 1653 with responses to Patriarch Nikon in defense of the old rites and in support of the priest Ivan Neronov, the first of the Old Believers to be arrested. Works written by priests and aristocrats devoted to the Old Belief, such as the "Tale of the Boyarina Morozova" ("Povest' o Boiaryne Morozovoi", 1675–77), a biography written by an eyewitness to the arrest and exile of the noblewoman Feodosiia Prokof'evna Morozova, were confessional and documentary in form rather than belletristic or hagiographic (despite the use of the label *zhitie* in some copies). The style of narrative, sometimes formal, but often colloquial and vivid, attested in tales of arrest and persecution their religious devotion and determination to resist the modernizing decrees of a theocratic tsardom they opposed. The Church councils of 1656, supported by Tsar Aleksei Mikhailovich, had approved Nikon's reforms, and pronounced an anathema on the supporters of the old rituals.

Old Believer writing began to appear in the mid-seventeenth century, peaked with the *Life* of the Archpriest Avvakum (published only in the 1861 for the first time), and trickled to a halt by the end of the eighteenth century. This religious literature, written in opposition to the Church and the state, circulated in manuscript in secret. The Old Believers were nervous of the printed word.[29] This distrust, not uncommon in Reformation cultures, was bred by the association of the printing press with government officialdom, and an anxiety about typography as a less reliable technology than scribal expertise. Manuscript production of their works was intensive and extensive. The facsimile edition of works written from the remote place of exile in Pustozersk shows how skilled Old Believer scribes were in fighting fire with fire: handwritten books use regular margins, precise lineation and letterforms to emulate the look of the printed page.[30] Among the monuments to the Old Believers, Avvakum's *Life* was immediately recognized as a work of great originality and historical significance, at once bringing to new heights the poetics of medieval Russian literature and giving new amplitude to the writer. It is Avvakum who remains one of the most eloquent writers on the clash between the old and new faith generally referred to as the Schism (*Raskol*), but his novelty lies in his fiery commitment rather than in his theological contribution to a controversy that began almost twenty years earlier in Moscow before culminating in the provincial's priest's martyrdom in 1682. Most other autobiographical texts before the eighteenth century, including both the long and short versions of the "Tale of the Boyarina Morozova", are documentary in style with little first-person narration and some dialogue.[31] Avvakum's work, by contrast, reads like a cross-section of all genres practiced in the period, blurring the boundary between fiction and history, autobiography and Biblical narration, realist observation and miracle accounts. Most fictional works of the period fold historical information of any kind into their episodic plots, obliquely conveying social upheavals of a period in which monastic authority and wealth were undermined, the peasantry formally enslaved and confirmed in their misery, and traditional elites at court made nervous by a sense that Russia's pre-modern intellectual life could not keep Western advances in natural philosophy at bay forever. No figure offers a more powerful account of Russia at a crossroads. The much-loved *Life of the Archpriest Avvakum as Written by Himself* demonstrates remarkable skill in assimilating hagiographic conventions, popular elements, and the rhetorical tropes of diatribe. No writer since Ivan the Terrible had spoken with an individual voice rooted in experience and fully alive to the shifts in the world in which he lived. The fusion of rhetoric, religious conviction, and personality results in something that feels entirely new for Russian literature because the sum of the familiar parts is highly original.

CASE STUDY **The *Life* of Archpriest Avvakum**

Originally a village priest, Avvakum was opposed to ritual and scriptural emendations that he and the other sectarians regarded as corrupting the purity of the Orthodox faith, and therefore, a breach of Russia's boundary as the last bastion of Orthodoxy after the fall of Constantinople in 1453. Avvakum's fight, as he described it, was intensely personal, and although he was the author of a number of doctrinal works, his account of his battle with the authorities and two periods of exile in the deep of Siberia remains a masterpiece of Russian literature because it combines a gift for storytelling and psychological portraiture. Avvakum's vocal support of other Old Believers brought him notoriety, arrests, and his first period of exile in Siberia in Tobolsk where his feisty character incurred the anger of the authorities, resulting in a further period of even more distant exile with his wife and children. From 1656 to 1662, as part of his exile, Avvakum accompanied the geographic expeditions led by General Pashkov, and casts his story as one of unflinching devotion to his faith despite physical and mental persecution.

For Avvakum, personal relations with the tsar were the key to his religious campaign, for the tsar was regarded as a possibly divine figure. His apostasy seemed to guarantee Old Believers the coming end of the world, whereas his return to the ancestral faith might result in redemption. From the beginning of his final exile, Avvakum sent the tsar a number of petitions or epistles. In them he assumes the charismatic authority of an alternative ruler and uses his skills as a writer to instruct the real ruler on the correct principles of kingship in a theocratic state. In the "Fifth Petition" ("Piataia chelobitnaia"), written in 1669, a year after his exile to Pustozersk, Avvakum expresses his pity for the tsar about whom he has had horrific visions, and whom he judges. Avvakum identifies with a kind of kenotic sainthood in the first part of his petition, thereby justifying his teaching to and judgment of the tsar on behalf of the community, which Avvakum sees as a historical expression of the mystical body of Christ. His "Fifth Petition" presents his solution to the breakdown of the theocratic state. Having found the tsar wanting, Avvakum looks to himself and to his spiritual family to fill the vacuum created by the ruler's apostasy from the traditional ideal of community. In his vision, he sees that the tsar's angelic body has been corrupted, and now resembles the beast from Revelation.

Avvakum was anything but naive and must have been well aware that the appeals would neither bring the tsar back into the fold nor alleviate Avvakum's situation. Indeed, the tsar never replied, and Avvakum was executed in 1682 after being exiled to Pustozersk, north of the Arctic Circle, along with a number of supporters who had been barbarically suppressed (Neronov, one such victim, had his tongue cut out only to see his faith miraculously rewarded when it grew back, as he recounted in his autobiography). Avvakum's *Life* recounts the story of how he and his fellow Schismatics had reached the point of no return. Composed in his underground cell in Pustozersk in 1675, Avvakum's *Life* went through numerous revisions before being copied by hand in two principal versions (to which he added his signature, see Figure II.02). Avvakum modeled his literary life after the genre of the saint's life. Oblivious to the arrogance of attesting to his own sanctity, Avvakum recounts miracles of healing which he performed; he recalls the vision of a figure that sets

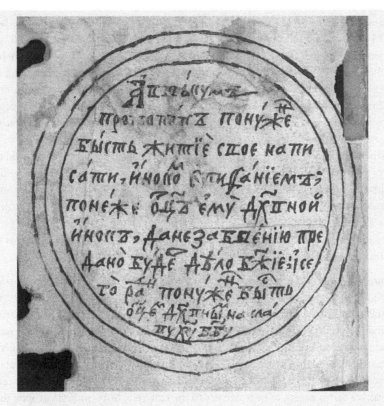

FIGURE 11.02. Avvakum, *Life of the Archpriest Avvakum* (c. 1682), colophon.

him on his course in life; he draws on the Biblical parallels that are adduced to demonstrate the conformity of the subject with the saintly type. The little dog that comes to him in prison and licks his wounds reminds Avvakum of the dogs that lick the wounds of the New Testament Lazarus. With its combination of didactic yet compelling stories, its proverbial style and Biblical quotations, and the complex time-management of its narrative, culminating in a final set of miracles that make Avvakum virtually a saint, this is a work which has no equal in Russian narrative art before the nineteenth century. It suspends the readers in eternal Christian time while also grounding them in both a cultural reality and a Christian ideal of time as an ahistorical constant. His mode of literary self-examination looks unusual in the context of other seventeenth-century Russian writing because of its introspection. Consider, for example, an account of lust that shades into religious parable in a specifically Russian landscape:

> When I was still a priest, a young woman came to me to confess; she was burdened with many sins, guilty of fornication and every sort of self-abuse; and with tears in her eyes she began to acquaint me with all her sins in detail, facing the Gospel there in the church. But I, thrice-accused healer, I was afflicted myself, burning inwardly with a lecherous fire, and I felt it bitterly in that hour. I lit three candles and stuck them to the lectern, and raised my right hand into the flame and held it there until the evil conflagration within me had been extinguished. After dismissing the young woman, putting away my vestments, and praying awhile, I went to my home deeply agrieved. The hour was as midnight, and having come into my house I wept before the icon of the Lord until my eyes swelled; and I prayed earnestly that God might

separate me from my spiritual children, for the burden was heavy and hard to bear. And I fell face down to the ground; I wept bitterly, and lying there sank into forgetfulness. Nothing could I know, as I was weeping, but the eyes of my heart beheld the Volga. I saw two golden boats sailing gracefully, and their oars were of gold, and the masts of gold, and everything was of gold; each had one helmsman for the crew. And I asked, "Whose boats are these?" And they answered, "Luka's and Lavrenty's." They had been my spiritual children; they set my house and me on the path to salvation, and their passing was pleasing to God. And lo, there was a third boat, not adorned with gold but motley colored—red, and white, and blue, and black, and grey; the mind of man could not take in all its beauty and excellence. A radiant youth sitting aft was steering. He raced toward me out of the Volga as if he wanted to swallow me whole. And I shouted, "Whose boat is this?" And sitting in it he answered, "Your boat. Sail in it with your wife and children if you're going to pester the Lord." And trembling seized me, and sitting down I pondered: "What is this vision? And what sort of voyage will it be?"[32]

Avvakum models the episodes in his "life," or *zhitie*, on Gospel parables, but in addition, the breadth of the canvas and the dynamism of his narrative style differentiate it from a more static Russian hagiographic tradition. Plotted according to a dynamic of detention and miraculous release, his entire text unfolds on a scale worthy of Leo Tolstoy's parables, encompassing a wide geographic range and a large cast of figures including holy fools, widows, the ill, sympathizers, martyrs, and his wife, who delivers a few memorable lines of brave encouragement. Avvakum regarded contemporary events as a great religious upheaval; his text is meant to bear witness to the concrete, historical catastrophe that was imminent.

Avvakum's *Life* creates a portrait of an exemplary individual who has one foot in his historical time and another in the world of the Gospels that subtly inform how Avvakum shapes the stories of his acts of bravery and miracles. Writing as a means of creating a complex sense of identity, as defined by the class (clergy), one's faith (Old Belief), and one's politics (dissent), was unprecedented. As singular as the pitch of his discourse is, his literary language is equally remarkable. A writer of Avvakum's period could draw on three related but very distinct literary idioms: the pure Church Slavonic of sacred texts; the Slavonic that had been cultivated by the bookmen of the Ukraine, admixed with Russian and with Polonisms, Latinisms, Ukrainianisms, and a more fluid syntax; and the spoken, colloquial Russian familiar from folklore or oral narratives. Avvakum's originality lies in the amalgamation of these different idioms. The historical subject matter and dense style—both colloquial and learned—take writing in a new direction beyond a polemical function already familiar from the ecclesiastical disputes of the sixteenth century into personality and individual lives.

When the censorship ban on this work was lifted in 1856, its publication could not have been better timed, and it acquired a eager readership among radical critics and writers whose Slavophile interests corresponded to Avvakum's sense that Russia had a particular mission and spiritual shape. Avvakum's staunch belief in his right to practice his faith made him a kindred revolutionary figure and, somewhat improbably, a prototype for a national ideal of the *intelligent*, selflessly devoted to a cause even at the risk of great hardship. For historians and younger writers intent on creating in prose a distinctive Russian landscape and sense of character, his story of persecution and torture was the source of psychological fascination as well as much period detail. Although inclusion in the canon and critical acclaim might not have pleased him, Avvakum's greatness as a writer is evident not only to adherents of the Old Belief. He claimed to despise eloquence, associating it with Latin learning and therefore Catholicism, but he is a master of all the arts of rhetoric, including persuasion, narration, diatribe and parable.[33] The strength of his style, the amazing variety of his powers of description, the range of emotions, poised between thundering denunciation and a beguiling domesticity, and his erudite Biblical learning, create a highly recognizable individual persona such as we have not seen in Russia until this point. It is impossible to understand him outside the religious controversy of his time, but his appeal as a personality and writer has a justifiable fascination of its own. In an age when the sermon had fallen into disfavor, when piety dictated complete self-effacement, the insistence of Avvakum's attention to the self and to the relation of that self to one's faith was an astonishing innovation. But Avvakum also looks very modern as a study in contradiction. He is a remarkably innovative writer dedicated to a highly conservative cause: the belief that he can preserve and transmit an essential spiritual truth about his nation.

2

Cultural interface:
Printing, Humanist learning, and
Orthodox resistance in the second half
of the seventeenth century

THE concept of professional writer did not emerge in the seventeenth century. However, a new vision of court culture, the expanding administration, and the implementation of ecclesiastical reforms created new opportunities for writing, leading to significant innovations especially in the theater and in poetry.

The emergence of a literary field is one indicator of a shift between the medieval and early modern. The "literary field" is a term coined and popularized by literary sociologists to describe institutional conditions—including modes of production, print culture and book history, literature, and pedagogy—that enable the emergence of an idea of authorship positioned notionally outside the direct control of the state and the Church. The term helps redirect attention to the less standardized contexts of production even at a time when neither the idea of literature nor the idea of author had become fully formed.[1] New trends in the second half of the seventeenth century suggest that, for the first time in Russia, some notion of authorship, as well as readership—albeit subordinate to the primary duties of the writer as monk, courtier, or clerk—conditioned the identity of individuals who wished to sign their works and be known as authors. While Church figures bridled at the suspicion of heresy, eventually cracking down after the death of the tsar in 1676, the politically powerful tolerated and fostered these Orthodox proponents of neo-Humanist culture because they appreciated the arts of flattery and tribute wrapped up in conspicuous rhetorical splendor.

Aleksandr Panchenko coined the term "Chancery School" (*prikaznaia shkola*, from *prikaz*, Chancery) to refer to a constellation of poets whose lyric experiments anticipated by several decades the court poetry of the 1660s. Among the Chancery poets, individual exchanges of verse or their circulation between personnel at the chanceries and monasteries had a practical aspect. Art was not practiced for its own sake though clearly the display of artistry was valuable in enhancing professions of friendship and cultivation of a patron. While these versifiers conceive of the reader only as the actual addressee, there practice is just one step away from a poet like Simeon Polotsky who makes of the reader a rhetorical construct. In "To the Distinguished Reader" ("K blagochestivomu zhe chitateliu," 1678), a verse preface to the *Rhymed Psalter*, Polotsky treats the reader as a searcher of wisdom, whose common sense, reason, and learning incline him not only to appreciate the theological value of the text but, above all, to understand that the point of the "new style" (*rechenie novo*) of poetry written "in measures inherited from wise men/acquired through the study of Greek books" as well as in other "pagan poems" is not to exacerbate religious strife, but rather to attain spiritual enlightenment (*svetlost'*).

The spaces represented in Russian literature in the seventeenth century were, as previously, the monastery and the church. The court moves into the limelight as a center of cultural production. The social reality of the period did not entirely foster civic spaces or an autonomous literary field, and writing had to accommodate the controlling authorities at least up to a point. Ritual opportunities for the performance of the liturgy in church and at court grew considerably during the last third of the seventeenth century under the aegis of Tsar Aleksei, aided by the Patriarch Nikon (whose staunch religiousness ultimately alienated the political elite) and his successors. Ceremonial occasions now included prayers recited on royal birthdays, accessions, and obsequies, all used to demonstrate adherence to Orthodoxy and to attack ritually the non-Orthodox (often lambasted as the Hagarites, meaning the sons of Hagar, considered by Islam the second wife of the patriarch Abraham and, as mother of Ishmael, a matriarch of Islam). With the state authorities tested from within by the Schism and famine, and from without by invasion and war, new alignments eventually became possible. Tsar Aleksei Mikhailovich (Figure 11.03) simultaneously affirmed his commitment to Orthodoxy and autocracy (*samoderzhavie*). He fought the Schismatics, even while he began the long process of containing the Church (continued by Peter the Great, his son) when Patriarch Nikon and his followers became a destabilizing force. Court culture created a platform from which to project an image of absolutist authority in which erudition and prestige played a role.[2] Just as monks and clerks could begin to write about themselves, to copy foreign novellas and entertaining stories, to switch between writing high liturgical works and stories of tricksters,

FIGURE 11.03. Anonymous, Portrait of Tsar Aleksei Mikhailovich, late 18th c.

so could the tsar allow writing to progress through the acculturation of means and messages that had already achieved success in Europe.

A Western European idea of authorship follows a broad trajectory from the medieval university to royal courts to academies in the seventeenth century and increasingly into the public sphere in the eighteenth century and its substantial book market and readership. In Russia, there were no universities or academies to serve as cradles of independent thought: scientific and medical knowledge were scarcely to be distinguished from superstition and folk medicine. Jesuit academies were confined to the south in Ruthenia until the second half of the seventeenth century.[3] By the seventeenth century, one legacy of the state apparatus created by Ivan III was a larger pool of literate functionaries, clerks, and copyists who had the learning and craft required to write in the various Chancery scripts.[4] Skilled writers, mostly anonymous, from whose ranks emerged individuals who identified themselves as authors, came from three areas: the state or the imperial bureaucracy, the court, and the monasteries. These clerks found in the Chancery language, a bookish vernacular used in Moscow from the sixteenth century for non-ecclesiastical purposes, a resource for their own expressivity.[5]

By the seventeenth century, Russia had technically moved into a print culture. Muscovite printing was largely if not exclusively ecclesiastical, and only a single set of presses was actually in operation initially. Differences of scale and infrastructure between Russia and Western centers of learning were enormous. Literary works might circulate in no more than dozens of manuscript copies rather than in the thousands of printed copies known in Western Europe. The publication in 1663 of a magnificent folio Bible in 2,400 copies is noteworthy for the quality of production and for the fact that hundreds of copies remained unsold, unused, and unopened; and it was not until 1751 that the next complete printed Bible appeared in Russia (the St. Petersburg "Elizabeth Bible").

The printing press proved a powerful technology for the dissemination of political and religious indoctrination. From the 1620s, more so from the 1660s when the Schism became a factor, and even more when the physical plant and number of presses churning out decrees and Church rescripts increased, printing was overseen and controlled in the Kremlin. The published books were religious and liturgical with a few exceptions such as military manuals, the first printed grammar of the Russian language by Melety Smotritsky (1577–1633), and the Law Code of 1649 (*Sobornoe ulozhenie 1649 goda*), as well as a collection of secular canon law called the *Book of the Pilot* (*Kormchaia kniga*). All publications had to be authorized, at least nominally, by the tsar or the patriarch, and carried an afterword addressed to readers—who were listed according to their rank from the tsar and nobles down to the "poor" and even "the endless multitude." The afterword attested to the suitability of the reading matter for the subjects of a "divinely chosen country."[6] The purpose of a basic education was in the first instance religious, and grammars and primers, like the psalter, were used to inculcate dogma.[7] As Smotritsky wrote in his preface to the 1648 Moscow edition, "I am like a wet-nurse to the young...and like a protector to children..." and "to adolescents I am a swift-sighted governess who does not ignore matters of number and quality but asks and obliges one to find out." The Printing Office (*Pechatnyi dvor*) published prayers, liturgical rites, rules of obeisance, sometimes individually or collected in the *Sluzhebnik*, as well as saints' lives, menologies (in print runs of 500 copies), breviaries (there is evidence of a double printing of a single edition in 1623 of more than 2,000 copies), historical summaries of the lives of famous people and incidents (such as the baptism of the land of Rus'), and works of dogmatic theology. For instance, an edition of the *Life of St. Sergii of Radonezh*, printed in 1,200 copies, went on sale in 1646, treating St. Sergii as a national figure.[8] Starting in the 1670s, the number of presses and typesetters (drawn from the clergy) grew to meet the demand for wider distribution of printed material through the church parishes, schools, and churches. Works that came off the presses now included homilies (as collected in the *Margarit*, an anthology of ancient provenance), new editions of the *Prolog* (a work attested in medieval Rus'), the Psalter, instructions on conduct aimed at regulating the enjoyment of games, consumption of alcohol, and other forms of behavior (although the question whether there is any evidence to suggest that parishioners assimilated these rules as meaningful or accepted rote compliance, is debatable).[9] By the 1670s, life outside the Printing Office spilled over into the extracurricular writing of some typographers, correctors, and scribes such as Efimy Chudovsky, creating a small and mainly versified sub-literature of anecdotes and reminiscences about their jobs, conflicts, and lawsuits.

But the seventeenth-century story does not move toward a book market and readership. As in the Western Reformation, writing in Russia straddled the fault lines of the country's own doctrinal controversies. Different pedagogical models and cultural affiliations reflected factions in the widening rift between parties within the Church concerned to maintain its doctrinal purity and adherence to the correct rite. The default mode both in monastic centers and in cities remained manuscript and scribal rather than print.[10] The establishment of print culture faced obstacles in poor infrastructure, the cost of materials, and tight oversight of content. Monastic workshops continued to generate saints' lives and even to appropriate the new technology of printing to their own end. For instance, the Monastery of the Caves in Kiev issued a first printed edition of the *Paterikon*, a prestigious and expensive artifact. Old Believers enjoyed higher rates of literacy. Nonetheless, they proved to be staunch defenders of scribal culture as the most accurate way to preserve scripture, and saw the printing press as an aspect of corrupting Westernization that needed to be warded off. A manuscript copy of one important Old Believer text shows how scribes could enter into competition with the printed book by emulating its page design without resorting to typeface. Such technological limitations, compounded by literacy being restricted to a tiny fraction of the population, clearly limited the potential for change in the literary field.

To understand the literary dynamics of court culture we need to consider the role of intellectual migration as a conduit for Western forms of expression. Advances in Russian literary culture in the seventeenth century depend on injections of exogenous talent. With the annexation of parts of the left-bank Ukraine and the dismantling of the Polish–Lithuanian Commonwealth, some alignment between the cultural outlook of the center and the periphery became important. Rus' was under Polish rule, but it was not Poland; it was East Slavonic, but it was not Russian; it was Orthodox, and not Catholic. For a Muscovite tsar intent on renovating court culture, there was a considerable talent pool to be tapped in the region, the equivalent of current-day Ukraine and Belarus, and made up of entities shaped by distinct traditions and different vernaculars. Again, in a world in which learning and cultural activity remained limited to the imperial bureaucracy, court, and monastery, the impact of a small number of individuals on even a restricted audience was outsized and decisive. Based in Moscow, these people also served outside their workplace as copyists and adaptors of popular, sometimes oral literature.

A critical role in the supply of an educated force was the founding of the Kiev–Mohyla College (sometimes also referred to as Academy).[11] Raised in Moldavia, educated in France, and based in Ukraine as a monk at the Monastery of the Caves, Petr Mohyla (1596–1647) established the College in 1632. The school was confirmed in 1635 by Wladyslaw IV (r. 1632–48), King of Poland and Grand Duke of Lithuania, whose policy was to refute Catholicism on its own terms by educating the Orthodox faithful in enemy dogma.

Mohyla's aims were not narrowly doctrinal. His curriculum exceeded that of the Jesuit confraternity school, which emphasized scripture alone. In the seventeenth century, Mohyla's

College remained faithful to scholastic traditions derived mainly from Latin–Polish Jesuit schools not only in rhetoric but with regard to instruction in ethics as well.[12] Students remained largely unaware of the new learning that grew out of the Reformation. They did not read contemporary philosophers like René Descartes or Gottfried Wilhelm Leibniz; although Feofan Prokopovich (1681–1736), one of the most significant figures of the next generation, knew the work of the Dutch Jurist Hugo Grotius (1583–1645) and the German political philosopher Samuel von Pufendorf (1632–94), among others. The curriculum, patterned on the Jesuit model, initially took five years to complete. Classes on poetics and rhetoric were conducted in Greek, Latin, Slavonic, and Polish. In Poland and Ukraine, classical imitation was a standard part of the teaching of poetics (piitika), offering to the lower and middle years (or classes) an education in the neo-Latin tradition and aspects of Renaissance style.[13] The poetics class taught literary genres and mythology since speeches, poems, and sermons used mythological allusions to energize examples and display learning. All manuals of poetics were written in Latin and Polish with examples drawn both from classical and Polish neo-Latin writers. Later on, alumni like Polotsky and Feofan Prokopovich would contribute to the textbooks used at the Kiev–Mohyla College.[14] Students learned the rules of composing speeches of thanks, greetings, and farewells, funeral orations, and sermons, genres that would gain some currency in seventeenth-century Russian poetry. As one historian of the school says, "Kievan poets delighted in linguistic subtleties, puns, and sensationalism... Evidence of these values can be seen in many genres, particularly in the acrostic and the 'curious' verse, which assumed a variety of shapes and forms, ranging from simple crosses and pyramids to exotic chalices and abstract designs."[15] All manuals of poetics were written in Latin and Polish with examples drawn both from classical and Polish neo-Latin writers.

Mohyla represents the heterogeneous strands out of which a new cultural attitude could be forged. His Orthodoxy, his command of Polish, and his love and championing of Latin culture were not easy to reconcile with one another or to transfer to Moscow. If the Eastern Church in general had been caught unprepared for the controversies of the Western Reformation, the problem was particularly to be felt in the Ukraine, where confessional identity divided the Uniates, Orthodox, and Catholics (or Protestants). Traffic between Moscow and the Eastern Ukraine necessarily created some cultural rapprochement. Certain Kievan bookmen, such as Lazar Baranovich (1616–93), author of The Spiritual Sword (Mech dukhovnyi, 1666), Innokenty Gizel (1600–83), an Orthodox convert from Lutheranism who edited the Paterik of the Kievo-Pechersk Monastery, and Epifany Slavinetsky (1600–75), were staunch Orthodox conservatives who defended the "true faith" from positions in Moscow. Following his transfer to Moscow in 1664, Polotsky took the teachings of Aristotle and St. Thomas Aquinas to the northern capital. His arrival marked the establishment of an alternative trend in literary culture. Muscovite conservatism had its stronghold in the Greek school based at the Chudov Monastery, headed by the monk Euthymius (d. 1705) and Slavinetsky, a pupil of Mohyla. Both occupied prominent positions in the Printing Office and at the court. They and others, often referred to as Grecophiles or the Greek party, supported the Church rites based on Byzantine theology as confirmed in the sixteenth century. Anything that smacked of Latinity and the Catholic Church aroused their opposition. In the Latin school based at the Zaikonospassky School, precursor to the important Slavo-Greco-Latin Academy, Polotsky taught Latin scholasticism, attracting only a small albeit highly active group of followers of which Medvedev was the most talented. Their brand of scholasticism, however novel in Russia, lagged behind developments in seventeenth-century European thought, confined as it was to points of doctrine and an old-fashioned style of disputation. All the same, their contribution to the expansion of thought in Moscow was noteworthy for transferring the repertory of Humanist poetics to the Russian language and creating forms of expression new for Russia.

Once he had secured a position of authority, Mohyla strengthened the educational system developed in Orthodox Rus' after Kiev had been revived as a cultural center in the wake of the Union of Brest (1596) when the Ruthenian Church of Rus' abjured the Eastern Orthodox Church and joined the Catholic Church. Mohyla felt that only an equal education could equip Orthodox clergy with the proper skills for checking the Latinizers. This did not sit well with all the clergy in Orthodox Ruthenian lands or in Moscow, who were hostile to the teaching of any Catholic dogma and wary of Latinizing in any form. The liturgical books printed by the Printing Office regularly spread the view that Russia needed to preserve through its sacred rituals the sanctity of the legacy of Byzantium as inherited through Kievan Rus' and now Moscow. The view was that "an attraction for Latin wisdom dishonors the simplicity and greater wisdom of God."[16] Anti-Catholic feeling also led Old Believers, already dissenters against the Church reforms of the 1650s, to see in the theory of Moscow as the Third Rome an ominous attraction to Catholicism.[17] Yet new forms of learning had much to offer a court eager for ceremonial splendor, and aware that new learning and verbal skill had a contribution to make to the celebration of a dynasty whose legacy looked shaky from the Time of Troubles. Aspects of the Latin–Polish curriculum earlier in the seventeenth century had begun to trickle in to Moscow. It had even been briefly possible to run a bookshop specializing in foreign books, including some Latin writers, until the anti-Latin faction put an end to the venture. With the success of Mohyla's school, it became possible to recruit teachers from among the Orthodox Ukrainians, a step that Tsar Aleksei Mikhailovich readily undertook to the distress of the Greek teachers who had been invited to Moscow by the Patriarch Filaret (1554–1663). The Kiev–Mohyla College educated many who found themselves at the forefront during the transitional period at the end of the seventeenth century. The College's students included Stefan Yavorsky (1658–1722), initially admired by Peter the Great for his brilliant rhetoric before Yavorsky's conservatism and hankering for Ukraine alienated the tsar in the late 1710s; and Feofan Prokopovich, who, partly educated in Rome, applied his learning in the area of natural law to the cause of better defining Russian absolutism. Learned figures and gifted poets who became established in Moscow practiced in the literary language of Russian, a mixture of Slavonic and Chancery idiom, a full range of poetics and rhetoric acquired as part of their Humanist education.[18]

But for each figure with broader horizons there were many more clergy faithful to the Orthodox establishment. Apart from a number of Polish treatises on political theory, few Latin texts were rendered into Russian, and certainly no ancient Roman authors were given their due.[19] If anything, Greek-inspired learning oriented toward an old ideal of Byzantium fueled a considerable body of anti-Latinizing literature, which persisted in regarding the Latin language as nothing more than a vehicle for heresy.

Toward the end of the seventeenth century, Latin-language learning received a boost from the influx of Greek students in Moscow spurred by Tsar Aleksei Mikhailovich's relative openness to the West. Many of these Greek students, well educated and well traveled, recognized the historical importance of the Roman heritage and the contemporary place of Latin letters in international discourse. They encouraged Aleksei Mikhailovich to overcome Greek prejudice in the system. The Greek brothers Ioanniky (1633–1717) and Sofrony Likhud (1652–1730) undertook noteworthy educational initiatives in seventeenth-century Moscow. Initially, they were based at the Bogoiavlensky Monastery and taught pupils from the Typographic School. They subsequently transferred to the school at the Zaikonospassky Monastery before moving to the newly opened Slavo-Greco-Latin Academy in 1687. Their Greek origin and affiliation with the Grecophile party awoke suspicion among the clergy who viewed them as Hellenizers and even heretics. Peter I employed these students as tutors of modern languages to novice printers. Polotsky negotiated this difficult environment with the support of a small group of acolytes; the most important was Sil'vestr Medvedev (1641–91), who followed Polotsky's example as a preacher and poet while also working for Patriarch Nikon in implementing his ritual and textual reforms. By dint of circumstance and learning, Medvedev thus found himself between two stools as a supporter of Latin learning inimical to the Russian Orthodox Church (albeit one who harbored reservations about the Likhudov brothers as potentially subversive) and as an aid to the patriarch in the implementation of Orthodox rites and textual changes.[20]

Polotsky and his followers were the first to make the case in Russia for the liberal arts and the first to advocate a need for secular literature; they also brought new thinking and literary style to Moscow under strictly controlled conditions. For the first time Plato was mentioned alongside Aristotle, and the works of Plutarch, Cicero, and Seneca began to be taught. Some private libraries possessed foreign books, and the bulk of Western books, including Latin texts, belonged to churchmen from Ukraine. After the death of these churchmen, their collections could become donations to the libraries of monasteries and seminaries.[21] For example, another ally, the pro-Latin Palladius Rogovsky (1655–1703), in 1732 possessed a library of 500 volumes, a considerable collection at the time even by European standards, which was passed on to the library of the Slavo-Greco-Latin Academy.[22] Rogovsky acquired many of these books in Rome, where he had studied before returning to teach in Moscow, where he conducted his classes exclusively in Latin. Ancient works that penetrated the Orthodox defenses did so by accident and individual sponsorship.

The position of Western learning and a baroque literary culture in Moscow, therefore, rested on a small group of advocates.[23] If the situation in Moscow feels closer to the Middle Ages than to contemporaneous European debates about new concepts of classicism—which would eventually reach Russia in the 1730s—such parochialism did not stand in the way of important individual achievements, which made the literary field a patchwork of familiar and new, institutional and individual, popular and absolutist. It would be an exaggeration to qualify the reign of Tsar Aleksei as a "tipping point," since only small steps were taken toward instruction in rhetoric and philosophy during the second half of the seventeenth century; nor is "transition" entirely accurate, either, since eighteenth-century literature set new trends in style and genre and, above all, in changes to the literary field that were largely independent of seventeenth-century innovations. But the intermittent relaxation of hostility toward European trends had an outsized impact even in such a short time. And while old forms of ceremony and pageantry survived at court from the medieval world, even there the halting receptiveness to Humanist poetics created a moment when clergy could flourish as poets, and clerks employed for their literacy could set their sights on literature.

3

Court theater

THE imperial palaces, extensive administrative chanceries (*prikazy*), influential monasteries, cathedrals, and churches were all located within the precinct of the imposing Kremlin walls built by Ivan III in 1485–95 (as famously designed by Italian architects). Power radiated outwards from this bastion. The court was the social, political, and administrative center of Muscovy (or the Russian state) in the seventeenth century. Court rank, obtained through favoritism and hereditary distinction, determined the proximity to the sovereign on public occasions as well as private access (the system was known as *mestnichestvo*). Apart from family members, few courtiers ever gained access to the tsar's private quarters: the ruler's charisma, as in the medieval period, emanated from a remote and inaccessible locus of power.[1] Public occasions, therefore, relied all the more on elaborate ceremonial ritual to translate the tsar's role within the Church and the state into symbolic images and language. On religious festivals, such as the Palm Sunday procession (abolished by the Peter the Great in 1696), the tsar demonstrated humble submission to the patriarch as the leader of the Church, a further form of piety from Tsar Aleksei Mikhailovich, renowned for his attendance at worship, a gesture of clemency and charity that communicated the idea that his authority stemmed from his service to Christ.

Theatrical spectacles at court, attended by richly dressed nobles, were a way for the head of government to project national authority and to advertise the prestige of the court; at the same time, the content of baroque drama with its emphasis on ceremony and pageantry, and on plots about kingship and court intrigue, dovetailed with the ritualistic elements of court life. Content and context mirrored each other. Behind this screen of ceremonial dignity, a rhetorical and ritual iconostasis of stability, political maneuvers, and complex rivalries played out without disturbing the image of the omnipotent autocrat.

The first theater dedicated in Russia opened at the court of Aleksei Mikhailovich in 1672, but the increase in entertainment was brief since the theater barely had time to formalize procedures before it was closed down after the death of Aleksei Mikhailovich in 1676, suggesting that no routines became established for actors. Theater as a regular component of court culture would not be institutionalized until the reign of the Empress Elizabeth (r. 1741–61).

Dramatic entertainments provided by actors were occasional contributions to spectacles that marked special court events like important anniversaries, foreign treaties, and royal marriages, and, above all, the monarch's birthday at which poems were recited in addition to religious ceremony. Popular theater as practiced outside the court mainly by itinerant minstrels (*skomorokhi*) consisted largely of mummers' performances, morality plays, and skits, often parodies of religious holidays. The Church had clamped down on popular practices, enlisting the aid of puritanical groups like the Zealots of Piety, to which Avvakum belonged, in order to consolidate its grip and also check social unrest and heresy.[2]

In 1672, the tsar commissioned Johann Gottfried Gregori (1631–75), a Lutheran pastor in Moscow and a school founder, to write and stage a play. He also suggested the plot of this play: the Old Testament's book of *Esther*. Gregori wrote the play in German; or perhaps compiled it, since in addition to the Bible, he used several German plays on this subject as his models. It was translated into Russian by officials from the Foreign Ministry (*Posol'skii prikaz*), which was the source of translators most adept in Slavic and European languages. The play, entitled *The Drama of Artaxerxes (Artakserksovo deistvo)*, was performed about six months after the commission.[3] Several further performances occurred in the coming years. Was the Biblical subject meant to be an allegory for Aleksei Mikhailovich's marriage to Natalia Naryshkina? Baroque theater reveled in the idea of life as a stage, but there is little basis for any concrete correlations other than specific allegorical plots. It is hard to measure Gregori's intentions: the book of Esther was not a novelty, and had long circulated in many copies; yet this does not contradict its thematic suitability to the occasion, even if the play falls short of equating the heroine with the tsarina.[4]

Another play, *Judith (Iudif')*, was staged shortly thereafter, and enjoyed several performances. The repertory included other works on Biblical and historical themes with allegorical potential, sometimes favoring mythological plots, such as now lost plays about Tobias, St. George, David and Goliath, Bacchus and Venus, a ballet *Orpheus*, and the extant "A Sad Comedy about Adam and Eve" ("Zhalobnaia komediia ob Adame i Eve"). Two one-act plays by Simeon Polotsky, "The Comic Parable of the Prodigal Son" ("Komidiia pritchi o bludnom syne," published in 1685) and *On King Nebuchadnezzar, his Golden Body, and the Three Youths Not Burned in an Oven* ("O Navukhodonosore tsare, tele zlate i trekh otrotsekh, v peshchi ognemne sozhzhennykh," 1673–74) were written specifically for the court according to the conventions of Jesuit school theater and staged; however, their performance histories have been lost.[5]

KEYWORD **Baroque**

In Europe, the baroque is defined by its intellectual underpinnings in Humanism, its relation to the cognate artistic style of mannerism, and its association with the religious poetry of Catholicism. Histories of Western Slavic literatures, such as Polish, justifiably treat the baroque as a full-fledged movement. Hostility in Muscovite ecclesiastical circles to these trends, however, severely circumscribed the transfer of baroque aesthetics to a Russian context, which nonetheless made a limited mark on the seventeenth-century literary and visual culture of the court of Tsar Aleksei. As a result of their Kievan education in neo-Latin and Humanist poetics, Medvedev and Polotsky amply applied baroque devices such as paradox, contradiction, repetition metaphor, and exclamation in their ceremonial poetry. When used adjectivally, the term "baroque" has enjoyed some critical currency in Russian culture to denote a style marked by verbal dynamism, abundant figurative language that privileges connotation over the nominalism and direct signification of neoclassical rationalism. There is a pronounced preference for self-reflexivity in which metaphors take on a dynamism of their own and images generate more images; but also for establishing through rhetorical tropes an isomorphic relation between the text and the world in which forms mirror content as in acrostic and maze poetry cultivated by seventeenth-century poets. These traits of baroque aesthetics can be attested in major Russian poets from Polotsky to Lomonosov to Joseph Brodsky and Elizaveta Mnatsakanova in the twentieth century.

The genre of plays was not narrowly fixed. The word "action" (*deistvo*) is often attached to a play without specific connotation. The labels "drama" (*drama*), "comedy" (*komediia*), "act" (*akt*), and "interlude" (*intermediia* or *mezhdorechie*) also occur, but theatrical nomenclature is obscure.[6] The terms used are broad, and they imply no rules about the unities of time, location, and action. A comedy was never a farce, but nor was it happily resolved, in the Shakespearian sense: the outcome of the "Comedy of the Parable of the Prodigal Son" is repentance and a lesson learned, which reflected the morals of popular prose and verse narratives about wayward children. There is no conclusive evidence to determine whether the "interlude" was part of a larger program and inserted between plays or performed perhaps during a meal; or whether the interlude was a stand-alone piece. The number of voices in an interlude implies between two and four players. The names of parts in dialogues such as "Old Man" (*Starik*), "Youth" (*Malets*), "Teacher" (*Uchitel'*), or "Deceiver" (*Obmanshchik*), "Glutton" (*Lakomets*) give a direct line to the subject matter, written in a mixture of short alternating speeches.

Playwrights included Simeon Polotsky and Feofan Prokopovich, both educated at the Kievan Mohyla College where school plays were performed regularly. Aleksei Mikhailovich observed a performance of one of Polotsky's plays when he visited Polotsk in 1660. The practice was transplanted to Moscow at the Slavo-Greco-Latin Academy and later at the medical school founded by Peter in 1706, the Hospital Theater. As in poetry, the stimulus for court theater was Western in origin and reflected the influence of Ruthenian figures, familiar with the tradition of student drama and declamation (sometimes referred to as school theater). In Ukraine, Jesuit or school theater, like the fictional tales of the period, treated didactic subjects as we see from titles such as "The Terrible Deceit of a Corrupt Life" ("Uzhasnaia izmena slastoliubivogo zhitiia"), "A Terrible Depiction of the Second Coming" ("Strashnoe izobrazhenie vtorogo prishestviia"), and "Russian Glory" ("Slava rossiiskaia"). School theater used a wide range of speakers and techniques consistent with a much broader Jesuit curriculum that exposed students in Ruthenia to the use of drama to perform spiritual and moral plots.[7] Locked in competition with Jesuits in Belorussia and Ukraine, the Orthodox clergy in Moscow tolerated court theater, at least briefly. Eventually, a Russian tradition of school theater would also emerge in Russian seminaries in the early eighteenth century.

On the evidence of the few extant plays known to have been performed, Moscow court dramaturgy was simpler and less overtly theological than Jesuit school drama, and did not go out of its way to refer to contemporary events or suggest tension between the spiritual and secular. Like Pastor Gregori's *Comedy of Artaxerxes*, Dmitry Rostovsky's "The Comedy on the Birth of Christ" ("Komediia na rozhdestvo Khristovo," 1702), is much more in the tradition of Humanist religious drama, and affiliations with the plays of the Dutch dramatist Joost van den Vondel (1587–1679) have been suggested.[8] This work features a large cast of allegorical figures, including "Life" (*Zhizn'*), "Death" (*Smert'*), "Nature" (*Natura*), "Fortune" (*Fortuna*), "Reason" (*Razsuzhdenie*) and "The Iron Age" (*Zheleznyi vek*), among others, who discuss in dogmatic terms the divine creation of man and human nature (*natura liudskaia*), man's fall from grace, and the possibility of redemption through Christ, all this in an anti-prologue before the story of the Nativity is enacted. Dmitry Rostovsky (1651–1709) deploys a wide range of discourses—his play features Herod and six senators who use the language of political ideology and show a mutual concern with gaining royal favor.

Plays did not have multiple plots. Stage directions were often incorporated into dialogue. A messenger in the "Comedy about the Parable of the Prodigal Son" announces, "Your son in tears enters your gates / And is ashamed of his tattered clothes." Polotsky's drama does not feature a chorus or other speaker to offer detached critical commentary on the static debating positions of the main characters. Very little, if anything, is known about stage techniques, such as how scenic and lighting effects were managed. The paucity of archival records might in itself raise an interesting possibility that actors did not have access to copied or printed playbooks and undertook the rote learning of parts. Initially a troop of German actors took the parts until Russian youths were trained to work as a company exclusively at court.

Like Restoration drama, although there is no evidence for specific influence, plays could feature terrifying scenes and did not shy away from depicting torture, execution, or murder. Surviving stage directions date to eighteenth-century copies with scant production notes.[9] Plays, whether written or staged, do demarcate the boundaries between player and spectator, and rarely mention any details of the play's performance conditions and audience or the performance space (in the prologue to *The Drama of Artaxerxes* the speaker suggests that Muscovite viewers will find in Biblical history relevant parallels). Shows were produced within the court itself. Performances took place in Preobrazhenskoe, the tsar's suburban residence, in a theatrical building (*teatral'naia khramina*), and in Moscow, in a much smaller space in the building where the court pharmacy was located. The tsar attended, seated in a special chair positioned in the middle of the room in front of the stage. One of the few notes about the stage production instructs musicians (*musikiia*) that their playing and singing are to accompany the traditional acclamation of the tsar at the end of the performance. Natalia, Tsar Aleksei's young second wife and mother of Prince Peter, sometimes also attended, and courtiers stood on stage as the royal children watched from behind a lattice screen. Speeches in plays make direct reference to the tsar and other patrons sitting prominently in front and standing around them, the closed community offered by the Russian court. There is no other information about acting modes or stage props, including sound, since we have no eyewitnesses to performances. In the Prologue to the "Comedy of the Parable of the Prodigal Son," the speaker alerts the audience that the play will be in six parts and, more interestingly, appeals for their attention and gives some instruction that the work will use the heritage of Christian parable to comment on the new secular outlook. The Prologue evokes an audience that will interpret what it hears and see in the issues it dramatizes a personal message. The playwright appears to take control of the performance space in order to captivate not only the vision, hearing, and hearts of the audience but in order to give them true delight (*sladost'*) by offering them spiritual salvation.

> Извольте убо милость си явити,
> Очеса и слух к действу приклонити:
> Так бо сладость будет обретенна,
> Не токмо сердцам, но душам спасенна.[10]

> Please kindly bear with us for a while
> And train your eyes and ears on the stage:
> For you shall find a source of great delight
> Not merely for your hearts but for your souls.

The language suggests that Polotsky believed that theater could achieve a fusion of a Christian message, serious social commentary, and the dramatic technique of catharsis, if we take the word "delight" here to signify relief that the spectator feels. At the end of *On King Nebuchadnezzar, his Golden Body, and the Three Youths Not Burned in an Oven*, the Epilogue expresses gratitude to the royal patron for casting a "gracious eye on our comic action" ("svetloe oko tvoe sozertsashe / komidiinoe sie deistvo nashe").

Muscovite dramaturgy put scriptural stories to secular use and was concerned mainly with worldly morality. Writing does not mingle different stylistic elements: the language is stately although the styled expression is not devoid of emotion. The monologue of the Prodigal Son which opens Act VI of Polotsky's play is a deeply felt statement of repentance full of wonder at the beauty of the world and grief at his betrayal of a cherished father. Great rhetorical plangency marks the treatment of a Biblical episode that is reinvented as a story of fathers and sons in which the older generation bears much of the blame and repentance. There is no necessity to read this language as allegorical commentary on court politics. Other works contain royalist statements that fall short of overt discussion of the ideology of absolutism: speakers simply place their trust in the virtue of the ruler positioned right in front of them, confirming the political order as it is.[11] King Nebuchadnezzar in Polotsky's play is given cere- monial pomp at the beginning where he asserts that his authority and righteousness stem from his monotheistic faith, unlike the pagans who have many gods.

It is questionable whether a speech of this kind reflects an understanding of the uncertain religious situation of the country in the aftermath of the Schism. Muscovite dramaturgy responds to its immediate context by using the moral and didactic language more generally adopted by the clergy and court figures like Polotsky in his sermons and pedagogical works. Issues of religion and Church politics are not touched on extensively or explicitly and plots do not raise problematic questions about doctrinal issues that might have caused controversy. Muscovite dramaturgy stays within the limits of modes of teaching and theological commen- tary endorsed by the Orthodox Church, and plays repeat the preoccupations found in secular stories that circulated among lay people. At the very least, if not much more, drama made a start by adding a new emotional dimension to didactic literature less static than familiar lessons about conduct and piety conveyed in sermons.

While no modern idea of what it meant to be a writer in the professional sense emerged at this time, aspirations for writing that differed from the ideals and modes of the scribe charac- terize interest in literature. While writing as an activity remained subordinate to the primary duties of the writer as monk, courtier, or clerk—it also became part of the identity of indi- viduals who wish to sign their works and be known as authors. This is certainly true for both Simeon Polotsky and Avvakum, who sought renown through writing: the first because the notion of posterity and glory is part of the former's ethos as a writer committed to the ideal Humanist poets learned from Horace of serving poetry and the prince (or emperor or tsar); and the second because he sees writing as an inevitable element of his own martyrdom in which bearing witness and testifying to his own self-sacrifice through a text his followers will heed and copy—and copies of the *Life* proliferated immediately and by the thousand—defines his mission. Both projects grow out of medieval values of service and piety. Yet their under- standing of writing as a means to fame, and through to the hearts of readers, represents a significant departure from the author-function model characteristic of the medieval world. They also look like forays into forms of expression characteristic of the early modern period rather than the Enlightenment.

4

Poets

THE reign of Tsar Aleksei Mikhailovich saw an initiation into literary genres, mainly drama and poetry, even before techniques for composing them were formally taught in Moscow. The concentration of power at the court, when mixed with the arrival of learned Humanists from Ukraine, was immensely important to the practices of writing. The rise of poetry emanated from the growth of complex bureaucratic structures (more than the social affiliations that will be important in the eighteenth century). This is the context in which writing for self-expression was synergistic with professional duties. If there were only a handful of writers of note—and Avvakum and Polotsky are the most considerable talents—there was a crowd of less able men who invested meaning in the act of writing. Russia had no real tradition of vernacular poetry (apart from oral song). From the 1620s onward the century saw a huge shift in the production of verse, but the scale and quality have historically remained hard to estimate because of the limited availability of texts. Many poems remain unattributed and unpublished, leaving a fascinating body of work relatively neglected since the 1970s; and some biographies remain entirely irrecoverable or sadly incomplete. In the nineteenth century there persisted the impression that seventeenth-century poetry was largely confined to *virshi*, *byliny*, and lyric songs. The hazards of archival retrieval associated with a pre-printing culture are to blame. Much of the poetry written in the seventeenth century survived solely in manuscript copies that were little known to the first generations of Russian literary historians, and are hard to read and expensive to reproduce. Anthologies and scholarly studies published since the 1970s now provide a significant corpus of representative works and extracts. These provide a much better sense of the status poetry acquired as a vehicle for a variety of purposes that can be described in outline.

Beyond folk verses, hymnographic texts, and rhythmic prayers, poetry as a type of written composition distinct from prose attracted practitioners. But did they think of themselves as poets? From the 1620s to 1650s versifiers were, like prose writers, mainly from the clergy, bureaucracy, and in small numbers from the educated aristocracy—perhaps no more than a few dozen figures in total.[1] From the 1650s to the early Petrine period, verse creation became concentrated at court where this small cluster of figures who thought of themselves as theologians, courtiers, and poets accounted for a massive output of poems numbering in the tens of thousands of lines.

All of the poets Panchenko identified as members of the Chancery School served as secretaries in chanceries, primarily in the Printing Office and Typography Office (*Knizhnaia sprava*).[2] Their activity spans the period from the final years of Patriarch Filaret, who died in 1633, to several years into the reign of Tsar Aleksei Mikhailovich and the Patriarchy of Iosif (1642–52). While Peter the Great would eventually separate government and ecclesiastical printing and put the former under the supervision of a new Printing Office, in the seventeenth century, the departments responsible for the publication of state and liturgical decrees, and liturgical books, came under the command of the Head Chancery (*Bol'shoi dvorets*). Chanceries were staffed by hundreds of petty functionaries; these clerks (*d'iaki*) and correctors (*spravshchiki*) appear to have constituted a separate group of intellectual elite and were recruited not from other chanceries, but from seminaries and Muscovite churches and were the pupils, and sometimes children, of the white clergy (that is the diocesan priests permitted to marry, unlike the black clergy or monks). Climbing the career ladder—a recurring topic in poetry—depended on reciprocal patronage and on service to the Head Chancery and the patriarch, since the clerks' job included correcting and publishing liturgical and religious texts.

Many poems in this corpus are verse epistles. But even these lyric poems were not just verse transactions. Clerks by profession, these writers applied their rhetorical skills to enhancing expressivity, and many devised clever tropes, word-games, and visual puzzles. Poetry created opportunities to mark private occasions and to show off one's ingenuity or invention (in the Latin sense of *ingenium*, a prized quality of Humanist verbal culture). Their output—Panchenko calls them a "school," although "coterie" seems better suited to their loose grouping—most likely comes to a total of several hundred poems; while many remain unpublished, the corpus of syllabic verse now in print amounts to several thousand lines.

The texts of the Chancery poets provide unprecedented insight into the world of educated figures, who negotiated between private ideals and state service. By dint of their intermittent literary production they were more versifiers than poets: their vocation is their work rather than their writing. They are original, however, insofar as they understand how to use literature as a vehicle for self-discovery. While the sense of self of these poets falls well short of a modern idea of subjectivity, identity construed as a function of their relation to work and service, the exploration of feeling as it arises out of circumstances sets them apart from monks. Copyists at work in the medieval tradition, they dabbled in authorship on the side. To the extent that their poems consider themes of friendship, aspiration, patronage, personal feelings, and even service itself, they are literary innovators as the first to write about these topics, and in verse form. While the poets applied their learning to the advancement of a bureaucratic career, they also showed some appetite for learning for its own sake in order to attract the praise of friends and colleagues. Learning also plays an essential role in the self-image of the cleric as a reasonable man who is both pious and worldly. Outside the Printing Office, figures like Petr Samsonov (*fl.* mid-seventeenth century), a chancellery secretary of the Patriarchal Palace Office, and Aleksei Romanchukov (*fl.* early seventeenth century), used poetry to forge a coterie. The latter was a diplomat who as ambassador to Persia enjoyed wide contacts among foreigners, and recorded occasional verses in the album of a doctor from Holstein as an expression of gratitude for medical services.

A number of figures emerge from obscurity. Semen Vasil'ev Bashmak, known as Savvaty (d. 1670s), served professionally in various chanceries in Moscow in the 1630s, becoming a monk in 1654. Later in life, at the request of the tsar, he corrected printed copies of sacred books before suffering persecution as an Old Believer, his endurance praised by Avvakum in his *Life*. In one verse epistle he refers to his service at the court where he cultivated connections with those close to the imperial family. Erudite, eloquent, and given to writing about his own life whether in prose sketches or syllabic verse, he collected some of his writings in the 1640s into a single album that contains reciprocal correspondence (originally published in 1862). These friendly letters are classic examples of advice literature that sometimes touch on everyday matters and reveal something of the author's personality. Savvaty, who admits to a penchant for sturgeon, also resorts to food metaphor for spiritual sustenance:

Ничто же честнее в человецех учения,
И тебе бы не преслушати сего нашего к тебе речения.
И аще не восхощеши сих наших словес себе слышати,
То не будеш семидална хлеба с сахары кушати.[3]

Among men there is nothing more honorable than learning,
Which is why you should follow our advice.
But if you decide to disregard it,
Why, you will not break heavenly bread.

The archpriest Mikhail Rogov (d. *c.*1650) worked alongside Savvaty as a typographic corrector. He was also a fellow poet who produced the first printed edition of the anthology called *The Book of Cyril* (*Kirillova Kniga*, 1596), named for its initial polemical article quoting St. Cyril. It originated in a manuscript pamphlet of religious polemical articles attacking "the Latins and Lutherans," after a Danish prince and suitor of the tsar's daughter refused to convert to Orthodoxy.

The career, position, and contributions of Simeon Polotsky, the greatest poet of the age and perhaps Russia's first and only full-time court poet, constitute a peak in the literary culture of the period and a case study in how the literary field operated. His origins and career reflect the main crosscurrents running through the period that can be conveniently summed up as an opposition between the theological and the secular, monastery and court, Russian and Western, Orthodox and Catholic/Latin, literature and propaganda. He was steeped in the Latin Humanist education offered by the Kiev–Mohyla College, and fluent in Polish and neo-Latin, which brought him a mastery of the classical and baroque traditions, including rhetoric, scholastic commentary, and a full range of poetic genres such as occasional odes, epitaphs, pastoral, allegory, and emblem poetry. Such mastery was typically acquired by Eastern Slavic bookmen, including other eminent writers who were Polotsky's followers and allies in Moscow: Sil´vestr Medvedev, Karion Istomin (*c.*1640–1717/1722?), and Stefan Yavorsky.[4] Polotsky had a total command of poetic craft of which the Chancery poets had only caught glimpses, and his training equipped him to write syllabic verse in Church Slavonic (with evidence of Ruthenian and Ukrainian dialect) and in Polish. Despite an education complete with all the worldly logical and rhetorical training often condemned in Moscow as Jesuit, Simeon was of Orthodox faith. In 1661, he caught the attention of Tsar Aleksei Mikhailovich by presenting him with poems on the occasion of the latter's visit to Polotsk. In 1664, he departed for Moscow where the learned Greek Patriarch Paisios, who found in him a useful helper and translator, served as his protector. It was not long before Aleksei Mikhailovich rediscovered the poet and appointed him as a court poet as well as a teacher of Latin at a school at the Zaikonospassky Monastery; it was a bold move at a time when religious discontent and resentment of the Latinizers were coming to a head.

At the Muscovite court, dominated by the upper echelons of the conservative Orthodox clergy even after the fall of Patriarch Nikon, Polotsky's origins, background, and literary affinities raised suspicions that he must have been a Uniate worshipper and crypto-Latinizer; these were unfounded charges since Jesuit schools in Ukraine taught pupils of different denominations. Within Tsar Aleksei's immediate entourage, which included the influential courtier Fedor M. Rtishchev (1626–73), Polotsky's eloquence in his sermons, plays, and poetry as an advocate of Russian autocracy, and his ingenuity as a writer of a purer form of literary Church Slavonic, overcame the suspicions of heretical belief and un-Orthodox literary practices. His enemies included Avvakum who referred to him as a "wolf in sheep's clothing" and castigated as rhetoric his type of Latin erudition. Only nominally a clergyman of modest rank, Polotsky identified himself as a "laborer of the word" (*trudnik slova*). Polotsky's cultural orientation, loyalty, and eloquence made him, implicitly and explicitly (in his treatise on government, the *Scepter of Rule* [*Zhezl pravleniia*, 1667]), an ally in the tsar's culture wars against Nikon and the Old Believers. The tsar subsequently made him tutor to Tsarevich Aleksei and, on his death, to his brother Tsarevich Fedor. In his letters to Tsar Aleksei Mikhailovich, Polotsky prides himself on the bookish cleverness of his poetic learning, expressing satisfaction in his belief that his poetry has afforded feeling consonant with his standing as Christian and poet.

Later, when oversight of the Printing Office was within the jurisdiction of Patriarch Ioakhim, he used his control to frustrate Polotsky in publishing his writings as freely as he and Medvedev had hoped. Polotsky, however, found a supporter in the new Tsar Fedor Alekseevich (r. 1676–82). On Fedor's accession to the throne in 1676, in the occasional poem "Harmonious Lyre" ("Gusl' dobroglasnaia", 1676), Polotsky considered the possibility of establishing a separate printing enterprise to be run for the tsar's "profit and glory" ("slavu i pribytok").[5] By February 1679, the new Upper Printing House (*Verkhniaia tipografiia*), was set up under the direct supervision of the tsar. It was equipped with four printing presses, and like the Printing Office, capable of producing engraved images based on its library of Western doctrinal and ecclesiastical works. Its first publication was an *Alphabet of the Slavonic Language* (*Bukvar' iazyka slavenska*, 1679). While its secondary function was to handle overflow from the Printing Office and increase the list and quantity of religious books, its primary purpose was to print educational works of a more secular cast and, expressly, the works of Polotsky, all of these in more luxurious editions. He saw his *Rhymed Psalter* into print (*Psaltyr' rifmotvornaia*, 1680; Figure 11.04 shows the frontispiece featuring King David the Psalmodist, and Figure 11.05 reproduces the front page signed by Simeon near the ornamental scrollwork at the top). His pupil Silvestr Medvedev, as authorized by Tsar Fedor, oversaw the posthumous publication of Polotsky's collection of homilies, the *Spiritual Repast* (*Obed dushevnyi*) and the *Spiritual Evening* (*Vecheria dushevnaia*, 1683), both of those books featuring emblem poems and engraved frontispieces. The resistance of Church officials to Polotsky was limited in his lifetime because of his position close to the tsar as tutor for the Tsareviches Fedor and Aleksei as well as the Tsarevna Sophia, eventually the regent between 1682 and 1689. After his death, however, the patriarch described his writing as "a disgrace and heresy" ("podzor i eres'") and deemed it unsuitable for the Orthodox, a sentence that consigned his greatest poetry collections to remain in manuscript.

Apparently the idea of translating the Psalter came to him as he worked on ordering the hundreds of poems in the *Many-Flowered Vineyard* (*Vertograd mnogotsvetnyi*, 1676–80). The result was the first collection of poems to be published as a separate book in Russian territory. In 1690, virtually a decade after Polotsky's death, and seven years after the Upper Printing House had been closed on the death of the tsar, the patriarch preached a sermon attacking Polotsky "for the arrogance of typesetting and printing his books, having taken advantage of our moderation and alleging that these books were printed with our permission."[6] Privileges of status, salary, and reward had accompanied his achievements. It was from this position of relative protection that Polotsky and his followers created what might be called their own literary micro-culture within a world still dominated by theological writings on dogma. Polotsky fits well into the larger context of the courtier-poet, not unlike the Elizabethan court poets, such as Edmund Spenser, for whom patronage and royal approval within the small court circle were a necessary compensation. This is still a far cry from the main definitions of professionalism as practiced within a print culture based on regular incentives such as royalty and intellectual property rights.

In composing his poetic garden, the *Many-Flowered Vineyard*, Polotsky sought to recreate in Russian the rhetorically artful structures, replete with tropes and figures, that featured in the elegant and elaborate poetry of baroque traditions. Framing poetic cycles within the complex structure of a verse garden, organized alphabetically yet full of criss-crossing motifs and

FIGURE 11.04. Simeon Polotsky, *The Rhymed Psalter* (*Psaltyr' rifmotvornaia*, Moscow: Verkhniaia tipografiia, 1680), plate opposite p. 17.

echoes, was a spectacular innovation of the Moscow baroque. He thought the best way to see Russia as "the richest vineyard" was by "imitating foreign idioms" and "domesticating them to the Slavonic language."[7] This boast mirrored Horace's famous claims about his own achievement in adapting Greek meters to the Latin language, and Polotsky's own practice, following the tradition of the Renaissance *poeta doctus*, was to exercise his affinities with Western traditions through allusion, imitation, and translation. His success was not to be taken for granted, and owed a great to deal to his prodigious productivity not only as a poet, but also as a polemicist and translator from Latin. Students of his religious writings—there are over 200 sermons—conclude that these writings reconcile a sound knowledge of Eastern Orthodoxy with an equally profound understanding of Catholic doctrine and ritual. His sermons reveal, apart from their rhetorical fluency, a zeal for religion and the sanctity of the Church as a social force. In 1680, Polotsky plunged directly into a theological controversy, when the Typography of the Upper Chamber printed his *Rhymed Psalter*, a work in which transposition was at cross

FIGURE 11.05. Simeon Polotsky, *The Rhymed Psalter*, title page.

purposes with the strict literalism to which clergy subscribed. Polotsky's intention to publish his other collections at his own press in the Printing Office was never realized (for one thing, the cycles designed to be performed and appreciated in their entirety may have exceeded the technical capacities of the printers).

Polotsky's lasting fame as a writer rests on three massive collections of verse: *The Many-Flowered Vineyard* (*Vertograd mnogotsvetnyi*), the *Book of Rhymes* (*Rifmologion*, unpublished) and the *Rhymed Psalter*. Completed in manuscript in the late 1670s, and written in a contemporary Russian version of Church Slavonic largely untainted by Belorussian, Ukrainian, or Polish, *The Many-Flowered Vineyard* consists of about 2,763 poems (20,000 lines) composed across a wide range of genres and rhetorical styles and laid out in a complex arrangement. Apart from issues of scale, the three extant manuscripts of this monumental achievement present considerable complications. In the authorial manuscript copy, Polotsky followed a thematic ordering full of digressions and cross-references: Jesuit poetics, emulated by Ukrainian acolytes, taught how to write echo poems and such effects here put this form of cleverness on display on an imposing scale.

Two fair copies of the *The Many Flowered-Vineyard* made by scribes, including a lavish presentation copy, adopted an alphabetical arrangement. This later internal order is followed in the first complete critical edition of the poem begun in the 1990s and completed in 2002.[8] This great florilegium of verse has many topics or poetic "flowers," sometimes arranged pictographically as labyrinths, sometimes etymologically as riddles, sometimes as emblem poems laid out calligraphically, or as rebus poems laid out geometrically as cubes, all formats Polotsky uses in his last book. The reader who enters the poetic garden, wandering through its cycles and sub-cycles, is meant to harvest learning and Christian virtue by reading poems that explain and illustrate religious, moral, and political concepts such as angelology, wealth, the Holy Spirit, the relation of body and soul, sin, luck, and many more. As a compendium of such definitional poems, *The Many-Flowered Vineyard* is an encyclopedia of spiritual and worldly issues. One pervasive phrase that defines its moral outlook is the third-person construction "it is befitting that" (*podobaet*) followed by predicates relating to the right conduct or the path of virtue that should be adopted by reason and emotion, mind and heart. What ties the entire compilation together, despite the sometimes bewildering, sometimes exhilarating variety, is its attempt to set out, illustrate, and cultivate didactic and moral precepts. Simeon viewed it as the task of the poet to enunciate a message of education and moral guidance. In *The Many-Flowered Vineyard*, the quest for the good life provides continuity.

Polotsky's final collection was the *Book of Rhythms* (*Rifmologion*), a vast compendium of ceremonial poems written for court occasions. It demonstrates the full extent of the poet's virtuosity and learning by matching a range of rhetorical tropes and poetic forms (often calligraphic) to its themes. The collection is on an unprecedented scale for a Muscovite poet (and has never been published in full). It represents a summa and repository of much of Polotsky's creative work written from 1659 to 1680, the year of his death. Simeon began assembling the *Rifmologion* in 1678. The autograph title page announces that the syllabic "rhyming verses in couplets" ("stikhi ravnomerno slozhennye kraeglasno") were dedicated to the glory of God. And while Polotsky professes that the poems were composed for the "benefit of the young and old, for religious and lay honorable people", this enormous folio book was conceived solely for presentation to Tsar Aleksei in a unique copy and never intended for publication, unlike his sermons, grammars, polemical pieces of the late 1670s directed against Protestantism, and works on absolutism (the *Scepter of Rule*). Rooted in court ritual and focused on topics relating to the royal house, all parts of the collection are microcosms of that larger cosmos of praise culture and spiritual enlightenment that was the court.

Even more varied by genre and rhetorical mode than *The Many-Flowered Vineyard*, the manuscript book contains emblem and zodiac poems, cryptograms, lyric poems, court masques written for musical accompaniment, and two plays (*On King Nebuchadnezzar* and *The Comedy of the Prodigal Son*). Miscellaneous works, arranged according to theme and occasion, surround the five poetic books that are the heart of this codex and positioned centrally in the folio sheets. The first two books are made up of poems of "greeting" ("Blagoprivetstvovanie"), written to Tsar Aleksei Mikhailovich on the birth of his son Simeon in 1665, and are the shortest of the set of five; the third book is the *Russian Eagle* (*Orel Rossiiskii*, 1667).[9] The fourth is the *Threnodies, or Lamentations of all the Ranks and Dignitaries of the Orthodox Russian Kingdom* (*Threny, ili Plachi vsekh sanov i chinov pravoslavnogo rossiiskogo tsarstva*), written from April 29, 1669 after the death of Tsaritsa Maria Miloslavskaia in March, poems in which Polotsky rises to great heights of eloquence and personal statement. The fifth and final book is the *The Final*

Utterance of Tsar Aleksei Mikhailovich to the Lord God (*Glas poslednii ko gospodu bogu*, 1676), a set of elegies full of historical and mythic analogy, composed on the death of Tsar Aleksei Mikhailovich on January 29, 1676. It is followed by a palinode, the "Beautiful-Sounding Lyre" ("Gusl′ dobroglasnaia") celebrating the coronation of Fedor Alekseevich in June 1676. Each of these books (Polotsky refers to them as *knizhnitsy*) is complex in structure, devised to display the art of variation by producing new forms in poems written around the same type of occasion. These genres include the greeting, in which poems apostrophize the ruler, the epithalamion, the prayer, and the epigram, to name only several. The intricacy of design is staggering. There are cycles within cycles, some extensive, some miniature, giving the impression of an imposing poetic architecture. We can gain some impression of the scale by noting, as an example, that a single cycle such as the opening work on "The Birth of Christ" ("Rozhdestvo Khristovo") contained thirty-two separately titled poems, some as long as seventy lines, reportedly taking up nearly 200 folio sheets. A subsection or separate cycle contained in this section is the "Verses on the Resurrection of Christ dedicated to the Tsar" ("Stisi na Voskresenie Khristovo ko gosudariu tsariu"). This set of 112 lines is followed by a set of verse greetings (*privetstva*) written for specific occasions, included in 1680 toward the end of Simeon's work on the compilation, and arranged by addressee, who are mainly boyars. These poems, all originally meant for oral performance and highly theatrical, are formally heterogeneous. Unifying this omnibus of works to the ruling house is the theme of patriarchal authority and loyalty to autocracy.

Textbooks as well as more recent specialist studies speak of Polotsky as the "progenitor of Russian poetry" (*rodonachal′nik russkoi poezii*).[10] We might turn the claim around by asking: How can a Ruthenian churchman immersed in the Latin and neo-Humanist literary arts, positioned between Catholicism and Orthodoxy, writing in Church Slavonic syllabics, and whose major works were never published, be said to relate to any native tradition, whether past or future?

However stunning this constellation of works may be, and whatever its considerable inherent value, the absence of direct links to later practice, or demonstrable examples of how Polotsky's precedence served as a compelling example to later generations, alters the picture. The growth of the printing industry was driven mainly by the utilitarian purpose of publishing ecclesiastical regulations and official decrees. Is Polotsky truly a transitional author, as Lydia Sazonova has argued, one straddling Latin and Slavonic literary cultures?[11] The present book aims to undermine stereotypes that suggest a seamless overlap between the seventeenth century as an opening of the mind and the fulfillment of that promise in eighteenth-century modes of writing. The idea of constant evolution does not fit with the world of a partial print culture strongly controlled by dogmatic prohibition and Church oversight because those conditions inhibited forms of continuity. Few eighteenth-century readers knew the seventeenth century or had access to texts and even a luminary like Prokopovich was best known for his public role rather than the treatise he wrote in Latin on rhetoric. The innovations of Polotsky, Istomin, and Medvedev, such as the cycle, the visual poem, the emblem poem, and the occasional ode, enjoyed little exposure in Russia or, indeed, failed to find any readership whatsoever.[12] The *Rhymed Psalter*, his metrical setting of the Psalms, a book inspired by the collection of the great Polish Renaissance poet Jan Kochanowski, was the only one of Polotsky's poetry collections to be published in his lifetime. It was the first verse setting of a Biblical book in Russian and envisaged for "use at home" but represented only a fraction of his enormous poetic achievement, which meant that his reputation scarcely outlived his lifetime.[13] Fifty years later, Polotsky's rhetorical skill, perhaps more than his religious fervor, might well have inspired the admiration of the likes of Trediakovsky and Mikhailo Lomonosov, two of the most important poetic innovators of the eighteenth century and accomplished scholars of Latin rhetoric. But Trediakovsky's knowledge of Polotsky's poetry was scant, and it was only the sight of his tombstone that occasioned a mention in the 1720s. Lomonosov's affinity to Polotsky is only attested in anecdote. It is said that when the young Lomonosov happened by chance to read some of his poems he was so impressed that, according to an eighteenth-century source (Nikolai Novikov's biographical dictionary), he decided on the spot to become a poet. But as it happens Lomonosov never mentions Polotsky, and the story is likely to be apocrypha inspired by the resemblance of two comparably hyperbolic court panegyrists rather than an example of Polotsky's legacy to a later generation. Ippolit Bogdanovich, a distinguished and charming eighteenth-century poet, too, discovered Polotsky's translations of the Psalms, called the him "un des anciens poètes russes," and declared that "this poet is not a personage to be forgotten," even though he evidently had been.[14] By the time more of Polotsky's original poems had come to light in an 1861 collection edited by the philologist F. I. Buslaev, they had already become examples of Old Russian literature written in a dead literary language.[15]

From a longer-term perspective, precedence does not seem sufficient to justify the term "progenitor," since there is little evidence for the ensuing influence on the generation of poets who began to transform Russian literature in the 1730s. None of the poets at the court of Aleksei Mikhailovich can be described as transitional, if the term is meant to suggest they represent stepping stones toward secular poetry. While many write non-liturgical verse, their understanding of enlightenment remains anchored in Christian thought with no reference to scientific reasoning or any other usual benchmark of progress and secularization. If his rhetorical practices to a degree anticipate the classicism of later seminal theorists and poets, most notably Antiokh Kantemir, Vasily Trediakovsky, and Mikhailo Lomonosov, the similarities stem from a common European poetic culture and education (Lomonosov finished the Slavo-Greco-Latin Academy), absorbed through the reading of the classics rather directly from Polotsky as primary influence.[16] Whatever their knowledge of the earlier syllabic poets, who were accessible only in manuscript, none of these three writers, collectively and individually credited with transforming eighteenth-century Russian literature, has any real debt to Polotsky's innovations, and they launched their poetic careers largely on their own merit, through their education and by emulating European models.

Nonetheless, the work of these seventeenth-century poets suggests that the traditional relationship between the tsar, the Church, and writers had entered a new phase, where literature can be practiced outside the Church provided it remains consistent with the political ideology. This anticipates a long-term trend to be consolidated with the reorganization of the Church and the loosened grip of Orthodox censorship on writing over the course of the eighteenth century. Furthermore, the entire cultural episode around Polotsky raises important theoretical questions about the relationship between the local and the distant, and the definition of the native in a geographical region defined by multiple cultural norms.

Readers, and historians of literature, always debate whether it is the norms or the exceptions that define a period. Should one speak of a Moscow Baroque or of exogenous effects of the baroque in Moscow? Furthermore, there is the question of tradition and originality, and the degree to which translation of innovative practices can initiate new trends in the target language. Within the culture of imitation, Western Renaissance and baroque poets flaunted their erudite manipulation of traditions, and Polotsky and his followers, especially Istomin, followed this example in their own writings. Polotsky's Russian works place him squarely within a Humanist tradition that measures poetic excellence more in terms of mastery and ingenuity than original invention. His sources lie largely in the writings of Jesuit theologians and a great medieval compilation, the *Magnum speculum exemplorum*, whose prose passages found reflection in syllabic poetry.[17] Most students of Polotsky's poetry see a close adherence to the sources he imitates. Quoting from Scripture and the Psalms, from diverse liturgical traditions, and from a range of neo-Latin emblem books (such as Andrea Alciati's influential *Emblematum liber* and the four copious collections of Camerarius), including plates, Polotsky fashioned a verbal art devoted to Christian allegory and moral *sententiae*. Pronouncements on subjects like luxury and sinful temptations situate him within the mainstream of homiletic culture, but the brilliance of his poetic adaptations lies in his pictorial translation of homiletic images.

The influence of a Latin-based poetics on Polotsky's style was profound. His surviving notes from his early career contain interesting passages on the nature of poetry that clearly shaped his attitude toward his vocation in Moscow. Many of his ideas are Horatian in origin, filtered through Jesuit theory. Polotsky's immediate source for his notes on rhetoric appears to have been the *Institutio poetica* by the Jesuit scholar Jacobus Pontanus, published in 1594. "What is the task of the poet?" Polotsky asks; and he answers: "The immediate or internal task is to transmit a method of fashioning connected speech. The long-term or eternal task is to teach, please, and move by means of connected speech, as is expressed in these verses."[18] Polotsky argues that poetry is the commingling of the beneficial and the pleasing, a sentiment that becomes a leitmotif of the introduction to *The Many-Flowered Vineyard*, which says:

> And so I, most sinful servant of God, having been enabled by his divine grace to see and visit flowering gardens of strange tongues and to experience soul-refreshing delights through their flowers so sweet and so beneficial to the soul, have applied every effort and no small labor so that I might bring thence the roots and seeds of divinely inspired flowers and plant and sow them again in my own domestic Slavonic language for the strengthening and protection of the Russian Church.[19]

Jesuit teaching had reconciled the use of pagan figures by Christians, and poets were free to access the myths and images of antiquity. This was a resource also open to Polotsky, and while he does draw on classical mythology he is sometimes apologetic about the references, perhaps more as a concession to the ignorance of his royal patrons than to religious constraints.

Polotsky's case is important because the juxtaposition of Christianity and paganism, acceptable in Kiev, could be rather risky in Moscow. While Polotsky enjoyed some level of royal protection, it did not extend to all aspects of his activity. The compositions of his follower Sil´vestr Medvedev were anathematized in the wake of Medvedev's execution on February 11, 1691 for his "opposition to our Mother, our Eastern Church," that is, for heresy. Medvedev began his career in a state of favor with the tsar twenty-five years earlier when he was invited to leave his position as a clerk at the Chancery of Secret Affairs and join Polotsky as a pupil and then secretary, inheriting his mentor's substantial personal library on his death in 1680. His "Epitafion," a work belonging to the cycle of quatrains of elegies commissioned by the tsar in memory of Polotsky and carved in stone on Polotsky's tomb, begins with the lamentation that "over the death of my great teacher I have wept" ("o smerti uchitelia slavna proslezisia"),[20] and focuses more on the relationship between the pupil and the master than that between a patron and a writer. It commemorates what must be the first instance of poetic discipleship in Russian literature. In 1678, Medvedev began his service at the Printing Office, eventually becoming close to the retinue of the Regent Sophia who provided ready admirers for his poems, including acrostic verses to Tsarevna Evdokia ("Pokhvala Evdokii"), declaimed in 1681 on the birthday of the tsarevna, as well as many religious poems. Medvedev had clashed with the Patriarch Ioakim on aspects of the ritual, such as the status of the sacrament of the Eucharist, and angered Grecophiles, including educators, namely, the Likhud brothers Ioanniky and Sofrony, founding figures at the Slavo-Greco-Latin Academy, and the monk Euthymius, an accomplished poet and polemicist. The downfall of the Regent Sophia left him exposed to reprisals, and his implication in a plot against Peter I led to his confinement and execution in 1691 on charges of sorcery and conspiracy.[21]

Istomin, a Russian-born pupil and sometime friend of Medvedev, served in the Printing Office (as head from 1698–1701) while holding office in the Chudov Monastery and teaching Greek in the typography school. As a Grecophile, he became embroiled in religious factions and may have participated in the discrediting of his former teacher and collaborator Medvedev. He was a court poet par excellence, the author of elegantly rendered if morally hackneyed syllabic poems for young princes. He also wrote genuinely more inventive poetry to mark various military campaigns and significant royal occasions. These include *A Book of Love to Mark a Noble Marriage: an Emblem Poem* (*Kniga liubvi znak v chesten brak: emblematicheskaia poema*: see Plate 9 for a sample allegorical figure), produced to mark the marriage of Peter I and Evdokia Lopukhina in 1689, and the *Alphabet of the Great Russian Letters...with Illustrations of Things and Moralizing Verses* (*Bukvar' slavenorossiiskikh pismen...s obrazovaniem veshchei i so nravouchitel'nymi stikhami*, 1694), an epithalamion, commissioned by the Tsaritsa Natalia Naryshkina, the mother of Peter I, for her grandson. Written in a calligraphic hand on vellum and hand-illustrated in gold and vermilion, this collection of visually spectacular poems physically communicates its status as a costly production, conferring as much prestige on the author as on the addressees.[22] In Istomin's poem, the Mind poses questions about the role of the five senses in a wedding and marriage. The answer follows on the subsequent page. The Mind and the senses are all personified, and represented on engravings. In each case there is close interplay between word and image: the departure point for the pictures are Biblical mottos that appear on the page, prompting the response. As a result, the images look out to the reader, giving the impression that the text is in dialogue with the reader. In the engraving reproduced here, the Mind is in dialogue with and instructs Vision (*Videnie*) to examine its "words used to honor the celebration of tsar" ("Slovesy smotri v chest' tsarsku otradno"). On the next page, not shown here, two astronomers follow the injunction of a citation from the book of Isaiah instructing one to raise one's eyes heavenward and examine the stars. Among the other engravings there are hands, representing the sense of Touch, shown weaving a "wreath of rejoicings," an allegorical symbol of a gift, again a response to a Biblical line from the Psalms. Istomin's contributions go beyond panegyric. Among his still unpublished works there are numerous poetic cycles on theological themes, versions of Biblical stories, and versified vituperation against the Old Belief. He was also adept at versifying moral systems as well as at writing pedagogical and didactic verse. The *Alphabet* (*Bukvar'*) appeared as a printed book with illustrations and ornamental woodcuts, and was subsequently reprinted several times in the early eighteenth century. In 1694, Istomin produced a brand new *Alphabet*, printed in twenty copies, which was bound together with an *Alphabet* authored by Polotsky in 1679. These works, dedicated to the education of "young men and women" ("for the teaching of youths and girls, men and women to write") reflect contemporary emphasis on rote learning as the standard pedagogical method but imply more than functional literacy as the expected level of their readers.[23] Like Polotsky, Istomin wrote for a small circle of elite readers and patrons, and, like Polotsky and Medvedev, he recycled much of his own poetry for comparable occasions and also for use in different genres.

New expressions and techniques

The period from the 1630s to the 1730s saw a gradual introduction of versified language arranged rhythmically and using rhyme. Epistles (*poslaniia*), petitions (*prosheniia*), and dedications (*posviashcheniia*), sometimes placed at the ends of prose works, were all written in verse. Scarcely any theoretical writing on the composition of poetry can be found in the period. In his pioneering printed *Slavonic Grammar* (*Gramatika*, 1619), which came to influence noteworthy grammarians including Vasily Adodurov (1709–80), the grammarian and lexicographer Melety Smotrytsky (1577–1633) included some notes on prosody and metrics, but he is the exception. The practice of poetry (referred to as *virshi*, generally meaning syllabic rhyming couplets) precedes any idea of poetry as a branch separate from rhetoric.[24] In a brief Latin pamphlet Polotsky wrote as a student ("Commendatio brevis Poeticae," 1646), probably synthesizing lectures he attended at the Mohyla College, Polotsky expresses the view that the poet is a creator who, like God, brings new things into being.[25] Such confidence might be thought to have informed his Horatian project of transplanting aspects of Humanist poetics to Moscow.

The emergence of a versification system organized syllabically (as in Polish) was defined by practice rather than theory.[26] Contemporaries energetically exploited a new system that was destined to be obsolete by the 1730s, which is another reason for seeing as much discontinuity as consistency between this period and the eighteenth century. In an early, pre-syllabic phase, lasting from approximately the 1630s to the 1670s, practitioners aimed at differentiating written verse from popular oral song. The shift was from the polysyllabic line of poetry with no fixed number of syllables and fixed distribution of stress toward the consistent use of a more regular verse line in which the number of syllables and frequency of stress stabilized. Toward the 1670s, practice settled on the standard use of a repertory of eleven-, twelve-, thirteen-, and fourteen-syllable lines (although six other syllabic variants were in use). About half of all of Polotsky's poetry, for instance, is in thirteen-syllable lines. What further differentiates written verse from oral is the tendency toward a more regular number of stresses per chosen number of syllables, and, increasingly, a more regular rhythmic structure that anticipates the pattern formalized in the establishment of the syllabotonic system in the eighteenth century. Whether the fixing of the stress pattern followed the natural tendency of the language toward an iambic or trochaic pattern has been the subject of modern debate.[27]

Readers of syllabic poetry—and the preponderate body of Russian syllabics comes from this time—will want to note a number of features. The first is a regular use of stress on adjoining syllables, something that becomes obsolete or exceptional in modern Russian poetry. As syllabic, rather than syllabotonic, Polotsky's poetry ignored word stress with the exception of the last word of the line where the penult was always stressed to reflect the influence of the Polish stress pattern. Another conspicuous feature is a tendency to split the line regularly into two parts (or hemistichs) through the use of a caesura. The thirteen-syllable line has a caesura after the seventh syllable, the eleven-syllable line after the fifth. The second hemistich of both the eleven- and thirteen-syllable lines contains six syllables and has a required stress on the penultimate syllable.

Such a division suited the tendency toward definition and aphorism adopted by many poets, evidence of a sometimes Latin rhetorical style prizing control and the manifestation of reason through cleverness. These features may be illustrated in representative couplets selected from Polotsky (in which the use of feminine rhyme remains a cast-iron feature) as in his celebrated description of spiritual concentration:

> Монаху подобает в келии седети,
> Во посту молится, нищетою терпети,
> Искушения врагов, сильно побеждати
> И похоти плотския труды умерщвляти.[28]

> It is appropriate for a monk to sit in his cell,
> To pray during a fast, to endure poverty,
> The taunting of enemies, to conquer decisively
> And to deaden the desire of the flesh through work.

Polotsky also varies management of his verse line through the use of internal rhymes, or Leonine verse. The Latin Leonine verse consisted of hexameters, or hexameters alternating with pentameters, where the final word rhymed with the word preceding the caesura. In Polotsky's Leonine verse, the number of syllables varies from poem to poem, but was always an even number: thus the rhyming hemistichs are of equal length. For an example of twelve-syllable Leonine verse we may turn to the epitaphs for Tsarevna Evdokiia:

> Аз бех Евдокия, роди мя Мария.
> Увидех свет, увядох яко свет.
> От царей рожденна, в гроб сей водворенна.

> I was Evdokia, Maria gave birth to me.
> I saw the light/world, I perished like light.
> Born of tsars, I am laid in this tomb.

Internal rhyme combined with rhyming couplets is one source of variation. This effect can be sampled in a quatrain from the *Rifmologion*, "A Song on the Delight of the World Translated from the Polish Dialect into Slavonic" ("Pesn' iz pol'skogo dialekta, perevedennaia na slavianskii, o prelesti mira," n.d.), with its commentary on the vanity of human wishes:

> Есть прелесть в свете, як в полном цвете, эту ты остави,
> Возлюбленная, душе грешная, от злоб воспряни.
> Преходит время, а грехов бремя тя угнетает:
> Демон же смелый, на тебе стрелы яд свой выпускает.[29]

> The world is delightful in full bloom, and this you reject.
> O beloved sinful soul, awaken from evil.
> Time passes, and the burden of sins weighs you down,
> While the brazen devil aims his poison arrows at you.

Caesura creates three intonational segments, offsetting the usual symmetry of hemistichs. This patterned style was in fact common to numerous poets, whether clerks without much formal training in poetry, adept at bureaucratic jargon, or the 1680s' masters, fully educated in classical poetics, engaged in private meditations and personal confessions. Their speech is erudite and their cadences are formal rather than folksy, although their locution is not specifically designated as poetic. None strive for metrical sophistication. In search of expressive means, they regularly employ tropes such as sound orchestration, exclamation, apostrophe, and metaphor, prosodic features much used in sermons, a genre in which the practice of word-weaving continued to be strong.

Invention and ingenuity appear in playful formal variation, associated with the baroque aesthetic of contrast and dynamic tension between control and variation. In a similar vein, many literary epistles composed by the Chancery poets are acrostics that spell out the names of the addressees. The device of the acrostic was regarded more as a sign of literary elegance than as a formal camouflage. The acrostic was known in Russian by the Greek word *akrostikhida* or the Russian *kraegranesie/kraegranie* (also used to refer to "rhyme"). Numerous ephemeral figures whose extant published work consists sometimes of single compositions made use of the device. Interest in testing forms is one feature that creates a semblance of a cohort or school (Panchenko's preferred term). Amplification, multiplicity, and intricacy were baroque stylistic features that even Orthodox monks assimilated. Even the monks of the New

Jerusalem Monastery, a bastion of Patriarch Nikon's Grecophile followers, wrote inscriptions abundantly.[30]

The ingenuity and sheer productivity of court writers marked a watershed. As poets, rather than just versifiers, they proved capable of dazzling displays of erudition, formal versatility, visual and rhetorical complexity. Whether in manuscript books intended for limited private circulation or in performance at court recitals of poetry, they pull out all the stops. In transferring the tropes, structures, and visual designs that had a long tradition in Western and Central European Renaissance courts into Russian, Polotsky and others achieved a great feat of originality.

Ceremonial or occasional poetry showcased both the new position of the poet at court and the position of the royal family. In terms of production, the situation of poetry in the 1680s was reverse to that of ode writers in the eighteenth century: in the seventeenth century, a handful of poets authored a large number of lines, whereas in the eighteenth century a large number of poets produced relatively little. Royal birthdays were the bread and butter of court poets everywhere. Polotsky excels at using the monumental structure as vehicles for more delicate structures devised for a ritual occasion, impressing with both grandeur and readability. A summary of one of his celebratory works is illustrative. On the birth of Tsarevich Petr (later Peter the Great), Polotsky composed a cycle of thematically linked mini-cycles. The first large section presents a series of twenty six-line epigrams of congratulation to and benediction (*zhelaniia*) upon the members of the court who would have been present when the poem was declaimed, including the Patriarch Ioakim, the tsar and family members, such as Peter Alekseevich, alluded to through wordplay as we see in this example:

> Петр имя камене толком знаменает,
> Камень же твердость собою являет.
> Петр убо, брат твой, тверду тебе быти,
> Непозыблему на престоле жити
> Радостно хощет и да победиши
> Вся Голиафы, егда я узриши.[31]

> The name Peter means rock,
> And rock embodies firmness.
> Thus Peter, your brother, wants you to be firm,
> Unshakably installed on your throne.
> He joyfully wishes that you vanquish
> Every Goliath whenever you see one.

The next poem in the sequence is a labyrinth poem based on the phrase "Long live Simeon" ("Mnoga leta Simeonu"), incorporating a tribute on his birthday to the late Tsarevich Simeon Alekseevich, deceased in 1669 at the age of four. Elegy for the dead child and celebration of a new birth are juxtaposed.

The term labyrinth has been applied to most of Polotsky's ornamental poems in which the words are laid out geometrically in the shape of a figure like a cube (by which a square or rectangle can be meant). Poems composed with this degree of formal skill (and this includes the use of acrostic) are examples of *carmina curiosa*, as they are called in rhetorical handbooks and Humanist manuals on poetics, and Polotsky's mastery is impressive. Exercises in cleverness (or *acumen*), poems written in this manner are devised to showcase the art of invention (*inventio*). Their project is to find new expressions for familiar sentiments and in doing so they adopt visual means. Poems that are calligraphic conceive the poem as a signifier whose shape ought best to match the signified. For poems about the heart Polotsky formats the poem to assume the shape of a heart on the page as in a forty-line poem that uses the heart as an emblem. As the poem explains, God desires a man's heart like his gold and silver, and wants to take up residence in the heart. At the same time, the poet is drawing the tsar's attention back to himself as the humble servant presenting his poetic offering, for the heart, as it transpires, is in fact Polotsky's own heart, out of the abundance of which his mouth speaks. The heart is an emblem and bears an appropriate symbol taken from the Gospels: "Of the abundance of the heart his mouth speaketh" (Luke 6: 45). Similarly, a poem written in the shape of a star corresponds to an image of New Testament Annunciation. Polotsky likens this star to the one that guided the magi to Bethlehem, and hopes that its function will be similar, namely to proclaim the tsarevich's birth far and wide so that from all four corners of the earth men might come and do him homage. Polotsky's emblem poems are designed to give pleasure and reveal the joy of creating special structures for the occasion.

In the case of calligraphic figures, words arranged consecutively follow the shape of the designated emblem. One glance suffices to know a key image. Labyrinth poems that are not calligraphic are cast as geometric shapes. Like all the puzzles implanted in Polotsky's verse, they are designed to intrigue and their meaning cannot be exhausted at a single glance since repetition is their main trope. Their starting point is often a single motto from which a pattern is built. Among the most used formulas is the phrase "many years" (*mnoga leta*) or its variants. The phrase is a motif in Polotsky's occasional verse including the original cantata that brought him to the tsar's attention, and its associated motto "Reign many years" ("Tsarstvui mnoga leta") also can form the nucleus of a labyrinth as is the case in Figure 11.06. "Many years" is used to express a wish for the longevity of the reign, to celebrate an occasion, and even to commemorate the dead. Lyrics written at the appearance of the tsar and his family use the phrase to apostrophize them at the start of a cycle of poems, and the phrase provides a building block for the verbal edifice that is the labyrinth, and an Ariadne's thread through the verbal maze for the reader.

It is the unusual arrangement of the words that makes these poems curiosities or exercises in ingenuity as the reader works out how many different combinations the poem uses to encrypt its meaning. In a labyrinth, the initial letter of the phrase may occur in the very center of the block, or in the top left-hand corner, or in the middle of the top line. These geometric poems are devised to increase the number of line combinations in which the motto is laid out. The eye is meant to follow the sequence of letters horizontally across a line, vertically down the first line of the block, diagonally from one corner of the cube to its opposite on a straight line, and often reading in reverse, like a palindrome. The line can spell backwards the same words spelled out when moving forward from the other end, and when the first word and the last word of the line are the same, this is serpentine verse, as the effect is called, a further example of cleverness (or *ingenium*). Other less obvious ways to combine the letters can also operate, and the reader must do some work to pick out the chess-like rules that guide the eye in forming combinations that can be ladder-like, moving one down left, one down right, and so on. Labyrinths may look dauntingly impenetrable but the poet does not want to defeat comprehension. As a courtesy or sign of condescension, Polotsky's practice is to position a short poem of instruction to the reader on how to proceed at the top.

Two examples can show us what can be built around a single phrase such as *mnogo leta*. With characteristic hyperbole, Polotsky's "Verses on the Advent" ("Metry na prishestvie," 1664) wish the tsar a reign commensurate with the number of the labyrinth's combinations. He then appends twenty-four separate greetings (*privetstva*) offering precepts expressed through analogy with Biblical episodes. The entire set begins with the following instruction:

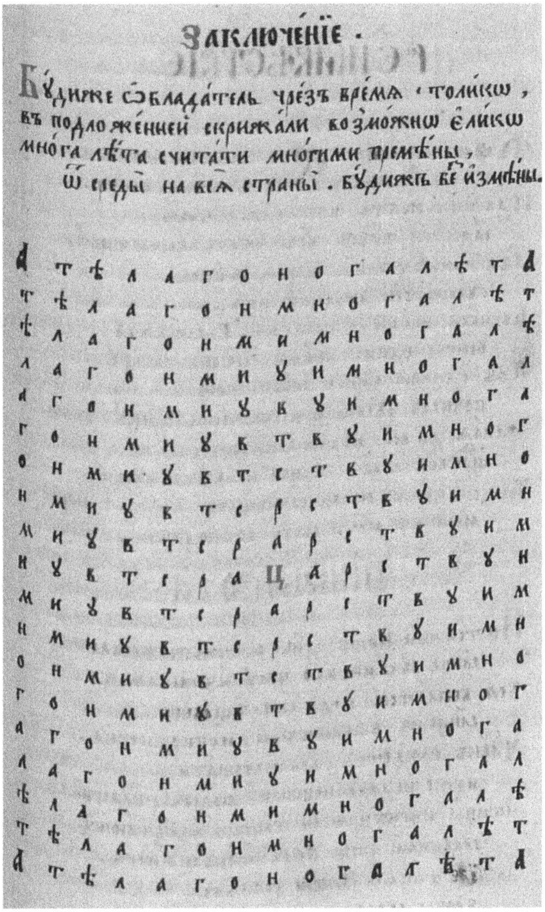

FIGURE 11.06. Simeon Polotsky, *The Harmonious Lyre* (Moscow, 1676), labyrinth.

Начало в кентре, чтется во вся страны,
От всех стран буди, Царь, почитаны.
Елики путьми лет есть се читати,
Толико лет ти даждь Бог царсвовати.[32]

Start in the center and read in any direction,
May you be, Tsar, honored by all nations.
As many years as it takes to read this,
May God grant you as many years of reign.

The sequence of advent (or salutation) poems come in varied form: an initial geometric labyrinth is followed by a poem patterned in the shape of an eight-pointed star, the contours of which are created by sixteen lines of verse. A thread through the poems can be a motto or phrase that recurs.

A more extensive example comes from a page from *The Harmonious Lyre*, a poem set out as a block of fifteen letters across and nineteen down (see Figure 11.06). At the center of the picture stands the capital letter Ц (colored in red) clearly intended as a starting point for the reader who can then pick out phrases in multiple directions: the phrase can be found by moving up or down that column vertically; the sense can be assembled by moving to the left or to the right of Ц; the phrase emerges when we read by moving one letter to the left and then up and symmetrically one to the right and one up; and it is even possible to trace the letters through a radius. If one chooses the corners of the cube as starting points then more possibilities unfold. As the verse instruction given in the header to the page says, it is possible "to read *mnoga leta* in many ways [*mnogimi peremeny*]." As in everything he did, Simeon's accomplishment was on a larger scale. But other poets also dabbled in these forms. For example, the monk Evstraty (*fl. c.*1700–25), one of many ephemeral versifiers, produced labyrinthine curiosities, while Polotsky's pupil Medvedev borrowed many ideas, forms, and calqued verbal phrases for his own elaborate poems from the works of his teacher.[33]

The use of ornament is an important feature of the poetry of the *Rifmologion*. The chief function of ornament is, of course, to adorn, but its relation to the overall structure of the collection is like that of architectonic decoration to a building in the baroque period. Embellishment helps to propel the poem forward and to give an impression of movement within the stasis of a huge poetic book. Like baroque architecture that combines mass with movement, weight with an upward thrust, and individual detail with the overall structure, Polotsky's use of poetic ornament creates an impression of movement and dynamics that relieve the potentially oppressive tone of the long poems. The funeral cycle "Threnodies or Dirges" on the death of Tsaritsa Maria stands in sharp contrast to the jubilation of *The Russian Eagle*. The poem consists of a series of twelve laments, each one followed by a consolation. The prevailing feeling is one of heaviness as one long section follows another, with all ornamentation reserved for the concluding pages. The first lament, written as though from the point of view of the tsar, is followed by the consolation of faith; the tsareviches are comforted by hope, the tsarevnas by charity, the clergy by piety, and so on; dark and light sections alternate. This series is matched in the second part of the ode, where the dead tsaritsa addresses parting words to each of those who have mourned her death. The work closes with two labyrinths, nine epitaphs, and nine emblems. Architecturally, it "could perhaps be compared to a mausoleum adorned with the usual symbols of death."[34] Polotsky's monumental verse also serves as scaffolding for conspicuous display of classical learning. The monumental structure of the odes was obviously deliberate and too elaborate for recitation.

The influence of Kievan Humanism is pervasive. Classical ornamentation freely intermingles with Christian themes and imagery. This is a recognizable feature of the baroque, an aesthetic taught at Mohyla's College, in which the classical and the Christian work together, regardless of any inherent doctrinal tension between paganism and Orthodoxy.[35] Ever the educator, Polotsky was not one to forfeit an opportunity to kindle interest in the rich heritage of classical antiquity.

Visual poetry added to the repertory of forms within larger cycles and as single works. Polotsky's *The Russian Eagle* uses the same emblems as the Bible of 1663, associating the tsar's titles and seals with deluxe book production. Simon Franklin concludes that Polotsky's work remained "a monument of elite manuscript production," and there was no analogous development in print culture until Magnitsky's lengthy acrostic verse in his *Arifmetika* of 1703.[36] Acrostics, typography, and graphic design were used as displays of cleverness but also to give a concrete form to an abstraction like a virtue (and therefore in the baroque tradition of making the intangible tangible).[37] Sil′vestr Medvedev's "Inscription to a Portrait of Tsarevna Sophia" ("Nadpis′ k portretu tsarevny Sof′i," 1687; Figure 11.07) takes the emblems of virtues embossed around the portrait as its theme. Surrounding Sophia's portrait are allegorical figures representing a mixture of Christian and classical virtues as attributes of the just ruler: moving clockwise from the top, they are Chastity (*Tselomudrie*), Justice (*Pravda*), Spiritual Hope (*Nadezhda Bozhestvennaia*), Courage (*Velikodushie*), Charity (*Shchedrota*), and Faith (*Blagochestie*). The inscription is printed as an inset poem in the base (perhaps altar) on which Sophia's

FIGURE 11.07. L. Tarasevich, Engraving of Sophia surrounded by the seven virtues, with inscriptions, 1687.

portrait rests, a clever device for creating a verbal icon out of iconography. The tribute intends to help legitimate the subject's claims to the throne.[38] She is praised as "ruling rightfully" ("pravdoderzhanna") because, on the one hand, she is wise and strong like Elizabeth I ("Elisavef Britanska skipetroderzhashchi") and, on the other, deserving of comparison to the Babylonian Empress Semiramis, as Catherine II would later be, since she is prepared to wage war.

Nobody was more prolific in this mode than Polotsky. Beyond their panegyric function, emblems could serve to represent the glory of God and divine attributes through objects. Hippisley has identified more than eighty separate emblems in Polotsky's work, of which at least thirty are drawn from the animal and insect kingdoms.[39] All derive from European emblem books, some of which had been translated into Russian and were kept in the Synod Typographical Collection to which Polotsky and fellow courtier-poets had access. Internal references and titles suggest that Polotsky nurtured a hope of producing his own book of emblems (in the event the first such book, *Symbola et emblemata*, was published in Amsterdam in 1705 for Peter the Great). While Polotsky's use of sources demonstrates the degree to which learning defined the poetic vocation, and scholars rightly admire his skill in assimilating sources to his own voice, his syllabic verse affords pleasure on its own terms for its evident skill in matching image and spiritual message. On occasion, emblem poems on the subject of the soul and spirit explored a more theological vein. Emblems also represented human qualities, and Polotsky produced his fair share of zoomorphic hieroglyphs to signify attributes such as the mole standing for the moral blindness of the venal, the lion a polyvalent symbol for bravery, Christ, and vigilance. Consider how the following verses about the "wisdom of tranquility" use the peacock to symbolize both vanity and humility:

> Елма перие пав свое смотряет,
> …зело кичиво весь ся надымает.
> Егда же ног си черность созерцает,
>   абие гордость свою оставляет.
> Ты аще дела благая узриши
>   в тебе, и того деля ся гордиши,
> Призри на злая, коль люта и многа.
> Отригни гордость, знай тебе у Бога.[40]

> When the peacock looks at its own plumage
> It puffs up most boastfully.
> But no sooner does it gaze on the blackness of its feet,
>   Than it abandons its pride.
> If you should see good deeds
>   In yourself and take pride in them,
> Consider your own evil deeds, wicked and many as they are.
> Cast off your pride, and find yourself in God.

In creating visual tropes of great complexity, often far more intricate than those provided by his sources, Polotsky excels in representing the hazards, such as poverty, that await the seeker of the Christian virtues of patience, humility, peace, faith, hope, and charity. An equal number of vices threaten salvation, and Polotsky does not hesitate to resort to classical mythology, normally shunned in Muscovite writing, in order to generate narrative momentum and dramatic effect. Like Polotsky, and possibly even more dramatically, Istomin sees no barriers between his visual emblems and their verbal expressions, and experiments with isomorphic expressions.

To the extent that certain emblems can be represented with words on the page or illustrated iconographically, the visual and the verbal become interchangeable. Poetry becomes a unique vehicle for spiritual perception (*zrenie dukhovnoe*). Perhaps the most spectacular calligraphic poems of the period are the distichs in Istomin's *Book of Love* arranged in the shape of a heart. Studies of the manuscripts have conjectured that later connoisseurs bound Istomin and Polotsky's works together as manuscript books in order to confer on Istomin a distinction equal to Polotsky's fame as a "learned poet" (*poeta doctus*), a Humanist ideal.

Paradise regained: Simeon Polotsky's poetic garden

We return to *The Many-Flowered Vineyard* in order to explore briefly the moral aspects to which Simeon, more than any other writer of the time, devoted his intricate art. His achievements in cultivating a poetic garden, the elaborate cyclical form widely popular in continental Europe, put Moscow poetry on par with the baroque style practiced in Ruthenia. At the same time as Polotsky elaborated his vast labyrinth of poems in Moscow, in Kiev, Antony Radivilovsky (1620–88; Antin Radyvylovsky, Ukr.) published the *Garden of Mary* (*Ogorodok Marii*, 1676) in which many poems are arranged according to Church feast days. Poetic gardens are allegorical spaces in which various virtues are put on display for the reader entering the purer world of the isolated garden in order to cultivate his own moral improvement.

What are the symbolic properties of this garden of virtue? The frontispiece to Polotsky's book, a magnificent hand-colored polychrome illustration, aptly depicts a beautifully cultivated garden of colorful flowers that is fenced off, and at the bottom of the fence the gateway is closed. An enclosure of scriptural quotation and Christian precepts keep entry to the garden exclusive. The baroque *hortus* is a virtual space that the reader, assumed to be devout and equipped to open the lock, enters with the intention of culling the moral lessons that "grow" in each poem, and in so doing eradicating vice. Whatever path the reader takes, whether to proceed through a maze of poems or alphabetically by topic, the promise is one of moral transfiguration because the garden, or especially the vineyard, represents a closed conceptual space that fosters certain ethical matters. Outside this space of contemplation, and inside the world where vice beckons with its temptations, man forfeits the proper environment in which to strive for his own perfection. Outside the garden, man is like a roadside tree, its foliage torn by passersby, and repeatedly the approved worshipper is promised the reward of beauty and goodness.

The notion of a garden of virtue owes more than a few allusions to the Old and New Testaments, for there it is also closely associated with the Passion of Christ and the parable of the bad vintners (Mark 12: 1–12) and with the world of Genesis. In the parable, the grapevine (*vinograd*) is the individual soul; the fence represents the rules that cannot be transgressed; and man is a gardener whose duty lies in spiritual cultivation. This parable seems to have enjoyed certain popularity among Ukrainian churchmen. It appears frequently in the sermons of Lazar Baranovich's *Spiritual Sword* (*Mech Dukhovnyi*) and Polotsky's posthumous *Spiritual Repast*. It is in the world of the garden of virtue that the transgressions of Eden and Gethsemane can be made right, at least symbolically. In the Garden of Eden, as Polotsky says, Adam succumbed to temptation, but in the new garden the devil must be vanquished by a second Adam who is Christ; man's fall transpired in a garden, and so his rebirth must also take place in a garden. Hence the vineyard signaled to the reader that the virtue that grows in the writer's poetry is like a garden of Christian variety.

As an image and as a form, the poetic garden perfectly unites the means and the message. Like virtue and the virtuous, the garden is a deliberately crafted medium, an orderly world: its structure is an aesthetic analogue of the ethical virtue it aims to convey. Just as gardens vary in their design, so does the poetic garden, as a collection of genres exhibit variety rather than uniformity. The baroque aesthetic delights in sharp contrasts between high and low, rough and smooth, light and darkness. The prolific image-making and the scale intended to rouse emotion are essential to communication. Polotsky did not believe in pruning his garden very much. By living up to the scale and intricacy of this aesthetic, and allying to it a message about the glory of Orthodoxy and absolutism, Polotsky showed confidence in a cultural turn he worked to secure in Moscow. On every page the reader encounters verse meditations on worldly themes such as power and politics (Augustus [*Avgustus*], citizenship [*grazhdanstvo*], worth [*dostoinstvo*], clemency [*milost' gospodskaia*], honor [*chest'*]); intellectual value (such as art [*khudozhestvo*], reading [*chtenie*], talent [*talant*]); ethics and psychology (such as drunkenness [*p'ianstvo*], moderation [*mernost'*], appetite [*lakomstvo*], love of fame [*slavoliubie*]); and the human predicament as affected by phenomena such as disaster (*pogibel'*), the vanity of human wishes (*prekhodiat vsia*), calumny (*kleveta*), marriage (*zhenit'ba*), and desire (*zhen blizost'*). Or, as Polotsky states in "Man" ("Chelovek"), one of the final mini-cycles in his *Many-Flowering Vineyard*:

> Мир малый человек есть, а конец познает,
> да изменою смерти вечность зачинает.[41]

> Man is a world in miniature that knows his bounds,
> So that death may alternate with eternity.

From the 1630s to the 1690s, poets certainly flaunt their cleverness and take pleasure in artful contrivance, often deployed in letters among friends. But these displays of wit link mental sharpness to a belief in rational conduct that is benevolent and consistent with the decorum to be ascribed to those who work in proximity to the tsar and the great men of the court.

Friendship

Most of the poets discussed here treat proper conduct as an essential topic, making it a matter of personal belief and confessional propriety. The motif of friendship runs through Chancery poetry—friendship is a tribute of respect earned through learning and position, and recognized through reciprocity extended to trusted allies as a form of protection. We may be reluctant to go along with the view that these writers form an "intelligentsia," a term that has been sometimes used to describe them and that seems anachronistic. Yet the individual writers in this network of epistolary exchanges and solitary poems exhibited the mentality of a coterie because they shared the values of moral virtue, religious faith, and personal loyalty. Chancery poets, and later writers at court, espoused Orthodoxy as a moral code rather than a matter of ritual. Bound by Christian love, friends could ponder the wickedness of man and exalt the importance of Christian morals. Moods brighten when poets write to one another. Learning and education comprise one of the key themes in these epistles. In an epistle to his young pupil, the prince Mikhail Nikitich Odoevsky, the monk and printer Savvaty conveys the message that learning and morality should be inseparable. His notion of learning exceeds mere knowledge of Scripture to encompass admiration for secular books, which were treated with suspicion by conservatives like the Old Believers in the 1660s. In this particular epistle, Savvaty warns against gossip, spite, and meanness of spirit.

Likewise, the workplace required reflection about correct conduct. The theme of favor and disfavor, and demotion and promotion, occupied these writers who understood how much depends on protection, here described as "grace" or "favor" (*milost'*). Many poems offered advice on how to stay on the right side of the powerful. The reasons for currying favor are not entirely self-interested because poets saw compassion for one another as an aspect of mentoring.

Chancery poetry can seem to send a mixed message: while urging their addressees to practice virtue, these poets also dispensed shrewd advice on how to climb the shaky career ladder, how to cultivate the favor of the mighty without compromising one's virtue. These writers were the first in Russia to explore the tension between reciprocity and dignity, and the potential contradiction between worldliness and virtue. Their concerns testify to the growing importance of the court, and to the greater social mobility that fiction of the period reflects. The rise of a merchant class and increasing urbanization came at a time when historic social hierarchies were under pressure, changes visible to Chancery poets at the heart of government. *Mestnichestvo* was the complicated system of seniority that regulated the allocation of government posts to boyars, determined precedence at state functions (see Figure II.08 for a modern image of tsar and courtiers) and also determined physical and symbolic proximity to the tsar on ceremonial occasions. It atrophied under the expansion of the chanceries and was abolished in 1682.

Epistles, written to friends bound to the author by Christian love and class ties, feature reflections on fate, morality, and ethical problems, sometimes offered as consolation in times of grief. In an epistle to the nobleman Semen Ivanovich Shakhovskoi, Savvaty comforts his correspondent, a man he praises as "learned in the way of ecclesiastical writing," acknowledging the "cloud of despondence" or trouble hanging over him at the office. More than a few poems are utilitarian petitions in which the author sets out his dissatisfaction with his lot, usually the result of disfavor, bad luck, youthful transgressions, and lack of status. These epistles hint at the poet's situation and give details of his working conditions: the authors are educated men, but neither financially independent nor secure in their posts, and therefore sensitive to patronage. Some addressees are people of great power, occasionally members of the royal household. The Chancery poets view the world as destabilized by ambition and deceit. The sole advice they give is to remain vigilant and ambitious for oneself. Savvaty, however, remains true to his emphasis on thinking and reason as the basis for good conduct. But obedience to the monarch is the ultimate standard as he advised the scribe V. S. Prokof'iev:

FIGURE II.08. Andrei Ryabushkin, *Zemsky sobor c.*1645 under Tsar Alexis (Aleksei Mikhailovich Romanov), consultation with a council of boyars, 1893.

Вельми преудивляюся твоему благоумию,
А не вем, как написати тебе по своему недоразумию.
Светлому бо царскому величеству предстоиши,
И рождьшее от него премудрому разуму учиши.[42]

I feel amazement at your intelligence,
And cannot write to you due to my own poor comprehension.
For when you appear in the holy presence of the tsar,
He imparts to you the highest wisdom.

Savvaty's poems repeatedly juxtapose the positive values of genuine wisdom (*mudrost'*) and reason (*um/razum*) with cunning (*lukavstvo*) and stealth (*zlokhitrost'*). Human error, impossible to avoid and often damaging, requires understanding as a passive flaw. But the two forms of piety, Orthodox faith and moral behavior toward others, are inseparable for many of these writers, whether the author be an aristocrat like Prince Shakhovskoy, writing to the Old Believer Prince D. M. Pozharsky, or Savvaty, a clergyman, who in his "Epistle to Mikhail" ("Poslanie Mikhailu") uses poetry to extol the virtue of candor. To aid a friend in his tasks and career is seen as morally right, especially when, as Savvaty puts it, "his heart crumbles from a great shame" and a friend is in a position to "help during a period of royal disfavor."[43]

In another epistolary poem, Savvaty cautions that "corrupted words" only barely hide the cunning of a flattering friend, while the value of an unflattering friend may be "high and stable," his value comparable "to the shining illumination of the solar circle." Prince Ivan Khvorostinin (d. 1625), earlier disgraced for abetting the Pretender during the Time of Troubles, speaks firsthand in uttering a prayer for the "many Christians who from the tsars and unreasonable rulers receive many ills" and denouncing "schemers." The initial letters of the first ten lines of his poem "A Prayer to Christ the Lord" ("Molitva Khristu Bogu," *c*.1620s) spell out the phrase "Overcome evil" ("PREVODI ZLA" [*ПРЕВОДИ ЗЛА*]). Like Savvaty, he underscores the importance of conscience (*sovest'*) as a moral touchstone although in Khvorostinin's case morality is more explicitly a matter of religious confession and strict adherence to Orthodoxy, unlike the position of Savvaty who pragmatically advocates success as the measure of loyalty and decency.

In twenty-five couplets of the "Request" ("Proshenie"), Mikhail Zlobin (*fl.* 1st half of the seventeenth century) elaborates the ethical criteria that deeds must satisfy to be truly moral. Sanction and reward, while seen as part of the economy of friendship, also speak to standards of reasonableness (*razum*) defined in terms of religious belief. "Can there be anyone who does not genuinely understand / How readily one invokes God in good deeds?" he enquires, and similarly announces that "Should anyone's unlimited favor be generous to us / Then truly God does promise to grant manifold reward."[44] These sentiments are not exclusive to Chancery poetry; they are expressed more broadly as part of the ethical component of didactic Christian poetry linking piety and virtue. For instance, Karion Istomin opens his poetic "Household Conduct" ("Domostroi," 1696) by announcing right thinking as the basis of personal conduct:

Сию книжницу возми в десницу,
Чти и помни стихи словни,
Младый, старый в разум правый.[45]

Grasp this book in your right hand,
Read and remember these verses,
Young and old, you obey reason.

The source of wisdom and reason remains the proper attention to prayer and good deeds described in the complete poem, fourteen twelve-line stanzas that cover a single day from morning till nighttime. The literary epistle as a genre goes on to have an illustrious career in modern Russian literature, starting in the eighteenth century and flourishing in the Pushkin period when the art of concealing one's anxieties behind polite formulae becomes much more elaborate.

Mortality

Poetry regularly expresses a preoccupation with mortality consistent with trends seen elsewhere in Europe, such as metaphysical poetry in Poland and England. The Russian theme of *memento mori* comes packaged in short forms. Few poets aspire to the grandeur Polotsky achieves in his ceremonial verse, *Threnodies*, or to be experienced in the elaborately moving sequences produced by a master of the Polish baroque, Jan Kochanowski (1530–84) in his *Laments* (*Treny*, 1580). Dozens of poems that treat the subject reveal an intimate handling of personal themes, and tend toward brevity and rhetorical simplicity. If none of the poets ever attain quite the heights or metaphysical complexities of a John Donne (1573– 1631) or the radiant simplicity of George Herbert (1593-1633), they constitute an impressive first chapter in the history of the Russian elegy. Istomin's "Verses on Remembering Death through a Welcome" ("Stikhi vospominati smert' privetstvom" 1696), a cycle of four poems, explore death as a contradictory predicament, a type of contradiction often described as typically baroque in its paradoxical contrasts. In the first three poems, twelve-syllable rhyming couplets use antithesis and balance to construct a sideways movement between lapses into the temptations of mortal life and intermittent spiritual awakening. No matter how hard writer and reader try to attain certitude and a breakthrough into salvation, the undertow of earthly life prevails. In the fourth and final poem, written in the manner of a song, Istomin splits twelve decasyllables into two columns: a strong caesura divides the hemistichs, and rhyme occurs internally between the last words of each half but not between the consecutive vertical lines. These internal rhymes have a semantic cogency, bringing together "appearance" and "wonder" (*iavliusia / nedoumliusia*), "grace" and "sweetness" (*blagost' / sladost'*), and "time" and "burden" (*vremia / bremia*).

Poems can also be worldly and use death as an occasion to rehearse secular achievements. At the Voskresenky New Jerusalem Monastery, the Abbot German (d. 1681) was an outstanding poet (as well as composer) at this center of monastic verse culture. An acquaintance of Polotsky and Medvedev, he experimented with different stanza forms. He was a past master of the acrostic verse, to which he set the hymnography of the *typikon*, or prayer book, used by the brethren. His "Epitaph to the Patriarch Nikon," ("Epitafii patriarkhu," n.d.) written in rhyming couplets and carved on Nikon's tombstone, begins by noting the "good six years" of Nikon's tenure amid religious strife, and then charts the career of the patriarch who after his fall from office retreated to the New Jerusalem Monastery and performed "many fine deeds" (*sovershal mnogikh trudov*).[46]

In its twelve quatrains, Sil'vestr Medvedev's "Epitafion" for Simeon Polotsky (Figure 11.09) combines biography, poetic conceit, and typical baroque images of *memento mori* by reviewing the facts of Polotsky's career and praising him for his moral virtues and for his creativity. Speaking as a "dignified monk, a lover of ingenuity" ("Ieromonakh chestnyi, liubitel' chestnoty"), he helps the reader rehearse the acceptance of death over all forty-eight lines. In the process, Medvedev coins the unusual compound noun "unremembered-malice" ("nepamiatozlobie"), and also integrates the titles of Polotsky's poetic works into the epitaph, rhyming the title *Rifmologion* with *Besedoslovie*, a homiletic collection, in the ninth quatrain of the poem:

FIGURE 11.09. Sil′vestr Medvedev, Funerary epitaph for Simeon Polotsky, 1680.

> Вечерю, Псалтырь, стихи со Рифмословием,
> Вертоград многоцветный с Беседословием.
> Вся оны книги мудрый он муж сотворивый,
> В научение роду российску явивый.[47]

> For the evening, the Psalter, verses that are Rhymes,
> The Many-flowered garden with the book of Homilies,
> All these books a single wise man created,
> Revealed them for the edification of the Russian people.

A syllabic elegy by the Chancery poet Petr Samsonov (*fl.* first half of the seventeenth century) declares that consolation is an essential gesture of friendship:

> Мужественно убо слово весть всегда печаль утешати,
> И беседа ближняго может твердость скорби разрушати.[48]

> For a brave word is always able to comfort grief,
> And the conversation of an intimate is able to dissolve the hardness of sorrow.

The entire poem is built around a definition of bravery and "brave-heartedness" (*khrabroserdie*) in the imaginative coinage of this clerk. Solemnity does not preclude verbal ingenuity, and seventeenth-century poets are highly accomplished and consistent in moderating the personal through consideration of the universal. This seems to be the legacy of their knowledge of the Psalter, but is hard to detach from the influence of foreign poetry, especially the Polish baroque with its strong tradition of lamentations and funerary verse. Like a preacher, the poet often

aims to suggest the grief of the larger community of readers of the epitaph and other mourn-
ers. Lamentation has a paradoxical quality of distanced intimacy.

In the "Epitaph for Dmitry Rostovsky" ("Epitafiia Dimitriiu Rostovskomu," c.1709) Yavorsky
celebrates a distinguished preacher, and begins with the universal declaration that "everyone
who is not stupid ['um imeia ne temnyi'] has need of verses of mourning" from which he
spins a brief moral on how mourning occasions a contemplation of death. To "people enlightened in faith" ("liudie v vere prosveshchenii") he attributes a monkish calm and passivity
("krotsy i smirenny") that will permit, beyond sorrow, prayer for the departed. Yet while the
Abbot German casts death as a "faithful proof / of the love of God" ("bozhiia liubvi dnes' /
pokazanie nelozhnoe"), hints of individual loss and personal loss can appear.[49] By contrast, in
his "Epitaph to P. T. Semennikov" ("Epitafiia P. T. Semennikovu,"1668), Istomin treats death as
the accomplishment of the sacraments, and therefore a cause to rejoice. The poet weaves into
his lines the exact date of his friend's death (he may not have known his age or the year of
birth), and uses deictic rhetoric to point out the tomb and the body of the deceased, evidence
of parting and grief.

At the end of the period, Feofan Prokopovich's short stanzaic lyric "O Vain Man, Threadbare
Slave" ("O suetnyi cheloveche, rabe nekliuchimy," n.d.), first published in 1769 by the learned
eighteenth-century antiquarian and polymath Nikolai Kurganov, invokes the tone of
Ecclesiastes in asking why the fear of death is dangerous. Grief, says the speaker, is "limitless,"
and then asks us to imagine death as a "pit," to find mortality "a terrifying truth," because life
is a sickness and robs mortals of the capacity to see God.[50] Yet the poem protests too much
in denying the fear of death and plays off an ironic gap between its posture of sangfroid and
its use of language to cause even greater terror. This degree of awareness about the psychological power of physical detail anticipates the technique the eighteenth-century poet Gavriila
Derzhavin will employ in voicing human truths.

One later exception to the tendency to brevity is Petr Buslaev's (fl. 1720s) Cogitation on the
Soul (Umozritel'stvo dushevnoe, 1734). While this work, dating to the eighteenth century, demonstrates how long baroque poetics lingered. Written in memory of Maria Stroganova, this
substantial cycle of sonnet-like poems forms a 200-line diptych in which the first part narrates
her decline and death, joining the language of a philosophical treatise with observations on
the body. The second part develops an extensive comparison between the dead subject and her
namesake the Virgin Mary, culminating in Maria Stroganova's ascension to heaven.

5

Prose

Popular fiction for a disrupted age: Social satire or literary fantasy?

As we have seen in the preceding chapters, the seventeenth century saw an unprecedented rise in narrative prose about historical events, visions, and national trauma that were not strictly scripted by medieval conventions. The period also witnessed the proliferation of works written more purely for enjoyment.

Throughout the seventeenth century, traditional centers of textual production, such as monasteries, continued to reflect the cultural domination of the Church, and to guarantee the continuing availability of familiar forms such as saints' lives and homilies. During the lingering unrest that beggared monasteries, monks and young clergy who had been dispersed to urban centers joined the growing ranks of educated functionaries. Copyists skilled in the transcription of urban tales and their composition now applied their understanding of storytelling conventions to plots suited to changing socio-economic circumstances.[1] The rise of the pre-Petrine novellas has been explained by two contentions put forward separately. The first posits a new relationship between production and demand. The second explains the increase in that demand. Dmitrij Tschižewskij assumed that "the appearance of a new class of readers... composed of merchants, townsmen and even peasants" explained new trends in fiction.[2] Much to the frustration of historians of the book, material evidence about reading practices of the period is too scant to corroborate conjectures about the motivation of copyists and the demands of the readership. Soviet historiography has seen fiction as a mirror to historical change. While literary representation may capture aspects of social history, a claim for verisimilitude would be tenuous. The plots and tone of Russian fiction are increasingly mediated through the devices of storytelling available from translated literature originating in often-distant contexts. This is not to deny the expressive appeal and occasional topicality of stories whose novelty lies in a better matching of universal themes and local predicaments. Debatably, Dmitry Likhachev goes so far as to see the seventeenth-century treatment of character as a long-delayed catching up with a Renaissance understanding of selfhood, a proposition that can only be measured by literary means rather than social or theological sources. Theories of personality or models of subjectivity were not available in early modern Russia.[3]

Imitation and translation were therefore critical to changes in narration. From the 1630s, an influx of foreign works increased the stock of fictions available for native adaptation.[4] The genetic history of these works, including short satirical stories, known in Latin as *facetiae*, and their multiple border crossings from Western Europe, often via Polish and Ruthenian versions, raise questions about the assumption that these fictions grew out of social discontent. Differentiation between native and foreign, original and copy, mattered very little in a culture that readily modified and adapted plots and characters in ways that seem designed to optimize the entertainment value of some works or the moral commentary of others.

Many questions about the history of seventeenth-century fictional tales—who wrote the tales, who copied them, how they came to be read, and what their standing was in relation to other cultural practices—cannot be answered in the current state of research. The relative neglect of more than a handful of texts, prose and poetry alike, is due in part to the absence of printed editions. In the seventeenth century, the tale, much more than had medieval chronicle and hagiographic writing, paid attention to specific details of the lives of ordinary people rather than warriors and saints. The tendency to insist on the mimetic realism of these works has also limited literary historical interest to a core canon that seems to corroborate an idea dominant in seventeenth-century studies that fiction suddenly became realistic. In the absence of a comprehensive survey of these works as they circulated in print and manuscript, an estimate made on the basis of entries in the *Dictionary of Writers and Writing* gives a total of well over 200 works, only a handful of which are regularly anthologized. There was no clearly demarcated genre system to set the rules of prose composition. In their own time, these fictions were referred to as "tale" (*povest'*) as well as using other terminology, such as "narration" (*skazanie*) and "discourse" (*slovo*); "history" (*istoriia/gistoriia*) seems to have been reserved for novel-length works of adventure. The term *povest'*, which originally designated a short tale, often narrated adventures and gradually encompassed works of various kinds featuring ordinary people. Old and new modes coexisted in these fictions, which is why folkloric and oral elements continued to contribute plot devices, dialogue, and tone to written tales, often produced as a woodcut or *lubok* with text and illustration (Figure II.10).

Do changes in fiction correspond to the changes in seventeenth-century attitudes to reality? Whether works of fiction actually represent mentalities is a topic that requires further research. Social and religious historians find in the historical dimensions of texts evidence of

FIGURE II.10. Illustrated tale, 17th c.

personal viewpoints and reactions of people to their environment.[5] There is room for debate on the question of whether characters enjoy the autonomy of ethical choice made by full-fledged individual selves, or whether plot reversals built into the ironical purposes of these fictions drive the action. Stories can overtly give the impression of being anchored in popular practice and represent entertainments, festivals, oral culture, and attitudes to money.[6] Yet arguably most of these works, if not all, have no real claim to be considered part of "popular" culture in any pure sense. Overall, we find that trends in prose fiction, whatever the haphazard attention to real situations, remain rooted in a world somewhere outside the book culture of the court yet not verifiable as documentation of real experience because they filter impressions through the inherited plot devices of foreign models and Russian folklore, while also sharing the Christian morality of more educated discourses.

Prose works achieved a balance of continuity and innovation, distancing or eliminating a historical frame in order to concentrate on plots and moral (sometimes comic) situations. Given the persistently low literacy rates among all classes and a relative shortage of skilled copyists and absence of modern book production, it would neither have been possible for many common laborers to have read them, nor for any but a small elite to have purchased them. It has been surmised, partly from the evidence of *lubki*, that original audiences were listeners in taverns and those attending public entertainments rather than readers, and therefore they were positioned lower on the social scale. Short fictions should not be taken to be unadulterated examples of popular storytelling, since they were transcribed and refashioned by literate scribes who had at least one foot in the higher reaches of the bureaucracy and a higher social milieu. It is possible that tales bear a rough resemblance to contemporary life. Highly stylized, these fictions put plot before causality and simple lessons before moral complexity, falling back on didactic tendencies when characters succeed and fail.

The subject matter of prose fiction occupies a narrow zone between moral stories on Christian themes of piety and obedience and satirical tales about the social order. The former type of narrative has the force of parable in its use of timeless stories for didactic ends. Moral fictions clearly aimed to reinforce traditional expectations. They repackage Christian precepts in a way that falls short of conduct-manuals, which would become popular in the eighteenth century; they also step back from implicating plots in tangible reality. Many stories have a cautionary element and, in the manner of a contemporary English work like John Bunyan's *Pilgrim's Progress* (1678), view life as a set of snares and delusions that can lead one astray from the right path unless the lessons are heeded. While both parables and satires have a didactic element, their solutions are mirror reflections of one another, since satire champions characters who revel in their capacity to engineer social subversion and comic reversal through wit and cunning. Satiric fictions that showcase the narrator's superior viewpoint convey, and sometimes also mock, the values of culture. Are these works carnivalesque in the sense that Mikhail Bakhtin famously argued in *Rabelais and his World* (1965), an influential study on the early modern world? It is easy to see the appeal of applying here the binary terms of low/high, popular/elite, and the equation of subversive humor with popular interest.[7] Behind this is the assumption that most tales, and especially humorous ones, articulate unofficial views. This supposition deserves to be questioned (and further substantiated) in a context in which so little is known about how tales were circulated and read. Carnivalesque situations involving acts of social subversion might follow the intrinsic workings of humor built into plots rather than genuine antagonism to the surrounding order. In the current state of knowledge about reading patterns and the history of the seventeenth-century Russian book, we might reserve judgment and see the relation between purpose, production, and genre as more complex than claims for realism allow. While the reader-response dynamic implied in works seems (albeit to an uncertain degree) to reflect a social context, essential features of style and plot often originate outside the immediate purview of the tellers of tales. Scribes, clerks, and monks worked in chanceries, monasteries, or in law courts in a highly regulated state: the skilled laborers who copied these tales were educated, and read not just for pragmatic reasons; they must have also read for pleasure, afforded by the intricacy of the plot and the interweaving of oral literature and urban storytelling. Would people in these occupational categories have consumed literature that was genuinely subversive? Or did demotic fiction and its humor offer some pleasure other than undermining traditional social values? Might subversive stories of rogues and upstarts be forms of wish-fulfillment and projection, not unlike the impossible pleasures of fairy tales and romance in a world in which too little social mobility occurred?[8]

A second reason to question the suppositions about intentionality concerns the extensive role of adaptation and translation in the evolution of fiction. The degree to which tales were specifically Russian or more international varied; the only helpful generalization possible is to accept that a spectrum of adaptation across languages (from Polish, Ukrainian, French, and Italian, at least) and genres characterizes new texts which are abundantly copied in the seventeenth century. Translated and adapted fictions achieved a hybrid form of mimesis: they told familiar human stories, sometimes in a fantastic way, but rarely adapted foreign features, such as names and places, to Russian life—and when they did, the veneer was thin. Details that look historically real are not necessarily signs of realism. Morality tales could include details of the everyday and attain a vividness certainly less stylized than in hagiography, yet they are hardly ironclad evidence of a documentary style. Events and details marked as realistic (such as genuine place names, Russian as opposed to foreign names, and legal terms) crop up even in saints' lives and tales where miracles and unnatural events regularly occur.

In 1676–77, Tsar Aleksei Mikhailovich, alert to the uses of didactic literature in promoting loyalty and piety and in expanding literacy, commissioned a team of five translators in the Foreign Chancery to produce the Russian work known as *The Great Mirror* (*Velikoe zertsalo*).[9] This collection of moral tales and legends was three times removed from any original source, having been adapted from Polish settings of Italian translations of Latin texts that were taught by Jesuits.[10] Its confessional origins by their very nature might have repelled the tsar, given the ongoing hostility in the Church and among court factions to all things Latin. Translation and a discriminating selection, commensurate with the new Russian context, effectively erased any traces of foreign provenance. The Russian *Great Mirror* was about a third the length of the original Polish anthology. Even this abridged form represented a substantial addition of a corpus of moral tales whose universal messages could be adjusted for Orthodoxy. Among the topics treated in these stories and legends—the generic terms used in the work include fairy tale (*skazki*), longer tale (*povesti*), and story (rasskaz)—are questions of sins, repentance, and divine mercy. Moreover, adaptation also moved in the other direction: in producing new versions, Russian copyists interpolated age-old stories from Orthodox sources such as the *Sinai Paterikon*, the *Prolog*, and other medieval works that harked back almost to the Christianization of Rus'.

Seventeenth-century readers would have perceived no gap between the value systems of this collection, a hodge-podge of prototypes unified by consistency of message about Christian virtue, and medieval Russian works similarly concerned with the human condition, especially under pressure from historical uncertainty and religious strife.[11] In the tales of this collection, much as in stories that originated in Russia, material and emotional hardships affecting ordinary folk, rather than the plight of the monasteries, dominate. Topics include "the burial of a rich man" ("O pogrebenii bogacha"), "the significance of repentance" ("O znachenii pokoianiia"), "the child who was punished for indebtedness to servants" ("O rebenke, nakazannom za to, chto zadolzhal slugam"), "why it is better not to weep too much for the dead" ("O tom, chto ne nado mnogo plakat' ob umershikh"), and "On the punishment of a merciless ruler"

("Nakazanie nemilostivogo pravitelia"). To be sure, Christian worship, veneration of the Virgin, and a belief in the presence of the saints and the possibility of miracles, all inhabit the world of these stories and condition the mentality of characters who must contend with conditions and states of mind like "chastity and purity" (*tselomudrie i chistota*), "charity" (*milostynia*), silence (*molchanie*), heretics (*otstupniki*), modesty (*skromnost'*), cunning (*lukavstvo*), homosexuals (*sodomity*), and dozens of others. But dogmatic theology of any kind is muted, erasing any real generic boundary between the "parable" (*pritcha*) and the story, and it is no wonder that some of the tales can also be found as the inscriptions to *lubki*. Co-ordinated translation achieved a consistent style in which an appealing narrative voice personalizes the universal dimension and adds allure to the extension of didactic literature from the realm of homily and liturgy into secular types of narrative about characters such as the greedy merchant, the lascivious wife, the corrupt priest, which recur in more famous fictions originating outside large collections and circulated independently.

In addition to the tales of the *Great Mirror*, many other works embroiled characters in complex situations that become baffling when the circumstances challenged moral verities. "The Tale of the Drunkard" ("Povest' o brazhnike") is one example of popular stories that also include the "Tale of Shemiakin's Judgment" ("Povest' o Shemiakinom sude"), the animal fabliau "Tale of the Rooster and the Fox" ("Povest' o kure i lisitse"), and the "Tale of Ruff the Ruff's Son" ("Povest' o Ershe Ershoviche"), all generally read as comic satires. Arguably, the human predicament and anguish of the hero in the "Tale of a Drunkard" outweigh the humorous dimension, a reading that does not undermine the skeptical challenge the tale presents to a Church establishment confident in the efficacy of wisdom literature. Like a mini-Job, the unnamed hero wrestles with suffering in his effort to give up drink. In some versions, the framing passage that introduces the narrative pays tribute to the wondrous works of the Virgin who responds to pious supplicants and aims to cure them (other redactions cut right to the story but note that "with every drop of booze" the hero still praises God). The Virgin is outmatched by the devil who skillfully "catches out the elderly parishioner in drunkenness." The story advances not through plot but as a set of interviews with Biblical figures. St. Peter, St. Paul, King Solomon, King David, and St. John Chrysostom admonish the drunkard either to mend his ways or forfeit entrance to heaven. Widely anthologized as well as copied in five highly productive versions, the tale attracted scholarly commentary in the nineteenth century because it seemed to side with the underdog and everyman, defending drunkenness, at least occasionally, as a necessary release, despite widespread strictures against all forms of decadence.[12] Variations frequently consist in expressions of sympathy included by scribes and in two different endings attached to the core tale. In one version, no less a figure than God himself intervenes and instructs St. Peter to "open the gates of the heavenly kingdom" to the drunkard, "and admit him to the place prepared for him by Abraham, Isaac and Jacob because he praised my name with each and every cup." In one version, St. John says, "The heavenly kingdom has not been readied for drunkards and ready wine-drinkers" ("Brazhnikom i vino-ranopiiashchim ne ugotovleno tsar'stvo nebesnoe").[13]

Morality tales reinforced a message of piety that took its lead from Scripture rather than directly from the tsar or monastic leaders. We have seen that medieval narrative attributed cause and effect to divine retribution for sin, sometimes representing it as the logical outcome of internecine strife between princes. Contemporary narrators of the Time of Troubles, like Palitsyn, accommodated human fallibility in their accounts without dismissing Christian teleology. Some fictions perpetuated this didactic mode and simply narrativized precepts familiar from homily. For instance, the short "Household Book. On Female Wickedness" ("Kniga domostroi. O zhenstei zlobe"), the five versions of which were much copied in the seventeenth century, is a cycle of stories on the topic of sexual temptation. One of these is

"A Conversation of a Father with His Son on the Wickedness of Women" ("Beseda ottsa s synom o zhenskoi zlobe"). This moral tale is a patchwork of quotations of Christian texts reworked in a narrative that begins with the Biblical Eve and her cardinal transgression in the Garden of Eden, and proceeds to illustrate forms of "feminine evil" (thievery, gossip, fornication), comparing women unflatteringly to insects and animals. Like the earlier "Tale of Good and Evil Women," this work accommodates an opposite argument as advanced by the character of the son who gamely adduces Biblical learning to parry each damning episode before filial piety compels him at last to confess: "O father, my ears are full of your instruction, my soul is now in a state of horror, and my reason relents, and my heart is shaken, as I stand before you."[14]

While stereotypes continue to dominate characterization, stories model a broader range of outcomes because plots endow characters with somewhat more agency than earlier protagonists were able to enjoy, creating a sense of nascent individualism that is something of an illusion. Depending on their reaction, the activities of the cunning merchant, the lovable rogue, the trickster, the wayward monk, and the virtuous maiden might—or might not—lead to moral salvation, or social success, or drunken oblivion. Sometimes the wicked prosper, sometimes the pious are not rewarded. Characters operate at a much more immediate emotional level than in medieval texts, where responses tend to be even more formulaic and stylized according to a narrower range of situations.

Caution should be exercised in attributing to first-person narrators, whether fictional or non-fictional, a psychological view of the self and subjectivity. Writing as a Church historian and cultural anthropologist, Viktor Zhivov has compared confessional practices for insights into the development of subjectivity. He notes that while Catholic and Reformation cultures have been associated with the development of subjectivity, he concludes that Russian confessional practices and the rote learning of the liturgy discouraged any practice of introspection.[15] The conclusion would seem to undermine Likhachev's search for the equivalent of a Renaissance self or a modern fictional self occupying its own autonomous world. At least this holds true in a large number of stories and novellas where plot outcomes consistently correspond to moral rewards and punishment for the good and bad Christian, respectively, rather than inner fulfillment. In this regard, there is an instructive contrast between the predetermined patterns of behavior that dominate in fiction and the spiritual autobiographies of groups like the Old Believers who face complex situations and exercise choice.

"The Tale of Savva Grudtsyn" ("Povest' o Savve Grudtsyne"), much anthologized from the nineteenth century onward as a classic work of the period, delivers a clear cautionary message about the hazards of dissoluteness that confront all who leave behind Christian virtue, both monks and laity.[16] The old evangelical theme of the Prodigal Son has been transposed to a setting that is less timeless, more historical, and more familiar to the Russian reader of its day; however, the narrator articulates a timeless conviction that there is only one right path in life. Plot structure serves the message well by assigning the cause for all the twists and turns in the hero's life to the intervention of the devil. "The Tale of Savva Grudtsyn" originated in the 1660s, and while over eighty copies with numerous variations of detail survive, the plot remains constant.[17] An internal date indicates that the story is set sometime between 1606 and the 1630s. Savva is the young son of a merchant. He falls in love with a married woman, the wife of another merchant, who has been corrupted by the devil. Their affair proceeds (the author's only formula for it is "to roll in the dirt of lechery like a swine") until the merchant banishes Savva.[18] Despondent to learn that a magic potion induced him to fall in love, Savva on the rebound proves vulnerable to the persuasion of a handsome youth who gets him to sign a document in which he renounces Christ in return for the love of the merchant's wife with whom he once again enjoys sexual bliss. The handsome youth then leads Savva to the kingdom of his own father. To Savva's surprise the youth's domain turns out to be the empire of the devil. As Savva declines, his father sets out in search for his son. But Savva has already joined forces with the devil in search of adventure. At the devil's prompting, Savva enters military service and becomes a hero. In the end, Savva falls ill in Moscow and confesses to a priest. Tormented by demons, he prays to the Virgin Mary who appears to him in a vision, accompanied by the Apostles Peter and John, and instructs him to visit a church on the feast day of the icon of Virgin Mary of Kazan'. During the church service, the document in which Savva signed away his soul falls from above, bringing about his cure. He acquires faith and enters a monastery. The absence of psychological motivation for Savva's actions is striking. The appearance of the devil (used sometimes by scholars to suggest that the tale represents a sub-genre known as demonological novel) is accepted not as a mental aberration, but as part of the order of things.

Although the mentality of characters in satirical and didactic fictions often operates within a Christian framework, plots also explore a broader engagement with worldly questions and motivations, including money, social status, erotic desire, and urbanization. The general, if subtle, loosening of class boundaries plays an important role in the genesis of these new plots, a tendency that social historians have read as evidence for shifts in social mobility. The religious controversies that convulsed the Church from the 1650s, stemmed from a fundamentalist attempt at reformation that targeted popular religion, sometimes seen as blasphemous and unorthodox in practice. It remains an open question how directly famine and invasion-driven exodus from monasteries and the countryside motivated new modes of storytelling. However, fictional plots focalized individual and class responses to the social, political, and religious fissures of the historical period. Storytelling became a widespread mode of both instruction and escapism, sometimes tinged with hints of documentary realism, sometimes utterly fantastic, and sometimes strictly moralizing.

Things are especially lively in half-serious and comic tales, which favor the everyday world (*byt*) over religious life, focusing on human activity without much reference to the divine. In this world, men and women live by their own wits and succeed by dint of their own cunning. Often social conflict is obliquely presented, rarely with commentary; the world of these tales delights in tensions between classes and irreverent reversals. In the "Tale of the Peasant Son" ("Skazanie o krest'ianskom syne," n.d., first published 1903), the lazy son of a peasant turns to theft. When he breaks into the house of a rich man, the master of the house mistakes him for an angel, since the thief manages to get out of a tight spot by quoting the Scriptures at length. As he makes his escape, he tells the foolish man that the portals of heaven are opening before him and then in an aside chuckles that the merchant thinks the fur coat he has stolen will cloak an angel, whereas in fact it will dress a peasant.

Perhaps the most celebrated work of this kind is the "Tale of Misery-Misfortune" ("Povest' o Gore-Zlochastii"), discovered in a single eighteenth-century copy in 1856. It displays great artistry as a blend of the written and oral and defies genre boundaries. Although written in verse of mixed stress patterns, its title is that of a *povest'* or prose tale, and we include it in this section because its narrative thrust and plot line counter aspects of versification, diction, and use of formulae that are poetic.[19] Beyond its generic ambivalence, the work has a complex thematic ambivalence. On the surface, the plot creates a false trail ostensibly leading the reader toward a message of monkish obedience. Yet when seen against the historical backdrop its main preoccupation is fear that in a period of economic and social instability tricksters will exploit the vulnerable. Its use of picaresque and moral dilemma aligns it with the mimetic conventions of seventeenth-century prose tales. This oscillation between realism and allegory, between human characters and exemplary ones, reflects the fluidity of genres, a productive and important literary feature of the period. That instability is further compounded by a marvelous folkloric shape-shifting episode.

The tale opens with a Prologue, retelling the fall of Adam and Eve, which in this version is blamed on their eagerness to taste the fruit of the vine. It is the knowledge of drink, more than carnal knowledge, that leads the hero to ruin. The Prologue sets the moral agenda for a story that professes to show that original sin is in essence a failure to follow parental guidance. The tale proper moves into the moral biography of the hero. Young and foolish, he is an anonymous everyman figure who fails to heed admonitions not to party, never to drink two cups in quick succession, not to let his eyes wander (meaning not to covet his neighbor's wife), and to avoid stupid people and gamblers. Consequently, he suffers repeated misfortunes culminating in the appearance of his nemesis, Misery-Misfortune, from whom the only escape is flight to a monastery. The second, main section disperses the narrative into three locations. In lines 51 to 164 the action unfolds in the main character's native land. In lines 165 to 429, his misfortunes take him abroad; in this section there is a further tripartite subdivision: (i) the character appears as a guest at a feast (lines 165–253); (ii) as the successful host at his own feast when temptation strikes again (lines 254–335); and (iii) at a river-crossing (lines 336–429). This leads to the third segment comprising the protagonist's return to his homeland, and his monastic retreat. The triadic structure conspicuously mimics the three-part pattern of folkloric plots.

Youthful indiscretion blinds the hero's judgment. He makes some money, is duped by a group of faithless friends, whereupon he is tempted to drink. He awakens from his stupor to find his friends gone, his clothes stolen, and rags left in their place; and instead of a pillow, he has a brick. Disgraced, this prodigal son (and the Biblical story provides a strong subtext) ventures abroad; and, like the hero of *bylina*, wanders into a feast where he is welcomed graciously and bares the causes of his sorrow. His hosts offer advice akin to his parents' precepts though they are designed to bring him worldly success. He takes their advice, gets rich, finds a girl, and throws a party. He is egged on by the devil, who prompts him to boast of his success. Hubris triggers the appearance of his nemesis Misery-Misfortune, who may perhaps be the true hero and who, now in a dream, now in the guise of the Archangel Gabriel, ensnares the Youth in a losing streak. In a series of magical transformations, shape-shifting typical of the magical tale, and completely departing from the realistic tone of the story, the Youth seeks to escape Misery who relentlessly dogs him. He becomes in succession a falcon pursued by Misery's gyre-falcon; a dove chased by a hawk; a wolf hunted by dogs; a blade of grass threatened by a reaper's scythe; a fish about to be caught in a fisherman's net. Despondent, the Youth resigns himself to Misery's attempts to teach him to steal and kill when he remembers the path of salvation and enters a monastery where even Misery cannot follow.

Whether or not of popular origin, the work looks like a deliberate seventeenth-century pastiche of the *bylina* adapted to express suspicion of new wealth and new heroes celebrated in roguery tales. The tale's complexity comes from the unexpected combination of form and content and meshing of fantastic and realistic detail. Scholarship has long been divided between source critics who detect popular origins in folkloric material, and scholars who see learned sources (such as the parable of the Prodigal Son) and a monastic provenance.[20] The "Tale of Misery-Misfortune" creates its own fictional canvas that subsumes hints of the real into the devices of storytelling used to create a self-contained invented world, a distinctly modern approach to fiction. The discourse of poverty has little in common, for instance, with a contemporary exposition like the essay on mercantilism written in the late seventeenth century by Ivan Pososhkov (1652–1726), *The Book of Poverty and Wealth* (*Kniga o skudosti i bogatstve*). The predetermined storytelling function of the *bylina* and *skazka* dictate that the hero must undergo a series of trials and repeat his errors, a structure that suits the prodigal son plot and leads the Youth to reach Christian salvation as he seeks refuge from sin.

Two value systems intersect in the figure of the Youth. Like the *videniia*, this work assumes that the world is rife with supernatural forces, but the elements of folk religion, pagan in their workings, and Christian morality, Biblical in origin, are made to coexist. Everything in the tale is generalized; no superfluous detail distracts from the fate of the hero and his inner life. As the Prologue suggests, he is an everyman of sorts.[21] Only the incidental mention of the hero's clothes suggests that the Youth may be from a family of the merchant class. An expert trickster, Misery exploits the Youth's weaknesses in a world that is more amoral than Christian, preying upon his anxiety that robbers will impoverish him. With characteristic cunning, he talks his victim into making this fear self-fulfilling. As Likhachev has argued, the author's values were worldly and materialistic (though it is still a leap to assume from this that the author comes from the merchant class).[22] To this author the loss of material well-being is a terrible fate, and he shares with the protagonist's parents and the common people (*dobrye liudi*) a respect for wealth and its concomitant status. The tale demonstrates no adherence to the Christian view, so prevalent in medieval Russian literature, that poverty is desirable because it removes earthly vanities and allows one to imitate Christ's humility.

Other works of the period slough off any sense of pessimism by endorsing luck and cunning. Two of the most popular picaresque or scabrous tales, often seen as precursors to the eighteenth-century fictions such as Mikhail Chulkov's novel *The Comely Cook* (*Prigozhaia povarikha*, 1770), are the "Tale of the Wealthy and Famous Merchant Karp Sutulov and About His Wise Wife and How She Did Not Defile Her Husband's Marital Bed" ("Povest' o nekotorom goste bogatom i o slavnom o Karpe Sutulove i o premudroi zhene evo, kako ne oskverni lozha muzha svoego") and the "Tale of Frol Skobeev" ("Povest' o Frole Skobeeve"), both dating to the late seventeenth and early eighteenth centuries.[23] The "Tale of Karp Sutulov" celebrates the wiles of the merchant Sutulov's wife Tatiana who keeps at bay three suitors: a merchant, a priest, and an archbishop. Before long, she invites them to her house, whereupon she persuades each one that her husband's return is imminent; each suitor takes refuge in a trunk. The trunks are then removed and the three suitors face the local marshal who praises the cunning and wit of the faithful wife. Virtue is rewarded but only barely, and the tale uses a widely known plot to satirize the prevalence of corruption and a heroine who fights fire with fire.

Sometimes tricks pay off. "The Tale of Frol Skobeev" is set in 1680, and concerns Frol Skobeev, a poor legal agent from Novogorod. His duties as a *iabednik* make him a go-getter who brings in business to his legal practice.[24] When Skobeev learns that a rich neighbor has an eligible daughter, Annushka, he decides to court her. He begins by bribing her nurse. When his sister is invited to pay Annushka a visit, he joins the party dressed as a girl and seduces the very willing Annushka who connives in later trysts. All of the antics, including cross-dressing, reversed morality, and the topsy-turvy outcome, reflect the story's explicit setting during Yuletide. With the complicity of the nurse, Frol follows Annushka and her family on a trip to Moscow, intercepts Annushka on her way to a convent to pay a visit to her aunt, and succeeds in marrying her to the great dismay of her father. At the urging of the tsar himself reconciliation is effected, and Frol, that "thief and rogue" (*vor i plut*), as the author calls him, ends his days celebrated and rich. The author's failure to condemn Frol, to say nothing of his scarcely hidden admiration, are essential features of the criminal picaresque or fiction of roguery (the category of *plutovskii roman* has been coined for tales of this sort to align them with an eighteenth-century taste for tales of brigands and the ilk) where the victory of the hero takes pride of place: in the world of the criminal picaresque, cunning and initiative conquer passivity, belief, and weakness.[25] The tale's delight in such adventures arises almost as a challenge to Church morality that favored strict adherence to doctrine and canon law, frowning upon any departures from sanctioned behavior. In the eighteenth and nineteenth centuries, the story remained in print and attracted adaptations as a work in tune with picaresque ups and downs of more modern fiction.[26]

A contemporary anecdote conveys nervousness about the real possibility that fiction may have broken loose from its didactic moorings. It concerns Ivan Begichev, who bears the title of *stol'nik*, indicating his right to preside at the table of the tsar. He reprimanded a relation for acquiring a taste for the new literary style:

> Despite the person you are, apart from the fabliau Bova Korolevich and the other stories, also fictional, that appear to you to be of benefit to the soul, including that story to which the souls of children are exposed, that of the Rooster and the Fox, and apart from some comic tales, really apart from all of this you've not read any holy book on the dogma of our religion.[27]

Disregard of the traditional instructional modes is clearly bad enough, but a positive enjoyment of satirical or escapist fiction adds insult to injury for this court official. It will always be open to question whether tales of this kind are pure entertainment or whether they blend the "timeless wisdom" of advice literature with realistic appraisal of new social realities. When seen from the later perspective of Bakhtinian carnivalesque or trickster literature, it cannot be excluded that the tendency of popular literature to create comedy out of disruption represents a reaction through storytelling to all overarching hierarchy, including Tsardom and Orthodoxy.

Petrine novellas and fantasy fiction

By contrast with fictions grounded in social reality, fantasy works of romance, often called "histories," distanced the readers from the world temporally, geographically, and by disruptions of normal causality. Works of a somewhat later origin, traditionally known as Petrine novellas and tales because they date roughly to the early years of Peter's reign, show considerable versatility in absorbing into the fabric of their Romance tale elements of the contemporary world that give the stories a more overtly Russian complexion. The romance story pursued far-flung settings in medieval or feudal times, frequently in exotic locales in the Orient. Seventeenth-century fictions of this kind narrate unusual journeys charged with difficult tasks performed through cunning tricks. These stories have one foot in an emotional world organized according to recognizable human feelings and the other in a fantasy land dominated by accident, open to magical and supernatural intervention (although structurally they do not unfold in the regular units mapped by Propp for the fairy tale). Like the roguery tale, romance stories or adventure tales appreciate individual cleverness as a means that will help a man move to the top of the social pyramid, but adventure and travel as well as a certain chivalry combine in this style.

In the "Tale of Vasily the Golden-Haired" ("Povest' o Vasilii Zlatovlasom"), set in the German lands (meaning Bohemia), virtually all other characters, apart from the eponymous hero, have pseudo-Greek names such as Queen Polymestra and Poklisarius. Plot details and distinctly chivalric behavior on the hero's part despite overt references to courtly codes of behavior align this more with the *bylina* such as the "Heroic Legend of Nightingale Budimirovich" ("Bylina o Solov'e Budimiroviche"), posited as one source. Does this sort of patchwork go back to the original tale or reveal later additions and editorial choices made by tellers or copyists? It is a matter of reasonable conjecture, in the absence of recorded comments by contemporaries, that readers of the period must have found a certain thrill in outlandish heroism, highly intricate plots, and unbelievable characterization. One fiction written with a sense of vivid fantasy and glamorous wish fulfillment is the "History of Meliuzina" ("Istoriia o Meliuzine"). Its totally fantastic plot concerns the adventures of Meliuzina's ten sons. A fairy-tale figure with magical powers, half wise maiden, half cunning sorceress, she marries the noble Prince Raymond, who eventually discovers that she is in reality a dragon.

The most popular of these adventure tales appears to have been the "Tale of Bova Korolevich" ("Povest' o Bove Koroleviche"), most likely derived from a medieval Italian tale, *Buovo d'Antona*, also attested in England as the story of Bevis of Hampton and in Anglo-Norman French as *Bœuve de Haumton*. The story concerns the valiant knight Bova Korolevich who escapes from the clutches of his evil stepmother Militrisa, who connived to send Bova's father and her husband to his death. Bova takes refuge with the nearby king Zenzivius Andronovich, whereupon he becomes smitten with his daughter Druzhevna. This liaison sets in train the quests that Bova will undertake to prove his worthiness, beginning with Bova's release of Druzhevna from captivity, rewarded by the birth of two children and later marriage. Through a further series of plot twists involving disappearances, shipwrecks (Sinbad the sailor makes an appearance), battle scenes, and temptations, their love triumphs. Most other secondary characters facilitate the plot intrigue by motivating each successive episode, and the serial vignettes tend to replicate the basic structure of the challenge plot.

More than one hundred seventeenth-century manuscript copies contain five different versions of the tale of the knightly Bova that vary in details such as names of subordinate characters and toponyms, inventory of subplots, and sometimes phraseology. Romance tales of this kind explore the courtly values and chivalric aims of an individual hero, blending elements of fantasy such as magic, monsters, and exotic location into the history of the hero and his circle—original or adapted from foreign sources, these works, just like folkloric tales, seem to express a basic human need to seek wish fulfillment through plot. Like popular fiction and folklore, romance tales such as "The Tale of Bova Korolevich" employ episodic structures, adding and dropping installments in series of actions. But these variations do not alter an overarching plot that charts the triumph of the hero over malicious schemers, evil sorcery, and battles. The third, and most copied, variant of the Bova legend contains six stories that unfold as a sequence, although time is a matter of internal progression rather than of historical or natural chronology. Virtually all the characters' names apart from Bova himself (an unusual name nonetheless attested from the fifteenth century in Russia) are Slavonicized versions of exotic, Greek- or Italian-sounding or simply outlandish names.

These patently fantastic features belie the dominant tendency in much Soviet scholarship—in part a legacy of Jacob Grimm's theory of popular, non-literary origins of fairy tales—to regard these and other Petrine tales as pure instances of Russian culture in its actual state.[28] Many stories and novellas are skillful adaptations of foreign models, sometimes twice removed, and integration of familiar tropes from the *skazka* and *bylina* into the foreign plot line suggests the universality of certain plot structures (such as magical transportation, the evil stepmother, and love rewarded) and motifs; it also suggests that the capacity of Russian storytelling for innovation depends strongly on an openness to external influences and a perpetual appetite to recycle and retell. Bova Korolevich is a case study in the longevity of romance. Initial versions began to circulate perhaps as early as the sixteenth century and later admirers included both Alexander Radishchev and Pushkin who attempted verse retellings of Bova, and Pushkin found it so delightful that he used names and some details in his "Fairy tale about the Tsar Saltan." It continued to be published throughout the nineteenth century—in "Oblomov's Dream" by Ivan Goncharov (originally 1849) the child-hero's nanny recites *Bova* to him as part of the oral tradition—and a version was recently published as a children's book.

Other works also seem to originate in native oral genres although written versions, which mainly date to the seventeenth century, superimpose on the plot an overlay of exogenous landscape features, sometimes drawn from Oriental as much as Western sources. This is an apt description of the "Tale of Eruslan Lazarevich" ("Povest' o Eruslane Lazareviche"), which gained popular appeal in the form of woodblock carvings in the seventeenth and eighteenth centuries. Later admirers include the young Alexander Pushkin whose burlesque narrative poem *Ruslan and Liudmila* (1820), his first critical and popular success, emulates this source. Numerous dates, ranging from the tenth century to the sixteenth, and a wide variety of sources, from Saadi's *Bustan* to Mongolian tales, have been postulated for individual features, and the hero is both cognate with Western chivalric types (but also distinctly related to a *bylina* hero like Ilya Muromets, depicted here in Figure II.11) and a Russian clone of Rustem, the hero of Oriental legends. Certainly on the surface the variety of foreign and invented proper names and toponyms add to the "Tale of Eruslan Lazarevich" a magical touch and sense of dislocation from Russian reality, which is also present in the use of precise terms to describe court rank.

The compilatory nature of the work, done over several stages, bedevils any attempts to categorize it neatly by subcategories, such as the "magical" or "wonder tale" (*volshebnaia ska-zka*) or chivalric or heroic tale (*rytsarskii roman*), differentiations that are sometimes too finely drawn since writers' intentions were shaped by a loose sense of genre conceived as plots nested within plots. Conformity to the chivalric plot lies in the extensive travels of the hero whose adventures and quest take him east as far as India (an itinerary not dissimilar to Afanasy Nikitin's fabulous journey); as well as in his princely status and in his marvelous, magical steed, the prophetic Arash. Numerous small details such as the use of the word *bogatyr'* for

FIGURE II.11. *Ilya Muromets and Nightingale the Robber (Il'ia Muromets i Solovei-razboinik)*, lubok print, 18th c. *Lubok* (plural *lubki*) were Russian popular prints with simple graphics portraying stories derived from literature, religion, and popular tales. A knight errant of Kievan Rus', Ilya Muromets is a hero of Russian folk poems.

the hero, the fixed epithet "good horse" (*dobryi kon'*) for Arash, the recurrence of the phrase "clear field" (*chistoe pole*) can all be regarded as phrases associated with the *bylina*. Their cumulative effect is more a matter of tone and stylization than precise imitation of the form as a whole.

Romance tales of this type combined chivalric aspects of characterization (honor codes, loyalty and fidelity, gallantry) with adventure tales and folkloric supernaturalism. In the "History of the Russian Sailor Vasily Koriotskii" ("Gistoriia o Vasilii Koriotskom," early eighteenth century), a young gentleman fallen on hard times recovers his fortune by exercising intelligence and wit, thought to be valued qualities in the new world of meritocratic promotion championed by Peter. The picaresque plot involves a shipwreck, pirates, a desert island, and multiple other adventures leading to the eventual triumph. This typical romance structure was to remain popular in Russian fiction until the late eighteenth century. Similarly, the rollicking "History of Alexander, the Russian Nobleman" ("Gistoriia ob Aleksandre, rossiiskom dvorianine," mid-seventeenth century) takes its hero on epic peregrinations and pits him against a formidable English knight. In Paris he falls in love with the fair Eleanor; they cope with pirates and brigands by escaping to South America (New Spain) and Africa before finally turning back to Russia during which final leg they drown. Because they are buried together, they remain united in death. Formally, this anonymous work looks quite innovative because it contains snippets of songs, poetry, and more extensive letters written by the lovers to one another. What was new in these fictions was neither the content, nor the plotting, but rather a fictional game of suspense that amused the readers before educating them in the ways of fortune.

Such a mix of messages and genres looks ahead to the more regular use of these devices in the epistolary exchanges in European fiction (which will find a Russian imitator in Fedor Emin's *The Letters of Ernest and Doravra* [*Pis'ma Ernesta i Doravry*], 1766). The history of the "Tale of Peter of the Golden Keys" ("Povest' o Petre Zlatykh Kliuchei," *c.*1650) provides as good an example as any of the complex process of domestication that turned foreign fictions into popular Russian works. The boundary between foreign and native was essentially rendered meaningless. Their production depended entirely on literate bookmen who exercised linguistic skills as translators and editorial skills in adjusting aspects of content to suit what they deemed to be the vernacular mode of storytelling. Many works originally foreign in origin were read in translation as authentically Russian because of folkloric stylization, often through the use of features from the *bylina*. Described in relation to prototype, the "Tale of Peter of the Golden Keys," widely circulated from the mid-seventeenth century, is a translation and adaptation of a Polish version of a French fifteenth-century chivalric *chanson de geste* based on a Czech translation.[29] The basic plot tells of a young French knight on whose helmet were embossed two golden keys. The Neapolitan princess Maguelone spies him during a joust, and they fall in love only to be accidentally separated when they travel to France. Petr ends up in captive service to the Turkish Sultan, while the heroine finds work in a hospital for sailors where she hopes to find her beloved. Among the patients she eventually finds Peter who had quit the Sultan and then fallen ill. She nurses him; they marry, and live happily thereafter. New and very different redactions of the Russian version of this tale appeared over the eighteenth century, splitting an original fiction into three related but independent tales.

This reworking as a sentimental story could not be more different from another contemporary redaction in which the introduction of homiletic material, prayers, and Biblical quotations, cast in a more ecclesiastical style, lays the emphasis on the story as a moral allegory with Christian meaning. The Russian reception, already quite tangled, took a new twist in the 1780s with the appearance of a version, possibly done by the courtier F. I. Dmitriev-Mamonov (1727–1805) who also adapted works by Jean de La Fontaine. This retelling takes the history of the work full circle. Based on a direct adaptation of the medieval French tale, it greatly expanded the original to read much more like a traditional chivalric novel in the Romance tradition. For example, a second manuscript redaction pared away the remaining traces of knightly decorum in order to de-emphasize the chivalric plot and concentrate on affective relations and love as a matter of eloquent expression in the manner of Trediakovsky's *Journey to the Isle of Love* (*Ezda v ostrov liubvi*, 1730). The last was an adaptation-cum-translation of the abbé Paul Tallemant's *Voyage*, one of a group of texts that derives from Madeleine de Scudéry's *Carte de tendre*, a masterpiece of *préciosité* that represented love and courtship according to the exquisite manners of the salon. Mistakenly characterized as "the first Russian novel," Trediakovsky's work evoked for the reader a new social paradigm by promoting the culture of the salon over the culture of Orthodoxy and the Church.[30] In literary terms, the work is an example of romance that looks at home in Russia but was already backward looking in the context of French fiction. This single example of an act of cultural appropriation is a fitting way to end this treatment of early modern literature. Trediakovsky's initiative in trying to update Russian literature by turning the clock back to the seventeenth century captures the dual dynamic of advancement and conservatism reflected throughout the century, often concurrently.

Conclusion

It is difficult to name eighteenth-century trends, other than the tendency of the novel to revive folkloric plots, that derive from seventeenth-century writing. Echoes of the seventeenth century are even less pervasive in the first half of the nineteenth century although later writers like Nikolai Leskov and Pavel Mel'nikov-Pechersky would find material for their stories and novels in the subject of the Old Belief. At what point does the attenuation of influence become less a matter of trend than an isolated fact of historical record? Responses to the seventeenth century constitute a disconnected patchwork of influences. Later writers such as Daniil Kharms (1905–42) and Aleksandr Vvedensky, (1904–41) and Joseph Brodsky (1940–96) and Aleksei Tsvetkov (b. 1947) all admired Russian syllabic poetry and turned to the seventeenth century for models. Dmitry Prigov (1940–2007) composed a large set of alphabetic texts as a series of ingenious installments (*bukvarnye opusy*) in more parts than letters available, conceived "according to the lax rules of this genre" in the manner of seventeenth-century authors such as Karion Istomin (1640–1722).[1] Solzhenitsyn emulated Avvakum, while Vladimir Sharov (b. 1952), an admirer of Avvakum in his *Resurrection of Lazarus* (*Voskreshenie Lazaria*, 2002), created a part for the Patriarch Nikon in his 1992 novel *Rehearsals* (*Repetitsii*). While the dynamism of the early modern period can be studied and enjoyed for itself rather than relegated to the category of the transitional, its influence arguably starts to flourish only in the twentieth century.

Part III

The Eighteenth Century

Introduction:
The innovation of the eighteenth century

T
HE eighteenth century was a period of technocratic and cultural modernization that had been launched in the reign of Peter the Great (r. 1689–1725) and greatly advanced during the rule of Catherine the Great (r. 1762–96). The discourse about the Russian Enlightenment that developed over the course of the eighteenth century regularly attributed the secularization of culture and growth to Peter. In fact, his reforms to the state were an early chapter in an ongoing dynamic of Westernization.[1] It would take several decades to lay the groundwork for the establishment of a modern literature and literary field. Important changes to the historical context included the expansion of schools, especially the seminaries, which produced a more worldly clergy, and the foundation of the Academy Gymnasium in 1724 (a part of the Academy of Science founded the same year, functioning until 1766), Russia's only establishment of higher education until the foundation of Moscow University in 1755. Through educational reform and political change, the gradual diminution of the influence of the Church saw ecclesiastical censorship diminish. Court culture radiated outwards from a new capital in St. Petersburg, built in 1703 and showcasing the ruler's cultural and literary policies. Peter the Great's initiatives largely concentrated on the pragmatic measures needed to modernize the state. The creation of a meritocratic bureaucracy gradually led to the rise of a literate body of state servitors who also became producers and consumers of literature within two generations after the tsar's death.

The eighteenth century saw far less continuity than the period spanning the medieval and the early modern eras, partly because Peter the Great's ecclesiastical reforms in the 1720s had undermined the authority of the Church. After some years of stagnation in the reign of Catherine the Great, this tendency found new impetus. Her patronage of writers, translating cooperatives, and encouragement of freedom of the press laid the foundation for changes that would alter the canons of taste, aesthetics, and the functions of writing well beyond her reign. Much of that initiative was top-down, but it is also clear that the creation of a readership and reader-driven literary economy begun in her reign responded to the existence of a critical mass of readers and fledgling writers. The evolution of new writing unfolded not as a binary opposition between Orthodox Russia and the secular state, but rather as a set of shifting attempts to define the boundaries of classicism understood primarily in the context of classical antiquity and French neoclassicism. The implementation of new norms was uneven and much less of a shared goal than one might think. The birth of Russian literary theory produced clear theoretical prescriptions that corroborated the work of various competing poetic schools. Poetry, more quickly than prose, assimilated new linguistic norms and prosodic systems, and from the 1770s was abundantly written and read outside the court. The last third of the eighteenth century witnessed systematic change in the literary language, in experimentation with a raft of new genres, from epic to idyll, and in the concurrent practice of literary taste. The debate about cultural models spilled over into the literary societies that were active from the 1770s into the 1810s and continued to reverberate during Alexander Pushkin's formative years.

While Peter modernized the state, it was left to the Empress Elizabeth (r. 1741–61), and then to Catherine, to advance patronage networks and royal support in publishing, launch translation projects, and manage public venues like the theater. These initiatives secured the creation of a literary field in which individuals, groups, journals, coteries, and private publication flourished.

Our approach to the eighteenth century is structured thematically and united by the common project in which generations of writers—and a purposeful ruler—worked to satisfy a desire to create a national literature that was the equal in polish and taste of older European models. For eighteenth-century Russian writers the means of achieving cultural parity with the West lay in the creation of a native canon written in the vernacular rather than in Slavonic, and stocked with the full complement of genres. In surveying the institutions of the literary field, the narrative of Part III is structured in five chapters. Chapter 1 seeks to explore how a new literary system developed, what its aims were, and how theory and practice, rule-giving and satire, normative composition and parody, originality and imitation defined the practice of literature. Chapter 2 examines the ways in which court culture dominated the practice of the most prominent lyric and dramatic genres, the ode, tragedy, and comedy. Chapter 3 then takes a look at how, once the literary field was established, writing became a source of personal self-expression and pleasure from the early 1770s. Over the ensuing decades that enjoyment fostered a belief in the value of literature and authority of the writer and gave rise to the idea of individual genius to be commemorated in posterity. In itself this would constitute one of the most significant breaks with the medieval anonymity of the author function and considerably expand on the tentative understanding of authorship inaugurated in the early modern period. Ideas that instilled new methods of critical thinking led writers to address questions of national self-definition and Enlightenment, and also to use poetry and theater in order to question class roles (monarch and service gentry), the limits on power, and the personal conduct of the monarch and courtiers. Chapter 4 examines how the experience of feeling and the cycle of life was channeled into poetry, written, above all, for small groups, whereas Chapter 5 focuses on prose writing, which remained keyed in to a different, fledgling book market in which the readership preferred Russian fiction to remain faithful to old models of storytelling and consumed the contemporary novel in translation. Like Part I, Part III follows a chronological order but does allow for some movement back and forth, sometimes in order to sustain the coherence of a topic within its single treatment, but also because the century itself showed delayed reactions to the rediscovery of earlier trends that were initially precocious failures.

I

Defining classicism:
The canons of taste

THE eighteenth century saw an intensified drive to create a national literature comparable in polish and expressive potential to the established modern European traditions. Imitation, translation, and adaptation dominated the literary production of the time. No national culture can be seamlessly mapped onto a foreign counterpart either in terms of time span or scope. By the end of the century, hundreds of poets, and thousands of pages of literary journalism, had fashioned a body of literature written in a modern idiom and consumed for pleasure as well as education. Over the course of the eighteenth century, Russia telescoped an eclectic range of practices, and while a French taste dominated, there was openness to other continental trends.[2] During the process of acculturating European genres, literature acquired great cultural capital in the cumulative shift toward secular values, marking the adoption of Western aesthetic and intellectual styles, such as classicism, and assimilating ideas and values associated with Enlightenment. While still relatively small when compared to Europe, a reading public had come into existence. And even European writers took note of these changes on the Russian scene. Consider as a straw in the wind the publication of an anthology of poetry of the Catherine period in French translation. The preface, unsigned, cites the favorable opinion of Voltaire (1694–1778), the greatest arbiter of taste, on the "genius of the Russians," and argues that Russian literature is a testimony now to the European "character and energy" of its people.[3]

We get an early sense of the growing Russian aspiration to match Europe's cultural prestige in the latter years of Peter's reign. In his "Discourse on the Power and Honor of the Tsar" ("Slovo o vlasti i chesti tsarskoi," 1718), Feofan Prokopovich (1681–1736), a rhetorician, poet, and clergyman famed for his learning and support of Peter's vision, used his mastery of ancient sources and classical rhetoric to support the concept of a new Russia that Peter the Great took forward. Prokopovich placed responsibility for the genesis of a new literary culture on the educated elite fostered by Peter's reforms. Among the first secular writers to come of age in the Petrine period is the diplomat and man of letters Antiokh Kantemir (1709–44). His career, publishing history, and literary works are a case study in the optimistic and perhaps thwarted hopes. Kantemir's most substantial literary work was his *Satires* (*Satiry*), a collection of nine syllabic poems written in the Horatian manner about contemporary subjects, such as the resistance of the Church to science and learning ("The First Satire"); the obsession of the old nobility and the newly ennobled with pedigree and social climbing ("The Second Satire"); the tension between reason and emotion, especially religious enthusiasm impeding enlightened judgment; the benefits of education and the true meaning of happiness (both of these in "The Seventh Satire"). Written and revised over more than a decade from 1729, his poetry circulated in manuscript in Russia. It was published first in translation in the Low Countries and France (in both cases with a title page giving London as the place of publication). Kantemir could have had no more than a handful of readers in St. Petersburg. The nine satires were equipped with notes and commentaries in Latin and French, far exceeding the competence of all but an exiguous number of erudite readers in Russia.[4] An habitué of *mondain* and literary Augustan circles in Paris and in London, Kantemir may have used his *Satires* to establish his cultural credentials during his career as a diplomat. The work evinces an admirable European style and learning, subsuming an entire classical and neoclassical tradition. The authorial persona in the *Satires* is a commentator capable of asserting his identity as a modern European imbued with the Enlightenment values of reason and tolerance—and both values are important themes throughout the *Satires*—as well as, more indirectly, intent on dispelling Russia's reputation as an uncouth country.

The Russian vision of European literatures could not move in lockstep with European trends, and had a fragile dependence on single advocates such as Kantemir for translating the Petrine legacy into the literary culture of a secular civilization. He had caught a trend, and was ahead of the next generation, whose achievements were lasting. The three main innovators, whose personal rivalry and principled quarrels became the material of satire and comedy, as well as later legend, rightly dominate any discussion because they changed the face of Russian literature. Vasily Trediakovsky (1703–68), Mikhailo Lomonosov (1711–65), and Aleksandr Sumarokov (1717–77) promulgated norms of diction, versification, and genre on the basis of abstract and universal precepts, but defended them on the grounds of taste. Their works of poetry and theater treated literary progress as a subject open to contestation through wit, parody, and theatrical lampooning. Didactic prescription, imitation, and translation were modes used to shift literary practice away from its ecclesiastical basis toward a secular expression of themes in a vernacular language refashioned according to a modern genre system.

As a Russian of the period, Trediakovsky could boast of an uncommon command of the scholastic and Humanistic traditions he learned at a Jesuit college run by Italian Capuchin monks (who taught him Italian), at the Slavo-Greco-Latin Academy, and later at the Sorbonne and Collège de France where he studied mathematics, theology, French poetry, and historiography in 1726.[5] He was born into a world whose cultural agenda had been set by a greater openness to humanist and Latin learning beginning with the reign of Tsar Aleksei Mikhailovich. Trediakovsky remains a figure of historical note because his work reflected a conviction that the time was ripe to articulate systematically for Russia literary conventions, including rules of prosody, equivalent to those that had shaped European literature, especially from the seventeenth century.

Aleksandr Sumarokov was the son of an aristocratic officer who rose to prominence under Peter the Great. In 1732, Sumarokov, who already knew French, Italian, and some German, was enlisted in the freshly organized Noble Infantry Cadet Corps (*Sukhoputnyi shliakhetnyi korpus*), an academy designed for the children of the nobility, a mixture of a finishing school, military academy, and institute of higher education. In 1740, Sumarokov made his debut on the literary scene with two odes written in honor of the Empress Anna Ioannovna (whose disrespectful treatment of the nobility would later be used by the poet Gavriila Derzhavin [1743–1816] in the poem "Felitsa," 1782, as a counterexample to Catherine the Great). Sumarokov wrote these early odes following Trediakovsky's rules of versification (which he was soon to reject).[6]

In this company, Mikhailo Lomonosov's origins look highly unexpected, and his sense of being an outsider may have contributed to the displays of self-assertion and even brawling that became the stuff of anecdote and legend in his own lifetime.[7] Born in Kholmogory, in the far north of Russia, the son of a state peasant fisherman and transporter, Lomonosov until the age of ten worked alongside his father, learning about desalination and pearl cultivation and exploring the geography of the region. He was taken under the wing of a parish priest, himself a peasant, who taught Lomonosov to read and write. His schooling included some knowledge of grammar, compiled by Meletii Smotrytsky (1577 or 1578–1633), as well as the *Psalter* in Simeon Polotsky's poetic version. In late 1730, Lomonosov left home, arrived in Moscow with a cargo of fish, and eventually enrolled in the Slavo-Greco-Latin Academy to study rhetoric and logic with a generation of well-educated, Humanist clerics, such as Feofilakt Lopatinsky. In 1735, he transferred to the Academy of Sciences in St. Petersburg, where he began learning German and studying mathematics. His time at the Academy was interrupted by an opportunity to study the natural sciences, as part of a cohort, in Germany, where the faculty included the highly influential philosopher Christian Wolff, who had been ousted from his chair at Halle in 1723 because of his views on determinism (again, Lomonosov may have found in his teacher's behavior a model for his own stubbornness).[8]

Committed to secular literature as a source of pleasure, instruction, and intellectual distinction, Trediakovsky, Lomonosov, and Sumarokov articulated cognate, if distinct, views on the notion of style. In theory, they strove in the same direction, namely toward the creation of a normative system. In practice, they produced concurrent versions of classicism, and because all three writers diverged, sometimes vehemently, on major questions of language and style, the literary system remained in flux. Nonetheless, their common critical practice established the importance of imitation as a form of creative expansion for individual talents, sometimes grouped as alliances by stylistic affiliation and social connection.

In outlining how a new literary system developed, critical literature has described Russian classicism primarily as the establishment of an ironclad system of rules of genre and style similar to those followed by other literary schools.[9] This is deceptive, because the actual process was incremental and involved continual revision and choice, rather than a sudden transformation. An exclusive emphasis on rules further distorts the picture of literary history happening "in real time." The theory of a stable eighteenth-century classicism evolved in the late nineteenth century: it is in fact a natural corollary to how Romanticism was conceptualized as superseding classicism by making its own rules or breaking rules altogether. To be sure, all the so-called classicists supported the idea of a normative aesthetic. But they changed their minds over time about what this aesthetic was actually to be like, in addition to debating the fundamental aspects of prosody (including versification), syntax, and diction. Classicism had guiding principles that tolerated diversity.[10] The recognition of its multiple sources informs more modern work on "classicisms," showing flexibility familiar from the scholarship on French classicism that also works well in the Russian context. And the reality was that it was only by means of imitation, translation, and adaptation, as much as by following some set of rules or another, that Russian writers worked out good style through trial and error. The period can also be seen as a constant search for expressivity. This involved cultivating taste and voice, the accomplishment of which was not guaranteed solely by compliance with rules. A sense of practical accommodation to the limitations of the language, and experimentation with individual voice, lent vitality and individuality to the best works of the period, which cannot be simply understood as departures from the norms of genre.

In his "Discourse on Rich, Varied, Tasteful, and Individual Eloquence" ("Slovo o bogatom, razlichnom, iskusnom i neskhodstvennom vitiistve," 1745), originally delivered in Latin ("De eloquentia") on the occasion of his receiving the title of professor, Trediakovsky marshaled all his considerable learning and philological sophistication to back up the message Prokopovich had articulated twenty years earlier. He followed the Europe-wide trend of turning to France for guidance on matters of literary decorum and on imitation as an index of progress. At the

Académie française in the 1680s, the famous Quarrel of the Ancients and Moderns (*la querelle des anciens et des modernes*) had created two opposing factions in the debates around the canons of taste and good style. The Ancients, led by Nicolas Boileau-Despréaux (1636–1711), argued that imitation of ancient authors, who were by definition unsurpassable, was the path to good art; whereas the Moderns, led among others by the distinguished natural philosopher Bernard de Fontenelle, argued that they were the standard-bearers of progress and would surpass the Ancients. The Ancients aimed to recreate the simplicity and the harmonious style of Greece and Rome by imitating their practice; the Moderns wished to build on the classical legacy, attempting to create a body of literature turned toward their own time and place and written in a more contemporary language. The Quarrel and the arguments deployed were highly influential all across Europe and, to a limited extent, influenced the positions of Russia's theorists.[11] Trediakovsky followed the example of European scholars when he directed his attention to questions of rhetoric and poetics. From a position of considerable authority at the Academy of Sciences, Trediakovsky argued that advancement could only occur if Russian writers, translators, and literary theorists responded creatively to the influences both of classical antiquity and of French and German neoclassicism. His handbook on versification, his essays on eloquence, comedy, the epic, and the ode attempt to explain the origin, goals, and rules of verbal art.

The recognition of imitation as its principal dynamic is one benefit of a more supple description of classicism. This was particularly important in the Russian case because of the need to build a secular literature virtually from scratch. Translation was the primary conduit of cultural transfer. Imitation of superior models as the basis of good art was a fundamental premise of neoclassical theory. Alongside those forms of normative imitation a vast amount of second- and third-rate literature was translated, mainly from French.[12] As had France a century earlier, Russia grappled with fundamental questions about imitation as well as whether rules and practices were to be transposed literally or adapted more creatively. The paradox of classicism is that the closer one comes to the classical Greek and Roman writers the more privileged one's own national version can be as it lays claim to being the definitive appropriation of a tradition. Versification and prosody were the obvious testing grounds. Should writers in the epic mode try to emulate the heroic hexameter of Homer in a language with tonic stress, whereas the Homeric meters are quantitative, since vowels in Greek have length? Should poets use rhyme when translating the Greeks and Romans who avoided it? Should writers substitute modern place names and proper names for the ancient originals?[13] In its concern to determine whether the arts could progress beyond the perfection of antiquity, the French Académie had debated whether strict imitation of the Greeks and Romans or imitation and modernizing was the right way to go. Or, to put the matter differently, was one writing as an Ancient in Paris or London or St. Petersburg, or writing in a new language as a Modern somehow transported back to Rome or Athens? The successful transfer of new elements of style was more than a matter of mechanics.

For Trediakovsky, particularly late in his literary career, and for others like Grigory Teplov (1716 or 1717–79; mainly known as a translator), the writers of classical antiquity, read in the original or mediated through French translation, were the fundamental canons of taste.[16] In practice, the choice between two ideals was more limited than in theory. Recognizing the importance of models, Trediakovsky translated treatises by both Horace and Nicolas Boileau, each a cornerstone of classical and neoclassical poetics. Trediakovsky's "Epistle to Apollo from Russian Poetry" makes poetry a vehicle of literary history. It provides a survey of ancient poetry by genre, gathering in chronological order a roster of the most influential writers from antiquity to seventeenth-century France and England, but also Italy, Spain, and Germany, folding in references to important movements like *preciosité*.

KEYWORD **Russian classicism**

In seventeenth-century Western Europe and in Russia from the 1730s onward, all the major theorists of literature and art acknowledged that the basic, eternal, and unchangeable literary models were all created in Greece, brought to perfection in Rome, and then revised in seventeenth-century France. Within this system, each genre operates according to the norms of practice, based on the immutable properties of the human heart and mind. Russian classicism refers generally to the literature produced during the reign of Catherine the Great, although its roots lie even deeper, and date from the 1730s. In theory, the literature of classicism is a period committed to stylistic clarity, universal emotion, and rules of genre, starting with Trediakovsky's "Epistle to Apollo from Russian Poetry" ("Epistola ot Rossiiskiia poezii k Apollinu," 1735) and ending with Pushkin's late poetry. Classicism serves as a catchword for a great diversity of European models behind Russian experimentation with forms of secular literature. The need to telescope continental literary history results in a motley and complex notion of classicism, sometimes based on the direct reception of the Greeks and Romans sometimes mediated through European neoclassical writing. While classicism is often thought to identify a clear orientation toward France, in fact it reflected the influence of diverse European models based on multiple literary and intellectual traditions (French, English, German, Roman, and Greek), confounding any neat account because different sets of rules vied for influence in determining good style. Neoclassicism refers more specifically to a direct imitation of ancient writers or their seventeenth- and eighteenth-century French admirers.[14] Despite advocates of imitating ancient Rome (early Trediakovsky, Lomonosov) and ancient Greece (Sumarokov, later Trediakovsky), Russian classicism merges features of antiquity, French neoclassicism, and English Augustanism. By the early nineteenth century, a notion of the classical affiliation had come to exist in the adjective "klassicheskii," describing works that aspired to the timeless values of beauty and emotional truth.[15]

Like Kantemir, Trediakovsky used poetry to establish his authority by setting a trend. The poem's learned allusions and its range of reference were intended to give like-minded readers confidence that Trediakovsky, as the author of a new versification system, proceeded from a deep understanding of the Western literary culture with which he advocates convergence. The poem's speaker sends "Russian poetry" to Mount Helicon with an order to pay tribute to Apollo and to apply for membership in the canon.[17] The question of which tradition should be chosen as the basis for a new Russian literature is a matter of choice, entailing advantages and risks. The purist in Trediakovsky would like to advocate the direct imitation of antiquity. If the French had set a standard through neoclassical imitation of the Greeks and the Romans, why should the Russians not strive for equal fidelity to the classics? The "Epistle to Apollo from Russian Poetry" argues that French tragedy was inferior to its classical model, and, consistent with that position, argues that dramatists should return to ancient theater as a source. But Trediakovsky takes the argument to an extreme to show confidence while being in full awareness that sidelining canonical writers like Racine (1639–99) and Voltaire (1694–1778), the most influential and popular tragedians of the age, was not viable or desirable.

Trediakovsky's own efforts to introduce Western literary models into the Russian language were far less uniform than his theories might have implied. He rendered in verse and prose

John Barclay's (1582–1621) political novel *Argenis*, originally published in Latin (1621; Trediakovsky's Russian translation published in 1751), and his translations of numerous French lyrics published in the 1730s offered the first generic models for poetic forms such as the sonnet, the rondeau, the elegy, and, most importantly, the epic. Trediakovsky's translation of Fénelon's *Télémaque* and the multiple book-length prefaces he wrote for his translation of the ancient and Roman histories of Charles Rollin (1661–1741) are a *tour de force* of metrical manipulation and creative word-coinage.[18] In 1745, in a speech he delivered to the Academy of Sciences, and in the introduction to his translation of *Argenida* ("A Preface from One Who Labors at Translation" ["Preduvedomlenie ot trudivshegosia v perevode"], 1751), Trediakovsky argued for literary translation as the best medium of transfer. His image of the translator as a defender of the language and protector of the national culture is important as perhaps the first expression of a unique role for the layman of letters in Russia. Trediakovsky put his linguistic prowess to use translating from many languages.

In the late 1720s, he wrote French libertine poetry; in 1730, he translated Paul Tallemant's 1663 allegorical novel *Voyage à l'île d'Amour* as *Ezda v ostrov liubvi* (*Journey to the Isle of Love*), and planned to translate Molière; in the early 1750s, he translated Roman comedies from the Latin; and in the 1760s he produced *Tilemakhida*, his verse translation of François Fénelon's prose epic *Télémaque* stylized in the manner of ancient Greek epic. His catholic taste hardly interfered with his staunch advocacy of direct imitation of the Ancients beginning in the 1740s. Lomonosov, whose writings (especially his imitation of Johann Gottsched, 1700–66) showed the influence of German baroque poetics, also subscribed to the widely held view that classical antiquity established an unachievable ideal of style and taste. Horace's *Ars poetica*, a treatise not only on Roman poetic taste but also on the influence of Greek aesthetics on poetry, commanded universal respect. After the pioneering translation by Trediakovsky, Nikolai Popovsky (1728–60), a pupil of Lomonosov, followed with a translation of his own. Russian proponents turn out to be both Ancients and Moderns in advocating mixed models for a classical style: allusions to ancient Roman and Greek writers sit alongside myriad contemporary examples. Trediakovsky and Lomonosov start with comparable premises and a similar engagement with preferences among contemporary national literatures, German in Lomonosov's and German and French in Trediakovsky's.[19] Trediakovky's views on the question of which European culture was authoritative varied over the course of his career.

Questions of language and style

The classical style defines literary decorum according to the conventions of language, form, and prosody. The question of the right style, however, occasioned a furious debate in Russia, as it did in France and England. Eighteenth-century Europe abounded with theories of the historical development of languages.[20] In Russia, as had been the case in seventeenth-century France, the critical issue in the development of new forms of literature was the development of an appropriate vernacular.[21] The ecclesiastical language was regarded as archaic and too bookish, while spoken Russian was too mundane and unpolished. The development of a new style of prose entailed a shift away from Slavonic and convergence with oral, spoken Russian. In his 1683 translation of the *Psalter*, probably from a Polish-language translation, Avraamy Firsov (*fl.* late seventeenth century) described his version as a rendering "into our simple, daily, Slavonic language" ("na nash prostoi, obykloi, slovenskoi iazyk").[22] In the preface to his 1718 translation of Bernhard Varenius's *Geographia generalis*, the lexicographer Fedor Polikarpov (*c.*1660–1731) noted that he had adopted not the high Slavonic dialect, but at the request of the patron who commissioned the work, Ivan Alekseevich Musin-Pushkin, the middle civic language.[23] Feofan Prokopovich, an expert on rhetoric and an accomplished practitioner of

Slavonic prose, called for writing in the "simple language" (*prostorechie*). In his *Ecclesiastical Statutes* (*Dukhovnyi Reglament*, 1721), he went so far as to say that Slavonic had become obscure. Similar assertions and aspirations are given prominence in Trediakovsky's preface to the reader in his translation of the abbé Paul Tallemant's *Voyage de l'île d'amour*. And yet a full sixty years later, in the 1790s, Nikolai Karamzin (1766–1826) was moved to complain of the paucity of good quality prose and the uncultured quality of the language.

The major theorists largely shared the goal of developing a new secular literature more than their personal rivalry would suggest, but diverged on points of prosodic, syntactic, and lexicographical practice. Their competition indicates the degree to which personal authority, based on charisma, stature at court, or learning, corroborated the "rightness" of their taste and attracted proponents. Their rivalry was significant because there was no reliable measure of success. Sales of books remained meager and literary criticism was undeveloped until the 1770s. It is arguable that when one takes into account the broadest set of major and minor works, and translations as well as original compositions, we see that imitation practiced by trial and error was the norm for scores of users of the literal vernacular more than any single benchmark set by one of the major theorists. In the 1780s Andrei Baibakov (1737–1801), a typical product of the Slavo-Greco-Latin Academy trained in scholastic rhetoric, compiled a handbook on poetics that confirms the basic principles of the new literary style. But the sheer breadth of his examples, drawn from Prokopovich, Trediakovsky, Kantemir, Lomonosov, and others, shows that the common features of style and practice overshadowed erstwhile distinctions well until the end of the century. Perhaps most striking of all is a comparison between Karamzin's language, praised as the most limpid literary version of the vernacular, and Trediakovsky's early style. Trediakovsky's writings until the 1740s contain passages of grace and elegance comparable to Nikolai Karamzin, who set the standard for prose from the late 1790s onward. The similarity is remarkable—it is perhaps no coincidence that Karamzin owned the second edition of Trediakovsky's translation—and reveals the fact that the language has come full circle after sixty years of trial and error and practical application rather than codification.[24] In this connection pedagogical lineage mattered: Trediakovsky's pupil Anton Barsov (1730–91) was Karamzin's teacher.[25]

Only specialist studies can address the more highly technical questions involving word order, sound orchestration, punctuation, and other aspects of style on which writers and translators tested their command of the language. Within the literary-historical context, there was a close connection between rules of style and practice because the key figures, especially Trediakovsky and Lomonosov, were also skilled grammarians and scholars of rhetoric whose original works discussed these questions in prefaces and embodied them in their own style.[26] In his treatise *A Conversation about Spelling* (*Razgovor ob orfografii*, 1748), Trediakovsky addressed questions of grammar; although his conclusions and suggestions were rejected and ridiculed, they stimulated important linguistic speculation and thought. Trediakovsky mobilized his learning in establishing systems of rules that he hoped would be followed scrupulously by a new generation of "those willingly practicing exquisite Russian verse," the dedicatees of his *New and Short Manual to the Composition of Russian Verses* (*Novyi i kratkii sposob k slozheniiu rossiiskikh stikhov*; first published in 1735; in revised form and under a new title, *Sposob k Slozheniiu Rossiiskikh Stikhov*, included in volume 1 of his *Sochineniia i perevody*, 1752).

Throughout the eighteenth century, the desire to develop a Russian literary language was driven by the need for a vehicle that would suit a wide range of genres, from the high-style epic to the love song. The basis of linguistic nationalism in the cases of both Lomonosov and Trediakovsky was confidence that from the reign of Peter the Great Russia had entered a long imperial age. Trediakovsky and Lomonosov both argued that, via Old Church Slavonic, Russia had inherited a language comparable in beauty to Ancient Greek. Diverging from Trediakovsky,

Lomonosov attributed to the modernized Russian the "liveliness of French," the "strength of German," and, above all, the "richness and powerful, incisive figurativeness of Greek and Latin."[27] Ultimately, what all three writers shared is a belief in best practice formed on the basis of imitation of the greatest models; and while they disagreed on the identity of those models, they are remarkably similar in establishing new systems by force of the examples they used in their work.

A striking feature of Trediakovsky's theoretical writings is their reliance on historical summaries of both Western and Russian traditions. The *New and Short Manual* is a guide to the composition of poetry according to sets of rules interspersed with both short and extensive examples. Readers may learn through precept and practice with the aid of commentaries on poetic models. Trediakovsky implicitly criticized syllabic verse by revising quotations from Kantemir's "First Satire" to move them closer to syllabotonic meters. He added examples demonstrating metrical schemes of his own invention in order to illustrate the regular distribution of accents as practiced in a range of genres such as the sonnet, the song, the rondeau, the poetic epistle, the elegy, the ode, and the epigram. Copious citations give proof of his talent and offered a practical demonstration of the feasibility of this style of writing: these were models that might, he hoped, as imitations of best practice, be suitable candidates for further imitation. Such an approach, exemplified in his "Epistle to Apollo," first published in his *New and Short Manual*, puts Trediakovsky in a line of theorists that, fancifully, stretches back all the way to the god of poetry.[28] Amid a welter of contradictory rules, the "Epistle to Apollo" helps us not to lose sight of the bigger picture. In enumerating exemplary writers and genres, Trediakovsky, like Lomonosov, turns to the history of literature in order to elucidate the relation between rules of style and what he calls "superior eloquence" (*prevoskhodnoe krasnorechie*) as the basis of neoclassical art: the premise underlying all his examples is that a skillful application of the rules of eloquence makes art universal and therefore capable of "igniting the passions." The recipes for formal perfection are by no means seen as antithetical to feeling, however stylized the neoclassical form and expression may seem to later generations. Prescription must be specific enough to guarantee stability of meaning but also flexible enough to allow originality (as conceived within the aesthetic). Writing reasonably (*razumno*), sweetly (*sladostno*), decorously (*prilichno*), and wittily (*ostrota*) is a matter of skill rather than mechanical application.[29]

In 1732, Trediakovsky was appointed translator at the Academy of Sciences where he steeped himself in scholarly and literary work, serving from 1733 to 1745 as Secretary of the Academy of Sciences (dominated by émigré German scholars) and becoming full professor in 1745. The question of whether to base vocabulary on the vernacular or on a bookish language was not the unique obsession of Trediakovsky and occupied all parties involved in the French seventeenth-century Ancients versus Modern debates, which attempted to define canons of taste, as well as similar debates in Russia.[30] In his "Speech on the Purity of the Russian Language" ("Rech' o chistote rossiiskogo iazyka," 1735), the first discourse ever delivered in Russian at the Academy of Sciences, Trediakovsky argued that it was in the vital interest of Russians to cultivate their native language; he appealed to the example of educated Romans who opted to write in Latin rather than in Greek, which had been the language of learning at the time. It was possible to be both a progressive Modern and imitate the Ancients. Trediakovsky provides a long list of writers straddling two cultures, and cites the historic reward they received when Latin became the *lingua franca* of scholarly and international discourse. Initially, Trediakovsky viewed vernacular Russian and Slavonic as two separate languages. At this time in his career, he was adamant that the literary language should be based on language spoken by educated people. To that end, he wished to reduce the role of Slavonic words either of ecclesiastical provenance or newly formed in the literary language.

Trediakovsky wanted writing to cultivate the virtues of speech: directness and simplicity free of archaic word choices and morphology.[31] He advocated a new version of the vernacular as the idiom appropriate to literary expression. In breaking with the ecclesiastical linguistic culture, Trediakovsky sought to create a situation in Russia similar to that in Europe where the language of the Church was Latin, but the vernacular was deployed in secular texts. In the preface to his translation of the *Journey to the Isle of Love*, Trediakovsky proposed that the basis of good writing should be the educated vernacular, the conversation of polite society (*izriadnaia kompaniia*). He confirmed his position in the "Speech on Eloquence" ("Slovo o vitiistve," 1745). The position of the Slavonic language (*Slavenorossiiskii*) in relation to spoken Russian, he maintained, was not the same as that of Latin to Romance languages. The speakers of those modern European languages have to study Latin in order to understand it, whereas, he continued, Russians understand the Slavonic language without formal study owing to its continuous usage in ecclesiastical literature and closeness to the modern language.

In translating the *Psalter* (1753), Trediakovsky's purpose, as he stated in the preface, was to provide alternative models to the ancient poets; it was also an attempt to renew the significance of the Psalms.[32] His views on style, held for nearly twenty years, had changed. As he modified his recommendations on prosody and verse syntax, Trediakovsky ascribed greater importance to Slavonic words and bookish syntax as hallmarks of good style. He objected to the trend, as he perceived it, of abandoning Slavonic-based words for new words calqued on foreign languages. In his "Three Considerations on the Three Principal Russian Antiquities" ("Tri rassuzhdeniia o trekh glavneishikh drevnostiakh rossiiskikh," 1757, published in 1773), he even argued that Slavonic and Russian were the same language at different stages of development. At the same time, in the preface to *Tilemakhida* (1766), published in 412 copies, Trediakovsky argued for a difference between written and spoken language. Abandoning his earlier premises, he now contended that the French wrote in a style different from their spoken language, and Russians should follow their example. In *Tilemakhida* he changed his orientation from Latin as the great ancient language to Greek as the basis on which to redevelop written Russian syntax, morphology, and vocabulary. Few, if any, followed this example before the 1810s, when acolytes of the Colloquy of the Lovers of the Russian Word, better known as Beseda (Beseda liubitelei russkogo slova), made a nationalist case for the reorientation of educated Russian away from the French norms of smoothness and vocabulary formation to an archaic Slavonic model. The entire process of assimilating foreign styles in a native idiom piqued cultural pride. Trediakovsky's defensive advocacy of an archaic idiom reflected a search for authenticity and national distinctiveness; he expressed it in "On Ancient, Middle, and New Russian Poetry" ("O drevnem, srednem i novom stikhotvorenii rossiiskom," 1755), a work which can lay claim to being the first history that acknowledges the existence and importance of pre-Petrine Russian literature and stretches from folk tales to the poetry of Antiokh Kantemir. In his *Conversation about Spelling*, Trediakovsky began to favor the use of adjectives drawn from Old Church Slavonic. He believed that the use of older East Slavonic words formed etymologically from Greek connected the Russians with the Ancients. In casting his epic *Tilemakhida* in this older idiom, Trediakovsky believed the work would be closer to Homer's epics than Fénelon's *Télémaque*, a celebrated didactic work much read by royals as a manual in noble ideals. Indeed, the title of the translation with its Greek ending (*-ida*) has a point to make by classicizing the French original. The works that reflect this new tendency are his adaptation in verse of the *Psalter*, published in full only recently, the theological poem *Theoptia* written partly in syllabics, and, finally, *Tilemakhida*.

Trediakovsky's influence was rarely acknowledged, and no single writer of importance applied his system wholesale. Taken together, his views became increasingly impractical and divorced from the educated vernacular. But some of his recommendations on the literary language and style gained traction. We have seen that his early style won over Karamzin, while his later attitude to archaic stylization appealed to Admiral Shishkov, a proponent of linguistic nationalism in the 1810s. Trediakovsky's version of the hexameter influenced the classicists Sergey Uvarov and Nikolai Gnedich in the early decades of the nineteenth century, and Aleksandr Radishchev favored this meter over Lomonosov's iamb. Vasily Petrov, the ode writer and translator of Virgil's *Aeneid*, imitated his syntactic inversions—all in all a substantial legacy for a writer who was much derided in his lifetime and posthumously. The eventual failure of his solutions to problems of grammar, language, and style should not obscure the value of a body of work that, more than any other in the period, produced a comprehensive and systematic statement on the struggle writers faced in elaborating rules and values of literary art.

Lomonosov made rules of eloquence the basis of his theory of style set out and illustrated in his *Short Handbook on Rhetoric for the Use of Lovers of Eloquence* (*Kratkoe rukovodstvo k ritorike na pol'zu liubitelei sladkorechiia*, 1743), which he revised extensively over the next three years. It drew widely on the repertory of Latin examples in prose and in verse from Jesuit manuals, and featured examples from Russian poetry, including Lomonosov's own. Based on extensive knowledge of key Renaissance and seventeenth-century texts, the *Rhetoric* was a cutting-edge anthology of European sources. After much of the first print run had been destroyed in a warehouse fire in 1747, new copies were printed in 1748, with reprints in 1759 and 1765. The book also formed the basis of a set of lectures he gave at the Academy of Sciences on versification and prosody, the first of their kind at the Academy. His supposition was that rules of literary decorum necessarily reflected a message and an idea of communicative appropriateness (as opposed to the philological premises on which Trediakovsky's positions rested). As a pupil of the Slavo-Greco-Latin Academy, Lomonosov had received a solid classical education. His *Short Handbook* provided a historical perspective on the utilitarian and persuasive functions of style and a wealth of examples of rhetoric from a living language composed in a supple vernacular that gave speakers a flexibility of register. Lomonosov believed the tropes used in ancient European literature to be transferable to his own context, and to this end he illustrated expressive techniques by adducing ample passages from Cicero and Virgil in the Latin with his own translations. Bilingual excerpts held out the promise of a modern Russian written language capable of the range of literary modes practiced by the ancient writers. His own poetic compositions implement the prosodic theories he outlined in his "Letter on the Rules of Russian Versification" ("Pis'mo o pravilakh rossiiskogo stikhotvorstva"), which he sent to the Academy of Sciences along with his "Ode on the Taking of Chocim" ("Oda na vziatie Khotina," 1739), which was modeled on the expositions of Nicolas Caussin (1583–1651) and Johann-Christoph Gottsched. In his work on rhetoric and grammar, in particular, Lomonosov aimed ultimately to regularize the literary language—in effect, its use in poetry.[33] He accepted that the formation of new words would necessarily be eclectic and that the structure of the Russian language, and above all the morphology of words, made the creation of calques based on modern European languages a highly productive way to expand the language and create new usages. He reserved Slavonic words as by-forms or alternatives to be used when writers wished to strike an elevated tone.

Variations in diction, more than any other single factor, were the basis of Lomonosov's adaptation of the theory of the three styles (*teoriia trekh stilei*) founded on his reading of Roman and seventeenth-century French rhetoricians. Lomonosov advocated the necessity of a correlation between genre and diction, which encouraged practices that, starting in the 1760s, would become the dominant norm (if not exclusive system) in poetry and drama. His theory restricted the low style, marked by colloquial speech and dialogue, to comedy and satire. The high style, in which Slavonic words supplanted their everyday equivalents, was the language of tragedy and solemn and spiritual odes, and he discussed its advantages in "A Preface on the Utility of Ecclesiastical Books in the Russian Language" ("Predislovie o pol´ze knig tser´kovnykh v rossiiskom iazyke," 1758).

Lomonosov's three-style theory was not a comprehensive solution to the difficult problem of Slavonicisms in Russian. He did not clearly explain the nature of the middle style or systematically coordinate the interrelation among the three styles. Yet while it would be an exaggeration to posit a "linguistic turn," trends in poetic diction and form stabilized quickly, and while debate would continue well into the nineteenth century—Alexander Pushkin's letters to friends are full of quibbles about word choice, for instance—a strong sense of poetic style, and the pleasure of poetic eloquence, crystallized around Lomonosov's lifetime.[34] Poets worked in far larger numbers than prose writers, and while it is hard to determine what was cause and what was effect, more versifiers meant a relatively rapid advance in the verse language.

CASE STUDY The creation of modern verse

Medieval Russian literature used prose genres almost exclusively. The absence of written poetry has been explained by various factors, such as the lack of knightly and courtly cultures, the scarcity of developed city life, and the absence of universities. The need for poetry in medieval Russia was satisfied by folk genres, some of which were recited (epic poems, or *byliny*; and funeral laments), others sung (ritual poetry, love songs, and lullabies), and yet others spoken (all genres employed by itinerant performers, or *skomorokhi*). The prosody of each of these poetic forms was markedly different from the others and from that of the Russian written poetry that began to appear in the seventeenth century. Furthermore, although a substantial amount of scholarship exists on folk versification, there remains little agreement on how different verse forms should be described and interpreted.

Written poetry emerged in Muscovite Russia in the early seventeenth century, when several cultural developments coalesced to encourage changes in the forms of literary production and thus facilitated its appearance. The social and cultural transformations that followed the so-called Time of Troubles, the years of interregnum between the death of the last Russian tsar of the Rurik dynasty and the establishment of the Romanov dynasty in 1613, brought Russians into closer contact with Europe. Russia's increased involvement in European politics required literate bureaucrats, which promoted the development of lay learning. This in turn led to changes in the venues of literary production: hitherto mostly confined to the monasteries, literature increasingly began to be produced by non-clerics.

In the 1630s, contacts with Poland and Ukraine resulted in the emergence of the practice of poetry among a group of men who were otherwise employed as bureaucrats (hence the collective name of the Chancery School: *prikaznaia shkola*). Influenced by Polish, Ukrainian, and Belarusian poetry, this first sizable cohort of secularly educated Russians employed verse traditionally called pre-syllabic; its lines as a rule were arranged in rhymed couplets, and the rhyming lines tended to be parisyllabic, that is, more or less of the same length. Unlike Polish poetry, where feminine rhyme predominated, these poets used all types of rhymes, from masculine to hyperdactylic. They also frequently used acrostics and other types of word play to structure their verse.

Simeon Polotsky brought regular syllabic verse to Russia. In Russian syllabics, modeled after Polish, rhythm was created by the count of syllables and by rhyme. Russians used syllabic versification up until the late 1730s, when they began to adopt syllabotonic (or accentual-syllabic) versification, a process mostly completed in the late 1740s. The adoption by Russians of the syllabotonics is usually called "the reform of versification," which implies a conscious effort, a deliberate rejection of the old system and embracing of the new one. Deliberate though it may have been on the part of a number of practitioners, it took place gradually and in stages, and the following milestones need to be acknowledged.

In 1735, Trediakovsky published a theoretical treatise *New and Brief Method for Composing Russian Verse*, in which he argued that the Russian ear, accustomed to the inherent stress pattern of the language, finds it hard to process the longer (thirteen- and eleven-syllable) syllabic lines, and they therefore must have a predictable distribution of stresses. His proposed modifications resulted in a verse-line that was closest to trochaic hexameters and pentameters, with obligatory feminine rhymes. Trediakovsky's treatise drew the attention of his fellow poets. Lomonosov, who studied his book thoroughly (the copy with his notes has survived), proposed more radical changes, making the requirement for regular distribution of stresses universal and introducing iambic and ternary meters. He also rejected Trediakovsky's ban on masculine and dactylic rhymes as well as on alternating rhymes. Lomonosov described his new system in the 1739 "Letter on the Rules of Russian Versification," which he sent from Germany, where he was studying mining at the time, to the Russian Academy of Sciences. As an illustration of his ideas, he included with the letter a poem in iambic tetrameter, "Ode on the Taking of Chocim," commemorating a minor Russian victory in the Russo-Austro-Turkish War of 1735–39. Lomonosov's proposed changes were far more comprehensive and radical than Trediakovsky's. In fact, they were so radical that he had to backtrack on some of his rules, such as his initial requirement that in binary meters every foot should carry a stress and therefore comply with the pattern of stress fulfillment posited in a line of verse as supposed in theory. This was not viable because Russian permits only one stress per word, and yet the average Russian word has three syllables. Such a rule would have severely curtailed the stock of words that a poet could have fitted into a line, and would have precluded any flexibility in the rhythm. Lomonosov jettisoned this restriction and revised his "Ode on the Taking of Chocim" in 1751, introducing "pyrrhics" and thus making the cadence of its verse more supple.

Kantemir attempted to defend syllabics in his 1743 response to Trediakovsky's proposal, "Letter of Khariton Makentin [*Antiokh Kantemir*] to a Friend on Composing Russian Verse" ("Pis′mo Kharitona Makentina k priiateliu o slozhenii stikhov russkikh," 1742) in which he, while rejecting Trediakovsky's modifications and arguing for keeping syllabics, proposed some changes of his own, such as enjambment, use of varied rhymes, and even unrhymed verse.

In response to Lomonosov's suggestions, Trediakovsky revised his *Method* and published the new version in his 1752 *Collected Works* under the title "A Method for Composing Russian Verse." He mostly accepted the changes proposed by Lomonosov; furthermore, he systematized them, stressing, however, his priority in initiating the reform. Aleksandr Sumarokov's contribution to the reform was primarily practical: while Trediakovsky continued to prefer trochees and Lomonosov, iambs, Sumarokov used all possible metrical variations the new system offered. He also experimented with verse forms not suggested by either Trediakovsky or Lomonosov, such as variable (or free) iambs, which he used to write fables, successfully making it a preferred meter for this genre. In the 1770s, Sumarokov wrote his own theoretical essay "On Versification" ("O stoposlozhenii," first published in 1781), in which he took stock of the changes Russian verse had undergone since 1735. Most importantly, in this essay he listed all five syllabotonic meters, two binary (iamb and trochee) and three ternary (dactyl, amphibrach, and anapest), thus describing for the first time the system to be used through the nineteenth century and to the present day.

While the syllabotonic system was taking shape and becoming predominant in Russian poetry, Trediakovsky was also experimenting with the tonic system, that is, a system in which the rhythm is created by the counting of stresses. He used as his models both ancient Greek and Roman poetry, as well as Russian folk songs. Trediakovsky's experiments resulted in the first Russian imitation of classic hexameter, which he deployed in *Tilemakhida*, an epic based on François Fénelon's *Les Aventures de Télémaque*. His contemporaries and immediate successors did not appreciate Trediakovsky's epic or its meter. Nonetheless, when Nikolai Gnedich (1784–1833) and Vasily Zhukovsky (1783–1852) later turned to translating *The Iliad* and *The Odyssey*, respectively, they both followed Trediakovsky in their imitations of epic verse.

The versification system that developed in the eighteenth century proved to be a stable foundation for the modern poetic tradition. Binary syllabotonic meters, and iambic tetrameter in particular, predominated in Russian poetic practice throughout the nineteenth century. However, ternary meters gradually began to gain in popularity as well. Prominent practitioners from the second half of the nineteenth century include Nikolai Nekrasov (1821–78) and Aleksei Tolstoy (1817–75).

In the early twentieth century, tonic meters provided new rhythmic possibilities. Foremost among these were the so-called *dol'nik* (in which the intervals between the stresses vary from one to two syllables) and *taktovik* (in which the intervals between the stresses vary from one to three syllables). Twentieth-century poets who drew immediately on these new resources included Aleksandr Blok, who used tonic verse to emulate folk idiom, and Marina Tsvetaeva, whose verse dramas adopted very complex polymetrical systems. Later, moving even further in the direction of the rhythmically loosened line, poets experimented with accentual verse in which the number of syllables forming the intervals between stresses is not regulated. Vladimir Mayakovsky, who was highly resourceful in his manipulation of stanza forms as well as metrical schemes, showed a marked preference for accentual verse as a vehicle for his dynamic, explosive narrations. While *dol'nik* and (to a lesser extent) *taktovik* have acquired a permanent place in the canon of Russian meters, accentual verse lost its popularity by the end of the avant-garde period in Russia. Together with tonic meters, free verse—or *vers libre*, a term that has been Russified as *verlibr*—was gaining some popularity at the turn of the twentieth century. Never as prominent as in French or English poetic traditions, it nonetheless has been taken up by a sizable group of contemporary poets. The flourishing of Russian poetry in the post-Soviet period has come in large part from extensive experimentations with free verse. Some of these poets have also shown considerable flair in experimenting with other rare or forgotten meters, such as accentual verse.

More conservative views of poetry still persist, and just as Russian poets have largely kept to traditional metric patterns much longer than most other European or American poetic traditions, Russians have been quite conservative in respect to rhyme. Some contemporary poets, for example, whose metrical experimentations can be impressive, rarely abandon rhyme. Although unrhymed verse was promoted already by Trediakovsky (who cited ancient Greek and Roman poetry as his models), it was used sparsely. Some meters have been more likely to drop rhymes, such as iambic pentameter. Under the influence of Shakespeare, it first was widely used in nineteenth-century drama (particularly by Alexander Pushkin and Tolstoy); however, it soon also became a popular choice for elegy. Other syllabotonic and tonic meters drop rhymes less frequently, but trochaic, iambic, and amphibrach tetrameters occasionally have been used, as has an extremely rare trochaic pentameter. Free verse also rejects rhyme, and it is in that form that most contemporary readers will encounter unrhymed poetry.

The reform of prose was a different matter altogether. The English man of letters and lexicographer Samuel Johnson (1709–84) advised writers to read Joseph Addison (1672–1719) in order to acquire a model of the "middle style"—chatty, polite, smooth, modern, and never vulgar. In Russia, the need for such a style emerged only in relation to the gradual development of an educated readership and a fledgling civic space: readers numbered in the low hundreds by contrast with the subscribers in the 1710s to Addison's daily periodical (with Sir Richard Steele) *The Spectator*, who numbered in the thousands in London, Edinburgh, and even the American colonies. For Lomonosov, prose was a tool of scientific exposition, homily, and speeches, and it largely followed the prescriptions he formulated for the higher genres: a formal bookishness that is Latinate and certainly not conversational. Attempts to fashion a literary vernacular created a welter of approaches, seen especially in the wildly divergent styles translators used in working with European literature.[35] Writers of Lomonosov's generation who wished to compose works in serious genres had no difficulty finding stylistic and linguistic models; there was no problem about lengthening periods and inflating one's rhetoric. But from the 1750s onward, and most particularly in the 1760s, the growth in taste for fiction, chitchat, wit, and narrative poems led to stylistic uncertainty.

In his early years, Trediakovsky's expository prose adopted a higher style by dint of register but he advocated a consecutive syntax unencumbered by subordinate clauses; his translations were even more closely attuned to the level of the spoken language. Later on, his inversions and difficult syntax proved to be a dead end, although they found an unexpected admirer and selective imitator in Aleksandr Radishchev (1749–1802). For Radishchev, who was a sophisticated and flexible stylist capable of writing a smoother, more colloquial prose, style could be a statement. In his most important and most famous work, *The Journey from St. Petersburg to Moscow* (*Puteshestvie iz Peterburga v Moskvu*, 1790), he deliberately fashions an archaic, cumbersome style in the manner of Trediakovsky, exceeding his model in the abundant use of complex subordinate clauses, replete with dative and genitive absolutes and a Slavonic-based vocabulary. The use of a difficult style was a deliberate rejection of the smoother style of writing that by the 1790s had finally become the norm.

Lomonosov's idea of syntactic decorum has its roots in the linguistic theories of the Port-Royal school. Until the 1760s, the Port-Royal model of prose was given a last lease on life in Russia by Lomonosov. The qualities that defined its style are force (*sila*) and elaborateness, and, because it was put to use largely in the service of such genres as the eulogy, sermon, and speech, this style emphasized the use of rhetorical effects: sharp contrasts, long periods, sound-play, among others. In his *Short Course* and his *Russian Grammar* (*Rossiiskaia grammatika*, 1755), Lomonosov sought to develop an expository style capable of expressing philosophical abstractions and ideas. Influenced as well by the psychological theories of the French philologist and grammarian Étienne Bonnot de Condillac (1714–80), Lomonosov treated word-placement as a means of mirroring the order of signifiers as they enter one's consciousness: thoughts ordered words and words ordered ideas of things in the mind. Lomonosov, and later Karamzin, tried to refine their prose to approximate the ideal of fluidity that Condillac had defined as follows: "Nous voudrions donner à nos expressions la rapidité de nos pensées" ("We would like to give the rapidity of our thoughts to what we write").[36] Nonetheless, Lomonosov hesitated between different syntactic paradigms, experimenting with using both German and Latin as models for prose. The formality of language and periodic syntax made his own prose much less influential than his writings on versification.

Lomonosov's exposure to Trediakovsky seems to have primed him to seek out other theoretical models, and he was especially well-read in the poetic theories of contemporary German writers, especially Johann-Christoph Gottsched, whose works on language and style he summarized in articles. Following on his "Letter on the Rules of Russian Versification," Lomonosov turned to other aspects of literary style in his *Short Handbook*. Lomonosov's innovative principles influenced Trediakovsky, whose two versions of a single poem, "Triumphal Ode on the Surrender of Gdansk" ("Oda torzhestvennaia o sdache goroda Gdanska"), are a case in point. The original version of 1734 was written in syllabic verse; for the 1752 edition of his works, Trediakovsky revised it in syllabotonic four-foot trochee. Furthermore, in the earlier version, Trediakovsky praises Feofan Prokopovich, a modern, as a second Horace, underscoring the value of an "Ancient" within the native culture. In 1752, he praises Boileau as equal to Pindar and Horace, and here Boileau stands for Trediakovsky as a Modern who writes poetry on par with the Ancients but in his own native language.[37]

During the 1750s, Lomonosov (himself widely dubbed the "Russian Pindar") had two forums to promote his vision of the literary system: the Academy of Sciences in St. Petersburg and the newly founded Moscow University.[38] In focusing on Roman and Greek authors in his *Rhetoric*, and in forging a seamless connection with remote ancestors, however artificial the link may be, Lomonosov also wishes to nudge out the claims of more proximate traditions. In his works on literary theory, Trediakovsky expresses his admiration for the Greek and Roman authors as models of style, while Lomonosov in his *Rhetoric* chose passages in Latin for translation into Russian in order to illustrate how equivalent figures of speech would sound in Russian. He eclipsed Trediakovsky as the key theorist of the new system because his rules about diction, meter, and syntax were easier to apply.[39]

Like Addison in England, it was the Russian satirists, above all Nikolai Novikov (1744–1818; portrayed in Figure III.01 by one of the most distinguished Russian painters of the age), who, in the 1770s, crafted a conversational voice—argumentative, jocular, folksy, and when need be, also educated.[40] In the next generation, Karamzin favored a more pared-down style, elegant and ostensibly "simple."

FIGURE III.01. D. G. Levitsky, *Portrait of Nikolai Novikov*, before 1792.

In the context of attempts to work out an educated prose style, simplicity stands for clarity and flexibility, and the means of achieving this effect lay in the use of immediately transparent syntactic relations and phrases. The goal of "writing simply" reverses the legacy of scholastic rhetoric still entrenched in schools whose curriculum was established on the basis of Jesuitical models. Karamzin's view of prose structure was highly influenced by three important French theoreticians of direct word order and the sentence as a progressive sequence—Claude Buffier (1661–1737), Étienne-Simon de Gamaches (1672–1756), the author of *Les Agréments du langage réduits à leurs principes* (1718), and Nicolas Beauzée (1717–89), the author of a *Grammaire générale* (1767). In their work, particular attention is given to the order and placement of verbal complements such as direct and indirect objects. Their argument is based on psychology and the assumption that syntax should reflect the logical sequence of apprehension. Furthermore, the premise behind the reform of syntax that Karamzin undertook was faithful to a tenet of French prose theory: that prose must be concerned with furnishing the reader with an easy textual experience, that it must always move forward and without surprise, and avoid the dislocations that require the readers to retrace their steps. Word order arranged in a strictly logical and progressive manner conformed to the then current ideas about the workings of the mind, and in the ensuing decades remained a model of an educated style. As Nikolai Koshansky (1784 or 1785–1831), the Russian rhetorician and Alexander Pushkin's teacher at the Lyceum, noted in his textbook: "Words and expressions must follow ideas and their actual sequencing."[41] If normalization leads to a loss of intricacy and variety, the assumption is that it is more than adequately compensated by gain in clarity. Achieving agreeability (*priiatnost'*)—a virtue Karamzin rated highly—depends less on the lexicon and simplicity than on fluidity and attentiveness to the act of reading. Karamzin's view was that ideally prose should have fewer words and more ideas. These are some of the technical decisions that paved the way for the smoothness of so-called "Salon style" (*salonnaia rech'*) of Karamzin's generation. Behind all of these initiatives and creative efforts was a unified belief that Russia, especially from the rule of Catherine the Great (r. 1762–96), had the requisite linguistic resources and human talent to produce a significant body of literature on par with that of Europe.

In his two important verse epistles on the subject of language and literature, written in 1747 and published the following year, Sumarokov outlined his program of good literary taste and usage.[42] In effect, he picked up the gauntlet thrown by Trediakovsky's "Epistle to Apollo" to the Russian letters. Was it possible to secure a place for Russia in European letters equal to the one occupied by French literature? Satire and precept combine in the two epistles, where Sumarokov asserts his claim to being a codifier of Russian literary practice. Sumarokov's two epistles address literary style as an integrated set of elements (prosody, diction, models) that define taste. The "Epistle on Versification" has been called the manifesto of Russian classicism. In it, Sumarokov carries out his ambition to follow Boileau's *Art poétique* in prescribing rules for genres and the literary system. (Sumarokov has often been called the Russian Boileau, which looks like another example of a spurious search for a single father-figure.)

In his didactic epistles Sumarokov put theory to work, demonstrating a combination of stylistic polish and erudition that lives up to the classical and neoclassical ideal of reconciling pleasure and pedagogy.[43] All a Russian writer needed to do, Sumarokov argued, was to assimilate these practices and avoid pitfalls such as contaminating one genre with another, "lest you irritate the muses with your ill-gained success; Thalia with tears and Melpomene with laughter."[44] For Sumarokov, the paramount prescription was the need for purity of style for perfect clarity of thought. Thus he opposes overcomplicated syntax and lexicon, archaisms and metaphor, and his criticism of these prosodic features sparked a quarrel with Lomonosov whom he also admired despite the rivalry to be the "Malesherbes of our land, the equal of Pindar." For the epistles' republication in 1774, Sumarokov gave them a single title under the rubric "an instruction to those who wish to be writers."

In his first epistle, Sumarokov opposes nature to art: poetic expression must be in harmony with his ideas about the nature of man. The principles of style are therefore determined not only by aesthetics, but also by philosophical conceptions about mankind and the world. In his article "On Human Understanding in the Opinion of Locke" ("O razumenii chelovecheskom po mneniiu Lokka," 1759), Sumarokov expresses the view of a philosophical sensualist that reason is empty when divorced from sensation: "What the ringing of bells sounds like and the roar of the cannon we know not from reason but from our ear."[45] All movements of the soul find their source in sensation. Nature does not reveal the truth to our souls and consequently offers no moral lesson. Yet imitating nature may create a union between the ethical and the beautiful, in keeping with the neoclassical aesthetic.

Clarity of expression and a logical exposition are the hallmarks of Sumarokov's program based on a theory of language that treats the word as a mathematical sign with perfect equivalence between signifier and signified. The ideal of rational clarity is far from being seen as the enemy of feeling. On the contrary, Sumarokov argues that expression marked by clarity, simplicity, and feeling will strike the right balance between the implication of intelligence (*um*) and the overt expression of passion (*strast'*). The contrast with the utterances of Lomonosov's odes is pointed. Sumarokov faulted them for an ambiguity of language and denseness of metaphor that, he felt, fell short of the classical ideal. He equates clarity with aesthetic satisfaction, attacking Lomonosov in his "Criticism of the ode" ("Kritika na odu," written in 1751), and mocking both him and Trediakovsky in his comedy *Monsters* (*Chudovishchi*, 1750). It is not surprising to find Sumarokov disparaging his two chief rivals for the lack of proportion in their syntax and regular use of vocabulary, for their use of archaisms and extravagant metaphor. Oriented toward France as a beacon of taste, the opening of Sumarokov's "Epistle on the Russian Language" ("Epistola II") argues that Russian must aspire to develop an idiom fit for an "educated people" (*slovesnyi cheloveki*). While he admits that other languages have achieved their perfection and polish thanks to their literatures, he is confident that Russia can simultaneously reinvent its language and found its literature anew. Sumarokov's preferred solution is to imitate the French syntax, develop coinages and calques based on the French, and to maintain a correlation between literary register and genre (high style for the epic, the ode, and tragedy; middle style for epistles and lyric poetry; and low style for comedy, fables, and epigrams). Much of Russian tragedy, a highly productive genre, would remain true to the classical unities, rules of diction, and declamatory verse exemplified by Sumarokov's practice of the high style, especially in his tragedies, beginning with *Khorev* (1747, staged 1750), *Sinav and Truvor* (*Sinav i Truvor*, staged 1750), *Semira* (staged 1751), *Iaropolk i Dimiza* (written c.1759, published in 1768) and *Vysheslav* (1768). These plays, as well as the tragedy *Mstislav* (completed 1772), were instrumental in establishing the genre of tragedy in Russia, which other writers, including Lomonosov, followed.[46]

It is therefore understandable that Trediakovsky and Lomonosov should clash with Sumarokov, who did not celebrate the classical tradition or employ established rhetorical formulas to the same extent. The appeal to nature and greater simplicity discernible in Sumarokov's writings repudiate Trediakovsky's archaist tendencies. Sumarokov's style adheres to the middle register described by Lomonosov. But his syntax is smoother and closer to the French ideal, consistent with his desire to establish French culture as the poetic and cultural norm rather than the Latin and German models favored by Lomonosov.

Literary quarrels and a culture of contest

It may have been his experience of the literary polemics of his own day in the 1920s that led Grigory Gukovsky (1902–50), a pioneering scholar of the eighteenth century, to observe that Russian literature had stepped out of its infancy in the mid-eighteenth century precisely when literary schools formed, when authors closed ranks around one leading figure, and set themselves in opposition to an alternative poetics promoted by rival authors.[47] Notions of taste and sensibility became an intense and contested business. Questions about imitation and originality, reason and passion, duty and autonomy increasingly polarized writers. For the articulation of every norm, there was a parodist ready and waiting to debunk it and advocate an alternative. The eighteenth century affords much pleasure if we appreciate how wit leavened serious philological purpose.

Russian literary historians tend to treat the antagonism between the three main protagonists as a series of personal spats or squabbles between schools. Quarrelling in itself enjoyed cultural valence as a competitive performance. However personal the stakes, disputes turned into literature aligned the Russian literary scene with the literary field of Europe, since battles of the books ruled the day across Europe.[48] In this respect, the rolling series of disputes over style that lasted from the 1750s until the 1820s moved Russia from the position of an outlier into mainstream practice.[49] After all, writers, translators, and grammarians found themselves undertaking a great experiment in which norms might be established only to be changed again because no authority was absolute. In practice, because the language was in such a flux, with norms of syntax, word formation, and register highly fluid, the application of any theoretical system did not determine success or guarantee loyalty.

The story of quarrels also illustrates not just the pitfalls threatening individual reputations, but it shows how vital were the assertion and the debunking of leadership roles in making the establishment of norms dynamic and therefore unstable. Gukovsky plausibly attributes the bitterness of the fighting to the aesthetic mentality of the period, namely to the belief in a single true artistic ideal, existing outside time and space. The creative act was understood to be rational and governed by a set of rules. Every artistic goal had in principle only one solution. Since the means of achieving the literary ideal were held to be rationally determined, representatives of alien schools were regarded as blockheads. Yet there was also a competing ideal of contest and witty exchange for their own sake as a demonstration of mental and linguistic panache, qualities that were taken as evidence of Europeanization and rational accomplishment.

A few snapshots capture the communal project to portray one another as witless dunces despite the fact that their individual artistic programs shared common features. After an initial alliance, Sumarokov repudiated Trediakovsky's program as too complex and regressive in order to side with Lomonosov. In 1744, the three writers arranged a translation contest of Psalm 143, a peaceful experiment rather than a heated argument. Trediakovsky, who previously advocated the trochee as the dominant meter, relented because he now concluded that no meter is intrinsically better suited to a given genre or theme. Nonetheless, he employed the trochee in his translation, while Lomonosov and Sumarokov used the iamb, consistent with their view that, since it is an ascending meter, its rhythm confers nobility. These translations provided a showcase for their styles. The three versions spanned the spectrum from literal translation (Lomonosov) to radical adaptation (Trediakovsky). Through their different use and weighting of archaic language or the smoother contemporary idiom, the translations provided a master class of a literary system in flux.

A veritable war was sparked by Trediakovsky's negative review of Sumarokov's plays *Khorev* and *Hamlet* (1748, staged 1750), highlighting their erratic style and grammatical mistakes.[50] Sumarokov repaid the criticism in kind in his "Epistle on the Russian Language," in which he alludes to Trediakovsky's foul style. In his "Epistle on Versification," Sumarokov speaks of Lomonosov as akin to Pindar, but likens Trediakovsky to the mathematician Michael Stifel (1486–1567), who loved complex calculations, saying "But you, Shtivelius, can only talk nonsense."[51] Trediakovsky's bitter enmity with Lomonosov and Sumarokov dates to the 1750s, when he became the satirical butt of their epigrams and plays. Sumarokov continued his attacks on Trediakovsky in the comedy *Tresotinius* (1750), mocking the author of *Conversation about Spelling* as a Trissotin, the mediocre scholar-poet of Molière's *Les Femmes savantes*.[52] Sumarokov publicly exposed Trediakovsky's Achilles' heel after his turn toward a more archaic style. Trediakovsky parried with a long treatise, which he called "A Letter Containing a Consideration on the Poem Recently Published by the Author of Two Odes, Two Tragedies and Two Epistles, Composed by One Acquaintance to Another" ("Pis′mo, v kotorom soderzhitsia rassuzhdenie o stikhot-vorenii, ponyne na svet izdannom ot avtora dvukh od, dvukh tragedii i dvukh epistol, pisan-noe ot priiateliu k priiateliu," [1750, pub. 1865]). The label "acquaintance" was a gesture of insincere civility: the author found numerous faults in Sumarokov's works, and charged him with incompetence in regard to Church Slavonic.[53]

In the early 1750s, Sumarokov sparred with Lomonosov. He had criticized the latter's "Ode on the Day of the Accession to the All Russian Throne of Her Majesty" ("Oda na den′ vossh-estviia na prestol imperatritsy Elisavety Petrovny," 1747) and defended his own style of dra-matic writing against Lomonosov's criticism. Sumarokov, nonetheless, continued to support Lomonosov in his attacks on Trediakovsky, although he was becoming irritated with Lomonosov over his ventures into tragedy, especially *Tamira and Selim* and *Demofont*, commis-sioned by the Empress Elizabeth in 1750–51 and performed in 1752. In 1756, Sumarokov, who had already made his mark as a dramatist, was appointed manager of the new Russian Theater, where he served until 1761, when various factions engineered his departure. Sumarokov mounted an assault on Lomonosov's poetic style in his highly amusing *Nonsense Odes* (*Vzdornye ody*, late 1750s), replete with caricatural odic devices and bombast. Sumarokov found an easy target in Lomonosov's grandeur. Nor did the poet's followers escape unscathed from Sumarokov and his acolytes' sharp tongues. In the "Dithyramb to Pegasus" ("Difiramv Pegasu," 1766) Sumarokov took aim at both Lomonosov, who had recently died, and Vasily Petrov (1736–99), an admirer of Lomonosov, whose expansive "Ode on a Carousel" ("Oda na velikolepnyi karusel′," 1766) set a new standard for rhetorical excess and use of amplification. In the article "On the Contemporary State of the Literary Arts in Russia" ("O nyneshnem sostoianii slovesnykh nauk v Rossii," 1757) and the poetic cycle "Conversation with Anacreon" ("Razgovor s Anakreonom," published 1774), Lomonosov staunchly defended the elevated genres, antagonized by Sumarokov's mockery of high styles and advocacy of *poésie légère*. By 1759, when Sumarokov inaugurated his journal *The Diligent Bee* (*Trudoliubivaia pchela*), Lomonosov's star was setting. Mikhail Kheraskov (1733–1807) and Aleksei Rzhevsky (1737–1804), in the new journal *Useful Entertainment*, parodied Lomonosov in print.

As in the Quarrel of the Ancients and Moderns in France and the Battle of the Books in England, factions determined to outwit one another deployed all the forms and arts of irony, parody, and satire in pitting one set of conventions against another.[54] Attempts to imitate Homeric and Virgilian epic had not met with much success, but mock-epic writers flourished. We see this in Vasily Maikov's burlesque celebration of drink, *Elysei, or Bacchus Disturbed* (*Elisei, ili Razdrazhennyi Vakkh*, 1771) and *Dushen′ka* (1783), a mock-epic revision of Jean de La Fontaine's novel in verse *Les Amours de Psyché et de Cupidon* (1669) by Ippolit Bogdanovich (1743–1803); and the brilliant reworking of the French Alexis Piron (1689–1773) in the "Ode to Priapus" ("Oda Priapu," 1750s) by Russia's first pornographic poet, the outrageously indecent and incredibly witty Ivan Barkov (1732–68).

The clash of 1753 deserves attention as classicism's first concerted contest and an exercise in the use of personal quarrels to articulate a literary system, a pattern that would persist into the 1810s, Pushkin's formative years. In 1753, Ivan Perfil′evich Elagin (1725–93; portrayed in Figure III.02 as a man of letters) wrote "An Epistle to Mr. Sumarokov" ("Epistola k g. Sumarokovu") which circulated in manuscript copies under the title "A Satire on the Petit-

FIGURE III.02. Jean-Louis Voille, *Portrait of Ivan Elagin*, *c*.1789.

Maître and Coquettes." An educated soldier and eventually a loyal advisor to Catherine, Elagin was an all-rounder who translated the Abbé Prevost, published works on the reform of serfdom, helped Sumarokov to publish his tragedies, wrote elegies, and participated in the empress's collective translation of Marmontel's *Bélisaire* (1767), a novel containing a celebrated chapter on religious tolerance.

Elagin also exercised a sharp literary wit in satirical verse. A polemical poem, the "Epistle" discriminates, on the one hand, between true and false neoclassical style and, on the other, implies that masters are not to be blamed for the excesses of their less talented followers. Despite Elagin's protests that he lacked facility in rhyme, the poem is an excellent example of well-honed Alexandrine couplets. (In 1770, an anonymous apologist of Elagin began an epigram with the ironical boast: "Every type of verse I love to make / As easy as frying a pancake.")[55] It was not for nothing that Elagin admired Alexander Pope (1688–1744), and he produced a satire worthy of that Augustan poet's elegant form and pungent wit.[56] Wrapping his discerning judgments in epigrammatic phrases, Elagin praises the effortlessness with which his old friend Sumarokov writes poetry imbued with reason, beauty, and wonder (*razum, krasota i divnost'*[57]). Elagin laments in mock-tragic tones the effort that writing costs him—the thanklessness of writing is a theme that goes back to Kantemir's "First Satire"—but then reflects on the empty smoothness cultivated by imitators of all things French at court, and the vanity of their self-deception in confusing facile mimicry with real style. Everything from fake beauty spots to foppish dress to speech (including bogus rhymes such as those Lomonosov devised in *Rosslia/IndIa* with the deliberate wrong stress) advertises a lack of genuine taste that suffers badly by comparison with true masters, such as Sumarokov and

Pope. In mocking these absurdly affected *petits-maîtres* who distort both genuine classicism and Russian common sense, he professes that he would prefer to "sweat over his rhymes" rather than be a laughing stock for his pseudo-Frenchness.

Elagin did not remain on the sidelines. His 1753 parody of Lomonosov's tragedy *Tamira and Selim* (1750) clearly hit a nerve. Lomonosov's ally, the courtier and translator Grigory Teplov, replied in an article, "Reflection on the Qualities of the Poet" ("O kachestvakh stikhotvortsa, rassuzhdenie," 1755), in which he attacked Sumarokov's followers for betraying the pedagogical mission of art. When Sumarokov published a fable, "An Ass in a Lion's Skin" ("Osel vo l'vovoi kozhe"), in which he alluded to Lomonosov's lowly origins, Lomonosov answered with the fable "A Pig in a Fox's Skin" ("Svin'ia v lis'ei kozhe"). Sumarokov ridiculed Lomonosov for his Homeric aspirations as a national poet. Eventually, in 1759, Lomonosov had the last word by having Sumarokov's journal, the *Diligent Bee*, closed down.[58]

A second round of exchanges followed in 1765, perhaps a final salute in the aftermath of Lomonosov's death. In another work, "An Announcement from Russian Theater" ("Ot rossiiskogo teatra ob"iavlenie," 1774), Elagin ignited a round of quarrels by targeting the pathetic language Lomonosov used in his tragedy *Tamira and Selim*. This was a negative way of affirming aesthetic affinities, since Elagin, together with Kheraskov, Rzhevsky, and Maikov, formed one of the first literary associations in Russia to support Sumarokov's artistic principles. Given the character of literary play and the amateur ethos of the time, it is more appropriate to think of these informal and open groups as coteries rather than schools, united by shared taste and a common sense of literary pleasure.

Widely seen as Sumarokov's defense by proxy and a repudiation of the styles of other leading poets, Elagin's epistle unleashed a storm of critical debate and sometimes scurrilous attacks. Authors of verse epistles and epigrams included major figures such as Lomonosov and Trediakovsky, their respective allies, Popovsky (Alexander Pope's Russian admirer and translator) and the moralist and courtier Mikhail Shcherbatov (1733–90), as well as anonymous verse pamphleteers. Wit and invective were the common stock of versified quarrels. The claim that Sumarokov had "taken poetry in our language to such a high level" was greeted with outrage. Elagin's detractors misquoted and rewrote his phrases, caricaturing his style and attacking Sumarokov as the "discoverer of the mystery of discordant phrases" rather than the pioneer of a "much loved lyre," thereby ridiculing his pretension to being the equal of Racine, Boileau, or Molière. One of Elagin's partisans chastised satirists for their "harmful banter" by accusing them of bawling. The anonymous author of "Verses on Verses in Praise of the Epistle" ("Stikhi na stikhi, pokhval'nye epistoli," c.1753) openly disparaged the battle altogether. Despite his misgivings about Elagin's satirical style, he took the view that quarrels were the greater evil because they allowed fools to sound off. Such a contention was of course devised to provoke a new round of response and outrage as can be seen in the "Satire on the Use of French Words in Russian Conversations" ("Satira na upotreblenie frantsuzskikh slov v russkikh razgovorakh"). Elagin followed with a mini-treatise of his own, "The Author" (1755), lobbing insults at Teplov as a hack. The dramatist Iakov Kniazhnin (1740–91) produced a mock-epic in two cantos of about 400 lines called "The Battle of the Versifiers" ("Boi stikhotvortsev," 1765), which catalogs the defects of virtually all the poets, major and minor, who furiously compete for fame as the ultimate reward and climb one over the other to the top of Mount Parnassus.[59] At the end of Canto I, Kniazhnin makes Elagin advise them to consider the possibility that there are alternative paths to glory. In response, the whole swarm shouts in unison "We shall continue to versify even if lightning strikes us."[60] Poets are not easily herded into the obedience of single literary masters.

The next generation, while less vociferous, continued to score literary points phrased as enjoyable literary satire. In his "Consideration of the Difference between the High, Grand,

Majestic, Loud and Pompous" ("Rassuzhdenie o razlichii slogov vysokogo, velikolepnogo, velichestvennogo, gromkogo, nadutogo," 1783), Mikhail Murav'ev (1757–1807), in many respects a follower of Sumarokov and a polished master of the smooth style, mocked the distortions that could result from an overly zealous application of his rules (as can be seen in Kheraskov's narrative poems, which were considered nearly unreadable by contemporaries). Aleksandr Klushin (1763–1803/1804), a friend of Ivan Krylov (1769–1844), an influential critic and a translator, author of prose fiction and plays, including the successful comedy "It's No Good to Be Short-Sighted" ("Khudo byt' blizorukim," 1790), as late as the 1790s believed that one had to be discriminating about the choice of classical style. He praised Lomonosov's work as a historic contribution, but lambasted Lomonosov's follower I. I. Zavalishin (1769–1844) for the style of his gigantic epic poem *Heroiade* (*Geroida*, 1793) as a tasteless application of Lomonosov's poetics.[61]

These disagreements, aired in literary works displaying cleverness as well as genuine rancor, exemplify the art of the literary quarrel as a type of play that ironized a new classical system, confirming it, albeit only through subversion. While all the major literary programs of the late eighteenth and early nineteenth centuries promoted features of the new or neoclassical poetics, perhaps it was above all the legacy of the witty contest that survived in different schools and in the practice of individuals who occupied various positions in contemporaneous movements like Sentimentalism and pre-Romanticism.

We see that no single set of rules can define the classical style. Despite the impersonality of its formal aesthetic, uncertainty and doubt marked classicism, making and undoing reputations within relatively short spans of time. Trediakovsky's life and reputation have come to represent a parable of the writer of the period and the hazards of fame in a dynamic literary context.[62] In the 1760s, Trediakovsky's prolific output failed to find a readership. Forgotten and insulted, Trediakovsky died in 1769, his literary legacy a farrago of published and unpublished works, his reputation in tatters, and his image an almost constant source of mirth and ridicule in Russian literature. Beginning with the works produced in the 1740s, and especially his translations, the complexity of his prescriptions for word order, his prosodic regulations about how to harmonize the verse line, syntactic rules concerning the relationships between parts of speech, and the placement of the caesura began to look unworkable to any other writer and off-putting to any reader, despite occasional sparks of beauty and intricacy. Yet Trediakovsky remains historically important, rather than a mere curiosity, because his early contribution to the Academy, his position as an irritant to his rivals, his poetic practice, and his theoretical writings proved vital. Lomonosov's position at the Academy of Sciences, his stature at court, the success of his stylistic prescriptions (rather more than his works of theater), and perhaps even his love of metaphor, a favorite trope of Russian poetry, made him a mythic figure. Yet, arguably, Sumarokov had shown greater skill as a lyric poet and dramatist. His crafting of the language of the elegy more directly influenced the development of lyric poetry with the next generation, while his mastery of the Alexandrine and forms of tragedy proved to be a long-lasting model.

Yet, as poets, neither Lomonosov nor Sumarokov would remain a live presence for the following generations. Higher genres lost favor, and were revived only on special occasions, such as the accession of Alexander I. Poets, including Karamzin, hastened to mark the accession by writing odes. We see a further vestige of the bygone era in neoclassical tragedy, which had a final lease on life in the plays of Vladislav Ozerov (1769–1816), whose last play *Polyxena* (1809), a vehicle for the actress Ekaterina Semenova (later mentioned in *Evgenii Onegin*), injected sentimental pathos into the immobile grandeur of a Corneille-style plot about love and duty. The archaic idiom and the valorization of tragedy, defended in conservative circles with a nationalist bias such as Beseda, was recognized as outmoded.[63] Individual reputations remained in flux, more subject to neglect than reevaluation. Gavrila Derzhavin (1743–1816) quickly eclipsed Lomonosov, Sumarokov, and Trediakovsky as the preeminent genius of the age. An unpublished essay on Russian literature, written by a nobleman in the early 1770s, accords much attention to a gallery of figures from Feofan Prokopovich to a long list of unknowns. The absence of Derzhavin from such a list reminds one that his renown only took off a decade later.[64] Partly thanks to his longevity, partly thanks to his creation of a personal voice that resonated with the new subjectivities of early Romanticism, Derzhavin enjoyed great esteem as the undisputed lyric genius of the Catherine period. In recent critical discussions, Derzhavin has acquired a reputation as a visionary poet with a clumsy style whose originality stems from his transgressive tendency to violate neoclassical rules.[65] The strict divisions between high and low styles, which fomented argument from the 1750s onward, were by no means the definitive criterion of taste in the 1780s when Derzhavin's celebrity began. Derzhavin's own benchmark of genius was a visionary state he associated with the sublime.[66] Deviation from the rules was neither a shatteringly unusual nor a necessary criterion of originality. His own contemporaries did not criticize him for stylistic solecisms or attribute his originality to tonal instability, especially his mixing of high and low registers. Contemporaries prized Derzhavin as a voice of individual genius and a frank personality.[67] But a consensus on his development and the periodization of his work has, to this day, eluded literary historians.[68]

2

Institutions of writing and authorship

Court literature and absolutism: The ode

Peter the Great needed civil servants to staff his expanding government. The structure he devised for creating a pool of qualified people was the Table of Ranks, instituted in 1722. Its function was to recruit literate and numerate men who were employed in the civil and military administration; they were incentivized with ennoblement and further promotion as designated by grades in the Table of Ranks. The system initiated a culture of service to the state among the gentry (or service gentry) and over time produced a new elite. "In practice," as the historian Geoffrey Hosking notes, "the Table of Ranks became part of the patronage networks [and] strengthened the power of existing elites while providing a mechanism by which they could be renewed."[1] Over the span of several decades, the criteria for social and professional advancement also motivated a demand for better education, leading to the growth of literacy, with all its consequences for a book culture. The monarch and the court remained central to Peter's vision of absolutism. During the reign of Peter the Great's daughter Elizabeth Petrovna (r. 1741–61), architecture and music flourished, and foreign theater companies found a welcome reception. Literature, on the whole, had lost impetus. Empress Elizabeth's remarkable construction program transformed St. Petersburg. Its new spaces of culture complemented the civic and academic institutions located on Vasilevsky Island and were within a close radius of the imperial palace. The newly established Academy of Fine Arts and the Academy of Sciences, a Petrine foundation, supported artistic and scientific activities.[2] The lasting legacy of these two decades was a small number of plays, translations of psalms, and Lomonosov's impressive odes and lyric meditations. While revisionist arguments have been made for court theater as a sophisticated form of commentary on current events, there is an abiding consensus that, by and large, the literary legacy of Elizabeth's reign—not much more than token poems of praise, some experimental translations, and scattered collections of songs—represents a lull by comparison with the dynamism of the last third of the century.[3]

Writers of the period pondered this gap between the flourishing of the arts and literary stagnation. In the 200 "Verses on Those Aspiring to Honor at Court" ("Stikhi na zhelaiushchikh chesti pri dvore," c.1730?), attributed to Kantemir, the speaker pulls no punches in describing the career path and the thrills and spills awaiting courtiers. "Naked truth finds it dangerous to broach the court," he says, detailing a system in which reward is the symbolic capital of status as much as material wealth.[4] This is a far cry from the ceremonial world of court ritual described by the seventeenth-century poets Simeon Polotsky and Sylvester Medvedev. While Kantemir's picture applied mainly to the new career class created by Peter the Great, writers also depended on the favor of the monarch and his entourage. Neither Peter nor Elizabeth had shown much of an interest in literature, and aspiring writers looked elsewhere for support. In 1740, Sumarokov took up a position as assistant to Count Golovkin. When Golovkin fell from grace at the beginning of Elizabeth's reign, Sumarokov entered the service of Count A. G. Razumovsky, a favorite of the empress and patron of European culture in Russia.

From the start of her long reign (1762–96), Catherine II seized every opportunity to use culture to create a new vision of civilization in Russia based on refinement, creativity, and national values.[5] Literature was central to projecting her brand of enlightened absolutism, not least because Catherine naturally gravitated to literary forms. Always a voracious reader, she was a gifted letter-writer and memoirist, and an assiduous playwright whose comedies and opera librettos featured topical material about family dramas, love intrigues, and masonic conspiracies. While by her own estimation her literary talent was modest, she was the essential enabler whose patronage, example, and participation oversaw the transformation of the literary field.

As in some of the German principalities, such as Dresden under Augustus the Strong (r. 1697–1706)—and we must not forget that Catherine was by birth Princess Sophie Friederike Auguste von Anhalt-Zerbst—the court and institutions under the protection of the sovereign became the focus of cultural activity and a center for patronage and service.[6] The example of the centralization of musical, theatrical, and literary culture at the court of Louis XIV (r. 1643–1715) was not lost on later European rulers, particularly Frederick the Great of Prussia (r. 1740–86) and Catherine the Great, his correspondent and sometimes rival. Court activities, and Catherine's own lobbying through her vast European correspondence, were intended to project power.[7]

In Russia, more than in England or France a century after the Sun King, literature written in the eighteenth century up to the 1780s was meant for consumption by the monarch, her entourage, and a relatively small group of well-educated figures, serving as private secretaries, like Denis Fonvizin, and in chanceries. Literature was also practiced by nobles outside state institutions as a matter of private pursuit. The diffusion of forms of court and urban culture outside the capital into estates and provincial towns was much slower. Among the wealthiest who could afford to maintain their own theater companies, the country estate became an important venue for performances.[8]

From the reign of Elizabeth, the court had been the home to imperial splendor on a lavish scale (the British ambassador Sir Charles Hanbury-Williams provides memorable vignettes in his correspondence).[9] During Catherine's reign, imperial birthdays, name days, and anniversaries were regularly marked, sometimes with firework displays, often with great banquets and masked balls. Such celebration conveyed an impression of commanding authority; diplomatic reports describing the scale of Catherine's lavishness earned her prestige abroad. Spectacle could travel, too. On the occasion of Catherine's visit to Novgorod on December 6, 1776, Mikhail Verevkin (1732–95) wrote an allegorical interlude called "Epilogue. Astreia", intended for performance. He depicts Catherine's mythic alter ego exchanging compliments with the citizens of the city, who pledge their loyalty even as she proclaims: "I am your leader from this moment on and forever."[10] The court also encompassed private space where different arts and refinements of civilization could be cultivated. Catherine laid down a famous and remarkable set of rules governing sociability when she was at home, requiring her friends (who were still her subjects) to set aside their rank and title, grudges and politics, and to enjoy the civilized pleasures of the salon. Apart from its expressive function, literature was another outlet for writers eager to play a part in the system. Ideology and personal gratitude were inextricable. Writers like Vasily Petrov, a vigorous odist, may well have felt an obligation to align their message to imperial policies.[11] Sycophants rose to the occasion regularly with florid displays of flattery like that of the provincial merchant Ivan Seletsky, otherwise unknown except as the author of an ode celebrating a general.[12]

Much writing could acquire an instrumental function calibrated to the rewards of a patronage network. Patronage as practiced in the court system was closer to what Raymond Williams calls "protection and support," which means that it was "concerned less with the direct retaining and commissioning of artists than with the provision of some kind of social protection and recognition."[13] Patronage could be symbolic, monetary, or personal, depending on the status of the poet-client. For individual writers, artful praise of the powerful was one strategy for managing a career, procuring advancement, staying visible (or alive), or possibly expressing true feeling. Fedor Kozel'sky (1734–c.1799), best remembered for the poems collected in the volume *The Daily Record of Fedor Kozel'sky* (*Dnevnaia zapiska Fedora Kozel'skogo*, 1771), made his financial straits and dependence on his patron, the influential minister Nikita Panin (1718–83), the subject of the poem "A Letter on Benefaction" ("Pis'mo o blagodeianii," 1776). In his "Letter to His Excellency Count Roman Larionovich Vorontsov" ("Pis'mo ego siiatel'stvu Romanu Larionovichu Vorontsovu," 1777), Kozel'sky begins by declaring his good faith in an effort to distinguish between genuine admiration and false praise. Having already been mocked as a toady on the pages of Novikov's satirical journal *The Drone* (*Truten'*, 1769–70), Kozel'sky praises Vorontsov for assistance in paying for his son's education. The posture of sincere motivation rather than praise for hire is more rhetorical than genuine: "Not vanity I praise, not the pretty verse of flatterers / Do I sing to you, o lover of the Muses, Vorontsov!" ("Ne suetnu khvalu, ne krasnyi stikh l'stetsov, / Poiu tebe, o muz liubitel', Vorontsov!")[14] It is still unclear how effective in this world of clientelism the ode was as a tool of praise.[15] Late in her reign, Catherine's government reintroduced controls on nobles, requiring passports to travel abroad (originally abolished in the *Charter to the Nobility*, 1785). On receiving permission from the empress to continue his studies in Göttingen, Aleksandr Klushin published "An Expression of Gratitude to Catherine the Great for Her Most Generous Furlough of Myself to Foreign Parts with a Salary" ("Blagodarnost' Ekaterine Velikoi za vsemilostiveishee uvol'nenie menia v chuzhie kraia s zhalovan'em," 1793) in the journal *Mercury*.[16]

In the 1780s, private and official presses, such as the Moscow University Press and the Press of the Artillery Company, printed no fewer than fifty books of odes. The genre of the ode is rhetorically manifold but tends to be ideologically delimited as imperial celebration (except when used to channel critique of absolutism and Enlightenment, as can also be seen in the period). Pretexts for praise also included religious ceremonies (like baptism), imperial arrivals and departures, the conferment of a title and promotion, election to a society; but sometimes more unusual occasions were commemorated, as in "An Ode in Defense of a Striped Tail-Coat" (n.d. [1789]), written to celebrate Catherine's inoculation with smallpox.[17] While it is reasonable to assume that in many instances there was an unspoken understanding that poetry had an instrumental potential, we should not neglect the pleasure afforded the writer and the audience in the fulfillment of ceremonial functions. The privilege of reading aloud, or having one's work read aloud at court, of being seen, and having one's verse published were status markers. Odes were churned out mechanically even by the most minor poets, and court lackeys provide evidence for rituals of court culture in addition to the much-studied rhetorical forms and performative qualities of odes. The triumphal or solemn ode was a performance, both on the page and literally on stage when delivered at court.[18] Performances of these poems whipped up drama by making immodest claims to divine inspiration, manifested in extreme physical symptoms. In "The Ode on the Taking of Chocim," for instance, the scale of victory earns comparison with no less than the eruption of Mt. Etna and an earthquake on the Black Sea and blood flows in vast quantities—effects underscored by emphatic prosody, rhetorical questions, repetitions, and comparisons. The poem gloats luridly over the defeat of the Turks. Just like printed authorial dedications in books recording gratitude, patronage, and intentions, the titles of odes can contain important rhetorical, theatrical, and performative elements. In the opening of the same ode, the speaker cites a "sudden upsurge of ecstasy" (*vostorg vnezapnyi*) that "captures his mind" (*um plenil*). The lines are noteworthy for bringing together sublime inspiration and reason, qualities that Kantemir celebrated in his "First Satire" and which, toward the end of the century, Derzhavin would unite in the faculty of poetic genius.

Titles of poems became more and more extensive, including not just the subject's name and the poem's occasion but also rehearsing formulaic expressions of obeisance. Ritual expression of abject devotion used hyperbole as a trope appropriate to a highly stratified society. The title alone can flatter by lending an air of celebrity to the dedicatee as in the seven-page anonymous ode of July 13, 1789 headed by a title of some fifty-odd words to "His Most Exalted Gavriil, the Metropolitan of Novgorod and St. Petersburg and Holy Archimandrite of the Alexander Nevsky Monastery, the esteemed Archpriest and Patron therefore and Most August Member of the Holy Synod."[19] Writers also outdid one another in the rhetoric of abjection and servitude. For example, in the full title of his 1762 ode on the accession of Catherine the Great, Lomonosov, using the accepted, obligatory (and empty) formula, signed off as "the most humble slave" (*vsepoddanneishii rab*).[20] Titles flaunting loyalty contributed to the performance here addressed to "Her most exalted majesty . . . from her most abject slave." Lomonosov is unlikely to have believed that inflated, disingenuous rhetoric, since he was famously proud and stubborn, and valued his own genius as poet, scientist, and educator above mere rank at court. Similarly, the unknown author of the ode to Gavriil may well have been equally disingenuous in his use of hyperbole. Such excessive self-abasement was part of the game of deference customary in much neoclassical literature written at court. The benefits of patronage, exercised through Catherine's courtiers, would have been clear to most writers, and especially to Lomonosov as a man of science, since his promotion depended on the hierarchies at the Academy whose director was appointed by the monarch. (Lomonosov's clashes with authorities such as the president, the German-born Ivan Shumakher, were the stuff of legend even in his own lifetime.)[21] The modesty topos, even when taken too far, should not, however, be regarded as ironic. Sincerity had no place in court culture, and hyperbolic self-abnegation was understood for what it was: a performance of humility with an ulterior motive.

All significant (and many minor) poets in eighteenth-century Russia wrote odes. Writers brought to the ode, the most prominent of the encomiastic genres, both seriousness and extravagant vitality, finding in the form's inherent rhetorical grandeur, in its love of metaphor, and in its pictorial features a license for verbal display.[22] Odes could adopt a highly rhetorical structure by following the outline of a classical speech. While the content varied, the opening and conclusion were reserved for an invocation, and a prayer or a formal coda, respectively (an arrangement that Pushkin adopts in the concluding section of the prologue to *The Bronze Horseman* (1833), replete with odic formulas). This is also true of Derzhavin's celebrated satirical-political ode to Catherine, "Felitsa." After the invocation, which sometimes establishes the qualifications of the speaker to deliver praise (vatic exaltation, uncommon devotion, and inspiring admiration are typical motifs), poems usually describe the occasion, illustrate its importance with vivid vignettes, convey a message, and draw a conclusion. Stanzaic patterns were maintained; while the standard stanza of an ode contained ten lines, writers exploited dozens of syntactic permutations and rhyme schemes. Just how many stanzas were required depended on energy and patience. Odes are capacious vessels that can accommodate a plethora of examples: sometimes organizing a stanza around a single comparison expressed as a simile, at other times narrating an illustration over a sequence of stanzas. Amplification is the standard trope of this poetic form. Sumarokov, ever moderate, kept his poems short, while others' exuberance filled dozens of stanzas.[23] Ingenuity was given much scope for use of novel metaphors and other effects. While few could match the young Lomonosov's loquaciousness, others such as Catherine the Great's librarian, Vasily Petrov, built on his style, using striking metaphors, elaborate syntactic structures within the stanza, and neologisms.

The central stanzas offered much freedom to combine eloquence and innovation, allocate more or less space to mythological and metaphorical comparison, or vary image and sound content. While the rules of high style were strictly observed in the solemn ode, since the correct register, word choice, versification, and tone were proof of literary competence, the genre allowed much expressivity: a combination between skillful conformity and uncommon visual and musical imagination marks the best examples of the form. Like Lomonosov, Petrov created a poetic persona endowed with supernatural powers of sight and therefore able to use the entire universe as a comparative basis for his hyperbolic claims of Catherine's accomplishments.[24] Grade inflation is an accepted feature of Pindaric style, and Petrov makes unstinting use of adjectives, some coined for the occasion; but above all he parades a seemingly limitless pantheon of heroes, from Romulus and Remus to Peter the Great, who is only outdone by Catherine.[25] Petrov resorted to ancient analogies to lend longevity and scale to Catherine's deeds, but also as a witty way of mirroring an occasion like a masked ball at court, where figures, dressed up in ancient costumes, laid tribute on an altar to Catherine's greatness. What is reality, what is illusion? As at the court of Louis XIV, the play between appearance and reality was part of the landscape to which poems like Petrov's "The Ode on a Carousel" and Derzhavin's "Felitsa" approvingly and somewhat critically belonged.[26]

Court circles and gentlemanly coteries dominated the practice of literature. For authors dependent on the wealthy and powerful, literature as a vehicle of celebrity was the currency writers could use to repay their patrons. For poets of noble descent, this meant that direct patronage was problematic and might be seen as compromising their sense of status and honor.[27] Figures like Klushin and Kozel'sky, both recently ennobled, would have been particularly sensitive to their standing at court. In the late 1750s, Sumarokov was fortunate in siding with the then Grand Duchess, expressing loyalty to her as a supporter of Enlightenment.[28] He greeted her accession with no fewer than six odes, a gesture that Catherine rewarded handsomely in August 1762 when she pardoned the printing debts he had amassed and transferred the expenses he incurred in publishing his works to her own office. Their relationship had soured by the mid-1760s. Catherine found Sumarokov something of a high-handed busybody in matters of state, and his tendency to ask her to intervene in his squabbles, aggravated by his disorderly behavior when intoxicated, clearly vexed her; she may also have resented his closeness to Nikita Panin and his ward, Catherine's young son Paul I (r. 1796–1801).

Documented cases of reward for poetic favor are infrequent but do exist, mainly as divulged by poets themselves who treat poetry as an act of reciprocity in exchange for a reward. As a rule, even when writers are less outspoken than Klushin, we can infer that those who celebrate their relationship with the addressee wish to convey the reality of some sort of transactional benefit. But, as at every court, appearances mattered as much as realities. Sumarokov would feel the loss of Catherine's favor or protection in connection with his entitlement to royalties from the Imperial Theater.[29]

Poets of gentry or aristocratic origin such as Yuri A. Neledinsky-Meletsky (1752–1829), a minor versifier of great facility, showed their class independence by not writing panegyrics. Other, lesser-born poets based at court certainly supported their position and earned their keep by using the arts of flattery. Vasily Petrov, the son of a priest, is frank about his rise from humble origins in his "Ode of 25 January 1771 to Grigory Orlov" ("Ego siiatel'stvu grafu Grigor'iu Grigor'evichu Orlovu, Genvaria 25 dnia 1771") when he thanks the subject on behalf of his own muse, who has been "rewarded generously by munificent fate" ("Ta muza, chto blagoi ushchedrena sud'boiu").[30] But the allusion to patronage, while staying just on the polite side of explicit, is part of a more elaborate game between courting praise and risking embarrassment. Petrov admonishes his listeners to shut their ears so that he can conduct a private conversation with Orlov, a "hero" praised for Stoic qualities that will outlive earthly symbols of vanity, such as wealth, luxury, and power. Building on a set of analogies between the Russian and Roman empires (a much used comparison in the period), the ode does anything but spare Orlov's blushes and likens him to the sun in its own trajectory. Praise of this kind would be worthless if it were kept truly private. Does Petrov ironize the transactional relationship he has with his patron in order to suggest genuine feeling?

Ermil Kostrov (1755–96), the son of a sexton, is another representative man of the age. Like other figures from a clerical background, Kostrov found it much easier to accept patronage than did members of the gentry. Educated at a seminary and Moscow University, he was competent in Latin and ancient Greek and seems to have become the semiofficial poet of the university, on hand for all occasions requiring a poem. Flattery came easily to this prolific versifier (and a colorful drunk) who also depended on the sponsorship of the President of the Academy of Fine Arts, Count Ivan Shuvalov (1727–97). He expressed gratitude to Shuvalov and Catherine in an epistle he wrote in 1786 on the anniversary of her accession to the throne. He wrote other solemn odes to celebrate such occasions as the anniversary of Catherine's rule in 1780, and again in 1781, as well as the quarter-century anniversary of Moscow University.

Like Petrov, who often used mythology to elevate contemporary figures, Kostrov adapted his poetic iconography to the ideology of his paymasters Grigory Potemkin (1739–91) and the Grand Chancellor Count Aleksandr Bezborodko (1747–99), the architects of the Greek Project in the early 1780s in Russia's second phase of expansion into Crimea. In collaboration with the Emperor Joseph of Austria the two nobles planned to partition the Ottoman Empire and symbolically asserted Russian interest over the Black Sea region (including Crimea) by devising Greek toponyms for new cities such as Odessa and Kherson in "New Russia." While Kostrov's translation of the first nine books of the *Iliad* in Alexandrines (1787, second edition in 1811) was a lumbering dud, destined to be eclipsed by the 1829 version of Nikolai Gnedich (1784–1833), to this day a classic of translation, Catherine's officials regarded Kostrov's version as a prestigious underscoring of a cultural continuity between Byzantium and Russia, which, in their view, helped justify Russian imperial claims on the Bosphorus. Kostrov dedicated the first six cantos to Catherine the Great and was handsomely rewarded by the empress's office.

Odes and verse epistles that appeal to the arts and sciences rather than to personal reward can use a veneer of altruism to "signal virtue." In his "Letter on the Use of the Sciences and on the Education therein of Youth" ("Pis′mo o pol′ze nauk i o vospitanii vo onykh iunoshestva," 1772), Popovsky opens this philosophical tribute to intellectual progress by addressing "benefactors," or the *metsenat*, a Russian term transferred either via the French *mécène*, or directly from the Latin name Maecenas, Horace's patron and dedicatee, who became a byword for arts patronage. Because Popovsky's own station is modest, he offers subscribers fame as an incentive to support his endeavor. Poetry promises the benefactor that his "name will be a monument praised by wondrous multitudes" ("imia chudnymi gromadami proslavit′"), and interjects further lines of encouragement ("You have selected, Maecenas, a sure path to glory").[31]

In "Ode I," Aleksei Rzhevsky dismisses the idea of praise as mere vanity destined to perish like all other mortal undertakings. His "Ode to the Ruler Peter the Great, the True Father of the Country and the First Emperor, Worthy of the Blessed and Eternal Memory" ("Oda blazhennyia i vechno dostoinyia pamiati istinnomu ottsu otechestva, imperatoru pervomu, gosudariu Petru Velikomu," 1761), written in the classic ten-line stanza, is offered as a gesture of commitment to the myth of Petrine progressive values rather than an act of flattery.

Ivan Barkov, a poet notorious for his libertine, pornographic verse, which circulated clandestinely in the eighteenth and nineteenth centuries, proved witty in every mode. In a 1763 poem dedicated to Grigory Orlov, Barkov argued that occasions for laughter rather than flattery were the greatest service the poet can afford a patron. He claims that the license granted to satirists to blame, mock, or praise was proof that in their age "politics has deprived one of freedom" ("Lishila vol'nosti politika v nash vek").[32]

Praising the accomplishments of the great, and sometimes the not so great, took considerable mastery. The aim was to match the actual splendor, or projected magnificence, of the ruler's court with commensurate performance.[33] The writer's immediate celebrity and lasting fame of the subject were the goal. Later on, writers came to appreciate the form as a model for new purposes. Yuri Tynianov (1894–1943), a Formalist critic and scholar, was the first to perceive how much his contemporary, the Futurist poet and revolutionary agitator, Vladimir Mayakovsky, admired the zany verbosity and perceived civic intent of the ode. Joseph Brodsky, who admired the syllabic verse of earlier writers such as Kantemir, generally appreciated and adapted the verbal wit and coinages, sublime postures and metaphysical grandeur of eighteenth-century poetics: his elegy for a Soviet commander, "On the Death of Zhukov" is an adaptation of Derzhavin's funerary ode-cum-elegy "The Bullfinch," written in 1800 on the death of Aleksandr Suvorov (1729–1800), the last Generalissimo of the Russian Empire. But given how many poets produced odes, it is by definition hard to pull away from the pack when everyone writes in an agreed mode and style with an official occasion in mind. Ironically, despite the vanity of their subjects, few panegyrics transcended the immediate context of the court.

Who was up and who was down was a function of the system of court patronage and favoritism open to relatively small numbers. Factions might vie for power and influence for pragmatic reasons, without any real appeal to theoretical or philosophical models of governance. In "Felitsa" and "The Representation of Felitsa" ("Izobrazhenie Felitsy," 1789) Derzhavin appropriates the plot of a fairy tale composed by Catherine the Great to create a contrasting portrait of oriental-style courtiers surrounding an enlightened monarch. What it means to be a poet as well as a statesman is a question never far from Derzhavin's mind. His poem is a double portrait of a ruler and a poet. The former is all seriousness of purpose and rational management, whereas the latter is a hedonist who serves as a foil to the industrious ruler. However, it is the poet who understands the relationship between individual happiness and a successful political order, and poetry that proves to be the vehicle for commentary.

Odes, epistles, and inscriptions cemented the reputations of poets at court, and no doubt also satisfied earthly vanity. But classicism prized the eternal in the local. Within the value system of neoclassical literature and art (such as academic painting) the figure of the exemplary leader—a philosopher, a general, or a statesman, or even a poet—occupied a prominent position. Leading Russians were no less keen than their European counterparts to secure their image and legacy for all posterity. It was the job of odists, however minor, to burnish the reputation of a courtier, and few exceeded conventional forms of expression. By the 1780s, as literary fashion gradually transitioned from classicism to early Romanticism, the vocabulary of poetic tribute began to celebrate accomplishments, military, political, and artistic, in terms of individual genius.

While many odes were clearly written for immediate performance in the service of a courtly "client," masterpieces of the genre emerged out of the mass of texts. The ode was an effective vehicle for contemplating the relation between the writer's own greatness, the endurance of art, and the endurance and extent of the addressee's own fame. Lomonosov, one of the earliest practitioners of the ode who learned much from the poetry of Johann-Christoph Gottsched, provides classic examples, starting with the "Ode on the Taking of Chocim." His first-person speaker assumes a position higher than Mt. Pindus, a vantage point from which he can survey the Muses. It is possible to speak of a topography of fame. From early Lomonosov to Derzhavin's mature verse, the 1794 "My Idol" ("Moi istukan") to Pushkin's "Monument

Poem" (1836), references to actual places map the poet's fame across the vast expanse of the ever-growing Russian Empire.[34]

The elegy as a poetic form of lamentation flourished in the eighteenth century. But there are a number of conspicuous cases where writers turn to odes instead of the elegy, because the ode presents historic figures as persons whose renown commends them to posterity. Odes written to commemorate the dead blur the boundaries between the praise function of the eulogy and the eulogizing component of the elegy. Poetry here stands aloof from the transactional service–reward relationship implicit in patronage. What are the dead worth to the living poet? Mourning provides an occasion to shine poetically and to harness the writer's own talent to the commemorated glory of the dead. After all, great subjects require great poets. Single individuals could rival monarchs if they impressed the right poet. Of all funerary odes written during Catherine's reign, the most imposing must surely be "The Waterfall" ("Vodopad," published 1798), the poem Derzhavin composed in tribute to Grigory Potemkin, who was Catherine's most beloved favorite, her steadfast ally, morganatic consort, and bulwark of her projects. A physical giant, with a larger-than-life personality, Potemkin inspired anecdotes and examples of court life that would live on in memoirs and historical collections, most notably Pushkin's brilliantly witty anthology *Table Talk* (1830–37).[35] Potemkin was famously spendthrift, infamously oversexed, notoriously melancholy, and prone to bouts of depression that sometimes paralyzed the government. None of these human flaws come across in the portrait painted by Derzhavin of a heroic "unvanquished leader" ("vozhd' nepobedimyi"), an "incomparable man" ("nesravnennyi muzh"), whose "image, name and deeds / Shine forth amidst gleams of brilliance" ("Chto obraz, imia i dela / Tsvetut ego sred' raznykh gliantsev").[36]

Court theater and tragedy

After its fledgling start in the Jesuit plays of the seventeenth century, it would be several decades before theater became a fixture in the culture of the court. In 1702, on the order of Peter the Great, a theater opened to the general public in a special building on Red Square. It was named the Kunst–Fuerst Theater after the two German directors of the company that also trained Russian actors. The German company brought with it its usual repertoire, the so-called "English comedies," popular in Germany in the seventeenth century. The plays were full of adventures, bloody fights, love, sorcery, and so on. The repertory often consisted of adaptations several times removed from the original. For example, the skit "Prince Pickled-Herring, or Jodolet" ("Prints Pikl' gerring, ili Zhodolet") can be traced (through Dutch, German, and French adaptations) to one of Calderón's plays. Molière was represented by "A Comedy about a Beaten Doctor" ("Komediia o doktore bitom," a version of *Le Médicin malgré lui*) and "Precious Amusings" ("Dragyia smeianyia," a version of *Les Précieuses ridicules*). The theater proved unpopular; nor did it satisfy Peter's desire for a propaganda medium, and it closed in 1706.

The Kunst–Fuerst theater stage sets and costumes were given to Princess Natalia, Peter's sister, who organized her own private theater on her estate near Moscow. That theater was later moved to St. Petersburg, and ran from 1707 until Natalia's death in 1716. Privately owned, it was open to the local public, and the repertoire included adaptations of European chivalric romances, such as "A Drama about the Spanish King" ("Deistvie o korole Gishpanskom"), "A Spanish Comedy about Hyppolite and Julie" ("Komediia gishpanskaia o Ipalite i Zhulii"), and a play based on a popular prose legend, "A Comedy of Peter of the Golden Keys" ("Komediia Petra Zlatykh Kliuchei"). The theater enjoyed some success, and its repertoire was adopted by numerous amateur troupes that sprang up not only in the capitals but also in provincial cities and towns. One such troupe, led by the actor Fedor Volkov (1729–63), was brought by a decree of the Empress Elizabeth from the town Iaroslavl', north of Moscow, to St. Petersburg. Actors were then enrolled in the Noble Infantry Cadet Corps, and in 1756 a public theater in the capital was organized on a permanent basis.

To fill the gap left by Natalia's theater, prior to the establishment of a public theater in St. Petersburg, companies from France and Italy, as well as a *commedia dell'arte* troupe, performed at the Empress Anna's court beginning in 1733. The Empress Anna welcomed foreign troupes, especially performers of *commedia dell'arte*.[37] Elizabeth continued the tradition of court theater. This was the venue for which Sumarokov wrote his first plays. From 1747, Sumarokov, who, as a cadet, had been routinely involved in the theater, now regularly served as producer charged with building the repertory. Trediakovsky also contributed as an Academy of Sciences translator, rendering foreign scripts into Russian. In addition, Elizabeth ordered Trediakovsky and Lomonosov to write a tragedy apiece. In satisfying the commission, Trediakovsky wrote the five-act tragedy *Deidamiia* (never staged, published 1775) and translated a comedy by Terence, *The Eunuch* (*Evnukh*, 1751). Lomonosov wrote *Tamira i Selim* (1750) and *Demofont* (1751); the former took the Battle of Kulikovo as a backdrop to its love plot, while the latter was based on a subject from Ovid's *Metamorphoses*.

The court and the Imperial Theater were the most prestigious venues for drama. From the time of Empress Elizabeth, and well into the reign of Alexander I, Russian playwrights found models for their own works in the perennial themes of French classical theater. Neoclassical tragedy had an extended life on the Russian stage from the 1760s until the 1820s, and, like the ode, also reflected the imperial ideology. Written in imitation of great French models, especially Corneille and Racine, plays interwove political master plots and marital subplots that focused on characters torn between loyalty to country and monarch and individual passions (*strasti*). Medieval Russian history proved a fertile source of plots. Loyalty to the ruler (who might also be a father, brother, or husband) is often compromised by passion for a foreigner or rival of the monarch, and characters struggle to reconcile personal and political virtues (*dobrodetel'*). A tyrant is frequently pitted against an enlightened monarch, juxtaposing the evils of uncurbed power with a voluntary respect for limited power. Prominent examples include Sumarokov's *Dimitry the Pretender*, Nikolai Nikolev's (1758–1815) *Sorena and Zamir* (1784), Vasily Maikov's *Agriope* (1769), and his *Themist and Ieronima* (1775). In Kniazhnin's *Vladimir and Iaropolk*, two medieval Russian princes, Iaropolk the Kievan son of Grand Prince Svyatoslav, and the Novgorodian prince Vladimir, vie for the hand of Rogneda, daughter of the Polovtsian tribal invaders who menace Kiev from across the steppe. Written in 1772 to mark the eighteenth birthday of Grand Duke Paul, and first performed in 1784, the play breathes life into episodes from the *Primary Chronicle*, much recounted in eighteenth-century Russian historiography, by creating extensive situational and verbal parallels with Racine's *Andromaque* (1668), a debt to a classic which also reflects Kniazhnin's experience as a translator of numerous plays by Corneille as well as Voltaire's tragedies. In Act I, scene i, the eponymous hero Vladimir and the nobleman Svadel confront the main dilemma, and debate the unenviable choices between the national interest and personal sacrifice:

> Но страсти их, когда граждан умолкнут стоны,
> Блаженству общему быть могут ли препоны?
> Рогнеде ль Ярополк, гречанке ли супруг,
> Не все ли то равно, коль обществу он друг,
> Коль прекратитель он нам пагубного рока?

> Свадель
> Кто страстен—слаб, кто слаб, тот близок от порока.
> Когда бы княжеский с гречанкою союз

Касался только лишь одних любовных уз;
Когда бы страсть его во сердце затворенна
К позору не была престола устремленна,
И если б он, любя, России не вредил,
Пускай гречанку бы на трон к себе взводил.

But will their passions, once the groans of citizens fall silent,
Be a hindrance to the happiness of all?
Whether Iaropolk weds Rogneda or a Greek woman,
Does it matter, as long as he is a friend to society
And can thwart a fatal outcome?

SVADEL´
He who is passionate is weak, he who is weak is on the brink of sin.
If the union between a prince and a Greek woman
Were merely a matter of their loving bond,
If passion rooted in his heart
Had not been aimed to disgrace the throne,
And if he, despite his love, were not harming Russia,
Then he might have elevated the Greek woman to the throne.

The profile of absolutism in its optimal and sometimes degenerate shape preoccupied Russian classical tragedians. The most notable treatments include Sumarokov's *Dimitry the Pretender* (*Dmitrii Samozvanets*, 1771), Kheraskov's *Borislav* (1772), and works by Kniazhnin, especially the *Clemency of Titus* (*Titovo miloserdie*, 1777), an opera set to the libretto by Antonio Caldara— made famous in an earlier version by Pietro Metastasio, whose *La Clemenza di Tito* (1734) had been performed in St. Petersburg in the 1750s in a translation by Volkov—and his final play *Vadim of Novgorod* (*Vadim Novgorodskii*, late 1788 or early 1789).

Historians of the period have naturally been sensitive to the interplay between theatrical performance, court politics, and attitudes to governance. By deploying a vocabulary of virtue, rational government, transparency, and justice, a vocabulary also used by poets such as Derzhavin and Vasily Kapnist (1758–1823), were playwrights offering a political critique of the government? Or were plays seen more as philosophical reflections on absolutism that might focus the minds of the gentry and nobility present in the audience? By its very nature, court theater had to use subject matter that flattered the attention of the spectators, and sometimes picked up on local intrigues that could be dressed up in universal language. Whether plays were read as allegories of contemporary politics depended on the circumstance and the mood at court more than on the actual handling of topical material. All playwrights of the time used standard universal themes and a vocabulary of patriotism and justice in conventional ways: their ideal monarchs were all exemplary in the same way, their tyrants, often portrayed as corrupt potentates from the East, were all equally stereotypical. Clemency remained a virtue of signal importance in a ruler, explored later in Vladislav Ozerov's *Dimitry Donskoi* (1807), Petr Plavilshchikov's (1760–1812) *Ermak, the Conqueror of Siberia* (*Ermak, pokoritel´ Sibiri*, 1803), and even in Pushkin's *Andzhelo* (1833), an adaptation of Shakespeare's *Measure for Measure*.

In and of itself, a production might not represent serious commentary—but it certainly represented a flattering gesture. While not all classical dramas allegorized contemporary circumstance, and a work like Sumarokov's first tragedy *Khorev* uses the standard tropes of the genre to focus on the internal dilemma of characters, theater did provide a chance, sometimes taken, to exploit topical resonances between issues of the day and action on stage, accidental or deliberate. On occasion, both writers and actors—who could themselves be courtiers like

General Petr Melissino (1726–97) or Petr Plavilshchikov, who had started out as an actor—used theater as a vehicle for putting their personal case before the ruler, much like ode writers who cultivated protection. Sumarokov's *Khorev* drew on a seventeenth-century history of Kievan Rus´ in fashioning a drama that took Voltaire's *Brutus* (1730) as a model of how to align a plot about the duties of kingship with a complicating subplot about passion. By 1790, the play's praise of rulers who behave as enlightened rulers rather than despots—a topic on which Derzhavin, for instance, had written earlier—touched a nerve, and the play was closed down— only to be revived within a decade when Alexander I still looked like a reforming tsar.

Neoclassical tragedy effectively used ancient props and trappings to attenuate connections that were potentially hazardous. Rzhevksy's *The False Smerdii*, staged in 1769 was based on a plot drawn from Book III of Herodotus's *Histories*. Andrei Nartov's first ever Russian-language version of Herodotus, written in 1763–64, well illustrates the crossover between translation and new works. The convoluted plots of tragedy often transpose national issues into domestic and dynastic drama. In Nartov's play, the Persian princess Fedima exposes her husband as an unscrupulous pretender to the throne. Noble and self-sacrificing, she wishes to remain true to the villain and accompany him into exile but he betrays her. He is killed and she is rewarded with a new husband who ascends to the throne. The play enjoyed considerable success, praised by Novikov and others for its excellent verse style, "powerful depictions" (*izobrazheniia sil´nye*), and the compelling quality of its heroine. Others were quick to detect parallels with Catherine the Great as the once foreign bride of an ill-fated prince whose claim to the throne was ultimately contested. An asymmetry between Rzhevsky's plot and actual political history was one fortunate way of maintaining a level of obliqueness.[38]

In *Dimitry*, a historical drama written in 1771 and reported to have been staged more than forty times in the eighteenth century, Sumarokov mined the theme of the Pretender and the Time of Troubles for a rich streak in Russian history.[39] The play uncannily anticipated the anxieties Catherine faced from 1772 to 1774 because of the Cossack rebellion led by Emel´ian Pugachev, the most recent in a line of pretenders, claiming to be Peter III who had miraculously survived assassination following Catherine's coup. There was never a more villainous specimen of autocratic excess to tread the boards than Sumarokov's hero, whose long monologues contained memorable aphorisms, such as his declaration in Act III "Not I was made for nations, nations were made for me" ("Ne dlia narodov—ia, narody—dlia menia"). The play repeatedly shows the horrors of tyranny (*tiranstvo*), which implicitly contrasts with autocracy (*samoderzhavie*) as an acceptable version of kingship upheld by Catherine. (The censorship regimes of Catherine's grandsons Alexander I and Nicholas I would not tolerate this vocabulary.) Tragedies such as *Dimitry the Pretender* enjoyed the advantage of elaborate plots and historical distance praising law-abiding monarchs.

The reform of comedy and comedy of reform

Comedy also flourished from the 1760s. The Enlightenment by any basic definition was ameliorative, and one did not have to be a *philosophe* to exploit the opportunities created by the rapid Europeanization of the gentry that followed the Petrine years. While satirical journals required a literary field in order to function and circulate, comedy was already well ensconced in public and private theaters from the reign of Elizabeth, and benefited from a stream of guest troupes hosted at court.[40]

In 1748, Trediakovsky set out guidelines for writers in his *Meditation on Comedy in General* (*Rassuzhdenie o komedii voobshche*). His view was that while the theater could secondarily aim at amusing and invigorating the mind, its primary goal was to "enhance reason and deter base thoughts," and both comedy and tragedy were suitable vehicles for such instruction in virtue.

His stipulations were that dialogue was to be spoken in correct language, costumes were to be plausible, and behavior was to be natural and realistic. Similarly, in his "Epistle on Versification," Sumarokov also placed emphasis on the notions of decorum and didacticism in comedy:

> Смешить без разума —дар подлыя души.
> Не представляй того, что мне на миг приятно,
> Но чтоб то действие мне долго было внятно.
> Свойство комедии —издевкой править нрав;
> Смешить и пользовать —прямой ея устав.[41]

> To amuse without reason is the gift of a base soul.
> Do not represent that which which pleases but for a second,
> But rather an action that will long be heeded.
> It is a property of comedy to improve morals with mockery.
> To amuse and instruct—that is the law it upholds!

Unlike tragedians who conformed to neoclassical theory, writers of comedy were slow to implement any of these principles. The nature of Russian comic writing was dictated by the native tradition of farce, reinforced by an influx of works in translation where uninstructive amusement and purposeless entertainment were the norm.[42] Indeed, Sumarokov himself took little note of his own advice and continued to produce either light-hearted vaudeville, spectacles of an ephemeral nature geared to popular success (*igrishche*), or vicious satires directed at personal enemies rather than human vice. Whether translated or original, fashionable comedy of the 1760s and 1770s generally either favored satire of a particular vice or perpetuated the popular Russian taste for interludes (*intermedii*) based solely on loosely plotted love intrigues and featuring characters drawn from French and Italian comedy with un-Russian names like Doront, Octavius, Oront, and Erast. Alongside stagings of translations and imitations of seventeenth-century classics like Molière's *L'Avare* and *Amphitryon*, Delisle de la Drevetière's *Arlequin sauvage* (1721), or works by Philippe Destouches and Marc-Antoine Le Grand, there were performances of Sumarokov's *Tresotinius* (1750) and *Narcissus* (*Nartsis*, 1769), both attacks directed at Trediakovsky's pedantry. Comedy as a vehicle of literary criticism never totally abated. In "The Vain Versifier" ("Samoliubivyi stikhotvorets," 1775), the precocious Nikolai Nikolev, best known for his comic opera *Rozana and Liubim* (1776), took aim at Sumarokov, later in his career lampooning other proponents of the so-called "smooth style," including Karamzin. Farce and vaudeville remained staples of theatrical life as forms of pure entertainment. These did not hinder the performance of dozens of new plays staged at the court theater in St. Petersburg and in provincial theaters. Writers found in topical comedy a way to address contemporary concerns and entertain, targeting the usual foibles of high and provincial society adjusted for local situation.

Comedy and satire had long treated superficial feeling as a symptom of Gallomania and shallow secularization. One of the most prominent proponents of comedy as a vehicle for moral improvement, entertainingly done, was V. L. Lukin (1737–94), author of numerous minor comedies of which *The Profligate Reformed by Love* (*Mot liubov'iu ispravlennyi*, 1765) remains the best known.[43] In a series of prefaces to his published works, Lukin articulated an opposing program to contemporary trends. He condemned wholesale the practice of literal translation of European comedies as irrelevant to a Russian audience. From a contextual point of view, the plots were alien; from a linguistic point of view, the translations were slavish; and from a psychological point of view, the endless parade of coquettes and *petits-maîtres* with their stilted names were of no personal interest to anyone. In Lukin's view, translation of derivative plots without any attempt at adaptation was pointless; and he advocated modifications ranging from minor changes, like the alteration of names, to more intrusive rewriting. The way forward, he argued, called for original composition, alongside imitation and transposition, provided that certain elementary conditions were met. Comedy should not rely on superfluous amusement: pointless laughter had become part and parcel of the genre, forcing writers to distort plots and undermine the serious purpose. Lukin applied his criticism even to his own most successful play, which mixed conversations about virtue with passages tacked on with the aim of "amusing the gallery."

Lukin fostered a new expectation that comedy should become adept at representing complex feelings rather than being limited to slapstick. The expression of sensibility through displays of emotion and empathy was naturally the stuff of theater. By the 1780s, under the impetus of a new sensibility, Russian drama expanded to include the *drame bourgeois*. Playwrights and spectators more interested in the complex social functions of individual characters discovered in this new mode of theater a chance to consider psychologically more complex plots. In the 1760s, Lukin had already championed this form of mixed sentimental drama, and Fonvizin and Plavil'shchikov both understood its compatibility with audience tastes and the contemporary style of theatrical composition of the 1770s and, increasingly, of the 1780s. In the introduction to the 1787 *Dramatic Dictionary*, the first Russian attempt to provide a history of stagecraft and performance, the editor cites the progress in theatrical writing from mere entertainment to a medium of psychological and moral characterization as a sign of enlightenment and the evolution of manners. In 1792, Pavil'shchikov published an essay *Theater* ("Teatr") in one of the journals he edited with Krylov, *The Mirror*. The author of some fifteen plays, Plavil'shchikov was also a reputable actor who played a title role in Sumarokov's tragedy *Sinav and Truvor* and acted in the premiere of Fonvizin's *The Minor*. Gifted at creating pleasant and positive types imbued with reason, sentiment, and virtue, Plavil'shchikov excelled at rousing spectators' emotions through gestures and put his ideas into practice in theater productions at Moscow University. His essay marked a watershed in the history of Russian drama because it advocated the creation of a truly national drama, rather than an imitation of French plays. Content, the essay argued, needed to be drawn from Russian life. He even deemed the subject of serfdom to be fit for discussion on the stage.

Informed by Diderot's writings on the theater, Plavil'shchikov's essay begins with a three-part discussion of theater, tragedy, and comedy, prolonged in a single epistolary exchange between an imaginary correspondent and Plavil'shchikov.[44] Much of his discourse is given over to the contemporary preoccupation with the question of whether a national culture is self-sufficient, or whether it can justifiably transmute foreign models. The specific sections on comedy, however, where Plavil'shchikov argues for a drama poised between comedy and tragedy, echo the position Diderot had espoused over thirty years earlier in both the *Entretiens sur le Fils naturel* (1757), his essay on his own play of that title, and the *Discours sur la poésie dramatique* (1758):

> *Drame bourgeois*, or civic tragedy, requires no less attention and care in composition and presentation, even though its characters are lowlier than those of heroic tragedy and, accordingly, have a style closer to the ordinary. It is for this reason that the action [of the *drame bourgeois*] penetrates the hearts of the spectators more quickly, since the plot mirrors their own circumstances. And I think that writing an accomplished *drame bourgeois* is as difficult as writing a tragedy, if not possibly even more heroic, since it is necessary in it to elevate feelings and passions, even while observing an ordinary style...I do not understand why bourgeois tragedy is distinguished from drama; I perceive no distinction [between them] apart from the fact that in drama a word or character may sometimes burst out and provoke a smile or laughter, even though the author's intention was to intensify sorrow; equally, in comedies, there may be instances that elicit tears.

Hence, it seems, one can dare to mix bourgeois tragedy with bourgeois drama, and leave it to depend on the will of the author: whether to write a drama that is entirely tearful or one that, here and there, achieves humor; or whether to determine it necessary that in drama laughter be a type of joy *that brings viewers relief from sensibility*, and this laughter or smile, while as pleasing, is very far from the laughter of comedy.[45]

The theater is now understood as a mirror (a common metaphor in advice and conduct literature of the period) in which spectators see themselves clearly because virtues and vices are compellingly displayed on stage. Many writers, including Kheraskov and Kniazhnin, wrote in this manner. This new style of play cultivated the affect of the audience by exploring the world of feeling and passions as a subject. Happy endings as a reward for virtue work well on stage because characters have greater depth than their slapstick avatars. Domestic comedy also acquires a psychological dimension (hence the label *genre sérieux*) as characters face choices that can involve sacrifice.[46] While still short of the realism of nineteenth-century characters, and more heavily defined by classical types (Starodum from Fonvizin's *The Minor* is the classic example of the *raisonneur*), they do come to life on stage as they find their way morally. In the Introduction to his translation of Diderot's 1757 play *Le Fils naturel* (translated and published in 1788 as *Pobochnyi syn*), an exemplary work in the genre, the translator Ivan Yakovlev provided a key to the affective and performance values of the work:

> The reader will find here only those properties that, given our natural weaknesses, will captivate the heart, charm the soul, and induce that pleasant state that arouses us to love and foster a greater attachment to virtue. This is drama! ... The chief intention of my author in composing this work was to make it a model for domestic tragedies and to bring them into fashion and performance. A praiseworthy intention! But do we still think that it is only the misfortunes of noble people, heroes, imperial soldiers, or the destroyers of nations, that deserves general feeling? That the fate of other good people is not worthy of our attention and could not produce in us any feelings?[47]

Physical gesture and bodily reaction were also necessary as coded displays of feeling. Weeping on stage and in fiction becomes a conventional necessity and a token of authenticity, a standard paradox of the neoclassical style in which emotional credibility derives from the use of conventional situations to generate a familiar response in the reader. Throughout the period, tears will serve as an index of sensibility; more tears are shed in the last third of the eighteenth century than in the entirety of medieval Russian literature. Emphasis now falls on the exterior depiction of feeling for its own sake and as a catalyst of the individual histories. All types of response can now be channeled through external expression and signs of emotion. In tragedy and theatrical soliloquies, tears serve as the ultimate expression of loyalty to the nation over the beloved, or the beloved over the nation. In these genres, few writers ever surpassed neoclassical expectations, but they largely succeeded in bridging the gap between Russian and European stagecraft and, in so doing, helped to create a new emotional vocabulary focused on the links between sensation, sensibility, and comportment.

The literary field: Writers and readership

Patronage and court literature were not the exclusive models and creative modes. Over the course of Catherine II's reign, a publishing boom tracked and eventually surpassed the slow growth of the reading public in the two main cities, Moscow and St. Petersburg. The literary field expanded through the efforts of amateurs, societies, institutions of higher learning (in the first instance, the Academy of Sciences and Moscow University), and university presses. To some degree, Catherine herself was responsible for this expansion by funding large-scale projects, patronizing the theater, participating in literary journals, and setting an example as a writer. In these circumstances, the longer-term trajectory altered the balance of the gentry from dependence on the court to less direct reliance on the monarch. The emergence of new audiences was predicated in large part on secondary education. The Petrine reforms made education compulsory for nobility, and everyone, regardless of their station in life, had to educate their male children, who were subjected to periodic examinations from the age of ten. Promotion along a career path required serious instruction. As a result, larger numbers of the gentry acquired a broader humanistic education, and a small portion of those came truly to believe in the value of culture.[48] The post-Petrine state required of its service elite a better skill set to administer economic growth. We see this, for instance, in the gymnasium established at the Academy of Sciences in St. Petersburg in 1724 and a feeder school (*blagorodnyi pansion*) founded by Mikhail Kheraskov in 1779 for Moscow University. The system of humanistic and general secondary education that had come into being by the mid-century also aimed to imbue the service gentry with a civilized secular outlook and a sense of moral duty. Until 1750, most educated people were the product of ecclesiastical academies and Church schools. This state of affairs changed in the middle of the century as new schools opened, previously existing ones expanded their enrolments, and a higher percentage of enrolled students graduated.[49] Enrolment figures vary enormously according to different sources, but there is consensus that Russia's seminaries had between 5,000 and 6,000 students annually by the mid-1760s and that the numbers rose sharply in the next twenty years.[50]

Home education also proved to be a significant mode of instruction and preparation for state service. The acceptance of formal education by the upper and middle gentry, sometimes mocked in comic writing as superficial, accompanied a gradual shift in values and also increased the reading public.[51] The creation of a reading public "took place in a culture in which literacy and reading remained highly exceptional and in which the struggle for the attention of the Russian public was directed and largely waged at the top of society, among the relatively small educated elites residing in Moscow and St. Petersburg."[52] While the civic spaces they created fell short of the institutions that the hero of Karamzin's *Letters of a Russian Traveler* (*Pis'ma russkogo puteshestvennika*, 1790–91) admires in Europe and Great Britain for their scale and quality, arguably, their Russian counterparts also enlightened critical reflection on social practice and values.[53]

Secondary-school graduates of the 1750s and 1760s played a decisive role in determining which books institutional presses published. In the words of the historian Marc Raeff, "it was believed that unless a Russian acquired a smattering of everything that the West had to offer, he could not be considered educated or even civilized."[54] The educated elites were encouraged to familiarize themselves with the cumulative wealth of ideas and information that European civilization represented. An analysis of sales of literature from the 1770s to the 1790s indicates that the social composition of the largest proportion of subscribers and purchasers of books was from the bottom half of the Table of Ranks (whereas the majority of buyers of Masonic books were clergy).[55]

In the 1720s, Kantemir thought the unthinkable in considering authorial aspirations and the possibility of a literary field populated by educated readers and writers. His "First Satire" acknowledges that in the world of the 1720s a "golden age" has yet to arrive, but insists that writing as a skill can no longer be confined to the chanceries and wielded only by bureaucrats.[56] In his "Second Epistle. To My Verses" ("Pis'mo II. K stikham svoim," 1743), written in the manner of Horace's Epistle I.20, Kantemir advised young writers that acquiring style, by which he meant primarily a command of verse form and "resonant" rhyme, is a difficult but worthwhile endeavor, since "such verses have sometimes been of use to people" ("chto polezny inogda podobnye byli liudiam stikhi").[57] While he remained true to the mission of satire to "improve morals," Kantemir held that writing must be its own reward. Reading, he acknowledges, affords pleasures for its own sake.

Kantemir portrayed the writer as "hunched over his desk" in endeavors that would never enrich him by "adding a sheep to his flock" ("Ovtsu ne pribavit on ottsovskomu stadu"); in fact, his foppish scribbler values authorship so little that he regrets wasting paper that might otherwise be used for curling his hair.[58] The satirist himself can praise the "use of science" and "wisdom" enjoyed for its own sake. It took several more generations for his fantasy to be realized. From the 1750s, the obstacles to secularization that thwarted Kantemir's satirical persona had disappeared, and perhaps for that reason the nature and purpose of reading and writing, whether utilitarian or pleasurable, remained a topic of less anxious commentary in literature.

Later, writers begin to perceive changes that indicate the emergence of a literary field. Best known as the author of *The Battle of Chesme* (*Chesmenskii boi*, 1771) and *Rossiada* (1779), lumbering epics on national themes, Mikhail Kheraskov deflects criticism of lyric poetry as a waste of time in the short poem "On the Importance of Verse" ("O vazhnosti stikhotvorstva," 1762). The poem identifies multiple merits in panegyric, scientific, legal, and religious uses to which poets have adapted their verse, and sees his "poetry fever" ("zhar moi k stikham") as a positive sign of the times.[59]

If we fast-forward a little more than a decade to the late 1770s, we find figures like Kheraskov, at the time Rector of Moscow University, and Derzhavin, rewarded for his service during the Pugachev Rebellion and newly promoted in the civil service, using their personal correspondence to complain that what we might call their day jobs crowd out time for writing, a vocation they would keenly like to see become full-time and professional.[60] When in the 1800s Derzhavin looked back at the period as he prepared to write his autobiography, he may have treated aspects of his biography creatively, de-emphasizing his service career, in order retrospectively to give the impression that writers, and himself above all, had more professional standing than was the case.[61] Novikov defended poetry (and literature more generally) as a fruitful occupation. With some irony, his essay "On the Poetry of Classicism" ("O poezii klassitsizma," published in *The Drone*) notes that prose writers earn more lucrative fees for less work, while poets are rewarded for superior art with lower wages. "I have only recently," he says, "attained common sense and am satisfied that ... glorious versifiers should chew green laurels as their exclusive source of nourishment."[62] In the lyric poem "Solitary Hours" ("Uedinennye chasy"), Princess Ekaterina Urusova (1747–after 1817) describes the pleasure of reading on one's own. Yet she also takes pleasure in writing for others. Acts of sharing one's poetry in manuscript, opening up one's album for inscription in a salon, as was the case from the late eighteenth century onward, and exchanging verse epistles spurred dozens of writers, rather than single individuals, to produce a significant body of lyric poetry that bears witness to the emergence, by the 1780s, of a common notion that literature must be attuned to contemporary manners and the sentiments of its readers.

At the beginning of Catherine's reign publishing opportunities were very limited, and small numbers of readers, rather than a sizeable reading public, could look to anthologies like the *Collection of Best Compositions* (*Sobranie luchshikh sochinenii*), which appeared in three parts from 1762, for information on economics, history, and literature as translated from German, English, and French (some by the soon-to-be celebrated playwright and satirist Denis Fonvizin).[63] Evidence points to difficult conditions for booksellers marked by inefficient distribution, bloated print runs, and financial problems. Top-down decisions about what ought to be published, rather than a reader-driven demand, characterize the embryonic book market. Writers had no royalty mechanism or professional status, yet piecemeal wages were paid to translators and contributors to journals.

The history of the Russian book trade is severely hampered by a paucity of archival material, uneven reconstruction of libraries, few publishers' inventories, and scarce references to the reception of texts. Yet despite the slender source material some generalizations of value can be made based on the current state of research. Because an economic model of literature had yet to emerge, no stable pricing structure based on a market existed, but the rudiments were present. Extant sales and inventory lists show that readers did pay to buy books either in shops (few though they were) or directly from university or academy presses. Between 1756 and 1775, Moscow University Press doubled the number of titles it published annually from forty to about eighty. The catalyst for making Moscow University Press into a creative intellectual force came less from the open market than from the students and teachers, such as the poets Kheraskov and Nikolai Popovsky, and the grammarians Anton Barsov and Johann Reichel (1727–88), whose translating and publishing duties were characterized as "morally uplifting."[64] Similar growth took place at the Academy of Sciences. Between 1755 and 1765, the Academy employed sixteen full-time translators, hiring a dozen more in 1766; recruits came from young men sent abroad for their education. This cohort formed the workforce of the Society Dedicated to the Translation of Foreign Books (Sobranie, staraiushcheesia o perevode inostrannykh knig na rossiiskii iazyk), founded by Catherine the Great in 1768 and managed by Novikov under the aegis of the Academy until 1783, when it was reorganized. The Translation Society (as it is known) published 112 separate translations in 174 volumes; by the time it ceased publishing, it had completed an additional twenty-nine translations for publication and had begun work on nearly one hundred more, including translations of the influential French philosophers like Mably, Montesquieu, Voltaire, and Rousseau. After 1772, the Translation Society's print runs ranged between 300 and 600; subscription lists, however, often numbered no more than in the low one hundreds.[65] Novikov, whose own operations relied on subsidies from Catherine II, feared that translations were crowding out homegrown talent and creativity. While they were a positive phenomenon, new institutions like lending libraries and book clubs eroded sales. Reprints and print run figures are unreliable indicators of market demand because entire print runs were sometimes warehoused and lost or accidentally pulped, and the cost of reprinting was borne by the author. Yet the rapidity of change is remarkable. The year 1783 saw the promulgation of the Free Press Edict. This had an immediate effect, as did a tacit relaxation of censorship. In St. Petersburg, the Gay brothers opened a bookshop. Within a few years some twenty shops imported and sold books from France and Switzerland. Some journals included updates on new publications.[66] For instance, the *Mirror of the Light* (*Zerkalo sveta*), which ran regularly in 1786 and 1787 and was initially edited by Ippolit Bogdanovich, featured a section "Book News" with bibliographic details of foreign and Russian publications. And the number of literary works translated into Russian increased massively.

Concurrent with the changes in the book industry, a gap opened up between the growth in the theater repertory, audience demand, and financial reward. Sumarokov had a contract with the Italian-born theater producer Belmonti stipulating his own involvement in the staging of his plays in Moscow. The unacceptable behavior of the lead actress, Elizaveta Ivanova, put her in the sidelines for the opening night of *Sinav and Truvor*. But Sumarokov's request that the performance be delayed, supported by Belmonti, was denied by Count Petr Saltykov, the commander-in-chief of Moscow. In late January 1770, Sumarokov appealed to the empress in two letters; she replied with a reprimand, sending a copy of her own response to Count Saltykov. He in turn circulated copies to a wide range of Moscow society, aiming to disgrace the playwright and put the upstart in his place. As Marcus Levitt puts it, "Catherine upheld the Moscow commander-in-chief's power to treat Moscow as his fiefdom over Sumarokov's legal rights, choosing to extend her patronage to an important political client rather than to an unruly literary one."[67] Sumarokov persisted in his ambitions only to be hindered again.

Despite a prior contract he had with a Moscow theater, Sumarokov *Dimitry the Pretender* was first staged in 1775, four years after its composition, by a third party. Sumarokov was thwarted by a pair of entrepreneurs who had purchased the privilege and royalty rights. On this occasion, and during the staging of *Sinav and Truvor*, Sumarokov attempted to reassert his author's rights but was accused of undermining imperial authority.[68] In the course of these skirmishes, he sorely tested Catherine's patience, prompting her to complain about his "ravings." More importantly, it is clear that she viewed the management of even private theaters as a lucrative perk in her own patronage network, which trumped the writer's aspirations for professional recognition.

Literary journals

In the period from 1700 to around 1755, no specialist literary journals were launched.[69] Newspapers existed solely in the form of court circulars with separate proceedings from the Academy of Sciences. From 1750 to 1800, however, at least forty-six literary journals came out. Many were ephemeral, lasting no more than several issues. In the second half of the eighteenth century, most educated figures depended on state service. For many dabblers in literature, journalism was no more than a gentleman's hobby, a bonding activity through which the cultural elite explored their own individual and collective identity. For others, like Nikolai Novikov and figures around Aleksandr Radishchev, writing served a cultural mission and philosophical purpose. It is no wonder that writers quickly seized on the attractions of the medium including the low cost of production, openness to miscellaneous material, and topicality.

Under the auspices of the Academy of Sciences, Lomonosov initiated the publication of the *Monthly Compositions* (*Ezhemesiachnye sochineniia*, 1755–64). He also lent his authority to an article "On the Duty of Journalists" ("O dolzhnosti zhurnalistov," 1754), which argued emphatically the more general point that print culture was an essential tool of progress, and that the periodical press was a more lasting and efficient means of disseminating ideas than the manuscript circulation of opinion. Literary journals soon became a publishing phenomenon of Catherine's reign, a product of a newly ambitious literary culture in which better-educated scions of the elite, some pupils at Moscow University, most fluent in French, could participate.

In 1761, the polymath Vasily Ruban (1742–95), thought to be the son of a Cossack and educated at the Kiev-Mohyla Academy and then the Slavo-Greco-Latin Academy in Moscow, brought out twenty-six issues of *The Diligent Ant* (*Trudoliubivyi muravei*). Best known as an odist and court client, this classicist, economist, and agronomist was critical of satire as merely frivolous carping. His journal advocated a high moral tone and turned to classical writers for examples of quality literature. Journals attracted fresh graduates of religious academies, employing them as rank and file of the new translation industry. Signed contributors include a large number of ephemeral figures. Even while circles of participation widened, aspiring writers faced a reality check when they confronted the economic conditions of the book trade. The very existence of these journals gives positive proof of a significant shift in the hopes for literature, confidence in a literary system that was in the process of modernizing, and the delight to be afforded to authors in publishing. Talent, interest, and debate were concentrated in small, sometimes overlapping groups whose belief in the cultural capital of literature as pleasure, antidote to boredom, and demonstration of taste migrated from one journal to the next.[70]

Journals served as a conduit for the literary production of amateur men of letters (rarely women) and a vehicle for establishing alliances based on taste. New journals devoted considerable space to poetry and prose, promoting literature as a leisure activity that went beyond the humorous critique of satire. Titles often reflect this advocacy as we see with periodicals such as *Idle Time Advantageously Used* (*Prazdnoe vremia, v pol'zu upotreblennoe*, 1759–60), *Useful Entertainment* (*Poleznoe uveselenie*, 1760), and *A Pleasurable and Useful Pastime* (*Priiatnoe i poleznoe preprovozhdenie vremeni*, 1794). In 1758, Sumarokov received permission to establish his own journal, *The Diligent Bee*, published in 1759 as the first private literary periodical in Russia. It showcased writers close to Sumarokov's own aesthetic ideals (meaning *not* Trediakovsky or Lomonosov), with an inclination toward pleasure over instruction. Among the better educated, writing poetry had caught on as a civilized pastime, and among Sumarokov's loyal fans and followers there were poets such as Ivan Elagin, Aleksei Vasil'evich Naryshkin (1742–1800), and Adam Olsuf'ev (1721–84). Under the sponsorship of Kheraskov and the publisher Vasily Sankovsky (1741–98), both collaborators in *Useful Entertainment* and *Free Hours* (*Svobodnye chasy*, 1763), the new journal *Good Intention* (*Dobroe namerenie*, 1764) attracted more than a dozen contributors positioned lower on the social scale. Some of these are canonical, like Vasily Maikov (see Plate 10), the subject of a splendid portrait by one of the best artists of the age; some are not, since their literary production was subsumed into translation rather than new composition.

Kheraskov also headed *Evenings* (1772–73), whose avowed purpose in fifty-two weekly issues was to satisfy lovers of lyric poetry and, as the title suggests, enable sociable ways of spending an evening. Some foreign authors appeared in Russian in these pages for the first time, including Edward Young's *Night Thoughts* (1745), a seminal text in the development of the Gothic. Among the contributors to *Evenings* can be counted the most productive elegists and writers of the love lyric: Bogdanovich, Maikov, and Elizabeth Kheraskov (1737–1809), wife of the editor and an accomplished poet in her own right. The contributors felt that the issues had a lasting value, and by assembling them in book form in 1788–89 followed a practice common in journal publishing in the second half of the eighteenth century. Other periodicals with a similar emphasis on non-satirical content, featuring original and translated material by Maikov and Ivan Krylov, included *Old and New* (*Starina i novizna*, 1772–73) and *Medicine for Boredom and Cares* (*Lekarstvo ot skuki i zabot*, 1786–87).

The organization of the contents of a literary journal was flexible. No certain formula applied to the proportion of translated and original material or to the distribution of prose and poetry. Rubrics followed no standard order, and the category of miscellanea (*smes'*) was used for works of criticism. Few journals restricted their content to a single topic, however. No doubt dependent on available material for copy, some journals relied on a variety of formats. For instance, the monthly journal *Innocent Activity* (*Nevinnoe Uprazhnenie*, 1763), printed by Moscow University Press, declared its mission to be the "mixing of the amusing and the useful." A whole range of short lyrics from epigrams to odes provided the amusement. On the "useful", or serious, side was a translation by Bogdanovich of Voltaire's *Poem on the Lisbon Disaster*, a highly influential work written in response to the earthquake of 1755.[71] Also on the serious side was a 1763 translation of a "dangerous" French philosopher by Princess Ekaterina Dashkova (1743–1810), who twenty years later was appointed president of both Imperial Academy of Sciences and the newly created Russian Academy (responsible for the *Dictionary of the Russian Academy* [*Slovar' Akademii Rossiiskoi*], 1735). The excerpt produced by this boon companion of Catherine (until her exile by Paul I after the empress's death in 1796) came from a work on the passions by the French philosopher and tax-farmer Claude-Adrien Helvétius. Helvétius's heterodox work, *De l'esprit*, later much admired by Radishchev, had caused a storm of controversy (leading to its suppression by the French Parliament). In the Russian context, Dashkova's modest introduction of a cutting-edge thinker reflects a haphazard interest in European thought typical of the early 1760s, rather than a subversive intention.

Journals of the 1770s could project a commitment to culture, although few were truly vehicles of any ideological or political message before the 1790s. They contributed broadly to the positive value literature acquired between the 1750s and the 1770s. That difference comes across vibrantly in "The Defamer of Poetry" ("Khulitel' stikhotvorstva," n.d.), a short work in which Ivan Khemnitser (1745–84) satirizes the satirists, concluding that writers devoted solely to criticism will be restricted to "lampooning idiots in satire."[72] Expectations had risen about entertainment and craft as well as instruction to be included in journals. In the 1770s, at a moment when attacks were directed at false Europeanization or Gallomania, the appreciation of truly cultivated taste became pronounced. In 1778, Bogdanovich published Book I of *Dushen'ka*, which begins by claiming that the writer's "own delight" in "idle hours" was his sole inspiration. The idea of idleness as a reward was a contemporary ideal of the gentry that harked back to the Roman virtue of *otium cum dignitate* ("indolence with dignity") affected by eighteenth-century aristocrats. For readers of Bogdanovich the reward of idleness was the pleasure of reading poems by a writer whose verse was a versatile instrument, capable of every effect, from literary parody to visionary evocations of happiness in civilization. Even a brief overview of just a few of the dozens of short-lived journals can give a feel for the trend. Ruban's *The Diligent Ant*, for instance, made wit and entertainment its purpose, and largely gathered translations of ancients (Horace, Theophrastus, Lucian) and Moderns (Voltaire), mixing light-hearted verse and anecdotes. *The Tatler* (*Pustomelia*, 1770) in its short life of two issues broke new ground by publishing a theater chronicle with reviews of performances and staging.

None of these journals had a long lifespan, possibly cut short by a lack of original content and subscribers. Yet their aspirations represent a stepping-stone toward the idea of a literary life, still an amateur pastime but recognized for its value as part of a cultivated elite life. This is precisely the point made by Kheraskov in the introduction to *Evenings*, in which he identifies the journal's audience as members of the gentry who, as commercially disinterested lovers of literature, are amateurs of the sonnets, idylls, eclogues, and light verse that they enjoy reading to one another.

Pedagogical intentions and virtuous ends were sometimes invoked to justify the pleasures of the imagination.[73] These went beyond the more modest pleasures that a writer like Sumarokov had made available in his popular songs and love elegies. Journals like the weekly *Idle Time* and *Free Hours* catered to this image of literary work as civilized recreation and a refuge from court intrigue and politics. Sumarokov contributed a number of epigrams and fables to *Idle Time*. The journal emanated from the Noble Infantry Cadet Corps, an elite military academy. Much of its material reflected the school's corporate values and was pedagogical and ethical in nature, focused on inculcating good behavior among the cadets. In advocating the virtue of reason among the educated, the magazine set the definition of enlightenment at a fairly low pragmatic level. At the opposite end of the spectrum, and at the tail end of the period, was the short-lived *St. Petersburg Journal* (*Sankt-Peterburgskii zhurnal*, 1798). One of the few journals with an explicit philosophical (if uncertain political) orientation, its twelve issues under the leadership of Ivan Pnin (1773–1805), poet and thinker, set the bar high in defining Enlightenment in terms of the political and social theory by Montesquieu, the materialist philosopher Baron d'Holbach, the brothers Pietro and Alessandro Verri—a Milanese economist and an author, respectively. The journal also featured Pnin's own work on the questions of citizenship, manifesting a clear connection to Radishchev's work (and therefore still dangerous in 1798).

Amateur writers, coteries, and readership

By the 1780s, literary groups had acquired another dimension. A language of friendship based on common interests and personal sympathy characterized these associations, channeling antagonism and a critical reflex, sanctioned by the querulous habits of the earlier generation, into more friendly banter. Forms of sociability were now to coterie poetry what questions of style had been to the generation of Lomonosov, Sumarokov, and Trediakovsky. Poetic circles were metropolitan, male in membership, and, while mostly drawn from the gentry, the sons of clergy such as Semen Bobrov (1763–1810), author of fine lyrics and narrative poetry such as the narrative poem *Tavrida* (1798) and contributor to the journal *The Chatty Citizen* (*Beseduiushchii grazhdanin*, 1789), augmented their ranks.[74] Amateur lovers of poetry and theater included government officials like Derzhavin, educators like Mikhail Murav'ev, the first rector of Moscow University; artisans like the architect N. A. L'vov (1751–1803); and landowners like the accomplished Horatian poet Vasily Kapnist. The Derzhavin–L'vov circle of friends was active from the beginning of the 1770s. Despite the fact that Derzhavin was the most prominent poet in this group—which also included Kapnist, Ivan Khemnitser, and Murav'ev—L'vov was its acknowledged leader. Called by his comrades "the genius of taste," he regularly corrected their poetry, including Derzhavin's. A poet himself, L'vov rarely published or, if he published, then did so anonymously, preferring to circulate his verse informally among his friends. In the late eighteenth century, the classicist Aleksei Olenin (1763–1843) joined the group. He served as a link between the Derzhavin–L'vov group and familiar circles of the early nineteenth century, among which his own "Olenin" circle was one of the most renowned.[75] Coterie members were generally content to circulate their lyrics and collections in manuscript anthologies, to publish occasionally in literary journals that enjoyed a tiny circulation, and to come together for debate and discussion in friendly associations (which by the mid-1810s were factionalized by literary politics). Many poems, and some handbooks, make the correct style of verse a subject of criticism, and revel in virtuoso displays of wit and polemic. Many poets, including the members of the Arzamas group that functioned in 1815–18, carried this model of literary community, based on social and aesthetic cohesion, over into the new century.

Coteries gathered on estates and in city residences, and these venues also housed private theaters. For instance, the aristocrat P. M. Volkonsky hosted Mikhail and Elizaveta Kheraskov (who had their own private theater) for performances at home; Vasily Maikov wrote works for the private theater of his friend, the eminent actor F. G. Volkov; and Nikolai Nikolev staged his own plays on his estate. In 1778, Mikhail Murav'ev mentions attending the premiere of Kniazhnin's first tragedy *Dido* (*Didona*, 1769) at the home of P. V. Bakunin, a noteworthy performance because the play made ambitious use of spectacular special effects, including Dido's immolation.[76] The richest families, such as the Sheremetevs, maintained their own private companies staffed by serf actors. D. A. Levitsky's joint portrait of the serf actors E. N. Khrushcheva and E. N. Khovansky, dressed for their parts in the comic opera "The Caprices of Love, or Nineta at Court" (1773), painted against a rustic backdrop, conveys the charm of these productions. Catherine herself was a prolific author of skits, charades, dramatizations of proverbs, and plays of which only *Oh! Time* (*O! Vremia*, 1772) and *The Deceiver* (*Obmanshchik*, 1786), about the Sicilian adventurer Cagliostro, have a claim to lasting merit. Within her private suite in the Hermitage, she gathered writers and noblemen (who obeyed a code of politeness shown in Figure III.03), both Russian and foreign, to write and stage private theatrical performances.[77]

By the end of the eighteenth century, the critical mass of printed literature attests to the consolidation of an amateur culture of letters. This is radically different from its beginning in the 1730s. By the 1770s, ideas of authorship had moved away from prescriptive efforts to establish norms of taste and art to a wide range of interests. At this time, print was not a means of creating literary reputations among a wider public beyond coteries, as would happen in the 1830s. In this connection, the rare extant subscription lists for published volumes are of interest to historians of the book as evidence of the limited diffusion of literature. Typically, such a list contained no more than several dozen names. Journal readers represented a demand for

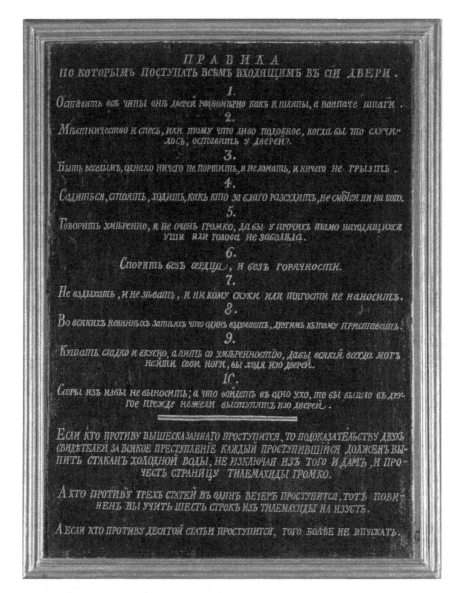

FIGURE III.03. Catherine the Great's Rules for Good Conduct, *c.*1760.

quality writing, but the subscriber base largely overlapped with the contributors. The literary field had begun to move only very gradually toward the creation of an anonymous book market, and readership began to snowball in the 1830s, becoming an important topic for Romantic writers. Consider that, in 1776, Mikhail Murav′ev assembled in *New Lyric Pieces of Mikhail Murav′ev* (*Novye liricheskie opyty Mikhaila Murav′eva*), works that had circulated in manuscript. Similarly, hand-copied anthologies of Derzhavin's verse also survive. Since both writers could easily have paid to have their poems printed, the preference for manuscript books of this kind indicates their value as gifts and tokens of friendship rather than commercial objects. In his "Letter to Aleksandr Alekseevich Pleshcheev" ("Poslanie k Aleksandru Alekseevichu Pleshcheevu," 1794), Karamzin spoke for many writers when he assumed that readers and friends were coextensive groups, perpetuating the model of readership networks as a class-based phenomenon.

The authority of the writer: Satirical journals, politics, and society

Seventy years after Addison and Steele had provided a model for British writers (and French imitators, like Voltaire) of how to create a satirical persona using the middle style, Novikov created comparable personae for a Russian readership. The bantering tone, applied to contemporary mores and literary polemics, suggested a real pleasure in literature for its own sake and the use of wit as a weapon of literary criticism and personal positioning. Didacticism and delight in equal measure characterized satirical journals. Between 1769, when Novikov began publishing, and the end of his career in the 1790s, about a dozen satirical journals aimed their wit and criticism at contemporary issues.[78] To this day, they remain the most anthologized and read journalistic works of the period thanks to Novikov's brilliant playfulness.

As a satirical writer, at his most relaxed, Novikov has the chattiness and sharpness of a pro-verbial man on the street. His journals include comic treatments of a host of contemporary topics, using a variety of lively narrative modes, such as anecdote, essay, and dialogue. The danger of individual satire, as Steele had argued in the English magazine the *Tatler* in 1710, was that it could descend into personal attack. In a mode he called satire on vice (*satira na porok*), Novikov uses a persona, a scoffer by nature and trade, to express concern over human conduct and its absurdity, articulating reasons to laugh, and issuing wake-up calls about vice while avoiding any finger-pointing.[79] Mankind must be stripped of its social veneer so that we can see our failings. Satirists, both ancient and modern, and across national traditions, generally share a know-it-all attitude. It is the privilege of the satiric persona to judge the norms of pub-lic and private behavior and to condemn, sometimes muting censure with a hope of improve-ment.[80] In Novikov's satire on individuals (*satira na litso*), real and invented persons become the fall guys for failings that typify the attitudes of their time, and while the satirist scores points, a certain affection reduces the excessive asperity.

The Drone has a particular claim to our interest because Novikov used his satirical persona to stage a contest with Catherine the Great. By and large, his jesting persona is that of a monarchist and conservative hoping to correct bad behavior. His criticism never targets sen-sitive political matters; nor does it truly upend the reader's poise. In a shrewd performance, Catherine responded to Novikov's sallies as a fellow satirist. In the aftermath of the *Nakaz* (*Instruction*, 1767), a legislative program that established Catherine's credentials as a progres-sive monarch versed in the social theories of Montesquieu and the Italian jurist Cesare Beccaria (1738–94), Catherine had instructed Count V. G. Orlov (1743–83) of the Academy of Sciences to keep the published satirical journals under the strictest surveillance possible—evidence that her tolerance was contingent on controlling public opinion rather than out-right repression. The test case proved to be a set of satirical journals published by Novikov that focused on social and political issues beyond the run-of-the-mill satire of manners to be found on the pages of a satirical journal like Mikhail Chulkov's (1743 or 1744–92) *Parnassian Peddler* (*Parnasskii Shchepetil'nik*).[81] Her participation as a contributor, however, was not a green light to direct criticism or even a sign that she felt entirely relaxed about the arrange-ment. The Empress sustained the momentum by participating in the new journal *This and That* (*Vsiakaia vsiachina*) starting in early 1769. (Figure III.04 shows her working on the *Nakaz* and facing a bust of Peter the Great.)[82]

This and That was a vehicle for her own satirical writing launched by Catherine to provoke rebuttals and critical response.[83] Installments of *This and That* appeared until 1770, and Catherine published in the journal anonymously or adopted a variety of pseudonyms (possibly a trick she picked up from Voltaire, her correspondent, whom she read and admired). Pieces attributed to her focus on the class system and personal satisfaction as an organic element in a harmonious state, an Enlightenment goal vitiated, she observes, by the vices that universally beset humanity. It is the purpose of satire to identify these vices and shame people into self-betterment.

In the best tradition of satirical journals from which she borrowed, Catherine eventually assumed her own persona as Granny ("Babushka") in order to chide courtiers on the subject of manners. Her identity was an open secret, a ploy seemingly calculated to pre-empt anything seditious while soliciting response. While Catherine preferred to take the high ground in her use of moral literature, she encouraged debate among her "grandchildren," that is, the editors of other magazines who roundly attacked Granny, sometimes in highly personal terms. In *Hell's Post* (*Adskaia pochta*, 1769), the editor and main author, the novelist Fedor Emin (1735?–70), applied lessons he had learned from Voltaire about satirizing literary opponents in order to increase his own notoriety and celebrity.[84] He had no scruples about pointing his

FIGURE III.04. *Catherine and the Nakaz*, miniature enamel.

satirical arrows at literary enemies like Sumarokov. Cast as a correspondence between a lame devil and a cripple, the journal, which was republished in 1788 and 1791 (by Ippolit Bogdanovich), took no hostages among literary foes and mocked the comic playwright Vladimir Lukin in the poem "What I Believe and Do not Believe" ("Chemu ia veriu i chemu ne veriu," September 1769).[85]

Novikov participated actively on the pages of his own journal, *The Drone*, which ran from May 1769 to the spring of 1770. With a bantering tone, *The Drone* took aim at all figures of authority such as judges who fell short of the empress's legislative ideals. His editorial persona defended the practice of personal satire, justifying the right to target recognizable (if unnamed) figures and to use mockery to improve morals because "the person who corrects flaws is more philanthropic than the one who treats them with condescension" (May 26, 1769). This directly contradicted the policy of *This and That* to target "common sin" and adopt a lofty tone "because it seems to us that love for one's neighbor extends to correction rather than condescension and philanthropy; and he who sees only faults, without love, is unable to instruct another" (*This and That*, May 1, 1769). Novikov's speaker sticks to his guns. He notes that "Madame Granny praises those writers who only try to please," but criticizes this as hypocrisy ("krivodushnoe prikazanie"), and professes to show restraint since "a beast is known by its claws."[86] *The Drone* engaged directly with the position of *This and That*, disputing articles presumed to have been written by Catherine. Novikov took a more bracing approach to satire, targeting a broad range of issues from serfdom to the mania for all things French, and while he rarely named his targets outright, the salient point was that the editors defended the tactic of speaking frankly about individual examples of vice, civic abuse, and corruption, rather than using euphemism and expressing disapproval generically. The titular Drone dispenses his wisdom to perplexed readers through a combination of wit, sarcasm, and trenchant morality. At the same time, the editorial persona of *The Drone* pulls no punches in attacking Granny's substantive positions. In another journal, *The Miscellany* (*Smes'*, 1769), articles supported the Drone and argued that while Granny criticizes vice, she is excessively lenient in assigning blame. Both Emin in *Hell's Post* and Vasily Ruban in his *Neither This nor That* (*Ni to ni sio*, 1769), a journal composed largely of translated extracts, mocked the Granny as a has-been in offensive terms. Through his adopted persona of the Drone, Novikov also supported a more aggressive legislative program to combat social injustice, and treated the highly sensitive question of how to reform serfdom as an economic system and social injustice.

The high-profile involvement of the empress has generated much debate about her ultimate purposes, and whether the exchanges were genuinely critical or a performance carefully managed to produce a simulacrum of candid speech at a time in her reign when she particularly wanted to impress thinkers abroad, especially following the publication of the *Nakaz*, with the image of Russia as a land of tolerance.[87] Even a century later, in the 1860s, the radical writer and critic Nikolai Dobroliubov drew inspiration from Novikov's boldness in his article "Russian Satire in the Age of Catherine" while also criticizing the accommodation he found with Catherine.[88] Was this posture merely a pantomime, a display of controlled criticism that did not give others license to do the same?[89] Bearing in mind the fact that Catherine was always in the position to discontinue exchanges and close down the press, the answer is ambiguous.

It is doubtful whether Novikov ever intended to adopt radical positions designed to subvert Catherine, who may have colluded with—or manipulated—him as a way to test the waters of opinion at court and among the gentry. Whether in closing down the journal for financial reasons Novikov actually feared he had gone too far, or was protecting his self-interest, is debatable. Catherine remained a supporter, financing the Society for the Translation of

Foreign Books and its successor, the Typographical Company, Novikov's powerhouse effort to bring all kinds of foreign literature to Russia. *The Drone* failed to cover its costs because of a poor subscription base and closed as a commercial failure. It is hard to know exactly whether Novikov was undermined by the indifference of noblemen averse to his castigations about the abuse of serfs, or simply by a dearth of readers. The well-established approach of Soviet scholarship that treats Novikov and others as proponents of social democracy wrongly presents their position as that of an intelligentsia group (or an equivalent to the Fronde) pitted against the empress, and exaggerates their intentions of implementing reform. What should not be underestimated, however, is the extent to which Novikov and others, including Derzhavin in some of his poetry, pushed against Catherine's comfort zone as they explored the boundaries of her approach to Enlightenment absolutism. On her part, encouraging frankness was one way to turn court gossip into opinion, channeling discontent into firm positions she could evaluate. In her correspondence, she confided to Voltaire that her boldness abroad in countering the Ottomans meant that her policy initiatives at home would be limited. She conceded that literature could only flourish if there were at least an illusion of freedom (and, conversely, that harsh measures might backfire). Cultural accomplishment mattered to Catherine— admittedly, less than survival, but still to a significant degree. To expect no criticism would have been naive, and she was never naive. The critical issue for writers prepared to defend interests and test the boundaries of candor was how they played the game without causing offense or suggesting fundamental disbelief in autocracy.

For Novikov, and later for Fonvizin in the 1780s, serfdom reflected directly on the moral and intellectual standing of the educated elite on whom Russia's economic prosperity and progress in all spheres depended. Until the mid-1780s, Catherine gave evidence of a desire to at least reform serfdom, stopping short of full emancipation of the serfs. Her instinct for self-preservation led her not to disrupt the economic interests of landowners, although she legislated against inhumane treatment in a period that saw numerous peasant rebellions and murdered estate owners. From 1772 to 1773, Novikov brought out a new journal, *The Painter* (*Zhivopisets*), which deserves to be regarded as his masterpiece. The extent of his authorship and the identity of the other writers for Novikov's journals remains unclear; some identified authors include M. I. Popov (1742–90), Fonvizin, Catherine II, N. I. Panin, and E. R. Dashkova. Editorials consistently seem to dialogue with the reader. Unrelenting in his concern about serfdom, Novikov published here a series of works targeting abusive practices, including four "Letters of a Provincial Landowner to his Son," known as the "Letters to Falaleius" ("Pis'ma k Falaleiu"), and a "Fragment of a Journey by ***I***T***" ("Otryvok puteshestviia ***I***T***,") possibly written by Aleksandr Radishchev, on the subject of economic ruin caused by serfdom.[90] Clever inventions rather than "real" documentary works by actual landowners, these exposés caused consternation among landowners and elicited an eventual response from Novikov ("An English Walk" ["Angliiskaia progulka"], 1784) in which he professed to be targeting disgraceful abusers rather than all landowners and the system as such. Characterization shifts from lampooning of individuals to the creation of types. Portraits grow out of anecdotes, scraps of information, and documents such as the story "The Consequence of a Bad Education," the kernel of which served as the basis for Ivan Krylov's play *The Coffee Girl* (*Kofeinitsa*, 1784).

The theme of Russia's progress toward genuine Enlightenment rather than superficial imitation of French ways provided material for Novikov's later journal *The Purse* (*Koshelek*, 1774). Its anti-French stance riled the French ambassador who forced the journal's closure. At least initially, Catherine may have assented or turned a blind eye to Novikov's technique of setting abstract principles, some of which were legislated on in the *Nakaz*, into satirical vignettes that tested moral choices and human nature. By 1774, she had clearly grown eager to find other uses for his talent as a literary entrepreneur.

While the great age of satirical journals was over, literary magazines would continue to serve as a showcase for new literary talent, as a conduit for foreign literature, and as a form of textbook in moral instruction and practical wisdom. *Medicine from Boredom and Cares* (*Lekarstvo ot skuki i zabot*, 1786–87) covered in each of thirty-two issues such topics as morality, enjoyment, husbandry, fashion, and "activities of virtuous men," covered by the likes of Krylov, Maikov, and Bogdanovich. Between 1785 and 1789, Novikov, Karamzin and his friend the Freemason A. A. Petrov (1763?–93) collaborated on the weekly *Children's Reading for the Heart and Mind* (*Detskoe chtenie dlia serdtsa i razuma*). Compiled in the spirit of Rousseau's pedagogical theories of child development, the journal printed a wide range of literary pieces (stories, anecdote, pastoral verse), essays on natural science, and translations by Karamzin from works of moral literature. And even during 1793, a difficult year when Catherine, goaded by the Terror in France, imposed stricter controls, the journal the *St. Petersburg Mercury*, edited by Krylov and Klushin, published translations of works of philosophy, satire, a portrait of Voltaire (by now dead but still a persona non grata as the free-thinker behind "Voltairism"[91]), excerpts from the *Histoire des deux Indes*, the important work of the Abbé Raynal on political economy, and even a review of Iakov Kniazhnin's *Vadim of Novgorod* (c.1788/89), this despite scandal surrounding the publication of the play in 1793 two years after the writer's death.

The pleasures of literature

During the reign of Catherine the Great, literary activity came to be seen as a form of refinement and an expression of sensibility. Two keywords of the period are "usefulness" and its variants (*pol'za, poleznyi*) and "pleasant" or "cheerful" (*priiatnyi, veselyi*). The Horatian dictum that the "ultimate goal of poetry is to please and to instruct" (*omne tulit punctum qui miscuit utile dulci*) was central to neoclassical aesthetics. That tenet acquired a new life in Russia.[92] Usefulness softened by pleasure, and pleasure made purposeful, express a commonly held ideal for moral instruction in a variety of literary modes.

Fables, a genre known in Russia from the seventeenth century onward, found a master in Ivan Krylov who abandoned journalism and playwriting in the early nineteenth century in favor of composing fables. His versions were much loved and widely read in the nineteenth century. The genre is a showcase for the aesthetic of attractive instruction or, as Derzhavin put it in "Felitsa," "delicious lemonade," combining moral pungency and aesthetic delight. A seventeenth-century translation into Russian of Aesop's *Fables*, done from a Polish translation, struggled to attract any readers. It was only the first generation of European secularizers, and initially Kantemir and Trediakovsky, who showed any interest in and flair for the form. From the 1760s, fables show staying power, appearing in separate books published by individual authors.

Like the epigram, the form of raillery and score setting par excellence, the fable excels in delivering moral judgments, cleverly wrapping up personal prejudices in impersonal stories. Narrated usually in the third person, these short anecdotes often amuse with their stock of animal characters yet can also hit the mark about human failings, combining the innocence of writing for children with the precept of wisdom literature. Thirty years after Trediakovsky and Kantemir, Sumarokov continued in the tradition with dozens of parables (*pritchi*), such as the "Mouse Who Renounced the World" ("Otrekshaiasia mira Mysh'," 1759), "The Fool" or "Idol" (the double entendre is intended in the Russian title "Bolvan," 1760), the "Monkey-Poet" ("Obez'iana-stikhotvorets," 1763), and the "The Ambassador Donkey" ("Posol Osel," n.d.), titles that give the flavor of these ironic doses of wisdom packaged in rhyme.

Most lyric poets tried their hand at didactic allegory in verse, and animal fables in particular were a popular vehicle for moralists with a light satirical touch. Of longer examples, highly noteworthy is Kniazhnin's "The Parrot, while not an Epic, Is a Fairytale" ("Popugai esli ne poema, tak skazka," 1788 or 1790). Vasily Maikov penned more than forty "didactic fables" (*nravouchitel'nyie basni*), including "Aesop Explains a Will" ("Ezop tolkuet dukhovnuiu," 1763 or 1767) about a predatory priest who swindles an inheritance out of a gullible young girl. Like *satira na porok*, fables targeted vices seen as universal, especially venality, vanity, ignorance, and miserliness. Catherine the Great chipped in with prose fables and oriental tales of her own composition, including the "Fairy Tale of the Tsarevich Khlor" ("Skazka o tsareviche Khlore," 1783), the story that formed the basis for Derzhavin's poem "Felitsa."

Many other poets, such as Maikov and the poet and educator Mikhail Kheraskov, are among the past masters in this area, often following the model of La Fontaine.[93] As an avowed imitator of the classic moralist poems from Aesop to Charles-Étienne Pesselier, Kheraskov used his fables to attack the corrupt legal system, and on occasion to denounce gossip and calumny. He devotes "The Mosquito" ("Komar") to the figure of the slanderer, a "professional" defamer who drummed up litigation:

> Что гнусен клеветник, так то пример не новой,
> Но бойся, злой язык, судьбины Комаровой.[94]

> That slanderers are vile, everybody knows,
> But beware, evil tongue, the fate of mosquitoes.

Foremost among poets specializing in moralizing verse was Ivan Khemnitser, now little remembered for anything other than his fables, starting with "The Two Families" ("Dva semeistva," 1779), apparently inspired by a visit to the studio of the French genre painter Jean-Baptiste Greuze. His first collection *Fables and Fairy Tales* (*Basni i skazki*, 1779) contained around thirty-three fables, augmented by a further thirty-five in a second edition of 1782. While his poems are mainly original compositions, Khemnitser, like many fable writers, also adapted into Russian works by French masters such as Voltaire, Jean-Jacques Dorat, Pesselier, and, above all, Jean de La Fontaine, the supreme master of the genre. Khemniter's work was the basis of a collective three-volume anthology of fables, published in 1799 and featuring contributions by Derzhavin, N. A. L'vov, Kapnist, and Aleksei Olenin. Generally, didactic animal fables (as distinct from fairy tales) pithily reinforce a message about good civic values and private morality to be found in the conduct literature of the period published in literary journals, the moralistic writings of Novikov and others, and in the educational writings of the statesman and pedagogue Ivan Betskoi (1704–95) and Catherine the Great.[95]

Satirists remained alert to the difference between genuine and false manners and affectations of civilization. In the "Ode to Those Seeking Wisdom" ("Oda ishchushchim mudrosti," 1778), the normally light-hearted Maikov touts wisdom, learning, and the improvement of manners as a bulwark against evil, hailing reason as a menace to the "gloomy clouds of ignorance" ("razum preziraet / Grozu nevezhestva mrachnykh tuch"). Like Kantemir fifty years earlier, Maikov rounds on his supposed "enemies" because they stubbornly nurse "thoughts full of eternal gloom." Fortifying these attacks with arguments from virtue leads to the positive conclusion, thinks Maikov, that wisdom is as "pleasant a reward for the wise / [and] gladdens their spirit" ("premudrym skol' priiatna / I skol'ku dukh ikh veselit").[96]

Poets remained highly alert to the service they were providing not just by entertaining but also by reflecting on issues in ways that were little addressed elsewhere. Well-read poets might fill a gap in an intellectual tradition conspicuously light on systematic philosophy. It is worth pausing here on the single example of Ivan Krylov's poem "A Letter on the Use of Wishes" ("Pi'smo o pol'ze zhelanii," late 1790s–early 1800s).[97] As an example of how far satire had come from Kantemir's use of broad caricature, it speaks volumes. Famed for his mordant wit, Krylov was a paradoxist who loved to put his readers in a double bind by finding every solution unsatisfactory. His implied reader is clearly capable of logic, humor, and making moral choices. The poem addresses the question of how to achieve contentment by controlling one's desires. Satirists, of course, love to tackle philosophical problems. In Russia, philosophy as a discipline did not exist outside scholastic academies where it was taught mainly as logic, leaving the field wide open to critical satire. In "A Letter on the Use of Wishes," Krylov begins by invoking advice from wisdom literature, citing and debunking the proverbial insights of the Songs of Solomon, Ecclesiastes, and other ancient moralists. To read about the appetites is one thing, to deal with them—another. Yet despite his criticism of other authorities, Krylov wants us to take his poem seriously, perhaps more to vent frustration than for the purpose of actual edification. Through a set of questions, he suggests we consider how appearances may confuse the assignment of value. If the value is uncertain, how do we know what we ought to want? Should the ancient pottery fragment necessarily be worth more than a clump of mud? If diamonds are priced according to their shininess, why is a piece of ice not worth as much?

> Чем худ кремень? чем дорог так алмаз?
> Коль скажут мне, что он блестит для глаз—
> Блестит и лед не менее подчас.
> Так скажут мне: поскольку вещи редки,
> Постольку им и цены будут едки.
> Опять не то—здесь римска грязь редка;
> Она лишь к нам на их медалях входит;
> Но ей никто торговли не заводит,
> И римска грязь—как наша грязь, гадка.[98]

> Why should flint be base? And a diamond so dear?
> If I'm told it sparkles in one's eye,
> Well, so does ice sparkle no less sometimes.
> Next they tell me, the rarer the thing,
> The more the price tag must sting.
> This ain't right, either—Roman dirt is rare around here,
> We get it only with their medals,
> Yet no one cares to buy it or sell it,
> For Roman dirt, like ours, is foul.

Krylov knows the answers to these rhetorical questions: value is arbitrary and assigned by human beings rather than nature. Objects are priced according to desire rather than intrinsic merit. To thwart desire—a laudable goal since the quest is to control desires—one must set aside objects of temptation. Yet the further we remove the object, the greater its value. Krylov's speaker reduces the argument *ad absurdum* by leveling out the difference between the extremes of coveting and renouncing in paired examples. While Krylov's speaker pretends to endorse this position, we can see through his indifference to indifference. A recognition dawns that Stoic renunciation might be worse than appetites themselves. If renouncing things only leads the speaker into a dead end of self-castigation, then the next step is to deaden feeling itself and stop desiring altogether. Indifference is the technique or attitude the Stoics counsel as defense against perturbation. Yet total indifference deadens feelings and robs one of judgment and the capacity to discriminate between the good and the bad. By implication, then, pleasure creates interest, disperses indifference, and leads to better ethical judgments. According to a final set of propositions, desire is not spoiled by being fulfilled; fulfillment is not spoiled by not having; and not having is not spoiled by not wanting.

As Krylov says, "He who possesses happiness is not fortunate; fortunate is he who anticipates happiness" ("Ne tot schastliv, kto schast'em obladaet: / Schastliv lish' tot, kto schast'ia ozhidaet"). But perhaps the real lesson of a poem that moves quickly through philosophical suppositions, the twists and turns of paradox and contradictory emotions, is the conclusion that systems are no match for a moralist writer for whom wisdom is purely a function of practical philosophy, disdaining "wise men who compose systems of happiness" ("mudretsy sistemy schast'iia pishut") and are stuck on "fruitless labors" ("besplodnye trudy").[99]

By the second half of the century, the association of wisdom (*mudrost'*) and writing, while frequent, was not to be taken for granted. The expectation that literature affords pleasure purely for itself without necessary didacticism took root. Increasingly, writers defined, and relished, the task of catering to a craving for civilized entertainment. Mikhail Murav'ev was one of the most refined of poets and essayists in the period, a man wholly European in his education and, as rector of Moscow University, remarkably progressive in his outlook. In his essay "The Amusements of the Imagination" ("Zabavy voobrazheniia," 1797), he uses a discussion of Sumarokov's tragedies to praise "invention" as an "honor" (*chest' izobreteniia*).[100] Delight in versifying, and reading poetry, gradually becomes its own topic. Or, as Barkov put it in the epigram "Eternal Study," ("Uchenie vechno," n.d.),

> Чем больше будешь знать посредством ты науки,
> Тем более учись, и не имей в том скуки.[101]

> The more you know because you study,
> The more you learn, and the less you're bored.

Journals took a clear line on the value of pleasure as a literary goal: in 1771, the weekly *The Diligent Ant* identified its mission as providing "enjoyable reading." Individual writers adopted the message. As the title of Ivan Barkov's short poem recommended, "Read a lot, but with discrimination" ("Chitai mnogo, no s rassuzhdeniem," n.d.). Poetry and essays from the 1770s characterize art as a form of refinement that brings its own pleasures and benefits to the individual and educated social circles. Reading is said to teach certain social skills of tact and above all how to suggest meaning without being explicit. We see some of the intellectual justification formulated in terms of civilizational models elaborated by thinkers such as Montesquieu, David Hume, and Jean-Jacques Rousseau. Novikov's essay "On the Principal Causes Relating to the Augmentation of the Arts and Sciences" ("O glavnykh prichinakh, otnosiashchikhsia k prirashcheniiu khudozhestv i nauk," 1781) made a systematic case (that also seems anti-Rousseauian) for how the arts lifted mankind out of the primitive state characterized by uncouthness (*grubost'*). He distinguished between the necessities of life, goods that are essentially useful, such as food and shelter, and the benefits of civilization, such as the products of human reason and pleasure (*razum, udovol'stvie*). It is on the basis of such advancements that the arts and sciences increase in their social utility, becoming as essential as the first category in the "multiplication of human pleasure and repulsion of need."[102]

The message of the essay falls squarely into the Enlightenment mainstream vision of progress. In the Russian context, Novikov refers to a national "awakening from slumber," and from a long incubation of values into an atmosphere of political stability in which the arts will "flourish in freedom."[103] Novikov, and other writers, too, repeatedly draw a distinction between Russia as a European and civilized country and Asiatic despotic nations in which terror reigns and the arts, when inhibited by fear, cannot flourish and achieve intellectual excellence. Civilized pastimes, as practiced in Paris, London, and, Novikov now presumes, in St. Petersburg, beautify (*ukrasit'*) these peoples. Yet M. I. Popov, a translator of French comedy and contributor to Novikov's satirical journals, asks in the opening line of a poem "whether theater" genuinely "purifies morals" and whether plays bring nothing more than entertainment ("Polezen li featr i chistit li on nravy, / Il' tol'ko chto odne prinosit nam zabavy").[104] He suggests in his satirical epigrams that didactic literature can be pointless when the morals of the readers have already been corrupted. Such attention to context suggests that writers are working with a model of a virtuous group in which the quality of literature will improve as the society improves (and conversely).

In the Preface to *Dushen'ka*, whose supple style and wit make it worthy of comparison with a masterpiece like Alexander Pope's *The Rape of the Lock* (1712), Bogdanovich pays tribute to his ancestors whose devotion to the service culture of the gentry was their principal occupation. In claiming that he is not among "established writers," Bogdanovich deliberately pretends to be a dilettante, ignoring the fact that he had a lifetime of service to the state and was also well known as an author. He notes the debt he owes to the generosity of his readers (*liudei blagodushie*) who are prepared to indulge his faults.[105] The Preface avoids the language of instruction, wisdom, and utility, evoking instead individual sensibility and a feedback loop between writer and readership.

These are types of virtue specific to poetry and to sociability, terms that were ubiquitous at the time. This is what we observe in Mikhail Murav'ev's poem "To I. F. Bogdanovich" ("K I. F. Bogdanovichu," 1782). The poet begins by suggesting that Bogdanovich has mastered a pictorial art worthy of the ancients or the Renaissance Italians, praising the author of *Dushen'ka* for a style so vivid that it sharpens in the reader the "liveliest feelings of existence" ("bytiia zhiveishi oshchushchen'ia"). References to "genius" and "talent" introduce a new language of appreciation. What Murav'ev finds stunning in the poem is the impression that he is witnessing "practically the discovery of the beautiful" ("prekrasnogo pochti ia videl otkroven'e"). And while the speaker confesses that in the past the attraction of art was an appreciation of virtue, he ends the poem exalted by aesthetic delight for its own sake. Art instills in Murav'ev "reverence of virtue" ("k dobrodeteli imel blagogoven'ie") and a "morality of spirit" ("moral'naia dusha"), but the virtue (*dobrodetel'*) he invokes here is a sense of service to poetry rather than the civic duty the term normally indicates. Implicitly, Murav'ev makes the more positive case for literature as enjoyment because it creates a personal bond based on taste and ideas within a small group.[106]

The idea of pleasure as literature's reward finds confirmation in the title of a journal that appeared in twelve substantial issues thanks to the energetic man of letters Andrei Reshetnikov (b. 1770): *Business from Un-busyness, or Pleasant Entertainment Bringing Smiles to the Faces of the Grumpy, Moderating the Excessive Joy of the Flighty and Each to His Own (Delo ot bezdel'ia, ili Priiatnaia zabava, rozhdaiushchaia ulybku na chele ugriumykh, umeriaiushchaia izlishniuiu radost' vertoprakhov i kazhdomu po ego vkusu,* 1792). Taking pleasure in poetry as a personal gift rather than a polemical statement on the rules of art distances us from those earlier debates in which poetry was a vehicle of attack. In "The Love of Pleasure" ("Liubov' udovol'stviia," first published in his collected works in 1820), Mikhail Murav'ev made the point that while all pleasures required the control of "reason," some pleasures like literature instilled a sense of virtue. Murav'ev was a great connoisseur of the traditions of European lyric poetry.[107] Lines written in the 1780s that refer to works of mid-century as classics use praise to affirm a canon and confirm an idea of taste. In his poem "An Essay on Versification" ("Opyt o stikhotvorstve," 1775), Murav'ev identifies virtue in the sense of service to poetry by finding in Russian poetry parallels with the European classics, pairing Lomonosov's *Petriada* with Homer and Sumarokov's fables with La Fontaine's classic works.[108]

Such intergenerational tributes were also forms of alliance consistent with the idea of coteries, lived and virtual. Poetry creates its own space of sociability based on shared bonds of taste and similar artistic values which constitute their own type of virtue (a point made by Bogdanovich in his "Lines on Friendship" ["Stikhi na druzhbu"], published in the journal *The Lyre* [*Lira*], 1773).[109] Journals put discussions of sociability as a function of literature and education in the public domain because a world in need of reform can be improved through laughter and friendship. For instance, *The Useful and Pleasant* (*Poleznoe s priiatnym*, 1769) published articles "On Manners and the Selection of Friends" (nos. 3–4, 6), as well as separate essays on types of emotions and behavior, such as foppishness (no. 5), envy (no. 8), and hypocrisy (no. 8). For writers like Murav´ev, Bogdanovich, and many others, the verse epistle by its very form demonstrated how effective poetry could be as a medium of friendship.

The republication of an early work like *Journey to the Isle of Love* also tells us something about changed circumstances. Like many "précieux" fictions, Tallemant's narrative is organized around the "carte du tendre," something like a board game of feelings in which the lover negotiates obstacles until he reaches the isle of love. This work of erotic utopia looks improbable in the context of Russian court culture of the 1730s. The republication of the novel with its simply worded love songs looked apposite in 1778, in the early days of sensibility and Sentimentalism. The appearance of the novel had been challenged by the Church officials as immoral, and Trediakovsky burned nearly the entire print run. Its reappearance in a new edition in 1778 captures the more relaxed atmosphere and new attitudes at ease with luxury, worldliness, and the erotic. In "An Epistle to the Russian Students Taught by the Free Arts" ("Poslanie k rossiiskim pitomtsam svobodnykh khudozhestv," 1782), the playwright Yakov Kniazhnin identifies art, including poetry, and also painting, as an ideal medium for self-fashioning and fashioning others according to the best values. The poem was a riff on a speech he gave at the Academy in 1779. Talent on its own is "weak to complete the path / When, unsupported by widespread enlightenment..." ("Talant edinyi slab k sversheniiu puti / Kogda, ne ozaren prostrannym prosveshchen'em..."), says Kniazhnin. He praises the "eternal beauties" ("bessmertny krasoty") revealed by art, and celebrates the "creative spirit" ("dukh tvorcheskii"). But a worthy artist must combine wisdom with technical skill and be a "philosopher in colors" ("v kraskakh filosof") in order to educate and please. Pleasure (*udovol´stvie*) and amusement (*zabava*) are to the fore here. In its conclusion, the poem strikes a cautious note about the danger of using art to promote a message. Kniazhnin's poem, which takes patent enjoyment in its witty couplets and fluency of argument, ends with an admonition directed at the writer and painter not to be seduced into compliance or complacency by the rewards of service to the state. A supporter of the Academy of Arts and coteries founded by like-minded people, Kniazhnin nonetheless fears the corrupting influence of official messages and patronage, and sees a civic space such as the Academy as a haven against careerism. The statement is more than a reiteration of a Horatian posture of retreat from court and the business of the city. It edges toward a confident assertion of literature as its own domain:

> Художник, своему способствуя незнанью,
> Желает чина лишь вдобавок дарованью
> И льстится звуками предлинных в титле слов;
> Но духом кто велик—велик и без чинов.[110]

> The artist only facilitates his own stupidity,
> By seeking to add rank to his talent

> And to be flattered by the noise of wordy titles;
> But he who is great in spirit is great even without promotion.

Individual genius produces good art and is its own pleasure, a message that provided a lasting theme of verse culture and contributed to the entire creative ethos of play and literature for its own sake that would prove to be formative in the 1810s. Kniazhnin's tribute to bookish occupations picks up where Kantemir left off. Kniazhnin lampoons not those who toil in vain but rather writers who sell out, and thanks to hypocritical posturing make worldly careers either by kowtowing to the powerful or by being artistically conservative. That same belief in art as a self-contained pleasure spills over into the "Epistle to the Three Graces" ("Poslanie trem gratsiiam," 1790) in which Kniazhnin hails them as "tender young sisters" ("nezhnye sestritsy") and "companions of everything beautiful" ("soputnitsy prekrasnogo vsego") to whom he is willing to sacrifice himself.[111] Ever the satirist, and ever accomplished as a versifier, Kniazhnin tackles the question of rules and their importance by poking fun at those who define success entirely in terms of conformity. Pity the dramatist obedient to all conventions, he intimates, since audiences equally accustomed to conventions and bored by them will know when to laugh and when to applaud.

The idea of poetry as a pleasurable art finds resounding endorsement in "To the Lover of the Arts" ("Liubiteliu khudozhestv," 1791), Derzhavin's birthday-cum-new year's celebration of Count A. S. Stroganov.[112] A polymetric extravaganza of almost 200 lines written in a variety of stanza forms and ingenious rhymes, this tour de force of variation and artistry was published immediately as a separate pamphlet before being reprinted in the same year in the *Moscow Journal*. The poem follows the pattern of many an ode in asserting the writer's sincerity ("the pure fire of his heart" ["chistyi serdtsa zhar"]) as he asks for blessings on his house and invokes a goddess, the muse of lyric poetry Erato, to send a whole flotilla of winds to fan a perfect conflagration of inspiration within his breast ("she ignites, burns, and strikes my soul to the core" ["Blistaet, zhzhet i porazhaet / Vsiu vnutrennost′ dushi moei"]). While the image and the scale of inspiration—nothing short of ecstasy (*vostorg*)—are worthy of Lomonosov at his most exalted and vatic, the subject this time is art, rather than a battle. Derzhavin creates poetic pleasure by matching the visual extravagance of the setting and collection: "little geniuses" or the *putti* of Italian baroque painting hover around him, the air is a jet stream of crystal, and the poet hears a remarkable symphony of drums, voices, and pastoral echoes. Such sensory overload leads him to the assertion that while "science enlightens mortals / Feeds and lightens their work / The arts beautify them / And lead to their eternal glory" ("Nauki smertnykh prosveshchaiut, / Pitaiut, oblegchaiut trud / Khudozhestvy ikh ukrashaiut / I k vechnoi slave ikh vedut′").[113] This poem celebrates Stroganov as a patron of beauty, while "To Angelika Kauffmann" ("K Anzhelike Kaufman," 1798), a poem written to celebrate a portrait of Derzhavin's second wife Milena done by the renowned artist, makes clear that for Derzhavin visual arts and poetry are comparable, and that a single language of art criticism can be applied to both. At their best, painting and poetry display "vitality, feeling, and taste" ("zhivost′, chuvstvo, vkus").[114] Derzhavin taps into a vocabulary of delight (*plenit′sia*) and beauty (*krasa*) that by the last quarter of the eighteenth century had become a signature of lyric poetry. His appreciation is for beauty imbued with positive feeling (as distinct from dissipation), well constructed or harmonious (*stroinyi*) and rational, yet still individual and therefore original. Pleasure has completely displaced didacticism.

Among amateur men of letters drawn largely from the educated nobility, the assumption that social polish and literary aptitude went together was unsurprising because social and literary forms of address rely on conventions of decorum. Lyric speakers newly regarded life as a network of social obligations and literary affiliations. They put to good use the obverse technique of making common friends by trashing enemies. In "From the Elder of the Parnassian Guild" ("Ot starosty Parnasskogo tsekha," 1799), Kapnist turns the receipt of a friendly commission to recite his verse into a poem about his anxiety to win over his listeners. Nikolai Karamzin's "Letter to Aleksandr Alekseevich Pleshcheev" creates its own space for a "free hour of chat" ("v svodobnyi chas pogovorit'") about the good life, mulling over whether happiness is to be found in philosophizing and bowing to fate; or in making discoveries; or whether the happiness found in talking about books comes at a price. In further considering the cost of isolation and loneliness to an author, Karamzin, like Kantemir before him, draws on the idiom of the moralist. The language of the great French and English moral satirists from La Rochefoucauld, Addison's *Spectator*, and Johnson's *Rambler* left a lasting impression. But writing affords a domestic pleasure, since Karamzin conjures how Pleshcheev "entertains himself, his family, and strangers in prose and poetry" ("Stikhami, prozoi zabavliaet / Sebia, domashnikh i chuzhikh").[115] Karamzin is more optimistic in arguing that literature also provides a way out of isolation through the connection made between the writer and the reader.[116] It turns out that the pleasures of friendship are also sweetened by poetry, since numerous writers draw an equation between aesthetic values of control, clarity, smoothness, and good social conduct. These same writers are also prepared to recognize individual gifts as a form of genius in the period sense of individual voice and, looking ahead to Romanticism, as a unique talent.

The genius of the poet

The energy with which Russians emulated European literary models had produced a large and diverse body of literature outside Church and state. After two generations of intense activity, Russia could finally boast of significant talents worthy of celebration and commemoration. The idea that recognition by posterity would be achievable, and that Russians could apply international standards of criticism to evaluating worth, itself marks a turning point. Between the 1790s and 1810s, the theme of posterity became prominent in elegies to poets, and fellow writers were concerned about perpetuating the names of admired figures in order to secure their immortal reputation. For instance, the members of the Free Society of Lovers of Literature, Sciences, and Arts (Vol'noe obshchestvo liubitelei slovesnosti, nauk i khudozhestv, 1801–26), an umbrella organization for informal subgroups aligned by political and intellectual affinity, saw memorial poems as a key to posterity. The early death of the learned and gifted Ivan Pnin (1773–1805) elicited a number of tributes that cast the social ideals of the deceased and his friends as his true monument.

This new vocabulary reflects new attitudes to writing as a psychological activity and its standing within culture. Before the 1780s, the emphasis on the correct application of rules as a mark of literary competence confined poetic talent to a species of artisanal ability rather than special talent. By the mid-1780s, the idea of genius as a special intellectual faculty that elevated individuals above most of mankind had become widespread in Russian writing, usually applied to figures in whom unique aesthetic powers and benevolence are fused. Appreciation for the poetic talent as a special cognitive power develops but falls short of the full-blown Romantic idea of the genius as a unique individual. The critical status of Lomonosov, for instance, gives a measure of the change in perception of literature and writers. While Lomonosov invoked divine inspiration at the beginning of an ode to demonstrate his poetic genius, his immediate contemporaries were well aware that Lomonosov owed his status to his renown as a scientist.[117] By the 1790s, tributes singled out the genius to be found in a comprehensive list of his accomplishments as a linguist, scientist, metallurgist, and poet.

The *Letters of a Russian Traveler* departs from the neoclassical depiction of the Great Man, based on Plutarch's exemplary lives, that was influential in the period (and had an impact on

Radishchev). Closer to the early Romantic celebration of individual ability, Karamzin sees genius as an innate gift and specifically associates it with philosophers rather than leaders and in the lyric "Poetry" ("Poeziia," 1787) with the poet. Among the exemplary figures of the age, Karamzin includes Gottfried von Leibniz, Benjamin Franklin, Charles Bonnet, and Moses Mendelssohn.[118] Each in their individual sphere devoted his genius to the benefit of mankind. The poem concludes that genius has a greater power than reason to conceptualize on a vast scale; and that poets are able to tap into this ability.

In Russia, it is mainly in connection with poets that the term genius comes into use. From the mid-nineteenth century, the poet as a figure of cultural authority plays a substantial role in Russian literary history. While, for complex reasons combining artistry and politics, Pushkin has stood above all others as a national genius, in historical terms, it is clear that ideas about the special nature of the poet developed over the preceding generation. Most citations given in the *Dictionary of the Russian Language of the Eighteenth Century* attest to the use of the term to denote "uncommon creative strength", which is linked to an element of craft and "an uncommon degree of persistence."[119] Unlike the Romantic notion of genius, as defined against the opinion of an unworthy anonymous public (a topic treated importantly by Pushkin in his poems of 1828), here, genius refers to the positive valuation conferred by the coterie and known admirers. In the period from the 1770s to the 1810s, a legion of minor amateur poets provided a critical mass of writers who wished to identify a generational figure in their own midst. They were the predominant arbiters of taste and success in the long transition to a broader-based readership. Of great importance to the identity that writers cultivated as part of their private self-image and public persona were trends in the representation of imagination and genius assimilated from the early stages of Romanticism. Literary circles ranked poetry and poets ahead of prose and prose writers based on their appraisal of the canon of Russian literature produced in the course of the eighteenth century. In the early 1810s, Kapnist wrote an "Ode on Poetic Praise" ("Oda na piiticheskuiu lest'," second half of the 1810s), which crowns the "poet-tsar" and darling of the Muses in recognition of his social conscience. In his famous ode "God" ("Bog," composed 1780, published 1784), Derzhavin argued for the eminence of the poet in terms of the Great Chain of Being, a hierarchy of species devised by naturalists. Based on superior powers of reason, Derzhavin places his lyric alter ego next to God.

It was the literary group that established critical reputation, and not the public at large or the court. In addition, the idea of the poet as a "braggart" (*samokhval*) has been coined to describe Derzhavin's occasional boastfulness. In that respect, as in so many others, Derzhavin looks unusual within his peer group.[120] In "A Turning to Look at Myself" ("Oborot na sebia," 1803), Mikhail Murav'ev evaluated his own poetry against the superior accomplishments, in his view, of Karamzin and Derzhavin. With a typical gentle modesty and pride, he concludes that he does, after all, enjoy some renown among his brethren and has a claim to lasting fame. Individual reputation, a newfound sense of satisfaction, and a positive commitment to literature as one establishment of the age are values that become hard to disaggregate.

Essays on the nature of the imagination and inspiration appeared sporadically and were not systematic investigations. In reality, Russia lacked a theorist like Samuel Taylor Coleridge (1772–1834) to bring together a mentalist description of poetic function. Instead the meta-discourse of poetic creativity—whether seen as mechanical facility or a divine type of epiphany—finds an outlet in lyrics rather than in theoretical exposition. Writers began to extend this principle to poets seen, as Murav'ev states in his poem "The Power of Genius" ("Sila geniia," 1785, revised 1797), to possess powers of perception that penetrate the workings of nature and "taste in its plenitude the full delight of existence" ("i v polnote vkushat' vsiu sladost' bytiia"). But the cult of sensibility also raised the profile of poets whose individual genius was recognized as exceptional: "everything serves genius" ("vse sluzhit geniiu"), says Murav'ev.[121] Foremost of his generation was Derzhavin, who as a theorist of the concept of genius described the near-divine powers of reason and feeling that set the poet apart.

From the late 1780s to the end of this period, the capacity of the poet to serve as a vessel of feeling and heightened consciousness emerged as a prominent motif. In his essay "Reflection on Lyric Poetry or the Ode" ("Rassuzhdenie o liricheskoi poezii ili ob ode," 1811–15), Derzhavin describes the imagination of the poet as a sublime gift.[122] From waterfalls that function as emblems (such as the Kivach Falls near Petrozavodsk in Derzhavin's magnificent elegy on the death of Prince Potemkin) to glaciers as moments of the sublime (in Karamzin's *Letters of a Russian Traveler*), to country graveyards (as in Vasily Zhukovsky's 1802 translation of Gray's elegy) or battlefields as in Konstantin Batiushkov's "On the Ruins of a Castle in Sweden" ("Na razvalinakh zamka v Shvetsii," 1814), landscapes inspire new powers of vision, introspection, and imagination.[123]

While the word "imagination" (*voobrazhenie*) appears rarely, poets display alertness to dreams, reverie, and fantasy, suggesting an emerging idea of subjectivity within which literary sensibility denotes a faculty for combining images into new representations. This combination of greater imagination and greater depth of vision—of the past, of their own age, and sometimes of a sense of the future—gradually leads writers to appraise degrees of poetic talent. Murav'ev differentiates between genius as an aptitude to satisfy the demands of good taste, and genius as a higher capacity to penetrate beneath the "magical veil" of life. In the lyric "The Strength of Genius" ("Sila geniia," 1785, revised 1797), he identifies the poet as the "child of a moral Grace" ("pitomets gratsii moral'noi"),[124] stopping short of Karamzin's encomium of Shakespeare, whose glory stems from "greatness and truth" of his characters and his "penetration into the human heart."[125]

By the end of the century, Russian poetry, fostered in coteries and through friendships, displayed a tendency to intertextual dialogue. Personal voices were in conversation with one another on a range of questions, including art as pleasure and entertainment, the best modes of instruction and communication, and the status of the poet. In "To Khrapovitsky" (1797), Derzhavin asked his addressee whether the role of the poet was primarily to stay close to the throne, expending enthusiasm on flattery and public messages. The question is unsurprising, since Derzhavin wrote the poem immediately after the death of Catherine the Great. Clearly, the search had begun for a figure who would satisfy this idea of genius based on the assumption, articulated by Karamzin, that "Men of genius are born in every country."[126] In 1792, the discovery of the *The Lay of Igor's Campaign* aroused great enthusiasm because this highly poetic account of a twelfth-century battle boosted the idea of an authentic Russian culture. In the age of Ossian, the bardic narrator struck many as the long-awaited example of a homegrown genius and validation of national pride, an extension to Russia of a pan-European craze for authentic bards.[127] Different candidates emerged, including Peter the Great and the scientist-cum-poet Lomonosov, whom the writer and philosopher Aleksandr Radishchev elevates to the status of a mythic, Promethean figure in the final section of his *Journey from St. Petersburg to Moscow*, a transformation anticipated twenty years earlier by Nikolai Novikov in his *Attempt at a Historical Dictionary of Russian Writers* (*Opyt istoricheskogo slovaria o rossiiskikh pisateliakh*, 1772). In "A Eulogy to Mikhail Vasil'evich Lomonosov" ("Pokhval'noe slovo Mikhaile Vasil'evichu Lomonosovu," 1774), Mikhail Murav'ev praises Lomonosov as a modern classic exemplifying the power of the imagination thanks to sublime effects of his odes in which "the tempestuous spirit races in the heavens: there every word is a new thunder-clap" ("burnyi dukh ego nosilsia v oblakakh: tam vsiakoe slovo est' novyi grom").[128] For Murav'ev, the source of Lomonosov's authority as a hero lies in his enriching contribution to the Russian language. He ends his speech by quoting the opening of Lomonosov's "Ode on the Taking of

Chocim" as an example of the poet's divine afflatus and of the posture of inspiration. Murav'ev regarded lyric poetry as the medium of poetic genius. In the deceptively titled "Epistle about Light Verse. To A. M. Brianchaninov" ("Poslanie o legkom stikhotvorenii. K A. M. Brianchaninovu," 1783) he argued that the lyric, rather than a narrative, could best deliver the "sensibility" ("chuvstvovanie"), "style full of ideas" ("polnyi myslei slog"), "the picturesque vision" ("zhivopisno oko"), the "charms of mind," ("prelesti uma") and "mastery of writing" ("masterstvo pisat'") that readers usually sought elsewhere. "Poetry is only sound," he opines, "when it contains no thought" ("No stikh est' tol'ko zvuk, kogda v nem mysli net").[129] By these lights the power to produce rapture (*vostorgi*) and beauty are nature's gift to the lyric poet. N. A. L'vov compared Derzhavin to the ancient bards while paying tribute to the "elect son of Russia" for combining Horatian wisdom with a Pindaric power of imagination. A renowned elegist, Derzhavin himself was treated elegiacally long before his death in poems that celebrated his lavish eloquence, his uncommon images, and his larger-than-life personality. In the 1830s Pushkin lightly mocked his uncouth diction and haphazard learning, but Derzhavin's admirers acclaimed him for a matchless expressivity of language and feeling, proofs of a unique sensibility. When Derzhavin was widowed, Ivan Dmitriev (1760–1837) wrote an elegy about disconsolation ending in paradox because he argued that only a poet with the powers of Derzhavin could produce the eloquence and wisdom required to console him.

Such aggrandizing belief suggests rapid advancement on the way to the full-blown Romantic cult of genius.[130] For the earlier generation, the authority of the writer rested in their standing at court and combined personal appeal and talent. Denis Fonvizin served as secretary to the minister Nikita Panin, and Radishchev was originally a member of the landmark Commission on Legislation (1767). In certain cases, and here Derzhavin is the outstanding example, the writer's gift for living well and being a moral guide on issues of life and death defined an ethos if not a social posture. Critical fashion in recent years has merged two distinct paradigms in Russian thought to synthesize a concept of the charismatic poet out of the medieval, divine status of the tsar and the poet as prophet familiar from its nineteenth-century Romantic incarnation. Yet Derzhavin was unusual in claiming to be a tsar (and the boast was infrequent), and he invoked charismatic sublimity as only one source of authority. In later, Horatian poems like "Invitation to Lunch" ("Priglashenie k obedu," 1795) and "Modesty" ("Skromnost'," 1791) Derzhavin adopts a thoughtful posture of praising country life away from the politics of court. His presentation of a philosophical self in retreat from the busy futility of metropolitan life fits within a Russian tradition that includes Kantemir's sixth satire "On True Blessedness" ("Ob istinnom blazhenstve," first published in 1762) and "Stanzas in Praise of Country Life" ("Strofy pokhval'nye poselianskomu zhitiiu," 1752), the verse adaptation Trediakovsky made of Horace's Epode 11.9.[131] Even in "God," a metaphysical poem that looks at religious questions from the point of view of natural philosophy, Derzhavin makes reason and poetic creativity, rather than sanctification, the measure of the poet. Among poets who come of age in the post-Napoleonic period, years that will prove formative for Alexander Pushkin, the idea of genius as a visionary talent becomes an operative concept.

In this vein, the first decades of the nineteenth century saw a proliferation of muse-induced epiphanies or yearnings after the naive powers of the nightingale. Among the most interesting is Vasily Zhukovsky's "I Met My Youthful Muse" ("Ia muzu iunuiu, byvalo," 1824), which equates poetic power not merely with sentimental feeling but rather with plasticity of imagination and involuntary power of fancy. Minor poets, now better remembered for their progressive views, celebrated the pure art of the songbird whose poignant warbles loosened in the mind and heart "the joy of pure sympathy" and the pure charm of song (A. G. Volkov, "To the Nightingale," 1799).[132] Instances of pathetic fallacy abound throughout lyric poems.

However, attitudes to nature still fall short of the mature Romantic, Schellingian theories of nature and poetic subjectivity that inform the early poetry of Fedor Tiutchev (1803–73) in the late 1820s. Numerous poems about memory as a type of poetic genius—of which Konstantin Batiushkov's "My Genius" ("Moi genii," 1815) is a typical example—celebrate the power of association, often when induced by sleep or brought on by a reverie, to unlock experience. In the "Speech on the Influence of Light Poetry on Language" ("Rech´ o vliianii legkoi poezii na iazyk...") that he delivered in 1816 to the Society of the Lovers of Russian Literature (Obshchestvo liubitelei Rossiiskoi slovesnosti), Batiushkov showed deference to the eighteenth-century writers, starting with Lomonosov, whose legacy (also explored by him in a separate essay) in his view had already begun to fade because "only a small number of poems have escaped general oblivion."[133] Batiushkov's preoccupation with posterity falls within the values of the period, but also reminds us how much the survival of texts, as well as the transmission of reputation, depended on the production of print editions. Semen Bobrov has a reputation as an "Archaizer" rather than an Innovator, to use Tynianov's categories for opposing literary trends. Yet he was a versatile poet in all moods and genres, a classicist as well as early Romantic, who produced an impassioned defense of the legacy of the eighteenth century in his article "An Incident in the Kingdom of the Shades, or the Fate of the Russian Language" ("Proisshestvie v tsarstve tenei, ili sud´bina rossiiskogo iazyka," 1805).[134] It is in the same spirit of conservation, respect, and admiration that printed anthologies of poetry finally begin to supplant the circulation of manuscript anthologies from the 1810s. This is thanks to the activity of younger luminaries like Karamzin, Zhukovsky, and Batiushkov, who organized the publication of new editions of eighteenth-century writers to establish them as classics.

3

National narratives

The myth of Peter the Great and the progress narrative

Peter's reforms undoubtedly modernized every aspect of Russia's bureaucracy, diplomacy, and military. While modern historians see cultural transformation as a long-term process, eighteenth-century literature and historiography worked to create a myth of Peter the Great and his reforms, cast as a big bang moment of unstoppable momentum.[1] This myth went on to be used as a convenient proof of continuity against the backdrop of dynastic crises; and as the century wore on, the topos served elites as a standard of national progress.[2]

In the decade or so following the tsar's death, despite the recognition of his achievements as a modernizer, contemporary opinion-makers abroad and at home treated Peter with ambivalence. Yet even during that first decade of backlash and continued Westernization, the foundation myth that would come to define Enlightenment progress as a cultural achievement began to take shape.[3] The preacher and bishop Gavriil Buzhinsky (1680–1713) was unequivocal in his praise of Peter; he was an accomplished translator from the Latin of political works of Erasmus and Samuel von Pufendorf, and was highly placed in the Holy Synod as the overseer of all publications. He commemorated the anniversary of Peter the Great's death in an oration delivered on January 28, 1726. A masterpiece of homily, the "Sermon on the Anniversary in Memory of Peter the Great" ("Slovo v den´ godishchnago pominoveniia vo blazhennoi pamiati...Petra Velikogo") immortalized his subject by appropriating Biblical and classical terms to an essentially secular portrait. Given Peter's Church reforms, the secular emphasis was appropriate but no less striking for its rhetorical use of the trope of apotheosis, a fixture of the myth as it will eventually develop. The tsar he portrays is powerful and mighty. Sacralization is entirely a matter of metaphor and the standard tropes of apotheosis were widespread in baroque and classical poetics. Buzhinsky compares Peter to conquerors from Greek mythology (Agamemnon and Ajax), equates his place in Russia's history to that of Moses in the Old Testament as the founder of a new state, and ultimately likens him to Christ because Peter will never die "in spirit." The evidence of his immortality lies in his "great governmental deeds" ("pri velikikh trudakh gosudarstvennykh"); and while the preacher extols above all Peter's Christian qualities, he also notes the "rebirth of Russia" ("vozrozhdenie Rossii") as an achievement that will continue to be meaningful after his death ("sia vsled tebe khodiat i vechno khoditi budut v mire sem"). The sermon ends with a resounding prayer that the "spirit of Peter lives on in his successor" ("Zhiv dukh Petrov v naslednitse").[4] Buzhinsky's thought-world stands out as resolutely Petrine and, despite the lip-service to religious traditions, his sermon marks a moment of secular apotheosis for Peter as a national icon.

Eloquence was something that Avvakum had disparaged as false; yet forty years later it reached an apogee in sermons on Peter. The eulogy composed by Feofan Prokopovich on the death of the tsar remains a celebrated landmark in the history of eloquence in Russia. A pioneer in the history of Russian rhetoric, a learned theorist of absolutism, Feofan deploys his considerable learning, both theological and historical, to create a legend of Peter as a secular visionary, a counter-image to the denigrations of his Westernizing reforms seen as incompatible with native Russianness. Printed in Russian immediately upon its delivery, Prokopovich's speech was translated into Latin, French, Swedish, and English to notify the international community that Peter had given Russia a new permanent self-image. The "Eulogy on the Burial of the Most Exalted, Most Powerful Peter the Great" ("Slovo na pogrebenie vsepresvetleishago derzhavneishago Petra Velikago," 1725) opens by casting his death as a national tragedy for all Russians; the whole nation shares in Feofan's grief because they have recognized Peter in his lifetime as an agent of change who has brought "endless benefits and joys...that have rebuilt Russia strong and full of joy."[5]

Framed by conventional lamentations, the sermon delivers a message about social, educational, and material benefits; it portrays the age as an epoch of progress and enduring transformation that is visible, and even tangible, in the form of the stones of St. Petersburg. Look around you, says Feofan, and consider the security Peter's diplomatic and military ventures have wrought (a frequent subject of historical painting, see Plate 11); look around you and see the city of St. Petersburg as a permanent proof of civilization—terms of appreciation that also became fixtures in the myth. Nearly thirty years later, the Academician Andrei Nartov (1737–1813) would refer to the city in his poem "Praise of St. Petersburg" ("Pokhvala Peterburgu," 1756) as an "open temple of the sciences" ("khram otverst nauk").[6] Like Buzhinsky, Feofan also compares Peter to Moses, but whereas the former lauds him for leading the country to the promised land in a phrase that is clearly just a high-flown conceit, for Feofan, the comparison is tangible because Peter is cast as the architect of a more rational state governed ostensibly by the meritocratic Table of Ranks. Statecraft, seen as a good in itself, also enables the cultivation of learning, the arts, and civilizing conduct ("chestnye obrazy zhiteiskogo obkhozhdeniia"), for the first time suggesting the importance in Russia of a new type of sociability marked by personal manners and a sense of social decorum.

The terms of the sermon draw on a vocabulary already familiar in European Enlightenment writing about progress: Peter is a "luminary" (svetilo), his works combine "utility" (poleznoe), "common sense" (smysl') and "wisdom" (mudrost'), and he knew how to apply the practical lessons of philosophy (filosofiia) and art (iskusstvo). Indeed, Feofan extols the tsar for his "unprecedented" commitment to learning (neslykhannaia ucheniia). The literal truth of these claims matters less than Feofan's intention to persuade his listeners at court of the need to perpetuate and secure this legacy.

There has been debate about whether Feofan's sermon was aimed to lend concrete support to a putative group of allies committed to the Academy of Sciences, the printing presses, and Peter's governmental structures. The evidence for this remains unconvincing. But the message about Russia remains resolutely outward looking: the endorsement of cultural attainment of an international kind is a source of pride. It is hardly surprising that Peter's new capital city was praised as the material embodiment of this new spirit, seen by Prokopovich as a new Rome.

Similarly, and like a true mondain, Trediakovsky also praised St. Petersburg as a city on its way to becoming as worldly (gradu svet) as Paris, where he spent two formative years of his education.[7] For the early eulogists of St. Petersburg, the city represents an aspiration to create a trading emporium and a place of cosmopolitan exchange on par with Amsterdam, London, and Venice. Time and again, works that consider the project of becoming enlightened authenticate their vision with reference to Peter's original project of modernization.[8] The backlash against the Petrine reforms, both from the Church and the small cabal who succeeded Peter, proved a serious threat to this cultural vision, and Feofan was determined to secure Peter's legacy by praising his "spiritual, civic, and military improvements" as permanent. "Such is the Russia that he made, and thus shall it be," declares Feofan, arguing that continuity depends entirely on the commitment of Peter's wife Catherine I, as the new autocrat, to "the good sense of a master" (*vladetel'skoe blagorazumie*).

It is not surprising to see the champions of the Petrine worldview express anxiety: writers of the period, and up until Pushkin, have attributed exceptional vision and agency to Peter himself rather than to institutions. The surviving fragment of Kantemir's unfinished narrative poem, started in 1730 and published only in 1859, *Petrida, or a Descriptive Poem on the Death of Peter the Great* (*Petrida, ili Opisanie stikhotvornoe smerti Petra Velikogo*) elevated onto a mythic plane the image of the reformer who imposed order on the state (*tsar' domostroinyi*) and immortalized it in his new city ("grad novyi szidati"). The poem uses personal grief to express repeatedly the speaker's inability to conceptualize the impact of the ruler's death.[9] Just as Kantemir opened his book of *Satires* by invoking an "immature mind" ("um nedozrelyi"), he once again finds the "mind" unprepared to convey to his audience the meaning of this "open wound" because the "loss will be grievous to prosperous Russia" ("skorbna budet Rossii tsvetushchei gibel' siia").

Much of the fragment addresses Russia's diplomatic and military vulnerability, understandable concerns given Peter's aggressive foreign policy and wars. Kantemir now fears regressing from light to darkness, apprehensions still haunting him a full decade later. In the *Satires*, Kantemir turns to the solar system and the Copernican order as a metaphor for the course on which Peter set Russia.[10] He predicts that once the principles of modern science have been accepted a new path will open to his country. He states his belief that a "second sun"—by which he means the legacy of Peter, embodied in his city—will arise to guide the country into the future. He pays tribute to the city, to useful laws and "charming customs," a sum total of dazzling "magnificence." "Satire IX. On the State of this World. To the Sun" ("Satira IX. Na sostoianie sego sveta. K solntsu," composed c.1738, published 1858), whose attribution to Kantemir remains contested, provides a selective commentary on superstitious beliefs that persisted despite educational reforms.[11] The poem personifies different viewpoints on Peter's contested legacy. Some characters, dismayed by changes to religious practices, dress codes, and education, bridle at heresy. Enemies of modernization target "learning" and the "learned" who "build palaces" ("palaty slavnye") at great expense, welcome "printed news" (*pechatnye vesti*) and foster "foreign scholars" ("uchiteli zamorski"). The voice of the satirist predominates, caricaturing the defense of pre-scientific thought dictated by ancient custom and superstition of a type that would have incurred anger worthy of the "wrath of Avvakum" ("zapal'chivost' Avvakuma"). But the speaker cannot contain his fear that "There is little good, and much evil in the world" ("Dobra malo, a polno vo vsem svete zlogo").[12] His sight—and vision is of course the Enlightenment's primary faculty of sense perception—becomes clouded at these thoughts, while the so-called "Philosopher" fears that the reforms will ban smoking and drinking beer. Overall, the conservative voices take the view that it is "impossible to please God and the world" ("Nel'zia Bogu i svetu vmeste ugoditi") at the same time.

Prokopovich and Kantemir were not alone. In the "Elegy on the Death of Peter the Great" (1725, revised for publication in 1752), Trediakovsky adopts the theme of cultural progress and wisdom to define the emperor's legacy. Fame declares that the Russian emperor is glorious and then asks a set of rhetorical questions that permit only an affirmative answer:

Паки Слава: "Российский император славный,
Кто когда во искусстве? кто лучший в науке?

Любовь ко отечеству дала ль место скуке?
Что же бодрость? что промысл? православна вера?"

Fame spoke again: "The Russian emperor is renowned,
But who excels in art? who in science?
Did love for the country give way to boredom?
What about courage? Providence? The Orthodox faith?"

When Trediakovsky refers to Peter's genius for politics (*politika*), he means, like Feofan Prokopovich, to praise him as the founder of a city (*polis*) as well as for polishing, or making polite, the manners of his subjects. In this lamentation the very sciences themselves—engineering, mathematics, politics—join the speaker in mourning the ruler.

The consolidation of the myth, and the cultural appropriation of Peter's legacy, soon occurred in poetry, historical writing, and iconography. The process took off with, first, the reign of Peter's daughter Elizabeth and then that of Catherine the Great. The former justified her coup as a return to the principles of Peter's reign, just as the latter would borrow a page from her predecessor's book by affirming her own commitment to Peter's vision, a useful step for a foreign princess who, unlike Elizabeth, had married into the royal house, but like her had won the throne by force.

In the early years of Elizabeth's reign, a corpus of poems accumulated around the Petrine theme, written for occasions and as verses inscribed on monuments. In the 1747 "Ode on the Day of the Accession to the All Russian Throne of Her Majesty" ("Oda na den´ vosshestviia na prestol imperatritsy Elisavety Petrovny 1747 goda"), Lomonosov uses place names to demarcate the vast region where the mineral wealth of the earth will be uncovered ("Bogatstvo, v onykh potaenno, / Naukoi budet otkrovenno"). Lomonosov, a physical chemist and member of the Academy of Sciences since 1745, heralds a new age of renewal of the sciences, or learning (*nauki*). As a reader of the ancient historians, above all Tacitus, he knew that the Romans believed that one proof of the sign of advancement was an increase in eloquence. He clearly believes that a new age of science will also be in Russia a new age of rhetoric, and that Russia's counterparts to Plato and Newton will be praised for discoveries leading to substantial social benefits ("The sciences are useful everywhere / Among nations even in the desert" ["Nauki pol´zuiut vezde, / Sredi narodov i v pustyne"]).[13] With Catherine's accession in 1762, the rhetoric of past and future accomplishments escalates: Lomonosov deploys images of a golden age, calling Russia a "beautiful paradise" ("prekrasnyi rai"). In looking back to the military successes of earlier reigns, which he had cheered on, the poet is revisionist. Earlier advances are steps toward the secular benefits of Enlightenment that have yet to come. The 1747 poem praises Elizabeth's reign for preparing the "fruits of the purest mind" ("chisteishego uma plody"), by which Lomonosov means practical accomplishments and culture ("poleznye trudy," "iskusstvo"). For Lomonosov, the current prosperity—measured by the boom in commerce (figured as ships laden with goods) and the wealth of natural resources exploited by the sciences of engineering and metallurgy—bears witness to the continuing legacy of Peter as a historic colossus.

Like many a solemn ode, the 1762 poem written on Catherine's accession seems, at first sight, to consist of exuberant celebratory figures of speech commensurate with Russia's increasing clout as a European power. The poem's underlying argument advances from an old-fashioned patriotic statement of military victory to a modern assertion that civilization and nationhood depend on science and poetry as the true measures of achievement. The ode is more wishful thinking than factual statement, intended to encourage royal patronage of the arts and sciences without which no progress is possible. But its terms of reference, while new to Russia, adopt assumptions about progress familiar from Augustan England and Regency France. There is a determination to apply Western benchmarks and values to Russia's cultural development. Advancements in this area, more than military success, are the source of glory (*slava*), and while Lomonosov characterizes it as a continuation of Peter's efforts (*trud*), he revives the sun as a metaphor for the illumination of science:

> Уже нам дневное светило
> Свое пресветлое лице
> Всерадостным очам явило
> Лучей прекрасных во венце.
> Туманы, мраки разгоняя
> И радость нашу предваряя,
> Поля, леса, брега живит...[14]

> Now the daily orb
> Reveals its brilliant visage
> To our overjoyed eyes
> Crowned with beautiful rays
> Dispersing the clouds, the darkness
> And preparing our joy
> As it enlivens the fields, woods, riverbanks.

Peter's city on the Neva will be a capital to model statecraft as well as to heroism. As a man of science, with personal ambitions and aspirations for the Academy of Sciences, Lomonosov praises the sciences last, and he sees them rejoicing under the aegis of a new Minerva, goddess of wisdom as well as protector of the empire.[15]

In the 1740s, Lomonosov and other poets jointly authored a set of verse inscriptions meant to adorn statues of Peter the Great and Empress Elizabeth (never realized). The statues, real or planned, for which poets wrote inscriptions, are said to endure, harder than metal, for as long as the cultural legacy to Russia of what Lomonosov calls "spiritual beauties" (*dushevnye krasoty*) remains active. The poems apply to the Russian rulers a definition of greatness that had wide currency across Europe in the eighteenth century. Inscription Two ("Nadpis 2," 1743) praises Elizabeth for having summoned Peter's ghost:

> Елисавета здесь воздвигла зрак Петров
> К утехе россов всех, но кто он был таков,
> Гласит сей град и флот, художества и войски,
> Гражданские труды и подвиги геройски.[16]

> Here is Peter's likeness as erected by Elizabeth,
> A delight to Russians all. Who he was is proclaimed
> By his city and his navy, the arts and armies,
> His civic deeds and heroic victories.

Writers continued in this vein by positioning Catherine's activities as the fulfillment of Peter's design, whether or not this was historically accurate. And the positive image of Peter was unstoppable because Catherine was dedicated to renewing its relevance, extending the poetic tradition into the visual sphere by erecting the equestrian state of Peter the Great (known as the Bronze Horseman), one of the defining monuments of the St. Petersburg cityscape and its literary images. The appearance of this dynamic and imposing statue left no doubt about Tsar

Peter's status at the heart of her own Enlightenment project. If she was Catherine *the Great* it was because Peter had defined the greatness required to modernize Russia. In the "Ode to the Blessed and Eternally Worthy Memory of Peter the Great, the True Father of the Nation" ("Oda blazhennyia i vechno dostoinyia pamiati istinnomu ottsu otechestva, imperatoru per-vomu, Gosudariu Petru Velikomu," 1761), Aleksei Rzhevsky recounts how Peter saved Russia "mired in darkness" ("vo tme Rossiia prebyvaia"), by upgrading its infrastructure, moderniz-ing its government, but above all by "enlightening our coarseness" ("grubost' nashu pros-vetiti").[17] Polished manners and courteous conduct are taken as evidence of civilization and a sign of permanent transformation. Even the less grandiose "Rondeau to the Blessed Memory of Peter I" ("Rondo. Blazhennyia pamiati gosudariu Petru Pervomu," 1796) by Nikolai Nikolev praises the "refinement of manners" as a heroic achievement (one of the points Derzhavin mocked in his parody "Na rondo Petru Velikomu," 1796).[18] In Rzhevsky's ode, the benefits of Peter's reign endure in the present as Peter, metaphorically, "extends his arms to the sciences" ("k naukam ruki prostiraet") and "pierces through the darkness with his gaze" ("skvoz' mrachnost' vzorom pronikaet"). If Kantemir spoke of reason as still "immature" at the acces-sion of Catherine I, the widow of Peter the Great, Rzhevsky, like Lomonosov, firmly believes that Peter "nourished reason with science" ("naukoi razum svoi pitaia") and that these are the hallmarks of progress.[19]

In the shift from the more technocratic language of pragmatic Enlightenment (or moderniza-tion), Enlightenment ideals of progress, scientific discovery, and reason become literary motifs, all features that marked the division between countries perceived as civilized or not.[20] In an absolute monarchy, the advancement of civilization cannot be divorced from the sovereign.[21] Over the course of Catherine's reign, poetry celebrated the ideas of accomplishment as much as actual events. In this context, Lomonosov's ode of 1762 heralded a new age in very precise terms of cultural vision. One of the canonical poems of the century, Lomonosov's "Ode on the Accession of Catherine the Great" makes the specter of Peter an embodiment of progress whose legacy will drive forward (and, to a degree, haunt) Russian literature. Written in the wake of the coup that brought Catherine to the throne, Lomonosov's poem is a spectacular example of the poetic art of the period: it is pictorially vivid, rhetorically sophisticated, and full of emo-tional tropes. This occasional poem in twenty-six ten-line iambic tetrameter stanzas (the stand-ard stanza form for the genre), deploys all the art of eloquence in order to usher in a new beginning for Russia. A celebration of political stability and a good-luck wish for her reign, the poem legitimates Catherine by positioning her as the natural heir to Peter's program. Lomonosov establishes his nationalist credentials, taking pride in the country's military might, praising Elizabeth for keeping peace, but also noting foreign policy objectives (the Ottoman Empire looms as a threat). Yet whatever careerist motivation on his part might have been suspected, in the "Ode on the Accession of Catherine the Great" Lomonosov personifies the nation's elite, and humbles himself, because the poem delivers a specific message of encouragement to Catherine II (portrayed in Plate 12 shortly after her accession to the throne) to resume the work of Enlightenment and science by reinvigorating the institutions founded by Peter.

Poems of praise can also be wish lists of favors attainable through patronage. Lomonosov combines national and self-interest first by imagining the benefits to the country that will accrue if the monarch rewards the interest of a group, including himself, who are "noble in spirit" rather than birth. Through her royal leniency (*oslaba*) Catherine as the true daughter of Peter will promote scientists and other modernizers whose fortunes had shone less brightly since the reign of Elizabeth. The poem casts Lomonosov as a personal defender of the sover-eign, attesting his loyalty as one of the heroes who wish to secure her rule. But that personal loyalty goes with a commitment to certain ideals associated with the "joy" (*radost'*) that comes from advancement. The poem's great stroke of imagination is to conjure in a baroque trope the ghost of Peter, the Great Shadow (*Ten' velikaia*) that rises from the grave and speaks to his successor to convey his dismay at the interruption in progress experienced in the 1730s.

Much historical writing about Peter is literary in character, and follows the European trend of using moral assessment as a measure of benevolent rule. Based on examples from Plutarch and other classical moralists, the period developed ideas about exemplarity along with rhetorics of praise and blame, whereby posterity could bring the ruler to account. Historical research, collections of anecdotes, and biographical material amplified rather than debunked the myth of Peter.[22] Until the reign of Catherine, the Petrine myth remained a topos for the consolidation, and a nervous affirmation, of the past. It combined nostalgia and aspiration. Over the course of Catherine's reign, commentators rated new forms of cultural achievement in relative terms (military, cultural, intellectual) in comparison to Europe, and in absolute terms, against new self-expectations and the fulfillment of the Petrine promise. This tendency will carry on into the 1830s. The resurgence of praise for Peter as the founder of Enlightenment defended his positive reputation against the evaluations of eighteenth-century European historians who were skeptical or downright hostile about Russia. Russian images of Peter cannot be dissociated from the complex and dynamic European treatment of the monarch and his nation, and at times respond to it, especially in the 1750s and 1760s when Lomonosov, among others, reacted to the highly influential historical portrait produced by Voltaire.

Among the first Russian efforts to contribute to the historical, and not just rhetorical, evaluation of Peter's impact was a comprehensive chronicle originally in twelve volumes by Ivan Golikov (1734–1801), *The Deeds of Peter the Great, the Wise Transformer of Russia, Compiled from Trustworthy Sources and Organized by Year* (*Deianiia Petra Velikogo, mudrogo preobrazitelia Rossii, sobrannye iz dostovernykh istochnikov i raspolozhennye po godam*, 1788–89). The book is a thesis-driven work of providential history. Born to a merchant family and educated by a priest in northern Russia, Golikov claimed that Fate had predestined him to praise Peter just as God had ordained Peter to transform Russia. Golikov made his living as an importer of spirits. After serving time for a financial misdemeanor, he was pardoned in 1782, just in time for the unveiling of Falconet's monument to Peter the Great. Biographers relate that, on the occasion, he fell to his knees before the statue and swore then and there to complete writing a history of the reign he had begun in prison. His highly readable narrative is of residual historical interest, because it draws heavily on popular anecdotes and stories about the tsar (on which Pushkin relied for his planned history of Peter's reign, sketched out in the 1830s). In the 1760s, Golikov interviewed survivors among Peter's staff and recorded their stories. He also collected popular legends and printed anecdotes (these take up the seventeenth volume of a supplementary six tomes he added in the second edition of 1798, reprinted in a third edition of 1807). Anecdotes with their private glimpses of the person offered an up-close perspective that was, in some respects, the antithesis of the mythic projection for which the Bronze Horseman stood. The vividness and positive character of these anecdotes pleased Catherine, who had granted Golikov access to state archives. A complete edition was published between 1837 and 1847, just before Russian history achieved serious academic status at national universities.

Foreign views also mattered because they eventually fed back into the Russian representations of the tsar and his legacy.[23] And as a matter of diplomatic standing, the courts of the Empresses Elizabeth and Catherine, sensitive to national context and the question of who controlled the reputation of a leader, kept a close eye on their nation's standing in European opinion. Kantemir's acquaintance in France, the great grammarian and natural philosopher Academician Bernard de Fontenelle, had published a florid *Éloge du czar Pierre Ier* (1727), praising his enterprise but condemning his personal behavior. Among foreign accounts of Peter's reign the most significant are the work by the Englishman John Perry, *The State of Russia, under the Present Czar* (1716), and an account in French by the German Friedrich Christian Weber, *Nouveaux Mémoires sur l'état présent de la Grande Russie ou Moscovie* (Paris, 1725). The latter contains many factual observations about the infrastructure, social structure, and modernization, including mining and trade initiatives. It also underscores the importance of printing as a relatively new technology and the ingenuity of Peter in designing a new alphabet, simpler than the "ancient letters" and adaptable for typesetting.[24]

The myth of Peter was also given shape by Voltaire working in concert with his Russian sources. This European account went on, in turn, to influence Russian views of Peter the Great all the way to Karamzin and Pushkin. In the late 1750s, Voltaire accepted a commission from the Russian government to write his *History of Russia under the Reign of Peter the Great*. Ivan Shuvalov was well aware that the reigning monarch, Empress Elizabeth, would not tolerate any criticism of Peter the Great, her father, and carefully controlled Voltaire's access to the documents and archival material that the philosopher requested be sent to France (Voltaire never traveled to Russia). Voltaire's *Anecdotes on the Reign of Peter the Great* and his *History* emphasize the uncivilized and barbaric nature of Russia before Peter, thereby helping to perpetuate the attractive but false notion in an age that worshipped Great Men that Peter created a whole world out of nothing in a country devoid of institutions and values.

Not everyone was persuaded by Voltaire, of course. The European image of Russia during Catherine's reign certainly attracted critics. In 1761, the celebrated French astronomer Chappe d'Auteroche travelled to Siberia to observe the transit of Venus. His account of his journey through Russia *Voyage en Sibérie, fait par ordre du roi en 1761* recorded his negative impressions of a country whose thin European veneer could not, in his view, disguise the undeveloped state of its infrastructure and regional governments.[25] The depiction stung Catherine personally, as it did senior figures at her court who placed great stock in Russia's European reputation as a realm of tolerance, progressiveness, and rapid modernization. Catherine's government responded furiously in a famous pamphlet known as the *Antidote*. Attributed to Catherine II and sometimes thought to be the work of her secretary G. V. Kozitsky (1724–75), the pamphlet rebutted the criticisms of Russia and of the country's infrastructure made by Chappe d'Auteroche. The *Antidote* circulated anonymously in 1770 as a systematic refutation of Chappe's charges. After this episode, Catherine proved highly skillful in maintaining useful friendships with European intellectuals, above all the French *philosophes* Denis Diderot and Voltaire (Diderot received a pension; Voltaire's library was purchased after his death), to disseminate her message that Russia was fully part of the European Enlightenment, a haven of religious toleration, and a rationally managed state (unlike the Ottoman Empire which she battled perennially in the southern confines of her multiethnic state, from the Black Sea region to the Caspian and into the Crimea). Yet other dissenting voices would always make themselves heard. Jean-Jacques Rousseau, admired by writers like Karamzin and Radishchev as an autobiographical writer as well as influential theorist of human rights, and much disliked by Catherine, condemned Peter for failing to see that the European trappings he imposed on his people were damaging to national identity.

In the neoclassical manner, poetry and history as a moral narrative of the ideal overrode skepticism. The myth paved the way for Catherine's commission in 1772 of the great equestrian statue of Peter the Great by Étienne Maurice Falconet. Unveiled on Senate Square in 1782, the Bronze Horseman has generated a cultural narrative and complex mythology.[26] Catherine the Great micromanaged the creation of the statue of Peter, which took more than a decade. She made clear in an important exchange of letters with Diderot and Falconet himself that she viewed the work as not just the portrait of a single individual but a representation of historical greatness.[27] Speaking of Falconet's monument, Derzhavin wrote: "Before us is the hero who illumined the Eagle" ("Se tot geroi, Orla kotoryi prosvetil"). He describes Peter as someone who is "led by great wisdom" ("vodim premudrost´iu"), as a "builder, sailor, worker" ("stroitel', plavatel', rabotnik"); Derzhavin then goes on to celebrate Catherine precisely because she raised a statue that serves as an "image of her deeds" ("obraz del").

The ruler, his city, and the idea of Enlightenment come to be used virtually interchangeably, especially in the second half of the century. It is during this period, of course, that Enlightenment government policies and trends in the arts were really put to the test.[28] In his prose cycle *Walks* (*Progulki*, published in the journal *The Spectator* [*Zritel'*] in June 1792), anticipating the later collection by Konstantin Batiushkov, Aleksandr Klushin ponders the statue and compares Peter and Catherine. In the "Letter to a Friend Living in Tobolsk" ("Pis'mo k drugu, zhitel'stvuiushchemu v Tobol'ske, po dolgu zvaniia ego,"1782), Radishchev captured the unveiling of the monument, describing its imperial grandeur and Catherine's emotional investment. This was the first piece Radishchev printed on his own hand press (which he used to eventually print the *Journey from St. Petersburg to Moscow*). His fascination with the statue and his hesitation as to whether it emblematized the timeless absolute virtue of the ideal ruler or a historical legacy, caught the attention of Karamzin who offered his own version on the same theme in the *Letters of a Russian Traveler*.

The focus of our discussion has been on a corpus of texts that show the tremendous durability and vitality of the discourse of the Enlightenment as a cultural topos associated with Peter, with the idea of national progress, and with a projection of cultural might intended to match Russia's newfound diplomatic prowess. When viewed from the perspective of the early eighteenth century, claims to a Europeanized literary culture are seen to combine wishful thinking with aspirational statements. From a later standpoint, and especially after 1762, there is greater validity and confidence in the repeated credit accorded to the post-Petrine vision of Russia's cultural orientation. There is a sense in which the discourse of the Enlightenment becomes its own reality, self-reinforcing and self-referential. We see how continuing tributes to Peter reflect a sense that his vision has come full circle. This is precisely the point made by an epigram by Maikov. Normally a wit, he is unusually sober in praising Feofan Prokopovich because the preacher's very greatness was a stimulus to find a suitable language.

> Великого Петра дел славных проповедник,
> Витийством Златоуст, муз чистых собеседник,
> Историк, богослов, мудрец российских стран—
> Таков был пастырь стад словесных Феофан.[29]

> Preacher of the glorious deeds of Peter the Great,
> Golden Mouth of Eloquence, interlocutor of the pure Muses,
> Historian, theologian, and sage of the Russian lands,
> Such was the pastor of the flock of literary men, Feofan.

Feofan stands for eloquence itself; he is a latter-day Golden Mouth. Other inscriptions praising Feofan and Kantemir by Fedor Kozel'sky, best known for his elegies, celebrate these figures and create a verbal pantheon of national heroes who sustained the Petrine vision.

In the 1830s, Pushkin, who had a far more profound understanding of historiographical principles, ridiculed Golikov while also drawing on anecdotes from his work (at the time, Pushkin himself had compiled two prose works of anecdotes about the eighteenth century and was working on a history of Peter the Great that he failed to finish by the time of his death).[30] Pushkin's work on the reign, and his interest in the anecdote, more generally, as a key to historical personality and the spirit of the age, owed a greater debt to Voltaire. Voltaire's portrait of Peter as a driver of change was more myth than fact; and as myth, it has an ideological purpose of producing a model for other European rulers, not just Peter's Russian successors. Together with Peter's statue and the legends surrounding the tsar, Voltaire's writings would contribute to Pushkin's thinking about the role of the Great Man and of causality in one of his greatest works, *The Bronze Horseman* (*Mednyi vsadnik*, 1833), a profound meditation with no answers as to Russia's future course or the meaning of Peter's legacy.

The Petrine legacy was both verbal and material. It generated images and words that were more than empty slogans, at least for the more progressive educated elite who had raised expectations about progress as well as about Catherine. Stephen Baehr has explored the development of the paradise theme expressed mainly in odes. Paradise as conceived in many of his texts is largely secular and aligned with contemporary notions of progress, defined as movement from superstition toward reason.[31] The reward offered to rulers was not only the happiness of the nation but a permanent monument in the form of glory and poetic celebration. Absolute rulers ideally should be law-abiding, but by definition even the enlightened despot could not be held to account, however much the body politic or nobles wished them to heed the rule of law. This is precisely the case Vasily Petrov made in a poem entitled "On the Composition of a New Legal Code" ("Na sochinenie novogo Ulozheniia," 1767, revised 1782).[32] Despite its topical title, the poem is virtually a handbook on neoclassical panegyric: it features comparisons to mythic gods (Minerva, most prominent as the goddess of wisdom and Catherine's accepted sobriquet; see Figure III.05), lavish metaphor, and hyperbole, and poses numerous rhetorical questions. Erudite flourishes bolster the impression that literature thrived in the age of a successful ruler. Accusations of bombast dogged Petrov's reputation. He found it hard to desist, because the ode itself, as a rhetorical genre, uses amplification and illustration by example in order to corroborate the main argument. Petrov's second version of the poem updated its references to include Catherine's success against the Pugachev Rebellion. In this version he likens Catherine's achievements as a lawgiver to the legal reforms of the fabled

FIGURE III.05. Jean-Pierre Ador, Catherine the Great as Minerva, snuff box after medallion of J. G. Waechter commemorating the accession of the Empress Catherine, 1771.

Spartan king Lycurgus. She is an Enlightenment ruler because she applies reason, because she exercises "most humble power" ("krotchaishaia derzhava"), and, above all, cares about social welfare—meaning she legislates to ensure "domestic peace" ("domashne spokoistvo"). But the social-political vocabulary of the poem also aligns the virtues of her statecraft with a wise application of the law.

It was precisely the issue of the rule of law and of natural law as a limitation on autocracy that was formalized in Derzhavin's "To the Potentates and Judges" ("Vlastiteliam i sud'iam," 1780). An adaptation of the 82nd Psalm (the 81st in Orthodox tradition) that also borrows imagery from the 1st and 145th Psalms, the poem riled Catherine when she first read it; what particularly upset her, however, was Derzhavin's plan to include it in a new edition of his poetry to be published in the 1790s at the time of the Jacobin Terror. Something of a social contract, the poem bluntly castigates rulers who fail to act according to the precepts of natural justice, and it stands in a direct line with Pushkin's incendiary "Liberty. An Ode" ("Vol'nost'. Oda," 1817), which quotes liberally from contract theorists and French revolutionary writing. Derzhavin's "To the Potentates and Judges" was unusually bold as a verbalization of wishful thinking.

In her public demeanor, and to the larger world, however, Catherine's image as an enlightened ruler was part of the soft power she exercised in enhancing the perception of Russia abroad, largely as filtered through her correspondence networks with European intellectuals.[33] Good government constituted a point of reference in public poetry, such as the ode. Writers describe culture as a manifestation of a well-ordered reign. This is why poets repeatedly emphasize the parallels between Russia's experience under Catherine and Augustus's Rome, and the association of Vergil with the monarchic state was exemplified in Vasily Petrov's majestic Russian translation of the *Aeneid* (1782–86). In overseeing the flourishing of culture, Catherine was well aware that a certain amount of leeway would encourage freethinking about the nature of the state. She was torn between, on the one hand, benevolent absolutism that would positively continue to foster progress and, on the other hand, an absolutism that might negatively lead to decay and corruption of a kind familiar from the reign of Anna Ioannovna in the 1730s. That period became a byword for oligarchy exercised to the detriment of the nobles (as late as the 1830s in the unflattering portrait of the period as a house of horrors depicted by Ivan Lazhechnikov [1792–1869] in his historical novel the *House of Ice* [*Ledianoi dom*]).

CASE STUDY Karamzin's *Letters of a Russian Traveler*

Antiokh Kantemir's *Satires* (1729–32, 1738) and Nikolai Karamzin's *Letters of a Russian Traveler* (1791–92; full publication, 1797) both reflect, in their respective periods, the changing nature of Russia's intellectual engagement with new forms of writing and new models of thinking. But each also represents the considerable difficulties involved in a knowledge transfer between cultures where the institutions of learning, the advancement of scientific thought, and the mentalities of cultural elites are less than equal. The *Satires* set a standard for forward-looking development toward a civil society governed by rules grounded in reason and the laws of the physical universe if it was not to remain a medieval state.

By the 1770s, nearly a half century after Kantemir's first publication, the reality had begun to catch up with the cultural achievement envisioned in his *Satires*. The foundation of a new major center of learning, Moscow University, in 1755; the increasingly rapid expansion of publishing; the acquisition of French as the preferred language of learning and social engagement among the urban elite; the development of a vernacular literary and technical language well suited to the translation of a variety of philosophical, scientific, fictional, and essayistic works from European languages, all created conditions in which minds could mature, the image Kantemir used as an emblem of Enlightenment to open his *Satires*.

Like Kantemir, Karamzin looks outward to Europe with the purpose of reflecting inwardly the examples of taste, creativity, and intellectual sophistication he would like to see his readers and fellow writers cultivate. Travel writing favors formal flexibility, blending fiction and documentary, the archeology of a place and the personal, the autobiographical, and the invented. To a high degree, the *Letters of a Russian Traveler* demonstrates how far Russian prose writing had advanced, indicating key changes in the perceptions of culture and the engagement with Europe.[34] Becoming European was no longer just a matter of shedding the caftan and the beard, to cite Peter the Great's famous sartorial reforms. Manners and savoir-vivre would make the newly Europeanized elite. While Karamzin's traveler might suggest at certain points that the Russian experience of ideas and emotions might still be a work in progress, and that intellectual life had yet to attain the same dynamism and originality to be found in European cities from Lausanne to London to Berlin, nevertheless, the Karamzinian traveler proves to be receptive to new ideas and experiences, and expert in packaging them for the Russian readership. Unlike the famous travelers in Montesquieu's *Persian Letters*, whose binocular vision of the East–West divide makes cultural difference and comparison a main theme of the text, Karamzin's work seems to emphasize the cosmopolitan narrator's at times seamless integration into different capital cities and different institutional contexts ranging from concert halls to meetings of Parliament and the Assemblée Nationale.

The itinerary of Karamzin's fictional alter ego, unfolding in 154 letters addressed to friends, tracks the traveler across the Baltic states, the kingdom of Prussia and the German principalities of the Holy Roman Empire, the cantons and cities of Switzerland, France in upheaval from Lyon to Paris, and then England as the final destination. Departing from Moscow, characterized as patriarchal and medieval, he returns to Russia via Kronstadt and arrives in St. Petersburg, Russia's European capital, a place he clearly views as part of the Enlightenment continuum. The whole journey represents a rather original version of a Grand Tour with the added twist that the traveler not only learns from his journey but gives Europeans a chance to learn about Russia (assuming the posture, tongue in cheek, of a Scythian, that is, barbarian to the Europeans as civilized Greeks). By the end of the eighteenth century, European noblemen, especially British and German, attracted to the classical world and the romance of ruins, favored southern Europe as their destination. While debate continues about how closely the journey replicates Karamzin's own travels in the same period, his fictional alter ego adopts a consistent *modus operandi*. In every city he visits, he seeks out the most distinguished intellectuals and locates the most famous sites, and often makes his conversations the centerpiece of his letters. In Königsberg, without any letter of introduction, he succeeds in making the acquaintance of Immanuel Kant and discoursing with him on metaphysics and other topics for over half an hour. Although Kantian philosophy was not taught in Russia at the time, and would remain suspect to the Russian authorities into the 1820s, the letter ends with a dense transcription of Kant's alleged thinking about moral law, in which the Russian reader would have found a mini-tutorial on Kantian ethics.

Letters frame their intellectual substance with descriptions of landscapes, customs, and costumes typical of travel literature. Because the *Letters* aim to capture a sense of being on the road, they record impressions of borderlands and border crossings, postal stations and inns, customs houses and the mores of coachmen. "A word is in order," says the narrator in Letter fourteen, "about Prussian interrogations."

> In every town and village, travellers are stopped as they enter and as they leave, and they are asked how they are, where they are from and where they are going. Some in jest take funny names, and different ones, —that is, they call themselves by one name when they come in, and another when they depart. As a result the reports to the supervisors are bizarre.... Sometimes, I was one Barakomeneverus who was travelling from Mount Ararat; at other times, I was Aristides in exile from Athens; then Alcibiades on his way to Persia; or yet Doctor Pangloss.[35]

The jumbling up of names might have stymied the officials, but playfully reminds the readers of the itineraries of fictional travelers in picaresque narratives of the period, such as Wieland's *History of Agathon* (*Geschichte des Agathon*, first edition 1766–67), a neoclassical utopian novel set in ancient Greece, or the ironical dystopia of Voltaire's *Candide* (twice translated into Russian). These are travelers who might be on the narrator's mind as counterparts but they do not determine the course of his own adventures or make Karamzin's narrative a philosophical fiction of an allegorical kind. Conversations that take place in coaches on the road often involve travelers of different nationalities, and afford Karamzin an efficient and often comic means of delivering comparative cultural commentary while also satisfying a traditional comic function since coachmen (like taxi drivers in modern English fiction) provide a stream of clichés about current affairs.

While letters from capitals like Berlin, Paris, Geneva, and London concentrate the most sightseeing and most intellectual content, notes on provincial towns scattered along the route provide local color. Place names help to supply verisimilitude used by travel writers to suggest authenticity, whether based on genuine experience or on other literary sources. Letter after letter crams in a delightful miscellany of information. A letter from Danzig (no. 10) provides standard topographical description, but also discusses the state of the herring trade, a *Last Judgment* by van Eyck, the local currency (which is the topic of continued preoccupation as the traveler exchanges promissory notes for cash), and a handbook of Greek grammar written by a local academic. This practice of observation and commentary is sustained throughout the narrative, down to the final letters from the London suburbs. Virtually all landscapes are saturated with artifacts or sights that elicit from the highly attentive observer factual reports or creative responses. When traveling in more rural parts, and especially in mountainous regions, the traveler hears tales of brigands, and records them, undoubtedly embellishing them with Gothic tropes. He reacts to iconic landscapes such as the Alps by breaking out into quotation of poetry. He thus incorporates different kinds of embedded text that give this work its variety.

The close connection between literary sensitivity and experience throughout this long and substantial work is unprecedented in Russian writing of the period. One function of the narrative seems to be to capture those moments when reality and expectation created by literature converge, and there is rarely a sense of disappointment that the reality falls short of its imaginary counterpart. Part-novelistic, part-documentary, Karamzin's text, like much travel literature, bridges fact and fiction. Such a combination stood a better chance than the novel of engaging the attention of Russian readers because the novel had been slow to catch on, engendering critical mistrust or losing out to superior foreign works. While Karamzin's itinerary ostensibly grounds him as a traveler in a specific time and place, Karamzin's narrator as a writer of place descriptions conveys a sense of the power of the literary imagination to conjure landscapes, objects, and feelings. It is part of the contract between the Karamzinian narrator and reader, based on a pact of sympathy, that what moves the narrator will have the power to move readers. The *Letters* are an inventory of places, collections of paintings, and proceedings of meetings, even transcribing entire speeches. There is a degree of research that no traveler could have possibly undertaken while on the road. Studies of Karamzin's sources show how heavily he relied on materials such as guidebooks. Yet this archaeology of knowledge never interferes with the experiential flow of a work that stays close to the narrator's sensibility and perception. The *Letters* can be read as a great experiment in recording how, through travel, an individual self can confront different identities and pick and choose among them. While the traveler is Russian by nationality, and border crossings remind us that national identity exists as a conceptual category in the period, he moves between cultures with cosmopolitan ease, conversing with the French on the merits of Corneille versus Racine, discoursing with the English on the merits of Handel, exchanging views on aesthetics with Platner.

To the extent that this enormous work is larger than the sum of its parts, and sustains a single protagonist over the course of his journey, the *Letters* use the devices of epistolary fiction, and exploit the very openness of the novel as a genre. The most fictional aspect of the work is arguably its creation of a hero who projects a cosmopolitan ideal. Attempts to equate Karamzin and his narrator seem exaggerated.[36] It is not surprising that the author equips his protagonist with the poetic skills and idiom that he commanded. But the differences in outlook and performance are as notable as the similarities. In his personal correspondence, Karamzin was restrained, as noted by his contemporaries, whereas the narrator of the *Letters* maintains the fiction of tender friendship throughout. As a historian working in the early nineteenth century, Karamzin favored an annalistic approach based on the chronicles he had studied and sometimes even rescued from neglect in monasteries. By contrast, the philosophy of history adopted by his fictional persona and alter ego in the *Letters* follows important Enlightenment historiographic theorists, such as Gabriel Bonnet de Mably and Montesquieu, who saw history in terms of cyclical rise and decline of nations. To be sure, the narrator's facility with short poems and stories reflects Karamzin's strengths, and the entire production reflects his ambition to see the novel, or prose writing, better established as a genre in Russian. But as travel writing, the *Letters* combine intellectual fields of inquiry to an unprecedented degree for European, and much less Russian, literature. There is no other work of travel writing that moves so easily between extended discussions of metaphysics, theology, the occult, and science, on the one hand, and literary pastiche, including a wide range of lyric genres, the discourse on the sublime, landscape description, pathetic fallacy, on the other. A language of sensibility structures the narrator's outlook and his use of the letter to suggest a friendship network back home. But an extrovert interest in the world at large keeps this narrator from sentimental brooding, and his attention to the political events, such as the French Revolution, as they unfold show him to be a philosophical traveler of rare intelligence capable of judging diverse cultural norms as well as a believer in a universal code of conduct.

With the *Letters of a Russian Traveler*, we have come full circle from Kantemir's original experiment in European-style writing to hold up a mirror to Russian society. This work's polyphony, its novelistic capacity to absorb multiple genres and discourses, foregrounds a Russian writer composing in the vernacular who now has all the tools at his disposal to describe Europe from a position of cultural strength. While Kantemir barely had a readership ripe for his message, Karamzin artfully creates a reader in the figure of the internal addressee to guarantee that his readership keeps pace with him. In reality, the work sold well among a public who no longer perceived a cultural commentary on Europe written by a Russian as an implicit critique of Russia's backwardness. If anything, the fact that Russian letters could now field a gifted commentator who could roll documentary history, art historical appreciation, poetry, scientific observation, social charm and conversation, and high intellectualism into one, meant that perhaps, for the first time, Russians could feel they had excelled in the European sphere.

Literary voices on civic virtue and absolute rule

Early in Catherine's reign, Russian satire maintained the traditional function of the genre from antiquity to lampoon manners and personal foibles. During a period of relative tolerance and freedom of the press from the 1780s, satirical writers, joined by playwrights (especially in comedy), prose writers, and poets, pushed the boundaries of the critique of society, with ethical implications for personal conduct as well as politics. Policing one's own manners, and questioning the function of political economy based on serfdom, became the direct subjects of literature. Yet even in a more promising atmosphere, raising questions about the nature of absolutism and the policies of a specific monarch could only be done indirectly with considerable tact.

Catherine's policies gave evidence of her practical commitment to Enlightenment.[37] She also actively encouraged public opinion on the pages of literary journals. This was the case in 1769 when, despite initiating a war with the Porte in the Crimea, she engaged Novikov in debate, giving license to him and others to raise sensitive matters of policy, such as serfdom, on the pages of satirical journals. Writers tested the boundaries of expression throughout Catherine's reign. For those whose status was already secure, at least to some extent, contributing to the literary and cultural life of the court did not oblige them to slavish praise, and it did allow some public reflection. Their aim may well have been to determine whether Catherine's commitments to ideas like freedom of the press and the principles set out in her legislative program were genuine or compromised by tactical considerations at court. Yet, when under pressure, courtiers and monarchs, and none more so than Catherine the Great, remained vigilant about implied criticisms. Loyalty had to be overtly absolute, but some critique intimated through literary irony, satire, and comic forms suggests that restrained critique was acceptable.

Writers remained keenly aware of the potential for political control over writing. But censorship had not been systematically enforced either by the state or the Church. From the autocrat's point of view, the balance between censorship and freedom of the press raises the question of the monarch's self-interest in permitting criticism. Censorship was rudimentary during most of Catherine's reign.[38] Although the Holy Synod intervened sporadically in the 1750s, and then in the late 1760s, the state largely did not act, possibly because there was little in the way of subversive writing to fear. Having engineered reforms to education, supported a huge expansion in publishing and translation from European literature, and having publicly entered into correspondence with some of the great minds of Europe and positioned herself as a champion of Enlightenment principles, Catherine expected writing to pose questions about the limits of absolutism. Succession depended entirely on the will of the previous ruler. Survival depended on the cooperation of the nobility and army who were made to serve the state but were opportunists when it came to their own interests. In the letter of August 2, 1762

Catherine wrote to her lover, the Polish king Stanisław Poniatowski, she made clear her keen grasp of the political reality she faced after the coup that put her on the throne. To be an absolute ruler was not to rule single-handedly but to negotiate competing interests and situations rife with faction, all of which limited her ability to implement ideals. In a famous riposte to Diderot, she reiterated that she governed in the real world while he devised ideal states on paper.[39]

Once a literary sphere was established outside the direct control of the court, writers were relatively quick to grasp the value of literature as a vehicle for reflection on social thought, short of outright subversion. Nonetheless, from the 1780s, and most especially around the time of the French Revolution, we find a willingness in literature to raise issues that imply social and political critique of absolutism. Doubts about absolutism are more often implicit than outright, expressed in terms of an underlying contrast between an ideal of progress associated with the Enlightenment and the shortcomings of the Russian political economy and its model of serfdom. Soviet scholarship imputed to the satirical journals an ideological function by grouping writers into official and unofficial, and by extension, into supporters or detractors of absolutism. These categories are anachronistic and too clear-cut to describe accurately the interrelation between a wider literary culture and the court. Like Prussia under Frederick the Great, though less advanced, Russia was a state that saw little contradiction between absolutism and its cultural achievements. The latter reinforced the impression of Enlightenment. European thinkers, most famously the *encyclopédistes* led by Diderot, identified tensions between the absolutist model and freedoms and forms of tolerance we would call progressive (and they called Enlightened). Even in St. Petersburg and Moscow, Russia lacked a full complement of public institutions, now seen as civic spaces central to the dissemination of the bourgeois identity in the European Enlightenment.[40]

In a "Speech on the Use of Education and the Arts" ("Rech´, govorennaia v publichnom sobranii imperatorskoi Akademii khudozhestv, pri vypuske iz onoi pitomtsev, v 1779," published in 1779), Kniazhnin saw no contradiction between didactic art and creative freedom and espoused the widely held view that art had a responsibility to produce a "useful citizen" ("poleznyi grazhdanin"), thus echoing the rhetoric of Catherine's own views on citizenship. He also argued that art encourages an "intelligent understanding of freedom" ("razumnoe vospriiatie vol´nosti"), an opinion held by a minority of more daring writers.[41]

Some works, now appreciated for their literary flair, were politically suggestive in their immediate context, and whether their connotations were acceptable, provocative, or too radical was ultimately for the authorities and especially the monarch to decide, regardless of the author's intentions. The politics of Catherinian Russia were highly fluid, sensitive to internal pressures at court and the monarch's perceived standing grew abroad, where her foreign policy was highly active. It is a matter for counter-factual speculation, but no less valuable for that, to wonder whether Radishchev's *Journey from St. Petersburg to Moscow* would have been deemed to be seditious if it had been published in the early 1780s rather than a decade later. What is certain is that Fonvizin's *The Minor* (*Nedorosl´*, 1782), Derzhavin's *Felitsa* poems, Novikov's satirical writings, and Radishchev's (not comic but often satirical) *Journey from St. Petersburg to Moscow* remain classics, All four writers were skilled in creating irony out of implied contrasts between traditional literary forms and messages that were subversive. In Fonvizin's plays, the social side overshadows comedy; in Derzhavin's odes, implicit challenge undermines panegyric; and in Radishchev's work, questions of law and justice cannot be separated from sentimental tales. All of these texts employ terms like "virtue" (*dobrodetel´*), "duty" (*dolzhnost´*), and "honour" (*chest´*), all used by Catherine herself, but the words become double-edged swords because they hint at expectations of greater freedom at least for nobles (if not for serfs) and practical Enlightenment than Catherine could deliver. Whether it is possible in this context to talk about a full-fledged political discourse seems questionable.[42]

Among the period's many comic writers, Denis Fonvizin was peerless at balancing the slap-stick and broad satire of comedy with ethical instruction. In 1769, Fonvizin scored an initial suc-cess at court when he read his satirical comedy *The Brigadier* (*Brigadir*) to Catherine the Great. In *The Drone*, Novikov praised both Fonvizin and Catherine, whose own comedy *O! Time* (*O! Vremia*, 1772), which satirized the tendency of the disgruntled gentry to blame the government for various ills and use rumor as leverage for increasingly absurd demands. Fonvizin's admirer Count Nikita Panin, then an indispensable Foreign Minister and Tutor to the Crown Prince, recruited Fonvizin to serve as his personal secretary, a position that enabled the playwright to observe the workings of the state up close; in his letters to his employer he expressed a keen sense that factional politics meant more at court than Enlightenment principles. Fonvizin's relationship with the monarch was never smooth sailing. For one thing, his thinking on the question of ideal monarchy had evolved toward a system that encouraged more accountability. Not for nothing did he translate in 1777 "A Eulogy to Marcus Aurelius" by the French writer A. L. Thomas. He was also the author of an incomplete work of political theory (his *Reflections on Inviolable State Laws* ["Rassuzhdeniia o nepremennykh gosudarstvennykh zakonakh," c.1784] were suppressed until produced for Paul I after his mother's death in 1796). In addition, his association with Petr Panin, one of a group of disgruntled courtiers, aroused some suspicion.

For a writer the relevant question was whether the moral critique of the satirist was a suit-able vehicle for questioning the state of affairs, including despotism, corruption, inequality, and laying the blame at the feet of officials. While many writers such as Novikov, Fonvizin, and Derzhavin addressed the definition and shape of Enlightenment autocracy, it is ques-tionable and debatable whether any had specifically political points to make to the ruler about the actual political structure of the government. In works that represent kingship, from Sumarokov's neoclassical tragedy *Dimitry the Pretender* (1771) to Radishchev's philosophical fiction *Journey from St. Petersburg*, the authentic ruler is one who promotes the good of the people and subjects the nobles to the rule of law. Tyranny, corruption, and self-interest are identified as the enemy but fundamentally no alternative political system is advanced against absolutism.[43]

When Fonvizin retired from state service in 1782 he had already written his comic master-piece, *The Minor*, which enjoyed a triumph at its premiere in Moscow and then in St. Petersburg, and was reprinted many times in the period (reports in the 1820s suggest that actors in a new production of the play, frightened that the play might be subversive, turned down parts).[44] Despite vestiges of old-style comic devices, and despite aspects of pedagogical comedy, such as a speaking name, which relate *The Minor* to other classics of the period, like Goldoni's *Il padre di famiglia* and Nivelle de La Chaussée's *L'École de mères*, the play achieves a thematic complexity well beyond any other comedy of the time. *The Minor*'s plot concerns the Prostakov family, members of the rural gentry whose pretensions do not hide a moral baseness: the mother, Prostakova, proves to be irredeemably cruel to her serfs. Their names would come to serve as a byword for the uncouth gentry, while the nearly uneducable son Mitrofan demon-strated the pitfalls of confusing superficial imitation with genuine education. A subplot, inev-itably based on a love intrigue, involves more positive characters, the most celebrated among whom is Starodum whose "speaking name" means Old Thought. As the traditional *raisonneur* figure of neoclassical comedy, the embodiment of reason and, in human dealings, reasonable-ness, he counterbalances the Prostakovs as a model of civilized behavior and cultivation.

In parallel to the comic love intrigue, where virtue and love are the dominant themes and are taken up in a series of great soliloquies, *The Minor* runs an equally important civic plot. Guided by an ethical vocabulary, characters are torn between their sense of duty and their impulse to follow their hearts. *The Minor* is an ethical comedy because it holds up a mirror to the gentry audience, subjecting their manifold shortcomings to gentle and sometimes harsh mockery through caricature. Catherine's own writings on duty and virtue are the direct source of the lines Fonvizin wrote for Starodum. But Fonvizin has also put in Starodum's mouth substantial monologues dealing with virtue and duty to the sovereign, which had political resonance. Starodum argues that moral improvement in an absolutist reign can only occur where virtue, an abstract ideal of civic and moral conduct, and responsibility toward society, are exercised by all members, monarch and nobles alike.

These arguments add a political dimension to the ethical satire of the nobility. The play presented to its immediate audience recognizable patterns of behavior that made them both laugh and squirm (the contemporary reaction to the play was mixed and earned Fonvizin more than a few enemies at court).[45] The play's countryside setting is no accident. The Prostakovs prove to be just as uncouth as their servants, reminding us that membership of the gentry did not automatically entail social polish. All the play's more attractive figures, however, are city dwellers. Periodically in Catherine's reign questions about noble self-definition of the service gentry would become a literary theme, often in response to legislative changes that could affect corporate privilege.[46] In the *Charter to the Nobility* (1785), Catherine confirmed Peter III's decree of 1762, which relaxed the requirement of state service placed upon the nobility. The law was meant to bring advantage by allowing the nobles to cultivate their estates. It also abolished corporal punishment for them and lifted other restrictions. Catherine clearly understood how status contributed to the corporate identity of the gentry; and as a legislator she knew the importance a portion of the service gentry and Senate assigned to their part in the running of the country. Emancipation from service looked on the surface like an extension of privilege. In the longer term, the language of the Charter potentially veiled a strengthening of the throne at the expense of the nobility's economic interests or their political involvement, or both.

Fonvizin was politically astute, and his writings overall display a moral concern over the behavior of the service gentry and the state of the nation, as well as a deep concern with the virtue of the monarch. If the discourse of good governance is always abstract, does that mean the writer does not have Catherine in mind? Fonvizin's plays show an aptitude for couching a topical response within the codes of drama, whether the issue was morality or, more cautiously, politics. Catherine planned to promulgate the *Charter to the Nobility*—a piece of unfinished business inherited from her husband's brief reign—and Fonvizin seems to have understood that the immediate gain to the gentry, however attractive dispensation from state service would be, threatened the dilution of that estate's influence. The monarch's favorites would be left to consolidate power with the throne. His comedy deftly revealed that the boon to the honor of the service gentry ("honor" [*chest'*] is a key word in *The Minor*) was potentially a snare.

Literature produced at court and for the Imperial Theater could never be immune from scrutiny. The degree to which plays on stage were allegories of court situations remains debatable and highly circumstantial. In this instance, there could be no doubt that just like Derzhavin in "Felitsa," Fonvizin was talking to Catherine in the terms of her own progressive discourse. No reprisals were forthcoming from Catherine at this point. Indeed, any critique implied by the language of the play could also work to her benefit since she positioned herself as a promoter of a partnership with the nobility. The play could be read largely as an admonition to the gentry not to go the way of the Prostakovs by burying themselves in the country (and Fonvizin himself was a landowner who supported a humane form of serfdom). The play draws a link between the politics of absolutism and the superfluity of the gentry. The prospect that the service gentry, once sent back to their estates, might suffer long-term decline was played out in the complex agrarian problems of the nineteenth century that led to the impoverishment of the landowners. While the manners of the gentry, and the corruption of institutions, provided suitable topics for entertainment, even entertainment with a didactic slant,

questions about the political standing of the educated gentry involved some writers in considerations of the nature of absolutism.

When works broached a critique, the degree of backlash depended on Catherine's internal
situation in balancing court factions and aspects of policy. In 1772–74, Fonvizin weathered
some unsettling scrutiny, which prompted him to leave for Europe in 1777. Past success did not
guarantee renewed performance. In 1782, Fonvizin faced delays in the staging of *The Minor*,
partly as a result of personal friction with influential courtiers, but more generally because the
didactic parts of his play dealing with the duty (*dolzhnost'*) of the gentry might have implied
challenges to Catherine's stewardship.[47] In 1783, Catherine and Fonvizin aired their differences
over autocracy. In the third issue of the journal *The Interlocutor* (*Sobesednik*), the editor Princess
Dashkova published a piece by Fonvizin with annotations and answers by Catherine, entitled
"Several Questions Able to Elicit in Smart and Honorable People Special Attention" ("Neskol'ko
voprosov, mogushchikh vozbudit' v umnykh i chestnykh liudiakh osoblivoe vnimanie"). In
1783, Catherine upped the ante by publishing in the same journal a more aggressive set of
responses in a series of installments titled "Facts and fictions" ("Byli i nebylitsy"). She remarks
tartly on an exchange between Pravdin and Starodum in *The Minor* as to whether ill members
of the court should be treated by a doctor. Pravdin advocates calling a specialist rather than
allowing the sick to leave, but Starodum disagrees because of the risk that the doctor himself
might catch the disease. Catherine had no trouble reading between the lines or picking up on
other hints of dissatisfaction that were potentially troublesome, if not entirely seditious. In
1783, the political content of *The Minor* was brought out in a document Fonvizin composed
under the guidance of his employer and patron N. I. Panin, "A Consideration of Inalienable
State Laws" ("Rassuzhdenie o nepremennykh gosudarstvennykh zakonakh"). Also known
as "Panin's Testament" ("Zaveshchanie Panina"), this critique of absolute power argued
that the law be used to fix firm limits to the power of the autocrat. What made the conclusions
more problematic and politically sensitive than similar ideas insinuated in the play was the
immediate context: Panin, who died shortly afterwards on March 31, 1783, as a loyal mentor
of Grand Duke Paul appeared to be putting the cause of the heir ahead of that of the
sovereign. Circulated clandestinely in multiple copies, the position paper openly criticized
an "enlightened and virtuous monarch who, finding her empire and her own laws in such
disarray and chaos," took measures to heal the state. If the description looked calculated
to praise Catherine for her early accomplishments, it did not flinch from raising the prospect that such a monarch then had gone too far and made things worse by abusing absolute
power. Catherine's ripostes thwarted Fonvizin, leading him to withdraw his questions and
acknowledge the "monarch as most wise and just."[48] We see in this episode how closely the
world of the stage and the world of politics overlap here, proof of Fonvizin's intentions to
write a universal comedy on manners and virtue whose more immediate ideological contentions were felt. And the consequences were real since the journal edited by Fonvizin and
Dashkova, *The Friend of Honest Folk, or Starodum* (*Drug chestnykh liudei, ili Starodum*) was
banned from print in 1788 although copies circulated clandestinely as Radishchev noted in his
Journey.[49]

Others fared worse. Kheraskov found his promotion blocked after he had voiced certain
criticisms. Mystery still surrounds Kniazhnin's clashes with the government from the 1770s
until his sudden death in 1791, shortly after his release from prison (at least until the mid-
nineteenth century, legends circulated that his death was brought on by interrogation and
torture). In 1772, he was accused of embezzlement, arrested, and initially sentenced to death
before the sentence was commuted and he was stripped of his rank and the right to own property. The trumped-up charge was thought to have been a reaction to the sentiments expressed
in his play *Olga* (1772) implying that maternal love was incompatible with monarchy. The poor

state of Catherine's relationship with her son Paul was common knowledge. It has been reasonably assumed that, in 1777, when Kniazhnin wrote for the Russian stage a musical version of Pietro Metastasio's *La Clemenza di Tito*, a work that had circulated in Russia since the 1750s, it was to secure the rehabilitation to his rank, granted him by an act of clemency from the empress that same year.

Nevertheless, Kniazhnin continued to use classical tragedy as a vehicle for political discourse. Whether his intention was to dramatize his views on forms of government, or to produce thinly veiled commentary on the present, mattered little since in the febrile atmosphere of the late *ancien régime* the effect was the same: namely, incurring the risk of irritating a ruler who had always tried to gain the upper hand in any potentially subversive exchange and had also shown a willingness to penalize mettlesome individuals. Like Radishchev, Kniazhnin tempted fate by exploring republicanism (as a noble failure) in the tragedies *Sofonisba*, performed in 1789, and most controversially in *Vadim Novgorodskii* (1788 or 1789). A posthumous printing of the latter play was confiscated and then publicly burned after an article by the minor writer A. I. Klushin, here a proxy for Kniazhnin's inveterate enemy Krylov, denounced it as politically hostile; and the ban on this play lasted throughout the remainder of the imperial period, a measure insufficient to prevent its clandestine circulation in the 1820s.

In practice, few thinkers and writers before the 1790s advocated radical limitations on the power of the autocrat or explicitly mounted any concrete alternatives to Catherine's style of rule. Catherine did take exception to some of Fonvizin's own more direct criticisms published in a dictionary of synonyms, accusing him of having a "loose tongue" ("svobodoiazychie"), to which the normally acerbic Fonvizin responded with a clarification and retraction. While fighting shy of Catherine, he defended the rights of authors to speak their minds in a *Petition to the Russian Minerva from Russian Writers* ("Chelobitnaia k rossiiskoi Minerve ot rossiiskikh pisatelei," 1783), which criticized ignorant courtiers (one target of attack was the Procurator of the Senate, Prince A. Viazemsky, an enemy he shared with Derzhavin).

We turn to two odes Vasily Kapnist wrote in 1783 in response to the changes in legislation that affected the peasantry and the nobility, and look at them as examples of literature that pits the voice of the writer against the state. Educated at home on the family estate Obukhovka in Ukraine, Kapnist moved as a teenager to St. Petersburg in 1771, and pursued a modest military career in the Preobrazhensky Regiment (the troop that put Catherine on the throne), during which time he struck up friendships with fellow officers Derzhavin and the poet and architect N. A. L'vov, as well as L'vov's friend, M. N. Murav'ev. Later he hosted his literary friends at Obukhovka, its landscape commemorated in his poetry. Their activities as a coterie include readings and collective composition, and reflect how sociability and literature occupied a private sphere in elite urban life with no compulsion to be performed at court. Kapnist published in the fashionable journals patronized by his circle, eventually including Karamzin's *Moscow Journal* (1791–92) and his own anthology *The Aeonids* (1796–99).

A highly accomplished lyric poet (especially noted for his translations of Horace), Kapnist honed his satire and social criticism on contemporary issues. His greatest comedy *Chicanery* (*Iabeda*, 1798) treats corruption in the judiciary, a topic on which he was an expert due to his involvement in a lawsuit that took over two decades before it was settled. He also showed considerable boldness in addressing serfdom and its abuses. Kapnist, who had quit his job in the Post Office under the minister Count A. A. Bezborodko, vented his fury in a great work of political invective in response to Catherine's decree of 1783, which had altered the terms of bondage of the peasantry to the state and in relation to the landowner. The decree abolished the freedom of the peasantry in Little Russia (now Ukraine) by imposing a poll tax and other forms of rent. Further decrees of 1785 and 1786 effectively bound the peasants to the land as slaves owned by landowners, and deprived the nobles of the flexibility they had enjoyed in managing the peasantry on terms suited to their rural estates. Kapnist's unstinting criticism of the empress would have been reckless were it not for two facts: until that point, the tone of the reign had been lenient (as Derzhavin notes in "Felitsa" when praising Felitsa for her willingness to disregard foibles); and Kapnist, although a Ukrainian landowner of considerable erudition and literary talent, was not a courtier or prominent figure.

The radical message of the "Ode on Slavery" ("Oda na rabstvo," 1783), admired by Radishchev and the young Pushkin (see his poem "The Countryside," 1819), begins on a note of humble self-mockery as the poet dusts off his lyre out of love for the fatherland and "sings of enslavement" ("otchizny moeia liubeznoi / Poraboshchen'ie vospoiu"). Against the cruelty of the earthly gods he implores the ruler of the universe to exercise justice. The poem reserves its central stanzas for a remarkable dystopian landscape in which the land is disfigured by suffering. His gaze, "washed by tears," alights on "misery" that has descended upon once happy fields, forests, and meadows. Arguing for freedom as a matter of right (he uses both the words *svoboda* and *vol'nost'*), Kapnist makes a republican argument and asserts the right of the poet to act in defense of the people. The argument he produces in the "Ode on Slavery" is one that Derzhavin had already summarized in "To the Potentates and Judges" and one that Radishchev would make again in his *Journey from St. Petersburg to Moscow*. The argument against despotism presupposes that a tacit contract between ruler and people governs the ruler's behavior:

> А вы, цари! на то ль зиждитель
> Своей подобну власть вам дал,
> Чтобы во областях подвластных
> Из счастливых людей несчастных
> И зло из общих благ творить?[50]

> And you, tsars! Did the creator of the universe
> Grant you power equal to his own
> So that in the land you rule
> You might make happy people miserable,
> And turn common good into villainy?

On the one hand, his argument oscillates between economic self-interest, as he questions the stability of serfdom and its economic viability, and a direct appeal to the empress, as he shames her for dashing the hopes for reform built up in an earlier part of her reign, and accuses her of "shackling [people's] hands" ("Ty tsep' na ruki nalagaesh'"). Given Catherine's ambitious social legislation in the 1780s, which looked like benevolent reform and included the founding of orphanages, hospitals, and schools, the accusation that enslavement will destroy families, create orphans, and impoverish the peasantry seemed calculated to wound. At the end, Kapnist holds out an olive branch in the hope that the ruler will reconsider, and extends a promise to sing her praises when she does.

Kapnist kept that promise after a fashion several years later. He sent the "Ode on Slavery" to his friend, the architect N. A. L'vov, with a request that he hand-deliver it to the empress. Kapnist was neither an advocate of the abolition of traditional land tenure, nor an opponent of absolutism. His poem "On the Abolishment of the Word Slave in Russia by Catherine II on February 15, 1786" ("Oda na istreblenie v Rossii zvaniia raba Ekaterinoiu Vtoroiu, v 15 den' fevralia 1786 goda") is signed by Her Imperial Majesty's "faithful subject (*vernopodannyi*)

V. Kapnist." In using the wording of a decree he abhorred in his title, Kapnist launches a provocation. He furthermore signals the ironic meaning of the ode written in condemnation, rather than as a celebration, by employing an obsolete epistolary closing in the title. In a poem written to denounce the enslavement of the peasant population, a writer who hardly sees himself as a "slave" (rab) revives the cliché in order to ironize the fact that absolutism entails his own servitude despite the rights and privileges of the gentry. No absolutist cliché escapes irony as the poet lavishes sarcasm on the ruler for "removing the chains from our hands," "the yoke from our neck," for "gifting life again" ("ona tebe vnov' zhizn' daruet") and "tying happiness to liberty" ("I schastie s vol'nost'iu sviazuet"). No less than a Golden Age, in his view, has been ushered in by a single change: "In the captivity of meekness we remained till now / And became a hundred-fold more imprisoned" ("V plenu dnes' krotosti ostalis' / I stali plennee stokrat"). Catherine will erect a monument to "her generous deeds."[51]

But in Russia, as in any other absolutist state such as Prussia, France, Austria, or Sweden, writers, and all subjects generally, were obliged to exercise caution on political and philosophical topics in order to avoid charges of subversion. The harsh reprisals of Catherine's last years, and the repressive atmosphere of Paul I's short reign, ending with his assassination in 1801, curbed political expression without killing off new ideals. In "Verses on Sleep" ("Stikhi na son," 1805), Ivan Pnin makes his ideals of Enlightenment political theory and radical materialism the content of poetic inspiration that sleep visited on the unconscious and turns social progress into the content of his "visions" ("videniia") and a "spark to the imagination" ("iskra voobrazheniia"). And in his unpublished "Essay on Enlightenment with respect to Russia" ("Opyt o prosveshchenii otnositel'no Rossii," 1804), Pnin bridges the interest in political theory, elaborated by older-generation figures such as Radishchev, concentrated around the journal Morning Light (Utrenii svet), and the younger generation's commitment to reforming Russia's political economy, which will directly inform Decembrist thought from the mid-1810s.[52] The air of danger might well have motivated an increase in interest: the journal's subscription figures were close to 1,000, a relatively large number by comparison with other periodicals. Among elite circles, the outspokenness of these writers and their ideals increased their moral authority and earned them sympathy.

Like many a thinker of the period, including Diderot whom he may have met in 1774, Radishchev approaches questions of power, justice, and absolutism in the abstract, and more from a moral position than with a pragmatic view to institutional reform. As a civil servant, Radishchev could have chosen to stay on the safe side of the law. Poor timing was one factor in the harsh penalty he faced. Between 1790 and 1792, 825 copies of sixty-seven titles, including works by Voltaire, were burned.[53] The most notorious repressive incidents of the reign included the scandal of Yakov Kniazhnin whose Vadim Novogordskii, a typical work of neoclassical tragedy, was banned from performance. Its representation of the historical republican values of the citizens of Novgorod (also treated by Radishchev in the Journey from St. Petersburg to Moscow) was misread as a gesture of solidarity with the French revolutionaries (as well as with restive Polish nobles before the second partition of Poland by Russia and Prussia in 1793).

Throughout Europe, the association of Freemasonry with radical thought led to crackdowns. Even Novikov, a great literary impresario and all-round man of letters, suffered badly because of his close Masonic affiliations. Arrested in 1792, allegedly for proselytizing for the Old Faith, he was accused of being a "fanatic" by Catherine, who eventually commuted his death sentence to a prison term "in accordance with our inherent love of mankind." Other court figures, like the senator and memoirist Ivan Lopukhin, had his book purchases closely scrutinized. Derzhavin was put under suspicion for Jacobinism, although he was left untouched. For the first time in her reign, Catherine established a special censorship committee to vet foreign books at customs; however restrictive the measure was, one must remember that the

French crown had kept its publishing industry under regulation, thereby helping to create a huge clandestine book trade in the more liberal Protestant Low Countries.

It would be a distortion to see the end of Catherine's reign as uniquely repressive or to misread Radishchev's reflections on social theory as a political program in a practical sense. Catherine's satirical exchanges with Novikov in the 1760s furnish one celebrated counter-example. Throughout her reign, and especially in the 1780s, when Catherine actively fostered literature, tensions were bound to build between a burgeoning impulse to independent thought among certain writers and the ruler's tolerance of even moderated criticism. Other examples of tensions can be found, above all, in the control she exercised over publishing. The Free Press Edict marked an important moment of liberalization that led to a publishing boom.[54] Only three years later, in 1786, the authorities closed Ivan Lopukhin's Free Typograph, a publishing house originally founded in 1783, for printing Masonic literature. In 1786, Novikov's publishing activities were again investigated by Petr Levshin, also known as Metropolitan Platon (1737–1812), a relatively liberal and well-educated clergyman.[55] He condemned twenty-three translations of writings by the French *encyclopédistes* as "mystical" works and therefore suspect. Catherine, nonetheless, granted permission for the publication of all but six. Novikov also obtained police clearance to publish his "Dialogues with God," with contributions by Karamzin and his friend Aleksandr Petrov.

Nonetheless, the persecution of Novikov, and especially Radishchev, only enhanced the radical intelligentsia's admiration for their works in the late nineteenth century: Radishchev was published abroad by Alexander Herzen (1812–70). The early Bolsheviks also admired their lives and legacies, and treated them as the ideological forefathers of future opponents to the imperial regime. Radishchev inspired a trilogy of historical novels by the Soviet writer Olga Forsh (1873–1961) published in the 1930s. Both Novikov and Radishchev were the subject of popular pamphlets that depicted them as heroes.

CASE STUDY **Aleksandr Radishchev and the philosophical life**

Aleksandr Radishchev's life, writings, and career make him a remarkable figure in the history of Enlightenment thought and literature. His status as a champion of press freedom, enemy of the slave economy, and, finally, a victim of political repression made him a figure of great interest throughout the nineteenth century and into the early Soviet period, but Radishchev is far more than a symbol of the daring of the writer against autocratic oppression. As a civil servant, legal advisor, and publisher, Radishchev regularly reflected on, and recorded, his activities, experiences, and thoughts in original writings and translations. Among the latter is a version of Book III of Montesquieu's *Considérations sur les causes de la grandeur des Romains et de leur décadence*, apparently done under the supervision of Catherine's secretary A. V. Khrapovitsy in 1773, as well as Mably's *Observations sur l'histoire de la Grèce, ou Des causes de la prospérité et des malheurs des Grecs*, translated the same year. These works give some idea of the basis of Radishchev's thinking about history, progress, the importance of law, and governance. While best remembered for the *Journey from St. Petersburg to Moscow* (1790), the sum total of his practical and literary contributions is of a distinction in scale, learning, and thoughtfulness comparable with the greatest French *encyclopédistes*. And like his older European contemporaries Voltaire and Diderot, Radishchev fell foul of the authorities for his subversive views. He used writing in all forms to provoke others into reconsidering fundamental premises underlying beliefs, institutions, and customs.

At every stage of his life, Radishchev found a variety of forms for his often highly original thoughts, including the essay, the biographical sketch, biography, fictional autobiography, travel literature, utopian fiction, and short and long verse forms. His writings about his student years reveal a permanent interest in areas of political theory and natural law, as well as in the mind–body dualism that featured so importantly in Enlightenment thought. In his later career as a customs official, Radishchev remained committed to the ideals of rational governance that also informed his work on Catherine's Legislative Commission in the 1760s. And his membership of progressive private societies and participation in the publication of literary-cum-philosophical journals demonstrated that, being widely read in French, German, English, and Russian literatures, one could, in the late eighteenth century, be an intellectual or something close to a *philosophe*. Arguably, and perhaps paradoxically, given their eventual antagonism, the only figure in the period who matches Radishchev's consistency in using writing for practical, theoretical, and creative purposes might have been Catherine II herself, the monarch whom he served and whom he eventually enraged by the perceived subversiveness of his writings.

Radishchev was born in Moscow in 1749; his father was a well-educated member of the service gentry who, according to family legend, was spared by his peasants during the Pugachev Rebellion thanks to his reasonable and humane style of running his estate in the Kaluga Province. Like many sons of the gentry, Radishchev was earmarked as a youth for service in the Page Corps, an elite school founded by the Empress Elizabeth with the mission of instilling reason in its students and encouraging noble behavior in accordance with Christian precepts and natural law. Catherine II, a keen student of pedagogy as a form of shaping social attitudes, restricted admission to the school to the sons of the gentry from the start of her reign. As one of a group of students, including five other handpicked pages, all supported by the imperial purse, Radishchev was sent by Catherine the Great to complete his education at Leipzig University, where he received tuition in a wide range of subjects, including jurisprudence, history, logic, and moral philosophy from such notable Enlightenment figures as Christian Gellert and Ernst Platner, both of whom Karamzin's traveler encounters in his *Letters of a Russian Traveler*. In May 1775, Radishchev married and suspended the career in state service he had embarked on after Leipzig. He returned to state service in 1777, occupying different posts in the Customs Office, sometimes in Narva and Kronstadt. He continued to move up the civil service grades, achieving the rank of collegiate assessor as well as obtaining a commendation; according to his son, in all matters he exhibited unflinching rectitude.[56]

In addition to his state service, Radishchev continued to work as a translator and writer. The *Life of Fedor Vasilievich Ushakov* (*Zhitie Fedora Vasil'evicha Ushakova*, 1789) is a major piece of life-writing of the Russian eighteenth century. Like Karamzin's *Letters of a Russian Traveler*, it deserves attention as an example of a skillful mix of prose genres deployed in order to represent intersecting philosophical, political, and personal ideas and convictions. Such a manipulation of prose genres constitutes a step-change in Russian literature of the period. Radishchev dedicated the memoir-cum-secular hagiography to his and Ushakov's mutual friend Aleksei Kutuzov (1749–97), a classmate from Leipzig and Radishchev's roommate when both men in 1771 returned to St. Petersburg. The *Life* contains Radishchev's extensive narrative of his Leipzig experiences, cast as a semi-hagiographical tribute to the title figure, a close friend and boon companion, who died prematurely young of venereal-like symptoms (Radishchev's fascination with the connection between erotic fantasy, sexual activity, and love for freedom persists as an object of highly expressive treatment elsewhere in writings that treat questions of political economy). On publication in 1789 some readers such as Catherine's friend Princess Dashkova noted that Radishchev wrote prose that was effortful rather than smooth in the style of elegant classical French; she also made note of expressions that were "dangerous."

In his various roles as a civil servant Radishchev was capable of producing routine bureaucratic prose of polish and clarity, whereas in his literary texts he deliberately cultivated a more difficult style marked by complex syntax, inventive neologisms, and pseudo-Slavonic register. Norms of prose style in the period remained in flux, with translators and original writers still experimenting with German and Latin syntactic forms as well as other prosodic features. But experimentation for its own sake seems less the cause for Radishchev's mannered style than his wish to create a distinctive and expressive voice in poetry and prose. Although a denser style than one would have encountered in prose fiction of the period, Radishchev's language is a tool for focusing the mind of the reader on his sometimes abstract philosophical vocabulary and on the highly visual element of his prose which relies on anecdote, episode, ekphrasis, and verbal painting as a way of aligning emotional and intellectual content.

Part One of the *Life* narrates the history of Radishchev's student group at Leipzig University, and concentrates on a student rebellion against the strict disciplinarian regime of their guardian and the local authorities. Part Two presents a set of essays or compositions and translations written in the manner of school assignments. It has not been determined whether Radishchev is the true author of all the pieces; he may well have written them and fabricated attribution in order to create a legacy for his subject. Two sets of "meditations" (*razmyshleniia*), first on punishment and the death penalty, and then on love, take the form of Socratic questions and responses. The conclusion consists of commentaries on Helvétius's *De l'esprit* cast as five letters. In the *Life*, Radishchev recalls studying *De l'esprit* and cites the encouragement of another Russian, the government official F. G. Orlov (1741–96), who was passing through Leipzig and just happened to have a copy to spare; Radishchev notes that the book "taught him to think."[57] The casual reference to Orlov who sanctioned the reading of a notorious radical thinker seems pregnant with implication for the history of freethinking at Catherine's court. (Many copies of the posthumous 1773 first edition of Helvétius's other scandalous work *De l'homme* appeared with a dedication to Catherine, of which she approved, as its publication was overseen by the Russian ambassador in The Hague, Dmitry A. Golitsyn.) While radical ideas had been widely debated in the early 1780s, Catherine later hardened her autocratic line as revolutionary turmoil swept France. Helvétius's writings had been condemned in France in 1758–59, and were still regarded as dangerous because, like all works labeled "freethinking," they subjected the social order to skepticism. One point of using the material in Part Two of the *Life* is to associate Ushakov with the materialism of the radical Enlightenment, and Radishchev uses it to create an opportunity to establish a legacy for his friend as a lover of freedom who is philosophically informed. Radishchev uses the *Life* to examine the relationship between personal ambition and altruism, and suggests that while Ushakov works for his own personal benefit rather than for the glory of posterity, he remains admirable because he turned a cluster of students into a political action group, now ready to take on oppressive authorities and improve their own lot. In his writings, Radishchev saw the events of 1767 in Leipzig as the start of a serious and lifelong engagement with questions of political reform. While the student rebellion itself was modest in scale and aims, it was unexpected and ill-timed. Catherine's protégés were a privileged group sent abroad to expand a skill set they were expected to use on returning to Russia in service to the monarch. Moreover, dissidence even against local authority struck a sour note because Russia at the time was embroiled in the Russo-Turkish War and facing opposition in

Poland. These seditious actions would not have played well at home, and after twenty years of service Radishchev recalled youthful idealism as still relevant in a Catherinian Russia stuck between the language of reform and the reality of a political economy governed by the interests of a powerful class. Freedom fighters and tyrants, republicans and misguided autocrats recur in Radishchev's writing. The ode "Liberty" ("Vol′nost′," 1783), for example, pays tribute to the regicide Cromwell and enthusiastically acknowledges the American Revolution. Radishchev's commemoration of Ushakov not only as an upstart but as a principled intellectual informed by Helvétius's *De l'esprit*, suggests continuity between the youthful reaction of the group to despotic rule and his now mature views on autocracy. Ushakov acted out what Radishchev would come to formulate in his *Journey*: a theory of society based on mutual respect and implied contract in which the aggrieved retained the right to rebel. The essay effectively amounts to Radishchev's political genealogy written from the perspective of 1789. The work as a whole, reprinted in 1811 and then banned, marks an innovation in Russian life-writing as an intellectual biography, creating out of Ushakov a man of reason (also driven by bodily passions) and a type of Enlightenment hero.

But the basis of Radishchev's affinity for Helvétius is not merely political. Helvétius inspired a line of enquiry in Radishchev that runs from the *Life* to the treatise *On Man, on his Mortality and Immortality* (*O cheloveke, ego smertnosti i bessmertii*), composed in exile in 1795. Radishchev was given to considering ideas about politics, free will, and duty in relation to theories about sensation and sensitivity. In his major works, he represents and explores the relation between material determinism and free will, and between sociopolitical structures and individual choice, and their novelty lies in how he combines extensive sentimental fictions with the expository form of the treatise. The genre of *Life* seems to represent an attempt to assemble fragments into something on the order of "complete works" to represent a mature author's attempt, despite Ushakov's tragically short life and modest accomplishments. The *vita*—the best equivalent of the Slavonic word "zhitie" used in the title—intertwines Radishchev's memories with reflections on human conduct. The conjunction of the personal and the universal raises fundamental questions of social and individual identity, from how to react against oppressive society to how to die well. The work is as much about Radishchev as it is about his friend who comes close to, yet ultimately fails to attain, an ethical ideal. Ushakov is a flawed hero of tremendous potential. And while his contribution is not on the same scale as those of the great men in history, such as Agricola or Montesquieu, celebrated, respectively, by Tacitus and Jean D'Alembert, Ushakov was a freedom fighter who stood out for his acts of bravery. Radishchev's reflection on his friend is also an occasion for introspection, so much so that the final pages turn the description of Ushakov's agony into a reflection on the ethics of euthanasia and suicide. When the tormented Ushakov is told that his end is near, he convenes his friends, asking them to preserve his literary legacy and begging them to provide him with poison to help end his sufferings. This staging of a death scene inevitably recalls the heroic death of Socrates, a subject of neoclassical genre painting, and further represents a variation on the type of brave Stoic suicide committed by a warrior, such as Cato (Addison's play put this noble ideal of an autonomous life on the stage in 1713), or by a philosopher. Yet while suicide is seen as a type of heroic emulation, Radishchev and Kutuzov cannot bring themselves to supply the poison. The final pages manage perhaps to justify their behavior and articulate at least the heroic potential of Ushakov's intentions, thwarted only by his friends' timidity.

On January 15, 1783, Catherine the Great issued an *ukase* that allowed privately owned presses. Radishchev acquired a hand press in 1789 and in 1790 printed his 1782 "A Letter to a friend living in Tobolsk," an examination of autocracy prompted by the dedication of Falconet's famous Bronze Horseman. The same year, he anonymously published his *Journey*, on which he worked in 1780–81. The censor approved the penultimate version of the book. Radishchev, however, expanded the original version by about 40 percent, adding passages that gave it a much more radical cast at a time when Catherine's patience for dissent had been stretched thin by the news from France. One can only wonder whether he had drawn a lesson from the famous Enlightenment scandals of 1759, namely the prosecution of Diderot over the *Encyclopédie* and the attack by the Parlement de Paris on Helvétius. Radishchev added a dedication to his friend, Aleksei Kutuzov, which contained a poignant sentence that aptly encapsulates the subject of the book: "I glanced around me, and my soul was wounded by the sufferings of mankind. I directed my gaze inward and observed that the woes of man emanate from man, and often only because he does not look directly at the things around him."[58] Radishchev also replaced the concluding chapter, which had originally recounted how the narrator witnessed a man committing suicide, with a panegyric to Mikhailo Lomonosov, the greatest eighteenth-century Russian poet before Derzhavin. Radishchev is supposed to have printed 600 copies of this new version—an astonishingly large print run for the time. The book went on sale anonymously in late May 1790; Catherine the Great acquired her own copy on June 25. She read it carefully, making many highly critical marginal notes. Radishchev was soon identified as the book's author, and on June 30 he was arrested and imprisoned in the Peter and Paul Fortress. Before his arrest, he ordered most of the printed copies to be burned; only about seventy survived.

Radishchev acknowledged his authorship and, possibly trying to play down the importance of his transgression, claimed that he did not have any ill intention, just wanted to achieve celebrity as a writer. His explanation did not persuade the authorities; the investigation was swiftly completed, and on July 24 Radishchev was sentenced to death. The Senate confirmed the verdict on August 7. On September 4, Catherine commuted the sentence, replacing it with a ten-year exile to Ilimsk, Siberia. On September 8, in chains and under guard, Radishchev began his long journey to exile. His influential friends (Count Semen Vorontsov, in particular) did everything in their power to ease his passage: his chains were removed in Novgorod, and Radishchev was allowed long stops along the way, spending weeks and even months in Moscow, Nizhnii Novgorod, Tobolsk, and Irkutsk. Eventually, he reached Ilimsk in January of 1792. During his stay in Tobolsk, he was joined by the sister of his late wife with two of his younger children, E. V. Rubanovskaia. She later became his common-law wife (the Church prohibited marriages between in-laws, and the three children born in this marriage were considered illegitimate until Alexander I granted Radishchev's petition to legitimize their status). Rubanovskaia accompanied Radishchev throughout the entire period of exile, but fell ill and died on their way back to European Russia in April of 1797.

After Catherine's death in November of 1796, her son and heir, Paul I, allowed Radishchev to live on his estate not far away from Moscow. Alexander I, who ascended to the throne after Paul's assassination in March of 1801, granted Radishchev a full pardon and offered him a position in the Legislative Commission that began its work on the codification of Russian laws soon after Alexander's enthronement. Radishchev enthusiastically accepted the position and produced several legal documents, attempting to introduce into the Russian legal code some personal freedoms, such as freedom of the press, religion, and commerce. Thanks to Radishchev's good knowledge and understanding of Western legal theory and practice, his legislative initiatives proved him unusually well qualified by comparison with the other members of the Commission. But they also seemed to alarm his colleagues and superiors. According to a biography written by his sons, Nikolai and Pavel, the head of the Commission, Count Petr Zavadovsky, ostensibly faulted Radishchev for being too lofty a thinker.[59] On September 12, 1802, Radishchev committed suicide by drinking nitrohydrochloric acid. The explanations of his suicide vary: some cite depression over the lack of positive response to his legislative initiatives; others suggest that Zavadovsky threatened him with another Siberian exile. One must remember, however, that the thought of suicide had occupied Radishchev since his youth and was linked in his mind with such heroic figures as Socrates and Cato the Younger. In this context, suicide becomes not an escape but a heroic act, potentially precipitating social transformation and regime change by causing a backlash against tyranny among like-minded, enlightened members of the gentry.

While in prison and exile, Radishchev continued to write in various genres. After receiving his death sentence, he began composing an autobiographical piece addressed to his children and intended to explain his actions to them. Not being able to write openly, he based his autobiography on a *vita* of an eighth-century Orthodox saint, Philaretus the Charitable, thus presenting his *Journey* as an act of self-sacrifice for humanity's sake. Radishchev did not finish the apologia, and the prison authorities did not pass on what he had written to his children; the manuscript survived among other papers pertaining to Radishchev's case.

Upon his return from the exile, while living on his estate, Radishchev carried on his literary work. Among the most interesting, even idiosyncratic, literary pieces is his unfinished long poem *Bova*. Written in blank verse (a rarity in Russia at the time), *Bova* imitated a popular low-brow adventure story of Italian origin, which at the time had the status of a folk tale. High-brow Russian literati assigned only modest value to folklore. Out of the planned twelve cantos, Radishchev finished eleven. Disheartened that his experiment with folk material was out of step with other trends, he burned them all except for the first one. Radishchev's interest in Old Russian and folk poetry can also be seen in his long poem *Songs Sung at the Competitions in Honor of the Ancient Slavic Divinities* (*Pesni petye na sostiazaniiakh v chest' drevnim slavianskim bozhestvam*, written 1800–02, published 1807), which was one of the first responses to the recently discovered *Lay of Igor's Campaign*. Another idiosyncratic work produced during this period was a parodic piece *Memorial for a Dactylo-Trochaic Knight* (*Pamiatnik daktilokhoreicheskomu vitiaziu*, written 1801, published 1811), in which, among other things, Radishchev discussed Trediakovsky's metrical experiment based on Friedrich Klopstock's version of Greek hexameter. Concerned that, following the powerful example of Lomonosov, iambics had begun to predominate in Russian poetry, Radishchev experimented with different meters in his own verse, and promoted Trediakovsky as a poet who had attempted to do the same. Radishchev's last poem, "The Eighteenth Century," greeted the arrival of a new age (and a new reign). Using the imagery of time as water flowing into the ocean of eternity, he attempted to make sense of a recently ended period that was full of social and political turmoil and yet bequeathed to subsequent generations great philosophical ideas about progress and the engines of historical development, still relevant in our time.

Throughout the nineteenth century, Radishchev's political and philosophical works were suppressed (his *Journey* was published abroad by Herzen in 1858 and in Russia only in 1905), and his poetry and literary prose were ignored. During the Soviet period, Radishchev was hailed as a revolutionary, a precursor of the Bolsheviks, and a harbinger of the October Revolution. Such a view greatly distorted the meaning of his legacy. Only lately has his literary oeuvre begun to be seriously reexamined, more so abroad than in Russia.

Enlightenment and Counter-Enlightenment:
A contemporary critique

While blaming the clergy for obscurantism and for "denouncing the intellect," Kantemir provided a positive definition of progressiveness: the application of reason in all spheres including religion and science. The narrative of progress, dovetailing as it did with the Petrine myth, resumed with the start of Catherine II's reign, picking up on the Europe-wide awareness of living in a special age.[60] *Prosveshchenie*, the Russian word for Enlightenment, calqued on the German *Aufklärung*, was not strictly secular in its uses and was applied in ecclesiastical writings to signify spiritual awakening. But in certain circles and discourses it privileged progress based on rational ideas about man, society, and nature rather than dogma.[61] Enlightenment entailed new ways of thinking, the examination of the self and society, new expectations of the state, as well as an implicit belief in an open exchange of ideas across borders, where cultural rivalry and emulation would also play a part. The question of the sustainability of progress had a staying power as a theme through the end of the century when, as Luba Golburt has argued, writers eulogized the end of Catherine's reign by hailing the period as the first epoch of remarkable accomplishments.[62]

In considering the image of Russia and of Peter that would emerge in his history, Voltaire faced the question of Russia's belated modernization. Voltaire defended his thesis that Russia was a paradox because its peoples were ancient, but dwelled in a land where the laws, manners, and arts were a new creation that could only be brought forward by a great man. Mikhail Shcherbatov, an aristocratic writer of utopian novels and an essayist, calculated, perhaps tongue in cheek, that, had it not been for Peter, Russia would have achieved the same degree of civilization, only a hundred years later.[63] European perception generally held that Peter was not genuinely committed to the Europeanization of Russia. The episode of his reign that had most damaged Peter's reputation was the alleged conspiracy of Tsarevich Alexis against his father and the mysterious circumstances of the Tsarevich's death following a secret trial over which Peter presided. Educated public opinion in the Age of Reason revolted at the thought of a father killing his own son for reasons of state. Those hostile to Russia—and it is important to realize that Russia had become a great power-player in European diplomacy, sometime stymying the ambitions of the French—used the episode to cast aspersions on the country as a whole.

In poetry of the period, science (*nauka*) and the sciences (*nauki*) are cited as evidence of progress and practical accomplishment. Just how pragmatism and theory might join forces and contribute to economic development and, in turn, to the refinement of manners, is the subject of Lomonosov's wonderful "Epistle on the Usefulness of Glass" ("Pis'mo o pol'ze stekla," 1752). In 220 heroic hexameter couplets, he treats manifold benefits of the applied sciences as a force for enlightenment and commercial prosperity.[64] Highly accomplished as a work of scientific poetry, the "Epistle on the Usefulness of Glass" describes the stages of glass manufacture, beginning with the mineral properties of lava, a wonder equal to the spectacular eruption of Mt. Etna. From here Lomonosov enumerates the manifold uses of glass in the manufacture of goblets for alcoholic beverages (wine and beer rather than a monastic brew like mead); vials for preserving medicines; fine table ware that drives lucrative trade; mosaics on which decorative "heroic faces" ("geroiskikh bodrost' lits") can be painted with no risk of decay; greenhouses that can be built to defy winter; and mirrors that reflect the image of beauty. He lists many other such uses that combine utility and beauty and facilitate technological advancement, sociability (glass, he opines, is really a lover's best friend), and adornment of private and public spaces. What need is there, asks Lomonosov, to travel colossal distances to mine metals when glass can be produced domestically, bringing a livelihood to local populations and "putting an end to their barbarity" ("varvarstvu konchinu")? Optical devices such as telescopes and spectacles are a further benefit and a joy to a natural philosopher like Lomonosov, because they enable reading and penetrating the mysteries of nature. In a modern age that has cast off pagan beliefs and myths, one can fearlessly "imitate Prometheus" ("I Prometeia tem bezbedno podrazhaem"), train a telescope on stars, other galaxies, and possible worlds, affirm the discoveries of astronomy and physics without reprisal from the Church, and bring modernization to peoples.

Over the course of the eighteenth century, secularization and modernization were sometimes cast as a betrayal of authentic Russianness.[65] We have seen that in the seventeenth century forms of narrative tracked the fate of the nation in terms of Christian piety. Visions, catastrophic stories, and tales of redemption focalize national events through the local and the personal. In the second half of the eighteenth century, we see the Enlightenment critically presented in some quarters as a betrayal of national values. With the achievement of a critical mass of secular literature, writers who wished to take stock of their ruler and their own society measured standards of decorum, reason, and progress, generally understood to be vouchsafed by the term Enlightenment.

While it was broadly assumed in the Age of Reason that science, education, and benevolent social policy would fuel progress (hence the famous Enlightenment optimism), an underlying awareness of the fragility of improvement, abetted at least in part by religious questions about the divine plan, tempered such optimism across national Enlightenment cultures. Progress and decline formed two sides of a single preoccupation in Russia as in Europe. The theme reflected twinned anxieties about slipping away from civilization and about progress and advancement being insufficient or slowed. The enemies of Enlightenment were corruption through luxury and, for some, Westernization itself, since the status of being a dependent, recipient culture had compromised the authentic core of the nation.[66]

Ippolit Bogdanovich poured his hopes into a long poem, *The Happiness of Nations* (*Blazhenstvo narodov*, 1765), originally published separately in 1765 as *Utter Happiness* (*Suguboe blazhenstvo*). Like Derzhavin's "Felitsa," this commentary on progress filters a view of the present through allegory. While Virgil famously sang of the "arms and the man," Bogdanovich sings of the "sacred regulations of government" ("pravitel´stva sviashchennye ustavy"), "power preserving the peace of earthy nations" ("I vlast´, khraniashchuiu pokoi zemnykh plemen") under the ruler susceptible to hearing the "reason" of the poet who draws inspiration from the state of the nation itself. The narrative concerns a quest for utopia, and Bogdanovich seeks to celebrate and protect the ruler's chosen path for the next generation in the figure of Catherine's heir, the poem's dedicatee Paul I. At the outset, confidence in the rational, progressive management of the state enables the poet to "be borne aloft by reason to you, Muses, in the places where eternal spring dwells."

Throughout the poem, images of light and dispelled darkness characterize the field of vision. An avowed empiricist, Bogdanovich claims to trust the evidence of his senses rather than abstract knowledge. Yet the picture he paints is not of an actual Russia, but rather a utopian idyll regulated entirely according to justice, marked by economic equality in which sufficiency rather than wealth dominates, guaranteeing a moderate, rather than exploitative, use of human and natural resources. This corresponds to a European vision of Russia. Thinly populated, newly Westernized, its people uncorrupted, Russia appealed to theorists imbued with ideal progressive schemes, including Giacomo Casanova and Denis Diderot (both of whom visited St. Petersburg: the former briefly in 1765, the latter for five months from the end of 1773 to March 1774). In this world, each is "full of love for his neighbor" ("ispolnen kazhdyi byl ko blizhnemu liubovi"), order is maintained without slavery, and social bonds are secured through mutual need. To this Edenic vision, the poem opposes a dystopian vision of the destructive force of tyranny, in which the "sciences become an instrument of revenge" and man hears neither "reason nor duty," two watchwords for gentry values of the eighteenth century. Where can one find the better of these two states? Is "benevolent power" ("blagotvoriashchaia vlast'"), as Bogdanovich calls it, possible? The question will recur nearly twenty years later in Derzhavin's political allegory, the ode "Felitsa" (1782) in which the speaker wonders where virtue lives and whether it can be achieved at little cost. In *The Happiness of Nations*, as in the later "Felitsa," praise is explicit, and criticism remains oblique. In 1765, two years before the proclamation of Catherine's *Nakaz*, Bogdanovich concluded that "You will long be happy, Russia / For as long as the voice of Catherine lives in the hearts of her people" ("Prebudesh' schastliva tak dolgo ty, Rossiia, / Kak budet zhit' v serdtsakh Ekaterinin glas'"). But the narrative of the poem counters that assertion with an alternative vision. The suggestion is that the best outcomes of Enlightenment are within Catherine's grasp, provided she remains true to fundamental values of rational political economy.[67]

Bogdanovich in *The Happiness of Nations* and Lomonosov in "On the Usefulness of Glass" represent cautiously optimistic voices. Their limited praise seems calculated to encourage Catherine to continue on the road of progress. In her letters to Voltaire, Catherine defended her war against the Ottomans (which led to her annexation of Crimea in 1783), having earlier deflected criticism of the first partition of Poland by Russia, Austria, and Prussia in 1772. She allied herself with Voltaire, famed as an enemy of religious bigotry, by juxtaposing her religious tolerance as a Christian ruler who defends religious freedom against the intolerance of the Ottoman Empire.

Taking a cue from the monarch herself, some writers like Vasily Maikov jumped the gun by proclaiming "a Golden Age in the North." Maikov's 1769 poem written in celebration of the Russian victory at Chocim against the Turks repeats Catherine's own manipulation of public opinion. Similarly, Mikhail Kheraskov adopted the court's position in his long and bombastic narrative poem *The Battle of Chesme* (1771). Elsewhere, comparisons to a Golden Age derive from the belief that improvements at every level, starting with individual happiness, mark the age. Derzhavin's great poem "On Happiness" ("Na schastie," 1789) draws together different strands of Epicurean and neo-Stoic thought to suggest that an orderly society is a precondition for personal satisfaction. Vasily Maikov's "Ode to Those Seeking Wisdom" ("Oda ishchushchim mudrosti," 1778) is another example. Grounded in the deist language of religion that combines reason and Christian morality, Maikov's poem endorses the individual who is spiritually and morally enlightened as a defender of human, progressive values. Stanza after stanza, the poem asserts the belief that a "ray of light" will disperse interchangeable forms of darkness (night, gloom, fog).[68] While Maikov's Masonic belief system suggests the possibility of improvement achieved through spirituality rather than scientific reason, his poem concludes on a vision of the triumph of wisdom based on Enlightenment progress. Like other elite literary figures, such as Novikov, who were Freemasons or Pietists, Maikov found in the movement a compromise between secular ethics, rational religion, and traditional Christianity, which proved acceptable to the Russian authorities. (Catherine's reign would see two repressive phases when Masonic lodges were closed, first in the 1780s and again in the early 1790s before Alexander I shut the lodges permanently in 1822.)

Literary works also pursued a second, more trenchant line of argument that articulated a critique of progress. One definition of progress emphasizes a successful assimilation of European norms, whereas a definition blames decline on excessive Europeanization. Indexing national achievement by external standards has an element of paradox. The 1760s' and 1770s' comic repudiation of French manners targeted excess and vanity. But in the last decade of the eighteenth century emerged a different kind of reaction against France.

Doubts about the extent and sustainability of Europeanization were not necessarily newfound. They originated in Russia with the backlash against Peter's reforms that followed his death, and with a much broader context of a counter-Enlightenment critique across Europe.[69] Even Kantemir contemplated elements of a counter-Enlightenment critique. In his modest lyric "On Wealth" ("O bogatstve," n.d.), Kantemir imitated Roman moralists whose thoughts about decadence and the corruption of wealth were fashionable among the Augustan poets he had met in London. The poem by Vasily Trediakovsky "Ode on the Inconstancy of the World" ("Oda o nepostoianstve mira," written in 1730) identifies change for the worse as evil (*zlo*) inherent in the natural world (flowers fade, bodies age). His concern is to use the language of deism to formulate a belief as a bulwark against the vicissitudes of fortune which are a part of the human condition. In Fonvizin's "An Epistle to My Servants" ("Poslanie k slugam moim," *c*.1762–63), the speaker inquires into the problem of "why this world has been created" ("Na chto sei sozdan svet?") and why he and his servants Shumilov, Vanka, and Petrushka were born into it.[70] Their answers offer little consolation, suggesting that existence is nothing more than a game; they also draw attention to social inequality as a flaw in design, forcing the speaker to reiterate his question as a negative statement: he does not know why the world came into being.

Questions about theodicy in response to the destructiveness of nature and war continually trouble thinkers throughout the period. Voltaire's influential *Poem on the Disaster of Lisbon* found Russian readers and imitators from the late 1750s. It undermined blithe assumptions that mankind "lived in the best of all possible worlds," as Voltaire's Leibnizian Doctor Pangloss opined in *Candide*.

Some found consolation in Masonic theories or in versions of Pietism or, as in the case of Metropolitan Platon Levshin, in traditional religion, without abandoning their faith in cultural progress and civilization. Sumarokov, in his "Dithyramb" (1755), similarly acknowledges the anxiety (*trepet*) that besets the individual spirit, employing the familiar metaphor of the shipwreck as a metaphor for life and fate. But the speaker foretells "future ages" ("Vizhu budushchie veki") in which progress will eventually prevail over decline.[71] In this vision, the settlement of frontiers and further urbanization seen as propitious for the sciences and arts will secure the modernization of a visionary like Peter the Great.

By the late 1760s, a backlash against the adoration of all things French gathered steam, and some literary works lavished sarcasm on forms of superficial Westernization as nothing better than pseudo-progress. Critics aimed their fire at the use of extravagant comic routine, disregard for verisimilitude, and characterization lacking any psychological plausibility. The worst excesses periodically fueled a satirical repudiation of Gallomania, namely, the satirical treatment of a superficial attitude to education as merely a smattering of French and sartorial fashions adopted in some circles. Novikov created comic vignettes in order to illustrate the pitfalls of Gallomania. For the invented persona of the female correspondent to the journal he composed an autobiographical letter published in the February 9, 1770 issue of *The Drone*. The woman looks back on her strict upbringing in the countryside. Skilled at raising chickens and planting crops, she has no notion of fashion or her own beauty until she escapes to St. Petersburg and comes to learn "what fashion is." She owes her new polish to a French lady who offers her her services and promises to turn a village boob into a fashionable *ingénue* in three months. "What gratitude we owe the French: they enlighten us and bestow such favors." The rags-to-riches story of a young *ingénue* became fashionable owing to the widely translated novel *Manon Lescaut* by Prévost (1697–1763). Novikov's correspondent similarly comes to grief in her love life.[72] In another of his satirical journals, *The Painter*, Novikov mocks fashionable people, their minds filled with French fashions, for treating books like "decorative headgear": everyone reads the same silly titles, enriching French authors rather than supporting Russian writers. Much blame is laid at the feet of the French tutor, who persuades his hapless Russian pupils that the ability to fight a duel and speak in passable French are proof of intelligence and who inculcates in them contempt for genuine understanding of practical and theoretical issues. In advocating the enhancement of his native culture, Novikov invokes the patronage of the empress who had endorsed a systematic program of translation as a way to bridge gaps between Russia and European elite cultures and to kick-start emulation for the sake of Russian achievements.[73]

Among the more than forty poems exchanged in the quarrel over Elagin's defence of Sumarokov, the "Epistle of Mr. Elagin to Mr. Sumarokov," and the anonymous "Defense of the Petit-Maître" ("Zashchishchenie petimetra,"1753) are noteworthy because of its implied criticism of both the Europhile and Euroskeptic trends in Russian culture. The sixty-four couplets build an argument that cultural attainment, always a matter of custom and fashion, is impossible to measure.[74] Castigating Ivan Elagin, a supporter of Sumarokov and gifted versifier, for his criticisms of fops ("you boil over spitefully like a fury"), the author counter-attacks by supporting cultural relativism over normativity. Different nations, he says, have different practices that can change in time and there is no a priori reason that Russians "disgusted by the barbarity of the old ways" thanks to "commerce with Europe" should continue to wear caftans and beards. The ironic defense of Europeanization picks on these two symbols of the Petrine revolution in gentry culture. The author's point, however, is that fault lies on both sides because Francophiles unconcerned about the substance of education are just as guilty of confusing manners and mentalities. Reformers, who believe that cultural progress can be viewed merely as a question of style, are vulnerable to a charge of superficiality, because the old ways do not look inherently superior: the foppish and the old-fashioned turn out to be bedfellows in self-deception.

Different sources stoked the abiding fear of decline through corruption. Corruption caused by failure of governance fuels satirical and comic treatments. The conceit of the social climber attracted attention in numerous plays, such Kniazhnin's The Braggart (Khvastun, 1786), which Petr Viazemsky once called the best Russian comedy. Age-old stereotypes found in seventeenth-century tales continued to enjoy currency. Kniazhnin's successful comic opera The Sbiten' Seller (Sbitenshchik, performed 1784) targeted the crafty marketing ploys of merchants just as Nikolev attacked corrupt estate managers in one-act The Bailiff ("Prikazchik," 1778), a theme that would run through nineteenth-century fiction. Comedy presented the traditional concern of moralists about the corruption of material success. A more specific worry in poetic culture was that the desire for riches would rob individuals of the equanimity necessary for individual happiness (a theme that extends from Semen Naryshkin's poems in the 1760s to Derzhavin's Epicurean poems of the 1780s).

In his satire on vice, Novikov's scoffer is concerned with human conduct and its absurdity, articulating reasons to laugh while issuing wake-up calls about vice. There is a direct line from Kapnist's play Chicanery, an incisive satire on the judiciary, to Gogol's Inspector General (Revizor, 1836). These works expose how individuals play the system, evading the rule of law and ignoring the civic virtue endorsed by the likes of Starodum in The Minor. Written between 1791 and 1798, prefaced by a dedication to Grand Duke Paul in the hope of the amelioration of "the morals of stubborn people" ("liudei stroptivykh nravy"), Chicanery concerns a dispute between a lieutenant Priamikov (Mr. Uprightman) and his neighbor Pravolov (Mr. Justice-catcher), a "malicious slanderer" notorious for his bribes and lies. The naive Priamikov expresses faith that the "Law is my support and shield" ("zakon podpora mne i shchit"). Abetted by the corrupt magistrate Krivosudov (Mr. Crooked-judge), Pravolov's machinations bring his opponent to the brink of disaster and the loss of his estate. As in Molière's Tartuffe, it is only at the last minute that justice is served through a royal intervention that sets matters right and punishes the judge and the entire court for their venality. Belief in the just monarch who triumphs over a corrupt system is the only resort against injustice. The play uses the language of law and its subversion, rather than the vocabulary of morality, as its measure of progress, sending the message that, while "laws are sacrosanct," in a country where the "practitioners are rabid apostates" ("ispolniteli—likhie supostaty"), society suffers.[75]

The eighteenth century abounds in moralists who tend toward pessimism. In Europe, the fear of Orientalizing luxury and corruption overshadows the narrative of civilization and Enlightenment. In Russia, the equivalent is an attack on Westernization as corruption of native innocence.[76] Anxiety about slavish dependence and the dangers of fashion as a distraction from true learning (*nauka*) started in the 1760s. In a short essay "On the Greatness of the Spirit of the Russian People" ("O velikosti dukha russkikh liudei," 1773), Novikov declared, "Thank God, not everything of ours has been infected by France," and praised the modest preservation of ancestral Russian ways, arguing that there was no contradiction between pride in a national culture and European Enlightenment.[77]

Novikov was certainly not alone in using lampoon to make a serious point about Westernization as a slippery slope toward the ruin of native virtue. A frequenter of court circles as a friend of Princess Dashkova and Nikita Panin (to whom he composed an important epistolary poem), he dabbled in many literary modes and authored the highly popular comic opera *Rozana and Liubim* (1778) as well as the much-lauded neoclassical tragedy *Sorena and Zamir* (1785). He identified his "Satire on the Corrupted Manners of the Present Age" ("Satira na razvrashchennye nravy nyneshnego veka," 1774, revised 1797) as one of his first serious efforts. Written with a wit worthy of Molière and in the denunciatory mode of Juvenalian satire, brimming with mock emotion ("I blanch, I tremble—what I fear, I do not know" ["Robeiu, trepeshchu,—chego boius', ne znaiu"]) and feigned indignation, the poem satirizes a range of stock figures for their vanity as social climbers. In surveying a "host of people of this corrupted age" ("sonm liudei sego razvratna veka"), the speaker laments the impossibility of finding a single person who "would apply his mind to the purpose for which the creator made him" and "wishes for Enlightenment to do good things" ("Na chto ego tvorets semu sozdan'iu dal? / Kto prosveshcheniia dlia dobrykh del zhelaet"). Instead, wherever the satirist turns, he sees evidence of superficiality taking root in the hearts and minds of his contemporaries, and condemns a society marred by "dissolute luxury" ("v besputnoi roskoshi"). He argues that Parisian vanity has migrated to Moscow where fops now multiply ("in the world of fashion there are a million follies" ["u mira modnogo durachestv million"]), and despairs of popinjays who have forgotten their Russian, squandered fortunes, and mistaken modishness for genuine good manners and taste, religious hypocrisy for sincerity, and chatter for conversation. Beneath the sparkling caricature, the satire observes that such flawed conduct saps reason and common sense, fostering prejudice and the delusion that nonsense is actually "philosophy," that "decoration" is "beauty." Paradoxically, at a moment "when we are becoming enlightened / We are only able to be rude" ("Net, net my prosvetias', / umeem lish' grubit'"). A society full of riffraff is of no use, opines the satirist, who concludes by exhorting reason to act ("Rassudki, deistvuite!").[78]

In the same spirit, yet harder hitting, is Ivan Krylov's satirical journal *The Post of Spirits* (*Pochta dukhov*, 1789–90), which contains the fictional correspondence of the Arab philosopher Malikulmumulk with a group of ghosts who, the poet says, can only survive in the Enlightenment world because they are invisible. The figure of the foreign traveler who provides a critique on a new culture was a time-honored device in the eighteenth century. Following the example of Addison and Montesquieu, Krylov invents observers who visit the "rooms of fops, the offices of grandness, [in order] to unmask the hypocritical and godless." He goes one step further in imagining a set of subterranean gnomes who attack the dissipation and corruption they observe on earth. In this fantasy a set of air spirits muse on morality, the responsibilities of the gentry, and the duties of the good king (it was long thought that the author of these particular letters was Aleksandr Radishchev). As the sylph Dal'novid (Mr. Farsighted) says in a letter to the magician Malikulmumulk, "we now live, thanks to the Enlightenment, in a world in which all forms of stupid sentimentality and prejudice have been left behind." He means the exact opposite, however. Despite their repeated tribute to science as the "light illuminating souls," the letters revel in all forms of gluttony, idleness (with much time spent on card playing and wig powdering), boorishness, and sexual excess that characterize so-called polite society. The conclusion that "a passion for theft is a feature of the locals" is amply borne out in forty-eight lucid, biting set pieces by a moralist whose material is part invention, part documentation.[79]

The underlying message of satire has shifted over the entire period. With Kantemir, the premise was that social change and institutions would reform individuals (rather than the other way around). Fonvizin, despite his personal pessimism, exudes rational optimism in constructing scenarios in which individuals initiate reforms that can lead to a better future. Krylov, however, seems to conclude that human nature remains the same *sub specie aeternitatis*. Here and in other well-crafted pieces like "Thoughts of a Fashionable Philosopher" ("Mysli filosofa po mode," 1792), Krylov excoriates blind optimists who are deluded by their own posturing. These include the uncouth bore fluent in the blithe formulas of politeness, the egotist convinced of his own philanthropy by boasts rather than deeds, and so on. In the tradition of Fonvizin in his *Brigadier*, Krylov takes aim at the French tutor or *petit-maître*, who teaches pupils to do all things fashionable to cut a figure in society.[80] This legacy of foppishness will be lightly mocked in Chapter One of Pushkin's *Evgeny Onegin* (1824).

Nikolai Karamzin's fictional and essayistic writings position him as a reconciler of both optimistic and skeptical trends. His belief in progress rests on a confidence that people can achieve an inner spiritual light through the contemplation of nature and the moral order. "A Note on the Sciences, Cultures, and Enlightenment" ("Nechto o naukakh, iskusstvakh i prosveshchenii," 1793), written as news of the Terror reached Russia, suggests that Karamzin's belief in the permanence of the Enlightenment was shaken. Despite this historical cataclysm, and despite his conflicted hero-worship of Robespierre, Karamzin's essay rejects Rousseau's claims in his *Discourse on the Arts and Sciences* (1750) that civilization has corrupted man in his natural state. Although an admirer of Rousseau's psychology and natural religion, he criticizes Rousseau for failing to discern, as other thinkers such as the Earl of Shaftesbury did, the operation of reason and logic (what Karamzin calls "science") in the original state of Nature. Karamzin affirms the view that far from spoiling man, the arts and sciences represent inherent tendencies felt by ethnic groups and individuals to create distinctive cultures that ward off chaos. To debate Rousseau, he devises a putative "thinking man" confident in the dawn of a new age of reason that will dispel "darkness" through philosophy. His belief in the reason of Nature leads him to conclude that intellectual figures of the caliber of Francis Bacon, John Locke, and Charles Bonnet (all mentioned in the *Letters of a Russian Traveler*) will bring yet further advancement, and that the "light of Prometheus will never expire."[81] In general, the *Letters of a Russian Traveler* pay extensive attention to philosophical systems, including Kantian ethics, and a broad range of institutions such as academies, libraries, and theaters that define a public sphere or civic space largely missing from Russia. This is a message that Karamzin explicitly confirmed in the essay "Pleasant Views, Hopes, and Wishes for the Present Time" ("Priiatnye vidy, nadezhdy i zhelaniia nyneshnego vremeni") that he published in his journal the *Herald of Europe* in 1802.

The most severe cultural critique came from the aristocratic courtier Mikhail Shcherbatov. He was a soldier, an amateur historian (who did important early work on the reign of Peter I), a novelist, a bibliophile with an impressive private library of more than 15,000 volumes, and a lexicographer active in the compilation of the *Dictionary of the Russian Academy*. A self-styled

Cato the Elder, Shcherbatov deplores Catherine's reign as the next chapter in the misguided policies of Peter the Great which led Russia away from her natural path. While this may sound like a proto-version of the nineteenth-century Slavophile cultural philosophy, it relies on, on the one hand, eighteenth-century theories of political economy which suppose that states have a natural form of government and type of culture based on their geography, size, and natural resources, and on Herderian attitudes to the specific character of the individual nation, on the other. Shcherbatov's now obscure literary legacy included the novel *A Journey into the Territory of Ofir of Mr. S., a Swedish Landowner* (*Puteshestvie v zemliu Ofirskuiu g-na S., shvedskogo dvorianina*, 1784), a political utopian fantasy on good kingship; a satire *A Clever Conversation* (*Umnyi razgovor*, written in the 1780s but only published in 1935) that stages a meeting of Catherine II, Grand Duke Paul, Frederick the Great, and the Cossack rebel and Pretender Emel'ian Pugachev; and other works that engage with Fonvizin.

Throughout his life, Shcherbatov took the opportunity to express in print his view on matters of morals and contemporary ethics, starting with his article of 1759 (published in the *Monthly Compositions*) "On the Need and Use of Civic Laws" ("O nadobnosti i pol'ze gradskikh zakonov"), well grounded in contemporary European discourse. Other essays on the reason of the law and aspects of governance use the vocabulary of civilization and polish also to be found in contemporary conduct manuals.[82] However, Shcherbatov is best remembered for a masterpiece of essayistic expression and argumentation that distils aspects of the debate on Russia's cultural direction. His *On the Corruption of Morals in Russia* (*O povrezhdenii nravov v Rossii*, written 1786–89) was too critical of Catherine's reign to be published in Russia; Alexander Herzen published it abroad in 1858. A survey of eighteenth-century Russian history, from the pre-Petrine years to the reign of Catherine II, the essay reviews the state of the nation with deadpan irony, caricature, and aphorisms, and reaches the ineluctable conclusion that Shcherbatov's own decline into old age coincided perfectly with the "ruination of all good morals" in Russia. While proponents of the court and Enlightenment celebrated the rational management of the economy, the growth of trade, the supposedly legal distribution of licenses for mineral wealth, and the applied sciences, Shcherbatov rues a legacy of dissipation (*razvratnost'*), prodigal expenditure, and a vain love of glory that have reached an apogee in the reign of Catherine whose own falseness and licentiousness he excoriates. He provides a contemporary perspective on literary history by attacking the culture of literary flattery enshrined in odes and plays.

Shcherbatov is one of the great portraitists of the age whose sketches of writers and political biographies fall into the tradition of anecdotal writing as a form of history that Pushkin would take to a new level in his essay "On Russian History of the XVIIIth Century" ("O russkoi istorii XVIII veka," 1822) and *Table-Talk* (1836). Like all great moralists and satirists—and he must owe a debt to the tradition of La Bruyère—Shcherbatov is wont to see evidence everywhere for decay, judging power and progress to be forms of corruption. As he surveys the century retrospectively, he pronounces Prokopovich "a man full of ambition," Kantemir "clever and enterprising but poor who sought honor and riches," and finally deems Count Sheremetev, the richest of Russian aristocrats, to be "of extremely mediocre intellect, lazy, ignorant of affairs and, in a word, a man who drag[s] down rather than [bears] his name." Ivan Betskoi, Catherine's advisor on many matters, "is a man of small intellect but sufficiently cunning to deceive her."[83] Shcherbatov's account of moral decline runs contrary to an Enlightenment vision of improvement and progress. His story is one descending arc from the death of Peter the Great in which ancestral Russianness has been undermined by foreign cultural practices.

Like the "Defense of the Petit-Maître," Ivan Elagin's comedy *Jean de Molle, or A Russian Frenchman* (*Zhan de Mole ili Russkii frantsuz*, 1764) is one of many plays that lampoon

Gallomania. Its critique is more subtle than most slapstick because the play identifies foibles and also suggests that adopting the moral high ground is itself a trap. To expose with equal vigor the bigotry and shortcomings of the anti-French is to leave oneself open to the charge that the idea of ancestral virtue is a cultural myth requiring adjustment and even deconstruction, preferably by using a dose of "English salt," known as a laxative and here meaning satirical wit.[84] As an admirer of Fonvizin's theater, in her comedies Catherine the Great displayed a zest for exposing charlatans and dupes, usually the foreign and pretentious. Her play *The Deceiver* treats the international celebrity and conman Cagliostro. Nonetheless, this type of comedy as cultural critique cuts two ways by showing how integral everything European was to the Russian mentality, for good and ill. The theme took on a life of its own and became particularly acute at the turn of the century. In the Lucianic satire "An Incident in the Kingdom of Shades, Or the Fate of the Russian Language" ("Proisshestvie v tsarstve tenei, ili Sud'bina rossiiskogo iazyka," 1805) Semen Bobrov's satirical traveler, a "Gallorussian," mocks the wave of cultural nationalism that broke out during the Napoleonic wars, and lampoons the ardent proponents of a "Russian only" attitude and the traditional slavish admiration of the French.[85] After more than sixty years of cultural immersion via literature, fashion, and architecture, the delusions of a blind rejection of Europe comes in for derision.[86]

Aleksandr Radishchev set out a vision of philosophical history in his poems "The Eighteenth Century" ("Os'mnadtsatoe stoletie," 1802) and "A Historical Song" ("Pesn' istoricheskaia," c.1793, first published 1807). "The Eighteenth Century" opens with a magnificent but almost nihilistic vision of time and history as unquenchable forces that through bloodshed can and do devour the most cherished values that society can secure, such as the happiness, virtue, and freedom. He positions Russia's two great Enlightenment figures, Peter and Catherine, as "two cliffs" ("dve skaly"), amidst this chaos. Like Karamzin, he believes in the renewal of the values of "truth, light, and freedom" ("Istinu, vol'nost' i svet") that will emerge from the revolutionary rubble precisely because the spectacle of Nature, sublime in its force and copiousness, convinces him of a cycle of renewal. Radishchev tends to overload idiom and image with as much conceptual material as possible. His sentences jam together in a ragged style the contradictions that he identifies as structural features of historical progress. He enjoins the reader to look, repeatedly linking the act of vision with enlightenment through experience. He concludes the poem symmetrically with an optimistic vision of the legacy of Peter and Catherine overriding the disruption of revolutionary collapse:

> Выше и выше лети ко солнцу, орел ты Российской,
> Свет ты на землю снеси, молньи смертельны оставь.
> Мир, суд правды, истина, вольность лиются от трона,
> Екатериной, Петром воздвигнут, чтоб счастлив был Росс.
> Петр и ты, Екатерина! дух ваш живет еще с нами.
> Зрите на новый вы век, зрите Россию свою.
> Гений хранитель всегда Александр будь у нас...[87]

> Russian eagle, fly higher and higher toward the sun,
> Bring light to the earth, thwart the deadly lightning.
> Peace, justice, truth, freedom pour forth from the throne
> Erected by Catherine and Peter for the happiness of Russians.
> Peter and you, Catherine! Your spirit still lives with us.
> Gaze on this new age, behold your Russia.
> Alexander, remain with us as a guardian genius...

Over the course of the century, different views would be espoused about cultural autonomy and the risk that Westernization posed to a distinct national profile. In 1814, to mark the opening of the Public Library in St. Petersburg, Nikolai Gnedich delivered a speech entitled "Thoughts on the Causes of Delay in the Success of our Literature" reinforcing the need to extend the tradition of translation into a new age.[88] Although ostensibly provoked by a controversy over the use of hexameter in Russian, his speech has a wider message and flatly contradicts Shcherbatov's conclusions. By refusing to accept a strict binary opposition between Russian and Western, he advocates further integration of Russian literature and Western models. For Gnedich, the job so far is only half done. Writers of his generation, while looking ahead to Romanticism, also looked back with curiosity and avidity to the eighteenth century and showed their awareness of continuity by publishing editions of all the key figures, including Lomonosov, Petrov, Murav'ev, and Fonvizin. Murav'ev's writings, edited by Zhukovsky and Batiushkov, and belatedly published in several volumes in 1820, contained a manuscript note on the opposition between the uncivilized and Enlightenment that cites the flourishing of literature as the best evidence of progress.[89] Murav'ev's essay "The Birth of Letters" ("Rozhdenie pis'men"), much influenced by his readings of Montesquieu and Herder, copiously mentioned in his notebooks, is a potted history of the rise of literature.[90] The essay makes clear that Russia had moved in his view from the category of the uncivilized to the category of the enlightened. No sense of anxiety obtains despite the recognition of the debt writers of his generation owe to European models. Given the critical mass of literature written in Russian that now existed, there was little mileage in differentiating on these grounds. In progressive circles, the precise origins of literary models mattered much less than quality. In 1815, Beseda staunchly defended a retrograde attempt to purge the literary language of foreign terms and recalibrate it on the basis of Russian words. Even later critics who become associated with the Slavophiles did not support cultural exclusivity, and Belinsky, briefly a Slavophile sympathizer, will be among jobbing critics the most ardent advocate of contemporary European fiction in translation.

4

Poetics and subjectivities between classicism and Romanticism

OR most authors at the end of the eighteenth century, identity remained largely a function of social and class status, even when membership in a coterie or circle defined the creative orientation. While the writer would gain independent economic status only gradually in the course of the nineteenth century, over the final decades of the eighteenth the educated elites' ardent participation in culture made literature attractive and respectable as a leisure pursuit. Amateurs who did not consider themselves primarily poets (and who despised the novel) began to devote much time to literature as a regular occupation. Numbering in the low hundreds, educated men and (a few) women turned to literature and most especially poetry as a mode in which to explore feeling, understand the self in relation to others and to society and nature.[1] In addition to ceremonial and national poetry, examined in previous chapters, the eighteenth-century corpus is considerable, and is available today in modern authorial editions, journals, almanacs, and anthologies. Writing for the sake of art and for posterity was no longer the main motivation of writers; instead, they were driven by the impulse to self-expression.[2]

The reorientation of elite culture toward Western models of behavior, introduced by Peter in the 1700s and given intellectual momentum by Catherine the Great from the 1760s, opened up new patterns of feeling and elicited recognition that the passions can act on men and women. This realization marks a great step toward subjectivity in a culture where prescriptions about conduct were more available than analysis of feeling. While ideas about sensibility, as a medical and psychological aspect of human identity, developed haltingly over the course of the Enlightenment, the translation and imitation of English, French, and German literature introduced new behavioral patterns and customs in literature as in life.

Representations of emotion tended to follow the opportunities created by genre. In medieval and early modern literature, feelings sought expression in the symbolic and the typical. By the late seventeenth century, a slow and perceptible attentiveness to sensation begins to take place in Russia. Initially, newfound attention to empiricism does not stem from experimental science or natural philosophy. The instruments of control established by Orthodox autocracy, while not engaged in systematic censorship, remained in place well until the end of the reign of Catherine the Great.[3] One result was that philosophical schools, from Cartesianism to Kantianism, failed to gain a foothold in Russia. In Russia, a dogmatic theology and the duties of service that bound the educated few to the ruler gave religion a tighter intellectual and affective hold than elsewhere. Rather, the cause was the imitation of foreign fiction that made available new codes of behavior and fashions in feeling.

In Russia, the development of new literary genres and the use of emphatic and performative language of sentiment and sensibility applied to family and friendship occurred in parallel and enhanced one another. Much Western literary depiction of feeling, from Richardson to Fielding and from Laclos to Diderot, derives from Cartesianism and Lockean empiricism whose fictional codes are synchronized with theories about the mechanical body and immaterial soul.[4] The scarcity of universities and medical schools, as well as of advanced theological academies in Russia, helped preserve the older notion of the exteriority of the self as it was understood in the early modern age.[5] By the 1780s, although hundreds of foreign titles had been translated, the educational system remained dominated by seminaries and military academies for the elite, which were no bastions of Westernizing thought.[6] In the 1750s, Russians were still little engaged with epistemological questions or metaphysics, and had little exposure to some of the most innovative thinkers who bridged disciplines and influenced literary works, such as Pierre Bayle, Anthony, the 3rd Earl of Shaftesbury, and David Hume. Yet from the 1770s, the practice of sensibility acquired some new grounding in theories of the body and sensation, confirming a general intellectual trend toward practical experimentation in the arts and literature over academic discovery. Emotion became a subject for frequent representation, initially as a reflex of literary imitation. Gradually, an understanding of theories of the physiological and medical basis of sensibility accustomed Russians to writing about feelings in terms of bodily phenomena, such as nervous responses and quickened pulse. The mutual reinforcement of feeling as a form of literary self-expression and curiosity about feeling as sensation governed by organic laws gained the attention of writers such as Aleksandr Radishchev and the diarist Andrei Turgenev (1781–1803), who treated the question of how to control sexual passion in fiction and diary-writing.

Writing a modern self: The discovery of feeling and the diary

The language of human emotions in Russian literature dates to the 1730s and gained momentum in the 1750s, long before the arrival in Russia of theories of emotions rooted in the various models of empirical psychology widely accepted in Europe as the basis for sensationalist philosophy (*chuvstvennost'*), the physiological basis underlying theories of sensibility (*chuvstvitel'nost'*), and, by extension, Sentimentalism. From the end of the Petrine period outbursts of frustration with the resistance to new systems of knowledge accompany representations of the self that hint at awareness, however incomplete, of more complex models of the self. Writers who address the questions "Who am I?" and "What is the self?" were not operating entirely in the dark or without an intuitive sense that the literary representation of what it meant to be human must seek to assimilate new scientific discussions of human psychology and physiology.

Kantemir's *Satires* systematically poked fun at obscurantism and religious prejudice by mocking the enemies of the Copernican Revolution. The Church as Kantemir's bugbear remains in view, but he advocates the benefits of application (*prilezhnost'*) and practical experience which will give "support to reason" ("iskus daet razumu podporu") and help one to understand the "causes of things" ("prichiny del"), a habit of mind that needs to be instilled early. In "The Seventh Satire" Kantemir produces novel arguments in favor of a secular education, citing good husbandry of estates, practicality, and virtue, but also affirming that:

> Главно воспитания в том состоит дело,
> Чтоб сердце, страсти изгнав, младенчее зрело
> В добрых нравах утвердить, чтоб чрез то полезен
> Сын твой был отечеству, меж людьми любезен
> И всегда желателен,—к тому все науки
> Концу и искусства все должны подать руки.[7]

> The main task of education
> Is to purge the young heart of passions
> And instill firm morals, so that your child
> May grow useful to the country, amiable to people,
> And everywhere be welcome—that is the goal
> Toward which all science and art must labor.

In one of the many lengthy notes attached to the poem, Kantemir assigns the satirist the responsibility to teach us to attribute the passions, dangerous as they are, to education and moral upbringing (*vospitanie*). The notion that there is a tension between the heart and the mind, and therefore that there is a world within as complex as the solar system without, remains implicit but is taken up repeatedly by later writers who rarely had access to the systematic philosophical exposition by thinkers like David Hume and Immanuel Kant. (This was not true of Karamzin and Radishchev, who were well-read in philosophy, or Lomonosov, whose library contained many works on the natural sciences and natural philosophy.) Better informed in the 1730s about European pedagogy than his Russian peers, Kantemir appeared much more contemporary in the 1760s. By then, pedagogical journals advocated the same principles, and his *Satires* were republished. In the next generation, a successor to Kantemir's advocacy, Nikolai Popovsky (1725/26–60) defended Newtonianism and treated poetry as a vehicle for rational religion, defending his views in a speech before the Academy in 1753.

The year 1753 saw the Holy Synod block the publication of Popovsky's translation of Alexander Pope's *Essay on Man* (Figures III.06a and III.06b). While a censored version eventually appeared after Ivan Shuvalov intervened, the original translation, with its heterodox views, circulated in at least a few rare manuscript copies.

Popovsky continued to write philosophical poetry. The very title of his "Epistle on the Use of the Sciences and on the Education of the Young" ("Pis'mo o pol'ze nauk i o vospitanii v onykh iunoshestva," 1756) makes him every bit the pupil of Lomonosov for whom utility was an essential principle. Dedicated to Shuvalov, the "Epistle" looks like a restatement of John Locke's views on education. The connection, while limited, is nonetheless significant because Locke's writings, while available in French, were not translated into Russian. But much of this snappy work in 120 couplets is a tribute not only to parents who educate their children properly, but to benefactors and patrons who understand that the development of the intellect forms the basis of the most lasting societal achievements. Reason, hailed by Kantemir in the very first line of "The First Satire" thirty years earlier, is now accepted as the proper check on corrupting appetites, an antidote to the narrow egotism of rulers that leads to warfare and political intrigue, and a scourge of superstition. So intent is the poem on extolling reason as the defining characteristic of the enlightened self that despite the self's presumed Lockean empiricism there is not a single reference to feeling or sensation. Nor is there any acknowledgment of the divine as a defining characteristic of human identity.

Popovsky's skepticism is well beyond the position espoused by Lomonosov, also a champion of reason. In his "Evening Meditation on God's Majesty on the Occasion of the Great Northern Lights" ("Vechernee razmyshlenie o bozhiem velichestve pri sluchae velikogo severnogo siiania," 1743), the speaker contemplates the Northern Lights and, awed by the wondrous sight, is moved to meditate on the nature of divinity. His response uses shorthand to run through all existing scientific theories to explain the phenomenon, essentially reaching a deist position. Ultimately, the touchstone for his belief is the deeply felt conviction that the design of the universe requires a supreme architect. In the poem "I long pondered and long in doubt" ("Ia dolgo razmyshlial i dolgo byl v somnen'e," 1761), Lomonosov restates his belief that "we are created by a divine force" ("Priznal, chto bozheskoi my siloi sozdany"),

FIGURE III.06A–B. Alexander Pope, *Essay on Man* (*Opyt o cheloveke*, trans. Nikolai Popovsky), illustration and opening page of Part III, manuscript copy by Ilya Savinov, c.1779.

FIGURE III.06A–B. (Continued)

but reluctantly hints at his doubt that "there is visibility from on high down onto the earth" ("chto est′ li na zemliu ot vysoty smotren′e"). The admission of the limits of scientific understanding seems to be the only true source of feeling. Lomonosov endorses this dynamic of feeling leading to reason and reason leading back to feeling to the exclusion of sensibility, because overall he views the human being as a mechanism made up of chemical and physical properties to which, it would seem, a divine sense has been superadded. His unique position in Russia at the time as both a scientist and a poet gives him an unusual perspective on defining the self.[8]

It is in the latter part of the eighteenth century that literary, scientific, and social trends come together to acknowledge a connection between personality and bodily sensation that looks modern and well suited to undergird characterization. By the 1770s, writers make poetry their favorite mode of self-exploration. But drama and prose, including memoir-writing, provide opportunities for the discovery of manifold aspects of emotional expressivity. Russia has a longstanding interest in autobiographical genres (memoirs, autobiographies, and diaries) which dates to the late seventeenth century. Most autobiographical works were written by men, such as Peter the Great's diplomats Count Petr Tolstoy (1645–1729; he was the ancestor of both Leo and Aleksei K. Tolstoy), who left a diary of his 1697–99 journey through Europe. Similarly, Prince Boris Kurakin (1676–1727) kept a diary and travel notes as well as writing an autobiography, *The Life of Prince Boris Kurakin, Described by Himself* (*Zhizn' kniazia Borisa Kurakina im samim opisannaia*). Semen Poroshin (1741–69), one of Grand Duke Paul's tutors, compiled a detailed account of the future emperor's childhood years. The most sustained act of autobiography of the period (and perhaps for all of Russian literature) belongs to Andrei Bolotov (1738–1833). A highly prolific chronicler of his daily routine as a landowner, Bolotov engaged in multiple autobiographical accounts, most notably *The Life and Adventures of Andrei Bolotov* (*Zhizn' i prikliucheniia Andreia Bolotova*), in twenty-six parts. Tolstoy's and Kurakin's travelogues are organized as diaries. Kurakin's chronological account of his life from his birth in 1676 to 1709 is organized by year, Poroshin's diary is focused on his charge's behavior and education, while Bolotov's account of his life uses epistolary form. The genre and focus can vary, but the author is always present, and it is his personality that shapes the narrative. The reader cannot help but learn about the author.

Even though men were the authors of the majority of eighteenth- and early nineteenth-century autobiographical accounts, there are quite a few notable exceptions. These include Catherine the Great and Ekaterina Dashkova (1743–1810), who, both writing in French, used the genre of autobiography to represent for posterity their public personas as independent, self-sufficient, and highly accomplished women. At the same time, Catherine and Dashkova could not help but let some information about their private lives seep into their memoirs: some very personal details can be gleaned from both Catherine's *Mémoires* (*Memoirs*, several versions written around 1756–94; first published abroad in 1859 by Herzen) and Dashkova's *Mon histoire* (*My History*, written in French in 1804–05; first published abroad in English translation).[9] We learn about Catherine's failed marital relations with her husband, the future Peter III, and about her lovers; she writes about giving birth to her illegitimate children—all details included for the purpose of shaping her public persona, but still intimate, at times shockingly so. Likewise, we learn about Dashkova's love for her husband (who died early) and about her difficult relations with her son Pavel—again, told with a view to relations at court, but opening some aspects of personal life to the reader.

The Russian historian Evgeny Anisimov has named the group "compassionate women." Other noteworthy members include Avvakum's wife, Anastasia Markovna, followed by Natalia Dolgorukaia and the wives of the Decembrists who follow.[10] Unlike Catherine and Dashkova, Natalia Dolgorukaia (1714–71) not only wrote her *Self-Written Notes* (*Svoeruchnye zapiski*, 1767) in Russian rather than in French, but also fashioned them as an artless account of the highly unfortunate life of a woman whose chief character trait was her devotion to her spouse. The presentation of this unfortunate life, however, is deliberate, and her mode of self-depiction places her in a group of women who followed a behavioral model strikingly different from Catherine's and Dashkova's, yet one that is no less heroic in its own way. Dolgorukaia is one of the very few women to tell her story in her own voice. She protests that her report is nothing but an artless and truthful account of what happened to her after she followed her beloved husband into his Siberian exile. Ivan Dolgoruky (1708–39) was a favorite of Peter II, and when Peter died unexpectedly at age 14, Dolgoruky was found guilty of forging Peter II's will. He was left at the mercy of the young tsar's successor, Empress Anna, who sent him into exile. Like the memoirs of Catherine and Dashkova, Dolgorukaia's memoir, which obscures her husband's misdemeanors, has an ulterior motive in building a particular version of her life story for posterity. Similar to Catherine's memoir, Dolgorukaia's text exists in two versions; the second, shorter one displays a particularly strong influence of hagiography in the way it portrays Natalia and, especially, her husband. In the first version, the emphasis is on Natalia's own sufferings as well as her love and devotion to her husband; in the second, she stresses her husband's Christian qualities, his sufferings, and his role as her religious teacher. In her analysis of the memoir, Anna Maria Summers (who treats the two versions as a single text), suggests that, having failed to rehabilitate her husband and to make him worthy of her everlasting love—he was after all a debaucher and a state criminal—"the best [Natalia] could do, at the end, is to finish her story with one last laudatory description of Ivan Dolgorukii's virtues."[11] Apparently, Dolgorukaia's attempt to use hagiography for this purpose also failed, and this version also remained unfinished.

Dolgorukaia's memoir was published in 1810 by her grandson, Ivan Dolgorukov (1764–1823; the family varied the spelling of their last name; she used both versions). A minor poet, the younger Dolgorukov was also the author of a memoir titled *The Temple of My Heart, or The Dictionary of all Persons with Whom I Had Various Kinds of Relations during My Life* (*Kapishche moego serdtsa, ili slovar' vsekh tekh lits, s koimi ia byl v raznykh otnosheniiakh v techenii moei zhizni*; compiled in 1818 on the basis of memoirs and travelogues that Dolgorukov had produced up to this date). The structure of his memoir is unique: the narrative is organized not by linear chronology, but the cyclic calendar: every day of the year is dedicated to a person the author chooses to commemorate on that day. Some of these persons are luminaries (Catherine the Great, remembered on January 1), others are reasonably well known (like the poet Mikhail Kheraskov, commemorated on January 21); still others are nonentities, significant only to the author of the memoir (January 10 is dedicated to Liubov Elagina, "an entirely insignificant girl, but comely enough to attract a twenty-year-old boy [*mal'chishka*]").[12] Dolgorukov's deliberate refusal to distinguish between famous and obscure people, his insistence that only those should be included who are important to him (curiously, his parents are not included, whereas his wife is) implicitly asserts that only his personal view of society is valid. What Dolgorukov says about those included is defined by his unique interactions with them; he is not trying to be objective or exhaustive: what the reader gets is his perspective of the person.[13]

CASE STUDY Radishchev and the experimental diary

Diary-writing, sometimes half-fictional, half-autobiographical, was a private complement to theatrical display. Aleksandr Radishchev's "Diary of One Week" ("Dnevnik odnoi nedeli"), one of the most notable, enigmatic, and controversial experiments in subjectivity, was a precursor to the full-fledged, psychologically rounded hero. "The Diary" appeared in the posthumous edition of Radishchev's works published in 1806–11 by his sons. Because Radishchev did not date the work, various conjectures have been made about the period of its composition, ranging from 1772 to 1802 without any firm consensus. Interpretations that stress its status as an autobiographical account attempt to connect it with different events in the writer's life, while the question of dating is less critical if we read it as a fictional or quasi-fictional exercise.

"The Diary" is a highly emotional account of the lyrical hero's anguish over his friends' or family members' (he calls them "the friends of my soul") departure from home. Even though their absence is supposed to last but a week, the hero's despair is so profound that he repeatedly thinks about suicide. An occasional glimpse of hope may temporarily alleviate his suffering, but it inevitably ends in even worse despair. When his friends fail to return on time, the hero once again invokes death but then decides to leave his home for a different city in order to force his cruel friends to experience similar pain and desolation ("let them await me"). As the hero prepares to leave, his friends return, to the hero's rapturous joy.

"The Diary of One Week" unfolds surprisingly in eleven rather than seven installments, the first written on the Saturday of his friends' departure and the last on the Tuesday ten days later. The title of each installment is the name of the day on which it is written. The "week" of the title thus refers not to the number of installments but to the initially supposed duration of the friends' absence. This discrepancy emphasizes the hero's distress and allows the reader to track his emotional life in smaller units than a day.

Students of this pseudo-diary tend to treat its subject matter as autobiographical. However, the correlations between Radishchev's description of events and actual circumstances are too slim to substantiate this reading. It is more productive to regard the autobiographical element in "The Diary" as psychological, rather than factual; or, in other words, the emotional turmoil that informs "The Diary" emanates from different circumstances in Radishchev's life than those described in the piece: while the real-life events most likely date to the second half of the 1780s, "The Diary" reflects the writer's emotional state prior to his suicide in September of 1802.[14] "The Diary" therefore was most likely written toward the end of Radishchev's life.

Even more remarkable than the work's equivocal autobiographical quality is the narrative technique that Radishchev devised to convey his intense interest in emotions, and the corresponding philosophical aim of representing man as a highly social creature unable to live in isolation. The diary form allows Radishchev to write in short entries of which none is longer than a page and several are just one paragraph long. This fragmentation creates the sense of disquiet and impatience, reflecting the hero's distress over his friends' absence and uncertain return. Furthermore, the narrative frequently switches from the past tense (used to describe the events of the day) to the present, and the use of the present tense is complex. Sometimes it expresses the narrator's thoughts and feelings at the time of writing—the present tense is thus literally present. For example, in the entry titled "Wednesday," the hero clearly chronicles the thoughts he is having as he writes in his diary: "They call me to dinner—can I dine? With whom? Alone!—no—leave me to feel all the burden of separation—leave me. I want to fast."[15] On other occasions, the narrator uses the historic present, as when he describes his visit to the theater: "Here is the assembly of carriages—the theater; they perform *Beverly*,—let us go in. Let's shed tears over the unfortunate" (first "Monday"). The occasional use of the future tense also further complicates the temporal structure of the work.

The heavy use of ellipses, dashes, exclamation points, and question marks disrupts the flow of the narrative even further, adding to the fragmentation and augmenting the sense of anxiety and uncertainty. The trope of apostrophe followed by an exclamation mark is particularly prominent and seems to be the main technique with which Radishchev experiments in crafting his language of emotion in "The Diary." Such non-verbal representation of emotions on the printed page can also be found in Nikolai Karamzin's prose, especially in his seminal short story "Poor Liza" ("Bednaia Liza"), but in "The Diary" this device is very intensively used. This device also works at the aural level, allowing the reader to hear the hero's voice and thus creates a sense of authenticity and sincerity. Influenced by the widely appreciated model of Laurence Sterne's sentimental traveler, the hero-narrator relies heavily on exclamation and apostrophe throughout the piece, and with his increasing despair they are used emphatically. If in the first installment he addresses his friends as "O my beloved!," toward the end of the "Diary" the apostrophes "cruel ones" relate his utter despair.

The hero also often converses with himself. In the very first paragraph of the work he wonders: "Why, why, didn't I go with them?" The next day, on his way home, he consoles himself: "[Going] home? Again you will be alone, —let [me] be alone, my heart is not empty, and I live more than one life, I live in the soul of my friends, I live a hundred times." It is notable that the narrator addresses himself both as "I" and "you." The second-person address continues to be used throughout "The Diary." The narrator also addresses himself in first person plural: "let's go," "let's go in," "let's shed tears," "Let's speed up [the sun's] progress, let's laugh at its enviousness, let's go to sleep," and so on. "I," "you," and "we" engage in passionate conversations with each other. The narrator's friends occasionally also join in these conversations in his imagination, as in the scene at the cemetery, where the narrator ponders the question of suicide. Remarkably, alongside the narrator ("I, you, and we") and his friends, an abstract entity, "sentiment," occasionally intervenes to play a part. In fact, the hero frequently talks to all kinds of abstractions: sleep, silence, solitude, dream, illusion, equanimity, joy, hope, doubt, and impatience. At the height of his desolation, he conveys a sense of hopelessness through a series of apostrophes: "O sorrow! O separation! Why, why did I part with them? If they have forgotten me, forgotten their friend, —o death! Come, o desirable...." Despite the fact that the hero is alone for the duration of the piece, he constructs his narrative as an ongoing conversation with different interlocutors: his friends, abstract ideas, emotions, and different humane states and conditions as well as himself, presented as "I," "you," and "we." It may be suggested that the narrator, by creating a group of interlocutors, attempts to alleviate his loneliness in order to endure the absence of his beloved friends. Yet the passage invoking death, just cited, demonstrates that this is a futile enterprise. Despite being in constant conversation, the narrator ultimately remains alone and all too aware of the fact that imaginary interlocutors, whether they are animate or inanimate, cannot replace the real friends whose community he craves. The ending of this passage explains why: "If they have forgotten me, forgotten their friend,—o death! come, o desirable,—how can man be alone, be solitary in nature!" The conviction that man can be happy only in society (*obshchezhitie*, or social/communal life) is one that Radishchev formed early in his life and which, perhaps, brought him to write "The Diary of One Week" and, eventually, to commit suicide. After surviving imprisonment, a death sentence, and Siberian exile, he could not—or rather did not want to—withstand the sense of isolation that, according to many scholars, he experienced in Alexander I's St. Petersburg.

Seen as a late work, "The Diary of One Week" is a philosophical validation of his decision to kill himself, rather than merely a description of his emotional distress. Understood as an earlier work, however, it is a sketch toward a theory of sociability and intersubjective relations to which Radishchev remained true until his death. And yet, despite all the references to the events in Radishchev's life and his philosophy, and despite all the passionate emotions that fill "The Diary of One Week," its tone is surprisingly abstract. We finish reading it without gaining any clear idea of who the ostensibly autobiographical narrator is, except for the fact that he, like all men, cannot exist without others. We learn about his philosophy but not about his personality. It is true that the self is elusive in all Sentimentalist writings, which can be explained by Sentimentalism's understanding of emotions as general, common to all persons, rather than individual. The question arises, however: what was Radishchev's purpose in selecting the autobiographical genre to represent not so much his own but generalized emotions? It may be argued that all his writings are to some degree autobiographical, but "The Diary" is the only work that announces its autobiographical status in its title and form. It remains open to debate whether Radishchev recognized the anti-autobiographical tenor of his "Diary."

The work of creating a new vocabulary of sensibility partly took place at the boundaries between natural philosophy and literature. Radishchev was, arguably, the first Russian thinker to provide a comprehensive treatise on the mind–body duality, a key area of enquiry since Descartes. Radishchev's treatise *On Man, Immortality and Mortality* (*O cheloveke, o ego smertnosti i bessmertii*, 1793), written during his journey into Siberian exile, is, like others of his works, a hybrid creation. Steeped in sources on the mind–matter dichotomy from Lucretius to contemporary Vitalist thinkers, Radishchev produced a synthesis of modern thought in essay form combined with fictional tropes (the description of the separation of body and soul uses the horror of Gothic fiction). His four-part, 40,000-word treatise is remarkable by Russian standards for its learning and range of reference. It distills a whole chapter of Russian writing and thought in which the concept of sensibility became central to the representation of literary character and human identity. Only a few writers had tentatively initiated such lines of pursuit. The treatise systematically, if sometimes chaotically, and with an almost desperate comprehensiveness, attempts to articulate positions on sophisticated ideas about the interrelationships between matter and energy, body and soul, vegetable and animal, the physical and the imaginary, the sexual and the mechanical. The treatise uses vignettes and fictional devices in illustrating these ideas. His text addresses some of the most problematic areas of natural philosophical thought, at the boundaries of science, philosophy, and theology, and in so doing stakes out positions on issues of fundamental importance in the period, including the nature of matter. It contains remarkable statements about sexual desire that, especially against the literary backdrop of Sentimentalism, the fashionable literary movement of the day, look transgressive and radical; it features highly prominent passages of political invective that look reckless and certainly are libertarian; it takes positions on religious issues that are certainly heterodox but not necessarily atheistic.

Readers of sentimental fiction of the period in all languages will recognize the symptoms of excitability and sensible pathology. References to nerves and juices abound. Excesses of sensibility were a problem that concerned Karamzin, who is often regarded as the founding father of the Sentimental movement in Russia, a strand in the pre-Romantic literary fabric from the 1770s to the end of the century. Karamzin's short fiction contains two notable examples of plots motivated by erotic and sexual mores. "Poor Liza" tells the story of a young peasant girl who falls in love with Erast (note the "speaking name", suggesting the Greek for "lover"), a member of the gentry (who may not be land- or serf-owner); he seduces and then leaves Liza, who drowns herself. The performance of the narrator is a lesson in Rousseauian natural feeling, demonstrating to Karamzin's reader at virtually every turn how to follow the narrator's empathy and close identification with the emotional lives of the characters, and possibly his valorization of emotional failure.[16] While canonical readings of the story have emphasized, in the words of a famous line from the story, that Karamzin taught his readers that "even peasant women are able to love," love across class lines occurred but could be problematic. It is only at the end of the story when Erast weeps on Liza's grave and tells his story to the narrator that the value systems and sensibilities of hero, formerly a rake, and heroine, now of course a suicide, match.[17] Although readers will have more sympathy for the heroine than Erast did, the question of bodily appetites is also of importance to the philosophical meaning of the work: the physical basis of Liza and Erast's desire intrigues the narrator.

But in his Gothic story "The Isle of Bornholm" ("Ostrov Borngol'm," 1793), Karamzin tackles the question of the limits of natural feeling by using an incest plot. The story deploys fiction to pose questions about the relationship between social norms and uncontrollable bodily desire, a theme that will later run through much of Russian literature, perhaps starting with Alexander Pushkin's *The Captive of the Caucasus* (*Kavkazkii plennik*, 1821), to be taken up from a different philosophical premise by Tolstoy in his mature writing.

Throughout the *Letters of a Russian Traveler*, Karamzin's letter-writer remains a familiar example of Karamzinian sensibility—affectionate, tender, highly responsive; he provides an education on contemporary European thought about the workings of body and spirit. Despite his own erudition in contemporary descriptions of the self from the biological theories of Bonnet to the physiology-based approach of Lavater, Karamzin never sets down his own theory of human subjectivity. Although their behavior is scripted according to sentimental codes of expression, his heroes never follow a single idea of sensibility. A tension between the head and heart, or reason and sensibility, repeatedly grips his invented lyric persona, a dilemma he dramatized outside poetry in the prose piece "The Sensitive One and the Cold One" ("Chuvstvitel'nyi i kholodnyi," 1803) which stages a debate ending in a stand-off between the two positions, an implicit repudiation of the simplistic value of a binary choice. Each in the extreme leads to misery. In the poem "To My Own Self" ("K samomu sebe," 1795) the speaker derides the emotional postures of elegy ("the river of bitter, vain tears") as useless and pathetic. In contrast he celebrates self-possession of a Stoic kind, holding up the Elder Cato as a paradigm of emotional resilience. The poem is a monologue that captures as rarely before in Russian lyric the workings of an inner voice that seeks to understand identity. The key line comes in an injunction to the self: "Buck up / And remember how you used to be / How you imitated the wise in feeling" ("Obodris' / I vspomni, chto byval ty prezhde, / Kak mudrym v chuvstvakh podrazhal"). Karamzin relies on reason to lead him to the right degree of sensibility.

By and large, poets attain a level of competence, proficiency, and often elegance lacking in prose written before the 1790s. Clarity of expression and keen rendering of universal emotions were typical features of the classical style. Sumarokov, more a trend-setter among lyric poets than Trediakovsky and arguably even Lomonosov, struck a key note in "An Insufficiency of Vividness" ("Nedostatok izobrazheniia," 1759): the writer who applies reason, and reason alone, as the fulfillment of rules is merely "coldblooded" ("kholodnuiu imeia krov'") and can never claim a place on the Parnassus because the capacity to awaken feeling in the reader requires feeling as much as reason and taste. Most writers, however, made the combination of virtue, sensibility, and expression, elegantly conveyed in the middle style, a source of satisfaction. Even lesser geniuses than Derzhavin derived pleasure from seeing their poems printed in literary journals, although some writers like L'vov preferred pseudonyms. Poems represent literature as an extension of the sensibility and sociability generally prized in the period as evidence of polish, intelligence, and civilized behavior. Publication confirms the idea that poetry has value. It offers evidence of emotional vitality, provides psychological benefit as a channel for emotions, and also confirms identity through the promise of a legacy that others might read.

Poetry and self-creation

The following discussion considers three thematic clusters of poems about the value of life, love, and death. They give a cross-section of the topics on which lyric poets of the period dwell when they are in modes of self-exploration. Each moment of pondering, sometimes triggered by an existential or aesthetic moment of reckoning, finds the first-person speaker turning inward to take stock of the emotional states. More than prose, versified language seems to be the default idiom in which this kind of self-analysis happens. Fundamental to these more personal and abstract musings is the idea of empathy. Until the end of the century, poets will invoke imagination not as a source of inspiration—they often rely on reason and the rules of art—but as an essential principle of empathy that allows them to establish connections with readers and allows readers to connect with them. Much poetry focuses on learning to live in the here and now, and on the quintessential ability of lyric poetry to distil the meaning of the present moment.

Lyric poets are preoccupied with questions about the value of life and the value of art, and values as in personal choices. A strong Stoic message, equally familiar from Ecclesiastes, about the vanity of human desires, guides poets who prize ephemeral pleasures: sixty years before Pushkin created in *Evgeny Onegin* a narrator able to expatiate on the wisdom of Epicurean pleasures and a *carpe diem* attitude, Sumarokov in "On the Vanity of Man" ("Na suetu cheloveka," 1759) called for poetry that juxtaposed worldly goods such as riches and glory (*pyshnost' i slava*) with the more modest reward of true feeling to which poetry could recall the reader. Overwhelmed by the vanity of human wishes, repelled by the corruption of the city (a Horatian motif), daunted by unhappy love, the speaker of Aleksei Rzhevsky's elegy "Fate Has Decided Everything, There Is No More Hope" ("Rok vse teper' svershil," 1760) swings between extreme states of despair and joy by imagining his fate and then reviving, as pictures of love and happiness produced by his imagination push his emotions to an opposite extreme. In nine couplets of Alexandrines, Rzhevsky's "Portrait" ("Portret," 1763) uses rhetorical antithesis and balance, typical of this French-inspired form, to mock the rat race of life:

> Спешить во всех делах, опять остановляться,
> Всё делать начинав, не сделать ничего,
> Желать; желав, не знать желанья своего.
> Что мило, то узреть всечасно торопиться;
> Не видя, воздыхать; увидевши, крушиться.
> Внимав, что говорят, речей не понимать
> Нескладно говорить, некстати отвечать,
> И много говоря, ни слова не сказать.[18]

> Doing everything in a rush, only to drop it,
> Beginning everything, and finishing nothing,
> Wishing without knowing what to wish for.
> Always hurrying about to see what we're after;
> Pining, when it's not there; despairing, when it's gone.
> Listening to people talk without comprehending,
> Blathering and speaking out of turn,
> Prattling on and on without saying anything at all.

Opposed to the daily routine that dulls feeling, the speaker relishes poetry that causes one "to feel a cruel stirring in the blood" ("volnen'e chuvstvovat' zhestokoe v krovi").[19] The memorable moment becomes a good in itself, and neither Rzhevsky nor Sumarokov aspires to individual fame as the goal of poetry: in a letter to Catherine the Great of February 25, 1770 Sumarokov speaks of his plays as "compositions written with care that promise me fame" ("sochineniia, pisannye trudom i obeshchaiushchie mne slavu").[20] Highly aware that suffering can be life-affirming by its very intensity, in many of his elegies Rzhevsky treats the lyrics as a playbook for feeling in which the poet simultaneously analyzes and acts out propositions about emotional intelligence as reason experiences the imagination. The seal of approval for Sumarokov is the "poetry that generates sad verse for others" ("Elegiia" ["Drugim pechal'nyi stikh rozhdaet stikhotvorstvo"], 1759).[21] This is the same "gift of the imagination" that Mikhail Murav'ev praises in "The Choice of the Poet" ("Izbranie stikhotvortsa," first half of the 1770s). Similarly, Karamzin's "To a Poor Poet" ("K bednomu poetu," 1796) says that while the poet may suffer materially, nonetheless, owing to heightened powers of sympathy and a capacity to visualize states of emotion (the idea of viewing mentally [*mechtatel'no*] recurs), he must revel in "the art of singing, a miraculous gift / To pour fire into golden strings, / And enchant hearts through harmony" ("Isskustvo pet', chudesnyi dar / Vlivat' ogon' v zlatye struny, / Serdtsa garmoniei pleniat'").[22] Karamzin identifies this as the gift (rather than genius) that makes poetry worthwhile for both writer and reader, each of whom benefits from the traffic of sympathy because "we can only be happy in our dreams and wishes" ("V mechtakh, v zhelaniiakh svoikh / My tol'ko schastlivy byvaem"). Similarly, in her lyric "Solitary Hours" Ekaterina Urusova ("Uedinennye chasy," 1796) refers to the "sweet pleasure" ("sladost'") that poetic discourse affords thanks to "feeling, heart, and imagination" ("chuvstvo, serdtse, vobrazhen'e").[23]

On the whole, then, sensation and sensibility increasingly complicate the relation between reason and emotion, and follow the tension between representation (*izobrazhenie*) and imagination (*voobrazhenie*). Poems capture the poet's reasoned arguments with himself in order to counter feeling, while sensation inspires strong powers of visualization that stimulate yet more feeling. Passion is not passion for its own sake, but is needed in order to recognize the meaning of a moment or, sometimes, to admit uncertainty. Such is the force of Derzhavin's belief in reason and his intellectual profile that as he lay dying he marked his final lines on a slate tablet. "The River of Time" ("Reka vremen," 1816) is an elegy written about the impermanence of memory and even the futility of mourning. And while it briskly shuns any false sentiment or consolation, the poem has of course survived (and provided the nucleus of Mandelstam's great "Ode on a Slate" ["Grifel'naia oda"], 1923). Words etched on a slate cannot be preserved any better than, in Derzhavin's view, the "peoples, kingdoms, and kings" ("narody, tsarstva i tsarei") washed away by the river of time, and nothing—not even poetry—will be immune to the "general fate" ("obshchei...sud'by") of destruction.[24]

That position of radical skepticism about art as a means of self-perpetuation is highly original in the Russian context not least because it reverses a pervasive striving for immortality. This position is best articulated by Derzhavin in his poem "My Idol," in which despair at the prospect of time's annihilation engenders doubt that the self can acquire reputation in posterity. The author tells us how, upon unveiling his own bust, he feels no pride or awe, but reasons instead that art in itself cannot immortalize a subject who otherwise has no claim to greatness. He goes on to rehearse at length fame as a reward for moral acts, which heroes such as statesmen, generals, or the ruler, deserve to enjoy. How can the poet ever hope to achieve everlasting fame in this company? His claim to glory combines modesty with genuine pride in arguing that great rulers, such as Catherine II, require commensurate praise. The excellence of the panegyrist depends on the celebrity of the sovereign. But then, once again, Derzhavin recoils as he thinks this idea through only to realize that it lays him open to charges of flattery. He remains caught in a double bind because, he argues, on the one hand, to praise oneself is meaningless unless self-praise accompanies praise of an even greater person; and, on the other hand, to praise the truly great undermines oneself and therefore the quest for posthumous reputation. Should one simply keep quiet instead? asks the poet. He cannot shake the feeling of vanity at the prospect of seeing the bust as an eternal image of himself. Fame, he concludes, is a necessary incentive because it spurs one to aspire to achieve greatness through service to one's country and monarch. But he cannot see how the argument applies to himself as a poet, and enjoins his wife to hide the bust, quipping that "To live in peace with one's conscience is immediate happiness" ("Schast'e nam priamoe / Zhit' s nashei sovest'iu v pokoe").[25] The recognition is one that most other poets might have understood intuitively, and it is a measure of Derzhavin's commitment to poetry, understood as a reasoned check on emotions, that he creates a memorable and famous work that undermines its very purpose and suggests to the reader that to do so is a virtue. The clever twist of the poem is to achieve all the effects of boastfulness and self-assertion moderated by modest refusal. Few, if any, other poets of the day explore the incentives of creativity with as much self-irony and psychological insight as Derzhavin. Virtually all poets, however, speculated on fame as a reward, a shift in sentiment away from patronage and praise to the inherent value of art.

Love and death

Medieval and early modern Russian literature knew marital love either for the sake of producing children or, better still, unconsummated. Both attitudes can be found epitomized in the *Life of St. Alexius, the Man of God* borrowed from Byzantium and very popular in medieval Rus'. No examples of romantic love or positive representations of sex can be found in medieval Russian texts. Sexual love began to appear in chivalric romances assimilated from the West beginning in the sixteenth century, such as *The Tale of Prince Bova*: Bova and the Princess Druzhnevna have a long love affair that ends in marriage. Their relations are openly sexual: even though sex is not described, their sexual encounters are carefully counted. Druzhnevna becomes pregnant with twin sons after sleeping with Bova three times (in some versions of the romance it happens before the marriage, in others, after).

Love and sex enter literature in the late seventeenth and early eighteenth centuries. In *The Tale of Frol Skobeev*, the social climber Frol seduces Annushka, the daughter of a high-ranking official; he manages to marry his well-born lover, gain her father's acceptance, and thus join the eminent and rich family. Bawdy tales continued to thrive throughout the eighteenth century and beyond. For example, Matvei Komarov's *Van'ka Kain, A Tale about the Adventure of the English Lord George* (*Povest' o prikliuchenii angliiskogo milorda Georga*), and *Invisible Man* (*Nevidimka*), from the late 1770s through the October Revolution of 1917 appeared in more than thirty editions.[26]

In highbrow literature, love first began to appear in eighteenth-century poetry. Its two modes are delight and suffering. Suffering from frustration and longing dominates expression as a component of a complex idea of happiness combining pleasure and pain. Libertine poetry dedicated to hedonistic pursuits extends from Trediakovsky well into the Pushkin era.[27] Aleksandr Sumarokov was a particularly active promoter and practitioner of this type of lyric. Several love songs are written in a woman's voice like "Don't be sad, my dear! I am sad myself...My jealous husband won't let me go anywhere" ("Ne grusti, moi svet! Mne grustno i samoi...Muzh revnivyi ne puskaet nikuda," 1770).[28] The love song was that rare literary genre open to the influence of folk poetry; and folk love songs were often composed for female voices. In general, Sumarokov solved the problem of gender type by using female speakers rather often, well ahead of the later Sentimentalist tendency to feminize expressions of sensibility.[29] He seems to be the only eighteenth-century Russian poet experimenting with the female voice and point of view.

The subjects of pastoral elegies and songs of the period—the best of them by Sumarokov, Andrei Rzhevsky, and Ivan Elagin—are experts on the physical symptoms of love and express emotion bodily rather than abstractly: weeping when loving, wooing, and parting. Love is not unremitting misery. Dozens of pastoral idylls written in imitation of *poésie fugitive*—short lyric snapshots of a moment—provide a platform for erotic importuning, pursuit, and conquest. Bogdanovich's *Dushen'ka* and his lyric poetry celebrate a capacity to express emotion. Like numerous other elegists, such as Sumarokov, Bogdanovich fetishizes the bodily symptoms of emotion (tears, sighs, trembling) of lovers and their beloved heroines who still bear artificial neoclassical names. But Bogdanovich moves a step further by identifying sensibility (*chuvstvitel'nost'*) as the definitive quality:

> Климена! научись чувствительною быть.
> Никто не избежал любовной страсти,
> И все подвержены любовна бога власти.[30]

> Clymene! Learn how to be sensitive!
> No one ever escaped the passion of love,
> And all are subject to the love of god above!

We find a typical example of the style in the Rococo "The Nymph's Repose" ("Otdokhnovenie nimfy," 1795) by Mikhail Magnitsky (1778–1844), a civil servant, future member of the group Beseda, and a minor poet lauded by his contemporaries. A short narrative whose pictorial equivalent would be a Rococo picture by Boucher or Charles Dorat, "The Nymph's Repose" has all the trappings of the genre of light lyric: "crimson roses" ("rozy alye"), a little "Cupid" sharpshooter with his arrow aiming through the "trembling leaves" ("trepeshchushchie listki") of the "pink grove," and the beauteous nymph whose "Carmine blood / Plays on the youthful roses of her cheeks" ("Krov', rumianaia igraet / V iunykh rozakh na shchekakh"), whose curls are tender, who sleeps soundly when "nature caresses" ("priroda laskaet"), unaware that dangerous pleasure lurks (a subject treated more concisely by Bogdanovich in his "Dangerous Occurrence" ["Opasnyi sluchai," 1763]).[31]

The body also has its more elemental side. Lomonsov's student, Ivan Barkov, was no less adept at writing pornographic verse than he was at translating Horatian odes. Banned throughout the imperial and Soviet periods, Barkov's libertine poetry takes a near childish delight in applying the rules of versification to smut. His desire to amuse and shock is sure proof of the degree to which the rules of decorum, in poetry as in life, had finally been established.[32] These poems about sexual organs parody elegiac style and celebrate the body and its pleasures over love, and create a space for the reader in which sensation obliterates sensibility. Less bawdy although still enthusiastic about "tenderest flesh" ("nezhneishaia plot',") is Fedor Dmitriev-Mamonov's "Ode to a Beauty" ("Oda krasavitse," 1771). From an erotic celebration, the poem moves to a tribute to Platonic Beauty, reminding us that this gifted aristocrat also translated La Fontaine's *Les Amours de Psyché et de Cupidon*, a famous neo-Platonic allegory about love and beauty. Desire could inspire clever formal contrivance such as Rzhevsky's "Sonnet Containing within Itself Three Thoughts" ("Sonet, zakliuchaiushchii v sebe tri mysli," 1761), a sonnet printed in two columns separated by a gutter. The lines can be read across with the words of each column a half-line (or hemistich); or each column can be read vertically as a separate stanza. Instructions on how to read the hemistiches, first vertically and then horizontally, precedes this poem on happiness, reason, and evil that seems to suggest that the delight of poetry is one medicine for despair, not taken too seriously.[33]

Another pertinent genre was the Anacreontic poem (or the *Anacreontea* in the neuter plural to indicate an entire cycle of songs), produced by virtually every eighteenth-century poet, from Kantemir to Sumarokov to Murav´ev to Nikolai L´vov to Derzhavin.[34] Most Anacreontic odes were translations or transpositions of Anacreontea popular throughout Europe, but some were original. Remarkable among these is a cycle of eight poems by Lomonosov titled "A Conversation with Anacreon" ("Razgovor s Anakreonom," written between 1756 and 1761). Four are translations of poems attributed to Anacreon and the other four are Lomonosov's responses, in which he disagrees with Anacreon's celebration of love, food, and wine, advocating instead celebration of heroic deeds and Mother Russia. However, it is Derzhavin's 1804 collection *Anacreontic Songs* (*Anakreonticheskie pesni*) that is the most substantial Russian contribution to both the genres of the love song and love lyric. Of its nearly one hundred poems (to which the poet later added another thirty-six), a few are transpositions of Anacreontea, some are translations and transpositions of other Greek and Latin poems (including Sappho and Horace) and even the *Song of Songs*, but the majority are original poems on Russian topics. The most innovative features of Derzhavin's "Anacreontics" are poems on Russian folk themes. The best known of these is "The Russian Girls" ("Russkie devushki"), composed as a series of questions addressed to Anacreon and describing dancing peasant girls; the concluding quatrain proclaims their superiority over the Greek girls extolled by Anacreon; and, especially, poems of personal significance, such as "Invoking and Appearance of Plenira" ("Prizyvanie i iavlenie Pleniry," 1794), addressed to Derzhavin's late first wife, Ekaterina Bastidon.

Most lovers only become aware of the strength of their attachment too late. Consequently, they languish, weep, rage, and eventually expire. This is consonant with the hyper-emotiveness of the age of sensibility when a shed tear enjoys uncommon value as a token of genuine feeling. Breaking up might be hard to do, but it is never hard to write about because there is a stable repertory of symptoms, expressions, and postures from the mid-1750s until the 1790s. Dozens of poets in a great number of poems repeat a similar cycle of suffering, weeping, regret, and desolation. As in so much else, Trediakovsky, whose first two elegies date to 1735, was decades ahead of trends made popular by more influential trend-setters such as Sumarokov, the pioneer of the smooth style; the effusive Fedor Kozlovsky, nimble Rzhevsky, earnest Murav´ev, and both Kheraskov and his wife Elizabeth. The elegy as a genre is not yet a poem written in mourning for the dead; instead, poems bearing the title of elegy are almost exclusively about the end of a relationship. The love elegy (*liubovnaia elegiia*) consistently attracted poets from classicism to Romanticism as a form well adapted to conveying extremes of suffering brought on by erotic passion. Eighteenth-century Russian lyric poets had available to them, above all, the example of French *poésie larmoyante* (*tearful poetry*) in which certain clichés shape emotional exhibitionism. For most poets, male speakers predominate and struggle to contain feeling, setting up a tension between Stoic reserve and the need to heave windy sighs for an absent beloved.[35] Love elegies are frequent among the longer poems written in the period, often exceeding one hundred lines. The length of the poem allows for amplification through repetition. This is an important trope, since poems tend to work as variations on a single theme, lavishing eloquence in the form of Alexandrine couplets on an obsession that does not develop because the tearful elegy exhausts the drama of separation and loss. Notwithstanding their prolixity, speakers pretend to fear that because of their anxiety language will fail them and create a vacuum of silence.

Love elegies tend to follow a standard performance. They begin with an acknowledgment of suffering in the present tense, the cause of which is separation from a beloved (who is either unnamed or given a conventional Greek or Russian name taken from pastoral poetry). The opening of Trediakovsky's "First Elegy" ("Elegiia pervaia," 1735) illustrates the point and also the degree to which a broken syntax can capture emotion: "It is impossible, ah!, for my heart not to feel sadness / And so have my eyes not ceased to weep!" ("Ne vozmozhno serdtsu, akh! Ne imet' pechali; / Ochi takozhde eshche plakat' ne prestali").[36] Memories associated with a once happy place flood the forlorn speaker as he recalls former scenes that were, inevitably, pleasant (the word "delights" [*utekhi*] usually sums this up). One recognized feature of the age of sensibility is the gendering of emotions as female: that is, men are expected to emulate the sensitive sex in the physical expression of their feelings and distress.

In keeping with the repetition of standard tropes, the love elegy pays little attention to circumstantial or realistic aspects. In drawing on standard pastoral situations, poems tend to open with dramatic declarations of loneliness, loss, hope, and confessions of love and even lustful attraction. The recurrence of emotional plots created a stable lexicon of feeling and symptoms. Speakers regularly exhort their souls to bear up, applying the language of equanimity and suffering (*terpenie*). Deprivation (*lishenie*) is a constant motif, as poems circle back to the original cause of breakdown. Tears, fevers, cries, gestures, and desperate searching give these monologues their theatrical nature. Apostrophe provides a pathetic intonation as speakers go from desperation to exhaustion until their sorrow regains new force.

The cruelty of the beloved or of fate (or both) are the causes widely blamed for erotic misery, and it is a rare speaker whose memory of happier days can stanch the endless tears. Desperate speakers find solace in imaging a reunion with the beloved and delude themselves by imaging how they will renew their suit and declare their passion. Love is an illness from which one can hope to recover, although it would defeat the purpose of such poetry actually to allow any speaker to get well. Hence the first-person speaker in the "Elegy" (1759) is typical in cataloguing the symptoms of an illness, marked by sighs, floods of tears, and other poems such as "Suffer, Most Sorrowful Spirit!" ("Stradai, priskorbnyi dukh," 1768) characterize the passions as a fever that invades or inflames the blood. Eighteenth-century Russian love elegies share these common elements to such a degree that differentiating between authors seems almost pointless when all strive for effects perfected by Sumarokov, whose supple middle style lent itself readily to an emotional fluidity and pained eloquence that followers could easily copy.

In the 1760s and 1770s, the vocabulary of suffering ("to suffer," "to tear apart," "to be sad" [*stradat'*, *terzat'*, *grustit'*]) and sickness is a standard feature, along with such symptoms as streaming tears, feverish burning (*goret'*), and paralysis (e.g., "mochi net"). Even Bogdanovich, a poet with a light touch whose narrative burlesque poem "Dushen'ka" is a masterpiece of hedonistic literature, attempts this darker mode in "Fear of Love" ("Strakh liubvi"), declaring, "Fever has entered my blood, and passion is renewed" ("Zhar v krov' moiu vstupil, i strast' vozobnovilas' ").[37] "You are suffering from illness," says the poet to his lyric hero in Sumarokov's "Elegy" ("V bolezni strazhdesh' ty," 1760). The poem provides a definition of love as illness that will become standard. Over time heated confessions will taper off into a more muted sadness, accompanied by a weary yearning.

The term "forlorn elegy" (*unylaia elegiia*) has been coined for the love elegy written during the pre-Romantic period through the 1810s, Pushkin's formative years when he and his Lyceum friend Anton Del'vig (1798–1831) particularly excelled at mimicking these tropes. Throughout the period, there is a somatic symptomology of love. In the 1760s, Fedor Kozel'sky and Aleksei Rzhevsky are the most persistent practitioners of amorous devastations. Kozel'sky is the author of an entire book of elegies capturing speakers who are already jilted or on the brink of being dumped. They make abundant and regular use of rhetorical tropes such as apostrophe and exclamation to create emotional intensity. In their formulaic approach to the subject, poems move from desperate outrage to bewilderment and then to disgust. Psychological nuance and individual emotion are not their goal.

When poets use the first person in the present tense they keep the spotlight on speakers who emote, a style of monologue that owes a great deal to neoclassical tragic soliloquy. Lovers invoke fate often at the beginning and end of their speeches. Fatalism opens Rzhevsky's 1760 poem "Fate has decided everything, there is no more hope" ("Rok vse teper' svershil, nadezhdy bol'she net"), a sentiment that permeates the entire book of Kozel'sky's elegies. The mind proves useless as a weapon against passion: Kozel'sky's "Elegy XXI" (1769) declares that "Having darkened reason in me, blind passion / Promised in vain a sweet fate for my soul" ("Rassudok pomrachiv vo mne, slepaia strast' / Votshche dushe moei sulila sladku chast'"). Recognition often gives way to denial as the lover reviews the history of the relationship, largely in terms of his own feelings with little sense of reciprocity since the love object is no more than a pretext for the performance of feeling. Typically anger subsides into guilt: "No matter how often I look on you favorably, / I still feel such harshness in you / That I dare not address myself to you" ("I skol'ko na tebia ia ni gliazhu priiatno, / To chuvstvuiu ia stol' surovosti v tebe, / Chto tebe dat' znat' ne smeiu o sebe").[38] But of course few speakers of this kind show restraint and the remaining lines of this and other poems become an exercise either in protracted renunciation or a guilt trip or both. At the end of Kozel'sky's "Elegy XXI," the speaker relinquishes the addressee but also punishes her by saying that, no matter her decision, his love remains true and that such is his devotion that he wishes her happy with another. As Sumarokov declared in his "Hymn to Venus" ("Gymn Venere," 1755), a poem written in a version of the Sapphic meter, there is no defense against this strong goddess, a conviction that Rzhevsky, most of all, made a common feature of his many elegies in which fate is "most severe" (prestrogaia).[39] Daringly, Sumarokov also authored a poem "Sonet," published in 1755, in the voice of an aborted fetus, a consequence of an illicit love affair.

Intimations of mortality did not even require a conventional landscape. Funeral elegy to a named individual in the last third of the eighteenth century extended the tradition of epitaphion poetry established in the seventeenth century. Such tributes stylistically and emotionally keep pace with the discovery of feeling and the entire culture of sensibility that promoted sociability and private bonds as the proper object of feeling, displays of empathy for friends and family, and also a tendency to make out of death an occasion to pay tribute to a creative talent or genius and identify for posterity qualities the mourner would like to perpetuate. Death occasions equally strong feelings—but to a surprising degree they have far less variety and individuality. This is because the death of a friend or loved one coincides with a fashionable Gothic obsession with memento mori. Elegies can remain very close to the lamented subject. The sentiment is palpable in Vasily Petrov's "The Death of My Son in March 1795" ["Smert' moego syna marta 1795 goda"], a bitterly personal commemoration of a young child. Elegies also channel loss into metaphysical questioning of death that leaves the original subject far behind, as is the case in Derzhavin's monumental "The Waterfall" ("Vodopad," 1791–94). The tension between the generic and the individual is resolved not in favor of greater biographical precision about the subject, but innovative and expansive meditations on mortality, often inflected by Christian belief. In 1763, Sumarokov mourned the death of the actor Fedor Volkov, the star in many of the playwright's tragedies. While couched in standard lachrymose language ("anguish tears me apart, my entire spirit is rocked"), his short elegy "To Mr. Dmitrievsky on the death of F. G. Volkov" ("K g. Dmitrievskomu na smert' F. G. Volkova") anticipates a later tendency in poetry to view death as an irretrievable loss. Some poets may boast of imperishable monuments, others confront the possibility that fame is ephemeral and ponder the need to let others make the claim for posterity rather than to rely on one's own claim. Sumarokov fears that their joint achievement of creating a Racinian theater in Russia will be in vain because their "temple" (khram, meaning their art) has been carried off into nonexistence (nebytie).

CASE STUDY Horatian monument poems from Lomonosov to Brodsky

The absence of a Humanist school or well-developed neo-Latin tradition in Muscovite culture retarded the development of lyric poetry based on the legacy of classical antiquity to which other literary cultures (even in nearby Kiev and Poland) had access. Yet the adaptation of Western cultural models that forms a part of the secular transformation of Russian literature in the eighteenth century found in the Roman poet Horace a figure worthy of emulation. During the heyday of European classicism, whether in seventeenth-century France, with its famous quarrel between the Ancients and Moderns, or among the English Augustan poets, Horace occupied an influential position as a teacher of poetic conventions and good style (as evidenced in his *Art of Poetry*); an important didactic poet in his *Satires* and *Epistles*; and as a writer of odes who was both close to imperial power yet managed, nonetheless, to praise the ruler and still cultivate a posture of independent wisdom.

A series of imitations and adaptations of Horace's famous ode ("Exegi monumentum," Ode III.30), known as the "monument poem," extends from the eighteenth century to the late twentieth century. Conceived as the final lyric in the third book of odes—a book that Horace anticipated would be his last, although he ended up writing a fourth—the poem boasts hyperbolically that the poet's work is a monument more durable than bronze, grander than the pyramids, resilient against natural erosion, and, above all, a pledge of the poet's own immortality despite the finality of his own human life. Its most startling twist comes near the end in which the claim for enduring reputation is made not on the basis of absolute originality but rather owing to his skill in adapting Greek (what he calls "Aeolian song") to the Latin language. The model of originality that Horace affirms is by its very nature imitative and privileges tradition and adaptation, values that speak to enthusiastic imitators in the eighteenth century.

As constituted by more than two dozen poets, some major, some minor, a tradition provides an index of the creative ambitions and meanings of imitation and originality that we encounter at different moments in the history of Russian literature. Ode III.30 made available to all lyric poets a vocabulary in which to evaluate their accomplishment and in which to trumpet their own fame and value. Poets did not have to be professed Horatians in order to latch on to the idea of the monument poem as an opportunity to issue a credo.

The measure of the Horatian poet's contribution, and therefore the basis of his claim to immortality, lies in the poet's capacity to renew a national poetry through imitation of earlier traditions and across linguistic barriers—a capacity that is both individual and shared. Horace lauds the monument, the poet's verbal lifework, which he has erected, for its durability and grandeur. The conceit of hyperbolic self-praise rests on the belief that truly great poets perpetuate and renovate the idioms they inherit from mother traditions, implying that poetry that truly matters to a national tradition is poetry that assimilates the best of alien practice (such as devising new meters for Roman poetry that derive from Greek versification, to give the example cited by Horace). The specific claim poets make in their bid for immortality mixes originality and imitation, the international and national. That balance suited Russian writers well at a time when the emulation of European practices through translation and imitation played an important role in a highly dynamic literary culture.

The three most important Russian imitations were Lomonosov's transposition of 1747, Derzhavin's poem of 1795, and Pushkin's restatement in 1836. These three genuine pioneers created a spectrum of assertions about the value of poetry and aspirations of longevity. Instead of arguing that only the most original poets will stand the test of time, each of the poets found inspiration in the exercise of accumulating voices and rewriting his predecessor.

In keeping with his preference for literal translation, Lomonosov's version in his preferred iambic meter faithfully transfers Latin terms, including place names and deities. While staying close to Horace's order of argument, Lomonosov in his "I erected a sign of immortality to myself" ("Ia znak bessmertiia sebe vozdvignul," 1747) at times departs from the original, omitting Horace's religious language in the middle of the poem, and instead underscoring that the poet's posthumous success will depend on the perpetuation of his language within an empire that is politically secure. Should Rome fall, the poet's immortality will be compromised; conversely the flourishing of the Roman Empire will ensure that his fame (*slava*) will increase. In the middle of the poem Lomonosov replaces Horace's allusion to religious ritual with a more personal declaration: "My fatherland will not keep silent / That my unknown origin was no hindrance" ("Otechestvo moe molchat' ne budet, / Chto mne bezznatnoi rod prepiatstvom ne byl"). Personal fame reciprocally enhances the individual and the nation, since Peter the Great's reforms enabled "new men," and not just the aristocracy, to succeed through talent. Arguably, in 1747, Lomonosov stood at the threshold of greatest success, but by then contemporaries would have recognized his combined scientific and literary gifts as well as his highly pugnacious career-driven personality.

Lomonosov's translation makes keen use of syntax for visual points. He uses interpretative circumlocution at essential moments, reminding us of his interest in the ideas fostered by Port-Royal logicians about the connection between the logical order of words as visual symbols and the way they appear in the mind and syntax. In his rendering, the word "monument" is deconstructed into a "sign of deathlessness" ("znak bessmertiia"); Horace's "series of years" and "flight of time," agents of destruction, has been compressed into a single instrument of destruction called "biting antiquity" ("edka drevnost'"). Like Latin, Russian does not require the first-person pronouns, but Lomonosov underscores the personal investment by using the pronoun several times. There is an inescapable sense of mortality to the declaration "Not in my entirety shall I die" because "death will spare the larger part of me."[40]

In 1795, the still robust fifty-two-year-old Derzhavin, by then the author of dozens of now classic lyrics, must have sensed that his epoch was in transition. Catherine II was in decline. In his titanic strophic ode "The Waterfall" Derzhavin had already commemorated Potemkin, a political colossus of the age, Catherine's former lover and court favorite, who died in 1791 at a moment when events in France seemed to threaten the *ancien régime*. From the 1780s, posterity as a theme, widespread in English Romanticism, had begun to occupy the imagination of Russian poets, a natural consequence of the rapid growth of a productive verse tradition cultivated in elite literary circles. In "My Idol," Derzhavin, with his usual mixture of grandeur and humor, created a poem in which the arts of statuary and poetry stand as rival forms in the perpetuation of the image of the poet. Which is the better vehicle, the marble of the sculptor, the paint of the portraitist, or the language of the poet? In "I erected a monument, miraculous and eternal" ("Ia pamiatnik sebe vozdvig chudesnyi, vechnyi"), Derzhavin shows no ambivalence: the poem as a verbal monument remains an imperishable object. But whereas Lomonosov exercised the restraint of the translator, Derzhavin's poem asserts his greatness with an exuberance that is in keeping with Horace's original boast that to be a memorable poet requires the adaptation of foreign idiom and expression into one's own newly coined poetic language. Unlike

Lomonosov, Derzhavin follows Horace's stanzaic structure, creating out of each quatrain single sentences that combine abstract statements about time verging on the metaphysical, and sharply etched, concrete images: time has "flight" (*polet*), the ruin of time is like a "swift-flowing storm or thunder" ("Ni vikhr' ego, ni grom...bystrotechnyi"). Derzhavin's monument is not merely a "sign of immortality"; it is "miraculous" and "eternal." The second stanza begins with a more emphatic declaration that "I shall not die entirely" ("ves' ia ne umru") and then paradoxically interprets the original by predicting that "after death" ("po smerti") that part of him, namely his poetry, will not only continue to live but actually flourish and grow as it becomes absorbed into the Russian language.

Modesty is not in the nature of this lyric tradition. But it would be crude to speak about it as boasting because the ambition to succeed here by its very definition obliges the poet to compete and pay tribute and to assimilate the words of the dead into the living. Derzhavin uses words like "fame" and "reputation," absent from Lomonosov, to characterize his aspiration far more frankly, and for the neutral "fatherland" he substitutes "the tribe of Slavs." The culminating stroke as he defines the extent of his fame is a list of names of Russian rivers in the third stanza, which cement the connection between language, the national tradition, and the poet—associations that remain true to the spirit of Horace. But where Derzhavin looks beyond Lomonosov and back to the Latin original is in firmly associating his accomplishment with the reign of Catherine, named here as "Felitsa" ("The Happy One"), a figure from the empress's prose that inspired four of Derzhavin's poems in the 1780s. In the early Roman Empire, eloquence and poetic accomplishment were held to reflect the quality of the political regime, a point on which writers from Horace to Tacitus were clear. Derzhavin, perhaps cautious lest he seem to be saying that his own fame would outstrip Catherine's, subordinates himself to her, a gesture that characteristically looks politic but is also ambiguous, open to interpretation about its sincerity. In the final stanza of his imitation Derzhavin achieves a rhetorical magnificence that exceeds the original, using antithesis and cadence and commanding the muse to do his bidding with a regal force.[41]

Pushkin's version, one of the late poems traditionally grouped in the Easter cycle written in 1836 at a time when he faced considerable financial and creative pressure, is typically more contained. For Derzhavin's abundant adjectives he finds single words: the monument is literally "not manufactured" (*nerukotvornyi*), a witty paradox coming from a writer with a quill in hand. As with Derzhavin, and sometimes quoting him directly, Pushkin sees that he will escape the oblivion of mortality and the corruption of death; and like Derzhavin, although much more obliquely, he links his distinction to a symbol of the imperial regime. His "unmade" monument will tower above "Alexander's column" ("Aleksandriiskogo stolpa"), a reference either to the famous column on Senate Square atop of which an angel stands as an effigy of Alexander I; or possibly one of the wonders of antiquity if the adjectival form refers to the colossus of the ancient city of Alexandria.[42] Whereas Derzhavin uses geography to map the extent of his fame, Pushkin identifies groups who will be the bearers of his fame, meaning the separate ethnic groups, such as the Kalmyks and "the people" (*narod*) in the popular sense. He also identifies a category he calls "the fallen," pinning his hopes of immortality on the recognition that he interceded on their behalf in seeking clemency—these, it is understood, first and foremost include the Decembrists. The political clarity of the message in which the poet asserts his authority as a singer of "freedom" (the precise connotation of the Russian *svoboda* as political or metaphysical is open for discussion) sits well with the tone of independent defiance Pushkin assumes in the larger Easter cycle and at a moment when his fortunes depended more and more on the credit and benevolence of the tsar. Pushkin's imitation of Horace ends on a note of bathos, and is more like *Hamlet* in its attack on potential detractors whom he derides as "fools" than it is like the serene Horace. While the poem projects confidence in his national and popular appeal, the concluding lines deflate epic aspiration by assuming that the moral vision of the poet will always put him at odds with the establishment. The poet wishes to separate his own moral distinction as a figure who aroused with his lyre "good feelings," by which he means "clemency for the fallen," from the standing of the government under which he wrote. The stance he adopts puts the imitation in ironic relation to its source since the tradition started with Horace's frank recognition of his debt to the imperial support of his patron, the Emperor Augustus.[43]

Other notable versions from the nineteenth century include an elegant adaptation of 1806 in a single stanza by Vasily Kapnist whose attachment to a Horatian ideal of self-cultivation informs his poetry; a metrically interesting translation by D. I. Khvostov (1757–1835), sometimes the butt of jokes by other poets, who winds up the self-praise to a feverish pitch; a version by Konstantin Batiushkov, already disturbed by mental illness, that openly copies Derzhavin but ends in gibberish; and a beautifully controlled, elegant translation in Alexandrines by A. A. Fet (1820–92) that underscores the sense of religious awe of the original and the hieratic power of the poet.

While a number of early twentieth-century poets, including the learned Valery Briusov (1873–1924), produced versions of Horace's poem, it is not surprising that the tradition dries up. Sublime displays of poetic egotism would have been alien to the official requirements of literary art in the Soviet period, and even poets who wrote "for the drawer," while sometimes, like Bulat Okudzhava (1924–97), echoing Roman themes, did not continue the tradition. The exception is Joseph Brodsky (1940–96) whose 1962 version, "I erected a monument to myself, a different one!" ("Ia pamiatnik vozdvig sebe inoi"), shatters with magnificent disdain all the pieties and subverts the original purpose of the poem. His monument, still to be built or written, is cast as "different" (*inoi*), depending on nobody else and predicated solely on his own individuality as an entity apart ("I am not about to change my profile" ["ia oblik svoi ne stanu izmeniat'"]). No price is worth paying for fame and any attempt to imitate other imitators would be getting carried away by "fatigue" (*ustalost'*) or repetition. Brodsky does not come to revive Horace, but to bury him, and while his poem follows the contours of the original, touching on time and destruction, region and fame, he turns his back on his "shameful century" ("K postydnomu stoletiiu — spinoi"). Yet like Pushkin, except in the extreme, he creates an occasion for defiant statement, and ends the poem with an image that synthesizes both Pushkin's deflationary rhetoric and Derzhavin's association of fame with a bust. If the speaker of this poem is to be remembered at all, it will not be by a "people" (*narod*) stretching from the Caspian to the Urals. Instead, he foretells that his bust will serve as a fountain in a playground, jets of water streaming out of his sightless, empty eyes. As a deconstruction of the tradition, and as a poem that refuses to assume automatically that a poetic canon can be reassembled or resumed after significant disruption, Brodsky's poem is a classic example of his unsentimental capacity through anti-statement to take a tradition to the next step even as he seems to erase it. Although his poem is not likely to be the last word on the subject, it conveys a sense of rupture with the past that had to be faced and dealt with by the writer for whom any declaration of self-perpetuation through poetry would have looked absurd at that moment in the Soviet state—or even suspect.

Broadly speaking, eighteenth-century reflections on mortality widely apply the language of practical or ethical philosophy to be found in the homiletic and didactic literature of the period. Much of it is rooted in neo-Stoic thought about bravery as an ethical virtue in response to suffering, and it shares affinities with Christian thinking on the nature of life, whether specific to Freemasonic or Pietist thought. The fact is that all these beliefs make use of the same vocabulary of fate, reward, justice, and tolerance, whether they are Stoic, or Christian, or even atheist.

Surprisingly few poems deliver a message of Christian consolation, and many convey the experience of death as a type of loss rather than rebirth. Always with an eye for symmetry and Christian belief, Sumarokov in "The Final Hour of Life," ("Poslednii zhizni chas," written in 1773, published in 1774) conceives of life as coming full circle in death, and he finds justice in the fact that "having received from heaven a soul for a mortal body / I return that soul to heaven" ("ot nebes priiav vo tlenno telo dushu, / Ia dushu nebesam obratno otdaiu"). This message of resignation to the inevitable recurs in other poems by elegists like Mikhail Popov, Ermil Kostrov, and many minor poets writing into the early 1800s, including Nikolai Smirnov (1767–1800), the remarkable son of a serf who refused emancipation by the Golitsyn family and who read Young, Ossian, Thomson, and Gessner.[44] Elizaveta Kheraskova's "Hope" ("Nadezhda," 1761) sees all hope for life beyond death as vain illusion, a consolation for the burden of facing up to death, while her husband Mikhail Kheraskov goes one better in his "Sonnet and Epitaph" ("Sonet i epitafiia," 1755) in which the deceased subject speaks from the grave.[45] To the passerby he admits that "I used to be covered by the sky, but now I am covered in earth, / My home was the entire world, but now it is a narrow coffin" ("Ia nebom byl pokryt, a dnes' pokryt zemleiu / Moi dom byl tselyi svet, a nyne tesnyi grob"). The English Gothic, largely through the novels of Ann Radcliffe and Edward Young's poetry, forms one strand running through Russian lyric well before Zhukovsky's translation of Thomas Gray's "Elegy on a Country Churchyard" (1751) earned celebrity.[46] In "Stanzas on Death" ("Stansy na smert'," 1790), Kniazhnin attains a lyric prowess equal to his stateliness as a tragedian, anticipating the rhetorical magnificence and abstractness of the metaphysical poems Evgeny Baratynsky (1800–44) wrote from the 1830s. Here Kniazhnin catalogues in thirty-eight quatrains the ruin and emotional devastation death causes. Seen as an "unavoidable boundary" ("predel neizbezhimyi"), and as a principle that turns existence into non-existence (*nebytie* is a word that Sumarokov also uses), Kniazhnin's vision of death as a leveling agent looks forward to the "daughter of darkness" ("dshcher' t'my") described in Evgenii Baratynsky's 1829 poem "Death" ("Smert'").[47] At several points the poet apostrophizes death, not in order to reason with it, but to acknowledge its power. The message of the poem, replete with vivid iconography of death in action, is a *memento mori* with no reference to an afterlife. Unlike later lyrics that grapple imaginatively with the question to what lies beyond, the poetry of 1750–1800 rarely ponders Christian ends in a way that dogmatic Christian thinkers like Platon Levshin or Masonic writers such as Ivan Novikov and Ivan Lopukhin consider in prose.[48] Poets remain focused on the prospects of grief and bodily disintegration bravely withstood by the lyric speaker and reader.

What Sumarokov mentions in passing Derzhavin elaborates into a great meditation on absence. The pain of loss thwarts the imagination of speakers who find language inadequate to their purpose. The elegy "On the Death of Prince Meshchersky" ("Na smert' kniazia Meshcherskogo," 1779) considers the mourner much more than the dead subject. Death, which the speaker admits he used to think of as a Biblical figure like a grim reaper, now seems all too close and personal. Derzhavin indicates that he is under the power of an impulse that confuses him and that terrifies him with the possibility of extinction. The force of disappearance shapes the opening stanza from which the title figure is absent. Hesitation and *aporia* produce a failure to commemorate an individual and an eloquent attempt to find language for the unknowable. More than an expression of grief over the death of a friend, "On the Death of Prince Meshchersky" dramatizes the poet's realization of his own mortality. This emphasis on the personal turns into a meditation on the universal significance of death in the next three stanzas, where the poet speaks in the first person plural. These lines do not express grief over the death of a friend, but capture and dramatize the poet's realization of his own mortality.

Derzhavin's poems often proceed through accumulation: they sustain an argument by creating verbal structures and associative chains. Yet on this occasion magnificent images convey desperate *horror vacui* in a poem that repeatedly juxtaposes life and death and comes to a complete halt in order to express puzzlement. Nothing prepares the reader for the apostrophe of the fifth stanza with its rhetorical address to Meshchersky.

> Сын роскоши, прохлад и нег,
> Куда, Мещерской! ты сокрылся?
> Оставил ты сей жизни брег,
> К брегам ты мертвых удалился;
> Здесь персть твоя, а духа нет.
> Где ж он?—Он там.—Где там?—Не знаем.
> Мы только плачем и взываем:
> «О, горе нам, рожденным в свет!»[49]

> Son of luxury, pleasure, and delight,
> Where, Meshcherskoi, are you hiding?
> You have left the shore life,
> You have gone off to the shores of the dead;
> Here your mortal coil remains, but your spirit is gone.
> Where is it?—It is there.—Where is there?—We do not know.
> We only weep and cry out:
> "Oh, woe to us, those born into the world!"

What is particularly striking here is the tone of bewilderment: is the series of questions the expression of a bewildered grieving friend? Or of a puzzled child? Or is it to be read as the speculation of a rational thinker accustomed to trusting the material world and puzzled by the disappearance of the quality that gives life and yet is invisible? Philosophical statement overshadows any attempt to create a portrait of his friend Meshchersky, the ostensible subject. Readers of Derzhavin know that all of his subjects, whether Nature as a system or Catherine the Great as an interlocutor, exist in relation to his formidable ego. In the end, he seems to reason that an elegy about a dead person is an occasion to write memorable thoughts that will outlast him. By honoring his friend with a poem deserving renown of its own, he will have created a vehicle for his own and Meshchersky's immortality. Derzhavin's own death in 1816 inspired elegists to pay him tribute in terms that use figures of speech Derzhavin coined: the poem "On the Death of Derzhavin" ("Na konchinu Derzhavina") by Mikhail Milonov (1792–1821), a modest Voronezh landowner, lover of Schiller, and graduate of Moscow University, echoes the poem on Meshchersky by asking where Derzhavin has hidden (he repeats the verb *skryt'sia*), and by reprising the theme of earthly success as a chimera.[50]

Not every elegy is self-elegy. The young Derzhavin began with a generic love lyric addressed to a conventional Plamida (meaning "the fiery one"; 1770, revised 1802) and to Nina (1770; both included in the *Anacreontic Songs* collection). "To the Bride" ("Neveste") was first addressed to the Grand Duke Paul's bride in 1776, revised in 1778, and readdressed by Derzhavin to his own bride, the future Plenira (his endearment for her). Despite the adjustment, this poem remains rather generic: the addressee is compared to a rose and angel; her breasts to lilies, her rosy cheeks to dawn. By contrast, the poem Derzhavin wrote on the occasion of Plenira's death, "On the Death of Katerina Yakovlevna that Happened in the Year of 1794 on July 15" ("Na smert' Kateriny Iakovlevny, 1794 godu iiulia 15 dnia prikliuchivshuiusia"), is one of the most strikingly original in Russian poetic tradition. It may well be the most personal poem in the entire eighteenth century, conveying the raw pain the poet experienced when his wife died. Furthermore, the poem uses a unique meter: it does not rely on the syllabotonic patterns that had become regularized by the end of the eighteenth century (educated friends tried to correct what they thought to be metric irregularities, but Derzhavin rejected their corrections). The rhythm could be interpreted as syllabics, however, with alternating ten- and nine-syllable lines. In this, it resembles the lament, the Russian *zaplachka*, which also tends to be isosyllabic. The strong folk component supports the resemblance: the poem employs negative anaphora, stock epithets in inverted position, refers explicitly to "the dead body" ("telo mertvoe")—which is almost always mentioned in Russian laments—and, most significantly, includes the image of a swallow, which in folk poetry (not only Russian) symbolizes purity, holiness, and femininity, but also is a chthonic creature that disappears in the fall and returns in the spring, thus mediating between the worlds of the living and the dead. The swallow image connects "On the Death" with Derzhavin's earlier poem "Swallow" ("Lastochka," written in 1792 but revised and readdressed to Plenira after she died), in which the lyric hero compares his soul to a swallow: like a swallow, the human soul also dwells in this world only temporarily, but it revives and returns every spring, which gives the lyrical hero hope to see his Plenira again. While less striking metrically than "On the Death," this is one of the earliest poems in a ternary meter with variable omission of stress. It is remarkable that metrical innovations mark the two most personal poems in Derzhavin's oeuvre.

Death as a theme inspires a search for greater expressiveness. Ruins and cemeteries are also part of poetry's Gothic legacy in the 1790s.[51] Among the most unusual evocations of death is Karamzin's "Graveyard" ("Kladbishche," 1792), a free translation from a minor German poet (L. Kozergarten [1758–1818], "Des Grabes Furchtbarkeit und Lieblichkeit"). The poem takes the form of a short dialogue between two disembodied voices belonging to the recently buried. With grim humor, the speakers note their awareness of the world above ground and fear that wanderers in the graveyard will fail to pause and read their epitaphs.[52] Their anxiety that the gravestones will not catch the attention of figures in the landscape and will not be read inverts the normal expectation that the passerby will stop and by reading aloud an epitaph give voice to the subject.[53] In this exchange, death does not obliterate consciousness, and Karamzin's use of a Gothic trope, originally to be found in Young's *Night Thoughts* (1742), creates a moment of dread. On this theme, Semen Bobrov and Magnitsky contribute two short lyrics, respectively "A Walk at Twilight" ("Progulka v sumerki," 1795) and "Night in the Countryside of 1795" ("Noch' v derevne 1795 goda") that typify the creation of the rural retreat as the location of country graveyards and other spots that attract the solitary, melancholic wanderer who contemplates death as the annihilation of life.[54] Zhukovsky's famous translation of Thomas Gray's "Elegy Written in a Country Churchyard" will consolidate this trend, eventually culminating in elegies by Pushkin in the 1830s such as "When I Wander Pensively beyond the City Bounds" ("Kogda za gorodom zadumchiv ia brozhu," 1836) which expresses a sublime disgust for the urban cemetery and envisions eternal merger with nature under the patriarchal protection of an oak.

Modes of landscape

Landscape poems encompass different prospects: pastoral and idyll, scenes of Horatian retreat, and rustic delight. Trediakovsky, Lomonosov, and Sumarokov, the great triumvirate of poets who dominated until the 1770s, do not make uniform contributions to this budding theme. Lomonosov, fixated on atoms or stars, and on nature as a physical system, takes little interest in the sensory world. Sumarokov turned most steadfastly to pastoral and cultivates the elegy as dramatic monologue, a style of emoting also practiced by others like M. I. Popov and Kozel′sky.

Both idylls and eclogues afford some distraction from emotions by attention to leafy groves, rivulets and streams, and banks on which the lover rests. The idyll as a poetic mode also allows some reference to agricultural labor, even if farming is not shown directly; and eclogues following Virgil's model "Ninth Eclogue" focus on inner states in contrast to an outer lushness of circumstances that is taken for granted. Lovers in pastoral poems have Greek names. This erotic *mise-en-scène* in which flora and fauna are mere props serves as the backdrop for Sumarokov's heroines, like Doriza, Clarissa, Kalista, and Melita, who frolic without inhibition, while the languorous male, generally tamer than his counterpart in the erotic elegy, adopts a ruminative pose: "In this grove / I had many pleasant days with her" ("V dubrove sei / Ia mnozhestvo imel priiatnykh s neiu dnei"), says the speaker of "Tormenting thought, cease to trouble me" ("Muchitel′naia mysl′, prestan′ menia terzati," 1755) as the beloved blithely collects a bouquet "like her beauty."[55] That speakers are two-dimensional characters is to be expected in poems where a premium is placed on surface decoration and the theatrical performance of love. No Romantic poet would address nature as does the speaker in the opening line of Sumarokov's idyll "Sing, little birds, freedom" ("Poite, ptichki, vy svobodu," 1756). Seen from a later perspective, poems of this type move a step closer to the pathetic fallacy that will become the norm with the generation of Zhukovsky and Batiushkov in the 1800s and 1810s.

The idea of the countryside as a retreat is an active part of the legacy of the Roman poet Horace to Russian eighteenth-century poets, seen in poetry from Kantemir in the 1720s to Kapnist, who was also an accomplished translator from the Latin. These works occupy their own niche between the numerous examples of the Rococo aesthetic of pastoral poetry and the pre-Romantic vision of the countryside as a *locus amoenus* in which communion with the landscape brings poets inspiration. Trediakovsky established his Horatian credentials in "Verses in Praise of Country" and produced a prose and verse translation of Horace's Epode 2 ("Beatus ille qui procul negotiis"), the famous praise of being "far from the madding crowd." Horatian poems make a virtue of the speaker's cultivation of simple pleasures and restraint over the hedonism and facile Epicureanism to be found in idylls. By putting distance between himself and the hustle and bustle of city life or the court, the speaker creates an opportunity to espouse the values of self-knowledge, friendship, and fundamental virtue to which a simpler life conduces.

Inner tranquility emanates from a set of harmonious relations between the speaker and his environment and circle, and poems regularly peg this sense of satisfaction at a higher price than worldly success. This is the "true blessing" described in Kantemir's "Sixth Satire." Based on a reading of both Horace and Boileau, Kantemir's work assembles in eighty-one couplets an inventory of topoi that endure in the Stoic description of the countryside.[56] He begins by rewriting the opening line of Horace, Epode 2, "Beatus ille qui procul negotiis," extolling figures who can retreat from urban temptations and then cataloguing with the jaundiced eye of the satirist the pursuits of wealth (*bogatstvo*), status (*vysokii chin*), and educational efforts (*trudy*) required to attain success defined by purely external criteria of consumption, display, and boastfulness. In "Stanzas in Praise of Country Life" ("Strofy pokhval′nye poselianskomu zhitiiu," 1752) Trediakovsky also opens by extolling as "Happy the one who lives in the world without cares / As in a golden age and even without enemies" ("Schastliv! v mire bez suet zhivushchii, / Kak v zlatyi vek, da i bez vragov").[57] These terms recur in Semen Naryshkin's version of Horace's epode ("Praise to Pastoral Life" ["Pokhvala pastush′ei zhizni"], 1756) where the poet sees a "tranquil spirit" ("dukh spokoinyi") as the ultimate good.[58] Given the purpose of

Kantemir's *Satires*, it is not surprising that the sixth poem tauntingly identifies with panache irritations that the unphilosophical person cannot slough off. While Kantemir devotes less energy to describing the "path to virtue," he praises self-sufficiency as a virtue over luxury. The merit of subsistence lies in freedom from want and hunger that only increases appetite, precipitating the individual back into the rat race. Subsistence enables Trediakovsky's vision of a life of simple husbandry, spent tying up vines, walking along country valleys, beekeeping, angling, shearing sheep, and harvesting. Any surplus, he suggests, can be shared as charity or spent on hospitality. For most poets, including Kantemir and Trediakovsky, the path to subsistence lay through frugality, praised as a virtue because obliviousness to wealth enhances ethical living. This philosophy is not a recipe for misery, but instead redefines pleasures in terms of things that cannot actually be estimated in terms of cost. Among these perhaps the greatest pleasure is friendship, and a more modest life serves as both a test of who one's friends truly are and as an opportunity to enjoy good company for its own sake.

Kantemir counseled restraint of appetite as a virtue, and poets in the last thirty years of the eighteenth century cultivated the theme.[59] In the Horatian manner, friendship was seen as a supreme pleasure, or as what Kantemir termed the means "to alleviating the burden of boredom together" ("v lishni chasy prognat' skuki bremia"). The theme also appealed to Trediakovsky, who delighted in the thought of a grateful friend. Seventy years later this is also the subject of Derzhavin's "An Invitation to Lunch" ("Priglashenie k obedu," 1795), four ten-line stanzas that begin by conjuring a meal of deceptive opulence, passed off as local produce, but for an addressee benefactor (possibly Count Ivan Ivanovich Shuvalov) willing to visit a humble house (unadorned by carving) and to grace a simple table (no gold or silver and service by the mistress of the house). Although the poem is cast as an invitation, the second stanza lays down the expectation that in return for hospitality the visitor will set aside questions of rank (*chin*) and dignity: the idea of knowing true value ("dostoinstvam ia tsenu znaiu"). Echoes of the Horatian theme of *tempus fugit* sound in the third and fourth stanzas, a universal condition that affects the mood even of a king. It is a measure of Derzhavin's acute use of rhetoric to psychological purpose that he puts the onus of whether to accept the invitation on the reader who in complying with these expectations will understand the moral stance behind the poem: namely, that

> Блаженство не в лучах порфир,
> Не в вкусе яств, не в неге слуха;
> Но в здравья и спокойстве духа,—
> Умеренность есть лучший пир.[60]

> Bliss is not in the shine of porphyry,
> Not in the taste of sweets, not in the pleasure of listening,
> But in health and calm spirit:
> The best feast is moderation.

Horace positively enthralls Kapnist, the most ardent of Horatian imitators, whose "Ode on Friendship" ("Oda na druzhestvo," 1796, revised 1806) creates a synthesis of the Russian (or Ukrainian) countryside and Roman names as the perfect venue for "forgetting calamties" ("bedstva zabyvaet"). The cult of friendship that Kapnist professes anticipates Pushkin's similar elevation of friendship to the status of a protective like-minded community—both poets refer to it as a "holy union" (*soiuz sviashchennyi*) only possible at a distance from a world "spoiled by malice," "the evil of cunning," and "odious self-interest" (*postylaia koryst'*).[61]

In his 1833 fragment "It is time, my friend, it is time!" ("Pora, moi drug, pora!"), Pushkin focuses tenderly and wistfully on the role of the friend (who is here his wife) as a companion on the road to a better world. Biographical readings of this work will argue that it reflects his wish to move to Mikhailovskoe after attempting, in 1834, to resign from his position as titular councilor at the Foreign College. Nicholas I responded by barring Pushkin from the imperial archives, which made Pushkin relent and ask for Zhukovsky's help in returning to service. Yet Pushkin uses the Horatian tradition to deflect any personal information and universalize the need to retreat. With brilliant concision, Pushkin reduces the usual sequence by omitting any description of cares, and dwells instead on the present anguish, the impossibility of happiness, and the need to take refuge in search of some perhaps transient illusion of freedom and relief. But the place of refuge is not a concrete countryside, whether described or implied, but some "distant dwelling of work and pure pleasures."

While poets spar elsewhere over diction and aspects of form, landscape does not serve as a battleground for competing visions of nature. These modes coexist and develop side by side. Serfdom and the reality of agrarian life generally do not break into rustic visions. A poetic critique of political economy, like Kapnist's "Ode on Slavery," is unusual, and only thirty years later will it find an equivalent Romantic response in Pushkin's depiction of a countryside ("The Countryside" ["Derevnia"], 1819) in which the human cost is so great that the only way to treat serfdom is by making it an absence whose humanity the reader can only ponder.[62] Poems about rusticity take an interest in the affective bonds forged between the lyric subject and a familiar scene and, in the case of Derzhavin, celebrate the countryside as its own economic and preindustrial world.

No poem better embodies the indolent vision of the bucolic than Derzhavin's "To Evgenii: Life at Zvanska" ("Evgeniiu. Zhizn′ Zvanskaia," 1807). The third and final poem on the theme alongside "Country Life" ("Derevenskaia zhizn′," 1802) and "Praise of Country Life" ("Pokhvala sel′skoi zhizni," 1798), this long and intricately worded evocation of the countryside divides the self into urban and rural, landowner or worker, and appreciated practical intelligence as well as theoretical knowledge. This is not the *locus amoenus* of the Romantic elegy, infused with psychological attachment; nor is it a pastoral world, since labor and technology abound, such as optical devices, a dam, a loom, and other English machines. In describing a single day, the poem creates an ideal ecosystem out of the working country estate that offers its own cosmos as man produces, consumes, works, relaxes, worships, ails, and recovers.

Derzhavin is among the most pictorial of poets, and country life fills the quatrains with visions seen up close through a telescope, a sign of luxury, trained on the picturesque prospect, and on the stars.[63] At court, Derzhavin's poet figure accepts luxury as his due without questioning its origins. Yet in the countryside he seems to find even greater riches. This vision of the countryside is characterized by an abundance rather than austerity, an embarrassment of riches rather than Stoic virtue, vibrant communities rather than solitary meditation, and, above all, activity. Derzhavin wrote the epistle to his friend, the distinguished clergyman Evgeny Bolkhovitinov (1767–1837), after Alexander I had forced the poet to retire. Derzhavin makes a virtue of necessity and takes pleasure in describing the countryside in terms of rural economy. Horticulture and rural manufacture exist side by side, as do artisans and shepherds, and the countryside itself is variegated thanks to lakes and hills and man-made monuments, and painterly evocations of historical figures. Late in the poem, having established the range and vigor of his activities, the retired statesman cannot resist an ironic comment:

> О славных подвигах великих тех мужей,
> Чьи в рамах по стенам златых блистают лицы,
> Для вспоминанья их деяний, славных дней,
> И для прикрас моей светлицы,

В которой поутру иль ввечеру порой
Дивлюся в Вестнике, в газетах иль журналах
Россиян храбрости, как всяк из них герой,
Где есть Суворов в генералах![64]

About the glorious exploits of those great men,
Whose faces shine in gold frames on the walls,
For the memory of their deeds, their glorious days
And the decoration of my salon,

In which morning and evening I am surprised
From time to time reading the *Herald*, newspapers, and magazines,
At the bravery of Russians, how each is a hero,
A veritable Suvorov among generals!

For all its command of agricultural techniques and the arts of husbandry, Derzhavin's poem is of course an idealization that shifts toward the world of things and away from the world of the mind. In its own context, Derzhavin's poem looks exceptional rather than a trendsetter for a new direction of lyric poetry. Viewed over a longer period of time it looks intergenerational, serving as a reminder that connections between the 1830s and the late eighteenth century were selectively productive. Here the link is with Pushkin's great poem "Autumn" ("Osen'," 1833), which looks back to Derzhavin's work for its epigraph. "What does not enter my slumbering mind?" ("Chego v moi dremliushchii togda ne vkhodit um?"), an anthem of sleep, that great Romantic theme, gives Pushkin his pretext to treat the world of Nature with the same lavish care as Derzhavin details his world of material objects and practical activity.

In the slipstream of Sentimentalism, other poets such as Mikhail Murav'ev, Anna Bunina, Pavel Golenishchev-Kutuzov (1767–1829), M. V. Milonov, and slightly later, the members of the Society of Lovers of Russian Letters at Moscow University, created landscape spaces that accommodate a shifting range of tone, better attuned to fluid states of mind, more deliberative, and seemingly less artificial. In contrast with Derzhavin's buzzing Zvanka, poems about winter such as Neledinsky-Meletsky's "The Gloomy Days of Winter Disappear…" ("Zimy dni mrachny ischezaiut…," 1796), Murav'ev's "Winter Wish" ("Zhelanie zimy," 1776), and Anna Zhukova's (died around 1799) "Winter Visions" ("Zimnie iavleniia," published 1799) ponder the stasis that sets in and wonder how to react. Like small Dutch-Flemish canvases, poems serve as snapshots of winter landscapes especially for Murav'ev who finds things to do "during the days of Boreas" and hopes that "love does not retreat into seclusion."[65] Zhukova laments that as nature fades (the "sweet rose" ["milaia roza"] has died off) and "her blood freezes" ("krov' stynet"), the only recourse is to sleep and occasionally imagine the coming of spring.[66] Pushkin takes a much more active approach to winter scenes. He will provide a wondrous winterscape on which to open Chapter 5 of *Evgeny Onegin*, two stanzas that are a medley of voices of earlier treatments of the season.[67] His truly memorable treatment comes in "Winter. What are we to do in the countryside?" ("Zima. Chto delat' nam v derevne?," 1829). Over the course of the soliloquy the speaker finds that his blood is still warm and that love has not retreated into seclusion: the poetic and erotic imagination never hibernates. Here we discover an introspective Pushkin finding value through the possibility of love, and that erotic charge in turn generates a sense of being alive that motivates the writing of the poem. A landscape that looked barren, a moment that looked empty, a life that looked flat have now all come to life in a lyric.

5

Prose Fiction

Entertainment literature, or the problem of the novel

The subjectivity and self-fashioning present in eighteenth-century poetry are absent from the Russian novel of the period. The eighteenth-century, and largely post-1770s, novel assumed a variety of forms: the first-person novel, the epistolary novel, the didactic novel, and the adventure novel. These forms appeared in parallel but in unequal numbers: the last two greatly outnumber first-person narratives. We have seen that prose forms, such as memoir, autobiography, and letter writing, began to emerge, and some important short fictions appreciative of subjectivity appeared in the last decade of the century.[1] None of the listed types of eighteenth-century novels can compete with the rich psychological and descriptive traditions the field of poetry had accumulated over the same period. Introspection, a prominent feature of French fiction at that time and later a hallmark of nineteenth-century Russian fiction, is absent even in adventure and pedagogical novels, two of the more successful novelistic forms practiced in Russia.[2] Hardly any Russian writer—Mikhail Chulkov's achievement in *The Comely Cook* has been much debated—used the form of the novel to capture the type of personal experience and inner life we find in diary-writing of the period. Nor did their works create a sense of interior domestic space that can be found in certain episodes of Karamzin's *Letters of a Russian Traveler*, which takes a particular interest in the middle-class family ideology of the English, whose novelistic tradition Karamzin admired.

Karamzin the critic provides us with a contemporary view of the educated reader frustrated by the peculiarly antiquated trends in Russian fiction and stymied by a puzzling absence of interest among the educated in the newer literary forms. As an advocate of quality literature, in 1792, he would have seen his efforts as a reviewer and author vindicated, but at the same time he would have felt dissatisfied with the kind of fiction Russians were writing and reading—if at all. There was an asymmetry between the openness to the European novel in translation, whether publisher-driven or led by readers, and the Russian preference for adventure tales and episodic plots—works that might essentially be regarded as throwbacks to seventeenth-century popular fiction—that continued among a lower-class readership. Karamzin's article "From the Publisher to Readers" ("Ot izdatelia k chitateliam," 1791) speaks of his wish to cultivate a taste for contemporary prose, such as *Tom Jones*, over older forms of storytelling.[3] Ever hopeful, but also nearing the end of his literary career, Karamzin wrote another article on the state of fiction. He notes in "On the Book Trade on the Love of Reading in Russia" ("O knizhnoi torgovle i liubvi ko chteniiu v Rossii," 1802) that novels had begun to sell, pegging his hopes for the novel on a new generation of readers who might stimulate the demand for Russian novels that would match French and English fiction in translation on which a small number of well-educated readers depended.[4] In his memoir *A Look at My Life*

(*Vzgliad na moiu zhizn'*, published 1893), the lyric poet Ivan Dmitriev recalled having once seen Karamzin admiringly holding up a two-volume edition of Fielding's *Tom Jones* in Russian translation by E. S. Kharlamov (1770–71). The original novel, however, went unnoticed, unsold, and unread, one small indication that, overall, the love of reading in Russia, hailed in Karamzin's pronouncement, did not extend to openness to the novel as a form grounded in the representation of social reality, a feature of both English and French novels of the eighteenth century. Nor were the audiences ready for the novel's capacity to narrate and create plot from a conflict between characters and their environment (one great achievement of Richardson's *Clarissa*).

The twist in all this is that the novel was not totally ignored as a genre. Before 1763, Russia produced no original novels and few translations. From the 1760s, the translation industry set in motion by Catherine and Novikov translated European texts at an impressive pace. While readers bought up the grammars, histories, and law books that were reprinted by the hundreds but rarely a thousand, the market for literary texts was smaller and confined to an urban elite that expanded substantially only after the 1820s. However, publishers and translators saw some commercial opportunity in the translation of dozens of novels from French, English, and German. In the period from 1763 to 1775, the Russian presses produced 123 novels in translation. The production of entertainment literature increased after the Free Press Edict dissolved the government monopoly on printing. Out of a total of 893 novels published between 1730 and 1800, more than 120 were published between 1792 and 1794.[5] Of this last set of novels, only twelve were original and written in Russian, a fraction so small that, in itself, it testifies to a lack of interest. Their print runs of around 600 copies were higher than average, although few sales figures are available to confirm a correlation between production and demand. Even the sporadic evidence of sales suggests that, as a rule, publishers failed to move their stock. Print runs, even for favorites like *Van'ka-Kain* (1779), a much-appreciated tale of a rogue by Matvei Komarov (1730–1812)—a work that inspired the Formalist critic and experimental writer Viktor Shklovsky to write an imitation—numbered in the low hundreds. Multiple reprints (*Van'ka Kain* went through seven) suggest continued demand for this potboiler, which corroborates the notion that, when priced affordably, entertainment literature will find purchasers.

A book market that is only semi-professionalized can neither promote quality translations of new works of European fiction, nor encourage original composition equal to the poetic production fostered among amateur coteries. Translations were commonly hack-work, poorly remunerated, and novels were often cheaply printed. There was little financial reward for novelists in a system where copyright had not been established and where royalty payments from the new private presses were precarious. Writers of prose for the masses achieved a precarious professional status by providing entertainment literature and catering to the less educated who comprised a lion's share of prose readership.

We can surmise that no novelistic tradition was sanctioned by the literary establishment partly because of the economic circumstances. The attitude of the reading public must also have been a factor. The latter remains harder to define because readers of fiction were also readers of popular fiction, and were generally less educated and therefore not inclined to record their reading habits as criticism or even privately in diaries. A bias against fiction, widely attested in Europe, was one obstacle, at least in the early 1760s, and may have deterred educated readers. Book reviews, the standard form of literary criticism published in journals, took a position against the novel. Among the educated classes, prose was considered to be pedestrian until the 1790s. Tragedy and epic enjoyed the most prestige as elite genres, while the novel elicited censure from the likes of Dr. Johnson in England or Sumarokov in Russia. Criticism of the novel as a morally suspect genre, in particular, was commonplace, especially in countries like England and France where fiction in general was successful. The absence of new critical benchmarks for prose stands in contrast to the heated debates concerning poetic style.

Yet throughout Europe, and in Russia as well, anxiety about the novel as a low genre whose plots encouraged moral turpitude did nothing to stymie the growth of fiction as a form of entertainment.[6] In his article "On the Reading of Novels," Sumarokov rehearsed familiar critical shibboleths. In his poetic treatises written in imitation of Boileau, Sumarokov had laid down rules governing poetic style, but as the author of popular songs and elegant elegies he had no time for "novels that weigh[ed] a ton, but [did] not have a pound worth of essence." "On the Reading of Novels" condoned only those novels that served a moral purpose, otherwise vilifying the genre because it instilled in "readers an affected and deformed outlook on life and [led] them away from what [was] natural." Yet Sumarokov's strictures may have deployed arguments about taste only to veil his chagrin, because material reward was skewed in favor of popular entertainment. As a playwright, he was frustrated by his small share of the box office takings. It may be that he could not contain his envy at the perceived commercial success enjoyed by another genre: despite "their lack of utility," "novels have multiplied so much in number that one could fill half a library the size of the world." And his disapproval of the artistic form of fiction led to the moral condemnation of a genre he viewed as "written by idiots" and as a "fatal waste of time" that "teaches readers false and base character."[7]

The predominant strand of eighteenth-century Russian fiction gravitated away from Western-style narrative to modes of storytelling rooted in an older tradition that persisted into the 1790s. A taste for old-fashioned morality and adventure tales fed into the newly expanded modes of the utopian, philosophical, and even political novel. Readers of Part II of this book will be familiar with the tradition of narrative fiction that flourished before and immediately after the Petrine period. Full of folkloric plots and popular wisdom, these fictions were popular and counter-cultural in orientation. They hark back to the seventeenth-century narrative tale and prolong the enormously popular tradition of the woodcut and the block-book (*lubok*)—a medium that might be thought of as the seventeenth-century Russian equivalent of an illustrated paperback—well into the late eighteenth century. Stories of oral and popular provenance, sometimes passed down anonymously in written form, sometimes originated in book form, generate new works in the eighteenth century. We see, therefore, a certain amount of continuity with the past, while there will be a more pronounced discontinuity between eighteenth-century Russian fiction and the nineteenth-century novel.

Russian versions of utopian, philosophical, and political novels looked contemporary and idiomatic as types of neoclassical fiction. These highbrow fictions were not a mainstay of readerships, however. Even more popular and productive well into the 1790s were adventure tales expanded into novelistic form. Eighteenth-century Russian fiction gravitated away from Western-style narrative and back to that older tradition of storytelling rather than ahead to the nineteenth-century novel. There was, it seems, an inherited taste for the remarkable, fantastic, and episodic narrative dressed up as romance, and variably known as *povest'*, *gistoriia*, *skazanie*, or, less frequently, *roman*. Mistakenly called the first Russian novel, while it might more plausibly be called a revival of the romance, Trediakovsky's *The Journey to the Isle of Love* was one of the first fictions composed in Russia with a view toward entertaining a secular, albeit rather small, elite audience. Trediakovsky's aspiration may have been first and foremost to introduce a new language of love and polite decorum to the post-Petrine society still unsure of its manners. Erotic fictions treating the passions as a form of upper-class game were an innovation in Russian literature. But the form of this novel, its plot, and the language of the French salon (*preciosité*), were a throwback to a mode of novel-writing that in France already looked quite old-fashioned.

Popular fiction continued to perpetuate the moralistic satire and burlesque humor found in seventeenth-century tales and appeared in lowbrow genres like calendar literature (*kalendar-naia literatura*). For example, in reworking the *Tale of Frol Skobeev* as *All Hallows' Eve of the Maidens of Novgorod* (*Novgorodskikh devushek sviatochnyi vecher*, 1725), Ivan Novikov (*fl.* 1780s) accentuated its original Yuletide elements, possibly catering to a taste for tales about the privileged who get their comeuppance. Nikolai Kurganov's *Pis'movnik* (1769), a ragbag of grammar tables, poetry, and versification rules, offered the readers of its ten reprints erotic tales of illicit love and models of behavior similar to the social climbing antics of Martona in Chulkov's *The Comely Cook*.

Ivan Novikov's *Adventures of Ivan, the Merchant's Son* (*Pokhozhdenie Ivana gostinnogo syna*, 1785), charts the descent of a respectable youth into the world of a thieving Muscovite underclass by way of warning parents of the material temptations of urban life and the dangers of luxury. After an elaborate series of adventures, containing multiple embedded narratives by a fleeting cast of characters, the merchant's son has a dream. It reveals the path of Truth leading to the Temple of Virtue. Similar to the seventeenth-century *Tale of Misery-Misfortune*, whose protagonist sought piety in a monastery and was thwarted by the devil wherever he turned, the anonymous novel *Unfortunate Nikanor, or the Adventure of the Life of a Russian Nobleman N******** (*Neschastnyi Nikanor, ili prikliuchenie zhizni rossiiskogo dvorianina N********, 1775, 1787–89) provided lessons on the inconstancy of fortune and the precariousness of social mobility.

In the ever-popular adventure novel, Russian fiction widened its geographic range to embrace Europe, often bypassing the home landscape. Adventure novels written in Russian can seem hardly Russian at all. Locations are often foreign or historical, characters have invented names, and, as fantasy fictions, narratives neglect social and political circumstance.[8] It is open to conjecture whether the purpose of these fictitious foreign itineraries was to generate an image to which the Russian readership were meant to aspire; more likely, the writers latched onto a formula that proved viable and marketable within a tradition where conventions of folklore lingered. Komarov's *The Story of the Adventure of the English Milord George and the Marquess of Brandenburg Frederica Louise* (*Povest' o prikliuchenii angliiskogo milorda Georga i brandenburgskoi markgrafini Frederiki Luizy*, 1782) was reported to have sold very well and been a popular success. This novel is more adroit than many an episodic narrative at integrating the frame-story and secondary plots spun around the amorous adventures of George, who travels around Europe in search of pleasure. Yet for all the pace of its plotting, the book's artificial air of make-believe is typical of a work of romance that makes no gestures toward observed reality.

Most successful of the frame-story novels was Fedor Emin's *Inconstant Fortune, or the Adventure of Miramond* (*Nepostoiannaia Fortuna, ili pokhozhdenie Miramonda*, 1763). From robbery to shipwreck, from military service in Egypt to marriage and baptism in Turkey—improbably meant to remind the reader of Emin's own strange biography—the episodic plot also proves a vehicle for a historical, geographic, and ethnographic commentary. To be sure, some works did more than maximize entertainment value by splicing together disparate features of the adventure tale and the travelogue. In *The Sad Love of The Marquis of Toledo* (*Gorestnaia liubov' markiza de Toledo*, 1764), Emin attempted to reform his archaizing approach to narrative by adopting a more realistic manner; he also encouraged readers to consider philosophical questions about the relation between man and nature, but again without reference to a Russian setting. Escapist and abstract, works of this type move against the grain of the realism cultivated by English novelists like Defoe and Fielding. The precise topography of the English novel, along with depictions of costume and architecture, were typical of the French fictions from which these works descended. Characters with names like Miramond, Saramond, Askalon, Gomalis, and Martsemiris are not conceived for verisimilitude. If these novels have an intellectual project at all beyond their debt to folkloric and picaresque plots, their openness to the exotic and new forms of experience might have tapped into the wider appreciation of Enlightenment writing and thinkers for cross-cultural contact and exploration. As the seductive and naked Queen Musalmina says to the hero of Komarov's *Milord George*, "Look, Milord, you certainly won't see such pleasant and tender forms as these in London, will you?" Impossible plots, hackneyed characterizations, and routine rhetoric mark imitations that nonetheless also managed for the first time to address social questions in a specifically Russian context.

The improving fictions of this period, whether the closely related allegorical, adventure, or didactic novels, drew heavily on the conduct books, rule books, and primers that enjoyed official sanction and publication. Moralistic passages, perhaps intended to diffuse the suspicion of the novel, sometimes subordinate entertainment value to their larger ethical purpose, which was typically expressed in monologues. Closer to the tastes of high culture and the principles of absolutism, the didactic novel combines moral conclusions with adventure plots. Most of the heroes of these fictions leave Russia far behind either by getting on a time machine to ancient Greece to experience republican values; or by undergoing, somewhat like Voltaire's hero Candide, mishaps and adventures, usually in the exotic Orient. Concern about the nature of the benevolent ruler had been made topical by Catherine the Great in her own writings and official decrees.

While tastemakers like Sumarokov despised the novel, as a whole, he and others made exceptions for allegorical, didactic fiction. Fénelon's *Télémaque* (1699), translated in 1734 by A. F. Khrushchev (1691–1740) as *The Adventures of Telemachus* (*Pokhozhdeniia Telemaka*), appeared in 1747, and was republished several times, and Trediakovsky's translation of the highly important novel *Argenis*, a generically complex ragbag of romance, tragedy, and political allegory, finally appeared in 1751, some twenty-five years after he began. Early Russian novels imitated neoclassical works such as the Abbé Barthélemy's *The Journey of the Young Anacharsis in Greece* (*Le Voyage du jeune Anacharsis en Grèce*, 1788), mentioned admiringly in Karamzin's *Letters of a Russian Traveler*, by featuring quests across the city-states of ancient Greece in search of the good king. As a literary subject, the formation of the ideal monarch inspired Fedor Emin's *The Adventures of Themistocles and Various Political, Civic, and Philosophical Conversations with His Son* (*Prikliucheniia Femistokla i raznye politicheskie, grazhdanskie, filosofskie...i ego s synom svoim razgovory*, 1763) where the expulsion of Themistocles provides a lightly veiled allegory for Catherine the Great's deposition of her husband Peter III and assumption of the throne. Mikhail Kheraskov's *Numa Pompilii, or Flourishing Rome* (*Numa Pompilii, ili protsvetaiushchi Rim*, 1768) is a fictionalized treatise on good government staged as dialogue. The novel's language of statecraft repeats the ideals presented in Catherine's own manifestos, breathing faltering life into an ancient monarch who is idealized as a prototype. Implicitly, these and other works endorsed or accepted the image of the Enlightenment ruler that Catherine had fashioned for herself; yet at the same time, while affirming the status quo, these books convey a neo-Stoic message typical of the neoclassical novel: virtue is to be sought through reason and mystical contemplation in the private cultivation of a quiet life in rustic retreat. Written under the inspiration of his Masonic ideals, Kheraskov's novels such as *Polydorus, Son of Cadmus and Harmony* (*Polidor, syn Kadma i Garmonii*, 1794) express the trend of combining inner piety with civic virtue.

This tradition informs the philosophical project of Aleksandr Radishchev's *Journey from St. Petersburg to Moscow* (Figure III.07). While seen historically as a classic work of Russian dissident literature for its radical views on serfdom and application of Enlightenment theories to the political economy of the Russian state, as a literary work, the *Journey* is much more than a political essay. Radishchev mined Western literary sources, from the ancient historians to

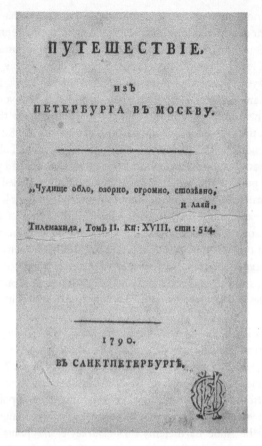

ПУТЕШЕСТВIЕ.

изъ

ПЕТЕРБУРГА ВЪ МОСКВУ.

„Чудище обло, озорно, огромно, стозѣвно,
и лаяй,,

Тилемахида, Томъ II. Кн: XVIII. спи: 514.

1790.

ВЪ САНКТПЕТЕРБУРГѢ.

FIGURE III.07. Aleksandr Radishchev, *The Journey from St. Petersburg to Moscow* (*Puteshestvie iz Peterburga v Moskvu*, St Petersburg, 1790), title page of first edition.

Rousseau, and his narrative has more in common with European fictions than Russian models. Once again, the single frame-story of the traveler forms the narrative axis carrying a series of vignettes illustrating the evils of serfdom, history, prostitution, censorship, court life, excess, and luxury. For the first time, a Russian work of fiction deployed the resources of the novel to create a polyphony of discourses in which the authoritative speech of the narrator and the fictional speech of the characters are independent. To the extent that the discourse of the characters reflects their own psychology rather than an authorial message, they fulfill the expectation that the literary theorist Mikhail Bakhtin would lay down for the novel as a genre in which characters come to life precisely through speech that exists apart from the control of the narrator, and sometimes is in conflict with the narrator's views. Written partly in imitation of Laurence Sterne's *Sentimental Journey*, Radishchev's *Journey* is an early example in Russia of a type of metafiction that calls into question the nature of reading and the artificiality of the novel.

The novels of Komarov and Mikhail Chulkov revel in comic reversals and sexual abandon, and consistently champion the poor over the privileged, the serf over the master, and even the reader over the author himself. Once singled out for its supposed strains of realism by the critical treatments of the late nineteenth century, Chulkov's enduring *The Comely Cook* has been noted as a landmark in the history of Russian fiction because it is written from the point of view of a Russian in a historically recognizable context (albeit full of anachronisms that militate against realism). Although it is self-consciously literary, *The Comely Cook* employs the conventions of the romance and fabliau familiar from other adventure and travel fictions, including Chulkov's own collection of fantastic tales *The Mocker* (*Peresmeshnik*, 1789). Within the devices and frame structures of an older form that excludes close mimesis of a represented world, a sassy heroine seduces her way from rags to riches and back to rags. She maintains an outrageous scorecard of her own ruses. This heroine Martona is a *pícara* (a female picaresque character) who uses her native wit and cunning to withstand misfortune while also letting the good times roll. Gifted with a proverbial wisdom and great verbal invention (the novel is often referred to as an early example of the technique of *skaz*), she is the first heroine in Russian literature to offer the reader a vicarious view of urban life: her numerous observations, including comments on custom, money, serfdom, and jail, provide a context in which the heroine's philosophy of life develops as part of the novel's lived experience instead of being imposed by the author through interpolated speech. Through her sayings, erotic daring, and lawless guile, Martona thrives on a clash between contradictory moral worlds of the subculture and the values of moralistic literature. Chulkov uses the novel as a celebration of the power of fiction to parody cultural institutions and conventions.[9] Amusement rather than self-knowledge or philosophical truth is the goal of Martona's subversive wit. In subverting a range of cultural fixtures, from the salon (depicted as a bordello) to the neoclassical novel (where characters with none of Martona's palpable experience moralize pompously), *The Comely Cook* creates an unstable world that perfectly illustrates the author's stated belief in the inconstancy of fortune that can best be revealed in the story of a character who cuts her moral cloth to suit those mutable circumstances and values.

Dubbed a parody of Rousseau's *La Nouvelle Héloïse*, Emin's *The Letters of Ernest and Doravra* (*Pis'ma Ernesta i Doravry*, 1766), was for all its tendentiousness the most successful of Russian sentimental novels. Although the attempt at psychological nuance is hampered by Emin's inability to differentiate between the discourse of the two characters, who sound identical, this first epistolary novel in Russia captured the emotional upheavals of Ernest and Doravra who, like Julie and Saint-Preux, remain separated by class and by sexual, if not emotional, fidelity to their respective spouses. Translations of Richardson's *Pamela* in 1787, *Clarissa* in 1791–92, and *Sir Charles Grandison* in 1793–94, may well have given impetus to the budding cult of sensibility and appealed to a largely female readership of fiction. Karamzin's treatment in "Poor Liza" of an unequal romance between members of different social classes, while justly celebrated, was not unique. P. Iu. L'vov's novel *The Russian Pamela* (*Russkaia Pamela*, 1789) addressed the same issue. Few of these sentimental fictions appear to have survived into the nineteenth century to judge by the catalogues of (relatively few) private libraries. The taste for Fielding and Richardson that persisted into the late 1820s (if we accept as evidence the reading list that Pushkin gives Tatiana in *Evgenii Onegin*) looks highly specific, and generated some moralistic novels such as Aleksandr Izmailov's *Eugene, or the Destructive Consequences of a Bad Education and Company* (*Evgenii, ili Pagubnye sledstviia durnogo vospitaniia i soobshchestva*, 1799–1801).

By the end of the century, the gap between native production of novels and foreign translations was glaring. When seen in the context of a literary environment so open to European models and accommodating to the demands of a readership that had been consuming English and French fiction, the explanation must lie not only in economics or in the canons of taste as an abstract system. Two mutually exclusive readerships coexisted in close proximity, the first avid consumers of entertainment literature, the second devoted to serious literature embodied in poetry, theater, and essays. The genre of the modern European novel was problematic for most Russian readers. But within that broad generalization lurks a further distinction between attitudes to fiction typical of each of these readerships. The less educated readers were comfortable with fiction, and could continue to satisfy a taste for narrative forms by reading works that looked distinctly old-fashioned. Prose fiction remained under-valued by educated readers, who could find in poetry ample formal and expressive innov-ation or turn to translation for quality fiction. In criticizing the continuing buoyant demand for fiction, Karamzin targeted some readers who, in his view, should have known better and realized that some fiction was no longer appropriate for people of a certain class, certainly not the better educated. Educated readers who enjoyed old-fashioned stories might not have classified them as novels in any modern sense, but thought of them instead as trad-itional tales that were acceptable because they were Russian, and discounted their status as novels.

The real problem was that educated readers did not appreciate fiction as such. When it came to acquiring a taste for the modern novel, they proved highly reluctant to accept the genre on its own terms. The most serious fictions of the period—serious in the sense of mimetic sophistication—met with little success among educated readers, a sign that this read-ership had reservations about this type of storytelling. In both his *Letters of a Russian Traveler*, and in his stories, Karamzin pretends to present truthful events; just as in poetry, speakers attained such a level of conviction that, however stylized, looked believable in the moment. Suspension of disbelief was not something educated Russian readers were obviously prepared to contemplate. Fictional novelistic events, invented rather than experienced and open to the analysis of the diary or letter, present a difficulty to readers whose idea of truth felt betrayed by invention. It is not for nothing that Pushkin's only novel, *The Captain's Daughter* (published 1836), is a historical novel and, even more telling, a work of memoir fiction presented by a first-person retrospective narrator.

For all its subsequent prestige and success, the Russian novel was slow to gain ground and lacked the backing of the class of readers and writers who had taken other areas of literature forward. The history of this reception illustrates the distinctness of national traditions, even in periods of intense cross-cultural sharing when there is broad synchronization among other forms. Such a fitful start captures the real impediments in the transmission between an idea of Western literary culture and the real literary field in search of different canons. Arguably, the broad divergence between native fictions and contemporary European models, despite some exceptions, dictated the slow establishment of the novel from the 1820s. Archaic fictions of all kinds, whether the bookish *Journey to the Isle of Love* or the extensive popular fictions that inspired forms like the chivalric and adventure novels, were not, in the long term, suitable models of narrative voice and style for modern topics. Given the attraction exerted by older forms of narrative, it is not surprising that in this context no talents emerged comparable to Richardson or Fielding or Diderot, and even if they had existed, it is likely that the time was not yet ripe for a major success comparable to *Clarissa*.

In the intervening period, from Radishchev to Pushkin, the novel found few followers among writers of Sentimentalism and pre-Romanticism. Karamzin and his supporters found shorter prose tales to be a better medium for boldly exploring the theme of sexual transgres-sion than the novel. And when seen purely in commercial terms as well as in terms of technical skill, the most accomplished extended narrative work of the period, and the most widely read (it sold over 3,000 copies) was Karamzin's *History of the Russian State* (*Istoriia gosudarstva rossi-iskogo*, 1818–29). Entertainment literature, however, continued to do well. In the 1820s and 1830s, the popular success of the works of Faddei Bulgarin, Osip Senkovsky, Ivan Lazhechnikov, and others, was a feature of the literary landscape in which Pushkin, like Karamzin before him, thought about the difficulty of establishing a tradition for quality prose.[10] Despite their popular success, the historical novels of the Napoleonic wars fell short of artistic distinction. Fiction was in a no-man's-land between the now-dated didactic and adventure-plot style of eighteenth-century fiction and the advances of Stendhal, Balzac, Scott, and other European masters who would serve as a departure point from the 1820s.

Conclusion

Historical continuity is not necessarily obvious to contemporaries. In the extended and magnificent discourse Karamzin pronounced in 1818, he celebrated the *Dictionary of the Russian Language* as the labor of the Russian Academy, observing the signal contribution made by imaginative writers to the development of style and rhetoric. To illustrate his points, he adduced Shakespeare, Schiller, and numerous Ancients like Cicero and Demosthenes, without ever looking back to the Russian eighteenth century.[1] Retrospectively, we can see that the legacy of the eighteenth century was massive and transformative. Its contributions included a new system of versification, a vernacular literary language of refinement, a complex understanding and language of sensibility and representation of the body, a genre system that was essential in perpetuating ideas of taste and forms of expression, and, vitally, an idea of authorship. The development of each of these, traced in our account, produced a literary field that now looked well established and open to further development.

The Russian eighteenth century was truly a long century in that its poetic culture lived on in print—and even in body. After all, Derzhavin died only in 1816. In "The Shade of Fonvizin" ("Ten' Fonvizina," 1815), the young Pushkin played with and mocked the neoclassical masters he had absorbed in his youth. Other poets put themselves in a problematic relationship with the previous generation without necessarily seeing themselves as innovators. In "To My Reason. Third Satire" ("K moemu rassudku. Satira tretiia," 1812), M. V. Milonov wittily denounced the pompous poetry and the Slavonic style advocated by the Beseda. His attack was a chance to flaunt the linguistic mannerisms of Arzamas, the rival literary group he preferred whose rules of literary play owed much to the eighteenth-century culture of literary sparring and epigram. The ethos of poetic groups and their culture of contest perpetuated the trends established in the 1770s well into the 1830s.[2] Vissarion Belinsky, the greatest critic of the 1830s and 1840s, a man highly appreciative of European fiction, even if better remembered perhaps for his later, narrower attitudes and a political mission of art, often invoked the memories of figures like Lomonosov and Derzhavin as evidence of a substantial Russian literary tradition.

A good deal of the legacy of the eighteenth century remained alive to the writers of the 1820s and 1830s, some of whom devoted their energies to the recuperation of the period. Viazemsky, for instance, in his study of Fonvizin, produced one of the first literary biographies in Russia based on documentary, archival research. Why, then, did the perception continue to persist among this generation, including Viazemsky, that Russia still lacked a national literature? This conclusion should not be taken literally as a dismissal of the achievements of the previous fifty years.[3] In these conditions, and with the rise of new trends like Realism, it is not surprising that eighteenth-century literature began to look remote very quickly, reclaimed more by antiquarian scholars in the second half of the nineteenth century. No period is taken over wholesale by the next generation, a point made by twentieth-century Formalist scholarship when suggesting that the pattern of skipping a generation occurs in literary history. The imperatives of Romanticism, the growth in print culture and newspapers, a rapidly changing readership, and the relative paucity of reading clubs and libraries, meant a highly selective approach to the legacy of the eighteenth century. Most of Krylov's earlier writings, including the brilliant comedy *Trumf, or Podshchipa* (1800), were quickly forgotten, whereas his fables, which he began writing in the nineteenth century, were read eagerly, and a statue was dedicated to "Grandfather Krylov" (as he was nicknamed by his new admirers). Furthermore, no other fable-writer sustained an enthusiastic readership (well into the Soviet period as a standard part of the school curriculum). Publishers issued his *Fables* separately, paying little attention to his eighteenth-century work, as in the case of an 1809 selection of twenty works; at a ceremonial meeting of the Russian Academy in December 1818, the poetry readings included only three of his fables presented as classics.[4] Fonvizin's plays continued to be seen as stage-worthy but his prose works looked too firmly rooted in their own time to be relevant.

The poetic traditions of the nineteenth century would have been unthinkable without the innovations of the eighteenth: there is no denying the assimilation of the systemic changes to language and prosody that produced the forms and the idea of voice that nineteenth-century writers could use. At over 180 pages, a contemporary *Florilegium of Selected Poems for the Use and Pleasure of the Young* contains no more than a handful of pieces written in the eighteenth century, including one psalm translated by Derzhavin, and instead gives precedence to contemporary figures who are now irredeemably marginal.[5] If anthologists of the nineteenth century preferred the works of contemporaries to older verse, it was because much new verse was being written. Cultural memory is shaped by the history of the book: the availability or, as was more often the case, the unavailability of works is partly responsible for maintaining continuities or, on the contrary, attenuating the sense of indebtedness that nineteenth-century writers post-Pushkin may have felt toward the eighteenth century. Here material factors exaggerated the generational difference: many print runs never reached wide circulation, prestige copies were treasured in private, and there were too few subscription or lending libraries to penetrate beyond small circles of acquaintances. In the absence of a royalty system, few publishers, writers, or their heirs and families had any commercial incentive to revive past legacies.

The appreciation of the past is a process mediated successively by next generations, and partly conditioned by the historic achievements of the previous period. While writers of the 1820s and 1830s responded vigorously to the writing of Catherine's reign, they also engaged in complex forms of assimilation and rejection. By the end of the eighteenth century, a growing Romantic expectation was that nations attested their worth through a national genius, a spur to a younger generation to satisfy the search for an outstanding single figure. In a way, in setting up a narrative of their time as a first epoch, eighteenth-century writers also determined a narrative of rupture. Ambitions for a national literature crystallized a Romantic need in the 1830s to identify a national genius—and strikingly few contemporaries write about Pushkin's "genius." The eighteenth century had produced changes to the literary system through accumulation and a large number of figures. Did Russians truly have in the figure of Peter I a Great Man, the favored agent of eighteenth-century historiography, who single-handedly modernized the Russian state? Trediakovsky, Lomonosov, and Sumarokov vied for preeminence—it is telling that Sumarokov went as far as likening himself as a poet-reformer to Peter the Great—but none had prevailed entirely. Derzhavin cast a long shadow over the early nineteenth-century literary scene as an honored relic of a previous age. A noteworthy and authorized anthology of his verse published in 1817 opened with a verse dedication by Derzhavin to Catherine the Great. Composed in 1795, the poem locates him firmly in the past. His lyre, says the publisher, was the instrument "of the glorification of three brilliant reigns for Russia" and was its own epoch.[6] The criticism Pushkin made of Derzhavin for a "barbarous" style needs to be seen in the context of his own generation's literary norms after decades in which the smoother style of Sumarokov and Karamzin had been assimilated, and from the individual perspective of a writer who had subsumed Romantic ardor into a cool language that was classical in expression and refinement.[7] While Derzhavin's genius seemed unequivocal to his contemporaries, there remains little consensus on where exactly his work fits in to the literary tradition, a problem that Pushkin is aware of.

If there is a tendency to exaggerate the gap between the literature of the eighteenth and nineteenth centuries, it is in itself a cultural construct conditioned by history and literary history. For one thing, the habit of thinking of the nineteenth century as the Age of the Novel compounds a sense of discontinuity built into the reification of that century as the Age of Realism to which the eighteenth century could scarcely contribute, given its relative failure to engage with fiction. The story would look different when viewed in terms of the history of lyric, the diary, autobiography, and between-genre writing, a whole set of aesthetic affinities and genres that contributed starting points for later developments, some continuous, some discontinuous, but all historically important in the longer term. And the legacy of the eighteenth century is quite profound if measured in terms of a cultural shift in consciousness and self-consciousness that literature stimulated and captured. The notion that there is a self of psychological complexity, made up of spirit and matter, originates in Russia in the Enlightenment period. It is also then that we find authors grappling with the complexities of ideas about empiricism, political identity, and anthropology. This commitment to employing literature as the best heuristic medium in which to pose questions about the human self and subjective feeling seems particularly Russian in its subordination of the abstract to the more tangible and immediately felt—and also vital to the new trends that will develop in and after the nineteenth century.

Part IV

The Nineteenth Century

Introduction:
Defining the nineteenth century

B
Y the end of the eighteenth century, the theme of Catherine's reign as a first epoch
had created a strong sense that Russia had closed the gap with European, and above all
French, literature. Yet few time periods expose more glaringly than the nineteenth century the fallibility of 100 years as a unit of periodization. For one thing, the calendar as an
objective demarcation was as much a symbol of the difficulties of synchronization as an index
of modernization. Peter the Great had decreed that January 1, 1700 would be the beginning of
the new century. Russians internalized this innovation only in 1800, and the country remained
on the Julian calendar, and thus twelve days behind the rest of Europe (thirteen days from
January 1, 1900), until adopting the Gregorian calendar in 1918.

Important historical changes, and above all dynastic confusion, rendered the calendar event
less noticeable. Insecurity caused by the death of Catherine the Great in 1796, and Paul's succession the same year, then Paul's assassination in March of 1801 and Alexander I's accession
to the throne, blurred the turn of the century as a boundary. Anxiety filtered through to literary works, which betrayed uncertainty about when a new epoch had truly begun. Scores of
poems marked the beginning of the nineteenth century—and qualified its advent. Even the
poems formally dedicated to the arrival of the new century were mostly written after Paul's
death and tended to treat the two beginnings—of the new century and of the new reign—as
concurrent events. Similarly, odes greeting Alexander's accession usually referred both to the
change of reign and to the calendar change of centuries.[1] Semen Bobrov (1765–1810) alone
dedicated to these events four poems: "To the New Nineteenth Century" ("K Novostoletiu
XIX," around 1800), "The Hundred-Year Song, or the Triumph of Russia's Eighteenth Century"
("Stoletniaia pesn', ili Torzhestvo os'mogo na desiat' veka Rossii," around 1801), "Query to
the New Century" ("Zapros novomu veku," 1802 or 1803), and "The Century's Foreseen
Response" ("Predchuvstvennyi otzyv veka," 1802 or 1803). Bobrov's poems evince his doubts
about the possibility of social progress. Nikolai L'vov's two poems greeting the new century,
both written in 1801—"The New Nineteenth Century in Russia" ("Novyi XIX vek v Rossii")
and "Popular Exclamation on the Entrance of the New Century" ("Narodnoe voskliknovenie
na vstuplenie novogo veka")—are less concerned than Bobrov's poems about mankind's
future, perhaps because of their nascent nationalistic sensibilities. Radishchev's "The Eighteenth
Century" ("Os'mnadtsatoe stoletie," 1801), while looking back at the troubled previous century, greets the new one with no more than cautious optimism.

The conceptual boundaries of the nineteenth century remain hard to demarcate because,
despite disruption caused by dynastic unrest, continuity with the eighteenth century prevails as does a sense of unfinished Enlightenment business brought about by the French
Revolution, acutely felt among the more progressive thinkers of Catherine's reign. The understanding of sensibility, the development of literature, which gained momentum in the 1790s,

and debates on language and style continued uninterrupted. A keen interest in the eighteenth century remained on the agenda. Lyric poetry, already strongly established, was attuned to the latest trends and attracted more poets and more venues such as the salon. Coteries, the model of poetic exchange from the 1770s, continued to thrive, expanding into larger groups that adopted formal rules; and the discovery of genius as part of early Romanticism inspired a continual search for Russia's own distinctive figure, leading eventually to the precocious (and ultimately justified) crowning of the young Alexander Pushkin (1799–1837) as the preeminent figure of his generation. Symbolically, politically, and artistically, therefore, it would be hard to pin down 1800 as a literal starting point.

The end of the nineteenth century is also blurred. The accession of Nicholas II, who was to be the last Russian emperor, occurred close to its end, in 1894, and his coronation in May of 1896 was marred by a stampede on Khodynka Field in Moscow, where nearly 1,400 people were killed and which was seen by many in an apocalyptic light. Furthermore, it can be argued that the new era in Russian history began in 1905, when, after Bloody Sunday (the shooting of petitioners near the Winter Palace on January 9) and subsequent uprisings in St. Petersburg and Moscow, the first Russian constitution was enacted in 1906. Finally, it might be asked whether the year 1917, with two revolutions that toppled Imperial Russia, might have been the real end of the nineteenth century.

The calendar helps to define a century at least formally. And the calendar nineteenth century in Russia saw the last imperial coup d'état (the assassination of Paul); the triumphant end of the long war with Napoleon, two bloody Polish uprisings; the first attempt at a revolution (the Decembrist Uprising on December 14, 1825); the conquest of the Caucasus, the disastrous Crimean War (1853–56); the liberal reforms of the 1860s, including the abolition of serfdom (1861); the rise of terrorism; and the last, victorious, war with Turkey (1877–78), which expanded Russian influence throughout the Balkans. The Russian nineteenth century was also the century of industrial growth and the upsurge of the bourgeoisie and liberal professions. By the end of it, Russia was much more in step with the West industrially, militarily, and culturally.

In literature, the Russian nineteenth century began with the dominance of poetry and its unprecedented flourishing (the so-called Golden Age associated with Pushkin and his contemporaries); then prose slowly emerged, first mass-entertainment literature, and eventually what is known as the Great Russian Novel. The 1850s can be seen as the time when the novel began in earnest to establish itself in Russia; works marked by unified plot construction and well-developed three-dimensional characters, explored against a broader social and political canvas of individual, family, and collective psychology. Prior to 1850, the most notable works might be thought of as fictions written in search of the novel—proto-novelistic cycles like Mikhail Lermontov's *Hero of Our Time* (*Geroi nashego vremeni*, 1840) or Ivan Turgenev's *Notes of a Hunter* (*Zapiski okhotnika*; stories were first published separately in *Sovremennik* in 1847–51 and collected in one volume in 1852; Turgenev continued to add an occasional story now and then)—rather than novels. In the age of the Great Reforms, the novel in its mature form sought to capture the chaos of Russia's social and agrarian revolution and the turmoil of its political economy by adopting a mimetic-realist approach to the historical context of linear plots experienced causally by characters who make choices and react to their environment or their own inner worlds. The structure of Russian society with its political fault-lines increasingly became a core issue of fiction. Prose attracted larger readerships than poetry, and while some of the greatest Russian poets—Fedor Tiutchev (1803–73), Nikolai Nekrasov (1821–77), and Afanasy Fet (1820–92)—were active and much admired, the dominance that poetry had enjoyed since the eighteenth century had abated.[2] Ultimately, toward the end of the century, poetry saw a popular resurgence that crested during the epoch known as the Silver Age.

Literary movements took shape, and a departure point was the Russian brand of Sentimentalism in the first decade of the nineteenth century, followed by Romanticism, the starting date of which became a matter of dispute in the mid-1820s—a reminder that demarcating the new and the old presents a challenge to the cultural producers themselves. No fixed date marks the end of Romanticism. The age of Realism begins in the 1840s; it persisted almost through the end of the century, to be succeeded in the 1890s by Decadence and early Symbolism, movements that reacted against the rational and practical view of life they took Realism to represent. The early twentieth century saw the rise of important modernist schools, most notably Symbolism, Acmeism, and Futurism, all remarkable for the high quality of poetry and prose. Throughout these interchanges in form, literature builds impressively on its repertory of techniques, mimesis, plotting, and characterization.

Impatience with the long-delayed rise of the novel, caused by formal problems in narrative technique and the tentative growth of a readership and a book market, should not obscure an essential earlier chapter in which sensibility contributed greatly to the idea of a hero in prose and poetry. Our story of the nineteenth century begins with Sentimentalism, the first literary movement truly interested in human emotions and their workings in the body and psyche. Not only were emotions described and analyzed in the works of Sentimentalism, but they also began to shape writers' lives, including writerly behavior, to which we turn now.

I

Institutions

Male poetic circles: Friendship and intellectual networks

In the last third of the eighteenth century, friendship becomes both a recognized part in the lives of producers of literature as well as a topic of literary exploration. The literary field moves gradually out of coteries into broader friendship networks that over the next thirty years, from the 1790s to the 1820s, foster a critical mass of writers with aspirations to become professionals. The treatment of friendship as an emotional experience deserving of description owed much to the literature of Sentimentalism, which focused writers' attention on feelings and their place in life and art. But friendship was also the organizing principle behind communities of readers, and represented an important stage on the way to the creation of a book market. The rise of an anonymous readership marked the next chapter in the shift from an amateur culture to the professionalization of writing, that is, a trajectory from tiny groups of friends, to networks held together by meetings and correspondence, and then on to the anonymous book market that is a constituent feature of the nineteenth-century story of how Russia learned to write and to read.

Friendship as an act of writing and reading grows out of a culture of sensibility. Among noteworthy examples of a homosocial bond we find the life-long friendship of Aleksandr Radishchev and Aleksei Kutuzov, which responded to Sentimentalist ideas. It lasted for over fifteen years, and eleven of those years they roomed together. As adolescents, both were pages at the court; as young men, they attended Leipzig University; as adults, they became interested in Freemasonry. While Kutuzov eventually eschewed other interests in favor of Rosicrucianism (a branch of Freemasonry inspired by the esoteric and mystical Order of the Rosy Cross, considered subversive at the time), Radishchev was influenced by masonic ideas more generally: the imagery of light and the metaphor of moral change as a journey, both fundamental for Radishchev's *Journey from St. Petersburg to Moscow* (1790), had roots in masonic philosophy as did the *Journey*'s notions of "inner man" and of moral growth.[1] Finally, both Radishchev and Kutuzov were literary men, which further deepened the friendship; Radishchev was likely interested in Kutuzov's translations of Christian Gellert's articles on emotions (including "On the Pleasure of Sorrow," 1747, Kutuzov's translation 1781), Young's *Night Thoughts* (1742–45, Kutuzov's complete translation in book form 1785), and especially Klopstock's *Messiah*. Radishchev expressed his feelings for Kutuzov by dedicating and addressing two major works to him: the *Life of Fedor Vasil'evich Ushakov* (1789), containing reminiscences about their time in Leipzig, and the *Journey*. In the *Life of Ushakov*, the dedication analyzes emotions, characteristic of young people, which, according to Radishchev, fostered their friendship. These emotions are complex and contradictory, yet happy. The mixture of spirituality and physicality in Radishchev's description of these emotions can be traced to the 1770 class taught by Ernst Platner, in which the philosopher advocated the soul's dependence on the body. Later, in the summer of 1789, Karamzin—or his traveling narrator—also encounters Platner's ideas: while in Leipzig, the traveler not only attends Platner's lecture but also pays him home visits.[2] The spirituality and physicality, as well as the continued presence of Kutuzov as the addressee of the *Life of Ushakov* make Radishchev's experimentation with hagiography in this work even more radical. In his dedication-cum-address to Kutuzov at the beginning of *A Journey*, Radishchev calls him his "most beloved friend" and someone with whom he shares deep feelings (*sochuvstvennik*), stressing the prevalence of friendship over differences of opinion. The primacy of emotions over abstract ideas is fundamental for the Sentimentalist view of human interactions.

In Karamzin's relations with Aleksandr Petrov (*c.*1763–93), the pedagogical element is prominent. Their friendship, as expressed in literary works, whether biography, essays, or poetry, takes the form of a set of ethical exchanges and a modeling system for self-betterment. Both Karamzin and Petrov were members of Novikov's circle; they participated in his masonic projects (including editing in 1785–89 the first Russian journal for children, *Children's Reading for Heart and Mind* [*Detskoe chtenie dlia serdtsa i razuma*]) and roomed together for several years in the house owned by Novikov's Friendly Learned Society. Petrov, about three years older than Karamzin, influenced his friend's development as a writer: he cultivated Karamzin's interest in Shakespeare and, as Karamzin acknowledged, corrected his early literary compositions. One of Karamzin's poems, "Anacreontic Verses for A. A. P[etrov]" ("Anakreonticheskie stikhi A. A. P[etrovu]," 1788) acknowledges his debt to Petrov. Their friendship produced extensive correspondence (of which only nine of Petrov's letters survived), instrumental in forming the style of Karamzin's *Letters of a Russian Traveler*.[3] It also anticipated the active letter-writing of the next generation and the rise of epistolary poetic genres.[4]

The familiar letter (usually called friendly epistle in the Russian tradition) proliferated in Karamzin's poetry. In addition to his epistles to Petrov, he addressed nine to Ivan Dmitriev who responded with several of his own. Often poetic epistles were included in actual letters, and occasionally they formed poetic exchanges. In 1793, Dmitriev sent Karamzin his "Stanzas to N. M. K." ("Stansy k N. M. K."), to which Karamzin responded with his 1794 "Epistle to Dmitriev, in Response to His Poem, in Which He Complains of the Fleetingness of Happy Youth" ("Poslanie k Dmitrievu. V otvet na ego stikhi, v kotorykh on zhaluetsia na skorotechnost' schastlivoi molodosti"). Unlike Dmitriev's rather traditional lamentations about the passage of time, Karamzin's epistle is a tragic contemplation on "terrible European events" (*uzhasnye proisshestviia Evropy*) of the late eighteenth century.[5] That elliptical phrase refers to the failure of the French Revolution, which drastically changed Karamzin's view of the nature of man; it also eventually resulted in his monarchist outlook, as is evident in his *History of the Russian State*.

As the author of about twenty verse epistles, Mikhail Murav'ev, already familiar as an elegiac poet and polemicist, was perhaps the most energetic practitioner of the genre. The selection of many friends and relatives rather than fellow writers as addressees is noteworthy because Murav'ev deliberately disregarded the boundary between everyday life and poetry, anticipating what the twentieth-century Russian critic Boris Eikhenbaum would call "literary domesticity" (*domashnost'*) in order to describe an important feature of early nineteenth-century literary life. Domesticity, in Eikhenbaum's usage, denoted the shift away from power structures (such as the court and the state) to informal domestic sphere and friendly circles.[6] The balance of public and private spheres had changed, as noblemen, the dominant producers of culture at the time, began to withdraw from the state structures in search of other means of defining their identity.

At the start of the nineteenth century, the Friendly Literary Society (Druzheskoe literaturnoe obshchestvo), which emerged out of an informal circle of friends, mostly students of the

Moscow University Gentry Pension (Vasily Zhukovsky, Andrei Kaisarov [1782–1813], Andrei and Aleksandr Turgenev [1784–1845], among others) was short-lived (from January to November of 1801) but influential. A prominent member of the group was Aleksei Merzliakov (1778–1830), a Moscow University student at the time and, later, professor of Russian literature at the same university as well as a literary theorist, critic, and poet.[7] The Society espoused pre-Romantic, anti-classicist ideas; its members admired Goethe, Schiller, Wieland, as well as Shakespeare. The epistle was one of their favorite genres.

Prominent among formally organized literary groups were the politically and culturally conservative Beseda liubitelei russkogo slova (hereafter Beseda) and the liberal Arzamas. Initially informal, Beseda's weekly meetings in Derzhavin's Petersburg home began in 1807; the official establishment of the society dates to March 1811; it dissolved in 1816, after Derzhavin's death. In addition to Derzhavin, the members included, among others, Aleksandr S. Shishkov (1754–1841), whose chief concern was to keep the Russian language free of foreign linguistic borrowings; Nikolai Gnedich, the future translator of *The Iliad*;[8] Ivan Krylov, who at the time was on his way to becoming the best known Russian fabulist; and Anna Bunina (1774–1829), the first Russian woman poet acknowledged by her male colleagues. In addition to poetry readings, the members delivered scholarly papers and led political discussions. The society published a periodical, *Readings in the Colloquy of the Lovers of the Russian Word* (*Chteniia v Besede liubitelei russkogo slova*, 1811–16).[9]

The fad for epistolary poetry remained central for this group, too. Perhaps the most famous poem of this genre is Derzhavin's "To Evgeny. Life in Zvanka" ("Evgeniiu. Zhizn' Zvanskaia," 1807), addressed to Metropolitan Evgeny (Bolkhovitinov [1767–1837]), a literary historian, Derzhavin's friend, and later an honorary member of Beseda. Anna Bunina chose to enter into a poetical dialogue with Derzhavin with her 1808 epistle "Twilight. To Gavriil Romanovich Derzhavin in his Village, Zvanka" ("Sumerki. Gavriilu Romanovichu Derzhavinu v ego derevniu Zvanku"). In this poem, Bunina imagines herself in Zvanka, listening to Derzhavin compose his poetry and witnessing the muse crowning him with a myrtle wreath.

The Arzamas Society of Obscure People (Arzamasskoe obshchestvo bezvestnykh liudei), known as Arzamas, was established in 1815 as a parodic counterpoint to Beseda. It brought together many of the most brilliant poets of the time: Zhukovsky, Konstantin Batiushkov (1787–1855), Petr Viazemsky (1792–1878), Ivan Dmitriev, and Vasily Pushkin (1770–1830)—whose famous nephew, Alexander, was admitted as a member at the very last meeting of the society, on April 7, 1818.[10] Arzamasians parodied the ceremonial assemblies of Beseda by holding their meetings over sumptuous dinners, underscoring their desire to operate in a private, "domestic" sphere. Every member had a humorous nickname derived from Zhukovsky's ballads (Viazemsky was Asmodeus; Batiushkov—Achilles; and Alexander Pushkin—Cricket [*Sverchok*]). The society adopted nonsensical bylaws, and the speeches they delivered at meetings were full of humorous gibberish they called *gallimatias*. But mockery of Beseda did not hinder Arzamas from considering serious matters, including quite possibly the constitutional changes they believed were about to be introduced by Alexander I.[11]

The humorous and informal nature of interactions among the Arzamasians invigorates their correspondence, and many epistles contain ample references to the group's ceremonies.[12] Even though few of these epistles merit inclusion in anthologies of Russian poetry (except, perhaps, Batiushkov's "My Penates: an Epistle to Zh<ukovsky> and V<iazemsky>" ["Moi Penaty: Poslanie k Zh<ukovskomu> i V<iazemskomu>," written 1811–12, published 1814] and Pushkin's "The Little Town" ["Gorodok," 1815]), collectively they created the vocabulary for the familiar epistle as a genre and for domestic poetry in general.

In the 1810s the number of literary societies, both informal and those connected with cultural institutions, such as universities, was in fact much higher than the few mentioned here, and they tended to proliferate. Toward the end of the decade, however, the government's lenient attitude toward unofficial forms of social life began to harden, and the familiar literary gatherings became targets of police harassment. This resulted in the emergence of secret societies, such as the Green Lamp (Zelenaia lampa, 1819–20). Because its members included future Decembrists, Soviet scholars felt justified in presenting the society as a predominantly political organization. In fact, the Green Lamp was a familiar society, focused not so much on politics but on so-called prankish behavior.[13] A prank (or *shalost'*, a root designating folly) was a prominent part of young people's behavior at that time. Pushkin's well-known habitual misconduct in the theater, such as booing and hissing in disapproval of a performance is one example of prankish actions (one such occasion, in December of 1819, almost led to a duel with one Major Denisevich, who objected to Pushkin's misbehavior). Pushkin's walking between the seats displaying a portrait of the republican Louis Pierre Louvel (who assassinated Duc de Berry in February of 1820) was another prank—granted, more dangerous, but still a prank. This culture of horseplay was a hallmark of social life that ran over into the swash-buckling military poems and drinking songs of the Napoleonic period. In the first volume of *War and Peace* (*Voina i mir*; written in 1863–69; the first three volumes published in 1868, followed by the other two in 1869; Tolstoy continued to revise and edit the book for subsequent editions), Leo Tolstoy (1828–1910) gives an accurate historical reconstruction of aristocratic behavior in the party scene at Anatole Kuragin's. Both Dolokhov's drinking rum while balancing on a window ledge high above the street and the subsequent cruel trick played on the policemen were typical pranks. In Tolstoy's historically correct description, prankish behavior is practiced by younger members of high society regardless of their character—both the morally suspect Dolokhov and the thoughtful and kind Pierre with equal enthusiasm tie a policeman and a bear together and throw the pair into the Neva River. Dueling—usually serious and dangerous activity—sometimes could border on prankish behavior, as Pushkin's conflict with Denisevich demonstrates.

CASE STUDY Dueling writers

Dueling was an institution transplanted to Russia, and its adaptation required the assimilation of foreign behavior and alien notions of the self as an independent entity. Dueling was crucial in fostering the idea of autonomy and, especially, physical inviolability among the nobles and, later, among educated commoners. Despite initial resistance to these foreign ideas, by the beginning of the nineteenth century, dueling had become established among the Russian nobility. It was not long before nobles were dueling with alarming regularity, often on the slightest pretext and under extremely dangerous conditions. Such fearless duelists became known as *bretteurs*. The emergence of dueling reflected the formation of notions of polite behavior and the duel's high cultural prestige in Russia originates in this period of reckless combat.

The behavior of the *bretteur* was a common feature of intellectual elite life of the early nineteenth century, including writers. Even friendship did not always prevent dueling: soon after graduating from the Lyceum, Pushkin and his classmate Wilhelm Küchelbecker (1797–1846) fought a duel, allegedly over a slightly offensive poem Pushkin wrote about his friend. Küchelbecker took his shot, whereas Pushkin did not. However, duels were usually triggered by more serious matters. In February 1824, Kondraty Ryleev (1795–1826), poet and future leader of the Decembrist Uprising, fought with Prince Konstantin Shakhovskoi (1802–67), the lover of his unmarried half-sister. Ryleev insisted on draconian conditions, and the duelists exchanged several shots at a distance of three paces, twice hitting each other's pistols. Ryleev was wounded in the heel by a ricochet bullet, which ended the duel. Aleksandr Bestuzhev (1797–1837), yet another Decembrist and a Romantic writer, publishing from 1830 under the name Aleksandr Marlinsky, was an ardent duelist who established dueling both as a feature of Romantic behavior and as a prominent theme in Russian fiction. Alexander Pushkin and Mikhail Lermontov (1814–41), representing successive generations, fully accepted the cultural importance of the duel in fiction as in life. Their deaths in duels, in 1837 and 1841, respectively, further elevated the status of dueling as a cultural institution. Their early deaths also reinforced the Romantic idea that males (poets in particular) were more heroic if they died young.

The literature of the second half of the nineteenth century continued to explore conflicts of honor: duels took place in a number of works by Ivan Turgenev (1818–83) (the stories "Three Portraits" ["Tri portreta," 1846], "The *Bretteur*" ["Breter," 1847—which is usually translated as "The Bully"], and "The Diary of a Superfluous Man" ["Dnevnik lishnego cheloveka," 1850], as well as his novel *Fathers and Sons* [*Ottsy i deti*, 1862]); in Tolstoy's *War and Peace*; and in *Demons* (*Besy*, 1871–72; also translated as *The Devils* and *The Possessed*) and *The Brothers Karamazov* (*Brat 'ia Karamazovy*, 1879–80) by Fedor Dostoevsky (1821–81). In real life, dueling between writers subsided: even when challenges were issued, those did not always result in duels (the conflicts of honor between Belinsky and Bakunin, or Tolstoy and Turgenev are good examples).

At least the idea of dueling, if not dueling itself, recovered its glamor among the early-twentieth-century modernists. Andrei Bely (1880–1934) attempted to challenge Aleksandr Blok (1880–1921) several times in the course of their rivalry over Liubov Mendeleeva-Blok (1881–1939). Bely's conflict with Valery Briusov (1873–1924) over Nina Petrovskaia (1879–1928) also nearly ended in a duel. In at least one case, dueling was not confined to men: in 1907, Marietta Shaginian (1888–1982) challenged Vladislav Khodasevich (1886–1939) to a duel with rapiers over his allegedly bad treatment of his first wife. The duel was an important means of self-creation for the modernists, allowing them to construct their images as poets. This is evident in Shaginian's challenge to Khodasevich: she asserted not only her right to what was seen as exclusively male behavior but also her status as a Russian poet.

In their life-creating behavior (*zhiznetvorchestvo*, life-creation or "fusing art and life"), the modernists often used Pushkin and Lermontov as their models.[14] In 1909, Nikolai Gumilev (1886–1921) and Maksimilian Voloshin (1877–1932) quarreled over Cherubina de Gabriak (the pen name of the poet Elizaveta Dmitrieva [1887–1928], a persona invented for her by Voloshin). They planned to duel at Chernaia Rechka, the site of Pushkin's fatal duel with Georges-Charles de Heeckeren d'Anthès as well as one of Lermontov's duels. In 1914, Boris Pasternak (1890–1960) chose to challenge the poet Yulian Anisimov (1886–1940) on January 27, the anniversary of Pushkin's mortal duel. Their contest was averted, but not before it was set for January 29, the day of Pushkin's death and Pasternak's birthday. In choosing the sites and timing of their duels, writers of the early twentieth century extended the established tradition and affirmed their status as Russian literati.

The violence of the post-revolutionary period and the changing views of class identity all but ended dueling, even though the tradition of the duel between writers continued for a while, as did symbolic choices of time and place. In 1922, Veniamin Kaverin (1902–89) challenged Mikhail Zoshchenko (1895–1958) in late January, again, on the anniversary of Pushkin's duel with d'Anthès; the duel did not take place. In his autobiography written the same year, Zoshchenko recounts a duel that he supposedly fought in 1913 in Kislovodsk, famous as the site of Pechorin and Grushnitsky's encounter in Lermontov's *Hero of Our*

Time. The notion that a duel, or at least a challenge, serves to assert oneself as a Russian writer survived until the late twentieth century, preserving, in new circumstances, the tradition of early-twentieth-century *zhiznetvorchestvo*: in the late 1970s, two Russian writers (whose names remain secret) in Jerusalem attempted to resolve their rivalry over a woman in a duel.

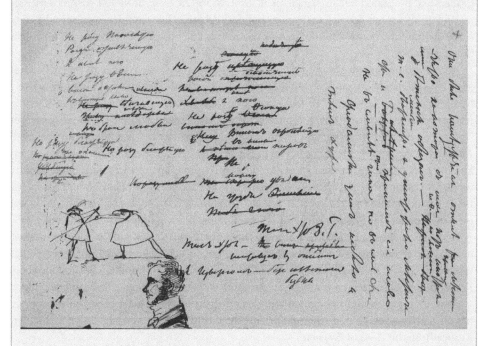

FIGURE IV.01. A. S. Pushkin, *Duelists*, 1830.

A prank could be an action (such as a duel or Dolokhov and Pierre's outrageous behavior, as described by Tolstoy); it also could take the form of a literary work and include, if not outright pornography, then obvious references to the sexual sphere. Both forms were practiced by Arzamasians. Military men dominated the membership of the Green Lamp (the most prolific practical pranksters), but many were poets, such as Pushkin, Anton Del'vig (1798–1831), and Gnedich. The literary works they read at the gatherings of the society often were literary pranks, containing allusions to erotic desire and sexual acts. One example is Del'vig's "Fanny: A Horatian Ode" ("Fani [Goratsianskaia oda]," 1814–17).[15] Normally, such playful poems were not intended for publication. One notable exception is Pushkin's first narrative poem *Ruslan and Liudmila* (published in 1820), which was written during Pushkin's participation in the Green Lamp and read at one of its gatherings; scholars have convincingly interpreted it as a literary prank.[16] Pushkin's participation in the Green Lamp shaped his poetic idiom no less strongly than did his association with the Arzamas members.

The use of banter and *gallimatias* can be found throughout the entire corpus of Pushkin's correspondence and in many of his poems addressed to friends as well as in their responses. This correspondence, both in prose and in verse, organized the circle of Pushkin's friends and acquaintances into a loosely connected but surprisingly durable network of like-minded associates and collaborators. In particular, the list of epistles in verse maps both the friendly and literary relations of this group of Pushkin's contemporaries: Pushkin writes to Wilhelm Küchelbecker, Evgeny Baratynsky (1800–44), Del'vig, Viazemsky, Gnedich (to name a few addressees of his epistles in verse); Baratynsky writes to Küchelbecker, Del'vig, Gnedich, and Viazemsky; Del'vig writes to Pushkin and Gnedich; and so on. The use of specific, sometimes coded language in this correspondence (both letters and poems) marked the participants as insiders and promoted free exchange on all kinds of topics, from news and gossip to friendly teasing, from serious literary matters to political debate. This extensive correspondence to some degree compensated for the lack of periodicals and criticism by providing a forum for free expression.[17]

Not all correspondence was banter, however. Pushkin's poetic epistles to Petr Chaadaev (1794–1856), a dandy hussar-turned-philosopher, present both the poet and his addressee in a heroic light. The 1818 poem "To Chaadaev" ("K Chadaevu") in particular portrays them as fearless rebels who will save their motherland from political oppression and whose names will be "written on the ruins of autocracy" ("I na oblomkakh samovlast'ia / Napishut nashi imena").[18] Although there is no evidence of actual involvement of either Pushkin or Chaadaev in any kind of activity against Russian autocracy, Pushkin again refers to their alleged intention to topple the throne in his 1824 epistle to Chaadaev. In 1836, Chaadaev's so-called "First Philosophical Letter" had appeared in the journal *Telescope* (originally written in 1829 in French, it was published under the Russian title "Filosoficheskie pis'ma k g[ospo]zhe ***. Pis'mo 1-oe"). A landmark in Russian thought, it argued that Russia's historical path as a non-European nation was erroneous and fruitless. Even though at this time Pushkin and Chaadaev still remained friendly, their views on national identity had diverged. Pushkin's sentiments about Russia turned patriotic and his view of the West was less accepting. In his unsent reply to Chaadaev's essay, Pushkin disagreed with his criticism of Russia as a historically irrelevant nation, pointing out, among other things, that Russia did have a historical mission in shielding Europe from the Mongol invasion.

Radical friendships and female networks

The next generation of Russian writers and intellectuals who came of age in the 1830s developed a different tone of friendly discourse, free of banter, and shockingly candid about feelings. This generation was deeply affected by German Romantic literature and philosophy, which determined to a large degree not only their ideology but also their behavior. One exponent and propagator of German Romanticism and philosophy was Nikolai Stankevich (1813–40), a minor poet and prose writer whose role in Russian culture was owed to his personality, to "the power of his influence on his contemporaries."[19] Romantic in his poetic production and, particularly, in his philosophy (promoting Schelling in the early 1830s, Hegel later in the decade), he propagated universal love as the only possible religion and ethical beacon in life. This philosophy presupposed a certain type of behavior—the behavior that prohibited moral and spiritual apathy and regarded friendship and love (particularly, love for a woman) as the most valuable life experience. His young acolytes in Moscow, the so-called Stankevich circle (founded in 1831, and most active in 1833–37), adopted and developed this new type of behavior. Among the circle's members were Vissarion Belinsky (1811–48), Konstantin Aksakov (1817–60), Ivan Turgenev, and Mikhail Bakunin (1814–76). Priamukhino, the estate owned by Bakunin's parents, was another important location where the members of the Stankevich circle spent time. The Bakunins had four daughters, Liubov, Varvara, Tatiana, and Aleksandra (the fifth and youngest, Sofia, died early), who variously attracted the members of the Stankevich circle, following the leader's philosophy of love. Stankevich and Liubov entered into an intimate relationship, becoming secretly engaged (1836–37); Stankevich, however, decided that his love for Liubov was not the true love he had heralded, and the engagement was eventually dissolved. Liubov died of consumption in 1838, and Stankevich died of the same illness two years later.[20] Since Nikolai's and Liubov's romance was of philosophical significance, their friends and relatives were actively involved, some promoting, others trying to oppose it. Similarly, Mikhail Bakunin was instrumental in his sister Varvara's "emancipation" from her supposedly unhappy marriage. Other companions and relatives were also involved in terminating her marital relations.[21] Such openness in affairs of the heart, entirely unacceptable to the members of previous generations, continued to be practiced by members of the educated class.

For Alexander Herzen (1812–70) it was the emotional pledge that mattered in relationships, and he was shattered when his wife Natalia (née Zakhar'ina), with whom he eloped in 1837 to be secretly married, betrayed their union with Georg Herwegh, a minor German poet of a revolutionary persuasion. Particularly striking was Herzen's insistence that his and Natalia's personal affairs be examined publicly and judged by the members of European revolutionary movement. Herzen told the story of his family tragedy in his memoir, *My Past and Thoughts* (*Byloe i dumy*, which he began to write in 1852, soon after Natalia's death, and left unfinished two years before his death).

The memoir, parts of which were published in mid-1850s, was dedicated to Nikolai Ogarev (1813–77), his lifelong friend and collaborator. The two met as adolescents and soon discovered common interests: both adored Schiller and admired the Decembrists. To cement their friendship, in 1827, they took an oath in the Sparrow Hills (Vorob'yovy Gory), a place near Moscow (now in Gorky Park), "to sacrifice [their] lives to the struggle [they] had chosen."[22] As they matured, they continued to share an ideology and cooperated in the publication of the radical newspaper *The Bell* (*Kolokol*, 1857–67). From 1857 they also shared a wife, Natalia Tuchkova-Ogareva. As Herzen explained to his friend, "In my pure-hearted intimacy with your wife, I saw a new pledge of our trio."[23] The triple union, based on both ideology and sexual attraction, would be conceptualized in the novel *What Is to Be Done?* (*Chto delat'?*, 1863) by Nikolai Chernyshevsky (1828–89).

Such friendships between men were formed alongside women's networks, which could also be vital and conducive to creative expression: if the women seem to readers even decades later to have lived largely in the background, it is in part because the form of writing men championed by the middle of the century, the novel, proved to be less popular as the genre of choice among women. Women did contribute as prose writers, however; and earlier in the century several made important contributions as poets. Incidental, occasional forms of expression, particularly the album, beginning in the late eighteenth century, but also poems, short fiction, and translations were important vehicles for women's writing. Their work has increasingly emerged to the forefront, as scholars have recovered more writings by women of the period and begun to reassess the significance of these contributions.[24] Women's writing followed an arc already familiar from the history of the nineteenth century, with poetry being more prominent in the early decades and prose achieving significance by the 1830s and onward. Over the course of the nineteenth century, women would go on to achieve parity with male writers both in poetry and prose, paving the way for writers of the fin-de-siécle, such as Zinaida Gippius (1869–1945), to forge distinctive female voices. It is a mark of Gippius's confidence in the independence of the female voice in the 1890s that she experimented by writing in a male persona.

Anna Bunina titled her first two-volume collection of poetry *The Inexperienced Muse* (*Neopytnaia muza*, 1809, 1812), as if aware that she was taking a remarkable, first solo step onto the public arena; but as Judith Vowles has noted, when Elizaveta Shakhova (1822–99) three decades later wrote the poem "To Women-Poets" ("K zhenshchinam-poetam," 1845), there was a sense of a tradition and of women who had come before her, even if the theme of women's isolation remained important.[25] Russian literature became professionalized, and while women moved more slowly than men into print, journals regularly featured women's writings beginning in the 1820s, and covering a wide range of subjects. One of Bunina's best-known poems, "A Conversation between Me and Women" ("Razgovor mezhdu mnoiu i zhenshchinami," 1812), mocked the idea that women's writings were best suited to tender feelings or a delicate style.[26] And there were more than a few poems, like this one, in which women poets spoke directly against expectations of how they should write, or whether indeed they should write at all. The child prodigy Elizaveta Kul'man (1808–25) has her "Corinna" ("Korinna," published posthumously, 1833) cry out "Is it not women from earliest times who have risen triumphantly over proud men in knowledge, thought proper to men alone?" ("Ne zheny li izdrevle / Nad gordymi muzh'iami / Pobedu oderzhali / Torzhestvennuiu,—v znan'i, / Odnim muzh'iam prilichnom?").[27] Kul'man is writing here about an imagined contest in the ancient world, but the contemporary reference is obvious, and her own level of knowledge more than proved her point: she mastered ten languages in her short life, starting with German, at age five, and could easily have read Corinna in ancient Greek or the popular novel *Corinne, ou l'Italie* (1807) by Germaine de Staël in French. She was taught by Karl Grossheinrich, one of several family friends who made it possible for her to gain an education (her father had died, and she lived alone with her mother). Kul'man was extremely unusual among women writers of the period, nearly all aristocrats, in that she grew up in poverty, and she also stands out for her steadfast aesthetic orientation toward Classicism in an era when Romantic norms were becoming predominant.[28]

The reassessment of nineteenth-century literature to include women's writing has also yielded a re-theorization of the feminization of literature, associated with the rise of Sentimentalism and with the Westernizing efforts of Nikolai Karamzin and others.[29] At least by 1779, when Nikolai Novikov's *Fashionable Monthly, or the Library for Women's Dress* (*Modnoe ezhemesiachnoe izdanie, ili Biblioteka dlia damskogo tualeta*) first came out, the power exerted by women readers gained recognition in certain forms of public discourse. The later *Ladies Journal* (*Damskii zhurnal*, 1806) was similarly created for a female audience, mixing fashions in sleeve styles and lace with prose and poetry women were thought eager to read. Plenty of stigma could attach to these publications, but discerning writers also recognized the salutary possibilities of women's presence in the salons and among the readership. Pushkin wondered, indeed, whether it would not be ridiculous to "consider women, who so often astonish us with the speed of their comprehension and delicacy of feeling and reason, as creatures beneath us?"[30] As always with Pushkin, layers of irony are possible in this deftly worded rhetorical question, but the poet was handing back to his rather masculine culture an image of intelligent, sensitive women that was being developed on the pages of novels eagerly being read in French and English and starting to appear in nascent Russian prose fiction as well. An influential interpretation of Pushkin's own heroine Tatiana by William Mills Todd III suggests that her emergence at the end of *Evgeny Onegin* (*Evgenii Onegin*, written in 1823–31; first edition in book form 1833) as the hostess of her dazzling salon presents a heroine "whose creative use of conventions comes closest to the author's."[31] But the claim that her status as a salon hostess "was the highest form of creativity open to a woman at this time" might require some modification now that we know much more about the publishing careers of women writers in the era.[32] By the middle of the nineteenth century, the third highest-earning writer, after Tolstoy and Turgenev, was Nadezhda Khvoshchinskaia (1824–89), publishing much of the time under the pseudonym V. Krestovsky.[33] In the years when she was writing and translating, a whole host of women prose writers would emerge, but in the age of Pushkin and earlier, women had begun to make a small but enduring mark on their culture as poets, against considerable odds given their tenuous access to education, assumptions about their fitness for literary work, and their reluctant acceptance by men as their intellectual equals.[34]

Karolina Pavlova (1807–93) was a successful salon hostess as well as a remarkably talented poet, and it was an uneasy combination. In 1837, she married N. F. Pavlov (1803–64), a writer and gambler who squandered her fortune and ruined her reputation. The marriage ended in separation, for which, ironically, society blamed the wife rather than the husband. Pavlova left a legacy in both poetry and prose, and she saw her work published in her lifetime beginning with a volume of poems she wrote in German, followed by another in French (born Karolina Jänisch, she was equally at home in German, French, and Russian). She is best known for a novella, *A Double Life* (*Dvoinaia zhizn'*, 1848), which mixed prose and poetry to suggest parallel worlds of the social whirlwind by day, the realm of desire and dreams by night. In its satiric revision of the popular form of the society tale (*svetskaia povest'*), *A Double Life* uses poetry as an emblem and a medium for the heroine, Cecilia, to experience an interval of spiritual and emotional freedom before the vise of convention tightens around her.

Pavlova also found ways to continue the project of Romantic poetry beyond the age of Lermontov, generally thought to be its final stage, perhaps most significantly in her long poem *Quadrille* (*Kadril'*, 1843–51, published 1859).[35] The foursome figuring in the poem's title refers to a group of four women who replace the usually lone male hero of the Romantic *poema*, and rather than charting their adventures or their search for marital happiness, Pavlova affords these heroines the luxury of a backward glance and the distanced perspective of judgment on their own behavior and that of their (high) society. In presenting them as independent women, capable of ethical and emotional clarity, Pavlova created the kind of heroines that readers of Mme de Lafayette or Jane Austen take for granted, but who were rare on the pages of Russian novels. Pavlova's lyric poetry is similarly unusual, reaching a high point by the later 1840s and continuing through the 1850s, when she traveled to what is now Estonia and then settled in Dresden.[36] Her earlier work offers a glimpse at the evolution of the poetic consciousness in a young woman. She tried out a number of lyrical forms, including ballads and elegies, and her experiments in what she called "Meditations" ("Dumy") are particularly revealing. Unlike Ryleev's cycle "Dumy" (written in the early 1820s), which throughout features historical personages as their heroes or heroines, several of Pavlova's "Dumy" take up the figure of the abandoned woman, drawing on Pavlova's own experience of her romantic relationship with Adam Mickiewicz, which he ended in 1827, and using it to continue a tradition of women's poetry begun by Sappho. In the first "Duma" poem, "Sadly the wind blows" ("Grustno veter veet," 1840), Pavlova conjures up the Sapphic image of a woman who sits alone, but also she explores the possibility of isolation as a source of poetic strength: the melancholy of the poem's opening gives way to a source of optimism in the ending. In a later "Duma" poem, "I am here again" ("Ia snova zdes'," 1847), she places herself in a landscape of other poets, only to note that they have fallen silent. Her own life was to end in isolation, and her work was recovered only years later by Valery Briusov at the beginning of the twentieth century.[37]

Countess Evdokia Rostopchina (1811–58), Pavlova's contemporary, also found appreciation only in the twentieth century, particularly among a rising generation of modernist women poets.[38] Like Pavlova, Rostopchina used the vocabulary of Romanticism in her poetry, wrote a successful society tale, "Rank and Money" ("Chiny i den'gi," 1838), and hosted a salon. Her guests, however, complained when she recited her own work instead of creating an atmosphere in which theirs could shine.[39] As a poet, Rostopchina was very much of her time, and many of her poems address the conventional themes, including love, friendship, and poetic inspiration. Nonetheless, she could also write perceptively about the ways her being a woman influenced her work, most notably in the poem "How Women Are Supposed to Write" ("Kak dolzhny pisat' zhenshchiny," 1840).[40] To give texture to her lyric poetry, Rostopchina successfully used frame narratives and deft external description to bring into relief inner complexity and to produce a sure account of the expectations about women's behavior.[41] She and Pavlova were enemies, but the friendship circles so important in the period did not fully exclude them. Each enjoyed some access to male friendship and the camaraderie that marked the aristocratic circles they frequented; each in her own way showed cognizance of the difficulty of writing in a culture that deemed them unsuited to creative work, even when they met with the approval of individual writers (Baratynsky and Lermontov among them).

The society tale (which we discuss elsewhere for its importance in the larger evolution of the Russian novel), in the hands of nineteenth-century women writers, proved exceptionally capable of accommodating the theme of a talented woman's isolation and sense of uselessness. In a way, these tales were exploring a version of the theme of the so-called superfluous man, which might otherwise seem to be so exclusively defined by its masculine privileges.[42] The prolific Maria Zhukova (1804–55) published a cycle of six tales entiled *Evenings on the Karpovka* (*Vechera na Karpovke*, 1837–38), two of which are society tales. The doomed romance in her "Baron Reikhman" oscillates between delicate psychological insights and an inclination to moralize, urging women toward humility and self-sacrifice—Catriona Kelly called it "melancholic fatalism."[43] Elena Gan (1814–42) gave life to "the bitter fate of the exceptional woman, especially in provincial society" in the several texts she produced in her short life, including "The Ideal" ("Ideal," 1837) and *A Futile Gift* (*Naprasnyi dar*, 1842).[44] Hers was a strong and idiosyncratic voice, and its excesses in tone make the stories a performance of the very complexity in social position that Gan's plots show women as occupying.

The ballroom was a prized venue and the backdrop to many society tales. Here, social hierarchies could be exposed and rule-breakers curtly punished by means ranging from gossip to more cruel forms of exposure. The ballroom could be the scene of deceit and artifice, and as a form of public space, its literary representations suggest a dangerous opposite of the salon. The nocturnal settings of balls came to seem unnatural and fatiguing as early as the description in the first chapter of *Evgeny Onegin*, one of numerous representations of dances in the period.[45] Many of these earlier texts were written by men, including the first chapter of *Evgeny Onegin* (1823) and Baratynsky's "Ball" ("Bal," 1828), which offered a dazzling heroine, Nina, modeled on the great beauty Agrafena Zakrevskaia, the "lawless comet" of Pushkin's lyric poetry.[46] The ballroom was a perfect locale for a contrasting play of sexual desire and social regulation, and many ballroom descriptions offer fewer details of dances and music than they do reports of heated gossip generated by a woman's aberrant behavior; Baratynsky's "Ball" exemplifies this well. An even more extreme instance is Lermontov's play *The Masquerade* (*Maskarad*, 1835), where a masked ball figures first as the setting for a performance of sexual betrayal; and then in a later act, an intermission from dancing and an ice-cream break, so often a moment of cool respite from too much waltzing and physical activity, instead offers the hero, Arbenin, a chance to poison his wife.

The rule-bound dances of the era were an apt metaphor for social regulation. Pavlova's "Quadrille," although its title was aimed at the four heroines of the poem, also pointed to the dance as set piece and included that favorite plot device, a young woman's first ball (best known from Tolstoy's *War and Peace* and *Anna Karenina* [serialized in 1875–77; first published in book form in 1878]). The innocence of a young woman, overwhelmed by the sights and sounds of the ballroom, is often contrasted with the reserved, if not bored, gaze of a (frequently sexually aggressive) older woman. Sexual tension remains a feature of ballroom scenes throughout the century, nowhere more memorably than in Tolstoy's novels. But Tolstoy's darkest ballroom scene, written sixty years after Pavlova, comes in the late short story "After the Ball" ("Posle bala," 1903; first published in 1911), where the contrast is not within the ballroom scene itself, but rather between the successive scenes. After the spectacle of highly stylized deportment, the readers witness, through the eyes of the narrator, a horrible military aftermath in which a Tartar soldier is made to run the gauntlet under the supervision of the very officer whose dancing had been so admired in the first half of the story.[47] Not coincidentally, the dance that defines the evening for the narrator is the quadrille, with its ritualistic verbal cues and formulas, but the dance fades from memory as the story reaches its brutal climax. Rather than the rules of the dance or the buzzing of women's gossip to curb or otherwise censure illicit desire, Tolstoy's story leaves the ballroom for another set of rituals, a military and entirely masculine one, where difference is defined by class and rank rather than gender. In another departure from many ballroom narratives, Tolstoy's story focuses not on the young woman, Varenka, who dances so prettily and who figures as the unnamed narrator's first love, but on the narrator's conflicted feelings of desire, tenderness, pride, and deep shame. The ballroom, no longer just a scene where women's fantasies play out, becomes for the late post-conversion and almost modernist Tolstoy the point of origin for a man's story of his own moral dilemma and reflection on his values.

Early-nineteenth-century elite society was the environment in which a national literature coalesced. Salons played a key role in organizing cultural conversations. Settings were created in which improvisation skills could be practiced, new works shared, and literary prestige attained. The atmosphere of friendly competition and flirtatious gamesmanship lowered the stakes, or seemed to: evaluations of others' social byplay or fresh recitation could maintain a light tone even as careers were managed and assessments of a new poem shared all around. The model for the salon in Russia came from Enlightenment France, and a good deal of French was spoken.[48] But not everywhere and not always: considerable intellectual banter occurred in Russian, and salons helped advance the language for a nascent modern literature and literary criticism; in the Moscow salon of Avdotia Elagina (1789–1877), Russian reigned, which was especially appropriate as the Slavophiles—friends and associates of her sons, Ivan and Petr Kireevsky (1806–56 and 1808–56, respectively)—became regular guests.

One distinctive feature of salons, despite their many differences, was a remarkable degree of unspoken regulation: invitations did not need to be issued, and activities required no announcement. Being casually in the know was a requirement for participation. It was common knowledge that Countess Ficquelmont's salon was frequented by diplomats, Baron Del'vig's by writers, and the guests of a salon knew as well that showy diamond necklaces or overly fashionable dresses were better saved for the ballroom.[49] In the salon of Sofia Ponomareva (1794–1824), where French was often spoken, flirtation was conducted by means of offering literary gifts in Russian to the discerning and brilliantly educated hostess.[50] In Elagina's salon, the more serious atmosphere put amorous byplay to the side; the warm embrace of friendship and family meant that those on warring sides of a philosophical debate could meet and converse on cordial terms. It was a measure of the salon's harmonizing function that such differences were frequently in the air but as if harmlessly, unlike the sarcastic, ugly intonations heard in published criticism by the 1830s.

Those who frequented salons kept diaries, wrote memoirs, and penned inscriptions in each other's albums often enough that the world of the salon has been well reconstructed and theorized by cultural semioticians, feminist historians, and literary historians.[51] In terms of literary history, the material is extensive and invaluable: we can imagine how guests felt privileged to hear strophes from *Evgeny Onegin* in versions some said surely could not get past the censors, how they were grateful when Aleksandra Smirnova (1809–82) asked Pushkin, who read too quickly to be understood, to just give the new poems to Petr Pletnev (1792–1865) to read, and how they might not have been sure whom to pay closer attention to: Nikolai Gogol (1809–52) reading from early drafts of *Dead Souls* (*Mertvye dushi*, 1842) or Pushkin pacing back and forth as he listened.[52] These examples foreground the contexts in which now-canonical writings were first shared and discussed; as we know from the extensive correspondences of the era, writers wrote back and forth to share and revise new work as well (Pushkin's years of exile are a treasure trove of this material, particularly his correspondence with Prince Petr Viazemsky). But the salons were also sites where para-literary texts were created, amateurs tested, and literary gossip shared. In an era when professional literary criticism was barely beginning, the informal atmosphere of the salon gave writers a sense of readership and readers a feeling for their role in the creation of a modern literary culture. And perhaps because it played by its own rules, the salon was also a space where women could have a place and a voice, often as a salon hostess, but also as writers and contributors to the literary performances and games.[53]

CASE STUDY Albums

Although album inscription was not limited to salons (within aristocratic family circles, albums could be collaborative scrapbooks recording domestic life and featuring drawings by family members and guests), the ritualized performance of an invitation to write some-thing in an album most frequently took place in the aristocratic salon. All of the norms of salon behavior were at play at such moments, and the gesture of inscription was charged with the expectation that it be executed with aplomb, mastery, and speed, whether it was a sketch or a few witty lines. This was routinely derided by writers as an empty social ritual, but many wrote poems that had much of the same virtues required of aristocratic literature in the early nineteenth century: wit, an air of improvisation, digressive jocularity, and pleasurable word play.

The forms of behavior around album inscription demonstrate the density of what the Formalists called "literariness" (*literaturnost'*) at social gatherings of the era. Poems were created on assigned rhymes, taking the form of charades, improvised poems, acrostics, and logographs, in an atmosphere of friendly competition.[54] The albums themselves may have drawn critical attention because of this concentration of force fields around literary innovation, and the fact that the Formalists were also working at a time when cinema was emerging as a new form of cultural expression, no doubt led them to see albums as struc-tured around montage: one of the introductions to the landmark 1920s republication of album material is in fact entitled "Montage and Literature." The Formalists saw their own publication as a form of montage, carefully selected from among the massive amounts of memoir material about salons and extant albums, but their attention was directed at the way that albums, like literary almanacs, were a collection of disparate bits of cultural material, both visual and verbal. Russian literary culture was at a time of transition in the early nineteenth century, moving toward a model of professionalization of authorship that would emerge mid-century.[55] The album was a legible sign of that transition, a model of accessibility and openness to quasi-literary forms and to new modes of self-expression.

Remarkably, study of the cultural significance of albums actually began in the 1820s. Two essays by Pavel Yakovlev (1796–1835), one written in an album and later republished in a journal, chronicled the evolution of the album toward serious collections of inscrip-tion by famous writers by the end of the 1820s, and he predicted that albums would be prized collector's items. His own album had a poem inscribed by Pushkin, who had studied at the Lyceum with Yakovlev's older brother.[56] His claim that the album was as significant in the advancement of culture as the invention of the printing press is perhaps a bit exaggerated, but the modes of flattery, flirting, redirecting, and recopying that made the album culture possible were all important elements in cultivating a sophisticated readership for the literary production that was flourishing in the nineteenth century.

Particularly noteworthy are the patterns of multiple dedications and inscriptions—writers found that a poem could be recycled sometimes with minimal if any changes. Evgeny Baratynsky was particularly adept at reuse—the albums of Sofia Ponomareva and Anna Lutkovskaia, for example, both have his 1821 poem which begins "You are loved by too many" ("Vy slishkom mnogimi liubimy"). Although flattery in the poem is tempered by insinuations of the flightiness of the addressee, it is the poet himself who quickly moves on, becoming another's admirer.[57]

Self-deprecation was a usual rhetorical gesture of the album poem, even when it was accompanied by faintly sarcastic doubts as to why the addressee would value the lines even as they are being written. As Baratynsky concluded another album poem:

> Я в ваших памятных листах
> Спокойно имя помещаю:
> Философ я; у вас в глазах
> Мое ничтожество я знаю.[58]

> In your leaves of memory
> I calmly place my name.
> I am a philosopher: I know
> My insignificance in your eyes.

Baratynsky does a deft movement of doubled self-characterization in this poem, presenting himself as philosophical, as one who is not deluded but who can think clearly, and as one who was, even in his lifetime, perceived as a poet who thought deeply. (Pushkin's famous characterization of Baratynsky as a poet *because* he was a thinker comes to mind.[59]) In this case, Baratynsky could be sure that his addressee was a sophisticated enough reader to catch his doubled meanings, as well as to recognize the affectionate humor in the earlier line of the poem, "An album resembles the graveyard" ("Al'bom pokhodit na kladbishche"), welcoming all mortals: the addressee was Karolina Pavlova, whose gifts Baratynsky appreciated from the first time he read her work.

In addition to the extensive opportunities for poets to write poems that were serious, light-hearted, and everything in between, albums were also important sites for authorial caricatures and quick sketches. As Figure IV.02 shows, some of Pushkin's most charming drawings come from the albums of his contemporaries, including this self-portrait from the album of Elizaveta Ushakova (1810–72).[60]

That same album has Pushkin's list of Don Juan's conquests and dozens of other drawings by the poet. One such drawing, which scholars have not successfully identified, has yielded an interesting pre-history on closer scrutiny: Pushkin transformed the coiffure of a woman, which was in the original figure of the drawing, into a man's hat and side-whiskers, and changed the lady's ample-sleeved dress into a sturdy frock-coat. The underlying narrative of this visual composition encodes the atmosphere of play and swift imagination that ruled in this particular salon.[61] It also suggests a quality of playfulness in gender roles, unlike the rather rigid expectations of the ballroom. In salons and private drawings rooms, in fact, a loosening of the strictures on women's roles could be observed. The mere fact that poems might be addressed to women whom one knew well, rather than to patrons or courtiers, marked a shift from dominant paradigms in the eighteenth century.[62] And while many albums belonged to women and many pages were filled with jottings and drawings by men, as if consigning women to the role of readers attentive to

FIGURE IV.02. A. S. Pushkin, Self-portrait, December 1828–January 1829.

the creative outpourings of men, the reverse was not impossible. A number of albums belonging to men have been preserved (Pushkin's father's, for example), and just as salon hostesses sometimes read or performed their own work, albums featured jottings and drawings made by women, sometimes in the position of a close friend and confidante of the album owner.[63] The collections of nineteenth-century albums preseved in museums, archives, and libraries are extensive, making them a valuable resource for cultural historians and literary scholars alike.[64]

2

The literary field:
From amateur societies to professional
institutions and literary alliances

A S writing became more professionalized in the nineteenth century, literary production, first predominantly of poetry, then prose, required new and more numerous
publication venues. Literature had been largely a domestic activity intended for private consumption, and out of the public limelight writers could play up their image among
the peer groups with like-minded values. Even a public prank presumed that some elements
of society would empathize with the prankster as an amateur performing in front of friends.
With the increasing professionalization of literature, public institutions such as censorship
and literary journalism put pressure on writers to conform to socially accepted behavior.
The young Pushkin made a virtue of his naughty pranks, while the mature man of letters,
especially from 1835, made a point of striking a serious note in his public pronouncements.
The habits of *domashnost'* had to move out into the public sphere and be made conventional
according to the practices of public institutions.

Many early-nineteenth-century familiar groups, troubled by the perceived scarcity of periodical publications, attempted to launch their own. They aimed to create periodicals independent from the government and from mass readers' tastes. Beseda brought out nineteen
issues of its *Readings* in 1811–16. The journal published works by Beseda members and articles
on history and the theory of literature. Arzamasians also thought about establishing a periodical but could not agree on its form or direction.[1] The Lovers of Wisdom (Liubomudry),
a familiar association that concentrated on philosophy, published four issues of an almanac,
Mnemosyne (1824–25). The co-editors, Vladimir Odoevsky (1803 or 1804–69) and Küchelbecker,
had different visions: while Odoevsky was interested in philosophy, Küchelbecker wanted to
spread ideas about literature's civic obligations (as shown in his 1824 article "On the Direction
of Our Poetry, Especially Lyrical, in the Last Decade" ["O napravlenii nashei poezii, osobenno
liricheskoi, v poslednee desiatiletie"]). Pushkin's circle was also eager to have a publication of
its own. In 1824, Del'vig started the almanac *Northern Flowers* (*Severnye tsvety*, first issue 1825),
which he continued until his death in January 1831; Pushkin edited the final (1832) issue. In 1830,
Pushkin and Del'vig received permission from the state to publish a weekly newspaper, *The
Literary Gazette* (*Literaturnaia gazeta*). The editors' lack of journalistic savvy, combined with
pressure from fiscally shrewd competitors, led to financial failure: despite contributions from
leading writers, the number of subscribers never exceeded one hundred.[2] The newspaper
closed shortly after Del'vig's death. Pushkin's *The Contemporary* (*Sovremennik*, 1836–37) was only
marginally more successful: the subscription numbers did not go over 600, and the publication

was perpetually troubled financially. After Pushkin's death, under Petr Pletnev's editorship, the number of subscribers fell to 233. The journal became profitable only after Ivan Panaev (1812–62) and Nekrasov acquired it in 1846 and turned it into a truly professional publication. *The Muscovite* (*Moskvitianin*, 1841–56) was perhaps the last journal that can be considered an amateur periodical. Edited by Mikhail Pogodin (1800–75) and Stepan Shevyrev (1806–64), the journal concentrated on history and was nationalistically oriented. It was Shevyrev, a former member of The Lovers of Wisdom, who, in 1842, wrote "an epitaph for the literature of familiar associations," condemning the commercialization of literature and rebuking real Russian intellectuals for their inaction in this critical situation.[3]

Professionalization of literature: Thick journals and literary criticism

The first attempt to professionalize journalism dates to *The Messenger of Europe* (*Vestnik Evropy*), when I. V. Popov (1774–1839), a minor writer, bookseller, and publisher, conceived the idea of publishing a journal and invited Karamzin to be its editor and leading critic. *The Messenger of Europe* succeeded financially under his editorship, with over 1,200 subscribers. Popov paid Karamzin 3,000 rubles a year (2,000, according to other sources)—a sum significantly larger than the salary of a middling bureaucrat in the state service, which allowed Karamzin to support himself and his family. But the writer left his post after two years and applied to Alexander I for financial support in order to write his multi-volume *History of the Russian State*, thus ending his stint as a professional writer. *The Messenger of Europe* continued to do well under subsequent editors (including Zhukovsky in 1808–11; in 1810–11 jointly with Mikhail Kachenovsky [1775–1842]) until the late 1810s, then began to fade during the 1820s, and closed in 1830. The publication reemerged in 1866 under the editorship of Mikhail Stasiulevich (1826–1911) as a new journal; by adopting the same name, it claimed a link to Karamzin's original publication. Another commercially successful periodical was *The Son of the Fatherland* (*Syn otechestva*), edited by Nikolai Grech (1787–1867) from 1812 to 1825. The journal counted the best writers of the time among its contributors. It was the first periodical to introduce illustrations, and it inaugurated the genre of yearly critical review (best known thanks to Belinsky's subsequent distinguished use of the rubric). The journal's success was reflected in the high number of subscribers: its print runs were between 1,200 and 1,800. *The Son of the Fatherland* continued to appear, with intervals and under different editors, until 1852. *The Northern Bee* (*Severnaia pchela*), a newspaper that Faddei Bulgarin (1789–1859) and Grech started in 1825 (it survived until 1864) was also popular and financially successful, in part owing to the support and protection from the Third Section.[4] This support from the section of the police in charge of secret operations resulted in the newspaper's losing the respect of the intellectual elite, but it continued to flourish because of its appeal to the mass reader with down-to-earth tastes.

Appeal to a broad readership also marked Nikolai Polevoi's *The Moscow Telegraph* (*Moskovskii telegraf*, 1825–34).[5] Polevoi (1796–1846) held his contributors to high standards. This was immensely ambitious for an autodidact coming from a merchant family, but it was a successful strategy. In its first year, the journal had some 1,500 subscribers, a figure that would grow to more than 2,500. Polevoi's determination to reach the mass reader, and his ability to achieve commercial success put his journal at odds with both elite and more popular journals. These disagreements caused what Polevoi himself called the "journal wars." In 1825–27, Grech and Bulgarin clashed with him over a fierce competition for readers. In 1830–31, similar discord erupted with Pushkin's circle concerning the professionalization of literature and, particularly, the rise of serious literary criticism. This second disagreement acquired political overtones, since Polevoi dubbed his opponents an "aristocratic party" opposed to the development of new trends in literature, particularly to democratization. In their turn, his opponents accused Polevoi of being a Jacobin journalist and a rabble-rouser. Eventually, *The Moscow Telegraph* was shut down on the grounds that it ostensibly menaced the social order. Polevoi's confrontation with the literary establishment cost him his career as a journalist, but his impact was enduring: the next generation of journalists and critics followed both his editorial practices and his principles as critic.

The Library for Reading (Biblioteka dlia chteniia, 1834–65) made further important steps toward professional journalism: its founder and publisher, the successful bookseller Aleksandr Smirdin (1795–1857), ensured its financial stability by paying the editor extremely well: Osip Senkovsky (Józef Julian Sękowski, 1800–58) knew Arabic, Persian, Turkish, and Hebrew, and in 1822 was appointed professor of oriental languages at St. Petersburg University. As the editor of *The Library for Reading*, he earned a very high yearly salary of 15,000 rubles, in addition to honoraria for published materials. Smirdin also established fixed royalty payments for contributors, between 200 and 1,000 rubles per signature (that is, per sheet), depending on the writer's reputation. Smirdin's choice of Senkovsky as the editor proved to be prescient: not only did Senkovsky issue the journal on schedule, he also attracted the best contributors (including Pushkin), and, most importantly, shaped and educated his readership.[6]

The success of Grech's *The Son of the Fatherland*, Polevoi's *The Moscow Telegraph*, and Senkovsky's *The Library for Reading* led to the emergence of the so-called thick journal. Considered to be a Russian journalistic phenomenon, the thick journal is defined by its size (300–500 pages) and by containing predictable, regular sections (such as literature, criticism, politics, science, and fashion). This desire to be encyclopedic is the embodiment "of the Russian urge to set journals at the very center of their culture."[7] The tendency to be encyclopedic can be traced at least to Karamzin's *The Messenger of Europe*, but the true precursor of the thick journal as such was Polevoi's *Moscow Telegraph*, which was both popular with mass readers and filled with high-quality diverse content. Later in the century, these journals actively debated the need for reform and renewal in all spheres of life, addressing such problems as the peasant question; freedom of the press and openly legal proceedings (*glasnost'*); women's liberation from inequality and family tyranny (the woman question); economic policy and the effects of modernization, including the railroad; and the implications of scientific developments. The writers of these journals were drawn from broader social strata than in the Pushkinian period, but the lifeblood of the talent were the so-called *raznochinnaia intelligentsia* (from *raznochintsy*), a group of university-educated, professional intellectuals of varied origins (mostly clerical and petit bourgeois) bound together by a spirit of opposition to the existing order. Less liberal, such as Dostoevsky's *Time* (Vremia, 1861–63) and *Epoch* (Epokha, 1864–65), and, beginning in the 1860s, increasingly conservative thick journals also existed (Mikhail Katkov's [1818–87] *The Russian Herald* [Russkii vestnik, 1856–87; also translated as *Russian Messenger*] in its later years), and they actively participated in the debates mentioned above, bringing in different perspectives.

Andrei Kraevsky (1810–89) is credited as the creator of the first thick journal, *Notes of the Fatherland* (Otechestvennye zapiski). The journal existed, with intervals, from 1818 to 1884, but it was under Kraevsky's editorship, beginning in 1839, that it grew in size to some 500 pages. Its coverage also expanded to accommodate a broad range of readers and their various interests with sections on current events, sciences, literature, arts, housekeeping (including agriculture and industry), criticism, and current bibliography. Financially savvy, from the very beginning Kraevsky was able to enlist the best contributors: Vladimir Odoevsky, Baratynsky, Viazemsky, Gogol; and later, Herzen, Nekrasov, Dostoevsky, Turgenev, and Ivan Goncharov (1812–91). Some of Russia's most celebrated works of fiction, including Dostoevsky's *The Double* (Dvoinik, 1846; subtitled "A Petersburg Poem") and Goncharov's *Oblomov* (1859), first appeared in Kraevsky's *Notes of the Fatherland*. It also published works by women writers, such as Maria

Zhukova, Elena Gan, and the highly regarded Nadezhda Sokhanskaia (1823 or 1825–84; published under the pseudonym Kokhanovskaia). Belinsky joined the journal as its leading critic and manager of the bibliography section in the fall of 1839. This was a turning point in the journal's history and that of Russian literary criticism; he remained with the journal until 1846 when he joined Nekrasov's and Panaev's *The Contemporary*. It was in *Notes of the Fatherland*, however, that Belinsky published the majority of his most important criticism, including his articles on Gogol, reviews of Lermontov's prose and poetry, and a series of eleven articles dedicated to Pushkin—still considered a milestone in the canonization of Pushkin as Russia's "first" poet (*Works of Alexander Pushkin* [*Sochineniia Aleksandra Pushkina*, 1843–46]). Belinsky also used *Notes of the Fatherland* to propagate his Westernizing views; he systematically reviewed European literature in translation, both serious prose (Balzac, George Sand, Hugo, Hoffmann, Dickens) and pulp fiction (Charles Paul de Kock, Eugène Sue). He did not reject entertainment literature as a genre: while often criticizing it as silly and implausible, he acknowledged its escapist appeal. He lavished as much care and critical discernment on Western as on Russian authors.[8] In 1840, Belinsky began to produce yearly critical reviews, analyzing contemporary literature and often discussing literary theory. His enduring reputation as the most influential literary critic in the history of Russian journalistic criticism is based mostly on his contributions to *Notes of the Fatherland*.

In the 1840s, *Notes of the Fatherland* was clearly the leading periodical: its print run rose to 8,000 copies, unprecedented for Russia, and the number of subscribers reached 4,000 in 1847. Even though *The Contemporary* eclipsed it in the 1850s and 1860s, in 1868, when Nekrasov assumed the actual editorship of *Notes of the Fatherland* (with Kraevsky as a nominal editor), its reputation grew again. Under Nekrasov—and, after his death in 1877, under Mikhail Saltykov-Shchedrin (1826–89; pen name Shchedrin) and his co-editor Nikolai Mikhailovsky (1842–1904), the theorist of Populism (*narodnichestvo*)—the best writers and critics of the period published in the journal, including Dostoevsky, Saltykov-Shchedrin, Dmitry Pisarev (1840–68), and Mikhailovsky himself. In 1884, because of its radical populist leanings, the journal was closed for good.

In 1846, after Nekrasov and Panaev took over the ownership of *The Contemporary*, and, two years later, its editorship, it became a leading thick journal. Belinsky moved there from *Notes of the Fatherland*, and although his term there had been brief (he died from tuberculosis in 1848), he had left his mark. He published in *The Contemporary* his last two yearly reviews and a disparaging article about Gogol's 1847 *Selected Passages from the Correspondence with Friends* (*Vybrannye mesta iz perepiski s druz'iami*), which criticized Gogol's turn to religion and monarchism. The article initiated an informal exchange with the offended Gogol, and concluded with Belinsky's famous "Letter to Gogol" ("Pis'mo k Gogoliu"; written in 1847, due to its allegedly subversive content, it was first published abroad in 1855). In 1853, Nikolai Chernyshevsky joined the editorial board of the journal and, in 1858, so did Nikolai Dobroliubov (1836–61), who first became a contributor two years earlier, in 1856. Both published their most important criticism in *The Contemporary*, including Chernyshevsky's nine *Sketches of the Gogolian Period of Russian Literature* (*Ocherki gogolevskogo perioda russkoi literatury*, 1855–56), in which he elaborated his theory of the social role of art; and Dobroliubov's influential "What is Oblomovism?" ("Chto takoe oblomovshchina?," 1859) and "A Ray of Light in the Kingdom of Darkness" ("Luch sveta v temnom tsarstve," 1860). The journal attracted the best writers of its day: Goncharov, Herzen, the young Tolstoy, and Saltykov-Shchedrin. Once again politics played a role in the journal's fate: in 1862, *The Contemporary* was halted for eight months for its supposedly harmful political tendency; it was closed for good in 1866 by personal order of Alexander II.

Mikhail Katkov's *The Russian Herald* took its name from two previous publications, first the patriotic journal edited by Sergei Glinka (1775–1847) in 1808–20 and 1824 (in 1821–23 only its supplement, "The New Reading for Children" ["Novoe detskoe chtenie"], was published) and financed by Fedor Rostopchin (1763–1826), the governor of Moscow at the time of Napoleon's invasion; and then Grech's and Nikolai Polevoi's 1841–44 publication supportive of the official nationality doctrine. In the beginning, Katkov's *The Russian Herald* was quite liberal, gradually becoming conservative only in the 1860s after the Great Reforms were initiated. In the last years of Katkov's tenure as its editor, it was considered by many to be far to the right, publishing a broad range of anti-nihilist novels, from Dostoevsky's *Demons*, to Vsevolod Krestovsky's (1840–95) virulent *The Flock of Panurge* (Panurgovo stado, 1869) and *Two Forces* (Dve sily, 1874; the novels were eventually combined into *The Bloody Bluff* [Krovavyi puf]) and even refusing to publish materials not in line with Katkov's views. Notoriously, Katkov refused to publish the epilogue to *Anna Karenina*, first serialized in his journal in 1875–77, because he did not accept Tolstoy's disapproval of Russia's involvement in the Balkans. Having among its contributors Konstantin Leont'ev (1831–91), a conservative thinker, writer, and critic; and Konstantin Pobedonostsev (1827–1907), the Ober-Procurator of the Holy Synod and powerful adviser to Alexander III, sealed the journal's reputation as a reactionary publication for years to come.

It was not only during its liberal years but also in the 1860s and 1870s that *The Russian Herald* published the most important writers of the period, the giants of the Russian novel (Turgenev, Tolstoy, and Dostoevsky) as well as a host of other outstanding writers (Goncharov, Saltykov-Shchedrin, Sergei Aksakov [1791–1859], Aleksandr Ostrovsky [1823–86], Nikolai Leskov [1831–95], Tiutchev, and Fet). At first, the radicalization of *The Contemporary* in the late 1850s helped Katkov to attract both moderately conservative and liberal-minded writers, including Tolstoy and Turgenev.[9] But the journal continued to appeal to the best writers because its large circulation enabled Katkov to offer substantial honoraria.[10] *The Russian Herald* made it possible for contributors to support themselves by writing, the final step in professionalization of literature in Russia. After Katkov's death in 1887, the journal moved even further to the right; it existed as such until 1906.

The Northern Herald (Severnyi vestnik, 1885–98) was one of the last nineteenth-century thick journals; it was also a precursor of avant-garde publications. After *Notes of the Fatherland*'s closing in 1884 and *The Russian Herald*'s reactionary turn after Katkov's death, it was *The Northern Herald* to which the Populist writers and critics moved and, at the same time, where many eminent writers, including Leskov, Tolstoy, and Anton Chekhov (1860–1904), began to publish. In the 1890s, it also became a primary publication for the early Symbolists, such as Dmitry Merezhkovsky (1865–1941), Nikolai Minsky (1855–1937), Zinaida Gippius, and Fedor Sologub (1863–1927; born Teternikov). Fully professional, the journal adopted a tolerant position in relation to writers whose views clashed. By encouraging the coexistence of different, even opposing, views, it ushered in the modernist movement.[11]

The late nineteenth century also saw the emergence (or reemergence, if one reaches back to eighteenth-century satirical journals) of a new journalistic genre, what could be called a monojournal: the journal produced by one person.[12] Its first practitioner was Fedor Dostoevsky, the sole author, editor, and publisher of *Diary of a Writer* (Dnevnik pisatelia, 1873, 1876–77, 1880, 1881). By the time he launched the *Diary of a Writer*, he was a consummate journalist: in the 1840s, he published feuilletons in various periodicals; in the 1860s, he and his older brother Mikhail published two journals, *Time* and, after it was closed, *Epoch* (after Mikhail's death in 1864, Dostoevsky continued to edit it alone). Both journals propagated a version of Slavophilism, *pochvennichestvo*, from *pochva*, soil, advocating with that metaphor for an organic connection to national tradition. In his journals, Dostoevsky published both his own works (*The Insulted and the Injured* [Unizhennye i oskorblennye, 1861]; *Notes from the House of the Dead* [Zapiski iz mertvogo doma, 1861–62; usually translated as *The House of the Dead*], *Notes from the Underground* [Zapiski iz podpol'ia, 1864]) and writings by Nekrasov, Turgenev, and Leskov, among many others. Criticism was contributed by Apollon Grigor'ev (1822–64), an exponent of what he called "an organic criticism" and a fellow *pochvennik* ("ideologist of the soil") and Nikolai Strakhov (1828–96), also a *pochvennik*.[13]

Dostoevsky's monojournal originated in a column titled *Diary of a Writer* that he published in the weekly *The Citizen* (*Grazhdanin*), which he edited for its publisher, the conservative journalist Vladimir Meshchersky (1839–1914), in 1873–74. In 1876–77 and in 1880–81, Dostoevsky issued the *Diary* as a separate monthly publication. In many ways, his monojournal resembled nineteenth-century thick journals (it had subscribers, covered domestic and foreign affairs, published criticism and literary works), but its various materials were united by Dostoevsky's authorial persona and thus reflected his preferences and interests. And it was shaped by his predilection for certain genres: the feuilleton, the utopian tale, and confessional narrative, which he considered conducive to his purposes. The feuilleton, in particular, was among Dostoevsky's favorite genres, going back to the beginning of his journalistic career. Written in the first person, responsive to contemporary issues, and allowing humor and satire, this versatile genre fitted Dostoevsky's purpose of reaching mass readership with his discussions of a variety of issues, including the successes and failures of the 1860s' court reform (in "Milieu" ["Sreda," 1873]), the state of Russian penitentiary system ("Correctional Institution for Underage Criminals" ["Koloniia dlia maloletnikh prestupnikov," 1876]), broken families ("A Future Novel. Again 'an Accidental Family'" ["Budushchii roman. Opiat' 'sluchainoe semeistvo'"], 1876), and suicide ("Two Suicides" ["Dva samoubiistva," 1876]), to name a few. Some of Dostoevsky's most celebrated short fiction, including "A Gentle Creature" ("Krotkaia," 1876), appeared in the *Diary*. Extraordinarily popular, *Diary of a Writer* engendered emulations, including the Symbolist Fedor Sologub's journal *Diaries of Writers* (*Dnevniki pisatelei*, 1914).

Having emerged from the mostly amateur publications put out, first, by familiar associations and journalists such as Grech and Bulgarin, and, later, by Nikolai Polevoi and Senkovsky who searched for ways to professionalize journalism and literature in general, thick journals achieved full professionalization in the second half of the nineteenth century. In addition, they worked out new forms of journalism that heralded the modernist journalistic practices of the early twentieth century.

CASE STUDY Imperial censorship

Censorship, absolutism, and Russian literature traditionally go together in people's minds, with writers seen as champions of free expression from the beginning of the imperial period to the collapse of the totalitarian Soviet Union. Terms like "samizdat" and "underground literature," long absorbed into English, surely serve for many people as portmanteau words for the contest between state control and the liberty of print culture. Political censorship became an important factor in Russian print culture with the establishment and rise of secular literature (which was not immune to intermittent religious censorship). Mechanisms of control and their enforcement developed in tandem with the huge increase in print culture that occurred over the course of the nineteenth century across the entire multiethnic empire.

In the imperial period, censorship by the state was initially sporadic; the authorities gradually evolved more systematic mechanisms, rules, and procedures for vetting, regulating, and curbing literary production. The licensing first of private presses in the 1770s, followed by the Free Press Edict (1783), fostered a substantial expansion of commercial presses. Gradually, a need for oversight became obvious to the government, and there are examples, even in the 1780s, a generally liberal decade, of individuals exercising self-censorship, presumably fearing rebuke or loss of favor. The most flagrant instances of state suppression of the freedom of the press, which was never a right granted by law, occurred late in Catherine's reign on the direct intervention of the empress herself. Her vitriolic reaction to Radishchev's *Journey from Petersburg to Moscow* showed how personal a reprisal could look, and how unsystematic the process was, since approval had been granted to a version of the book prior to its publication (admittedly, Radishchev's extensive revisions added inflammatory material). In 1796, Catherine closed the private printing presses permitted by the Free Press Edict and established censorship offices in Moscow, St. Petersburg, and, briefly, in Odessa. There were to be three censors in each office, one for ecclesiastical and two for secular works. The ecclesiastical censors were selected by the Holy Synod, the secular censors by the Senate, and academic censors by the Academy of Sciences and Moscow University.

Catherine's son and successor, Paul I, ordered an embargo on the import of foreign books. Alexander I relaxed these measures, but also initiated a gradual move toward a more regular system, issuing the first censorship statute in 1804. The new law established a procedure for preliminary censorship, which was to be implemented by committees staffed with university professors, among others.[14] In the early years of Alexander's reign, whose liberalism petered out with the Napoleonic campaigns, the new vetting system aimed to guarantee that only books promoting "the true enlightenment of the mind and the promotion of morals"—values that one censor, A. V. Nikitenko (1804–77), repeatedly endorsed in the diaries he kept for more than thirty years—would be allowed to appear in print. The so-called "Cast-Iron Statute" ("Chugunnyi ustav"; officially, "Ustav o tsenzure"), promulgated in 1826 by the new Tsar Nicholas I, represented a step change in government regulation of the journalistic and literary press, codifying in 240 paragraphs the rights of the censors to amend authors' language and style and also establishing tighter rules for periodicals. An even more stringent 1828 statute would remain in force until 1917, with periodic emendations.[15] The 1828 statute required that works be evaluated in terms of their presentation of the Russian Orthodox Church and Christianity as well as the tone of references to autocracy. Nicholas I restored the authority of the Holy Synod over all writings broadly classifiable as religious, with ecclesiastical censorship committees in St. Petersburg, Moscow, Kiev, and Kazan'.[16] When a new statute was passed in 1865, all censorship matters, except ecclesiastical, passed to the Chief Administration of Press Affairs in the Ministry of the Interior. A new statute of 1867 aimed at improving the 1865 statute urged that the civil censorship absorb the ecclesiastical censorship agency. It was only in 1905 when the imperial government declared religious toleration and freedom of the press that most forms of censorship, including ecclesiastical vetting, ceased.

The workings of censorship laws and their administrative implementation have been investigated in minute detail. In summary, it is clear that the authorities exercised vigilance by issuing year in and year out hundreds of new instructions, via circulars, containing punctilious guidance to censors in metropolitan and provincial centers, thereby keeping pace with the huge increases in literacy and publishing. Circulars could ban books and periodicals, native or imported, or impose partial bans by limiting print-runs and distribution on political grounds or in public interest. The Ministry of Education, through its local censorship committees, monitored the book trade (as well as book production by issuing licenses to printers), checking the stock of publishers as well as libraries. These restrictions proved much harder to enforce in provincial Russia, where censors, who were part-time and belonged to the staff of vice-governors, were poorly briefed and insufficiently resourced to exact compliance, especially given the boom in print culture. Enforced through censorship or administrative action when a publication slipped through the net, restrictions could apply to issues ranging from matters of state, such as diplomatic and economic policy, to personal affairs of the royal household. Writings that challenged the legitimacy of state censorship itself were censored, as were other ideas perceived as subversive or blasphemous.

The reign of Nicholas I, especially from the early 1840s, was quite strict in policing literature through the Third Section and suppressing any hint of sedition or irreligion. While the government did not insist that literature had to promote actively the ideals of the state formulated by Sergei Uvarov, the Minister of Education at the time, as "Orthodoxy, Autocracy, and Nationality," it was clear that it would brook no challenge to Uvarov's policy. Reports on the censorship of literature issued in 1858 and 1863 express a concern over the circulation of Russian émigré journals and clandestine material. Ecclesiastical censors remained alert to sacrilegious treatments of the historical Jesus, including works by Ludwig Feuerbach, Ernest Renan, and David Friederich Strauss, whose writings influenced many writers, including Dostoevsky. Osip Senkovsky, a pioneer journalist and publisher of serialized fiction, complained bitterly in an article of 1857 (published only posthumously in 1880) of the damage that preliminary censorship caused to all parts of the literary system with its capricious, ruthless, and subjective standards. Nikolai Ogarev, the exiled émigré political journalist, recalled that in the late 1840s the circulation of clandestine literature, much harder to regulate and to which the authorities often turned a blind eye, nonetheless completely dried up in the oppressive atmosphere. There were periods of hardening: 1848, for example, saw the establishment of a super-censorship committee in the aftermath of fresh political unrest in Europe. There were also instances of considerable license, depending on how writers negotiated the system, and contingent on the leniency of more sympathetic functionaries, some of whom were distinguished writers. *Quis custodiet ipsos custodies*: censorship proved only as strong as its weakest link, namely, the personal approach and degree of tolerance, as well as intelligence, brought to the job by individual members.

In his "Epistle to the Censor" ("Poslanie tsenzoru," 1822), Alexander Pushkin mercilessly ironized both the rules and his addressee, A. S. Birukov, who was known for his bureaucratic narrow-mindedness and stupidity during his twenty-five year chairmanship of the Foreign Censorship Committee. Pushkin analyzed the censor's skill set, namely his capacity to read between the lines and to appreciate literature in order to catch more subtle forms of subversion.[17] Both writers and readers had to devise highly sophisticated, elliptical, and oblique strategies of truth-telling, strategies that were by their very design clever and artfully wrought evasions. False imprints, false binding (of banned workings under approved titles), or burying of a suspect work in a compilation, the inclusion of "mistaken pages" were just some of the ruses used to evade the system, and the circulation of works in manuscript (of which some famous examples would include Pushkin's blasphemous *Gavriiliada* [c.1821] and Lermontov's "Death of the Poet" ["Smert' poeta," 1837, published 1858]) thwarted the authorities. Ultimately, the sheer scale of the empire, and its ramshackle administrative culture, defeated the centralization of bureaucratic control in the Directorate of Censorship.

Pushkin argued that competence required interpretative skills and taste that could provoke ambivalence and even compromise his work in filtering out subversion by potentially blinding the censor to problematic aspects of a work out of appreciation for artistic merit; and in any case, Pushkin mused, one failsafe against a ban on printing a work was its circulation in manuscript. His conclusions were borne out in due course by the examples of poets such as Tiutchev, Apollon Maikov (1821–97), and Yakov Polonsky (1819–98), and the novelist Ivan Goncharov, who were lauded in their role as censors for exhibiting discretion and professional judgment (although critics of Polonsky questioned how enlightened he truly was since he apparently allowed his mistress to do his censorship job for him).[18]

After the Great Reforms, the penal character of censorship, rather than the pedagogic side, became more overt. Authority was transferred from the Ministry of Education to the Ministry of the Interior and was run through a series of committees established in various cities of the empire, sometimes staffed by university professors under the aegis of the Directorate of Censorship, based in St. Petersburg, and headed by the presidents of the Academy of Sciences and the Russian Academy. New press laws of 1865, in force until the political crises of 1905, relaxed preliminary procedures but granted censors the right to initiate court cases against offenders, and, in response to a flourishing periodical scene, permitted the censor to suspend, fine, or take preemptive action against journals perceived to have "dangerous tendencies." Some variant of these rulings was applied about 500 times before the end of the nineteenth century.[19] Despite its well-developed infrastructure, censorship in the imperial period was rarely a matter of the strict application of legislation. Much depended on the political atmosphere and the willingness of the personnel who served on the committees tasked with reviewing submissions.

One noteworthy pattern concerned the use of censorship to maintain orthodoxy and the values of the Church. Works supportive of religious dissenters, like the Old Believers, were banned. Tolstoy's mass-produced editions of his didactic tales and religious tracts provoked repressive measures (circumvented by the publishing activities of his disciple Vladimir Chertkov [1854–1936] in more tolerant England).

Eforts to control domestic literary production found a counterpart in the Foreign Censorship Committee, established in 1828 to guard against subversion from imported works, including landmarks of émigré literature produced by so-called Russia Abroad. Among its most illustrious members was F. I. Tiutchev, briefly a career diplomat until 1839 and ardent nationalist, as well as a brilliant lyric poet. Tiutchev was the author of a number of memoranda, including "On Censorship in Russia" ("O tsenzure v Rossii," 1857), prepared for the Third Section, on how to reorganize his division. Tiutchev shared the doubts of another distinguished writer who was to serve on his committee, Vladimir Odoevsky (author of the article "On Measures against Foreign Russian Press" ["O merakh protiv zagranichnoi russkoi pechati," 1827]), about how effectively foreign literature could be screened, arguing that a relaxation of rules at home and more tolerance toward polemic would eliminate the demand for clandestine literature.

The mechanisms and pragmatics of censorship systems are not uniform in the history of reading and in the writing of literary history. The unofficial circulation of clandestine literature at home and abroad in Russian is one complicating factor that deserves thorough consideration. As J. C. Coetzee has rightly written, "the history of censorship and the history of authorship—even of literature itself, as a set of practices—are intimately bound together."[20] In Imperial Russia, authors and publishers quietly and defiantly got their works out either without permission or sometimes remarkably legally. The production of literature in these circumstances required individual authors to react to inhibitions by exercising choice that might involve silence (or "writing for the drawer"), self-censorship, stylistic concessions, increased opacity, implication—in a word, the whole panoply of techniques often referred to as Aesopian.

Literature framed according to the strategies of Aesopian language, developed a meta-discourse that included code words and euphemisms that writers drew on to allude to their awareness of constraint; and constraint itself paradoxically inspired literary response, sometimes philosophical, sometimes satirical, and sometimes outright defiant. Writers displayed irrepressible humor and creativity in coining euphemistic code names. Euphemisms, such as "Old Lady," or "my Dear Old Acquaintance," or a "Famous Madam," denoting censorship, occur in many pieces of literary correspondence, a wink to the addressee to read between the lines. A number of authors, including Turgenev and Chekhov, depicted censorship figuratively as a mythical or biblical beast, whether the three-headed Cerberus or a hydra. Saltykov-Shchedrin referred to the waiting period while a work was reviewed as being in the "belly of the whale." Journey metaphors also abound, with Turgenev calling a veto on a play a "shipwreck" on a "hidden reef."[21] Weather-related images were also used to represent the censorship environment: when conditions deteriorated, the weather was "stormy" and the "wind was from the north" (Turgenev); alternatively, when conditions improved then the ice melted in a "censorship thaw."[22] Code words for every stage of the process also proliferated. The tradition of writing about censorship in letters— letters between writers, letters between writers and publishers and other networks— spawned a virtual sub-genre.

Even more substantially, writing about being censored comprises a literary theme of considerable vitality expressed in a range of modes, from polemical essays to epigrams. In "Torzhok," a chapter from the *Journey from St. Petersburg to Moscow*, Aleksandr Radishchev included a quasi-essayistic, quasi-fictional piece on the history of censorship and arguments against it. Incited to write this defense of press freedom by the restoration of censorship in revolutionary France, Radishchev took advantage of the relative license under Catherine's reign, as he perceived it, to review the history of printing in Russia, including an excursus into censorship from antiquity to the modern age. His account identifies the fundamental enlightenment value of printing, and its downside for governments that fear criticism based on free thought. Such fear, he argues, rather than respect for religion or social conservatism, lies at the base of most censorship. We see the impact of this piece on the formulation of the idea of authorial rights and freedom of speech in the figure of Nikolai Ogarev. Co-publisher with Alexander Herzen of the London-based journal *The Bell*, a mainstay of Russian literature abroad, Ogarev edited and introduced the seminal anthology *Hidden Russian Literature of the Nineteenth Century* (*Russkaia potaennaia literatura XIX stoletiia*, 1861) containing classics of clandestine and erotic verse such as Pushkin's *Gavriiliada* and works by the eighteenth-century libertine poet Ivan Barkov. In the spirit of Radishchev's *Journey* (also published on those pages), in their introduction to the anthology Herzen and Ogarev mounted a detailed attack on the regulation of press freedom. The works they published are now canonical and mainstream, yet in their day were clandestine and, if known, deviating from the sanctioned tradition. Within Russia, other writers tread a fine line in the fight to eliminate government intervention. Works of poetry such as Konstantin Aksakov's "The Free Word" ("Svobodnoe slovo," 1854) glorify press freedom as "the miracle of divine miracles" ("chudo iz Bozh'ikh chudes"); sections of Nekrasov's *About the Weather* (*O pogode*, Part One written in 1858–59, Part Two in 1863–65; published in *The Contemporary* in 1859 and 1865, respectively) deride the censors of Pushkin's era.[23] Nekrasov's scathing "Songs on the Free Word" ("Pesni o svobodnom slove," 1865–66) is a cycle of poems organized according to the function of all workers involved in the production of literature, from what Nekrasov calls a "Grub Street grub" ("Fel'etonnaia bukashka") to the "Public" ("Publika"). Sections titled "Typesetters" ("Naborshchiki"), "Literary people," ("Literatory"), and "Carefulness" ("Ostorzhnost'") set the life of the author and his work within the more complex world of the literary field with its newly developed culture of criticism. But poems are especially attentive to censorship as an obstacle and reveal how easily a single veto can destroy the labor of many people, from the author to the typesetter, who collaborate in the production of literature. An epistle by Aleksei K. Tolstoy (1817–75) lampoons the government for its fear of Darwinism as the philosophy of nihilists (1872), satirically exposing the obscurantism of the official policy at a moment when scientific circles progressively debated evolution. In all of these cases, and many more, the publishable defense of freedom of the word afforded each writer a chance to talk about precisely the subject that had been banned. Historians of the book in the West, such as Robert Darnton, identified the role of banned works, literary sub-cultures, and ideas in the long gestation of political movements leading to events like the French Revolution.[24] In Russia, too, this repressive dynamic contributed to a political contest with the Old Regime.

As journalism was coming of age, and the "thick" journals began to enjoy the respect of intellectuals and popularity with general readership, subscriptions made them financially sound and underpinned a new economic model that made the honorarium the wage on which writers could live, thereby enabling professional literature. Serialization of longer works made possible by the "thick journals" provided a new way for writers to achieve financial success. Arguably, the first Russian writer who experimented with publishing a novel in installments was Pushkin, who printed his *Evgeny Onegin* chapter by chapter over the course of seven years, 1825–32. If his experiment was driven by a desire for financial gain—and an argument has been made that it did—then it failed, which does not vitiate his contribution to professionaliza-tion.[25] Pushkin's elegant and idiosyncratic novel in verse eventually lost in competition for money to contemporary writers of adventure novels in prose, such as Bulgarin's *Ivan Vyzhigin* (1829) and Senkovsky's *Fantastic Travels of Baron Brambeus* (*Fantastiheskie puteshestviia Barona Brambeusa*, 1833; Baron Brambeus was Senkovky's own pen name). Pushkin was dejected by this failure, as is evident from his letters of the mid-1830s and from his unfinished novella *Egyptian Nights* (*Egipetskie nochi*, published after his death, in 1837).

Dostoevsky gradually (and at times painfully) managed to earn his living and, toward the end of his life, achieve stability: the modicum of financial independence gave him a broader creative license as a writer of quality fiction. From Western authors—and Dickens's use of serialization was his main model—Dostoevsky learned the art of publishing in installments, for which the thick journals were the best medium. Serialization helped him to turn his writ-ing into a professional occupation.[26] Saltykov-Shchedrin followed in his footsteps in serializing his works at solid pay.

Even though Tolstoy also occasionally serialized his novels (most famously, *Anna Karenina* in *The Russian Herald*), he in fact did not depend on honoraria as badly as Dostoevsky, at least not until his family had grown and his wife insisted that the children had to be educated in Moscow, rather than at home in Iasnaia Poliana. By that time, however, Tolstoy had arrived at the idea that taking money for his literary works was immoral. He and his wife Sofia worked out a loophole: Tolstoy transferred the rights to all works written until 1883 to her name. Even though Tolstoy was unhappy about this arrangement, blaming his wife for forcing him to betray his principles, Sofia's publishing activity financed his continued life on his estate and in his newly acquired Moscow house. Neither Dostoevsky nor Saltykov-Shchedrin believed that selling their writings to journal editors and publishers was immoral. On the contrary, it was precisely earning their living by writing that, in their own eyes, made them truly profes-sional—and thus independent—writers.

An important question is whether serialization affected the architectonics of the novel as genre, and if it did, how. Publishing in installments had given Pushkin freedom to change any plan of his novel, assuming he had one, in the process of writing. Arguably, a built-in flexibility turned the author's capacity to change his story at will into an artistic principle. Dostoevsky initially seemed to use serialization rather traditionally in order to pique his readers' further interest by breaking off episodes at a crisis in the plot. Later, however, Dostoevsky moved closer to Pushkin's approach, and published the initial chapters without knowing what would come next. Financial need compelled Dostoevsky to sell to journals works he had yet to write. While concessions to circumstances may well have been a factor, it remains valid to consider whether Dostoevsky found this writerly strategy of open plotting attractive: he may have seen advantages in being free to alter a story at will in order to reflect his changing intentions or relevant real-life circumstances.[27] The story of Saltykov-Shchedrin's serial publication of *The Golovlev Family* (*Gospoda Golovlevy*, 1875–80, first edition in book form 1883) is particularly noteworthy. First producing and publishing a series of sketches, halfway through the publication Saltykov-Shchedrin changed genres, and the sketches coalesced into a novel, giving it a unique form.[28]

In discussing the professionalization of literature, it is useful to consider the teamwork that made up writers' labors, and how uncredited help was often the crucial element in success. Avdotia Panaeva (1820–93) was instrumental in making Ivan Panaev's and Nekrasov's *The Contemporary* a profitable and thus professional journal.[29] Dostoevsky's wife, Anna Snitkina, was indispensable in her husband's work. With her help as stenographer, he submitted *The Gambler* (*Igrok*, 1867) on time to the publisher F. T. Stellovsky. After their marriage, she continued to transcribe her husband's dictated novels, including *Crime and Punishment* (*Prestuplenie i nakazanie*, 1866), and gave him substantial aid in fulfilling his obligations to publishers and journal editors. Most importantly, "beginning with the first separate edition of *The Devils*, the intrepid Anna Grigor'evna took over the republication of Dostoevsky's major fiction, contracting with printers and selling his books from their own apartment," eventually becoming her husband's publishing agent.[30] When Leo Tolstoy granted Sofia Tolstaya the rights to publish his work, Anna's reputation for success inspired Sofia to ask her for advice, which was readily forthcoming and helpful.[31] The work of writers' wives as de facto literary agents was a further element in the professionalization of Russian literature, and it remains to be studied how women writers, largely deprived of these partnerships or supporting staff, compensated for their absence.

In the last twenty years of the nineteenth century, a number of factors changed the publishing scene. Journals that had formed around old battle lines folded. The long-simmering split between liberal and radical journals turned bitterly confrontational, and a more reactionary government closed down many radical publications. Yet new journals without an obvious ideological line began to appear, such as *The Messenger of Europe* in 1866–1908 under Stasiulevich. Around this time, comic journals popular with mass readership also emerged and flourished, such as *Alarm Clock* (*Budil'nik*, 1873–1917), *Fragments* (*Oskolki*, 1881–1916), and *Dragonfly* (*Strekoza*, 1875–1908). Anton Chekhov began his literary career by publishing in these journals. For him, participation in mass journals served both as a source of needed income (the young writer was his family's main breadwinner) and an opportunity to work out and refine his prose style. No doubt writing for these journals was hackwork in the full sense of the word: Chekhov wrote to order, under deadlines, and in quantities requested by editors. For example, for *Fragments*, where Chekhov published in 1882–85, he wrote more than 270 pieces. Chekhov owed his concise style and his ability to concentrate on only the most important details to the years he spent toiling for these publications. He also made a name for himself while publishing in mass editions. This was the kind of professionalism that would repulse not only the likes of Zhukovsky, but also Pushkin and perhaps even Dostoevsky.

Landmarks in criticism

Thick journals were also excellent and essential forums for the development of professional criticism. A mature critical review was long overdue. In the early decades of the nineteenth century, Karamzin and the future Decembrists Kondraty Ryleev, Aleksandr Bestuzhev, and Wilhelm Küchelbecker were among the ranks of literary critics. Their criticism, although incisive at times, was still addressed to a relatively small group of readers, often friends and acquaintances. Characteristically, Pushkin's quite bitter "Refutation of Criticism" ("Oproverzhenie na kritiki," 1830), polemicizes exclusively with the people he knew, including Ryleev, Viazemsky, and Ivan Kireevsky. He did not publish the piece apart from an excerpt dealing with his long poem *Poltava* (1829), which he printed in 1831 in order to express his surprise at the negative critical response to this narrative poem. Once a darling of the critics, in the 1830s, Pushkin was becoming more and more resentful of what he perceived as unfair attacks on his works. His fury, vented in "Refutation of Criticism," was all the more vehement because he found himself in the crosshairs of the second of the "journal wars" started by Nikolai Polevoi and joined by Grech and Bulgarin. Pushkin's literary antagonists detected among the members of his circle a tendency to address each other and ignore a broader readership; they attacked him sharply for what they perceived as snobbishness typical of "literary aristocrats." Pushkin was deeply hurt. In April of 1834, he wrote to Mikhail Pogodin, explaining his reluctance to publish: "Who cares to appear before a public that does not understand you, only to be cursed by four fools in their journals for six months all but obscenely [*tol'ko chto ne pomaternu*]."[32] Pushkin's own journal, *The Contemporary*, could not compete with the flourishing professional journals. No matter its bravura wit and incisiveness, the implied (and actual) reader of his critiques was still a circle of friends and not the mass reader. The swiftness with which the change to more professional criticism occurred is astonishing. In 1834, the same year when Pushkin complains about "four fools," Belinsky publishes his "Literary Reveries" ("Literaturnye mechtaniia"); in 1839 he joins Kraevsky's *Notes of the Fatherland*; in 1846, Panaev and Nekrasov acquire *The Contemporary* and turn it into both an intellectually influential and profitable publication. In less than ten years after Pushkin's untimely death, the literary landscape underwent a radical change, having embraced both criticism intended for diverse readership and profitability.[33]

The leading critics of the period saw their role as multifaceted: in addition to providing an overview of past literary developments (what later would become a separate field of literary history), a critic was supposed to judge contemporary literary works, thus shaping the literary process and forming the national literary canon by identifying the most important writers of the period—or even the one most prominent writer, "the leader of literature" [*glava literatury*]—as well as assigning suitable places to the rest of the contemporary writers.[34] Belinsky was the first critic who regarded himself as charged with these tasks. Influenced by German Romantic ideas (particularly, by Schelling's *Naturphilosophie*) about criticism as a leading force in developing and shaping national literature, he took up the role of the organizer and coordinator of Russian literature already in his first significant essay, "Literary Reveries." He opens his essay with the announcement (by that time quite familiar to Russian readers) that Russia still does not have literature. And yet he follows with a broad—if not entirely positive—overview of what has been written in Russia from the early eighteenth century up to his time. It is significant that Belinsky divides his review into periods, naming each after the writer he identifies as most important, from Lomonosov to Pushkin. Concluding his overview with Pushkin, he praises him, but talks about his achievement as confined to the past: for Belinsky, the time of Pushkin's leadership has passed. Furthermore, he unfavorably contrasts the poet's earlier works with his latest compositions: "Pushkin, predominantly a poet in Russian, ... whose playful and diverse talent Rus' loved and cherished so much... the author of *Poltava* and *[Boris] Godunov* [written in the 1820s], and the author of *Andzhelo* (*Angelo*) and other dead, lifeless tales [written in the 1830s]!..."[35]

When Belinsky returned to the topic of Pushkin in 1843 and began publishing a series of eleven articles about the late poet, he considered this series to be a part of a larger project that would include two articles on Derzhavin (both 1843) and articles on Lermontov and Gogol (which remained unwritten), and thus constitute a history of Russian literature. Accordingly, Belinsky begins with Pushkin's predecessors, Derzhavin, Karamzin, Batiushkov, and Gnedich, and turns to Pushkin's early lyrics only at the end of the fifth essay. The series concludes with an essay about Pushkin's later works, which Belinsky had discarded as "dead" in his "Literary Reveries." In the 1846 essay, Belinsky's appraisals of these works are mixed: in general, he praises Pushkin's poetry (including his dramas in verse, written in 1830 and traditionally called "Little Tragedies"), but consistently disparages his prose: *The Tales of the Late I. P. Belkin* (*Povesti pokoinogo I. P. Belkina*, 1830), "The Queen of Spades" ("Pikovaia dama," 1834), and *The Captain's Daughter* (*Kapitanskaia dochka*, 1836). Belinsky thus emphasizes his earlier opinion that Pushkin gave Russia its poetry and that this is his claim to fame, but once he had turned to prose, the poet's time was over.

From Belinsky's point of view, first expressed in "Literary Reveries," the time of poetry (of which Pushkin was the best practitioner) has ended, and the time of prose is coming: after "the period of Pushkin," "the period of Smirdin" the publisher of novels and tales follows in Belinsky's review. While Belinsky does not quite approve of an era of commercial literature, he greets this change as the beginning of something new. And although he devotes only one small paragraph in the discussion of prose to Gogol, Belinsky's note, referencing Gogol's first successful collection of tales in two volumes (*Vechera na khutore bliz Dikan'ki*, 1831 and 1832), which is told in the voice of the beekeeper Rudyi Pan'ko, has remarkable force: "Mr. Gogol, who so charmingly disguised himself as a *Beekeeper*, is among phenomenal talents. Who does not know his *Evenings at a Farm near Dikanka*? How much wit, merriment, poetry, and national spirit [*narodnost'*] they have! May God let him fulfill the promise he shows!"[36] He makes no secret of his hopes that Gogol will be "the next" (and an even better) Russian writer after Pushkin. Indeed, Belinsky's subsequent significant essay is "About the Russian Tale and about Mr. Gogol's Tales (*Arabesques* and *Mirgorod*)" ("O russkoi povesti i povestiakh g. Gogolia [*Arabeski i Mirgorod*]"; the date for Gogol's collections and Belinsky's article is 1835). Having discussed and praised all the tales (apart from "The Portrait" ["Portret"]) included in these two collections, Belinsky concludes that Gogol offers immense promise of future success: "These hopes are great, since Mr. Gogol has an extraordinary, powerful, and lofty talent. For now he is the leader of [Russian] literature, the leader of [Russian] poets. He has taken up the place that Pushkin had left."[37] The new term, "the leader of literature," that has replaced the term "genius" is important here: it signals that Belinsky is beginning to form a Russian canon. Canons presuppose hierarchies, with promising writers ranged from minor, secondary talents to first-class wordsmiths; by contrast, the notion of genius is absolute. The term "the leader of literature" also makes it possible to think about literature as a process, even progress: one leader of literature is necessarily replaced by another, and often a better one.

In the early 1840s, Belinsky continued to praise Gogol as the best prose writer of his generation. He joyfully greeted the publication of Gogol's four-volume *Works* (*Sochineniia*, 1842) in his article "Works of Nikolai Gogol" ("Sochineniia Nikolaia Gogolia," 1843): "In respect to literature, the end of the old year and the beginning of the new year could not be marked more brilliantly than by the publication of Gogol's works. God grant that this would be a lucky portent for the new year...."[38] Gogol seems to have fulfilled Belinsky's earlier hopes that he would continue to be the leader of Russian literature. Four years later, however, Gogol's notorious *Selected Passages from the Correspondence with Friends* appeared, and Belinsky first responded to it with a relatively mild criticism: in an essay dedicated specifically to this book and published in *The Contemporary*, he limits his disapproval to a regret that "even a man with tremendous talent can fall just like the most ordinary man."[39] Gogol, however, was offended; he replied with a private letter to Belinsky which attempted to explain the criticism by Belinsky's being personally offended by the book. Belinsky retorted with his famous "Letter to Gogol," and now he no longer held back his indignation at what he saw as Gogol's betrayal of all his ideals (mostly ascribed to him by Belinsky himself) and as "propagation of lies and immorality" "under the cover of religion."[40] Belinsky's frustration was amplified by the fact he felt forced to retract Gogol's title of the leader of Russian literature, the subject of his last article, "A View of Russian Literature of 1847" ("Vzgliad na russkuiu literaturu 1847 g.," published in 1848). Since by that time "a new Gogol," Dostoevsky, had also disappointed Belinsky, Russian literature turned out to be without a leader. Belinsky attempted to make it right by arguing that this was an indication of a high average level of literature, making it stable in the absence of a leader.[41] Even though, as Belinsky states in "A View of Russian Literature of 1847," "after *Dead Souls* Gogol did not write anything," it was crucial that he had created the Natural School (*natural'naia shkola*) that inherited his achievements: "On the literary scene there is now only his school."[42] In Belinsky's view, although Gogol did not leave a successor, he did create a movement, the Natural School, which, from the critic's perspective, is more important, and signifies considerable progress in the field of Russian prose.

To portray Gogol as the progenitor of the Natural School, Belinsky evoked a trend that already existed in Russian prose of the 1840s—a trend created by prose writers whose style and subject matter brought them closer to documentary realism. The term "school" should be loosely understood to refer to writers who shared techniques of representation without formally being members of a movement. In the 1830s, Nikolai Polevoi encouraged writers to shift the social orientation of literature onto more popular material by imitating modes like the feuilleton and physiological sketch as practiced on the pages of French literary almanacs such as *Les Français peints par eux-mêmes*. Polevoi's entreaty worked, and in 1841–42, A. P. Bashutsky (1803–76), a professed imitator of the French physiological sketch, published a series of fourteen slender illustrated almanacs, *Our People, As Copied from Nature by Russians* (*Nashi, spisannye s natury russkimi*), portraying urban types according to social category, profession, and ethnicity (his own contributions were "The Water Carrier" ["Vodovoz"] and "The Coffin Maker" ["Grobovoi master"]). Depictions of city types combined the veracity of economic hardship with an affectionate and sentimental tone. Hardly bestsellers, the almanacs did attract significant interest from writers and critics, and most importantly, a mixed review by Belinsky. He praised the quality of book production as a milestone in contemporary printing, but concluded by criticizing excessive fidelity to the French prototypes, which stood in the way of genuine verisimilitude and made Bashutsky's almanacs only intermittently successful in producing recognizable Russian types. I. I. Panaev's 1841 essay "The Petersburg Feuilletonist" ("Peterburgskii fel'etonist") explores the education and circumstances that motivate people (essentially of mixed-estate background) to write sketches and become this type of "scribbler" (*sochinitel'*). Other notable contributors to the trend include Vladimir Dal (1801–72) ("The Life of a Man, or a Walk along Nevsky Prospect" ["Zhizn' cheloveka, ili Progulka po Nevskomu prospektu"] 1843), Ya. P. Butkov (1820 or 1821–56) ("Petersburg Heights" ["Peterburgskie vershiny," 1845]), V. A. Sollogub (1813–82) (*Tarantas*, also translated as *Travel Notes*; first seven chapters 1840; first edition in book form 1845), the future playwright Aleksandr Ostrovsky ("Notes of a Zamoskovretsky Inhabitant" ["Zapiski zamoskvoretskogo zhitelia," 1847]), and Ivan Kokorev (1825–53) whose focus on the figures in urban landscapes in pieces like "Moscow

Markets" ("Moskovskie rynki," around 1848) used vaudevillian humor to alleviate the misery of reports on poverty. N. A. Nekrasov's *Physiology of Petersburg* (*Fiziologiia Peterburga*, 1845) was a landmark two-volume anthology containing twelve seminal chapters by Nekrasov, D. V. Grigorovich (1822–99), Panaev, and Belinsky. The aim, in Nekrasov's words, was "to expose all the secrets of our social life, all the springs of the happy and sad scenes of our domestic life...and the course and direction of our civic and moral education."[43] The idea that this trend is a school originates with Belinsky, who in his "View of Russian Literature for 1847" writes that the "Natural School now stands at the forefront of Russian literature."[44] The remark was largely meant as a rebuke to Faddei Bulgarin, who in one of the 1846 issues of his newspaper *The Northern Bee* used the term "natural" to denigrate writers whose transcription of reality he dismissed as vulgar. Belinsky, determined to promote the social utility of literature, aimed to bridge the gap between high and low modes of realism by identifying Gogol as the leading writer of the Natural School. Together with Belinsky's earlier essays on Gogol, this title to a significant degree shaped Gogol's image in Russian cultural memory.

CASE STUDY Nikolai Gogol

The image of Nikolai Gogol in Russian cultural memory is unusual since it is linked to the standing of another writer, Alexander Pushkin, which explains Gogol's somewhat ambivalent reputation. On the one hand, Gogol cannot rival Pushkin's preeminence, not being "the sun of our poetry," as the Romantic Vladimir Odoevsky called Pushkin in an obituary; nor is he "our everything," as the critic Apollon Grigor´ev described Pushkin;[45] and his anniversaries have never occasioned extravagant national celebrations, as did the centennial of Pushkin's death in 1937 or his birthday in 1999, and to a lesser extent in 1899. On the other hand, Gogol remains for some readers and critics a more important figure than Pushkin—more significant for the development of Russian prose and more spiritually inspired and inspiring.[46]

Gogol's reputation as an exemplary prose writer overshadowing Pushkin's was first crafted by Belinsky. He portrayed Gogol as a social critic whose masterful representation of Russian reality undermined the stability of the imperial order, its bureaucracy in particular. Belinsky's view was developed by another prominent critic, the radical Nikolai Chernyshevsky, in a series of articles he wrote in the 1850s, tellingly entitled *Sketches of the Gogolian Period of Russian Literature*. In the twentieth century, Soviet literary critics, working to appropriate Gogol as a precursor of Socialist Realism, also espoused this view.[47]

Fedor Dostoevsky, whose prose was strongly influenced by Gogol's, was the first writer to pay serious attention to Gogol's eccentric use of the language. Dostoevsky's polyphony, as described by Mikhail Bakhtin, may be seen to originate in Gogol's play with diverse narrative voices. Toward the end of the nineteenth century, the Symbolists extolled Gogol as a prose writer, downplaying, as had Dostoevsky, his ostensible social criticism and concentrating on the idiosyncratic language of his prose. Beginning with Boris Eikhenbaum's 1918 article "How Gogol's 'Overcoat' is Made," the Formalists further dismantled the view of him as a writer engaged in social criticism. Twentieth-century writers as different as Mikhail Zoshchenko, Mikhail Bulgakov (1891–1940), Vladimir Nabokov (1899–1977), and Andrei Sinyavsky (1925–1997; writing under the pen name Abram Tertz) continued to build on Gogol's stylistic extravagance and on the exuberant mix of linguistic registers that was his trademark.

Gogol's status as a spiritual authority emerged more slowly. From the very beginning of his literary vocation, Gogol, like other writers of the Romantic period, was drawn to the idea that literature (and art in general) had to have a higher meaning, similar to that of religion. Nonetheless, his first attempt at asserting the religious purpose of art, the story

"The Portrait" (two redactions, 1835 and 1842), was not met with enthusiasm, and his last work, the moralizing *Selected Passages from Correspondence with Friends*, was strongly condemned, most significantly by Belinsky. Gogol's reputation as a religious thinker began to emerge soon after his death in 1852. By the late nineteenth century, this side of his reputation was fairly well established, particularly among the Slavophiles. The post-conversion Leo Tolstoy, too, while rejecting Gogol's support of the Russian Orthodox Church, the monarchy, and serfdom in *Selected Passages*, was impressed by the book's religious ideas and especially by Gogol's views of literature as a means of religious teaching. Symbolists also extolled Gogol as a religious figure, attracted by what they perceived as the mystical nature of his religiosity.

Gogol's claims as a spiritual authority and his religious views were disregarded during the Soviet period, only to reemerge in the 1990s. Church officials, school teachers, and even television producers have joined efforts by scholars to reestablish and further Gogol's status as a religious thinker.[48] *Selected Passages* has been rehabilitated and is treated as an important contribution to Russian theology still relevant to today's readership.

It is remarkable that this image of Gogol as the progenitor of Russian prose and as a spiritual authority arose despite the fact that in many respects he looks like a quintessentially peripheral figure in Russian literature and culture. He is marginal in many senses. He came to St. Petersburg, the acknowledged center of cultural, particularly literary, life from what was then "the" Ukraine or Little Russia. As his debut Gogol chose to publish a long narrative poem, *Hanz Kuechelgarten* (1829), in which he not only displayed what Vasily Gippius, a prominent Gogol scholar of the past century, called "stupendous ineptitude and bad taste," but which also was stylistically outdated and awkwardly Germanized. The pretentious pen name V. Alov ("Crimson") completed the picture.[49] When the young Gogol did achieve recognition as a Russian writer, he did so in the narrative guise of Rudy Panko, a socially marginal and barely literate Ukrainian beekeeper. His first successful work, *Evenings at a Farm near Dikanka*, is set in Ukraine, features Ukrainian characters, and uses an imitation of the Ukrainian language: Gogol creates an image of Ukrainian by adding real and pseudo-Ukrainian linguistic elements to the speech of both his narrators and his characters. Gogol artfully exploited his cultural and pretended linguistic marginality in his *Dikanka Tales* and, later, in the collection of stories *Mirgorod*, in order to attract attention and to start moving from the literary periphery to the center.[50]

If in literature Gogol eventually managed to move to the center, his social marginality was more difficult to overcome. A low-ranking provincial, he initially had much trouble in obtaining any service position in St. Petersburg, and when he finally succeeded, it was only at the lowest rank, with boring duties and a meager income. Owing to his literary success, Gogol eventually found high-ranking patrons (Vasily Zhukovsky, the poet and the tutor of Grand Duke Alexander, was perhaps the most important of them). Through them he gained access to decent service positions, first as a teacher of history at the Patriotic Institute, a school for daughters of fallen officers; and later, as an adjunct professor of world history at St. Petersburg University. Characteristically, he proved a failure both times: at the Institute, he was replaced after he overstayed a leave; and at the university, he was dismissed ostensibly on the occasion of the restructuring of the university, but actually for being an uninspiring teacher who neglected his duties.

Even more vexing, however, was Gogol's inability to be accepted as an equal by the St. Petersburg literary elite—the high-society writers like Prince Petr Viazemsky, Zhukovsky, and Pushkin (Zhukovsky was the only one of these three who eventually befriended Gogol). Pushkin's reluctance to accept Gogol as a friend was particularly hard to accept.

To be sure, Pushkin took a favorable view of Gogol's writings (he praised the *Dikanka Tales* and some of his later works, including "Nevsky Prospect") and invited him to collaborate on *The Contemporary* (the collaboration was ephemeral and ended in yet another disappointment), but Gogol never managed to become Pushkin's personal friend despite his obvious eagerness; and while the patronage was welcome, the social rebuff seems to have wounded him deeply. To compensate, he began to present himself first to his friends and later to the public as accepted by his socially superior acquaintances and patrons. After Pushkin's death in particular Gogol vigorously portrayed his relations with Pushkin as a close and ardent friendship. He also resorted to tacit mockery of Pushkin under the guise of admiration.[51]

This brings us to what can be called Gogol's moral marginality: his proclivity for lying, falsification, and pretense. His regular and elaborate lies told to his mother are well documented in their correspondence, and the fact that he lied to others is well established by memoirists and biographers. In a way, Gogol resembled his own character Khlestakov of *The Inspector General* (*Revizor*, first staged 1836), a liar, pretender, and inventor of stories, who, among other things, also claimed to be a close friend of Pushkin. As a result, it is notoriously difficult to write a credible biography of Gogol or to present his views with any degree of confidence. His image fluctuates between that of a high-minded, sincere, and—later in life—deeply religious individual and that of a swindler and a con artist, without ever completely coming into focus. Abram Tertz, in *In the Shadow of Gogol* (*V teni Gogolia*, written in 1970–72, first published in 1975), artfully represents Gogol's remarkable lack of psychological consistency.

Gogol's fiction is no less difficult to interpret, most especially because it pretends to be more realistic that it actually is. The presentation of Ukrainian villages and towns (about which, at least in part, Gogol learned from his mother's letters or thought up on his own) is no less an invention than his presentation of the world of Russian bureaucracy in the Petersburg Tales, or of Russian provincial space in *Inspector General* and *Dead Souls*. The case of *Dead Souls* is particularly illustrative. In 1836, Gogol went abroad and spent about twelve out of the sixteen remaining years of his life outside Russia, mostly in Italy. Paradoxically, it is while in Europe that he wrote his most significant work, *Dead Souls*, in which he presented an image of the Russian provinces. For a century and a half, this image of life outside the capitals as monotonous, outdated, and corrupt replaced in the minds of Russians any actual picture of life in the provinces. Just to illustrate how ignorant of Russian provincial life Gogol must have been, we point out that, according to the calculations of S. A. Vengerov, the writer spent in the Russian countryside altogether about fifty days, most of them on the road, observing from the window of his carriage.[52] Only recently, both in Russia and abroad, have scholars begun to deconstruct Gogol's mirage and discover the actual diversity and richness of Russian provincial life at the time.[53]

Gogol's disastrous entry onto the literary arena was matched by a no less disastrous exit: his last published work, *Selected Passages*, caused a spectacular scandal: the book enraged everyone, foes and friends alike. Whether it deserved such harsh censure remains a topic for debate. But when it appeared, *Selected Passages* marginalized Gogol not only as a writer, but as a person as well: he was suspected of having gone mad, and was accused of having betrayed his progressive social ideals. In this context, it is significant that Gogol failed to complete his magnum opus, *Dead Souls*, despite years of fervent labor. Having published the first volume (see Figure IV.03 for the cover of the first edition designed by Gogol himself), he promised to produce two more, but could not: he reportedly burned two drafts, first in June of 1845 and then again in February of 1852, ten days before his death.

Figure IV.03. N. V. Gogol, *Dead Souls (Mertvye dushi)* (1842), cover of the first edition as designed by Gogol.

Yet neither *Selected Passages* nor Gogol's stymied sequel to *Dead Souls* hindered the explosive growth of his fame immediately after his death (his funeral was attended by thousands). This celebrity no doubt lent its name to the next, most influential literary trend—*gogolevskoe napravlenie*—which survived well into the twentieth century. Paradoxically, it was precisely Gogol's marginality and ambiguity that shaped his image in Russian cultural memory as one of the most enigmatic and, at the same time, brilliantly creative of Russian writers.

Toward the end of his life, Belinsky's position in *The Contemporary* had weakened. It was none other than Pavel Annenkov (1811 or 1813–87), his chief antagonist, who succeeded him as the leading critic of the journal. As a proponent of freedom of art, Annenkov opposed the aesthetic principles supported by Belinsky and, later, Chernyshevsky and Dobroliubov. He was the first Russian critic to produce a significant analysis and critique of the movement that was becoming known as Realism. In one of his early essays published in *The Contemporary*, "Notes about Russian Literature of 1848" ("Zametki o russkoi literature 1848 goda," 1849), he attempted to define Realism and, at the same time, to point out its possible weaknesses. While Annenkov did not deny the value of realism, he indicated how easily mimetic conventions can become ossified, declining into what he calls pseudo-realism, by which he means narratives that are repetitive, predictable, and tendentious.

In 1853, Nikolai Chernyshevsky joined the staff of *The Contemporary*. Starting as a contributor, he became the co-editor in 1859 and remained in this position until 1862 when he was arrested and the journal temporarily closed. Between 1855 and his arrest, Chernyshevsky was the most influential Russian radical critic. His master's thesis, *The Aesthetic Relations of Art to Reality* ("Esteticheskie otnosheniia iskusstva k deistvitel'nosti"; defended and published in 1855), assigned art the utilitarian function of explaining life. Chernyshevsky also propounded this view in his critical essays, particularly *Sketches of the Gogolian Period of Russian Literature*, which further developed Belinsky's take on Realism. Chernyshevsky took a unitary view of truth, arguing that there was nothing separating the real and the ideal, truth and reality. He held that writers were obliged to seek the ideal in reality, although he had little faith that art can be much more than a pale imitation of the real. True to this dogma, and blind to the shape of individual talents, in his critical essays he isolates in fiction elements of realism that look like the basis of a social critique. His essays present Gogol in particular as a Realist writer and a social critic. Chernyshevsky expressed a positive view of Turgenev's 1850s stories, too, and hailed the appearance of Tolstoy's early works. He pinned his true hopes for the future correct development of Russian literature on Nikolai Uspensky (1837–89), a minor writer known for frank portrayal of peasants as drunk, cruel, greedy, and ignorant. Chernyshevsky considered these depictions to be more compassionate and honest than the idealization of peasantry exemplified, in Chernyshevsky's view, by Grigorovich and Turgenev.[54] The hopes Chernyshevsky placed in Uspensky as a truthful portrayer of peasant life is evident in the title of the essay he wrote about him, "Is Not This the Beginning of a Change?" ("Ne nachalo li peremeny?", 1861). This sadly erroneous essay was one of the last written by Chernyshevsky: his arrest in June of 1862 on the suspicion of sedition and subsequent Siberian exile ended not only his career as a critic but deprived him of all semblance of a normal life.

Between 1855 and 1860 intellectuals addressed fundamental questions about the nature of art and literature. "Art," "aesthetics," and "realism" become watchwords in the critical debates about artistic ideology and in the discussions of whether art obeys its own laws as an independent object or whether reality is superior to art. In addition to Chernyshevsky, other influential voices were raised in debate. Nikolai Dobroliubov began contributing to *The Contemporary* in 1856. His best-known reviews are "What is Oblomovism?," which discusses Goncharov's novel and the social and psychological characteristics of its hero; and "A Ray of Light in the Kingdom of Darkness," on Ostrovsky's *The Storm* (*Groza*, 1859). Chernyshevsky considered Dobroliubov to be the future leader of Russian literature, and when he died of tuberculosis at the age of twenty-five, Chernyshevsky attempted to attribute this title to him posthumously.[55] In the 1860s, Dmitry Pisarev, the leading reviewer of *The Russian Word* (*Russkoe slovo*, 1859–66), was the most radical critic and earned a reputation as the only "true" nihilist in Russian criticism. He was the only one to accept Turgenev's Bazarov as a faithful portrait of a nihilist. In his 1864 essay "Realists" ("Realisty"), Pisarev rejected the aesthetic significance of art, and in "Pushkin and Belinsky" (1865, two parts) he demonstrated that Belinsky's attribution of social significance to Pushkin's works was entirely unfounded. It followed from this for Pisarev that Pushkin as well as Gogol and Lermontov had no value. By contrast, in the article "The New Type" ("Novyi tip," 1865), he praised Chernyshevsky's *What Is to Be Done?* as a novel that was "created by the labor of a strong mind," a novel which shows "the hallmark of profound thought."[56] Pisarev's last article before his untimely death (probably by suicide) was the 1868 "Old Gentry" ("Staroe barstvo"), conceived as the first in a series. It reviewed the first three volumes of Tolstoy's *War and Peace*, which Pisarev calls "an exemplary work about the pathology of Russian society." Pisarev does not deny Tolstoy's talent, but, in his view, it is exactly this talent that allows him, unintentionally, to portray people who can live without "knowledge, without thinking, without energy, and without working."[57] At the same time, it is obvious from Pisarev's essay that he had not begun to fathom the originality and uniqueness of Tolstoy's historical novel. He regarded it as a typical novel, and nothing exposes his mistake more cruelly than his view that Boris Drubetskoi, a minor character and social climber, is the work's protagonist.

Alongside the radical critics of the 1850s and 1860s there were a number of moderate and conservative critics. Apollon Grigor'ev, a Slavophile and, later, a *pochvennik*, was a proponent of "organic criticism"; he described its principles in such essays as "Some Words about the Laws and Terms of Organic Criticism" ("Neskol'ko slov o zakonakh i terminakh organicheskoi kritiki," 1859) and "Paradoxes of Organic Criticism" ("Paradoksy organicheskoi kritiki," 1864). The gist of his aesthetic theory was that criticism should regard art as an organic outgrowth of the life of the nation. In "A View of Russian Literature since Pushkin's Death" ("Vzgliad na russkuiu literaturu so smerti Pushkina," 1859), Grigor'ev names Pushkin as the writer whose works, such as *The Captain's Daughter*, most organically grew from the national soil. It is in this essay that he famously called Pushkin "our everything" ("Pushkin—eto nashe vse"). By contrast, Grigor'ev argued, Lermontov's *Hero of Our Time* with its Byronic hero is alien to Russian culture. Grigor'ev also was the first to give a positive assessment of Gogol's *Selected Passages* (Sergei Aksakov and Tolstoy would later follow suit). His interpretations of Oblomov the character and *Oblomov* the novel were in sharp disagreement with Dobroliubov's "What is Oblomovism?": Grigor'ev appreciated Oblomov's Christian qualities, such as his quietness and resignation (seen by Dobroliubov as passivity) as well as his marriage to a simple Russian woman. However, the most important writer of his time, in Grigor'ev's view, was the playwright Aleksandr Ostrovsky, whom he valued for his skillful representation of Russian life in all its aspects, including social and professional groups often ignored by Russian writers of the time, such as merchants or actors.

The name of Nikolai Strakhov is most closely associated with Dostoevsky and Tolstoy. Grigor'ev's and Dostoevsky's fellow *pochvennik*, Strakhov began his career as a critic in Dostoevsky's journals *Time* and *Epoch*. He devoted two positive reviews to *Crime and Punishment* (both 1867) and published many biographical materials about Dostoevsky after his death in 1881.[58] In 1870,

Strakhov produced a series of essays on *War and Peace*, later reworked into *A Critical Analysis of "War and Peace"* (*Kriticheskii razbor "Voiny i mira,"* 1871). After that, he and Tolstoy became personal friends. Deeply religious, Strakhov critiqued Chernyshevsky and Pisarev, and wrote against nihilism (see his *Letters about Nihilism* [*Pis'ma o nigilizme,* 1881]). Strakhov also produced a three-volume work critical of the West, *The Struggle with the West in Our Literature* (*Bor'ba s Zapadom v nashei literature,* 1882–96). The title is somewhat misleading: the three-volume edition, a collection of Strakhov's articles, is only partly devoted to Russians' views of the West: there is a part on Herzen and his disillusionment with the West (vol. 1, pp. 1–144); an overview of Russian literature from Lomonosov to the 1850s, with an emphasis on Russian writers' disagreements with the West (vol. 1, pp. 1–44); and an article on Belinsky (vol. 3, pp. 356–84). The rest of the collection contains Strakhov's critical discussions of Western philosophers, such as John Stuart Mill, Ernest Renan, David Friedrich Strauss, Charles Darwin, and Hippolyte Adolphe Taine. Strakhov's articles on various subjects—the Paris Commune, spiritism, nihilism, and natural sciences—are also included. The collection was popular and was republished several times in the late 1880s and 1890s.

Konstantin Leont'ev is another conservative philosopher, writer, and publicist, whose brilliant criticism considered aesthetics. His most significant essay is *Analysis, Style, and Import: On the Novels of L. N. Tolstoy* (*Analiz, stil' i veianie. O romanakh grafa Tolstogo,* written in 1890, published in 1911); it is one of the first works in Russian literary criticism to insist on the importance of form in a work of art. It is noteworthy that in writing about formal aspects of literature Leont'ev used the word "device" (*priem*), critical at a later date for the Formalists. It is probably no coincidence, given the fact that his essay was published around the time when the Formalist movement began to take shape. His work was one of the pivots on which the turn toward aesthetic considerations in literary judgments would come to stand.

3

Subjectivities

Diary-writing and autobiography:
Documentary and fictional self-presentation

Sentimentalist attention to emotions, evident in the late-eighteenth- and early nineteenth-century literature—in travelogues, sentimentalist tales, and in verse epistles so popular at that time—as well as the masonic interest in the "inner man" manifested itself in a strong urge to analyze one's own character. It is no wonder therefore that the posthumous publication of Rousseau's *Confessions* (the first volume appeared in 1782 and the second in 1790) generated vigorous responses from the Russians, especially from Freemasons who were both attracted by Rousseau's energetic and sincere self-examination and disagreed with his acceptance of his own shortcomings as natural and thus forgivable. Unlike Rousseau, the Freemasons saw human nature as corrupt and in need of improvement, and it is the acknowledgment of one's depravity and striving to become a better man that comes to the fore in autobiographical accounts produced by Freemasons and other writers who were close to masonic circles and thus affected by their ideas.

One such autobiographical account was penned by the playwright Denis Fonvizin. Paralyzed by a stroke at the age of forty, the former skeptic and admirer of Voltaire turned religious and responded to Rousseau's pseudo-confession in the unfinished *Open-Hearted Confession about My Deeds and Thoughts (Chistoserdechnoe priznanie v delakh moikh i pomyshleniiakh*, written in the early 1790s, before Fonvizin's death in 1792; partially published in 1798; fully in 1830), filled with regret and repentance. Contrary to Rousseau, who celebrates human nature in all its manifestations, Fonvizin follows St. Augustine's idea of man as inherently sinful; he therefore sees the main purpose of his confession (*priznanie*, acknowledgment) in conceding that he had sinned, focusing not on who he was as a person (as Rousseau did), but on his inherent sinfulness.[1] Although there is no documentary evidence that Fonvizin himself was a Freemason, many of his close friends were, and his novel views on the human nature as being in need of improvement suggest he had assimilated masonic ideas.

Introspection and self-scrutiny—habits of mind already cultivated in the eighteenth century, partly owing to religious movements like Pietism and the influence of Freemasonry—increasingly encouraged individuals to turn to confessional writing in the early nineteenth century. The diary of Andrei Turgenev reflects the trend. The older son of a prominent Freemason, Ivan P. Turgenev (1752–1807), Andrei began his diary in November of 1799, the same year in which he wrote and published the first Russian biography of Benjamin Franklin; he kept his diary until his untimely death in May of 1803. Freemasons encouraged diary-writing as a means of self-knowledge and self-improvement. They were following the example of Franklin, whose collected works, including his autobiography, were published in Russian in

1791; Freemasons also took inspiration from John Mason, whose 1745 treatise *Self-Knowledge* was translated and published in 1783 by Andrei's father.[2] Following both Franklin's and Mason's examples, Andrei did not spare himself, writing with repentance about all his transgressions, such as his visit to a brothel and the resulting gonorrhea, his infatuation with an actress, and his insincere behavior toward the woman he had claimed to love. His dissatisfaction with his behavior was so strong that his unexpected death was seen by some as a suicide.[3] In 1804–06, Vasily Zhukovsky, Andrei's friend and, like him, a member of the Friendly Literary Society, also kept a diary in which he analyzed his behavior and tried to understand and to better himself following both Franklin and Mason.[4]

The masonic influence can also be detected in the memoir of Anna Labzina (1758–1828), who, as a young woman, spent five years in the family of Mikhail Kheraskov, a poet and a prominent Freemason. After her first husband died, she married another Freemason, Aleksandr Labzin. It was during her years as his wife, in 1810, that she produced her memoir. It exists in two versions: a short, unfinished "Description of life of One Noblewoman" ("Opisanie zhizni odnoi blagorodnoi zhenshchiny"), focused on the death of her father, which she actually did not remember, as she informs the reader in the first lines of the second, much longer but also unfinished (it breaks off in mid-sentence), memoir titled "1810. I will describe all my life, as much as I can remember" ("1810. Opishu vsiu zhizn', skol'ko mogu vspomnit'"). The title of the latter memoir provides the apparent reason for abandoning the former attempt: Labzina wants to stress the eyewitness nature of her piece and thus its authenticity. Despite her striving for authenticity, her memoir—which describes her first unhappy marriage to a libertine fifteen year older than his thirteen-year bride—is far from being free of influences of contemporary debates on Enlightenment and, as Gary Marker points out, "offer[s] a running commentary on the prevailing oppositions of male/female, public/private, freedom/discipline, and—most critically—faith/reason."[5] More importantly, Labzina did not shy away from opening her private life to public view and, while remaining in the feminine sphere, from showing firmness and power.[6] She resisted her well-educated yet dissolute husband who urged her to behave in the same way. It is noteworthy that even though all her spiritual advisors (her dying mother, her supportive mother-in-law, and even Mikhail Kheraskov who provided a modicum of protection from her husband's demands) urge her to be patient with her husband's libertine behavior, she could not help but rebel, showing remarkable independence. In terms of style, Labzina's memoir shows influences of Sentimentalism, "sentimentalism that surrounded her," but which she most likely did not read.[7] But it was also influenced by devotional literature, such as the Gospels, with its focus on the Holy Virgin as a sufferer and intercessor and with its masonic vocabulary.[8] Both traditions provided models of strength and self-reliance, which formed her character as a firm and autonomous woman. Yuri Lotman, in his *Conversations about Russian Culture*, portrays Labzina as resisting the sound guidance of her well-educated husband, who was trying, as Lotman argues, to introduce her to his libertine philosophy— even though, in Lotman's view, she naively perceived his behavior not as a philosophical alternative to her faith, but as sheer depravity.[9] However, Labzina's self-reliance is obvious in her memoir and is even more obvious in her 1818 diary that is very informal, shows no literary influences, and reveals her as a strong woman involved in her second husband's masonic affairs and impatient with his detractors.

Not all autobiographies and diaries produced at the turn of the century were inward-looking and confessional. Among women's autobiographical accounts, Varvara Bakunina's (1773–1840) "The Persian Campaign of 1796" ("Persidskii pokhod v 1796 g.," first published in 1887) stands out as a rare record of military operations offered by a woman. Varvara was allowed to accompany her officer husband on Platon Zubov's (the last of Catherine's favorites) expedition against the Persian invasion of the Caucasus in 1795. Written in French in the form of a letter to her sister, the memoir covers the first three and a half months of the campaign; it provides a competent "commentary on the army leadership," descriptions of daily life in military camps, and discerning ethnographic observations.[10]

Later in life, from January to August of 1812, Bakunina kept a diary that described the society's reaction to important events of this time: the exile of Mikhail Speransky, the invasion of Napoleon, and the appointment of Barclay de Tolly as the commander of the Russian army.[11] Her diary captures the mood of contemporary society, particularly its apocalyptic bent, extraordinarily well.[12]

CASE STUDY Nadezhda Durova

The writer we know as Nadezhda Durova (1783–1866) has left us multiple autobiographical texts, including a brief "Autobiography," two accounts of her childhood, and a much longer narrative known as *The Cavalry Maiden* (*Zapiski kavelerist-devitsy*; the first full publication of 1836 was entitled *Kavalerist-Devitsa, proisshestvie* [occurance] *v Rossii*). Dressed as a man and renamed by Alexander I as Aleksandr Andreevich Aleksandrov (she had previously introduced herself as Aleksandr Vasil´evich Durov or Sokolov), Durova served in the Napoleonic Wars, first in the East Prussian campaign (1807) and later, when Napoleon had invaded Russia, in the Patriotic War, retiring from service in 1816. Durova also published a series of fictional tales in the 1830s, which is when her entire writing career was concentrated (after 1839 she retired to an uneventful life in the country, in the Elabuga region). Her best-known work is *The Cavalry Maiden*, not least because a substantial excerpt was published by Pushkin in his journal *The Contemporary* in 1836.

It is easy to be distracted by Pushkin's involvement in this publication—and his own autobiographical notes leave us a charming account of how he met Durova and of his earlier, equally unusual, encounter with her brother—but the most striking aspect of this publication history is that *The Cavalry Maiden*, as well as several other autobiographical writings, appeared during Durova's lifetime and at her initiative. All other extant autobiographies predating the 1830s were published posthumously, as if public forms of self-writing were somewhat unseemly. Durova, by comparison, appears to have known that she had quite a tale to tell, although it is in keeping with a common practice that Durova first approached Pushkin with the offer that he use her story as the basis for his own writing. Pushkin, however, felt that no further adornment was necessary; his judgment was all the encouragement Durova appeared to have needed, and within a few short years she published other autobiographical texts as well.

The Cavalry Maiden recounts the central, defining episodes of Durova's life: her service, wearing a male costume, in the military, including her participation in the defense of Russia with its exciting moments of battle as well as extensive, enervating periods of inaction. Durova's writings form a strong precursor to the representation of war found in Tolstoy's *War and Peace*, perhaps not going so far as his striking gestures of defamiliarization, but nonetheless conveying to the readers a canny, unsentimental, and straightforward sense of the repetitive rhythms of daily life in the military. It is likely that her memoir served Tolstoy as a source. The resemblance is most evident in a passage entitled "Tilsit" in which her description of Alexander I's bearing as he surveys the troops with "compassion and pensively" ("s sostradaniem i zadumchivost´iu") is mirrored in the way Tolstoy captures Nikolai's impressions of the tsar after the battle of Austerlitz has been lost. Tolstoy's affective vocabulary ("gentleness," "pensiveness," "adoration") seems to come directly from Durova's memoir.[13]

Mary Zirin has noted that *The Cavalry Maiden* functions "as a true autobiography, tracing [Durova's] development from eager recruit to disillusioned veteran and from a woman uneasy in her masquerade to one comfortable in an androgynous sense of self."[14] Yet the narrative elements rely on the conventions of fiction, and Durova's sure sense of the shape, pace, and point of view in the narrative shows that this insightful story of one individual's evolution is also largely understood and conveyed by means of ideas drawn from Enlightenment philosophies of reason and sense, as well as later notions of sensibility and emotion. What is more, Durova omits some key facts and distorts others in recounting the decision to leave home and serve in the military: even the tsar, with whom she met in 1807, knew she had been married in 1801, and Durova also bore a son in that marriage in 1803. Nothing in Durova's own writings suggests these facts, however, thus depriving the readers of what is surely the strongest element of contrast in the biography—the transition from the decidedly feminine roles of wife and mother to what was, in nineteenth-century Russian society, the masculine role of military officer. It is impossible to know what motivated this omission, but gestures of obfuscation and reinvention often mark autobiographical writing, and Durova's self-transformation across gender boundaries may have been sufficient motivation for her to exclude any references to her having given birth to a child. The one remnant of that feminine gender, however, is striking: the titular word "maiden" ("devitsa"), which is a word that marks the author not just as a woman but also as a virgin (perhaps in that gesture further repudiating the fact of motherhood, and allying herself with the traditional warrior woman who has rejected sexuality). On its telling, all of Durova's biography seems to converge toward the destiny of warrior, with the earlier episodes retrospectively reinforcing the claim that Durova was meant for a life on horseback and on the move. When writing about childhood, Durova finds her face possessed of martial features. And because the years of marriage are omitted, Durova describes herself as much younger than in fact she was: she entered the military in her early twenties, not her teens, as the notes suggest.

Durova's "Autobiography" purports to tell a more straightforward story than her *Cavalry Maiden*, but from the opening sentence, one mustn't read it naively or trustingly. The announcement of her birth reads: "I was born [*rodilsia*] in 1788, in September."[15] Russian past-tense verbs are marked by gender; therefore the sentence is explicitly masculine. Perhaps we would wish to argue that such a gesture of self-reference, by a transgendered individual (to put it in twenty-first century terms), is not needed. From a certain point in her life, Durova presented herself and experienced herself as a man, so that the cited sentence should, one could argue, be less marked by gender confusion. The indications of gender transformation, however, do not disappear, no matter how determined we are to read Durova's writings with an open mind. "Autobiography," for instance, describes with a sense of despair the time following her military service, when the military order and the dress codes were gone—and the description emerges in terms that call to mind nothing so much as a heroine's distress uttered in a mode of sentimental fiction. Durova writes:

> Constant sadness lay deeply within my soul, and I could not withstand it. Within a year I went to the provinces and to my father, a district police chief. Here my days flowed by peacefully and monotonously; from morning to evening I either rode or walked through our picturesque lands, which are filled with the wild beauty of northern climes.[16]

In *Cavalry Maiden*, Durova can speak boldly for a few paragraphs (as if she were a man) only to suddenly blush with embarrassment (which is a markedly feminine sign), and the

Russian grammar abets this tendency to move between genders. When we read Durova nearly two centuries later, in an era when women join the military and when gender transition and reassignment is a fact of social life, we are perhaps most intensely struck not by the gendered contours of the story as by the fact that a life story so unusual for its time was written in such memorable, distinctive prose.

The next generation of male writers of autobiographical accounts was more reluctant to use the confessional mode characteristic of Andrei Turgenev, Zhukovsky, and Labzina. Viazemsky and Pushkin did not open their inner lives "either in friendly conversations, or in letters and diaries."[17] Viazemsky's notebooks, which he kept (at intervals) from 1813 until his death, represent a unique genre that combines aphorisms, historical anecdotes, memoirs, portraits of his contemporaries, pieces of literary criticism, description of political events, and, particularly enthusiastically, gossip. Viazemsky called the material of his notebooks "everyday" (*obikhodnaia*) literature; later, the critic Lydia Ginzburg defined it as an "intermediate" (*promezhutochnyi*) genre in her introduction to the partial publication of *The Old Notebook* (*Staraia zapisnaia knizhka*, 1929).[18] Both terms stress the combination of the factual and the literary features of Viazemsky's narrative and exclude emotions.

Pushkin tried to write his autobiography several times: in 1821–25, around 1830, in 1833, and again, most likely in 1834. According to Pushkin himself, the 1821–25 attempt was substantial, but he burned the manuscript in late December of 1825, when, after the December 14 uprising, he expected his papers to be searched. The two subsequent attempts never progressed beyond outlines. The first outline is relatively detailed, but ends in 1815 with the word "Examination"— the famous yearly examination at the Lyceum when Pushkin read his poem "Reminiscences in Tsarskoe Selo" ("Vospominaniia v Tsarskom Sele") in the presence of Derzhavin and reportedly received his blessing. The second outline is less than four lines long and mostly relates to his time in Kishinev. The third piece, untitled by Pushkin and traditionally called "The Beginning of an Autobiography," starts with a paragraph about the memoir burned in 1825. What follows is his family's history, from the legendary Ratsha or Racha who arrived in Rus´ in the thirteenth century to the death of his maternal grandfather (1807) and grandmother (1818). In between, Pushkin relates the historical significance of the Pushkin line, stressing his ancestors' independence and loyalty to the oath they ostensibly kept to their own detriment. He also presents his version of the life of his African ancestor, Ibragim (Abram) Petrovich Gannibal (d. 1781; the name and surname reportedly given by Peter the Great; the patronymic derives from Peter's own name who reportedly was Ibragim's godfather; Gannibal's place of birth is contested).[19] While Pushkin does not conceal problematic—sometimes outright ugly—family behavior of his grandparents on both sides, he exaggerates his ancestors' historical prominence and their political independence, particularly from the Pushkin line.[20]

Pushkin's diary-writing was more consistent, especially in the 1830s. It is possible that not all of his diaries survived, but a substantial portion of the 1815 diary is extant. It is a heterogeneous text that includes anecdotes about his contemporaries; poetry, both by Pushkin and other poets; some remarks about his life and plans; a description of one of the Lyceum tutors; and a critical piece on the playwright Aleksandr Shakhovskoi (1777–1846). Also extant are fragments of diaries for 1821, 1822, 1824, and 1826–33. Some of these fragments are likely to be the only entries for a particular year. For example, the two notes for 1826 are about the deaths of people important to Pushkin (Amalia Riznich and the five executed Decembrists). Other entries are more extensive. In 1827, Pushkin tells about his substantial loss at cards in a provincial inn and the subsequent chance meeting with his Lyceum friend, the Decembrist

Küchelbecker, who was being transported from one place of incarceration to another. The friends had a chance to embrace before they parted forever. The records of 1826 and 1827 discuss events in Pushkin's life that had extraordinary emotional significance for him, and it is remarkable how terse they are. It is in fact more productive to look at Pushkin's doodles and marginal drawings in his manuscripts to gauge his emotional life. His thoughts and feelings can be deduced from the portraits of historical figures he drew: Jean Paul Marat (see Figure IV.04); the Decembrist Pavel Pestel (1793–1826); Wilhelm Küchelbecker and Ivan Pushchin (1798–1859)—both Pushkin's classmates, poets, and the Decembrists (see Figure IV.05); women whom Pushkin

FIGURE IV.04. A. S. Pushkin, A portrait of Jean-Paul Marat, 1823.

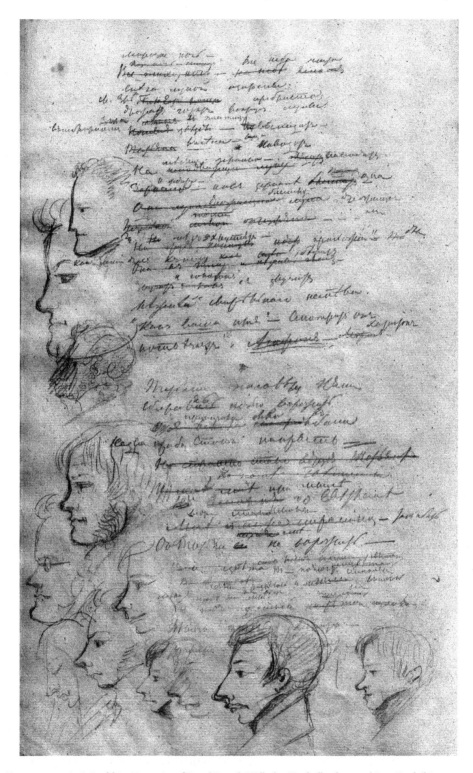

FIGURE IV.05. A. S. Pushkin, Portraits of Pavel Pestel, Wilhelm Küchelbecker, and Ivan Pushchin, 1826.

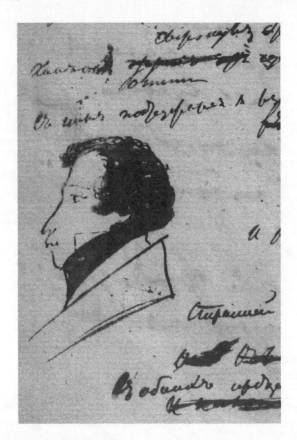

FIGURE IV.06. A. S. Pushkin, Self-portrait, 1823.

like or loved; and numerous self-portraits, both serious and humorous (see Figure IV.06). In the years following the execution of the Decembrist leaders, time and again Pushkin drew gallows with the bodies hanging—sometimes five bodies, representing the executed Decembrists (see Figure IV.07). Next to one such drawing he wrote "And I also could, like a jester...[*I ia by mog kak shut*...]." A comment suggests that Pushkin could not help but ponder what his own fate would have been had he joined the Decembrists.[21]

In November of 1833, Pushkin began keeping a relatively regular diary in a special notebook; he continued until the early 1835. The entries vary in content: Pushkin writes about his life (he names people he visits, comments on family affairs, writes about events at court and about the emperor); all of these entries are laconic. He also records St. Petersburg's high society news and rumors, and he jots down historical anecdotes. Again, emotions are almost entirely absent. Only occasionally can we guess at his irritation or anger—when he receives the title of *kammerjunker*, which he considered below his status as a famous poet and paterfamilias; or when he writes about poor critical response to his *History of Pugachev* (*Istoriia Pugacheva*, 1834). As we know, the years when Pushkin kept the diary were not easy for him, but almost none of his worries and discontents find their way into words.

Whereas men of Pushkin's generation did not trust their diaries with their emotions, women's strategies varied. Two diaries by women, both ladies-in-waiting, are strikingly different as to what their authors choose to record. Anna Olenina (1808–88) was the daughter of Aleksei Olenin (1763–1843)—a friend of Derzhavin, an artist, the director of the Imperial Public Library (1811–43), and the president of the Imperial Academy of Arts (1817–43). She kept a diary (in

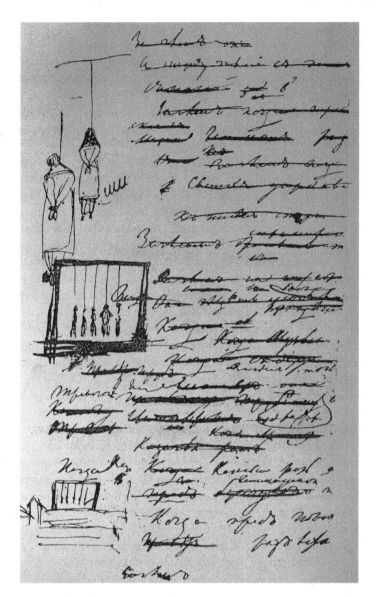

FIGURE IV.07. A. S. Pushkin, Five executed Decembrists, 1826.

French and Russian) in 1828–29, adding some entries in 1830–31 and 1835.[22] Her diary is almost entirely devoted to the life of her heart: the twenty-year Olenina is always thinking about marriage, in part, she explains, because she does not want to be a financial burden to her family. She therefore evaluates men she meets in her father's house and at his estate, Priiutino, as well as in high society, as possible future husbands. Focused on getting married as she is, Olenina is sensible and cautious: when Pushkin renewed his acquaintance with the Olenins after returning from his Mikhailovskoe exile, Olenina could not help but notice him and his obvious attraction to her. Being a love interest of a renowned poet was flattering; nonetheless, discussing her marital options with her father's friend, the fabulist Ivan Krylov, she names both Pushkin and the journalist Kraevsky as unsuitable matches, and Krylov agrees. On the same day (July 17, 1828) Olenina described her short romance with Pushkin, which had started in the fall of 1827 and was already fading. The entry (written in the third person) also presents Pushkin's portrait and a description of his character. The diarist was content with the results: "I reread my description of Pushkin and am very satisfied with the way I portrayed him. One can recognize him among a thousand of others."[23] Despite her active search for a husband, Olenina did not marry until 1840, and her family life with Teodor Andrault de Langeron, the President of Warsaw, was not particularly happy. Toward the end of her life, Olenina-Andrault worked on a memoir (the first installment dates from 1881, the second from 1884), but it did not progress beyond a brief history of her family.

In contrast, the diary that Maria Mörder (1815–70) kept in French in the 1830s is mostly devoted to the everyday life of the imperial family, which she could closely observe as a lady-in-waiting to the Empress and as the daughter of Karl Mörder, the tutor of the Grand Duke Alexander. Maria writes about things both trivial (walks and excursions, conversations with the members of the imperial family and courtiers) and important (the devastating fire in the Winter Palace in December of 1837). She observes what everyone believes to be the love affair between Pushkin's wife and Georges-Charles de Heeckeren d'Anthès. She remarks on Natalia Pushkina's beauty, on the couple's apparent happiness, and on the ugliness of the resentful husband. After the duel, Mörder records the information about it that is available to her. In doing so, she is rather methodical: she collects three versions and chooses the one that she likes most—which is sympathetic to d'Anthès. Mörder's judgment is harsh: "Pushkin is, undoubtedly, a great poet. I do not know whether he was anything else. They speak of him as a rude (brutal) man. But in the end, who is not brutal? Especially if one is foolish enough to marry a raving beauty while oneself being so unsightly."[24]

Members of the cultural elite were not the only ones to write autobiographical narratives. Aleksandr Nikitenko was born a serf, but received a good initial education thanks to his father's being a scribe on one of the estates of Nikolai Sheremetev (a notable grandee and also a musician and the owner of a renowned serf theater) and an educated man. In 1824, with the help of the poet and future Decembrist Kondraty Ryleev, Nikitenko was manumitted and allowed to enter the university. In 1832 he became adjunct professor of political economy and in 1834 also professor of Russian literature at the Petersburg University. He was appointed censor in 1833 and remained in this position until 1848. Nikitenko began keeping a diary when he was thirteen years old, and even though the diary did not survive, he used it to compose a memoir about his early years. The memoir was published in 1888–92, along with Nikitenko's diaries covering the years 1826–77. They remain one of the richest sources about intellectual life in nineteenth-century Russia. Furthermore, as a censor, Nikitenko was obliged to read all the works submitted to him, regardless of their quality, and his tendency to document his opinions is one of the most valuable aspects of his diaries. Even more interestingly, positioned as he was between the censorship board and the writers, Nikitenko could judge the behavior of both sides. Well-educated and generally liberal as censors go, he often provides important corrections to the view that writers were always in the right and the board always wrong. At the same time, he never missed a chance to criticize his overzealous colleagues or register absurd demands for censoring, particularly coming from Metropolitan Filaret (1782–1867).

Nadezhda Sokhanskaia is another example of a cultural outsider who used a form of auto-biography to document her life. Born into a middling gentry family, Sokhanskaia spent most of her life on a poor estate in the Kharkiv district, leaving only for schooling and for one visit to St. Petersburg. Her *Autobiography*, which she wrote in 1847–48 (published in 1896) on the suggestion of Petr Pletnev, describes her childhood in the countryside, first in the Kursk district, then near Kharkiv, and her years in the Kharkiv Institute for Noble Maidens, where she was very unhappy but from which she graduated with distinction. Returning to her estate, where she was to remain for the rest of her life, Sokhanskaia wrote mostly about the provinces, which she presented, contrary to the general trend in the era's literature, in a poetic light. Idealization of provincial life and Sokhanskaia's philosophy of humility recommended her work to Slavophiles, with whom she developed close ties in the 1850s. They considered her the most talented rising writer of their persuasion.[25]

In her conservatism, religiosity, and devotion to the solitary provincial life, Sokhanskaia stands out among the women writers of her time, who were mostly progressive in their views and often transgressive in their behavior. Avdotia Panaeva—the wife of Ivan Panaev, who was, with Nekrasov, the co-owner and co-editor of *The Contemporary*—for about twenty years was also Nekrasov's common-law wife. Beginning in 1846, the Panaevs and Nekrasov lived in the same apartment, prefiguring and likely inspiring the *ménage à trois* portrayed in Chernyshevsky's *What Is to Be Done?*[26] Panaeva was actively involved in Panaev's and Nekrasov's journalistic life, helping them manage the journal's affairs. As an informal member of the editorial board of *The Contemporary*, she was able to meet the important critics and writers of the time, and her retrospective memoir—written toward the end of her life and published in 1889—contains a wealth of information about the life and activities of this important circle of intellectuals. It also offers a glimpse into the psychology of one of the first "new women," later eulogized in Chernyshevsky's novel.

Both Sokhanskaia's memoir and Nikitenko's diaries are particularly valuable thanks to their immediacy: the former wrote her *Autobiography* in her early twenties, very soon after the events she described; the latter, as a diarist, wrote down what had happened earlier in the day or the day before. Such immediacy is absent from memoirs written retrospectively, for example, Panaeva's memoir. The same applies to the extraordinarily rich memoir by Filipp Vigel (1786–1856), one of the central figures of Pushkin's time. Vigel began writing his memoir in 1840, when the social life of which he was such an important part had already come to an end. Likewise, Stepan Zhikharev (1788–1860) compiled his valuable *Notes of a Contemporary* (*Zapiski sovremennika*) in the 1850s. Granted, Zhikharev based his memoir (in two parts: *A Diary of a Student* [*Dnevnik studenta*] and *A Diary of a Bureaucrat* [*Dnevnik chinovnika*]) on his diaries and letters to his brother, and, regardless of whatever editing he did, his memoir contains perceptive observations about the early nineteenth-century life, particularly about the literary circles (Zhikharev was on good terms with the members of both Beseda and Arzamas) and the theater (a passionate lover of theater, Zhikharev was an insider and thus provided a unique perspective on the events both on and off stage).

Just as Tolstoy's *War and Peace* can be called the most formidable historical novel in Russian, so can Alexander Herzen's *My Past and Thoughts* be considered the most remarkable and influential of all Russian memoirs. Furthermore, the genre of *My Past and Thoughts* is as difficult to define unequivocally as is the genre of Tolstoy's book. Consisting of eight parts (and taking four volumes of his collected works), it covers the time from Herzen's birth in 1812 to 1868, that is, two years before his death in 1870 (part eight was left unfinished, in fragments). The memoir emerged in a non-linear fashion: the first segment written, which eventually became the conclusion of part five, covers the years 1848–52 and describes what is traditionally known as Herzen's family drama: his wife Natalia's love affair with a minor German poet Georg Herwegh; the drowning of Herzen's mother and his deaf-mute son in a shipwreck in November of 1851; and Natalia's death, along with their newborn son, in May of 1852. Natalia's love affair is the center of the family drama: unlike Panaev before him and Ogarev after him (who welcomed his wife's union with Herzen), Herzen refused to accept a *ménage à trois* in his family life with Natalia, and he issued this refusal openly, calling on the European progressive community to render judgment and decide in his favor. By making the intimate—and deeply painful—events of his family life public, Herzen laid claim to their historical significance.[27] Equating private and historical events required placing family affairs in the context of Herzen's entire life, also presented as having historical significance. In literary terms he is a child of the century: his notions of sensibility derive from Sentimentalism, his understanding of the self as a heroic subject comes from Romanticism, and his commitment to political writing flows out of utopian socialism. Historically, Herzen makes much of the fact that as an infant born in 1812—a fateful year for Russia in which the country waged the Patriotic War—he was in Moscow during Napoleon's occupation and destruction of the city. Moreover, it was Ivan A. Yakovlev, Herzen's natural father, whom Napoleon chose to send to St. Petersburg with a letter to Alexander I offering negotiations. Consequently, other events of Herzen's life (his friendship with Nikolai Ogarev, his years at the Moscow University, his arrest in 1834 for attending a gathering where suspicious songs were sung, his internal exile, his marriage to Natalia, and the death of his premature baby) are portrayed as historically significant. Most importantly, his union with Natalia (his second cousin with whom he eloped) is presented in the loftiest terms and also as an affair of historic importance. The elevation of the private to the level of the public and historical defined the unusual genre of memoir: Herzen makes it heterogeneous, supplementing his own narrative with political and philosophical essays as well as documents (letters and diaries). He further subjects these documents to literary treatment by editing, rearranging, and rewriting them, sometimes even changing the facts as he sees fit.[28] The result is not the story of a man but the story of one man's role in history, the story of his "life as an integral part of Russian and pan-European history."[29]

CASE STUDY   Leo and Sofia Tolstoy as diary-writers

Perhaps surprisingly to the lovers of Leo Tolstoy's fiction, autobiographical works comprise over a half of his writings.[30] Moreover, Tolstoy valued autobiographical genres far more than what he often scornfully called *littérature* and which he attempted to renounce several times in the course of his life. Autobiographical and fictional genres were complementary for Tolstoy: when he was writing fiction, as a rule, he did not keep diaries and did not write any other kind of autobiographical narratives.

Tolstoy used autobiographical genres to explore what interested him the most: himself. Not only did he seek to answer the questions that were central throughout his life—"Who am I? What am I?"—but he also attempted to observe and analyze his own mental and psychic processes and to commit them to paper. Fully realizing the utopian nature of this project, he nonetheless attempted to fulfill it throughout his adult life, from age eighteen, when he began writing his first diary, and until his death (the last diary entry is dated from November 3, 1910, four days before he died).

All of Tolstoy's diaries (none was published in his lifetime) make for a fascinating reading, but his earliest, adolescent diaries are extraordinary in their sincere desire both to understand and reform himself.[31] Fittingly, Tolstoy began his first diary while in a hospital for treatment of gonorrhea. This experience prompted his first investigation into his own character, the most important task of his lifelong diary-writing. Tolstoy was methodical in this task: he would identify a flaw, make rules that would help him overcome it, break them, and then analyze with brutal honesty the reasons for his failure. And then he would start anew. In his desire to improve himself, he consciously followed Benjamin Franklin: the "Franklin Journal" was the other name he used for his 1851 "Journal for Weaknesses." Tolstoy's drive to investigate and better himself was very powerful, perhaps unique in its sincerity and perseverance. One still can detect the same urge in one of his last diary entries made on October 29, 1910: "If only I could refrain from sinning. And not to have wickedness [zlo]. Now I do not."[32]

The most fascinating aspect of Tolstoy's mature diaries is his handling of the problem that every diarist confronts to some degree: who is my addressee? Do I really write as if no one will ever read what I am writing? Can I trust my diary? Can I be completely honest if I do not? It seems that in his early diaries Tolstoy is entirely candid because he truly writes for himself, to figure out what kind of a person he is. This changed drastically in 1862, when, aged thirty-four, he married an eighteen-year-old Sofia Bers (1844–1919). Tolstoy made a decision to open his soul to his bride and offered her his diaries to read, including his records of sexual encounters with prostitutes and a love affair with a peasant woman with whom he had a son. Apparently, Tolstoy believed in complete honesty within a marriage: two of his fictional characters, Sergei Mikhailovich of *Family Happiness* (*Semeinoe schast'e*, 1859) and Levin of *Anna Karenina*, do the same with their respective brides. Sofia was deeply affected and, it seems, never forgot her shock upon realizing that her bridegroom was far from being celibate before marriage. Nonetheless, the practice of reading each other's diaries (Sofia was an avid and talented diarist herself) continued throughout their married life. Judging by how the wife and husband reacted to each other's diaries, this practice of full disclosure became a source of profound discontent for both of them, especially when their marital relations became strained. Eventually, Tolstoy attempted to reclaim his privacy, and his wife perceived it as a betrayal. He began keeping several diaries, some accessible to his wife, others not (in 1908 and in 1910, for example, he kept two diaries, one open and another secret). This further embittered the conflict. Some of their children became involved (in particular, the youngest daughter, Aleksandra, who was supportive of her father and hostile toward her mother). It must have been a torture for Tolstoy not to be free in what he wanted to write in his diary; it was as painful for his wife to be excluded from the inner life of her husband to whom she was sincerely devoted throughout their marriage.[33] Granted, the reasons for Tolstoy's leaving home to die at a small railroad station in Astapovo are numerous and complicated, but the last straw seems to have been his overhearing as Sofia rummaged around at night looking for his secret diary.[34]

Even though the diary entries are made after the events, they capture the present as closely as possible. Tolstoy's diaries can be understood as manifestations of his desire to create a synchronic account of himself, even though in one of his early diaries the pages are "divided into two vertical columns," one titled "The Future" (to make plans for the next day), another "The Past" (to take stock of the previous day), thus excluding the present.[35] Still, it was as close as Tolstoy could get to recording what was happening to him in the present. He was also interested in recreating the past—not so much for the sake of preserving the memory of the events, but as a way of understanding himself diachronically, in the process of living, feeling, and thinking. The first such attempt was "A History of Yesterday" ("Istoriia vcherashnego dnia," 1851), an endeavor to describe a day in his life in as much detail as possible. The experiment failed as a linear narrative: after a simple beginning ("I rose late yesterday"[36]), the narrative begins to digress (to explain, to judge, to record thoughts and emotions, to provide the narrator's analyses of these thoughts and emotions, and so forth); it eventually fails due to "internal multiplicity" of the narrating self.[37]

Later in life, Tolstoy attempted to recreate his past by looking at his earlier years from a distance. In 1878, on the request of Nikolai Strakhov, a critic and Tolstoy's friend, Tolstoy wrote a short factual account of his life that begins with the date of his birth and ends with his marriage. In the concluding paragraph, he lists his literary works: *War and Peace*, *The ABC* (*Azbuka*, 1872), *Primer for Reading* (*Pervaia russkaia kniga dlia chteniia*, 1875), and *Anna Karenina*. Working on this formal and strangely abbreviated autobiography, Tolstoy became interested in a different project: recreating life from memory. He titled this 1878 narrative "My Life" ("Moia zhizn'"), and attempted to base it on his personal recollections. However, as with "A History of Yesterday," he quickly ran into trouble: he could not arrange his memories chronologically and, moreover, could not sort out real memories from dreams. He abruptly dropped the project.

Tolstoy's next attempt at an autobiography, "Reminiscences" ("Vospominaniia"), dates from 1901, although the actual writing (or, rather, dictating: Tolstoy was seriously ill at the time) began in December of 1902. The plan was to write about four periods of his life and the corresponding stages of the self: innocence (up to the age of fourteen), sensuality and vanity (up to his marriage), family life and literary success (up to the time of his spiritual rebirth), and self-abnegation (up to his death, he hoped). Between 1902 and 1906, Tolstoy produced several installments, but was never able to fulfill his original plan: if in "My Life" he could not credibly reconstruct his earliest memories, "Reminiscences" gave rise to troubling thoughts about imminent death, which forced him to abandon this project as well.

Tolstoy's *Confession* (*Ispoved*'), on which he worked in 1879–82 and which was first published in Geneva in 1884, is not strictly speaking an autobiography, but a conversion narrative. And yet, like his diaries and reminiscences, it is focused on the question "who/what am I?" and "what should I be?" Even its original title, "What Am I?," points to the impulse not only to describe how the author has found faith, but also to discover what kind of a person he is. Reading Tolstoy's *Confession*, we learn a good deal about his life and his personality—granted, from a certain bias, but still we do, no less, perhaps, than from his "My Life" project and certainly no less than from a short 1905 piece "The Green Stick" ("Zelenaia palochka," first published in 1911), titled after the game Tolstoy and his brothers invented as children and which he described in his "Reminiscences." In this last piece, biographical only in its title, Tolstoy posits the familiar questions of all his self-narratives, beginning with "What am I?" He concludes that autobiographical narratives do not offer the answer to these questions, only faith and acceptance of God's will do.[38]

Sofia Tolstaya (1844–1919) began keeping a diary at age eleven, but, in contrast to her husband, she destroyed this early diary before getting married on September 23, 1862. She started a new diary two weeks after the wedding; the last entry dates from November 9, 1910, the day of Tolstoy's funeral, two days after his death. In between, she wrote irregularly, occasionally skipping a year or two, sometimes writing once or twice a year, but sometimes every day. Most often she turned to her diary in difficult periods of her life, writing about her sense of loneliness, her difficult pregnancies (sixteen altogether, with three miscarriages), loss of children (only eight reached adulthood), and, especially, about her increasingly strenuous relations with her husband. One of the two longest diaries dates to 1891 (eighty printed pages): it was the year when their relations became particularly strained over many things, including *The Kreutzer Sonata* (*Kreitserova sonata*, 1891; 1890 on the title page), in which many readers and critics saw a description of their family life; a disagreement over Tolstoy's decision not to accept honorariums for reprinting of his literary works; a conflict over her choice to educate their older sons in Moscow. Another long diary covers the year 1910 (110 pages), describing the last tortuous year of their life together. Beginning in 1905, in addition to her regular diary, Sofia Tolstaya started what she called "Dailies" ("Ezhednevniki"). She kept them until 1919, the year of her death (the last entry was made two weeks before she died). The entries in "Dailies" are regular, short, and factual, except for the entries that cover the days between Tolstoy's abandoning his home and his death.

On February 4, 1904 (that is, almost simultaneously with Tolstoy's work on his "Reminiscences") Sofia began writing her memoir *My Life* (*Moia zhizn'*); she continued working on it for more than ten years, covering the period from her birth to 1901. The memoir remained unpublished (except for several excerpts) until 2011–12 (the English translation appeared in 2010). It provides a more nuanced and balanced account of the couple's married life, but the main thrust of the narrative is similar to the one in her diaries: her devotion to her husband and her family; her sacrifice of her—indeed, quite considerable—talents to their good; and the high price she paid for this choice.

After Radishchev's experimental "Diary of a Week," the category of fictional autobiographies—that is, first-person accounts of an invented narrator who may or may not resemble the actual author—remained productive. Writers took advantage of the opportunity for self-exploration and self-expression, and accounts of this type increased particularly toward the middle of the nineteenth century. Avdotia Panaeva's *The Talnikov Family* (*Semeistvo Tal'nikovykh*; written in 1847 under the pen name of N. Stanitsky) is the story of a girl from childhood to marriage, told in the first-person voice. This first and the most successful of Panaeva's fictional works describes the difficult and lonely life of a patently autobiographical heroine-narrator. Like Panaeva, she has an unkind mother who likes to play cards, while her father is remote and quick-tempered; and like Panaeva, she marries a young man from a socially superior family. *The Talnikov Family* was supposed to appear in *The Illustrated Almanac*, a supplement to *The Contemporary*, but the censor banned the entire almanac because he judged Panaeva's work to be an immoral attack on parental authority. *The Talnikov Family* was first published only in 1928.

Tolstoy, too, turned to the genre of fictional autobiography after many failed efforts to produce a documentary record of his life: his first literary work, *Childhood* (*Detstvo*, 1852), is a story told by a young boy who resembles Tolstoy. Tolstoy, however, strongly disagreed with its interpretation as autobiographical and was annoyed when the first publication in *The Contemporary* came out under the title *My Childhood*: he saw it "not as a personal history but as a picture of a distinct stage in human life," the first part of the tetralogy *The Four Epochs of Development* (*Chetyre epokhi razvitiia*).[39] Even though Tolstoy never completed the fourth part of the tetralogy, he found in the pseudo-autobiographical, or "autopsychological," genre an effective transition from documentary autobiographical writings (diaries and "A History of Yesterday") to fiction.[40] *Childhood* can be seen as a "threshold work"—generically ambiguous and lending itself to double decoding, both as an autobiography and fiction.[41] In the next installments, *Boyhood* (*Otrochestvo*, 1854) and *Youth* (*Iunost'*, 1857), Tolstoy separated himself from his first-person protagonist more obviously (even as he preserved some autobiographical features). With his mastery of fictional characterization assured, he left the tetralogy unfinished and abandoned the genre of pseudo-autobiographical fiction. Autobiographical elements may have also sapped Tolstoy's will to finish *The Cossacks* (*Kazaki*; the first and only part published in 1863). Having worked on it from 1851 to the early 1860s, Tolstoy eventually abandoned and published a shorter version in order to satisfy a contractual obligation. It is remarkable that Tolstoy returned to the autopsychological mode of narration in his first post-conversion work of fiction, the unfinished 1884 "Notes of a Madman" ("Zapiski sumasshedshego"). The title refers to Gogol's 1835 story of the same name and it may be gesturing to Gogol's eventual religious conversion in the late 1840s. In his story, Tolstoy connects his own turn to Christianity with the 1869 episode he described in his September 4, 1869 letter to Sofia:

The day before yesterday I spent the night in Arzamas, and something out of the ordinary happened to me. It was two o'clock in the morning, I was awfully tired, was sleepy, and not in any pain. But all of a sudden I was seized with anxiety [*toska*], fear, terror of a kind that I had never experienced.[42]

In his "Notes of a Madman," he retells the episode recounted in the letter as lightly veiled fiction adding, however, an important detail: the terror is the fear of death: "'What kind of silliness is it?' I told myself. 'What I weary for, what I am afraid of.'—'Me,' the voice of death responded soundlessly. 'I am here.' I shivered. Yes, death."[43] Tolstoy obsessively revisited the piece in 1887, 1888, 1896, and 1903, but never completed it. According to Tolstoy's "Notes of a Madman," it is only by turning to God and Church that one may find freedom from the fear of death, something that Tolstoy's character accomplishes in the story, but that Tolstoy the writer never managed to achieve for himself.[44]

Unlike the young Tolstoy who declined to acknowledge the biographical origin of his trilogy, Sergei Aksakov embraced it. In fact, he approached his *Childhood Years of Bagrov the Grandson* (*Detskie gody Bagrova-vnuka*, 1858) by first writing memoirs: *The Family Chronicle* (*Semeinaia khronika*, first published in full in 1856) and four sketches about his own adolescence. *The Childhood Years* is obviously autobiographical (the full title points out that the piece is "*a Continuation of the Family Chronicle*"), and yet Aksakov chose to fictionalize the account of his early childhood. Possible reasons include his desire to give the work a more general character as well as his need for the freedom to change the details and write about his protagonist's earliest memories, now beyond Aksakov's own recall. Aksakov imagined his reader to be around twelve years old. Addressed to children, although not conceived strictly as a work of children's literature, Aksakov's portrayal of the inner world of a very young boy is extraordinarily perceptive. It captures myriad aspects of this boy's life in which his narrator-protagonist communes with nature; struggles together with his better educated mother, both treated as outsiders, to find a place in his grandfather's family; accompanies his father on trips to supervise peasants' work in the fields—descriptions that may have instructed Aksakov's young contemporaries in the task of running an estate.

Aksakov's was the first attempt by a Russian writer to write for children using a child's point of view. Another such literary work was Vladimir Korolenko's (1853–1921) story "In Bad Company" ("V durnoi kompanii," 1885; the same year the writer adapted it further for even younger readers and published it under the title "The Children of the Underground" ["Deti podzemel'ia"]), which he based on his own life in Rovno (Rivne, Ukraine) in 1866–71. It is a story of the narrator's friendship with a group of paupers living in a subterranean vault of a ruined castle. The boy's kindness toward a dying young girl, a member of the group, eventually leads to a rapprochement between him and his distant father. Aksakov and Korolenko paved the way not only for the enormously popular works for girls by Lidia Charskaia (1875–1937), many of which feature young first-person female narrators; but also for a masterpiece of children's literature, Boris Zhitkov's (1882–1938) *What I Saw* (*Chto ia videl*, 1939), told in the voice of a five-year-old boy.

As prose fiction began to gain popularity in the 1830s, purely fictional autobiographies and diaries also began to appear. Gogol's "Notes of a Madman" ("Zapiski sumasshedshego," 1835) uses a diaristic form to give the reader access to the protagonist's intensifying madness. Pushkin's *The Captain's Daughter*, a historical novel set during the Pugachev uprising (1773–75), is written as a memoir of its protagonist, Petr Grinev—of which the reader learns from a note appended to the narrative by the purported publisher. This note looks almost like an afterthought, the author's justification for using the first-person narrator: all of Pushkin's attempts to write a novel in the third person failed. Lermontov included "Pechorin's Journal" ("Zhurnal

Pechorina") as a significant part of his novel *A Hero of Our Time* (*Geroi nashego vremeni* [1838–40, first published 1840]): together with two chapters (or novellas united by their central character, Pechorin), "Bela" and "Maksim Maksimych," in which Pechorin is viewed and described by other characters, the journal (or diary) provides an important perspective on Pechorin's personality as seen and reported by himself. In the second, 1841, edition of the novel, Lermontov included an unsigned introduction, in which Pechorin is presented as a member of his generation, thus providing yet another perspective on the character. Ivan Turgenev's 1850 *Diary of a Superfluous Man* (*Dnevnik lishnego cheloveka*) is both a diary and a memoir: a dying young man recalls his past—mostly unhappy and unlucky (hence his self-definition as a superfluous man)—in about ten daily entries. The diary is framed by the concluding note from "the editor" that adds some stranger's negative and ungrammatical comment. The comment feels like a rude intrusion, forcefully reminding the reader that an intimate document can be examined by a hostile outsider, thereby problematizing the reader's position vis-à-vis the diary.

Nineteenth-century writers also experimented with autobiographical fiction without using the form of a diary or memoir. Some of Ivan Turgenev's works, such as his collection of short stories *Notes of a Hunter* and, especially, the novella *First Love* (*Pervaia liubov'*, 1860), have an autobiographical basis, but the first-person narrators in these works are farther removed from their prototype, and the reader, even if aware of the narrator's link to the author, will not be inclined to regard these works as true autobiographies. Nikolai Leskov's numerous works written in the first-person and autobiographical in detail are even more idiosyncratic: sometimes the narrator's voice is so peculiar that no number of biographical allusions can convince the reader that it is Leskov who is speaking ("The Devil-Chase" ["Chertogon," 1879]). In other cases, in contrast, Leskov's first-person stories read as documentary accounts of real events in the writer's life ("A Flaming Patriot" ["Plamennaia patriotka," 1881]; and "Concerning 'The Kreutzer Sonata'" ["Po povodu 'Kreitserovoi sonaty,'" 1890]). Tolstoy's *The Kreutzer Sonata* presents a particularly perplexing case: it features two first-person narrators—one in the novella's frame and the other in the embedded story told by Pozdnyshev—and both can be perceived as autobiographical by the reader. Perhaps the more apt term would be "autophilosopical," because Tolstoy lends both the murderer Pozdnyshev and his listener his own views on the problem of sexual relations and family life. In his "Afterword to *The Kreutzer Sonata*" ("Posleslovie k 'Kreitserovoi sonate,'" first published 1891), Tolstoy acknowledges the ownership of the ideas articulated by Pozdnyshev and approved by the narrator of the frame, thus confirming the readers' intuitive perception.

Elegy, love, and self-expression

The first-person voice defines the elegy as a lyric expression of feeling. The elegy's concern is the private world; its manner is as personal as the ode's was public. Unlike the ode, which was little practiced in the nineteenth century and discussed more for historical and rhetorical value than as an active model for imitation, the elegy remained one of the most productive genres in Russian poetry from the late eighteenth century on.[45]

In eighteenth-century Europe (including Russia), the definition of elegy depended on the content, tone, sentiment, and voice rather than on formal criteria such as a standard verse form. Around the mid-eighteenth century, writers used the Alexandrine as a form for elegy (in Russian tradition, a six-feet iambic line with a caesura after the third foot), indicating the emotional seriousness of the genre. That formal choice, however, proved temporary. By the 1770s, the elegy joined the trend toward shorter lines. Most significant elegists of the Romantic period, such as Pushkin, Del'vig, Baratynsky, and Lermontov, not to mention a host of minor poets, used iambic and trochaic tetrameter and pentameter (the blank verse was a stylization of Shakespearean soliloquy). Poems with the title "elegy" are not uncommon: for instance, Aleksandr Sumarokov (1717–77) wrote entire books of poems in which each separate numbered poem has this title. But these poems constitute only a small subset of a much larger group of elegies by virtue of their content, style, and use of the personal voice. In fact, Zhukovsky's translation of Thomas Gray's "Elegy Written in a Country Churchyard," a touchstone for landscape elegy in Russia from the 1810s, is one of very few of his elegies to use the term even as a subtitle: "Sel'skoe kladbishche. Elegiia" (1801, revised and published 1802).

Pushkin is one of the most prolific writers of all kinds of elegies (love, landscape, psychological). Yet he affixed the title "elegy" only to eight poems. When preparing an edition of the *Poems of Alexander Pushkin* (*Stikhotvoreniia Aleksandra Pushkina*, 1826), he compiled a handwritten list that organized lyric poems into genre-specific sections within which the texts are printed chronologically. His first genre category was *Elegies*. None of the works listed therein is called an "elegy," although many are classic examples. Lermontov used the title only twice in two early poems, but he is the author of a significant number of poems of this kind, such as "Hebrew Melody" ("Evreiskaia melodiia," 1836), "I regard the future in fear" ("Gliazhu na budushchnost' s boiazn'iu," 1838), "How often surrounded by a motley crowd" ("Kak chasto, pestroiu tolpoiu okruzhen," 1840), and "It's dreary and sad" ("I skuchno, i grustno," 1840). And what has been said here for Lermontov is also true for Baratynsky, whose actual titles often indicate elegiac subject-matter: "Hopelessness" ("Beznadezhnost'," 1823), "Dejection" ("Unynie," 1821), "Separation," ("Razluka," first published in 1820 as "Elegy"), "Discontent" ("Ropot," 1820), and many more. The fact that Baratynsky would later publish revised versions of the poems with the titles removed does not diminish the titles' usefulness as earlier markers of elegiac content.

Such topical indicators define elegiac practice. Yet the boundaries between the types of statement are more porous than fixed because the self-preoccupations of the lyrical speaker often overlap and spill over from some form of regret into a recognition of loss. The distinct trends of Russian elegiac writing favor the themes of love, mortality and death, and landscape. Here as elsewhere in the history of Russian poetry an important factor is openness to foreign trends. The influence of prominent European and English poets, including Tibullus and Horace, Parny, Hugo, Chénier, Lamartine, Gray, Byron, Goethe, and Novalis, enriched the efforts of Russian poets who balanced the demands of craft and conventional expression against their efforts to put a personal stamp on feelings that needed to seem both universal and still individual. Many elegies carry subtitles that announce their affiliation to poets like Delille and Chenier, implying a tribute to a poetic master or using the affiliation to suggest the mood of the poem. Although a first-person emotive lyric should, by its very nature, appear autobiographical, the feeling of intimacy is cultivated and artificial, and expression abides by impersonal codes that characterize how writers and readers expect feeling to be styled in poetry.

By the 1790s, the various trends that converged in pre-Romanticism elicited departures into new modes of poetic expression (which would in turn themselves fossilize into clichés over the course of the next twenty years). The trend is toward a wider spectrum of emotions handled in shorter forms and explored with greater psychological finesse in which poetic language uses more connotation and nuance to convey mixed feeling than the extensive repetitions of the earlier style could achieve.

In addition to commemorations of past loves, retrospection serves as a common factor in elegies. Landscape elegies engage in reverie about a cherished place that carries intimate personal associations or evokes hallowed feelings toward the family and even the nation. One typical situation places the speaker in a *locus amoenus*, a paradisiacal setting that is strongly associated with the formation of character and sometimes of poetic talent (or genius, in the eighteenth-century sense of individual ability). Tributes to the classic "lovely place," whether a country estate, or a wood, or a brook, momentarily revive the spot as it was in youth or childhood and engage in a quest to reverse time and recapture some essential sense of self. Retrospective association often leads to meditations on the passage of time and, therefore, mortality. Intimations of mortality, however, also spur poets to seek forms of continuity either by identification with Nature as spirit (a form of Schellingian association that runs through the lyrics of Zhukovsky and Lermontov) or by the pious veneration of the family and the acknowledgment that worshipping one's own ancestors provides continuity beyond death: in the fullness of time, later generations will also pay homage to the family graveyard, where the poet will lie buried as well.

The year 1802 marks an important moment in the development of the landscape elegy. Russian writers seem not to have absorbed the lessons of Wordsworth's *Lyrical Ballads* or his influential *Essays on Epitaphs* until the 1830s, when awareness of the Lake Poets increased. But Zhukovsky's translation of Thomas Gray's "Elegy on a Country Graveyard" crystallized for Russian writers and readers the early Romantic representation of subjectivity under the pressure of memory as well as intimations of mortality made recoverable through an evocation of the countryside. Composed in iambic hexameter and elegiac quatrains (AbAb), Zhukovsky's verse was notable for its melodious assonance, each vowel sound seemingly weighed to create a musical mood that enhanced the poignant feeling. Twilight is the time of day when the poem opens, a fitting moment for the speaker's hesitation between past, present, and future. He observes the pastoral labor of the countryside, remembering its rituals and the harvest cycle as timeless activities; and, like the English poets who were sensitive to the way land ownership and distribution impoverished the peasantry, he notes candidly how "slaves" (or serfs) work the land. This is a point that will not be lost on the young Pushkin who, in his 1819 poem "The Countryside" ("Derevnia"), intensifies indignation about the political economy of place and decries the forced labor that spoils the landscape. Zhukovsky's speaker, by contrast, does not overly dwell on the plight of serfs, nor does he level accusations. Alongside the laborers' suffering, the prospect also contains old oaks and gravestones. These emblems stand for a *memento mori*, leading to the poem's extended meditation on the vanity of human wishes, the noble failures of heroic men, and the value of the retreat into the countryside as a space in which one can hear the voice of conscience, recover from the world, and take stock of one's place in the world and one's legacy.

A tendency to read landscape in this way had already featured in Karamzin's poetry and prose, reflecting the influence of Rousseau and his belief that moments of reverie in nature were valuable because one heard an inner voice of truth. In Gray and Wordsworth, the direction of thought was inward, as in Rousseau, but it was also outward, directed at forms of community. Zhukovsky's "Elegy on a Country Graveyard" is a classic example of epitaph poetry. Plunged in thought, the visitor to the *locus amoenus* looks for the ploughman he remembers as a hard worker but also a "wanderer" on the land. He scans in vain—"My gaze sought him—sought—and did not find" ("Moi vzor ego iskal—iskal—ne nakhodil") until his eyes alight on a gravestone and read the inscription dedicated to the dead man.[46] The elegy employs standard terms of regret for an early death, praising a character marked by "meekness" ("krotok"), "sensibility" ("chustvitelen"), "generosity to the downtrodden" ("daril neschastnykh on...slezoiu"), and an "air of melancholy" ("melankholii pechat'") that the "Muses did not neglect" ("muzy ot nego litsa ne otvratili"). The final quatrain of the poem reproduces an imaginary inscription that enjoins, as actual gravestones did, the passerby to stop, utter a prayer over the grave, and to acknowledge the Christian truth that the dead man has gone to a better place.[47] Like many works that appear to set a trend, Zhukovsky's translation is a landmark—not because it is the first Russian poem to discover links between landscape and commemoration: the earlier poems, Karamzin's "Melancholy" ("Melankholiia," 1800) and Dmitriev's "Elegy" (1795), written in the style of Tibullus, both encapsulate these motifs (albeit on a smaller scale) and include all the themes of regret, mortality, and oblivion—but rather because, in addition to the beauty of its construction, Zhukovsky's imitation succeeded in concentrating a larger set of motifs and visual emblems, and, even more, in demonstrating how an elegiac speaker could experience the landscape visually and then internalize its truths.

In various configurations, the motifs of a familiar prospect, a beautiful grave, a monument, a mournful visitor, a vanished beloved, and sympathetic nature will define the strand of elegy-writing that remained fashionable into the 1830s. Evdokia Rostopchina's "Autumnal Leaves" ("Osennie list'ia," 1834) employs virtually all of these motifs; the total effect is startlingly fresh because her speaker revisits the beloved place only through an internal vision instead of dwelling on an actual prospect. The standard topoi can be touched on allusively and economically, leaving the speaker to dwell on expressions of feelings rather than on descriptions of the outside world. From the opening salutation of the ancestral land, Baratynsky's "I will return to you, fields of my fathers" ("Ia vozvrashchusia k vam, polia moikh ottsov," 1821) revels in all these elegiac props, including the oak, the figures of plowman and worker, the cherished home, the grave tucked away in a leafy corner, and the vision of a distant descendant drawn to pay homage to the speaker who by then rests in that spot, a visitor who will erect not a marble stone but leave in the place a "peaceful set of pipes" ("mirnuiu tsevnitsu").[48]

By the mid-1820s, Pushkin knew how ripe the elegy was for parody: the evocation of Lensky's grave in *Evgeny Onegin*, while full of feeling, does not stint on all of these clichés, partly in keeping with Lensky's own poetry as typical of a certain overly poetic style. A decade later, Pushkin revisited the graveyard theme in earnest in "When I am pensive and wander outside the city" ("Kogda za gorodom, zadumhiv, ia brozhu," 1836). The poem does deliberate violence to the landscapes of commemoration, creating a speaker who, haunted by the specter of death and alienated from city life, enters a public graveyard. Dismayed by the poor state of care and the vandalized funerary monuments, and repelled by the standard inscriptions on stones that rehearse generic virtues, he "wishes to spit and flee."[49] Does he flee? The second part of the poem leaves it unclear whether the evocation of the country graveyard is a real visit or a memory. This hardly matters because it is clear that the speaker views any landscape through the lens of its literary stereotype and finds consolation in the "majestic tranquility," created by the sleeping dead, by the evening calm, by the prayer of the passing farmer, and by the rustling of the oak that lends majesty and, through its own age, a sense of duration to the scene. The juxtaposition of the rejected urban graveyard and the hallowed rural space enables Pushkin to reanimate a classic elegiac locus that had, he perhaps felt, become overused in treatments by minor poets like Ivan Kozlov (1779–1840) ("Elegy," 1830), Ivan Borozdna (1804–58) ("The Dying Virgil" ["Umiraiushchii Vergilii," 1826]), Viktor Tepliakov (1804–42), and others. Petr Pletnev, in his poem "The Grave of Derzhavin" ("Grobnitsa Derzhavina," 1819), uses elegy to assert beyond any doubt that Derzhavin's place in posterity is assured because genius is imperishable. Just as the passerby in the landscape will have to read the inscription and imagine communing with the spirit of the deceased buried there, the reader of Derzhavin's poems ought to respond to what he called his "lyre of immortality." Genius, a word frequently applied to Derzhavin in the early Romantic period, is seen to be imperishable because, as Baratynsky wrote in his elegy "On the Death of Goethe" ("Na smert' Gete," 1832), it "encompassed the world with its rapid thought / And defined the limit to the unlimited" ("Krylatoiu mysl'iu on mir obletel, / V odnom bespredel'nom nashel ei predel").[50]

An English penchant, popularized by Byron, for wistful regret about premature aging enjoyed a vogue from the 1810s. Pushkin's "I shall soon fall silent" ("Umolknu skoro ia," 1821) and Baratynsky's "Do not demand feigned tenderness from me" ("Pritvornoi nezhnosti ne trebui ot menia," 1824; also known by the title "Confession," "Priznanie"), written when each writer was in his early twenties, typifies the tendency to self-pity. But there was also the discovery of an unlimited world of consciousness, far less closed in on the self or reliant on literary self-fashioning. Poets expressed their newfound awareness of the interplay of memory, feeling, and imagination through projection onto nature via pathetic fallacy, through meditation on posterity, and also using elegy to create moments in which to take stock of their identity. As a time of dreams and visions, nighttime became the setting for elegies full of regret. Over time, poets outgrew juvenile posturing only to find in maturity further material for self-elegy as a mode of anxious introspection. Elegy used in this way is no longer necessarily a poem about lost love, mourning, or commemoration. It has departed from its traditional subject matter and become a convenient lyric vehicle for short monologues in the first person: preoccupations with negotiating feelings about past and future, life and death, pleasure and pain tend to invade consciousness. This is how Nikolai Gnedich characterizes the state of mind in "Thoughtfulness" ("Zadumchivost'," 1809), an elegy that also ponders the dilemma of self-consciousness as a trap:

> Но ты, о задумчивость, тяжелой рукою
> Обнявши сидящего в грусти немой
> И думы вкруг черные простря над главою,
> Заводишь беседы с его лишь тоской;
> Не с тем, чтоб усталую грудь от вздыханий
> Надежды отрадной лучом оживить.[51]

> But you, o Thoughtfulness, with a heavy hand
> Embracing one who sits in silent sorrow
> And extending black thoughts over his head,
> Initiate conversations only with his yearning,
> Rather than enliven a breast tired from sighing
> With a ray of joyous hope.

In some landscape and graveyard poems the poetic speaker is engaged in a drama of contradictions provoked by nature, memory, and self-scrutiny. The ongoing cycle of extinction and renewal in nature presents the posterity's challenge to the speaker and leads to a revulsion over death or to a suspended anxiety typical of a moment of what John Keats called Negative Capability, the incapacity to find language to express the unimaginable. Memory collapses the past and the present, which creates a sense of continuity and bemusement about identities then and now. The self-scrutiny that results can be a moment of reckoning, either moral or imaginative, that leads to self-assertion or bitter disappointment.

All of these situations represent a speaker caught between the desire to exist in the world, where living is, as Pushkin wrote, a matter of "thinking and suffering,"[52] and the alternative desire to inhabit a magical realm free of these anxieties; between the desire to exercise critical faculties in self-conscious assessment—which, through the mind and sensibility affirms the speaker's sense of existence and his power of rational self-determination—and the yearning for a state of mind where all contradiction is erased and the flux of circumstance vanishes. For the Romantic poet, social estrangement is a mode of being and part and parcel of his rejection of a social definition of the self. A philosophy of existential alienation leads to a rejection of social engagement and a psychological conclusion to be explored in a verse conversation with the self. Yet looking inward poses a challenge because emotions are not to be trusted and the labels affixed through language betray feelings as lived in the here and now.

The escapist longing may take different forms: from transport into aesthetic perfection to, paradoxically, what Jerome McGann describes in Byron as flight "not into the future, or into art, but into the flux of everything which is most immediate, a flight into the surfaces of poetry and life."[53] Pushkin's "God forbid I should go mad" ("Ne dai mne Bog soiti s uma," 1833) transcribes a present fear of circumstances overwhelming reason. Just as the speaker's imagination leads him to a terrifying vision of incarceration and torture, the train of thought snaps and releases him into a vision of flight. Escapism here is hardly serene, but self-knowledge can only be borne for so long before the poet rediscovers a need to cut out and engage with his unconscious thoughts like a "child of nature." Baratynsky confronts unabashedly a tension between freedom as an internal ideal and a tormented surrender to determinism in "After A. Chénier" ("Iz A. Shen'e," 1828). It is paradoxically in contradiction, rather than as a resolution, that his speaker finds the stimulus to live, saying at the end: "And I search far and wide, however stern my lot / For a fitting reason to live and to suffer" ("I daleko ishchu, kak zhrebii moi ne strog, / Ia zhit' i bedstvovat' usluzhlivyi predlog").[54] Lermontov, a model Romantic by virtue of his emotional extremes, self-involvement, and alienation, owes his views on identity to other writers such as Byron, Heine, Lamartine, and Goethe (especially *Werther*). In "Do not believe yourself" ("Ne ver' sebe," 1839), a conversation between the poet and himself frames the problem of identity and self-knowledge, making radical skepticism the root of an impossible problem. For a self that trusts nobody with his intimate thoughts, the temptation to allow one's feelings to guide one's behavior is treacherous. As the poem rehearses inner states, whether melancholy ("the heavy delirium of a sick soul" ["tiazhelyi bred dushi tvoei bol'noi"]), anger ("blood boils" ["krov' kipit"]), passion, sadness, suffering, turbulence, and pity, the speaker returns to affective relations to which he has no access.[55] To be alone means not to express that self. Yet in arguing for solipsism the speaker, of course, shares the turmoil of a self that must not be known. In Tiutchev's "Silentium" (1829) the inhibition of speaking the self comes out of a mistrust toward language as a medium that cannot capture an inner essence. Without disclosing the feelings that might be voiced, thus giving form to identity, the poem vetoes confession. Only the self can speak to itself, protected from the outside world by silence. Ambivalent feelings are widespread, and the more positive sentiments partly relieve the existential anguish of elegists. In "The extinguished joy of my mad years" ("Bezumnykh let ugasshee vesel'e," 1830), Pushkin—mindful of the old adage that to a poet, *in vino veritas*—goes one better by comparing the memories that assail him to a hangover, meaning that the critical judgments that invade his imagination when he reviews his life are an excess of truth that must be tolerated. The speaker clears his head by imagining how full the anguishes and pleasures of life and love seem in contrast to the annihilation of death.

The meaning of life and death are issues addressed lucidly in the elegy, making it also a species of philosophical poetry. Lyric poetry is philosophical when its content raises speculative questions. It is in the nature of lyric poetry to see content in relation to personal reaction expressed through the voice of the speaker, most often in the first person. When they are being philosophical, lyric poets in the Russian tradition have a way of finding an emotionally vivid response to issues that could be construed as impersonal (death, fate, history) and a detached way of reacting to the personal (love, loss, age, fate). Universal themes, such as identity, nature, death, or the meaning of existence, elicit individual reactions. Philosophical lyric often tries to do the work of an argument, sometimes by embedding concepts in rhetorical and formal features rather than by explicitly using syllogism. Three rhetorical postures characterize philosophical poetry: (1) self-questioning; (2) interrogation or definition of another entity; (3) a sense of amazement or radical uncertainty. While the three are often distinct, they can and often do overlap.

Few poems measure up to Pushkin's bleak existentialism in "A vain gift, a futile gift" ("Dar naprasnyi, dar sluchainyi," 1828). Elegies like Radishchev's "Why, my friend, why does a tear fall" ("Pochto, moi drug, pochto sleza iz glaz katitsia," published 1807) and Pushkin's "The extinguished joy of my mad years" offer no consolation to the speaker crippled by feelings of doubt and waste; yet in the course of the poem a resolution leads to what Radishchev calls a "renewed life" ("vozobnoblena zhizn'").[56] What is philosophical is the development from a feeling of melancholy through introspection to the assertion of will. One pattern of response to faltering confidence in life is closer to the position of the stoic endurance Pushkin himself articulates in "Should life disappoint you" ("Esli zhizn' tebia obmanet," 1825).

Poets who came of age in the late 1830s and 1840s perceive in Nature immanence and spirit. Lermontov is a transitional figure between an earlier generation dominated by Byronic imitators and the next one influenced by German Romanticism. For him, as for Tiutchev, the poetic self remains subservient to consciousness and in retreat from the world. The elegy "I walk out alone onto the road" ("Vykhozhu odin ia na dorogu," 1841) was one of Lermontov's last poems before his death in a duel. It provides a classic case of the figure of a wanderer, who finds every path to escape blocked. He hears the music of the stars and would like to merge with the nighttime sky, to which Lermontov devotes a rapturous description. Yet the stars communicate with one another rather than with him. That sense of a gap between his own awareness and the universe's awareness of him creates a sense of unease: "Am I waiting for something? Is there something I regret?," he asks ("Zhdu l' chego? Zhaleiu li o chem?").[57] The third stanza rejects any sense of expectation and affirms that the journey embarked on is a metaphysical search for some better state outside space and time.

A yearning for absolutes is typical of much Romantic writing and theory.[58] While Baratynsky never allows himself such escapism, the impulse pushes Lermontov's speaker to extremes of feeling and imagining. Here the speaker conceives of death as a realm of escape, but this is not death as a physical extinction, because he imagines that while the "sleep of the grave" ("son mogily") will offer him respite from the turmoil that causes him to wander, he nonetheless will be sentient, his breathing will continue rhythmically in tandem with a song of love that he hears against the background rustling of an "eternally green oak tree" ("Nado mnoi chtob, vechno zeleneia, / Temnyi dub sklonialsia i shumel").[59] This vision of life-in-death makes the poem both an elegy to a past that has been cast off and a self-elegy for a life that needs to end in order to offer a fantasy of a posthumous life. It is a novel twist in the history of the genre (later to be taken up by Osip Mandelstam [1891–1938] in the poems he wrote in Voronezh).

For Yakov Polonsky in "I walked and did not hear" ("Ia shel i ne slykhal," 1862) and Nekrasov in "A Knight for an Hour" ("Rytsar' na chas," 1862) there is a productive tension between the model of a poetic self rooted in solipsistic interiority and the attentiveness to the sensory world to which another poetic self gravitates. Polonsky shuts off his senses in order to focus on an inner self. Like Lermontov, he makes his disbelief and mistrust of the world around him a starting point. But the divided ego of Lermontov's poem is externalized here into a "double" who stalks the poet and chastises him as an anti-poetic self that hampers the "nocturnal harmony" ("garmonii nochnoi").[60] In both of these poems, the mise-en-scène is a nondescript world, grey and gloomy, through which the speaker precedes. Nekrasov's equivalent of Polonsky's double is "conscience" (*sovest'*), and once again there is antagonism between a mental faculty such as inner vision and actual sensation through which the poet appreciates the smallest details whether assembling "large outlines of pictures" or viewing "the smallest filaments of the spider web" ("Ot bol'shikh ochertanii kartiny / do tonchaishikh setei pautiny").[61] Here as elsewhere there is a tension between sensibility in retreat and poetic identity open to the world. While an inner voice counsels the human subject to withdraw in self-protection, the voice of poetic identity prevails. In "This morning, this joy" ("Eto utro, radost' eta," 1881), Fet defines the spring by listing associatively its physical qualities. The mind of the subject remains on the edges of the poem, hinted at in effects such as "joy" and "tears." Under the influence of German Idealism and Schelling's *Naturphilosophie*, Tiutchev's poems of the 1830s and 1840s evoke Nature endowed with the power to match the subjectivity of the poet's own mind. The full-on interpenetration of nature and subjectivity comes to the poet sometimes through unconscious thought, as in "Dream at Sea" ("Son na more," 1830), or through intense listening, as in "Insomnia" ("Bessonitsa," 1829). In these moments, the external world of phenomena and the internal world of the mind exist in perfect reflexivity, mirroring one another seamlessly. Nikolai Zabolotsky (1903–58) is another, later Schellingian who sees Nature as an extension of his inner consciousness: that is why the storm in a poem by that name turns night into a "night of inspiration" (*noch' vdokhnoven'ia*; "Thunderstorm" ["Groza," 1946]).[62] Yet in 1869 Tiutchev recoiled from the philosophized Nature of his youth and pronounced it a "sphinx," wondering whether, in fact, it actually lacked all mystery.

The poems written as elegies in the nineteenth century laid the foundation for future work in lyric poetry, all across the twentieth century and into the twenty-first. Some patterns of thought and meditation persisted: poems like Lermontov's "Prayer" ("Molitva" ["V minutu zhizni trudnuiu," 1839]), Tiutchev's "Cicero" ("Tsitseron," 1829 or the early 1830s), and Pavlova's "More than once I ask myself" ("Ne raz sebia ia voproshaiu," 1844), for example, take stock of life in the present tense in order to reaffirm life through prayer, assertion, and reflection as positive acts when life seems aimless; or, as in the case of Petr Viazemsky's "In old age our life is a worn out bathrobe" ("Zhizn' nasha v starosti ponoshennyi khalat," between 1874 and 1877; first published in 1896), to shelter oneself in layers of protection, however flimsy. Viazemsky's desire for shelter was echoed much later in Elena Fanailova's (b. 1962) "I want to live like a snail in cotton" ("Zhit', kak ulitka, khochu, v vate khochu," from a cycle dated 1994–97). Viazemsky's "Epitaph on oneself while alive" ("Epitafiia sebe zazhivo," 1871) sees the self as an energy that gets depleted: the gap between the old man and the younger self is too great to bridge and therefore "that [younger?] Viazemsky is no longer" ("Togo uzh Viazemskogo net").[63] Pavlova, in one of her "Duma" poems (1844), fearing that life might be an "empty dream" (*pustoi son*), like Viazemsky, sees death as an ineluctable process of decline. Outwardly, the disappearance of others corresponds to an inner angst: "the joyous force of the heart / Yields to life's fate" ("serdtsa radostnaia sila / Ustupit zhiznennoi sud'be").[64] Viazemsky and Pavlova, like Pushkin in the 1830s, share a belief in dispassion or equanimity (*ravnodushie*) as the only attitude to take.

Baratynsky's "The Last Death" ("Posledniaia smert'," 1828) is an extended meditation on death as a destructive principle. It begins with a declaration: "There is a higher existence [*bytie*]; but how should it be named?" ("Est' bytie; no imenem kakim / Ego nazvat'?").[65] Since death itself cannot die or be limited, the poem wonders about the balance in nature between the destruction and creation of life. The speaker in Baratynsky's poem rises above time and place to survey the world, appreciating the human capacity to dominate nature, invent afresh ("fantasy" is the human talent par excellence), and to persevere. Nonetheless, the poem vwwsurveys humanity with an eye primed for destruction worthy of late Goya or Tolstoy on the battlefield of *War and Peace* and casts death as a universal power of limitation inherent in all things. But since death must always feed off life, it also guarantees a terrible continuity. The quality of Baratynsky's reflection lies not in the articulation of a law but in a magnificent set of stanzas and images filled with a terrible sublime. The poet seems to stand up to death and say, "I have the measure of you." In "Whether I walk along noisy streets" ("Brozhu li ia vdol' ulits shumnykh," 1829), Pushkin's speaker ruminates on the uncertainty of life and tries to exert control over his anxiety by imagining posthumous scenarios of a world from which he is absent. This is a much more intimate vision of death as a principle of self-extinction. Yet the poem ends with an evocation of "indifferent nature" (*ravnodushnaia priroda*), against which beauty and a new generation will arise, and the philosophical connotation of "indifference" as a term of Stoic theory of fate or simply practical concession is unmistakable.[66] Pushkin's poem folds into itself the main rhetorical forms of philosophical lyric: the act of self-questioning about fate and feeling prompts the speaker to address fate and time before resolving the radical uncertainty about the meaning of death within a vision of nature. While Baratynsky and Pushkin might be thought to have reached similar conclusions about death, the former puts death in the foreground as the universal without ever mentioning an "I"; to the latter, nature appears to be a neutral realm, which operates according to what, in "Once again I visited" ("Vnov' ia posetil," 1835), Pushkin calls "the general law."[67]

While eighteenth-century masters of the love elegy created erotic mini-dramas worthy of the classical stage, the younger generation learned from different examples. Konstantin Batiushkov, for instance, finds in Petrarch and his methods of contradiction a more concentrated way of handling love. In Batiushkov's hands, the love elegy is not a transcription of repetitive suffering but a crystallization of a paradoxical state of pleasure and suffering. Mixed feelings occasion surprise, gentle regret, and recollection tinged by hedonistic satisfaction. As Mikhail Milonov writes at the opening of "Dejection" ("Unynie," 1811), "I love in my soul to cherish dejection" ("Liubliu v dushe moei unynie pitat'"), pithily expressing a dominant idea that the lover is a victim of his own subjective feeling rather than being governed by a "cruel fate," and that he can derive pleasure from adverse circumstances.[68] Elegiac lovers in this vein remain true to the anonymity cultivated by the earlier Classicists.

In the 1800s, lyric poems shift concentration to the quality of suffering, dwelling on the nature of the feeling itself rather than on its rhetorical exposition. Greater use of pathetic fallacy replaces the high artificiality of the pastoral mise-en-scène. Konstantin Batiushkov's love poetry, for example, had little connection to his personal life, but nonetheless was highly sensual, even erotic. This feature was due to the neoclassic nature of Batiushkov's poetry about love, his attempt to recreate the ancient Greek spirit as he understood it.[69] A brilliant example of his neoclassic eroticism is "Bacchante" ("Vakhanka," 1815), a transposition of Parny's ninth tableau of *Les Déguisements de Vénus*. Written in the trochaic tetrameter typical for Russian anacreontea, Batiushkov's poem changes the descriptions: whereas Parny had stayed within the boundaries of gallantry with his young bacchante's running and dancing, Batiushkov offers a highly erotic presentation of a wild chase that likely ends in a sexual act: "I caught up with her—she fell! / ... / Evoe! and the shriek of [carnal] pleasure / Resounded in the grove" ("Ia nastig—ona upala! / ... / I po roshche razdavalis' / Evoe! i negi glas").[70] Batiushkov does not shy away from a description of sexual love or from presenting the bacchantes as wild and uninhibited, as they appear in Euripides's *Bacchae*: in their frenzy, they moan, howl, and shriek. The unrestrained eroticism of Batiushkov's poem shocked some of his contemporaries, Mikhail Murav'ev among others; however, it delighted Pushkin, who wrote that the poem is "an imitation of Parny, but is better than the original, more lively."[71]

While most of Vasily Zhukovsky's poems about love seem generic, often being transpositions of European originals, many of them were addressed to Maria Protasova, the woman he loved but could not marry because they were blood relatives (he was her mother's half-brother). Hiding his love behind other poets' poetry, Zhukovsky would tweak the originals to make them convey his own emotions. In "To Her" ("K nei," 1811 or 1817), a transposition of Hermann Wilhelm Franz Ultzen's poem "Ihr" (1786), Zhukovsky changes the opening sentence from a declarative one ("Namen nenne dich nicht") to the interrogative, "Where is the name for you?" ("Gde imia dlia tebia?"), turning the poem into a dialogue with the addressee.[72] Bringing the addressee explicitly into the poem, Zhukovsky at the same time diminishes the presence of the lyrical hero: "I" is mentioned three times in the original, and only once in the transposition, at the beginning of the concluding stanza:

> Я могу лишь любить,
> Сказать же, как ты любима,
> Может лишь вечность одна.[73]

> I can only love,
> But only eternity can tell
> How much you are beloved.

This change emphasizes the lyrical hero's forced silence, his inability to talk openly about his love for the addressee that permeates the poem.

Zhukovsky abandons the disguise of other poets in only one love poem addressed to Protasova, "March 19, 1823" ("19 marta 1823"), written the day after she died in childbirth.[74] Like Derzhavin's poems on the death of Katerina Yakovlevna, this poem employs an unusual form: two eight-line stanzas are written in two-footed iambs, a rarely used meter; then the last stanza consists of two nominal sentences, both in two-footed dactyls, providing a striking conclusion that takes the reader from earth to heaven: "Heavenly stars, / Quiet the night" ("Zvezdy nebes, / tikhaia noch'"). The poem also uses blank verse, which is rare in the Russian poetic tradition.[75]

KEYWORD **Romanticism**

Even though the chronology of the Romantic period varies greatly between different countries, ranging from the 1770s in Germany to the late 1840s in France, as a coherent movement Russian Romanticism generally coincided with the European movement, lasting from the early nineteenth century to the 1850s. Due to the late survival of classical aesthetics in Russia, the rejection of rules and insistence on the right of individual expression, as well as the idea of the writer as a genius, were particularly relevant for Russian Romanticism. Its earliest, strongest, and the most prolonged influence was German Romanticism (particularly German philosophers and, later, E. T. A. Hoffmann), followed by English (especially Lord Byron), and, finally, French Romanticism (above all, Victor Hugo). Vasily Zhukovsky, Petr Viazemsky, the young Alexander Pushkin, Mikhail Lermontov, and the young Fedor Tiutchev were among major Romantic poets. In the 1830s, Romantic prose writers predominated: Aleksandr Bestuzhev-Marlinsky, the young Nikolai Gogol, and Vladimir Odoevsky. Prominent genres included elegy, narrative poetry (*poema*) in the Oriental or exotic style, historical prose, Romantic and fantastic tales, and society tales. The Romantic period bequeathed to the subsequent Russian literary tradition the figure of the superfluous man: a person of high intellectual abilities and broad education who, nonetheless, can find neither personal happiness, nor a proper place in society. Romanticism was also the first movement that consistently showed profound interest in human interiority and began looking for ways to represent it (the society tale, influenced by the late French Romantics, was particularly important in this respect).

Evgeny Baratynsky's contemporaries recognized in his early love poetry the influence of the eighteenth-century French tradition: Baratynsky imitated Parny, Millevoye, La Fare, and Voltaire, among others. It is not surprising that his contemporaneous readers found the poems more rhetorical than emotional, devoid of true subjectivity, even the hidden forms of self-expression that can be found in Zhukovsky's love poetry. This is evident in his 1819 erotic poem "Parting," ("Proshchanie") with its "secluded alcove" where the lyrical hero takes "a young maiden under the cloak" ("Mladuiu devu pod plashchem"). In Baratynsky's untitled poem, which begins with the line "The signs of love" ("Liubvi primety," 1822), the speaker claims to be able to read in his addressee's psyche, observing the outer marks of love and claiming that he learned about them in previous love encounters. Like Lermontov toward the end of his life, Baratynsky's poems generally focus less on the decisive moment in a relationship than on the emotional reckoning that takes place after the relationship has failed, that is, on the end-stage moments in love as a process that has already caused disappointment. Poems serve as places in which the speaker relives and absorbs an emotional trauma, intensifying grief through analysis rather than by indulging in false comfort. Consider for this quality of the introspection a poem first published in 1820 as "Elegy" ("Elegiia") and then as "Separation":

> Расстались мы; на миг очарованьем,
> На краткий миг была мне жизнь моя;
> Словам любви внимать не буду я.
> Не буду я дышать любви дыханьем!
> Я всё имел, лишился вдруг всего;
> Лишь начал сон...исчезло сновиденье!
> Одно теперь унылое смущенье
> Осталось мне от счастья моего.[76]

> We have parted; for a second, enchantment
> —For a short second—was my life;
> I am not going to heed words of love.
> I shall not breathe the breath of love!
> I had everything, suddenly I lost it all;
> The dream had just begun...the dream-vision vanished!
> Now only despondent confusion
> Remains from my happiness.

As a true Romantic, Baratynsky tends to project individual feelings onto a cosmic scale, and disbelief in a single lover becomes therefore disbelief about Love. The ostensible acknowledgment of Baratynsky's "Confession" (written in the early 1820s, published without the title in his collection of 1835) is that a relationship has ended and the speaker refuses to be let down gently. But the poem's real admission lies in the emotional decision the speaker reaches. Always an aphorist, Baratynsky rarely shies away from drawing categorical conclusions: "But I will not love again, / Will not forget myself again: / Only a first love truly causes us rapture" ("No ia liubit' ne budu vnov', / Vnov' ne zabudus ia: vpolne upoevaet / Nas tol'ko pervaia liubov'").[77] Once that conclusion has been reached, the speaker envisages moving on to relationships that, while fully conventional, will by his definition fail, and he begs his addressee not to try to dissuade him, since he has chosen a new path (and bids her choose her own). Is the poem a reproach aimed at the woman who has crippled him emotionally? Is it more cathartic than bitter? Different answers are possible, but what is clear is that a poem of this kind not only buries dead love but also commemorates a part of the poet's self. The legacy of love in "Dissuasion" ("Razuverenie," 1821, Baratynsky's best-known love poem, set to music by Mikhail Glinka and usually recognized by its first line "Do not tempt me needlessly" ["Ne iskushai menia bez nuzhdy"]), as the poem's speaker explains, is an aging of the soul, also characterized in "Dejection" as the loss of an ability to enjoy society and the company of friends.

Later in Baratynsky's career, his love poetry becomes psychologically more complex, absorbed in tracing the dynamics of love and its different phases.[78] His untitled poem, "Do not demand feigned tenderness from me," is a history of love relationships, written retrospectively from their inception through to the eventual fading of sad reminiscences of former feelings. The poem describes love that has ended and cannot be revived, reflecting the poet's pessimistic conviction that love cannot last, that emotions must not be allowed to prevail, and that instead of yielding to "the whims of the soul" ("Dushevnym prikhotiam my voli ne dadim"), lovers should use "reason to subjugate futile sadness" ("Pechal' besplodnuiu rassudkom usmiri"). This, he finds, is the aftermath of every love.[79] Pushkin called this poem "perfection" (sovershenstvo), while the critic and writer Lydia Ginzburg thought that Baratynsky had condensed a novel's worth of analysis into a short lyric about an emotional episode.[80]

Out of an oeuvre of more than 600 lyrics, no fewer than sixty of Pushkin's poems talk about love, affection, and, on occasion, sex. Pushkin's poems about love rarely end the way they begin. If they start with a declaration of seduction, then the drama of the poem lies in the speaker's eloquent plea and the prospect of success. If they begin in a state of dejection, by the end there is some prospect either of resignation and future happiness apart or of a future togetherness. Because inconclusiveness is axiomatic to the presentation of the psychology of the Pushkinian speaker, ambiguity and ambivalence feature as important elements. Whether his speaker is wooing, rejecting, brooding, or embracing, poems create a sense of spontaneous flow and immediacy that contains but does not entirely hide glimpses of contradictory feelings and hints at complications. To a degree rarely seen before in Russian writing about love, in a poem ostensibly involving two people, a lover and beloved, Pushkin triangulates the relationship by implicating the reader who examines the authenticity of the speaker's emotions and evaluates the possibility of irony in every profession of deep feeling. While reading Sumarokov's love elegies, nobody will ask whether the sorrow is real in his poems, because they stage performances of grief according to codes that, when fulfilled, testify to the effectiveness of the performance and nothing more.

In Pushkin's mature love poetry, however, it would be rare not to stop and wonder whether statements are more disingenuous than genuine, which means that poems that deny suffering might actually camouflage deep feeling; and, conversely, professions of ardor might be tactical seductions rather than statements of love; and feelings of guilt might be manipulative statements of blame. At times, especially early in Pushkin's career as a writer, the speaker is simply in love with love rather than the love object. In "K***" (1817) bruised feelings about a precise rejection are less important than the sense that failed love dictates renunciation ("Who loved once, will not love again" ["Kto raz liubil, uzh ne poliubit vnov'"]), which forces the speaker to bid farewell not to a love in particular, but to love generally.[81] Elsewhere, the poet remains more resilient and attuned to a less static pattern of despondency following a rejection. Yet there are poems that dismantle clichés so effectively that they cannot but be read as breathtakingly frank. The danger of self-delight in recognizing love, requited or not, is self-hate, which is precisely the conclusion of the 1818 fragment "Kak sladostno!..." ("How sweet!.."), where beguilement turns to apprehension at the transitory nature of pleasure ("And I grew to hate my happiness" ["I schastie moe voznenavi-del"]).[82] Surrendering to emotional attachment is not something the speaker wishes to represent as easy. In the poem "I have outlived my wishes" ("Ia perezhil svoi zhelan'ia," 1821), it takes just three quatrains to move through the grim espousal of alienation, disillusion, and self-hate, whereas many earlier poets would have needed several dozen lines to get through these stages.

In Pushkin's early poems falling in love is a one-sided event, where a quasi-narcissistic subject confronts only an egotistical fading of love construed entirely as pleasure in the beautiful.

By 1820, love in the Pushkinian poem often involves an addressee. There is a sense of a one-sided dialogue. As a result, the role of the reader is much more critical at an interpretative level than previously, since readers will want to engage in psychologizing by thinking through the motivations and associating the poet's biography with first-person declarations. Pushkin was expert at cultivating the persona of a Don Juan, partly by using dedications to create mystery, partly by using his correspondence to stir up gossip. An argument about a long tradition of biographical reading of his love poems might contest the relevance of more literal-minded interpretations, since poems never limit the identity of a beloved by giving a name. Nonetheless, the very fact that love poems have inspired this type of reading demonstrates how involving the subject of love can be.

Despite a nineteenth-century sentimental tradition of reading Pushkin, later picked up by Soviet scholarship, Pushkin's lyric persona contains much contradiction, juxtaposing authenticity with hypocrisy, tenderness with sometimes shocking coarseness. More recent scholarship reminds us of the complex nature of sensibility in Pushkin and his libertine attraction to breaking boundaries, especially through erotic transgression.[83] This reflects Pushkin's technique as much as his subject matter. Poems often begin with a form of direct address that creates an immediate bond between lover and beloved, and simultaneously raises the question of what that bond means. "Do not ask why with forlorn thought" ("Ne sprashivai, zachem unyloi dumoi," in "K***"), "Was it you I saw, sweet friend?" ("Tebia l' ia videl, milyi drug?"; in "Recovery" ["Vyzdorovlenie," 1818]), "You find pleasure in the most bitter passion" ("Ty v strastnoi goresti nakhodish' naslazhden'e," in "To a dreamer" ["Mechtateliu," 1818]), "Will you forgive me my jealous fancies, / The mad disturbance of my love?" ("Prostish' li mne revnivye mechty, / Moei liubvi bezumnoe volnen'e?"; 1823): all of these first lines—and examples could be multiplied—instantly raise the questions as to what next, why and how the speaker will bring the addressee along and how much remains pure guesswork for the reader.[84] Consider the first of these poems, "Do not ask why with forlorn thought," and how the use of the question would affect declaration. "Do not ask," bids the speaker; yet of course the bidding indicates that the speaker wants her to ask him, that the poem, on the one hand, is overtly diffident and, on the other, indicates that the addressee may learn anything she wants, she only need to ask. "Do not ask" means, therefore, you do not need to ask in order to be told that, since you are rejecting me, I am "often gloomy amidst festivity," or that "the dream of a sweet life is not dear to me," or that "I have fallen out of love with love" ("Sredi zabav ia chasto omrachen"; "ne mil mne sladkoi zhizni son"; "Ia razliubil veseluiu liubov'").[85] An aspect of Byronic disaffection also prominent in Baratynsky's and Lermontov's love lyrics. And yet, says the speaker, despite the present bleakness and the conviction that he can never love again, because to have truly loved once precludes the possibility of another such happiness, he recognizes the good fortune that to have loved once is better than to have never loved at all. Yet this Shakespearean sort of resolution brings its own stinging rejoinder. Can he believe it? Does she believe it? Does he want her to feel guilt and renew their relationship? Or does he gently decline this possibility? How can the speaker be sure that the poem as a performative statement does not disturb the beloved and stir up her feelings? How certain can the reader be that a statement of such ringing sincerity betrays its own vows indeliberately? In the 1824 "Let [he / I] be crowned by the beauty of love" ("Puskai uvenchannyi liubov'iu krasoty") renunciation is a fait accompli and the poet catches the speaker in a state of resigned commemoration, pondering tokens of love like letters and a portrait.[86] Like the others, this poem, too, is a performative utterance because it enacts the cyclical process described in the poem: anguish moves the subject to gaze at the image in the frame, opening an inconsolable wound that once again compels the speaker to seek solace in the image of the former beloved even though it reinforces the cause of pain. Inconclusiveness and openness to unending sorrow or some possibility of renewal characterize the variations on this scenario nowhere more movingly than in "Under the azure sky of her native land" ("Pod nebom golubym strany svoei rodnoi," 1826), a love poem that is also a commemorative lament for a woman who died in Florence while Pushkin was in exile.

Pushkin's 1825 "K***" (also known as "I recall the beautiful/miraculous moment" ["Ia pomniu chudnoe mgnoven'e"]), traditionally considered to be addressed to A. P. Kern, is both among the most rhetorically perfect (several cleverly placed repetitions, including anaphoras in the last stanza, make its harmonious structure stand out, which does not happen very often in Pushkin's love lyrics) and among Pushkin's most playful, even mischievous, poems. It does, as do his many other love lyrics, depict love and the presence of the beloved as a necessary condition for creative inspiration. On the other hand, it is known that in this poem Pushkin is playing Choderlos de Laclos's Vicomte de Valmon to Anna Kern's la Présidente Tourvel.[87] Granted, the mischievous play is hidden behind the surface charm of the poem; furthermore, it can be argued that the possible double reading makes the poem even more fascinating. One of Pushkin's other best-known poems, "I loved you" ("Ia vas liubil," 1829), is often cited as an expression of the lyrical persona's generosity, as it ends "I loved you so sincerely, so tenderly, / God grant you be so loved by another man" ("Ia vas liubil tak iskrenno, tak nezhno, / Kak dai vam Bog liubimoi byt' drugim.")[88] And it does treat the addressee generously, despite the fact that the past tense underscores that the love had ended, which is not necessarily pleasant news to the addressee. Furthermore, the genuine value of the kind well-wishing in the poem depends on its circular structure and thus on the true nature of the lyrical persona's love. As with the poem "K***," the possibility of the double reading does not interfere with its acceptance by the reader at the face value.

The two poems Pushkin addressed to Natalia Goncharova, whom he married on February 18, 1831, are markedly different from both his love lyrics in general and from each other. The 1830 "Madonna," written in a form of a sonnet, compares Goncharova to Raphael's "Bridgewater Madonna," which Pushkin saw in a copy.[89] The virginal purity of the addressee is stressed in the concluding lines of the poem, the double meaning of the word "charm" (*prelest'*) notwithstanding: "The creator / Has sent you to me, my Madonna, / The purest example of the purest charm" ("Tvorets / Tebia mne nisposlal, tebia, moia Madonna, / Chisteishei prelesti chisteishii obrazets").[90] This purity, however, is problematized in Pushkin's striking love poem apparently addressed to the same woman: "No, I do not value riotous pleasure" ("Net, ia ne dorozhu miatezhnym naslazhden'em," 1831 or 1832). Michael Wachtel rightly calls it "unique among Pushkin's love poems."[91] The subject matter of the poem is a sexual act—the one to which the female addressee of the poem seems to submit somewhat unwillingly or, at least, not eagerly. Paradoxically, this reluctance is welcomed by the speaker who is made "painfully [*muchitel'no*] happy" when, after his long entreaties, she does reluctantly submit, remaining "modestly cold" throughout the act, and only at the end sharing "finally [his] ardor involuntary" ("I delish' nakonets moi plamen' ponevole").[92] It is remarkable that the simultaneously painful and sweet aspect of love that was present in Pushkin's adolescent love poetry is still present in this description of the seemingly happy, but clearly problematic, act of love.

While a continuous presence of certain motifs and themes is evident in Pushkin's love poetry, in Lermontov's oeuvre, including love lyrics, scholars usually see two distinct periods: up to 1833, when he virtually stopped writing lyrical poetry upon entering the military school; and after 1836, when he returned to writing poetry. During the first period, his lyrical persona is usually seen as derivative, consisting of Romantic (predominantly, Byronic) clichés—not simply appropriated but thoroughly internalized, transformed, consolidated, and used to create a recognizably Romantic but also distinctive autobiographical "I."[93] Conversely, this unity of the lyrical hero and the authorial figure is ascribed to Lermontov's life-creating experiments:

he shaped his behavior in accordance with Romantic models, both as presented in the literature of the time and in real-life behavior of Romantic poets, particularly Byron.[94] It is not to say that Lermontov abandoned life-creation in his later years, but the persona he created changed from outright transgressive, if vulnerable, to more nuanced in its refusal to fit in, if still unhappy and alienated. In addition, "Lermontov's early love poems focus less on his feelings for the love object than on his desire to inhabit her memory and discourse."[95] As the 1830/1831 poem "To ***" ("K ***" ["Ne ty, no sud'ba vinovata byla"]) declares, "My reproach will follow you / And will dig into your soul" ("Vosled za toboi pobezhit moi ukor / I v dushu on budet vpivat'sia").[96]

By contrast, Lermontov's mature love lyrics concentrate on the speaking subject's emotion in response to the neglect of the love object who can often be absent. Lermontov's acknowledged masterpieces, such as "There are words..." ("Est' rechi...," 1840) and "It's dreary and sad..." ("I skucho, i grustno..."), are good examples of this tendency toward solipsism: in the first poem, the beloved is present only as a sound that is impossible to understand but equally impossible to resist; in the second, the object of love does not exist at all, only the feeling of love itself is explored: "To love... but whom?... to love for a while is not worth it, / And to love forever is impossible" ("Liubit'... no kogo zhe?... na vremia—ne stoit truda, / A vechno liubit' nevozmozhno").[97] Even when the beloved is present, her presence is negated, as in "No, this is not you that I love so ardently..." ("Net, ne tebia tak pylko ia liubliu...," 1841); she is only the means to reconnect with the past love: "It is not you with whom my heart speaks" ("No ne s toboi ia serdtsem govotiu").[98]

And yet, despite the obvious differences between the early and the late love lyrics, there are also important continuities. Significantly, as in Baratynsky's and often in Pushkin's love poetry, love is unhappy. In contrast to Baratynsky, in whose poetry love is unhappy ontologically, Lermontov's lyric persona perceives love as unhappy as a matter of his fate. His 1838 poem "I look to the future with dread..." ("Gliazhu na budushchnost' s boiazn'iu...") ends as follows: "[My soul] withered in the storms of fate / Under the torrid sun of existence" ("uviala v buriakh roka / Pod znoinym solntsem bytiia").[99] In contrast to Pushkin's lyrical persona, who, despite his declared unhappiness, is, at least rhetorically, generous to the object of his love, Lermontov's speaker is adamantly possessive: he refuses ever to set free a beloved from his love. Ekaterina Sushkova, Lermontov's love interest in the early 1830s, whom he cruelly punished for not falling in love with him right away by first feigning love for her and then disappearing, quotes in her memoir his commentary to Pushkin's "I loved you," which ends with "I loved you so sincerely, so tenderly / May God grant you to be loved the same way by another." According to Sushkova, Lermontov exclaimed: "No, this needs to be altered; is it natural to wish the beloved happiness, and with someone else to boot? No, let her be unhappy; I... would prefer her being in love with me to her being happy. If she were unhappy because of me, this would bind her to me forever."[100] Remarkably, one of Lermontov's last poems, "The Love of the Dead Man" ("Liubov' mertvetsa," 1841; a transposition of Alphonse Karr's "Le mort amoureux") forbids the dead lyrical persona's beloved to love another: "You should not love another, / No, you should not!" ("Ty ne dolzhna liubit' drugogo, / Net, ne dolzhna").[101] Perhaps only one poem, "The Pact" ("Dogovor," 1841), seems to give the woman addressee the same agency as it does to the male speaker: both are free to love or not to love, and this makes them invulnerable to the pain of unrequited love. The price, however, is steep; the joy of love is gone together with the pain: "Love was without joy, / Separation will be without sadness" ("Byla bez radostei liubov', / Razluka budet bez pechali").[102]

Similar to Lermontov's pessimistic treatment of love, in most of Fedor Tiutchev's mature love lyrics love is a fateful, even fatal emotion. In his poem "Twins" ("Bliznetsy," 1850–51), alongside the traditional pair of twins, Death and Sleep, another pair is named: Suicide and

Love. In contrast to Baratynsky, who regarded love as tragic because it inevitably ended in pain, and unlike Lermontov, who believed that it was his fate not to experience happy love, Tiutchev's portrayal of love as tragic can, perhaps, be linked to his biography. His early love poetry is, in fact, light and happy (such as *"Cache-Cache,"* written in the late 1820s). But after having twice in his life experienced love that was socially unacceptable, Tiutchev began to see love as inescapably tragic. First, in the late 1830s, while married to his first wife, he fell in love with another woman who became his mistress and had an illegitimate child with him. Tiutchev married her after his first wife's death and remained married to her throughout his love affair with Elena Denis′eva, a young unmarried woman whom he met in the late 1840s and who became his mistress and the mother of his three illegitimate children. Denis′eva died in 1864 of tuberculosis. The poems that Tiutchev wrote during their affair, addressed both to her and to his wife, Ernestine, constitute his best-known and most extraordinary love lyrics.

These poems are often called "the Denis′eva cycle," although the title does not belong to Tiutchev. The cycle's content is not firmly established, but it likely begins with the poem "Though the sultry heat of midday" ("Kak ni dyshit polden′ znoinyi," 1850) and ends with "I stand again above the Neva" ("Opiat′ stoiu ia nad Nevoi," 1868), in which the concluding quatrain refers to Denis′eva's memory:

> Во сне ль всё это снится мне,
> Или гляжу я в самом деле,
> На что при этой же луне
> С тобой живые мы глядели?[103]

> Do I see all this in my dream,
> Or do I actually look
> At what by this very moonlight
> You and I, then still alive, looked?

The last line implies with just one word that the speaker is as dead as his deceased beloved, thus emphasizing all the unbearable tragedy of the speaker's loss.

Between 1850 and 1868, Tiutchev wrote about a dozen poems that are among the best examples of Russian love poetry: "O, how ruinous our love is" ("O, kak ubiistvenno my liubim"), "You have heard my confession more than once" ("Ne raz ty slyshala priznan′e"), "Predestination" ("Predopredelenie"), "Do not say: he loves me like before" ("Ne govori: menia on, kak i prezhde liubit"); "Last Love" ("Posledniaia liubov′"; all poems written in the early 1850s). Of these, "Do not say: he loves me like before…" is remarkable: its "I" is not that of the authorial persona but of his beloved. In this poem, Tiutchev assumes his subject's position and thus is able to describe himself as if objectively and honestly. He ascribes to her expressions of the deepest affection for her lover and, at the same time, the bitterest reproaches possible:

> Он мерит воздух мне так бережно и скудно…
> Не мерят так и лютому врагу…
> Ох, я дышу еще болезненно и трудно,
> Могу дышать, но жить уж не могу.[104]

> He measures out the air I can breathe so carefully and meagerly…
> They do not measure it like that even for the worst enemy…
> Oh, I still breathe, painfully and with difficulty,
> I yet can breathe, but I cannot live anymore.

Strikingly, the adverb "carefully" (*berezhno*) applies to the lover, not the beloved: it is himself whom he is protecting. The word clashes with the following adverb, "meagerly" (*skudno*) that recreates the point of view of the beloved, who is the one who cannot breathe as the result.

The poems written after Denis´eva's death form a separate group, which includes "All day she was unconscious…" ("Ves´ den´ ona lezhala v zabyt´i…"), "The bise has calmed down…" ("Utikhla biza…"), "Oh, this south, this Nice…" ("O, etot Iug, o, eta Nitstsa…"; all three written in the late 1864), and the 1865 "On the Eve of the Anniversary of August 4, 1864" ("Nakanune godovshchiny 4 avgusta 1864 g.," that is, the day of Denis´eva's death). The last poem addresses the dead beloved's soul, asking whether she can see him as he walks along the road: every one of the three quatrains ends with the insistent question "Do you see me?" ("vidish´ li menia?"). The poem uses trochaic pentameter—the same meter Lermontov used in his 1841 "I go out on the road alone." Both poets bridge this world and the otherworld, and Tiutchev's speaker transcends the physical environment of the poem, with its references to mundane events and sensations:

> Вот бреду я вдоль большой дороги
> В тихом свете гаснущего дня…
> Тяжело мне, замирают ноги…
> Друг мой милый, видишь ли меня?[105]

> Here I am walking slowly along the highway
> In the quiet light of the fading day…
> It is hard, my legs are growing numb…
> My dear friend, can you see me?

Half the words in this quatrain have both concrete and figurative meaning: thanks to the metrical link to Lermontov's metaphysical poem, the highway becomes also an existential life path; the expression "it's hard" connotes both the physical difficulty of movement and deep sadness; even the purely physiological "my legs are growing weary / numb" acquires a spiritual meaning. The poem portrays a feeble old man, but also conveys the unbearable despondency that the authorial persona experiences.[106]

During his love affair with Denis´eva, Tiutchev also wrote several poems for his wife, Ernestine. One is the 1851 "I do not know whether [God's] grace…" ("Ne znaiu ia, kosnetsia l´ blagodat´"), where she is addressed as the poet's "grace" and "earthly Providence." Tiutchev's wife did not find the poem until after the poet's death. A poem that is often included in the Denis´eva cycle, "She sat on the floor" ("Ona sidela na polu," no later than 1858), could have been addressed to Ernestine as well.[107] One of the last poems ("Vse otnial u menia kazniashchii Bog…," 1873), written by the dying poet, was also addressed to her. It begins:

> Всё отнял у меня казнящий Бог:
> Здоровье, силу воли, воздух, сон,
> Одну тебя при мне оставил он,
> Чтоб я ему еще молиться мог.[108]

> In punishment, God has taken everything away from me;
> My health, my will power, air, sleep.
> He left me only you alone,
> So that I could still pray to him.

All of Tiutchev's love poems transcend biography, and because, like Nekrasov's and Fet's love lyrics, they explore the openness of subjectivity and the fluidity of the inner self, these poems can be seen as a testing ground for the nineteenth-century Russian novel with its profound interest in human psychology.[109] It is remarkable that the lyric was the main (if not the only) genre at the time that provided direct access to human (lyric persona's or his addressee's) consciousness. Prose acquired this ability only when it became comfortable with third-person omniscient narration; only then human consciousness and thus psychology became fully open in the novel.[110]

Nikolai Nekrasov, who as a poet is best known for his poetry that protests economic and political inequality, oppression of the peasantry, and other social evils, also wrote extraordinary love poems, marked by what scholars identify as its "orientation toward prose"—a focus on "characters, story, direct speech, and circumstances."[111] Most of Nekrasov's poems are addressed to Panaeva, his common-law wife from 1846 through the early 1860s. Often centered on moments of conflict, they reflect an uneasy, tempestuous relationship. The 1847 poem "If, tormented by the rebellious passion..." ("Esli, muchimyi strast'iu miatezhnoi...") urges the beloved first to respond in kind but eventually to take pity on her lover's torments and forgive him. Several poems mark the lovers' temporary separation; one poem—which exists in two versions, "Letters" ("Pis'ma," 1855) and "Burning Letters" ("Goriashchie pis'ma," 1877)—is about the addressee's committing to flames their entire correspondence, and in both versions the burning letters are compared to their love: gone irretrievably.

Quite a few poems of this kind are written as conversations, such as "We—you and I—are dim-witted people" ("My s toboi bestolkovye liudi," 1851), in which dim-wittedness results in frequent and senseless quarrels. The male speaker suggests that his beloved be sincere when displeased: "Let us, my friend, be angry openly / It would be easier to make peace and [quarrelling] would bore us sooner" ("Budem, drug moi, serdit'sia otkryto: / Legche mir i skoree naskuchit"). Many words and expressions as well as syntactical constructions used in this poem are truly prosaic (like the word *bestolkovyi* in the first line). And the word "prose" is used to characterize their love:

> Если проза в любви неизбежна,
> Так возьмем и с нее долю счастья:
> После ссоры так полно, так нежно
> Возвращенье любви и участья...[112]

> If prose is inevitable in love,
> Let us take from it a share of happiness:
> After a quarrel, the return of love and attention
> Is so full, so tender...

Nekrasov gets something of the more relaxed rhythm of conversation into these rhyming lines, but he also invokes one of the tersest love lyrics in the tradition with his description of the lover's reconciliation as "so full, so tender" ("tak polno, tak nezhno"). Readers cannot help but hear Pushkin's line that ends "so truly, so tenderly" ("tak iskrenno, tak nezhno") from "I loved you"; and Nekrasov, like Pushkin, uses the epithet *nezhno* in rhyme position. It is wonderfully ironic that Nekrasov would write of love while turning to prose, even as he refers to the love lyric that presents love most poetically.

The poems addressed to Panaeva sometimes use unusual prosody. They are often written in Nekrasov's signature trisyllabic meters (dactylic trimeters and tetrameters, sometimes with variable anacruses), variable iambs, and iambs with lines that begin with spondees. Nekrasov also experiments with stanzaic structure: one poem is an unusual inverted sonnet variation: two three-line stanzas are followed by two quatrains. The famous "I do not like your irony" ("Ia ne liubliu ironii tvoei," 1850) consists of three five-line stanzas, with variable rhyming. Both the prosaic intonations of Nekrasov's poetry and his prosodic experimentation strongly influenced the poetry of Russian Symbolists.[113]

While both Tiutchev and Nekrasov wrote openly about their socially unacceptable love affairs, the lyrics of Evdokia Rostopchina and, especially, Karolina Pavlova often made the impossibility of love their overt theme. Not writing openly about their plight may be a gendered factor since married male poets do not show in their poetry concern that their clandestine love affair may become known. For Rostopchina, love by definition is not only unhappy but also dangerous. In her 1837 poem "Encounter" ("Vstrecha"), the lyrical persona keeps repeating "What for?" (*Zachem?*)—what was the reason for their encounter, if the male addressee of the poem can freely leave and have a meaningful life, whereas the female lyrical persona cannot and thus has no future?

> Тебя вся жизнь, младая жизнь манит,
> И будущность раскинулась широко
> Перед тобой; на мне же цепь лежит!
> Надеяться мне разум не велит…
> Любить - ни бог, ни свет не разрешит![114]

> Life, young life entices you,
> And your future spreads out wide
> In front of you; but a chain is upon me!
> My reason does not let me to hope…
> Neither God, nor society allows me to love!

In her 1840 poem "I Am Afraid!" ("Boius'!"), Rostopchina writes about the danger of being in love: "I am afraid, I am afraid!…I am not accustomed to happiness / I have always met grief after joy" ("Boius', boius'!…ia ne privykla k schast'iu / Vsegda za radost'iu vstrechala gore ia").[115]

Pavlova similarly—and perhaps more bitterly—writes about encounters that cannot be sustained. In her 1855 poem "Two Comets" ("Dve komety"), the two lovers never can be together and must rely on the occasional tryst. And yet they derive a deeper love from their sporadic meetings than couples who are together:

> И, в розное они теченье
> Опять влекомые судьбой,
> Сойдутся ближе на мгновенье,
> Чем все миры между собой.[116]

> And, again drawn by fate
> To different courses, they
> Will come together for an instant,
> Closer than all other worlds between themselves.

A similar theme of silent recognition is the center of Pavlova's 1854 poem "We came together strangely…" ("My stranno soshlis'…"). The interdiction against revealing their love is even stronger and more painful in this poem. Its central stanza compares the situation of the lovers to the agony of the Spartan boy hiding the stolen fox on his body:

И каждый из нас, болтовнею и шуткой
Удачно мороча их всех,
Подслушал в другом свой заносчивый, жуткой,
Ребенка спартанского смех.[117]

And each of us, successfully tricking
Them all with our banter and jokes,
Overheard in the other one's own arrogant and eerie
Laughter of the Spartan child.

The idea of love as a forbidden secret survives in Russian poetry at least until "The First Little Song" ("Pervaia pesenka," 1956) by Anna Akhmatova (1889–1966), which begins with the reference to "enigmatic non-encounter" (*tainstvennoi nevstrechi*). But it is elsewhere in Akhmatova's work that Pavlova's example pays off, including the early love poems, where Akhmatova, too, offers her reader a memory of a past love without revealing the "exact nature of what used to happen," as one scholar put it.[118]

As an adolescent, Afanasy Fet learned that he was of illegitimate birth. He had to relearn who he actually was in the most painful way; and these traumas that may well have contributed to the evasive psychology of his lyric speakers, even in rare works that name an addressee. Such poems often emerge long after incidents. The greater the emotion, the stronger the tendency we find in Fet to mask the biographical impulses. Of enduring interest are the poems commemorating Fet's love for Maria Lazich (who burned to death in 1850, having ignited her dress either inadvertently or on purpose); in these poems, the psychology of love and guilt was more important to Fet than specific evocations of the beloved. Only some of the poems to Maria Lazich were written in the 1850s (such as "I cannot sleep. Let me light a candle" ["Ne spitsia. Dai zazhgu svechu," 1854] or "Old Letters" ["Starye pis'ma," 1859]). Most appeared much later, such as the 1878 "Alter ego" and "On the Swings" ("Na kacheliakh," 1890). Two lines in "Alter ego" aptly describe the biographical undercurrent in Fet's poetry: "That grass, far away on your grave, / Gets more fresh here, on my heart, the longer it ages" ("Ta trava, chto vdali na mogile tvoei, / Zdes' na serdtse, chem stare ono, tem svezhei").[119] Even in his memoirs Fet tries to disguise the reality, giving pseudonyms to many people about whom he writes, including Maria Lazich (her name in Fet's memoir is Elena Larina, which combines the first name of Maria's sister with the last name of Pushkin's heroine in *Evgeny Onegin*). But Fet's reticence cannot be fully explained by his desire to protect Lazich's posthumous reputation, because she is not the only one hidden behind a pseudonym. It seems that Fet's reluctance to allow biographical reading of his love poetry had to do with his being interested more in writing about love itself than about himself in love or about objects of his love.[120] As Emily Klenin puts it, affect is what these poems are about.[121]

In many poems, an image of the beloved is barely present. One of Fet's most famous poems, written in nominal sentences, depicts the woman only as "whisper, timid breathing," and "magical changes of her dear face" ("Shopot, robkoe dykhan'e," which is the untitled poem's opening line, and "Riad volshebnykh izmenenii / Milogo litsa"; 1850). This virtual absence of the addressee is particularly striking because the poem in all probability describes orgasm, which is especially evident in its last stanza:

В дымных тучках пурпур розы,
Отблеск янтаря,
И лобзания, и слезы,
И заря, заря!...[122]

> The dark clouds reflect the red of rose
> And a gleam of amber.
> And the kissing and the weeping,
> And the dawn, the dawn!...

In another of Fet's poem, which begins "Today all stars are so splendidly" ("Segodnia vse zvezdy tak pyshno," 1888), the woman's presence is even less obvious: "And you have dashed by silently / Your eyes cast down" ("A ty promel'knula neslyshno, / I vzory tvoi preklonia-lis'").[123] The woman is often dissolved in nature that is depicted in far more detail than her, as in "I have come to you with greetings..." ("Ia prishel k tebe s privetom...," 1843) or "Willow" ("Iva," 1854), in which the nameless addressee appears only as a reflection in the water:

> В этом зеркале под ивой
> Уловил мой взор ревнивый
> Сердцу милые черты...
> Мягче взор твой горделивый...
> Я дрожу, глядя, счастливый,
> Как в воде дрожишь и ты.[124]

> In the mirror beneath the willow
> My jealous eye has caught
> Features dear to my heart...
> Your proud gaze is tenderer...
> I tremble happily looking
> How you too tremble in the water.

Occasionally, Fet compensates for his reticence to name or describe the beloved by composing poems in a woman's voice. "The Irresistible Image" ("Neotrazimyi obraz," probably 1856) provides a description of the male addressee seen from the perspective of a woman who is seemingly dead yet still remembers her beloved and relives both the happiness and the mortification she experienced during their relationship. The poem, while surprisingly kind to the beloved, is honest about the male character who is remembered by the speaker as provoking "terror of shame" (uzhas styda) in her. Fet thus allows the woman to verbalize his own torturous memory. In "All night the nearby ravine grumbled..." ("Vsiu noch' gremel ovrag sosednii," 1872), the male is asleep and the woman faces the night and nature alone, by herself, without the usually present male mediator. She voices the possibility of leaving—and perhaps even wishes to leave—but stays with her beloved by her own choice. Of course, it is the poet who imagines her staying, but it is important that in the poem the agency is hers. Two other poems contain both female and male voices. "The candle has been snuffed out..." ("Svecha nagorela," 1862), which begins from man's point of view and then switches to his beloved's point of view in the last stanza, to allow the woman to decide whether to come out to the man awaiting outside. "Why, my dear one, you are sitting lost in thought..." ("Chto ty, golubchik, zadumchiv sidish'," 1875) begins with an inquiry addressed to a man by a woman and then provides his response, in which he describes what seems to be the process of creating a poem—the poem that ends with the mention of the reproaching female voice. The two women blend together: the questioning woman can explain what the reproaching woman says. The form of the poem complicates the dialogue: in each of the three stanzas, the first two verses rhyme and the last two do not. It seems that when a woman is given a voice in the poem, the poetic persona's situation becomes more complicated, harder to interpret, and dependent on the woman's decision to remember him or not, to forgive him or not, to stay with him or not, and to explain to him the voice he hears or not.

After the deaths of Nekrasov and Tiutchev, and with Fet not publishing between 1863 and 1883, poetry was generally felt to be in decline and eclipsed by prose. Against this depleted backdrop Semen Nadson (1862–87) became a favorite of his contemporaries. Born an orphan and afflicted at seventeen with the tuberculosis that killed him at twenty-four, he poured out the miseries of his ill-fated life in ultra-romantic poetry influenced by Lermontov and Nekrasov. Modestly talented, he concentrated on themes of personal unhappiness and social injustice in tune with the spirit of the time. His love poetry for the most part lacks not only individuality and subjectivity but for the most part also any connections to the events of his life. Grigory Bialy writes about a certain theatricality of Nadson's poetry, pointing out that his poems "are not private contemplations, but public discussions, addressed to a large audience, sometimes meant to be read from the stage."[125] The 1883 poem "Only the morning of love is good" ("Tol'ko utro liubvi khorosho") is a good example: using banal tropes, the poem offers a clichéd argument that consummation of love inevitably kills it. Furthermore, in striving for a language of love that could be appropriated by any of his readers, Nadson achieves a faceless universality. The blandness of his lyrical voice likely explains his poetry's popularity with the mass readers and even connoisseurs: his only collection, the 1885 *Poems*, earned him the Pushkin Prize from the Academy of Sciences and enjoyed a total of twenty-nine reprints before 1917, five in his own lifetime. His poetry influenced the early Symbolists as well as the young Anna Akhmatova, while Osip Mandelstam wrote about the mania for Nadson as evidence of a gap between the popular taste for poetry and the high art of elite groups.

4

Forms of prose

The emergence of prose and the genres of fiction

Both throughout the eighteenth century and in the early nineteenth century, Russian literary production was predominantly in verse. Karamzin, who was the first Russian writer to produce prose fiction acceptable to the cultural elite of the time, abandoned it in 1803. Nevertheless, his travelogue, Sentimentalist short stories, and two historical tales, "Natalia the Boyar's Daughter" ("Natal'ia, boiarskaia doch'," 1792) and "Marfa the Governor, or the Subjugation of Novgorod" ("Marfa-Posadnitsa, ili Pokorenie Novagoroda," 1803) had inspired followers. The early novelistic tradition established in the eighteenth century (and despised by the cultural elite) also continued, cultivated by lesser writers, popular with the growing group of middling readers.

By the mid-1820s and early 1830s, as some reputable writers took up writing fiction, this tradition began to earn respect among better-educated readers. Writers of historical fiction, influenced by both Karamzin and Sir Walter Scott, made their mark. Aleksandr Bestuzhev, a future Decembrist, debuted in the early 1820s as the author of historical tales set in medieval Livonia (today's Baltic states). Mikhail Zagoskin (1789–52), with his 1829 *Yuri Miloslavsky, or Russians in 1612* (*Iury Miloslavskii, ili Russkie v 1612 godu*) and 1831 *Roslavlev, or Russians in 1812* (*Roslavlev, ili Russkie v 1812 godu*), became the most successful writer of historical novels before Tolstoy. Ivan Lazhechnikov's (1792–1869) novel *The House of Ice* (*Ledianoi dom*, 1835) was received well by readers, including Pushkin. Aleksandr Vel'tman (1800–70), one of the most popular writers of his time (although forgotten soon after his death), published historical novels of striking originality, such as *Koshchei the Immortal* (*Koshchei bessmertnyi*, 1833) and *Sviatoslavich, the Enemy's Fosterling* (*Sviatoslavich vrazhii pitomets*, 1835). Rather than trying to reconstruct the historical past, Vel'tman's historical novels freely combine the worlds of the chronicle, folk epic, fairy tale, and *Bova* and *Eruslan Lazarevich*, chivalric romances that had come to medieval Russia from the West and eventually converged with original Russian magical tales. The effect of his technique was not to produce any sense of historical authenticity, but rather that of a runaway—and clearly ironic—fantasy. It seems that Vel'tman in fact mocked and parodied the very genre of historical fiction in existence in contemporaneous Russia.[1]

Less prominent prose writers also experimented with the genre of adventure novel. In 1814 Vasily Narezhny (1780–1825) produced *A Russian Gil Blas, or Adventures of Count Chistiakov* (*Rossiiskii Zhil' Blaz, ili prikliucheniia grafa Chistiakova*) modelled on Alain-René Lesage's picaresque novel *Gil Blas* (1715–35). Due to its satirical bent, the Minister of Education A. K. Razumovsky stopped the publication of Narezhny's novel in mid-production. As a result, only the first three parts were published in 1814, with the last three appearing in 1838, long after the author's death. In 1824, Narezhny penned another adventure novel, *The

Divinity Student (Bursak), considered his best. Another prolific if ultimately minor writer of fiction was Faddei Bulgarin. A skillful and successful journalist of the liberal persuasion, he began to collaborate with the Third Section in the late 1820s and was involved in a series of ongoing and often personal disputes with Pushkin. For this reason his reputation has suffered disproportionately among his contemporaries as well as literary historians. He published his most successful novel, *Ivan Vyzhigin*, in 1829; it satirized the use of guile and deception to build a career (the name of the protagonist openly signaled its main idea: *vyzhiga* means a "cunning fellow"). In the early 1830s, Senkovsky—another successful journalist, the editor of *The Library for Reading*—debuted with his ironic adventure cycle, *Fantastic Travels of Baron Brambeus*.

These successes were important, but most Russian poets of the Golden Age were reluctant to move to prose fiction. Those who experimented with it were slow to acquire a technical command of prose genres. Aleksandr Bestuzhev (who in the 1830s took the pen name of Marlinsky, to be able to publish while in exile in the Caucasus for his participation in the Decembrist uprising) was one notable exception, gaining striking popularity both with his so-called Caucasus tales (such as "The Red Veil" ["Krasnoe pokryvalo," 1831], "Ammalat-bek," 1832; and "Mulla-Nur," 1836) and his society tales ("A Test" ["Ispytanie," 1830] and "The Clock and the Mirror" ["Chasy i zerkalo," 1831]). He became the most widely read Romantic writer. Ivan Turgenev confessed that he kissed the cover of the journals which featured Marlinsky's writings.

Another successful prose writer who emerged in the 1830s was of course Gogol. After his disastrous debut with the narrative poem *Hanz Kuechelgarten*, he firmly turned to prose and quickly made a name for himself with tales populated by grotesque characters undergoing strange metamorphoses and told by unreliable narrators using extravagant language—all of which brought him lasting fame. Belinsky's reading of Gogol as a social critic and the creator of the Natural School (and thus a precursor of Realism) was questioned as soon as he came up with these definitions. Slavophiles, Leo Tolstoy, Symbolists, Formalists, Abram Tertz (Andrei Sinyavsky), and the overwhelming majority of scholars outside of Russia disagreed with Belinsky's view. Indeed, none of Gogol's so-called Ukrainian tales, which comprise his two-volume collection *Evenings at a Farm near Dikanka* and *Mirgorod*, are in any way realistic nor do they include social criticism. Some claim to be based on Ukrainian folklore and include the supernatural ("The Fair at Sorochintsy," "Christmas Eve," "A Terrible Vengeance," and "Vii" ["Sorochinskaia iarmarka," "Noch' pered Rozhdestvom," "Strashnaia mest'," "Vii"]), while others only pretend to describe contemporary life in Ukraine ("Ivan Antonovich Shponka and His Auntie," "Old-World Landowners," or "The Tale of How Ivan Ivanovich Quarreled with Ivan Nikiforovich" ["Ivan Antonovich Shpon'ka i ego tetushka," "Starosvetskie pomesh-chiki," "Povest' o tom, kak possorilsia Ivan Ivanovich s Ivanom Nikiforovichem"]). On a formal level, in these collections, Gogol experiments with narrative voices and cyclization, as did many of his contemporaries.[2] On the level of content, the tales are so rich and idiosyncratic that they continue to lend themselves to various interpretations, from the existential, to narratological, to Marxist, to Freudian, to name but a few.[3]

Gogol's "Petersburg tales" (as they are often called) were written between the mid-1830s and the early 1840s. In standard editions, they follow the arrangement Gogol gave them in the 1842 collection of his works, namely: "Nevsky Prospect," "The Nose," "The Portrait," "The Overcoat," and "Notes of a Madman" ("Nevskii prospekt" [1835], "Nos" [1836], "Portret" [1835, 1842], "Shinel'" [1842], and "Zapiski sumasshedshego"). All take place in St. Petersburg and present state servants of various ranks (between "The Overcoat" and "Notes of a Madman," Gogol inserted a story, "The Carriage" ["Koliaska," 1836] that is not about St. Petersburg or bureaucracy; however, like the other stories, it pays attention to hierarchy of rank). The

Petersburg tales better conform to Belinsky's view of Gogol's works as criticizing social injustice and defending the so-called little man, that is, a socially insignificant, downtrodden, and humiliated character. Belinsky was one of the first to use the term in his 1840 essay on Aleksandr Griboedov's (1795–1829) comedy *Woe from Wit* (*Gore ot uma*, 1824; first staged in 1831; an expurgated version was published in 1833; integral version only in 1861).[4] Yet Belinsky's critical evaluation of Gogol's characters does not entirely reflect Gogol's own representation, and exposes a tendentious side to Belinsky's method. The Petersburg tales contain the fantastic and the absurd, vitiating their purported social criticism. Moreover, "little men" as portrayed by Gogol are so bizarre and implausible that it is difficult to feel much compassion toward them.[5] Gogol's famous play, *Inspector General* and his magnum opus *Dead Souls* are similarly grotesque and unbelievable, despite Belinsky's arguments to the contrary.[6] Belinsky's view of Gogol, nonetheless, should not be dismissed as simply erroneous: elusive and duplicitous, like their author, Gogol's works lend themselves to Belinsky's interpretation for some readers, and the legacy of Gogol scholarship bears this out.

Pushkin, by contrast, struggled to gain recognition as a prose writer. One reason was his reluctance to address the mass reader. In addition, he arguably had trouble mastering the conventions of prose fiction. This may be why Pushkin completed only four of about thirty contemplated prose works: *Tales of Belkin*, "The Queen of Spades," "Kirdzhali" (1834), and *The Captain's Daughter*. The rest remained in fragments of various length—some of them, perhaps left unfinished on purpose, others abandoned for various reasons, including difficulties with prose form.[7] It is noteworthy that numerous early nineteenth-century writers had trouble negotiating a passage from first-person narratives to omniscient third-person accounts and from fictions organized more loosely, such as cycles (Pushkin's *Tales of Belkin*, Gogol's *Evenings at a Farm near Dikanka* and *Mirgorod*; and Lermontov's *A Hero of Our Time*), to the novel.[8] Along the way, they experimented with such genres as the novel-in-verse (Pushkin's *Evgeny Onegin*) and the epic poem in prose (Gogol's *Dead Souls*). Setting aside the old contentions about the character of the superfluous man, nobody will now wish to argue that *Evgeny Onegin*, formally a throwback to *Tristam Shandy* as a metafictional masterwork, was an essential step toward *War and Peace* or *Crime and Punishment*. Yet nobody should now wish to argue that *Evgeny Onegin* is anything less than a novel (despite its verse form) because of its engagement with form and with conventions of storytelling, codes of representation, techniques of defamiliarization, and social institutions. In playing catch-up with European models and trying to generate their own brand of prose, Russian writers of the 1820s and 1830s produced formally diverse fictions that represented different modes of prose narration and various genres. Those experiments with narrative voice and form, and the attempt to use the lessons of lyric and narrative poetry to create new genres of prose, show Russian culture moving in a pattern similar to what was seen slightly earlier in England, France, and elsewhere. The influence of Romanticism lingered, and finding ways to accommodate its norms in prose was an important cultural challenge.

One genre that proved essential in establishing the reputation of Russian prose was the so-called society tale, which flourished in the 1830s and 1840s. The term was first used by the historian and critic Stepan Shevyrev, in his review of Nikolai Pavlov's (1803–64) collection *Three Tales* (*Tri povesti*, 1835).[9] As Elizabeth Shephard suggests, it "is the first important response in Russian prose fiction to French romantic realism." It was also the first genre that moved from description to analysis, that is, from portraying external events to revealing "internal events and [their] underlying causes," which shifted the readers' point of interest from action to human behavior and increased verisimilitude. The society tale was therefore an important precursor of the prose produced in the Age of Realism and an essential stage in the emergence of the novel. But it also had plenty to offer on its own terms. It attempted to represent interiority, to read the character and the character's motivations—in Shepard's formulation, it internalized "narrative interest."[10] Furthermore, the society tale opened the doors for women, to Belinsky's chagrin and the women's joy: it put women at the center of the narrative interest, which not only allowed women to read about characters who had similar concerns, but also inspired them to write about those concerns themselves. The society tale ushered in a new generation of women writers, including Elena Gan, Nadezhda Durova, Maria Zhukova, and Evdokia Rostopchina.[11]

Through its exploration of the world of interiors, both psychological and domestic, the society tale searched for ways to gain access to the characters' motivation in the home and the world at large. More than their predecessors, the authors of society tales devised techniques that combined character and plot development. Shown to be attentive to other people's behavior and facial impressions, alert to gossip, and privy to personal documents—letters and diaries—characters obtained their aims by using chance or through cunning. Yet in the final analysis, as Victoria Somoff argues, these fictions lead to a dead end. The society tale, for all its earnest efforts, ultimately failed to find the means to represent interiority in a believable way. Somoff's "exhibit number one" is Lermontov's unfinished "novel," "Princess Ligovskaia" ("Kniaginia Ligovskaia," begun in 1836, abandoned in 1837, and published only in 1882). "Princess Ligovskaia" served Lermontov as a stepping stone to *A Hero of Our Time* (the name of the main character, Pechorin, migrated to the later work). Pechorin in "Princess Ligovskaia" uses close observation and analysis as his main instruments for reading other characters' inner emotions, but his efforts prove ineffective. As a result, Lermontov abandoned "Princess Ligovskaia" and turned to a cyclical form for his successful novelistic experiment in *A Hero of Our Time*. By subjecting Pechorin to the scrutiny of several observers (one of whom clearly is the authorial figure), endowing him with an understanding of other people normally reserved for the author, and giving the reader access to Pechorin's self-descriptions—and self-analysis—through his diary, Lermontov largely succeeded in credibly portraying Pechorin's inner self. Nonetheless, Pechorin's thought processes and inner impulses fall short of complete transparency. Even though Lermontov made the enigma of Pechorin's character part of the novel's appeal, the fact remains that *A Hero of Our Time* is not a novel of the kind the mid-nineteenth-century Russian Realists would produce—that is, the novel in which the third-person narrator not only has free access to the characters' consciousness and provides similar access to his readers, but this entirely "fantastic" ability is perceived by the reader as entirely realistic.[12] However, *A Hero of Our Time* paved the way for such a novel.

For most readers outside Russia the so-called Great Russian Novel stands for Russian literature in general. The Great Russian Novel connotes a group of narratives of a considerable length and exceptional quality written roughly between 1856 (Turgenev's *Rudin*) and 1899 (Tolstoy's *Resurrection* [*Voskresen'e*]). Caryl Emerson has called the "aggressively long, thematically untidy Tolstoyan novel" a "trademark" of the tradition, and it is hard not to see why this perception remains broadly true.[13]

How many canonical works does it take to make the Great Russian Novel? Since the boundaries of the "Golden Age of the Russian Novel" (Dmitry Mirsky's term) are often challenged—particularly, its earlier chronological margins—the list is also open to debate, and the number may be disproportionately small in relation to impact on the canon. The scholarly consensus seems to be that, when particular novels produced during this time are counted, it turns out that there are surprisingly few of them in comparison with the Western novelistic production: "In a career that spanned roughly twenty-five years (allowing for his imprisonment and exile), Dostoevsky published only seven full-length novels; Turgenev—six in forty years; Tolstoy—only three in sixty years; Goncharov—three in twenty years."[14]

Could it be true that there was no novel before *Rudin* (which, by the way, was subtitled "a novella," *povest'*, in the first edition)? Do we really recognize Gogol's *Dead Souls* as a novel, if the author himself insisted that it was an epic poem and the narrative is in the form of a travelogue? Do we include among Great Russian Novels Herzen's *Who is to Blame* (*Kto vinovat?*, serialized in 1845–46; published in book form 1847) and Goncharov's *A Common Story* (*Obyknovennaia istoriia*, 1847), both subtitled "A Novel in Two Parts" and both good but, arguably, not great? Furthermore, how do we qualify such works as Nikolai Leskov's *Cathedral Folk* (*Soboriane*, 1873)? Even though it is subtitled "a chronicle," many narrative devices are novelistic, and Russian readers consider it among the period's masterpieces. However, *Cathedral Folk* never impressed Western admirers of the Russian novel: for them, it simply does not exist. Finally, what do we do with Chekhov who succeeded, both with the Russian and Western readers, as a writer of short stories and a playwright (his one attempt to write a longer novel-like narrative, *A Shooting Party* [*Drama na okhote*, literally, *Drama at the Hunt*, 1884] was a disastrous failure). His short prose and drama displays the same enigmatic (apparently "Russian") charm that moves non-Russian readers to work through not only a relatively transparent Goncharov's *Oblomov*, but also through such acknowledged "large, loose baggy monsters," to use Henry James's famous phrase, as Tolstoy's *War and Peace* and Dostoevsky's *Brothers Karamazov*.

The genre of the novel as an art form, social commentary, and a vehicle for character creation stands at the intersection of aesthetics, literary history, and psychology.[15] None of the disciplinary contexts underlying fiction were static: the conventions of realism altered to keep pace with new technologies, and descriptions of the self embraced new theories of the mind and personality. Two systemic changes in the study of the Russian novel relate to broader working descriptions of realism and to the redefinition of the creation and function of character. Richard Freeborn voiced a traditional view that all the great classic novelists share a common commitment to describing the world and expressing the truth of Russian life as they saw it.[16] However, more recently, far greater differentiation has been suggested in how we see their individual approaches to the genre and how we understand the relation between their formal innovation and their moral outlook and ideas. Donna Tussing Orwin sees the 1840s as a period of gradual development of subjectivity and the creation of an "I," with Herzen's essays "Dilettantism in Science" ("Diletantizm v nauke," 1843) and "Letters on the Study of Nature" ("Pis'ma ob izuchenii prirody," 1845–46) as seminal statements on the importance of the individual that defend the value and reality of the individual personality (*lichnost'*).[17] Gary Saul Morson and Caryl Emerson contend that Bakhtin's concept of the novel justifies prosaics (as opposed to poetics), that is, the aesthetics of the ordinary and mundane, with its decentralizing and anti-Romantic effects.[18] The best examples of the prosaics these scholars find not in Dostoevsky, but in Tolstoy's *Anna Karenina* ("the urtext of prosaics," in Morson's words[19]) and Chekhov's plays. At the level of the psychological, the question of what realism means depends on the sum total of how characters, who are complexly conceived and conditioned by the plot, act plausibly not because their acts necessarily comply with external standards of truth but rather seem truthful with reference to their personal history and sense of identity.[20]

The literature of Realism, the realism of literature: Fiction, class, society

The advances in literacy, Europe-wide growth of the bourgeoisie and the rise of the *raznochintsy* in Russia, the development of a literary field and the emergence of professional writers, and the growth of serial journals were conditions that made the project of the

Realist novel capable of tackling big contemporary questions of commerce, empire, manners, individual, and society. Out of a much larger critical mass of work published in the second half of the nineteenth century, some of the defining works of the Realist novel include Turgenev's political fictions (*Rudin*, *Fathers and Sons*); Dostoevsky's spiritual and legal thriller *Crime and Punishment*; Goncharov's psychological portraits, especially *Oblomov*; and Tolstoy's studies of the landed gentry, as well as his sprawling historical novel *War and Peace*. These works have been seen as landmarks of fiction because their heroes are both types and singular individuals who emerge as three-dimensional within a fully realized context that encompasses the local and national, socioeconomic and political, class-based and familial.

Yet while all of these great authors contribute to the tradition, because their visions of society and reality differ, and each shapes the novel as a genre to his own purposes, we must acknowledge the plurality of realisms available in the age of Realism. In the seminal article "Discourse on the Criticism by Professor A. Nikitenko. First Article" ("Rech' o kritike… A. Nikitenko," 1842), Belinsky asserted that "reality" was to be the watchword of the contemporary world, and that Realism was to be cultivated culturally, spiritually, and psychologically as the "first and last word of our age."[21] The theory and purpose of the real was, for Belinsky, rooted in the positivist description of human activity that the growth of science had imported to Russia. He aimed to make this mission of literature a foundation for the practice of Realism as embedded in a frank description of human existence in society in a given time and place. Other historically important contemporary examples of the Realist novel in Russia arguably favored type over individual, and subordinated artistic concerns to a programmatic purpose.

The question of the purpose of the novel was actively debated in Russia, especially in the 1860s, on the pages of the thick journals. In the 1860s, many writers grouped with the radicals responded variously to the call Belinsky had made in the 1840s. Chernyshevsky, both as a theorist and novelist, was a central figure. He is self-consistent in writing the novel *What Is to Be Done?*, which illustrated his theory (set out in his doctoral thesis *The Aesthetic Relations of Art to Reality*) that fiction must produce an enhanced reality to serve as a modeling system in which readers would find pragmatic guidance. Chernyshevsky's tenet that "the beautiful [i.e. aesthetically valuable] is life"[22] later endeared him in the Soviet period to Marxist-Leninist critics of the novel and, separately, became the subject of a famous lampoon by Nabokov in *The Gift* (*Dar*, 1937–38). Despite their avowed common purpose, the novels of the radical critics diverged in artistic practices. Some writers—such as Leskov—were less tendentious about mimesis. Leskov provides an instance of Realism that is not put to the service of radical politics, and he advances the project of Realism with his notable use of *skaz*, that is, an imitation of speech of an incompetent narrator.[23] Another important example is Aleksei Pisemsky. His *Thousand Souls* (*Tysiacha dush*, 1858), while more workaday than memorable, features techniques of realism (attentiveness to dialect and local speech, costume description, plausible time management of the plot) to capture the scale and experience of change sweeping through Russian life on the eve of the Great Reforms. His later novel, *The Turbulent Sea* (*Vzbalamuchennoe more*, 1863), is a notable realist study of young radicals. Pisemsky's negative description of the younger generation of radicals, whom he blamed for ignoring what he believed to be common sense, earned this novel the reputation of an anti-nihilist novel.[24] While Pisemsky did not hesitate to make literature a vehicle for contested ideals, his combination of documentary description of daily life (including dress, manners, social conventions, money, and modes of transport,) and the representation of individuals exceed (and depart from) Chernyshevsky's didactic approach to imitating life.

PLATE I. Leaf from the Ostromir Gospel, The Evangelist Mark, mid-11th c.

PLATE 2. Icon, Saints Boris and Gleb, Novgorod, 14th c.

PLATE 3. Icon, St George the Victorious (Pobedonosets), Novgorod, 14th c.

PLATE 4. Blessing of Grand Prince Dmitry Donskoi by Sergii of Radonezh, from the *Tale of the Rout of Mamai*, early 17th c.

PLATE 5. Icon, Prince Dmitry of Thessalonike, Vladimir-Suzdal, early 13th c.

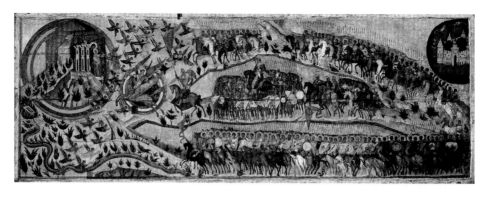

PLATE 6. Icon, The Church Militant, detail of Archangel Michael and Ivan the Terrible, mid-16th c.

PLATE 7. Icon, Virgin Orans [Bogoroditsa], Suzdal, c.1224.

PLATE 8. View of fortified city of Solovki on White Sea, detail from Panel of Saints Sabazio and Zosima, *c*.1645.

PLATE 9. Karion Istomin, *A Book of Love to Mark a Noble Marriage*, 1689.

PLATE 10. Fedor Rokotov, Portrait of Vasily Maikov, 1760.

PLATE 11. Johann Gottfried Tannauer, *Peter I at the Battle of Poltava*, 1724.

PLATE 12. Vigilius Eriksen, Equestrian portrait of Catherine II, *c.*1762.

PLATE 13. Dmitry Levitsky, Portrait of Alexandra Levshina from the series *Smolianki*, portraits of young women students from the Smolnyi Institute for Noble Girls, 1772–76.

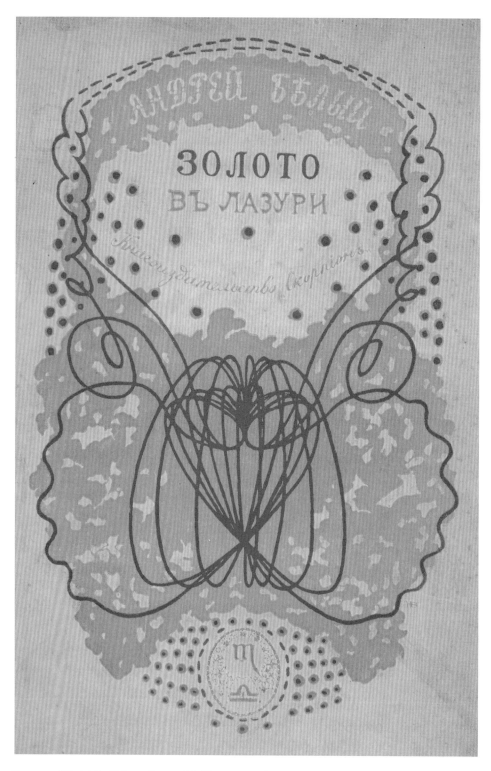

PLATE 14. Nikolai Feofilaktov, Cover of *Gold in Azure* (*Zoloto v lazuri*, 1904) by Andrei Bely.

PLATE 15. Aleksei Remizov, *A letter of credit for the Monkey Designation of the First Degree.*

PLATE 16. L. Baskin, Poster "Greeting to the Congress of Soviet Writers," 1934.

PLATE 17. Elena Guro, *A Woman in a Headscarf*, 1910.

PLATE 18. Erik Bulatov, *Sunrise or Sunset*, 1989.

PLATE 19. Komar & Melamid, *The Origin of Socialist Realism*, oil on canvas, 1982–83.

CASE STUDY Realism/realism

It is helpful at the outset to distinguish *realism*, associated with practices of mimesis independent of any particular school, movement, or genres, from the Realism characteristic of prose forms (especially the novel) and theatrical works produced in the second half of the nineteenth century. The first is a term of aesthetics and reception theory; the second is broadly content-based and a key term in literary history. Both are important in the Russian tradition, perhaps more than in any other European country.

As a necessarily broad term of aesthetics, *realism* refers to representation aimed at verisimilitude. It is a vexing term in art and literary history—indispensable, and more user-friendly when delimited, as in Donald Fanger's claims for Romantic realism.[25] In 1921, Roman Jakobson wrote a seminal piece "On Artistic Realism," where he sought to fix the definition and function of the term by linking the basic principles of artistic technique and the psychology of art to focus on the way writers, and especially painters, execute description.[26] Consistent with the Formalist aesthetics, Jakobson felt that, over time, the styles of description generative of verisimilitude grow stale in the perception of the reader. These conventions come to seem more about art imitating art than about art imitating life. Art therefore tends toward set pieces until a fresh vision disrupts the system by using descriptive techniques and deploying detail in a new way, sometimes stimulated by the examples of other media, like photography and film. Other theorists of mimesis, from Erich Auerbach to Jonathan Culler, agree that realism in the broadest sense achieves solidity by establishing a relation between appearance (such as dress) and symbolic codes. In their view, realism also differentiates between a narrator's language and the characters' discourse as part of characterization; organizes behavior according to contemporary social paradigms true to known character types; and filters the discovery of the world through the personality of characters.[27] In the hope of adding precision to these requisite features, twentieth-century critics have used adjectives in differentiating modes of realism, such as photographic, Romantic, and psychological. Such nuances suggest how much the "reality effect," or verisimilitude, depends on the larger context of culture, including other media such as painting, photography, and cinema that condition the norms of perception and aesthetic conventions. Once works of literature give the impression of imitating other artifacts, rather than seeming to get as close as possible to life, then works that break with these conventions are perceived as achieving a freshness equated with the real. Perception, essentially of a comparative kind, is at the core of judging realist intentions and effects. Shifts in the selection of detail have been a standard way of identifying how texts peel away layers of stylization that seem automatic in order to achieve an alienation effect that seems more real, sometimes shockingly so.

Two examples from literature can make the point quite concretely. Nobody in the twenty-first century is likely to find the depiction of love in Nikolai Karamzin's "Poor Liza" explicit or sensual, because the conventions of Sentimentalism as applied there are long out of date. But when seen against the norms established in pastoral verse of the 1780s, Karamzin's disruptive gestures are apparent: his description moves beyond the habitat of shepherds and shepherdesses and endows a figure from outside the genteel class with sensibility. The famous line that "Even peasant women are capable of love," a truism that seems almost offensive when uttered, was a bold departure that registered a reality effect at the time.

To turn to a much later example: Vladimir Sorokin's (b. 1955) novella *The Snowstorm* (*Metel′*, 2010) is reminiscent of nineteenth-century stories, such as Pushkin's "The Station

Master" ("Stantsionnyi smotritel'," 1830, published 1831) and Tolstoy's "Master and Worker" ("Khoziain i rabotnik," 1895; more commonly translated as "Master and Man"), both featuring a postal station. But Sorokin's narrator raises the description of horses and equestrian paraphernalia to a new level of microscopic detail that, while inessential to the plot, surpasses anything found in even ethnographic writers, such as Vladimir Sollogub (in his *Tarantas*) or Vladimir Dal (*Scenes from Russian Life* [*Kartiny iz russkogo byta*, 1848–57 in periodicals, 1861 in book form]). Is Sorokin's exaggerated use of detail meant as a parody? Or is it an even more aggressive truth about realism—as observed by Roman Jakobson long ago—that perception of the real becomes habitual and automatic, requiring new detail in order to seem fresh?[28] The excessive piling on of detail in Sorokin is also a reminder of the abundance of lists in the nineteenth-century tradition, and yet he so overdoes the visualization that this story seems anything but realist. Whereas defamiliarization of the kind practiced by Tolstoy reveals reality, Sorokin makes it impossible to move from the page to a plausible reconstruction of the object. Such an example may serve to remind us that, while nineteenth-century Realism is often praised for its omniscience and transparency as though life were unfolding on the page, in fact realism as a technique works with readers willing to enter into an illusion conveyed by imitation that is constantly being revised.

Realism and Realist, as used in standard phrases like "the Realist novel" (still in circulation) and "the age of Realism" (now perhaps old-fashioned), are shorthand designations for fiction with social content open to a broader mix of classes and experience than earlier chivalric or picaresque novels and romance fictions that flourished in eighteenth-century Russia. Realism in fiction can be seen as consistent with the nineteenth-century positivist quest, visible in economics, sociology, and the natural sciences, to define and catalogue a core reality underneath the surface messiness of life. The novel, always open to multiple discourses, kept pace with other explanatory modes by refracting the social reality uncovered in these areas of knowledge through individual perspectives that often challenged systems. It is not for nothing that Hayden White, writing largely on the philosophy of history, saw Marx and Flaubert as key to the styles of Realism.[29]

Literary identity and social structure of the imperial period

INETEENTH-CENTURY Russian prose paid keen attention to the structure of the society it described, including forms of address and language markers. Social groups in post-Petrine Russia are usually listed as nobility, clergy, townspeople, and peasants. Presented this way, they seem similar to the European estate system. The degree to which Russian social structures can be mapped onto a model of European estates continues to be hotly debated among historians.[1] However, these groups were different in many respects from their European analogues: while they represented a social structure that was no less complex, in some ways they were more fluid. Furthermore, other factors further divided the Russian population, both within and across the four main categories. One such factor was the legal right to own land and serfs: for most of the imperial period, only the nobility (in addition to the state and the royal family) had this right. Another factor was taxation. The entire population was divided according to their individual state tax obligations: most townspeople and all peasants were obliged to pay a tax (*podushnaia podat'*, applied only to males), whereas the nobility and the clergy as well as some groups of townspeople were not. The tax-paying groups endured other legal inequities: their mobility was restricted and they were subject to corporal punishment. In addition, peasants were liable to military service. A last dividing factor was cultural orientation: a small portion of Russians (mostly the nobility, but also some among the clergy and the townspeople) were oriented toward Europe in the ways they were educated, dressed, prepared their meals, worshipped, and generally organized their everyday lives. The rest of the population preserved pre-Petrine ways of life. Toward the end of the imperial period, the legal distinctions diminished, but these classes never closed the cultural gap between them.

Perhaps most important, none of the four groups was homogeneous or fixed. The post-Petrine nobility, in particular, as a newly created estate, was heterogeneous and open to new members. It encompassed all kinds of elite groups, as well as commoners who were able to enter the noble class thanks to successful state service or imperial favor. Movement within the Table of Ranks, the list of positions in the military, civil, and court services introduced by Peter the Great in 1722, was the easiest means for non-nobles to enter the noble estate: achieving a certain rank provided, first, the so-called personal nobility, which could not be passed on to one's children; and then, once higher rank had been achieved, hereditary nobility, which legally made one equal to nobles with pre-Petrine roots. With time, it was more and more difficult for a commoner to attain the noble status, especially hereditary: from 1722 to 1845, it was the rank of the lowest 14th class that afforded hereditary nobility in the military. Civil servants attained hereditary nobility by reaching the rank of the 8th class. In 1856, the barrier was raised to 6th class for the army and 4th class for the civil servants. However, all members of the estate tended to remember the origin of the nobility of individuals, which stubbornly defined one's status among peers. Those ennobled through service held lower status, whereas those ennobled through their connections with the monarch oftentimes enjoyed a higher status than some representatives of old pre-Petrine families.

The Table of Ranks created a hierarchy within the nobility: in every service category, ranks were divided into fourteen classes in decreasing order of importance, one being the highest. The hierarchy reflected in forms of address: officials in classes 1 and 2 were addressed "Your High Excellency" (*vashe vysokoprevoskhoditel'stvo*); in classes 3 and 4, "Your Excellency" (*vashe prevoskhoditel 'stvo*); in classes from 5 to 8, "Your High Honor" (*vashe vysokoblagorodie*); and 9 to 14, "Your Honor" (*vashe blagorodie*). All titles were also used in the third person, for example, "His/Her Excellency" (*ego/ee prevoskhoditel'stvo*).

The clergy consisted of two main groups: the "white" (or parochial; they were obliged to marry) and "black" (or monastic; had to remain celibate). However, the level of education was also an important status marker: the parochial clergy, who were educated in seminaries, had a lower status than the upper echelons of the Church officials, who mostly comprised monastic clergy educated in ecclesiastical academies. Monks and nuns living in the monasteries had their own internal hierarchies, sometimes dependent on their education and, in other cases, on personal charisma.

Townspeople were a motley group that included five different subgroups, some of them with further subdivisions: honorable citizens, or *pochetnye grazhdane* (split into two groups: hereditary and personal), merchantry (divided into three guilds allocated by the size of their capital), townspeople proper (*meshchane*), artisans, and workers. The relations among these subgroups were hierarchical, with honorable citizens and merchants of the first two guilds enjoying the highest status and workers the lowest. The upper subgroups had many privileges comparable to those of nobility, including the right to travel as well as freedom from taxation and corporal punishment.

The peasantry, which comprised a vast majority of the population of Russian Empire, was not homogeneous either.[2] Up until 1861, when serfdom was abolished, it included serfs who were obliged to work on the estates of noble landowners and were considered to be their property, which meant that they could be bought and sold—by law, only with the land to which they were attached, but the law was frequently disregarded. Most serfs tilled the land, while some worked as domestic servants (*dvorovye*) for their owners. State peasants were personally free but were obliged to work on state land. Finally, there were peasants who belonged to the imperial family. A group that paradoxically bridged the gap between nobility and peasantry were smallholders (*odnodvortsy*): like noblemen, they could own land and serfs; like peasants, they tilled the land, and their way of life was similar to that of peasants.

Both before 1861 and, especially, after, members of all groups of peasantry could change their status by becoming prosperous. Different pathways to prosperity were available, but wealthy individuals existed in all groups, including serfs. Sometimes serfs' owners sent them to urban centers to learn a skill (cooking, sewing) and allowed them to reside in these centers, paying their quitrent (*obrok*, as opposed to corvée, *barshchina*, which was required unpaid labor for a fixed period of time) from the money they earned; the serfs could keep the difference. Occasionally these serfs would save enough money to buy themselves out of serfdom. In other cases, if the landowner was reasonable and the estate was managed well, serfs could prosper while living in the village, working hard, and managing their money well.

Two groups of populations stood outside the described system. One was the *raznochintsy* (people of miscellaneous ranks). For about one hundred years the word designated low-ranking state servitors who comprised a taxable estate. After this estate was abolished in the mid-eighteenth century, the term acquired a new meaning and began to denote persons of non-noble origin who, thanks to their education, were excluded from the taxable status and could join upper social groups. Eventually, the *raznochintsy* gave rise to the Russian intelligentsia. The other group comprised people of liberal professions. This group grew significantly toward the middle of the nineteenth century, when it began to draw members from upper estates and especially from among the *raznochintsy*.

Even though the described system collapsed after 1917, it survived in cultural memory. The nobility as a group were remembered especially well, although not always favorably: in the early post-revolutionary decades they were stripped not only of their former privileges, but also of many civil rights, such as the right to higher education and the right to vote. After the collapse of the Soviet Union, however, those descended from the high nobility regained considerable cultural status (but no privileges) and even acquired a certain mystique in the Russian cultural imagination.

Cultural spaces

The places of residence of members of all classes had a very telling cultural significance. Russians experienced their country as divided into roughly three types of space: there were the two capitals, St. Petersburg and Moscow, different in important ways; the provinces, organized around distinctive provincial towns; and there was the countryside, which consisted in estates, where the gentry dwelled, and the country proper, *derevnia* or the village, populated by peasants.[3] In Russian literature, each space carried specific cultural associations. Many were first codified in the nineteenth century, and these associations long persisted. The social and political disruptions of the twentieth and the early twenty-first centuries complicated, and in some cases eroded, these meanings, but did not eliminate them completely. It is therefore supremely important in a literary text where a given character lives and how that character moves through space.

The meaning assigned to space was, of course, also generated by literary texts. In any given work or literature, the location of the plot had a decisive impact. Dostoevsky's major novels, for example, fall into two groups: the Petersburg novels (*Poor Folk* [*Bednye liudi*, 1846], *Crime and Punishment*, *The Idiot* [*Idiot*, 1868], and *The Adolescent* [*Podrostok*, 1875]) and the provincial novels (*Demons* and *The Brothers Karamazov*). The Petersburg novels are part of Russia's broader Petersburg text, which can be traced back to Vasily Trediakovsky's 1752 ode "Panegyric to the Land of Izhora and the Sovereign City St. Petersburg" ("Pokhvala Izherskoi zemle i tsarstvuiushchemu gradu Sanktpeterburgu") and to a passage from Konstantin Batiushkov's "Stroll to the Academy of Arts" ("Progulka v Akademiiu Khudozhestv," 1814). Batiushkov, like Trediakovsky before him, imagines Peter the Great making a willful decision to create a new capital on the empty banks of the Neva River.[4] The next steps in building a Petersburg mythology were taken by Pushkin, in *The Bronze Horseman* (*Mednyi vsadnik*, written in 1833; published in 1837, after Pushkin's death, with Zhukovsky's amendments) and in "The Queen of Spades," and by Gogol, in his tales featuring St. Petersburg bureaucracy. Pushkin and Gogol consolidated and developed the idea of Petersburg as a space that was artificially constructed by the will of Peter the Great. Built in an inhospitable location—swampy, cold, and prone to disastrous floods—Petersburg hovers on the verge of disintegration, dependent on constant human effort to contain rebellious nature. Its precarious equilibrium puts its inhabitants at risk, threatening them with calamities, sickness, madness, and death. Petersburg is also a place where strange things happen: statues come alive, the dead rise from their graves, and noses walk in the streets wearing uniforms of high-ranking officials. More often than not, because the fantastic events are also susceptible to rational explanation—as a hallucination, a dream, or rumor gone wild—the Petersburg uncanny conforms to the classic definition of the fantastic understood by Tzvetan Todorov as an event whose cause could be either explicable or inexplicable.[5] The ambiguity leaves the readers unsettled, unable to decide whether they are dealing with truthfully described events of ordinary life, in which reality is distorted by mental illness or an error in judgment, or with a world that allows the supernatural by definition and should be accepted as such. Andrei Bely's novel *Petersburg* (serialized in 1913–14, first edition in book form 1916; revised and abridged version 1922) created a definitive modernist version of the Petersburg text, to which later poems, films, memoirs, and fictions would also add further embellishments.

Although St. Petersburg became Russia's official capital in the early eighteenth century, Moscow never completely lost its status as the cultural and administrative center. Tsars were still crowned there, and the city retained its significance as the religious heart of Russia. More important, Moscow stood in stark contrast to Petersburg, which was built after Western models and according to a preconceived plan; in contrast, Moscow looked to Russians like an authentic city that had grown gradually and thus organically. Accordingly, life in Moscow was seen as less formal and less bureaucratic; it was associated with traditional family life, even with an opposition to the official Petersburg. The Slavophiles set up shop in Moscow and exhibited such devotion to the city that Konstantin Aksakov went so far as to break with the Western-leaning Belinsky for taking a job in Petersburg at the journal *Notes of the Fatherland*. Belinsky later addressed the question of the two capitals in his 1845 sketch "Petersburg and Moscow" ("Peterburg i Moskva").[6]

The opposition between Moscow and Petersburg itself became a literary theme. In Tolstoy's *War and Peace*, Moscow is home to the Rostov family—they are warm and hospitable people, and, for all their Western dress and modes of behavior, they understand and uphold Russian traditions. They rely on intuition rather than on cold reason in their judgment of people and events. In *Anna Karenina*, the Shcherbatskys and Levin, likewise, represent Moscow. By contrast, Petersburg is where the court and bureaucracy reign, and warmth and sincerity are hard to find. In *War and Peace*, the corrupt Kuragin family emblematizes the ambitious, self-centered Petersburg norm. The Petersburg–Moscow opposition engendered its own web of ironic, witty commentary. Nikolai Leskov makes a tongue-in-cheek claim in his story "The Devil-Chase" that its supposedly miraculous spiritual resurrection of the two main characters, so deeply rooted in national traditions, could only have happened in Moscow.

Russian provincial novels harken back to Gogol's imagined towns in *The Inspector General* and *Dead Souls*. These provinces are drab, undifferentiated, and stagnant; the population is uneducated (or undereducated), dim-witted, and corrupt. Provincial space acquires a tragic meaning in many of Chekhov's stories, such as "My Life (The Story of a Provincial)" ("Moia zhizn' [Rasskaz provintsiala]," 1896) and "A Case History" ("Sluchai iz praktiki," 1898), as well as in his play *Three Sisters* (*Tri sestry*, 1901). This tradition reaches a point of extreme decadence with Fedor Sologub's 1907 *Petty Demon* (*Melkii bes*). Later in the century, its Gogolian origins come full circle in Leonid Dobychin's (1894–1936) *The Town of N.* (*Gorod En*, 1935). The novel's narrator is a young boy growing up in the early-twentieth-century provincial "Everyplace," which he accepts as a given and thus as authentic and warm. His favorite book is *Dead Souls*, which he reads with sympathetic eyes, naively identifying with its characters.

On the whole, however, Russian literature tended to manifest a strong aversion to the provinces. Any healthy and productive cultural life that did exist outside the capitals (as testified by the surviving provincial library collections, museums, and archives) was almost entirely ignored.[7] The rare exceptions to this aversion often occur in works by women. In contrast to their male counterparts, who perceived the provinces as a featureless place, women writers saw the provincial space as diverse and consisting of various elements: a *gubernia* town is different for them from a district (*uezdnyi*) town; a village is different from the natural environment;

and nature is presented as full of various types of flora that narrators and heroines recognize and know by name; provincial space is pleasant, alive, and diverse.

The estate, described as an idyllic space in eighteenth-century poetry—and in *Evgeny Onegin*, Tolstoy's *Childhood*, and an early chapter of *Oblomov*, "Oblomov's Dream," published separately in 1849—gradually began to receive more authentic treatment while retaining an idyllic tonality. Sergei Aksakov's *Family Chronicle* and *Childhood Years of Bagrov the Grandson* played a signal role in that transformation. The latter, told in the first-person by the protagonist looking back at his boyhood, is beautifully balanced: it includes idyllic vignettes of nature and of happy countryside pursuits, as well as detailed descriptions of agricultural activities to which the boy's father introduces him. At the same time, the memoir does not shy away from descriptions of problematic characters and situations: it includes a stern (if loving) grandfather, conflicts that tear at the fabric of the narrator's family, and even a truly sadistic landowner with whom the narrator's family is acquainted. Vladimir Nabokov, in *Speak, Memory* (1966), writing about his pre-revolutionary childhood, will indulge his nostalgia for this vanished life by replicating the idyllic chronotope of the estate.

Still in the nineteenth century, long before Nabokov could write with such longing, the space of the literary estate had, in some texts, disintegrated into a place of murder, conflict, and blight. Dostoevsky's *Demons*, Saltykov-Shchedrin's *The Golovlev Family*, and some of Chekhov's stories display examples of this confined, ruined sense of the country estate. Unhappiness reigns in two of Chekhov's stories whose titles draw attention to the importance of space: "At the Manor" ("V usad′be," 1894), where a tyrannical father torments his daughters who have no place where to escape; and "At Home" ["V rodnom uglu," 1897], where the heroine cannot bear the stifling life on her estate and leaves it behind as soon as she can find an eligible husband. The estate in Chekhov's *Uncle Vania* (*Diadia Vania*, 1896) is a trap for the only truly likeable characters in the play, Sonia and her uncle, Ivan (Uncle Vania of the title). They remain on the estate and work hard to make it profitable to support the rest of their loafing family members. The death of the estate is emblematically portrayed in *The Cherry Orchard* (*Vishnevyi sad*, written in 1903, first staged in 1904): unable to pay the interest on their mortgaged estate and unwilling to turn it into a profitable enterprise, the owners are forced to sell to a developer. For the older generation, Liubov Ranevskaia and her brother Gaev, parting with the estate is painful, whereas for Ranevskaia's daughter, Ania, it is a chance to begin a new, more meaningful life.

The Russian cultural imagination first represented village life according to the norms of the pastoral (Nikolai Karamzin's "Poor Liza" is a well-known example). Exceptions were rare and politically charged, including some chapters in Aleksandr Radishchev's *Journey from St. Petersburg to Moscow* or Pushkin's poem "The Countryside." In the late 1840s, sympathetic and often naturalistic portrayals of the village began to appear. Dmitry Grigorovich's "The Village" ("Derevnia," 1846) and "Anton Goremyka" ("Anton the Unfortunate," 1847), published in *The Contemporary*, created the trend; they were followed by Turgenev's *Notes of a Hunter*. Aleksei Pisemsky's 1856 *Sketches of the Everyday Lives of the Peasantry* (*Ocherki iz krest′ianskogo byta*) also included three stories about village life. The collection appealed to both proponents of socially responsible art and believers in art for art's sake, and became a point of contention. Each group tried to claim the collection as an expression of their own views.

The emancipation of the serfs in 1861 and, even more, the failure of the "Going to the People" movement (*khozhdenie v narod*) in the late 1870s, engendered a more sober portrayal of village life. Even Tolstoy changed: in his writings, peasants usually serve as positive foils to the upper classes (as in "Three Deaths" ["Tri smerti," 1859] or "Master and Worker"), but he took a more critical look at village life in his 1886 play *The Power of Darkness* (*Vlast′ t′my*), which acknowledges the brutality of the peasants' living conditions and the existence of evil in their midst. Chekhov (who never forgot his non-gentry origin—his grandfather was a serf and his father an unsuccessful merchant) saw both beauty and ugliness in village life, as did Ivan Bunin (1870–1953), a nobleman who strongly felt his connection to the people. In *The Village* (*Derevnia*, 1910), Bunin reveals his unhappiness over the disintegration of the traditional village space, which he understood and loved.

The natural world complemented, and often communicated with, the cultural spaces. Almost non-existent in eighteenth-century literature (except for the highly artificial idylls and pastorals), nature begins to appear in the poetry and prose of Pushkin and Lermontov. Sergei Aksakov made nature an important theme in his *Family Chronicle* and *Childhood Years of Bagrov the Grandson*, and devoted an entire book to fishing (*Notes on Fishing* [*Zapiski ob uzhen'e ryby*, 1847]), two books to hunting (*Notes of a Rifle Hunter of the Orenburg District* [*Zapiski ruzheinogo okhotnika Orenburgskoi gubernii*, 1852]; and *Stories and Memoirs of a Hunter about Different Types of Hunting* [*Rasskazy i vospominaniia okhotnika o raznykh okhotakh*, 1855]), and an essay on butterflies (eventually sternly criticized by Vladimir Nabokov as unprofessional). Into his narrative poem *Sasha* (1855), which treats the theme of the superfluous man and his inability to love, Nekrasov inserted a long passage describing how an old forest is cut down and mourned by the heroine. But it is in the works of Turgenev, beginning with his *Notes of a Hunter*, that nature truly comes to life; it is not merely a setting where the action takes place, but almost a character in its own right. This is particularly evident in "Journey into Polesye" ("Poezdka v Poles'e," 1857), in which the forest is portrayed as "a personified female Nature who addresses man" and, at the same time, is an immense and inhospitable entity.[8] In poetry, the group of poets who firmly placed themselves in the "art for art's sake" camp (Apollon Maikov, Fet, and Polonsky) produced the best poetic descriptions of nature in the Russian tradition, as did Tiutchev when he was not writing socially conscious Slavophile-leaning poetry. Imbued with a pantheistic sense of wonder, these lyrics explore a sense of subjectivity originally inspired by Schelling and *Naturphilosophie* in the Romantic period. Although dismissed as self-indulgent by the radical critics of the time, the poems had great formal ingenuity and thematic depth, particularly in the work of Fet and Tiutchev. They initiated the creation of a new poetic language which in turn made possible the flourishing of poetry beginning in the late nineteenth century. The chain of inspiration extended through the twentieth and twenty-first centuries, with representations of the natural world marking the early poetry of Pasternak, the later work of Zabolotsky, and the entire oeuvre of poets they both influenced, including Gennady Aygi and Olga Sedakova.

KEYWORD **Regional literature**

In medieval Rus', regional literatures flourished in such cultural centers as Novgorod, Pskov, Vladimir, and Tver' up until Moscow gained supremacy. In post-Petrine Russia, despite the primacy of St. Petersburg and Moscow, old regional cultural centers continued to prosper (Arkhangelsk, Yaroslavl, Tver') even as new ones sprung up (Kazan', Irkutsk, Saratov). Nevertheless, most provincials with literary aspirations moved to the capitals and abandoned their regional affiliations. Some, however, continued to write about their native regions (S. T. Aksakov, F. M. Reshetnikov [1841–71], Leskov). Others stressed their connections to them by taking pen names suggestive of place names (Mamin-Sibiriak, Mel'nikov-Pechersky). The first cohort of Russian women writers who lived and wrote in the provinces (Elena Gan, Maria Zhukova, Sofia Zakrevskaia [1766/67–no earlier than 1865]) occasionally positioning themselves as regional writers.

Two Russian writers who worked with regional material were Pavel Mel′nikov (1818–83; pen name Andrei Pechersky) and Dmitry Mamin (1852–1912; pen name Sibiriak). The novels of Mel′nikov's diptych *In the Woods* (*V lesakh*, 1871–74) and *In the Hills* (*Na gorakh*, 1875–81) focus on the popular life (including peasantry, merchantry, and Old Believers) in the region between the Volga and the Ural Mountains. As a government official, Mel′nikov worked hard to force the Old Believers' incorporation into the official Orthodox Church. Nonetheless, he closely studied their culture and collected their folklore, which he then used as the material for novels that are plotless. To unite the descriptions of different characters and various events Mel′nikov uses a naive narrator, Andrei Pechersky, and the narrative technique of *skaz* based on local vernacular. *In the Woods* includes among other folk material the utopian "Legend of the Underwater City of Kitezh"; Mel′nikov's version was used by N. A. Rimsky-Korsakov for his opera *The Legend of the Invisible City of Kitezh and the Maiden Fevronia* (*Skazanie o nevidimom grade Kitezhe i deve Fevronii*, completed in 1905). The action of Mamin's works, on the other hand, takes place in the Urals, on the border with Siberia. Among his best novels are *The Privalov's Fortune* (*Privalovskie milliony*, 1883), *Mountain Nest* (*Gornoe gnezdo*, 1884), and *Wild Happiness* (*Dikoe schast′e*, 1884), all of which criticize greedy merchants and sympathize with the working masses.

As an empire, Russia—and later the USSR—also had colonial space. In the mid-sixteenth century, Russia (then called Muscovy, *Moskoviia*) embarked on expanding eastward, first conquering the Khanate of Kazan in 1552 and then gradually advancing into Siberia. In the early eighteenth century, the empire absorbed territories that are now independent Baltic republics of Latvia and Estonia; Lithuania followed in 1795, during the last partition of Poland. In 1809, Finland was conquered, and in 1812, Moldavia (today's Moldova) became part of the empire. In the late eighteenth century, Russia began to penetrate the Caucasus, a long process that took the best part of the nineteenth century. The advance into Central Asia took place in the second half of the nineteenth century. The USSR retained most of these colonial territories until its disintegration in 1991.⁹

In the nineteenth century, it was the Caucasus that was seen by Russians as the space where an exotic Other dwelled.¹⁰ The myth of an oriental place inhabited by both noble and ignoble savages and beautiful exotic maidens was formulated during the Romantic era in the works of Pushkin, Marlinsky, and Lermontov; it survived well into the second half of the nineteenth century, when Tolstoy began to deconstruct it first in his unfinished novella *The Cossacks*, then in the 1872 story "The Captive of the Caucasus" ("Kavkazskii plennik"), and, especially, in his novella *Hadji Murad* (written in 1896–1904; first published in 1912). Set in 1851, at the time of the long war to conquer the Caucasus, *Hadji Murad* is a story of one of the leaders of the resistance who, at the same time, entered into a conflict with Imam Shamil, the political and religious leader of the Muslim tribes of the Northern Caucasus. Shamil captured Hadji Murad's sons, and the novella recounts the father's failed attempt to free them. To accomplish his goal, Hadji Murad comes to the Russians for help, but soon realizes that they are not planning to free his sons. He attempts to flee the Russian fortress and is hunted down and killed. The novella presents a complex picture of the Caucasian war: both the Russian conquerors and the Caucasus insurgents (see Figure IV.08 for a portrait of one) can be good and bad, kind and cruel. It is noteworthy that Hadji Murad is pursued and killed by both Russian soldiers and locals: both groups join in triumph over his dead mutilated body.

Central Asia acquired significance in the Russian cultural consciousness toward the end of the nineteenth century. One way of appropriating Asia was to represent it as Russia's cultural, linguistic, and genetic counterpart. This view was developed artistically by the poet Velimir

Figure iv.08. M. Iu. Lermontov, *A Caucasian Mountaineer*, 1830s–1841.

Khlebnikov (1885–1922) and philosophically by the group of twentieth-century intellectuals known as Eurasianists. Another approach was exemplified by Andrei Platonov (1899–1951), who presented Asia in his story "Takyr" (1934) and in the novella *Dzhan* (1933–35; unexpurgated version 1999) as a primordial, liminal space where human beings exist on par with beasts and plants, barely subsisting but fiercely persevering.

Since the collapse of the Soviet Union, the topos of colonial space has been internalized, thus resurrecting significant themes from the nineteenth century. On the one hand, the post-Soviet war for the control of Chechnya and Northern Caucasus revitalized motifs echoing Lermontov, Marlinsky, and Tolstoy. However, Vladimir Makanin's (b. 1937) neo-Naturalist style is in dialogue with Russian classical authors ("The Prisoner from the Caucasus" ["Kavkazskii plennyi," 1994] and the 2008 novel *Asan*), in Zakhar Prilepin's (b. 1975) *Patologii* (*Pathologies*, 2005), and in Arkady Babchenko's (b. 1977) *Alkhan-Iurt* (2002) reveals a radical difference between the sensibilities of the nineteenth-century colonization and the present-day colonial war, in which the invading "others" and the native dwellers are united by the Soviet past. The mirror relationship between "us" and "them" emphasizes the futility of this new colonization: while present-day Russian soldiers typically do not know what they are fighting and dying for, their opponents have clear goals in defending their motherland and their freedom.

Another important tendency in post-Soviet literature could be defined as alternative regionalism (in parallel to "alternative history"). A number of contemporary writers reinvent traditional Russian areas as if they were foreign spaces colonized by Russia, and endow them with original lore, mores, hidden historical memory, and cultural specificity. For example, Denis Osokin's (b. 1977) short novel *Buntings* (*Ovsianki*, 2008; see also Aleksei Fedorchenko's eponymous film of 2010) depicts the rites of a Finno-Ugric tribe of Meria (extinct since the tenth century) that the author places in a contemporary setting of central Russian regions. He invents the tribe's folklore, mythology, and rituals purported to have survived until the present times. In a series of books, beginning with historical fiction, *The Heart of Parma* (*Serdtse Parmy*, 2003) and *The Gold of Rebellion, or The Gorge Downstream* (*Zoloto bunta, ili vniz po reke tesnin*, 2005), and continuing with the novels set in the present day (*The Geographer Has Drunk His Globe Away* [*Geograf globus propil*, 1995, published 2003]) as well as with non-fiction (*Message* [*Message: Chusovaia*, 2007], *The Ural Matrix* [*Ural'skaia matritsa*, 2008]), Aleksei Ivanov (b. 1969) develops the theme of the Urals as a distinct civilization, different from "central" Russia and having its own specific identity. The reason for this tendency and the corresponding depiction of Russian regional spaces as isolated and exotic lands may be found in the crisis of the (former Soviet) national identity based on the imperial pride and wounded by the collapse of the USSR. At the same time, this tendency might lead to a new conceptualization of Russia compatible with Michel Foucault's definition of heterotopia, that is, places and spaces that function in non-hegemonic conditions. Such regions "remember" their ancient past and are able to transform it into the foundation of unique collective identities, resisting unification and multiplying the notions of "Russianness" and Russian space.

Educated elite

The characters surveyed in this section come from one strata of society and are described according to the aesthetic canons of successive aesthetic movements (Sentimentalism, Romanticism, Realism). Group identity is not, however, the be-all and end-all in the construction of a character's identity. This is particularly true for Sentimentalist and Romantic writers. Readers will note the disparity between Erast's status as a nobleman and Liza's position as a peasant girl. And yet the explanation of her tragic end does not entirely reside in the differentiation of the lovers' social groups. Despite his hope of becoming a gypsy and living out the dream of a Rousseauian primitive in nature, Pushkin's Aleko of *The Gypsies* (*Tsygany*, written 1824, published in full 1827) remains an outsider to the gypsy tribe that adopts him. And who is he socially? It is hard to tell beyond the fact that different norms of behavior govern his conduct. Likewise, Pushkin never says how Dunia in "The Station Master", obviously undereducated and poorly brought up as she is, manages to lead what seems to be a happy life with Minsky, her socially and culturally superior lover. Only as Russian writers began to strive for realistic (even if not yet Realist) representation of their characters did they begin to mark their heroes and heroines more decisively as members of particular social groups. Readers still disagree about what went wrong between Onegin and Tatiana and at what stage. Did their ultimate failure to love stem from his rejection of her when he played the dandy and trifled with her feelings? Was the gap between an urban sophisticate and a provincial gentry girl unbridgeable? Or, in the end, was the source of their estrangement, ironically, the fact that her standing as a high society lady empowered her to spurn him, suspecting that he only wanted her now because of her high status? The answers to these questions may matter less than Pushkin's care in portraying his characters as representing a particular social class. The narrator tells us that Tatiana has a Russian soul, while personality traits like her belief in folk superstition reinforce her provincial identity. Yet there is no doubt that Tatiana is a noblewoman and has a noble ethos. Her sympathy for the peasantry and its practices does not make her a peasant. The function of Tatiana's nanny as a secondary character is to serve as a foil in this regard: Pushkin inserts the nanny's story of her marriage, which was devoid not only of Eros but even of sympathy between the mismatched bride and groom to juxtapose it with Tatiana's naive and derivative, but undoubtedly real and cultivated, emotions.

Within the nobility, Pushkin also distinguished different groups: the Petersburg elite; the Muscovites who were less sophisticated, a bit comical, but perhaps more sincere; and the provincial gentry, a mixed lot that included (albeit temporarily) a Petersburg fop, a Heidelberg-educated idealist, the well-read Tatiana, the simpler Olga, and a host of local nobles resembling Denis Fonvizin's comical characters in *The Minor*, an important and still popular satire on the shallow education of the middling landed gentry. All these characters move between different cultural spaces and strata, and Pushkin takes pains to show his heroine negotiating behavioral expectations as she moves from the garden—the site of a rendezvous—to the ballroom, where she maintains the singular reserve demanded by society. Pushkin never lets his reader forget who the characters are in terms of their social and cultural identity.

Other writers follow suit in underscoring the role of social institutions in conditioning characterization, a fundamental aspect of realism that Erich Auerbach identified long ago in his classic *Mimesis*. In Lermontov's *A Hero of Our Time*, the characters' social standing is as clear as it is important. The old veteran Maksim Maksimych may have a military rank superior to Pechorin's; however, Pechorin hails from St. Petersburg high society, whereas Maksim comes from the provincial middling nobility. The two may be friends when Pechorin is forced to serve in the Caucasus, but when they meet in a new context, Pechorin emphasizes their class difference. Grushnitsky, too, mistakenly thinks that only rank separates him and Pechorin as fellow officers, whereas in fact Pechorin, ever self-conscious about status, never acknowledges him as his peer. While the military rank might have leveled differences in status (or even established new hierarchies), it did not always work as an equalizer, especially in the civilian setting of a Caucasian spa, where Pechorin's confrontation with Grushnitsky takes place.

In *War and Peace*, the reader confronts a cross-section of Russian society, from members of the royal family to the humblest soldier hailing from the peasantry, epitomized in Platon Karataev. The majority of characters come from the noble class. Tolstoy portrays some members of high society as shallow and idle, gossipy and egotistic, first exemplified in Anna Scherer and Prince Vasily Kuragin, whose salon chatter opens the book. Kuragin's children, particularly Hélène and Anatole, are even worse, because their egotism is pure evil. We have seen that Pisarev condemned them as useless, a stilted characterization that does not entirely coincide with Tolstoy's portrait of his own class: other high society members in *War and Peace* are well-educated, intelligent, and look for ways to live meaningful lives. Prince Andrei Bolkonsky has Napoleonic dreams early in the novel, but he and his younger friend, Pierre Bezukhov, wish to better themselves and to serve mankind. While members of the Moscow nobility, represented by the Rostov family, are not intellectual, they are kind and sociable, and often exhibit incisive understanding and keen powers of intuition superior to their more intellectual counterparts. Furthermore, Princess Maria, Andrei's spiritually inclined sister, combines both intellect and intuition. The middling nobility is mainly represented by military officers, usually portrayed sympathetically because Tolstoy encourages the view that it is they, rather than the great generals, who enable Napoleon's defeat. The figure of Captain Tushin, essentially an extra in the vast military panorama, exemplifies the heroism of the Russian officer class.

In *Anna Karenina*, Tolstoy's representation of St. Petersburg high society is much more negative: almost all of its members are depicted as shallow, gossipy, and evil. Because Tolstoy focalizes the portrayal of Aleksei Karenin through the character of his wife, Anna, his disagreeable traits distort our perception of a man who is a gifted and erudite statesman, also capable in private life of compassion and forgiveness.[11] He is willing to divorce Anna, and it is her decision not to accept his offer.[12] As in *War and Peace*, Moscow society, represented by the Shcherbatskys, is kinder, more cordial, and family-oriented. Being part of a caring family in *Anna Karenina* is as important as in *War and Peace*: the novel takes pains to indicate that Anna, Stiva Oblonsky, and Vronsky all lacked proper families in their childhood. Supremely sensitive as a reader of Rousseau to the role of the environment in conditioning sensibility, and well aware of contemporary pedagogical theories, Tolstoy's developed sense of characters as personalities implies an important back-story to their behavior. This also explains why Levin strives to create a good family with Kitty. Being domestically inclined, however, can make a person blind to the pain of others. Anna, on the verge of committing suicide, seeks Dolly's help and receives none—Dolly spurns her because she is distracted by Kitty's difficulties breastfeeding her newborn son. Levin, too, is contemplating suicide at this very time, and Kitty, absorbed in caring for her son, is oblivious to his drama.[13] Levin is the most well-rounded of all characters; searching, troubled, volatile, and a dreamer, yet practical, he is therefore the most complex. It is crucial for the reader's understanding of him to note that he is looking at peasants to find the answers to the questions that torment him. Tolstoy seems to be unique in allowing his character to cross social boundaries in search of behavioral and moral models.

In *Resurrection*, high society, whether in St. Petersburg or Moscow, is presented grotesquely: they are seen through Nekhliudov's eyes, and, because he is undergoing profound spiritual change, they seem monstrous to him. The only positive members of the nobility are revolutionaries, men and women who left their social class to devote their lives to its destruction in the name of justice. These are characters capable of kindness toward any human being who needs it: be it the former prostitute Katiusha, a child, or Nekhliudov looking for the right path. It is crucial that Tolstoy, the propagator of non-resistance to evil, never presents these strong characters as the destructive force they actually were: everything that has to do with their radical activity is left out of the novel.

CASE STUDY Intelligentsia

The intelligentsia has a more prominent role in Russian cultural history than that of any Western European counterpart. Like the saint, the poet, and the revolutionary, the *intelligent* remains a figure closely associated in popular perception with the national identity. The true emergence of an intelligentsia dates roughly to the 1860s and 1870s, a time of critical social and educational changes that gave momentum and lent cohesiveness to trends in intellectual life dating to the 1830s. However, arguments have been made, by the historians Marc Raeff and Michael Confino as well as the literary scholar Dmitry Likhachev, that the intelligentsia originated in the Enlightenment as secular education expanded and a literature showing a critical attitude to society developed.[14] To be sure, there are single individuals such as Novikov, Karamzin, Radishchev, and in the 1830s the historian Nikolai Nadezhdin (1804–56) and the philosopher Petr Chaadaev, who fit the profile of the *philosophe* as a believer in Enlightenment precepts of reason and tolerance and a promoter of scientific knowledge. These individuals also attempted to define the distinctiveness of Russian culture, often in relation to European literary models and philosophical trends. But the pattern of a group devoted to certain ideals and public issues comes into its own in later decades. By 1855, the year of Nicholas's death, the younger generation was ready to apply critical thinking to the social world.

Nobody quite knows whether the term *intelligentsia* was coined from a Latin, French, or German noun but it was rapidly taken up by writers and commentators. Zhukovsky used it in a diary entry of 1836, and the word is attested in dictionaries and encyclopedias in the second half of the nineteenth century, including the second edition of Dal's dictionary of the Russian language (1880–82), a watershed in native lexicography, which defined the *intelligentsia* as a "rational, educated, intellectually developed segment of the population." However, as with the term "nihilist," supposedly coined by Turgenev, it is a novelist, the prolific but now obscure Petr Boborykin (1836–1921), who applied the term *intelligent* to fictional characters motivated by ethical and political purpose and who gave the notion currency. By the 1870s, the word began to appear regularly in fiction. In *Anna Karenina*, Levin's half-brother, the political economist Sergei Koznyshev, is described as a "leading representative of the Moscow intelligentsia."[15]

The significance of intelligentsia comes down to questions of activity and membership; the latter is the harder to define conclusively. For that reason, it is a matter of open discussion whether the intelligentsia comprises a social class, a group, or a stratum. Historically, its members differed in terms of class origin and status; they were sometimes professionals, sometimes belonged to the gentry or to the *raznochintsy*, or may have had urban or provincial roots. Yet despite those social differences, the intelligentsia had *esprit de corps* imbued with lofty ideals, an empirical method of observation, and a moral passion for improving Russian society. What gave the group its identity, as Michael Confino noted, was a sociological idea, a moral code, and, in literature and autobiography, a psychological profile.[16] Nikolai Berdiaev (1874–1948) in his *Russian Idea* (*Russkaia ideia*, 1946) perceptively defined the intelligentsia as "an idealistic class" whose devotion to liberal ideas and the philosophy of materialism rendered them akin to a monastic order, despite a generally atheistic outlook: "Materialism was a matter of religious faith and its opponents were treated at a certain period as enemies of the emancipation of the people."[17] To be an *intelligent* meant, in practice, taking seriously issues of national interest; feeling responsible for the justice and injustices of the state and the political system; applying reason rather than religion to the resolution of those problems; and taking action. Moreover, members of the intelligentsia were self-conscious about their values and their own value to society, and saw themselves as the bearers of a progressive national idea.

Not every writer was a member of the intelligentsia: the aristocratic Leo Tolstoy, most conspicuously, kept his distance from urban societies. And not every *intelligent* was an aesthetic and political radical: the Slavophiles, active from the late 1820s, added much to the discussion of Russia's national identity and forms of art while remaining staunchly monarchist and opposed to the literary politics of the radical critics.

In Russia, the establishment of an intelligentsia, positioned outside the government and outside the private sphere of the family, had to contend with strict governmental oversight of civic spaces, which in European countries belonged to a sphere in which the public as well as the intellectual avant-garde exercised public opinion and civic behavior. The constraints imposed by the tsarist state set limits to the open expression of ideology; however, that very pressure endowed the banned ideas with a sense of value. A comparison between two generations, the older "fathers" of the 1840s and the younger "sons" of the 1860s and 1870s, has been a time-honored way of illustrating the emergence of an intelligentsia. Both the fathers and the sons shared a love of literature and an openness to new liberal ideas. While Turgenev was the first to portray the two groups in his eponymous novel, Dostoevsky, a critic of the intelligentsia, represented them satirically (including Turgenev himself) in *Demons*.

Despite adversity, philosophical groups were to become a more regular feature of urban life, with some individuals enjoying membership in multiple groups. Such were the circles of Nikolai Ogarev (Herzen's great friend) and, above all, the Stankevich circle in Moscow, which brought together the literary critic Vissarion Belinsky, the Slavophile theorist Ivan Kireevsky, the future novelist Ivan Turgenev, the budding Slavophile Konstantin Aksakov, the future theorist of anarchism Mikhail Bakunin, and many others, all bound by ideas and friendship. Members of the gentry intelligentsia were worldly people, a far cry from both the Byronic burned-out hero of Romanticism and the déclassé student radical of the political novels later in the century. The men of the 1830s and 1840s could afford to retreat into German Idealist philosophy. Some, like Herzen and Bakunin, clashed with autocracy in the pursuit of their intellectual freedoms, escaped abroad, and fought against censorship across the border. They also fought for political ideals inimical to autocracy.

Over time, the focus of intelligentsia would shift from autonomous intellectual activity to planning reforms. From the 1850s, several simultaneous factors formed the generation of sons as a distinctive class of men (and later women) committed to a life led according to principles derived from philosophical thought. The growth of the university-educated *raznochintsy* as an urban class—estimated at about 5,000 students per annum, and therefore relatively small—as well as increasing numbers of gentry professionals provided an expanded social base for the rise of an intelligentsia who were avid readers of and contributors to the thick journals. Educational reforms passed by the government in the late 1840s privileged the sciences over the humanities (the latter were assumed to be contributing to subversion). Steeped in science, the generation of radical critics, perhaps the quintessential examples of the intelligentsia in this period, brought rational expectations to questions of social progress. But while they dismissed art for its own sake, many were also committed to literature and art as tools of progressive politics, exposing the government's policy as futile. The intelligentsia's values were no longer only a matter of theoretical ideals but applied thought and practical schemes to implementing utopian solutions of social problems. Lofty conceptualizations had offered the previous generation of post-Decembrist men of the 1840s comforting illusions about nature, history, and consciousness that offset their frustration with the stagnation of Nicholas I's reign. Such abstractions were not enough for the intelligentsia of the 1860s, who believed that liberty was as much a political issue as it was a matter of philosophical transcendence. Nikolai Chernyshevsky's life, career, and impact serve notice that the *intelligent* had arrived as a figure of cultural significance. Chernyshevsky's master's thesis at St. Petersburg University, *The Aesthetic Relation of Art to Reality*, expounded the principles of his doctrine of realism, while his *Sketches of the Gogolian Period of Russian Literature* refashioned the reputations of Gogol and Belinsky as radical realists and political writers, filling a void in the history of thought in Russia. His novel *What Is to Be Done?*, written in prison and published in *The Contemporary*, came to serve as a lifestyle manual for the next generation of young readers. On a much larger public scale than Stankevich, Chernyshevsky stimulated a vigorous debate on the question of how, or whether, art could provide active benefit to society. He also attracted readers to the figure of the author as thinker, activist, and social critic. His novel served as a model for the new unconventional sexual and emotional relationships cultivated by the intelligentsia within their own communal arrangements; the nihilists, a subgroup of the intelligentsia, extended their radicalism to all aspects of their life. The intelligentsia circle Land and Will (Zemlia i volia) incubated the revolutionary society headed by N. A. Ishutin (1840–79), who argued that the role of the intelligentsia was to pave the way for a peasant revolution. In the latter half of the nineteenth century, *intelligenty* also supported populist measures and the ideology of "going to the people," which promoted the idea that they should teach in schools for peasant children, work in countryside hospitals, and, most importantly, spread propaganda against the government. The peasants distrusted the populists agitating against the tsar, and the movement suffered a defeat. Turgenev and Chekhov, among other writers, represented the weaknesses of the movement in their work.

By the late nineteenth century, much of the intelligentsia had become radicalized and sold on the idea that Russia could circumvent capitalism and implement socialism without going through the development of capitalism and a bourgeoisie that Marx had envisaged. This idea of a "special path," or *Sonderweg*, extended the earlier theories of Petr Chaadaev (in his "Apology of a Madman" ["Apologie d'un fou," 1837; first published in French in 1862, twelve years after Chaadaev's death]) to the economic sphere, while Slavophile thinkers argued that Russia's strength lay in its unspoiled separateness. In "Intelligentsia and Revolution," a famous article published in the collection *Milestones* (*Vekhi*) in 1909, the Russian political economist and philosopher Petr Struve identified contradictions in the intelligentsia's belief, on the one hand, in its populism and, on the other, in its support of an economic model that did not satisfy the masses' expectations of how property would be divided in a new socialist Russia.

Peasantry

Beginning with Radishchev's *Journey from St. Petersburg to Moscow* and Karamzin's "Poor Liza," noblemen are often portrayed in their interactions with the peasantry. The largest estate in Russia and the least Westernized, peasants rather early began to serve as representatives of genuine pre-Petrine culture and thus as custodians of a national cultural heritage. This view began to gain currency in the 1840s, first among the members of the Natural School and later more broadly. Grigorovich stands at the beginning of this trend with his novellas *The Village* and *Anton the Unfortunate*. Both works follow the terribly hard life of a serf: the former, that of an orphaned girl Akulina and the latter, that of a poor peasant Anton. Both end badly: Akulina, brought up by a hostile and randomly chosen step-mother and then forced by her owner to marry a man also chosen at random, dies young, leaving an orphaned daughter to live a life that is likely to be very similar to her own. Anton, burdened by a large family and plagued by bad luck, is arrested at the end of the novella for a crime he did not commit, and faces prison. Both novellas were published in *The Contemporary*, were well received, and influenced subsequent portrayals of peasants, starting with Turgenev's *Notes of a Hunter*. But Turgenev's depictions, although compassionate, do not concentrate on misery to the degree that Grigorovich's novellas do. Turgenev's peasants, like anyone else, lead different lives: some are miserable, others less so, while some are quite ordinary. In the story "Bezhin Meadow" ("Bezhin lug"), five peasant boys are portrayed, and each has its own character, his own story, and his own fate. Turgenev's collection helped him make his name as a prose writer and was admired by his contemporaries, including Tolstoy.

In Tolstoy's *War and Peace*, Platon Karataev is the novelist's most memorable peasant. Meek, naive, but wise, he teaches Pierre by example to accept what life has in store for us, including death. Tolstoy returns to the portrayal of an ideal peasant in 1886, both in his novella *The Death of Ivan Ilyich* ("Smert' Ivana Il'icha," 1886), in which the only truly humane character is Gerasim, a house servant of peasant origin who kindly and patiently takes care of the dying title character; and in the play *The Power of Darkness*, in which Akim, deeply religious and just, is trying to stop the bad behavior of his son Nikita; it is hard to tell whether he succeeds—Nikita repents on his own—but Akim certainly rejoices in Nikita's repentance.

In Dostoevsky's *The Adolescent*, the title character is a natural son of a nobleman Versilov and a peasant woman, Sofia, whom Versilov seduced while visiting the estate of his relative. Atypically for literary seductions of peasant women, Sofia was married to the peasant Makar Dolgoruky. As Versilov explains later to his son, everything happened somewhat unintentionally, under the influence of two literary works, Aleksandr Druzhinin's (1824–64) *Polinka Sachs* (*Polin'ka Saks*, 1847) and Grigorovich's *Anton the Unfortunate*. This accidental union between Versilov and Sofia, however, lasts for more than twenty years and by the end of the novel it is clear that it is likely to last a lifetime. Both peasant characters are better and wiser than the rest, including Versilov and his son, Arkady. Makar is virtually a saint: he spends all his life as a pilgrim, returning to his wife only when she needs him, and finally he comes back to her to die. His kindness and wisdom help Arkady mature and find peace with his natural father and his mother. Sofia's devotion to Versilov and her love for her son have a similarly curative effect. (While working on The Adolescent, Dostoevsky left a drawing of a peasant face on the margins of his drafts for the novel; see Figure IV.09.[18])

The best-known peasant in Dostoevsky is Marei from the eponymous story ("Muzhik Marei," published in *Diary of a Writer* in 1876). The story is structured as a recollection of a recollection: while in a Siberian prison camp more than twenty years earlier, Dostoevsky recalls an episode from his childhood, which he then publishes in his *Diary*. Dostoevsky apparently needed the prison camp as a background or contrast to this story of kindness shown by his

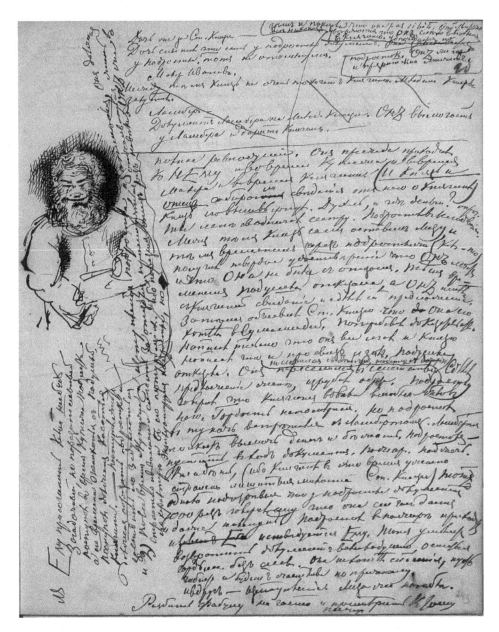

FIGURE IV.09. F. M. Dostoevsky, A face of a peasant in the rough drafts of *The Adolescent* (1874).

father's serf to the nine-year-old Fedor, who imagined being chased by a wolf and was terribly frightened. Marei calmed the child down, smiled at him (Dostoevsky calls his smile "motherly"), made the sign of the cross over him, and watched the boy as he went home to make sure that he was not frightened anymore. Recalling the episode in the prison camp helps Dostoevsky look at his fellow inmates with kinder eyes: any one of them, he realizes, could have been Marei.

Unlike most of his predecessors and contemporaries, Chekhov did not idealize the peasantry, probably because he did not feel the guilt of a former serf-owner, since he was of nonnoble birth. His stories show much complexity in his presentation of the peasantry. The story

"In the Ravine" ("V ovrage," 1900) features a peasant woman capable of utter cruelty as she scalds an infant whom she perceives as her rival in the fight for inheritance. In the 1897 story "Peasants" ("Muzhiki"), Nikolai, who has lived in Moscow working as a lackey in a hotel, falls ill and returns to his native village together with his wife and daughter. They are shocked by what they find: not only utter poverty, but also people indifferent and even cruel to each other. Nikolai's religious wife, Olga, finds consolation in religion, frequently visiting the local church and other neighboring churches. When Nikolai dies, she and her young daughter leave the village to become pilgrims and beggars. Olga pities the peasants of the village she has abandoned; rude, dishonest, and cruel as they are, they are still people: "they suffer and cry like humans, and in their life there is nothing that could not be excused."[19] "The New Dacha" ("Novaia dacha," 1899) stages a conflict revolving around the difficulty of establishing connections and understanding between people. The family of an engineer who supervises the construction of a new bridge, builds a summer house (*dacha*) in the vicinity, but has a hard time being accepted by the local peasants. Both the engineer and his wife try to be neighborly, but fail even to attain a state of neutral coexistence with the locals. The peasants' hostility seems to be groundless, but it looks like it is the family's very attempt to establish communication that causes the conflict and forces the newcomers to sell the dacha and leave. Chekhov shows that no one can communicate: the different classes literally do not understand each other, often on a purely grammatical level. It is significant that the new owner of the dacha does not communicate with the peasants at all, and they coexist peacefully. Who is to blame for the failure of communication? Is the new owner's way of behaving toward peasants preferable? Chekhov as always does not provide any answers to these questions. At best, he indicates that there exists a rift between the simple people and the educated classes, and both sides share responsibility.

Ivan Bunin considered himself to be the last in a long line of nineteenth-century writers of noble descent. This makes his 1912 novella *Dry Valley* (*Sukhodol*) particularly interesting because its main idea is that Russian noblemen and peasants are not as different and alienated from each other as the nineteenth-century tradition asserts. To begin with, the Russian words for "nobleman," *dvorianin*, and for a serf who lives in the nobleman's house doing all the necessary work, *dvorovyi*, derive from the same root, *dvor* (yard, homestead). Furthermore, after centuries of living under the same roof, *dvoriane* and *dvorovye* share blood: some peasants have their owners' blood in their veins, and more than a few noblemen have the serfs' blood in theirs. In Bunin's view, the peasants and their owners were also close culturally, singing the same songs and telling the same stories and legends. Notably, Natasha's uncle in *War and Peace* (in fact, her older distant relative, whom she calls "uncle" [*diadiushka*]), who not only has a peasant lover, but also is a virtuoso performer of folk music, obviously is of the same opinion. The relations between these two classes are not idyllic, and when a serf needs to be punished, the punishment is promptly meted out. But there is a sense of family in the household described by Bunin—perhaps a dysfunctional family, but still a family.

CASE STUDY *Narod*/The people

The term *narod* ("the people"), in addition to meaning "nation," "crowd," and "the populace," developed in the nineteenth century a specific set of meanings that had to do both with the circumstances of the post-Petrine cultural change and its interpretation by the educated classes. This new meaning is best illustrated by Konstantin Aksakov's 1848 essay "An Attempt at Synonyms: The People and the Public" ("Opyt sinonimov: Narod i publika"; first published in 1857), in which this prominent Slavophile portrays the Russian nation as split into two unequal parts: the people (*narod*) that comprises the majority of the nation, and the educated classes (*publika*), a thin upper layer of the nation. Contrasting the Russian *narod* and the Latin *publicus*, Aksakov presents the public as foreign and thus unnatural, unoriginal, imitative, and, ultimately, irrelevant; they are a part of the Russian nation that came into being as a result of Peter's Westernizing reforms. Initially consisting of the gentry (*dvorianstvo*, a new service class formed in the wake of the Petrine reforms), it also came to include the *raznochintsy*, the educated individuals of various social groups. The non-Westernized part of the nation comprised the peasantry (both serfs and state peasants), the townspeople (*meshchanstvo*), craftsmen (*tsekhovye*), lower strata of the merchant class, and most of the clergy, with the exception of its upper echelons. Aksakov's sarcastic piece illustrates the Slavophiles' concern about the lack of cultural homogeneity in the Russian nation and their own resulting marginality. First voiced in the eighteenth century (most forcefully, by Mikhail Shcherbatov and Aleksandr Radishchev), the concern persisted throughout the nineteenth century.

Toward the second half of the century, many among the upper classes, troubled and guilt-ridden by their break with the national tradition, began to idealize the *narod*, a group that they gradually came to equate almost exclusively with the peasants. Both Dostoevsky and Tolstoy contributed to this process. For his participation in a liberal intellectual group (the so-called Petrashevsky Circle named after its leader, the utopian theorist Mikhail Petrashevsky [1821–66]), Dostoevsky spent four years in a Siberian prison camp in close proximity with convicts of all social classes, but mostly peasants. His experience led him to formulate a Slavophile-type ideology, *pochvennichestvo*—the ideology that leaned toward the idealization of the peasantry as a repository of traditional Russian moral and religious values. Tolstoy formulated the idea that the peasantry is the only truly moral class in Russia as early as his 1859 story "Three Deaths." Levin of *Anna Karenina* goes even further in trying to join the peasants in their agricultural work. Tolstoy's own search for unity with the people eventually led him to a partial adoption of the peasants' lifestyle (*oproshchenie*). It is remarkable that being in contact with real peasants—and occasionally providing some unsentimentalized portraits, such as the rebelling peasants in Bogucharovo in *War and Peace*, Dron in particular; or the peasant beating his horse in Raskolnikov's dream—both Tolstoy and Dostoevsky never abandoned the idea that in general peasantry was morally better than the upper classes.

Maxim Gorky (1868–1936) stands alone in his fierce distrust and dislike of the Russian peasantry. Influenced in his youth by the Populist movement (*narodnichestvo*), he became disillusioned with the peasants whom he saw as inherently passive and uncivilized. His 1922 essay *On the Russian Peasantry* (*O russkom krest'ianstve*; published in Berlin) is particularly critical: it accuses peasants of orchestrating a famine as a means of their struggle against Soviet Russia, and calls for their extermination. Later, after he returned to the Soviet Union from emigration, Gorky became an avid supporter of Stalinist collectivization.

Russia's revolutionary ideology, and the Soviet literature inspired and censored by it, from the start looked to the *narod* for positive ideals. Despite this, controversial and even critical depictions did appear frequently in the works written and sometimes published in the 1920s and in those, typically unpublished, from the 1930s to the late 1980s. Mikhail Bulgakov's *The Heart of Dog* (*Sobach'e serdtse*, 1925) depicts a "simple man" Sharikov—a byproduct of a scientific experiment that has turned a dog into a human being—as an uncultured, smug, aggressive, and obnoxious creature, hardly a human, who nevertheless, due to the support from Soviet ideologues, promptly rises to power and becomes a source of danger to his "makers," the intelligentsia members. Bulgakov's manuscript was banned in the USSR until 1988. Mikhail Zoshchenko's short stories were widely published in the 1920s, although their characters and narrators, depicted by the writer with extraordinary humor, are hardly different from Sharikov. Yet Zoshchenko emphasizes that attempts by the people to pose as "new Soviet men" were ridiculous, and their inevitable failure, sometimes bombastic, more frequently pitiful, was invariably comical. Andrei Platonov, in his short stories and novels of the 1920s and 1930s, creates protagonists who try to conceptualize and philosophically explain the revolutionary and post-revolutionary world through their rather limited worldview, contaminated by the insertion of Soviet ideological and quasi-scientific lingo. Such protagonists (as, for example, in "Doubting Makar" ["Usomnivshiisia Makar," 1929]) naively reveal how rife with contradiction the Soviet world was. Elsewhere, as in *Chevengur* (1926–28; published in full in 1978 in London) and in *The Foundation Pit* (*Kotlovan*, 1930; first published in 1969 both in Frankfurt and London), this technique of naive irony also constitutes a philosophical and tragic critique of the absurd.

If in Socialist Realism the *narod* was idealized as an agglomeration of "progressive classes" with the backing of the Party's ideology, in the literature of the 1960s, beginning with Aleksandr Solzhenitsyn's (1918–2008) "Matryona's Household" ("Matrenin dvor," written 1959, published 1963 in *Novyi mir*) and continuing in the works of the so-called Village Prose writers (Vasily Belov [1932–2012], Vasily Shukshin [1929–1974], Fedor Abramov [1920–1983], Valentin Rasputin [1937–2015], and Vladimir Soloukhin [1924–1997]), simple peasants were again depicted as morally superior, but for reasons opposite to the Soviet ideological dictum. It is not their class origins, but rather their deep recognition of the catastrophic result of collectivization and Soviet history in general, as well as their holy foolishness and inability to conform to repressive social conditions, that justified their depiction as the ultimate victims of the Soviet regime and bearers of the long-lost cultural and moral traditions of the pre-revolutionary Russian village. While tolerated as an opposition in the late Soviet period, this discourse eventually contributed to the emergence of a spectrum of nationalist narratives and doctrines that took a radical turn after 1991.

Merchants

Unlike post-medieval Europe, Russia never regarded merchants as fully positive figures. Their money and power alienated them from the people, who regarded them as venal and cruel; while the often-impoverished nobility envied them. Furthermore, since Peter the Great exempted merchants from adopting non-Russian clothing and behavior, their clothes, food, type of dwellings, education, and ethos, all set the merchantry apart from the nobility, giving the merchant the status of the Other. Consequently, through the imperial period, literature represented the merchant predominantly in a negative light. Sartorial distinctions alone contained clues of fundamental otherness. A classic illustration of this point would be Rogozhin in Dostoevsky's *The Idiot* whose sheepskin coat (*tulup*), usually worn by non-nobles, offsets Prince Myshkin's light European-style cloak (incongruous with the Petersburg winter weather). It is by no means an accident that the Rogozhin family are Old Believers, which only accentuates their dissimilarity, since there were more Schismatics among the merchants than in any other estate in Imperial Russia. Yet their wealth and focus on business more than their dress and religion elicited lasting dislike.

Tolstoy paid scant attention to merchants or to any other estate besides the nobility and peasantry, but when he did, he usually took a dim view. Yet his story "Master and Worker" constitutes an exception: while a prospective good deal (read: greed) forces the merchant

Brekhunov to go on a business trip despite the approaching snow storm, the ensuing ordeal leads him to save his freezing coachman by covering him with his own body. The self-sacrifice he exhibits—he dies in the process—represents a remarkable change in a person who, until then, had been utterly consumed with profit.

Chekhov, born to a merchant family headed by a cruel father, usually casts merchants in an unfavorable light. Matvei, a righteous storyteller in "Peasant Women" ("Baby," 1891) is one vivid example. Chekhov is also the creator of Lopakhin of *The Cherry Orchard*, whose victory over the nobility is one of the most remarkable demonstrations of the changeover in economic power as nobles lose their position of dominance because of the declining crop prices, incompetent estate management (the corrupt bailiff is a notable figure in fiction), and reduced assets as they sell off their forests (Tolstoy's Brekhunov is actually on his way to negotiate such a purchase when the snowstorm strikes). Aleksandr Ostrovsky's plays often portray the merchant class, usually with humor and sometimes with sympathy. Even *The Storm*, with its vivid descriptions of the merchants' cruel disregard for human emotions, features positive characters: the religious and honest Katerina, the kind, if weak Boris, and the independent Varvara.

Nikolai Leskov was a blood relation to three estates through his father, a trader, who was born to a priest family, and his mother, whose father was a nobleman and whose mother came from a merchant family. Furthermore, business brought him frequently into contact with members of all classes. Many of his characters are of the merchant class, and he regarded ironically the idea that the Russian nation was irreparably split along class lines. Some of Leskov's merchants are portrayed with warmth and humor (as in "A Robbery" ["Grabezh," 1887]), others with mild irony ("A Small Mistake" ["Malen'kaia oshibka," 1883]), yet others with almost brutal directness ("Lady Macbeth of Mtsensk" ["Ledi Makbet Mtsenskogo uezda," 1865]). In "A Robbery," respectable members of the Orel district merchant class, including the narrator—raised well by his widowed mother—mistakenly become involved in a series of robberies and fistfights, but are eventually exonerated (the odd bribe also helps). Even the narrator, whose mother cannot forgive him for his unwitting participation in the robberies and defies any good woman to marry him, finds himself a bride, and they live happily ever after. In "A Small Mistake," misfortune visits a respectable Moscow merchant family: their unmarried daughter becomes pregnant. Her sister's husband (an icon painter of somewhat libertine persuasion) convinces her parents that this is their fault, because they made a mistake while asking a local holy fool to pray for their married daughter to become pregnant: apparently, he claims, either they or the holy fool mixed up the names and prayed for the wrong daughter. The story ends well: the lover marries his pregnant beloved and, furthermore, seeing that the daughters of the family are so visibly fertile, young men begin to pay attention to the third sister. The question that is posed at the beginning of the story (do miracles exist?) is answered somewhat tongue-in-cheek: all depends on one's point of view.

Negative descriptions of merchants continued to the end of the imperial period.

The clergy

Peter the Great's anticlerical policies caused all but highly ranked Church officials to become culturally marginalized. Cut off from a European education, linked to the pre-Petrine tradition by their way of life and modes of dress (including obligatory beards and prescribed clothing), often poor, even destitute, the parochial clergy were despised by the educated elites and disrespected by the peasants.[20] It is not for nothing that, according to superstition, meeting a priest was a bad omen. Feelings of hostility persisted even toward well-educated members of this estate, including those who left the priestly life. In *War and Peace*, Tolstoy portrays

Mikhail Speransky, the son of a priest who became one of the most progressive reformers under Alexander I.[21] As seen by Prince Andrei, he is "alien": attractive and repulsive at the same time. The power Speransky has achieved fascinates Prince Andrei, but the fact that he is different from the members of the nobility unsettles Andrei. Similarly, in his notebook for 1876–77, Dostoevsky writes about seminarians as a group standing apart from the rest of the society ("*status in statu*," as he calls them), and names Speransky as a statesman whose abstract, and thus erroneous, ideas about Russia "did a lot of harm" (*nadelal mnogo vreda*).[22]

The parish clergy understandably seemed even more alien to many Russian writers. In "Tale of a Priest and his Servant Balda" ("Skazka o pope i rabotnike ego Balde," 1830), Pushkin offers his version of a folk tale about a rapacious, foolish priest (called blockhead or fool, *tolokonnyi lob*, but considering himself shrewd) whom Balda (himself a dolt, judging by his name) cleverly, if cruelly, punishes for his excessive greed. In the rare cases when Gogol presents the parish clergy, he also follows the Russian folk or Western fabliau tradition, as in some of the stories in his *Evenings at a Farm near Dikanka*.

Distrustful of religious institutions throughout his life, in his early story "Three Deaths," Tolstoy negatively portrays a priest who is summoned to administer the last rites to a young woman dying of tuberculosis. The priest behaves as falsely and artificially as the rest of the family and the dying woman herself. He is more superstitious than truly religious, advising the dying woman who had just received the last rites to turn for help to a quack. The story is not so much anti-Christian (the psalm read over the dead woman represents true wisdom and teaches acceptance of the approaching death) as it is against the clergy (characteristically, the deacon reading the psalm does not understand it significance).

In the mainstream literary tradition, one can find only a few examples of sympathetic portrayal of the parish clergy. In Pushkin's *The Captain's Daughter*, Father Gerasim is kind and courageous, risking his life to save the heroine, Masha, both from Pugachev the imposter and from the evil Shvabrin. An even friendlier attitude toward parochial clergy can be seen in Nekrasov's long narrative poem *Who Is Happy in Russia* (*Komu na Rusi zhit' khorosho*, 1863–76, unfinished). A group of peasants sets out to find a happy estate, and one of the persons they encounter and interview is a parochial priest. After listening to the story of his sorry life, the peasants acknowledge their previously mistaken views and bow low to him in respectful tribute. Some of Turgenev's writings portray priests kindly, especially his "Story of Father Aleksei" ("Rasskaz ottsa Alekseia," 1877), an account of a village priest whose gifted son becomes possessed by evil and dies in a futile attempt to regain freedom. It is not clear what interests Turgenev more, the grief of the father or the mystery of his son's death, but the first-person frame narrator, to whom the priest tells his story, deeply sympathizes with him.

It was Leskov who wrote both most prolifically and most kindly about the parish clergy. Characteristically, Leskov's truly religious people can be found both inside and outside religious institutions. Furthermore, his clergymen can disregard religious prohibitions and still remain truly religious in Leskov's (or his narrators') view. In *The Little Things in Bishops' Lives* (*Melochi arkhiereiskoi zhizni*, 1878–79), Leskov distinguishes between those of the clergy for whom Christianity is a dead letter (and presents them satirically) and those for whom to right a wrong is more important than to follow lifeless traditions. One example is an archbishop advising a couple who, according to the Church law, could not marry as a brother- and sister-in-law, to disregard the prohibition. From his point of view, it is better to allow people who love each other and expect a child to marry than to follow an artificial rule.

Leskov's *Cathedral Folk*, a chronicle-like account of the life of a provincial priest and his deacon, likewise emphasizes that the living spirit of Christianity is more important than institutional conventions. As Leskov's other best religious people, Father Tuberozov of *Cathedral Folk* exercises free will in matters of faith, refusing to follow the established rules blindly.

Having had a mystical experience, he delivers a sermon in which he criticizes the "internal rottenness of believers who have forsaken the living spirit of Christianity."[23] For his supposedly heretical views, Father Tuberozov is arrested and punished by his superiors. He is forced to repent, then is allowed to return to his parish, where he soon dies. On his deathbed he confesses that he cannot forgive his persecutors: "As a Christian, I forgive them my humiliation in front of everyone, but their following the dead letter…their ruining the live God's work… [I cannot forgive]."[24] Deacon Akhilla, passionately devoted both to the faith and to Father Tuberozov, is also portrayed with warmth, despite his never-ending antics for which Tuberozov has to admonish and punish him. In general, Leskov's clergymen find their duties supremely important and edifying, if often difficult because their office requires them to put their family members' needs second to their duties (as Father Tuberozov finds himself doing).

It is not necessary to be formally Christian to behave in a truly Christian way. In "At the Edge of the World" ("Na kraiu sveta," 1875), the best Christian is a semi-pagan, who risks his life to save a missionary during a snowstorm. Baptized by a visiting priest, this member of an indigenous Northern tribe may forgo the Christian rites, but he firmly knows right from wrong. This moral compass is what makes him a real Christian. Furthermore, Leskov entertains the possibility that even a priest may go unbaptized and still do good. The "unbaptized priest" in the story by that name ("Nekreshchenyi pop," 1877) not only retains his position upon discovery that he was not baptized as a child, but is made archpriest by the wise archbishop who understands that the Christian spirit, not the letter of canon law, is most important. The archbishop instructs the congregation not to distrust their unbaptized archpriest: "Your priest Savva who is good for you is also good for me and is pleasing to God. Go home without a doubt."[25]

The monastic clergy fared better in nineteenth-century Russian literature than did the secular (or "white") clergy. Gogol's story "The Portrait" (two versions, 1835 and 1842) represents a painter who achieves true artistry only by becoming a monk and (in the 1842 version) spending years in seclusion and religious contemplation. Dostoevsky shows deep respect for monastic clergy in his writings. Archbishop Tikhon in Chapter 9 of *Demons* (meant to be part of the novel, but cut by the censor and never restored by Dostoevsky) and the Elder Zosima of *The Brothers Karamazov* are the most prominent examples of Dostoevsky's wise and truly pious monks. Observant as they are about the shortcomings of religious institutions—Zosima is particularly astute—neither monk denies their importance.

Tolstoy's view of monastic life was less forgiving, but he allows the title character in his 1898 story "Father Sergius" ("Otets Sergii") to find the right path. Even though spending years in different monasteries and eventually in a hermitage proves insufficient for him to attain true goodness, Father Sergius continues to strive and eventually finds real faith and genuine humility outside religious institutions, among pilgrims and vagabonds. The spiritual teacher who shows him the right path is his childhood acquaintance, Pashenka, now a widow supporting her daughter, her drunkard husband, and her grandchildren. Looking at her, Father Sergius finds the answer to the question that had tormented him during all his years as a monk— whether he acts out of his love for God or to impress the people who watch him. As he finally formulates it for himself, Pashenka "lives for God, thinking that she lives for people."[26] Becoming a tramp, having learned to disregard other people's opinions, Father Sergius achieves true humility and begins to feel the presence of God within him.

Chekhov's Bishop Petr of the story "The Bishop" ("Arkhierei," 1902) may have allowed the letter to overshadow the spirit, and this makes him one of the most tragic religious figures in nineteenth-century prose. A good person and a learned cleric, he wants to be kind to people, yet he has forfeited his connection not only to his congregation but to humanity in general. Even his own mother seems to be afraid of him. Chekhov allows the reader to follow the dying bishop's thoughts. His majestic position has left him isolated and vulnerable when he needs mankind the most, and it is only the reader who stands outside the text who can proffer him sympathy. At the same time, we witness the bishop's gradual realization that his high rank in the Church hierarchy is entirely unimportant (and even burdensome, since it stands between him and other people, including his mother); he also realizes that he is gradually losing his individuality. He disappears into the realm of death, where we cannot follow him.[27] Whether this deindividuation is good or bad remains unclear, but it is certainly disconcerting. Like his mother after his death, who cannot truly be sure whether she ever had a son who was a bishop, the reader is also left disoriented: "The text's expeditious disposal of the Bishop's remains dramatizes one aspect of our perplexity about death: our complete lack of access to how the story continues without us."[28]

The legacy of negative characterizations of the clergy survived until the end of the imperial period and beyond. The Symbolist Aleksandr Blok in his 1918 long poem *The Twelve* (*Dvennadtsat'*), despite its Christian imagery (the twelve revolutionaries who represent the apostles, Jesus Christ at the lead of the revolutionary march), still includes a mocking address to the priest unhappy with the drastic social changes brought by the revolutions:

> Что нынче невеселый,
> Товарищ поп?
>
> Помнишь, как бывало
> Брюхом шел вперед,
> И крестом сияло
> Брюхо на народ?[29]
>
> Why are you sad,
> Comrade priest?
>
> Do you remember how
> Your potbelly used to lead the way?
> And the cross on your belly
> Shone at the people?

Whether the address expresses the feelings of the twelve revolutionaries or the reader can hear the authorial voice here, does not matter much: the image of a fat, aggressive, and antagonistic priest summarizes the post-Petrine tradition of portraying clerics.

State bureaucrats (*chinovniki*)

While they do not legally belong to any of the five estates, the *chinovniki* are tantamount to a sixth because of the widespread attitudes toward bureaucrats as a group. For instance, Ivan Vasilievich, one of the two travelling characters in Sollogub's *Tarantas*, regards the state officials as a separate estate, one that is particularly corrupted by the Western influence. He expresses an utter hatred for them: "I hate with all my heart officials and that ugly nameless estate that appears in our country [*u nas*] because of their dirty pretension to some kind of pathetic, incomprehensible enlightenment."[30] He changes his view, however, when, toward the end of his journey, he meets a station master, a paralyzed father of three children, who is able to keep his position only thanks to his eleven-year-old son who performs his duties for him. The hater of state officials leaves the post station almost in tears, grieving for this low-ranking clerk.

Arguably, prose fiction about petty bureaucrats forms a generic category of its own. One common point of that sort of fiction is that main characters in these stories all are "little men," poor and socially insignificant. Another is in that these stories defy logic and feature the fantastic. The third is that they often touch on the problem of writing and reading. Pushkin's "The Station Master" belongs, perhaps, to the first category: its main character is Samson Vyrin, the lowest-ranking official (fourteenth class, according to the Table of Ranks), a typical little man, despised and insulted by everyone. While the main interest of the story seems to be Vyrin's daughter, who runs away with a handsome rich officer, there is considerable aesthetic interest in storytelling itself. The story presents a complex system of narrators, and Pushkin further inserts a paragraph into the introductory part, in which the story's main narrator claims that literary ability is inversely proportional to one's rank: the lower the rank, the better the storyteller. The theme of writing is also prominent in Gogol's stories featuring insignificant men: Poprishchin of "Notes of a Madman," even while losing his ability to write official papers, keeps a diary and, apparently, the dogs' correspondence; he also frequently points out that he is a great writer. In contrast, Akaky Akakievich Bashmachkin can only copy official papers: when ordered to make small changes, he is flustered to the point of incompetence.

The world of petty bureaucrats, steeped in mechanical behavior and strict hierarchies, provided an unlikely locus for supernatural occurrences, yet they were an important theme in the fiction. Vladimir Odoevsky, in his *Motley Tales* (*Pestrye skazki*, 1833), was probably the first to connect the world of bureaucrats with the fantastic. In "The Tale of a Dead Body, Owner Unknown" ("Skazka o mertvom tele, neizvestno komu prinadlezhashchem"), a hapless foreigner, while travelling along one of the notoriously bad Russian roads, decides to abandon his body, in order not to suffer physical discomfort. Subsequently, the bureaucratic formalities prevent him from reuniting with it, and he remains forever a bodiless ghost. Gogol followed suit with the Petersburg tales, particularly "The Nose" ("Nos," 1836), which never convincingly explains the unexpected separation of the nose from Kovalev's face or its equally unexpected return; "The Overcoat," which leaves Bashmachkin's ghost to wander the city; and "Notes of a Madman," which does not completely exclude the existence of the epistolary exchanges between dogs.[31]

Dostoevsky built on Gogol's legacy in his treatment of state officials, developing the character of the low-ranking bureaucrat. In contrast to Gogol, he endowed his low-ranking bureaucrats with self-awareness and interiority, adding a modicum of humanity to the character of the insignificant and pathetic clerk, but also uncovering in them unpleasant traits.[32] The protagonist in *Notes from the Underground* is a particularly interesting example. The Underground Man is much more complex than Gogol's low-ranking clerks, and, by Dostoevsky's design, much harder to like. The use of first-person monologue gives the reader access to his inner world. The unfiltered experience of his aggressiveness and shamelessness is bracing and also challenging. Unlike another of Dostoevsky's alienated functionaries, Goliadkin, the Underground Man is intellectually the reader's peer. Morbidly self-aware, he also induces self-awareness in readers, forcing the unsettling possibility that one has a similar capacity to behave badly.[33]

Leskov's 1879 story "Singlemind" ("Odnodum") significantly departs from the traditional treatment of petty bureaucrats by presenting a destitute, yet self-aware, honest, and dedicated clerk. The character, Aleksandr Ryzhov, is the only official in his town who does not take bribes, supporting his family on his meager pay. He cannot afford the required uniform, but out of honor refuses (unlike Makar Devushkin) any financial help, considering it a bribe (*dar*). He believes that good service is more important than a proper uniform. The governor visiting the town in which our protagonist lives cannot believe that he does not take bribes: "There is no such man in all of Russia," he says.[34] But after talking to this extraordinary person, the governor is astonished at the truth, and sends him a medal, a Cross of St. Vladimir. In contrast to Leskov's dignified and principled petty official, Chekhov's Cherviakov in "Death of a Clerk" ("Smert' chinovnika," 1883) is petty in the literal sense: he has no dignity at all. Chekhov takes the official's pettiness *ad absurdum*, depriving him of all humanity. In this exaggeration, Cherviakov is a precursor of the dreadful town officials in Sologub's *Petty Demon*.

Alongside the low-ranking Bashmachkin, Devushkin, Goliadkin, and Cherviakov, high-ranking officials also appear in nineteenth-century Russian prose. In fact, beginning with Gogol, they are often paired with their inferior colleagues. In "Notes of a Madman," the director of Poprishchin's Department, "Your Excellency" the general is mentioned (officials of third and fourth class were to be addressed as "Your Excellency"; they also could be referred to as "His Excellency"). He is not very active in the story: his role is primarily to make Poprishchin's tender feelings for his daughter appear futile. In "The Overcoat," "Your Excellency" has a much more important role: it is his stern rebuke of Bashmachkin who applied to him for help in finding the stolen overcoat that leads to the titular councilor's death. At the same time, Bashmachkin and his superior are strangely similar: both have trouble expressing themselves, both appear to be meek by nature (Bashmachkin's superior, having received his high rank, needs to learn how to speak sternly); both lose their overcoats while in pursuit of sexual pleasures.

Overall, it was Gogol who paid the most attention to the world of civil servants: his Petersburg tales as well as *Inspector General* and *Dead Souls* are populated with all kinds of bureaucrats, from the lowest- to the highest-ranking. It is tempting to believe that they accurately reflect the hierarchy of ranks established by the Table of Ranks, and reading Gogol's texts may seem a pleasurable way to learn about Russian bureaucracy and its structure. Gogol, however, is an unreliable source. All the names of the ranks in his works about bureaucrats seem to be correct, but very often the way these bureaucrats are portrayed is entirely misleading: in effect, he replaces the hierarchy of ranks created by Peter the Great with his own. For example, Akaky Bashmachkin in "The Overcoat" (even though the narrator informs us that he was born into the rank of titular councilor) in no way could have had this rank, which was of the relatively high ninth class and required certain bureaucratic skills. Akaky Akakievich, however, is so feebleminded that he can only copy papers; copyists normally had the title of collegiate registrar (fourteenth class). Nor does Gogol's other story featuring a titular councilor, "Notes of a Madman," describe historical practice accurately. Poprishchin's rank is more appropriate, since he is a desk chief—a position that would have made Poprishchin responsible for at least ten subordinates. Yet all we see him doing is sharpening quills for the head of his department. The incongruity leads to speculation about hidden layers of meaning. Is this because he is already mad? Perhaps, but then why is he still in service? The figure of titular councilor in Gogol's stories is thus a distortion of what historical sources suggest to us about this rank. It is easy to multiply examples of Gogol's playing with the Table of Ranks and it is worth keeping in mind that his original readers, versed in the details of the state service, could appreciate Gogol's playful distortions of reality.

Among later masters, Tolstoy ignored the low-ranking civil officials entirely. He did occasionally portray the upper bureaucracy, but mostly from a distance. The rare exceptions are Speransky in *War and Peace* and Karenin in *Anna Karenina*. The only work by Tolstoy with a bureaucrat as its protagonist is "The Death of Ivan Ilyich," but to largely conventional ends. Ivan Ilyich's concentration on his career throughout his life served as a useful background for showing the futility of career aspirations in comparison with the inevitability of death. Dostoevsky, in contrast, found perennial material in the world of high bureaucracy, especially for his shorter fictions. As with titular councilors, his portraits of high-ranking officials followed, and also complicated, Gogol's legacy. In *Poor Folk* "His Excellency," angry over Makar Devushkin's making a mistake in an important document, forgets his anger when he sees the clerk's completely worn-out uniform, and gives him 100 rubles from his own pocket to mend it. Dostoevsky continued to play with the characters of high-ranking officials. One newly minted "His Excellency" is portrayed in Dostoevsky's story "A Nasty Business" ("Skvernyi anekdot," 1862; also translated as "A Nasty Story" and "A Nasty Anecdote"), where a conflict between a low-ranking clerk and his superior ends in "His Excellency's" defeat that is more dramatic than that enacted by Akaky Akakievich's when his ghost snatches the general's overcoat. The story reflects Dostoevsky's doubts about the consequences of the Great Reforms of the early 1860s. A high-ranking official, Pralinsky, attempts to live according to the new principles of equality and humanness ostensibly promoted by the reforms: to prove that he can treat Pseldonimov, a low-ranking clerk serving under him, as his equal, he appears at Pseldonimov's wedding banquet uninvited. The generous act fails miserably: nobody is happy to see Pralinsky at the wedding and nobody is shy about showing it, so Pralinsky gets disgustingly drunk. At the end of the story, Pseldonimov asks for a transfer: it is he, the low-ranking clerk, who does not want to be Pralinsky's "brother."

Where do the *raznochintsy* fit?

The *raznochintsy* or "people of various ranks," form a heterogeneous social group: most left their original estates (clergy, merchantry, and occasionally peasantry) and joined lower ranks of the nobility through civil service; others became *raznochintsy* through education, since a university education accorded graduates either personal or hereditary nobility, depending on the degree received. While the first group can be seen as the real-life model for the type of the little man, the second group formed an influential faction around the middle of the nineteenth century and began to share the cultural center stage with the nobility. The three most important literary critics of this period, Belinsky, Chernyshevsky, and Dobroliubov, were *raznochintsy*, as were Leskov and Chekhov, among other writers.

Raznochintsy produced the majority of radicals active in literature, criticism, and, later, revolutionary movements. Chernyshevsky is one example. Ennobled through education and a brief stint in state service (he taught at several educational institutions), in the early 1860s Chernyshevsky was suspected of writing subversive leaflets, arrested, and imprisoned in the Peter and Paul Fortress. After being convicted for anti-government activities, he was publicly stripped of his nobility in a ceremony that included breaking a sword over his head, and sent to Siberia, where he spent almost twenty years, first in hard labor, then in exile. The *raznochintsy's* radical leanings also earned them the reputation as nihilists.

KEYWORD **Nihilism**

The history of the term illustrates the complex interactions between literary typology, ideology, and sociology. Originally used by Nikolai Nadezhdin in 1829 to castigate educated (and "between-states") gentry "who know nothing and understand nothing,"[35] in the 1860s the nihilist begins to denote an *intelligent* emboldened by a rational skepticism aimed at the landed gentry and the ruling political class. In Turgenev's *Fathers and Sons*, a conversation between characters identifies the rational, science-loving, and anti-establishment hero Bazarov as a nihilist. Some of the more radical intelligentsia members of the liberal journal *The Contemporary* repudiated as defeatist the critical portrayal and death of Bazarov (tragic, according to Turgenev) and they endorsed Bazarov's iconoclastic outlook as basic for a new generation of revolutionaries. Turgenev also had his defenders, such as Pisarev, who claimed that Turgenev had given an exact description of the feelings of the materialist younger generation.[36] Pisarev meant that the main function of the revolutionary intelligentsia was one of criticism and corrosion, the overcoming of a bitter disappointment, and the desire to turn an ideal into reality. Turgenev's brand of nihilism, still more a literary than sociological reality, quickly became a passing phase: Saltykov-Shchedrin regularly refuted the idea that the younger generation, while gripped by other ideals, worshiped nihilism. The series of articles entitled *Our Social Life* (*Nasha obshchestvennaia zhizn'*, 1863–64), examining the subject of nihilism and ridiculing Pisarev, caused a row with the radical journal *The Russian Word*.[37] But the character lived on, morphing into a sinister projection as a lurid anti-Christ figure for politically and religiously conservative writers such as Goncharov (*The Precipice* [*Obryv*, 1869]), Leskov (*At Daggers Drawn* [*Na nozhakh*, 1870–71]), Boleslav Markevich (1822–84) (*A Quarter of a Century Ago*, *The Turning Point*, and *The Void*, [*Chetvert' veka nazad, Perelom,* and *Bezdna*; 1878–84]). The character Petr Verkhovensky, in Dostoevsky's blistering political satire *Demons*, represents nihilism as an extreme denial of the basic structures of government and family. The godlessness of the nihilist is embodied by Dostoevsky in Stavrogin in the same novel, and expressed in the notorious confession (suppressed by the censor) of a child rape.

Turgenev paid close attention to *raznochintsy*. Bazarov in *Fathers and Sons* is the most prominent example. To make his reader ironically compare his new hero with the previous tradition, Turgenev gave Bazarov the same first name as the original superfluous man, Evgeny Onegin, playing on its transparent etymology, "well-born." The description of Bazarov's emphatically plebeian appearance is in sharp contrast with Lermontov's portrayal of Pechorin in "Maksim Maksimych" (Bazarov's large ungloved and thus red, weather-chafed hands could not be more different from Pechorin's aristocratic hand, thin and pale in its glove). Significantly, Bazarov is proud of his plebeian origin: "'My grandfather tilled the soil,' Bazarov replied with arrogant pride." At the same time, he omits mentioning that his mother was "a true Russian noblewoman [*dvorianochka*] of the olden times" (that is, of pre-Petrine origin).[38]

Dostoevsky (whose father was a *raznochinets*, ennobled through service) also portrayed *raznochintsy* albeit not according to any fixed formula. One is Razumikhin in *Crime and Punishment*, Raskolnikov's friend and foil. As poor as Raskolnikov (if not poorer), he supports himself by a variety of jobs and does not see poverty as humiliating, unlike Raskolnikov. Razumikhin tends Raskolnikov during his illnesses; he takes care of Raskolnikov's mother and sister when they show up in St. Petersburg; most importantly, like Sonya, but in his own, non-religious way, he helps Raskolnikov realize and admit his guilt. Razumikhin eventually marries Raskolnikov's sister, Dunia, supports Raskolnikov during his trial, and plans to join him in Siberia after his liberation from the prison camp. Unlike Razumikhin, whose easy character means he can be (and is) genuinely kind, Rakitin in *The Brothers Karamazov* is mean-spirited and manipulative. Rakitin is introduced as Alesha's friend who, like him, lives in a monastery ostensibly preparing for the vocation of a monk. He turns out to be falsely religious and a truly malicious person. Alesha, even though he is attached to him, considers him to be dishonorable: Rakitin, in Alesha's view, might not steal but he would do anything to advance his social standing (the title of the chapter devoted to Rakitin is "A Seminarian Careerist," *Seminarist-kar'erist*). Gradually, Alesha's intuition proves to be correct, since Rakitin's successive actions expose him as an ignominious person: he attempts to "sell" Alesha to Grushenka; he publishes slanderous reports about Dmitry's trial; and he pretends to be Dmitry's friend and then testifies against him. One scholar has suggested that Rakitin is a caricature of radical journalists whom Dostoevsky found both distasteful and dangerous to society.[39] The class-based attack on Rakitin conforms more broadly to Dostoevsky's representations of this type.

Not every major nineteenth-century writer saw the usefulness of portraying the *raznochinets* as a social type. Tolstoy, so focused on the goodness and misery of the peasantry and the guilt and good fortune of the gentry, entirely ignored *raznochintsy* in his writings. Significantly, when he rewrote Turgenev's 1848 story "Death" ("Smert'") as "Three Deaths," he disregarded the only character who, according to Tolstoy's own rules, dies well, and this character is a *raznochinets*. In Tolstoy's case, we might conclude that he was not particularly interested in the way people could move between social ranks or in the consequences those changes might have for the notions of personal identity and social responsibility. In general, however, toward the end of the imperial period the difference between the nobility and the educated *raznochintsy* was gradually disappearing both in life and in literature.

Where all classes meet

Most nineteenth-century novels and stories reflect the reality of Russian life by accommodating one or more classes in their multifaceted traditions of representation. There are, however, works whose themes or main ideas encouraged writers to bring the entire spectrum of social classes together. One genre is prison narratives, such as Dostoevsky's *Notes from the House of the Dead*, a semi-autobiographical account of life in a Siberian prison camp. Crime, like death, can be all too egalitarian, and the house of the dead brings together men from all walks of life, of various religions and nationalities. This often creates tensions between the inmates: Polish political prisoners dislike Russians and avoid them; commoners despise former nobles (stripped of nobility as part of their punishment, as was Dostoevsky himself); Christians detest Muslims and Jews. But there also are moments of communion, as when inmates organize theatrical performances during holidays: everyone relaxes and enjoys a temporary freedom from usual restrictions and pressures. In Tolstoy's *Resurrection* we also see the barriers between the prisoners come down, but to a lesser degree than in Dostoevsky's work: in Tolstoy's novel, prisoners of different classes are transported and housed separately on their way to Siberia and thus have fewer opportunities to mingle. Furthermore, by following his protagonist, Nekhliudov, Tolstoy focuses on political prisoners. Only now and then do prisoners of different classes interact. Most importantly, Katiusha, a commoner and a former prostitute, is allowed to spend nights among political prisoners, which protects her from sexual harassment by common criminals and facilitates her intellectual and spiritual growth.

Some works can include representatives of all classes to express a certain idea. One example is Turgenev's story "Death," included in his *Notes of a Hunter*. Its main thesis is that Russian people die "strangely" or "amazingly": they are not afraid of dying, and are more concerned with putting their earthly affairs in order than about the impeding death. Turgenev's examples include two peasants, a miller, a *raznochinets*, and an old gentry woman. He sees no difference in their manner of dying: all die calmly, without fear, trying to finish the business at hand. At the end of his report, the narrator concludes: "Yes, Russian people die in an amazing way!"[40] He needed to provide examples from every estate to make this general statement about the Russian national character.

Another work that includes characters of different social classes in a pointed way is Nekrasov's narrative poem *Who Is Happy in Russia*. Seen from a class-based perspective, the poem looks like an interesting experiment because it describes an assortment of individuals met by peasant characters travelling on foot in search of a happy Russian person. They meet a priest, a landowner, a peasant woman, and a *raznochinets*. They discover that every social class has its own problems. Nekrasov never completed the poem, and it remains unclear whether the peasants would have ever found a person or a social group that can be called happy. *Who Is Happy in Russia* appears to be Nekrasov's only work in which he gives some thought to the lives of other classes, besides peasants and the urban poor. The very idea that members of every class can face problems that make him or her unhappy is unique not only in Nekrasov's oeuvre, but in the radicals' literary production in general.

CASE STUDY Corporal punishment

In Muscovite Russia, all social groups were subject to corporal punishment, and there was no shame attached to being beaten by an executioner. Throughout the eighteenth century, the newly emerging post-Petrine noble class gradually acquired the idea that corporal punishment caused dishonor. This new awareness was partly fueled by the adoption of Western notions of personal inviolability (which gave rise to dueling in the West) and partly by some articles of Peter's legislation that encouraged the formation of an honor code by proclaiming certain punishments dishonorable. Catherine's 1785 *Charter to the Nobility* legally freed the nobility of corporal punishment and torture. The same year, *Charter on the Rights and Privileges of the Towns of the Russian Empire* (*Gramota na prava i vygody gorodam Rossiiskoi imperii*, or *Zhalovannaia gramota gorodam*) abolished corporal punishment for honorable citizens and merchants of the first two guilds. In 1801, the clergy was also freed from corporal punishment. Commoners ennobled through the state service or higher education also ceased to become subject to corporal punishment.

All other social groups could be physically punished until 1863, when, in the course of the Great Reforms, corporal punishment was generally abolished, with the exception of peasants, prisoners of common origin, and lower ranks in the navy and army. The liberal-minded members of the Russian intelligentsia were ashamed of the fact that large groups of their compatriots continued to be subject to physical violence by authorities. Most drastically, the populist (*narodnik*) Nikolai Mikhailovsky, to show his solidarity with the masses, expressed willingness to be flogged, because "peasants are flogged" (*muzhika sekut zhe*).[41] In 1878, Vera Zasulich (1849–1919) attempted to assassinate the governor-general of St. Petersburg ostensibly for ordering the flogging of an imprisoned fellow radical. Tolstoy's story "After the Ball," contrasts a high-society ball, with its rows of dancers and spectators, with a scene of brutal gauntlet-running. Corporal punishment in Russia was finally abolished for everyone in 1904.[42]

The nobility was thus the first estate to receive legal protection from corporal punishment. However, many believed that the law was frequently violated. A substantial number of rumors about nobles who had been beaten and tortured—most of them obviously false—began to circulate in the late years of Catherine's reign and continued to appear well into the nineteenth century. It is impossible to ascertain when these rumors reflected reality and when they exposed the Russians' general distrust of laws. One such rumor claimed that the playwright Yakov Kniazhnin ostensibly died under the birch while being punished for writing the tragedy *Vadim of Novgorod*, which Catherine allegedly saw as antimonarchical. Even though Kniazhnin died of illness in 1791, well before Catherine paid attention to the tragedy or banned it, the legend survived and was written down by Pushkin. The rumors also circulated that Nikolai Novikov and his fellow Freemasons were tortured when arrested in early 1790s. Aleksandr Radishchev's sons claimed in their biography of their father that he escaped torture only because his sister-in-law bribed the head of the Secret Chancellery who conducted the investigation.

Distrust grew substantially after Paul's 1797 *ukaz*, according to which nobles could be stripped of their nobility for serious crimes, thus losing their immunity against corporal punishment. For example, Dostoevsky, in 1849, forfeited his nobility as part of his sentence for participating in the Petrashevsky Circle, a discussion group of progressive intellectuals. His fear of being flogged while in the prison camp can be clearly seen in his semi-autobiographical *Notes from the House of the Dead*. Furthermore, the rumor circulated that he in fact was flogged and that his epilepsy was caused by the shock of the punishment. Petrashevsky, too, became subject of a particularly bizarre rumor, according to which he was tortured by Nicholas I himself, who did it from a distance, using a telegraph machine attached to Petrashevsky's forehead. The torture ostensibly left painful marks on Petrashevsky's forehead and also drove him half-mad.

As these rumors demonstrate, by the end of the eighteenth century Russian nobles had assimilated Western notions of physical inviolability so fully that even the suspicion that the law against physical punishment had been infringed was cause for horror and dismay. A mere rumor of having been flogged was sufficient to cause dishonor. Alexander Pushkin considered both a duel and suicide when a rumor began to circulate around 1820 that he had been flogged by the police.

6

Types:
Heroes and anti-heroes

TYPE has been historically sanctioned as the chief principle of character construction. Inspired by French masters—above all de Vigny, Balzac, and Stendhal—to demonstrate how social codes of class and education conditioned the attitudes of the hero, prose works like Pushkin's *The Captain's Daughter* and Lermontov's *A Hero of Our Time* found it harder to plot sequentially, along a developmental arc, stories of an alienated Romantic hero and a scion of the gentry. The contradiction between the programmatic principle of natural, unmediated mimesis advocated by realism and the awareness that literature is a construct was resolved with the help of the concept of type. In aesthetics of realism, the concept of type synthesized the sociological category of a representative member of a class and the Hegelian notion of ideal. A gravitation toward the mimetic-realist principle of the later nineteenth century is evident in the Russian novel. But no less evident is its built-in tendency to play with form and refuse to settle down—and to make of that very instability a working definition (rather than a theoretical description) of what the novel is. The greatest masterpieces, whether of historical fiction such as *War and Peace* or family chronicle/detective novel such as *The Brothers Karamazov*, exploit generic flexibility and openness of the form (to the point of disintegration) in order to create a historical panorama and capture convulsive social change.[1]

For Belinsky and his followers among the radical critics, type is an isolated fact of reality that, having passed through the imagination of the poet, acquires a universal significance.[2] More modern critical approaches regard the literary type as an aesthetic generalization based on reality. Characterization based on type is not random but selects material that reflects the social conditions thought to create such personalities.[3] The history of the novel has sometimes been cast in terms of the search for a positive hero (essentially in terms defined by Belinsky). Conditioned by class and their representative function within texts, characters were seen to fulfill certain roles and promote certain ideas. Like Rufus Mathewson in *The Positive Hero in Russian Literature*, Richard Freeborn in *The Rise of the Russian Novel* sees the trajectory of the novel as a rise toward creating characters equipped to participate convincingly in ideological debates about art and life, society, and political change.[4] Freeborn sees the novel as a mimetically stable form in which types of heroes can live out the destinies prescribed for their type as Romantic hero, superfluous man, revolutionary, or nihilist. For Freeborn, the special quality of the Russian novel lay in this capacity to move between the rounded but tightly controlled personality of the characters and an engagement with larger systems of thought rendered as private drama.

Romantic outcasts, "superfluous men"

From the perspective of the later nineteenth century, the first generation of male novelistic heroes seems to predetermine the shape of subsequent protagonists as either "little men" (following Pushkin's Samson Vyrin of "The Station Master" and Gogol's Poprishchin of "Notes of a Madman") or "superfluous men" (following Pushkin's Evgeny Onegin and Lermontov's Pechorin of *A Hero of Our Time*). Arguably, this contention tells us less about the characters themselves and more about the radical critics, who required prototypes and foils to advocate their program of socially progressive literature. The affinity between the Romantic outcasts in Pushkin and Lermontov appears inevitable in retrospect but less certain when seen from within the period. Evgeny Onegin is a composite figure that synthesizes earlier heroes, including the protagonists of François-René de Chateaubriand's *René* (1802), Benjamin Constant's *Adolphe* (1816), Charles Nodier's Gothic romance *Jean Sbogar* (1818), Charles Maturin's sensational and much-read *Melmoth the Wanderer* (1820, French translation 1821), and Samuel Richardson's *The History of Sir Charles Grandison*, first published in 1753, and belatedly popular in Russia. Curiously, however, in comparison with his literary prototypes, Onegin's role in the novel was much greater in draft versions; as Pushkin's work progressed, he pared down the central character, demoting the Romantic hero in favor of Tatiana and the narrator, who both undergo moral growth and show an ability to live in harmony with the values of society and accept the biological imperatives of aging. From the perspective of Pushkin's contemporaries, that displacement of Onegin from his own text looked like the natural result of Pushkin's impulse to parody all literary types rather than an intention to inaugurate the figure of the superfluous man as an influential argument has maintained. Characteristically, Tatiana wonders, while perusing Onegin's library, whether he is not a parody ("Uzh ne parodiia li on?").[5]

From the perspective of later generations, who took their lead from Belinsky's organic criticism with its emphasis on the Hegelian laws of progress, Onegin looked strikingly like an ancestor of the heroes of their own novels, who confronted the political oppression and the bourgeois torpor of Russia under Nicholas I.[6] Whether Pushkin, Lermontov, and their original readers would recognize them as such or not, the cohort of "superfluous men" kept growing, from Turgenev's Rudin in the eponymous novel, to Goncharov's Oblomov, and even to Turgenev's Bazarov in *Fathers and Sons*. Among common traits, superfluous men "share a radical alienation from society and an inability to take personally meaningful or socially useful action."[7] In addition, while they shy away from personal commitment, superfluous men, beginning with Onegin and Pechorin, are more active than the stereotype suggests: they do seduce women and fight duels. Judging by these similarities, one can say that Pushkin's Onegin is a prototype for Turgenev's Bazarov: they share the first name, Evgeny; they both fight a duel; they try to seduce women (Onegin successfully conquers society women, and Bazarov attempts to seduce Fenechka, his host's younger and socially inferior lover). At the same time, they cannot secure a marriage, and they are entirely useless to their respective societies. It is ironic, in this context, that the very practical and well-educated positivist Dr. Bazarov nicks himself the very first time we see him practicing medicine (besides using his tongue to take a speck out of Fenechka's eye) and succumbs to blood poisoning. Yet when we look beyond the category of the superfluous man, the differences between the two characters are conspicuous. The two Evgenys belong to different classes of Russian society and to different epochs in Russian history and literature. In fact, the term for this ostensibly homogeneous cluster of characters gained currency only after the publication in 1850 of Turgenev's novella *The Diary of a Superfluous Man*, whose protagonist Chulkaturin does not quite fit with the rest of the characters bearing the name of a superfluous man: even though he does fight a duel and fails in love, socially and psychologically he has little in common with the stock character.

It is unlikely that either of the original superfluous men—Onegin and Pechorin—would socialize with him, since he stands significantly below them on the social ladder. They would rather keep company with his rival, Prince N.—who duels, is reluctant to marry, and contributes little to society. Bazarov, too, would shun the passive and reflective protagonist of Turgenev's novella. Chulkaturin seems superfluous mostly because he is dying of tuberculosis, which makes him a rarity among his purported fellow characters who simply vanish (Onegin), or die either mysteriously (Pechorin) or heroically (Rudin and, arguably, Bazarov).

Overall, the cast of characters known as superfluous men surpasses a single type, because Russian literature was receptive to broader trends of European Romanticism and not just local circumstance. Crosscurrents, rather than unidirectional trends, shape the picture, and the superfluous man should not be seen as the only type in a gallery of disaffected heroes. The Cain-like figure, Lermontov's Pechorin, revived the legacy of Byron in the atmosphere of alienation pervading European fiction after Napoleon's disappearance, amplified in Russia by the aftermath of the Decembrist Uprising. While Pechorin may look like a kindred soul of the heroes of Stendhal and Chateaubriand, he can also be read as a subversion of Romantic types. It is not for nothing that Lermontov created Grushnitsky alongside Pechorin: Grushnitsky serves as the protagonist's double, but is a much clearer parody of a Byronic Romantic type.

In their other works, especially in poetry, both Pushkin and Lermontov produced different figures of Romantic alienation: homeless spirits cast out of their social milieu and, seemingly, the universe. Pushkin's narrative poems *The Captive of the Caucasus* (*Kavkazskii plennik*, 1821) and *The Gypsies* (*Tsygany*, 1824); Lermontov's *Demon* (final version 1841) and *The Boyar Orsha* (*Boiarin Orsha*, written in 1835–36, published in 1842) all include this type of a Romantic outcast. Pushkin's outcasts cannot participate in polite society where they belong by birth, but they also cannot live with simpler folks, causing death and destruction among them. Lermontov's outcasts are even more destructive: their beloveds die horrible deaths and barely escape eternal damnation.

In his portrayal of a Romantic outcast, Vel'tman stands out. His most significant work of fiction, *The Wanderer* (*Strannik*, 1831–32), features a kind of outcast, who leaves his habitual life to wander the earth. At the same time, the hero often comes across as a veritable philistine, more interested in food and a good place to spend the night. Indeed, it is not even clear whether the wanderer actually leaves his home and is not simply tracing his movements on a geographical map. The novel, written in combination of prose and verse, narrated by the wanderer himself, and consisting of chapters that are often only a couple of sentences long, both further ironizes the tradition of imaginary travels, from Sterne's *A Sentimental Journey through France and Italy* (1768) to Nikolai Brusilov's (1782–1849) "My Travel, or Adventures of One Day" ("Moe puteshestvie ili Prikliuheniia odnogo dnia," 1803) and anonymous *My Cousin's Journey into Pockets* (*Puteshestvie moego dvoiurodnogo brattsa v karmany*, 1803). If, however, Vel'tman's novel describes an actual journey, then it is a parody not only of Karamzin's travelogue but also of Pushkin's "Excerpts from Onegin's Travels" ("Otryvki iz puteshestviia Onegina," partially published in 1827 and 1830): both the places visited and the fragmentary form point to Pushkin's example.

Another outcast who does not conform fully to the type of the superfluous man is Aleksandr Griboedov's Chatsky in his comedy *Woe from Wit* (fully published only in 1861, it was widely read in manuscript). Initially an accepted member of Moscow high society (which, unlike St. Petersburg high society with its high-ranking bureaucrats and courtiers, was comprised of old noble families bound by kinship), Chatsky goes abroad. Upon his return, he finds himself alienated from the previously friendly circle of families. His beloved Sofia has a new beau—a "new man," in a fashion: he is not a member of the old nobility but a self-made man who advances by guile. Sofia's father, Famusov, in whose house Chatsky grew up, is now suspicious of his former charge's new ideas and views. Chatsky's old friends also do not understand him anymore. He does not fit in, and the more he speaks, the less acceptable his behavior is to other characters. When he finally realizes that he is no longer embraced by his former milieu and that Sofia is not interested in him anymore (which he sees as a betrayal), he leaves Famusov's house, Moscow, and, it seems, Russia. He exits, exclaiming:

> Вон из Москвы! Сюда я больше не ездок.
> Бегу, не оглянусь, пойду искать по свету,
> Где оскорбленному есть чувству уголок!...
>   Карету мне, карету![8]

> Out of Moscow! I'm never coming back again.
> Without a second thought, I'll scour the world
> To find a home for my injured feelings!...
>   Carriage! bring my carriage!

His plans for the future unclear, he disappears from the play forever. Despite Chatsky's seeming paralysis of will, the play and its protagonist are among the most memorable to the Russian public.

Unlike Pushkin's Onegin, displaced as the protagonist by Tatiana and the narrator, Lermontov's Pechorin firmly remains at the center of *A Hero of Our Time*. Furthermore, the novel places him in a series of different situations: among contrabandists in whose business he meddles and who, accordingly, try to kill him; among high society at a Caucasian spa, where he disturbs everyone's peace and leaves in his wake a trail of broken hearts, ruined reputations, as well as a dead body, a victim of his skill and ruthlessness as a duelist. Furthermore, Pechorin is examined through a number of different viewpoints: through the eyes of Maksim Maksimych, his commanding officer, an experienced soldier but not a member of polite society; through the eyes of the novel's narrator, who is Pechorin's social equal and is able to understand his psychological makeup; and finally, though his own eyes, as the reader is given direct access to his diaries. The reader thus gets to know Pechorin far better than he ever gets to know Onegin, who remains an enigma to the very end of the novel.

There are two other characters in Lermontov's novel who prefer to stay in the shade but who could be viewed as Romantic outcasts. They are the narrator and the author of the "Preface" (if they are in fact separate characters). Both are uncannily similar to Pechorin and other Romantic outcasts: they travel without any evident goal, they are disillusioned in life, and they feel superior to other people. In this way, the novel is constructed in layers or, as Rebecca Stanton puts it, as a set of nested autobiographies. Read this way, the novel turns out to be not only more complex but also more tragic: "Although we have seen Pechorin reveal himself over time, there is no possibility that he will ever change; he is trapped in a moment that is simultaneously the end and the beginning. It turns out, then, that both the terms in the novel's title denote absences: *A Hero of Our Time* is not only devoid of a definite 'hero'—it is also devoid of 'time.'"[9]

Ivan Goncharov's Oblomov is also sometimes viewed as a superfluous man. The radical critic Dobroliubov, in his essay "What Is Oblomovism?," was the first to include him in this group, and, indeed, Oblomov does share certain traits with other superfluous men. As Dobroliubov points out, Oblomov sees no purpose in life and is unable to find any suitable activity for himself. In addition, he is passive in love: in Dobroliubov's view, he does not know how to love. Although he eventually acquires a common-law wife and fathers a son—the only one to do so among the character of this type—Agafia is socially so far beneath him that society does not acknowledge their union. Moreover, after Oblomov's death, Agafia voluntarily gives up their child to Oblomov's former fiancée Olga, now married to Oblomov's friend and foil Andrei Stolz, convinced that they would be better parents than she. Oblomov's ability to procreate, however, is not the only trait that distinguishes him from other superfluous men. He is not demonic or evil in any way; on the contrary, he is kind and caring. Furthermore, his national identity seems more important than his social identity: he is contrasted to Stolz, who is half-German. Oblomov's passivity thus turns out to be a Russian trait (supported by the Russian Orthodox belief that faith is more important to salvation than deeds), whereas the energetic and well-accomplished Stolz represents Western business sense.

While the novel's original readers, including Dobroliubov, almost unanimously disliked the passive Oblomov and praised the active Stolz (Grigor'ev and Druzhinin were notable exceptions), later scholars are divided in their interpretations of Goncharov's intentions, arguing that in his presentation both characters are deficient.[10] Some argue that, by problematizing the character of Stolz, the writer forces the reader to doubt whether he is a real friend to Oblomov and whether Olga is better off with him than she would have been with her first fiancé.[11] More generally, they ask an important question: in Goncharov's eyes, is being active necessarily better than being passive? This question is particularly relevant in the context of Eastern Orthodox emphasis on faith over deeds.[12]

Fedor Dostoevsky's underground man of *Notes from Underground* can also be seen as another variation on this type (although he can be also interpreted as a "little man")—or rather, Dostoevsky's parody of it. Like others in this category, he attempts to fight a duel, seduces and cruelly abandons a woman, and lives according to literary examples, which, to make things worse, he usually misinterprets. There are many literary references in the novel, but those to Pushkin and Lermontov are particularly relevant. The underground man's awkward attempts to behave like Pushkin's Silvio (from his story "The Shot" in *The Tales of Belkin*) and Lermontov's Pechorin (Dostoevsky, strongly disliking Lermontov's character, does not deign to distinguish between the two Pechorins: the one in *Princess Ligovskaia* and the other in *A Hero of Our Time*) clearly cast him in a parodic light: his lack of understanding of the psychology and behavior of these characters is ridiculous.[13] Nikolai Chernyshevsky's *What Is to Be Done?* is an important intertext for the underground man's twisted attempt to save a fallen woman. (Chernyshevsky is Dostoevsky's main interlocutor in *Notes from Underground*, not only on this issue, but, most importantly, on the issue of rational egoism.) The underground man's propensity to reflect makes him a somewhat sympathetic character while, at the same time, it underscores the fact that he is a parody of a superfluous man: the underground man's propensity for reflection makes him hesitant, unsure of himself, and unable to act in the very situations where superfluous men act decisively, as in fighting a duel.[14]

While Dostoevsky's mature approach to the problem of the hero, such as Raskolnikov (the Napoleonic figure in *Crime and Punishment*) or Prince Myshkin (the "ideal man" in *The Idiot*), varies, it completely sidelines the superfluous man. Once he had parodied the type, Dostoevsky lost interest in it. Nor is that type important in *The Brothers Karamazov*. Dostoevsky himself calls Alesha a "new man"—no doubt, to polemicize with Chernyshevsky's "new men" in *What Is to Be Done?* Dostoevsky's "infernal" characters, Stavrogin and Petr Verkhovensky of *Demons*, unlike superfluous men are ferociously destructive. Although marginal as conspirators, they are at the center of explosive scandals that destabilize everyone around them.

Tolstoy, too, abandoned the figure of the superfluous man rather early on: he experimented with it in his unfinished *The Cossacks* and never returned to it again. Tolstoy's examination of heroism in *War and Peace* must be considered in conjunction with his views of history at the time: in fact, they challenge most conventional ideas of heroism. Turgenev, too, attempted to move away from the type of the superfluous man. This is evident in Rudin, seemingly a typical superfluous man who, nonetheless, dies heroically in the French revolution of 1848. Turgenev added the scene of Rudin's heroic death several years after the initial publication of the novel in 1856, in the version included in his collection of works published in 1860–61. This addition illustrates well Turgenev's disillusionment with the superfluous man. Turgenev's next male character, Insarov in *On the Eve* (*Nakanune*, 1860), in his incarnation as a man of action, a freedom fighter, and revolutionary bears no resemblance to a superfluous man.

The Romantic outcasts, first created by Griboedov, Pushkin, and Lermontov in the 1820s–40s and then rejected by the younger generation of Russian writers such as Tolstoy and Dostoevsky, returned to populate Russian prose fiction of the later part of the nineteenth century. While the type had begun to lose its luster in new literary contexts and cultural circumstances, these later superfluous men retained certain character and behavioral features and continued to encounter struggles somewhat similar to those of Onegin and Pechorin in their fictional lives. In a way, it was Turgenev's Chulkaturin of *The Diary of Superfluous Man* who not only provided the name for his predecessors but also presaged men of smaller caliber, such as Turgenev's N. N. in "Asya" (1858) or Anton Chekhov's Astrov in the 1896 play *Uncle Vanya*. Both N. N. and Astrov are incapable of reciprocal love; they also are unable to find meaning in life. N. N. initially seems to respond to the young Asya's affection, but shrinks from emotional commitment. She departs, and N. N. immediately realizes his mistake, but now she is nowhere to be found, and he remains alone and without any meaningful reason to continue living. Astrov is somewhat different: he has both an occupation (medicine) and a calling (a passion for saving and restoring the receding forest). Yet he does not notice Sonia's devoted love and, when he learns about it, he is unable to reciprocate. As other superfluous men, he is able to love a married woman, because this does not require commitment. Laevsky of Chekhov's 1891 story "The Duel" ("Duel'") is an even more interesting variation of the type. Chekhov clearly marks him as a superfluous man: Laevsky cannot sustain his love for the woman he has seduced; he does not have any purpose in life; he fights a duel, and, most importantly, identifies himself as a superfluous man and believes that this absolves him. Von Koren (characteristically, like Goncharov's Stolz, a German), Laevsky's foil in the story, believes that people of his sort should not be allowed to live. When the two confront each other in a duel, von Koren is prepared to kill his opponent, and only the intervention of a deacon, who secretly watches the combat from a far, makes von Koren miss his mark. Unlike other superfluous men, Laevsky reforms: he realizes the iniquity of his life and the pain he has inflicted on his mistress. He marries her, radically changes his way of life, and works hard to pay his debts. He comes to the realization that life is not a game or the enactment of a literary tradition, but a constant struggle that requires commitment, patience, and perseverance. Furthermore, Laevsky's transformation affects von Koren, who loses his conviction that he truly knows right from wrong and thus has the right to decide who should live and who should die: "Nobody knows the real truth," he admits to Laevsky.[15]

Critics of various persuasions, from champions of art for art's sake (Druzhinin, Annenkov), to radicals (Chernyshevsky, Dobroliubov), to conservatives (Katkov), recognized the superfluous man as a type. Among radical critics, Chernyshevsky, anticipating Dobroliubov's "What is Oblomovism?," used his 1858 article "A Russian at a Rendezvous" ("Russkii chelovek na rendez-vous") to condemn, with reference to Turgenev's story "Asya," the class that supposedly produced superfluous men. The critic begins with ridiculing the superfluous man's inability to respond adequately to love. As his examples, in addition to the narrator-protagonist N. N., Chernyshevsky mentions Lermontov's Pechorin, Herzen's Beltov of the novel *Who Is to Blame?*, and Turgenev's Rudin. Describing these characters' reluctance to accept the love offered them by attractive women, the critic is wonderfully sarcastic. And yet he makes the paradoxical claim that Turgenev's N. N. "is one of the best people in our society, and we hardly have any better people than him."[16] Chernyshevsky pretends that he does not blame N. N. for his behavior, arguing that he has been shaped by Russian society and thus is not guilty but unfortunate (*ne vina, a beda*). In Chernyshevsky's interpretation, N. N.'s behavior is "a symptom of an epidemic that has taken root in our society."[17] His timidity and indecision, and his cruelty toward Asya are blamed on the social conditions in Russia. That is not to say that Chernyshevsky absolves N. N.: the point of the article is that N. N.'s failure in love is important as a warning sign of the general shortcoming of the "best people" in Russia, because it indicates that they are likely to be as weak when faced with far more important trials. It is remarkable how easily Chernyshevsky appropriates characters created in different social and cultural situations, and with different literary goals in mind, to make a purely political point he perceives as relevant for his time. It is even more remarkable how easily he disregards the boundary between literature and life. The same year, Pavel Annenkov responded to Chernyshevsky's article with his own essay "The Literary Type of a Weak Man" ("Literaturnyi tip slabogo cheloveka"), in which he disagrees with Chernyshevsky's thesis that the type of superfluous man is a reflection of Russian educated class in general. He sees the superfluous man as largely a literary phenomenon, whereas in real life one can easily find what he calls "integral" (*tsel'nye*) or strong (*sil'nye*) people. He asserts: "The best way to see the importance of the 'weak' person is to look away from him for a minute and to look whether there is something else in the educated class, behind [the 'weak' person] or next to him. We suggest that every conscientious researcher should conduct this experiment." Annenkov also believes that literature did not entirely miss the existence of "strong" characters, and they can be found in Turgenev's *Notes of a Hunter*, in Mikhail Saltykov-Shchedrin's works, and in Aleksandr Ostrovsky's plays. Annenkov thus rejects both Chernyshevsky's interpretation of Russian literary tradition and his criticism of Russia's educated class.[18]

The genius

Like the outcast, the genius, a classic figure of European Romanticism, enjoys a complex Russian redaction into poet-prophets, musical visionaries, mystics, and lunatics.[19] The figure of the genius first became important in poetry. Pushkin, in one of his so-called little tragedies, *Mozart and Salieri* (1830), presents his version of a true genius as intuitive, generous, and almost childlike in his apparent unawareness of his clearly God-given gift, or, perhaps, reluctance to take it seriously. Of all geniuses created by Russian writers of the Romantic period, Pushkin's Mozart is the most harmonious, enjoying in equal measure his art and his life.[20] Pushkin seems to contrast this understanding of a man of genius with another one, represented by Salieri and arguably modeled on Jean-Philippe Rameau as portrayed in Diderot's *Le Neveu de Rameau*. Like Rameau, who employed mathematics in his study of harmony, Pushkin's Salieri "verified harmony with algebra."[21]

Pushkin's other figure of genius appears in his unfinished prose piece *The Egyptian Nights*. The Italian *improvisatore* (whose character to a large degree is based on Adam Mickiewicz[22]), an unpleasant character who earns his living by producing beautiful poetry to order, is contrasted with Charsky, an aristocrat who writes poetry, but apparently does not publish it and probably does not even share it with his friends. What is the right behavior for a genius, to hide his literary production or to sell it at the open market? Pushkin's unfinished piece does not provide an answer.[23]

In the same year that Pushkin produced his *Mozart and Salieri*, Prince Vladimir Odoevsky wrote his first novella portraying a genius, "Beethoven's Last Quartet" ("Poslednii kvartet Betkhovena"), which he later included in his most significant work, the philosophical novel *The Russian Nights* (*Russkie nochi*, 1844). Odoevsky, an admirer of Friedrich Schelling, a trained musician and musicologist, and, in literature, a follower of E. T. A. Hoffmann, devoted several chapters ("nights") of his novel to the problem of genius: in addition to "Beethoven's Last Quartet," he also offered stories about Giovanni Battista Piranesi and Johann Sebastian Bach. All of his geniuses are similar in that they are misunderstood by their contemporaries, and their innovations are treated as products of insane minds (Bach is the luckiest in this respect, since he achieves fame as an organist); moreover, none of them experiences what Odoevsky calls "the fullness of life" (*polnota zhizni*): absorbed by their art, they do not see anything beyond it. Even Bach—the only one who, in Odoevsky's portrayal, in addition to his art, has a wife and children—discovers by the end of his life that he has not fully lived: "Half of his soul was a corpse!," that is, his life as a husband and father was sacrificed to his art.[24] Furthermore, in Odoevsky's presentation, insanity often is not just in the eye of an observer. Geniuses do tend to go truly insane—witness his narratives about Piranesi and Beethoven.

Nikolai Gogol examines the problem of genius in his story "The Portrait." It exists in two different versions, both composed of two parts: first, a Faust story, in which a talented artist— Chertkov in the first version, Chartkov in the second—buys a mysterious portrait of demonic origin, falls under its spell, and squanders his talent by becoming a high-society portraitist. Here Gogol taps into contemporary discourse about the tension between commercial gain and art for its own sake. But he also asks about the essence of art and the roles of imitation and invention in creating original art. At the end of the first part, Chertkov/Chartkov sees a painting at the Academy of Arts produced by a former classmate who, following the right path, has learned how to transform imitation into an original creation, the chaos of nature into the cosmos of art. Recognizing now his own mistake, Chertkov/Chartkov goes mad and dies. The second part of the story in both versions explains the origins of the portrait and also presents Gogol's idea of the true artist. Told by the son of the artist who painted the mysterious portrait, the story is basically the same in both versions: a modest God-fearing artist paints a portrait of a vicious moneylender right before the latter's death. This brings destruction to the artist's family, and he takes vows at a distant monastery where he paints a beautiful icon. The two stories, however, differ in details. Most importantly, in the second version, the artist who paints the diabolical portrait is self-taught: his genius is innate. But he is able to produce a truly miraculous piece of art, an icon of Nativity, only after he cleanses himself by years of life in the wilderness.[25] This is the only work by Gogol in which he openly talks about two possible sources of the highest artistic achievement, divine and diabolical, a problem that deeply concerned him throughout his life.

The same year Gogol published his first version of "The Portrait" he also published one of his best-known stories, "Notes of a Madman." The protagonist, a mid-ranking bureaucrat who goes mad as the story unfolds, is convinced of his gift as a writer. While Poprishchin does not produce literary works, he diligently keeps a diary, recording his life down to the minutest detail; in addition, he apparently produces the correspondence between two dogs, which he believes to be real. Pathetic as he is, he nonetheless is a writer, and the way Gogol describes his graphomania has an autobiographical ring to it. A parody of the figure of a genius, Poprishchin still displays such Romantic traits as obsessive writing and madness.

Madmen

If Poprishchin's status as a genius can be easily contested, his madness is beyond doubt: by the end of the story he is taken off to an insane asylum because he claims to be the king of Spain, Ferdinand VIII. The reader can also observe the character's gradual descent into madness: as Donald Fanger argues, "the twenty diary entries enact a process, each of them representing a stage of Poprishchin's dementia."[26] It is difficult, however, to determine whether he is truly mad when the story begins. Granted, Poprishchin reports in his first diary entry that the head of his division has rebuked him for erratic behavior and poor performance. The same day he overhears two talking dogs (one of them belonging to the daughter of the Director of his Department, the general) and learns that they write letters to each other. Several days later he follows one of them to the apartment where the dog lives and confiscates a bundle of letters. All this seems to be pointing to Poprishchin's being insane at the time when the reader meets him: talking dogs would seem to be a product of his inflamed imagination and their letters are invented by him, rather than discovered. However, as often happens in Gogol's stories—particularly in the Petersburg tales—what is real is harder to separate from what is imagined than one might think. Does Major Kovalev of "The Nose," another of Gogol's Petersburg tales, really lose his nose or does he only dream about it? If he can lose his nose, then surely dogs can write letters. Only after Poprishchin learns (from the dogs' correspondence, if we believe him) that his beloved is to be married to a high society man, the signs of his insanity increase dramatically. When he dates an entry in his diary "April 43rd, 2000," it becomes clear that he has indeed lost his mind. On the "30th Februarius" Poprishchin is confined. What he continues to write in his diary is clearly a product of an insane mind—until the very last entry, in which Poprishchin abandons his identity as Ferdinand VIII, switches to the present tense and, using a poetic style much different from his usual pedestrian prose, complains most flowingly of the suffering he is subjected to in the insane asylum. Furthermore, he seems to have escaped, flying through the night high above the ground in search of a safe place, which he finds in his childhood home, in his mother's arms: "Dear mother," he pleads, "save your poor son! Shed a tear on his aching head! Look how they torture him! Press to your breast the poor orphan! There is no place for him in the world! He is being chased away! Dear mother, take pity on your sick little child! ..." It may seem that all of a sudden Poprishchin is not insane. But then comes the concluding line of the diary entry: "Do you know that the Dey of Algiers has a bulge right under his nose?"[27] Interpretations of Gogol's comic absurdity suggest that a range of meanings emerge even from insane utterances: Robert Maguire, for example, reads the bulge under the nose as phallic and the suggestion of a venereal disease. He argues that frustrated sexuality and social displacement explain Poprishchin's insanity.[28] Simon Karlinsky reads Poprishchin's sudden mention of the bulge as a "comical grimace of pure insanity."[29]

Pushkin's "The Queen of Spades" is another Petersburg tale featuring a character that goes insane. It is also constructed in such a way that the real and the fantastic are difficult (if not impossible) to disentangle: does the protagonist, Hermann, receive the information about the three lucky cards from the dead Countess who comes to him at night or are the cards a figment of his deranged mind? Does the Countess come to him as a ghost or in a dream? Is Hermann's eventual catastrophic loss at cards due to his mistake or to the Countess's posthumous vengeance? One can easily find convincing evidence for either set of suppositions. What is, however, uncontestable is that Hermann ends up in an insane asylum—driven mad either by Tomsky's anecdote about the three lucky cards ostensibly known to his grandmother the Countess, or by accidentally causing the Countess's death without learning her secret, or by the loss of all his money.

A fascination with insanity as a pathological condition fueled the growth of a literature of madness, associated with St. Petersburg, which was, in the word of Dostoevsky's Underground Man, "the most abstract and intentional [*otvlehennyi i umyshlennyi*] city on the entire globe."[30] This association of the city with madness had given writers the opportunity to create an indigenous type that took on a life of its own. Goliadkin, Dostoevsky's protagonist in "The Double," suddenly acquires a double, Goliadkin Jr., who elbows the original Goliadkin out of his apartment, his job, and finally his life. As in "Notes of a Madman" and "The Queen of Spades," the appearance of the double in Dostoevsky's story can be explained by Goliadkin's insanity or taken as part of the tale's fantastic landscape. Either way, like Poprishchin and Hermann, Goliadkin Sr., ends up in an insane asylum. In his haunting 1873 story "Bobok"—another Petersburg tale—Dostoevsky again turns to the theme of insanity. The protagonist, like Poprishchin, writes poorly and seems to be losing his mind: he has recurrent aural hallucinations—a disembodied voice that keeps pronouncing the word "bobok" (little bean). Furthermore, having attended a funeral at a St. Petersburg cemetery and having drunk a glass or two of vodka at a nearby restaurant, the nameless protagonist dozes off on a gravestone and is awakened by a conversation carried on by the dead. Once again, it is not clear whether the conversation is imagined or real. One of the dead in fact ventures the opinion that after death a person's consciousness continues to exist for several months, allowing the dead to converse. What the protagonist hears awakens his mind to a higher consciousness or the fantastic perception that, posthumously, people enjoy another chance to repent of their sins and change for the better. Insane or not, he finds a kind of truth (and as a result, learns what his hallucinatory "bobok" means: this is what one of the dead repeats whenever he awakens during his allotted time of posthumous existence). Dostoevsky called "Bobok" a fantastic story—the designation he gave to works in which he tested a philosophical idea.[31] What would people do, he asks, if they were given another chance at moral improvement? The deranged and half-mad protagonist helps him conduct this experiment.

In Dostoevsky's novel *The Idiot*, Prince Myshkin's alleged idiocy caused by epilepsy is more important as the sign of his charisma, an indication that he is different—a holy fool rather than a wise man.[32] Having initially experimented, as the rough drafts and Figure IV.10 show, with an "infernal" character, in the final version Dostoevsky attempted to create in the figure of Myshkin an ideal man, able to navigate difficult societal and moral problems without compromising his integrity. He is the only one of Dostoevsky's characters who twice declines to fight a duel and suffers no loss of face. It is notable that Dostoevsky's ideal man cannot survive among ordinary people and goes truly insane (or refuses to deal with the outside world) after Rogozhin has murdered Nastasia Filippovna.

It could be argued that Stavrogin of Dostoevsky's *Demons* is also not quite sane: some of his actions, such as dragging a fellow gentleman by the nose or biting the governor's ear, beg to be explained by mental illness. And yet, his behavior cannot be fully ascribed to insanity. Nor is he a holy fool: his attempts to behave as one when he marries a feeble-minded invalid Maria, and refuses to defend his honor after being slapped in the face, ultimately lead to debauchery and disaster for everyone around him and not to spiritual enlightenment. If Myshkin's idiocy marks him as God's man, Stavrogin's abnormal behavior is of demonic nature.

Like Dostoevsky's "Bobok," Chekhov's "Ward No. 6" ("Palata № 6," 1892) can be read as a philosophical experiment, attempting to answer the question what is the foundation of empathy. Interrupting Chekhov's work on *Sakhalin Island* (*Ostrov Sakhalin*, 1893–94)—a report on his 1890 trip to the penal colony in the Russian Far East—the story depicts another space of forcible confinement, an insane asylum.[33] "Ward No. 6" is set in what seems to be an emphatically apocalyptic space: as Liza Knapp points out, the ward resembles Dante's Inferno; and as Cathy Popkin demonstrates, its space is warped, so the reader cannot arrive at a correct count of the inmates.[34] It is also an inhumanly cruel place, and the story tests the value of stoicism as a philosophy that accepts suffering—one's own and, by extension, others' suffering as well. Dr. Ragin, the hero, is an admirer of Marcus Aurelius, which helps him rationalize his failure to perform his duties as a physician and his indifference to the suffering of others. He has never experienced pain or fear in his life and therefore can dismiss the pain of others—until he himself becomes an inmate in the ward, and Nikita the guard beats him up for insubordination. The experience of pain awakens him to the pain of his fellow sufferers; it also wakes him up to the realization of how immoral his former indifference was. He dies of stroke the next day.

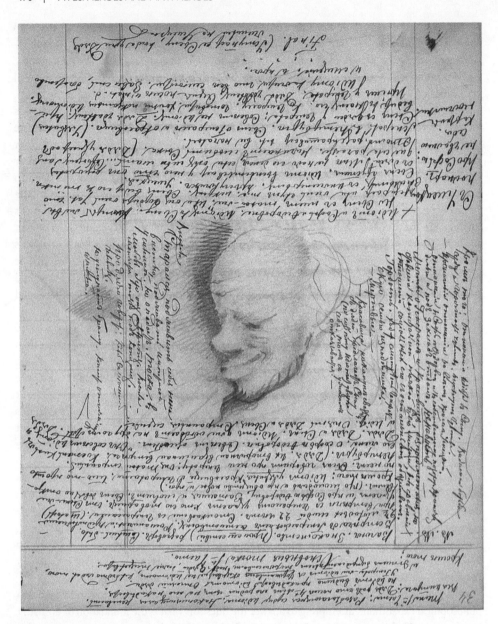

FIGURE IV.10. F. M. Dostoevsky, A portrait with "infernal" features in the early rough drafts of
The Idiot (1867).

Chekhov's other story that features an insane character, "The Black Monk" ("Chernyi
monakh," 1894), as some scholars suggest, harkens back to the literature of the 1830s and its
interest in the blurred line between the fantastic and madness. "Notes of a Madman" and
"Queen of Spades" are two obvious precursors, but Vladimir Odoevsky's "The Sylph"
("Sil'fida," 1837) is even more pertinent: like Chekhov's Kovrin, Odoevsky's protagonist moves
from St. Petersburg to the countryside to restore his mental health; like Kovrin, he decides to
marry a local girl; and like Kovrin, who begins to see and have conversations with the black
monk, Odoevsky's protagonist enters into a relationship with a fantastic creature, a beautiful
sylph he had ostensibly created following a recipe he had found in his late uncle's library.[35]
However, the endings of the two stories differ. The protagonist of Odoevsky's story returns to

the world of sanity, marries his fiancée, and lives happily ever after, even if he does drink too much. In contrast, Chekhov's Kovrin refuses treatment, abandons his wife, and dies of consumption following his last meeting with the black monk. In allowing the invisible world to prevail over reality, Chekhov's story foreshadows the arrival of modernism.

Across all these examples we see how writers maximize narrative technique to create distinctive visions and voices of madness. To be mad from within the text (like "Notes of a Madman"), with patches of narration floating in and out of the zone, is different than the Pushkin-like crystalline clarity of the narrator's voice in "The Queens of Spades," and different yet again from the sheer horror of "Ward No. 6."

"Little men"

Romantic interest in the figures of genius or madness waned as the Natural School began to pay attention to the everyday and the unremarkable, and even more so later, when Realism focused on the typical rather than exceptional. One of the types that socially progressive critics, beginning with Vissarion Belinsky, defined as central for this literary period was the so-called little (or insignificant) man (*malen 'kii chelovek*). For Belinsky, this type was a socially low-ranking person who deserved sympathy and attention; he commended Gogol for paying such attention to his little men, Poprishchin in "Notes of a Madman" and Akaky Bashmachkin of the 1842 story "Overcoat." The subsequent critical tradition, especially Soviet criticism, accepted Belinsky's definition enthusiastically and broadened its application: any poor or socially unremarkable character became a little man deserving universal sympathy.[36] In addition to Gogol's Poprishchin and Bashmachkin, the group began to include Pushkin's Samson Vyrin of "The Station Master," Dostoevsky's Makar Devushkin of *Poor Folk*, Goliadkin of *The Double*, and Mr. Prokharchin of the eponymous story ("Gospodin Prokharchin," 1846), and even Chekhov's Cherviakov in "Death of a Clerk." Influenced by their concerns for justice, critics of this persuasion see little men as helpless victims of societal cruelty. This view tended to simplify the type, overlooking their less sympathetic features. Samson Vyrin, for example, allows his young and pretty daughter to deal with irate male customers at the post station, blissfully unaware of the risks she faces; it is no wonder she eventually runs away with one of the handsome travelers. Even though Vyrin is an "inspector," *smotritel'* (from the verb *smotret'*, to look), he does not look out for his daughter. Boris Eikhenbaum in his article "How Gogol's 'Overcoat' Is Made" argued that the portrait of Bashmachkin was for Gogol an experiment in verbal performance rather than a representation of a pitiable literary type—which, to be convincing, needs to resemble a real person, which Bashmachkin hardly is. Eikhenbaum's analysis implicitly asks whether it is possible to pity a caricature. Many scholars now find in various representations of this type other features that contradict its image of helplessness. Poprishchin, for example, has a position in the bureaucratic hierarchy that no little man could have: he is a desk chief, a significant position that makes him a supervisor of roughly ten people.[37] In addition, he does have the embryonic qualities of a sexual predator: he walks under the windows of his beloved Sophie, and he also dreams about entering her bedroom to watch her undress. Likewise, Makar Devushkin, despite all his apparent meekness, is if not a stalker then certainly a lurker, prefiguring "the most complex and sinister figures of Dostoevsky's later fiction."[38] Goliadkin's inner world, accessible thanks to the complex narrative technique for which this story is famous, is shown to be twisted; the reader shudders in disgust and feels only relief when Golyadkin is finally taken to the insane asylum. Chekhov's character, Cherviakov (from *cherv'*, a worm), asks the general to forgive him for a minor infraction so many times that the general finally explodes, chasing him out. The clerk's subsequent death is not the result of the general's cruelty, then, but an effect of his own obsequiousness.[39] These readings follow the lines of complexity that the writers themselves embedded in their characters, and which the proponents of the little man theory were reluctant to acknowledge.

The provincial

Like the little men, superfluous men are predominately dwellers of St. Petersburg. Exceptions who leave the capital do so against their own will: Pechorin is sent to the Caucasus—apparently, for fighting a duel; while Onegin first leaves St. Petersburg to live on his inherited estate and then travels even further after killing his friend Lensky in a duel, returning to St. Petersburg only at the end of the novel. When superfluous men travel, they usually go to exotic parts of the Russian Empire, such as the Caucasus, Crimea, and Bessarabia (today's Moldova), as Onegin and Vel'tman's Wanderer do; or abroad, like Turgenev's Rudin and N. N. They journey across boring, provincial Russia to get to their more interesting destinations. As the narrator in *The Fragments from Onegin's Travels* says of his reaction to Nizhny Novgorod: "Boredom!" (*Toska!*).[40]

Travelers within Russia belong to different categories. One of the first such characters was Bulgarin's rogue Vyzhigin of the eponymous novel. Gogol's Khlestakov, the trickster protagonist of the comedy *The Inspector General*, and Chichikov, of *Dead Souls*, are also rogues who travel. The provincial dwellers these rogues meet are invariably strange and often grotesque. In *The Inspector General*, we encounter the indistinguishable Bobchinsky and Dobchinsky, who mistake Khlestakov, a nobody, for an important figure and thus initiate the play's comical action. Gogol also provides a host of corrupted provincial bureaucrats with impossibly comical surnames; and female characters, a mother and daughter, both ludicrously enamored. The common feature of all these characters is gullibility: the bureaucrats unanimously believe that Khlestakov is the inspector general, despite the fact that his behavior is obviously incongruous with such a role; and the women fall in love with him blindly even though it is obvious that he courts them at the same time. The characters in *Dead Souls* are also grotesque and gullible: they fall for Chichikov's self-portrait as a wealthy landowner in search of peasants to resettle on his land. Only gradually do they discover that he is buying the dead serfs who are still on the books until the next census, in order to mortgage them for cash.

Unlike Gogol, who was not very familiar with the population in the provinces and invented grotesque provincials, Saltykov-Shchedrin's representations of provincial types are based on his experiences during his lengthy service, first in Viatka (where he was exiled to serve for eight years, having displeased Nicholas I with two of his stories) and later in Ryazan' and Tver', where he served as a vice-governor, and after that in Perm', Tula, and again in Ryazan', where he held the position of the head of the treasury department. He had considerable experience with all categories of provincial population, from governors to paupers. *Provincial Sketches* (*Gubernskie ocherki*, published in 1856–57 under the penname N. Shchedrin), his first substantial work on the subject, portrays characters from all walks of life—local high-society ladies, low- and high-ranking bureaucrats, merchants, children, retired military men, pilgrims, holy fools, and prisoners. Virtually all of them are at least slightly bizarre: there is an underage alcoholic, an old maid who behaves inappropriately with very young boys; and a low-ranking official who courts the said old maid, hoping to use her to get a promotion. As is characteristic for most portrayals of provincials in Russian literature, they are all viewed and described by an outsider. When the narrator leaves Krutogorsk (which is Viatka) for St. Petersburg, he exclaims: "Oh provinces! You debauch people, you exterminate any kind of independence of mind, you freeze all outbursts of the heart, you annihilate everything, even the very capacity to desire!"[41] In a word, nobody living in a provincial town can escape some kind of perversion. Saltykov-Shchedrin continued to represent provincials in the same vein in his later writings, from

Innocent Stories (*Nevinnye rasskazy*, 1857–63), to *The Diary of a Provincial* (*Dnevnik provintsiala*, 1872), to *Poshekhonie in Days of Old* (*Poshekhonskaia starina*, 1887–89). His *Pompadours and Pompadouresses* (*Pompadury i pompadurshi*, 1863–74) and *The History of a Town* (*Istoriia odnogo goroda*, 1869–70) are populated by such ugly, nonsensical, and grotesquely distorted characters that they cannot be taken for real people.

Dostoevsky represents provincial characters in *Demons* and *The Brothers Karamazov*, and they are a mixed lot: some are created following Gogol's and Saltykov-Shchedrin's traditions (recall the grotesquely portrayed party attendees at the governor's house in *Demons* or Fedor Karamazov in *The Brothers Karamazov*), while others resemble ordinary people. His provinces and its inhabitants are described by insiders, that is, the provincials themselves: narrators in both novels reside in the towns where action takes place. It is even more significant that evil is often embodied by outsiders, those who come from the capitals or from abroad: Petr Verkhovensky in *Demons* and, arguably, Ivan Karamazov in *The Brothers Karamazov*. At the same time, there are characters who leave the reader with hope for a better future, such as the book-hawker Sofia Matveevna in *Demons*, who helps Stepan Trofimovich in the last days of his life; or Grushenka and the servant Grigory in *The Brothers Karamazov*.

Provincial residents are at the center of several Chekhov stories. In "My Life," written at the time when Chekhov was most strongly influenced by Tolstoy's ideas of *oproshchenie* (embracing the simple life), the protagonist escapes the morass of provincial life precisely by means of that philosophy, and becomes a craft worker—a painter. Even though provincial life causes his sister's death, the protagonist survives and lovingly brings up his young niece. There is hope for him and his niece as well as the young woman who loves him. In "Ionych" (1898) and "The Teacher of Literature" ("Uchitel' slovesnosti," chapter one 1889, chapter two 1894, in book form 1894) the characters moving into provincial towns suffer a crueler fate: in the first story, a young and talented doctor turns into an apathetic and insensitive man interested only in money; and in the second, a teacher is destroyed by the banality of the provincial town and its inhabitants. The last thing we read are the desperate words the teacher writes in his diary: "My God, where am I?! I am surrounded by vulgarity and more vulgarity [*poshlost' i poshlost'*]. . . . There is nothing more terrible, more offensive, more stultifying than vulgarity. I've got to get out of here! I've got to get away this very day, or else I will lose my mind!"[42] The heroine of Chekhov's "The Bride" ("Nevesta," 1903) saves herself by abandoning her vulgar fiancé and moving to Moscow. In his play *Three Sisters*, however, the titular characters, well-educated and talented young women who also strive to move to Moscow, fail completely: they cannot change their lives as radically as did Nadia of "The Bride."

The writers who worked outside this tradition were not numerous, but their contributions were significant. One is Turgenev, whose many novels, including *The Nest of the Gentry*, and stories, such as the 1876 "A Watch" ("Chasy"), portray likeable characters who live in provincial towns. Another such writer is Nikolai Leskov, who sympathetically describes not only residents of his native Orel, in the stories "A Robbery" or "Deathless Golovan" ("Nesmertel'nyi Golovan," 1880), but finds good people in all regions of the Russian Empire: from the Baltic provinces ("The Kolyvan Husband" ["Kolyvanskii muzh," 1888]), to Ukraine ("The Sealed Angel" ["Zapechatlennyi angel," 1873] and "Figura" [1889]), to central Russia (*Cathedral Folk* and "Singlemind"), to Siberia ("Siberian Pictures of the Eighteenth Century" ["Sibirskie kartinki 18 veka," 1893]), to the far east ("At the Edge of the World").

The characters who populate Leskov's stories may be somewhat odd (his famous use of the narrative device of *skaz* partly accounts for this oddness), but never grotesque; usually they are as bad and as good as people generally are; and often they represent the best of humanity: many of them are righteous people (*pravedniki*), that is, secular people who genuinely behave according to the spirit of Christian teaching. They do not transgress not because they are afraid to break the law, but because it is against their nature. They may suffer because of their righteousness (as Odnodum does, because he refuses to take bribes and therefore lives in utter poverty) but this does not deter them. It is noteworthy that, in contrast with virtually all other nineteenth-century Russian writers, there is no difference in Leskov's writings between the inhabitants of the capitals and the provinces. (Only Moscow is occasionally marked as the Slavophile cultural sphere, as it is in "The Devil-Chase" and "The Kolyvan Husband").

A significant number of women writers were viewed as "provincial" by their male contemporaries, both for their purported cultural inferiority and their frequently preferred subject matter. Many of them also actually lived in the provinces. Therefore, as Irina Savkina puts it, for these women writers, the provinces were "their own rather than an alien space"; as a result, "the provincial woman was the *subject* of representation and not its object. Not only do women authors prefer a provincial town as a setting to the countryside...they make a provincial woman their heroine, and as narrators also assume the identity of provincial dwellers."[43] It is not where they live that causes the unhappiness of heroines in the fiction of Zhukova, Gun, and Durova. The eponymous heroine of Zhukova's story "Nadenka" believes that "a person can be happy in any situation."[44] Prevalent in the prose works of women writers in the 1830s and 1840s, this positive view changed in the later part of the century. In a subgenre that emerged in the late nineteenth century and that Catriona Kelly defined as a "provincial tale," the heroines dislike their lives in the provinces, which they see as stifling and which they desire to abandon.[45]

7

Heroines and emancipation

Status of women

The lives of fictional women in Imperial Russia are much better known than the lives of real, historical women: even historians occasionally refer to Pushkin's Tatiana or Tolstoy's Anna to illustrate their points. However, since the 1970s or so, a number of historical accounts have appeared that elucidate non-fictional women's social and legal status as well as their everyday lives.[1] Scholars have recognized a contradiction between women's strong property rights and their status within the family that, in the absence of developed family law, was defined by patriarchal norms supported by the Church. Furthermore, it has been pointed out that women's social rights largely depended on social stratum: much was determined by whether one was a peasant, a priest's wife, a middling urban dweller, or a noblewoman.[2]

Even though the law made women dependent on husbands (or, if they were unmarried, on fathers), some managed to find ways around the patriarchal norms to achieve a degree of freedom. A few were very successful in becoming independent and living as they wished, like Nadezhda Durova who spent part of her life serving in the military and had a successful if short career as a writer. Many women, mostly from the nobility, lived separately from their husbands by mutual agreement, but they could obtain real freedom only if their husbands agreed to give them permission to receive a passport or get a job. As the century progressed, however, such things began to happen more frequently, at least among the educated classes. Avdotia Panaeva lived with a man who was not her husband, Nikolai Nekrasov, with her husband's blessing. Examples like theirs inspired the marital arrangements described in Nikolai Chernyshevsky's *What Is to Be Done?* The novel also reflected another practice, the fictitious marriage a woman could enter to obtain freedom from her birth family. Historical sources provide many examples of such marriages, and the number grew in the later nineteenth century. More and more frequently this practice was used by women to obtain education, often abroad.[3] Gradually even marriage became not strictly necessary, and unmarried women would leave their families to pursue whatever life they wanted, including that of revolutionaries and terrorists. Nineteenth-century literature reflected these changes in full.

Around the mid-nineteenth century a middling urban class began to emerge, bridging to some degree a gap between the Westernized nobility and the peasantry still largely living according to pre-Petrine traditions.[4] These social changes affected women no less than men, both negatively (the urban environment exposed them to sexual exploitation) and positively (it provided more freedom of choice, giving them access both to gainful employment and education). Nineteenth-century Russian literature paid far more attention to women's sexual exploitation in urban environments (Liza in Dostoevsky's *Notes from Underground*, Aniuta in Chekhov's 1886 eponymous story, Katiusha in Tolstoy's *Resurrection*) than to the opportunities it provided.

The freedoms the peasant women could enjoy in the nineteenth-century countryside are not very well studied, even though they clearly existed. For one, they could move more freely, particularly to visit places of religious significance, such as monasteries. They could also find gainful employment more easily, for example, as wet-nurses or nannies.[5] They could have enjoyed more sexual freedoms than noblewomen both before and after marriage, although there are no comparative studies of these behaviors to support this point. Nineteenth-century literature portrays women pilgrims (Princess Maria of *War and Peace*, for example, welcomes them in her father's house), nannies and wet-nurses (but rarely as having free agency to find their own employment, to come and go), and—particularly toward the end of the century—sexually transgressive unmarried and married peasant women. It is noteworthy that for the latter, the tradition begins early, with Karamzin's "Poor Liza," and goes all the way to the end of the century, when Tolstoy created his Katiusha in 1899 *Resurrection*. But most examples of transgressive women from the peasantry are found in the later part of the nineteenth century, when the idea of the moral purity of the people began to fade.

In what follows, several typical women characters that populate the nineteenth-century literature are discussed. Some of them appear in their respective works as male characters' partners and counterparts, while others are independent, sometimes replacing men as main characters.

"The necessary woman"

The superfluous men (if we accept this somewhat dubious term for the sake of the argument) are always accompanied by women. But most of these men cannot commit themselves to any lasting relations, particularly marital (Onegin, Pechorin, Rudin). Others resolve to get married, but then get cold feet and retreat, often quite unexpectedly (Goncharov's Oblomov and Turgenev's N. N. in "Asya"). Still others cannot win a woman to whom they are attracted. Interestingly, this last category includes both weak characters (Turgenev's Chulkaturin in "Diary of a Superfluous Man") and strong ones (Bazarov in *Fathers and Sons*). Scholarly interpretations of these characters' inability to maintain relations with women vary. Lotman explains the Russian male protagonists' failure to marry as well as to achieve any kind of success in life by the nineteenth-century Russian novel's idiosyncratic plot construction: "The Russian novel, beginning with Gogol, was concerned not with the problem of changing the hero's status, but with transforming his inner essence or with renovating the life around him, or, finally, with both." In other words, while the Western novel tends to be a "family novel," the Russian novel, Lotman says, is "social."[6] It has also been suggested that Russian male protagonists never really grow up, perpetually remaining in a liminal state between childhood and maturity. Their liminality explains both their inability to marry and their difficulties finding a meaningful occupation in life. It is telling that Tolstoy, who planned his first significant literary work, *Childhood, Boyhood, Youth*, to be in four parts—apparently intending to describe his protagonist's maturing and marrying at the end—never wrote this last part, ending what remained a trilogy at the moment when the protagonist fails his university exams, with no clear career path or a wife at the horizon.[7]

Jehanne Gheith aptly dubbed the heroine rejected by the superfluous man the "necessary woman," since she is not only invariably present alongside the superfluous man, but also defines him as a type. Critics agree that the necessary woman functions as his foil; however, they disagree in their assessments of her as a character. Some see her as stronger than her male counterpart (Turgenev's heroines—Odintsova in particular—are pertinent examples); others argue that, since it is a superfluous man who is the main character, being a necessary woman in fact limits this heroine, assigning her an auxiliary role and depriving her of any possibility to develop and change.[8] Of all women characters who are created to exist alongside the superfluous men only Pushkin's Tatiana is not limited by her assigned role: in the course of the novel, she becomes an independent character that grows and changes.[9] In contrast, Lermontov's necessary women in *A Hero of Our Time* (Bela, Princess Mary, and Vera) are all there only to define Pechorin—to demonstrate his inability to be any kind of a "significant other." Their characters are barely outlined; their main function is to be the victims of his inconstancy and thus to establish his status as what the later critical tradition will call a superfluous man. Dmitry Pisarev was the first to point out this feature of the necessary woman in his 1861 essay "Women Types in Novels and Novellas by Pisemsky, Turgenev, and Goncharov" ("Zhenskie tipy v romanakh i povestiakh Pisemskogo, Turgeneva i Goncharova"). He argues that women's characters are abridged in novels featuring superfluous men: they appear fully formed and remain as they are throughout the work. Abram Tertz (Andrei Sinyavsky) and Barbara Heldt from their very different points of view also "focused on the ways these texts limit the heroine's role."[10] It is noteworthy that Olga, the necessary woman in Goncharov's *Oblomov*, begins to change and grow when she marries Oblomov's opposite in the novel, Stoltz. She even outgrows her husband spiritually, making him worry that she may become dissatisfied with their marriage.

Gheith suggests that the dominant tradition of presenting the necessary woman as limited and unable to develop was subverted by nineteenth-century women writers, first of all Evgenia Tur (1815–92; the penname of Elizaveta Salias de Turnemir), whose novella *Antonina* (1851) was likely written in response to Turgenev's *Diary of Superfluous Man*.[11] *Antonina* is a first-person narrative, which allows Tur to make it Antonina's story, relegating male characters to secondary roles. Of the two significant male characters in the novella, Michel B., Antonina's first and only love, is a true superfluous man: when the two lovers encounter obstacles, he gives up, whereas Antonina (unlike the traditional necessary women) resists. Faced with various kinds of misfortunes and difficulties, Antonina does not isolate herself (as Turgenev's Chulkaturin does), but maintains connections with other people. Furthermore, she is not afraid to choose emotions over reason and, unlike her counterparts in tales of superfluous men, she does this consciously. Most importantly, Tur's *Antonina* gives an independent voice to the female character that hitherto existed only as the male character's foil.

Mothers

The role of the mother is surprisingly ambivalent in Russian nineteenth-century literature. While a superfluous man always has a young woman at his side—a potential partner whom he fails or who refuses him—he does not necessarily have a mother, and when he does, she is often inadequate. Evgeny Onegin has a father: his squandering of his estate and his death are mentioned. Not a word is said about his mother. Tatiana, in contrast, has a mother, thanks to whom she becomes an avid reader and marries up (whether this is good or bad for Tatiana is, of course, open for debate). Lermontov's Pechorin, like Onegin, is motherless in the novel. The only time we hear about Pechorin's (imaginary) mother is in Maksim Maksimych's explanation of his obduracy when he wants to get something (Bela or a wild boar) by his hypothetically indulgent mother: "Evidently, he was spoilt by his mommy as a child."[12] How Oblomov was spoiled by his mother is obvious from his dream. Beltov's mother in Herzen's *Who is to Blame?*, although attentive to his upbringing and education, is too lenient to provide him with adequate guidance in choosing his path in life. Chulkaturin's mother is cold, moralistic, and excessively judgmental, which kept her son at a distance: "She loved me, but I did not love her," Chulkaturin confesses.[13] Bazarov's mother, while certainly loving, is not his intellectual equal and her nurturing cannot explain why he has turned out as he does. None of the authors who portray superfluous men investigate their hero's "mother problem," but the problem's existence bespeaks a deeper cultural anxiety about the representation of women as mothers, which is to say as potentially powerful figures in the domestic worlds they inhabit.[14]

The absence or presence of a mother as well as her role in her children's life is also relevant in other types of narratives. In Karamzin's "Poor Liza," the father is dead, but the mother is present, and she obviously cares for her daughter in her own way, instructing her in religion and finding her a suitable bridegroom. At the same time, her role in her daughter's perishing is significant: she is instrumental (albeit unwittingly) in bringing Liza and Erast together; she is blind to Liza's love for Erast as well as to her distress after he abandons her. As a result, Liza faces her misfortunes alone, which no doubt contributes to her death. In Pushkin's "The Station Master," which is in part a response to "Poor Liza," the mother is absent, and the heroine, the young Dunia, performs the motherly role in the household, cleaning, cooking, and caring for her father. There is no mother to caution Dunia against the young men passing through the station, which eventually leads to her eloping with a dashing young officer.

Dunia's situation is prevalent in nineteenth-century Russian literature, and the list of motherless heroes and heroines is too long to enumerate. However, briefly considering those particularly affected by the absence of their mothers is instructive. In Dostoevsky's *Poor Folk*, the death of Varenka's mother leaves the girl defenseless, at the mercy of Anna Fedorovna, a procuress who sells her to Bykov. Varenka's entire life, including her eventual marriage to Bykov, is determined by this vulnerability. Goncharov's Olga in *Oblomov* and Tolstoy's Anna Karenina are both wards, but it is noteworthy how differently they are affected by this circumstance. Olga shows independence and moral strength; Anna, for all her charm, is portrayed by Tolstoy as lacking some important core qualities to guide her.[15] But it is Dostoevsky who makes the most of the significance for children of losing their mother. The four Karamazov brothers are orphans, and their orphanhood affects each of them differently. Dmitry is abandoned by his mother (who dies soon after her flight from Fedor Karamazov) when he is three years old and is first cared for by the family servant Grigory and his wife Marfa, and later taken in by his late mother's family members, a not too attentive and thoughtful lot. Consequently, Dmitry is badly educated and, it seems, the least self-aware of the brothers, including even Smerdiakov—which circumstance no doubt contributes to Dmitry's woes. Smerdiakov, Fedor Karamazov's natural son, never knew his mother: the stinking (*smerdiashchaia*) Lizaveta died while giving birth to him, and he was brought up by the same Grigory and Marfa to be Fedor's servant. Smerdiakov, however, could never forget his mother or, rather, shake off the shame of having a mother nicknamed "Stinking," since his last name, given to him by Fedor, derives from the same root "smerd-" ("to stink"; the root also means a "peasant"). Ivan's and Alesha's mother, a meek and deeply religious young woman, was the ward of a cranky old general's widow who mistreated her so badly that she, having failed to kill herself, had the misfortune to elope with Fedor. Fedor, in turn, treated her horribly, driving her to insanity and eventual death. She died when Ivan and Alesha were very young. Grigory promptly took them in, but soon the general's widow arrived and briefly assumed their care. Before her death she found a decent guardian who provided them with good education. Both brothers remember their mother: when Alesha has an epileptic fit while listening to his father's recounting pre-intercourse rituals with her (including spitting at an icon) and Fedor exclaims that he is "just like her, just like his mother," Ivan angrily points out that she was his mother, too.[16] However, the reader is told only what Alesha remembers: her hysterical religious ardor and her "frenzied but beautiful" face.[17] Ivan and Alesha's mother is not shown by Dostoevsky to have any autonomy or means of protecting and sustaining her own children, yet she leaves powerful emotional legacies for her sons, giving them a kind of imaginative presence.

The maternal figure is also generally very important for Tolstoy, beginning with his first published work, *Childhood*, in which the loving mother is the center of the young Nikolenka's life, and her early death strongly affects his further development. In *War and Peace*, the presence or absence of maternal feelings—and even the ability to be mother—are used to judge women characters. From the evil Hélène, who dies of a botched abortion, to Lise Bolkonsky, who dies in childbirth, to Sonya, called a barren flower (*pustotsvet*) by her friend Natasha, we see women whose inadequacy is marked by their refusal or inability to become mothers. In contrast, Princess Maria first becomes an excellent surrogate mother to her nephew and then, after her marriage to Nikolai, is portrayed as a conscientious, intelligent, and loving mother. And then there is Natasha, who, married to Pierre, becomes consumed by her motherly emotions—which is presented in a positive light by Tolstoy's narrator. In *Anna Karenina*, once again we see how being a good mother reflects on women characters. The reader is made not only to pity but also respect Dolly for her devotion to her children. Kitty obviously is developing into Natasha's double. And the reader is meant not to forgive Anna for her abandonment of Serezha, her indifference to Annie, and, especially, for her use of contraceptives.

Arina Peterovna Golovleva of Saltykov-Shchedrin's *The Golovlev Family* is perhaps the worst of all nineteenth-century mothers. She seems to be entirely devoid of maternal feelings, consumed by her desire to increase her wealth. Even her favorite child, Porfiry (nicknamed "Little Judas," *Iudushka*) inspires more fear in her than love. He is the only one who is able to outlive her, whereas all his siblings perish of various types of neglect. Arina is so inadequate as a mother that the curse of her cruel mothering survives her and continues to destroy what is left of the Golovlev family.[18]

It is remarkable that in nineteenth-century literature mothers, present or absent, almost never are the main characters. One exception is Nekrasov, who wrote several poems about mothers. His poem "Orina the Soldier's Mother" ("Orina, mat' soldatskaia," 1863) was written, as Nekrasov claimed, about a peasant mother whose son returns home after many years in compulsory military service, only to die. Nekrasov's "Mother" ("Mat'," 1868) is dedicated to the wife of a political prisoner and mother of three adolescent boys still at home; their fate is to become revolutionaries and also perish in prison. Between the late 1850s and his death, Nekrasov worked on a narrative poem about his own mother, recounting her unhappy marriage, her importance in his life, and her early death. The first-person protagonist of that poem (a stand-in for Nekrasov himself) arrives too late to say goodbye. He reminisces about her, imagines her reappearance in the garden at night, and rejoices that death has delivered her from suffering. Nekrasov published several fragments, but never finished the poem.

A rare work in which mother is central is Chekhov's "In the Ravine." It portrays the young Lipa whose aunt arranges her marriage into a rich and enterprising peasant family (significantly, her own mother is so meek and passive that she plays no role in this arrangement). Lipa's husband, Anisim, is a police detective and does not live at home. He comes to his native village for the wedding and leaves five days later. He is soon arrested for counterfeiting money. Lipa meanwhile gives birth to a son, Nikifor. The story describes her love for the newborn and her playing with him affectionately. The intensity of her love for her infant surprises Lipa: "Who is he? What is he like? He's light as a feather, or a little crumb, but I love him, love him like a real person."[19] Anisim is sentenced to six years of hard labor in Siberia, and his father makes little Nikifor the heir of his business. His other daughter-in-law, the greedy and opportunist Varvara, is so mad that she pours scalding water over little Nikifor. In horror, Lipa utters such a scream "as never before had been heard" in the village.[20] The little boy dies the same evening in the district hospital, and Lipa carries him home in her arms. Her bewilderment over her baby's suffering is as unanswerable as Job's laments about his woes. At the same time, "Chekhov's portrayal of Lipa . . . invokes the theme of Madonna and child"; her grief thus invokes Mary's.[21] And yet, in Chekhov's representation, Lipa eventually comes to terms with the fact that life brings both happiness and suffering. On her final appearance in the story, she is seen returning from a day of work with a group of women, singing. In fact, "she is *leading* [the] group of working peasant women and girls, *leading* the chorus of singers in song." No longer timid and sad as she was when she was a bride, no longer grieving and questioning God's justice as she did after Nikifor's death, Lipa triumphs "over sorrow and death."[22] It is through experiencing both a mother's love and a mother's grief that Lipa is able to accept the world in which she lives. The characters' names in this story are meaningful: Nikifor means "triumphant," and Lipa, if derived from Alipia, as Robert Louis Jackson suggests, means "free from pain and grief"; if, however, it derives from Olimpiada, as the list of Russian Orthodox saints submits, then the name means "lauding/singing the sky." This disturbing story thus provides catharsis if not transcendence.[23]

Wives and mistresses

The predominance of narratives in which men are either more socially conscious than family-oriented (in Lotman's terms) or never grow up (in Blank's terms) also affects the way wives are presented. The need to deal with a superfluous man inevitably alters the necessary woman. In *Evgeny Onegin*, Tatiana matures and becomes independent; in deciding to marry a man whom she respects rather than loves, she exercises her free will.[24] Introduced by her husband into high society, she excels in her new role. Her resolution to remain faithful to her husband despite her love for Onegin is also a decision based on the moral code she works out for herself, which includes, as she famously declares, a refusal to build happiness on someone else's pain. Vera in Lermontov's *Hero of Our Time* demonstrates the alternative choice and its consequences: she cheats on her husband with Pechorin, whom she loved before her marriage (in fact, two marriages) and continues to love. We know too little about her to judge her decisions (she is, perhaps, the most elusive woman in the tradition, despite her letter to Pechorin, included for our perusal), but it is clear that her choices do not make her happy. On the contrary, they bring her pain, shame, and, perhaps, death (her terminal illness seems to be the result of her unhappiness). Turgenev's Liza in *A Diary of Superfluous Man*, seduced and abandoned by Prince N., as limited as her character may be, follows in Tatiana's steps, making her own decision in marrying Biz´menkov rather than Chulkaturin. It looks like she prefers him precisely because he is, in Chulkaturin's sarcastic description, "a blond, kind, and meek little man." Chulkaturin expresses his sarcasm by using adjectives in diminutive form: *belokuren´kii, dobren´kii i smirnen´kii chelovek*.[25] Natalia in *Rudin* also marries after Rudin leaves her despite her readiness to elope with him. Turgenev does not show the reader how exactly she arrives at this decision; we learn about it from her fiancé's letter to a friend. In an interesting variation of the usual plot, Herzen's superfluous man, Beltov, of *Who Is to Blame?*, ruins a married woman: Liubinka, happily married to Krutsifersky, cannot resist the advances of this charming man, so handsome and well-educated, so unable to find his place in life. At the same time, she cannot forgive herself for her unfaithfulness (a kiss given to Beltov) and succumbs to tuberculosis. Turgenev's Elena in *On the Eve* is a different type of heroine, largely because her male counterpart is unlike Onegin or Rudin. In the eyes of his contemporaries, Turgenev's goal was to present a hero who is not a superfluous man. Ironically, his anti-superfluous man is not even Russian: Insarov is a Bulgarian patriot, seeking to free his native land of Turks. Elena chooses him precisely for his heroic determination and revolutionary zeal. After he dies, she continues his fight, abandoning Russia forever.

One of the first Russian works to directly address the woman question is Druzhinin's novella *Polinka Sachs*. It was Druzhinin's literary debut and remains the work by which he mostly is remembered. Influenced by George Sand's *Jacques* (1833), a novel about an unhappy marriage between an older retired soldier and a younger bride, *Polinka Sachs* discusses both the wife's right to choose freely whom to love and the husband's dilemma: should he set his wife free or is he responsible for guiding her? Druzhinin ably transplants the dilemmas of his model into a specifically Russian situation and portrays characters familiar to Russian readers, which perhaps explains the novella's success among the reading public. Konstantin Sachs is a state official of German descent (St. Petersburg bureaucracy was populated with Germans from the Baltic provinces, and Russian literature reflected this). A well-educated man in his thirties, he marries a very young woman who is a graduate of a boarding school (*institut* or *pansion*). First introduced by Catherine the Great, these schools (of which the most famous was the Smolnyi Institute in St. Petersburg) were given the task of educating ideal Russian gentlewomen who, in turn, were expected to educate their sons as ideal Russian gentlemen. But years of isolation at these boarding schools and the lack of any practical kind of instruction produced young women entirely unfamiliar with everyday life. Reactions to this pedagogical experiment varied: some found the graduates (*institutki*) charming, but others thought them ridiculous. Institute girls appear in Russian literature throughout the nineteenth century, in works by Bestuzhev-Marlinsky, Gogol, Ivan Bunin, and Aleksandr Kuprin (1870–1938).[26] Polinka is a typical institute girl: inadequately educated, childish, impractical, and naive. These features both attract and bother her husband, who attempts in vain to stock her mind with knowledge. Far more consequential than her poor education is Polinka's emotional immaturity. She is so childish that she is unable to interpret her own emotions. This proves tragic: when her old flame Prince Galitsky reappears, he easily convinces her that it is he whom she loves, not her husband. Sachs, believing this, gives her freedom. Polinka marries Galitsky—only to discover that, after all, it is Sachs whom she really loves. The discovery leads to sickness that eventually kills her. Numerous questions arise, and the novella gives no clear answers. Was Sachs right in giving Polinka her freedom? Was it not his duty to help her develop emotionally and learn to understand her own feelings? What is the husband's role in helping a young wife to become a mature woman who can handle her freedom? Herzen's Krutsifersky could be judged according to these criteria as well: when Liubinka falls in love with Beltov, instead of providing support and guidance, he takes to drink, heightening her unhappiness and thus contributing to her death.

Tolstoy's 1859 novella *Family Happiness* was also written in response to vigorous discussions, both in Europe and in Russia, of the woman question.[27] He was also likely influenced by the historian and cultural theorist Jules Michelet's ideas of marriage and womanhood, as expounded in his 1858 treatise *L'Amour*.[28] Tolstoy follows Michelet's concept of the stages that love necessarily undergoes in a marriage (changing from erotic to familiar) as well as the French historian's idea that the husband's duty is to form his wife's character. In the course of the novella, the young Masha's much older husband Sergei does precisely this: he changes Masha from a vivacious young woman enjoying erotic relations with her husband and (chastely) the attentions of other men, into a mother completely devoted to her child, while her husband becomes merely "an old friend."[29] But, knowing the larger picture of Tolstoy's representations of family life in his novels, we might put it differently: incapable of accepting the fact that his wife is a sexual being, Sergei banishes Eros from their marital relations. Only then do the wife and husband achieve a modicum of family happiness. To prove his points, Tolstoy employs a female narrator, Masha herself, who develops these views on marriage and female sexuality. Tolstoy's narrative structure makes her collude with the author in implying that the heroine herself is to blame for her marital troubles and the eventual departure of Eros from her marriage.[30] In *War and Peace*, while Tolstoy presents a number of married women, from the morally corrupt Hélène to the saintly Princess (Countess, in marriage) Maria, he does not spend much time on expounding his views on marriage or the woman's place in it. One exception is Natasha, who rather shockingly metamorphoses from a spirited slender girl who charms men with her singing into a stout mother indifferent to her looks and neglecting music to concentrate on her children and husband. Nonetheless, erotic love apparently is present in her marriage: when the reader meets her and Pierre for the last time, they are talking in bed after sex. Unbridled Eros, however, is evil. Hélène is Tolstoy's primary example, but even the young Natasha, pining for the absent Prince Andrei, is easily led astray by Hélène and her depraved brother Anatole precisely because they are able to use her awakening sexuality.

Anna Karenina from the opening lines presents itself as a family novel. Indeed, we observe several different women's behavior within marriage: one family is falling apart due to the wife's succumbing to erotic feelings for another man; another is enduring utter chaos at some times and enjoys relative peace at others thanks to the wife's patiently—almost heroically—tolerating her husband's infidelities; and yet another family is forming up nicely—experiencing growth pains but overcoming them because both the wife and, especially, the husband are willing to work things out. And then there is a pseudo-family: Anna's and Vronsky's cohabitation, which fundamentally cannot work, and leads to Anna's suicide.[31] It is instructive to contemplate what may have contributed to the success or failure of each marriage in the novel. Obviously, the causes are multiple, but it is, perhaps, no coincidence that the female character whose behavior is most destructive to family happiness, Anna, grew up as a ward.[32] Vronsky too, as the novel informs the reader, "never knew family life" due to his mother's dissipated lifestyle.[33] In contrast, Dolly and Kitty grew up in a loving family, which taught them how to be good wives and mothers—in Dolly's case, how to keep her family together despite her husband's disloyal behavior (he is Anna's brother, after all).[34] At the same time, it is important to remember that, however variously women's behavior may be presented in *Anna Karenina*, the central female characters, in contrast to "necessary women," are not limited—they are, like male characters, "full-fledged human subjects, free and unfinalizable."[35]

In contrast, *The Kreutzer Sonata*, which also centers on the relations of men and women within a marriage, is narrated in such a manner that the reader knows almost nothing about Pozdnyshev's murdered wife: it is even impossible to tell whether she really was unfaithful to him. All information comes from Pozdnyshev, a narrator of questionable trustworthiness. At the same time, his views are oddly feminist: he blames men, who objectify women sexually, for women's misbehavior. The idea of radical chastity, which Pozdnyshev offers as the best solution to the "woman question" (and to the "man question" as well), is supposed to free women from sexual slavery and give them dignity and space to grow as persons.[36] In his "Afterword to *The Kreutzer Sonata*," Tolstoy goes even further and advocates chastity for everyone, even to the point of the extinction of the species. In proposing universal chastity as a spiritual goal that he recognizes as an unachievable ideal, Tolstoy echoes the book of Genesis (the phrase "And I believe that it is not good," criticizing relations between sexes, is repeated with variations four times in the opening paragraphs), implying that by following his proposition, humankind can return to the prelapsarian state.[37]

Nikolai Chernyshevsky's *What Is to Be Done?* became a major text in the debate about women's roles and rights. It has been read as a rejoinder to Turgenev's *Fathers and Sons*. In particular, Chernyshevsky objected to the novel's presentation of the nihilist Bazarov, in contrast to whom Chernyshevsky created his "new men," Lopukhov and Kirsanov. Unlike Bazarov, they are successfully practicing physicians; they also arrange their family lives rationally and thus happily. Even more significant, however, is Chernyshevsky's portrayal of a new woman, Vera. Oppressed by her parents, she enters a fictitious marriage with Lopukhov and moves in with him. The marriage remains unconsummated, while he continues his medical studies and she works to organize a co-op of seamstresses, earning her own living and helping other women become independent. When Lopukhov's friend and colleague Kirsanov moves in with the couple, Vera falls in love with him, and he reciprocates. Not quite understanding her own feelings, Vera consummates her union with Lopukhov. Kirsanov withdraws, but eventually their love for each other becomes apparent. Lopukhov proposes a ménage à trois, but Vera is reluctant, and Lopukhov fakes suicide—while, in fact, he has left for America. Eventually he returns, marries another "new" woman, and the two couples live together under one roof. This, Chernyshevsky suggested, is a rational solution to marital problems; and his readers enthusiastically agreed.

What Is to Be Done?, although poorly written, was eagerly read, and its ideas enthusiastically implemented by generations of new men and women, including Lenin.[38] Chernyshevsky was drawing on behavioral models that already existed: some contemporary women had achieved independence by means of fictitious marriages, and some of them entered ménage-à-trois arrangements.[39] His novel served as a powerful vehicle for making these examples available for imitation. It also generated negative responses from those who saw the novel as a threat to monogamous marriage. Dostoevsky in *The Idiot* presents two love triangles: one, involving Myshkin, Aglaia, and Nastasia Filippovna, which leads to Aglaia's bitter disappointment; and another, involving Myshkin, Ragozhin, and Nastasia Filippovna, which leads to murder and destruction. And Tolstoy's *Anna Karenina* includes a horrific dream where Anna imagines herself in bed with both Vronsky and her husband.

Chekhov also addressed the woman question, and both his timely entrance into the debate and his ability to change his view were important. Taken with Tolstoy's philosophy early in his career, he gradually became more skeptical, doubting Tolstoy's vision of women's place in society and family. Chekhov's trip to Sakhalin was a critical step in his rejection of these ideas. We find traces of his evolution in his changing responses to *The Kreutzer Sonata*. Before the trip, Chekhov appreciated the novella's artistic qualities and believed that it was useful because it made the reader think. It was afterwards that his opinion of the work changed drastically: "Before the trip, I saw *The Kreutzer Sonata* as an [important] event [*byla ... sobytiem*], and now it looks ridiculous to me and seems confused [*bestolkovoi*]."[40] Three of Chekhov's stories written in the 1890s—"Anna around the Neck" ("Anna na shee," 1895), "About love" ("O liubvi," 1898), and "The Lady with a Little Dog" ("Dama s sobachkoi," 1899)—clearly respond to Tolstoy's treatment of the woman question with vigorous disagreement: all feature married women named Anna who are unfaithful to their husbands. These stories question and complicate Tolstoy's presentation of women's unfaithfulness, but the plot plays out quite differently in each case. In "Anna around the Neck," the young and poor Anna—who marries an old and well-to-do high-ranking official in the hope of providing support to her alcoholic father and two younger brothers—initially elicits readers' sympathy with her apparent meekness and devotion to her father and brothers. But after she realizes that her sexual attractiveness gives her power over men, including her husband's superior, she becomes ruthless in her relations with her husband, spending his money freely and leading a self-indulgent life. Although the story does not openly state that she is unfaithful, she probably is, and her husband uses her likely liaison with his superior to advance his career. Chekhov portrays here a world like that of Betsy Tverskaia in *Anna Karenina*: devoid of love, morals, and compassion.[41] Accordingly, Chekhov's Anna forgets about her father and brothers as soon as she achieves her own version of family happiness. Anna in "About Love" is quite different: although she is also married to an older man, she seems to love him or, at least, as the narrator of the story, Alekhin, puts it, she lives "in harmony and comfort" with him.[42] In contrast to "Anna around the Neck," the characters in "About Love" exercise restraint: having fallen in love with each other, Anna and Alekhin not only never consummate their relationship but behave in such a way that nobody, including Anna's husband, can suspect their love exists. However, when, about to part forever, they finally kiss, they realize that their reluctance to be happy at the expense of Anna's husband may have been a mistake. They did what they thought was right, and yet they are profoundly unhappy and regretful. In Chekhov's world, bad things happen to good people who behave nobly.[43] Or, to put it the other way around, good deeds do not necessarily constitute correct behavior. At the beginning of "The Lady with a Little Dog," the two main characters, Anna and Gurov, remind us in some ways of Tolstoy's Anna and Vronsky: Gurov is a womanizer and Anna is unhappily married to a state bureaucrat; furthermore, she succumbs to Gurov's seduction. But as their love affair continues, it becomes clear that they belong together despite their being married to other people. Paradoxically, carrying on their illicit affair makes them better human beings, in Chekhov's view: their affair's "very stability becomes a moral achievement."[44]

Married women from the merchant and peasant classes also appear in nineteenth-century literature.[45] The question of their representation was complicated by ideological debates within the educated classes. First the Slavophiles, then the *pochvenniki*, such as Dostoevsky and Apollon Grigor´ev, and later Tolstoy, held that the peasantry, by preserving the traditional lifestyle, also preserved traditional good morals. The same logic, however, did not apply to merchants: despite their manifest attachment to old ways, their traditional practices often were presented in a negative light. The playwright Aleksandr Ostrovsky, whose plays often focused on the life of the merchant class, was one of the few who offered a less rigid view of this class. Born in the Zamoskvorech´e district of Moscow predominantly inhabited by merchants, the extraordinarily prolific Ostrovsky dominated the nineteenth-century Russian theater repertoire. Among his numerous plays in different genres and on various topics, *The Storm* stands out both because of its artistic power and the polemics it provoked among contemporary critics. The play takes place in the imaginary town of Kalinov on the Volga River and focuses on two quite traditional merchant families: one headed by a man with the telling surname Dikoi (wild or savage) and another by the widow Kabanova (from *kaban*, boar). Both dominate their households, demanding total submission from the younger generation. The main heroine is Katerina, given in marriage by her family to Kabanova's weak-spirited son Tikhon. Oppressed by the suffocating environment of the household and unsupported by Tikhon, whose main goal in life is to get drunk when his mother is not watching, Katerina falls in love with Dikoi's nephew Boris. Boris reciprocates, and Tikhon's sister, the rebellious Varvara, brings the young lovers together. Katerina, however, is a deeply religious and moral person. She is unable to conceal her infidelity from her husband and his mother, and she expects divine retribution for her sin: she believes she will be killed by a thunderbolt and punished in the next life. Unable to withstand the pressure, she commits suicide by throwing herself into the Volga.

Dobroliubov was the first to respond to the play with his essay "A Ray of Light in the Kingdom of Darkness" in which he portrays the traditional life of the merchant class as a "dark kingdom" and presents Katerina's suicide as an act of heroic protest against this darkness, making her, symbolically, "a ray of light." Several critics disagreed. Pisarev saw Katerina not as a bold protester but as a victim of the "dark kingdom"; the *pochvennik* Grigor´ev, in his 1860 essay "After the 'Storm' by Ostrovsky. Letters to Ivan Sergeevich Turgenev" ("Posle 'Grozy' Ostrovskogo. Pis´ma k Ivanu Sergeevichu Turgenevu") argued that Ostrovsky's intention was not to condemn the milieu he portrayed, but to present it as it was, in an unbiased way. He even saw "daring poetry" and "joyous passion" in the scene in which Katerina decides to give herself to Boris.[46] Despite the fact that Ostrovsky, leaning toward Slavophilism, tended to present the oppressive atmosphere in some merchant families as an aberration, as a distortion of traditional family relations, Dobroliubov's interpretation of *The Storm* is still dominant among Russian critics.

Leskov's "Lady Macbeth of Mtsensk" also portrays a merchant family destroyed by passion. Katerina, married to the well-to-do merchant Zinovy Izmailov, lives with her much older husband and his father, Boris. The couple is childless, which greatly distresses both Zinovy and Boris. Bored by her idle life, Katerina takes a young lover, the clerk Sergei. Their torrid love affair leads to pregnancy. When her affair is discovered, Katerina first poisons Boris, then kills Zinovy with Sergei's help, and finally, also with Sergei's help, smothers little Fedor, Zinovy's and Boris's relative who is a lawful heir to their business. The murderers are discovered, arrested, tried, flogged in the marketplace, and sentenced to hard labor in Siberia. While on the way to Siberia with a large group of other prisoners, Sergei abandons Katerina and begins an affair with another woman. Unable to endure their teasing and insults, Katerina uses the opportunity when the party is crossing the Volga on a ferry to grab her rival and jump with her into the water, drowning her and perishing herself in the process. Unlike Ostrovsky's Katerina, Leskov's heroine is not meek, or religious, or morally sound. Like Shakespeare's Lady Macbeth, she is stronger and more decisive than her male partner and does not hesitate to get what she wants. It is noteworthy that Leskov does not present his heroine as purely evil: she is simply a woman who does not have a sense of right and wrong. Katerina inspires mixed feelings of horror and admiration, while the weak and opportunistic Sergei pales in comparison to her display of willpower and self-determination. It is perhaps Katerina's extraordinary (one may say, Shakespearian) single-mindedness in achieving her goals that inspired Dmitry Shostakovich's 1934 opera *Katerina Izmailova*.

Throughout most of the nineteenth century, peasants are portrayed both as suffering and moral. Tolstoy, too, mostly presents peasants as models to emulate. In his play *The Power of Darkness*, however, Tolstoy portrays the misbehavior of peasants, particularly women, and its disastrous consequences. His play tells the story of a peasant family destroyed by a series of immoral and criminal acts. The majority of its characters lack any sense of right and wrong, and it is hard to say who begins the chain of misdeeds. Anisia, married to the rich and sickly Petr, cheats on him with their hired hand Nikita. With the help of Nikita's mother, Matrena, she poisons her husband in order to inherit his money and marry Nikita. Nikita, in turn, cheats on her with different women, including her stepdaughter Akulina. Akulina becomes pregnant and gives birth. To preserve her marriageability, Anisia and Matrena force Nikita to murder the baby and bury it in the cellar. Nikita, bad as he is, does so only reluctantly. This act wakes him up and, tormented by the memories of the baby's cries, he comes to his moral senses and publicly confesses on the day of Akulina's marriage, taking all the crimes committed in the course of the play upon himself. It is hard to say who among the culprits is more to blame: the lustful Anisia, the greedy Matrena, or the womanizing Nikita. Nikita's confession, however, reveals that his ruin began when he seduced and abandoned an orphan, Marina. The subtitle of the play ("If a Claw Is Caught the Bird Is Lost," that is, "Kogotok uziaz, vsei ptichke propast′") and its epigraph from Matthew 5:28–29 on the dangers of lust confirm that it was Nikita's sin against Marina that triggered the criminal chain of events. His confession, however, gives hope for his salvation. As his God-fearing father Akim says, embracing him before his arrest: "God will forgive you, my dear child. You haven't had mercy on yourself, He will have mercy on you!"[47] In contrast, neither Anisia nor Matrena show any remorse and, presumably, will burn in hell. The play is the grimmest of Tolstoy's works: the murder of the baby happens right before the spectators' eyes; for this reason the play was not allowed to be staged for nearly ten years. At the same time, it is his most moralistic work, since there is no clear reason for Nikita to repent. His confession is needed to teach the spectators ethically right behavior and to demonstrate the innate potential for goodness in all people, including peasants.

In contrast to Tolstoy, Chekhov is much less dogmatic in his views on sexuality and morality. Two of his stories—which, incidentally, brought him recognition as a serious writer, "The

Huntsman" ("Eger'," 1885) and "Agafia" (1886)—treat marriage and love in idiosyncratic ways. The first describes an encounter between the huntsman Egor and his wife Pelageia. They were married against his will, never consummated their marriage, and Egor intends to keep it this way despite Pelageia's obvious deep and tender love for him. He is proud of his status as a huntsman and of his reputation as the best shot in the district. He cherishes the privileges that his position as the huntsman employed by the local landowner affords him—he loves the freedom and the communion with nature that comes with it. He despises Pelageia for being just a peasant woman, working hard to feed herself. He is blunt, even cruel when explaining the difference between them: "Do you really think we are a couple? I am an idler, I am spoiled and free to roam, but you are a laborer, a peasant; you live in filth and you're always bent over double."[48] In the scene of their parting, Egor's contempt for Pelageia is blatant: he starts to leave, then pauses and looks back, cruelly raising her hopes that he might have changed his mind. Instead, he presses a ruble into her hand and walks off, leaving her distraught but still in love with him.

In "Agafia," the heroine seems to be in a better situation: her husband, a railroad switchman, "a young and rugged fellow ... came off the line every night to be with her."[49] And yet, she is attracted to Savka, a man similar to Egor of "The Huntsman": he does not want to lead a life that involves any kind of real labor, either. He loves fishing, hunting, catching nightingales with his bare hands, and just enjoying nature. To make him useful, the village gives him a job normally reserved for old men: to be a watchman at the communal gardens. It suits Savka very well. Not only is he left alone to do what he enjoys the most, but it also allows him to receive the village women with whom he is very popular. The narrator of the story likes to visit him—ostensibly, to fish, but actually, as he confesses, just to enjoy "the peaceful tramping-about, the eating off-schedule, the chats with Savka, and the prolonged contacts with quiet summer [night]."[50] On the night of the visit described in the story, Agafia is to come to Savka for the first time. Savka is as contemptuous of her as Egor of Pelageia, but is ready to oblige her as he obliges every woman who shows up at his door. In order to conceal her adventure from her husband, Agafia has to return home as soon as she hears the mail train coming through. Savka, however, suddenly disappears in the woods, to catch a nightingale that sings every night and eludes his capture. Agafia awaits his return, lets the train pass, and stays with Savka until the morning. When she finally leaves, her husband is awaiting her on the other side of the river, ready to beat her in revenge. The narrator and Savka observe her hesitant progress, until she musters the courage to approach her wrathful husband with "a firm step."[51]

The freedom-loving Egor and Savka resemble Ermolai, the narrator's companion on the hunting trips in Turgenev's Notes of a Hunter, who, like them, refuses to live in the village, rarely sees his wife, and has affairs with local women. Aleksandr S. Dolinin suggests that Egor and Pelageia can also be usefully compared with Turgenev's Viktor and Akulina from "The Tryst" ("Svidanie," 1850; included in Notes of a Hunter): the women are meek, the men arrogant. But Dolinin uses the similarity to stress the difference between Turgenev's and Chekhov's narrative techniques: Turgenev presents an emotionally subjective description of his characters, whereas Chekhov keeps his narrator removed, creating an "illusion of objectivity."[52] Dolinin argues that the differences in point of view and tone betray fundamental differences in artistic method.

Chekhov's heroines differ vividly from Turgenev's also because they display sexual desire far more openly and even boldly (as in Agafia's case). Furthermore, Chekhov often represents this desire as irrational and irresistible. Significantly, in this his peasant women do not differ from upper-class women. In his story "A Calamity" ("Neschast'e," 1886), an upper-class heroine, like Agafia, married and seemingly content, cannot resist her sexual attraction to a family friend, knowing full well that this is wrong and that she will be sorry. Chekhov anticipates the new, freer, more tolerant attitude toward sexuality characteristic for emerging modernism, and shows that Eros trumps morals and rational thinking equally for peasant and aristocratic women; his narrators do not pass judgment on his characters' behavior.

The problem of passing judgment is at the center of Chekhov's story "Peasant Women." It is a story within a story, and the frame is as important as the internal narrative. The story's title (that stresses the low-class origin of the female characters) may refer more to three peasant women of the frame than to the heroine of the inserted narrative.[53] Both the inserted story and the frame address the question of marriage, love, and unfaithfulness. The inserted story is told by a businessman, Matvei, who had an affair with his ward's late mother, Masha, while her husband, Vasia, was conscripted to the army. When Vasia returns, Matvei is eager to part with her (he is looking for a suitable bride), but she refuses to go back to her husband. Vasia, unable to contain himself, gives Masha a brutal beating. Remorseful, he pleads to God to take his life; he soon dies of what is presumed to be cholera. People begin gossiping, his body is exhumed, and arsenic is found in his stomach. Masha is arrested and tried, and Matvei is the star witness against her. Convicted and sentenced to hard labor in Siberia, Masha dies on the way, and her son is sent back, to be taken in by Matvei "for the salvation of [his; that is, Matvei's] soul."[54] Matvei's listeners in the frame, both men and women, do not doubt Masha's guilt. The women in particular have reasons to pity Masha, because their life experiences are similar to hers. And yet they believe her to be guilty.

Like these listeners, until recently critics and scholars did not question Masha's guilt. There is a good reason for that: the narrator of the inserted story, the despicable Matvei, leaves no doubt that Masha is guilty, and the narrator of the frame does not challenge his assertion in any way. The attentive reader and critic can suspect that she may be innocent, but cannot prove it.[55] Unlike Tolstoy in *The Power of Darkness*, Chekhov refuses to give the reader grounds for judgment. Furthermore, the harshest "judge" of Masha's purported crime, Matvei, is so vile in his condemnation of her that he makes the very idea of judging another's misdeeds repulsive. And yet most readers do believe that Masha poisoned her husband, even if they do not blame her for the crime. This result is disturbing—it certainly bothered Tolstoy who wanted to have his publishing house Posrednik publish the story. As a compromise, the story appeared in the Posrednik edition without the most disconcerting passages—those where Varvara, one of the women listening to Matvei's story, suggests murdering the men of the house. Chekhov's tacit claim that, most often, people, including writers, do not know the real truth—and should not pretend they do—was difficult for Tolstoy to accept. It also seems that in this story Chekhov examines (and doubts) his own philosophy of withholding judgment as a writer: in the end, the readers cannot help but judge—not Masha, perhaps not even Varvara, but most certainly the chief judge and accuser, Matvei.[56]

Chekhov's refusal to pass judgment in general is one of the most important features of his writing style. This restraint is most striking in his stories about sexuality. He writes in such a way that a clear-cut answers to the questions of who is good and who is bad, who is right and who is wrong are almost impossible to tease out. There are a few exceptions ("The Grasshopper" ["Poprygun'ia," 1892], "Ariadna," 1895), but for the most part Chekhov not only leaves it up to his readers to make their decisions, but also frames his narratives in such a way that these decisions are inevitably ambivalent.

Fallen women and seductresses

The first love story in the modern Russian prose tradition, Karamzin's "Poor Liza," portrays a fallen woman: betrayed by her earnest love for Erast, Liza succumbs to his seduction;

abandoned by him, she drowns herself. The story contains a frank description of their sexual encounter (something unheard-of again in high-brow Russian prose until Turgenev's *On the Eve*, in which Elena and Insarov consummate their love before the marriage). "Poor Liza" generated a host of imitations by middling Sentimentalist writers, such as Aleksandr Izmailov's (1779–1831) "Poor Masha" ("Bednaia Masha," 1801), anonymous "Unfortunate Margarita" ("Neschastnaia Margarita," 1803), and even a retelling of *Daphnis and Chloe*, "Poor Chloe" ("Bednaia Khloia," 1804), published under the pen name Karra-Kakuello-Gudzhi. All these stories feature unlucky love, but not all follow Karamzin's formula: poor Masha unknowingly marries a bigamist, while the unfortunate Margarita is prohibited from marrying her beloved, commits a crime after his death, and ends up in a convent.

A more serious engagement with Karamzin's story is Pushkin's "The Station Master," in which Dunia, the young daughter of a lowly clerk, runs away with Minsky (whose last name signals his aristocratic birth), a dashing cavalry captain. Pushkin follows Karamzin in making the lovers socially unequal; Dunia's father, telling her story to the tale's narrator, several times calls her "poor Dunia." The father fully expects her adventure to end badly; dejected, he drinks himself to death. Pushkin, however, rejects Karamzin's (and the station master's) pessimism. He hints at the possibility of a different ending early in the story, when his narrator looks at pictures on the walls of the station master's home: they tell the parable of the prodigal son, which, of course, ends in return and reconciliation. Dunia, too, eventually comes back, and she is now well-off: she arrives in a carriage, richly dressed, and with several children in tow. Pushkin does not tell the reader whether she is married to Minsky or simply is supported by him; another possibility, suggested by Pushkin's reference to Ivan Dmitriev's 1791 ballad "Caricature" ("Karikatura"), is that Dunia has become rich on her own, like Grunia, a character in Dmitriev's poem, who kept a den for robbers. One thing is clear: Dunia is rich. In contrast to the story of poor Liza, the story of prodigal Dunia thus offers a payoff for being adventurous, even though Dunia returns home too late to reconcile with her father.

Pushkin also plays with Karamzin's plot in another of his *Tales of Belkin*, "The Squire's Daughter" ("Baryshnia-krest'ianka," also translated as "Mistress into Maid"). Liza, a young gentry girl (the *baryshnia* of the title) dresses as a peasant girl, Akulina, in order to get to know Aleksei, a young gentleman, whom she cannot meet undisguised because their fathers are on bad terms. Aleksei promptly falls in love with the pretty and bright Akulina (she "learns" to read and write surprisingly quickly) and decides to marry her regardless of the social obstacles. Only then does he find out, to his joy, that Liza and Akulina are the same girl, and his father, who has mended fences with his former enemy, has no objections to the marriage. The social differences that prevented Karamzin's Erast from marrying poor Liza turn out to be nonexistent in Pushkin's playful story.

Karamzin's "Poor Liza" thus created a tradition with which Russian fiction about love had to reckon.[57] Lermontov's Bela in *A Hero of Our Time* (the chapter was first published separately in 1839); Dostoevsky's Varenka in *Poor Folk*, Natasha in *The Insulted and Injured* (*Unizhennye i oskorblennye*, 1861), Nastasia Filippovna in *The Idiot*, Dasha in *Demons*, and Liza in *The Adolescent*; Turgenev's Zinaida in *First Love*; Chekhov's Aniuta; Tolstoy's Katiusha in *Resurrection*—all these heroines are, like poor Liza, fallen women used by the socially superior men. Their fates differ, however. Bela, a Circassian kidnapped, seduced, and half-abandoned by Pechorin, dies at the hands of her former Circassian admirer. Varenka marries her seducer; Natasha, abandoned by her lover, returns to her family. Nastasia Filippovna, even though she frees herself from her seducer, is so psychologically damaged that she cannot believe herself deserving to be loved by anyone decent; she is murdered by Rogozhin, whose lover she becomes to punish herself. Both Dasha in *Demons* and Liza in *The Adolescent* are strong enough to survive seductions and carry on. Turgenev's Zinaida apparently has a child by her seducer, but later marries an aristocrat and dies in childbirth. Tolstoy's Katiusha—who turned to prostitution after having been seduced by a young aristocrat, was falsely accused of murder and sent to Siberia—finds new love among political prisoners. Chekhov's Aniuta, a live-in lover and breadwinner for a series of university students who graduate and abandon her, is likely to continue her sad subservience.

The most idiosyncratic response to the Karamzinian tradition is Ivan Bunin's "Light Breathing" ("Legkoe dykhanie," 1916). It is the story of a fifteen-year-old girl Olia Meshcherskaia, seduced by her father's friend. But Olia is a seductress herself—she flirts not only with her first much older lover, but also with her peer, whose head she turns to such a degree that he attempts suicide. Even more shockingly, she seduces and abandons a socially inferior older man, a Cossack officer with a plebian appearance. Despite all the differences from her predecessor, Olia ends up as badly: provoked by Olia, the Cossack officer shoots her to death. The question remains: is Olia a shallow girl overcome by her own sexuality or is she just too young to contend with Eros? Or is it Thanatos, which underlies her vivacity and tendency to cross all sorts of boundaries, that leads to her death?[58] At the same time, her essence, her gentle breathing, a clear symbol both of Olia's triviality and of life, escapes death, rejoining the sky and the cold spring wind in the story's rich closing description.

Pushkin's Dunia in "The Station Master" is seduced, but she is an adventuress herself: even if she cries while leaving her old life behind, she does it by her own choice. And when her father comes to St. Petersburg to bring her home, she does not follow him and allows Minsky to throw him out of her apartment. Pushkin's Liza in "The Squire's Daughter" also crosses boundaries of proper behavior, as does Masha in "The Snowstorm" ("Metel'," also included in *The Tales of Belkin*): she elopes to marry her beloved Vladimir, only to marry a stranger by mistake. Sheer luck brings her and her mysterious husband together; they fall in love with each other and find out that they are already married and can live happily ever after. Turgenev's young Zinaida in *First Love* is even more inclined to risk-taking: she flirts with a whole crowd of men (including the young son of her lover), encouraging their amorous feelings for her. She becomes a lover of a married man and gets pregnant by him. Bunin's Olia, despite her young age, is perceived by some readers as a seductress in her own right: why should she flirt with Maliutin? Tease a boy Shenshin? Deceive the Cossack officer? However, a real seductress is Maria Polozova of Turgenev's "Torrents of Spring" ("Veshnie vody," 1872): ruthless and pitiless, she makes men fall in love with her, using her uncanny charms to attract them and causing them to forget their previous attachments—as Sanin, the protagonist of Turgenev's novella, does in abandoning his bride Jemma. The heroine of Chekhov's "Mire" ("Tina," 1886), the Jewess Susanna, possesses the same terrifying magic ability to attract men. Furthermore, she uses this ability not only to make men abandon women they love, but also to fleece them.

Viktor Pelevin's (b. 1962) "Nika" (1999) cleverly deconstructs the traditional representations of fallen women. It begins with references to "Light Breathing"; allusions to other love stories follow (Tolstoy's *Anna Karenina*, Gaito Gazdanov's [1903–71] 1930 novel *An Evening at Claire's* [*Vecher u Kler*], Aleksandr Blok's 1906 poem "The Stranger" ["Neznakomka"], Nabokov's 1928 poem "Lilith"). Pelevin's heroine, Nika, is not the narrator-protagonist's equal: unlike him, she is ignorant and sensual (at one point, the narrator observes her engage in a wild sexual act with a stranger). The narrator is annoyed by her shallowness, but also intrigued by it: he yearns in vain to see the world the way Nika does, without the interference of cultural references. At the end, when she is killed by a speeding car, the readers realize, to their shock, that Nika is a cat. In his story, Pelevin introduces layers of visible and invisible intertexts, but the literary game also has the goal of tricking the reader into thinking that this is just another story of a fallen woman. "Nika," which seems to be a glib joke at the expense of the high-brow Russian convention of writing about love, in fact posits important questions that confront contemporary writers and readers alike: Is it possible to write without using intertexts? Is it possible to read without looking for them? If yes, how can this be done? Pelevin leaves the questions unanswered.

Revolutionaries

With the rise of revolutionary and then terrorist movements in Russia, women began to participate in these political activities, and literature reflected it. Elena of Turgenev's *On the Eve* is attracted to an exotic and heroic man outside her social circle: Insarov is a Bulgarian fighting to chase the Turks out of his native land. Elena becomes his lover, then marries him against her parents' wishes, leaves Russia with him to share his dangerous and heroic life, and carries on his struggle after he dies. She is the first heroine in nineteenth-century Russian literature who chooses such an activist path. Later, Turgenev responded to the participation of women in terrorist activities. His poem in prose, "Threshold" ("Porog," 1878; illegally published 1882 or 1883; first legal Russian publication 1905), was written in the wake of the trial and acquittal of Vera Zasulich. It presents a generalized image of a young woman about to leave her comfortable life behind to join the terrorist movement. The poem is allegorical, beginning with the title that indicates a radical change, following with the description of the heroine's future life as "dreary haze/darkness" ("ugriumaia mgla"); and ending with the mention of the "heavy curtain" ("tiazhelaia zavesa") that falls as she steps over the threshold, cutting her off from her past. The ending reflects the split in attitudes to women revolutionaries: some call such a heroine a fool, but others disagree and see her as a saint.

The tendency to sympathize with women who have been punished for political crimes is also evident in Korolenko's story "A Strange One" ("Chudnáia," 1880). It is a story within a story, and the interpolated tale is narrated by a gendarme, whose duty is to escort political prisoners to Siberian exile, including the narrator of the frame story. On one of the stops, he tells his prisoner about a young woman he had to escort to Siberia years ago. Despite the woman's hostility, he pitied her, particularly when he realized that she had tuberculosis. The gendarme violated his duty out of sympathy: he told her where her place of exile would be, manipulated his supervisor, a drunken and cruel boor, for her sake, and offered her food. The young prisoner, however, did not respond to his kindness, remaining distant and even spiteful. Yet the gendarme could not help caring for her, and even visited her during his next tour to Siberia. The young woman remained steadfastly hostile, but at the end of his visit she agreed to shake his hand even as she re-emphasized that they must be enemies forever. She died shortly thereafter. Returning to St. Petersburg, the gendarme met her elderly mother who was on her way to join her daughter in her exile. The gendarme did not have the courage to tell her that her daughter had died. The experience has profoundly changed him: even though he continues his service out of necessity, he cannot forget the "angry girl," as he calls her: "And now too: sometimes I see her as if she stood right before my eyes" (*tak i stoit, byvaet, pered glazami*).[59]

Tolstoy's *Resurrection* features a large number of prisoners sent to Siberia for political crimes, many of them women. Almost all are portrayed with respect and sympathy. Seen through the eyes of the fallen aristocrat Nekhliudov, they deserve help, compassion, and often admiration. Two women stand out in particular. One is Vera Bogodukhovskaia, whom Nekhliudov long ago provided with money to attend courses on midwifery. At the time when the novel's action unfolds, she is held in the same prison where Katiusha is confined, having been arrested and condemned as a member of the People's Will Party (Narodnaia volia, founded in 1879). She writes Nekhliudov a note asking him to help a young colleague who is in solitary confinement in a St. Petersburg prison. Nekhliudov fulfills her request (as he does with all requests coming from prisoners). Vera also gives him good advice on how to make Katiusha's life easier. It is following her suggestion that Nekhliudov succeeds in placing Katiusha with political prisoners during overnight stops. Association with them allows Katiusha to grow spiritually and leave behind the tormenting memories of her time as a prostitute. She also meets her future husband, Simonson, among the political prisoners. Another female political prisoner, portrayed with even more sympathy, is Maria Pavlovna Shchetinina, a general's daughter and a revolutionary who is condemned for shooting a policeman (actually killed by someone else). She is kind to everyone, particularly children; a virgin, she is initially wary of Katiusha because of her past as a prostitute; but she makes an effort to be kind to her, and the two women become friends. It is Maria who helps Nekhliudov and Katiusha sort out their relationships and thus frees Katiusha to choose Simonson as her partner and turns Nekhliudov toward the Gospels and spiritual revival. Remarkably, describing political prisoners of both sexes with sympathy and showing both married and unmarried women, Tolstoy singles out for particular approval not only a virgin, but a virgin who has aversion to sex. Both chaste and caring, Maria is a living example of the moral benefits of radical chastity, advocated by Tolstoy in *Kreutzer Sonata* and, especially, in an afterword to it. It seems like Tolstoy finally managed to create an ideal heroine who resolved his conflicted feelings about sex.

CASE STUDY Terrorism

The emancipation of the serfs on February 19, 1861 marked the beginning of changes in Russia traditionally known as the Great Reforms. Whether the emancipation precipitated other reforms is debatable, but liberalization of other institutions—education (1863), judiciary (1864), local government (1864), and censorship (1864)—quickly ensued. It is amid these liberal changes that the terrorist movement began in Russia with Dmitry Karakozov's attempt at Alexander II's life in April of 1866. The Investigative Commission directly attributed Karakozov's act to the pernicious influence of Chernyshevsky's *What Is to Be Done?* and even suspected that Chernyshevsky knew in advance about Karakozov's planned assassination attempt.[60] Acts of terrorism would continue on and off until the revolutions of 1917 and right after, succeeded in 1918 by the so-called Red Terror, a campaign of mass arrests and executions administered by the Bolshevik government.

As Lynn Ellen Patyk points out, historians "credit revolutionaries in mid-nineteenth-century Russia with the 'invention' of modern insurgent terrorism." Insurgent, or terrorism "from below" (as opposed to state terrorism or terrorism "from above," as practiced in 1790s France or communist Russia) seeks to change the course of political events and, in doing so, it "differs from instrumental violence in its form (it is 'repeated') and its goals (communicative and affective)." It relies on memory and therefore has to be spectacular, that is, to have actors and spectators. Whether it is the terrorists who are spectators of the public reaction to the violent act (as Vera Figner [1852–1942] suggests), or the public for whom the violent act is staged, an act has to be repeated to be remembered.[61]

This is precisely how the events unfolded in Russia. Karakozov was hanged in September of 1866, but government reaction in the form of "White Terror" only temporarily slowed the radicalization of the opposition. Sergei Nechaev, the author of the ruthless *Catechism of a Revolutionary* (1869), founded a secret revolutionary society People's Reprisal (*Narodnaia rasprava*) that same year. The society's one and only action was the murder that November of I. I. Ivanov, who had left the society over a disagreement with Nechaev. After the arrests of some of the participants, Nechaev fled abroad, was arrested in Zurich in 1872, and handed over to the Russian police as a common, rather than political, criminal. He was sentenced to twenty years of Siberian exile, but was instead secretly incarcerated in the Alexei Ravelin in the Peter and Paul Fortress and died in prison in 1882. Nechaev was the first to formulate a program of large-scale political terror and to begin practicing it, albeit with the sordid murder of a fellow conspirator.

That murder temporarily discredited Nechaev's tactics in the eyes of the revolutionaries. Instead of embracing violence, politically minded young men and women espoused the movement of "going to the people." They began migrating to the countryside to help the peasants ("the people" of the movement's name) and working as teachers, agronomists, or doctors, but would also put on the traditional peasant attire and agitate against the government. The peasants, however, did not trust the young propagandists and regularly denounced them to the police. The government responded with mass arrests, which by the late 1870s turned the activists back to terrorism.

In January of 1878, Vera Zasulich attempted to assassinate Fedor Trepov, the governor-general of St. Petersburg. At the trial, she claimed that she wanted to punish Trepov for ordering an imprisoned fellow-radical to be flogged. Zasulich was found not guilty by a sympathetic jury. In addition to her skillful lawyer and her youth and sincerity (she spoke briefly on her own behalf), the nature of Trepov's transgression helped acquit Zasulich: the Russian elite was highly sensitive to the issue of physical violence; the dishonorable act could be redeemed only by challenging the offender to a duel, which the imprisoned radical was obviously unable to do. By shooting at Trepov, Zasulich—as her defense lawyer, Petr Aleksandrov, put it—symbolically cleansed the dishonor of the corporal punishment, something her flogged comrade could not do himself. It is remarkable how strongly the public, including Dostoevsky and Turgenev, supported Zasulich's acquittal. Discussing the upcoming verdict with a liberal journalist G. K. Gradovsky, Dostoevsky expressed his conviction that the verdict should be "Go, but do not do that again."[62] Dostoevsky's opinion was influenced by Zasulich's statement during the trial: "It is terrible to raise your hand [to kill] a person...but I believed I had to do this." Dostoevsky, who attended the trial and heard these words, quoted them in his notebook: "Zasulich: 'It is terrible to raise your hand to spill the blood'—this hesitation was more moral than the actual spilling of the blood."[63] Ivan Turgenev's prose poem "The Threshold" was another sympathetic treatment of a woman terrorist, likely based on Zasulich. The last lines of the poem portray Russian society as deeply divided between sympathy and condemnation.

In August of the same year, Sergei Kravchinsky (1851–95) sought to reprise Zasulich's act by stabbing the chief of Russian secret police, Nikolai Mezentsov. Kravchinsky escaped arrest and left Russia. Under the pseudonym Stepniak ("the son of the steppes"), he became well known in the West as a journalist and writer. Living as an exile in England, he became friends with many English intellectuals, including Constance Garnett, whom he encouraged to finish her first attempt at translating from Russian (Ivan Goncharov's novel, *A Common Story*) and thus started her on her remarkable career as a translator.

Ever since Karakozov's attempt, Alexander II remained a prime target for the terrorists, escaping two more attempts (in which both Vera Figner and Sofia Perovskaia [1853–81] participated), until March 1, 1881 when the members of the People's Will finally succeeded at planting a lethal bomb. The Executive Committee of the People's Will addressed a letter to Alexander III, justifying the assassination—and violence in general—as a means of political change. The letter promised to disband their organization if the demands for basic civil liberties enjoyed in Western nations were met. In response, the entire Executive Committee was arrested, tried, and hanged, including Perovskaia, the first woman executed in Russia for a political crime. Ironically, earlier on the day of the assassination,

Alexander II signed an *ukaz* creating commissions to prepare reforms in various branches of the administration (the so-called Loris–Melikov constitution); the *ukaz* was repealed by Alexander III. Perhaps because of Alexander II's increasingly liberal policies, his assassination had little public support, especially among the deeply monarchist peasantry, and the regicide prompted retaliatory pogroms against the Jews in the Pale, who were made scapegoats. Nonetheless, the People's Will continued its activity. In 1887, the organization's radical wing attempted to assassinate Alexander III. The would-be assassins were swiftly arrested and executed, including Lenin's older brother, Aleksandr Ul'ianov. This failure, the severe repressions, and the absence of public support led to the demise of the People's Will.

Terror as a mode of political change returned under Nicholas II. Especially active was the Socialist Revolutionary Party (SR, 1902–11), particularly its Combat Organization (Boevaia organizatsiia). Its first leader was Grigory Gershuni (1870–1908), and under his leadership, the minister of interior, Dmitry Sipiagin, was assassinated, and an attempt was made on the life of the ultra-conservative Procurator of the Holy Synod Konstantin Pobedonostsev. In 1903, Gershuni was replaced by Evno Azef (1869–1918), a double agent who collaborated with the Okhrana since 1892. Under Azef's leadership, the Organization assassinated the new minister of interior, Viacheslav Pleve, and Grand Duke Sergey Aleksandrovich. In 1908, Azef was exposed as a police agent and fled the country, leaving the Combat Organization in disarray. Its last leader, Boris Savinkov (1879–1925), failed to rebuild it, and it was suspended in 1911.

Some historians consider the year 1911—in which Petr Stolypin, the major statesman of the time, was also assassinated by a probable double agent, Dmitry (Mordekhai) Bogrov (1887–1911)—as the end of the Russian terrorist movement. However, there was a further burst of terrorist acts even after 1917, when a series of terrorist acts were committed, mostly by Socialist Revolutionaries, and these too should be taken into account. In July of that year, the German ambassador Count Mirbach was assassinated; on August 30, Moisei Uritsky, the first head of Petrograd Cheka, was killed; and on the same day, in Moscow, Fanny Kaplan (1890–1918) attempted to assassinate Lenin. The Red Terror was proclaimed by the Bolshevik government on September 5, 1918, ostensibly in response to this wave of violence. The tsar and his family were shot in July of 1918, and this killing can be considered the last terrorist act by the radicals against the Russian monarchy and, at the same time, the beginning of state terror. The murder also harks back to what some historians consider to be the first stirrings of Russian terrorist impulses: the plans by some Decembrists to assassinate the Imperial family in order to precipitate social and political change.

Both literature and religion provided powerful behavioral models for Russian terrorists. Turgenev's *Fathers and Sons* portrays a young radical, Bazarov, who preaches nihilism, which he presents as the only rational outlook for a rational person. In *Underground Russia: Revolutionary Profiles and Sketches from Life* (original in Italian, 1882), Stepniak-Kravchinsky writes about nihilism as the precursor of terrorism.[64] But he makes an important distinction: "The Nihilist seeks his own happiness at whatever cost. His ideal is a 'reasonable' and 'realistic' life. The Revolutionist seeks the happiness of others at whatever cost, sacrificing for it his own."[65] Nikolai Chernyshevsky's *What Is to Be Done?* was another powerful influence. Its minor but memorable character, the rationalist Rakhmetov, was nicknamed "rigorist" (the rigorous one) by his comrades. In order to prepare himself for arrests and imprisonments, he leads an ascetic life: he sleeps on a bed of nails, eats only foodstuffs accessible to the poor and even those in small amounts, and does not waste time on friendship, love, and reading—unless they serve his cause. Not a terrorist himself, Rakhmetov offered the future terrorists useful patterns of behavior. *What Is to Be Done?* was Lenin's favorite book, which he reread after his brother's execution in 1887. Even though Lenin dismissed individual political terrorism, he did not hesitate to implement state terror when he came to power.

Religion provided terrorists with models of behavior that were an alternative to rationalism, and the influence of religion was remarkable. This is not to say that terrorists were religious, although some were fervent Christians as children. In her memoirs, Vera Zasulich writes how, as a child, she was deeply affected by the plight of Christ. She did not seek salvation, but rather "wanted to serve Him, to save Him."[66] This love for Christ was transformed into a desire to sacrifice herself for human sufferers, including political prisoners. A readiness for martyrdom was evident in Zasulich's behavior in the courtroom and engendered widespread public admiration. She was not alone in her longing for self-sacrifice, and for many radicals it became "a goal in itself."[67] Religious modes of behavior served as both inspiration and justification. Stepniak stressed that a revolutionary's "ideal is a life full of suffering and a martyr's death."[68] Whenever the public in Russia and abroad expressed sympathy for the terrorists, they imagined them as sacrificial lambs, regardless of their actual actions and behavior. A striking example of religious models' shaping the public's imagination is the reputation of Maria Spiridonova, the member of the SR party who assassinated the Tambov governor G. N. Luzhenovsky in 1906. According to accounts that began to circulate soon after her arrest, she was severely beaten by the Cossacks who arrested her, sexually assaulted, and (according to some reports) infected with syphilis. The accounts originated with Spiridonova herself and were embellished and disseminated by the liberal press. Her young age (she was twenty-one) and purported sexual innocence made the myth all the more poignant. But the story proved to be highly exaggerated: her beatings were real but not severe, there was no evidence of sexual assault or infection with syphilis.[69] Nonetheless, the verifiability of the charges was less important in the mythologizing of terrorists than the widespread belief in the state's brutality.

Literature not only inspired the terrorist movement but also reacted to it, both negatively and positively. In Dostoevsky's *Demons*, the murder of Shatov is modeled after Ivanov's murder by Nechaev's People's Reprisal, and the characters Petr Verkhovensky and Shchigalev espouse some of Nechaev's views. Leskov produced several so-called anti-nihilist novels, *At Daggers Drawn* among them. This novel is a grotesque portrayal of the nihilist movement becoming increasingly violent. It underscores the total lack of moral principles among the terrorist leaders: they are presented as ruthlessly violent common criminals. Dostoevsky's treatment of terrorism and its destructive influence on society has more depth than Leskov's: Dostoevsky emphasizes both the inviolability of each individual life and the unscrupulousness of the terrorist leaders' tactics.

There were also positive literary reactions to the terrorist movement, and they portrayed the revolutionaries as martyrs. One is Turgenev's poem in prose "The Threshold." Another is Vsevolod Garshin's (1855–88) story "Nadezhda Nikolaevna" (1885), in which the heroine, a prostitute, serves as a model for the portrait of Charlotte Corday painted by the artist Lopatin; she finds salvation in Lopatin but is killed by a jealous former lover. Artists and writers of the time, unable to depict terrorists openly, found ways to represent them indirectly.[70] Ilya Repin's painting *Ivan the Terrible and His Son Ivan* (also known as *Ivan the Terrible Kills His Son*) was interpreted by both the public and Pobedonostsev as "an allegory for state and revolutionary terrorism" (Pobedonostsev banned the exhibition of the painting in Moscow). Similarly, Garshin's story about a young educated woman with the face of Charlotte Corday was understood as an allusion to present-day Russia. The 1908 story by Leonid Andreev (1871–1919), "The Seven Who Were Hanged" ("Rasskaz o semi poveshennykh") presents terrorists as saintly characters. The story describes the last days of two common criminals and five terrorists. The revolutionaries, with one exception, display heroism and compassion before execution. Their behavior impresses one of the common criminals so much that he recognizes the two women terrorists as saints who not only will enter the kingdom of heaven themselves, but will help him, a thief and murderer, be admitted as well. Andrei Bely's *Petersburg* (1916) also addresses the problem of contemporary terrorism in Russia, although with greater complexity and ambivalence.

Several terrorists were writers themselves, including Stepniak, Figner, and Savinkov. Stepniak's two most important works are the documentary account of the terrorist movement, *Underground Russia*, and the novel *The Career of a Nihilist* (1889; *Andrei Kozhukhov* in Russian translation, 1898). Both were addressed to the sympathetic public outside Russia, therefore were originally written in Italian and English, respectively. *Underground Russia* is a collection of essays on the history of Russian revolutionary movement, biographies of Russian radicals, and descriptions of terrorist acts. The second follows the main character's life from the time of his return to Russia from abroad up to his unsuccessful attempt at the czar's life. His failure, uncharacteristically for a terrorist, is caused by emotions: thinking about his young wife destined to become a widow, Andrei forgets to test his pistol and misses his target as a result. Savinkov's most famous work, *The Pale Steed (Kon' blednyi)*, was published in 1909 under the pseudonym V. Ropshin. Savinkov participated in Symbolist literary culture by that time, and his novella shows elements of self-fashioning under its influence. It is a story of a brutal terrorist, George, disappointed by the cause: he kills out of inertia. Unlike his comrade-in-arms, Vania, who fully understands the seriousness of his offense against Christ's teachings, George kills in hatred. The character of George is autobiographical, and Savinkov himself believed that terror was based on hatred.[71] Figner wrote poetry and prose, but is mostly remembered for her three-volume memoir that covers the radical movement from 1876 to 1917. In her memoir, she remarks upon the profound influence of literary critics such as Chernyshevsky and Dobroliubov, but reserved special mention for Nekrasov's narrative poem *Sasha* as inculcating an ethic of concordance between word and deed demanded by revolutionary terrorists.

Having focused on the connections between literature and social identity, and having examined representation of different literary types, we turn in the next chapter to the interrelation of literature and national identity. Just as nineteenth-century literature found moral and psychological categories in which to present socially diverse characters, so it articulated conceptual maps of the Russian Empire as it expanded and worked out the terms in which to describe and understand itself.

8

Narratives of nation-building

URBANIZATION and the consolidation of a multiethnic empire ushered a new stage of cultural development in Russia, with the expansion of universities, the growth of the print industry, and the rise of cultural institutions. State and ecclesiastical education was reorganized at all levels, while scientific societies enjoyed greater freedom of teaching and research, although still operating within the limits imposed by the government. Through book publications and on the pages of thick journals, prominent writers, scientists, and intellectuals contributed to the discussions about the seismic social and economic transformations set in motion by the Age of the Great Reforms. At the same time, ideological battles were waged within various intellectual groups about the tasks of literature and its role in representing Russia's social reality and class structure. The intelligentsia and writers channeled the "accursed questions" of Russian society into forms of writing that flourished in a newly expanded cultural marketplace as a publishing boom made literary production accessible to ever-larger audiences across swaths of the Russian Empire that were marginalized in the past. Literature responded to the disintegration of old patriarchal, agrarian lifestyles under the pressures of modernity; the expansion of state bureaucracy; and the emergence of new revolutionary figures like the nihilist and terrorist. The position of the writer had changed markedly from a gifted amateur to a professional with an essential sociopolitical role. The writers' artistic challenge, and responsibility, was now to adapt the norms of Realism to the representation of the social structures of the Imperial period and to fashion types—which initially, in the 1830s and 1840s, had imitated more mechanically the characters of the physiological sketch—into individualistic heroes that would crystallize the Russian experience as well as live up to the standards of Western fiction.

From the 1800s onward, if not earlier, the project of Russian literature had been to create an independent literary culture, comparable with the traditions of Western Europe, which could succeed on its own merits. To that end, drawing on the genius of Dickens, Balzac, and Stendhal in prose, and Byron, Lamartine, and Heine in poetry, Russian writers created their own gallery of memorable characters, thereby forging a formidable counterpart of the Western models which similarly transcended type as the primary device of psychological realism. It was only natural that a national literature, newly aware of its own maturity, would attempt to work through the negative political and social conditions, turning questions about the state of the nation into a source of creative material.

The dramatization and fictionalization of history

Attention to folk art and historical past gave Russians one way to measure the emergence of a national consciousness—as the need to define what it meant to be Russian.[1] The quest for authenticity reflects the widely held belief of the Romantic movement that the distinctiveness of national cultures is expressed most truly at the popular level. An interest in Russian folklore began to emerge in the late eighteenth century even as cultural pundits and writers worried about national enlightenment and a possible corruption of native values. In 1770–74, Mikhail Chulkov and Nikolai Novikov published *A Collection of Various Songs* (*Sobranie raznykh pesen*), which included both folk and literary songs; in 1790, Ivan Prach (Jan Bohumír Práč) and Nikolai L'vov published *A Collection of Russian Folk Songs with Their Melodies* (*Sobranie narod-nykh russkikh pesen s ikh golosami*). With the rise of Romanticism, and especially after the War of 1812, the interest in native Russian culture grew. It was inevitable that the emphasis in the discourse of cultural identity would shift to features that differentiated Russia from other countries. The first imitations of the Ancients appeared in a series of poetry collections by a number of early nineteenth-century poets (Derzhavin, Merzliakov, and Batiushkov, among others), culminating in the great translation of Homer's *Iliad* by Gnedich. This generation, and the following, also valued native song as a source of inspiration and imitation. In his later poems on Russian folk themes, published in his collection of Anacreontics, Derzhavin explored the pleasures of the countryside, anticipating the attention to native customs and folkloric plots that mark out a national narrative. Dmitriev and Merzliakov also experimented with recreations of Russian folk songs, and some of their imitations acquired the status of genuine folk poetry, such as Dmitriev's "The grey dove moans" ("Stonet sizyi golubochek," 1792) and Merzliakov's "In the middle of the level plain" ("Sredi doliny rovnyia," 1810). Vasily Zhukovsky similarly strove to give ethnographic authenticity to his ballads: even though both his "Liudmila" (1808) and "Svetlana" (1813) are transpositions of Gottfried Bürger's "Lenore," the trappings are Russian, including the names of the heroines (Svetlana being a Russian-sounding poetic name, a translation of Fotina[2]) and the description of Yuletide divination rituals. (In 1831, Zhukovsky translated Bürger's ballade in earnest, publishing it under its original title.) Pushkin's *Ruslan and Liudmila* (1820) followed suit, giving the hero an invented, Russian-sounding name (borrowed from the Russian version of a chivalric romance "The Tale of Eruslan Lazarevich") and the heroine a real Slavic name. The plot, although pseudo-folkloric, sounds authentic as well. In his ballads, Pavel Katenin (1792–1853), in turn, attempted to present Russian peasant life as more genuine and to use an idiom that imitated actual peasant speech. In particular, "Olga" (1816)—another transposition of Bürger's "Lenore"—in its language, imagery, and tropes emulates Russian folk poetry. In his later imitations of Russian folklore, Pushkin began to follow Katenin's lead, rather than Zhukovsky's. Although many of Pushkin's ballads, and virtually all of his fairy tales, had Western origins, the manner in which they were written made his readers believe that their origin was Russian, coming from Pushkin's nanny who lived with him during his exile to his father's estate in Mikhailovskoe. Petr Ershov's (1815–69) fairy tale in verse *The Humpback Horse* (*Konek-gorbunok*, 1834) is perhaps the best literary imitation of folklore, superior both to Pushkin's imitations and to Sergei Aksakov's 1858 Russified Cupid and Psyche story, "A Scarlet Flower" ("Alen'kii tsvetochek").

The sure sign of advancement in defining a particular nation's identity is the ability to reflect on its history through narrative, a feat achieved by Karamzin in his magisterial *History of the Russian State*. Despite his awareness of other models, Karamzin essentially gave future generations a new primary source, a super-chronicle based on massive archival research. Unlike Edward Gibbon's *Decline and Fall of the Roman Empire*, this is not a philosophical history that weighed good and evil over the course of a nation's progress; unlike Montesquieu's *De l'esprit des lois* (1758) or Adam Ferguson's *An Essay on the History of Civil Society* (1767), Karamzin's history does not privilege geographic or anthropological factors. Instead, Karamzin's *History* is a lucid narrative of political activity, closer in design to David Hume's *History of England* (1754–61).[3] The twelve volumes of Karamzin's history paved the way for post-1812 historical fictions: inspired by Sir Walter Scott, Russian writers borrowed plots and characterizations of historical figures from Karamzin's *History*. For example, Karamzin's *History* provided material for Pushkin's *Boris Godunov* (or, as the initial 1825 version of the play was titled, *A Comedy about Tsar Boris and Grishka Otrep'ev* [*Komediia o tsare Borise i Grishke Otrep'eve*]; the title reprises the diction of seventeenth-century Russian plays, in which "comedy" meant "drama") as well as for Aleksei K. Tolstoy's novel *Prince Serebryanyi* (*Kniaz' Serebrianyi*, 1862) and his dramatic trilogy *The Death of Ivan the Terrible* (*Smert' Ivana Groznogo*, 1866), *Tsar Fedor Ioannovich* (1868), and *Tsar Boris* (1870). It is noteworthy that all five works concentrate on the historical period from the reign of Ivan the Terrible to the period known in as the Time of Troubles (from 1598, the death of the last tsar of the Rurik dynasty, to 1613, the election of the first Romanov)—one of the most dramatic and painful in all of Russian history.[4]

The Time of Troubles provided the backdrop to dramas and narratives about Boris Godunov, whose life was transposed from history to drama to opera in the relatively short span of fifty years, from 1824, when volume 11 of Karamzin's *History* that included the narrative of Boris Godunov's reign came out, to 1874, when Modest Mussorgsky's opera was first staged.[5] He was an inherently interesting historical figure, a ruler whose own right to rule was suspect and whose authority was challenged by the False Dimitry, the most notorious of the many Russian pretenders. In the age of Romanticism and in the decades to follow, when ideas of personal authenticity and charismatic power were contested, a writer like Pushkin, wrestling with his own authority as a poet, found a perfect foil in the figure of Boris Godunov. His play about Godunov takes on the era's doubts about how stories might be effectively told; the unsettling confusion over whether Boris Godunov was responsible for the death of Tsarevich Dimitry, the youngest son of Ivan the Terrible, put ethical questions at the center of the play, even as it dramatized the frustrating limits of historiography.[6] Boris's life was a tale, as Monika Greenleaf has said, that could "hijack history."[7]

By the second half of the nineteenth century, historical narrative reached maturity and began to produce scholarly historical treatises: Sergei Solov'ov's (1820–79) *The History of Russia from the Ancient Times* (*Istoriia Rossii s drevneishikh vremen*, 1851–79; 29 volumes) and Vasily Kliuchevsky's (1841–1911) *A Course in Russian History* (*Kurs russkoi istorii*, vols. 1–4, 1904–10; vol. 5 came out posthumously, in 1921), among others. It also produced parodies of historical discourse. One such parody is Saltykov-Shchedrin's *The History of a Town*, a chronicle of the town Glupov ("Foolville") from 1731 to 1825 written by four town record-keepers. It parodies the *Primary Chronicle*, particularly its account of the origin of the Russian people and its report about the invitation to the Varangians to rule over Rus'—the foundation myth of contested veracity that persisted in the Russian historical consciousness and at times dominated the debates on nation-building.[8] *The History of a Town* proceeds with descriptions of all the town's administrators (*gradonachal'niki*), each one of whom is deficient in some grotesque way. The last of them, Ugrium-Burcheev, decides to implement Paul's and Alexander I's statesman Aleksei Arakcheev's (1769–1834) idea of military settlements, built on a grid, with straight streets and identical houses. The original town is demolished, but the new one cannot be built, because the nearby river keeps destroying the new buildings. The unsuccessful project brought about the end of the story. And it is no accident that the history of the town ends in 1825, the year of the Decembrist uprising and Nicholas' accession to the throne; moreover, the name of Ugrium-Burcheev (meaning "Gloomy Grumbler") has political undertones that are not very subtle.

If Saltykov-Shchedrin's *History* is grotesque and satirical, Aleksei K. Tolstoy's long poem *The History of the Russian State from Gostomysl to Timashev* (*Istoriia gosudarstava rossiiskogo ot Gostomysla do Timasheva*, 1868), written in light and merry iambic trimeters, is humorous and amusing. It also begins with the account of the invitation to the Varangians: in some chronicles, it was Gostomysl, the mythical elder (*stareishina*) of Novgorod, who was instrumental in summoning the Varangians to Rus´. The idea of disorderly Novgorodians who needed Varangians to keep order comes from the *Primary Chronicle*, from the entry for the year of 862. The phrase "there is no order in Rus´" is repeated throughout the poem as it wittily retells Russian history up to 1868, when the conservative Aleksei Timashev was appointed minister of interior affairs to keep order.

CASE STUDY *War and Peace*

The burgeoning variety of historical discourses informs Tolstoy's *War and Peace*, allowing the writer to create a uniquely intergeneric work equally at ease in treating historic and human events. Tolstoy arrived at the form of his book only gradually. At first, he planned to write a novel about a Decembrist returning from Siberian exile in the late 1850s, when the participants of the December 14, 1825 uprising against Nicholas I were pardoned by his successor, Alexander II, and began to come home. Feeling that, for the sake of historical accuracy, he needed to start his narrative earlier, Tolstoy began writing a family novel, a story of several families unfolding against the backdrop of the historical events of 1812. The historical part, however, began to grow, and Tolstoy moved the beginning of his narrative to 1805. He also changed the status of the war scenes, making them a part of the action, not just the background. At this point he began thinking about *War and Peace* as a work similar to *The Iliad* and *The Odyssey*; accordingly, he began to call it a "poem" (*poema*, like Gogol's subtitle to *Dead Souls*). Then Tolstoy began to include passages containing his views of historical writing. At this point he began to call his work an epic (*epopeia*), meaning a narrative about important historical events and their national significance. This put the War of 1812 at the center of the work, stressing the patriotic spirit of the book in general. However, ultimately, Tolstoy sought to produce a work that would intertwine human stories with the accounts of military events in order to present a picture of life in all its complexity.

In the end, Tolstoy refused to define the genre of his masterpiece, famously writing in "Some Words about the Book *War and Peace*" ("Neskol´ko slov po povodu knigi 'Voina i mir' "): "It is not a novel, even less is it an epic poem, and still less a historical chronicle. *War and Peace* is what the author wished and was able to express in the form in which it is expressed."[9] For all its provocative thrust, this apophatic definition reflects Tolstoy's own understanding of his idiosyncratic oeuvre. The term "book," which Tolstoy uses in the title of what can be called his afterword to *War and Peace* and repeats in the text of it, being excessively general, almost self-effacing, at the same time refers, with Tolstoy's characteristic impertinence, to the Good Book, the best-known and the most sacred historical account that he and his compatriots could imagine. In his search for the appropriate form for *War and Peace*, Tolstoy thus ended up with a work that aspires, often quite successfully, not simply to convince its readers of the veracity of its version of social, historical, and human developments, but also to make them believe that this work embodies a higher truth. In setting out to write a novel, Tolstoy produced a narrative that, for Russians—as well as generations of readers worldwide—has become the most convincing and credible account of the War of 1812; more importantly, to many readers, it also has come to represent life itself and thus serve as a source to which one turns in order to learn about the essence of the human condition.

Strangely enough, Tolstoy's knowledge of the historical material that could shape his narrative was not particularly profound.[10] It seems that he did not need it, because he obviously did not strive for historical accuracy. For one thing, his account drastically diminished Russia's actual military achievements.[11] Even more strikingly, Tolstoy changes at will the personalities of key historical figures. Napoleon, to take the most conspicuous example, is a caricature of the historically attested charisma and military genius. The character of Kutuzov not only distorts what we know from history, but also changes in the process of the book's elaboration: in accordance with historical reality, Kutuzov began as a clever and even cunning courtier, but became the personification of the Russian national character, as wise and authentic as the fictional Platon Karataev.[12] Soon after the book's publication—and regardless of its initial poor critical reception—Tolstoy's version of events and persons began to replace both the memories of the war and the documented historical accounts.

To achieve the effect of imposing verisimilitude in his narrative, Tolstoy relies on several skillful rhetorical devices. First, the narrative voice is invested with authority that precludes any challenge. Gary Saul Morson calls such declarations "absolute language."[13] Most often, Tolstoy resorts to it when presenting his views on history, for example: "The movement of humanity, arising as it does from innumerable arbitrary human wills, is continuous."[14] The sense of commanding authority is heightened by the fact that this sentence comprises the entire paragraph, that is, stands alone and is not supported by evidence—because it does not need evidence to persuade its readers. This type of language is used throughout the second part of the epilogue and in many passages throughout the novel. Tolstoy also employs absolute language in statements about human nature. To use Morson's example, "Rostov knew by experience that men always lie when describing military exploits."[15] Such a statement does not allow for a single honest account of wartime experiences, and by giving the lie to one participant's account, it reminds the readers just how powerfully true the author has made his fiction in War and Peace.

The other device that prevents Tolstoy's readers from questioning his narrator's statements is the persistent assertion that something is a general rule: "as is always the case," "as it always happens," "as it often happens," and "as it usually happens." Speaking about human behavior, Tolstoy uses these expressions over fifty times in the course of War and Peace. Sometimes they correspond to the readers' own experiences, and thus ring true: "Princess Marya—reluctantly, as is always the case—began telling of the condition in which she had found Prince Andrei."[16] At other times, when viewed critically, these statements turn out to be questionable: "Pierre's physical condition, as is always the case, corresponded to his mental state."[17] And occasionally they are simply nonsensical. Witness the remark about Hélène's ostensible power of speech: "It always happens in contests of cunning that a stupid person gets the better of cleverer one."[18] Cumulatively, these interpolated declarations of supreme authorial confidence are meant to convince the reader that universal rules of human behavior exist and the narrator knows them. And yet the vast narrative itself, with its multitude of individuals and its delight in the particulars of behavior, speech mannerisms, and realia, builds up an equally powerful sense that, if there is any truth at all, it is in the local, the specific, the seemingly unique. That, too, teaches readers to believe in Tolstoy's ability to create an illusion of the real.

The most famous device used by Tolstoy to convince his readers of the veracity of his narrative is defamiliarization (ostranenie). Viktor Shklovsky, in his 1917 article "Art as Device," was the first to classify ostranenie as a rhetorical trope and to establish it as Tolstoy's signature technique. In War and Peace, Tolstoy creates the effect of ostranenie when he shows events through the eyes of a person who is not an expert in what he observes (Pierre in Borodino) or whose expertise has temporarily lapsed (Natasha at the opera). The only civilian among military professionals, Pierre consistently misinterprets his perception of the battle of Borodino. The artillery fire and the movement of regiments seem merry to him, and he wishes "to be there with that smoke, those shining bayonets, that movement, and those sounds."[19] Likewise, he misjudges the importance of Raevsky's famous Redoubt, "which the French regarded as the key to the whole position," seeing it simply as the "spot, on which small trenches had been dug and from which a few guns were firing."[20] Most often, however, Pierre defamiliarizes the experience of death: "Suddenly something happened; the young officer gave a gasp, and bending double sat down on the ground like a bird shot on the wing. Everything became strange, confused, and misty in Pierre's eyes."[21] He views another dead officer with a similar feeling of incomprehension: "He saw the senior officer lying on the earth wall with his back turned as if he were examining something down below."[22] As observed by Pierre, the boundary between life and death becomes blurred, and the dead appear to be going about their daily tasks: sitting down, examining something only they can see. Pierre's refusal to understand scenes of death forces the reader to view war scenes as senseless slaughter.

Natasha's sudden inability to comprehend the operatic conventions on the evening of her first meeting with Anatole Kuragin has become the most often cited example of *ostranenie* since Shklovsky first described the phenomenon. As Natasha watches the stage from the box in which she's seated, the actresses and actors seem to her not the characters they represent but ordinary people doing strange things on the stage: "In the centre of the stage sat some girls in red bodices and white skirts. One very fat girl in a white silk dress sat apart on a low bench, to the back of which a piece of green cardboard was glued. They all sang something."[23] This misapprehension of operatic conventions represents Natasha's ability to see and judge correctly, which she would lose by the end of the evening under the evil influence of Hélène and Anatole: "Natasha no longer thought this strange. She looked about with pleasure, smiling joyfully" and answering in French Hélène's question whether she likes the performance: "Oh, oui."[24]

Tolstoy, however, uses *ostranenie* much more generally and pervasively by often making his narrator a non-expert, who, nonetheless, possesses common sense. We hear this defamiliarizing voice most often when Tolstoy criticizes professional historical accounts of the Napoleonic wars or describes what he considers to be wrongheaded attempts to control and direct historical events. Napoleon frequently becomes the object of defamiliarizing descriptions. His orientalizing and ignorant gaze, directed at Moscow from the Poklonny Hill, is perhaps the most vivid example of this technique. It is used to deflate Napoleon's sense of superiority.[25] Repeatedly assailed by the defamiliarizing mode of narration, the reader develops skepticism toward experts (historians, generals, and, particularly, Napoleon) and learns to trust far more the pseudo-naive authorial point of view or the perspective of unsophisticated observers.

In her book *From the Shadow of Empire*, Olga Maiorova describes yet another narrative technique that helps Tolstoy enhance the veracity of his narrative. By switching to the present tense in his descriptions (particularly, of battle scenes) and by employing the inclusive first-person plural, he collapses "the distance between the text and the reader," which opens the reader to the full impact of the narrator's point of view.[26] It may be added that by doing so Tolstoy also collapses the distance between his narrator and the narrated events, making him a participant in these events. This effect is described by Vasily Grossman (1905–64), in his Tolstoyan epic novel *Life and Fate* (*Zhizn' i sud'ba*, completed in 1960, first published abroad in 1980). One of the Russian generals negatively contrasts journalists reporting on the Battle of Stalingrad to Tolstoy:

Those sons of bitches never see any action themselves. They just sit on the other side of the Volga and write their articles. If someone gives them a good dinner, then they write about him. They're certainly no Tolstoys. People have been reading *War and Peace* for a century and they'll go on reading it for another century. Why's that? Because Tolstoy's a soldier, because he took part in the war himself. That's how he knew who to write about.[27]

When told that Tolstoy was born long after the Patriotic War, the general "flatly refused to believe" this incredible bit of news.[28] The sense of authenticity that Tolstoy creates in his book makes actual chronology irrelevant.

Finally, the very genre of Tolstoy's book, which allows historical and fictional characters to coexist, also helps him present his version of history as correct. The third-person narrator of fiction by definition knows what is true and what is false in his world, and earns the reader's trust many times over in Tolstoy's long novel. When a historical figure enters this fictional world, the laws of fiction begin to apply, and psychological depth, physical detail, and revealing social contexts can come into play. Thus Tolstoy's Kutuzov is a more satisfying, and in some ways more plausible, version of the Russian commander-in-chief than the one we can glean from historical documents; and Tolstoy's petty Napoleon supersedes the brilliant self-made military leader we know from other accounts. This approach works especially well when fiction invades a historian's account. When the veracity of Adolphe Thiers's report on Napoleon's conversation with a Cossack is undermined by way of inserting the fictional Lavrushka into the scene, the device of fiction pushing historical facts is at work. Thiers, writing his *Histoire du Consulat et de L'Empire*, naturally did not know that the man introduced to Napoleon as a Cossack, in Tolstoy's *War and Peace* is Nikolai's drunken orderly. Thiers's ignorance marks him as incompetent, whereas Tolstoy's narrator is revealed as a repository of true knowledge:

> "Le cosaque ignorant la compagnie dans laquelle il se trouvait, car la simplicité de Napoléon n'avait rien qui pût révéler à une imagination orientale la présence d'un souverain, s'entretint avec la plus extrême familiarité des affaires de la guerre actuelle," says Thiers, narrating this episode. In reality Lavrushka having got drunk the day before and left his master dinnerless, had been whipped and sent to the village in quest of chickens, where he engaged in looting till the French took him prisoner. Lavrushka was one of those coarse, bare-faced lackeys who have seen all sorts of things, consider it necessary to do everything in a mean and cunning way, are ready to render any sort of service to their master, and are keen at guessing their master's baser impulses, especially those prompted by vanity and pettiness.
>
> Finding himself in the company of Napoleon, whose identity he had easily and surely recognized, Lavrushka was not in the least abashed but merely did his utmost to gain his new master's favour.[29]

Tolstoy creates the effect of knowing "the way it really was," mocks both Thiers's ignorance and Napoleon's gullibility, and invites the reader to enjoy this insider knowledge.[30]

As historians note, Tolstoy's Russo-centric version of the War of 1812 conformed to Russia's self-image as a nation at the time of the book's publication.[31] Undoubtedly, this ideological overlap also persuaded readers to accept Tolstoy's account as truthful. However, without Tolstoy's narrative strategies, aimed at making the reader believe and trust him, such a smooth substitution of myth for history could not have happened.

Readers, Russian and Western alike, have long become accustomed to the book's idiosyncratic form: if its first readers as well as critics were perplexed by it, "it is by now a
commonplace to regard *War and Peace* as one of the greatest novels—if not the greatest—
ever written, as a book that virtually defines its genre."[32] While the readers simply "famil-
iarized" (in Morson's apt observation) the work, the theorists of the novel wrestled with
its generic description, trying to find the appropriate designation. For Georgy Lukacs, the
epic qualities make *War and Peace* the modern version of Homeric epic because of the
larger-than-life role of the hero. Whereas the novelistic hero, in his view, has to contend
with the falsity of the modern age and the hypocrisy of society and its stale conventions,
the epic hero is an agent of history who rises above the divisions of his time. While this
theory of the epic might accommodate Prince Andrei, whose view of the categorical
imperative is a glimpse of the eternal, there can be much more debate about the figure of
Napoleon whose sense of historical control is exposed as hollow. In contrast, Mikhail
Bakhtin saw *War and Peace* as the epitome of the novel as a genre, capable of grounding
characters in the lived reality and the prosaic detail of everyday life. Novels make the hero
central and none more so than historical novels. Tolstoy's technique of cutting to scenes
in *medias res* and attaching physical details and epithets to characters undoubtedly harks
back to the devices of the ancient epic. But it also suggests that what is seemingly random
actually creates patterns that are part of the fabric of life only a novel can successfully
capture. The Homeric epic ultimately stood above reality, whereas the novel does not free
the hero from the triviality of his milieu but enlarges its scale and depth.

The problem of the work's genre continues to be debated. Gary Saul Morson provides
a detailed overview of different attempts to grapple with the genre of *War and Peace* from
the time of its publication to the 1980s, and, at the same time, demonstrates the futility of
such attempts: he suggests accepting Tolstoy's masterpiece as is and learning from it to see
"in a new way what we have always regarded as too ordinary and unremarkable to attend."
Tolstoy teaches us to see "new truths."[33]

The interest in history continued and, perhaps, even grew toward the end of the nineteenth
century, although very few names of historical writers of that time survived in Russian cultural memory. Evgeny Salias de Turnemir (1840–1908) wrote a number of novels from the
time of Catherine the Great, including a novel about the Pugachev rebellion in 1773–75,
The Pugachev Rebels (*Pugachevtsy*, 1874). *The Burned Moscow* (*Sozhzhennaia Moskva*, 1886) by
G. P. Danilevsky (1829–90) shows clear influence of Tolstoy's *War and Peace*. Other writers
treated the themes traditionally popular in Russian historical fiction, such as the Time of
Troubles (*The False Dimitry* [*Lzhedimitrii*, 1879]) by D. L. Mordovtsev (1830–1905), the life of
Peter the Great (*Tsarevich Aleksei Petrovich* [1885]) and execution of Artemy Volynsky (*150 Years
Ago* [*150 let nazad*, 1883]), both by P. V. Polezhaev (1827–94). A number of novels described
Novgorod's prolonged fight for its independence from Moscow, which it eventually lost. It can
be suggested that the social instability of the last decades of the nineteenth century encouraged
the writers to turn to history for answers to their questions about the present. The growing
number of scholarly historical accounts likely stimulated the writers' interest in historical
themes.[34]

In tandem with the interest in the Russian past we can observe a great explosion of editorial
projects and academic research on medieval texts. Following the complete publication of
Karamzin's *History of the Russian State*, a commission was founded under the patronage of
Nicholas I and charged with publishing the complete chronicles of Russia. Such a compilation

of manuscripts, which profoundly altered the image of medieval Russia, was made possible by the fieldwork undertaken by archeologists and historians, such as Fedor Solntsev (1801–92), Aleksandr Neustroev (1825–1902), and Kliuchevsky, among others.

This academic phenomenon brought medieval works for the first time into the literary domain. Scholars such as Fedor Buslaev (1818–98), a learned philologist at Moscow University, tapped into a popular vein in post-emancipation Russia by treating disparate texts, from treatises to songs, as a single field unified by folk origins. Newly published works of folklore and folk poetry contributed to the image of Russia as a "fabulous" and "mythical" realm.

There was a conservative political dimension to the way in which scholarship positioned newfound texts. At the opposite end of the spectrum from medievalism-as-fairy-tale were the discoveries of the late-nineteenth-century philologists, which captured the scale of scribal culture by publishing editions of saints' lives. Hagiographies, available through mass publication, provided evidence of timeless, continuous patriarchal culture that writers such as Ivan Turgenev and Nikolai Leskov reflected in their fiction. The publication of the writings of Old Believers, including the *Life* of Avvakum made possible thanks to the relaxation of a censorship, showed that sometimes religious zeal pitted certain groups against the state and Tsar.

Aleksandr Pypin (1833–1904), a literary historian, ethnographer, and journalist, differentiated between writing (*pis'mennost'*) and literature (*slovesnost'*) in terms of production criteria by classifying literature as oral and popular while affiliating writing with works produced under the aegis of the state and Church. As a follower of the influential French critic Hippolyte Taine, who organized his model of literary history around the three-pronged system of "race, milieu, and moment," Pypin took an interest in the notion of Russianness.[35] Despite his own radical politics, his vision of popular culture helped him shore up the idea of a sacred bond between tsar and nation.

The critique of monarchy made by the nineteenth-century intelligentsia fostered the recovery of forms of popular culture appropriated as national and native. The study of medieval writing did not accentuate alterity, and found in chronicle-writing a confirmation of Russia's political economy (autocracy), in saints' lives a confirmation of its natural religion (Orthodoxy), and in its folkloric works evidence of popular genius (nationality). New accounts of the medieval period perpetuated the idea of Holy Russia as a unifying concept from the Kievan state to the end of the Imperial period in 1917. As Laura Engelstein has noted, in Russia, "the nineteenth century produced the story not only of Europe as the land of reason and progress but also of Russia as a land of Christian endurance and cultural inertia."[36] The interest in history thus reflected the continued preoccupation with the question of Russian national identity.

The search for national identity

The search for national identity in literature inspired repeated bouts of self-criticism and castigation from the late eighteenth century and well into the nineteenth century. Eventually, fiction found in family plots and intergenerational conflict a means to reflect on progress, but this took several decades of self-doubt and intensive debates. In his 1812 "Discourse on Russian Literature in Its Current State" ("Rassuzhdenie o Rossiiskoi slovesnosti v nyneshnem ee sostoianii"), Merzliakov asserts the importance of highly developed literature and language as proof of the maturity of a nation, and Russians in his view were only halfway there. Even in the 1830s, it was fashionable among writers and thinkers like Chaadaev and Kireevsky to contend that Russia had yet to produce world-class writers who were manifestations of native genius. Yet it would be a mistake to read the rhetoric as an objective index of actual accomplishment. To a large extent, the theme of authorial inadequacy, rather than signifying inertia or stagnation, indicated a growing momentum and important cultural turning points. The literary quarrels of the 1810s between Archaizers and Innovators (to use the terms Tynianov employed in his eponymous 1929 book, *Arkhaisy i novatory*) formed a backdrop to the work of Pushkin and his contemporaries. Batiushkov allegorized it as the quarrel between Ancients and Moderns in his poetry. Widespread concern existed that Russian literature habitually faltered, lapsing back into imitation rather than original creation. Reservations about this start-stop dynamic in a national literature were voiced in the mid-1820s by Küchelbecker in his "On the Direction of Our Poetry, Especially Lyrical, in the Last Decade," in which he lamented harmful Romantic tendencies in poetry; and Aleksandr Bestuzhev in "A View on Russian Literature in 1824 and the Beginning of 1825" ("Vzgliad na russkuiu slovestnost' v techenie 1824 i nachale 1825 goda," 1825), which famously declares that Russia has criticism but no literature. Their assertions were a pretext for Pushkin's aggressive critical performances in mapping out the terrain for his allies and literary enemies. The theme was picked up by others, such as Viazemsky and Ksenofont Polevoi (1801–67)—who saw the age conventionally as an arena for competition between literary parties—and later by Lermontov, who used Pushkin's death in 1837 to chastise society for its conservatism and falseness in his poem "Death of the Poet." Like Pushkin before him, Lermontov knew that writers could complain about indifference to literature and art even as they proved the power of the written word by their works. Nostalgia for a bygone age of better manners and gentility, such as we find in Pushkin's poem "To a Grandee" ("K vel'mozhe," 1830), prove the point that changes to social structure of Russia were underway and that one role of literature was to record change—and to precipitate social transformation. Finally, Belinsky, having also lamented the absence of literature in Russia in his "Literary Reveries," gradually began formulating a positive definition of Russian literature. He also began to compile its history. Many of his articles, including "Literary Reveries," begin with overviews of previous literary developments. His approach to writing a history of literature was consistently marked by his belief that it undergoes development (*razvitie*). This idea became particularly pronounced during his so-called Hegelian period. His knowledge of Hegel was second-hand (he did not read German and was introduced to Hegel's philosophy by Stankevich and Bakunin) and often seriously distorted, but Belinsky's influence was strong enough to shape contemporary thinking about literature and about social processes in general. The Hegelian notion of progress included the idea of conflict as its driving force, and its influence can be seen in the Russians' tendency to imagine transitions in terms of conflicts, particularly between generations.

The tendency to record transitions as a matter of generational conflict crystallized in the fiction of the 1850s. Many of the disagreements over the perceived obligation of literature to address social ills were generational—and even when they were not, that perception remained. In *Fathers and Sons*, the young nihilist Bazarov despises Pushkin's poetry, admired by the father and uncle of his friend Arkady, as socially useless. He advocates objective knowledge instead. As the century progressed, the younger generation of radicals grew to see their own predecessors, the liberal Westernizers of the 1840s, as dreamy and passive. Aleksei Pisemsky, clashing with his younger radical contemporaries, defends this generation in his novel *People of the 1840s* (*Liudi sorokovykh godov*, 1869), but even this defense can be halfhearted. His semi-biographical narrative presents the 1840s as a time when serfdom dominated and when the best people (including the protagonist) were not strong enough to confront effectively the evil of the time.

In Turgenev's *First Love*, love is an intergenerational battleground: the adolescent male hero vies with his father for the love of a young woman. He learns about love and violence when he witnesses his father strike her with a whip. She does not protest, but kisses the welt and then welcomes her lover into her bedroom. In *Fathers and Sons*, the ideological generational conflict is underscored by the rivalry between Bazarov and the elder brothers Kirsanov, Pavel, and Nikolai, over the young Fenechka, Nikolai's lover and, later, wife. Both ideology and love rivalry equally lead to a duel between Bazarov and Pavel. The generational lines in *Fathers and Sons* are not clear-cut, however: Bazarov loses his disciple, the young Arkady Kirsanov, who ends up siding with the older generation and marrying a family-minded young woman, Katia.

Family conflicts are present in most of Dostoevsky's major novels. In *Demons*, Dostoevsky describes the split between the generations of the 1840s and 1860s as a serious threat to the nation's stability and health. The elder Verkhovensky (whose character is thought to be based on the prominent professor of history Timofei Granovsky [1813–55]) and Karmazinov (a parody of Turgenev) are weak and narcissistic; they cannot withstand the new crafty radicals, such as Verkhovensky's son Petr. *Demons* is a political novel rather than principally a tale of families, but the generational conflict is presented as a rift within the family. Elsewhere, such splits can take a surprisingly violent turn. There is perhaps no better example of the congruence of generational and family discord than *The Brothers Karamazov*, Dostoevsky's final novel which tells stories of parental and brotherly neglect culminating in parricide. The patriarch is the Falstaffian Fedor Pavlovich Karamazov, a grasping, lecherous buffoon who neglects all four of his sons, sending them to be raised by the servant Grigory. His illegitimate son, Smerdiakov, fares the worst of all. Three of his sons grow up to be violent: Dmitry beats up his father, and Ivan hates him so deeply that his hatred inspires Smerdiakov's parricide. Only the younger son, the religious Alesha, remains unscarred by the violence and hatred that reigns in the family. Not all families, however, are equally unhappy in *The Brothers Karamazov*. Alesha brings the gift of love to the book, and the late subplot of the ill-fated young Iliusha and his family, the Snegirevs, offers a glimpse of one exemplary father–son relationship. Within its tale of intergenerational violence, murder, suicide, and penalty, the novel leaves the reader with a grain of hope for the future. The family conflicts in *The Adolescent* are intense, if less violent. They also allow reconciliation: Arkady loves and respects his legal father, Makar, and, having passed through many ordeals and committed many mistakes, he finds a way to connect with his natural father, Versilov.

In Saltykov-Shchedrin's *The Golovlev Family*, these ties are tested to their limits. In this grim and hopeless three-generation chronicle of a landowning family, the younger generation is completely wiped out by the malevolent mistreatment by their elders, first by Arina Petrovna, the mother of the family, who is entirely concentrated on the expansion of her estate; and then by her son, Porfiry, who keeps sending his illegitimate children to orphanages where they promptly die, and who tries to seduce his niece Anninka during her short stay on the estate. When Anninka returns to the estate after her twin sister's suicide, both she and her uncle take to drink, until one Easter, following a Good Friday Church service, they both begin to grasp the horror of their lives. The epiphany, however, comes too late: Porfiry, shaken by the realization of his sins, goes out and freezes to death that same night; and Anninka dies shortly thereafter, apparently of alcoholic delirium.

Another societal rift ran along national lines. Mistrust of foreigners or persons of different faiths (including non-Orthodox Christians) could be observed even in the medieval period and it survived well into the nineteenth century, despite the fact that Russian literature had continually demonstrated a productive openness to European literary traditions. Peter the Great's Westernizing reforms attenuated but did not eliminate the Russians' distrust of the Other. The Westernizer/Slavophile controversy well illustrates the sustained ambivalence toward the West. Foreigners residing and working in Russia, some for long periods of time, were also regarded with suspicion. Throughout the Imperial period, Germans from the Baltic provinces— who were Russian subjects—entered state service in significant numbers and were not always welcomed by the Russian nobility.

These and other foreigners were frontline targets for literary fiction. One of the first Baltic Germans ever portrayed is Hermann, the protagonist of "The Queen of Spades." Not only did Pushkin pick a name that conveys his Germanic origin (Pushkin spells it Germann), but the narrative also emphasizes his ostensibly typical German disposition. Reserved and circumspect, he is determined not to spend the 40,000 rubles inherited from his father. Since Madame de Staël's *De l'Allemagne*, Germans were considered the quintessential Romantics, Pushkin used the name possibly to hint at the fantasy that explains why Hermann believes a story about three magical winning cards. Hermann exercises remarkable control over his passion for cards and never gambles until the episode of St. Germain, the main turning point in the plot, ignites his uncontrollable desire to gamble and to win. What is important for the discussion of foreigners' social status is the way Pushkin positions his protagonist vis-à-vis other characters: Hermann is accepted by the Russian aristocrats with whom he mingles, but he is not quite their peer. He is reduced to his nationality by the Countess's grandson, Tomsky, who explains him away without hesitation: "Hermann is a German, he's thrifty, that's all." In the Russian original, this characterization sounds even more reductive, because of its trochaic rhythm: "'Gérmann némets, ón raschétliv, vót i vsé,' zamétil Tómskii."[37] Baltic Germans such as Hermann, even though they serve alongside Russians, are not quite what Russians call *svoi* (our people, one of us); they remain *chuzhoi* (alien, not one of us).

In Tolstoy's description of the military in *War and Peace* the divide is more emphatic: Germans in high command are always wrong in their military decisions, whereas Russians are always right. The most prominent example is the contrast between Michael Barclay de Tolly, a Baltic German of Scottish origin who was commander-in-chief during the first two months after Napoleon's invasion of Russia in June of 1812, and Mikhail Kutuzov, who replaced him in the late August. Historically, Barclay de Tolly was a talented military commander, and the strategic retreat from Napoleon's army was his original plan. Pushkin acknowledges Barclay's role in winning the war with Napoleon in the 1835 poem "The Commander" ("Polkovodets"), but Tolstoy, in his description of Barclay, does not, and instead depicts the Russian army retreat as a helpless flight from the enemy caused by Barclay's military mistakes. Likewise, Tolstoy never mentions that Barclay was asked by Alexander I to come out of retirement when Napoleon was approaching Moscow, and Barclay was not only obliged, but agreed to serve under his rival, Kutuzov, and took active part in the Borodino battle, during which five of the horses he rode were killed. In Tolstoy's representation, however, it was the Russian, Kutuzov, who acted wisely and made the end of Napoleon inevitable. In Dostoevsky's *Demons*, another German in Russian service is portrayed. It is the governor von Lembke, who, while not truly vicious, is so childish and incompetent that he allows a string of catastrophes to happen on his watch.

Leskov, with his usual self-awareness and irony, examines somewhat different aspects of the Russians' attitude toward foreigners. In "Iron Will" ("Zheleznaia volia," 1876), he describes a German engineer who comes from his native land to work at a Russian plant. The German is proud of his "iron will" and believes that it will help him conquer all possible difficulties and achieve anything he plans. And it does, to a degree: he learns Russian fluently and all by himself; he earns enough money to bring his bride to Russia; he establishes his own enterprise. But his iron will also hurts him: since he is determined to stick to his decision not to consummate his marriage until he earns a particular sum of money, his wife cheats on him and eventually leaves him; he quarrels with his neighbor, stubbornly refuses to compromise, takes him to court, and, this being a Russian court, loses his case. In the end he dies having eaten too many bliny pancakes, only because he claims that he can eat more than the local priest, and his iron will does not let him acknowledge defeat. The assertion made by Leskov's narrator at the beginning of the story that Russian flexibility and lack of rigor are more effective than German orderliness and rigidity, is thus confirmed, but the confirmation is rather ambivalent, because the narrator feels sadness about the German's unfortunate demise. A similar ambivalence can be observed in Leskov's 1881 story "The Left-handed Craftsman" ("Levsha"). The title character is a truly talented craftsman, perceptive and clever. After he wins a competition against the English in metalwork, he is taken to England for a visit. While there, he observes that in the English military they polish the barrels of their guns differently than in Russia, and their method does not damage the barrels. Lefty returns to St. Petersburg, eager to inform Alexander I of his important discovery. However, on his way, he drinks so much that by the time he gets back to Russia he is in alcoholic delirium, and nobody wants to listen to him. He dies, and the secret dies with him—which, the narrator claims, certainly tongue in cheek, in due time causes Russians to lose the Crimean War because their guns are damaged from being polished the wrong way. Clearly (if comically), Russian disorderliness is the target of Leskov's derision.

In another story written the same year, "The Flaming Patriot," Leskov mocks the Russian sense of superiority by contrasting the Russian aristocratic lady's haughty behavior and the Austro-Hungarian Emperor's friendly interaction with his subjects: he drinks beer with the commoners in the *Biergarten* and takes part in their simple entertainments. The aristocratic Russian lady, who intrudes on the scene to observe it without participating, is oblivious to the arrogance of her conduct. Her woman servant, in contrast, is so ashamed that she leaves her service. When the narrator inquires why she did so, she explains that she found her mistress's unseemly behavior (*neobrazovannost'*, lack of education or polish) offensive, especially because it made Russians look bad in the eyes of Austrians. It is noteworthy that it is a member of the Westernized elite who does not know how to behave properly in Europe, whereas a servant, supposedly untouched by European education, is observant enough to notice her mistress's insensitivity to foreign culture and insightful enough to deem it shameful.

In addition to Russian Orthodox Christians, many individuals of other faiths (*inovertsy*), both Christian and non-Christian, resided in the Russian Empire.[38] Baltic Germans were predominantly Lutherans; the Poles were Catholic; and there were Jews living in the Pale of Settlement and, later in the century, in the capitals. Many indigenous peoples in the conquered territories were Muslim; others throughout the land were pagan, and the efforts to convert them to Russian Orthodoxy that began in the Middle Ages were only partially successful. Sensitive to the local circumstances, the Imperial government did not impose Russian Orthodoxy on groups strongly affiliated to other religious traditions.[39] From the point of view of the official Orthodox Church, Old Believers were another problematic group, as were various sectarians. All these peoples of different faiths appeared in nineteenth-century Russian writings creating opportunities for writers to explore alternative modes of being in the world and also to display either imaginative sympathy with these others, or to show their own prejudices— or both, as more than a few examples show.

Leskov, always interested in portraying the Other, produced numerous works about people of different faiths, and unlike Dostoevsky's anti-Catholic and anti-Semitic depictions, his portrayals are usually sympathetic. His "The Sealed Angel" is a story about Old Believers trying to protect an icon particularly dear to them. It is characteristic that the Old Believers are helped in their task by the English, that is, by non-Orthodox Christians. Leskov's "At the Edge of the World" portrays an indigenous dweller of the far North, a half-pagan who is ugly, smelly, and seemingly dumb but proves to be a far better Christian than a missionary sent to convert him. "The Kolyvan Husband" is a comical story about a Russian who marries a Lutheran girl living in Revel (today's Tallinn, Estonia; *Kolyvan'* was an old Russian name of the city). His Slavophile father eagerly awaits the birth of a grandson who, he is sure, will be baptized into the Russian Orthodox faith and called, after him, Nikita. But every time the main character's wife is about to give birth, the husband is sent away, and the child is baptized Lutheran and named accordingly. The father-in-law is informed of a stillbirth, and the husband is helpless to change anything. Moreover, when the Lutheran wife dies, the widower marries her strong-willed sister and continues to bring little Lutherans into the world. In this story, Leskov gently mocks Slavophiles, but it is noteworthy that the main character's sister-in-law, and eventually wife, Lina, who is the main initiator of the events, is German: she comes from Germany to organize each act of deception and, when she marries her brother-in-law, they move to Germany.

As Jews began to abandon the Pale of Settlement and move from the margins of Russian society toward its center, Jewish characters began to appear on the pages of literary works, portrayed either negatively or sympathetically, often by the same authors. Dostoevsky's controversial treatment of Jews continues to attract scholars.[40] There is a Jewish moneylender in *Notes from the House of the Dead*; there are some unsympathetically portrayed Jews in *A Diary of a Writer*. However, Dostoevsky's attitude toward Jews was not unambiguously negative, as is evident from other materials in *A Diary of a Writer*.[41] Many scholars argue that his treatment of Jews should not be taken out of the historical context, and its complexity should not be reduced.[42]

Leskov's portrayal of Jews also could be considered ambivalent. For the most part it was positive. His 1886 "The Tale of Fedor the Christian and His Friend Abram the Jew" ("Skazanie o Fedore-Khristianine i o druge ego Abrame-zhidovine"), set in Byzantium at the time when Christianity was first recognized as an official religion, tells a story of friendship between the two title characters, the friendship that overcame the hostilities between their faiths. "The Bishop's Judgment" ("Vladychnyi sud," 1877) is also philosemitic, criticizing the practice of forceful enrollment of Jewish children in military schools. Filaret, Metropolitan of Kiev, saves one boy from such a fate. Leskov discusses the fate of Jews in the military in "Yiddish Tumblecollege" ("Zhidovskaia kuvyrkollegia," 1882); this story elicited accusations of anti-Semitism with its opening paragraphs which record various opinions about the Jews, including negative ones. However, the story itself defends Jews forced into the military service.

Chekhov also demonstrates ambiguity in viewing his Jewish characters. In "Mire," he paints the main character, a Jewish businesswoman, with cruel and even malevolent brushstrokes. The description of her as a deceiver and a pitiless seductress draws on multiple stereotypes: she is rapacious, dishonest, sickly, hypersexual, and weirdly repulsive with her big-nosed beauty suffused with heavy fragrances.[43] The Jewish stereotypes in this story—the Jew as greedy, sexual, aggressive, deceitful—strangely undermine what is likely the typical Chekhovian theme of indolent Russian noblemen leading meaningless lives who can be temporarily energized by an outside force; by making the jolt of energy in this story a demonic Jewess, Chekhov leaves the readers feeling mired in hopelessness which justifies the titular metaphor.[44] In another story, a converted Jew is described without sympathy: the title, "The Tumbleweed" ("Perekati-pole," 1887), warns the reader that this character is rootless: he abandoned his original faith, but can he be trusted to be a true Christian?

Chekhov's 1894 "Rothschild's Fiddle" ("Skripka Rotshil'da") has an anti-Semitism layer: the Jew Rothschild is called the usual volley of offensive names, mostly by Yakov, from whose point of view the story unfolds. Yakov is a coffin-maker, whose life is so miserable that he has lost all ability to love, sympathize, and express his feelings—except by means of music. And music turns out to be his and Rothschild's common language which helps Yakov regain his humanity. Before his death, he leaves his violin to Rothschild, and now Rothschild plays the melody he first learned from Yakov and moves his listeners to tears.[45]

Indigenous people (*inorodtsy*, which literally means "people of a different race") were even more alien to mainstream Orthodox Russians. How Russians evaluated them is a familiar tale of empire and conquest. The process started in medieval times, accelerated in the eighteenth century, and continued through the nineteenth. Along with new territories, the empire acquired their native populations. As Russians migrated into the newly secured regions, they came into contact with various indigenous people, officially called *inorodtsy*. Most of these peoples did not want to assimilate or be integrated into the general population; they continued to live according to their traditions, however uncultured they may have seemed to their conquerors. In some cases, the state allowed the local governing structures to remain in place as useful instruments in ruling the aborigines.[46] In other cases, particularly when the region became part of the empire voluntarily, partial integration did occur. One example is Georgia, which in the late eighteenth century found it advantageous to become part of the Russian Empire: most (but not all) of its population was of Eastern Orthodox faith, and joining the Russian Empire offered protection from Ottoman Turkey. While they shared beliefs with their Russian rulers, the Georgian Christians retained a permanent flavor of otherness in the Russian cultural imagination. Their social status could be high: according to a 1782 treaty, the Georgian aristocracy received the same rights as their Russian counterparts. The treaty did not hold and at the end Georgia, once conquered by Russia in the 1790s, did not received the promised autonomy. The special status of the Georgian aristocracy continued, and Georgians could and did enter Russian state service. One of the most prominent was Petr (Petre) Bagration, who, unlike Barclay the Tolly, was accepted by his Russian colleagues as *svoi*. Tolstoy, in *War and Peace*, portrays Bagration as a Russian national hero, despite his accented Russian and his dark complexion. Other nationalities whose elites were recruited successfully into Imperial power structures included Tatars, Poles, and, as mentioned before, Baltic Germans.[47]

Other peoples living in the lands conquered by the Russian Empire were rarely regarded as equals. Oftentimes, they were portrayed as savages—clinging to a pagan religion, unwilling and unable to learn the "civilized" way of life. Only occasionally do the *inorodtsy* appear in Russian literary works as peers. One example is Pushkin's 1829 poem "To a Kalmyk Girl" ("Kalmychke"), in which the poet, for a quarter of an hour, is ready to put her "barbarous beauty" (*dikaia krasa*) and unaffected behavior above those of high society Russian women.[48] Pushkin's epithet *dikaia* connects the addressee with his Romantic narrative poems, such as *The Captive of the Caucasus*, *The Fountain of Bakhchisarai* (*Bakhchisaraiskii fontan*, 1824), and *The Gypsies*—that is, Pushkin is attracted to her as an exotic other. But, as one critic suggests, the poem is "almost an album madrigal, addressed, however, to a girl who did not and could not have an album." Arguably, she is thus elevated to a higher status than Pushkin's other exotic beauties.[49] A similar potential equality is found in Sergei Aksakov's *The Childhood Years of Bagrov Grandson*. The story's narrator's family lives in Ufa, where the majority of indigenous people are Bashkirs. The narrator's father buys land from them, on which he wants to settle his Russian peasants and create an estate that the protagonist-narrator would inherit. While the relations between the buyer and the sellers are described as more or less equal, the deal itself goes awry, and it remains unclear whether the narrator could ever be the rightful owner of the land. In addition, while traveling from Ufa to the estate of the narrator's grandfather, the family meets other indigenous peoples, such as Mordovians, Tatars, and Chuvash, and the narrator's descriptions of the family's interactions with them are lively and informative, particularly when he resorts to ethnographical descriptions of their houses and everyday items.

Later in the nineteenth century, frank and, at the same time, compassionate portrayals of indigenous people appeared. One is *The People of Podlipnaia* (*Podlipovtsy*, 1864) by Fedor Reshetnikov, which describes the miserable life of a Finnish people, Komi (also known as Zyrians). The description of their life is brutally direct: the land they try to till is barren; in order to hunt they need gunpowder which they cannot afford; and their woodcrafts cannot find any buyers. As a result, they are destitute, sick, and so hungry that they are barely able to experience emotions for each other, or even care for themselves. Still, two of them, Pila and Sysoiko, find enough strength and willpower to leave Podlipnaia together with Pila's sons and travel on foot to the Kama River where they become barge haulers. In the end, Pila and Sysoiko die violent deaths, but the sons find a modicum of prosperity. The most remarkable aspect of the novel is its language: what the contemporary critics considered to be Reshetnikov's unpolished style, was in fact the best means to tell his story: it is "stark and sparse at the same time, as if matching the bleak bareness of the world it strove to convey." As Andrei Platonov would find the linguistic way to communicate the horror of collectivization, so Reshetnikov, by using ungrammatical and clumsy expressions, was able to portray the unbearable life of his characters.[50]

Korolenko's "Makar's Dream" ("Son Makara," 1883; published 1885; subtitled "A Yuletide Story") is one of his so-called Siberian stories, which are based on his experience living near Yakutsk, where he was exiled for refusing to swear allegiance to Alexander III. All of the stories in this cycle are centered on one local peasant or another, and "Makar's Dream" is the best of them. The story tells of a destitute Yakut, who manages to find enough vodka to get drunk on Christmas Eve; he gets lost in the woods, and then recounts his drunken dream—or perhaps his last visions before death. In the dream, he journeys to meet the big Toion, the Supreme Being who judges people after their death. Based on a mixture of local pagan mythology and whatever distorted Christian beliefs Makar had managed to internalize, the dream conveys the idea of the Supreme Being's mercy toward the unfortunate people He is judging. In this representation of an alternative belief system that is both comforting and morally right, Korolenko conveyed his own sense of modest respect for *inovertsy* and conferred on those he represented a degree of human dignity.

All literary works featuring *inorodtsy* and *inovertsy* forcefully advanced the image of Russia as an empire necessarily hosting different nationalities and faiths.[51] At the same time, writers from Chaadaev to Dostoevsky made the exceptionalism of the Russian people a focal point of the discourse of Russian identity. Even though *War and Peace* implies that Russia defeated Napoleon thanks to its chief military commander, Mikhail Kutuzov, whose genius, which included his ability to do nothing and wait, allowed him to commune with the spirit of Russian people and thus lead them to the victory, Tolstoy never presented military superiority in terms of Russian exceptionalism. Others, however, did, and Pushkin ironically formulated this idea in Chapter 10 of *Evgeny Onegin*—the chapter that he destroyed after December 14, 1825 and which survives in fragments: "The storm of 1812 came; / Who helped us then? / The rage of the people, / Barclay [de Tolly], the winter, or Russian God?" ("Groza dvenadtsatogo goda / Nastala—kto tut nam pomog? / Ostervenenie naroda, / Barklai, zima il' russkii Bog?").[52] Originating in medieval Russian texts (the tradition ascribes it to Mamai, the Golden Horde military commander defeated by Russians in the 1380 Battle of Kulikovo[53]), the formula gradually began to imply that God protects the Russian people as His chosen nation. During the 1812 war, this formula became quite popular: Kutuzov used it in his reports from the battlefield (in his variant, "rossiiskii Bog"), and Zhukovsky did as well in his immensely popular poem "The Singer in the Camp of Russian Warriors" ("Pevets vo stane russkikh voinov," 1812): "O Russian God, be our shield!" ("O! bud' zhe, Russkii Bog, nam shchit!").[54] Under Nicholas I, the formula was absorbed by the doctrine of Orthodoxy, Autocracy, and Nationality. Even in 1828, before the doctrine was formulated, Petr Viazemsky used it ironically in his poem "Russian God" ("Russikii Bog"), in which the Russian God is the god of everything that is unpleasant and inconvenient in Russia: snow storms, bad roads, cockroaches, and paupers. The formula gradually fell out of fashion during the second half of the nineteenth century.[55]

The phrase "Russian God" was not the only manifestation of the idea that Russians were God's chosen people. The notion of Russia's exceptional status dates back to the fall of Constantinople in 1453, which left Russia the only relevant Orthodox Christian nation. In the nineteenth century, as other European cultures were entering the early stages of industrialization (an Iron Age, in Baratynsky's formulation from his 1835 poem "The Last Poet" ["Poslednii poet"]), some theorists contended that Russia's usually deplored cultural belateness was in fact a sign of its freshness and promise. It is ironic that the first philosopher to propose this idea was Chaadaev, a fierce critic of Russian isolationism, in his so-called "First Philosophical Letter," in which he laments Russia's religious split from the rest of Christianity and argues that it led to Russia's exclusion from the universal brotherhood of Christian nations, which in turn resulted in backwardness. For this view, Chaadaev was harshly rebuked by the government and declared insane; the *Telescope*, where the "Letter" appeared, was closed, and its editor, Nadezhdin, exiled. Chaadaev's ideas were also criticized by future Slavophiles, whereas future Westernizers agreed with him. His letter, in fact, helped the two groups to formulate their positions and to organize as two separate ideological movements. While criticizing Russia's isolationism and backwardness, Chaadaev nonetheless insisted that Russia had its mission in history, and to fulfill it, Russians had to begin their cultural development anew. Fortunately, from Chaadaev's point of view, this was possible owing to Russia's unique geographical and cultural position between the West and the East: "We belong neither to the West, nor to the East, we are the exceptional people."[56] His conclusion is that Russia's historical mission is to be an example to the world. From here, there was only one step to proclaiming Russia a chosen nation, which Chaadaev did in his "Apology of a Madman," in which he asserted that Russia is "called to answer the most important questions that concern mankind."[57]

In his first important essay "The Nineteenth Century" ("Deviatnadtsatyi vek," 1832), Ivan Kireevsky, like Chaadaev, lamented Russia's isolation—not from Catholicism, but from classic antiquity: while Europe discovered and assimilated its heritage, shaping its cultural and political development in enduring ways, Russia missed this opportunity. However, as Kireevsky argues, since Europe broke with its own organic development in the mid-eighteenth century, turning to a new direction in science, art, and literature, Russia now can and should join Europe. The essay incurred the wrath of the government, and Kireevsky's journal *The European* (*Evropeets*) was closed. Kireevsky's mild Westernizing position changed by the end of the 1830s, which can be seen in his 1839 article "In Response to A. S. Khomiakov" ("V otvet Khomiakovu"), written in reaction to Aleksei Khomiakov's (1804–60) essay "On the Old and the New" ("O starom i novom," also 1839). Both essays were instrumental in formulating the Slavophile ideas of Russia's uniqueness and its superiority over the West. Later Khomiakov formulated the idea of *sobornost'*, central for the Slavophile claim of Russia's exceptionality.

KEYWORD **Sobornost'**

The term *sobornost'* or social collectivity was coined and popularized by the writer and thinker Aleksei Khomiakov as an essential element in his Slavophile-Christian interpretation of Russian history. Combining the words for council and cathedral (*sobor*) and for actions of unity or gathering (*sobirat'*), the notion stands as a spiritual and spatial equivalent to the communal peasant land tenure known as the *obshchina*. Khomiakov regarded this idea of unity in multiplicity as one feature, along with *dukhovnost'* (spirituality), that differentiated Russia from the West. According to the theory of *sobornost'*, individual self-realization comes not through isolation but is achieved through solidarity with others. Essentially a religious idea, it was elaborated as a social theory that advocated forms of communalism, explicitly Orthodox in nature. Slavophiles such as Khomiakov, Ivan Kireevsky, and Ivan Aksakov regarded it as an organic feature of popular life and one of the indigenous institutions of Russia's religious and historical traditions. This ideal of popular governance, allegedly reflected in the values and procedures of the village community, was seen to favor consensus over selfishness, and was deemed by conservatives to be a quality that had enabled Russia to remain on the right path of Christianity and avoid the rationalism and atheism that had spiritually impoverished Western societies. The image of collective action to defend the nation is attested in medieval works such as the *Igor Tale*, the *Will and Instruction of Monomakh*, and *Zadonshchina*, but mainly referring to the need of the princelings to unite under the leadership of the Grand Prince of Kiev or Vladimir. The view of *sobornost'* as a primordial indigenous expression of the popular will is dubious, more a mythic retrojection of Slavophile values into the past than a historical fact. Neither Karamzin's *History of the Russian State* early in the nineteenth century nor Kliuchevsky's *Course in Russian History* mentions the idea.

Proponents of *sobornost'*, captivated by the notion of the group rather than the individual as central to rural life, found some corroboration in legal discourse and ethnographic research. Both Ilya Orshansky (1846–75), an expert on customary law, and Aleksandra Efimenko (1848–1918), a historian and ethnographer who did original fieldwork on peasant culture, viewed *sobornost'* as a critical element of peasant and natural justice, seeing this as evidence of the innate sense of moral justice they attribute to the Russian people independent of a formal code of law. From the 1840s, Dostoevsky had subscribed to this brand of Slavophilism and, allied with major socialist thinkers like Herzen and Chernyshevsky through their populist belief, regarded the commune as the embodiment of *sobornost'*. Stimulated to skepticism by the economic blight of post-emancipation Russia, when agricultural productivity declined precipitously under communal management, other theorists of the peasant economy such as Aleksandr Engelgardt (1832–93) challenged the Slavophile opinion, questioning it from the viewpoint of Darwinian theories of survival.[58] It would take the full force of Realist writers, including Gleb Uspensky (1843–1902) and Chekhov in his most naturalistic mode, to dismantle such a glamorous populism and reveal the more backward and even brutal reality. Tolstoy, permanently inclined in his fiction and pedagogical writings to see in the peasant a model for potential moral perfection, manifests an interest in collective responsibility such as *krugovaia poruka* or communal guilt, as in the story "Polikushka" (1863), but *sobornost'* is absent in his representation of peasant government or relations with landowners.

In poetry, the idea of Russia as a chosen nation was most forcefully expressed by Tiutchev, first in the poem "These Poor Hamlets" ("Eti bednye selen'ia," 1855), which declares that the foreign gaze cannot appreciate and understand poor and humble Russian villages, its "meager nature" (mentioned in the second line of Tiutchev's poem), whereas in fact it is a place favored by Christ. As Christopher Ely puts it in his book on the role of landscape in Russian national identity, "The outward emptiness and lack of beauty in the countryside became a sign of inner, spiritual richness."[59] Tiutchev's poem of 1866 proclaims this idea even more vigorously:

> Умом Россию не понять,
> Аршином общим не измерить.
> У ней особенная стать—
> В Россию можно только *верить*.[60]

> One cannot understand Russia rationally,
> One cannot measure it with a common measure.
> It has a special character—
> One can only *believe* in Russia.

While Dostoevsky's version of Slavophilism, *pochvennichestvo*, was different from the main-stream doctrine in its greater openness to the West, he was also a believer in Russia's special mission. It was Dostoevsky who first used the term "Russian idea" (*russkaia ideia*). His understanding of Russia's special mission was, however, universalist rather than exceptionalist. Writing in his journal *Time* of 1861, he announced:

> We know that we cannot fence ourselves from the mankind with Chinese walls. We foresee that the character of our future activity should be panhuman [*obshchechelovecheskii*], that the Russian idea, perhaps, will be the synthesis of all those ideas that Europe, in all its separate nationalities, develops with such courage and perseverance.[61]

The religious philosopher Vladimir Solov'ev (1853–1900), in his 1888 "L'Idée russe" (Russian translation 1909) also suggests that the Russian mission is in the unification of the nations on the basis of Christianity.[62] When the fascination with Russian messianism reemerged first in the 1970s and then later, after the fall of the Soviet Union, it returned as a strictly nationalistic movement stripped of the ideal of unification with the West.

CASE STUDY **The national poet**

Pushkin is Russia's national poet, on par with Shakespeare in England or Goethe in Germany in terms of reputation and centrality, but also politicized, perhaps to an unusual degree, depending on the historical moment. Popular and elite cultures have enshrined him as a figure of universal appeal, Western to Westernizers, Russian to Russian national-ists. Nowadays in Russia his face stares out from billboards, vodka labels, and posters. His monumental figure dominates many public squares in major cities; his words cram librar-ies in millions of copies of innumerable editions; and his lines are quoted as a matter of habit. He entered the colloquial language long ago not only as a much-memorized poet but as a quasi-deity of a very domestic kind. "Who will close the windows?" "Pushkin will!"; "Who will pay the tax man?" "Pushkin will!"; "Who will cook dinner?" "Pushkin will!" Pushkin is pervasive in Russia and in Russian, at home in the former Soviet Union and abroad among émigrés alike; and his cultural status has not flagged since the 1990s. In the Russian cultural imagination he is credited with virtually everything from the inven-tion of the literary language to the discovery of love.

But the story of his legacy in literature and culture was not straightforward. In retro-spect, the famous declaration "Pushkin is our everything," made by the nineteenth-century Russian critic Apollon Grigor'ev in 1859, looks premature. It was only in the Soviet period that Pushkin's standing in the eyes of the nation became inseparable from the state of the nation and its culture. In the post-1917 period, anniversaries of all kinds, including Pushkin's death, birth, and even his first arrival in Odessa, were seized as occasions for public ritual attended by the masses. Immediately after the Revolution, Pushkin ranked fourth in popularity behind other writers like Tolstoy. The Bolsheviks' early need for cultural legitimation began with crude assertions, like that of Comrade Sosnovsky who observed that Lenin resembled Pushkin, "in his simplicity, optimism, love of nature, and respect for the common people."[63] Yet in the transitional period of the 1920s, Pushkin was deemed to be suspect because of his class origins. Debaters in Vladikavkaz were uncertain whether he was a bourgeois or a counterrevolutionary.

The creation of a Soviet Pushkin became a national issue with the celebration of 1924, which officially linked the cult of the poet to the foundation of a new order. Lunacharsky, the commissar of education, predicted that Pushkin "[would] live as an instance of the present and as a great teacher of the new life."[64] Images as well as words shaped public affection and taste. In 1937, against the backdrop of the Terror, Stalin and the state-run literary organizations mobilized a huge cultural apparatus for the centennial of Pushkin's death. By the time of the 1937 jubilee, any uncertainty as to his status had disappeared. Pushkin outranked all other authors put together; one émigré journal reported that every fifth book in a Soviet library was by Pushkin.[65] Marked by thousands of lectures and presentations across urban and rural Russia, in schools, factories, farms, the festivals and rituals provided a veneer of optimism and progress that concealed the traumas inflicted by the Terror. While the state boasted that unprecedented love for Pushkin was a measure of the widespread literacy achieved in the Soviet period, the cult of the writer was also an instrument of ideological conformity. The Central Committee of the Communist Party hailed Pushkin as the creator of virtually everything Russian, and his portrait was displayed right alongside pictures of Marx, Lenin, Stalin, and members of the politburo in the Moscow parades. Busts of Stalin and Pushkin shared an alcove in the vestibule of the poet's flat in Leningrad.

The cult of Pushkin as a national writer was never on this scale in the imperial period. Despite the devotion of individual writers to Pushkin, admired as a writer's writer by the likes of Fet, Turgenev, and Tolstoy, he looked marginal with respect to contemporary national issues. His critical and public reputation may have been a casualty of the history of editions of his works, highly imperfect as they continued to be long after his death.[66] Works now deemed to be classic reflections on Russian history, like *The Bronze Horseman*, originally censored by Nicholas I, were incompletely known. *Evgeny Onegin*, which had not sold well in his lifetime, finally achieved popularity and critical acclaim by the mid-nineteenth century. But it also became the focus of attacks by radical critics who criticized Pushkin for his failure to serve a social purpose of art, as laid down by Belinsky, and to produce an active protagonist whom later generations could emulate. Because of Onegin's superfluity to the plot, the generation of Pisarev, Dobroliubov, and other socially oriented critics relegated Pushkin to a second-tier "art for art's sake" role, out of date and out of touch with the mainstream direction of prose and, especially, the Nihilist novel. Reactionary Slavophiles, such as the critics Avksenty Martynov (1787–1858) in the 1840s and Viktor Askochensky (1813–79) in the 1860s, targeted Pushkin as offensive to Orthodoxy and, like Peter the Great, an upholder of the abhorrent European values that had, in their view, corroded the national heritage.

Representing the other end of the spectrum from these anti-Westernizing cultural conservatives, the Radical critic Nikolai Dobroliubov held that poets like Pushkin and Lermontov were of significance only for the time in which they lived and worked; Nekrasov, despite his continued reverence for Pushkin's verse, no longer cited him in his critical articles from 1857 to 1870. In 1865, Pisarev published a two-part essay, "Pushkin and Belinsky," in the summer issues of *The Russian Word*, which begins with a lengthy discussion of *Evgeny Onegin* and criticizes Pushkin for not addressing the social cause of Onegin's malaise. Pisarev claims that the novel had no intellectual content because it did not include any of the serious arguments of the time, and "dulls the social consciousness which a true poet should stimulate and guide through his writings."[67] He then turns to Pushkin's poetry, which he paraphrases in prose in order to discredit the poems as politically contemptible: "None among Russian poets can inspire his readers with such limitless indifference to people's sufferings, such profound contempt for honest poverty, and such systematic rejection of useful work as Pushkin."[68] Pisarev's interpretation was appropriated by both sides of the dispute about the function of art. But for no one in the 1860s and

1870s, whether Populists, Radicals, or Slavophiles, did Pushkin represent an unassailable authority.

To the literary establishment, the absence of a national genius around whom all sides could rally was a gaping hole. The nineteenth century was a great age of national literary festivals that consecrated writers, and not just poets, as cultural lawgivers. Cultural memory was embodied in statues all across Europe. In 1840, Scotland celebrated the inauguration of the Scott monument, the locus of the 1871 National Festival in Celebration of the Centenary of the Birth of Sir Walter Scott. In between, the Scots had a Burns Celebration in 1859. In 1864 Britain feted Shakespeare. In 1870, a week after the Prussian army besieged Paris, an open-air statue of Voltaire was erected. In 1878, the year of the Universal Exhibition, commemorations of Voltaire (whose heart had been presented to the Emperor Louis-Napoleon in 1864) were orchestrated amid fierce debates on the role of religion in national life, the economic structure of the state, and the meaning of citizenship. None other than Victor Hugo, an object of Dostoevsky's "worship,"[69] delivered a speech hailing Voltaire as the spirit of modern political and cultural values ushered by the French Revolution.

From the mid-1850s, the Russian intelligentsia deemed its cultural mission to be progressive. Pushkin seemed to concentrate and synthesize in his work all the contradictions that had come to polarize the different groups that split along the Slavophile/Westernizing axis, a dichotomy that was further complicated by differences between the nationalist programs advocated by the Populists and the Slavophiles. The Pushkin question became the battleground for these antagonisms. Proponents of Pushkin's legacy believed that the erection of a statue would revive Pushkin's reputation and also affirm his centrality to the tradition. Despite his negative judgments of Pushkin, Belinsky legitimated this point of view as progressive and not just nostalgic: in the fifth of his eleven articles on Pushkin, Belinsky identified him as more of a national genius than his predecessors. The initiative to build a monument to Pushkin first came from the alumni of the poet's alma mater. In 1861, on the fiftieth anniversary of the school's foundation, the Lycée graduates wished to promote the establishment's academic reputation, its liberal values, as well as its most celebrated graduate. In the early 1870s, after the Lycée group failed to raise sufficient funds, there was new momentum and a backlash against the opposition to Pushkin. Other proponents of the statue resented the negative treatment of Pushkin in the radical press and wished to counter Chernyshevsky's utilitarian literary doctrines with Pushkin as the symbol of an alternative ideal. The publication of Annenkov's biography encouraged the cultural critic Nikolai Strakhov to hope that a revival of interest in Pushkin would curtail the influence of the radical critics, baleful in his view. He deemed the failure to erect the monument as a sign of the decay of public taste and values.

As it turned out, factionalism and financial difficulties stymied initial planning. In 1871, Ivan Aksakov, the historians Petr Bartenev, Mikhail Pogodin, and others resumed the initiative; a location in central Moscow was chosen and approved by Alexander II, and a statue was commissioned from the sculptor Aleksandr Opekushin in 1875 and funded through public subscription (comparable to twenty-first-century crowd-sourcing). After nearly a decade of planning and construction, the unveiling of the monument on Tverskoi Square (now Pushkin Square) finally took place on June 6 (Old Style), 1880, Pushkin's birthday. As two great men of letters, Turgenev and Dostoevsky were invited to speak by the Society of Lovers of Russian Letters. (Tolstoy had refused to participate on principle: he objected to the festival while famine gripped parts of rural Russia.)

Dostoevsky delivered his address ("Pushkinskaia rech'") on June 8, 1880, the second day of the event. Immersed in the final stages of writing *The Brothers Karamazov* and visibly unwell, he nonetheless galvanized the audience. Eyewitness accounts note the passionate delivery of a substantial text of about 5,000 words, subsequently published in the *Diary of a Writer* with a further essay in preface. Marcus Levitt has rightly observed how involved Dostoevsky's rhetoric is. By building his argument on a close reading of Pushkin's works, replete with verse quotation, Dostoevsky compellingly turns questions of national definition into a function of aesthetic appreciation and emotional identification.[70] Intellectually, the speech represents the culmination of a virtually lifelong, passionate admiration for Pushkin about whom Dostoevsky had been writing sporadically from the 1860s. Consistently Dostoevsky based his admiration for Pushkin on a literary appreciation of both the poetry and the prose. As recently as 1877, in the *Diary of a Writer* Dostoevsky had lauded "The Gypsies," "The Queen of Spades," and *Evgeny Onegin* as masterpieces of psychology. From the preeminent practitioner of the psychological novel this was high praise.

Despite the failure of contemporaries to understand him, Pushkin's "greatness was a guiding genius," and Dostoevsky, following Gogol, championed him as a "great, remarkable phenomenon"—in fact, nothing less than "the first Russian."[71] In the 1880 speech, Dostoevsky repeated many of the terms of his own earlier appreciation. They included quite an unhistorical assertion of Pushkin's "reverence" for the Russian people, by which Dostoevsky meant all social classes, including serfs in their natural state, rather than the upper classes spoiled by Europeanization. Dostoevsky located Pushkin's closeness to the Russian people—he characterized it as a love of everything the *narod* loved—in heroes who embodied traits of character that Dostoevsky declared were national, namely, a capacity for suffering, selflessness, and pious devotion.

The Pushkin speech moves from an appreciation of the essence of the national character, as Dostoevsky sees it, to a panegyric of Pushkin as Russianness itself and an emblem of *narodnost'*. Such a claim stands in a double relation to the legacy of Belinsky by rejecting his conclusions about Pushkin and at the same time accepting some of his views regarding the trajectory of Russian culture. Belinsky was convinced that, as a reflection of the spirit of the age and as a builder of a single, unified national consciousness, Russian literature would become an important part of world literature. When Belinsky said that Pushkin's poetry was in many ways "outdated," he meant that the preoccupations of the Russian intelligentsia had changed in the 1840s. The new generation of Russian intellectuals, to whom Belinsky was a mentor, was interested in politics, although to a man like Dostoevsky Pushkin was not old-fashioned but eternally relevant. He is indispensable to Russians, true, but his genius, asserts Dostoevsky, elevates him above even Shakespeare and Goethe. Starting with Gogol's praise of Pushkin as "an exceptional phenomenon and perhaps the sole manifestation of the Russian spirit," Dostoevsky describes Pushkin as a "prophetic phenomenon."[72]

Dostoevsky's argument for Pushkin's greatness is thus both historical and absolute since he celebrates his innovation while praising him as the epitome of Russian self-knowledge (*samosoznanie*) through which other nations can discover much about their own humanity. In his *Philosophical Letters*, Petr Chaadaev had characterized Russia's backwardness as the advantage of innocence and promise, implicitly lending authority to its separate path (now thought of by cultural theorists as *Sonderweg*). In his 1880 speech, Dostoevsky navigates between the more radical conservatism of the Populist movement, with its primitivist myths of an ancestral Russia, and the stubborn liberal belief that even in the 1880s Russia remained behind. After all, on June 7, 1880, Turgenev, who in his own essays had identified Cervantes, Shakespeare, and Goethe as geniuses because their literary types captured universal human types, refused to call Pushkin a universal genius.

Arguably, Dostoevsky fought fire with fire by applying Belinsky's own acid test of great-ness. Belinsky and his followers regarded a psychological type as the result of an aesthetic organization of reality: only a poet's imagination could impart to it universal significance of mythic proportions. Dostoevsky delivered an emphatic rejoinder to the Belinsky position by basing his argument for Pushkin's relevance and universality on literary portrayals that captured human essence in representations of the philosophical "searcher" or "truth-seeker" (skitalets, iskatel'). For Dostoevsky, the figures from Aleko in The Gypsies to Onegin and Tatiana of the novel in verse embody a search for truth, meaning, and identity, a quest in which all people join and which Russians, he believes, pursue most ardently of all. Pushkin represented the national genius as a gift to all nations, evidence that not only had Russia closed the gap of cultural attainment, an anxiety often expressed in the nineteenth century, but was now a world leader.

It was Dostoevsky who put Pushkin as a national genius on the map. But it would be misleading to suggest that the Pushkin enshrined in Soviet culture descended directly or solely from Dostoevsky's final public act. Dostoevsky's hope of bridging and even unifying factions across the political and cultural spectrum was not realized. Among the Populists, notable left-wing theorists like Nikolai Mikhailovsky and Mikhail Protopopov (1848–1915; often published under the pen name Aleksandr Gorshkov) objected perhaps most vociferously to the idea, inherited by Dostoevsky from German Romantic philoso-phy, that a single man could embody the national spirit, because their goal was the eradication of national insularity. Regardless of how acceptable Dostoevsky's vision of a universal genius may have seemed, the streak of nationalism in the evaluation of Pushkin as specifically Russian looked regressive, and Dostoevsky's idealization of the people was a fantasy devoid of economic or social truth. As it turned out, none of the nationalist groups particularly endorsed Pushkin any more than the Westernizers who disputed Dostoevsky's equation of politics and morals. Notably, once the dust had settled, the ensu-ing debate about Russia's direction largely neglected Pushkin. Nor did Dostoevsky's word carry much weight among the later leaders of Soviet culture, who saw him as a conserva-tive reactionary. Gorky, for one, repeatedly excoriated Dostoevsky as an enemy of Socialism. Commenting on the Pushkin Speech, Gorky said that he knew no more "offensive slogan" than its call for "humility" (smirenie), and while the literary establish-ment toned this objection down after the 1930s, later critics took exception to Dostoevsky's reading of Pushkin. Aleksandr Tseitlin for one mocked the focus on "these Russian home-less wanderers," characters who looked like the antithesis of the positive heroes required by Socialist Realism.[73]

Conclusion

Signs of the crisis of Realism were already visible from the 1880s. In Turgenev's later works the strain of mysticism that can be occasionally seen in some his earlier stories (for instance, the 1856 "Faust") blossomed. In "A Song of Triumphant Love" ("Pesn' torzhestvuiushchei liubvi," 1881) and "Klara Milich (After Death)" ("Klara Milich [Posle smerti]," published 1883), mysticism and the fantastic dominate. A newly found synthesis of psychology and allegory plays a significant role in the work of Garshin; it is a pronounced feature in novellas like "Attalea Princeps" (1880) and "The Red Flower" ("Krasnyi tsvetok," 1883). Tolstoy's treatise "What Is Art?" ("Chto takoe iskusstvo?," 1897–98) proposed a radical reconceptualization of art as a communicative activity: "The activity of art is based on the fact that a man, receiving through his sense of hearing or sight another man's expression of feeling, is capable of experiencing the emotion which moved the man who expressed it."[1] While this idea does not always apply to Tolstoy's own novels, it does anticipate modernist and avant-garde theories of aesthetic reception.

In this respect, it is especially noteworthy that in the 1890s Chekhov, who had declared his loyalty to the sober use of realism uncontaminated by ideology, created works that would come to be read as harbingers of Russian modernism. Foremost among them is the story "The Black Monk" and the play *The Seagull* (*Chaika*, 1896). The story appears to ground in physical symptoms hallucinations in which the hero Kovrin sees a black monk. Yet by assuming the viewpoint of the character, Chekhov provides an overwhelmingly convincing demonstration that fantasy can supplant reality. The triumph of the invisible over the visible is confirmed by the psychological subject, and by the narrative in which the black monk, the garden, and a violin serenade acquire a symbolic meaning. In *The Seagull*, Chekhov on the surface parodies Symbolism, a movement that was gaining momentum, in the form of Treplev's play; however, he devotes equal if not greater vigor to attacking the representatives of conventional art, embodied by the melodramatic prima donna Arkadina and the realist (or impressionist) Trigorin whose characterization is transparently autobiographical. Added to this feature of the poetics of *The Seagull* is a plot development that is non-linear and "atmospheric" (in the expression of the great theater director Vsevolod Meyerhold[2]), unfolding more through the speeches and emotional states of the characters than through causality. These constituent features of the new language in Chekhov's writing exercised a decisive influence on the aesthetics of modernist theater. The initial performance history of *The Seagull* testifies to its disruptive novelty in fin-de-siècle Russian culture. The opening night at the Aleksandrinsky Theater (1896) was a total flop. But the staging at the Moscow Art Theater by Stanislavsky, which Chekhov regarded as "incorrect" and excessively naturalistic, had a sensational success and became a manifesto for a new type of theater.

A lecture course by Dmitry Merezhkovsky, entitled "On the Causes of the Decline and on New Trends in Contemporary Literature" ("O prichinakh upadka i o novykh techeniiakh sovremennoi russkoi literatury"), appeared in pamphlet form as a manifesto in 1893. Merezhkovsky determined that a crisis in positivism had led to the birth of a new idealism. In his view, modernism was supported by three pillars of idealist art: mystical content, reliance on symbols understood as images that permeated all of world culture, and an expansion of artistic receptiveness ("khudozhestvennaia vpechatlitel'nost'") to include "the obscure and unconscious" ("temnoe i bessoznatel'noe") in the new art. Merezhkovsky found hints of this new art in Turgenev, Goncharov, Tolstoy, and especially Dostoevsky, and its first full manifestations in the prose of Garshin, and poetry of Nikolai Minsky (1856–1937) and Konstantin Fofanov (1862–1911).

What initially looked like an amusing curiosity turned out to be a symptom of a change in the cultural paradigm. In the *History of Russian Literature* edited by Dmitry Ovsianiko-Kulikovsky (1911), Petr Kogan, a literary scholar with a sociological orientation, treats the birth of Russian modernism as a new aesthetic of the philosophy of freedom: "In essence, modernism is poetry of the paths by which personality, without seeking any compromises with the external world and completely rejecting the social principle, can achieve complete independence from the world and attain total freedom."[3] In the history of Russian literature he published in 1926, the émigré Dmitry Sviatopolk-Mirsky observed:

> With the growth of this new "civic" idealism, a more subversive attack was launched against the very foundation of radical intelligentsia-ism, and of civic morality. Aestheticism substituted beauty for duty, and individualism emancipated the individual from all social obligations. The two tendencies, which went hand in hand, proved a great civilizing force and changed the whole face

of Russian civilization between 1900 and 1910, bringing about the great renascence of Russian art and poetry that marked the decade.[4]

The genealogy of modernism lay in a shattered belief in a rational image of the world brought about by a new interest in the unconscious, a philosophy of transgressive freedom, debates about sexuality, and the search for new representations of religious consciousness, such as the occult and theosophy, conducted outside established institutions. The birth of modernism indicated Russia's entry into a modern age marked by colossal historical catastrophes and revolutionary cultural movements like the avant-garde that swept away old boundaries.

The end of the nineteenth century was marked by several parallel developments: the disillusionment with both realism and Realism, the consequent diminished interest in prose, and the surge of attention to poetry. These changing preferences did not affect the actual publication figures: prose still dominated the market, but its prestige fell, whereas the status of poetry was in the ascendancy. Another important change that occurred at the end of the century was a renewal of interest in Western cultural innovations: new trends in literature and art came to Russia from the West.

New developments in arts and literature, which migrated to Russia from France, were perceived by a significant part of the public as a form of cultural degeneration and received the name of Decadence. Simultaneously with Decadent art, Symbolism arrived in Russia, also from France. Decadence and Symbolism ushered the era of modernism in Russia. Early Russian modernism was characterized by deep interest in religion and mysticism and by sexual experimentation. However, its most radical experiments concerned art and literature in the first place. Russian literary culture would be remade by modernism, producing literature of enduring value and, some would say, considerable shock value as well.

Part V

The Twentieth and Twenty-First Centuries

Introduction:
The shape of the period

THE twentieth century brought a period of radical change, beginning with the Workers' Uprising in 1905, the First World War, the two Revolutions of 1917, the Civil War and the famine that followed it, the collectivization of agriculture, the Great Terror, and culminating in seventy-three years of Soviet rule. During those decades, the Second World War was fought, the Cold War endured, Stalin's cult rebuked, the Communist ideology transformed into a set of dead clichés, and late Soviet society, based upon utterly cynical attitudes and practices, came into being. With the dissolution of the Soviet Union, a strange mix of democratic rhetoric, staggering disparities in wealth, and widespread corruption prevailed; many forms of censorship relaxed, but as of the early 2000s, formats with wider audiences, such as television and journalism, remained strictly controlled.

These historical stages meant that literary culture has had many shocks to absorb, alongside virtually constant arts regulation and state control. The decades of Soviet rule have inevitably defined the twentieth century, and most ways of thinking about cultural mechanisms during that period, particularly in terms of literature, are oriented around whether or not a phenomenon fits into the rather capacious category of "Soviet." In keeping with the design of our *History*, which presents a narrative that unifies the different strands of Russian culture often seen as separate, we integrate the Soviet, underground, and émigré examples even as we also devote close attention to each phenomenon; and we contrast pre- and post-Soviet texts as much as we show the similarities between them.

While the Russian twentieth century may be dominated by efforts to break with the past, some cultural and historical continuities are inescapable. Those include the role of literary groups, whether official or unsanctioned; the inclination of theater toward social commentary; the authority of literature as a "second government"; and the role of women not only as essential consumers of literature but as important writers in all genres. Poetry remained an essential creative force, widely read and memorized; and the cumulative appreciation of the poetic traditions feeds into modes of writing and academic criticism that generate a complex relationship between theory and practice. Literature continued to shape national narratives and form the identity of the intelligentsia.

An important gesture of mediation between literary poetics and cultural processes was performed by institutions and infrastructures such as magazines and almanacs; formal and informal writers' unions; institutional concepts (such as Socialist Realism or literary underground); literary scholarship; and ways of producing and distributing literary texts (such as *samizdat* and *tamizdat*; and, by the end of the twentieth century, internet portals and blogs), in which group identities could be formed and debated. The first chapter, devoted to "Institutions," addresses these forms of mediation, as well as other aspects of the literary world (the social position of the writer, generational shifts, and culture wars), while laying out the thematic groupings that define the period.

In addition to institutions (Chapter 1), our examination of the twentieth and twenty-first centuries is structured around six themes: new subjectivities formed in poetry, on the one hand, around the concept of the self (Chapter 2) and, on the other, around the idea of language (Chapter 3); utopia / dystopia (Chapter 4) and the grotesque (Chapter 5) as formative elements of Russian and Soviet modernism in prose and drama; national narratives, including catastrophic narratives of political terror and war (Chapter 6); and narratives associated with the intelligentsia's cultural and historical self-identification (Chapter 7). The logic of Part V is thus defined by the transition from socio-cultural structures, through the transformed and newly invented subjectivities that required a new poetics for their manifestation, and from them to the large-scale narratives that embody a vision of Russia, its tragic experience, and its historical identity, in epic or neo-mythological, symbolically charged forms. As with earlier periods, we present a rough chronological progression within each section, but permit ourselves to jump ahead or to look back when needed. That capacity of writers to identify with earlier moments or to have belated readerships is an especially marked feature of twentieth-century and twenty-first-century Russian literature, and so our focus is less on the sequential march of literary history than on the leaps, bounds, reversals, and delayed enthusiasms of the era.

I

Institutions

Defining the Silver Age

The very name is problematic: Russia's Silver Age is one of many contested terms (alongside decadence, modernism, and the avant-garde) for defining the explosion of cultural creativity that occurred roughly between the 1890s and the 1920s. The origins of the term "Silver Age" ("Serebrianyi vek") are disputed and obscure, and the value judgments attached to it are diverse.[1] Describing Russia of 1913 in her *Poem Without a Hero* (*Poema bez geroia*, composed in 1940–62), Anna Akhmatova (1889–1966) famously set the mood for the era with a silver moon "brightly losing its heat" ("I serebrianyi mesiats iarko / Nad serebrianym vekom styl").[2] Even as the creative energy of the Silver Age seemed to wane, the term persisted thanks to the enduring Soviet-era nostalgia for pre-Revolutionary freedoms.

We continue to use the term because its history tells us something important about Russian culture: it presents the image of an era when cultural activity intensifies, when innovations outpace one another, when movements and groupings are quickly forming and recombining. The Silver Age considered explosive activity to be a feature of Pushkin's era, or the Golden Age, against which it sought to define itself.[3] An emphasis on poetry aimed at restoring the primacy of an aesthetic form that had seemed to recede before the flood of nineteenth-century novels. Amid striking innovations, the era reconstituted the virtues of the earlier period—its valorization of individual genius (Pushkin) and its status as a turning point in Russian culture. In proclaiming its debt to the classical, Golden period of Russian literature, the Silver Age was enacting a return not unlike that of the Renaissance.

Implicit in all these gestures of self-definition are assumptions that periods like the Golden Age represented a supreme achievement against which other periods are to be measured. The nearsightedness of contemporaries is never to be underestimated. Even some of the most astute leading writers of the turn of the century saw the modernists as decadent, frivolous troublemakers (the play within the play in Chekhov's *Seagull* [*Chaika*, 1896] ridiculed Symbolism's abstraction). Well into the Soviet period, the narrative of Russia's cultural decline would surface repeatedly in the views of émigré critics, who saw the decline as a sad consequence of a set of historical catastrophes, including the Revolution, Stalinist Terror, Socialist Realism, and rigid cultural bureaucracies. After the fall of the Soviet Union, that narrative of failure returned in the laments that Russians read less, write worse, or have fatally borrowed too many tricks of the trade from their Western counterparts. It remains a valuable lesson, then, to historicize these complaints and to recognize them as an enduring element in the cultural process. In setting out the range and qualities of the era's institutions, we can begin to see how they too survived and thrived, albeit in changing forms and locations, through to the late twentieth century. In a later section on poetics, we will consider the specific trends and movements that divided up the modernists; first, however, we will take a look at the institutions that brought them into close and productive contact.

Unlike the thick journals that were the fundamental means of disseminating realist prose in the nineteenth century, the journals and the publishing houses of the Modernist age did not uniformly cultivate a mass readership (although some did). They wanted to be a part of the fast-paced present. Even well-established journals changed with the times: *The Northern Herald* (*Severnyi vestnik*), taken over in 1891 by the publisher Liubov Gurevich (1866–1940) and the editor Akim Volynsky (1861–1926), soon began to feature such modernists as Paul Verlaine and Gabriele D'Annunzio in translation, and Russian poets such as Zinaida Gippius (1869–1945), Fedor Sologub (1863–1927), and Konstantin Bal'mont (1867–1927). Volynsky especially sought to introduce the works of Friedrich Nietzsche to the Russian reader. Nevertheless, *The Northern Herald* retained many of the features of the earlier thick journals (and continued to publish writers like Leskov and Tolstoy). A more radical break could be seen in the case of *The World of Art* (*Mir iskusstva*, 1898–1904), edited by Serge Diaghilev (1872–1929); *The New Path* (*Novyi put'*, 1902–04), inspired and led by Gippius and Dmitry Merezhkovsky (1865–1941); *Libra* (*Vesy*, 1904–09);[4] *The Golden Fleece* (*Zolotoe runo*, 1906–09); and *The Crossing* (*Pereval*, 1906–07), created because its publisher, S. A. Sokolov, quarreled with the leadership of *The Golden Fleece*; and *Apollon* (1909–17), edited by Nikolai Gumilev (1887–1921) and Sergei Makovsky (1877–1962). For nearly all these editors, the ideal reader was well versed in the principles of the new aesthetic forms and theories, although various modes of outreach were used in their book and almanac publication series. Journals were meant to be artistically complex, carefully assembled, and inevitably, with smaller print runs, more costly. One publication, *The Crossing*, took as its subtitle the identifying phrase "a journal of free thinking." Most journals had fairly firm ideas about the aesthetic innovations they hoped to advance.

Skorpion (1899–1916) was founded by the entrepreneur and translator Sergei Poliakov (1874–1943) along with poets Valery Briusov (1873–1924) and Jurgis Baltrušaitis (1873–1944). Managed by Briusov, it was the first publishing house exclusively devoted to the Symbolists, whose work was also promoted by the journal *Libra* and by the almanac *Northern Flowers* (*Severnye tsvety*, 1901–05; 1911; the almanac reprises the title of a Pushkin-era publication). The books and journals published by Skorpion over sixteen years sought a new unity of format and aesthetic credo, and particularly by means of accessible illustrations and cover designs, Skorpion hoped to attract readers for whom the ethos of Symbolism might be strange. The motifs and design elements made concrete and material some of the abstract concepts of the poetry. The cover of *Gold in Azure* (*Zoloto v lazuri*, 1904) by Andrei Bely (1880–1934) offers a splendid case in point. The words "gold" and "azure" in the book's title inspired the coloration of the cover design (see Plate 14). Jonathan Stone has suggested that the cover represents a classical mask, although the superposition of the golden arabesque over the amorphous cloud of blue might also hint at the mysteries contained in Bely's verse.[5]

Other publishing houses also sought to advance a specific new aesthetic: Hyperborea (Giperborei), founded by Gumilev in 1912, promoted Acmeism and rejected some of Symbolism's more high-flung ambitions, and it was associated with a journal with the same name. Knowledge (Znanie, 1898–1913), another house that flourished at the time, was more of a throwback to the nineteenth century's realist norms, and Maxim Gorky (1868–1936) joined shortly after its founding and radically reorganized it. It resisted the emerging modernist trends of the Silver Age, and within little more than two decades, its insistent realism would find renewed prominence. Unlike modernist publishing houses, it appealed to a mass readership, selling books with large print runs at low prices and paying high fees to its authors. Under Gorky's management, Knowledge Publishers was the most financially successful literary project in Silver Age Russia.

Key modernist journals and their publishing houses were supported by patrons, some of them quite wealthy: for example, Savva Mamontov and Princess Maria Tenishcheva subsidized *The World of Art*. At the same time, close interactions between writers and artists meant that some of the great art collectors of the era, such as Sergei Shchukin and Ivan Morozov, had an enormous influence on artistic exchanges and collaborations: their tastes and preferences affected what was exhibited and which publishing houses or journals flourished. Salons and social gatherings, where the art collectors exerted their influence, were also a sign of the times.

Russian culture had had a long history of ritualized social contexts for cultural expression, ranging from the glittering salons of the Pushkin era to the more politically motivated circles (*kruzhki*) of the later nineteenth century. Russian modernism fused the subtle social networking of the earlier nineteenth century with the seriousness of the *kruzhki*. Zinaida Gippius and Dmitry Merezhkovsky sought nothing less than a religious revolution in their Religious-Philosophical Meetings (1901–03), which were sanctioned by the church as long as attendance was limited. They talked of religion, celibacy, procreation, and marriage; Gippius thought the meetings were the only site of free speech in Russia.[6] Unlike gatherings in private homes and apartments (including frequent, less formal social events at the home of Gippius and Merezhkovsky), the Religious-Philosophical Meetings were held at a public venue, the Imperial Geographic Society, and versions of the transcripts were published in Gippius's journal *The New Path*.

A legendary gathering was at the Tower (*Bashnia*), hosted by Viacheslav Ivanov (1866–1949) and his wife Lidia Zinov'eva-Annibal (1866–1907), after they returned to Petersburg in 1905 following a decade abroad. Their Wednesday gatherings in rooms overlooking the Tavrichesky gardens were a dazzling setting for poets, artists, actors, and impresarios who stayed late into the night for readings, performances, and ardent debates. Drawing like-minded Symbolists to an environment in which terms like "mystic anarchism," "mystic realism," and "neo-Christianity" could be enthusiastically promoted, Ivanov's Tower hosted an eclectic group: the future Acmeist Osip Mandelstam (1891–1938) recited a poem on his first visit, and it was here that he met Akhmatova;[7] Meyerhold staged a drama by Calderón and hatched plans for his startling production of *Puppet-Show Booth* (*Balaganchik*, 1906, staged in 1907) by the Symbolist Aleksandr Blok (1880–1921); Andrei Bely introduced Blok to Ivanov at one of the very first Wednesdays, which featured an "impromptu symposium on the subject of love."[8] Not yet a Futurist, Velimir (born Viktor) Khlebnikov (1885–1922), who had met Ivanov in Crimea, was also an enthusiastic participant.[9] These were all modernists in their own way, but despite their separate artistic programs, the collective effort behind poetry readings, manifestos, and social gatherings created the impression of a committed avant-garde group. The Ivanovs' Wednesdays lasted a mere two years, cut short in 1907 by Lidia Zinov'eva-Annibal's illness, but their impact was enduring.

Sporadic gatherings centered around performances and exhibits that were also of signal importance. The World of Art group, which featured art, music, and theater on the pages of its journal as often as it did literature, connected artists across different media and forms of expression. Some writers foregrounded these connections in their work, like Elena Guro (1877–1913), who mixed visual art in to her books and whose husband, the artist, color theorist, and composer Mikhail Matiushin (1861–1934), kept her in close contact with the musical world. Vladimir Mayakovsky (1893–1930) was linked to the world of the visual arts early in his career, and, particularly after the Revolution, to the theater. Boris Pasternak (1890–1960), whose mother and father were, respectively, a pianist and an artist, had considered music and philosophy as vocations before settling on the written word. For Mikhail Kuzmin (1872–1936), music and literature went "hand in hand."[10] He set poems to music and performed them; he also wrote theater plays as well as prose and poetry, and had a life-long connection with the worlds of theater and cabaret. He was one of the founders of the best-known cabaret of the period, the Stray Dog (Brodiachaia sobaka, 1912–15).[11] The competitions, conversations, and performances at the Stray Dog Café were vital stimuli to the multifarious artistic creativity of the Silver Age. With its basement location and scruffy name, the Stray Dog set itself apart from the hieratic temple of Ivanov's Tower, yet it assembled many of the same literary figures: Akhmatova, Mandelstam, Khlebnikov, Gumilev, and Mayakovsky, to name a few. Sergei Esenin (1895–1925), another café regular, would go on to create a similar venue in Moscow, called the Poet's Café. The Stray Dog was memorialized in Akhmatova's lyric, which declares, "we are all boozers and hustlers here" ("Vse my brazhniki zdes´, bludnitsy," 1913), and less laconically in her later *Poem Without a Hero*. With the Cassandra-like powers for which she would later be celebrated, Akhmatova represented their 1910s revelries as doomed.

In the aftermath of the Revolution and the Civil War, many surviving modernist cultural institutions atrophied, particularly after the 1920s, although the pranks and performances of the OBERIU group carried the hope for artistic innovation into the early Soviet period.[12] Another exception was the circle surrounding the poet Maksimilian Voloshin (1877–1932), which he reconstituted in Koktebel in Crimea: what had been an unofficial literary salon before the Revolution and a shelter for many modernist writers during the Civil War became one of the first writers' retreats (*dom tvorchestva*) under the protection of the Ministry of Education (later these retreats would be controlled by the Soviet Writers' Union).[13]

Despite these few notable exceptions, the emigration of key figures, the tragic death of Blok, and the execution of Gumilev in 1921 were perceived as the symbolic end of an era. But was it a genuine ending? It can be argued that the emigration preserved, if not the energy, at least the spirit of Russian modernism abroad, and visual arts and music easily found a new home in foreign cultures (principally Paris and Berlin, the two main hubs of Russian emigration). Europe had already had a powerful whiff of the Russian revolution in art and culture when Diaghilev presented *The Firebird* in Paris in 1910, and then even more so after the scandalous Parisian staging of the *Rite of Spring* in 1913. Scholars of the music, art, and performance practices of the era, including John Bowlt, chronicled the events in Petersburg and Moscow that set the stage for those later exports.[14] Art exhibits by groups like the Jack of Diamonds (Bubnovyi valet, 1910, 1912, and 1913) and Donkey's Tail (Oslinyi khvost, 1912), which featured the work of Mikhail Larionov (1881–1964), Natalia Goncharova (1881–1962), David Burliuk (1882–1967), and Kazimir Malevich (1878–1935); performances, like the Futurist opera *Victory Over the Sun* (*Pobeda nad Solntsem*, 1913); and the cabarets, cafés, and salons would become inspirations for those in emigration.

Literary groups of the 1920s

The Silver Age of Russian culture had no precise end-point. Even the Red Terror (beginning in 1918), the Civil War, and the ensuing disasters could not immediately derail the innovations and energies of modernism. Bolshevik politics provoked dire forebodings, but the 1920s witnessed an unprecedented diversity of literary styles and trends. The heterogeneity of literature can be seen tangibly through a listing of various literary groups and associations. Some were short-lived and left only manifestoes and one or two slim collections, but others acquired solid institutional footing.

Among the organizations intended to promote cultural growth and creativity within the proletarian masses, the most important was Proletkult (Proletkul´t), created prior to the October Revolution but then financially and organizationally supported by the Bolshevik Minister of Education Anatoly Lunacharsky (1875–1933), a critic and writer and himself one of

Proletkult's founders. (Lunacharsky also extended his support to pro-Communist Futurists, placing them in state-sponsored propaganda jobs and backing their publications.) The ideology of Proletkult was shaped by Aleksandr Bogdanov (1873–1927), a former active Bolshevik and writer, and by Aleksei Gastev (1882–1939), a talented poet and theoretician. According to Bogdanov, each class has its own culture, and the task of Proletkult was to help the proletariat produce a new, pure proletarian culture free of the intelligentsia's interventions. Bogdanov and Gastev treated art and literature instrumentally as a form of class organization and education, considering aesthetic pleasure to be a bourgeois atavism.[15] The Proletkult grew exponentially, operating twenty magazines by 1920 and enlisting some 80,000 members, but Lenin categorically opposed its independence; it formally existed until 1932, but Lenin's scathing attack in 1920 (the directive "On Proletkults" ["O Proletkul'takh"]) channeled their members into organizations that were more firmly under party control.[16]

With the dissolution of Proletkult, a number of new literary groups emerged, including the Russian Association of Proletarian Writers (Rossiiskaia assotsiatsiia proletarskikh pisatelei, RAPP), its successor, the All-Union Association of Proletarian Writers (Vserossiiskaia assotsiatsia proletarskikh pisatelei, VAPP), and its subsections—The Forge (Kuznitsa), The Young Guard (Molodaia gvardiia), and October (Oktiabr'). Their members published in *On Guard* (*Na postu* [1923–25], later *Na literaturnom postu* [1926–32]), and in two other journals named after the literary groups they represented: *The Young Guard* and *October* (the latter was the organ of VAPP's Moscow section from 1926 to 1932). The RAPP ideologues Leopol'd Averbakh (1903–37), Grigory Lelevich (1901–45), Ilya Vardin (1890–1941), Semen Rodov (1893–1968), and Aleksei Selivanovsky (1900–38) also promoted the interpretation of literature as an instrument in class struggle. For them, the writer was mostly the medium of his class, which meant that a proper Soviet literature could only be created by writers of proletarian origin. They would inherently represent reality according to Marxist class theory, although on closer inspection their writings suggest a poorly disguised desire to guess at party ideological politics. At the time, however, this subjugation of literature to party ideology was defined as "the primacy of content over form." Conservative art forms were promoted: Proletkult and The Forge poets tried to inject proletarian pathos into the worn-out poetry of late nineteenth-century populism, and RAPP prose-writers tried to imitate Lev Tolstoy by replacing psychological complexity with a sense of "class instinct."[17]

Proletarian writers competed with Futurist organizations for the role of the "most revolutionary" literary group. The self-identified revolutionary groups included Left Front of Arts (Levyi front iskusstv, LEF, 1922–28), later transformed into a short-lived Revolutionary Front of Arts (Revoliutsionnyi front iskusstv, REF, 1929–30); it published the magazines *LEF* (1923–25) and *The New LEF* (1927–28). The LEF theorists and practitioners, most prominently Vladimir Mayakovsky, Sergei Tret'iakov (1892–1927), Osip Brik (1888–1945), Nikolai Aseev (1889–1963), Viktor Shklovsky (1893–1984), Nikolai Chuzhak (1876–1937), and Boris Arvatov (1896–1940), were unlike their RAPP counterparts in their quest to develop avant-garde forms able to connect art with everyday life. They wanted to use art as a practical tool for social innovation and they promoted close collaboration between literature and Bolshevik politics. They did resemble RAPP theorists, however, in one way: their fondness for statements about art's service to the interests of the proletariat and the Revolution. But instead of blindly subjugating literature to politics, they elevated the avant-garde artist as a producer of new forms of life, so that while fulfilling a "social command" (*sotsial'nyi zakaz*), art could shape the future by constructing new social relations and phenomena. For LEF, a new literature would engage consumers of their poems, posters, or the "literature of fact" in the process of creative, revolutionary construction.[18]

There were also groups of fellow travelers (*poputchiki*, in Trotsky's term): writers of a non-proletarian origin who were loyal to the Revolution. The two most prominent groups were The Crossing (Pereval, 1923–32), allied with the journals *Red Virgin Soil* (*Krasnaia nov'*, 1921–42) and *The New World* (*Novyi mir*, 1925–present); and the Leningrad-based Serapion Brothers (Serapionovy brat'ia). The Crossing was created by a critic, Aleksandr Voronsky (1884–1937), and two poets, Mikhail Svetlov (1903–64) and Mikhail Golodny (1903–49), who had just left the RAPP-dominated group The Young Guard. Eduard Bagritsky (1895–1934) joined The Crossing in 1925, but in 1927 became a leader in the Literary Center of Constructivists. Whereas RAPP treated literature as a vehicle for party ideology and LEF proclaimed the constructivist functions of art, The Crossing insisted on the heuristic powers of literature and emphasized the role of the writer's individuality, as opposed to social command or Marxist method. Major figures were literary critics: Voronsky, Abram Lezhnev (1893–1938), and Dmitry Gorbov (1894–1967). Viacheslav Polonsky (1886–1932), editor-in-chief of *Novyi mir* and *Press and Revolution* (*Pechat' i revoliutsiia*, 1921–30) also had views close to those of The Crossing. For them, the writer's ideology and class origin meant nothing in comparison with his or her sensitivity to the spirit of the times. They treated the artist as an unconscious instrument of historical cognition, and for that reason paid greater attention to literary style than to content or theme. The Crossing critics brought that method to an unlikely selection of writers, including Isaac Babel (1894–1940), Yuri Olesha (1899–1960), Vsevolod Ivanov (1895–1963), Boris Pil'niak (1894–1938), Sergei Esenin, and Boris Pasternak. The Crossing's slogan, "forward to the classics" (*vpered k klassike*), later hijacked by RAPP, in fact disguised their preference for modernist narratives: they valued the non-linear and thematically complex over traditional realist discourse.[19]

RAPP, LEF, and The Crossing competed for dominant influence over the state's literary policy in the 1920s. Divisions into warring factions were not categorical: some of Babel's stories first appeared in *LEF*, for example, even though Babel enjoyed the greatest support from The Crossing's critics Voronsky and Lezhnev. The most famous transition from one rival group to another is associated with Mayakovsky: after many years of leadership in LEF, he joined the RAPP group October, shocking his LEF friends and eliciting a stream of disparaging speeches and poems. (Mayakovsky's pained reaction was cited as a reason for his suicide two months later.)

Eventually the three groups suffered defeat. The death dates of their leaders are stunningly similar: between 1937 and 1939. These are the years of the Great Terror, which claimed countless lives, including Tret'iakov and Voronsky, Babel and Pil'niak, Averbakh and Lezhnev, Gastev and Chuzhak. This catastrophe could not have been imagined in 1925, when the party declared neutrality in literary battles. Prominent party officials—including Lunacharsky, Lev (Leon) Trotsky (1879–1940), and Nikolai Bukharin (1888–1938)—could voice their support for various literary associations. The LEF circle was most in favor in the early 1920s; however, the creation of *Red Virgin Soil* in 1921 (followed by *Novyi mir* in 1925), on direct orders from Lenin and Trotsky, suggested that The Crossing's moderate strategy was more appealing to party leadership. After Voronsky was fired from *Red Virgin Soil* during the anti-Trotsky campaign in 1927, RAPP and its followers gained the upper hand; pervasive bullying of non-proletarian writers ensued.[20] Many in the literary world, anticipating the creation of the Union of Soviet Writers, greeted the disbanding of all literary groups in 1932 with approval.

Beyond these conflicts, Russian literary life of the 1920s saw many other literary groups flourishing outside of the mainstream. The Imaginists, Emotionalists, Literary Constructivists (not to be confused with the Constructivist artists grouped around LEF), Expressionists, Fuists, Nichevoki, Biocosmists, the Leningrad Futurists (not affiliated with LEF), Group 41°, and OBERIU all sprang up, alongside many other informal groups and salons. While some were dead-end experiments, the diversity and the energy they generated caution us against accepting the usual triad of RAPP/proletarian writers, LEF/revolutionary avant-garde, and The Crossing/fellow travelers.

The Serapion Brothers offer an interesting case in point. In the group's 1922 manifesto, the young Lev Lunts (1901–24) declared: "We believe that literary chimeras are a separate reality and we oppose utilitarianism. We do not write propaganda. Art is as real as life. And like life, art has no goal or meaning: it exists because it cannot not exist."[21] This organization of fellow travelers was named after E. T. A. Hoffman's collection of novellas *Die Serapionsbrüder* (and after the eponymous literary circle of German Romantics). Its members included Evgeny Zamiatin (1884–1937), Mikhail Zoshchenko (1894–1958), Konstantin Fedin (1892–1977), Veniamin Kaverin (1902–89), Vsevolod Ivanov, Nikolai Tikhonov (1896–1979), and Nikolai Nikitin (1895–1963). The group was active in Petrograd-Leningrad from 1921 to 1926. In Soviet criticism, despite Gorky's support, it served as a poster child for apolitical art that "ignores revolutionary reality." One of the leaders, Evgeny Zamiatin, created the first political dystopia *We* (*My*, completed 1921), and Mikhail Zoshchenko authored sensationally popular, tragicomic short stories of everyday life (*byt*), but writings by the Serapion Brothers did not meet the expectations about appropriate representations of revolutionary reality, and were either ignored or denounced (*We* was banned). Yet it was precisely such fictions that grappled with the realities of revolutionary life, including the psychological and social consequences for individuals who tried to survive the process of the world's remaking.

The Serapions and minor avant-garde groups confronted, each in its own way, the utilitarian approach to literature. The seemingly incompatible strategies produced hybrid solutions. For example, the Literary Center of Constructivists (1924–30), which included Ilya Sel'vinsky (1899–1968), Vladimir Lugovskoi (1901–57), Eduard Bagritsky, and Vera Inber (1890–1972), combined the LEF programs with Neo-Romantic aesthetics. Much like supporters of LEF, they saw literature's active participation in the construction of new subjectivity as a process of radical modernization, even Westernization. But they resisted demands to subjugate poetic individuality to social command and popular taste. In Ilya Kukulin's formulation, they believed that the revolutionary intelligentsia, rather than party functionaries, would have a leading role in designing the new Soviet order. They saw pro-Soviet intelligentsia poets as the true engineers of a new civilization (the famous phrase about writers as "engineers of human souls" would appear only later).[22]

Some groups declared their commitment to collectivist and utilitarian values, variously interpreted.[23] A group of Neo-peasant poets, which included Nikolai Kliuev (1884–1937),[24] Sergei Esenin, Sergei Klychkov (1889–1937), Petr Oreshin (1887–1938), and Aleksandr Shiriaevets (1887–1924), envisioned a collectivist worldview; they drew on the language of sensibility and a mythology of peasant culture rather than on ideology.[25] The group was founded in the 1910s, when they were dubbed Neo-peasant (*novokrest'ianskie*) poets—as opposed to "old" peasant poets, such as Aleksei Kol'tsov or Ivan Nikitin—by the critic Ivanov-Razumnik (1878–1946).[26] The circle survived until the early 1930s when several were labeled "kulak poets": Kliuev, Klychkov, Oreshin, and Pavel Vasil'ev (1910–37), who joined in the late 1920s. At various points in the 1930s each was arrested, and all were executed.

Collectivist self-identification also marked the Biocosmists, who sought to extend Nikolai Fedorov's (1829–1903) "philosophy of the common task" and the Futurist Velimir Khlebnikov's cosmic visions. They tried to inscribe the social revolution within a large-scale utopian transformation of the entire cosmos through what they called "active evolution." The ideas of Biocosmism filtered through to the work of Andrei Platonov (1899–1951), whose science-fiction trilogy (*The Descendants of the Sun* [*Potomki solntsa*, 1922], *The Lunar Bomb* [*Lunnaia bomba*, 1926], and *The Ethereal Tract* [*Efirnyi trakt*, 1927]) draws on its principles.

Polemics among the different literary groups further reflected the disintegration of age-old ideas of what literature should be.[27] Manifestos and debates revealed the desire to invent literature appropriate to the new era. A surge in literary theory was inevitable, but the focus on trends in *contemporary* literature is notable. Theorists used the literature of their contemporaries to construct arguments for rebuilding all of Russian culture. Sociological theories of literature, mainly Marxist, dominated the cultural scene and were advanced by thinkers as different as Trotsky, Valerian Pereverzev (1882–1968), Vladimir Friche (1870–1929), Pavel Sakulin (1868–1930), and Boris Arvatov. For these theorists, literature was a manifestation of social and class ideology, psychology, and even the unconscious. Through analyses of plotlines, characters, and formal elements, they emphasized literature's function as a vehicle of social analysis. They reduced literary texts to illustrations of ideological doctrines or unwitting confessions of writers as the representatives of a given class. However, not all literary theories of the day were driven by ideology.

A strong challenge to any direct causal relationship between literature and social change came from the Formalists, whose starting point in thinking about literary creativity, influence across generations, and the elements of literary specificity reoriented theory. Seeing form as the interaction between mechanisms of perception, cultural inheritance, and everyday life (literary *byt*), the Formalists tried to capture the logic of cultural production as an independent political force. In their view, form did not reflect specific ideologies; rather, it generated new vision by producing a new apprehension of discourse. These ideas daringly informed the Formalists' approach to literature, producing new genres and styles of writing. Formalism proved to have great staying power as a set of theories best able to analyze the most profound and most radical literary innovations of the first quarter of the twentieth century and of later periods as well.

CASE STUDY Formalism

Formalism, based on a theory of literary texts as a collection of devices and on a theory of literary history as a process of non-linear shifts, was one of the twentieth century's most intellectually stimulating critical methods.[28] It offered paradigm-shifting theoretical concepts as well as practical interpretations of literary works and cinematic techniques. Although Viktor Shklovsky's paper "The Resurrection of the Word" ("Voskreshenie slova," 1914) provided an early manifesto, the true development of Formalism is inseparable from the St. Petersburg Society of Studies of Poetic Language (Obshchestvo izucheniia poeticheskogo iazyka, OPOIaZ), active from 1916 to 1925, and the work of its leading representatives: Shklovsky, Yuri Tynianov (1894–1943), Boris Eikhenbaum (1886–1959), Roman Jakobson (1896–1982), and Osip Brik. Their intellectual range was vast: from *Don Quixote* and Laurence Sterne to the history of nineteenth-century Russian literature; from folklore to the poetry of their contemporaries and to film (in which Shklovsky, Tynianov, and Brik also worked as practitioners). They sought a new concept of art and literature able to effectively interpret the most recent artistic innovations, even as they offered new strategies for reading literary classics and literary history.

The Formalists openly confronted the schools of cultural/historical and psychological commentary that had dominated Russian scholarship, as well as more recent impressionistic and Symbolist approaches. They wished to isolate what they called "literariness" (*literaturnost'*), giving priority to identifying the constitutive elements of literature as an art form. More radically, they rejected ideas ascribing to literature specifically poetic vocabulary and syntax (as the nineteenth-century philologist Aleksandr Potebnia had argued). Although almost all were graduates in Philology at St. Petersburg University, the intellectual sources of their theories lay elsewhere, including Bergson's theories of perception and Nietzsche's philosophy of history.[29]

A central Formalist concept is *ostranenie* (defamiliarization, estrangement), introduced by Shklovsky in the essay "Art as Device" ("Iskusstvo, kak priem," 1917) and developed in *Theory of Prose* (*O teorii prozy*, 1925). It locates the specificity of literature not in the language or themes, but in a new perception of the real, implicating the reader in the process of co-creation. Formalists termed "devices" (*priemy*) the various methods that could cause shifts or dislocations in perception, including changes to the meaning of words and the evolution of taste and style. Form was understood as a system of devices organized by a dominating device (*dominanta*). The history of literature (and of literary culture perceived as a system) was thus a transition from one sequence of devices to another. This conceptualization does away with the age-old opposition between form and content, where form emerges as the culmination of all shifts, both technical and semantic, in the literary text. In Eikhenbaum's words, Formalists bestowed on the concept of form "a new set of meanings: not as an enveloping structure, but as a sense of fullness or completeness, as something concrete and dynamic, with its own content outside of alignments to something external."[30]

The principle of *ostranenie* is best illuminated in the Formalists' studies of poetic language: they traced the semantic changes produced by syntagmatic links (Tynianov), rhythm (Jakobson), poetic syntax (Brik), and melodic structure (Eikhenbaum).[31] Shklovsky drew his material mainly from prose, focusing on works that bared the device (*obnazhenie priema*), including *Tristram Shandy*, *Don Quixote*, and Vasily Rozanov's (1856–1919) *Fallen Leaves* (*Opavshie list'ia*, 1913–15). Shklovsky's now famous distinction between *fabula* (the story line) and *siuzhet* (the narrative) further extended the opposition between device and material and emphasized the primacy of the former.

Formalists found examples of discontinuity and defamiliarization throughout the history of literature in individual creative practice and, more broadly, in literary traditions. They concluded that literary history moves along broken trajectories (parody, discussed by Tynianov, served as a paradigmatic example), where rejection and critique create forms of continuity. They demonstrated how eccentric and marginal tendencies of one epoch become dominant in the next, and how cultural inheritance is passed as if from uncle to nephew, rather than from father to son. (The masculine categories were unmarked, to use the structuralist parlance, although Formalist theoretical texts rarely treated women writers; Akhmatova was an exception.)

Formalists consciously emphasized the parallels between their own conceptualization of literary history, their assessments of modernity, and the experience of revolution.[32] Nevertheless, throughout the 1920s, they were attacked by Marxist critics for their lack of political engagement and by more conservative thinkers for their disregard of historical positivism. In 1936, the party launched an official ideological campaign, using "Formalism" as a derogatory umbrella term for the entire spectrum of modernist and avant-garde trends. Shklovsky, Tynianov, and Eikhenbaum, however, preserved a secret allegiance to their theoretical beliefs, transforming them into methods of literary writing or historical research. Formalism's legacy outlived its practitioners, surviving in the study of Formalist principles and their use in analyzing literary processes, texts, and traditions.

CASE STUDY Mikhail Bakhtin

Attention to form followed a different trajectory in the work of Mikhail Bakhtin (1895–1975), who focused on the philosophical teleology of form. Bakhtin saw literary form as a means to test ideas, philosophical concepts, and colloquial discourses. His ear for multi-voiced conversations between various systems of ideas in fictional texts effectively undermined sociological theories and their understanding of literature as a direct reflection of class ideology and/or psychology. In and after the 1970s, Bakhtin would emerge as one of the most influential literary and cultural theorists of the century. Although he was prolific and deeply admired by small circles of friends and colleagues, this fame would have struck him as improbable, given his profound marginalization for nearly his entire working life. The force fields in his thought that made their impact posthumously can be grouped around his writings on carnival and the grotesque, his notion of the novel as modernity's most expressive genre alongside a definition of novelistic discourse as polyphonic and unfinalizable, and his effective use of the concept of the chronotope as a way to typologize literary texts and genres. Bakhtin demonstrated great freedom in applying ideas of European philosophy, especially Kant and German phenomenologists. Scholars East and West have also emphasized the Judeo-Christian sources and implications in Bakhtin's thought, and the spiritual assumptions of these traditions balance the twin materialisms of Marxism and Formalism, also recognizable in his work and in that of his circle.[33]

Bakhtin belonged to several intellectual circles (in Nevel and Vitebsk), eventually creating an informal school of his own. After his move to Leningrad in 1924, his circle included the literary scholar Pavel Medvedev (1891 o.s.–1938), the musicologist and linguist Valentin Voloshinov (1895–1936), the music critic Ivan Sollertinsky (1902–44), the pianist and religious activist Maria Iudina (1899–1970), and the writer Konstantin Vaginov (1899–1934), among others. The tightness of this circle and the constant exchange of ideas led to persistent questions of authorship regarding some of the early writings. Although some have argued that Bakhtin had a share in the writing of V. N. Voloshinov's *Freudianism* (*Freidizm*, 1927), P. N. Medvedev's *The Formal Method in Literary Scholarship* (*Formal'nyi metod v literaturovedenii*, 1928), and Voloshinov's *Marxism and the Philosophy of Language* (*Marksizm i filosofiia iazyka*, 1929), most scholars now agree that these works were written by their stated authors. Co-authorship has not been entirely ruled out, but it is sensible to treat the clusters of ideas in all these books in productive conversation with one another and with Bakhtin's works in progress at the time.

Greater prominence has been attached to Bakhtin's study of Dostoevsky, *Problems of Dostoevsky's Poetics* (*Problemy poetiki Dostoevskogo*, first published in 1929 as *Problems of Dostoevsky's Oeuvre* [*Problemy tvorchestva Dostoevskogo*], revised extensively for the 1963 edition; scholars consult both, but the latter is the basis of Caryl Emerson's influential 1984 translation). Bakhtin's essays have also had a broad resonance, particularly "Discourse in the Novel" ("Slovo v romane," written 1934–35). Four of Bakhtin's essays on the history and theory of the novel were translated by Michael Holquist and Caryl Emerson as *The Dialogic Imagination* in 1981, which brought the essays a wide Anglophone readership eager for theoretical alternatives to structuralism and post-structuralism. The scholarly apparatus of the volume and of Emerson's translation of *Problems of Dostoevsky's Poetics* gave readers a broader context for appreciating Bakhtin's larger cultural project grounded, according to Holquist, in a distinctive approach to language: "The conception has as its enabling a priori an almost Manichean sense of opposition and struggle at the heart of existence, a ceaseless battle between centrifugal forces that seek to keep things apart, and centripetal forces that strive to make things cohere."[34] That metaphor of struggle characterized the competition of discourses within novels and defined the space of carnival, in Bakhtin's view.

In the 1930s, Bakhtin focused on the novel as a literary genre. In "Discourse in the Novel" and "From the Prehistory of Novelistic Discourse" ("Iz predystorii romannogo slova," 1940, published 1975), he relates the genre of the novel to specific historical and cultural formations. At the center of his argument is always a notion of language use, of a novelistic word or discourse (*slovo*) that is polyphonic in its distribution of distinct voices. More important, the narrative mode of the novel is dialogical, so that not only the characters, but the very forms of narration provide utterances that anticipate the response of another. That expectation of response, both from fictional characters and of the reader, is built into the novel, Bakhtin suggests, by means of another rhetorical feature with which his work has become associated, heteroglossia. Michael Holquist defined it as "the situation of a subject surrounded by the myriad responses he or she might make at any particular point, but any one of which must be framed in a specific discourse selected from the teeming thousands available. Heteroglossia is a way of conceiving the world as made up of a roiling mass of languages."[35]

One further philosophical inference about the nature of human existence follows from Bakhtin's understanding of the novel, which has been termed unfinalizability. It was emphasized in the scholarship of Gary Saul Morson and Caryl Emerson, and in their account of how Bakhtin understood language: "It is a *task*, a *project*, always ongoing and ever unfinished; and it is always opposed to the essential messiness of the world."[36] Such "ongoing and ever unfinished" language informed the novel; it was again being praised as the most significant and freedom-bearing literary form, one that could give us an aesthetic framework for understanding the open-ended nature of our lives.

The first of six volumes of Bakhtin's collected works in Russian appeared in 1996, the last in 2012.[37] With the help of its thorough apparatus, cultural historians such as Craig Brandist and Galin Tihanov began to restore Bakhtin to his European (largely German) contexts.[38] A further aspect of Bakhtin's legacy, pursued by scholars in Great Britain and oriented more toward Marxist thinking, centers on the phenomenon of carnival.[39] Here, his book *Rabelais and His World* (*Tvorchestvo Fransua Rable i narodnaia kul'tura srednevekov'ia i Renessansa*, 1965) has been crucial. In it, Bakhtin evoked an embodied notion of experience, theorizing everything from eating, drinking, and defecating to sweating and sneezing. The carnival body swallows up the world, as Bakhtin put it, and he used the temporal frame of the carnival to amass grotesque bodily experiences and map them onto a world becoming modern. These theories also enliven the important essay on "Forms of Time and of the Chronotope in the Novel" ("Formy vremeni i khronotopa v romane," written 1937–38, published 1975) and the term chronotope (time-space matrix) has since become a standard investigatory tool of narrative analysis, effective for ancient as well as modern narratives, and as a point of access to the cultural environments in which those narratives arose. Since 2014, there has been a resurgence of interest in aspects of Bakhtin's work only now being translated into English: his dark views on Shakespearean tragedy as a product of degenerate carnival, and his somber meditations on word and image during the bleakest months of the Second World War.[40]

The theories articulated by the Formalists and Bakhtin and his circle effectively challenged the reliance on a direct causal relationship between literature and social change that was to become dominant in the Soviet period. Unlike Bakhtin's theories, though, the Formalists' writings enjoyed an immediate impact on literary production: they affected the work of such disparate groups as LEF, the Serapion Brothers, and OBERIU, perhaps because of their understanding of literature as capable of changing readers' perception and ultimately even their worldview. Bakhtin's cult status was eventually assured, but only belatedly. The phenomenon of interaction between writers and theorists that was paradigmatic for the Formalists, however, could be observed later in the twentieth century, as practitioners of postmodernism and Conceptualism were to demonstrate in Moscow in the late Soviet period and as the activists and poets of the Chto delat'? (What Is To Be Done?) group would show in post-Soviet St. Petersburg.

Literary life of the emigration, 1918 through the 1980s

As Soviet literary institutions were being formed after the Revolution, cultural centers for those in emigration also emerged. Russian writers who had left because of Civil War, instability, and cultural intolerance, or because they had found the emerging Soviet state loathsome, gravitated toward a handful of destinations, and where they ended up had consequences for the literature they wrote. The major émigré centers across the twentieth century were Prague, Berlin, Paris, Belgrade, Sofia, Warsaw, and Harbin, and eventually New York, Tel Aviv, and Jerusalem. Most who fled the new Soviet Union did not remain in their first place of refuge. Marina Tsvetaeva (1892–1941) left Prague for Paris; Roman Jakobson ended up in the United States after a productive period among the Czech structuralists; and Vladimir Nabokov (1899–1977) settled in the United States after living in Berlin and Paris. Others returned to the USSR, including Ilya Erenburg (1891–1967), Maxim Gorky, Aleksei Tolstoy (1882 o.s.–1945), Viktor Shklovsky, and eventually Tsvetaeva. The pattern of return repeated itself after the fall of the Soviet Union in 1991, when open borders permitted cross-traffic: Joseph Brodsky (1940–96) joked that he would go back only in a US military uniform, but others took advantage of the eased travel restrictions to contribute to the more fully integrated literary culture of the post-Soviet period. Some returning writers resumed their Russian citizenship, even if they did not all return to Russia immediately or permanently, including Aleksandr Solzhenitsyn (1918–2008), Yuri Mamleev (1931–2015), Vladimir Voinovich (b. 1932), Evgeny Grishkovets (b. 1967), and Fedor Svarovsky (b. 1971). But even as borders had become more permeable, and differences between those who left and those who stayed became less absolute, the practice of emigration continued well into the twenty-first century. An exodus of writers and thinkers intensified in the 2010s, when cultural freedoms seemed suddenly very fragile and an increasingly capricious authoritarian rule began to reassert itself. The emigration has been slighter than in earlier generations, but it includes some figures of great symbolic importance, like the influential editor, poet, translator, and cultural entrepreneur Dmitry Kuz'min (b. 1968), who moved to Latvia in 2015.

In the 1920s, Paris and Berlin, in particular, created the kind of rich cultural environment in which writers and thinkers could flourish. As Marc Raeff observed, "the major tasks of bestowing a sense of unity and coherence to Russia Abroad fell to publishing;"[41] and, while publishing was certainly going on elsewhere, writers were most drawn to these two capitals where works and ideas could circulate freely. Berlin was a first destination: Germany and the Soviet Union had restored diplomatic relations in 1922, and Berlin, the capital, welcomed Russians; some 100,000 of them were present in the city in 1922.[42] Many arrivals had imagined their stay would only be temporary: surely, order would be restored in still-tumultuous post-Civil

War Russia. Most émigrés had moved on from Berlin by the mid-1920s, but rarely to return to Russia. Equally short-lived was their confidence that a connection between writers left behind in Russia and émigrés (the "pure" and the "impure," as Erenburg was to call them) would survive. But while it flourished, the Berlin community was a lively and remarkably tolerant center for sharp political and aesthetic debate, and the openness of Germany to arriving Russians made for easy passage back and forth.[43] Many notable writers spent some time in Berlin in the early 1920s, including Mayakovsky, Pasternak, Khodasevich, Remizov, Tsvetaeva, Severianin, Gorky, Esenin, Bely, as well as painters like Marc Chagall and Vasily Kandinsky. A major exhibit of Russian contemporary art was mounted in 1922. There were visiting theater companies, operas, and chamber theater and cabaret performances, with participants ranging from Stanislavsky and Kachalov to Chaliapin. There was a House of the Arts (Dom iskusstv), with more than 140 active or associate members, and sections on literature, music, and the visual arts; a Writers' Club was founded by Yuri Aikhenval'd in 1922.[44] Individual writers held forth at events devoted to their work (Mayakovsky and Pasternak together on a single evening, October 20, 1922), and texts that would enter the canon of Russian literature were first heard in Berlin, whether in their entirety or as excerpts (including Aleksei Tolstoy's *Aelita*, Shklovsky's *Zoo*, and Bely's *Kotik Letaev*).

Berlin offered a hospitable environment for literary publication, with its solid infrastructure and thriving book market. Germany had signed the Berne Convention on copyright, and writers— even pre-Revolutionary Russian writers like Lev Tolstoy and Ivan Turgenev—had long been willing to see their work published in Germany. As a result, Berlin was the acknowledged publishing capital of Russian literature in the 1920s. The Russian bookstore *Moscow* opened in 1919; the publishing house Petropolis flourished until the Gestapo shut it down in 1938. As had been true in Russia, periodicals were a more important publishing vehicle than books.[45]

Some writers used their short stays effectively. Aleksei Remizov published prolifically in his two years in the city. Marina Tsvetaeva was in Berlin for less than three months, during which time she published a second edition of her folktale poem *The Tsar-Maiden* (*Tsar'-Devitsa*, 1922), and worked on a volume of poems, *Craft* (*Remeslo*, 1923), that would appear a year later. Here she met Andrei Bely, remembered vividly in her later essay "A Captive Spirit" ("Plennyi dukh," 1934), and first read Pasternak's volume *My Sister, Life* (*Sestra moia zhizn'*, 1922). Tsvetaeva recorded her intense reaction to Pasternak's poems in the essay "A Cloudburst of Light" ("Svetovoi liven'"), which Bely published in his journal *Epopeia* in 1922.[46] Remarkable Russian journals and publishing houses flourished, including *Changing Landmarks* (*Smena vekh*), which was later called *On the Eve* (*Nakanune*) and eventually enjoyed a significant presence in Paris under its former name; *Russian Books* (*Russkaia kniga*, later *Novaia russkaia kniga*); *The Word* (*Slovo*); and *Colloquy* (*Beseda*). The links among publishing house, bookstore, and journal were tight: the first issue of *Russian Books* in January 1921 features the bookstore *Moscow* at the bottom of the cover as a kind of credit line.[47] Some books began to appear with a dual place of publication (Berlin–Petrograd, for instance, in the series created by Maxim Gorky and subsidized by the Soviet government: Mandelstam's *Tristia* read "Petersburg–Berlin" in its 1922 edition). The openness to Soviet writers was to remain a distinctive feature of Berlin émigré culture, in stark contrast to the anti-Soviet positions assumed in Paris in the 1920s and 1930s.

Among those who would return to the USSR from Berlin was Viktor Shklovsky. During his short two-year stay in Berlin, he wrote two non-fictional novels that are as unusual as any of the great modernist prose texts, including those by the Serapion Brothers whom he saw often in Petrograd in 1921: the novels are *A Sentimental Journey* (*Sentimental'noe puteshestvie*, 1923) and *Zoo, Letters Not About Love, or The Third Eloise* (*Zoo, Pis'ma ne o liubvi, ili Tret'ia Eloiza*, 1923). The first makes good on its allusions to Laurence Sterne in the title with its huge dose of Sternian irony, but the text presents readers with a memoir of catastrophe and revolution. *Zoo* is more personal, an experiment in the modernization of an eighteenth-century epistolary form, which turns its taboo on erotic topics to powerful advantage. Shklovsky uses his encyclopedic command of literary discourses to replace words of love with portraits, elegy, landscape description, dramatic fantasy, and an entire gallery of Russian writers then living in Berlin.[48] Some letters in *Zoo* were not authored by Shklovsky at all but by the object of his unrequited love, Elsa Triolet (1896–1970), the younger sister of Lilia Brik (1891–1978). Shklovsky and Triolet had a tryst in Bad-Saarov, a spa town outside Berlin, where they had both been invited by Gorky.[49] Shklovsky assembled his text by cutting it into pieces and moving them around on the floor to form a montage.[50]

As economic and political unrest intensified in 1923, many left Berlin for Paris. The City of Light was a powerful magnet for Russian writers, and Ivan Bunin (1870–1953), Konstantin Bal'mont (1867–1942), Nadezhda Teffi (pseud. Nadezhda Buchinskaia, née Lokhvitskaia, 1872–1952), Gippius, Merezhkovsky, and Mark Aldanov (1886–1957) were among those who went there directly from Russia. The enduring, formative role of French language and culture in Russia's intellectual history made the country a destination of choice.[51] Many writers had a superb command of the language, and they were able to connect with their French counterparts in ways that mitigated the isolation of émigré writers within their own linguistic communities.

Publishing enterprises in Paris were extensive and in some cases very long-lived. Daily newspapers that lasted more than a decade included *Renaissance* (*Vozrozhdenie*, 1925–40) and *The Latest News* (*Poslednie novosti*, 1920–40); both published literary material and were widely respected. *Contemporary Notes* (*Sovremennye zapiski*, 1920–40) was by any standard the most significant periodical of the emigration, and its title was meant to remind readers of two great nineteenth-century journals, *The Contemporary* and *Notes of the Fatherland*. Like its models, this classic "thick journal" offered hundreds of pages of poetry, prose, reviews, and philosophical essays. It took some positions, not always rigidly, so that its pages featured secular rather than metaphysical writing or nationalistic prose; in its final issue of 1940, which Ardis reprinted in full in 1983, the religious thinker and historian Georgy Fedotov (1886–1951) can be found contrasting the dangers of Nazism and Western-style democracies but also, in the end, favoring the latter for their capacity for improvement and reform.[52] That same issue features work by Sirin (soon to sign his name in full, Vladimir Nabokov), Gaito Gazdanov (1903–71), and the poetry of Viacheslav Ivanov and Vladislav Khodasevich (1886–1939), among others. One of the journal's strengths was that it did not hew to a specific orthodoxy.[53]

Contemporary Notes featured younger writers who drew inspiration from French culture. The premature death of Boris Poplavsky (1903–35) sealed his reputation as a controversial and mysterious figure.[54] His work shows vividly the impact of Baudelaire, Rimbaud, Apollinaire, and the Surrealists. Leonid Livak rightly describes him as maturing "at the crossroads of Soviet, émigré, and French letters."[55] Poplavsky continued the logical disruptions and linguistic experimentation of the Futurists, and he also drew on Aleksandr Blok's strange brand of Christian mysticism. Elements of automatic writing and explorations of the unconscious linked him to the Surrealists at least until the end of the 1920s, when he deliberately simplified his writing style.

The strong influence of Marcel Proust can be seen in the work of Gaito Gazdanov, best known for the novels *An Evening with Claire* (*Vecher u Kler*, 1930) and *Specter of Alexander Wolf* (*Prizrak Aleksandra Vul'fa*, 1947). Often cited as one of the two most promising prose writers of the emigration (the other being Nabokov), Gazdanov has been studied for his deep affinities to existentialism.[56]

Russian Paris was also well populated by established writers, including Nadezhda Teffi. Her short stories, feuilletons, plays, and character sketches featured characters slightly out of place in both a rapidly changing Russia and in Paris, as she found it upon emigration in 1919. Extremely popular in Russia, Teffi also discovered a ready audience in the Paris émigré community, and she often published in the Russian-language journals and newspapers. Her stories can be funny or tragic, or both, and they are rife with irony. Teffi's memoirs (*Vospominaniia*, completed 1928, published in Paris in 1932) recount the dramatic story of her flight from Russia with a steadfast determination to find humor in even the most horrifying and desperate moments of those months.[57]

The leading figures in the Paris émigré community also included Zinaida Gippius, who had worked with Teffi on the Bolshevik newspaper *New Life* (*Novaia zhizn'*, 1905–06) in Petersburg. Together with Merezhkovsky, starting in 1926, Gippius hosted a new version of their Petersburg salon, now called the Green Lamp in tribute to the literary group of the Pushkin era. These émigrés constituted close-knit groups, and some members, particularly critics, strenuously argued for the émigré writer as the true heir to Russian culture. A vocal advocate of this position was Georgy Adamovich (1884–1972), as amply attested in the volume of criticism reissued in 2002.[58] Adamovich was the standard bearer for a Paris School of Russian poetry called The Parisian Note (Parizhskaia nota), joined by Georgy Ivanov (1894–1958), a forceful voice as a poet and a notoriously unreliable memoirist. Ivanov's volume of poetry *The Roses* (*Rozy*, 1931) imitates the melancholic tones and prosaic language of Innokenty Annensky (1856–1909), who had been an earlier poetic inspiration to the Acmeists.[59] Other members of The Parisian Note included Irina Knorring (1906–43), whose diction and themes were like Akhmatova's but suffused by a deeper sadness; Lidia Chervinskaia (1907–88), who explored the poetics of expressive psychology and personal restraint with great musicality; Anatoly Shteiger (1907–44), whose poems remarkably mix aphoristic sharpness and a sense of longing; and Igor Chinnov (1909–96), whose first poems appeared in Paris in 1933, but who was mostly known for his later works, some marked by the school's verbal restraint and pessimism, others by expressions of irony and the grotesque.[60]

Other émigrés took polemical positions against Adamovich (as Tsvetaeva did in her essay "The Poet on the Critic" ["Poet o kritike," 1926]) and against the pessimistic nostalgia of The Parisian Note. The poet Vladislav Khodasevich, no enemy of pessimism, had come to Paris in 1925, and became an active critic. He embodied a neoclassical ideal, and was admired by Vladimir Nabokov perhaps in part for his acerbic assessments of literary gaffes and his stern taste. In Khodasevich's disputes with Adamovich, one can discern a strident note and more than a little bitterness on both sides. To Khodasevich, the de-emphasis on poetic craft in Adamovich's pronouncements was anathema; while Adamovich, during the Pushkin anniversary publications in 1927, insinuated that Pushkinian formal perfection was suspect.[61] Khodasevich's publications in emigration included his biography *Derzhavin* (1931), the essay-memoirs in *Necropolis* (*Nekropol'*, 1939), and a volume of poetry, *Collection of Verses* (*Sobranie stikhov*, 1927), which, along with already published texts, included his fifth book of poetry, *European Night* (*Evropeiskaia noch'*, 1927), its resonant title reminding readers just where he was.

A number of writers were quite productive in the emigration, often keeping apart from any particular school or group. Marina Tsvetaeva, despite staggering hardship, wrote a great deal, including the remarkable poems of *After Russia* (*Posle Rossii*, 1928), as well as passionate essays on contemporary writers, family members, Pushkin, and Pushkin myths. Ivan Bunin, who received the Nobel Prize for Literature in 1933, had completed many of his most famous stories prior to emigrating—including "Antonov Apples" ("Antonovskie iabloki," 1900) and "A Gentleman from San Francisco" ("Gospodin iz San-Frantsisko," 1915). But the complex eroticism of "Sunstroke" ("Solnechnyi udar," 1925) and the stories collected in the volume *Dark Avenues* (*Temnye allei*, 1946) are compelling examples of the lyrical, psychologically piercing narratives for which he is admired. His *Life of Arseniev* (*Zhizn' Arsen'eva*, written over many years, first published 1952) looked back on many events in his life but was a work of fiction. It summed up the meaningful events of those in his generation who experienced revolutionary change in Russia and then a life lived very far from the new Soviet reality.[62]

Another modernist who also wrote prolifically in emigration is Aleksei Remizov (1877–1957). He spent nearly four decades in Europe, largely in France, and even though he went for years with none of his work appearing in print, he continued to produce remarkable tales that fused dreams with reality, folklore with precisely observed details, archaic language with folk Russian, and expressionistic metaphors with a rhythmic syntax. Tsvetaeva called him "the universe's storyteller" ("vselenskii skazochnik").[63] His accounts of the Revolution and Civil War included the stunning "Lay on the Ruin of the Russian Land" ("Slovo o pogibeli Russkoi zemli," 1917); *Russia in a Whirlwind* (*Vzvikhrennaia Rus'*, 1927), which appeared in Paris; and "Along the Cornices" ("Po karnizam," 1929), published in Belgrade. His idiosyncratic later writings ranged from autobiographical vignettes, like *With Clipped Eyes* (*Podstrizhennymi glazami*, 1951), to imaginatively recast seventeenth-century tales about Solomonia and Savva Grudtsyn, published together as *Demons* (*Besnovatye*, 1951). Remizov was himself compared to a little demon by Andrei Bely, so perhaps the dreamy self-portraiture of the earlier works played some subterranean role in these demon tales. His engagement with pre-modern Russian culture, as for so many of his generation, meant preserving Russia's stories and cultural patterns, adapted to the modern age. Remizov's writing is often combined with elaborate drawings, and his certificates of membership in his fanciful Great Free Order of the Apes (*Obezvelpopal* in one abbreviation) show beautifully his fantastically detailed attention to calligraphy, spacing, and visual flourishes (as is shown in Plate 15).

Remizov's artistic legacy included drawings of his contemporaries from the worlds of literature and theater. Sometimes those images veered toward caricature, but in other cases the expressions were slightly exaggerated, as in his collage depicting the round-faced cabaret performer Nikita Baliev (see Figure v.01). The album *Theater*, from which the Baliev image comes, used brown wrapping paper, reminiscent of Futurist books. Its plainness contrasts the stylized, decorative border; that border provides a visual equivalent for the ornamental prose in which Remizov excelled.[64]

Paris reemerged as an émigré center in the late Soviet period, when the so-called third wave of emigration brought large numbers of Russians to the city. They produced an important newspaper, *Russian Thought* (*Russkaia mysl'*, 1947 to the present), featuring strong reporting on cultural events and book reviews. Natalia Gorbanevskaia (1936–2013) was its long-time editor. Paris was the home to *Continent* (*Kontinent*, in Paris—1974–92, in Moscow—1992–2013) and the *Messenger of the Russian Christian Movement* (*Vestnik russkogo khristianskogo dvizheniia*, abbreviated as *Vestnik RKhD*, 1925 to the present)—smaller-format thick journals where Soviet writers could publish abroad, albeit illegally. Andrei Sinyavsky (1925–97, also known as Abram Tertz) and his wife, the editor Maria Rozanova (b. 1929), settled in Paris in 1973, and founded the journal *Syntax* (*Sintaksis*, 1974–2006), in part to create a home for less orthodox (and less Orthodox) work. Writers as different as Andrei Bitov (b. 1937) and Elizaveta Mnatsakanova (b. 1922) appeared on its pages. YMCA Press (founded in 1921 in Prague), which had moved to Paris in 1925, continued for decades to publish theological and philosophical writings, and also brought out significant literary and cultural publications, including the first editions of Nadezhda Mandelstam's memoirs and Lydia Chukovskaya's three volumes on Anna Akhmatova.

The United States proved to be the destination of choice for late Soviet and post-Soviet writers, thinkers, editors, and scholars who either emigrated voluntarily or were exiled. Journalism in Russian found new outlets, including the New York-based *New Journal* (*Novyi zhurnal*), founded in 1942 and still in existence in the 2010s. Publishing houses included Ardis

FIGURE V.01. Aleksei Remizov, Baliev from the album "Teatr," collage with India ink and colored paper, 1929.

and Russica, which turned out enormous amounts of *tamizdat* literature. An independent press created in 1971 in Ann Arbor, Michigan by Carl Proffer, Professor of Russian Literature at the University of Michigan, and his colleague and wife Ellendea Proffer, Ardis became the major place of publication and translation of non-conformist contemporary Russian literature as well as reprints of forgotten treasures of Russian modernism. It released the first complete editions of major texts by Platonov, Kuzmin, Iskander, and Bitov, and republished (in Russian) all the Russian novels of Nabokov as well as Brodsky's books after his emigration.[65] Other important publishers for *tamizdat* included Inter-Language Literary Associates, Victor Kamkin Books in Washington, DC, and Chekhov Publishing House in New York. Comprehensive editions of the works of Mandelstam, Akhmatova, Khodasevich, and Gumilev were issued, based on archival holdings available at the time; these editions were treasured points of access to the poetic tradition of the Silver Age, which the émigré critics believed was being squandered in the Soviet Union. Such formerly *tamizdat* works were eventually published in post-Soviet Russia, often in superb scholarly editions, building on the foundation of publications by émigré editors from the 1960s–80s, and improving on it as additional archival material became available.

In addition to these important print venues for publication, the radio played an enduring and significant role in émigré cultural life. Radio Free Europe and Radio Liberty (Radio Svoboda), founded in 1951, had the mission of providing up-to-date news information to communist countries during the Cold War, but its cultural branch was also a significant part of its work, and it provided employment to a number of émigré writers at bureaus in the United States and in Europe, including Aleksandr Genis (b. 1953), Petr Vail (1949–2009), Igor Pomerantsev (b. 1947), Aleksei Tsvetkov (b. 1947), and Sergei Dovlatov (1941–90), who also briefly published the New York newspaper *The New American* (*Novyi amerikanets*, 1980–82). There were intersecting circles of friendship among some émigré writers and other cultural leaders, perhaps best imaged in a photograph of an unusually radiant Joseph Brodsky, Mstislav Rostropovich, and Mikhail Baryshnikov dancing in a New York restaurant.[66] Émigré writers adapted to their new environments in different ways: Solzhenitsyn and Brodsky represented polar opposites, the former confining himself to his glorious isolation in Vermont so as to remain a neo-Slavophile judge of the West, the latter keeping an eye on Russia even as he acculturated himself fully to life in Europe and the United States.

After the collapse of the Soviet Union, new émigré writers emerged in France, Germany, Israel, and the US, writing not in Russian, but in the language of their adopted countries, and to considerable acclaim. Among the most prominent are Andrei Makine (b. 1957) writing in French; Vladimir Kaminer (b. 1967) famous for his works in German; and the Anglophone writers Gary Shteyngart (b. 1972), David Bezmozgis (b. 1973), Olga Grushin (b. 1971), Michael Idov (b. 1976), and Lara Vapnyar (b. 1976).[67] Like Ilya Kaminsky (b. 1977), Eugene Ostashevsky (b. 1968), and Matvei Yankelevich (b. 1973) who write in English, the Belarusian Valzhyna Mort (b. 1981) has enjoyed great success as an English-language poet.[68] In different ways, these writers have reached a readership that recognizes the Slavic themes and intonations in their work as a mark of difference. It may be too early to say whether this new generation indicates a paradigm shift for Russian literature in emigration, and certainly many writers have continued to write in Russian, rather than switching to English, French, German, or Hebrew, even when they come to know the new language well. Yet there is a perceptible difference in terms of proportion: rather than the occasional writer whose exceptional linguistic facility permits a switch to a new language, as was the case with Nabokov and Brodsky, the bilingual capacities of a larger number of writers, many of whom left the Soviet Union as children and thus learned the language of their adoptive country early on, may mean that, in the twenty-first century, a global Russian literature will increasingly be written in multiple languages. It is stunning to realize how implausible that might have seemed to émigré writers who went to Berlin and Paris in the 1920s.

Creation of the Union of Soviet Writers

The cultural institutions of the emigration, although multiple and significant, look positively fluid when one compares them to the institutionalization of literature in the Soviet Union in the 1930s.[69] On April 23, 1932, the Central Committee of the Communist Party issued a resolution "On the Restructuring of Literary and Arts Organizations," which in effect launched the centralization of Soviet literature. In the aftermath of this resolution, a new cultural institution was created—the Union of Soviet Writers, with its compulsory artistic method, Socialist

Realism. Many writers happily interpreted this document as a license to avoid the dictatorship of RAPP. The result, however, proved to be far from liberation: the Soviet Writers' Union became a ministry of literature, controlling magazines and presses, and ideologically supervising all literary work before, during, and after publication.

The resolution of 1932 effectively disbanded all literary groups, above all the Association of Proletarian Writers (RAPP). The logic held that proletarian literary organizations had outlived their purpose as independent entities. They were said to have degenerated into "a means for cultivating exclusive circles, for detachment...from significant groups of writers and artists who sympathize with socialist construction."[70] More generally, groupings were seen as obstacles to the development of creative thought: the Central Committee decided to "to unite all writers who support the platform of Soviet power and who strive to participate in socialist construction into a single Union of Soviet Writers that includes a Communist faction."[71]

The First All-Union Congress of Soviet Writers followed in August 1934, and the Union of Soviet Writers was established as a necessary institutional mechanism facilitating the merger between the Soviet party-state and literature. Of the 1,500 members in 1934, some 800 would perish during the Great Terror in 1937–38. Despite bylaws (*ustav*) requiring regular meetings, the second Congress of the Writer's Union would not take place until 1954. During the period bracketed by these two congresses, in 1934 and 1954, high Stalinist culture unfolded.

The strange mixture of fear and reverence lavished on writers in Stalinist culture in many ways resonated with pre-revolutionary esteem for the writer as the voice of Truth and with Herzen's view of writers as a "second government." But Soviet ideologues valued literature for another reason, as well: as a discursive medium, it proved the most efficient vehicle for ideological messages. The restructuring of literature set the parameters for Soviet culture at large. The doctrine of Socialist Realism was first tested on literature, before it was extended to other forms of cultural expression. Designating writers as "engineers of human souls," the Stalinist state expected literature to perform a systemic reconstruction of reality and create a coherent, optimistic mythology that would develop and support a Soviet interpretation of moral values, social life, and history. In order to achieve this goal, literature had to be collectivized and industrialized in parallel with major political reforms in the 1930s.

Maxim Gorky played a central role in the organization of the Soviet Writers' Union and became its first Chair; in Plate 16, Gorky's beneficent image rises over the new card-carrying members at the First Congress. In the keynote address delivered at the First Congress, he defined Soviet writers as "judges of a world doomed to die" and as promoters of "true humanism, humanism of the revolutionary proletariat, humanism of the force invoked by history for the liberation of the entire world."[72] The messianic terms of his prediction expose a key feature of the Soviet literary project. According to Gorky, this project had to be radically different from both nineteenth-century realism and any form of modernism. Realism was created by "superfluous men," he argued, but "in our Union of Socialist Soviets, there cannot be superfluous men." Especially dangerous, in his opinion, were realist forms of social critique, which could not "serve to educate socialist individuality, for in criticizing everything, they asserted nothing.... Realism is necessary for us only for throwing light on the remnants of the past, for fighting them, and extirpating them."[73] As for modernism, Gorky unambiguously wrote off all its diverse forms as symptoms of bourgeois degeneration and "creative impotence." He described Dostoevsky as a main source of modernist degradation. The assault on Dostoevsky portrayed him as an individualist rebel and vilified him as the epitome of "philistinism" and "fascism."[74] This condemnation led to an unspoken near-ban on popular publication and interpretive study of Dostoevsky that was lifted only in the 1960s.

Gorky glorified folklore as a prototype of Socialist Realism. He had quite fantastic ideas about folklore, arguing, for instance, that folklore rejected pessimism (thus ignoring its tradition of laments and sad lyrical songs). He maintained that folklore was created by the toiling masses, and therefore was inherently suited to the needs of Soviet literature. Hidden beneath layers of cultural references, Gorky's elevation of folklore and myth as aesthetic models for Socialist Realism was little noticed at first. Yet his intentions became evident as Socialist Realism was being universally and exclusively promoted. Like folklore, Soviet literature was to be measured by popular taste; it had to be intelligible to the masses as if it were written by a "fellow toiler." The taint of so-called bourgeois individualism, associated with older forms of realism, was to be avoided, as were the complexity and experimentation of modernism. Gorky imagined Soviet literature as a new folk art that would fabricate a mythology adapted to the needs of the state and the party.

Never again was the essence of Socialist Realism formulated with such directness. No one at the Congress questioned Gorky's vision of Socialist Realism, although the former Politburo member and editor-in-chief of *Izvestia* Nikolai Bukharin offered an alternative set of priorities for Soviet literature. In his address "On Poetry, Poetics, and the Tasks of Poetic Work," he tried to correlate a Marxist approach to literature with scholarly theories, from Wilhelm von Humboldt to the Formalists (criticized but not demonized). Bukharin also presented a survey of contemporary Russian poetry, with respectful profiles of Blok, Esenin, Mayakovsky, Svetlov, Bagritsky, and especially Pasternak, along with the Serapion poet Nikolai Tikhonov and a member of the Literary Center of Constructivism, Ilya Sel'vinsky. He reserved his criticism for *agitprop* poetry written by Dem'ian Bedny (1883–1945), the author of popular political satires, and for Mayakovsky, the author of a significant body of propaganda poetry and slogans. Unlike Gorky, Bukharin interpreted Socialist Realism as a synthetic phenomenon, able to fuse realist analysis of social contradictions, romantic striving for the ideal, and universalism in philosophic thought. Goethe's *Faust* offered a perfect example of this synthesis. Bukharin's program for the new Soviet literature was no less utopian than Gorky's. But unlike Gorky's advocacy for folklore and its apparent simplifications, Bukharin confronted ideological poetry as overly primitive. He gave preference to forms adequate to the complexity of the new epoch.

His speech overshadowed Gorky's keynote address, as attested in NKVD reports about the reactions of prominent writers. However, Bukharin was forced to apologize for his criticism of "some comrade poets," which signaled the demise of his alternative viewpoint. This outcome was inevitable: the Congress was meticulously orchestrated, with the presidium consisting of party and state leaders, ecstatic applause at every mention of Stalin's name, and ritual greetings to the Congress from kolkhoz peasants and representatives of the working masses. RAPP had ceased to function, but the Congress perpetuated its theory of social command (*sotsial'nyi zakaz*). A speech by Andrei Zhdanov (1896–1948) unambiguously described literature as a form of class struggle; Zhdanov also provided a list of requirements: writers must reflect "heroic features of our everyday," "see positive aspects in our people," and "expose our enemies."[75]

Many writers felt deeply discouraged by this spectacle: "There's no place for me in this servile gathering" (Valerian Pravdukhin [1892–1938]); "The period of literature's total bureaucratization is upon us" (Aleksei Novikov-Priboi [1877–1944]); "We have to demonstrate to the world the unanimity of the Union's literary forces. But seeing as how all this is being done artificially, under the stick, the congress feels dead, like a tsarist parade" (Isaac Babel).[76] Even Gorky, appalled by the composition of the Union's Board, wrote: "Apparently, illiterate people will lead those who are much more cultured than they are."[77]

The Union of Soviet Writers acquired a monopoly over literary journals and presses. Under its auspices, a Literary Institute for the education of "literary cadres" (*kadry*) and a Fund for Literature of the USSR (Litfond SSSR), meant to provide material support to writers, were created, respectively, in 1933 and 1934. The Union had a Board (*pravlenie*), with the Chair and

Secretariat elected from among the members. Plenary meetings of the Board would take place annually, while the Secretariat ran all routine business. The actual control over the Union belonged to the working Secretariat, made up of party functionaries who were only nominally writers. This structure was later reproduced in Writers' Unions in each national republic of the USSR; in addition, there was a local organization of writers in every region.

For all this bureaucracy and centralized control, membership in the Soviet Writers' Union had its perks: it lifted a writer into the ranks of the Soviet elite. Writers were entitled to single-family apartments (in Moscow, there were special apartment buildings for members of the Union); they had access to dachas (in Peredelkino and elsewhere) and to pleasant seaside resorts and sanatoriums (*doma tvorchestva*) in places like Komarovo, Koktebel, and Yalta. In addition to generous honorariums for publications, writers enjoyed privileges similar to those reserved for party functionaries, including access to exclusive stores, holiday gift packages, and other luxury items.

Along with incentives for loyal writers came strict political control exerted through the Union's functionaries. A writer expelled from the Union for an ideological error or any other transgression would lose access to considerable privileges and risk being banned from professional literary activities. The Writers' Union would play a significant role during the Great Terror and afterwards, organizing informal trials and supplying compromising materials as well as direct denunciations to the NKVD/KGB.

The process of exclusion, to use the title that Lydia Chukovskaya (1907–96) gave to her book about her 1977 expulsion from the Writers' Union, changed over time. Still, it had some predictable steps, particularly from the 1930s until Stalin's death in 1953: it could include arrest, imprisonment, and possibly death, but it could also be limited to coercion and economic deprivation. To cite a famous case, Anna Akhmatova and Mikhail Zoshchenko were expelled from the Writers' Union but spared further persecution after Zhdanov's attack on them in 1946; they were in effect deprived of the right to earn a living. Similar methods were used to punish writers for their political activism in the 1960s through the 1980s; writers were banned from publication, their books were removed from libraries, and their names were deleted from new editions of encyclopedias and literary histories. Rendered invisible, they supported their families by menial jobs; for some, emigration (unthinkable and unavailable in the Stalin years) was a way out.

CASE STUDY *Prorabotka*, or political rebukes of writers

Prorabotka, literally a working over, or a public political rebuke of a writer, was a defining feature of Soviet culture. *Prorabotka* could target a single publication, the writer's entire oeuvre, or a literary school or movement. It exemplified the industrial production of enemies and scapegoats, a foundational element of the Soviet regime of violence. In Stalin's time, *prorabotka* could be a radical step towards the writer's stigmatization (Akhmatova and Zoshchenko), or it could lead to arrest within a few years (Kharms and Vvedensky, Zabolotsky, Pil'niak). But a tragic outcome was not inevitable; some victims of brutal public scolding were forgiven, allowed to resume publishing, and sometimes even rewarded with significant new positions.[78]

In the 1920s, *prorabotka* was mainly used by factions competing for influence in the party leadership and seeking domination over other groups. In the 1930s, it became a public ritual that included several phases. It typically began with an article in one of the main newspapers, where a literary work or its writer was castigated for ideological mistakes; ample use of recognizable political clichés served as a clear signal that a smear campaign was now underway. The article would be followed by a series of attacks—individual and collective—in many other newspapers and magazines. The ritual involved at least one public gathering where other writers criticized the accused; any lack of enthusiasm in the denunciations would put the speaker at risk of becoming a fresh defendant. The victim had to admit to his or her mistakes, and insufficient self-criticism could launch a new round of accusations, precipitating further consequences, including arrest and execution. One early victim was Leonid Dobychin (1894–1936), author of the novel *The Town of N* (*Gorod En*, 1935), who disappeared (a presumed suicide) after a public attack on March 25, 1936. There were cases when repentance headed off further persecution (Viktor Shklovsky and Kornei Chukovsky); but in other instances, writers were arrested despite their profuse admissions of guilt (former RAPP leaders Leopol'd Averbakh and Vladimir Kirshon). These dealings were heavily bureaucratized and formalized, and their ritualized nature is evocative of the mechanisms of Christian exorcism followed by repentance.

The 1929 campaign against two novels published abroad, Zamiatin's *We* and Pil'niak's *Mahogany* (*Krasnoe derevo*, 1929), marked the emergence of a new, systemic form of *prorabotka*. It constituted a literary analogue of the infamous Shakhty Affair (1928).[79] That trial against engineers signaled the end of Trotsky's politics of collaboration with the "bourgeois intelligentsia," and was then transferred into other spheres including fellow-travelers among Soviet writers. Pil'niak and Zamiatin were selected for *prorabotka* in this connection as the respective leaders of the Moscow and Leningrad branches of the independent All-Russian Union of writers (a major organization of fellow-travelers). But the brutal attack against the two writers did not damage their careers, at least not immediately: Pil'niak's *Mahogany* was incorporated into his 1930 novel *The Volga Streams into the Caspian Sea* (*Volga vpadaet v Kaspiiskoe more*) and published in the USSR, while Zamiatin was allowed to flee abroad with his Soviet passport in 1931. The campaign had broader institutional consequences, however. First, in 1931, new regulations regarding censorship were adopted which effectively banned Soviet writers from publishing their works abroad, outside official (i.e. state-controlled and censored) channels—unlike in the 1920s when a number of émigré journals and presses published Soviet writers and those publications were legally distributed in the USSR. By the same token, the 1931 ban severed émigré literature from the literary process in the USSR. Second, the campaign against Pil'niak and Zamiatin served as a springboard for the Central Committee's Resolution of 1932 that would disband all literary organizations and form the state-sponsored Writers' Union. Third, in Aleksandr Galushkin's words, "in the course of this affair a peculiar type of literary 'discussion' emerged, one characteristic of the Soviet epoch and resembling political show trials."[80] As of 1929, such discussions, often built on *prorabotka*, had become a powerful, formative element in Soviet literary politics.

In the late 1940s–early 1950s, the ritual of *prorabotka* was, as it were, industrialized, and ideological flagellation happened with ever-increasing regularity. This conveyor belt of persecution acquired the name of Zhdanovshchina after one of its top practitioners, Andrei Zhdanov, Secretary of the Communist Party Central Committee responsible for ideology and culture in the 1940s. Literary life resumed after the war with the ideological assault against Akhmatova and Zoshchenko, who were selected as the main targets of Zhdanov's wrath. The public humiliation was launched in the Central Committee's resolution "On the Journals *Zvezda* and *Leningrad*" (1946).

The 1940s and early 1950s also saw orchestrated campaigns against Western influence on Soviet philology in various universities, which went hand in hand with campaigns against "rootless cosmopolitans" (a euphemism for the Jewish intelligentsia).[81] Such campaigns included a crusade against so-called Jewish nationalism, leading to the destruction of Soviet Yiddish literature, as well as to the arrest of Jewish critics accused of badgering Russian playwrights. Other victims of *prorabotka* included Andrei Platonov, for his short story "The Return (The Ivanov Family)" ("Vozvrashchenie [Sem'ia Ivanovykh]," 1946); Vasily Grossman (1905–64), for his Stalingrad novel *For a Just Cause* (*Za pravoe delo*, 1952); Olga Berggol'ts (1910–75), once a powerful voice of the Leningrad Siege, for her support of Akhmatova; and the Sovetskii pisatel' publishing house, for reprinting Il'f's and Petrov's novels (both authors were already dead by the time of the campaign in 1949).

The mechanism of *prorabotka* did not spare the Writers' Union elite, including those who played leading roles in the public dressing-down of others: Aleksandr Fadeev (1901–56) was upbraided for diminishing the party's role in his novel *The Young Guard* (*Molodaia gvardiia*, 1946, revised in 1951), as were Konstantin Simonov (1915–79) for his novel *The Smoke of the Fatherland* (*Dym otechestva*, 1947), and Konstantin Fedin for his memoir *Gorky Among Us* (*Gor'kii sredi nas*, 1941). Certainly, the consequences of *prorabotka* for Fadeev or Fedin were incomparably lighter than for Zoshchenko and Akhmatova. The latter lost access to publishing their own writings and took on translations to earn a living, but the writers of the party elite, after passionate repentance, rewrote their erroneous texts and sought to confirm their loyalty by attacking new scapegoats with intensified energy. The main effect of this pedagogy of terror was universal fear: nobody was protected from *prorabotka*, and anybody, no matter how loyal, could become its next victim.

In the relatively liberal period of Khrushchev's Thaw (1954–64), the instances of *prorabotka* were rarer but still intense. In 1954, Zoshchenko (whose membership in the Writer's Union, revoked after Zhdanov's assault, had been restored) once again became a target, this time for refusing to admit that the party critique of his work had been just and useful. In 1956–57, Vladimir Dudintsev's (1918–98) novel *Not by Bread Alone* (*Ne khlebom edinym*, 1956), was disparaged for ideological mistakes; in 1958, Pasternak was expelled from the Writers' Union because of the publication abroad and the subsequent Nobel Prize for *Doctor Zhivago* (*Doktor Zhivago*, 1955), an honor he was forced to reject. Khrushchev nervously sought to keep limits on the relative liberalization launched by his secret speech against Stalinist excesses and mass terror at a closed session of the Twentieth Party Congress in 1956. Hence, he held regular "meetings with the creative intelligentsia" (twice in 1957, and then again in 1960, 1962, 1963), which turned into endless attacks on liberal writers and non-realist artists. Ilya Erenburg, Viktor Nekrasov (1911–87), Margarita Aliger (1915–92), Evgeny Yevtushenko (1932–2017), Andrei Voznesensky (1933–2010), Vasily Aksyonov (1932–2009), Boris Zhutovsky (b. 1932), Ernst Neizvestny (1925–2016), and Ely Beliutin (1925–2012) were among Khrushchev's many targets. Such meetings rarely led to prison terms, much less to execution, but the reprimands were widely reported and could seriously affect careers and the fates of journals and publishing houses.

But some of the most brutal attacks did not employ the ritual of *prorabotka* at all. Vasily Grossman (subjected to *prorabotka* in the 1940s and 50s) soon fell victim to a much more vicious assault. In 1960, his novel *Life and Fate* (*Zhizn' i sud'ba*, completed 1958) was submitted to *Znamia* (*Banner*); however, after being denounced by the editorial board, the novel was "arrested" by the KGB. In other words, the novel's manuscript and all related materials were confiscated (luckily one copy was secretly preserved by a close friend). The author was not publicly scolded but the private punishments were hardly benign: in Grossman's words, "They've strangled me in a dark alley…" ("Menia zadushili v podvorotne").[82] The tragic story of Grossman's novel became famous among the Soviet intelligentsia and in the West. Some acts of harassment or violence were known, however, only after considerable delay: in 1957, the poet Anna Barkova (1901–76), who had already spent years in the Gulag, was rearrested for "anti-Soviet agitation" that supposedly appeared in a manuscript not intended for publication. She was permitted to return to Moscow a decade later after some writers intervened on her behalf.

The years 1964–65 were a turning point in the history of *prorabotka* as a disciplinary device. In 1965, authorities clamped down on Andrei Sinyavsky and Yuli Daniel (1925–88) for illicitly publishing satirical works abroad. The trial signaled the end of the Thaw-period liberalization and a full-force return of the *prorabotka* ritual, with the imprisonment of criminal writers as its inevitable outcome. But Sinyavsky and Daniel defied the established ritual: they did not admit their guilt. They defended themselves as authors of literary texts that could not, they argued, be judged as political proclamations. Their closing statements were not published in the Soviet press, but they circulated quickly in *samizdat*. Reacting to these statements, Varlam Shalamov (1907–82) wrote in "The Letter to an Old Friend" ("Pis'mo staromu drugu" [1966], also distributed via *samizdat*): "The Sinyavsky trial is the first openly political trial under the Soviet regime where defendants, from the very beginning to the very end—from the preliminary investigation to the closing statements—did not admit their guilt and faced the verdict as real men."[83] In Shalamov's opinion, the unprecedented behavior of Sinyavsky and Daniel was closely associated with equally unprecedented support on the part of the intelligentsia. Not only Western media (as in Pasternak's case), but also Soviet writers and scholars sent the court and other official organs individual and collective statements of support. Many were themselves subjected to *prorabotka* and lost their jobs and access to publication as a result. Although the intelligentsia's backing of Sinyavsky and Daniel did not change the verdict or diminish the sentence (seven and five years of imprisonment, respectively), the uproar generated by the trial and by the resistance of some Soviet citizens gave rise to the dissident movement. The same refusal to feign contrition could be seen in another case, involving Joseph Brodsky: accused in 1964 of being a "social parasite" because he had allegedly broken the law requiring employment, he was sent into internal exile. But powerful support on the part of the intelligentsia eventually shortened the term of exile.

The use of *prorabotka* had now become a risky business for the authorities, as the outcome was proving increasingly unpredictable due to possible publicity abroad. Worse, *prorabotka* became a superb advertisement: readers were determined at all costs to read the poem or the story savaged in the official press, and victims became celebrities thanks to Western radio stations and *samizdat*. Soviet denunciations ended up promoting subversive literature. This paradox was epitomized in the campaign of 1979–80 against the uncensored almanac *Metropol* (1979), edited by Vasily Aksyonov, Andrei Bitov, Viktor Erofeev (b. 1947), Fazil Iskander (1929–2016), and Evgeny Popov (b. 1946). The scandal attracted enormous international attention, eliciting protests from Kurt Vonnegut, William Styron, and John Updike; the targeted writers did not repent. The almanac was promptly published in Russian by Ardis and in English translation by Norton; and the Russian text widely circulated in *samizdat*. Even the expulsion of two younger writers, Erofeev and Popov, from the Writers' Union backfired when two esteemed writers resigned in protest: Semen Lipkin (1911–2003) and Inna Lisnianskaia (1928–2014).

Nevertheless, *prorabotka* continued to be used against the ideologically suspect, with more brutal consequences. This mechanism of retribution and coercion exacted a high price—sometimes stunting a writer's talent, sometimes precipitating mental illness. It broke lives. The fear of *prorabotka* led to self-censorship: the presence of internal editors (*vnturenniaia tsenzura* and *vnutrennii redaktor*) shaped many Soviet writers, and compromised creative work. At the same time, stories of writers' behavior (as victims, witnesses, advocates, or silent supporters) gave rise to legends and anecdotes, which in turn solidified the cultural reputations, for better or worse, of countless Soviet literary luminaries.[84]

Literature and politics after Stalin: Aesopian language and ideological divisions

Soviet literature was so heavily monitored by party censorship that even slight variations in themes, imagery, or tone, barely visible to an ordinary reader, could signify enormous changes in political direction. This was especially true in the short period between Stalin's death in March 1953 and Khrushchev's secret speech in February 1956 when massive cultural changes were underway, as evidenced by several, otherwise quite ordinary, pieces of writing. Ilya Erenburg's novel *The Thaw* (*Ottepel'*, 1954) suggested a new atmosphere of doubt, for instance by the quiet mention of a person arrested in 1936, even as the book maintained the conventions of Socialist Realism, with its stock characters, bookish conversations, and a predictable plot. It became the symbol of a new epoch, to which it lent its name: the Thaw (1956–65). Vladimir Pomerantsev's critical article "On Sincerity in Literature," published in *Novyi mir* in December 1953, relied on party rhetoric and anti-Formalist jabs, but it was perceived as the first powerful attack on the Socialist Realist "varnishing of reality." Vladimir Dudintsev's novel *Not by Bread Alone*, despite its hackneyed plot (an undaunted inventor fights conservative bureaucrats), caused a sensation: it represented the party *nomenklatura* as a new exploitative class (in line with the portrayal in Milovan Djilas's *The New Class*, published abroad only a year later).

These deviations marked a radical change in the cultural atmosphere, but the results of this change were mixed. "Central to the Thaw and its historic impact was the drastic reduction of political violence in Soviet society," note Denis Kozlov and Eleonory Gilburd.[85] The release of Gulag political prisoners contributed to a "domestic climate of exhilarating optimism."[86] But the critique of Stalin's "cult of personality" (to use Khrushchev's euphemism), coincided with the analysis of political violence elsewhere in influential treatments of Nazism and the Holocaust like Günter Grass's *The Tin Drum* (*Die Blechtrommel*, 1959) or Hannah Arendt's *Eichmann in Jerusalem: A Report on the Banality of Evil* (1963). However, the Soviet situation was unlike post-Nazi Germany in a significant way: Kozlov and Gilburd argue that "the political order that had brought collectivization, the terror of 1936–38 and the Gulag not only survived 1945 (1953, 1956), but also proclaimed itself even more stable and successful."[87] This insistent stability produced egregious and unresolvable contradictions: the political discourse criticized Stalinism but defended its achievements. It declared an end to political terror but denounced those who deviated from renewed political dogmas.

The Thaw's inner contradictions contributed to its untimely demise: Khrushchev was removed by hardliners who perpetuated aggressive cultural policies in order to thwart genuine liberalization. Khrushchev's scandalous attacks on avant-garde artists of the Manezh exhibition (1962) and on young writers (1963) as too liberal climaxed in the trials of Sinyavsky/Daniel and Brodsky. The military assault against the Prague Spring in August 1968, the firing of Aleksandr Tvardovsky as editor of the most liberal literary journal, *Novyi mir* (1970), and, finally, the exile of Aleksandr Solzhenitsyn after the first volume of *The Gulag Archipelago 1918–1956: An Experiment in Literary Investigation* (*Arkhipelag GULAG 1918–1956: Opyt khudozhestvennogo issledovaniia*, 1973–75) was published abroad (1973), all signified the beginning of a new era, retroactively designated as the years of Stagnation. Despite its conservative and neo-nationalist cultural climate, this period was not a return to Stalinism (as many feared after the invasion of Czechoslovakia). Instead, it preserved and even intensified Thaw-era contradictions, hiding them under a cloak of lavish celebrations, mind-numbing congresses, and military parades.

The Thaw set in motion a debate about the political past and present, masked as a discussion about literature and the arts. By the 1960s, the literary field was divided between liberal and conservative publications (liberal *Novyi mir* and *Youth* [*Iunost'*] vs. orthodox and neo-nationalist *October, Ogonek, The Young Guard*) and institutions (the anti-Stalinist Moscow Writers' Organization vs. the newly created Writers' Union of the Russian Federation). Leaders of both the liberal and conservative camps, such as Tvardovsky (*Novyi mir*), Nikolai Gribachev and Anatoly Sofronov (*Ogonek*), and Vsevolod Kochetov (*October*) enjoyed personal favors from Khrushchev.[88] Differences between these camps involved attitudes toward Stalin and the Gulag, and more generally to Soviet history and ideology. From these fundamental positions stemmed radically different attitudes toward the role of the party, *nomenklatura* privileges, and intelligentsia freedoms. By the end of the 1960s, the debate had been refocused: the discussion of Stalinism was suppressed, while manifestations of Russian nationalism, coupled with attacks on liberal (or simply Jewish) intelligentsia, moved center stage. Some taboos persisted: it was forbidden to question Communist ideology or Lenin, and one could not compare Stalinism and Nazism or openly discuss contemporary political repressions. But these topics animated kitchen conversations, since after 1956, people no longer feared arrest for speaking their minds in the privacy of their homes.

In the literary sphere, critics debated class-based morality and the renovation of the Socialist Realist canon; there was disagreement about whether the depiction of social and economic problems meant focusing on the negative, to the detriment of other ideological goals.[89] The expansion of the official canon was notable: many authors previously banned as victims of the Great Terror (Babel, Mandelstam, Kharms), as ideologically harmful (Akhmatova, Zoshchenko, Esenin), or as émigrés (Bunin and Tsvetaeva) now appeared in print, as did marginalized and forgotten figures like Bulgakov and Olesha. But others (Nabokov, Gumilev, Khodasevich, Erdman) remained banned until the late 1980s.

In terms of their aesthetics, both literary camps gravitated toward realism, although *Novyi mir* tried to resurrect *critical* realism, while the more conservative *October* stood firmly for *Socialist* Realism. Realism as such was effectively being rethought. Traditional Socialist Realism meant loyalty to party-sponsored mythologies and a representation of idealized, flawless characters as if they were typical. Conversely, *Novyi mir* authors and editors valiantly moved away from conventional political mythologies and literary idealization in search of new conventions within realist aesthetics. Both camps remained suspicious of all modernist styles, and were repelled by the fantastic, the grotesque, and the absurd; they looked down on what they deemed excessive intellectualism. Yet those suspect forms of writing increasingly appeared in print. A censored but still remarkable version of Bulgakov's modernist, fantastic novel, *The Master and Margarita* (*Master i Margarita*, 1928–40), was published in 1966–67 in the journal *Moscow* (*Moskva*, later a conservative organ). The magazine *Youth*, founded in 1955 and edited by Valentin Kataev (1897–1986) until 1961, also took a more relaxed approach to art. Intended as a lab for young writers, it tolerated some modernism-inspired experiments by writers like Vasily Aksyonov, Andrei Voznesensky, Viktor Sosnora (b. 1936), and Anatoly Gladilin (b. 1935). Kataev himself was an interesting example of modernist experimentation: he considered Bunin his mentor, Olesha a personal friend, and Nabokov his competitor. His fragmented writing was driven by a carefully designed illusion of spontaneous memories and associations; it was a style that he had ironically designated as "mauvism" (from the French "mauvais," "bad").[90]

The Soviet intelligentsia of the Thaw period was in intellectual ferment. Events like the Picasso exhibition in 1956 or the newly established Moscow film festival, and publications such as the journal *Foreign Literature* (*Inostrannaia literatura*, created in 1955) were bridges to Western culture, which provided fresh sources of inspiration. A successor to *International Literature* (*Internatsional'naia literatura*, discontinued in 1943), *Foreign Literature* featured works by Hemingway and Fitzgerald, Beckett and Kafka, Sartre and Camus, Ionesco and Salinger, William Golding and Tennessee Williams in excellent translations by Nikolai Liubimov, Ivan Kashkin, Rita Rait-Kovaleva, Natalia Trauberg, Solomon Apt, and Liliana Lungina, to name a few. The culture of the 1960s thus generated alternative discourses and institutions that compensated for some limitations in official culture. This configuration survived the Thaw and fully developed during the period of Stagnation.

The principal alternative discourse was so-called Aesopian language, a system of hints and allusions that allowed forbidden subjects to be raised in the official press. In addition to smuggling a political message, Aesopian language served as a powerful artistic device of estrangement.[91] It met Shklovsky's definition of *ostranenie*: by heightening the reader's perception of motifs and details, it functioned as a cultural rite with a cathartic effect. Because of its dependence on the immediate context and tacit mutual understanding, Aesopian communication risked becoming unintelligible once the context had changed.

These risks, however, were not obvious in the 1960s, when Aesopian games among writer, censor, and reader became a sign of authentic literature. Arkady Belinkov (1921–70), a brilliant literary critic and a former Gulag prisoner, transformed Aesopian language into a contemporary version of sarcastic, multi-strand word-weaving saturated with cultural and historical references. His critical biography of the versatile Formalist Yuri Tynianov (1961) was a case in point, inspired by Tynianov's own historical novels about the absurdities of authoritarianism. Belinkov wrote about Tynianov and his characters (Pushkin, Griboedov, Küchelbecker, the Decembrists) as suggestive embodiments of the drama of the entire Russian/Soviet intelligentsia, creating parallels between the times of Nicholas I and Stalin's Terror. Belinkov's book about Yuri Olesha, *The Surrender and Death of the Soviet Intelligent* (*Sdacha i gibel' sovetskogo intelligenta*, begun while Belinkov was still in the USSR and completed in emigration, published 1976), was written in a more direct style than *Tynianov*, and lacked its semantic richness and aphoristic power.[92] The comparison shows how effectively Aesopian language could strengthen literary performances.

As exemplified by Belinkov's writings, the genre of historical or semi-fictional writing about revolutionary figures became a popular form of Aesopian literature. These were safe topics, drawing on the pantheon of Soviet heroes. Many such books were commissioned for a series of fictionalized biographies entitled *Fiery Revolutionaries* (*Plamennye revoliutsionery*, 1968–90). Its subjects were true nonconformists fighting against a conservative regime, whose behavior easily compared to that of 1960s and 1970s dissidents.[93] The biographies became allegories of contemporary dissent against the stale, aggressively conservative Soviet regime. A quintessential book in the genre is a novel by Bulat Okudzhava (1924–97) about the Decembrist Pavel Pestel (first published as *Poor Avrosimov* [*Bednyi Avrosimov*], 1969, then as *The Gulp of Freedom* [*Glotok svobody*], 1970). No less noteworthy were Yuri Trifonov's (1925–81) novel about the People's Will movement, *Impatience* (*Neterpenie*, 1973); numerous books about the Decembrists by Natan Eidel'man (1930–89); and books by Yuri Davydov (1924–2002) about late-nineteenth-century revolutionaries. The genre was also adopted by playwrights, including Edvard Radzinsky (b. 1936), who wrote *Conversations with Socrates* (*Besedy s Sokratom*, 1973), *Lunin, or the Death of Jacques* (*Lunin, ili smert' Zhaka*, 1979), and *Theater in the Time of Nero and Seneca* (*Teatr vremen Nerona i Seneki*, 1982); and Grigory Gorin (1940–2000), who created politically charged versions of famous literary texts and legendary biographies, such as *Till Eulenspiegel*

(Til', 1970), *To Kill Herostratus* (*Ubit' Gerostrata*, 1971), *The Most Truthful* (*Samyi pravdivyi*, 1974), and *The House That Swift Built* (*Dom, kotoryi postroil Svift*, 1982).

The 1960s and especially the 1970s also witnessed the transformation of science fiction into an Aesopian sub-genre. Science fiction had been a major, if underappreciated, contributor to the earlier post-Revolutionary project, in effect helping to shape Russia's culture of modernity.[94] It reemerged as a significant cultural force after the Thaw. Extremely popular among the scientific intelligentsia, it was more political than scientific by design: most typically, it employed socio-political parallels between distant planets and political processes in the Soviet Union. Launched by Ivan Efremov (1907–72), the genre included utopian representations of a communist future in *Andromeda Nebula* (*Tumannost' Andromedy*, 1957) and the more dystopian *The Bull's Hour* (*Chas byka*, 1967).[95] The genre was perfected by Arkady Strugatsky (1925–91) and Boris Strugatsky (1933–2012), who wrote together, and their work in turn inspired a whole generation of followers: Viacheslav Rybakov (b. 1954), Andrei Lazarchuk (b. 1958), and Mikhail Uspensky (1950–2014), among others.

Concurrent with these modest moves toward freer if coded literary expression, the official literary milieu witnessed a growing compartmentalization. Typically writers joined unofficial factions of like-minded authors. Within the Writers' Union, the antagonism between liberal and nationalist writers escalated with time. The liberals tended to publish in *Novyi mir* and *Youth*: many belonged to the 1960s' generation (*shestidesiatniki*, born approximately between 1927 and 1940), but they also had quite a few allies in the war generation (born between 1918 and 1926). The liberals were consistently anti-totalitarian even after the end of the Thaw, when anti-totalitarianism fell out of political favor; they walked a thin line between publishable literature and *samizdat*. The leading liberals included Yuri Trifonov, Fazil Iskander, Andrei Bitov, and David Samoilov (1920–90). Some writers in this circle would eventually emigrate: Viktor Nekrasov, Aleksandr Galich (1918–77), Vasily Aksyonov, Vladimir Voinovich, Georgy Vladimov (1931–2003), Anatoly Gladilin, Anatoly Kuznetsov (1929–79), and Fridrikh Gorenshtein (1932–2002); others were forced into inner emigration, like the Gulag survivors Varlam Shalamov and Yuri Dombrovsky (1909–78). A very few liberals found their way into the highest ranks of the literary *nomenklatura*, including Robert Rozhdestvensky (1932–94) and Yuri Bondarev (b. 1924), a promotion that required a vocal repudiation of former convictions. A unique status was reserved for Yevtushenko and Voznesensky: they were supposed to show Western critics of communism that both ideological liberalism and formal experimentation (not too wild) were encouraged in the USSR.

Yevtushenko and Voznesensky's position within liberal circles in the late Soviet period was thus always ambiguous. Nothing shows that ambiguity better than an anecdote recounted by the émigré writer Sergei Dovlatov. The story goes that Brodsky (long in emigration) was visited by friends after his heart bypass surgery in 1986. They tried to cheer him up with news about changes in the Soviet Union associated with Perestroika. They mentioned that Yevtushenko bravely spoke out against kolkhozes, or collective farms. To which Brodsky immediately retorted in a weak voice, "If Yevtushenko is against kolkhozes, then I'm for them."[96]

Alongside the strata of liberal-minded writers, a tight circle of Russian nationalists was grouped around the journals *The Young Guard* and *Our Contemporary* (*Nash sovremennik*, created in 1956 as a socio-political almanac, but as of 1964 converted into a monthly that played a role in literature). Their ideology openly attacked the liberal intelligentsia and quietly subverted official Marxist orthodoxy. They had influential supporters in the so-called informal Russian Party, which grew out of an alliance between nationalist writers and some members of the Komsomol and party leadership.[97] Expressing their views in fiction, poetry, and literary criticism alike, the nationalist circles developed ideas that resonated with Slavophilism and Dostoevsky's *pochvennichestvo*. They frequently amplified these intellectual traditions with aggressive rhetoric borrowed from the anti-cosmopolitan (anti-Semitic) campaign of late Stalinism. This was not a surprise, since many nationalists had launched their careers in the 1940s–50s. They promoted an anti-Western attitude, and were anti-modern and anti-intellectual. They interpreted all cultural, social, and political phenomena in terms of a single struggle: the forces loyal to national traditions (embodied by the peasantry and by classical Russian literature) versus the malevolent distortion and destruction of this tradition by the Jews, the Western-oriented intelligentsia, and other agents of modernization. Their leaders included the literary critics Vadim Kozhinov (1930–2001), Petr Palievsky (b. 1932), Yuri Seleznev (1939–84), Mikhail Lobanov (1925–2016), Vladimir Bushin (b. 1924), Viktor Chalmaev (b. 1932), and Vladimir Bondarenko (b. 1946).[98]

In the 1970s, the nationalist circle grew after co-opting some leading representatives of a trend known as Village Prose (derevenskaia proza). Initially divided between *Novyi mir* and *The Young Guard*, the Village writers included Vasily Shukshin (1929–74), Vladimir Soloukhin (1924–97), Valentin Rasputin (1937–2015), Vasily Belov (1932–2012), Viktor Astaf'ev (1924–2001), Fedor Abramov (1920–83), and Boris Mozhaev (1923–96). They saw village culture as morally and economically ruined by Soviet rule, starting with forced collectivization. The generative text was Solzhenitsyn's "Matryona's Home" ("Matrenin dvor," 1963), which was to Village Prose what Gogol's "Overcoat" was to the Natural School. These talented writers also opened literature up to a fresh influx of dialect speech that disturbed the hegemony of official language with its authoritative discourses.[99] Groundbreaking publications included *How Things Are* (*Privychnoe delo*, 1966) and *The Carpenter's Tales* (*Plotnitskie rasskazy*, 1968) by Belov; *The Final Stage* (*Poslednii srok*, 1970), *Live and Remember* (*Zhivi i pomni*, 1974), and *Farewell to Matyora* (*Proshchanie s Materoi*, 1976) by Rasputin; *The Last Bow* (*Poslednii poklon*, 1968) by Astaf'ev, as well as Shukshin's short stories. Comic and tragic peasant characters were portrayed by these writers as the victims of a modernity destructive of traditional values; they seemed lost and desperate without their connections to the soil, the people, the village. The Russian Party ideologues sought to reeducate these writers in the spirit of militant nationalism, but were only partially successful. Shukshin, Abramov, and Mozhaev resisted. Astaf'ev was repelled by his peers' growing infatuation with Stalin as the defender of the Russian nation, and he broke with them.[100]

Poetry of the 1980s, especially the so-called "quiet lyrics," closely tracked the direction of Village Prose. Nostalgia for traditional culture permeates the sentimental laments of Nikolai Rubtsov (1936–71), a latter-day imitator of Esenin. It was only a short step to the neo-Gothic poetry of Yuri Kuznetsov (1941–2003), who combined folkloric and surrealist motifs with pseudo-Nietzschean ideas of national superiority.

A similar confrontation between nationalists and liberals reemerged in the émigré literature and criticism of the 1970s–80s. After being exiled in 1973, Solzhenitsyn started a crusade against the liberal members of the Russian emigration and intelligentsia, accusing them of Russophobia and hostility toward national traditions, as defined principally by Orthodoxy and ardent statism. Using the term "pluralists" in a derogatory way (in the essay "Our pluralists," 1982), Solzhenitsyn attacked liberalism as imbued with a foreign spirit of destruction. In rebuttal, Andrei Sinyavsky accused him of promoting new intellectual uniformity. He contended that Solzhenitsyn and his followers' attack against "pluralists" replicated the patterns of Soviet nationalism that also accused the intelligentsia of being anti-Russian and presented "bourgeois democracy" as alien to Russian national culture. Sinyavsky's point of view on Solzhenitsyn resonated with Vladimir Voinovich's novel *Moscow 2042* (*Moskva 2042*, 1986). Here, Solzhenitsyn was satirically depicted as Sim Simych Karnavalov, the spiritual leader of a new Russia where Orthodoxy has replaced Communist ideology but preserved the totalitarian power structure. These debates continued as a matter of course in and beyond the

Perestroika period. Post-Soviet cultural and political debates have added new acuity to long-standing conflicts.

Samizdat, tamizdat, and the literary underground in the 1960s through 1980s

Even in the darkest years of the Soviet period, there was literary production outside official channels of publication. One has only to recall the fate of Evgeny Zamiatin's novel *We*, or *Master and Margarita* by Mikhail Bulgakov (1891–1940), Akhmatova's *Requiem* (1936–40) and Mandelstam's *Voronezh Notebooks* (1935–37). The OBERIU members Daniil Kharms (1905–42) and Aleksandr Vvedensky (1904–41) produced their most mature work in the 1930s when publication was unthinkable. This was also a period of activity for unsanctioned poets like Alik Rivin (1915–42), Georgy Obolduev (1898–1954), Andrei Nikolev (1895–1968), Ian Satunovsky (1913–82), and Evgeny Kropivnitsky (1893–1979). Nonconformist prose was written and distributed clandestinely; notable examples include Andrei Platonov's novels *Chevengur* (1928) and *The Foundation Pit* (*Kotlovan*, 1930), Lydia Chukovskaya's novella *Sofia Petrovna* (1939–40), and the mystical treatise *The Rose of the World* (1950–58) by Daniil Andreev (1906–59). It was only belatedly, in the 2000s, that *The Puppies* (*Shchenki*), written in the 1940s by Pavel Zal'tsman (1912–85), and the novella *Manon Lescaut of Turdei* (*Turdeiskaia Manon Lesko*, 1946) by Vsevolod Petrov (1912–78) saw the light of day.

In the 1960s, diverse, unaffiliated pockets of nonconformist literature found a shared outlet in samizdat (self-publication; typically retyping) and tamizdat (foreign Russian-language publications smuggled into the USSR). *Samizdat* circulated as individual copies passed from hand to hand among friends; wider dissemination occurred when a reader had access to a typewriter and could produce additional copies. Ann Komaromi has compellingly argued that *samizdat* was the key to Soviet political and cultural dissent, providing a new mode of existence for texts that navigated between private and public spheres and reflected individual, rather than group or party-bound, forms of dissent.[101]

Tamizdat made its way to readers in the Soviet Union in the luggage of foreign visitors and especially diplomats; but writing was also freely distributed (allowed to be stolen) during international book fairs. The material available in samizdat and tamizdat frequently overlapped, including unpublished poetry by Mandelstam, Tsvetaeva, Gumilev, and Akhmatova (especially *Requiem*), Zamiatin's *We*, Platonov's *The Foundation Pit* and *Chevengur*, Bulgakov's satirical novellas from the 1920s, Pasternak's *Doctor Zhivago*, Kharms's prose and poetry, and Nabokov's novels, especially *Lolita*. Remarkably, samizdat and tamizdat served as channels for the circulation in Russia of masterpieces that had become international bestsellers. The fact that all were banned in the USSR reflects a paradox of Soviet culture, which produced powerful works of literature that changed the face of modern literature only to be excluded from legal circulation in their home country. The divide between impoverished official literature and robust unofficial literature facilitated the split of the nation into (at least) two segments with few common values or shared aesthetic tastes.

Not limited to politically engaged, openly anti-Soviet texts, samizdat and tamzidat included aesthetic dissent—discourses of modernism, the avant-garde, and postmodernism marginalized by the norms of Socialist Realism. Modernist prose and poetry from the pre-Stalinist years circulated alongside contemporary underground or émigré literature: Venedikt Erofeev's (1938–90) *Moscow to the End of the Line* (*Moskva-Petushki*, 1970), Varlam Shalamov's *Kolyma Tales* (*Kolymskie rasskazy*, written 1954–73), Joseph Brodsky's poetry, Sasha Sokolov's (b. 1943) *A School for Fools* (*Shkola dlia durakov*, 1973), Andrei Bitov's *Pushkin House* (*Pushkinskii dom*, 1978), and the almanac *Metropol* all became recognized nonconformist classics. These texts combined political critique and aesthetic experimentation with elements of both modernism and (as yet unrecognized) postmodernism.

A third channel for the circulation of uncensored texts used tape recordings, sometimes called *magnitofonizdat* or *magnitizdat*.[102] The tapes featured poet-singers (bards) such as Aleksandr Galich, Bulat Okudzhava, Vladimir Vysotsky (1938–80), and Yuz Aleshkovsky (b. 1929), along with their numerous followers. This medium also transmitted political satires by Mikhail Zhvanetsky (b. 1934), a form of stand-up comedy heard at private gatherings. Tapes circulated widely (alongside recordings of Western rock music) and their possession was rarely subject to prosecution.[103]

In addition to the growing diffusion of *samizdat*, *tamizdat*, and *magnitizdat*, post-Stalinist culture witnessed the emergence of the literary underground as a sub-culture in its own right. The term "underground" (a loan-word Russified as *andegraund*) was adopted for self-identification by unofficial culture in the 1960s–80s. Representatives of the literary underground did not seek publication in the Soviet Union, positioning their work as an alternative to official discourses (hence, the currency of such synonyms as "second" or "parallel" culture).[104]

Although the underground consisted of disparate groups and circles (mainly in Moscow and Leningrad, but also in Kharkiv, Sverdlovsk, Eisk, and Rostov-on-Don), by the 1970s its authors were shaping their own cultural institutions, including regular readings and discussions, circulation and production of *samizdat* journals and almanacs, stable channels of publication abroad (especially through Ardis in the US), and even a literary prize (the Andrei Bely Prize, established in 1978, and still awarded in the twenty-first century). Far less persecuted than political dissidents, underground authors were nonetheless watched by the KGB, and subjected to sporadic detentions; there was systematic harassment of some individuals, including forced psychiatric treatment.[105]

Writers and critics from this unofficial milieu typically stayed away from literary-political debates between liberals and nationalists. They largely saw official publication as a path to corruption and self-destruction through compromise. They were shaping a new cultural modality, according to the anthropologist Alexei Yurchak, who calls this non-ideological mode of being "living *vnye*" (beyond, outside). He illustrates his thesis with such diverse examples as a community of theoretical physicists, teenagers' intellectual clubs at the Palace of Pioneers, Leningrad's Café Saigon, and the nonconformist artists' collective known as Mit'ki. As Yurchak argues: "Within these publics Soviet reality was not resisted but deterritorialized. Not surprisingly, for members of these milieus critical debates about Soviet political and social issues were considered 'uninteresting.'"[106]

The underground tended to create isolated circles, each with its own aesthetic. Some circles were formed around survivors of the 1920s–30s, such as Anna Akhmatova, Nadezhda Mandelstam (1899–1980), Lydia Chukovskaya, Lydia Ginzburg, as well as Yakov Druskin (1902–80), a former member of OBERIU. Through these charismatic figures the young generation found fully developed systems of cultural coordinates on which they could model their own behavior.

An early Moscow group coalesced around the poet Leonid Chertkov (1933–2000); one of its members, the celebrated translator Andrei Sergeev (1933–98), would later receive the Russian Booker Prize for his memoir-novel detailing the group's activities.[107] Another influential center of nonconformist literature and art formed outside Moscow in Lianozovo; its members included Vsevolod Nekrasov (1934–2009), as well as a pioneer of concrete poetry, Ian Satunovsky. In the early 1970s, the group of experimental nonconformist lyrical poets SMOG (The Youngest Society of Geniuses [Samoe molodoe obshchestvo geniev]) was organized by Leonid Gubanov (1946–83). Vladimir Aleinikov (b. 1946), Yuri Kublanovsky (b. 1947), Sasha Sokolov, the prominent dissident Vadim Delaunay (1947–83), and the future sociologist and translator Boris Dubin (1946–2014) were among its members. In the 1970s, several circles of artists and poets emerged who later would call themselves Conceptualists; the most famous among them was Dmitry Prigov (1940–2007). In the next decade, a group of Neo-Acmeists called Moscow Time (Moskovskoe vremia) emerged; it included Sergei Gandlevsky (b. 1952), Aleksei Tsvetkov, Bakhyt Kenzheev (b. 1950), and Aleksei Soprovsky (1953–90). Independent of group affiliation but famous in the nonconformist milieu were Venedikt Erofeev, author of the legendary poem in prose *Moscow to the End of the Line*; and Evgeny Kharitonov (1941–81), the originator of the first queer discourse in Russian literature since Kuzmin.

The communication among Moscow's nonconformist groups and individuals was sporadic, whereas Leningrad's circles were more tightly connected if no less diverse. The most conspicuous among the Leningrad underground groups was the circle of Joseph Brodsky, known as "Akhmatova's orphans," which comprised Evgeny Rein (b. 1935), Anatoly Naiman (b. 1936), and Dmitry Bobyshev (b. 1936); and the group of poets calling themselves the Philological School (Filologicheskaia shkola), which included Brodsky's future biographer, Lev Losev (1937–2009). A group of prose writers, known as the Urban-dwellers (Gorozhane), also emerged in Leningrad. Among its members were Sergei Dovlatov, Boris Vakhtin (1933–81), and Vladimir Maramzin (b. 1934). Offering an eloquent testimony to the enduring close connections among these disparate groups, Brodsky, once in emigration, wrote an open appeal to support Maramzin after his arrest in 1974.[108] Leningrad was famed for its almanacs, which published provincial, Muscovite, and Leningrad authors. These periodicals included 37 (published by Viktor Krivulin and Tatiana Goricheva), *The Clock* (*Chasy*, published by Boris Ivanov), *The Bypass Canal* (*Obvodnyi kanal*, published by Kirill Butyrin and Sergei Stratanovsky), and *Mitia's Journal* (*Mitin zhurnal*, published by Dmitry Volchek and Olga Abramovich).

The underground also facilitated new or radically renewed ideas of authorial identity. While the spectrum of official literature and writers' sanctioned roles ranged from the writer-prophet (revamped and cultivated by Solzhenitsyn) to the state's loyal, if cynical, servant (for example, Sergei Mikhalkov [1913–2009]), the underground writer was a self-styled outsider or even outcast. The epitome of the writer-outlaw was Abram Tertz (Andrei Sinyavsky's penname), but the image was also projected in Brodsky's poetry, Kharitonov's queer poetics, and Prigov's version of Conceptualism. A special case was the collective identity created by the group Mit'ki. It was founded and chronicled by the artists Vladimir Shinkarev (b. 1954), Dmitry Shagin (b. 1957), Aleksandr Florensky (b. 1960), and Olga Florenskaia (b. 1960). Their name came from the diminutive from Shagin's first name; Shinkarev's 1985 book *Mit'ki*, written while he was working in a boiler room, played an important role in shaping the group's counter-ideology. In their gestures of life-creation, drunkenness became an aesthetic act, and ironical self-mythologization is pervasive:

> The *mityok's* face alternates between two affected submissive expressions: tenderness that borders on idiocy, and sentimental dejection. All his movements and intonations, although very tender, are also energetic, and therefore the *mityok* always appears to be a bit drunk. In general, every sign of life that the *mityok* exudes is maximally pitched so that the word or utterance sounds like an undivided growl, while his face remains just as touching.[109]

Mit'ki were emphatically passive, recycling motifs derived from Russian holy fools and folk-loric simpletons. Their vocabulary contained only a limited number of expressions and they liked to use lines from Soviet movies to communicate emotion. Their repertoire paradoxically became a political gesture, because it replaced ritualized official slogans with no less ritualized yet silly discourse. In Alexei Yurchak's apt characterization, "However small and isolated the world of Mit'ki was, the lifestyle was so densely aestheticized that the living itself turned almost into an art project."[110]

Daily life was similarly aestheticized by the Moscow Conceptualists. In addition to Prigov, its leaders included Lev Rubinshtein (b. 1947), Andrei Monastyrsky (b. 1949), and Vladimir Sorokin (b. 1955). In Conceptualist terminology, the desired mode of behavior was *nezalipanie*, that is, not sticking to any ideologized discourse, and preserving a critical distance from it.[111] This gesture of distancing represented a new anti-totalitarian position, since it was based on the presupposition that any language, when perceived as the vehicle of unquestioned truth, becomes a source of totalitarian repression: "'totalitarian' was understood to mean Soviet language, the language of Soviet myth, and any significant discourse supported by complex institutions (the discourse of a great culture, nationalist discourses, etc.)."[112] This was an original version of what Lyotard called the "incredulity toward metanarratives," which in Western theory became the foundation of postmodernism.[113] Prigov later tended to interpret this principle as foundational for the function of the intellectual in any society, whom he characterized as "a being specially bred for the testing and experimentation of the durability of all possible myths and discourses of power. Like, for example, a dog trained to sniff out narcotics."[114] Intellectuals, in other words, should detect the falsities and fabrications of power and, as Prigov's poetry demonstrated, variously and endlessly entertain their readers with these revelations.

CASE STUDY The Moscow–Tartu School

The most significant academic manifestation of underground culture, broadly construed, was the Moscow–Tartu School, which reinvigorated Russian intellectual life and flourished alongside the rise of structuralism. The conditions within academic circles were ripe for a turn to the human sciences marked by rigor and universality. The actual creation of the Moscow–Tartu School was also made possible by strong personalities and individual brilliance, and by groundbreaking interdisciplinary collaborations, making the phenomenon of the Moscow–Tartu School an example of precisely the kind of random factors amid predictable structures and historical readiness that semiotics scholars sought to study.

Semiotics thrived as an academic discipline within literary and cultural theory, philosophy, and linguistics. Building on a structuralist foundation, semioticians interrogated the historically and culturally determined relationships between sign and signified: What patterns obtain among possible relationships? How are they conditioned or disrupted by internal and external factors? Soviet semiotics was at first closely linked to linguistics, as was originally structuralism, and it had strong ties with the sciences, in part because some of its scholars trained in mathematics. That affinity with the sciences affected the discursive register of Soviet semiotics, leaving a powerful inclination toward logic, categorization, and the search for invariants—as opposed to the ideologically polarized literary scholarship that held sway in many Academy of Sciences institutes and university literature departments in the 1960s. But there were undercurrents in such institutions, and semiotics absorbed important influences from innovative schools of poetics and literary studies in Leningrad.[115] It soon developed its distinctive focus on what it called "secondary modeling systems."[116] Regarding language as the primary set of signs, and thus as the primary modeling system, Moscow–Tartu scholars focused on the secondary modeling systems of literature and the arts. As their work progressed, several theorists sought to address cultural mechanisms more broadly (hence the frequent use of the term "semiotics of culture"); some began to work as well in the cognitive sciences. There was also a discernible shift in interest from signs to texts, with text standing in for the whole domain of culture.

The first deliberate steps toward Soviet semiotics were taken in 1962 in Moscow (hence the word-order: the Moscow–Tartu School, rather than the Tartu–Moscow School, giving preeminence to Tartu, or simply the Tartu School, which, however, were also in use). The 1962 Moscow symposium on the structural study of sign systems brought together leading scholars who hoped to create new forums for scholarly exchange and collaboration, and to found an institute for the study of semiotics within the Academy of Sciences, as had been called for in a 1960 resolution issued by the Academy. However, the institute was not created because the political winds shifted. Even so, semiotics work continued outside official settings, and the informality of association in apartments or available public spaces would forever define the Moscow–Tartu School's atmosphere. The subsequent attacks on semiotics in the Moscow press were deflating, but scholars were heartened when Professor Yuri Lotman (1922–93), newly established at the University of Tartu, sought to forge connections with them. Lotman had been at the University of Tartu for more than a decade and he was in the process of independently arriving at similar critical perspectives on the potential for developing semiotics out of structuralist poetics.[117] His overtures to Moscow scholars were successful, and an enduring collaboration began. The stigma associated with the term semiotics led Lotman and others involved in this new joint effort to refer in many public forums to sign systems (*znakovye sistemy*) rather than to semiotic theory. In 1964, both the journal (*Trudy po znakovym sistemam*) and the summer school in Kääriku near Tartu with that name were launched. The summer school convened each year until 1974 and then, in a slightly different form, through 1985. The participants necessarily changed when a number of the earlier stars emigrated in the 1970s and as superb students rose to the ranks of senior scholars. The research and publication efforts persisted in the post-Soviet period, particularly in Tartu, but also in universities across Europe and the United States.

Even an abbreviated list of the first generation of participants in the Moscow–Tartu School and their fields of interests demonstrates the capacious reach of the school. Among the most formidable was Viacheslav V. Ivanov (1929–2017), with his extensive knowledge of Indo-European languages, literature, and mythology. These areas of study were also central to the work of Vladimir Toporov (1928–2005). Boris Uspensky (b. 1937) brought knowledge of Russian literature, history, and culture, particularly of the medieval period. Aleksandr Piatigorsky (1929–2009) was a philosopher and scholar of religion. Boris Gasparov (b. 1940) was trained as a linguist and musicologist, and he would also emerge as a major scholar of literature. Tatiana Elizarenkova (1929–2007) worked on Indian ritual, literature, and culture. Yuri Levin (1935–2010) studied mathematics as well as literature. Zara Mints (1927–90) focused on Russian literature, particularly Symbolism. The Moscow–Tartu School also continued to flourish in its informal Moscow settings, reaching an ever-broader group of thinkers. An important poetics circle was led by the folklorist Eleazar Meletinsky (1918–2005) and Alexander Zholkovsky (b. 1937). Zholkovsky had studied Somali linguistics and machine translation; the poetics circle led by Zholkovsky and Meletinsky also reflected a wide range of personalities and interests. In addition to some of the scholars just listed, it included the linguist and poetics specialist Yuri Shcheglov (1937–2009) and the linguist, linguistic anthropologist, and literary scholar Tatiana Tsiv′ian (b. 1937). The list could go on, reminding us that the Moscow–Tartu School was the work of many people besides its much-admired leader, Yuri Lotman.[118]

Lotman's publications are emblematic of the Moscow–Tartu School's range of interests; republications and new editions of his work have appeared during the post-Soviet period at an impressive pace. They are almost equally divided between overarching, theoretical studies and works that draw on Lotman's training as a philologist specializing in the eighteenth and early nineteenth centuries in Russia. In *The Structure of the Artistic Text* (*Struktura khudozhestvennogo teksta*, 1970) Lotman first introduced a topic that was to be of lifelong interest, namely the impact of chance events and individual human agency on systems of meaning and artistic genres. He was influential in directing attention to the value of studying historically documented behavioral practices against the background of the grammars of culture or structures of representation. His book *The Creation of Karamzin* (*Sotvorenie Karamzina*, 1987) exemplified the detective work of a scholar able to reconstruct the lived experience of the past from scant records as well as the self-organizing system of one writer's self-creation as a "Russian European."[119] One could argue that Lotman found models of behavior pertinent to his own compromised era in the long life of Karamzin, and (as had Akhmatova before him) in Pushkin's life as well.

Lotman also invented the term "semiosphere" to study spatial modeling of culture, where hierarchies of sign systems could be analyzed as if in three dimensions and thus with ever-expanding points of interaction.[120] That problem is explored repeatedly in later works, including his last book, *Culture and Explosion* (*Kul'tura i vzryv*, 1992). This far-reaching work examined the larger patterns of cultural memory affected by seemingly random events, the semiotics of unpredictable systems, and the consequences of mobile boundaries between self and other, culture and nature, stasis and dynamism. These binaries—a stable model of thought advanced by structuralists that never disappeared from semiotics research—were under great pressure in the early 1990s. Lotman makes reference to these new instabilities in *Culture and Explosion* and optimistically reads the present moment as propitious for much-needed ternary models of cultural expression in Russia.

Reconstructions of mythological archetypes and a general interest in the archaic were important in the Moscow–Tartu School's research on cultural mechanisms and cultural transmission. Mythology, seen as a tool for interpreting and understanding historical consciousness, was studied by Meletinsky, Ivanov, Sergei Nekliudov (b. 1941), Toporov, and others. Efforts to describe the formal properties of complex texts led to projects focused on fictional and poetic worlds (Zholkovsky and Shcheglov),[121] and to the poetics of subtexts. The latter had seemed entirely pragmatic—adducing subtexts as a means to interpret difficult poems—but semiotics took up the challenge of theorizing the saturation of modernist poems with subtexts as a revealing cultural paradigm. The poetry of the Acmeists—particularly of Osip Mandelstam, whose poems were becoming more available at precisely the time semiotics was evolving—was central to that project.[122]

The Moscow–Tartu School was active over such a long period of time, and involved so much contact with other theorists and schools of thought, that one detects a wide array of influences and interactions, from post-structuralism to Ilya Prigogine's work on self-organizing systems. The School's openness to such a variety of sources of stimulation and challenge may be one reason for its unflagging vitality, and another is surely its ethics of collaboration and informality. A stunningly high percentage of major essays and books are co-authored. It encouraged differing approaches and methods, and created an atmosphere of ease and conviviality which fostered life-long friendships. In the words of Boris Gasparov, "the mere fact that this particular world could exist gave one the feeling of inner independence, of an opening onto a spiritual space that was protected against the hostile surroundings."[123] The history of the Moscow–Tartu School is still being written (and made); it awaits a broader cultural study in the context of Russian intellectual circles from the eighteenth century onward.[124]

Perestroika and post-Soviet transformations of the literary field

The democratic reforms launched by Mikhail Gorbachev in the mid-1980s created the policies of Glasnost (openness) and Perestroika (restructuring), which enabled a public critique of Soviet ideology and the publication in Russian of previously banned literary works. An avalanche of masterpieces swept through Soviet journals: the novels of Zamiatin, Platonov, Nabokov, Solzhenitsyn, Shalamov, Sokolov, Venedikt Erofeev, and the poetry of Mandelstam, Akhmatova, Gumilev, Kharms, Vvedensky, and Brodsky. In many cases, these publications made available previously censored or unpublished work that had circulated in *samizdat* or *tamizdat*. The most heated critical discussions were triggered not by aesthetically challenging works, but by more conventional novels like Anatoly Rybakov's (1911–98) *Children of the Arbat (Deti Arbata*, 1989) and Dudintsev's *White Robes (Belye odezhdy*, 1986), which dealt with Stalinist repressions and offered an anti-totalitarian revision of the Soviet past.[125]

More surprising was the new course taken by the authors associated with Village Prose. Largely assumed to support Perestroika, given their anti-Soviet stance, a number of them, including Rasputin, Belov, Soloukhin, and Leonid Leonov (1899–1994), became vocal defenders of Soviet literary hierarchies. They participated in various anti-liberal campaigns and signed open letters, including the infamous *Letter of 74* (1990) protesting against Russophobia in contemporary Russian media and literature, lamenting the reduction of Soviet military might, and expressing anger over such issues as the reunification of Germany and the idealization of what they called "the fascist state of Israel" by the liberal (i.e., Jewish) intelligentsia. This evolution might seem paradoxical—after all, Village Prose had gained popularity among the intelligentsia as the advocate for traditional peasant values destroyed by the Bolsheviks. Its proponents, however, were unable to accept radical cultural changes such as the liberalization of cultural norms or increasing Western influences: they feared that alien influences would weaken Russian national identity and lead to political and cultural "colonization."[126]

The Russian literary scene experienced a drastic political polarization. Criticism of Stalinism and the Brezhnev era of Stagnation, attacks on Soviet ideology and its founders (including Lenin and Marx), a pro-Western orientation, and intense opposition to Russian nationalism were the principles uniting one group of newspapers and literary journals, most prominently *Novyi mir, Znamia, Literary Gazette (Literaturnaia gazeta), Ogonek*, and *Youth*. By contrast, journals such as *Our Contemporary, The Young Guard, Moscow*, and the newspapers *Literary Russia (Literaturnaia Rossiia)* and *Tomorrow (Zavtra)* joined forces in support of the Soviet empire and Stalinism. They attacked what they saw as Russophobia and "rootless cosmopolitans" (a euphemism for Jews, harking back to the rhetoric of Stalinist anti-Semitic campaigns). Their fierce defense of the Soviet past against liberal besmirching coexisted with a cult of Russian monarchy and Orthodoxy.

During this period of polarized debate, readership of new literary publications soared; the subscription base for literary journals in 1987–92 reached a peak of up to several million per journal. However, after the failure of the pro-Communist coup in August 1991, which put an end to the seventy-four-year rule of the Communist Party, the "journal wars" ceased almost instantly. The one-party political system and unified cultural politics with clearly opposed blocs vanished as well; the struggle for influence over the political leadership lost any meaning.

The economic crisis of the 1990s also took its toll. In 1997, the cultural analyst Boris Dubin diagnosed "the twilight of the civilization of thick journals": "Neither events, nor reputations are created here [in thick journals] anymore."[127] The George Soros Foundation "Open Society" introduced a program that provided all provincial libraries with free subscriptions to major journals. This measure saved this cultural institution from complete extinction in the 1990s. Literary life nevertheless became decentralized, which in its own way reflected the dispersal of political and cultural power, elevated the status of publishing houses, and sped up the development of mass literature, both translated and home-grown. Readers' preferences became more diverse and even atomized, once the polarizing discourses had abated.

As a result, many critics in post-Soviet Russia lamented the disappearance of what they called the "literary process." It seemed to be fragmented into a multitude of disconnected phenomena, the success or failure of which was determined by accidental, if not commercial, factors. In 1990, Viktor Erofeev, one of the co-editors of the earlier nonconformist almanac *Metropol*, published a scandalous article entitled "Wake for Soviet Literature."[128] He claimed that the three branches of Soviet literature (official, liberal, and Village Prose) were now at a dead end, if not already dead. The crisis of official literature was self-evident and inextricable from the collapse of Soviet ideology. Village Prose had dissolved into sheer hatred of the contemporary world: it dreaded women, who threatened with their sensuality, and youthful subcultures, which posed the threat of a radically changed future. But above all it feared ethnic groups, primarily Jewish agents of Western corruption, who seemed to represent modernization in general. Liberal literature, in turn, suffered from hypermoralism, which consigned it to archaic redundancy. Erofeev retained hope only for a new alternative literature built on the legacy of the nonconformist underground.

Erofeev's article elicited immense hostility, but it did accurately reflect a profound crisis in literary institutions and a longing for new cultural forms. The establishment of private literary awards, distinct from state-sponsored literary prizes, offered one example of changing literary institutions. These private (and often generous) literary awards sought to support talented writers in a time of economic hardship, and also assumed important roles in the literary process. In addition to the long-existing Andrei Bely Award, launched in the Leningrad underground, the era saw the emergence of the Russian Booker Prize (established in 1991), the Anti-Booker Prize (1995–2001, awarded by *The Independent Newspaper* [*Nezavisimaia gazeta*]), the Apollon Grigor'ev Award (1997–2004), the National Bestseller Prize (in 2001), the Big Book Prize (Bol'shaia kniga, established in 2006), the Poet Prize (in 2005), and NOS (New Writing [Novaia Slovesnost'], a prize for innovative literature established by the Prokhorov Foundation in 2009). Very quickly, the culture of prizes attracted criticism: there emerged a significant track record of arbitrary or obviously mistaken decisions; the Anti-Booker and the Apollon Grigor'ev Award lost their sponsors; and the revelation of barely concealed state financing for heavy-weight awards like The Poet and The Big Book Prizes further discredited the process. Yet the number of prizes continues to grow amid economic fluctuations (there were about 300 literary awards nationwide in 2013), and the laureates continue to enjoy a level of prestige. The Andrei Bely Award, which had never offered lavish monetary compensation, has retained its considerable prestige.

Literary institutions stabilized in the early 1990s in several ways. Renewed, unimpeded connections to writers in emigration put Russian literary life on a new footing. The writer's country of residence was no longer a factor in eligibility for publication in Russia, and works of literature could travel across the border in either direction. Former writers-in-exile, such as Brodsky, Dovlatov, and Voinovich, acquired fresh cult status. A few writers returned to Russia, most notably Solzhenitsyn, who left Vermont in 1996 and traveled by train from Vladivostok to Moscow, giving speeches along the way.

Major figures of the literary underground began to receive public acclaim. Prigov, Rubinshtein, Sorokin, Viktor Krivulin (1944–2001), Elena Shvarts (1948–2010), Olga Sedakova (b. 1949), and Liudmila Petrushevskaya (b. 1938) gained full access to publication and public readings in Russia and travelled extensively abroad. Readings, social gatherings, and improvised competitions, which were typical of the underground, became integrated into newly created public spaces, especially in large cities where literary clubs and cafés flourished. The legitimation of underground literature launched a radical revision of literary norms, including the de facto assimilation of obscene speech (*mat*), and the adoption of the previously forbidden subjects of female sexuality, homoeroticism, and the occult, as well as philosophical discourses associated with Nietzsche, Freud, Jung, Bataille, and later Foucault and the post-structuralists (all translated into Russian in the 1990s).

Popular literature flourished: translated and pseudo-translated literature gave way to original and prolific new work. The sheer abundance of texts transformed the publishing industry. Within a decade after the fall of the Soviet Union, a whole multi-genre economy developed, producing mystery novels (mainly written by women, such as Aleksandra Marinina, Polina Dashkova, Tatiana Ustinova, Daria Dontsova, Marina Iudenich, Viktoria Platova), sci-fi and fantasy (Sergei Luk´ianenko, Nik Perumov, Max Frai, Viacheslav Rybakov), and glam literature (Oksana Robski).[129]

Boris Akunin (pseud. Grigory Chkhartishvili, b. 1956) represents a special case within popular literature. A professional translator from the Japanese and English, literary scholar, and deputy editor-in-chief of the journal *Foreign Literature* (1994–2000), he devoted himself to creating popular literature for the intelligentsia reader. His stylized historical mystery novels about Erast Fandorin have been extremely well received by critics and scholars. Critics have noted that Akunin's Fandorin was conceived as a cultural hybrid.[130] First, the character combines mutually exclusive paradigms of intelligentsia behavior: liberal values and personal dignity as opposed to state service, especially as represented by the notorious Third Section of the Imperial security service (best remembered for keeping Pushkin under surveillance). Second, Fandorin constantly moves among various locations in Russia, the West, and the East: he both belongs and does not belong to Russia. He typically comes back to Russia after a long stay abroad in order to solve a crime and then immediately departs. He mediates between Western values (freedom, progress, civility, and modernity) and Asian, or more specifically Japanese, traditions (honor, self-abnegation, and meditation).

Akunin's criminals frequently enhance Fandorin's function as a mediator between social, cultural, or ideological binaries. Akunin constantly plays with the post-Soviet desire to detect and to demonize the Other in the figure of a Chechen, a Jew, a German, a capitalist, a gay man, a feminist, or a foreigner. The writer undermines these stereotypes by deploying enthocentrism, homophobia, sexism, and xenophobia as clues to the suspect's identity only to subvert these judgments as false. Akunin's villains never stand for a clear-cut opposition between good and evil, and their concerns are frequently prophetic: they foresee the horrors of the Revolution and the ensuing totalitarian regime, and they try to prevent them by any means, including criminal.

Akunin's playful methods of postmodernist didacticism stand out in contemporary Russian pop-fiction, whose texts reinforce rather than problematize nationalist and conspiratorial scenarios. They exude homophobia and admiration for brutal force, patriarchal gender norms, and sexism; they are infused with anti-intellectual and imperialist sentiment, contributing to the neo-conservative transformations of the cultural and political climate of the 2000s and especially 2010s.[131]

Russia's social and cultural life continued to undergo dramatic change in the 2010s. Fueled by the rapid improvement of the country's economy thanks to high oil and gas prices early in Putin's second term, his success in politics has been accompanied by conservative cultural tendencies. Mass disillusion with seemingly chaotic democratic politics and nostalgia for Soviet-era stability fostered a new cultural mainstream, which combines neo-traditionalist devotion to Soviet imperial power with aggressive anti-Western and anti-liberal rhetoric.[132] This cultural atmosphere reflects an acute identity crisis, and its various manifestations are indicative of a quest for new or revived collective values such as nation, empire, and religion. Growing nationalist ambitions have escalated these tendencies, bringing about the neo-imperialist and conservative turn in politics in 2014–15. Cultural unity, however, has proved elusive, particularly in the face of ongoing schisms and wars in the Caucasus and Ukraine.

In 2012, several critics identified two parallel literary processes that privilege different genres and discourses and attract radically different readerships. Natalia Ivanova noted that the confrontation between writers claiming to be heirs to the realist tradition, including Socialist Realism, and those who gravitate toward modernist/postmodernist aesthetics, reproduces the political split in society between a neo-conservative/nationalist majority and a liberal minority.[133] The young critic Igor Gulin has pointed to a sharp contrast between the ideological novel, the novel of ideas, innovative poetry, unusually formatted prose and, one might add, new drama. In his view, these genres are mutually incompatible and possess different genealogies.[134] The sprawling novels of the Soviet epoch, from *The Quiet Don* to *Children of the Arbat*, sought to appeal to (and even create) a mainstream readership. The opposite trend can be defined as "post-underground," oriented towards connoisseurs, based on experimental and transgressive models of writing inherited from Platonov, Vaginov, Kharms, and Vvedensky. The former trend relied on journals and large publishing houses, while the latter resides predominantly on the internet and in select publications (such as NLO [Novoe literaturnoe obozrenie] Publishing House, New Press [Novoe izdatel´stvo], and Ivan Limbakh's Press).

Certainly, this divide is not absolute, nor does it correlate with the ideological schisms of previous eras. The post-2000 mainstream includes the works of Viktor Pelevin (b. 1962), Ludmila Ulitskaya (b. 1943), Tatyana Tolstaya (b. 1951), Dmitry Bykov (b. 1967), Olga Slavnikova (b. 1957), Aleksei Ivanov (b. 1969), and Leonid Yuzefovich (b. 1947), who balance quasi-realistic verisimilitude with modernist phantasmagoria. Published by the largest presses such as AST and Eksmo (who own nation-wide bookstore chains), these authors are broadly publicized, frequently televised, and often perceived as the face of contemporary Russian literature. Most of them have adopted greater aesthetic simplicity in their post-2000 publications, and they gravitate toward liberal ideologies. At the same time, the mainstream of the 2010s has absorbed the majority of New Realist writers, including, first and foremost, Zakhar Prilepin (b. 1975), whose narratives are marked by neo-imperialist and anti-liberal rhetoric.

The mainstream has its cultural opponents, to whom Boris Dubin has convincingly applied Deleuze and Guattari's concept of a minor literature. As he notes, limited readership and division into groups and sub-groups are not the defining feature of post-underground literature. What matters more is the potential for a political position: "everything experimental in culture and everything repressed from public life has gained an induced political significance."[135] The successors to the underground writers have become the center of political resistance to neo-imperialist and neo-conservative politics of the 2010s. In St. Petersburg, a circle of new left artists and writers (joined by some Moscow-based authors) has sought innovative ways to combine artmaking and activism. This circle includes the notorious performance artist Petr Pavlensky (b. 1984), the performance group Chto delat´?, and the poets Aleksandr Skidan (b. 1965), Kirill Medvedev (b. 1975), Roman Osminkin (b. 1979), and Pavel Arsen´ev (b. 1986).[136] In this group, the borders between theory and art practice are porous, as between writing and activism; many of the members may be best described as poet-theorists. They define politics in deeply theorized terms: Skidan has characterized political art as that which "through the caesura, alienation, self-reflection, fragmentariness and splintering of the narrative, allows us to discover non-semantic gaps—folds of meaning that have not yet been seized by ideology."[137] Medvedev adds:

Politicizing poetry means, apart from anything else, doubting the integrity of one's own conceptions of it; doubting not only at the level of discourse, but also on the level of social functions, distribution, the place of poetry in society. It means opening the poetic text to the contradiction that can only be resolved through action—not individual, but collective action; the action of history.[138]

These writers, and like-minded activists elsewhere, have effectively utilized the internet as a new multifunctional institution for sharing innovative or experimental Russian literature. Since the early 2000s, several portals, journals, and blogs, such as *Babylon* (*Vavilon*), *The Literary Map of Russia* (*Literaturnaia karta Rossii*), *TextOnly*, and *Post(non)fiction*, have been established, all promoting and archiving experimental writing.[139] Two of these projects, *Vavilon* and *The Literary Map of Russia*, are the work of the poet, translator, and editor Dmitry Kuz'min, who also launched several book series (ARGO-Risk; Vozdukh; and the Diaspora series for NLO), journals (*Vavilon* and *Vozdukh* [*Air*]), awards (the Nora Gal Prize in Translation), and festivals (perhaps most notably the young poets' festival, first held in 1991). Having moved from Moscow to Ozolnieki (Latvia) in 2015, Kuz'min has continued that work and emphasized the connections among Russian poets in and beyond the political borders of Russia, something he had in fact long championed.

The print and digitally archived journal *New Literary Observer* (*Novoe literaturnoe obozrenie* or *NLO*) has been an enduring presence on the contemporary Russian literary scene. It is coupled with an influential and innovative publishing house headed by Irina Prokhorova. Important literary competitions, especially for first-time authors, are also held on the internet (*Teneta*, *Debut*, and *Eurasia*; initially *New Drama* was also an internet-based competition). Lively literary and political debates have unfolded online as well, starting in the magazines *Russian Journal* (*Russkii zhurnal*) in the late 1990s and early 2000s, then on *Openspace.ru* and its successor *Colta.ru* in the 2010s, and via the platform *LiveJournal* (*ZhivoiZhurnal* or as it was typically called, *ZhZh*) and Facebook, which has radically expanded the possibilities for communication among writers and their readers.[140] All literary genres, but especially poetry, have thrived on the internet, allowing animated, real-time conversations and arguments as well as instant publication and review.[141]

2

The poetics of subjectivity

WE will now shift our focus from institutional culture of the twentieth and twenty-first centuries to an account of texts that tried to understand, as if from the inside, the sweeping historical changes of the era. The genre that most intensely concentrated and experimented with these changing notions of subjectivity is poetry. That is where we begin, with attention to prose and drama to follow. We will offer two approaches to poetry and poetics in twentieth- and twenty-first-century Russian literature: first, poetics of the self; second, poetics of language. Some poets and writers fit into both categories—or neither; we will address the phenomenon of "misfits" in an Interlude inserted between the sections on "The Poetics of Subjectivity" and "The Poetics of Language."

We are treating each poetic dialect, each system of devices and strategies developed within a group or a poetic trend, as a manifestation of subjectivity. There are multiple theories of subjectivity, and the concept should not be considered outside history or cultural context. For Foucault, subjectivity is formed by the interplay of power and freedom:

> This form of power applies itself to immediate everyday life which categorizes the individual, marks him by his own individuality, attaches him to his own identity, imposes a law of truth on him which he must recognize and which others have to recognize in him. It is a form of power which makes individuals subjects.[1]

This "form of power" is embodied in every aspect of literary form, yielding intensive experimentations especially but not exclusively in poetry. These experimentations will define the trajectories of Russian literature over the course of an entire century. They also present a spectrum of new models of subjectivity called to life by modernity and thoroughly tested in the ages of revolution, war, terror, and the collapse of the Soviet system.

The different poetic systems invoked by the turbulent century fall into two types determined by their approach to subjectivity. The first type is centered on the figure of the self, that is, the individual who confronts the forces of history through his/her sense of freedom, feelings and thoughts, cultural memory, beliefs, and aspirations. In the dramatic struggle, the poet's empathy extends fully to this self—in fact, in most cases, it is difficult to draw a line between the poet and the lyric subject. These formulations—by Symbolists, Acmeists, Neo-Acmeists, Neo-Classicists, and Neo-Romantics—can be summarized in Yuri Tynianov's characterization of Blok as the most significant lyric theme of his own poetry: "This theme draws us in as the theme of a novel that is new, newly born or perhaps as yet unrealized. This is the lyric hero that we are focused on now."[2]

The second type of poetic system takes language, not the self, as the starting point. Poets for whom language is the core of poetic experiment and expression were central figures in the historical avant-garde, which gave rise to neo- and post-avant-gardes. For these avant-garde authors, the self is elusive, if not fictitious, and it can be a byproduct of language games. To return to Foucault's terms, we could say that these poets treat language as the medium of power, showing the power of history, and the power of subjectivization itself. At the same time, the revolutionary vector subverts everything stable and authoritative, mocking anything posing as absolute. These avant-garde poets explored the power of language to make and unmake subjectivities, myths, and even history itself. The varieties of avant-garde poetics that arose at the turn of the twentieth century were subdued in the 1930s–40s, eventually to be resurrected in old and new forms in the 1960s. They remained a significant factor in the literary process at the end of the century.

Symbolists and Acmeists

Symbolism and other forms of modernism produced a radical transformation of the aesthetic possibilities and philosophical underpinnings of literary expression in the early twentieth century, creating new notions of subjectivity. These movements reordered Russia's literary traditions: Realist writers like Turgenev and Tolstoy receded from importance, and Dostoevsky and Gogol exerted far more influence. An increasing preference for fantastic and fateful elements in literature meant that "The Queen of Spades" and "The Bronze Horseman" were preferred among Pushkin's writings.[3] Influences stretched across the literary spectrum, and visual arts demonstrated new possibilities, supplying new designs for books and inspiring controversial exhibitions. Many of the aesthetic gestures and philosophical principles of Symbolism were learned from the French and German examples, and translations of such poets as Arthur Rimbaud and Stéphane Mallarmé (particularly by Valery Briusov) were crucial in forging a new approach to art, much as had been the translations of Chateaubriand, Constant, and Gray by Pushkin's contemporaries a century earlier.

Innokenty Annensky shared the Symbolists' appreciation for the French masters, and particularly for the ethos of ennui associated with Baudelaire; and yet he never joined the Symbolist movement and was repelled by its mystical urges. Like the Symbolists, however, he was attuned to the art of music, and there is an elliptical and psychological flair in his verse that marks him as a modernist.[4] Annensky's poems were collected in *Quiet Songs* (*Tikhie pesni*, 1904), *The Cypress Chest* (*Kiparisovyi larets*, 1910), and a posthumous volume. He was also known as the translator of the complete plays of Euripides and as the author of lyric tragedies, but it was his lyric poetry that most impressed his contemporaries and the succeeding generations of poets. Indeed, it might be argued that the Acmeists absorbed many Symbolist ideas through Annensky, whom they revered.

Symbolism as an aesthetic movement and poetic practice saw its first stirrings in Russia as early as the 1880s; it was given definitive form in an 1892 lecture by Dmitry Merezhkovsky, "On the Causes of the Decline and on the New Trends in Contemporary Russian Literature"; it withstood a crisis in 1910, and survived as late as the 1917 Revolution. Russian Symbolism spanned two generations: first—Merezhkovsky, Konstantin Bal'mont, Valery Briusov, Zinaida Gippius, and Fedor Sologub; second—Andrei Bely, Aleksandr Blok, and Viacheslav Ivanov, to name key figures. The movement flourished in both St. Petersburg and Moscow, particularly in Petersburg.

The Symbolists opposed Realism's emphasis on verisimilitude and objectivity, and rejected the nineteenth-century novel's idea of personhood as grounded in social mechanisms, such as class or nation, in favor of more transcendental values. They were not entirely apolitical, however, as evidenced in Viacheslav Ivanov's writings for the theater, which were imbued with ideas of the national and the communal (based in *sobornost'*). The perfect balance between the individual and community had been achieved in Dionysian theater, Ivanov felt, and he sought in his tragedies *Tantalus* (1905) and *Prometheus* (written in 1916) to recreate that balance for his contemporaries.[5]

Ivanov, as well as other Symbolists, emphasized the spiritual aspects of artistic practice and of being itself. Although most also wrote fiction or other forms of prose, they revered poetry, believing that its musical, non-representational qualities were invaluable in reaching an understanding of the ideal world. Their poetics were innovative and fresh, often preferring to Russian syllabotonic meters the freer form of the *dol'nik* (where either one or two unstressed syllables could occur in a metrical foot). They also worked extensively in some traditional forms, like the sonnet, and in dramatic and narrative forms. Symbolist poetry strove to captivate or seduce through a skillful deployment of rhetorical features, rather than to convince the reader through logic. They wrote extensively about verse theory, with important work by Bely and Briusov.

Bely's legacy was his creation of a new form of modernist prose, but one could argue that his innovative, richly poetic narratives were made possible by his experiments in poetic forms and subjectivities. Poetry was his laboratory, which may account for his extensive, not to say obsessive, revisions (although these are not confined to verse). His cycle of spider poems, included in his second volume of verse, *Ashes* (*Pepel*, first edition 1909), is particularly striking, with its grotesque imagery and self-representation. Bely shows the brutality and ugliness of life through a series of masks and personae: the poem "Bacchanalia" ("Vakkhanaliia," 1906), for instance, juxtaposes a dreamy speaker with a demonic alter ego but makes the two uncannily interchangeable and intertwined. The poem's increasingly ominous sound orchestration, following the rules later set out in Bely's essay "Lyric Poetry and Experiment" ("Lirika i eksperiment," 1909), bring it to the brink of the apocalypse that the poet so often contemplated.[6] Bely's next volume of poetry, *The Urn* (*Urna*, 1909) was more philosophical; among the poems that had a lasting interest for readers was the long reflective poem *The First Rendezvous* (*Pervoe svidanie*, 1921), which mixed memoir, near stream of consciousness, and vivid sound patterning. Bely, who was knowledgeable about music as well as linguistics (and mathematics), carefully crafted musical structures in his four prose *Symphonies* (*Simfonii*, 1899–1908).[7]

Bely's writings reflect his early interest in anthroposophy, and he shared with the second generation of Symbolists an enthusiasm for the philosophical theories of Vladimir Solov'ev (1853–1900). Russian Symbolists were also conversant with broader European literary movements, and many were strongly influenced by the French Symbolists. Their poetic texts aimed for transcendence, even when their work showed, as did Bely's spider poems, that it could not be attained. The belief that an ideal world could be represented through images of concrete objects or beings goes back to Plato. Baudelaire and French poets of the nineteenth century sought to represent ideal worlds without mysticism or religion; but Russian Symbolist poets embraced metaphysical thinking, mystical diction, and a range of theologies. The first generation of Symbolists, in particular, assigned their poetry a theurgic function, aiming to bring humans closer to cosmic harmony. Art was meant to seek a higher form of reality. Balancing these lofty aesthetic ambitions was an undercurrent of sensationalism and decadence, and the label Decadent had as wide a currency as the term Symbolist. The legacy of Romanticism, particularly in its German strains, persisted, legitimating in aesthetic terms the strong expression of emotion, mystical aspirations, otherworldliness, and ideas of beauty.[8]

Personal alliances and collaborations supported the writing practices of the Symbolists, individually and as a group. The volume of poetry offered new aesthetic possibilities, and Symbolist poets' books were often arranged as complex cycles of poems. Cultural institutions provided a hospitable environment for Symbolism, which flourished in cabarets and salons. Partly because a wider range of poets and writers frequented these gatherings and presented their works to journals for publication, the rise of Symbolism also facilitated the larger cultural project of introducing modernism to Russia.

The most charismatic of the Symbolists was Aleksandr Blok, a magnetic spiritual presence in his lifetime and legendary thereafter. From the appearance of his first volume of poetry, *Poems on a Fair Lady* (*Stikhi o prekrasnoi dame*, 1904), he was a singer of love poems, first addressed to an elusive, idealized beloved, and then to the terrifyingly complicated women who were his muses in the later volumes. The transformation of his unrequited love into a tragedy of cosmic, unattainably mystical significance—and one that had a degenerate, dismal underside—marked Blok as a maker of myths for the new century. Dramatic historical events across his lifetime, the peripeteias of his personal relationships, as well as the stimulating environments of Petersburg and the Italian cities he visited, supplied Blok with ever-changing new material, turning his poems into vignettes of urban dissonance, laments of cosmic despair, and wondrous harmonic compositions. Real persons and the objects of daily life never lost their ability to serve as allegories across these many forms; Blok expressed his foreboding about national destiny and an irrevocable historical catastrophe in his poetry and essays. His dramas also played an outsized cultural role, including the acclaimed staging of his most successful play, *The Puppet Show Booth*, by Vsevolod Meyerhold (1874–1940). The play's mix of parody, mystery, and tragedy showed the emerging self-critique of the Symbolists, and also the capacity for its leading poets to develop creatively long after the original manifestos of their movement (as would be true for the Acmeists, the Futurists, and their heirs). Andrei Bely similarly outgrew the achievements of his early prose symphonies, extensive lyric poetry, and essays to write novels, memoirs, studies on verse rhythm, and *Gogol's Craft* (*Masterstvo Gogolia*, 1934). Viacheslav Ivanov and Zinaida Gippius, who emigrated after the Revolution, also outlived Symbolism, flourishing as poets and as writers of philosophical, literary-critical prose (Ivanov) and memoir and fiction (Gippius).

The boundaries among genres were often permeable, encouraging the Symbolists' fascination with self-creation and performance. Their public statements, interactions, writings, and records of each other's words and deeds prefigure later studies in the semiotics of behavior by Lotman and others. Yet early twentieth-century poets did not invent ideas of behavioral codes or cultural syncretism.[9] The modes of behavior found across decades of writers in the nineteenth century presented valuable, lasting models for the emerging modernists. More than their predecessors, though, the Symbolists created cultural mythologies out of lived experiences, love triangles, literary experiments, and social gatherings. They established rules and norms for daily life that regulated their practices of self-creation (*zhiznetvorchestvo*). The theurgic impulse discernible in their writings also inspired forms of behavior, as did a looming sense of apocalypse. In their programmatic statements they pressed one another to ever more ambitious symbolic acts; an extreme example was that of Aleksandr Dobroliubov (1876–1945), who lived for decades as a religious wanderer among sectarians or in a monastery. The greatest fascination was exerted by the love triangle among Blok, Bely, and Liubov Mendeleeva, whom Blok married in 1903 and to whom he dedicated his *Verses on a Fair Lady*. This was a much-mythologized and mystical marriage, as Olga Matich has persuasively written: its "task was to bring history to an end by proclaiming the new word of apocalyptic transfiguration."[10] Participants were unfazed by the possibility that an obsessively theorized marriage could find its ultimate meanings in cosmic history.

KEYWORDS **Life-creation and self-construction (*zhiznetvorchestvo*)**

The artistic practice of *zhiznetvorchestvo* in Russian modernist circles of the 1900s–10s stems from Romantic and Neo-Romantic concepts of the poet's life as a self-contained work of art, and includes a system of cultural practices theatrically representing a public image of the poet in everyday life. From the Romantic era, the poet as subject of legend and myth became inseparable in the minds of readers from the experience of reading poetry. Practices of life-creation were especially widespread among the younger Symbolists (including Bely and Blok). New versions emerged among Russian avant-gardists, beginning with the Futurists and members of OBERIU, to be reinvented by the Conceptualists in the 1970s–80s (Prigov and Monastyrsky). For the Futurists and, later, for members of OBERIU, the poet's self-mythologization flaunted transgressions such as eccentric costumes, make-up, scandalous drunkenness, or sexual escapades. Such transgressive practices in the poet's public and private life confronted bourgeois tastes and expectations.[11]

In the 1920s, former Futurists transformed modernist life-creation into socialist life-construction as members of LEF, suggesting that the artist's task was to create a reality-based vision of a new socialist life ("literature of fact"). They also presupposed the writer's active engagement with social life (Sergei Tret´iakov working on a collective farm, for example). But whereas Symbolist life-creation enacted a poet's individual myth, LEF life-construction paved the way for Socialist Realism, subordinating individual talent to the demands of an emerging collective society.

Modernist life-creation did not fully disappear even in the repressive, fearful atmosphere of the 1930s–50s. Numerous anecdotes about pranks and witticisms by Daniil Kharms, Yuri Olesha, Nikolai Erdman, and Mikhail Svetlov kept alive the performative mythology of the artist challenging social mores. Anna Akhmatova exemplified a different model of life-creation: she cultivated her image as one who remains faithful to the modernist culture of the Silver Age, despite the pressures of Soviet culture and society. A new surge of modernist *zhiznetvorchestvo* emerged in the 1960s–70s. It flourished in underground circles (with examples ranging from Brodsky to Mit´ki), and in official and semi-official culture (from Vysotsky to Yevtushenko and Voznesensky). Solzhenitsyn's self-representation as the writer-prophet single-handedly confronting the oppressive political system, as promoted in his autobiographical writings, was also supported by his theatricalized behavior.

During the late Soviet period, the self-mythologizing acts of poets and writers supplied models for the intelligentsia's lifestyle. The tradition of modernist and avant-garde life-creation also laid the foundation for the performance art born in the 1970s (Collective Actions), and the post-Soviet period (The Prigov Family group, E. T. I., Voina, Pussy Riot).

The Symbolists made an enduring contribution to the Russian tradition in their poetry, although they wrote in many forms: they extended the traditions created in the eighteenth and nineteenth centuries, when writers as different as Derzhavin, Pushkin, and Nekrasov used poetic texts to create alternative views of Russia's history and its destiny. For modernist groups of all stripes, revulsion at nineteenth-century materialistic values and a rejection of positivism created a space in which a range of thinkers could provide inspiring alternatives, most especially Friedrich Nietzsche (1844–1900). Nietzsche's rebellion against multiple traditions, his embrace of new values and creative energies, and his reorientation toward the future had a broad impact. It penetrated the erudite, formal poems and the theory of tragedy developed by Viacheslav Ivanov as well as the euphonious, sense-laden poems of Konstantin Bal´mont; some poets also wrote directly about Nietzsche, including Bely and Merezhkovsky.[12] Redeeming mankind aesthetically through his darkest experiences, as Nietzsche envisioned, was a powerfully appealing response to the historical crisis of the era; it came eventually to seem a terrible harbinger of the October Revolution. That art should be both decadent and refined was a paradoxical but seemingly indisputable aim, concretely imaged for example by Gippius's

"Spiders" ("Pauki," 1903): their endless labor of spinning represents the poet's act of creation, joining distant points into a unified web of sticky, foul-smelling, sulfurous words. Her spiders may have inspired those of Andrei Bely, although both likely drew on other common sources, including Dostoevsky. Gippius's distinctive contribution to Russian Symbolism also comes from her blend of post-Nietzschean and intensely erotic decadence with a strand of metaphysical, even religious poetry that had its origins in Tiutchev.[13]

A different version of this sensory paradox infuses the poetry of Ivanov, particularly in *Cor Ardens* (1911), the very title of which conjoins the destructions of fire with the life-affirming organ of the heart. Dedicated to the memory of his dead wife, Lidia Zinov'eva-Annibal, *Cor Ardens* seeks to bring about her resurrection, reaffirming at once the theurgic aims of art and an unyielding notion of the Eternal Feminine. Ivanov also stands out among the Symbolists for his devotion to specific poetic forms, above all the sonnet—which flourished in the period— and the sonnet cycle known as a wreath of sonnets, each poem's last line providing the start of the next and all the first lines then collected into a crowning last (or sometimes first) sonnet. Ivanov wrote several such cycles, and dozens of individual sonnets besides. The sonnet suited his esoteric inclinations because of its formal complexity, and its long association with the love lyric let Ivanov write of love as both a human emotion and an idealized way to apprehend the world.

One of Ivanov's sonnets takes up a different object of affection and investigation, the theater. He worked from a deep understanding of theatrical performance as a ritual—his doctoral dissertation was on the cult of Dionysus—and in addition to writing plays of his own, he translated Aeschylus, among others. Ivanov's theory of Dostoevsky's creative work as a series of "novel-tragedies" also reflected his fascination with Nietzsche (tragedy as the signifier for the Dionysian).[14] The rituals of ancient drama are the context for his early sonnet "Taormina." Its title names the site of a celebrated ancient theater and ornately describes the Sicilian landscape and the theater's ruins. The sonnet ends with the following beautiful lines. The Russian, with its archaic diction and spelling, bears quotation in the old orthography, the more to appreciate Ivanov's high style:

> Въ обломкахъ спитъ ѳеатръ, орхестра онѣмѣла;
> Но вѣчно курится въ снѣгахъ твоя ѳимела,
> Грядый въ востокѣ дня и торжествѣ святынь!
>
> И съ твоего кремля, какъ древле, Мельпомена
> Зритъ, Эвій, скорбная, волшебный кругъ пустынь
> И Тартаръ, дышащій подъ вертоградомъ плѣна![15]

> In remnants the theater sleeps, the orchestra has gone dumb,
> But your altar burns eternally amidst the snow,
> You who come with the east of day and in the triumph of shrines!
>
> In ancient days, from your citadel, Evius,
> Sorrowful Melpomene views the deserts' magical circle
> And Tartarus breathing beneath the garden's lure!

Ivanov presents a stunningly optimistic account of this ancient site: the ruined theater retains the mystery of its performances, as if Melpomene, the muse of tragedy, could yet look over its "magic circle" and hidden, divine habitats, down even to the gardened captivity of Hades (Tartarus).

While the orientation toward mystery and magic retains the distinct flavor of Symbolism, Ivanov's insistence that the values of the ancient world (or of humanistic aesthetics more broadly) were waiting for modernists to revive them is also a guiding principle of the Russian Acmeists. (Ivanov's fellow classicist Innokenty Annensky was a significant force in this direction for the Acmeists as well.) Acmeism and Symbolism shared many of the same salons and publication venues, and continuities must be acknowledged within these forms of modernism. In founding one of the most famous journals of the period, *Apollon*, Nikolai Gumilev and Sergei Makovsky created a space in which Acmeism could be defined and defended, and the new journal also showcased the webs of connections between different modes of aesthetic expression now generally associated with modernism. The essay "On Beautiful Clarity" ("O prekrasnoi iasnosti," 1910) by Mikhail Kuzmin appeared in *Apollon*; along with Gumilev's letters on Russian poetry, it stood as a manifesto of a new poetic movement. The clarity advocated by Kuzmin was a challenge to the obscurity of the Symbolists. Like Gumilev, Anna Akhmatova, and Osip Mandelstam, who were more explicitly a part of the Acmeist group, Kuzmin shared the Symbolists' passionate commitment to aestheticism, but the tone of his work, like that of the Acmeists, tended to be cooler and more logical. The original polemical purpose of Acmeist manifestos was to criticize the Symbolists for directing "their main energies into the realm of the unknown" (Gumilev).[16] Rather than the Symbolists' idealistic philosophy that promoted transcendental longing, these poets wrote of concrete, even prosaic phenomena of daily life, although it has to be said that their idea of the everyday might extend to Chablis and oysters on ice or to Gothic cathedrals with their heavenly vaults.[17] The spiritual truths that informed the imagery and diction of their poetry evinced a programmatic nostalgia for world culture. The minor Acmeist poet Mikhail Lozinsky (1886–1955), for example, chose to spend his waking hours translating into Russian one of the greatest religious and humanist texts of world literature, Dante's *Divine Comedy*; Mandelstam's habit of carrying with him a volume of Dante sprang from the same devotion (and also reflected his sense of the Great Terror as a new Inferno).

Acmeism adopted the idea of cultural memory as its fundamental precept, and saw the Acmeist poet as its living vessel. Intertextual and intercultural allusions and quotations turned the word, saturated with associations from past usages, into a vehicle for historical memory. The Acmeist writer, in constant dialogue with cultural memory, would construct an identity at once infused with the present moment and committed to trans-historical continuity. By intertwining cultural and personal memories, the Acmeist subject pits the persistence of culture against the erasure and disruption caused by historical catastrophes. Capable of resisting the whirlwind of modernity, the Acmeist finds within historical and personal experience a reality constituted by art and language that can survive.

Acmeist texts were thus built on the artistic word in its historical and contemporary connotations: "For the Acmeists, the conscious sense of the word, the Logos, is just as magnificent a form as music for the Symbolists."[18] Eschewing the mystical and musical, rather than verbal, insights of their predecessors, this generation of poets valued words above all; indeed a whole school of literary criticism would eventually be built on their use of subtexts and intertexts.[19] Not that these poets rejected all nonverbal art forms—Mandelstam created his first volume of poetry, *Stone* (*Kamen'*, 1913) around church architecture, Akhmatova would use multiple forms of sculpture and the Tsarskoe Selo gardens as significant points of reference, and Kuzmin's poetry is beautifully enriched by his knowledge of music, especially opera and the theater. Theirs was not an isolated form of poetic expression, but it did elevate the status of the word as a carrier of traditions, values, and cultural history, so much so that the freedom to transform those received values—to rearrange the household gods, as Mandelstam put it in an early poem—was imagined as a bold gesture of aesthetic maturity. Akhmatova would write her Pushkin essays in the Soviet period not only because the state was commissioning all manner of Pushkiniana in the run-up to the 1937 Jubilee, but also because she was engaged in her own private act of preserving the highest expression of Russian culture. The notion of subjective expression in Acmeist poetics is inextricable from this commitment to cultural identity: the self could not be imagined apart from the cultural legacy it inherited.

Mandelstam's first book of poetry, *Stone*, remains an outstanding example of how a poet might imagine a self whose greatest aim was to carry forward a daunting cultural legacy. As published in March 1913, it included only 23 poems; it was hailed by fellow Acmeists but ignored by the literary press. In 1914, Mandelstam personally financed and published a second edition, with over 70 poems, and this is the version read today. This time reviews were widespread, citing the poet's ease and freedom with verse form, and his natural musicality. Sophia Parnok called Mandelstam a "sculptor of the word" ("vaianie iz slova"), while Maksimilian Voloshin found Mandelstam's voice to be "unusually resonant" ("neobyknovenno zvuchen") and "rich in nuance and intonations."[20]

Many poems in *Stone* express the quest for a poetic identity through an implicit repudiation of Symbolism. The poetic persona is both anxious and resilient in his rejection of a movement whose sound textures he emulates and whose somewhat precious postures of *enfant terrible*, outsider (as a bohemian and a Jew), and aesthete he adopts. Even as Mandelstam alludes to the poets of the previous generation, and even as his sound play is as rich as Bal'mont's, his cityscapes as impressionistic as Blok's, and his wistful melancholy highly reminiscent of Annensky's, he moves away from the otherworldly quality of Symbolism. As *Stone* unfolds, the speaker is reborn as a new Adam who finds his own idiom and assigns names to his feelings and to the visible world around him (but not to the invisible realm of a higher, mystical reality). In so doing, he establishes his modernist credentials as a writer who believes in the power of the poetic word, saturated with connotation, and the power of the poem, built from historic images, emblems of culture, and citations, to perpetuate the past into the here and now. The poems are meant to build a new version of the beautiful using traditional elements, for which stone serves as a metaphor. The best-known poems in the collection, such as "Hagia Sophia" and "Notre Dame," are about buildings, and translate into highly visual stanzas the views that Mandelstam had set out in programmatic essays like "The Morning of Acmeism."[21] "Hagia Sophia" and "Notre Dame" are attentive to the dynamics of destruction and recycling that can be embodied in a single structure that synthesizes pagan and Christian, old and new, East and West. The conservation and transformation of material—here the reuse of the precious marble columns from the Temple of Diana at Ephesus—is, for Mandelstam, a guiding principle of civilization which, in literature, corresponds to the salvaging techniques of quotation, allusion, and rewriting employed by Mandelstam as well as other modernist poets, like T. S. Eliot and Ezra Pound. In architecture and nature, just as in poetry, tensions between contraries, such as might and meekness, the fantasy of ornament and the depth of reason, provide a structure that will survive the test of time.

Mandelstam found a different way of accessing the past in his second volume of poetry, *Tristia* (1922). Nevertheless, continuities with his first book were discernible even in the initially proposed title, *New Stone* (*Novyi kamen'*). The poet settled on a title borrowed from Ovid, whose *Tristia* already figured as the title of one poem in the collection. Semantically, the title *Tristia* points unambiguously toward the theme of loss, which would become a mainstay of Mandelstam's poetry, as well as of the writings of so many others of his generation. The poem "Tristia" represented to its readers a model of cultural synchronism that could sustain them through times of crisis; it offered the idea of adopting a new persona for a "new life" ("novaia zhizn'") that dawned on the horizon of the 1920s as much as it did when Christianity itself was born.[22] "All happened long ago, all will be repeated again," the poem intoned, leaving on readers' lips the sweet taste of recognition.

CASE STUDY Anna Akhmatova

Among celebrated poets in the twentieth century, the poet who named herself Anna Akhmatova (b. Anna Gorenko, 1889–1966) stands out for a long, productive, and dramatic literary career and for a compelling and sometimes controversial personality. Readers esteemed her early love poetry, complex civic poems, and the later poetics of memory, while state officials and literary critics of all stripes sought to rein in her poetic production or to pick apart its apparent merits and deficiencies.

Anna Akhmatova thrived amid a generation of great poets—Pasternak, Mandelstam, Tsvetaeva, Khodasevich, Kuzmin, and Khlebnikov—which left an imprint of self-conscious legacy-building if not competitiveness on her work. Akhmatova's life spanned from the era of the Symbolists to the rise of 1960s' unofficial culture, and the stages of self-creation in her career reflect the cultural milestones in twentieth-century poetry.

Her earliest poetry featured love lyrics that struck many readers, including the young literary scholar and critic Boris Eikhenbaum, as novelistic psychological portraits compressed into the space of a few quatrains.[23] Some of the most famous poems featured a man, a woman, and a few bits of dialogue, with the conversation so pared down that a single imperative, for instance the famous command not to stand outside in the wind, resonated with the full force of its erotic violence.[24] Abandonment and argument moved through the poems as recurring plots, making the love poems into records of the inevitable pain of intimacy and desire. The First World War brought new civic themes into Akhmatova's poems, and then, with the Revolution, Civil War, the New Economic Policy (NEP), the Soviet consolidation of power, Stalin's Terror, and the Second World War, her poetry turned away from personal dramas toward the epic. But those more consciously historical poems—and there were to be many of them—retained the psychological depth and emotional richness that marked Akhmatova's early work. In writing about loss during wartime, for example, or about the uncertain fates of the Terror's victims, she could conjure up an entire elegiac tradition with deft choices in meter, imagery, or allusion. Yet she also put that private elegiac tradition into the service of the epic: in one 1921 poem, "Fear, turning over things in the darkness" ("Strakh vo t´me perebiraia veshchi"), the poet calmly reveals her readiness to submit to a public execution rather than suffer the private horror of constant fear creeping into the barely illuminated spaces of daily life.[25]

Beginning with her first volume of poems, *Evening* (*Vecher*, 1912), Akhmatova was associated with the poetry of Petersburg and Tsarskoe Selo, and with the poetic movement of Acmeism. Her poems would never lose the concreteness, clarity, and "nostalgia for world culture" that defined Acmeist poetry. Among all the Acmeists, she was perhaps the most consistently exemplary of its poetics of restraint and precision.[26] Yet her personal connections to her fellow Acmeists were equally significant. She was married to the movement's intellectual leader, Nikolai Gumilev, and although their marriage had broken up by the time he was arrested and shot by the Soviet authorities in 1921, Akhmatova mourned his death and commemorated it often in her poetry; she so powerfully assumed the emotional position of a widow that few readers would easily guess that she and he were essentially remarried to others by 1921. As important was her friendship with Mandelstam, attested in the loyal, mutual representations in their poetry and in the memoirs of Mandelstam's widow, Nadezhda Mandelstam. Acmeism also connected Akhmatova to Mikhail Kuzmin, resulting in many intertextual motifs in her poetry; his long poem *The Trout Breaks the Ice* (*Forel' razbivaet led*, 1927) provided Akhmatova with a formal and rhetorical model for *Poem Without a Hero*.

Loyal friendships mark Akhmatova's poetry, and a form of cultural loyalty motivated her extensive writings about Pushkin in the 1930s. The essays were a form of concealed autobiography; for example, in her study of Pushkin's play *The Stone Guest* she encrypted references to the Don-Juanesque Gumilev. She also probed the memoir and epistolary legacy from the Pushkin period in search of models for behavior and ethical norms. She pointedly praised Pushkin's honorable conduct in the most challenging years of Nicholas I's Russia, implying that it might stand as an inspiration to those living in later, more desperate times.

Akhmatova's own behavior has been questioned by a few later scholars who found her domineering, for example in her treatment of her loyal friend and amanuensis Lydia Chukovskaya.[27] Narcissism and earnestness were thought by these critics to be an especially unattractive combination. Akhmatova's formally conservative poetry might hold a limited appeal for those readers who prefer the explosive linguistic experimentation of Khlebnikov and Tsvetaeva, or the expressive minimalism of OBERIU. But she was widely acclaimed by other scholars and critics;[28] and many have insisted that no twentieth-century poem comes even close to her *Requiem* (*Rekviem*, dateline 1936–40) in its encapsulation of the psychological and spiritual experience of the Terror. The sequence of prefaces, dedication, lyric texts, and epilogues creates a structure that demonstrates the difficulty of recounting this history; the poem epitomizes the lasting values of human integrity and moral courage. *Requiem* articulated in an unprecedented way the special horror reserved for those who were not arrested, tortured, deported, or executed, but "merely" left behind as witnesses to disappearance and loss. In the emerging field of memory studies, Akhmatova's poetics is exemplary, and her myth-making is culturally productive and historically significant.[29] *Poem Without a Hero*, her most complex and enigmatic piece of writing, also enacts a poetics of commemoration even as it recreates the lost world of pre-revolutionary Russia. Both poems rely on a network of subtexts, and the many citations, some of them encrypted, from Kuzmin, Blok, Pushkin, Mandelstam, and others, lend substance to the theme of memory.[30]

One of the distinctive features of *Requiem* is its implicit narrative of a woman's loss of her son and her husband to the deranged legal system of arrest and imprisonment in the late 1930s. The heroine of *Requiem* shares biographical traits with Akhmatova, whose third husband, the art historian Nikolai Punin, was arrested in 1934; her son, Lev Gumilev, was arrested in 1934 and again in 1937. But *Requiem* is insistently universal and its lament explicitly refuses to be confined to the speaker's own losses. "No, it is not I, it is someone else who suffers": this is the claim not merely of a woman whose grief is so terrible that she denies it, but the voice of a woman for whom "someone else" is always present to the mind.[31]

Akhmatova's poetry before *Requiem* had readied her for this focus on the voice of another. Her capacity to project her lyrical voice, indeed to speak with uncanny persuasiveness and originality as Lot's wife, as Cleopatra, or as Dido mark some of her most memorable poems. Her transfiguration as Dido has been seen as the framework of the late cycle "Sweetbrier in Bloom" ("Shipovnik tsvetet," 1946–64).[32] These dramatic poems were also tremendously influential, enabling, for example, the later ventriloquisms of Elena Shvarts, speaking as Lavinia or Cynthia or Arno Tsart. Akhmatova's fierce integrity and emotional lucidity also inspired the lyric poetry of Inna Lisnianskaia (1928–2014); the clarity of diction and the brilliant use of folkloric, religious, and traditionally metered forms may be felt in the background of the work of poets as different as Maria Petrovykh (1908–79) and Olga Sedakova. That all these heirs are women is no accident, but Akhmatova also enjoyed the attention of a coterie of young male poets in the 1960s, including Joseph Brodsky. Just as Pushkin had set for Akhmatova an exemplary path of noble, detached behavior in the face of vulgarity (*poshlost'*) and evil, so Brodsky would later say of Akhmatova that she was a model for him and his contemporaries. Brodsky added, however, that the behavior would have been worth nothing without the quality of the poetry. For him, as for so many later readers, Akhmatova was always, even in her most public, historical verse, "a poet of human ties: cherished, strained, severed"; she left as her legacy a form of personal lyric marked by "the note of controlled terror."[33]

Women's writing as a modernist legacy

Akhmatova's legacy as a Russian poet cannot be separated from her status as a woman poet. She found the means in her poetry to articulate both vulnerability and strength. It was as if she also knew that the subtle self-characterizations and the verbal precision of her delicate poems would seem to do women's work, and could be made to speak to and about women in unexpected ways. In bequeathing her legacy to later women poets, Akhmatova rarely abandoned her acerbic wit or irony, crystallized in a late lyric that asks archly what might now be done to stifle the voices of women she had taught to speak.[34]

And speak they did—and do.[35] Women had contributed to Russian poetry since the eighteenth century, including such figures as Ekaterina Urusova, Anna Bunina, Karolina Pavlova, and Evdokia Rostopchina. The era of modernism saw a fresh emergence of women poets, Mirra Lokhvitskaia (1869–1905), Lidia Zinovieva-Annibal (1866–1907), and Poliksena Solov'eva (pen-name Allegro) (1867–1924) among them.[36] Valery Briusov's 1921 soirée of women poets might be seen as a positive development, had the event not been savagely critiqued by its most famous participant, Marina Tsvetaeva, in her essay "A Hero of Labor" ("Geroi truda," 1925). The essay exemplifies a deep ambivalence about whether the category of women's poetry has any validity—and if so, who stands to put it to use. In addressing the topic in 1931, Vladislav Khodasevich rather mockingly put "women's" verse between quotation marks. He was reviewing several now nearly forgotten poets of the emigration, including Irina Knorring, and the review suggested a canon of women writers: he mentioned the salutary influence of Akhmatova on one poet, and the underlying reliance on Gippius's aesthetic principles by another.[37]

Symbolism, with its poems to the Fair Lady and an unearthly, spiritual symbolism of the divine Sophia, was permeated with dreamy fantasies of a feminine voice softly whispering in the ear of a male poet. Russia's women poets found different ways of solving the dilemma of whether women might also hear the promptings of a muse. Some played with gendered identity or bypassed the idea of the muse altogether; the closer they were aesthetically to the Symbolists, the more radical their solutions. Zinaida Gippius adopted at times a masculine persona who could hold forth like a sexual libertine in one poem or go off on a quest as a spiritual knight-errant in another; her poems sought pleasure as earnestly as they did truth. Before Gippius, there was Elena Guro, who cultivated a childlike persona but also spun the story of a dead child, which resonated with such quiet force that some critics took the central fact of her life to have been the loss of a child. Both Gippius and Guro still stand a bit outside mainstream feminist accounts of Russian poetry, despite an impressive body of theoretical work on Gippius and retrieval of valuable archival materials by and about Guro.[38] Akhmatova has been more central, and a source of multiple guises for the woman poet. She could speak as a scorned or scornful lover, a reveler in a cabaret, a loyal poet determined to preserve the poetic tradition, or as the defiantly courageous voice of multitudes. Nothing seemed beyond her: she could, as she did in her *Requiem*, unflinchingly describe the massive traumatic "this" of war, terror, and public deception.

Marina Tsvetaeva represented the foremost alternative model of a modernist woman poet. Her modes of address to her lovers, family members, and anyone who fell within her orbit, achieved a passionate intensity that had few antecedents in the Russian tradition.[39] Folkloric, impersonal speech serves as a counterpoint to the direct form of appeal; this is true particularly of Tsvetaeva's prose writings and drama, but also comes across in her long poems. A precarious balance between the fiercely personal and the relentlessly analytical is one of the many challenging aspects of her legacy, and it should have complicated attempts to read Tsvetaeva as simply speaking either as a woman or for women. Her dramatic biography became an enduring subject of scholarly interest, and the catastrophic losses and ruptures in her life have often been interpreted as the foundation of the powerfully tragic elements in her work.[40] Her writings show her preoccupation with mythological stories and folktales (Ariadne, Andromache, Orpheus, Psyche, amazons, sibyls, the Pied Piper) as well as historical figures who had attained a mythic status, like Casanova or Pushkin.

Catriona Kelly noted "how inimical the Tsvetaeva icon is to the anxious gentility which is prevalent in Russian intellectual culture"; yet she went on to observe that the quirky elements in the poet's biography "enhance her reputation as the quintessential Romantic genius."[41] Feminist enthusiasm for Tsvetaeva is matched by the dry-eyed admiration of her poetic successors, many of them men, and by the impressive efforts of scholars who have analyzed her virtuoso metrical patterns.[42] One senses an almost envious admiration for her poetic inventiveness, for her brilliantly rhymed and almost supernaturally compressed lines of verse. Her life made some nervous, as evidenced by an essay published by the pioneering Mandelstam scholar Clarence Brown, "On Not Liking Tsvetaeva";[43] but there were also those, like Brodsky, for whom her writings provided an inspired framework within which to understand the poet's complex life. Brodsky also saw her work as a unified whole; he refused to elevate her poetry, because the prose was "nothing but the continuation of poetry by other means."[44] Among Tsvetaeva's most striking essays were two magnificently transgressive texts about Pushkin, written in the 1930s when others were busy building the myth of the canonical Pushkin. Tsvetaeva wanted to have nothing to do with the grandiosity of these myths, which she associated with the Empress Catherine's bland presence in "The Captain's Daughter," or worse, with the demure femininity of that novella's young Masha Mironova. Instead, she much preferred the passion and dark violence of the rebel leader Pugachev. Tsvetaeva matched the fervor of her essays with her cycle of "Poems to Pushkin" ("Stikhi k Pushkinu," 1931), which exalted an embodied representation of Pushkin: in one passage, she fantasizes about the poet's strength allowing him, were he ever imprisoned, to climb down any tower using the rope of his own veins.[45]

Signs of rebellion against gender norms were to be found across Tsvetaeva's works, and they also marked her biography. Her long marriage to Sergei Efron proved anything but conventional. Her first biographer, Simon Karlinsky, set the example with his forthrightness for later accounts of what another scholar was to call her "transgressive eros."[46]

The transgressions associated with Tsvetaeva's love life, which spilled over into such writings as the poem cycle "The Girlfriend" ("Podruga," 1915) or the prose text "Sonechka's Tale" ("Povest' o Sonechke," 1937), paled in comparison to the legacy of the poet to whom "The Girlfriend" was addressed, Sophia Parnok (1885–1933).[47] Tsvetaeva's cycle of love poems to Parnok coyly hides the gender of their addressee, or toys with disclosing it, as in the famous final lines of the first poem in the cycle, which note the "ironic charm" that the addressee cannot be designated by a masculine pronoun ("Za etu ironicheskuiu prelest' / Chto Vy—ne on").[48]

But Parnok was bold in announcing her love for women. She was ready to challenge the stereotypes about lesbians that prevailed in even the most progressive circles of the age: she neither concealed her sexual identity nor conformed to conventions of decadent representations of lesbian sexuality as tinged with depravity or death.[49] Her joyful figuration of women's desires would stand in vivid contrast to the aesthetic practice of Gippius, for example, who arranged many of her amorous texts addressed to women into apparently heterosexual patterns by using speakers grammatically identified as male.

How to represent women's sexuality was something that also challenged male writers of the period. Creative use of ventriloquism provided one solution to the problem. Valery Briusov went further than many of his peers in writing the poems of a woman whose biography he also invented. He named her Nelly, and in 1913 published a volume of her poems. Vladislav Khodasevich found them to be superior to the work of other women poets of the time in that they were more profound in thought and more harmoniously composed. Was Khodasevich slyly displaying his awareness that they were written by a man when he added that the poems were inferior in one way: their slavish imitation of the poetry of Valery Briusov?[50] Briusov's hoax is all the more interesting because of the hyper-masculinity of his poetry and his reputation. He would later be parodied by Tsvetaeva (who knew how to hit her mark) as a "hero of labor": for Briusov, making poetry was a form of exertion (aggressively explained in his polemical response to Bal'mont in 1913, the same year the Nelly poems appeared).[51]

Another appropriation of the feminine was perpetrated a few years earlier by Maksimilian Voloshin (1877–1932), who was one of Tsvetaeva's earliest champions: he also facilitated the publication of the poetry of Cherubina de Gabriak (pseud. Elizaveta Dmitrieva, 1887–1928) in 1909, seeking to tantalize readers—and above all perhaps male readers. These poems were not exactly a hoax (although at the time, when the truth first came to light, some assumed that the poems were the work of Voloshin, because they were thought to exhibit too much talent to be the work of a provincial young woman), but they were advanced by him in what retrospectively may be thought of as a brilliant marketing campaign. Voloshin targeted the journal *Apollon* for having rejected some of Dmitrieva's poems, and he wrapped her work in an aura of mystery, sending the poems on perfumed sheets of paper and taking advantage of the new technology of the telephone to have a seductive feminine voice captivate *Apollon*'s editor, Sergei Makovsky. When it was revealed that the poet was not a Catholic prodigy of Italian-Polish descent with a secret past, as Cherubina de Gabriak had made herself out to be, but rather a disabled schoolteacher with the very plain name of Elizaveta Dmitrieva, Makovsky made quick peace with the news and published further work by Dmitrieva. But Nikolai Gumilev, a co-editor at *Apollon* and, more important, a man who had had a passionate attachment to Dmitrieva before her transformation into Cherubina de Gabriak, was outraged. Gumilev and Voloshin even fought a duel, making it all the more palpable how control over this woman's career was an affair between men. As for Dmitrieva herself, she seems to have come into her own as a writer. She was able to pose as a European émigré because she had in fact been extremely well educated. Her poems on the theme of dual identity are the best indication that she was far from a pawn in Voloshin's or anyone else's hands.[52] But Dmitrieva's later fate sadly showed how little writers could control their own lives in the Soviet era. She experienced the tragedies of the era, including surveillance, arrest, exile, and early death; but she continued to write through the 1920s, finding a distinctive voice against considerable odds.

One other woman poet, who is something of an outlier in the modernist legacy, must be mentioned: while Anna Barkova's proletarian origins and early enthusiasm for the Soviet cause set her apart, her poetry and drama incorporated historical material and made use of dramatic alter egos, as was common in the work of Akhmatova and others. Barkova displayed an understanding of the significance of gender throughout her career. Her first book, *The Woman (Zhenshchina)*, published in 1922, proclaimed the poet's awareness that her poems were broken, craggy, unlovely and hard to grasp (as one poem puts it, "obryvochna, nevniatna"; "Two Poetesses" ["Dve poetessy," 1921]).[53] She embraced the identity of a criminal, a holy fool, an amazon, and an incendiary who blows up churches. Barkova was subjected to three prison terms and a period of exile, and wrote poetry and prose through it all. The poems moved easily between traditional meters and *dol'nik* rhythms, dispatching assonance rhymes that emphasized the poet's insistence on her freedom to write as she wished. Later poems returned with renewed bitterness to the theme of what it meant to write as a woman, perhaps most expressively in "A Few Autobiographical Facts" ("Nechto avtobiograficheskoe," 1953), where the poet imagines herself dead, lying in a mass grave. Her bones retain the power of speech: "I was listed in death as male / But I was always, my whole life, a *she*" ("V pol muzhskoi za grobom zapisali... / Ia vsegda, vsiu zhizn' byla *ona*").[54] Scholars have found that Barkova's writings, particularly the late poetry, were "fiercer and more cynical than most poetry written by Russian women."[55] She was a strong contributor to the diversity of voices within Russian women's writing, and her work can be seen as a precursor to the poetry of Elena Shvarts and to the plays and prose of Liudmila Petrushevskaya.

Late modernism: Neo-Acmeism and other classical poetry

Like other strands of modernism, Acmeism had a long and uneven legacy in Russian culture, marked by interruptions and renewals. No institutional backing guaranteed its legacy within the Soviet Union, where Acmeism's aesthetic values of beauty, clarity, and freshness of perception were overwhelmed in official cultural life by the doctrines of Socialist Realism. But vestiges of Acmeism survived through the 1930s, both in the later work of Kuzmin (who died in 1936) and in that of Andrei Egunov (1895–1968), who was a friend of Kuzmin in the 1930s and who, like Mandelstam (and Nabokov), had studied at the Tenishev School in his youth and assimilated its humanist values. Egunov was a classicist, which provides another point of contiguity, if not with Acmeism itself, then with two of the Acmeists' early maîtres, Innokenty Annensky and Viacheslav Ivanov, both also trained as classicists. Like Annensky, Egunov was a long-time teacher, and his knowledge of ancient languages gave him the means to earn a living even in exile. His novel *On the Other Side of Tula: A Soviet Pastoral (Po tu storonu Tuly: Sovetskaia pastoral'*, 1931) appeared under the pseudonym Andrei Nikolev—a humorous gesture toward the minor eighteenth-century poet Nikolai Nikolev—and its publication history epitomizes the various ways in which Neo-Acmeism survived. *On the Other Side of Tula* turned the emerging Soviet production novel on its head, fusing it with the remnants of classical romance (in this case between two men), and lacing the descriptions of landscape and factory floor with darkly funny dialogue. The novel was Egunov's only published literary work in his lifetime, and it was rescued from obscurity by the efforts of late Soviet and post-Soviet critics to champion some peripheral figures of the Silver Age.[56]

Egunov also wrote poetry, which was known in some *tamizdat* publications, but his collection *Elysian Pleasures (Eliseiskie radosti)* was published only in the 1990s, and it shows his enduring affinities with the writings of both Kuzmin and Vaginov.[57] Later poets who upheld the values of the Acmeists include Arseny Tarkovsky (1907–89), David Samoilov (1920–90), Aleksandr Kushner (b. 1936), Lev Losev, Oleg Chukhontsev (b. 1938), and Joseph Brodsky. Although the span of these poets' birthdates means that they came of age at different times, most wrote their early poems or rose to prominence by the 1960s, and variously benefitted from the relaxed censorship during the Thaw. One whose fate is representative of broader trends in poetry of the era is Arseny Tarkovsky. Known for decades as a translator, he was unable to publish his poetry until later; his first book was *Before the Snow* (*Pered snegom*, 1962), published when he was 55. He might be taken as a signal figure for those who, in their own way, continued the legacy of Acmeism: he was a fierce exemplar of poetic integrity, and he faced renewed obstacles to publication for signing a letter in support of Sinyavsky and Daniel in 1966. And he was an exponent of lyrical, often elegiac, poetry that retreated from the triumphant intonations of Soviet literature. Rather than exploring the experimental pathways of poets he deeply admired, such as (early) Pasternak and Tsvetaeva, Tarkovsky pushed the boundaries of classical, harmonious, and deeply philosophical poetry, in a manner reminiscent of Tiutchev and Fet. Tarkovsky's poetry reached a new audience after he read four of his poems in the film *The Mirror* (*Zerkalo*, 1975), directed by his son Andrei. Those four poems typify the themes of love cherished and lost, of the endurance of the natural world, and of the meaning of the cosmos. Through concrete imagery and precise language, the poems address large philosophical themes. One poem is titled after the most expansive theme of all, "Life, Life" ("Zhizn', zhizn'," 1965). It affirms the power of death to set boundaries and meaning to life. A similar paradox is felt in another of the poems recited in *The Mirror*, a short, asymmetrical, and untitled poem that begins, "I was waiting for you all yesterday" ("S utra ia tebia dozhidalsia vchera," 1941). Here, the arrival of the beloved brings no consolation, and drops of rain flowing over the trees suggest that the waiting poet's own body remains cold and uncared for.[58]

Oleg Chukhontsev, in the next generation, also saw his work receive only belated publication. A Moscow poet, he became the poetry editor for *Novyi mir* in 1986, as Glasnost was reaching its peak, and then the deputy editor of this influential monthly magazine. Chukhontsev has never been prolific, and his poems are well crafted. They can be sprawling and conversational (to the point of including *skaz*), with *dol'nik* rhythms and loose narrative shape, or, on the contrary, compressed into meticulously constructed rhymed quatrains. Meter and rhyme have remained consistently important (an appreciation for strict form being a marker of Neo-Acmeism). Chukhontsev's poetry contrasts the forms of containment and constraint with images of flux, fluidity, even chaos.[59] His untitled poem about a crematorium, a cemetery, and other forms of death, "A hybrid of bakery with bell tower" ("Gibrid pekarni s kolokol'nei," 1963), exemplifies the contrast at the levels of both theme and form, and it also shows him as an heir to the traditions of the philosophical lyric, which in its sternness and focus on the inescapable fact of death traces back to Baratynsky.[60] A formidable post-Acmeist aesthetic affects the poem's sheer materiality of imagery, however, which is evidenced in its rootedness in the earth and the physical world ("before the living I am obliged / to lie down in the earth and to become earth myself"; "pered zhivymi ia obiazan /lezhat' v zemle i stat' zemleiu").[61]

The earth as a repository of human remains also sets in motion a short poem by Lev Losev. In contrast to Chukhontsev, Losev reminds us of Acmeism's Petersburg roots: Losev lived in Leningrad until his emigration in 1976. His untitled poem that begins with the line, "The poet is humus, within him dead words / ooze" ("Poet est' peregnoi, v nem mertvye slova / sochatsia," published 1987) takes the Acmeist theme of connection to the earth almost to the point of the grotesque.[62] Like Chukhontsev, Losev was a stern judge of his own work. He came to poetry late, and was influenced by his colleagues in Leningrad's Philological School, and above all, by Brodsky.[63] His poetry began to flourish in emigration. A professor at Dartmouth College and a critic of modern literature whose work includes a biography of Brodsky as well as the first large-scale edition of Brodsky's poetry with commentary, Losev brought to his own poetry a dry, unsentimental sense of aesthetic, social, and ethical judgment, including self-judgment.[64] Poems, as he says in the cycle "A Journey" ("Puteshestvie," 1984), should be measured by their effectiveness as clocks: they should "tick and tell time," an image, as one critic noted, that "admirably suggests the finely wrought resilient and tradition-tested craftsmanship" of his verse.[65] His emotional restraint puts him squarely in the Acmeist tradition, as does the stunningly easy formal mastery and the intense intertextuality of his verse. A question that future scholars will have to address is how much the Acmeist tradition was mediated for Losev by Brodsky, as it was for many others. Losev wrote in the introduction to his first book of poems in 1985 that the impulse for him to start writing poems was Brodsky's departure from the Soviet Union in 1972.[66]

CASE STUDY Joseph (Iosif) Brodsky

Russia's last Nobel laureate of the twentieth century, Joseph Brodsky was an internationally acclaimed poet when he won the prize in 1987, and he was not a surprising choice: he had the biography of a persecuted poet that the state manufactured for him, as Anna Akhmatova mordantly noted after his 1964 trial; his work was prestigiously published in English translation and he had begun to write essays in English, including the volume that most likely attracted the Nobel Committee's attention, *Less Than One* (1986). The intonation of moral certainty in those essays (and in no small portion of the poetry), which prize committees admire, would complicate his reputation for some readers. Perhaps winning a Nobel Prize for Literature is bound to bring out detractors, but Brodsky, as the best-known Russian writer in the West in the last decades of the twentieth century, drew a range of reactions that did not stem from sheer jealousy. Russian poetry had changed dramatically during his lifetime, so whether or not he was your hero said a lot about what counted for you as poetry in the first place.

From some of his earliest work, Brodsky showed himself as a poet of tremendous ambition and as a writer to be reckoned with. The first volume whose publication he supervised or authorized, *A Halt in the Desert* (*Ostanovka v pustyne*, 1970), opened with two poems that announced his ambitions: the first, "Christmas Romance" ("Rozhdestvenskii romans," 1961), dedicated to the poet he called his mentor, Evgeny Rein (b. 1935), was a personal, even intimate lyric ballad, evocatively describing a wintry Moscow evening on which the wandering poet lightly registers sparks of eros or perhaps simply human interaction. But the poem's mood is lifted by its framing imagery, wrapping it in the promise that every New Year brings rebirth; enfolding lines of balladic refrain also shape the stanzas. Hypnotic repetitions register at a formal level the possibilities of verbal renewal and reinvention, even as the repeating words pull both poet and reader back to the stasis of the present. Brodsky read "Christmas Romance" in Russian in a recording from 1966, one of the most melodious of his performances.[67]

The second poem in *A Halt in the Desert* takes the metaphysical glimmers of "Christmas Romance" and expands them into a seemingly infinite spatial and formal arrangement, "The Great Elegy for John Donne" ("Bol'shaia elegiia Dzhonu Donnu," 1962). Here the repetitions again stand out: "John Donne sleeps" ("Dzhon Donn usnul"), the poem intones, but rather than the tight, rhyming eight-line stanzas of the "Christmas Romance," this elegy uses rhymed iambic pentameter in free-flowing verse paragraphs; and, rather than repeating the rhythmic phrase compulsively, the elegy spreads out into a somnambulistic series of worldly objects and entities that sleep alongside John Donne. David Bethea, in the first major English-language study of Brodsky, published in 1994, has shown that the lessons learned from Donne's metaphysical poetry seeped into Brodsky's lyrics, including love lyrics that could be among "the most cerebral, mathematically formulated, and intellectually teasing description[s] of love's demise in all modern Russian poetry."[68] Erotic elegy was to be one of the genres in which Brodsky excelled, particularly in the large group of poems he collected as *New Stanzas to Augusta* (*Novye stansy k Avguste*, 1983).

In *New Stanzas to Augusta*, Brodsky brought together all the poems addressed to a woman identified in the dedications as "M. B.," as well as poems inspired by her or otherwise related to their love affair. She is identified in many places as Marianna or Marina Basmanova, and Losev, in the biography, calls her "the central event of his life."[69] Losev vividly describes Brodsky's under-education by the Soviet system—an education that the poet more than compensated for thanks to his own quick assimilation of languages, cultures, and modes of knowledge. Basmanova, knowledgeable about the visual arts and much else, was one of the many who opened whole new worlds to the poet. Losev calls *New Stanzas to Augusta* Brodsky's account of his sentimental education. Particularly striking among poems to M. B. is "Six Years Later," the poem David Bethea had in mind as encapsulating Brodsky's metaphysical poetics. Losev notes the poem's ability to "recast [the poet's] personal drama in terms of classical and Christian culture."[70] The expansion of the context to include European culture was a move Brodsky would have known well from Mandelstam's poetics.

Although Brodsky became comfortable on the world stage as a poet engaged with other cultural traditions and discourses, as evidenced by texts as different as the long poem "Mexican Divertimento" and the essay "A Place as Good as Any," he was perhaps always a supremely Petersburg poet.[71] And a Leningrad poet, too, of course: born in 1940, he cannot have much remembered the Blockade, as he and his mother were evacuated to Cherepovets a year into the Siege, but he grew up in the city where ruined buildings stood next to remnants of imperial architecture. The sense of an empire marked by both triumph and failure can be felt in much of his poetry. A much-admired example is the poem that gave the title to his 1970 volume of poetry, "A Halt in the Desert" ("Ostanovka v pustyne," 1966). A signal work in blank verse, it was modeled after Khodasevich's foundational long poem, "The House" ("Dom," 1919, 1920), and, more distantly, on Pushkin's "Again I visited" ("Vnov' ia posetil," 1835).[72] Brodsky takes the razing of a Greek Orthodox church to make way for a concert venue as an ironic triumph of a low-brow art form over religion in the atheistic Soviet era, and thus as an occasion to ridicule the replacement of church cupolas with raw brutalist architecture. The poem ends with rhetorical questions about the state and the fate of contemporary civilization, and the jettisoned values of both the Hellenic and the Christian worlds. The poet sounds an elegiac note that was to be heard often in his mature work.

"A Halt in the Desert" also marked a formal transition for Brodsky in the late 1960s, showing him some pathways around the potentially overwrought metaphysical conceits of the earlier work in lines that could still reach for eternal themes. It is no accident that the conversational tone of a blank verse poem would occasion such a shift; Brodsky would bring great prosaic discursiveness into his later poems. There is another innovation in "A Halt in the Desert," as well: as Losev has noted, the complexity of argument in the poem shifts from metaphors or tropes to the potential for hidden meanings in words or details. The Tatar family walking past the scene of demolition, for instance, telescopes the whole history of violence that has beset the Russian people.[73] Those historical gestures will allow Brodsky to make grand arguments about the fate of Russia in the pensive lines of "New Life" ("Novaia zhizn'," 1988) or the more political poem "On the Negotiations in Kabul" ("K peregovoram v Kabule," 1992).[74]

Brodsky wrote poetry for nearly forty years, long enough for scholars to propose phases or stages of development, but no such structure has emerged convincingly. Instead, a sequence of milestones serve as biographical markers, nearly all of them because of events brought upon the poet by exernal forces rather than actively sought: his trial for parasitism in 1964, and the resulting period of internal exile in the region of Arkhangelsk; his emigration in 1972; the Nobel Prize in 1987; and so forth.[75] The idea of exile is one the poet himself repeatedly calls attention to, most eloquently in his essay "The Condition We Call Exile," but it is a transition for him more than a sharp divide. As Losev notes, he resisted starting his first American book with a poem that would invoke the year 1972 directly.[76] Still, the transformation is unmistakable: we see the vivid new landscapes evoked in his work—from Cape Cod to Rome, to Venice and Cappadocia, and beyond; we also hear a recurring sense of lost home, echoing Odysseus at some times, Robinson Crusoe at others.

The volume *A Part of Speech* (*Chast' rechi*, 1977) sets out the range of possibilities that later work will extend, brilliantly exemplified in the cycle of twenty short poems that gave the volume its title. The poems display what became the poet's signature choice of *dol'nik* lines with anti-grammatical rhymes; radical enjambments; and bold aphoristic assertions held together by metonymy and metaphor. As the seventh poem in the cycle (seventh in the Russian version; in English, Brodsky moved this poem to the beginning) says:

> Я родился и вырос в балтийских болотах, подле
> серых цинковых волн, всегда набегавших по две,
> и отсюда—все рифмы, отсюда тот блеклый голос,
> вьющийся между ними, как мокрый волос;
> если вьется вообще.[77]

In Brodsky's English translation:

> I was born and grew up in the Baltic marshland
> by zinc-gray breakers that always marched on
> in twos. Hence all rhymes, hence that wan flat voice
> that ripples between them like hair still moist,
> if it ripples at all.[78]

The striking rhyme of a preposition with a prepositional phrase (*podle* / *po dve*); the assertion that the foundational prosodic element of poetry (for Brodsky, it is rhyme) comes from the natural world's rhythms of paired Baltic waves; and the deflating tone that casts doubts on the rippling, wreathing movement described here—these elements turn the opening lines of this poem into a kind of signature, the signature of someone who grew up in the North, and whose voice may be harsh or flat, but always mercilessly true. That alienated speaker will continue to be heard until the final summing up in what is likely the last poem Brodsky completed, "August" ("Avgust," 1996).[79] All but one of the poems in "A Part of Speech" are twelve lines long; they are collected into a group of short poems that call back and forth to one another across the pages. Brodsky excelled at creating stanzaic patterns that could become effective motors to generate energy for longer sequences. Often the stanzas were large and built on unusual rhyme patterns: in *A Part of Speech*, splendid examples include "December 24, 1971" ("24 dekabria 1971 goda," 1972); "1972"; and "The Butterfly" ("Babochka," 1972), its twelve-line stanzas centered on the page like splayed butterflies opened up for inspection; and, still more spectacularly, "December in Florence" ("Dekabr' vo Florentsii," 1976), with its rolling sets of triple rhymes.[80]

Brodsky published in Russian with Ardis Press in the United States; after the fall of the USSR, he saw his work in print in Russia as well. The final two books with Ardis are thick and seem to be bundled presentations of what might have been smaller collections. *To Urania* (*Uraniia*, 1987) features some of the poet's greatest poems, both long and short: "A Hawk's

Cry in Autumn" ("Osennii krik iastreba," 1975), "Eclogue IV: Winter" ("Ekloga 4-ia [zim-niaia]," 1977) and "Eclogue V: Summer" ("Ekloga 5-ia [letniaia]," 1981), "Letters of the Ming Dynasty" ("Pis′ma dinastii Min′," 1977), "Lithuanian Nocturne: to Tomas Ventslova" ("Litovskii noktiurn: Tomasu Ventslova," 1973–83), and "The Fly" ("Mukha," 1985), to name a few. The volume reprised poems that had appeared in *New Poems to Augusta*, rearranging them to a different effect, and, unlike earlier books, it mixed in recent poems with older ones. The Russian press paid the book little notice, but Brodsky's friend Derek Walcott staked out the largest possible claim for the work:

> The intellectual vigor of Brodsky's poetry is too alarming even for his poet-readers, because it contains the history of the craft, because it openly reveres its inheritance, but, and here comes the payoff, this wit is founded on what poets used to advance the craft by—intelligence, argument, an awareness of contemporary science, and not so much a sense of the past as a certainty that the past is always parsed in the present tense.[81]

Walcott emphasized the volume's longest poems, but in the final Russian collection, *Landscape with a Flood* (*Peizazh s navodneniem*, 1996), in preparation at the time of Brodsky's death, shorter lyrics also show powerfully what has rightly been seen as an intense, prolific final period of work. There are many poems of 16 or 20 lines, sometimes in quatrains and with end-stopped lines, some retreating from his favorite *dol′nik* to the iamb. A splendid example is the poem "On the Akhmatova Centenary" ("Na stoletie Akhmatovoi," 1989), with its stately quatrains in rhymed iambic hexameter with caesura. Brodsky, who had risen in stature among his peers with Akhmatova's approval, conveys in this poem, written on the centennial of her birth, the quality of her voice and the cadence of her diction. The poem expresses directly his gratitude for all she taught him. Gratitude had long been a key word in Brodsky's poetics, but here it sought to fill all of cosmic space. Brodsky had said of Akhmatova that her work would survive "because language is older than the state and because prosody always survives history."[82]

That statement about Akhmatova came from a 1982 essay. Brodsky, whose talent was best shown in his Russian poems, almost certainly reached far more readers internationally through his essays in English, which could in their own way inhabit virtuoso heights. As a teacher, he came to write long essays on the poets he taught, including Thomas Hardy, W. H. Auden, and Robert Frost; and as an increasingly famous Russian poet, he wrote introductions to translations of Russian literature, or intense, occasional pieces generated by his own ideas, for example, on Tsvetaeva, Mandelstam, and Platonov. He demonstrated, as if on a dare, that anything could propel an essay, even a postage stamp depicting Kim Philby in his mischievous and deadly serious piece "Collector's Item" (1991).[83] He would claim that he wrote the essays in English because he found the language more analytical, more appropriate to expressing distance and irony. The essays joked about the author's English, but Brodsky bemoaned the choice to adopt a foreign tongue in the piercing essay about his parents, "In a Room and a Half" (1985). As he noted, it was written "in a language they didn't understand," because to do so is "to grant them a margin of freedom" and because "English offers a better semblance of afterlife." Brodsky's bitterest invective against the state that kept him from seeing his parents as they were dying comes in this essay as well: "No country has mastered the art of destroying its subjects' souls as well as Russia."[84] It was his "job," to use his own favorite self-deprecating way to refer to the poet's high calling, to record the soul's rebellion against such an assault, and his successes and failures alike left readers with poems to memorize, and essays to reread.

A counterweight to the outsized influence of Brodsky in contemporary poetry may be found in the work of Leonid Aronzon (1939–70). Little known outside of Russia, Aronzon has been seen by some as Brodsky's potential equal, had his life and work not been cut short prematurely (he died from a self-inflicted gunshot wound).[85] Aronzon's use of classical forms and his clear diction ally him with Acmeist traditions, but there are strong influences from more radical poetic trends as well. He wrote a dissertation on Zabolotsky and valued the innovations of Khlebnikov's poetry very highly. Aronzon resisted joining any groups, although he maintained friendly relations with a number of poets, including Brodsky (they parted ways by the early 1960s) and those in the Khelenukty group (the Malaia Sadovaia circle). Aronzon was an avid traveler but journeyed even more into his inner world, a world imprinted with landscapes reminiscent of Tiutchev's poetry, which he loved. A master of the sonnet, Aronzon wrote in both strict form and in formats that were unusual for the 1960s. One of his sonnets is a kind of early experiment in Conceptualism, entitled "Two Identical Sonnets" ("Dva odinakovykh soneta," 1969), which presents the same sonnet twice, one after the other, inviting readers to hunt down some difference in wording or punctuation between the two sets of fourteen lines. Another reimagination of this strictest of poetic forms is Aronzon's "Empty sonnet" ("Pustoi sonet," 1969, Figure v.02), shaped as a frame around the empty space within.[86]

Love, a popular theme of sonnets, was among Aronzon's constant topics, and he dedicated many poems to his beloved wife and muse, Margarita Purishinskaia. In "Empty Sonnet," the intensity of the poet's love is the poem's point of departure, and given the poem's format, where the opening line reads clearly across the top of the page, it stands out from the poem's other lines. A superb example of Aronzon's nature poetry is "Morning" ("Utro," 1966), which brims with emotion like the love poetry, but records the wonder of climbing a hill. The ascent transforms the climber into a child, or into one of God's first creations, now able to name the flowers and to identify the signs of God's goodness. The poem is rich in word and phrase repetitions, as if wonder at the universe could renew language itself.[87]

It was Viktor Krivulin who made the sharp contrast between Aronzon and Brodsky. Krivulin's own poetry, with its deep engagement with history and theological reach, was also written in the wake of Acmeism. Like Aronzon and Brodsky, Krivulin grew up in Leningrad, in the shadow of Silver Age Petersburg poetry. He was a prolific poet, ready to try new things in his work, but also endlessly engaged in intertextual dialogue with the poetic tradition. One of his best long poems begins with the exclaimed pleasure of drinking the "wine of archaisms" ("P'iu vino arkhaizmov," 1973). Krivulin played a social role in unofficial culture of the late Soviet period, hosting a series of discussion groups with his then wife Tatiana Goricheva (b. 1947), with whom he co-edited the journal 37; he also collaborated as an editor on the key samizdat journal Bypass Canal. Michael Molnar, one of Krivulin's best translators, has called him a domovoi, or house spirit, of unofficial Leningrad culture.[88]

Krivulin lived independently in the margins of Soviet culture, moving freely among Leningrad's cultural institutions and residences, and this freedom of physical and intellectual movement was his particular form of resistance, since Krivulin suffered from a lifelong physical disability and walked with difficulty. As if to defy that challenge, many of his poems chronicle a pedestrian's passage through the space of the city, and record how the city—that mythic city of Leningrad/Petersburg—takes on cultural meaning in the process. In true Acmeist fashion, the meaning of monuments and landmarks comes from the words written about them, as if stones were not solidified minerals but sounds (his phrase is "hardened words," zastyvshee slovo).[89] Krivulin was able to draw on other art forms to transmute the urban environment into the poetic word, as is seen in his striking long poem "Gobelin Tapestries" ("Gobeleny," 1972).[90] Not only does the poem resonate with echoes from Acmeist poets, but its overall aesthetic also evokes their "nostalgia for world culture," even as it moves beyond it: the poem

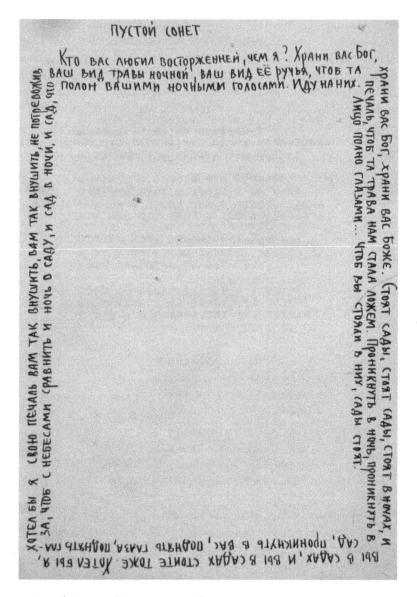

FIGURE V.02. Leonid Aronzon, "An empty sonnet," 1969.

shows the disharmony and vacuity of the present, more like the "pale creations" ("blednye sozdan′ia") seen in the fading tapestries.

No less prolific, Mikhail Eremin (b. 1936) is a poet who was part of the Philological School alongside Lev Losev, Sergei Kulle (1936–84), Vladimir Ufliand (1937–2007), and Aleksandr Kondratov (1937–93).[91] Eremin quickly settled into a writing pattern that has remained unchanged for decades: eight-line poems, almost always untitled, collected in volumes published every few years and entitled *Poems* (*Stikhotvoreniia*, starting in 1998; by 2016, there were six of them), displaying a single-minded commitment to a poetic form unrivaled in the history of Russian poetry. Eremin is regarded as a difficult poet, and yet the hermetically sealed world of his eight-line poems opens out linguistically and even formally, in the frequent use of dedications, epigraphs, and authorial footnotes. Some of those notes perform the function of a dictionary, and Eremin collects obscure words with the zeal of a paleontologist assembling animal bones from disparate sites; the imagery of the poems is often biological, chemical, and especially botanical. The poems themselves resemble museum exhibits, showcasing curious words and thematizing the semantic density of lexical items with images of geodes, owl pellets, or the entrails of birds to be interpreted by augurs. This verbal intricacy makes the lines resistant to translation, but the poems themselves often perform acts of translation between languages or codes, scientific systems, and forms of typology or classification.[92]

Less resistant to readers is the harmonious, inviting poetry of Vladimir Gandel′sman (b. 1948). He shares Brodsky's language-focused aesthetic (he is a poet who might say, as did Brodsky, that he works for the dictionary). That hyper-valuation of the enduring word resounds in an untitled eight-line poem first published in 1995:

> Дай бессмысленного слова нежного,
> свежего, как ветвь с надломом,
> связка жил древесных неизбежная
> в воздухе дрожит бездомном.
>
> Из двоих привязанность
> сохранить последнему страшней,
> ясный ужас ветви, темносказанность
> сил, еще пульсирующих в ней.[93]

> Give me a word, meaningless, tender,
> fresh like a branch that is cracking up,
> a bundle of tree vessels, inevitable,
> is trembling in the homeless air.
>
> Between the two it is more frightening
> to be the last one who feels attached,
> it's the sheer horror of the branch, the dark speech
> of the forces still pulsating there.[94]

It is a richly musical poem, written in trochaic verses of variable length, with dactylic rhymes in odd-numbered lines and feminine or masculine rhyme in the other two pairs. Despite those formal demands, the poem achieves a remarkable naturalness of tone typical of Gandel′sman's poetry. The trochaic rhythm flows freely thanks to the pyrrhic feet—the unstressed syllables in the long, even elongated words, as in the lovely neologism *temnoskazannost′* (dark speech). The word is, for Gandel′sman, even while tenderly "meaningless," still a potent form of dark speech, which is to say magic speech, that pulsates even in the cracked branches of the poem's endangered, unyielding tree. Gandel′sman emigrated to the United States in 1990, which is where this poem was written, capturing the émigré poet's awareness of the fragility of a language that must be protected and preserved. Gandel′sman became a distinguished translator from English to Russian, and has published numerous books of poetry. A popular poet, he has had a sizable role in the flourishing Russian poetic culture in the New York area.

Aleksei Tsvetkov has played a similar role; he and Gandel′sman have both translated Shakespeare, publishing in a single volume their respective versions of *Macbeth* and *Hamlet* in 2010. Tsvetkov is a brilliant formal poet, whose range includes not just innovative riffs on syllabotonic and rhymed verse, but revivals of older forms and extensive work in *dol′nik*, the meter favored by Brodsky and others. Born in Ukraine, Tsvetkov was active as a Moscow poet until his emigration in 1975. He lived in Prague and then in the United States, and received a

PhD from the University of Michigan (with a dissertation on Platonov). Tsvetkov has been a prolific writer, although with a seventeen-year hiatus, which ended in 2004. After 2004, Tsvetkov rejected punctuation marks and capital letters in his poetry, not just at the start of poetic lines but also for most proper names. The result is modern-looking poems built on traditional forms. Tsvetkov openly engages with work in other languages, perhaps most strikingly in the intensely American poem "kennedy kennedy king and similar victims" ("kennedi kennedi king i prochie zhertvy," 2005).[95] Tsvetkov takes strong political and ethical positions, and his poetry is clearly stimulated by conversations about politics and social justice (he was an active blogger on LiveJournal through 2014, and posts vigorously on Facebook). He has said that the absence of interest in the political is "not the result of a conscious choice by an individual, but a form of social illness," a symptom in fact of slavery.[96] He wrote a bitter lament on the 2004 Beslan school massacre, "it was september 3" ("bylo tret′e sentiabria," 2004): the poet compares the security forces as well as the hostage-takers to the servants of Herod, and declares that if there is still a heaven that welcomes a select few, he not only no longer believes in it, but chooses to live in hell.[97] Tsvetkov writes with a piercing sense of immediate history: his is a concrete and personal aesthetic, attuned to the injustices of contemporary life in and well beyond Russia.

Before he emigrated, Tsvetkov was a leading member of the Moscow Time group in the 1970s, which included Bakhyt Kenzheev (b. 1950), Aleksandr Soprovsky (1953–90), and the most prominent poet of the group, Sergei Gandlevsky (b. 1952). Gandlevsky's poetry has the group's fierce precision, its everyday language, and its mastery of traditional poetic forms. The poem "To land a job at the garage" ("Ustroit′sia na avtobazu," 1985) exemplifies both the superb sound play of Gandlevsky's poetry and his signature masculine, easy bravado.[98] Gandlevsky elicits affection from a broad swath of readers for his mix of boldness with very human vulnerability and warmth, especially in his prose: *Trepanation of the Skull* (*Trepanatsiia cherepa*, written in 1994) and *Illegible* (*[nrzb]*, 2002).[99] His unerring eye and ear for the way that everyday late Soviet life might be captured in its shabby ordinariness are also endearing to readers. He turns sights and sounds into lines of rhyming iambs, an unmarked formal choice that makes the work seem all the more effortless. Here are the opening lines of a 1980 poem that thematizes that sense of the ordinary:

> Вот наша улица, допустим,
> Орджоникидзержинского.
> Родня советским захолустьям,
> Но это все-таки Москва.
> Вдали топорщатся массивы
> Промышленности некрасивой—
> Каркасы, трубы, корпуса
> Настырно лезут в небеса.
> Как видишь, нет примет особых...

> Here's our street, let's say—
> Ordzhonikidzerzhinsky.
> It could be any Soviet province,
> But this is Moscow also.
> In the distance the blocks bristle
> With the ugliness of heavy industry—
> Building skeletons, pipes, complexes
> Stubbornly crawl to the heavens.
> As you can see, nothing special here—[100]

With his characteristic dry tone, the poet sketches a cityscape of massive buildings as "nothing special," yet, at the same time, a setting where the pressure of Soviet culture on an ordinary passerby is palpable. Gandlevsky, like his admired Khodasevich, practices an asceticism that makes every poetic line pay its way.

Similarly ascetic is the work of Gandlevsky's Moscow contemporary, Mikhail Aizenberg (b. 1948), whose poetry is as emotionally restrained, even as it conveys a strong sense of the personal.[101] Aizenberg makes that paradox palpable on the page through a kind of self-consciousness that gets close to, but never fully embraces, the rhetoric of irony. The lead poem in his book *Other Things, As Formerly* (*Drugie i prezhnie veshchi*, 2000) begins:

> Что я тебе скажу
> как частное лицо частному лицу—
> открываешь глаза и видишь свои ладони.
> Что за сон такой?

> What can I say to you
> as one private individual to another—
> you open your eyes and see the palms of your hands.
> What kind of dream is this?[102]

The speaker feels a need to remind himself and the other that they are both private individuals. Aizenberg reveals this need as a kind of remnant of the unofficial poetry world of the late Soviet Union, when the idea that a poet writes as an individual, not as a member of any collective or even as a citizen, held sway. The tone has changed, however, and we can hear celebratory inflections that emerge alongside the elegiac in another poem from 1990, when the poet seems to proclaim his desire for success to all of nature, as if his command, "do not despair" ("ne unyvai") were all the encouragement any person or creature could need.[103]

Aizenberg has published essays about contemporary poets in addition to his multiple volumes of poetry.[104] That capacity to record and analyze poetic innovation informs his lyric persona. This is also true of a slightly younger poet, Grigory Dashevsky (1964–2013), who joined in a late-1980s revival of the Moscow Time group.[105] Trained as a classicist and revered as both a poet and a translator, Dashevsky published very little and seemed to polish each poem like a rare gemstone. The poetics of concrete if minimalist description, virtuoso stylization, formal precision, and a kind of intimate basis for invoking the worlds of myth or antiquity defined his work. Each poem created a strong, distinctive voice, and yet the fading or disappearance of the subject is a repeating if largely implicit narrative (the imperative to "melt" in one poem, for instance, is the locus of that disappearance).[106] The poems' surface possesses an ethereal quality, but their sound orchestration and structure lend them a density of thought that is at once ontological and phenomenological. Dashevsky was perhaps the most Mandelstamian of contemporary poets (and his near-cult status is a further similarity to Mandelstam, beyond those of aesthetics, ethics, and temperament). While other Neo-Acmeist or near-Neo-Acmeist poets of the younger generation might be mentioned, for example Maxim Amelin (b. 1970), Dashevsky stands out. In writing about his work, Mikhail Aizenberg used metaphors that define him brilliantly:

> The word-whistles and word-rustlings out of which Dashevsky made his poems can be formed (and are formed) into meaningful sentences, but their nature is unchanged: made of thoughts and impulses, they are in essence prior to speech. They are the arrows of breath, hitting a single target.[107]

Russian spiritual poetry

It has been argued that philosophical and religious thought flourished in the nineteenth-century Russian novel as much as it did in philosophy proper.[108] It makes sense, as Russian literature re-entered an age of poetry at the end of the nineteenth century, that the poem would absorb these spiritual questions; philosophical meditation and interrogation had long been a part of the lyric genre.[109] The poetry of philosopher Vladimir Solov'ev constitutes an important body of transitional work, including both his short lyric poems and the expansive, visionary "Three Meetings" ("Tri svidaniia," 1898). For Solov'ev, the encounter that mattered most was with the divine Sophia; as the grandson of an Orthodox priest, he found the work of centering his life around religious practice and mystical vision a meaningful struggle. That question, what difference belief makes to life or to writing, is an enduring theme in Russian spiritual poetry. Many writers reframed it in terms of a quest for the sacred: a desire for experiences imbued with a sense of awe, and a durable belief that the transcendence of daily sensations and impressions could make sense of modern life.[110]

Russian poets have been drawn to several distinctive genres and themes. Most engage in a dialogue with the language and forms of liturgy; this often means the Orthodox liturgy, but other faiths and other forms of Christianity are important as well. Those inclined toward Christianity draw freely on the Old Testament, and poetry by Jews or poets interested in Judaism has been a visible strand running through the tradition.[111] Less prominent but increasingly important are poems that look beyond the Judeo-Christian tradition, often toward Buddhism. Its principles have attracted poets interested in more passive, absorptive modes of poetic subjectivity. It has also drawn those for whom Buddhism offered a kind of stylized, zoned-out contemplation of the universe, particularly in the late Soviet-era. Examples come chiefly from the Conceptualists, including Andrei Monastyrsky's experiments with Buddhism and Dmitry Prigov's chanting performances of the opening stanzas of *Evgeny Onegin* in what he called "the Buddhist manner."[112] The performances may seem parodic, but they were also a way for apparently secular poetry to reach out to the divine on its own terms.

Across the modern Russian tradition, some genres of religious and quasi-religious poetry have been especially productive: songs, prayers, hymns, and imprecations recur. The rhetoric of address can be intense; the trope of apostrophe is fundamental to the lyric, but poems to or about God use forms of address with special urgency, even when they do no more than echo the ancient, weary question of why the Lord has forsaken His beseecher. These poems draw on archaic diction, whether stylized Church Slavonic or Hebraic prayer. There are recurrent references to Biblical books or scenes, such as the Crucifixion, the parable of the Prodigal Son, the burning bush, or psalms. Pushkin's poem "The Prophet" is a frequent point of orientation, perhaps because it fuses the quest for divine recognition and poetic self-definition.

Among poems that attained a broad public presence, the cycle of poems that Boris Pasternak appended to *Doctor Zhivago* (first published 1957) stand out. The scandal around the Nobel Prize for Literature in 1958 sealed the novel's fame, and over the years, while some have questioned aesthetic or political choices in the narrative, readers, including poets, have attested to the importance of the poems.[113] There is a consensus that the Zhivago poems reflect a deep knowledge of Orthodox liturgy.[114] In addition to poems that derive plainly from Biblical stories ("Gethsemane," "Magdalene," "The Miracle" ["Chudo"], for example), Biblical motifs and images course through other poems, creating the suggestion, for example, that a dinner with friends is like a communion (in "The Earth" ["Zemlia"]), or that the heroic, humble action of a secular prince is modeled after Christ's passion (in "Hamlet"). Studies of Christian images and theological principles in the poems have also led to substantial new reinterpretations of the novel, including a rereading of its Marxist materialism in the context of Christian asceticism.[115]

Doctor Zhivago's poems also demonstrate the Russian tradition's greater emphasis on the Passion of Christ and the Resurrection than on the Nativity. The vivid presence of Christian theology in these late poems encourages readers to seek it in Pasternak's earlier work; and Christian motifs have been seen even in works that sought to join with the spirit of the Revolution. Blok's "The Twelve" ("Dvenadtsat´," 1918) is perhaps the most famous example, but in Pasternak's "Lieutenant Schmidt" ("Leitenant Shmidt," 1926), the hero is also compared to Christ. The historical project, buttressed by Christian theology, that Pasternak undertook in *Doctor Zhivago*, finds its counterpart in the historical impulse of his earlier work.

Such recourse to religion in order to understand history was not exclusive to elite writers. As has now been well documented, uneducated Russian workers wrote extensively in the early decades of the twentieth century, and their prose and poetry was marked by complex expressions of religion. They used a "symbolic language of the sacred" to try to "read the disjointed fragments of everyday experience as part of a meaningful and purposeful narrative."[116] Although their writings have no literary pretensions, the themes and forms of self-expression they used are continuous with the work of poets across the century.

Among the most unusual Russian religious poets is Nikolai Kliuev, a complex figure whose work combined profound spiritual quest with impressive acts of self-fashioning. Kliuev styled himself as a peasant poet and as a sectarian. His poems were steeped in the vernacular and in the symbols of folk religion, including the Old Belief, and borrowed religious ritual imagery to lend meaning to the simplest nature scenes. Kliuev's self-mythologizing has itself been a subject of scholarly dispute.[117] The contest over authenticity and identity may be as much an effect of the kind of spiritual poetry Kliuev wrote as it is an effect of his forms of self-fashioning. His lament "The Charred Debris" ("Pogorel´shchina," 1928) recounts the loss of spiritual values and the destruction of the Russian folk. This poem depicts an Old Believers' village as a symbol of peasant Russia: here icon-painters create their visual prayers from the elements of surrounding nature, and the northern village hosts fairy-tale birds and animals. The epic destruction of the village, whether due to a Saracen invasion, mythical dragon, cannibalism, or icon-burning, is set in 1919, making the advent of the Soviet era a new apocalypse. This monumental mythological poem was one of the reasons for Kliuev's arrest in 1934 and execution in 1937.

Vera Merkur´eva (1876–1943) shared with Kliuev a loose connection to the Russian Symbolists (Kliuev addressed important early poems to Blok, and Merkur´eva was close to Viacheslav Ivanov in Moscow beginning in 1917); and she, too, drew not on Symbolism's esoteric theosophies so much as on popular religion. Merkur´eva deeply admired Kliuev, and once jokingly called herself Vera Kliuevna. The sense of cosmic abandonment that marked Kliuev's "Charred Debris" is also felt in her poetry, but the elegiac lament has ironic undertones. Merkur´eva's work was little known in her lifetime, when she published barely over a dozen poems. But the philologist Mikhail Gasparov gave it a new visibility in the post-Soviet period.[118] The belated publication has proven paradoxically appropriate, since her mix of faith, doubt, good and evil, and stern self-appraisal has a contemporary feel. Gasparov also collected and helped bring to a new generation the poems of Maria Shkapskaia (1891–1952); her poetry more vividly emphasized the body than that of any other spiritually inclined Russian poet before Elena Shvarts.[119]

Merkur´eva's work encompasses many themes, including love poems and intense responses to revolution and war: hers was one of the most strongly voiced poetic reactions to the first violence of the Revolution, which she witnessed in Moscow, particularly in her poem "Explosion—in Assumption Cathedral" ("Proboina—v Uspenskom sobore," dated November 11, 1917). Perhaps even more remarkable is her wreath of sonnets "Approaching Moscow" ("Na podstupakh k Moskve," 1942), written in evacuation and as she was dying.[120] Some of her most daring poems include "Snowy Vespers" ("Snegovaia vechernia," 1919), a cycle structured around Orthodox ritual, with its mix of prose and poetry keyed in to regularly repeating prayers and hymns; "Mystical Adventure" ("Misticheskoe prikliuchenie," 1918), with its atmosphere of wounded blessedness; and many poems featuring demons, beginning with "My Demon" ("Moi demon," 1918).[121] Miracle and mystery (*chudo, taina*) were, as Gasparov noted, the key words in her poetic world.[122]

Pavel Zal′tsman has also reached a belated readership thanks to extensive publications, helped by a generally renewed interest in OBERIU. Zal′tsman was an artist and cinematographer as well as a prose writer and poet; he belonged to Pavel Filonov's circle in Leningrad in 1929, and thus became acquainted with the members of OBERIU and attended their events.[123] While the Expressionistic aesthetics of Filonov's art did not influence Zal′tsman's visual work, it permeated both his poetry and prose. This means that the most obviously religious of his poems, like his series of psalms written before, during, and after the Blockade, are as rife with blasphemy as with prayer. This kind of audacious search for sacred meanings through brutal confrontations with the divine recurs in post-Soviet Russian poetry. Having survived the brutal first winter of the Siege, Zal′tsman wrote a cycle of anti-psalms full of anger at God for leaving humans to be tortured; among these psalms is a four-line verse that juxtaposes the absence of food to sustain life with the equally starved need for divine sustenance, "Give me a dinner, give it" ("Daite, daite mne obed," 1942).[124]

The catastrophic experiences of the Blockade motivated Zal′tsman's poetry in ways that are similar to the work of Varlam Shalamov, whose decades spent in the Gulag had an equally wrenching effect on his mind and spirit. Shalamov's poetry is marked by the same fierce courage as his better-known prose, and by the same intense will to set down the details of psyche and vision precisely, as if that were the only act of integrity left to a Gulag prisoner. Most of Shalamov's poems are written in the first person, but a few portray heroic figures, such as "Boyarina Morozova." Avvakum, another great figure of the Schism, is at the center of one of Shalamov's most memorable poems, "Avvakum in Pustozersk" ("Avvakum v Pustozerske," 1955).[125] The forceful amphibrachic short lines convey the determination that had never left Avvakum. The poem also shows how, for Shalamov, the unambiguous belief in a true cause and the will to fight the brutal power of the state were far more important than the elements of ritual or consolation. Avvakum might not have agreed with the lines that have him asserting that his struggle is not spiritual or a matter of church doctrine: "Our quarrel is about freedom / About the right to breathe" ("Nash spor—o svobode, / O prave dyshat′").[126] Shalamov keeps faith with the integrity of his art, a commitment in which he resembles other secular poets of his generation—Arseny Tarkovsky, for example, or Maria Petrovykh and a poet for whom Petrovykh was a mentor, Inna Lisnianskaia.

For Shalamov, there was never anything redemptive about suffering, but the familiar Russian conviction that suffering defines spiritual life informs the poetry of Veniamin Blazhenny (pseud. Veniamin Aizenshtadt, 1921–99), for whom the struggle against God (*bogoborchestvo*) and the search for the experience of the sacred are crucial.[127] Blazhenny was born a Jew in a Galician shtetl, and lived out his long life in Minsk. In writings that have strong affinities with Orthodox theology, particularly in his unusual embodiment of the figure of the Holy Fool, he also explored traditional Jewish themes, including the sense of having been chosen to do God's work. A poet who claimed a deep kinship with the language of birds and angels, Blazhenny, a sufferer of mental illness, spent his fair share of time among the mad, and his poetry reflects an identification with those relegated to the margins of Soviet society. In the post-Soviet period, Blazhenny's work began to be published, including *Heart's Hearing* (*Slukh serdtsa*, 1990), and the substantial collection *Co-Crucifixion* (*Soraspiat′e*, 1995, reissued 2009). Among writers, he admired Shalamov and Boris Chichibabin (1923–94).[128]

Blazhenny's work shared Chichibabin's willingness to speak with the urgent, truth-telling tones of a prophet; it is replete with the images, personages, and stories of the Old Testament and the Apocrypha, and underpinned by a deep identification with figures not of prophetic strength but, as his pseudonym makes clear, with the marginalized, impoverished figure of the Holy Fool. He was willing to be irreverent in asking God why it was so hard to find a common language: "We speak to you in verse / But you respond with invectives."[129] Mostly, though, the poems use simple terms, relying on structures of parallelism and repetition, and often in rhymed, rhythmic quatrains, speaking as the Holy Fool. One such poem begins:

> Я живу в нищете, как живут скоморохи и боги,
> Я посмешищем стал и недоброю притчей для всех.
> И кружусь колесом по своей бесконечной дороге,
> И лишь стужа скрипит в спотыкающемся колесе.[130]

> I live in poverty, like gods and wandering jesters,
> I have become a laughing stock, a parable that bodes ill,
> I spin like a wheel on endless roads,
> And the cold creaks in the wheel as it sticks.

In these long lines, with their regular anapestic rhythm, Blazhenny suggests the forward movement of a wheel that is the poem's dominant metaphor. It may recall the folkloric bread roll, Kolobok, or even something like a wheel of fortune, but because of the poem's rhetorical reliance on simple diction and syntax, the wheel actually starts to seem like the fundamental device of physics, that first machine created by mankind to do work. The poet goes on to say that, having once called himself a man, he now goes only by the name of wheel, accumulating dust as he moves along the ruts in the soil.

A similar ethical force can be keenly felt in the stern, moving work of Sergei Magid (b. 1947).[131] Magid participated in unofficial literary work in Leningrad in the late Soviet period, before moving to Prague in 1990. He is a prolific writer of both poetry and prose. His later poetry has tended toward free verse, with some interesting experiments in fixed forms in *The First Century* (*Pervaia sotnitsa*, 2013), a variation on the two sets of 100 short meditations penned by Maximus the Confessor (580–662). Rather than a collection of quotations from the Bible or other scriptures, Magid offers 100 quatrains of his own devising, with reflections on lived experience, the quest for God, and poetry. Old Testament sites, images, personages, and narratives play an important role in Magid's work, particularly in the volume *In the Valley of Elah* (*V doline Elakh*, 2010). The title poem retells the story of David and Goliath, while another narrates a strange fusion of gullible passivity and argumentative speechifying as people are taken to gas chambers.[132] Magid's lyric hero is sometimes identified as the despised Jew, cast to the margins of history: "I will be a Jew, solitary despised puny" ("budu zhidom odinokim prezrennym nichtozhnym"), one poem begins.[133] Magid draws on Christian imagery and ideas, often rewriting New Testament parables alongside work based on modern historical experience. Like Pasternak, he insists on a strong connection among the principles of ethics, religion, and politics, and his unsparing gaze may call to mind late Tolstoy. He is determined to judge himself and others for private as well as public actions.

Magid's poetry brings us to the contemporary moment. The generation born after the war includes poets who variously found their way to a poetics of deep spiritual search. The Leningrad underground featured a number of poets who developed the traditions of Russian spiritual verse, and some felt that the main distinguishing feature of their work, as opposed to that of Moscow's unofficial circles, was a stubborn reliance on a theological vocabulary, often as a way to write about the creative act. Krivulin, Aleksandr Mironov (1948–2010), Oleg Okhapkin (1944–2008), Elena Shvarts, and Sergei Stratanovsky (b. 1944) are key poets in this trend; all participated in some way in the religious-philosophical seminars founded by Krivulin and Goricheva in the 1970s.[134] Shvarts would emerge as the most significant in the group, but all possess strong, distinctive individual voices.

CASE STUDY Elena Shvarts

For decades, Elena Shvarts commanded attention with her wild poems of impersonation and mystical revelation, of formal beauty and distorted invention, of ecstasy and pain and every other emotion in between. She was an unofficial poet in the 1970s, and began publishing in Russia by the late 1980s. Her once clandestine Leningrad audience grew substantially, winning her major prizes, wide publication in journals and books, and translation into many languages. She was a prolific, undaunted poet, even a bit feared for her passionate temperament, her firm opinions, and her sublimely high standards for what counted as genuine poetry. She generated many myths about herself, claiming to write carelessly and to live outrageously.

We read Shvarts's poetry, however, as if none of this existed; indeed, her intense capacity in each new poem to create a superbly differentiated and imagined world means that her readers become utterly absorbed in her work, shutting out everything else. Shvarts can seem a strongly religious poet, and much of her work bears out this view, not because she hews to doctrines of the Church or because she seems theologically wise, but because the ways of belief clearly fascinated her. She explored a divinely ordered but also violently disrupted cosmos, and she never ceased to imagine a world larger than what our minds can grasp. Her poems reach beyond the horizon of the visible with a formal confidence and lexical agility that gives even her wildest fantasies improbable powers of persuasion. As if to balance those acts of hopeful imagination, she wrote two books of shattering meditations on the death of her mother in 1998: *Solo on a White-Hot Trumpet* (*Solo na raskalennoi trube*, 1998) and *Wild Writing of the Recent Past* (*Dikopis' poslednego vremeni*, 2001). The poems of the 2000s use fantastically created worlds to delve deeper into the inner experiences of pain, loss, and transcendence.

Such a richly imagined world occupies the poet in a late cycle, "The Big Bang Rondo" ("Rondo bol'shogo vzryva," 2008). It is an example of a form she practiced throughout her life, the miniature long poem (*malaia poema*). The component sequences project a story across shorter poems in a way that reminds one of narrative poetry (which is what *poema* designates in Russian), although without providing the satisfactions of a developed plot. Yet undoubtedly there is an underlying story or drama that shapes her miniature long poems, as their titles often announce: "An Englishman Roasted in Moscow" ("Zharenyi anglichanin v Moskve," 1989) or "The Holy Fools' March on Kiev" ("Pokhod iurodivykh na Kiev," 1994). Shvarts gave these poems prominence in her published volumes of poetry, often using a longer sequence to start things off. "Big Bang Rondo" is not given that prominence in *Bird in Migration* (*Pereletnaia ptitsa*, 2011), but that may be a tactful gesture on the part of Kirill Kozyrev, who placed the poems in rough chronological order when he assembled the volume, and to whom this cycle was dedicated. Perhaps the dedication to Kozyrev, who cared for the poet during her final illness and who was her chosen executor, signals that Shvarts saw this poem as the signature or keynote to the last months of her life.

"Big Bang Rondo" is one of Shvarts's most ambitious miniature long poems, and it thematizes the paradox of size inherent in the form. Its title tells us to expect a poem about the cosmic origins of the universe, but the poet wishes to imagine not just the infinitesimal particle from which the vast universe could have burst forth, but also the reverse process of implosion. As she writes in a terse prose introduction to the poem:

(There are two hypotheses about the possible endings of the Big Bang that created our cosmos—our cosmos, in which we are rushing headlong with all the stars and galaxies: either the Universe will shatter against the kingdom of the dead, or it will return to its compressed point of birth. I believe the latter.)[135]

Representing the explosive origin of a universe in words is no small challenge. But "Big Bang Rondo" is almost entirely interested in how the world will end, not how it began. Returning all matter back to a pinpoint of origin is the poet's task, and she seems fully aware that her project is spatial—and thus she places her short prefatory remarks in parentheses, enclosing them as if to demonstrate the act of holding, compressing—and, following the logic of Einsteinian relativity, the compression is both spatial and temporal. If matter is rolling itself up into the tiny ball from which it once exploded, then time must turn itself backwards as well.

These binaries of space and time return again and again in the tropes and rhetorical gestures of "Big Bang Rondo." Many of the oppositions are familiar from Shvarts's other poems, where we often see the dichotomies huge/tiny, cosmic/individual, plant/animal, concrete/spiritual, or human/divine. In this poem, with its basis in theoretical physics, there is a further point of contrast between science and art. Shvarts compares science as a form of knowledge to mythology or theology. She offers references to mythological accounts of the origin of the universe, referring us to Maia, a mountain nymph identified with the Earth, and Pegasus (in fact a whole herd of flying horses); sparks of divinity are seen most prominently in God's inspiration that is said to cause the cracking open of the egg of the cosmos—ovoid in shape, but also suggesting the nucleus of a new life.

"Big Bang Rondo" is a sizable work, comprising 82 lines of poetry, plus the prologue in prose. The 82 lines are divided into seven poems of thirteen to fourteen lines (poems 1, 2, 3, 4, 7) or seven to eight lines (poems 5 and 6). The controlled freedom in the act of structuring the work is typical of Shvarts: she wants a patterning that could emerge from a seven-poem sequence, but also the flexibility of poem length. Essentially, she is working with two kinds of short poems, both deriving from something like sonnet form, with its bipartite structure and ability to develop and then challenge an argument. Seven-to-eight line poems tend toward the octave, which some have seen as the first part of, or even a truncated, sonnet, but which has come to be developed brilliantly in its own right, particularly in the twentieth century, by poets as varied as Osip Mandelstam, Natalia Gorbanevskaya, and Mikhail Eremin. Shvarts would have known these antecedents, but, as always, she developed the possibilities in idiosyncratic ways and strayed very far from anything immediately recognizable as a sonnet.

Thus, in the first poem in the sequence, "The Gardener" ("Sadovnik"), the thirteen lines are divided into three groups (5 + 4 + 4). In a way, the poem is a flipped sonnet, with the first five lines acting as something like a six-line conclusion, offered before anything else is said. But there is no contrast of specific with abstract in the poem's parts; rather, the contrast is offered multiple times across the text of the thirteen lines—the image of a flower bud's opening as a form of cosmic explosion repeats three times. Here, physics and metaphysics seem to originate in the plant world:

Каждый год в начале мая,
Медленно почку вскрыв,
Лист распухает, воздух бодая
И повторяя
Большой космический взрыв.

Every year in early May,
When flower buds slowly unfold,
Leaves burst open, and thrust into the air,
Repeating
The cosmic Big Bang.

In these lines, Shvarts forges a primeval allegory, suggesting a parallel between the botanical logic of springtime flowering and the astrophysics of the origins of the universe. Those parallels flow so nicely that they distract us from the temporal systems they imply. But Shvarts hides nothing about time's strange behavior. The very first words of the poem are "every year," as if flaunting her willingness to compare a one-time event like the Big Bang with the regularity of seasonal flowering. The poem's claim, after all, is that the end of the Big Bang is the return of all matter back to its minuscule point of origin, which is to say, what seems like a forward progression in time and space is in fact a kind of circling back. The seasons, in such an event, become a structurally apt comparison for cosmic explosions—the difference would be one of frequency rather than temporal shape. Many other poets have played with ideas of cyclic time, perhaps most famously Yeats and his gyres, but Shvarts points us not just toward poetic models but also musical ones. In this case, the circular, "round" nature of the rondo is also part of her poetic logic.

The gardener introduced in this poem initiates a series of human presences in "Big Bang Rondo," all defined by their activities: a shepherd, a poet, a passerby, a singer and, in the final poem, nobody. Each will lend its name to a poem; the sequence also features a chorus of molecules. In the second poem, "The Shepherd" ("Pastukh"), a compressed bit of elemental matter cracks open, and out fly not particles of energy but fully formed mythological figures. The shepherd appears as Maia, chasing an androgynous form that combines the figures of her son, Hermes, and his offspring, Hermaphroditus. When Maia shrieks the androgyne out to pasture, her command reverses a famous action of Hermes. He stole Apollo's sacred cattle, a theft that recalls the exchange of the cattle for the first lyre crafted by Hermes and coveted by Apollo. Shvarts's spare lines thus turn the cosmic explosion of primal material into poetry's point of origin. The shepherd Maia also stands as a figure for the earth, but it is an earth under threat from its very inception— she walks, with time and space tugging at her garments ("Vremia-prostranstvo tianut ee plat'e vo vse storony"). Yet she is not defenseless, as if incarnating something of the poet's own fierce will to live: she protects herself with her sharp nails and her ability to lash out.

The "Big Bang Rondo" contains a bold allegory of the origins and ends of the universe reenacted through the making of poems. Two poems in the sequence, No. 3, "The Poet" ("Poet"), and No. 6, "The Singer" ("Pevets"), imagine sound rising forth from the throat and traveling across the universe as if it were poetic melodies. Those "hundreds of unknown vowels" ("sotni nevedomykh glasnykh") resound as ecstatic, creative outbursts; indeed, as another form of explosion or "big bang." Each poem in the sequence brings the tale of universal ending one step closer to realization. The images summon the dead out of their graves and restore youth to the old, turning back the clock of time as if progress toward the world's end implied regression to a point of universal and individual birth. Hearts begin to beat backwards, and mature bodies are thrust back into an embryonic state. It is an extraordinary sequence of images, observed at one point by a nameless passerby who senses that the bodies now lying upon the surface, rather than in the earth, like flowers on the sands of time, show themselves to be made of light with the glow of their wide-open eyes. The bodies are in fact stardust, and their souls shine with the light they have swallowed.

The ending of "Big Bang Rondo" projects a sense of resignation to the fact that the limits of the universe must remain unknowable. Poem No. 7, entitled "Nobody" ("Nikto"), also offers the consolation that the universe is filled with exit points. The last eight lines are as follows:

> Одно хорошо—в ней повсюду есть выходы,
> Столько их, что, по сути,
> Всё скользит из космической мути
> И весь Космос—огромный Исход.
> И ведёт
> Всю Вселенную
> В Точку нетленную
> В огненном облаке невидимый Моисей.

> One thing is true: the world is full of portals,
> So many at work
> That all slide out of the cosmic murk
> And the whole Cosmos is one great Exodus.
> And one man leads
> The whole Universe
> To an immutable Point:
> Moses, hidden in a fiery cloud.

The "immutable Point" into which all matter returns is represented by Shvarts as deliverance. Moses leads forth the known world as he had led the Israelites out of Egypt. The image of the fiery cloud is a stunning transformation of the burning bush through which God spoke to Moses; it is all that is left of the botanical imagery with which "Big Bang Rondo" began.

The image of Moses is reprised here from an earlier poem, "Moses and the Bush in which God Appeared" ("Moisei i kust, v kotorom iavilsia Bog," 1970s). To use that image more than thirty years later is a rare instance when the poet, known to fill her poems with an endless succession of new objects, animals, plants, and myths, goes back to an earlier vision of the divine as if to test its potential for further revelation.[136] Bringing Moses into "Big Bang Rondo" lets Shvarts reaffirm her belief in the power of theological explanations: she shows her enduring preference for the laws of the Five Books of Moses over the laws of Newton or Einstein. Moses stands forth in the cosmos, transforming a tale of physical implosion into a fantasy of deliverance into safety and freedom. Shvarts's Rondo returns "the Universe" to the dream of imperishability. Her poem has ventured to imagine the end of the world, but it is an ending that shows the pathways toward cosmic redemption, the dream that has filled the imagination of writers from the times of medieval Rus´ well past the end of the Soviet Union.

Aleksandr Mironov remained close friends with Elena Shvarts until the end of their lives (they both died in 2010); in fact, she edited the first substantial publication of his poetry.[137] Mironov's poetry, however, has quite a different texture from her dramatically intense and often ventrilo-quizing work, despite some important elements of shared heritage. Like Shvarts, he built an idiosyncratic poetic edifice on the foundation laid down by Kuzmin and other modernists; like Shvarts, he explored multiple fields of knowledge and culture, not as an expert, but as someone taking pleasure in myths, stories, and alternative identities thus uncovered; and, perhaps most characteristically, like Shvarts, Mironov could irritate some of his sterner and more prudish readers by his frequent evocations of sexuality, the body, and death.

Valery Shubinsky had his reservations about Mironov's poetry, but still described him as "faithful to the traditional Christian hierarchy of flesh-psyche-spirit, while spurning the prin-cipled norms of the bodily, the psychological or the spiritual. In his world, 'God is possible all around.'"[138] That last phrase is a citation from an OBERIU poet who inspired Mironov, Aleksandr Vvedensky. Mironov's encounter with the divine had a kind of pervasive, spontaneous quality, resulting in poems akin to Zen koans. These are contemplative metaphysical riddles in which divinities seemed to wander about waiting to be noticed.[139] His deity could be a laughing god or one surrounded by demons.[140] Like Kliuev and Blazhenny, Mironov was drawn to the sectarian, itinerant side of religious life. His vast cycle of Gnostic poems exem-plifies his desire to be associated with heresy and defiance. Mironov's best-known poems include "I have stopped lying" ("Ia perestal lgat'," 1965), "The Skomorokh's Wives Tale" ("Skaz o zhenakh skomorosh'ikh," 1978), and "Autumn of the Androgyne" ("Osen' androgina," 1978).[141] But the epithet "best-known" is relative: in the Leningrad underground, Mironov seemed to cultivate a kind of invisibility, even within that self-consciously marginalized culture of the underground.

The concentration of poets pursuing the tradition of spiritual verse in Leningrad/Petersburg remains a distinctive feature of the city's culture. But devotional poetry also flourished in pro-vincial towns and distant urban centers. Some poets may have found slightly greater freedom outside the big metropolitan areas; for example, Svetlana Kekova (b. 1951), who was born on Sakhalin, lived in Tashkent and Tambov, and then remained in Saratov after graduating from the local university; or Boris Khersonsky (b. 1950), who has spent his entire life in Odessa. Kekova's poems can include the errant thoughts of one at prayer, and yet as aware of birds singing outside as of the church service itself. Her psychological portraits are subtle, the penitence and humility touched by rare but gratefully received grace.[142] When asked whether her poems were conversations with God, or conversations with her readers about God, Kekova answered by quoting a line from the Psalms, "Every breath praises the Lord." This, she said, is "the real task of poetry."[143]

As an inspiring figure for her work, Kekova has named Olga Sedakova, a much-honored contemporary poet who has been accorded prizes from the Vatican, France, Italy, Germany, and Russia. Sedakova has become an outspoken critic of the Orthodox Church, seeking to hold it to high standards of integrity and humanism, just as many canonical writers did before her, from the radical positions taken by Avvakum and Tolstoy to the more moderated argu-ments implicit in the writings of Leskov and Solov'ev. In her prose and poetry alike, Sedakova addresses fundamental theological and ethical questions; however, church institutions and its rituals are not a structural element in her verse.[144] She has written a number of poems about saints, notably Aleksy, the Good Man of Rome, and about Biblical figures, particularly Jacob and the Prodigal Son.[145] These parables of errancy and forgiveness sustain one of Sedakova's great themes. An enduring contribution to the poetry of faith in her work is the absorption of a simple, daily lexicon and the steadfast, inspired, and utterly ordinary world in her *Old Songs* (*Starye pesni*, 1980–81).[146] Although much of her poetry is built on recognizable poetic forms—from troubadour and Renaissance forms to odes—the *Old Songs* cycle is distinctive in its reliance on free verse. Its unfussy language and plain imagery are enriched by the layered meanings embedded in familiar words.[147]

A poet, translator, teacher (among others, of a seminar on Dante), and essayist of great erudition, Sedakova had strong ties to two of the most prominent humanist thinkers of the late Soviet period: Vladimir Bibikhin (1938–2004), who bridged Russian thought and the European philosophical tradition, introducing many philosophers thanks to his translations (Heidegger first and foremost); and Sergei Averintsev (1937–2004), whose work is marked by a more pronounced Christian humanism. Averintsev has also made a modest contribution to the poetic tradition with his spiritual rhymes, hymns, and translations.[148] These thinkers—Bibikhin was a great friend and she often referred to Averintsev as her mentor—not only acquainted Sedakova with a philosophical and philological tradition that was imperiled during the Soviet era, but also imbued her with a spirit of open debate and optimistic faith in ideas.[149] Sedakova is the creator of poetry that only rarely sounds the notes of fear or despair that can be so prominent in twentieth-century poetry—especially the poetry "after Auschwitz"—and it often feels as if she reserves her sterner judgments for her prose.[150] The predominant tone in her poetry is joy. As one of her poems concludes—a poem that speaks in the voice of an angel: "I say unto you: / are you / ready / for unbelievable happiness" ("Ia govoriu: ty / gotov / k neveroiatnomu schast'iu?").[151]

That joy can also be found in Joseph Brodsky's *Nativity Poems*, a volume created and published posthumously that brought together poems written over several decades. His practice of writing a poem every New Year all the more deserves mention because he is not usually thought to be a religious poet. Some of these poems strike firmly secular notes in their pleasure at the renewal of a new calendar year. They often also celebrate the promise of renewal marked by the birth of Christ, and there is a generosity of spirit in them as well—one begins "when it's Christmas we're all of us magi."[152]

Brodsky was born a Jew, although like Mandelstam and many others born to Judaism but not active practitioners, it was Christianity that almost invariably provided the imagery and themes for his poems that were even tangentially religious. The work of another Jewish poet, Boris Khersonsky, presents a more complex picture. He converted to Orthodoxy, and much of his work closely reflects a Christian perspective: for example the series of poems "In the Icon Shop" ("Ikonnaia lavka"), the cycle "The Holy Week" ("Strastnaia sedmitsa"), and the title sequence in his 2009 book *Spirituals*.[153] But the work that brought wider fame to Khersonsky, who had been writing and publishing in unofficial circles in Odessa for years, is *Family Archive* (*Semeinyi arkhiv*, 2006). This celebrated book recreates the whole history of the Jewish people in the era of pogroms and displacement, of Holocaust and persecution, not just in his native Odessa but throughout the Pale of Settlement.[154] The collection is structured around recurring genres, such as tales of families broken by violence or assimilation; sayings of the Rabbis; lists of ritual objects sold at auction; and, perhaps most remarkably, short poems based loosely on the prayers that would be uttered in any daily Jewish service but rendered strange and beautiful through the poet's alterations. Russian words are interspersed with transliterated Hebrew vocables, and contemporary references place the timeless prayers in historical time—a temporality when prayers seem to go unanswered. Khersonsky's writings are striking for their determined, persistent faith, whether in a Christian Holy Trinity or in a Jewish God, coupled with a clear-eyed realism about history and especially politics. Residing in Ukraine in the 2010s, he has been witness to the violence and discord created by Russia's annexation of Crimea in 2014 and by the war in Eastern Ukraine. He has not been silent on this subject, speaking out on behalf of Ukrainian sovereignty and reinforcing his strong connections to Ukrainian-language poets.[155] As is the case with Olga Sedakova, Khersonsky's writings make clear that religious belief may compel a poet to take a political position; like hers, his is a passionate voice for tolerance.

While peaceful coexistence between Jewish and Orthodox traditions is not exactly a hallmark of Russian cultural history, Khersonsky has been able to accommodate and flourish within both idioms as a poet. He has also collaborated with an Orthodox priest, the poet Sergei Kruglov (b. 1966), on a book publication featuring poetic cycles by each poet and concluding sections in which each writes poems in the voice of a dramatic character invented by the other.[156] Kruglov's hero is Nathan, a Jew who converts to Orthodoxy and becomes a priest, serving a congregation that includes violent anti-Semites; Khersonsky creates an elder of the Church, Bishop Gury (Petrov), who reflects on his entire life in a way reminiscent of Chekhov's story "The Bishop" ("Arkhierei," 1899). Both heroes are, in a sense, heretics;[157] when Kruglov writes poems in the voice of Khersonsky's Gury, or when Khersonsky creates the poems Nathan might have written, both are giving voice to rebellious believers who see the church as having failed in its obligations. The result cannot but be political, particularly at the contentious moment when the book appeared (2012), a time of powerful alliance between the Orthodox Church and the Russian state. There are many overtly political moments in their poetry, including references to elections, to tanks, to sites of conflict. But the power of the dialogue within the book comes from its insights into the minds and spirits of the heroes.

Kruglov's poetry can veer toward irony and the grotesque. Khersonsky answers with Nathan's poems of prayer and disbelief; his final poem, as imagined by Khersonsky, takes him back to his Jewish origins: he asks, like a penitent at the High Holidays, to be inscribed into the Book of Life.[158] Khersonsky's Gury poems have their own jagged edges, and Kruglov answers with words that seem to speak to and for all Russians, believers and atheists, Christians and Jews. He speaks of God as beyond description, neither angry nor gentle, yet filled with self-assurance and a sense of righteousness: "He—is us" ("On—eto my").[159] That astonishing assertion shows the great distance traveled by poetry of the spirit in the twentieth century: rather than a quest to transcend daily life, Kruglov asserts that the divine is embodied in daily life, in people's attitudes toward one another. Metaphysics has been superseded by the demands of ethics, and as Russian poetry faces the challenges of the twenty-first century, it seems hard to imagine that these ethical pressures will lessen.

Neo-Romanticism

Literary scholars have rarely identified Neo-Romanticism as a self-contained poetic system in modern Russian literature.[160] Although not an independent movement or school like Acmeism, Symbolism, or Futurism, the term is routinely used to foreground often-unexpected lines of affiliation among writers of prose, poetry, and drama. Neo-Romanticism featured stylization, imaginative fantasy, and often a dose of irony.

A staggeringly wide range of writers incorporated elements of Neo-Romanticism into their work, from Gorky and Nikolai Gumilev to Konstantin Paustovsky (1892–1968) and Evgeny Shvarts (1896–1958). Neo-Romanticism provided a highly versatile mechanism for negotiating between a commitment to individual freedom and the depersonalizing political or cultural forces required to satisfy apparent state interests. A number of techniques and tropes can be bundled under the term Neo-Romanticism, such as intense stylization that replaces the earlier Romantic quest for a transcendental ideal. Openly playful, stylization also permits nostalgia for that ideal by hiding it under the layers of irony. Characters in ballads and narrative poems are often surrounded by an aura of romance, as in the case of Gumilev's captains, conquistadors, and travelers to exotic lands; Nikolai Tikhonov's and Pavel Kogan's (1918–42) sailors and heroic soldiers; Bagritsky's sea smugglers and Till Eulenspiegel; Mikhail Svetlov's (1903–64) Don Quixote, Joan of Arc, and musketeers; Okudzhava's "commissars in dusty helmets" and pirates. Esenin's "hooligan poems" (1920–22) inspired the much later poetry of Boris Ryzhy (1974–2001), who could make petty thugs from Sverdlovsk's industrial neighborhoods seem alluring. Neo-Romantic poems also had frequent recourse to folkloric and religious motifs. Esenin, for example, as well as like-minded "peasant" poets, employed stylizations based on Old Believer, rather than official Orthodox, motifs. They created an idealized image of Holy Russia. Esenin was able to use it as a source of utopian fantasies about revolutionary Russia (*Inoniia*, 1918), and as a form of nostalgic critique of destructive modernity (in his long poem *The Forty-Day Commemoration* [*Sorokoust*, 1920]).

Stylization offered a powerful means for estrangement. By inverting Shklovsky's notion of defamiliarization (*ostranenie*) to create freshness of perception, Neo-Romantic authors represented the natural and mundane as if they were acts of art and poetic design. They blurred the borderline between fiction and reality by problematizing the solidity of the real and materializing the dream of an alternative. A vivid example comes in Aleksandr Vertinsky's (1889–1957) boastful claim in his poem "The Halfbreed" ("Polukrovka," 1930): "I can create poems from carrion, / I love to turn housemaids into queens" ("Ia mogu iz padali sozdavat' poemy, / Ia liubliu iz gornichnykh delat' korolev").[161] The baroque metaphor of life as a theatrical performance reinforces the Neo-Romantic fascination with fantasy and deception, as Gumilev proclaimed in "The Theater" ("Teatr," 1910): "All of us, saints and thieves, / From the altar and the barracks, / We are all ridiculous actors / In the theater of the Lord God" ("Vse my, sviatye i vory, / Iz altaria i ostroga, / Vse my—smeshnye aktery / V teatre Gospoda Boga").[162] This logic of estrangement also explains why live toys of all kinds, tin soldiers, paper ballerinas, Christmas ornaments, marionettes, as well as fairy-tale characters, actors, and clowns unable to remove their masks, inhabit Neo-Romantic texts. The masked or toy alter egos provided ventriloquized forms of self-expression and dramatic fantasies of alternative personae.

Yet this strategy is inherently contradictory: *The Pillar of Fire* (*Ognennyi stolp*, 1921), Gumilev's last book and in many ways the foundational text of Russian Neo-Romanticism, contains two powerful poems with mutually incompatible meanings. "The Sixth Sense" ("Shestoe chuvstvo," 1920) places aesthetic imagination at the top of the evolutionary process, as its distant, inevitable goal. But in the poem "The Word" ("Slovo," 1921), Gumilev praises a bygone era when "the Word could stop the sun, / the Word could destroy towns" ("solntse ostanavlivali slovom, / slovom razrushali goroda"), while condemning contemporary culture: "And like bees in an emptied hive / dead words have a bad smell" ("i, kak pchely v ul'e opustelom, / durno pakhnut mertvye slova").[163]

The idea of stylization as a futile, even while desperately needed, gesture explains its frequent coupling with irony to indicate the chasm between the realm of stylized subjectivity and reality (as in many of Vertinsky's songs, especially "Tango Magnolia," 1931). Aleksandr Galich's invocation of the images and rhythm of Zhukovsky's translation of von Zedlitz's poem about Napoleon "The Night Parade" ("Die nächtliche Heerschau" ["Nochnoi smotr," 1836]) in his ballad "Night Watch" ("Nochnoi dozor," 1962–64) also produces an ironic effect, although it is tragic irony: popular nostalgia for a despot able to raise corpses and animate monuments has an uncanny power. In Aleksandr (Alik) Rivin's (1915–42) poems, irony typically stems from a kind of secondary stylization applied to recent and popular poetic formulas. For instance, he takes a phrase from a popular song about a brave captain (it appeared in the 1936 Soviet film *Captain Grant's Children*, based on Jules Verne's novel, which explains the quotation's quasi-romantic aura), and transforms it into a metaphor of bitter distance from his own era. His words enact a radical deflation. So, the Yiddish phrase meaning "kiss my ass" is inscribed on the pennant of the romantic captain's boat:

Капитан, капитан, улыбнитесь,

кус ин тохес—это флаг корабля.

Наш корабль без флагов и правительств,

во вселенной наш корабль—Земля.

Мы плывем, только брызжем звездами,

как веслом мы кометой гребем . . .[164]

Captain, o captain, give us a smile,

"kish-mir-in-tukhes" flies on our flag.

Our ship has no flag and no nation,

in the universe, our ship is the earth.

We sail, splashing by the stars,

we row with the comets as oars . . .

(late 1930s)

As the poet gains distance from the contemporary world by means of ironic stylization, the subject is placed in a fragile and precarious position. That sense of precarious existence is a valuable contribution of the literature of Neo-Romanticism, and it stands as an expressive alternative to the two-dimensional self championed by Socialist Realism.

The oxymoron, another staple Neo-Romantic trope, corresponds to the poet's attempts to lend substance to fantasy and foreground the instability of any imagined reality; oxymoron becomes inevitable in these emphatically prosaic manifestations of lofty themes. In Bagritsky's "Smugglers" ("Kontrabandisty," 1927), stars shed their celestial light on the stolen booty—"cognac, nylons, and condoms . . ." ("kon'iak, chulki i prezervativy . . .").[165] Okudzhava's poetry, as Alexander Zholkovsky has observed, presents a version of paradise disguised as a Moscow backyard,[166] and Leonid Dubshan speaks about the "total dominance of oxymorons" in Okudzhava's oeuvre.[167] Timur Kibirov's (b. 1955) later epistles to friends similarly combine the flourishes of a high poetic style—frequently inspired by Blok, who was also a source for Okudzhava's ironies—with comical naturalistic details.

The rhetorical use of oxymoron inevitably affects the poetic subject, who enacts incompatible scenarios and embodies multiple personalities: literary and fictional alongside real and mundane. These selves contradict each other while being mutually dependent and ultimately inseparable. Each of the personas manages to transcend various internal limits, leading toward moments of liberation from restrictive identities, both historical and social. One of the first to explore this path was Gumilev, who declared: "The words 'I, myself' sound strange to me" ("Mne stranno sochetan'e slov 'ia sam'" in "Two Adams" ["Dva Adama", 1917–18]).[168] In the poem "Memory" ("Pamiat'," 1921), he subverts Christian doctrine to claim: "we change souls, not bodies" ("my meniaem dushi, ne tela"). Gumilev can present a range of identities, from a melancholic child-sorcerer able to stop the rain with a single word to one who loves "freedom's favored son, / the seafarer and the archer" ("ia liubliu izbrannika svobody, / moreplavatelia i strelka"). While some of these identities seem repellant to the poet and others are treasured, his power to create them never wanes. He remains "the pensive, stubborn architect / of a temple rising from the gloom" ("ugriumyi i upriamyi zodchii khrama, / vosstaiushchego vo mgle").[169]

A somewhat different treatment of multiple personalities is found in the work of Sergei Esenin, who could pose as a young monk or hooligan, a folksy good lad, or the prophet Sergei Esenin. In his "hooligan" poems, he creates the image of a person who has already absorbed the experience of death into his everyday existence: "I am just the same as you, the goners / And there is no turning back" ("Ia takoi zhe, kak vy, propashchii / Mne teper' ne uiti nazad," from the poem "Yes! Now It's Decided..." ["Da! Teper' resheno...," 1922–23]); and "I am terrified: after all, the soul comes to an end / Like youth and love" ("Mne strashno,—ved' dusha prokhodit, / Kak molodost' i kak liubov'," from the poem "Farewell to Mariengof" ["Proshchanie s Mariengofom," 1922]).[170] In transforming death into an everyday psychological state, Esenin revives traditional Romantic motifs of anti-normative behavior and ennui, which in the Soviet context struck a jarring note. The resurrection of the Doppelgänger in the narrative poem *The Black Man* (*Chernyi chelovek*, 1925), written a month before Esenin's suicide, converts the Neo-Romantic fascination with multiplying personae into the theme of self-destruction as a form of existential incompatibility with (contemporary) life.

For late Soviet Neo-Romanticism, the genre of song or ballad developed by poet-performers like Galich and Vysotsky was of singular importance, and the form enjoyed enormous popularity. These songs relied on the creation of distinctive, memorable characters. In Galich's ballads, the perspective of an ordinary person reveals grotesque transformations of a living person into an automaton ("Kolomiitsev at His Best" ["Kolomiitsev v polnyi rost"], 1968–70), or alternatively, puts timeless plots of miraculous love and betrayal into the rough speech and humiliating rituals of daily Soviet life ("Merry Talk" ["Veselyi razgovor," 1963], "The Urban Romance (Tonechka)" ["Gorodskoi romans (Tonechka)," 1962], "The Red Triangle" ["Krasnyi treugol'nik," 1964], and "Lenochka," 1959). Vysotsky's poetry comprises poetic monologues delivered by pirates, thugs, alcoholics, space travelers, psychiatric patients, prisoners, as well as by a jet-plane and a wolf, but all these characters represent manifestations of the lyric self. Some have argued that the encyclopedia of voices channeled by Vysotsky represents a new, multi-voiced and many-faced poetic subjectivity.[171] From a Bakhtinian perspective, Vysotsky's poetry becomes a carnival of grotesque personas that undermine the notion of any monologic truth and offer the audience the joy of self-recognition in the experience of otherness.

Many Neo-Romantic poets explore extreme, life-and-death situations as moments of ultimate freedom from social and cultural conventions: the logic of banality is destroyed, and unusual, instant reactions are demanded. This is why they favor the genre of the ballad, with its extreme dramatic situations; and several practitioners, including Gumilev, Svetlov, Simonov, Tikhonov, Okudzhava, and Vysotsky, also enjoy renown for their war lyrics. Extreme situations reinforce the striving for moral clarity and a more unified personality, which evokes timeless oppositions between good and evil, heroism and treason.

The seductions of extreme situations can lead to dangerous forms of life-creation and to an aestheticization of violence (and even the adoption of hate speech, as in the later work of Eduard Limonov, b. 1943). Boris Ryzhy, who killed himself at age 26, expresses the self-destructive bent with naive, if stylized, straightforwardness: "I've been killing, and you're playing Doom, / until your weak members felt exhausted. / ... You lived, because you kept playing, / I played because I was alive" ("Ia ubival, a vy igrali v dum / do chlenov nemoshchnykh iznemozhen'ia. / ... Vy zhili, potomu chto vy igrali. / Ia zhil, i lish' poetomu igral," 1997).[172]

The representation of extreme situations polarizes Neo-Romanticism. To one pole gravitate those poets who glorify masculinity, chivalry, self-sacrifice, and heroic death—Gumilev, Tikhonov, Simonov, Vysotsky, and Ryzhy. To the other, those who choose sentimentality over heroism and present compassion and tenderness as the sole dignified response to inhuman conditions: Esenin, Rivin, Okudzhava, Galich, and Kibirov. Most illuminating in this respect is the example of Okudzhava, with his persistent pacifism, consistent with his autobiographic novella *Be Well, Student* (*Bud' zdorov, shkoliar*, 1961). He shows war as senseless and indiscriminate killing. In the words of Leonid Dubshan, Okudzhava "took the risk to rehabilitate weakness as the truth that cannot triumph and conquer...."[173]

Paradoxically, the greatest authority is attained through transgression. In crossing lines, breaking rules, and subverting expectations, poems spectacularly embody a form of freedom.

Gumilev's "tram that lost its way" from his eponymous poem ("Zabludivshiisia tramvai," 1919) travels across ages and connects the mundane with the fairy-tale, Pushkin's *Captain's Daughter* with "the India of the Spirit." It serves as a metaphor for poetry, and retrospectively the lost tram reads as a prophetic sign of impending violent death (in 1921, Gumilev would be executed by the Cheka). The poet's freedom in Neo-Romantic poems frequently joins with martyrdom; in Vysotsky's adept formulation: "Poets walk on the edges of knives / And slice to bloody bits their barefoot souls" ("Poety khodiat piatkami po lezviiu nozha / I rezhut v krov' svoi bosye dushi"; "On Fatal Dates and Numbers" ["O fatal'nykh datakh i tsifrakh," 1971]).[174] Such poets can be raised to near sainthood for actions that, from another standpoint, look like failure or mere caprice. For example, Galich depicts Akhmatova writing a cycle of Socialist Realist poems ("Glory to peace!" ["Slava miru"], 1950), hoping to alleviate the suffering of her imprisoned son. In Galich's view, this transgressive self-betrayal turns into solemn self-sacrifice, and his lines stylistically echo her *Requiem*: "The sun sparkled as they led him before the firing squad / On the banks of a sparkling river / And Her son watched them walk away / To the very edge of the line" ("Po belomu svetu veli na rasstrel / Nad beregom beloi reki / I syn Ee vsled ukhodiashchim smotrel / U samogo kraia stroki"; "Untitled" ["Bez nazvaniia"; the poem begins "Ei strashno. I dushno. I khochetsia lech'," 1967]).[175] Poetry appears as something unquestionably vital in extreme conditions like war, as we see in Bagritsky's "A Conversation with Komsomol Member Nikolai Dement'ev" ("Razgovor s komsomol'tsem Nikolaem Dement'evym," 1927) or Slutsky's "Prose-Writers" ("Prozaiki," 1956)—a poem about the Gulag:

> Весь барак, как дурак, бормотал, подбирал
> рифму к рифме и строку к строке.
> То начальство стихом до костей пробирал,
> то стремился излиться в тоске.
>
> Ямб рождался из мерного боя лопат.
> Словно уголь, он в шахтах копался.
> Точно так же на фронте, из шага солдат,
> он рождался и в строфы слагался.[176]

> The barracks were muttering, nattering like a fool,
> assembling the rhyming lines.
> They pierced through to the truth about power,
> Then poured out their anguish in verse.
>
> Iambs were created to the even rhythm of digging into earth.
> Digging deep as if into mines, searching out coal,
> And just the same way, using the marching rhythm of the soldiers,
> verse was born, and formed into lines of words.

Poetry took on an existential role as the sole, if fragile, alternative to non-freedom and banality; by creating distance between the subject and the bloody calamities of the epoch, Neo-Romanticism as an aesthetic discourse kept open channels of expression and self-assertion through decades of inhospitable, dangerous public life.

For that reason, Neo-Romanticism flourished largely in the Soviet period, but it left valuable traces in the work of writers who emerged after 1991. The most significant is Fedor Svarovsky, whose work attained popularity in the 2000s. His science-fiction adventures and battle-weary heroes are steeped in Neo-Romantic irony. As Ilya Kukulin has observed, describing Svarovsky's ballads and narrative poems, "cosmic battles, robot assistants, and so on, take on the function that in romantic ballads was played by a 'gothic' setting." Kukulin adds that the resulting mythology turns out to be "a contemporary version of the sublime," but "as if placed between quotations marks, subjected to defamiliarization."[177] Svarovsky's poem "Glory to Heroes" ("Slava geroiam," 2006) provides an excellent example. It takes the conventional paean to Soviet heroes and changes it first by according praise to citizens of other countries, and then to an imagined inter-galactic warrior who, at the sight of the watery blue earth, turns his attacking space ship around and, in his own way, performs a similar act of salvation.

Слава героям

четыре канадца спасли мир от генетической катастрофы
один армянин изобрёл новый вид ракетного топлива
и лекарство от рака
один русский пожертвовал собой
отключил реактор и спас международную космическую станцию
один англичанин отдал свою печень раненой журналистке
вернувшейся после переворота в Калифорнии
один татарин во время этнического конфликта
в Юго-Восточной Азии спас 240 малайских младенцев
одна француженка умерла за свободу Фобоса в застенках Деймоса
один картадианин
должен был атаковать землю на корабле с нейтринным приводом
но
увидев синюю планету
он развернул корабль в сторону солнца

жизнь есть любовь
люди бессмертны
и слава
слава героям[178]

Glory to Heroes

four Canadians have saved the world from genetic catastrophe
one Armenian has invented a new form of rocket fuel
and medicine to cure cancer
one Russian sacrificed himself
unplugged a reactor and saved the international space station
one Englishman gave up his liver to a wounded journalist a woman
who returned after the Gypsy coup in California
one Tatar in the midst of ethnic violence
in Southwest Asia saved 240 Malaysian infants
one French woman died for the freedom of Phobos in Deimos prison
one Kartadian
was meant to attack earth aboard a neutrino-powered ship
but
at the sight of that blue planet
turned his ship in the direction of the sun

life is love
people are immortal
glory
glory to heroes[179]

The heroic acts are half-plausible, half-fantastic, and the latter injects irony into the former along with some tenderness. The poem has the flat tone and seemingly undifferentiated list-like organization often found in Svarovsky's work, and, in another typical turn, it builds up to a moment when pathos undercuts irony. A banal slogan like "life is love" carries an alienated force of conviction. In many other Svarovsky poems, "the invisible, the unnoticed, and the downtrodden" are brought to visibility and shown to have a profound presence in the life of all people.[180] There are Christian undertones in such poems, often tinged with irony. Many of his poems manifest the hyper-masculine ethos of cinematic adventures, but others present subtle challenges to patriarchy.[181] Svarovsky's tenderness marks a splendid point of contrast to the violence of other Neo-Romantic poets (the later work of Limonov, for example); it may hold possibilities for new modulations of Neo-Romanticism long into the future.

Interlude
Misfits in Russian poetry

I N this space between the Poetics of Subjectivity and the Poetics of Language, we want to pause briefly to consider several otherwise unrelated poets who, for a portion of their careers, did not fit into the reigning poetic movements of their age, or do not smoothly align with the critical trends that dominated Russian literary studies in the twentieth century. These poets straddle the two types of poetics we have foregrounded in this part of our *History*, that of subjectivity and language. By putting the notions of self and verbal expression into a problematic relationship with one another, the poets also stand as significant innovators. Some are canonical, some not, for reasons that bear further thought. We begin with Boris Pasternak and Nikolai Zabolotsky as complementary cases. It is not that they shunned all associations or movements. Pasternak flirted with Futurism, and in the 1920s he was associated with the writers of LEF; Zabolotsky participated in OBERIU.[1] Yet neither is delimited by those phases in their work. Both were to go through multiple stages of development and to change their manner of writing, partly in response to the historical cataclysms of the age. Religious and ethical themes rise to greater importance in their later work, in language and form that was simpler and aimed for an unattainable aesthetic purity. In their early work, Pasternak and Zabolotsky shared a mesmerizing, almost surreal imagery, a lush, idiosyncratic diction, and a resistance to forward-moving poetic logic (how one line follows from another) by means of dense metaphor.

Pasternak's early poetry, as John E. Malmstad has put it, attempts "to renovate the pictorial and verbal language of Russian art."[2] The saturation of color and the formal disjunctions of modern art are translated into verbal terms, in poems with vivid visual imagery like the black birds clustered on trees in a poem of 1912 that are compared to charred pears.[3] It is the third book of his poetry that made Pasternak's reputation as a poet, *My Sister, Life* (*Sestra moia— zhizn'*, 1922). Here, as Andrei Sinyavsky was to observe, the landscape "becomes the subject of the action, the main hero, the mover of events," and it is the landscape that has the "heightened sensitivity" that we would normally expect the poetic subject to exude.[4] What results is a "draughty, reshuffled world, intersected and united by metaphors," to again cite Sinyavsky, and theorists would go on to pay special attention to Pasternak's figurative language, including a strong case for his distinctive reliance on metonymy.[5] The substitutions and acts of displacement that are at the heart of the rhetoric of metaphor also characterize the subject who speaks in the poetry, a subject who can be displaced or dispersed onto the rain, the horizon, the grassy expanse. In the untitled poem whose first three words gave the volume its remarkable name (the poem is six stanzas, of which we cite the first two), Pasternak writes:

> Сестра моя—жизнь и сегодня в разливе
> Расшиблась весенним дождем обо всех,

Но люди в брелоках высоко брюзгливы
И вежливо жалят, как змеи в овсе.

У старших на это свои есть резоны.
Бесспорно, бесспорно смешон твой резон,
Что в грóзу лиловы глаза и газоны
И пахнет сырой резедой горизонт.[6]

My sister is life and today overflows,
It splashes spring raindrops on everyone,
But monocled people are haughtily snooty
They hiss and sting like snakes in the grass.

The grownups possess a reasoned view.
But surely, surely your reason is foolish:
That eyes and lawns turn purple in storms,
And the sweet mignonette perfumes the horizon.

The ternary meter (amphibrachic tetrameter) gives the poem a melodic urgency that resounds elsewhere in the volume, for example in "The Mirror" ("Zerkalo," 1920, 1922).[7] The music is amplified by the verbal repetitions (*bessporno, bessporno*) and sound orchestration (the *b*, *v*, and *l* sounds intermingle beautifully in ll. 3–4, for instance). The rhymes are built on internally consonantal repetitions, particularly in the second stanza (*rezony, rezon, gazony, gorizont*). The visual imagery is casually stunning in the claim that a storm can turn both one's eyes and the lawn seen with those eyes to a fine shade of violet; this interest in the weather, a great Pasternak theme, and its capacity to alter perception, is a residue of the poet's earlier work in philosophy.[8]

Music, the other rejected career path of the gifted Pasternak, was to give formal shape to his next major collection of poems, *Themes and Variations* (*Temy i variatsii*, 1916–22). Unlike the singularly brilliant poems in *My Sister—Life*, this volume features poems in groups, using the conceit of musical variations on a theme by offering five poems on a "Winter Morning" ("Zimnee utro"), another five on "Spring" ("Vesna"), and so on. But the volume opens with what Pasternak called five "tales" ("Piat' povestei"), variations on *Faust* and on Shakespeare. The first of them is "Inspiration" ("Vdokhnovenie," 1921), and its metapoetic foregrounding of the creative process is in some ways the theme on which all the volume's variations will play. A memorable continuation is provided by the untitled poem that begins with its own self-conscious notions of origin, "Thus they begin. At about age two" ("Tak nachinaiut. Goda v dva," 1921). With its gorgeous echoes of Pushkin's *Gypsies* as well as Goethe's *Faust*, the poem spins a fable of maturation, language acquisition, and the power of poetic creation. The poem is in quatrains but its famous final line stands alone: "Thus they begin to live for the sake of verse" ("Tak nachinaiut zhit' stikhom").[9]

To live for the sake of art could mean many things, and in the Soviet period it was a particularly risky life path. Nikolai Zabolotsky shared with Pasternak a quality praised by Lydia Ginzburg—utter fearlessness before perfect, beautiful diction.[10] But the poets' starting points differ. For Zabolotsky, there is even more intense displacement of the lyric subject in his work, and a kind of wildness to the passing imitations of mental consciousness that creates the fleeting images of a poetic self as holy fool, farm animal, childish observer, or drunken reveler. He held his poem "Red Bavaria" ("Krasnaia Bavariia," 1926) in high regard, putting it first in his volume of poems entitled *Columns* (*Stolbtsy*, 1929), a major collection of his early verse. By naming his poem after a brand of beer and setting the poem in a raucous tavern of the same name, Zabolotsky pulled his readers down from the ethereal heights of poetry into the chaos of inebriated perception. The poem's 64 lines (in rhymed iambic tetrameter) open out the confined space of a lyric like Blok's "Unknown Woman" ("Neznakomka," 1906), which the poem partly reprises, into a densely populated site for the aesthetics of sensory and verbal overload.[11] Although the opening description of a "backwoods bottle paradise" ("V glushi butylochnogo raia") leads quickly to the flat declaration that none of this can be described ("No eto opisat' nel'zia"), a dynamic description determinedly ensues, one that sustains the clashing stylistic registers heard in the juxtaposition of beer bottles and paradise in the first line. In keeping with OBERIU aesthetics, material objects—bottles, fan blades, guitars, glasses—pile up as so many shapes and reflecting surfaces; any possibility of an automatic response to these sights is eliminated when they are offered up as a jumbled list.[12] The world of "Red Bavaria" is out of control, as if the very place were as inebriated as its patrons, and suffused with a kind of unreal dreaminess.[13] Yet this clangorous description is strangely list-less, and the revelers' boredom is explicitly mentioned, as if the deathless atmosphere of Petersburg were wafting through open windows. In the poem's last stanza, we read:

> Там Невский в блеске и тоске,
> в ночи переменивший кожу,
> гудками сонными воспет,
> над баром вывеску тревожил;[14]

> There Nevsky in its glitter and anguish,
> having changed its skin in the night,
> its praises once sung in dreamy hooting,
> disturbs the sign above the bar;

Zabolotsky has the Russian poetic tradition agitate the signs of modernity in this setting: his subtle *Onegin* reference (to Chapter 1, verse 35, containing a description of the city awakening as Evgeny goes home from the ball) lets the poem reverberate with a high cultural intonation (signaled by the archaic term "vospet'," itself straight out of *Onegin*, irony intact) that shows his readiness to depart from OBERIU aesthetics.

There is also a Pushkinian echo in a more deeply strange poem of the same year, "The Horse's Face" ("Litso konia," 1926), where the poet contemplates what would happen if a person, gazing on the magical face of a horse, would tear out his tongue and give it and the gift of language to the horse. This rewriting of Pushkin's "Prophet" leads to a form of poetic speech as astounding as Pushkin's own prophetic fantasy: the horse would be able to speak, uttering "big words, words like apples. Thick, / Like honey or raw milk" ("Slova bol'shie, slovno iabloki. Gustye, / Kak med ili krutoe moloko").[15] The thick, juicy, wet words crunch like the apples a horse might eat. Zabolotsky transforms gustatory pleasures into aesthetic produc-tion. The words may be those about which songs are to be sung ("slova... o kotorykh pesni my poem"), but the horse by the end of the poem is a workhorse, burdened by the shaft as he heads to the fields. With "his submissive eyes," he gazes on the "secret and immobile world" ("Gliadit pokornymi glazami / V tainstvennyi i nepodvizhnyi mir").[16]

That mysterious world can be seen with extraordinary calm and fathomless depth in the poems that Zabolotsky would write during his stay in the labor camps and after his release in 1946, many of which exude an undying quest for universal harmony despite grotesque obstacles. Olga Sedakova has described a special sense of trust and integrity in writings where the "music of misfortune" is "experienced humbly and chastely," and she praised his extraor-dinary sensitivity to the suffering of others.[17] The poem "Forest Lake" ("Lesnoe ozero," 1938), composed while Zabolotsky was in transit to the camps, transforms a scene of nature's aggres-siveness and predatory habits into the poet's motionless observation of wild beasts drinking at the lake's edge as if at a sacred font. The poet who wrote "The Triumph of Agriculture" ("Torzhestvo zemledeliia," 1929–30) and other works which engaged with the rhetoric of collectivization and the new Soviet order (even if in ways that brought on sharp official criticism) became someone who sought out glimpses of a cosmic harmony that was surely in short supply. Zabolotsky's work "abounds in anachronism," writes Sarah Pratt.[18] In a sense he did not fully fit into the chronology of his era, and unlike Pasternak, whose reputation may have been complicated within the Soviet Union by his Nobel Prize win (1958) but was nonetheless vouchsafed internationally as a result, there was nothing at the end of Zabolotsky's life to crown his achievements. A quiet reassessment of Zabolotsky's poetry and fuller appreciation of his work have been helped by heightened interest in OBERIU poetics in the twenty-first century, however.[19]

No such late reassessment of one other important misfit poet was needed: Marina Tsvetaeva's poetry has been the subject of intense scholarly attention and poetic appreciation for decades, and yet there remains little consensus on where exactly her work fits in to the literary tradition. As is the case for Zabolotsky and Pasternak, her mature work defied conventions of language use and traditional poetic practice; the term "innovation" scarcely describes what she was doing in the long poems, which, even more than her lyric poetry, challenge critical interpretation.[20] The tradition of the long poem (*poema*) in Russian literature, with forward-moving narrative and often the shape of familiar, rhymed iambic tetrameter, feels like a distant memory, left behind in the poetry of Nekrasov or Aleksei Tolstoy, when one is confronted with the jolting music and rapidly changing scenes of Tsvetaeva's long poems.[21] Traits found elsewhere in her work are accentuated in these longer texts, including the ruptured syntax, the elimination of most verbs, and the jarring rhythms, all of which combine to create what Michael Makin called her "discontinuous discourse."[22] Makin was referring to *The Swain* (*Molodets*, 1920), and other scholars have productively turned attention to *Perekop* (completed in 1929) and especially *The Pied Piper* (*Krysolov*, 1926), regarded as one of Tsvetaeva's supreme poetic achievements, by Pasternak among others.[23] Remarkably, *The Pied Piper* is almost completely built around voices: the Piper himself and the townspeople, the rats, and the children he leads to their death. The representation of distinct voices stands out all the more in the poem's intense staccato rhythms, alliterations, anaphora, and rhymes. Tsvetaeva gave the subtitle of "lyric satire" to *The Pied Piper*, and the poem enacts a blunt assault on the social duplicities and false reasoning of the townspeople. Although the poem is based on a folktale, Tsvetaeva uses its material to offer a sarcastic social commentary. She rejects the pieties and false hopes of radical social change and, although she allied herself with rebels (and misfits) throughout her life, we know that she found little to praise about the Revolution and the Civil War. Her political views, complicated as they were, come through strongly in the poetry; however, hers is always the longer view, that of history. In that sense, her long poems share the aesthetic project of Blok's *The Twelve* and Mayakovsky's *150,000,000* (1919–20); although her ambivalence about the political project of the Revolution has more in common with Pasternak's *Sublime Malady* (*Vysokaia bolezn'*, 1924).[24] The long poem also attains mastery in Tsvetaeva's hands in two poems about the disastrous end of a love affair published in 1926: *Poem of the Mountain* (*Poema gory*) and *Poem of the End* (*Poema kontsa*). The shattered syntax and fierce intonation of the two poems embraced the subject identity of a triumphant outcast. That combination of linguistic fireworks with a strong articulation of subjectivity marks the poetic achievement of Marina Tsvetaeva, who employed the poetics of self and the poetics of language in equal measure.

Innokenty Annensky might be called a misfit even among misfits. He is most often mentioned in relation to some other writer who became more important, Acmeist poets in particular. He fits badly even in this context of misfits, treated after poets whom he in fact preceded historically; nor is he exactly straddling the boundary between language and subjectivity in the way that Pasternak, Tsvetaeva, and Zabolotsky do. Annensky forged a point of connection between Symbolism and Acmeism, movements to which he did not belong. By any standard, Annensky is a poet's poet, the creator of refined and memorable poems, a poet and translator who transmitted the most elite elements of French Symbolism (Mallarmé, Rimbaud, Verlaine) as well as the creator of his own versions from the classical tragedy tradition and the author of important essays. Arguably, however, Annensky's real impact is as an emblem of insufficient critical appreciation, a poet whose work is praised but under-theorized, and who was never fully absorbed by succeeding generations (beyond those who immediately followed him—it is clear that the Acmeists learned a great deal from him). But Annensky often seems a lost poet, a fate which links him to such unlikely figures as Vladimir Nabokov, revered as a writer of prose and as an arbiter of critical judgments, and yet someone whose poetry is rarely given much attention. The same claim may be made about Georgy Ivanov (1894–1958), whose late poetry has a philosophical element that ought to make him seem a successor to Tiutchev or a predecessor to Brodsky, and yet he too stands curiously alone.[25] Ivanov's exaggerations and imprecisions in his memoirs, written in emigration, also contributed to the disdain of some later critics and scholars (he is famously the target of Nabokov's satire in "Spring in Fialta"). That fate is its own success in some corners of the critical tradition. Idiosyncratic and querulous essays (and not a few dissertations) have been penned by those who come to champion any one of these misfits; Ivanov in particular has drawn fresh attention from those who praise his later verse.[26] To claim that a poet would write his best work at the end of a long life and in emigration is provocative within the Russian tradition, and Ivanov is a poet who could substantiate such claims.

One of the further contributions that a study of misfits might yet offer, in fact, is a reconsideration of how the "life and works" account of a poet has led to overly conventional narrative accounts of more than one literary figure. Examples here have been chosen entirely from among those who lived earlier in the twentieth century, but there can be no doubt that patterns for understanding the trends, groupings, alliances, and battles of the late Soviet and post-Soviet periods will leave some interesting poets oddly adrift. We can anticipate, given the striking diversity of contemporary poetry, that more than a few poets active in the twenty-first century will look like misfits when a backward glance is cast in their direction many years hence. Should they begin to outnumber the poets who fit more easily into the narratives of literary history, future theorists may also want to reconsider how misfits might subversively be doing the work of canon formation inside out. A test of this theory may come when we look back, decades into the twenty-first century, at the immediate post-Soviet years: will such hard-to-categorize, but clearly significant poets as Arkady Dragomoshchenko (1946–2012), Mikhail Gronas (b. 1970), or Sergei Magid, be misfits? Or will the label apply far more aptly to writers of prose or drama?

3

The poetics of language

THE domains of poetics and subjectivity collide in unprecedented ways in the texts, public gestures, and performances of the Russian avant-garde, and the collisions exploded in a poetic practice of verbal rupture. Avant-garde texts, theories, and life-creating adventures have had a lasting legacy internationally. Just as the novels of the nineteenth century drew a wide readership to Russian literature, so the radical writings, performances, and artwork of the Russian avant-garde would inspire creative work across disparate decades and places, from Vienna to San Francisco. The first burst of avant-garde energy in the twentieth century was associated with the Futurists, who insisted more forcefully than had any before them that poems and prose were made of verbal material and nothing more.

Futurism

Futurism is the first and most prominent avant-garde movement in Russian literature to join what has been termed by Marjorie Perloff the "Futurist moment" in European literature.[1] Cognate with Italian Futurism, Cubism, and the development of collage in French and German art, as well as Guillaume Apollinaire's and Ezra Pound's poetic experiments, Russian Futurism comprised several overlapping groups (Gileia, Cubo-Futurism, Mezzanine of Poetry, Centrifuge, Ego-Futurism, 41°) and a very large number of poets, artists, and theorists: David Burliuk, Velimir Khlebnikov, Aleksei Kruchenykh (1886–1968), Natalia Goncharova, Kazimir Malevich, and Roman Jakobson, among many others.[2] Outrageous manifestoes were a hallmark of a movement in which Futurist poets and theorists emphasized the self-sufficient qualities of the word (*samovitoe slovo*; word as such). They focused on the poetic potential concentrated in sounds (*zaum´* or transrational poetry) and morphemes (*korneslovie* in Khlebnikov's poetry). Along with the experimental treatment of language and a turn to neo-primitivist poetic form, Futurists introduced into Russian poetry highly emotional, expressive tropes of anarchic rebellion, sexuality, violence, war, urban life, and revolution. They also pioneered experimentation with performance art (before it was defined as such), frequently to the point of scandal. They took to provincial cities in the winter of 1913–14, demonstrating that art presented a revolutionary challenge to the "public taste" they slapped in the face. The performance style of the Futurists would influence the later antics of OBERIU.

The focus on the "word as such" paralleled the efforts of Futurist painters to eschew representation for the formal elements of painting, although allegiances to the Italian poet, prose writer, and theorist Marinetti proved divisive for members of the Russian avant-garde. The affinities between verbal and visual creative work led to innovative book design, so it is not surprising that many scholars date the emergence of Futurism to the publication of the first volume of *A Trap for Judges* (*Sadok sudei*, 1910), with its idiosyncratic revisions to orthography, its pages made from repurposed wallpaper, and its free-flowing mix of poems and images. Contributors included David Burliuk, Elena Guro, Vasily Kamensky, Velimir Khlebnikov, and Aleksei Kruchenykh. Several went on to publish a manifesto in the second volume of *A Trap for Judges* (1913), whose dainty format still registers as a strange setting for their aggressively stated set of rules and principles. In advancing a claim for the significance of how letters are shaped, and in arguing that there is an expressive function to handwriting, the proponents of a new mode of literature were in a sense simply following through on the initial impulse that saw verbal and visual creative work as inseparable.[3] Book production continued to advance a radical agenda by means of format and typeface, vividly shown in Kamensky's *Tango With Cows* (*Tango s korovami*, 1914), where the wallpaper's bright colors are set off by a spray of different fonts and variously sized letters, creating a collage effect that challenges the reader as to where to begin and how to proceed.

Kamensky was proud of using this mix of "ruptures, dislocations and a stair of stressed lines of versification."[4] The dynamism of words on the pentagon-shaped page had a modern look, as did many avant-garde book productions that used irregular pages, deliberate mistakes, and handwritten words, perhaps most famously in the books assembled by Kruchenykh, including *A Game in Hell* (*Igra v adu*, 1912) and *Worldbackwards* (*Mirskontsa*, 1912–13), with artwork by Mikhail Larionov and Natalia Goncharova.[5] Publishing formats emphasized the materiality of the word as signifier and object: it is what we have come to call *faktura* (a term borrowed from the visual arts) and what the Futurists demonstrated to their readers in textured, patterned, and playful uses of typeface and handwriting. Futurist *zaum*, its language of trans-sense (or, as Paul Schmidt translated it, beyonsense),[6] is but the rhetorical equivalent of these radical forms of book publications.

Futurists manifested their trademark energy in prolific creativity during the early 1910s. Both collective actions and publications remained significant, like *A Slap in the Face of Public Taste* (*Poshchechina obshestvennomu vkusu*, 1912), which included a manifesto urging readers to throw Pushkin off the ship of modernity, and a brilliant selection of texts (Khlebnikov's "Bobeobi," poems by Kruchenykh, Burliuk, and Mayakovsky, and prose by the painter Vasily Kandinsky). Several figures emerged into the foreground within these publications and collective events, particularly Mayakovsky, a great crowd favorite at the performances.

Vladimir Mayakovsky seems to have taken to heart David Burliuk's announcement to him when they met in 1911 that he was a genius, and he played the *enfant terrible* role to the hilt, casting himself in the tragedy *Vladimir Mayakovsky* (1913) as the suffering, tragic, brazen hero of a doomed culture; it was performed in repertoire with Kruchenykh's opera *Victory over the Sun*.[7] His first book of poetry was published in the same ego-futuristic spirit, with its bold title *I* (*Ia*, 1913). But as Clare Cavanagh has emphasized, he was not "simply a poet of the self": like the American poet Walt Whitman, to whom she perceptively compares him, Mayakovsky "houses his monumental ego in a suitably oversized body, and this body is the tortured hero of all his early work."[8] Mayakovsky's most admired work includes two narrative lyric poems of 1915, "A Cloud in Trousers" ("Oblako v shtanakh") and "The Backbone Flute" ("Fleita-pozvonochnik," 1915), which feature themes of unrequited love and a kind of existential despair at the alienation of the bourgeois world. He was, as Roman Jakobson put it, the lyric voice of the avant-garde.[9] Mayakovsky's poetics, whether based on conventional syllabotonic forms, pure accentual verse, or a form of *dol'nik*, derive great innovative energy from unusual word choices and sentence structure, and from the visual rupture of the lines into his famous stair-step (*lesenka*) arrangement. Unexpected rhymes abound, as do clangorous, shocking metaphors alongside strangely gentle intonations of lyric poetry. As Victor Terras wrote, "the emotions of Mayakovsky's lyrics range from sneering, jeering, swagger, and épatage to hyperbolic, and hence parodic, self-glorification, plaintive self-pity, unbearable pain, raging despair—all expressed in ingenious and wildly overstated conceits."[10] Many of the texts are long gallops through these emotions, but Mayakovsky can cover considerable terrain in short bursts, too, as in a passage from *A Cloud in Trousers*:

> Я,
> златоустейший,
> чье каждое слово
> душу новородит,
> именинит тело,
> говорю вам:
> мельчайшая пылинка живого
> ценее всего, что я сделаю и сделал![11]

> I,
> the most golden of mouths,
> whose every word
> gives new birth to the soul
> and christens the body,
> I say to you:
> the tiniest speck of living life
> is more valuable than everything I will do or have done!

Not all readers have enthused over this range of exuberant personae; even before Boris Groys attacked the avant-garde for setting the stage for Socialist Realism,[12] some critics had noted in Mayakovsky's poetry a strand of sadism far more unsettling than the poet's masochistic revelations.[13] Mayakovsky was involved in revolutionary political activity in his youth, and he fuses the anarchic poetic energy of the earlier work with the idea of the Revolution after 1917. The outsized heroic status accorded him after the Revolution further complicated Mayakovsky's reputation. Soviet tastemakers favored Mayakovsky and criticized him when he wrote poems the workers could not understand. His agitationist pieces are complicated by their sarcasm, and he was not silent about the lingering philistinism he found in the post-Revolutionary world. Key texts include the plays *Mystery-Bouffe* (*Misteriia-Buff*, 1918), *The Bedbug* (*Klop*, mostly completed by 1928), and *The Bathhouse* (*Bania*, mostly completed by 1929).

One of his final works, "At the Top of My Voice" (*Vo ves' golos*, 1930), shows Mayakovsky echoing the *épatage* of the earliest Futurism as well as its unrelenting confidence in its ability to set its own artistic agenda. The long poem begins:

> Уважаемые
>   товарищи потомки!
> Роясь
>   в сегодняшнем
>   окаменевшем г...,
> наших дней изучая потемки,
> вы,
>   возможно,
>   спросите и обо мне.
> И, возможно, скажет
>   ваш ученый,
> кроя эрудицией
>   вопросов рой,

что жил-де такой

          певец кипяченой

и ярый враг воды сырой.

Профессор,

          снимите очки-велосипед!

Я сам расскажу

      о времени

             и о себе.[14]

Respected

      comrades of posterity!

When you start digging around

           in today's

              petrified sh . .

and studying the darkness of our days,

you,

   possibly,

      will come to ask about me, too.

And, possibly, your scholars

                 will declare,

as they cover their erudition

           with a swarm of questions,

once there lived a certain

          singer of boiled water,

and a raging enemy of water from the tap.

Professor,

         take off your bicycle goggles!

I myself will tell the tales

       about that time

            and about myself.

The denunciation of scholars, to whom curious future readers may desperately turn as they try to understand the murky reality of the past, is mostly Futurist swagger, but it also lets the poet declare himself a reliable expert witness for historians to come. Mikhail Vaiskopf shows how Mayakovsky builds his megalomaniac self-image out of Symbolist narcissism and hyperbolic panegyrics of the eighteenth century, "projecting the Baroque glorifications of God or King to his own person."[15] Ultimately, Mayakovsky's self-image absorbs Christian and demiurgic motifs, combining the challenge to God with God-like functions ascribed to the poetic self. These themes are fully present in his early work. Mayakovsky's poetry of the Soviet period, frequently perceived to be radically different from his early writings, perpetuates the same themes but links them with a "humbled and rapturous self-dissolution in the party or class as depicted in *Vladimir Ilich Lenin*."[16]

Mayakovsky's promise to tell his own story about his era suggests the epic side of his work (fully shown in his long poem about Lenin), but epic more precisely defined the work of Velimir Khlebnikov. Yuri Tynianov called him "our only epic poet of the twentieth century."[17] Khlebnikov's preferred label for the Futurists was a coinage based on Slavic word formation, *budetliane*, and neologisms were his specialty. By 1910 he had published a poem that created a virtuoso series of words based on the root meaning "laughter," "Incantation by Laughter" ("Zakliatie smekhom"). With Kruchenykh, he wrote the best-known Futurist manifesto, "The Word as Such" ("Slovo kak takovoe," 1913). The same year, the two poets also co-authored a less well-known manifesto, "The Letter as Such" ("Bukva kak takovaia," 1913), which called attention to the appearance of alphabetic signs. Khlebnikov's sound play seems like the key to what Viktor Grigor´ev called his idiosyncratic style (*idiostil´*), but "The Letter as Such" reminds us that the visual elements are also crucial: the poems' look on the page, the manuscripts filled with charts and drawings, and Khlebnikov's use of rich visual imagery, particularly of faces.[18] The face that is created by the *zaum* poem "Bobeobi" is one such vivid visual image.

Khlebnikov left a vast legacy still being decoded and interpreted by scholars; his "Tables of Fate" ("Doski sud´by," 1922) appeared in the form in which he had hoped to publish them only in 2000.[19] Khlebnikov's carelessness about his own publications was much mythologized; readers owe a great debt to those who brought his works to posthumous publication, beginning with Tynianov and Stepanov in the 1920s (editors of a five-volume set of collected works, 1928–33), continuing with Nikolai Khardzhiev and then Aleksandr Parnis and R. V. Duganov in the late Soviet period, and culminating in a full edition with commentary.[20]

Khlebnikov left an individual legacy dominated by historical and mythological impulses, which in turn defined his modes of self-expression. Many of his longer narratives unfold with high drama; yet they are often committed to the principles of word formation, neologism, and *zaum* even as they seek a universal cosmic language or the mathematical principles of cosmic unity. Figures from Russian history, from Sten´ka Razin ("Razin," 1920) to the Red Guard of "Night in the Trenches" ("Noch´ v okope," 1920), had as much place in his work as did the *kamennye baby* (in the poem "The Stone Women," 1919, but they also stand guard in the poem "Night in the Trenches") and the magnificent seer Zangezi in Khlebnikov's final super-saga (*Zangezi*, 1922).[21] More than any such obviously difficult poet, Khlebnikov has had a significant presence in other national literatures, thanks in part to the superb translations into English by Paul Schmidt.[22] We cite below his version of the 1912 lyric "Numbers," which draws together so many of Khlebnikov's themes:

Я всматриваюсь в вас, о, числа,
И вы мне видитесь одетыми в звери, в их шкурах,
Рукой опирающимися на вырванные дубы.
Вы даруете—единство между змееобразным движением
Хребта вселенной и пляской коромысла,
Вы позволяете понимать века, как быстрого хохота зубы.
Мои сейчас вещеобразно разверзлися зеницы:
Узнать, что будет Я, когда делимое его—единица.[23]

I see right through you, Numbers.
I see you dressed in animals, their skins,
coolly propped against uprooted oaks.
You offer us a gift: unity between the snaky movement
of the backbone of the universe and Libra dancing
overhead. You help us to see centuries as a flash
of laughing teeth. See my wisdom-wizened eyes
opening to recognize
what my I
will be
when its dividend is one.[24]

For all the energy that goes into word creation in his poetry, Khlebnikov was to display more confidence in numbers than in words, particularly in "Tables of Fate." But he felt no joy in having predicted the year of the Russian Revolution.[25] Whereas Mayakovsky's legacy was complicated by his collaboration with the Soviet cultural establishment, Khlebnikov, even when he wrote of the Revolution as public history, saw tragedy all around him.

Aleksei Kruchenykh is central in any account of Futurism because he forged extensive net-works with figures across the arts, providing leadership on issues of principle, public stance, and publication. Having by far outlived many of his contemporaries in the avant-garde, Kruchenykh had the last word in shaping their legacy. But even early on, Kruchenykh had the idea of writing a book about Futurism.[26] He may have been regarded by his contemporaries as something of a wild man, but he was also "a systematic archivist and bibliographer."[27] Kruchenykh's own writings, aside from the many co-authored public statements and later memoir accounts, show him as a radical thinker determined to explode the logic of verbal utterance. He admired as poetic the sounds suggested by an itemized laundry bill.[28] His *zaum* poems appeared in 1913, the most famous of which begins with the stunning nonsensical syl-lables "Dyr bul shchyl," preceded by the poet's announcement that these poems' words are in a language of his own making (*na sobstvennom iazyke*) and that the "words have no definitive meaning."[29] Writing a poem entirely of unknown words was a way of acting out the Futurists' radical break with tradition, yet readers have consistently found referential meanings and aesthetic pleasure in the text (with some exceptions—Briusov found the lines flat), including the philosopher Pavel Florensky, who found something "foresty, brown, gnarled, disheveled" here.[30] Kruchenykh remained remarkably true to his radical aesthetics. In 1922, he produced some of his most programmatic writings, including "The Texture of the Word" ("Faktura slova") and "The Shiftology of Russian Verse" ("Sdvigologiia russkogo stikha").

Two further poets more loosely associated with Futurism should be mentioned. The first is Igor Severianin (1887–1941), whose reputation is ripe for fresh study.[31] He began as an heir to the Romantic poetic traditions, and wrote verse that could be skillful if sentimental; in the 1910s, however, his poems took on a satiric edge and welcomed a brash vulgarity. He was a consummate performer of his poetry, half singing or chanting what he called a *poeza*: he beat out Mayakovsky as King of the Poets in 1918 and Tsvetaeva admired his Paris reading in 1932. His first great success had come with the volume *Goblet Seething with Thunders* (*Gromokipiashchii kubok*, 1913), one of the bestselling books of its time, and Severianin's reading/performance tours were overwhelmingly popular—so much so that some looked on his achievements with suspicion. The word "phony" appears in Vladimir Markov's account of Severianin's success, where he aptly captures the atmosphere of the performances:

> [Severianin] poured champagne into a lily, and in his verses, his heroines yielded on rugs made of lilies of the valley...[A]ll this was silly and often cheap and easy to parody, but it was also garishly colorful and full of contrasts, and, like a good tenor, Severyanin was capable of producing a high C on demand and without much strain.

Markov is also quick to note Severianin's innovations in rhyme and his neologisms, especially when combined with the use of foreign words.[32] The quality of the verse has been overshadowed by Severianin's grand self-fashioning: his name was a pseudonym, and the poet who some-times signed himself "Igor-Severianin," as if making of his first and last names a bulwark against the world, also wrote multiple autobiographies, some in third-person, some as conver-sations between Igor Lotarev (the name he was born with) and Igor Severianin.[33] The conver-sations include one written late in his life, when he was living in Estonia, forgotten or disparaged.

Severianin's was an unusual trajectory for an avant-garde poet: it was not uncommon for Soviet official cultural to denigrate the work of such experimental or outré poets, but Severianin seemed questionable even to those who once thought him worthy of notice. One senses a nervous patrolling of the borders around poetry when critics write about Severianin, with zealous guards insisting on certain standards that Russian poetry is obliged to maintain. In the nineteenth century, Benediktov and Nadson had come in for this kind of scrutiny; later in the twentieth century, Dmitry Aleksandrovich Prigov rose to the implicit challenge of such critics with an unrivaled performance of graphomania.

Another poet who has obvious affinities with the early avant-garde but who most dramatically outgrew its categories was Boris Pasternak. Depending on how one regards his poetics and his politics, he fits either just barely into multiple categories of twentieth-century literature—Futurism (specifically the Centrifuge group), avant-garde, early Soviet (with some affinities to LEF), mature Soviet, *tamizdat*—or not at all (and is in fact treated in our *History* as a misfit). Pasternak's early work stands as an extraordinary creative outburst in both prose and poetry, as if the young man who had considered philosophy and music as serious pursuits, and now turned to literature, could only work restlessly in multiple forms. The density of figuration in the early work conveys a singular absorption in a world of emotional intensity. In the narrative prose of *The Childhood of Luvers* (*Detstvo Liuvers*, 1918, published 1922), Pasternak gave a sequential account of what was experienced as simultaneity, but in the early poetry he used dense metaphor, sound play, and synesthesia to suggest that temporality was bested by intimate apprehension of other people and the natural world. Osip Mandelstam would say of his poetry that it cleared the air passageways of the body, renewing the lungs.[34] The salutary properties of the verse seemed to take form because of the poet's unfailing wonder at the external world and at words themselves.

CASE STUDY Elena Guro

Elena Guro (1877–1913), frequently mentioned as Russian Futurism's only woman,[35] created lovely visual and verbal works of delicate imagination, at times mournful but also suffused with joy. She had been long eclipsed from view in the USSR, with posthumous publications appearing in the West, until her rediscovery in post-Soviet Russia. Still, she may now seem a minor modernist, and an inscrutable one at that. The image of her face drawn in 1910 by Vladimir Burliuk (1886–1917) suggests a certain mystery, as if the one eye turned toward the viewer emblematized the inadequacy of all eyes trained back on Guro (see Figure v.03).

FIGURE v.03. Vladimir Burliuk, Portrait of Elena Guro, 1910.

Despite important publications from her archive, Guro's work remains mysterious and less fully contextualized than that of most other Russian modernists. Some of the mystification was of her doing, making her one of the most successful practitioners of *zhiznetvorchestvo*—albeit one who would likely have rejected the label. But its appropriateness should also press us to see her affinities with Symbolism, and we have an approving review by Viacheslav Ivanov to suggest further connections to the ethos of Symbolism. Her longing for another world evidences a further trait of Symbolism, but Futurism remains a valuable context even if the tone of her writing is far from its aggressiveness: Guro's fascination with the world of the child, her use of fragmentary language and plot structures, and her representations of the city are typical Futurist features.

She left a small body of work, much of it unpublished at her death. Her collaborations, some with her husband Mikhail Matiushin, a composer, artist, and publisher, were numerous, and she contributed to important modernist publications, including *A Trap for Judges* (in the volumes of both 1910 and 1913). Guro wrote poetry, narrative prose, drama, and diary notation, and her work is especially rife with texts that cross the boundaries between prose and poetry. Her artistic legacy includes many drawings, gouaches, paintings, and illustrations; an exhibition of her work in 1994 in St. Petersburg featured some 300 items.[36] She trained as an artist, and incorporated visual imagery into her verbal texts. The challenges to understanding her work include defining the productive intersections between sight and sound, the lettering and the line in books that she designed carefully. Archival holdings of her notebooks show the same juxtapostion, at times confounding, of text and image.

Guro's years of publishing her own work were compressed into the period from 1905 to 1913. In those eight years, she produced illustrations for a volume of George Sand's *Contes d'une grand-mère* in Russian translation (*Babushkiny skazki*, 1905); illustrated other authors' books and two books of her own poetry, drama, and prose, *The Hurdy Gurdy* (*Sharmanka*, 1909) and *Autumn Dream* (*Osennii son*, 1912), and she contributed to various collective projects. Guro's first publication in prose was a story entitled "Early Spring" ("Ranniaia vesna," 1905). The prose brims over with energetic perceptions about a vividly colorful natural scene, one so marked by the season's changes that the narrating child-like voice barely contains her excitement and deep impressions. She is thrilled to have escaped the city for a wide-open expanse, and her desire to sink into the pleasures of the sensory impressions produced by the scene is nearly overwhelming:

> One feels the urge to rush off somewhere, to run, to leap up, and with the vigor of the needle-strewn earth, just losing its winter's thaw, one brims with the desire to do something great, to be great. How interesting to think that the future's greats may have started out precisely this way, destined to create great things, and that my sister and I, without a doubt, are meant to be just those people.[37]

What is striking about this passage is the speaker's assertion that the deep connection to the natural world, enabled by this moment of springtime arrival in the village, itself promises great achievements in an unspecified future. Within a few paragraphs, on arrival at the dacha, she reflects: "we did not yet know then that for grownups it was all much more prosaic and everyday, they felt nothing of what the children experienced."[38] Guro has chosen the point of view of a child as the privileged vantage point, as if to get as far from the pious exegete of Symbolism as she could.

Equally important in Guro's creative universe is her pantheistic sense of joy about the flora and fauna of the natural world. "Early Spring" emanates pleasure possessed of a kind of visual energy that makes the prose sketch feel like an impressionist painting. Guro's

own artwork often has the vivid coloristic moods or expressive pencil lines of the impres-
sionists, and many of her texts qualify as poems in prose because they are so fully given
over to this kind of painting with words. In a four-line sketch entitled "Winter" ("Zima,"
undated), all but the final line are devoted entirely to visual imagery: consider only the
first, which reads, "Icicles hung from the rooftops like iced-over curls of a horse's mane."[39]
Guro's descriptions are an education in forms of attention to the natural world.[40]

This absorption in the world of nature is balanced by her attention to the urban
environment. Although impressionist in tone and spirit, and "refracted through her highly
subjective personal vision," Guro's city is "conveyed in cinematic flashes that depict the
city's color, mood, rhythm, sounds and atmosphere."[41] The city is St. Petersburg, and the
key texts are *The Hurdy-Gurdy* and the poem "The City" ("Gorod," 1910). Baudelaire and
the Symbolists had made the city an appealing subject for literary representation, and the
Futurists embraced the clash and clangor of the city's noisy sights. Guro was especially
drawn to the urban world's capacity to offer constant new objects of attention, both seen
and heard. The city was staged in her writings, seen through windows that acted as frames.
The motif of the window appears often in her writings, and shows up in some of her
artwork as well, including the striking figure of a woman depicted in bright blocks of
color, sometimes referred to as the Scandinavian Princess (see Plate 17).

Guro's posthumously published work includes *Baby Camels in the Sky* (*Nebesnye verbliuzhata*, 1914), which mixes prose and poetry as well as titled and untitled works to create a
free-flowing set of texts with intertwining themes. There are occasional neologisms, some
of them beloved by the Futurists, and a splendid mix of fantasy and a kind of journalistic
reportage. The first text, "A Newspaper Ad" ("Gazetnoe ob"iavlenie"), reports the sky-
borne baby camels that give the book its title. The newspaper seems to announce the best
means of gathering camel fluff, and reassures the readers that no camels need be harmed
in the process. Subsequent publications include the unfinished text *There Lived a Poor
Knight* (*Zhil na svete rytsar' bednyi*), critical sketches, and other prose from the archive.[42]
Guro's criticism is particularly interesting for its attention to the visual arts, where she
sought the same "intuitive, emotional, immediate experience of reality" as she did in her
writings in prose or poetry.[43]

Guro's reputation has a further complicating factor, however, one which makes it hard
to understand why she has not been taken up by feminist theorists with the same zeal that
has reset scholarly agendas in studying figures like Tsvetaeva and Gippius. One of the
books Guro published in her lifetime, a slim book, with her own delicate wispy illustrations and rippled pages, *Autumn Dream*, is dedicated to the memory of her one and only
son, V. V. Notenberg. The authorial inscription on the flyleaf of the volume gives a dual
name, Elena Guro and Eleonora von Notenberg. The mystification was sufficiently successful that one can still find online biographical accounts of Guro that offer "Eleonora
von Notenberg" as her given name, as if Guro were a pseudonym (it is not). The astute
Vladimir Markov, who wrote one of the first serious appreciations of her work, also
accepted the false name and registered the poet's grief for her dead son as profound, and
the son as so deeply loved that Guro imagined him still alive long into the future.[44] There
was no son, as there was no original Germanic name masked by the pseudonym Guro.
But the real question is why the fantasy of a son who died was proffered in the first place.
The invented son is himself a remarkable double for the poet: thin, delicate, feminine, a
lover of *Don Quixote*, and a man of many names. Wilhelm, Willy, Prince Guillaume, as he
is called in the play "Autumn Dream" (which makes up most of the book), he is a young
man who refuses military service and at one point expresses the overwhelming sense of

love that emanates from Guro's own writings: "I always love. Do you have any idea what love can be? Let me tell you. It can be everywhere and in no one image. It is the autumn sun. It has the right to forgive everything."[45]

We can, however, begin to offer at least one provisional answer as to why Guro created the myth of a dead son. Presenting herself as a grieving mother in the format of *Autumn Dream* performed the same kind of blocking maneuver that Gippius engineered by styling herself either as a man (signing her work at times as Anton Krainy or writing lyric poems in the masculine) or as a person of indeterminate gender. (One has to think that the rumor that Gippius was a hermaphrodite might have been her own doing, on such a reading.) In both cases, women writers like Guro and Gippius were casting themselves in roles very far from the figure of woman-as-muse, so fetishized by the male Symbolist poets. Their reinventions of poetic personae have provided potential alternative models for subsequent poets of all genders and sexual identities.

Avant-gardists of the 1920s

The avant-garde underwent significant transformations in the 1920s. To many, 1922, the year of Khlebnikov's death, seemed the endpoint of Futurism (and it was the final year that the last Futurist group, Centrifuge, existed). Although hostility toward all forms of creative rebellion and aesthetic experimentation was to solidify in the 1930s, avant-garde innovations survived in clusters of individuals and in efforts by some who worked in quiet isolation to be rediscovered much later.

Several groups bear mentioning. Continuing the Futurists' emphasis on the word as such, and in a way deeply resonant with the Formalist theory of *ostranenie*, the Imaginists—Anatoly Mariengof (1897–1962), Sergei Esenin, Vadim Shershenevich (1893–1942) among others—used shocking oxymorons and dissonant metaphors as tools for breaking through automatized perception. The Imaginists and their followers in the Nichevoki (from the Russian word *nichego*— "nothing") associated the principle of estrangement with the shock effects they produced in their texts and in public antics (which frequently got them arrested). They replaced street names with their own names and conducted trials of contemporary poetry in a comical and offensive manner. For good reason, some scholars call Nichevoki the Russian Dadaists and predecessors of OBERIU. Their ironic, self-deprecatory performances exposed nothingness as a negative remainder of individuality and individual perception, and exposed as well the "internal meaning of things and events (meaning is nothing…)."[46] Akin to them were Fuists (from the French for "crazy," *fou*), whose poetry, in Igor Vasil'ev's words, "displayed elements similar to Surrealism…their fragmented language and confused articulation appeared as a pre-programmed method of reaching for new horizons of the poetic utterance."[47] The group of poets calling themselves the Expressionists focused on what they defined as "transcendental naturalism":[48] following the lineage of Mayakovsky's early poetry, they created exalted hyperbolic images as micro-myths designed to be the "essence" of present-day apocalypses. A group of Emotionalists (Emotsionalisty, the most prominent among whom was Mikhail Kuzmin, previously close to the Acmeists) saw the meaning of art in the "production of unique, unrepeatable emotional acts by means of unique, unrepeatable emotional perception."[49] They rejected all forms of universality and collectivity, including "types, canons, laws of psychology, history and even nature," for the sake of the phenomenal and exceptional. Both the Expressionists and Emotionalists gravitated towards Neo-Romanticism with its emphasis on individual perception and its interest in the transcendental concealed in everyday life and masked with irony.

The Imaginists, Nichevoki, Fuists, Expressionists, and Emotionists all placed autonomous, subjective, and individualistic languages above the collectivist, universal, and "objectivist." Their understanding of art directly confronted RAPP and LEF theories as manifestations of debilitating utilitarian and collectivist approaches to literature. By means of this insistence on subjective experience as enduringly valuable, avant-garde artists of all orientations made their most radical contribution to modernist culture, and it is a legacy that their late post-modernist successors paradoxically picked up on, even as debates about the plausibility and sustainability of theories of the subject raged. Most radical were the members of OBERIU in claiming to be the direct heirs of Futurism.

OBERIU

An innovative and rule-resistant group of writers in Leningrad in the 1920s and 1930s, who called themselves Chinari, released a manifesto in 1928 that created the Union of Real Art (the acronym OBERIU is based on the Russian name, Ob″edinenie real′nogo iskusstva) and the name OBERIU prevailed. The acronym is slippery: the meaning of "real art" was a constant topic of OBERIU conversation, textual exploration, and performance art. The manifesto sought a new poetic language; a new relationship to life and its objects; and a means to strip both things and the words that named them of the thick protective shells that obscured their essence. The metaphor may remind one of Potebnya's understanding of the word as a nucleus with an outer shell (a meaning encased in its usages); but for the writers and thinkers of OBERIU, philology and semantics were at best a springboard to a dramatic or even absurd performance. The manifesto declared words to be objects in their own right—at one point, it famously advocated forging words of such durable substance that they could shatter windows. But their texts defied the rules of cause and effect, which in turn makes the manifesto function less as a set of rules than as an admirable performance. As one text had it, speaking of tooth extraction: "here comes the word *suddenly*, and then comes the event, filled with foreign content."[50]

The best-known writers of OBERIU are Aleksandr Vvedensky and Daniil Kharms. Nikolai Oleinikov (1898–1937), Igor Bakhterev (1908–96), Yakov Druskin, and Leonid Lipavsky (1904–41) were key presences as well. Although the poetry of Nikolai Zabolotsky would later depart considerably from OBERIU principles, he was an author of the 1928 manifesto and a crucial figure within the group. Also named in the manifesto was Konstantin Vaginov (1889–1934). Among all these writers, Vvedensky, Kharms, Zabolotsky, and Vaginov would exert the strongest influence on later unofficial Russian literature (and on avant-garde writing in English as well), beginning with *samizdat* publications in the 1970s. Substantial, well-edited collections of their writings have appeared in the post-Soviet period, as have many superb translations, particularly of Kharms and Vvedensky.

OBERIU artistic practice investigated the relationships among time, space, and objects. It produced writing as a kind of performance art, and the poets of OBERIU were indeed performers, as exemplified by the 1928 show "Three Left Hours" ("Tri levykh chasa") as well as by Kharms's and Oleinikov's numerous pranks. The silly behavior hid an underlying seriousness of purpose and an anti-authoritarian stance. The philosophical underpinnings of OBERIU ran deep. Readers were meant to experience writing as an event that makes reality happen, rather than as a record of some external reality. For Kharms, writing was the main event.[51] OBERIU texts feature dramatic formal and stylistic shifts; a love of humor and the absurd; linguistic experiment that cleaved apart sounds from semantics; and affinities with children's literature. This last element, the valorization of the child's viewpoint, could deflate all the others, and it is the source of both the charm and sometimes the deepening horror of their writings: by taking a naive or foolish position in observing the world, or by fashioning speech acts out of simplified verbal expressions, the poems, prose, plays, and essays of OBERIU challenge rational responses and throw audiences off balance time and again.

Several OBERIU writers composed texts for children. This orientation toward the child was deeply congenial to their poetics, and also a way to earn a living. Oleinikov, for instance, worked as an editor in the children's department of Leningrad's state publishing house (Gosizdat), and he was a frequent contributor to the *Ezhemesiachnyi zhurnal* or *EZh*, *The Hedgehog*. Vvedensky also worked at Gosizdat, and he published several children's books elsewhere. Kharms, although he claimed to detest children, contributed to several books for young readers, including *The Game* (*Igra*, 1930). His poem "Ivan Ivanych Samovar" (1928) is still one of his best known. The verbal horseplay of writing for children defines much of OBERIU's work.

The foolishness has strong philosophical underpinnings. The purpose of art, as poet, scholar, and translator Eugene Ostashevsky has noted, is an "active non-understanding of reality" or, as Vvedensky called it in "The Gray Notebook" ("Seraia tetrad'"), "wild non-understanding."[52] Wild non-understanding also meant resistance—resistance to rigid forms of social thinking and to narrow notions of how best to live in the world. As Vvedensky commanded in one poem, the way to make everything clear was to live backwards.[53] The notion of autonomous personhood is singularly disrupted in OBERIU texts, a good example of which is Kharms's short "Blue Notebook No. 10" ("Golubaia tetrad' No. 10"), with its red-haired man all of whose physical attributes are checked off as absent, so that by the end of the text it's not clear who could even be the subject of the sentences. Often, a literary character in an OBERIU poem or narrative has a descriptive designation, but actions are improbably predicated on nouns with no concern for logic (a knight swims like a cod in Vvedensky's "Elegy" ["Elegiia," 1940]; Oleinikov writes of "Zeroes" that are crippled, yet curative; Lipavsky begins "Water Tractatus" ["Traktat o vode"] with the assertion that "when in a restaurant, you involuntarily think of space.")[54] The narrative does not depend on the character, and the character may be a number or an abstract concept, rather than a proper noun suggesting distinct identity. In Vvedensky's "Fact, Theory, and God" ("Fakt, teoriia, i Bog," 1930), the three-noun title names the characters in the text, rather than the themes; in other poems, the hours of the day or a clock have speaking parts. The lyric subject does not occupy a privileged, authoritative position, and poems often feature polyphony as well as a cacophony of sounds and stylistic registers. Vvedensky's work, in particular, exploits the devices of drama, such as soliloquy and dialogue.

OBERIU texts can exaggerate a feature of poetic language, the weakening of the referential capacity of words. A poem or mini-story can use the hints found in the semantic properties of the words as obstacles rather than as useful interpretive pathways. Kharms's prose text "Thing" ("Veshch'"), for example, gives no meaningful clue in its title, especially as the text consists entirely of conversations among persons, not descriptions of objects: a series of knocks at the door does not lead, as one expects, to the arrival of a guest through the door but, instead, announces an unidentified monk who flies up through the floorboards. Many OBERIU texts are built as a series of misadventures or mistakes, and the characters are frequently oblivious to the incongruity. The power of error extends to the use of language itself, where phonetic misspellings and messed-up morphologies create language games with constantly changing rules. The logic of verbal disruption is well named in a line from Zabolotsky's "Battle of Elephants" ("Bitva slonov," 1931): "The general ruckus in the tower of Syntax" ("V bashne Sintaksis—razboi").[55] A new reality emerges, based on absurd principles—a reality that liberates experience from mundane existence, revealing its hidden horror. OBERIU texts create a purely metaphysical language that is situated outside common rationality, and that can have theological implications. The atomization of life is also realized in the texts' many acts of

FIGURE V.04. Daniil Kharms (1905–42), Russia, early 1930s.

physical violence and implausible conversations, where humans seem able to connect only by bumping into one another or through chatter that leads nowhere.

Despite their silly jokes and illogical sequences, OBERIU writings have often been read as historically astute commentaries on early Soviet life. Their absurdity has struck readers as a weirdly accurate reflection of an illogical social world. Their tales of frequent disappearances and acts of physical violence seem terribly like the omnipresent violence of the encroaching Terror; hunger is prevalent like a terrible background noise to many tales; and the undercurrent of destabilized identity and opportunities for violence in Russia in the 1920s and 1930s are there as well. Such readings work best for the writings of Daniil Kharms (Daniil Iuvachev's best-known pen-name), where social realities find many forms of skewed reflection (see Figure V.04 for a typical image of Kharms calmly smoking a pipe and yet looking vaguely alarmed).

Consider as an example this untitled text by Kharms from 1936–37:

One man fell asleep a believer but woke up an atheist.

Luckily, this man kept medical scales in his room, because he was in the habit of weighing himself every morning and every evening. And so, going to sleep the night before, he had weighed himself and had found he weighed four poods and 21 pounds. But the following morning, waking up an atheist, he weighed himself again and found that now he weighed only four poods and thirteen pounds. "Therefore," he concluded, "my faith weighed approximately eight pounds."[56]

As is often the case in Kharms, some details follow logically—this man has a scale in his room because he is in the habit of weighing himself, and in other tales we read of those who go out because they are hungry or drop in on an acquaintance to repay a debt. But any notion of cause and effect occurs in an estranging context; here, the scale for daily weighing is used to measure faith. OBERIU texts often resort to numbers as deluded forms of counting (compare Kharms's "Sonnet," where the sequence of numbers is in doubt) and as incongruous measurements. Here the mix of poods and pounds, so brilliantly euphonious in the English translation, makes the weights a kind of macaronic language (they are "pud" and "funt" in Russian, compactly similar words linked by assonance). But the real resistance to logic hides in the first sentence of the narrative, before any weighing can happen. The man draws an inference, certain that the weight reduction is an effect of the narrative premise: that a former believer woke up as an atheist. Kharms is estranging us from spiritual processes by the very idea that belief can become faithlessness overnight, even as he gently parodies what was in fact an omnipresent expectation of early Soviet daily life—the requirement that the faithful convert to atheism. Philosophical curiosity about the material nature of immaterial abstractions is also well exemplified in this story. Where else would someone get the idea of a scale that could pick up the presence or absence of religious belief? Kharms is mixing metaphysics with mathematics in a vignette made of nothing more than sleeping, waking, and stepping onto a scale.

OBERIU writers perished during the Terror (Kharms, Vvedensky, Oleinikov), died at the front (Lipavsky), or survived arrest (Bakhterev) and the labor camps (Zabolotsky). Vaginov died of tuberculosis in 1934. Druskin miraculously survived these dangerous years and thus preserved a suitcase full of writings, mostly by Kharms, with some, although considerably fewer, by Vvedensky (much of Vvedensky's work is presumed lost). OBERIU texts began to circulate in Leningrad and Moscow circles in the 1960s and to appear in the West in the 1970s, owing to archival work by a small group of dedicated scholars, including Mikhail Meilakh and Anatoly Aleksandrov. Authoritative editions are appearing in Russia, and the writers of OBERIU have attracted a new generation of readers. Scholarship on their work has deepened and expanded in scope, extending to comparisons to other movements in modernist aesthetics as well as to investigations of the philosophical, theological, and aesthetic implications of their work.[57]

Neo-avant-garde

In the post-OBERIU period, it seemed that there could be no room left for avant-garde literature under the monopoly of Socialist Realism, and yet important continuities between the first generations of the avant-garde and their successors persisted.[58] Some members of the earlier wave survived, and were known in Leningrad or elsewhere, like Kruchenykh and Bakhterev; Vasilisk Gnedov (pseud. Vasily Gnedov 1890–1978) was living in Kherson, where the poet Sergei Sigei (1947–2014) met him.

An unusual transitional figure in the history of avant-garde writing is Nikolai Glazkov (1919–79), a man of multiple trades (he appears as an actor in the hot-air balloon sequence at the start of Andrei Tarkovsky's film *Andrei Rublev*, 1966). In an ironic twist on the word-creating impulses of the Futurists, Glazkov coined one of the most famous neologisms of the twentieth century, *samizdat*, when he jokingly made up fake points of publication for the books and pamphlets he assembled over his decades of writing; Samizdat was one of his feigned publishing houses. Glazkov's personae of joker, rhymester, translator, and prodigious consumer of alcohol place him squarely within the traditions of writers at the perimeter of the permissible, from OBERIU to Venedikt Erofeev.[59] His writings could foreground that insistence as well, for instance in his pithy description of the poet as eternally enslaved by his freedom (*vechnyi rab svoei svobody*). Glazkov indulged in the simplest play with words and sounds in the poetry, pressing consistently toward what he regarded as fundamental truths. As he wrote, in an undated poem:

> Не все, что сложное—
> Ложное;
> Не все простое—
> Пустое![60]

> Not everything that's complicated
> Is false.

> Not everything that's simple
> Is hollow.

Another linking figure is Vladimir Kazakov (1938–88), whose life was changed when he met Aleksei Kruchenykh in 1966. He had written poems and plays throughout his life spent at the margins of Soviet society (including a stint working as a logger in Siberia), but on Kruchenykh's advice he started writing prose.[61] His novel *The Living Make a Mistake* (*Oshibka zhivykh*, 1976) took its title from Khlebnikov's play *Death Makes a Mistake* (*Oshibka smerti*, published 1917), but its absurd plot, animation of objects, and paratactic structure recall the writings of OBERIU.

Two of Kazakov's Munich publications contain introductions by another remarkable figure working within the avant-garde by the 1970s, Elizaveta Mnatsakanova. Designer and creator of her own books, Mnatsakanova has carried forward the Futurist tradition of book-making into an age when access to copying technology allowed for complete control of the look and format of her books. Her independence makes for a more autonomous form of creative work than the collective efforts of the earlier avant-garde. Mnatsakanova's poetic orientation is not toward the fanciful neologisms of *zaum*, although her melodic, haunting lines of morphological reinvention build on the lessons of earlier word creators, and she has written compellingly about Khlebnikov.[62] Mnatsakanova's best known text is her Requiem: "Autumn in the

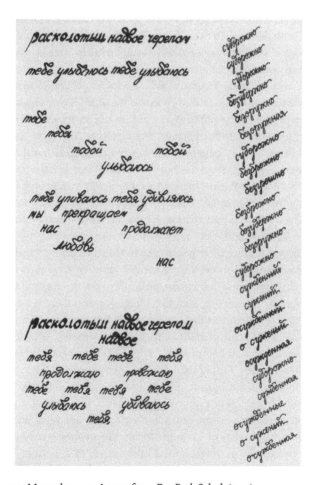

FIGURE V.05. Elizaveta Mnatsakanova, A page from *Das Buch Sabeth* (1979).

Infirmary of the Innocent Sisters: A Seven-Part Requiem" ("Osen′ v lazarete nevinnykh sester. Rekviem v semi chastiakh"), at once a searing critique of substandard, cruel medical care in the Soviet Union and a musical tour de force, using a Requiem Mass structure to recreate the sufferings of modern-day, all too human bodies.[63] Her most beautifully illustrated handmade book is one to which she gave a German title (Mnatsakanova emigrated to Vienna in 1972), *Das Buch Sabeth*, which includes pages of carefully arranged calligraphy (see Figure v.05).

Such ornate handwriting reminds readers of the personal work of bookmaking, as do the poet's photographs of her own hand that also appear in some books. The repetition of words on this page from *Das Buch Sabeth* is typical of her poetry, in which sound plays as significant a structuring role as the visual arrangement of words on the page.

The visual poetry practiced by Mnatsakanova can also be found in the work of Ry Nikonova (pseud. Anna Tarshis, 1942–2014) and Sergei Sigei. The two poets originated from the so-called Uktus School—a circle of nonconformists (including the artists Evgeny Arbenev, Valery D′iachenko, Aleksandr Galomaga, and Feliks Volosenkov) active in Sverdlovsk in 1965 to 1974; they published the *samizdat* magazine *Nomer (Number)*.[64] After Sverdlovsk, Nikonova and Sigei, who were married in 1967, moved to the town of Eisk in the Krasnodar region where they put out the *samizdat* journal *Transponans* (1979–87). They emigrated to Germany in 1998, and continued experimenting with both sight and sound; several of their books were published in elegant editions by the Madrid publisher Editiones del hebreo errante. Nikonova's texts alternated simply typed neo-primitivist small texts with airy word and line drawings or careful grids, for example in the excellent collection assembled in 2001, with the one-letter title that in English would be pronounced *You (Iu)*.[65] Their publishing and creative work was honored with an Andrei Bely Prize in 1998. They affirmed a strong link back to the avant-garde efforts of the earlier modernists: Sigei, who was also active as a critic, prepared the work of the ego-futurist Vasilisk Gnedov for publication in 1992 (Gnedov's most famous creation was the blank page entitled "Poem of the End" ["Poema kontsa"], 1913).[66]

The best-known representative of the avant-garde in late Soviet and early post-Soviet literature, measured by his fame outside of Russia, was Gennady Aygi (1934–2006), winner of the 1987 Andrei Bely Prize. Widely published in French and English translation, Aygi himself translated extensively, especially from the French—not into Russian, the language in which he wrote his poetry, but into his native language, Chuvash. His own poetry showed the lessons he learned from the French surrealists and from Paul Celan, whom he also translated; and his work brought a new freedom in punctuation, syntax, and diction into Russian poetry. Meeting Boris Pasternak in Moscow in the late 1950s was a turning point for Aygi's work, and it was Pasternak who advised him to write poetry not in Chuvash but in Russian. The sustained attention to the natural world shows a thematic link between Aygi and Pasternak, but similarities mostly end there. Aygi's minimalist diction evokes the natural world in a fiercely stripped-down linguistic framework, and, like Mnatsakanova, there is a tough and idiosyncratic poetic principle that animates the work, a nearly Romantic reverence for the word and its sublime potential, and a sense of spiritual protest as the impulse even for poems on topics as seemingly benign as snow or hills or love.[67] Olga Sedakova wrote of his poetry as seeking to meet the public's hunger "for elevated, serious, perspicacious, 'mysterious' poetry."[68] A sense of mystery inhered in the disarmingly simple and severely limited lexicon of the poems, and Aygi intensified it by means of expressive and dynamic spacing on the page (some poems use horizontally centered lines, some not; some are spaced out vertically, some more compressed) and especially by means of his punctuation. The hyphen is used often to link nouns as if creating a conceptual or metaphorical compound, in a gesture that feels akin to Khlebnikov's neologisms. Aygi also relies on webs of parentheses that create complex nests of subordination and on colons that do precisely the opposite: they put words or phrases into adjacency but as if on equal footing. The colon appears often in poem titles (for example, "And: Schubert" ["I: Shubert," 1981]), or "And: The One-Ravine" ["I: Edino-Ovrag," 1984].[69]

A few poems use equal signs or other non-alphabetical means of communication, and Aygi can masterfully use white space between minimalist poetic lines, as in this poem from 1987:

Снова: воздух в вершинах—берез

светлее:

:

свобода

:

(давно)[70]

Again: air in the summits—of birch trees

more light:

:

freedom

:

(long ago)

There is a Zen-like quality to the space for contemplation that Aygi opens up for the reader of such a poem; its birch trees make it perceptibly Russian in orientation, and its longing for a freedom that existed long ago makes it far more than a poem of nature.

Less well known in the West but also a distinctive and long-lived heir of the avant-garde is Viktor Sosnora (b. 1936). It was entirely apt that Andrei Ar′ev entitled a large review essay about Sosnora "No One's Contemporary."[71] Futurist influence can be felt in Sosnora's work; he picks up an archaic strain in Khlebnikov's poetry, for instance, in his texts based on the *Igor Tale* and *byliny*, but in his own strongly idiosyncratic sound orchestration.[72] His link to the Futurists was made visible when Nikolai Aseev wrote the introduction to his first volume of poems, *January Rainstorm* (*Ianvarskii liven′*, 1962); Aseev was also probably responsible for getting Sosnora quickly into the Writer's Union. Sosnora kept alive the early avant-garde's advocacy for the poetic book: when his work was collected in 2001, he wrote a short preface that insisted that the way to read him was not as the creator of individual poems but as the creator of books, and so the collected volume is called *Nine Books* (*Deviat′ knig*).[73] Many of Sosnora's most impressive poems are long, epic narratives. There is a display of virtuosity, for example, in a poem from the late 1970s, "The Ballad of Edgar Allen Poe" ("Ballada Edgara Po"), in which the poet is visited by Poe—beloved of the Russian Symbolists—and his arrival brings hints of both Blok and Bal′mont (translator of Poe's "Raven"). And it is no accident that Sosnora would associate himself with the *poètes maudits*, Poe among them.[74] The "Ballad" gives a vivid sense of Sosnora's pungent wit, edgy sarcasm, and sheer verbal power, with the Raven's "nevermore" played with in multiple ways: cited in English, turned into an aggressive and antithetical "always" (*vsegda*), radically enjambed in one stanza's end as "Nev- / ermore!" (*Nikog- / da!*).[75]

Born in the same prewar generation as Sosnora, Andrei Voznesensky was still more renowned. In performance with Evgeny Yevtushenko and Bella Akhmadulina, he could fill stadiums. All three poets flirted with ideologically risky topics (the mass murder of Jews in Yevtushenko's "Babi Yar" [1961] being the best-known instance). Voznesensky's "Anti-Worlds" ("Anti-miry," 1964) was transformed into a drama performed at the Taganka Theater, a place where some experimentation, as well as material with political themes, was common. What sounded, if not experimental, then at least fresh in Voznesensky's early poetry was the replacement of conventional rhyme, that mainstay of Russian poetry, with sound patterning, assonance, internal rhyme, and rhythmic patterning. His "Goya" (1959) offered a daringly intense version of that sound play, particularly with the "g" sound of Goya's name, to write about the anguish and violence of war. It was one of the poems performed to great acclaim during his tours abroad. That he was permitted to travel, indeed that he was sent on what were at least in part hopeful propaganda missions, made Voznesensky seem compromised in the eyes of some, and to be sure his could be a publicistic voice. But it could also be argued that he was merely following a tradition set forth by Mayakovsky. His own chosen mentor was Pasternak, who had of course his own complex relationship to the state, although in a more fraught era. In his skill as a performer, Voznesensky also carried forward a valuable element of the avant-garde, where performances were a central part of the culture. Among later poets, Mnatsakanova might be emphasized as a powerful, rhythmic reader of her own work, and one for whom performance has existed as significantly on the page, where she relies on calligraphy and illustration.[76]

Another, and very different, poet-performer was the man known simply as Khvost, Aleksei Khvostenko (1940–2004). He lived in Leningrad, then Moscow, finally in Europe; he was a central, beloved figure in unofficial poetry, art, and music circles until his emigration to Paris in 1977. There, he continued his creative work in a thriving mixed-media artistic culture. Khvostenko embodied a style of life and art more or less uniformly penetrated by performance and pleasure; his work across all media was astonishingly joyful even when its rhetorical force was skeptical of all values, especially bourgeois values. As his friend Vadim Alekseev said of him, "Khvost poisoned us with the sweet potion of bohemian life, he became our narcotic, our medium."[77] For Alekseev, Khvostenko was the first Russian hippie, and tales abound about his failures at multiple jobs, his drinking, and the parties he enlivened. It is hard to imagine that any text Khvostenko authored could be as colorful as the story of his being fired from a job at the zoo for eating a turtle.[78] But Khvostenko did join some traditional literary enterprises, co-editing the journal *Echo* with Vladimir Maramzin, and publishing a number of volumes of poetry, including *The Fables of A. V. Kh.* (*Basni A. V. Kh.*, Paris, 1984, co-authored with Anri Volokhonsky [1936–2017]) and *The Suspector* (*Podozritel': 2-oi sbornik Verpy*, Paris, 1985, meant as a follow-up to the *samizdat* publication in 1965 of the first *Podozritel'*).[79] Some of those books include drawings, handwritten poems, and other visual material; the musical connections and performances continued as well, resulting in multiple recordings and videos.[80] Khvostenko's work shows an indebtedness to Khlebnikov, OBERIU, and other avant-garde poets: Khlebnikov inspired Khvostenko's most compelling musical performance, the collaboration with the rock group Auktsyon on the CD *Summit Dweller* (*Zhilets vershin*, 2000), with its songs based on Khlebnikov poems; the OBERIU connection is best seen in the fragmentary, self-consciously impoverished aesthetic of much of the earlier work, and the affection for plots of absurdity. The poet and activist Kirill Medvedev praised the childlike pleasure of the work, even as he emphasized connections to the earlier avant-garde; Medvedev was undecided whether the best metaphor for Khvostenko as a poet was a child seeing an elephant for the first time or an old man discovering a unicorn.[81]

Khvostenko associated with the Khelenukty group when he was still in Leningrad; some of its members, like Aleksandr Mironov, were close to the city's Neo-Acmeists, but others had in common with Khvostenko a determination to carry forward the innovations and experiments of the Futurists and of OBERIU, to the extent that they knew about OBERIU's writings and behavior;[82] a flair for the absurd marked them all. The group flourished in the late 1960s and early 1970s, and some of its members went on to enjoy long careers as writers, most importantly Vladimir Erl (b. 1947). Members of Khelenukty played with personas and pseudonyms, including Dmitry Makrinov (b. 1946, Dm. M.; after 1980, a monk, Aleksy), Viktor Nemtinov (b. 1947, VNE [a preposition denoting "outside" or "beyond"]), and Nikolai Aksel'rod (1945–2011, A. Nik.). They specialized in "happenings," engaged in forms of eccentric behavior that turned all those present into actors and spectators at once, and created a theatrical genre to which they gave the neologism "dramagedy." Epistolary genres were also important, demonstrating the enduring bonds of friendship and strong interconnections that marked many unofficial groups at the time; for Khelenukty, however, the use of letters and rhetorical forms of address ran deeper. In the short period of 1972–74, for example, Makrinov sent more than 60 letters to Erl, creating what might be called a forerunner to "mail art."[83] Their connections to other performers were strong, and Nemtinov became the photographer traveling with the rock group Aquarium. Nemtinov was also an editor, bringing to publication a number of books by fellow poets; Erl compiled the beginnings of a history of the Malaia Sadovaia group, a forerunner of Khelenukty (in 1989).[84]

Valuable scholarship has illuminated the performance and behavior practices of these later avant-garde groups, including study of subject-formation and theory of the event in their work. Aleksandr Zhitenev has seen a tendency toward the aesthetics of nullification in poems that manufacture non-events and in the lyric speaker's disbelief in his own real existence in the world.[85] Excellent examples come from the work of Erl, and the skepticism of the speaker and of the speech act also informs the neologism that named Khvostenko's early book of poetry, *The Suspector*. One of its short poems asserts the full force of such negations:

Сил моих нет
Лет моих нет
Рыб моих нет
Рук моих нет
Ног моих нет[86]

Strength—none
Years—none
Fish—none
Arms—none
Legs—none

The grammatical structure and presentation as lines of poetry are different, but the phenomenological force of the text is straight out of Kharms's "Blue Notebook No. 10."

The legacy of OBERIU had a further and surprising impact in a geographical setting far from its Leningrad/Petersburg home: in Siberia. The scholar and poet Igor Loshchilov (b. 1965), a Novosibirsk resident, has devoted his research to Zabolotsky, and published several books of poetry and prose; his own expressive manner of reading resounds as an extension of OBERIU performance practice, and can be heard in his reading of his poem "The Theater" ("Teatr").[87] Viktor Ivaniv (1977–2015) also lived in Novosibirsk, where he defended a dissertation on philosophical concepts and iconic signs in the Russian avant-garde and published extensively in both poetry and prose. Ivaniv was awarded the Burliuk Prize in 2003 and the Andrei Bely Prize in 2014 for his prose; the esteem with which fellow poets regarded him showed through in the outpouring of grief at his untimely death. Ivaniv wrote densely metaphorical yet immensely playful poetry, mixing imaginary place names with the sites of Siberia and mythological topoi. His free verse and remarkably open form combined with remnants of classical genres; simple quatrains and straightforward rhymes increasingly mark the later work. His prose bears the same precision in diction, the same unsparing glance in the alarmingly transparent "metaphysical mirror," as one critic has called it.[88] The dazzling range of images can be seen in a poem entitled, in Latin letters, "Rùt." Its first three stanzas are these:

> Голубиноглазая девочка с красным бантом
> и с глазастой перламутровой ниткой
> завивает дымки в городе идёт дождь
> а по городу клоуны и собаки и птицы
> ну а дети другие лицом ко мне хотят обратиться
>
> одноногий священник танцует с женой
> получает письмо озерцо кот наплакал
> там красотка и чудище и пёсик сторожевой
> кто-то каркал и крякал и квакал
>
> и слеза солона ждёт от моря одна
> роза мне что весною досталась
> а у девочки кровь горяча водяна
> и волшебное слово осталось

> Pigeon eye girl ribbon
> pie eye pearl string
> little smokes twist through towns rains
> but around town clowns and dogs and birds
> and kids all gravitate to me well
>
> one legged priest dance
> wife letter tomcat cry me a river
> bombshell and wildebeast and watchdoggy
> somebody croaked and quacked and cackled
>
> spring rose and a saline tear left me
> anticipating ocean delivery
> and the blood of the girl is hot watery
> and a mystic word remains[89]

In the claim that a "mystic word" endures amid this strange mix of dreamy tropes and insistently real-world objects, the poem shows well its OBERIU inheritance. Ivaniv created vivid imaginative worlds, perhaps especially in "Daydream Insurrection" ("Vosstanie grez," 2009). His legacy, not fully published at the time of his death, includes a broad range of texts, from love poems to mythic epics, from mock diary to traumatized lyric.

Important avant-garde traditions have also been carried forward by Natalia Azarova (b. 1956), a Moscow poet and scholar who shares with Loshchilov, Ivaniv, and others, a serious, professional interest in the literary tradition—in her case, the philosophy of language. She is a researcher at the Institute of Linguistics at the Academy of Sciences, and her doctoral dissertation became a substantial book on the languages of philosophy and poetry.[90] Azarova hosted many gatherings in a salon-like setting during the 2000s, engendering collaborations with other poets, philosophers, theorists, and artists. She has also published a number of books of poetry, some with her own visual illustrations, others with photographs and graphic art by Aleksei Lazarev; a distinctive instance of this work is the volume that combined her poetry with that of Anna Al'chuk

(1955–2008), *57577* (2004). The book identified itself as "A Correspondence in the Form of Traditional Japanese Poetry" to explain the numerical title: the sequence *57577* tells the required number of syllables for each of the five lines of verse that make up the traditional Japanese *tanka*. One of Azarova's signature poetic devices is drawing the reader's attention to specific letters and syllables in a poetic text, spreading out the words in a way also seen in the poetry of Mnatsakanova and, to a lesser extent, Aygi.[91] Like Mnatsakanova, she reads her own work in a highly musical, distinctive way. Several of her books, including *Letters of the Sea* (*Bukvy moria*, 2008), are instances of visual poetry.[92] But like Mnatsakanova, and before her, Guro, Azarova has come a good distance from the stylized poverty of Futurist book art. In her work, the arrangement of letters and words creates rhythms of visual spacing that complement the rhythms of sound patternings.[93]

Perhaps it is appropriate, if slightly out of chronological sequence, to conclude this account of Russia's avant-gardes with a poet who draws together many of the strands shown in others' works, the editor, critic, actor, teacher, and curator Sergei Biriukov (b. 1950). He was born and educated in Tambov, and since 1998 has lived in Germany. As unlikely as its very existence sounds, the International Academy of Zaum was created thanks to Biriukov's enterprising labors, and more than anything else exists as a website he was still updating as of 2016.[94] Although some of the individual poet pages offer little beyond links to pages easily found on Google, the repository of the website taken as a whole is significant, with video and audio links, photo and event catalogues, and extensive listings of pertinent print and web publications. In addition to this pioneering work of documenting and preserving records of late Soviet and post-Soviet avant-garde culture, Biriukov's own publications are also extensive. His poetry has a flavor of Conceptualism in its canny references to cultural institutions and quickly changing technologies of poetry and communication. It can be intensely, even parodically metapoetic, particularly in the aptly named volume *ΠΟΕΣΙΣ ПОЭЗИС POESIS* (2009). Biriukov's contribution to the art of the avant-garde may be even more significant, however, in his tireless efforts to make texts available to a broader readership and to study the nature and the impact of the texts themselves.[95]

Concrete and Conceptualist poetry

We turn our attention to a further legacy of the avant-garde, a group of poets and writers who sought to disrupt aesthetic traditions beginning in the 1960s. They understood that art exists in a complex social context that it can neither escape nor control. This attitude toward public power shows an important difference from the more utopian aspirations of the earlier avant-garde. These poets all associated themselves with unofficial literature, even those who had access to official publication (often as translators or children's writers). And not all entirely fled the traditions of high modernism, particularly those poets who had grown up in Leningrad, with its many sustaining connections to the Silver Age. But the first flourishing of this new wave of creative work occurred in Moscow.

It was Moscow, though, in the broadest sense of the place name: in the outskirts of the city, in the district of Lianozovo, an important group of poets and artists emerged in the 1950s. Lianozovo was the home of the artist Oskar Rabin (b. 1928), whose studio became a gathering place for artists as well as for the writers Genrikh Sapgir (1928–99), Vsevolod Nekrasov, Igor Kholin (1920–99), and Evgeny Kropivnitsky.[96] The Lianozovo poets were inspired by the public persona and poetic work of Ian Satunovsky, who was also a precursor of Conceptualism. For the Lianozovo group, the poet's voice was not idiosyncratic or distinctive or even all that interesting; what mattered was the language heard all around them. Satunovsky said of his work that it was based on an accidentally overheard or invented phrase, and that its distinctive feature was an absence of pauses. He meant that the poem was to seem as if uttered in one breath.[97] Nekrasov, by comparison, relied on the pause, a defining trope in his poems built out of colliding monosyllables, clashing intonations, and strange bits of verbal detritus amid an otherwise impoverished vocabulary.[98] Kholin's poems had something more like a plot, and his quickly sketched tales caught the vulnerable spirit of lives lived in the margins. The resulting work was minimalist in form and diction, giving poetic shape by means of lineation and repetition to speech acts and impressions that seem to have been passively gathered on the urban streets.[99] The environment itself had a kind of weird randomness, and the label "barracks poetry" has been attached to the group for its use of temporary postwar housing (in Lianozovo and elsewhere) as a backdrop in many poems and as a metaphor for the fragile equilibrium of inhabitants' lives. The rejection of utopian aspirations could be heard most vividly in poems that drew on the language of slogans or public discourse, rendered either as grotesque repetition or as fragmentary delusion, but almost always as radically minimalist utterance. The deformation of language studied by the Formalists and practiced by the Futurists was also a distinctive feature of Lianozovo poetics, but its force was ontological, expressing the very essence of post-Stalinist experience.[100]

Nekrasov covered much of this terrain, but the expansive grasp of the work emerged from poems whose rhetorical gestures and formal elements are astonishingly slight. Nekrasov could make a poem out of next to nothing, as epitomized in one of his most famous poems, "Freedom" ("Svoboda," 1964), which repeats the phrase "freedom is" six times to conclude with a final, seventh line containing the balanced assertion "freedom is freedom."[101] Some poems are a single word, like the white sheet of paper that has a period in the middle and the word "however" (*odnako*) just below it, to the right.[102] The poems, even the most minimalist, lend themselves to many interpretations, even though one critic has suggested that Nekrasov is seeking to "lay open the path toward semiotic kenosis, a transformative hollowing out of meaning effects."[103] To be sure, many of Nekrasov's poems seem to pull away from social or political content: a poem made entirely of the word "however" may be its own form of dissent, a gesture, crystallized into its purest form, of demurring from another's point of view or from official views.

Nekrasov also wrote many poems that engage with social norms and particularly with official rhetoric. A good example is the following:

> Стой
> Чувствуй
> Гордись
>
> куда денешься
>
> вот теперь и гордись
> столица
> и столица гордится
>
> вечным памятником
> великим нашим
> начальникам
>
> как они стучали
> на нас
>
> каким большим большим
> Кулаком[104]

> Stop
> Feel it
> Be proud

there's nowhere to hide

right now be proud
capital
and the capital is proud

of its eternal monument
of our great
leader

how they banged the table
at us

with their big big
Fists

The image of a leader pounding with his fist evokes the behavior of any number of General Secretaries of the Communist Party, including the notorious incident when Mr. Khrushchev banged his shoe on a table at the United Nations, but the poem seems less directed toward an individual than toward the very idea of public leadership. That Fist displays a vividly capitalized initial letter, as if both the initial letter and the fist itself were big, and the Fist rises up as a motivating threat to elicit the pride demanded in the poem's opening line. The poem's language and its images of public culture (capital, monument) are the stuff of Moscow Conceptualism, a movement to which Nekrasov had many affinities.

The term "Moscow Conceptualism" was introduced by Boris Groys in 1979 to name a circle of underground artists and poets, mainly residing in Moscow, whose aesthetics of mockery and critique radically diverged from other representatives of late Soviet nonconformist art. Groys's original term was Moscow Romantic Conceptualism, but the plainer label seemed to accommodate more readily such varying artistic practices as visual art by Ilya Kabakov (b. 1933), Erik Bulatov (b. 1933), and Viktor Pivovarov (b. 1937); the Sots-Art work of Vitaly Komar (b. 1943) and Aleksandr Melamid (b. 1945); performances by Andrei Monastyrsky, particularly his Collective Actions, and by Dmitry Prigov, including his "Appeals to Citizens" (1985–86); as well as literary works by Prigov, Nekrasov, Lev Rubinshtein, and Vladimir Sorokin. For a photograph that includes Sapgir, Sorokin, Monastyrsky, and other members of this group, see Figure v.06.

These artists and writers were united by a spectrum of cultural interests and a set of irreverent attitudes, rather than by specific principles. Moscow Conceptualism belongs to the sphere of Russian postmodernism: the consistent critique of all authoritative discourses, including the anti-Soviet discourse of liberal intelligentsia and the tradition of the avant-garde, and the avoidance of describing one's own position as universal or axiomatic, define its aesthetic. The second generation of Conceptualists featured groups with colorful names: The Medicinal Hermeneutics Inspection; the group Mukhomory (named after the poisonous fly amanita); and The Blue Noses group. Along with the performance artist Oleg Kulik (b. 1961), these later Conceptualists variously engaged religious themes, the aesthetics of psychedelic art, the commercialization of culture, and motifs of popular culture and the occult. Conceptualist aesthetics also resonate with political actionism of the 2010s (groups like Voina and Pussy Riot). The boundaries between performance art and poetry were particularly porous for Prigov, whose experiments with aesthetic freedom had far-reaching influence.

The poetry of Lev Rubinshtein incarnated that mobile boundary at the level of the text: his poems, even when formatted as books to be read, were always designed as performances. First written as short sets of words on the backs of canceled library catalogue cards, Rubinshtein's insistently ordinary lines had a relationship to the book that, in an age of digitization and com-

FIGURE V.06. The First Group Exhibition of Moscow Conceptualists in the Moscow gallery AptArt, 1982.

puterized research tools, may seem quaint. The production of a poem on library cards was revolutionary in the 1980s, however, modeling a notion of the text as a world as complete as any library, collected according to laws at once random and logical. Most book publications of Rubinshtein's work do not try to reproduce the presentation of library cards (although some facsimiles exist).[105] Instead, numbered sequences of lines run down the page, the numbers slowing a reader just enough to notice the sly humor and delicious ironies. Many sequences give the appearance of a dialogue, as if the lines were shaped by call and response, assertion and reaction, as in these lines from "Sonnet 66" ("Sonet 66," 1987):

> 102.—Неужели больше никогда?
> 103.—Да-да!
> 104.—Другу будет трудно без меня
> 105.—Да-да!
> 106.—Неужели больше никогда?
> 107.—Да-да![106]

> 91.—Surely this is not the last
> 92.—Yeah!
> 93.—When I am gone my friend will be downcast
> 94.—Yeah!

95.—Surely this is not the last
96.—Yeah![107]

Those affirmative responses continue for a while, and at the end of the poem, the question/
answer rhythm persists, but instead of "Yeah!," the answers are the words for punctuation
marks or poetic pauses (caesura, period): an utterance elicits nothing more than a statement
about the nature of the pause that should follow. Rubinshtein turns the language of poetry
into a self-conscious performance about syntax and prosody. There is a ritualized quality to
both the language and the format of his poems on library catalogue cards; earlier in "Sonnet
66," slightly longer lines use quotation marks, rendering ironic any possibility of the transcendental (the phrase used is "linguistic mystery"/"iazykovaia misteriia"). Shklovsky's defamiliarization is at play here, not only in the way that words are made strange, but also in the
defamiliarization of the lyric hero. Persons speak in the poems, but they are all filtered through
layers of public discourse that becomes its own engine of defamiliarization. In that process,
Rubinshtein deploys an important trait of Conceptualism, whereby language, one might say,
uses its user, rather than the other way around.[108] No Conceptualist poet reproduced that
paradox to greater effect than Dmitry Aleksandrovich Prigov.

CASE STUDY Dmitry Prigov's "Militsaner"

Starting in the late 1970s, at private readings of poetry—typical events in the life of
Moscow underground culture—Dmitry Prigov would appear in a militia cap and introduce himself as the poet of the Soviet cop or militiaman (see Figure v.07).

This "image" (*imidzh*, as Prigov called it) was well grounded in Prigov's poems about
the policeman, or *Militsaner*, which promptly became his poetic trademark. The demonstrative misspelling of Militsaner (as opposed to the correct *militsioner*) clearly signified
that this symbol belonged to the sphere of vernacular language and mythology, with
which Prigov was seriocomically engaged from the early 1970s. In the Preface to
Militsaner and Others (*Militsaner i drugie*, 1978), Prigov defines his Militsaner as a quasi-
mythological hero, and a preferable hero at that.[109] He represents the Militsaner "as a
mediator between the earthly and heavenly states; since the ideas of the earthly state
cannot be implemented, he is also a suffering cultural hero."[110]

In public readings that included these poems, Prigov invariably began with "When a
Militsaner stands here at his post…" ("Kogda zdes´ na postu stoit Militsaner," 1976):

> Когда здесь на посту стоит Милицанер
> Ему до Внуково простор весь открывается
> На Запад и на Восток глядит Милицанер
> И пустота за ними открывается
> И центр, где стоит Милицанер—
> Взгляд на него отсюда открывается
> Отовсюду виден Милицанер
> С Востока виден Милицанер
> И с Юга виден Милицанер
> И с моря виден Милицанер
> И с неба виден Милицанер
> И с-под земли…
> Да он и не скрывается[111]

FIGURE V.07. Dmitry Prigov in a militiaman cap, late 1970s.

> When a Militsaner stands here on guard
> An entire prospect opens up for him as far as Vnukovo
> The Militsaner looks East and West
> And behind them a void opens up
> And the center is where the Militsaner stands—
> From any point the sight of him opens up
> From everywhere the Militsaner can be seen
> From the East the Militsaner can be seen
> And from the South the Militsaner can be seen
> And from the sea the Militsaner can be seen
> And from the sky the Militsaner can be seen
> And from beneath the earth . .
> And he is not hiding at all

At first glance, this poem seems stylistically facile, with no obvious ruptures or gaps in its fabric. A verbal statue or fresco of Militsaner rises as a symbol of authority, or, to quote another poem of the same cycle, as "the pillar and symbol of the State" ("kak stolp i simvol Gosudarstva").[112] The poem is divided into two symmetrical parts: lines 1–5 are about *what* Militsaner sees, and lines 6–13 about *where he is seen from*. The reader expects an opposition or incongruity, but in vain: the opposition is replaced by tautology, emphasized in the last line.

Ironically, the lack of paradox constitutes the central paradox of the poem's structure. The utterance about the central position of the authority figure, the policeman, excludes, or at least conceals, any contradictions in the object of description or in the utterance itself. Consequently, tautology rules: Militsaner as the manifestation of authority occupies the central position because he is situated in the center—such is the poem's circular logic. The tautological nature of this statement is emphasized by tautological rhymes.

The repression of contradictions reveals a very important quality of the Soviet political unconscious: state power is perceived not in political, historical, or social terms, but rather in metaphysical/mythical terms (heaven, earth, the underworld) and in natural categories. It is no accident that the spatial coordinates of the poem only superficially suggest the topography of Moscow. In the second line, "An entire prospect opens up for him as far as Vnukovo," but later East and West appear, then the sea and sky, and finally, the nether world. In other poems of the cycle, Militsaner embodies eternity: "Militsaner represents / immortality in and of himself" ("Militsaner zhe predstavliaet / Bessmertnoe samim soboi"); "[He's] permanently fixed between heaven and earth" ("konstanten mezh nebom i zemlei"), "He rises to the standard equal to those of Rome / And he bests the forces that are invisible / He rises high as a visible example of / Governmentality" ("vstaet ravnodostoinym Rimom / I dazhe bol'she—toi nezrimoi / On zrimyi vysitsia primer / Gosudarstvennosti"); "And the day's eternal revolutions / And the transformation of summer into autumn / Do not leave any marks on him…" ("I sutok vechnoe vrashchen'e / I leta v osen' prevrashchen'e / Na nem ne ostavliaiut met…").[113]

As a mediator connecting East and West, heaven and earth, sea and shore, Militsaner is the axis on which a mythological worldview turns. As Prigov suggests in the preface to *Militsaner and Others*: "While fulfilling his functions as a mediator on a vertical axis connecting heaven and earth, Militsaner meets various enemies (sometimes not even knowing what they're doing). This is the dramatic arc of the character's development and representation."[114] But Militsaner also confronts the emptiness concealed by the world around: "The Militsaner looks East and West / And behind them a void opens up." He represents the cosmic order, and chaos/emptiness turns out to be *everything* that is *not* Militsaner.

Prigov applies this logic, with comical directness, in another famous Militsaner poem:

Вот придет водопроводчик
И испортит унитаз
Газовщик испортит газ
Электричество—электрик

Запалит пожар пожарник
Подлость сделает курьер
Но придет Милицанер
Скажет им: Не баловаться![115]

The plumber will come
And break the toilet
The gas master will cut off the gas supply
And the electrician—the power

> The fireman will start a fire
> And the messenger will do something base
> But the Militsaner will come
> And tell them all: Stop fooling around!

Here representatives of every profession, except for the police, destroy whatever they are supposed to protect or provide. The order of things, as embodied by a plumber, electrician, or fireman, is indistinguishable from chaos. And only Militsaner fulfills his proper function: the adult able to restrain misbehaving children, putting chaos under the control of a higher order.

If it is Militsaner (actually the state behind him) who is solely able to reveal order, what remains for the rest of the world? Nothing. Emptiness. The absolute center saturated by power and harmony paradoxically generates chaos and emptiness outside itself. Having accumulated in itself all conceivable perfection, it deprives the governed world of independent meaning, leaving it empty and chaotic. A world dominated by a power that substitutes tautologies for contradictions becomes a wilderness.

In this paradoxical transformation of order into a generator of chaos, one detects the first steps towards what later Moscow Conceptualists will define as the "emptiness canon" (*pustotnyi kanon*): the interpretation of emptiness as a trace left over from the destruction produced by the state-centered cultural order. The destructive effect of Militsaner's tautological power is well seen in "At the bar of the Writers' House" ("V bufete Doma Literatorov"), which ends:

> Он представляет собой Жизнь
> Явившуюся в форме Долга
> Жизнь кратка, а искусство долго
> И в схватке побеждает жизнь[116]

> He represents Life
> Manifested in the form of Duty
> Life is short, but art endures
> And in the conflict triumphs life

While comically extending Horace's famous line "Ars longa, vita brevis," Prigov's victory of life over art sets up the opposite: if Militsaner represents Life, and Life is brief (and interrupted by death), but Art is long (because it avoids death), then Militsaner's victory over Art means that it ceases being immortal, and death defeats all.

Militsaner also symbolizes logocentrism and the transcendental center of structural binary oppositions. Prigov's Soviet texts, which the Militsaner poems brilliantly exemplify, deconstruct the metaphysics of the center. His subversive affirmation outlandishly elevates the center (Militsaner) and maximizes its effects, among which the most prominent is "closing off free play" (to use Derrida's term), which transforms the center, i.e., Militsaner's presence, into a powerful tool for establishing the "fundamental immobility" of the system, equal to its emptiness and death.[117] As Prigov demonstrates to grotesque effect, binary oppositions, when permanently stabilized, cease to generate new meanings and effectively erase and empty existing ones.

It is doubtful that Prigov was then familiar with the terms of Derrida's deconstruction, but his Conceptualist works of the 1970s–80s resonate with the larger project of deconstruction. They were subversive not only in a political sense but culturally as well: they assassinated the very idea of the stable center. His Soviet texts thus reinvented the traditions of the avant-garde and, at the same time, laid foundations for the radical lines of inquiry that Russian postmodernism would develop in the 1990s–2000s.

Metarealism

An approach to creating innovative and sometimes formally untraditional poetry emerged in parallel to Conceptualism. It came to be called Metaphorism, Metarealism, or by some practitioners and critics, Metametaphorism. Among these possibilities, Metarealism is the most expressive name, in that these poets worked to complicate an idea of the real, to expand it into the "realm of things unseen" and to show "multiple realities, connected by a continuum of internal passageways and interchangeabilities."[118] These connections make Metaphorism an apt name as well: the rhetorical figure of metaphor becomes a cognitive or epistemological structure, within which poems of layered realities can be built. Unlike Conceptualists or the Lianozovo poets, the Metarealists or Metaphorists were not united by anything like a school or common set of poetic principles, although there are bonds of friendship and affinity among many of the poets: Vladimir Aristov (b. 1950), Arkady Dragomoshchenko, Aleksandr Eremenko (b. 1950), Viktor Krivulin, Aleksei Parshchikov (1954–2009), Olga Sedakova, Elena Shvarts, and Ivan Zhdanov (b. 1948). While the religious or spiritual reality in the writings of poets such as Sedakova, Shvarts, and Krivulin may make them seem quite distinct from the others, the boundaries between groups are porous, and the rhetorical effects they use in their spiritual quests align them with emphatically secular poets like Dragomoshchenko and Parshchikov.

Dragomoshchenko stayed on the outside of many established poetry circles in Russia, but his significance snapped into clearer focus after his death in 2012, when fresh appreciations and tributes poured in. His relentlessly curious mind, his knowledge of philosophy and other poetic traditions, and his prolific poetry as well as prose had already made him an important poet for the younger generation in post-Soviet Petersburg. He modeled a kind of wide-ranging poetic creation, poetic translation (notably of American LANGUAGE poets), deployment of free verse, and absorption of contemporary theory that is particularly well carried on in the poetry, theory, and translation work of Aleksandr Skidan and Anna Glazova (b. 1973).[119] Dragomoshchenko also exemplified a notion of poetry not as a continuation of any prior traditions, even the most avant-garde, but as a fierce engagement with the contemporary. In a poem that explicitly named Khlebnikov, or Vvedensky, or, for that matter, Wittgenstein or Baudelaire, Dragomoshchenko directed his readers' attention to the now of the poem, to its ontological and phenomenological insights, and to the performance of its own words on the page.[120] Dragomoshchenko's poetry is defined by its gaze and by the sense of touch, in the formulation of Mikhail Iampolsky, who writes that the poetry is porously open to the sensory world.[121]

Ivan Zhdanov's poetry, like Dragomoshchenko's, features layers of visual metaphors, metaphorical associations, and abstractions (both poets took up photography as more than a passing hobby, as did Parshchikov). Zhdanov was the first poet in the post-avant-garde to get a book of poetry into print in the USSR, *Portrait* (*Portret*, 1982). The title poem in that volume is a good example of his rather formally conservative work, which perhaps helped it into print, but there was no mistaking the radical nature of Zhdanov's rhetoric, tropes, and modes of self-presentation. "Portrait" (the poem) is structured around repetitions of a scene: a woman before a mirror, a sense of falling into that mirror as into a landscape. Zhdanov orients his readers by mythological references (in this poem, to Aphrodite), but disorients by means of a moody, uncertain atmosphere. The poem ends:

> Ты вспомнишь: ты чья-то невеста,
> чужая в столь зыбком краю.
> И красное марево жеста
> окутает руку твою. [122]

> You'll recall: you are someone's betrothed,
> Alien in an unreal land.
> And the red mist of the gesture
> Will enfold your hand. [123]

Zhdanov's lines are in a ternery meter that has a hypnotic effect; they conjure up the idea of a person without any actual representation of a lyric subject. Yet, as in the work of other Metarealists, the gestures and affect of identity waft through the poem. Zhdanov titled a later, slim volume *Composite Photograph of a Forbidden World* (*Fotorobot zapretnogo mira*, 1997), taking that phrase from a poem in which a city is described by means of such a composite photograph. It is a good metaphor for his artistic process, where identifying features are clipped out and reassembled, producing an unreal image of an absent person, place, or thing.

Visual imagery is also important to Parshchikov, and, as with Zhdanov, his poems can be formally conservative, organized by rhyme and including extensive use of some fixed forms, including a number of eight-line poems and longer poems set in quatrains. The texture and mental orientation of the poetry, though, is more like Dragomoshchenko's, in part because of the way he fixed on objects or phenomena in the visible world (oil, estuary, dacha, dogs, bottles) as simultaneously physical entities and mental abstractions. The descriptions often sound as if the natural world could not possibly accommodate them. To see this oxymoron in action, consider some lines not by Parshchikov, but by Aleksandr Eremenko, which Parshchikov cited and explicated in his book of prose *Paradise on a Low Flame* (*Rai medlennogo ognia*, 2006):

> Взлетает косолапый самолетик
> и вертится в спортивных небесах.
> . . .
> Пропеллер—маг и косточка в компоте
> и крепдешин, разорванный в ушах. [124]

> The pigeon-toed airplane lifts off
> and spins in the athletic skies.
> . . .
> The propeller is a magician and a cherry pit in compote
> and torn up beats of crêpe de chine.

Parshchikov explains the image in this Eremenko poem as a contrast of speed and stasis, the latter congealed as images from late Soviet public life: women in crêpe de chine gazing at such spectacles as new achievements in aviation or the thin compote offered as dessert. The stilling of movement interests the poet, turning the poem into a verbal photograph: frozen language where all movement has been brought to a halt, removing from the objects represented here any sign of syntax, phonetics, and morphology, as Parshchikov explained in his commentary on this poem. And it is one reason we get metaphors of boggy, soggy, muddy landscapes in Parshchikov's own work, natural elements in which linguistic elements can surface in slowed, thickened, observable form. These bits of language then take on a life of their own in the poetry, motivating the strange tropes and combinations.

Among foreign poets to whom Parshchikov and others were drawn, Michael Palmer exemplified precisely this version of American LANGUAGE poetry; and Parshchikov, Dragomoshchenko, Aristov, and Skidan wrote about and translated Palmer at various times.[125] Palmer in turn has commented on and celebrated the work of several Metarealists, and he joined with others in translating Parshchikov. A fine example of Parshchikov's work is the second of three poems he entitled "Flight" ("Begstvo-2," 1996), which nicely picks up images from Eremenko's text just cited. The poem begins:

> Пыль. Пыль и песок. Медленно, как
> смятый пакет целлофановый шевелится, расширяясь,
> замутняется память. Самолёт из песка
> снижается, таковым не являясь.[126]

> Dust. Dust and sand. Slowly, the way
> a crumpled cellophane wrapper crinkles as it unfolds,
> memory grows dim. An airplane of sand
> descends, though hardly even a plane.[127]

Dust and sand, those metonymically linked tiny particles, appear often in the poetry of the Metarealists, like the debris of a crumpling lived reality (sometimes a recognizable Soviet environment, sometimes the more anonymous, universal debris of metaphysical dislocation). Dragomoshchenko's poems are liberally sprinkled with dust, which spreads out to create countless tiny points of contiguity between disparate substances.[128] Parshchikov assembles the particles into strange shapes: the airplane in the poem "Flight" rises over the sand and is as if made of sand, so impossible a constructive substance that it is "hardly even a plane." That recoiling from the assertion that something "is" recurs in the poem's final lines and now regards the lyric subject himself: "I seek you, not being myself; / The earth dissolves us, possibly."[129] The speaker and the addressee are themselves as if turned to dust in that rather tentative final line, but instead of a simple evocation of the Biblical dust returning unto dust, the poem has the dirt of the world act as the agent of dissolution. Memories are not made by such poems; instead they are blurred, turned muddy and resistant to visual inspection.

Writing about Parshchikov's long masterpiece "I Lived on the Battlefield at Poltava" ("Ia zhil na pole Poltavskoi bitvy," written in 1984), Andrew Wachtel observed that metaphors serve to connect "various spaces and gaps between natural and manmade, present and past, self and world."[130] That effort to bridge, to connect, aptly describes the metaphors of Metarealist poems, and this is the reason they were also called Metametaphorists: they were assembling metaphors that would do the work of carrying-over suggested by the etymology of this term. That privileging of metaphor extends beyond even the list of poets considered here: the vivid metaphors of Elena Shvarts, for example, were one reason why she was seen as a member of the group. Among later contemporaries, in addition to Skidan, one finds similarities in the work of Viktor Ivaniv and Aleksandra Tsibulia (b. 1990).[131]

Post-Soviet poetic languages

The period following the demise of the Soviet Union has seen the emergence of a host of post-avant-garde poets, ranging from those who employ recognizable poetic forms for sometimes unpredictable ends (Maria Stepanova, b. 1972; Polina Barskova, b. 1976) to others who draw on popular culture to invent narratives of chaotic daily life (Stanislav L'vovsky, b. 1972; Fedor Svarovsky). Critics and poets have been writing about trends and patterns of this work all along, recording in real time the impressions based on the publication of significant volumes, the awarding of prizes, the rise and fall of journals and websites. Dmitry Kuz'min has chronicled many of these phases and events,[132] and advanced the work of contemporary poets by compiling two massive anthologies. The anthologies introduced dozens of new writers and framed the debate about what is new in post-Soviet poetry in terms of geographical range and aesthetic variety: the volume *Ulysses Unbound* (*Osvobozhdennyi Uliss*, 2004) presented nearly 1,000 pages of poetry by poets living outside the territory of the Russian state; and *Literature Outside the Capitals* (*Nestolichnaia literatura*, 2001) offered 600 pages of poetry and prose from provincial cities where unofficial literature had long thrived.

The riches to be found on those pages make a strong case for the vitality and variety of contemporary Russian poetry. Among the poets whose work has drawn special attention, beyond those just named, are Nika Skandiaka (b. 1978), Shamshad Abdullaev (b. 1957), Vasily Lomakin (b. 1958), Elena Fanailova (b. 1962), Nikolai Zviagintsev (b. 1967), Faina Grimberg (b. 1951), Anna Glazova, Mikhail Gronas (b. 1970), Grigory Dashevsky, Linor Goralik (b. 1975), Aleksandra Petrova (b. 1964), Gali-Dana Zinger (b. 1962), and Kirill Korchagin (b. 1986). Several of these poets have also written narrative and essayistic prose, or extensive criticism (Barskova, Grimberg, L'vovsky, Stepanova, Petrova, Dashevsky, Korchagin), and Goralik has written drama and created graphic novels as well. The fluid boundaries around poetry are significant, both because the poets draw so freely on the inspiration of other aesthetic forms, and because many, although not all, of them have continued the Conceptualists' efforts to keep poetry off an aesthetic pedestal. In their view, poetry flourishes best when it is down to earth, and in contact with the prose of lived experience. That does not mean renouncing the possibility that poetry could reach for sublime forms of expression—it is enough to read Grimberg's haunting poem about Andrei Ivanovich and Barskova's Blockade poems to notice that there is no falling off of intensity here.[133]

Some of that intensity is created by means of narrative, a strong trend in post-Soviet poetry, led by Svarovsky, Stepanova, L'vovsky, and others who have been seen as creators of a "New Epos." Stepanova has published several books featuring ballads and tales that incorporate vampires, ghosts, and revenants, but in settings so recognizably a part of daily Moscow life or a vestige from the historical traumas of the Soviet past that there is a weird reality effect even as supernatural entities flit past.[134] Stepanova, like Barskova, displays a mastery of traditional forms but drives their rhythms toward disturbed psychological and metaphysical speculations, so that the result feels more like fragmentation than the unity that fixed form typically brings. Even more fragmented is the work of Skandiaka, perhaps the most radical (and mysterious, as emphasized by the eloquent pseudonym: no personal appearances or readings, no recordings online). Her poems imprint the shock of digital communication on the languages of poetry, spreading words, graphic symbols, and punctuation marks across the page (or screen: she is a prolific blogger), taking words and syllables apart along the way so that the energy of verbal activity displaces all initial semantic possibilities.[135] Aleksandr Zhitenev described her as a poet of ellipsis: her poetry journeys back toward a kind of pre-verbal state of being, he says.[136] Yet it does so by means of an ecstatic profusion of words, splattered and spliced, joined by strings of idiosyncratic punctuation marks or remnants of computer code that are then recombined with superscripts and non-alphabetic signs.

Skandiaka, also a significant translator, writes her poems in the spaces between languages; reviewing her work, Aleksey Parshchikov noted that among the many pleasures it offered was the possibility of imagining the linguistic impulses from which the poem at hand might have sprung, as well as the languages into which it seemed poised for translation (actually, the same is true of Dragomoshchenko's work).[137] Contemporary Russian poetry features a number of other poets who have distinguished themselves as translators (Glazova, Sedakova, Kuz'min, Skidan, Dashevsky); the originality of their work has nearly wiped away the taint of translation as alienated labor that lingered from the Soviet era, when it was the only livelihood available to Anna Akhmatova and others. In fact, some poets in the Soviet era also used translation as a means of personal expression and aesthetic experimentation.[138] A visible mark of the rising status of translation is the inclination of some contemporary poets to mix translations prominently into their books of poetry.[139] Indeed, one could argue that just as the blurring of boundaries between poetry and prose or drama has intensified in contemporary Russian poetic practice, so has the boundary been shaken between translation and "original" poetry. That blurring is a legacy of postmodernism or of Moscow Conceptualism, in some ways: a consequence of the view of all language as always already someone else's. But given the rhetoric of insularity and nationalism that has been a formidable component of official Russian culture, the insistence on translation as a vital part of contemporary poetic practice is also a political statement.

4

Prose and drama:
Negotiations with history

THE aesthetic modes of narrative prose and dramatic theater, as in earlier periods, offered special opportunities in the twentieth century for the examination of conflicts between the individual and society. Increasingly, these conflicts became a clash between a man or a woman and ongoing historical processes. Prose and drama, like poetry, were engaged in the formation and testing of new subjectivities brought about by the historic shifts and catastrophes of the twentieth century. Much more than poetry, however, these genres necessitate a focus on conflict and on the *other*—psychological, sexual, cultural, political, historical. The novel, in particular, acquired greater complexity to encompass the multiple networks in which individuals lived. Its focus on the relationships between self and other opened new pathways for understanding individuals, society, and Russia's dramatic historical transformations.

The enormous prestige and many innovations of the Russian novel in the nineteenth century meant that it had an enduring impact on a range of other forms, and even as we turn principally to short prose and dramas of varying lengths, we cannot fully leave the novel behind. At the end of his essay "Epic and Novel," Mikhail Bakhtin speculated that the novelization of other genres was already taking place and that it involved not making other genres "like novels," but allowing them to absorb its plasticity.[1] But it is equally observable, particularly if one uses a narrower, genre-specific idea of the novel than did Bakhtin, that whatever was happening in prose involved a determined effort to explore narrative alternatives to the novel, particularly to its realism. Many critics and writers had argued since the turn of the twentieth century that the novel had run its course, opening the space for new possibilities. Mandelstam suggested that biography and circumstances had lost their deep connection in the age of modernism and revolution:

> ...both the stock value of the individual in history and the power and influence of the novel declined, for the generally accepted role of the individual in history serves as a kind of monometer indicating the pressure of the social atmosphere. The measure of a novel is human biography or a system of biographies.... The future development of the novel will be no less than the history of the atomization of biography as a form of personal existence; what is more, we shall witness the catastrophic collapse of biography.[2]

"The catastrophic collapse of biography" appears as a scenario for the novel's (as well as drama's) development, but only one. This was a discourse of Socialist Realism focused on the dispersal of everything personal, everything that was not integrated into the collective body. However, despite Socialist Realism's decades-long monopoly, literature of this period generated ever greater diversity of discourses and artistic dialects, either formed in confrontation with Socialist Realism and its normative system, or undermining it from within. These discourses resist all attempts to describe a unifying style or artistic method. The confrontation between personal and impersonal values, existential and political worldview, individualized and "collectivized" (i.e., clichéd) language, utopian perspectives and the experience of the everyday, ideological formulae and poetics of transgressions—such dichotomies define the trajectory of Russian prose and drama in the twentieth century.

The lack of biography in the nineteenth-century sense stimulated twentieth-century prose and drama to become a source of added reality, or rather, added history. It was not an escapist or fictitious history, since it constantly reworked actual events and circumstances as its material. Yet it was an invaluable alternative to uncontrollable and traumatic lived history, breaking through social alienation and compensating for denied freedoms. Socialist Realism offered an idealized and parallel history, cleansed of contradiction, one that enabled the reader's rite of passage into a shared utopian worldview—at the price of accepting anti-humanistic and anti-individualist ethics. In other types of writing (modernist, grotesque, existentialist, etc.), prose and drama created conditions specifically designed for the negotiations between self and others, and through them with the inhuman or alienated history. These negotiations involved personal freedom and dignity, individual space and nonconformism, a critique of societal projects and collectivist values. Taken together, major works of prose and drama performed the multi-voiced realization of all that was repressed and expelled from the public sphere during the Soviet period.

New forms of prose and drama

The career of Anton Chekhov epitomized the coming together of prose fiction and stage drama. His dramas, internationally regarded as a high point in the history of theater, also well exemplify the impact of novelistic narrative. In both drama and narrative, Chekhov explored the new ideas of subjectivity that arose with modernity. Identity is a problem for practically all his characters. They are forced into a type and therefore deprived of a distinctive identity (the "Kievan philistine"/Symbolist author Treplev, the eternal student Trofimov, the clown Charlotte); or they live through the disintegration of traditional class- and culture-based identity (Uncle Vanya and Sonia, the Prozorovs, Ranevskaia); or are in the process of creating themselves afresh (Tuzenbach, Lopakhin). In this context, the idea of the everyday and its seemingly nugatory components acquire a new meaning. Chekhov's tendency to relegate events to the background and foreground trivialities is well known.[3] The rituals of tea-drinking, conversations leading nowhere, and daily problems including domestic finances raise the image of an existence that is on the brink of crumbling under the pressure of dawning historical catastrophes, hinted at off-stage.

Chekhov's poetic system replaced the dominant grand narratives of social justice, "popular truth" (narodnaia pravda), enlightenment, and revolution no less than it undermined the idea that one can reduce life to any sort of straightforward scheme, as Aleksandr Chudakov has demonstrated.[4] Chekhov's characters are reluctant to impose their will on the course of their lives, which are complicated and chaotic. That Chekhov attempted to write a novel is well known. Arguably, his plays come closer than his stories to satisfying his novelistic ambitions, although the lack of a governing idea in his prose might well have led him to compose a recognizably modernist novel.

His writing for the theater turned out to be quite radical: his dramas intentionally subverted and mocked the system of dramatic conventions employed in the classic theater from the eighteenth century (and mastered by Chekhov in the early vaudeville he wrote) and commonly thought to define the structure of a well-made play. In the manipulation of these devices, commonplaces for theatergoers of the 1880s through 1900s, Chekhov found a way to innovate. His characters and his audiences recognize the types of roles that they are meant to instantiate. But they drop out of their assumed roles or deliberately cast them off. For example, the explanations that never quite occur between Astrov and Sonya in *Uncle Vanya* (*Diadia Vania*, 1896) and between Lopakhin and Varya in *The Cherry Orchard* (*Vishnevyi sad*, written in 1903, first staged in 1904) are all the more powerful because the logic of the well-made play dictates that they ought to take place. Gary Saul Morson has commented on the continual interplay between Chekhov's dramatic character and his role as a type of "reverse mimesis":

> His plays center on histrionic people who imitate theatrical performances and model themselves on other melodramatic genres. They posture, seek grand romance, imagine that a tragic fatalism governs their lives, and indulge in utopian dreams while they neglect the ordinary virtues and ignore the daily processes that truly sustain them.[5]

In Morson's view, this technique is particularly important to Chekhov in his critique of the intelligentsia and its responsibility for massive waste—of productive time and energy, of cultural tradition, of the country's potential, and eventually, of the future—which "results from the lack not of great ideals but of daily care."[6] Such serious, philosophical readings of Chekhov have somewhat outweighed attention to the comic aspects of the work. *The Cherry Orchard* was Chekhov's final play, and it was performed only after his death; perhaps for that reason the performance tradition has favored a melodramatic and tragic tonality. Svetlana Evdokimova argues that the gap between the demands of daily life and the idealism of the intelligentsia has in fact a blatantly comic character, foregrounding the motive of the intelligentsia's infantilism and irresponsible behavior as they lose control over their lives.[7]

CASE STUDY   Maxim Gorky and Leonid Andreev

Two of the most popular writers of fiction and theater in the first two decades of the twentieth century, Maxim Gorky (1868–1936) and Leonid Andreev (1871–1919), pictured together in Figure v.08, developed in logical if somewhat unexpected ways key tendencies in Chekhov's work: attention to everyday life; the framing of mundane gestures as philosophical motifs; and detection of subtle signs of social conflict. They created original versions of expressionist writing decades before Expressionism established itself in European literary modernism. For both writers, a human character or a social phenomenon had to be embodied by an eccentric, sometimes even grotesque detail, gesture, or phrase, which served as an emblem of social or philosophical conflicts. Like the Expressionists, Gorky and Andreev were deeply influenced by Nietzsche, stylistically and conceptually. Following his lead, they passionately explored paradoxes of the rebellious mind: the price of freedom, its dark underside, its relative value.

They were close friends, and uncanny parallels mark their biographies.[8] Each attempted suicide in his youth; both became literary celebrities at a relatively young age (and Gorky significantly contributed to Andreev's success among the reading public); each one was imprisoned during revolutionary events of 1905; and both enjoyed triumphs as dramatists of the Moscow Art Theater. Initially, they disagreed with the Bolshevik regime and preferred emigration to collaboration. But Andreev died in Finland in 1919, while Gorky returned to the USSR in 1928 to become the spokesman for Stalinist transformations of Soviet literature. Despite comparable early literary strategies, Andreev and Gorky eventually developed in different directions.

Gorky featured characters thrown away to the margins of society and rendered them poetic: homeless bums and petty criminals ("Makar Chudra" [1892], "Chelkash" [1895], "Old Woman Izergil" ["Starukha Izergil," 1895], "Malva" [1897]), and those who break

FIGURE V.08. Maxim Gorky and Leonid Andreev, 1901.

with social conventions, such as the millionaire Foma Gordeev (in the eponymous 1899 novel). In Gorky's early stories, déclassé characters rebel against societal norms; it is little wonder that critics heard echoes of Nietzsche's supermen in Gorky's *bosiaki* (literally, barefooted creatures).[9] These stories and their protagonists revolted against *meshchanstvo* (bourgeois philistinism) and against the values of the middle class, a target of Gorky's anger and satire in numerous works, most explicitly in his essays "Notes on Philistinism" ("Zametki o meshchanstve," 1905), "On the Grey" ("O Serom," 1905), and plays *Philistines* (*Meshchane*, 1902), *Barbarians* (*Varvary*, 1905), and *Vassa Zheleznova* (1910). The war against *meshchanstvo* remained a central theme of his entire career. For the writer who spent his childhood in the depths of a low middle-class milieu (see his *Childhood* [*Detstvo*, 1914–15]), *meshchanstvo* was more a philosophical than a social category. He perceived it as a form of debilitating inertia, full of cruelty and suffering. These Neo-Romantic sensibilities pushed Gorky towards the socialist movement (he was a member of the Bolshevik faction of the Russian Social-Democratic Party as of 1905), and also explain his deep attraction to various utopian projects, Stalinism included.

Gorky channeled his critique of *meshchanstvo* through ugly, bizarre, and twisted characters and situations that represented this phenomenon. He depicted *meshchanstvo* as hatred and envy towards life and as a desire to denigrate anything beautiful. Many of his story collections, including *Along Russia* (*Po Rusi*, 1912–17), make a mosaic of such bizarre and grotesque scenes. Often *meshchanstvo* is decoupled from the middle class per se; for example, in the story "The Watchman" ("Storozh," 1922), a lesser-known programmatic text, he depicts an abject, sexually explicit ritual of initiation into a circle of disenfranchised drunkards as the height of *meshchanstvo* in a philosophic sense. Similar motifs permeate his novels: *The Town of Okurov* (*Gorodok Okurov*, 1909), *The Life of Matvei Kozhemiakin* (*Zhizn' Matveia Kozhemiakina*, 1910–11), *Among People* (*V liudiakh*, 1915), *My Universities* (*Moi universitety*, 1923), and, of course, his monumental *The Life of Klim Samgin* (*Zhizn' Klima Samgina*, 1925–36).

Rebellion against *meshchanstvo* triggers Gorky's search for an "anthropological" rather than social revolution (to use Dmitry Bykov's formulation),[10] which explains the continuities with Nietzsche's themes of transcending the human, exposing moral hypocrisy, and vitality as the means to freedom.[11] Gorky tirelessly collected examples of the life force that should demolish social barriers, leading to the triumph, albeit temporary, of beauty, eroticism, and political energy. In "The Watchman," the drunkards' rite of passage parallels another ritual—an orgy of town officials, which the narrator praises as a life-affirming celebration. Gorky is equally excited by a variegated cast of others, including a ruthless market strongman, Artem ("Kain and Artem," 1899); a performer of folk songs (*Life of Klim Samgin*); assorted revolutionaries (*Mother* [*Mat'*, 1906]); sectarians (*Confession* [*Ispoved'*, 1909]); and talented entrepreneurs (*Vassa Zheleznova*; *The Artamonovs' Business* [*Delo Artamonovykh*, 1925]). His special fondness, however, is reserved for prominent writers and artists, such as Leo Tolstoy, Chekhov, Chaliapin, Korolenko, and Leonid Andreev, and other celebrities of his time, including Lenin, about all of whom Gorky left brilliantly expressive memoirs. He sees people blessed by the vital force as true revolutionaries, even if their political views do not directly advocate revolution—insofar as they transcend boring, repressive norms and create new pathways for self-realization. Such heroes are often degraded and traduced. But in his best works, all from the early 1920s, Gorky resists idealizing them: he discovers that the manifestations of the vital force do not exclude monstrosity, and the word "monster" even appears in the first version of his memoir about Lenin. Key works here include the astoundingly Dostoevskian (despite Gorky's avowed hatred of him) "Short Stories of 1922–24" ("Rasskazy 1922–24 goda," 1924) and "Notes from a Diary" ("Zametki iz dnevnika," 1924).

Admiration for the life force also laid the foundation for Gorky's critique of the intelligentsia, most tangibly in his plays *Summer Folk* (*Dachniki*, 1904), *Children of the Sun* (*Deti solntsa*, 1905), and *Oddballs* (*Chudaki*, 1910). Gorky believed in the high mission of the intelligentsia and criticizes it for a lack of vitality, seen in the rejection of transgressive heroism and desire to live a comfortable life. (Gorky would build *The Life of Klim Samgin* around a character who tries to combine the intelligentsia's clout with comfortable conformity). Reprising the setting and methods found in Chekhov's plays, Gorky's dramas are much harsher in their attitude towards the intelligentsia, frequently bordering on caricature. Dmitry Mirsky wrote sarcastically but not without justification:

> As a dramatist Gorky...is nothing but a bad disciple of Chekhov....His dramatic style is exactly the same....The only thing Gorky did not notice in Chekhov's dramatic art was the only thing that justifies it: its hidden dynamic structure. The only thing he added...were "conversations on the meaning of life," which would be capable of killing even the greatest drama of Shakespeare.[12]

The most original of Gorky's plays was *The Lower Depths* (*Na dne*, 1902), which, along with Chekhov's *Seagull*, became a signature production at the Moscow Art Theater. The play sheds considerable light on Gorky's vision of the intelligentsia's mission—despite the fact that there are no actual members of the intelligentsia among its characters. *The Lower Depths* is perhaps the first Menippean satire in Russian drama: a homeless shelter becomes the setting for open-ended and provocative philosophical discussions in full accordance with Bakhtin's definition: "The idea here fears no slum, is not afraid of any of life's depravity, baseness, and vulgarity in their most extreme expression. The man of the idea—the wise man—collides with worldly evil."[13] Gorky's wise man is the itinerant Luka, who speaks words of kindness and consolation to the depraved and desperate inhabitants of the shelter. He reminds them of their human dignity, extolling the value of life and individuality. His hope-inspiring effect is routinely interpreted by critics as delusional happiness followed by bitter disappointment and protest, and in his later statements Gorky supported this interpretation. However, the final monologue of Satin, the déclassé rebel, which is frequently cited as an anthem of humanism, in fact recycles and augments ideas and even phrases initially pronounced by Luka.[14] Gorky does not downplay the role of Luka's hopeful lie; through him he implements Nietzsche's dictum about the aesthetic justification of reality from *The Birth of Tragedy*. That gesture perfectly fits *The Lower Depths*: Luka's hopeful humanistic discourse lets the shelter's inhabitants justify their catastrophic lives aesthetically. Luka's beautiful dream recasts Gorky's presumed notion of the intelligentsia's mission: to lift up the value of individual human life through utopias that would console the downtrodden and inspire the desperate.[15]

This philosophical conviction underlies both Gorky's perennial admiration for world literature, philosophy, and the arts, and his dedication to educational projects and institutions like the publishing house Knowledge, the World Literature (Vsemirnaia literatura, 1918–21) and other book series, and the journals that he initiated and curated in emigration and in the USSR. In the words of Viktor Shklovsky, Gorky's "most developed pathos is the pathos of preservation, quantitative preservation of culture—all of it."[16] The defense of culture from revolutionary barbarism is fundamental to Gorky's conflict with Lenin and his emigration in 1921.

From Gorky's concept of the intelligentsia's mission follows his understanding of socialism, which he interpreted as a new secular religion meant to bring aesthetic and teleological justifications to the working class's deprived existence (the so-called God-building also promoted by Aleksandr Bogdanov and the future Soviet commissar of education Anatoly Lunacharsky). His novel *Mother*, later the sacred text of Socialist Realism, was written to show the transformation of the workers' movement into a new religion. At the center of the novel is a downtrodden woman, Pelageia Vlasova. She cannot perceive revolution rationally, but a religious perspective comes easily, and she elevates her revolutionary son, Pavel, as a new Christ. This new faith seems to resurrect her own soul, destroyed by daily humiliations. Similar motifs mark Gorky's novellas *Confession* and *Summer* (*Leto*, 1910). As Richard Stites has demonstrated, Lenin harshly criticized this vision of socialism, but it reemerged as a driving force of cultural construction in the USSR in the 1920s.[17] After Gorky's return from emigration, he implemented it in his cultural activity, and God-building became the unmentionable foundation of Socialist Realism.

Leonid Andreev, by comparison, takes a godless metaphysics as his starting point, creating a neo-mythological outlook suited to the post-traditionalist world. As against Gorky's fragmented epic of vital forces fighting *meshchanstvo*, Andreev ponders the tragic loneliness of modern man, "naked man on the naked Earth" (as the protagonist of his 1906 play *Savva* says). Gorky's expressionist poetics eventually leads him to Socialist Realism, while Andreev becomes the first fully accomplished existentialist writer in Russian literature, whose poetics and philosophy foreshadow those of Camus and Sartre. His disappointment in the revolutionary movement follows from his philosophical rather than political pessimism.

Emblematic of Andreev's expressionist style is his novella *The Red Laugh* (*Krasnyi smekh*, 1904), inspired by the events of the Russo-Japanese War and openly in dialogue with Garshin's story "The Red Flower." Garshin's insane protagonist imagines all the world's evil concentrated in the red flower which he tries to destroy, but Andreev's protagonist and narrator, shocked by war's horror, absorbs its insanity into his mind and body. His post-war recovery is illusory, as the novella's finale suggests when the narrative perspective shifts to that of his brother. *The Red Laugh* reads as "the story of the gradual capitulation of all mankind to the insanity unleashed by modern warfare."[18] The surreal world exposed by the war is concentrated in the novella's signature motif—the red laugh, connoting something completely irrational and yet highly expressive. The story ends with the hyperbolic materialization of this immaterial symbol of global chaos: "Behind the window, in the dark red and unmoving light, stood the Red Laugh itself."[19]

The difference of this method from Symbolism was pinpointed by Dmitry Merezhkovsky, who wrote in 1908, "Andreev's literary work is problematic for me not only because he depicts ugliness, horrors, and chaos (on the contrary, such depictions demand the highest artistic creativity), but because while contemplating ugliness, he agrees with it, and while observing chaos, he becomes chaotic himself."[20] Merezhkovsky disapproves of Andreev because his symbols do not point at a hidden harmony; instead, they serve as concentrated embodiments of disharmony and of the cacophony of existence.

Andreev's poetics always balance psychological analysis with expressionist hyperbole. This is especially true in such short stories and novellas as "The Abyss" ("Bezdna," 1902), "The Governor" ("Gubernator," 1906), "Eleasar" (1906), "Darkness" ("T'ma," 1907), and "The Story of Seven Who Were Hanged" ("Rasskaz o semi poveshennykh," 1908). He explores what in existentialist discourse will be defined as a borderline situation, when a subject facing death undergoes a profound liberation from societal restraints and conventions. Andreev does not overlook the negative aspects of his characters' existential freedom. In "The Abyss," a protagonist is attacked by a group of thugs who rape the girl he loves; after regaining consciousness, he also takes advantage of her senseless body.[21] In "Darkness," a terrorist-revolutionary hides from the police in a brothel, where he undergoes a crisis: the prostitute with whom he spends the night asks, "How do you dare to be good when I am bad?" Her question pushes him to devalue the revolutionary struggle, seeing in it pride and self-aggrandizement, rather than care for the oppressed. This story caused an outcry among Andreev's liberal (and not only liberal) readers.

He offended the religious feelings of his readers still more pointedly. In the story "Eleasar," he depicts Lazarus raised from the dead, but as one whose restored sight devalues life for everyone who encounters him. "Eleasar" was the first in the cycle of Andreev's "Biblical" stories and plays, among which the most famous is the novella *Judas Iscariot* (*Iuda Iskariot*, 1907). It provocatively depicts Judas as a rebel and a true martyr who betrays Christ in order to elevate his words and deeds; Judas's sacrifice of a good name and his love for Christ appear comparable to Christ's passions. In the words of A. V. Tatarinov, this novella "forms a unified trope of 'Judas-Christ,' which in Andreev's universe serves as the possibility for a new salvation; a blasphemous fusion of two Biblical antagonists, it opened the way to a new concept of subjectivity."[22] Praised by Innokenty Annensky and condemned (if misunderstood) by Merezhkovsky and Yuri Aikhenval'd, this novella opened a long lineage of transpositions of Biblical myths into post-religious modern conditions—not by modernizing mythical events, but by making the participants think and feel like modern people. This literary discourse is exemplified by Thomas Mann's *Joseph and His Brothers* (*Joseph und seine Brüder*, 1933–43) and by Bulgakov's *The Master and Margarita*.

Andreev penned other ambivalent interpretations of ancient myths: in the 1910 play *Anathema*, he inverts the story of Job and places at its center the Devil-Anathema, who tests a poor Jew, David Leizer, with incredible wealth; in his last novel, *Satan's Diary* (*Dnevnik Satany*, 1919), the Devil learns that his cynicism is naive in comparison with that of ordinary people.

Ambivalent dialogues with ancient myths reverberate through other dramas by Andreev: *Tsar Hunger* (*Tsar'-Golod*, 1907), *Savva, The Life of a Human* (*Zhizn' cheloveka*, 1907), *Requiem* (*Rekviem*, 1915), *He Who Got Slapped on the Face* (*Tot, kto poluchaet posh-chechiny*, 1915), and *Dogs' Waltz* (*Sobachii val's*, 1915, published 1922). They either psychologically destabilize mythological narratives or, on the contrary, reveal mythological patterns in the depth of mundane experiences. All bear the trademark of Expressionist poetics.[23] As produced by various directors from Nemirovich-Danchenko to Tairov, stagings were often cruel and always spectacular dramatic experiments testing the limits of the modern subject, prototypically represented by Judas-Christ. Each of Andreev's protagonists is in a state of constant internal and external conflict. They perform rebellious and self-destructive acts, although despite first impressions, they mostly try to preempt or overcome the impending catastrophe—all in vain. With the notable exception of David Leizer in *Anathema*, Andreev's protagonists fail to save themselves, let alone the world; their provocative actions instead knock down the last pillars of an already shaking world.

The ups and downs of literary history have not spared Gorky and Andreev. Dmitry Mirsky wrote in 1926: "At first the Gorky-Andreev group obscured the Symbolists almost completely; but with time the situation was reversed and today the first decade of this century appears as the Age of Symbolism."[24] This situation was reversed again when Gorky became the central object of Soviet literary scholarship for decades, almost entirely overshadowing the achievements of the Silver Age and early Soviet modernism in official publications. Most Soviet scholarship about Gorky is heavily ideologized and barely readable, and the representation of his legacy was partial: his *Untimely Thoughts* (*Nesvoevremennye mysli*, 1917–18) and other texts critical of Bolshevism were long censored or published only during Perestroika. Critical interest in Andreev was revived in the 1960s, when Soviet literary scholars saw him as a permissible representative of Russian modernism (due to his friendship with Gorky), although again the writings remained partially published and heavily censored.[25] In the post-Soviet era, critical work on these writers, both in Russia and abroad, has radically diminished. The only exceptions are literary biographies, curiously enough.[26] Are we on the verge of another change in Gorky's and Andreev's posthumous legacies? If so, the next step would be a rediscovery of their innovations in poetics as idiosyncratic and under-valued contributions to Russian modernism.

Although Ivan Bunin once belonged to the same community of allegedly realist writers as Andreev and Gorky (Wednesday [Sreda, the 1890s–1900s]), his prose stylistically constitutes a contrast both to Andreev's tragic and theatrical expressionism and to Gorky's socially oriented Neitzscheanism. His prose, however, also conveys the sense of impending catastrophe and the loss of control over events. The deeply tragic worldview of his characters attempts to muffle that near doom with the distractions of day-to-day business or amorous attachment. Bunin would develop further as a writer in the emigration, but his first steps as a writer, particularly his unsentimental tales of peasants or the declining gentry, bear mention for their compression of a number of aesthetic traits of modernism (somewhat anecdotal or episodic plot lines, atmosphere built up more fully than character, a pervasive pessimism) with a lingering after-effect of populist realism. The short novel that brought him first fame, *The Village* (*Derevnia*, 1909–10), gives a grim example of such portraiture, and the admired novella *Dry Valley* (*Sukhodol*, 1912) offers a panorama of ruin. Bunin's love stories are celebrated, in the early work perhaps none more than "Light Breathing" ("Legkoe dykhanie," 1916), but the pleasures of erotic connection inevitably lead to doom. The final collection, *Dark Avenues*, featured many such stories, with the paralyzed emotional lives of male heroes more often than not sweeping across the lives of a range of women. His was a peculiarly repressed version of modernism, perhaps best seen in contrast to the later developments found in Nabokov's stories and novels; Nabokov admired Bunin enough to send him his early writings and ask his advice, although his later recollections of meeting Bunin are hilariously unkind, perhaps because Nabokov found him "basking in the Nobel prize he had just received."[27]

Alternatively, one might contrast Bunin with writings by women of the era who were reimagining the erotic liaisons and triangles that had become standard literary fare. A number of women writers were cracking the fairly rigid codes of gendered behavior; the resulting new kinds of female characters provided another impetus to narrative innovation in the first decades of the twentieth century. Zinaida Gippius's "The Madwoman" ("Sumasshedshaia," first published in 1903) has a narrative frame and set of thematic concerns very much like those of Tolstoy's "Kreutzer Sonata." Gippius's tale gives us not a man driven to jealous murder, as in Tolstoy's story, but a woman driven to declare herself insane; the heroine's coerced retreat from her family life and particularly her beloved child is chilling. The feminist theme in this account of her madness will likely remind English-language readers of Charlotte Perkins Gilman's story "The Yellow Wallpaper" (1892). Gippius shares with Gilman a sharp analysis of a woman's spiritual and social paralysis in a sexist culture, but she also launches an attack on the excessive rationalism of bourgeois, provincial Russian society. Her narrative's conflict between husband and wife contrasts his stern confidence in reason and science with her deep commitment to faith. Gippius is continuing traditional nineteenth-century themes, whereas other writers in this period were more likely, if they wished to build a narrative around the struggle between spirit and matter, to represent the spiritual world not as Orthodoxy with its institutional rituals but as a more mystical and obscure force in nature. Elizaveta Dmitrieva, for example, who wrote as Cherubina de Gabriak, was deeply affected by anthroposophy, the tenets of which electrified many a Russian Symbolist.

One of the most famous and, at the time, infamous short novels of early modernism was by Mikhail Kuzmin, *Wings* (*Kryl'ia*, 1906). Its undisguised representation of homosexual love shocked some readers. Astonishment greeted its focus on a hero's discovery that love between men could become a part of his own life, and its adult conversations about same-sex love in history and culture are devoid of censorious judgment and portentous doom. *Wings* created a kind of mosaic narrative picked up in much later modernism. The juxtapositions and quick cuts between settings and events asked readers to create narrative continuities and absorb the surprises of some scenes, like the suicide of a young woman that ends Part 1. Kuzmin's biographers John E. Malmstad and Nikolay Bogomolov see the narrative development as perhaps not the novel's greatest strength, but a weakness balanced by the absorption of elements of the philosophical treatise, making *Wings* into an "analogue to the Platonic dialogues." The title, in fact, comes from Plato's *Phaedrus*: the deeper themes of the novel thus become "the quest for freedom and beauty, the soul's journey to perfection through love, and Hellenism's vision of male love as the agent of personal and cultural transformation."[28] It should not surprise us that the admiration for Hellenism coexists in the novel with the representation of Old Believers, who are brought forward as exemplars of a venerable, genuine spiritual tradition. In *Wings*, the young hero Vanya is variously seeking pathways to an authentic, meaningful life, and the religious tradition shows him that choosing against one's true nature is a betrayal of God's plan.

Erotic attachments are also at the center of *The Petty Demon* (*Melkii bes*, 1907) by Fedor Sologub. Himself a former provincial schoolteacher, Sologub created characters based on children whose innocence can never be assumed. Such narrative fantasies were not uncommon at the time—one thinks of the siblings at the center of Henry James's tale "The Turn of the Screw" (1898)—but there was an air of terrible decadence in Sologub's character portrayals. The mental deterioration of his hero, Peredonov, mixed the descent into madness and paranoia with weird flashes of beauty and innocence, and with an unsettling undercurrent of banality (the novel's famous *poshlost'*). Sologub also takes to its logical extreme standard representations of provincial life, where everyday pettiness provides ample material for ethical reflection. Has Peredonov brought evil to the town, with his eventually murderous acts, or is he provoked to insanity and violence by the spectacle of innocence seduced, in the form of the adolescent Sasha Pyl'nikov? The decadent themes of *The Petty Demon* make it precisely emblematic of its age, but later writers were to find inspiration in its depiction of provincial vulgarity and pre-pubescent curiosities in works as different as Leonid Dobychin's *Town of N* and Nabokov's *Lolita* (1955).[29]

It can be argued, however, that the most significant innovator in the poetics of Russian modernist prose was Andrei Bely. Having absorbed many influences, from Nietzsche to Steiner, and being a prominent theorist of Symbolism and sensitive interpreter of Russian classics (Gogol, Dostoevsky, Tolstoy), Bely sought a synthesis of philosophical, artistic, and cultural opposites in his writings, a synthesis which constituted the essence of Symbolism. In his early "symphonies" (1902, 1904, 1905, 1908), he fused principles of musical composition and literature, prose and poetic rhythm; in his mature works—the novels *The Silver Dove* (*Serebriannyi golub'*, 1910) and *Petersburg* (*Peterburg*, publication in the almanac *Sirin* 1913–14, and two book editions of 1916 and 1922—all different from each other)—he integrates Gogolian grotesque, Dostoevskian psychological analysis, Tolstoyan motifs, autobiography, and Symbolist mythological constructions. An innovative poetic language results, which in Bely's writings becomes a sensitive tool for the comprehension and foreseeing of the historical destiny of Russia shaken by revolutionary energies. In the 1920s, Bely's style had formed what became known as "ornamental prose," eventually the most influential style for the representation of revolution in Russian prose. It was adopted and creatively transformed by such diverse writers as Evgeny Zamiatin, Boris Pil'niak, Vsevolod Ivanov, and Leonid Leonov.

Bely's novel *Petersburg* saw revolution as the collision of two insanities: in the words of Konstantin Mochulsky, "two crazy ideas crash against each other: political reaction embodied by the senator Ableukhov and the revolution epitomized by the party-activist Dudkin.... Yet the chilling air of death exhumes both from the old and dying world and from the new one that brings destruction with it."[30]

In Bely's novel, Senator Ableukhov has to be killed by his son Nikolai. The assassination fails, and Ableukhov Sr. lives after the accidental explosion of the bomb; although the blast happens despite the son's will, the father cannot forgive his potential crime, and family unity is shattered. Senator Ableukhov is depicted by Bely with obvious reference to Tolstoy's Karenin and to the real-life Ober-Prosecutor of the Orthodox Church and reactionary jurist Konstantin Pobedonostsev (also depicted in Blok's *Retribution*). He is the Russian state incarnate, and he is directly responsible for the gap separating him from his son, Nikolai, who becomes an unwilling terrorist.[31] But for Bely, the most important task is to avoid fratricide—symbolic and literal alike—by escaping from the blinding phantasms of Petersburg itself.

In Bely's logic, the bomb hidden in Nikolai's desk drawer serves as a metaphor of revolution. Its explosion is prepared by various factors, especially by the general atmosphere of insanity, provocations, and brain games. In the almanac version, one of the novel's most profound characters, the terrorist Dudkin (he kills the grand provocateur Lippanchenko) receives a mysterious letter expressing the author's own views that revolution is similar to modernist art. Both stir unconscious forces in the collective strife, and both have a decadent charge of violence and eroticism.[32] Tellingly, the name of senator Ableukhov is Apollon Apollonovich, which—along with his demeanor and life style—makes him the symbol of the Apollonian dictate of order which has to be confronted by the Dionysian striving towards unrestrained freedom and creativity.

In *Petersburg*, one cannot prevent the revolutionary blast—as the mythologically inevitable event—because the Russian state system is already pregnant with its apocalypse. Revolutionary terror emerges in Bely's novel as the extension of the metaphysical horror associated with St. Petersburg itself, the embodiment of the rationalist project mercilessly applied to reality. As noted by Lotman, Bely is one of the first Russian writers to fuse neo-mythologism with irony and thus liberate it from its dogmatisms: he emphasized instead "the multiplicity of perspectives" and "the relativism and incomprehensibility of the world" as foundational principles of neo-mythologism.[33] The myth of Petersburg (harkening back to Gogol and Dostoevsky) created by Bely fully embodies these principles. *Petersburg* thus opened the way for Boris Pil'niak's *Naked Year*, Andrei Platonov's *Foundation Pit* and *Chevengur*, Bulgakov's *The Master and Margarita*, and Pasternak's *Doctor Zhivago*, not to mention their numerous epigones.[34] In general, the interaction between two major influences, expressionist prose shaped by Andreev and Gorky, and its Symbolist versions exemplified by Bely and to a lesser extent Sologub, would become formative for the entire spectrum of prose experiments in the 1920s–30s.

Utopia and dystopia in early Soviet literature

Modernist subjectivities also took form in texts that fantasized possible futures. In the immediate aftermath of the Revolution, when dreams about a communist future were given very practical, state-authorized encouragement, the challenge to writers thinking about new forms of identity was obvious. How to imagine the people of the future? How to create stories and plays that could project possible futures in all their promise but also, to some writers, dismal threat? Utopian discourse awakened in the early twentieth century as a secularized version of the mythology of a heavenly kingdom. Widespread apocalyptic interpretations of the Civil War and ensuing economic and social collapse, as well as the millennialist character of communist ideology, all contributed to the popularity of the utopian genre, including dystopia. This spectrum of utopian discourses granted writers a sense of synergy with the revolutionary era, while at the same time offering a map of the new cultural terrain organized as positive or negative according to binary oppositions. An unsurprising backlash in the form of critical narratives was aimed at utopian visions in general and at specific formulations. By 1921 Evgeny Zamiatin had completed the landmark novel *We* (*My*), and by the end of the 1920s, various forms of writing, from science fiction and experimental modernist novels to exaggerated forms of drama, had assimilated utopian motifs.

Utopian discourses had multiple sources. As Richard Stites, Leonid Geller, and others have demonstrated, the surge of utopian discourses in the 1920s cannot be explained solely by the influence of Marxist ideology; rather, there was a fusion of Marxist and anarchist utopian ideas with ancient folk beliefs preserved by the Old Believers and sectarians.[35] The post-revolutionary avant-garde, particularly Constructivism, served as a vehicle for utopian daydreaming. Another wave of utopian thinking arose from administrative dreams of rationalized and militarized social bodies (from Petrine dreams to Arakcheev's Military Colonies). Nikolai Fedorov's "cosmic" utopias ("the philosophy of the common task") also gained new popularity in the 1920s, as did socialist-populist utopias of the 1860s–70s.[36]

This contradictory, explosive combination of discourses generated multifaceted utopian texts in the 1920s. Among them were popular Marxist books, such as *The ABC of Communism*

(*Azbuka kommunizma*, 1920) by Nikolai Bukharin and Evgeny Preobrazhensky, as well as the Proletkult manuals on the mechanization and rationalization of the communist future promoted by Aleksandr Bogdanov, Lenin's former friend and later opponent, and the author of the first Russian Marxist utopian science fiction, *The Red Star* (*Krasnaia Zvezda*, 1908). Also important is the work of Aleksei Gastev, an original poet, veteran of the Revolution, the organizer of the Central Institute of Labor and The League of Time, and an avid follower of Taylor's and Ford's ideas of efficient management.

A veritable encyclopedia of utopian beliefs and their consequences may be found in Evgeny Zamiatin's ironic and stylized *Fairy Tales for Grown-Ups* (*Bol'shim detiam skazki*, 1922). Among other characters, here the reader meets *poshekhontsy*—the traditional nincompoops of folkloric tales and nineteenth-century satire (especially Saltykov-Shchedrin's characters), who in their search for fresh water made a hole in the earth ("naskvoz' zemliu prokolupali") because the water they encountered was too ordinary. Next to them stands the angel Dormidon, who pulls the "saved" human on a rope to heaven with such force that he delivers only a dead body; or a horrible monster named Khriapalo, who can only move along a straight line, leaving behind burned desert. The cycle ends in a micro-dystopia about Fita, a bureaucratic monster (reminiscent of Saltykov-Schedrin's Organchik), who establishes total happiness through a series of orders. With one order he "defeats" cholera by declaring all sick people state criminals, and fires all doctors. By another, he establishes "unbent freedom of singing and marching in national costumes." With his final order, he demands that everyone become a complete fool: "And they lived happily ever after, because no one in the world is happier than complete fools" ("netu na svete schastlivei petykh").[37]

Utopian influences were prominent in popular genres, children's literature, journalism, and public discourses of the period, less so in major literary texts. Utopian sensibility found its most effective expression across all genres when tinged with doubt. This paradoxical position looks true of both pro-communist and anti-communist ideological productions. Even the Proletkult poets, who became famous for their glorifications of the class-based "we" and the "Iron Messiah" (Vladimir Kirillov), expressed deep ambivalence, as Mark Steinberg noted: "ecstasy and terror, good and evil, death and salvation are combined in these images of modern factories and machines, and of modern change and progress."[38] However, neither Khlebnikov's utopian poem *Ladomir* (1920), with its opaque prophecies about the world spearheaded by the revolution of creative minds, nor Mayakovsky's utopian poems *150,000,000* and *The Flying Proletarian* (*Letaiushchii proletarii*, 1925) had an impact comparable to that of Mayakovsky's satirical play *The Bedbug* (*Klop*, 1928–29).

First produced by Vsevolod Meyerhold (1929) and accompanied by Dmitry Shostakovich's original score, Mayakovsky's *Bedbug* enjoyed renewed popularity in the 1960s through 1980s. The play's main laughingstock is a degraded proletarian, Ivan Prisypkin, who sells out his class origin and his party card in exchange for acceptance into a nouveau riche family brought to wealth by the New Economic Policy (1921–28). However, the wedding feast ends with a fire, in which the drunken groom and his entire future family perish. In the second part of the play, Prisypkin is resurrected in the communist world fifty years after his death. Mayakovsky's intention is to test current social phenomena by their projection onto the future where vast improvements are to be anticipated; the same principle will be used in his last comedy, *The Bathhouse*.

The communist future in *The Bedbug* is more than a little ambivalent. Reflecting some Constructivist ideas, it presents the super-rationalist organization of society as the state of perfection. On the one hand, in a global direct democracy all decisions are made by universal vote through advanced communicative technologies, and every individual life is venerated and endlessly extended. On the other hand, the future is emotionless: rationality and the cult of efficiency have obliterated such negative practices as alcoholism and foul language, and also love and poetry, art and kisses. But Prisypkin, silly and vulgar as he is, effortlessly seduces this sterile world, causing "an acute attack of an ancient disease they called 'love,'" which results in an "epidemic of oceanic proportion."[39] His remonstrations undo the rationalized utopia by exposing its repression of the emotional and irrational. This will prove to be the Achilles heel of the communist future.

The learned experts in that future define Prisypkin as an "anthropoid simulator," i.e., a subhuman creature, similar in his parasitic nature to the bedbug unfrozen together with him. In this respect, *Bedbug* resembles *The Heart of a Dog* (*Sobach'e serdtse*, written in 1925), despite radical ideological differences between Mayakovsky and Bulgakov (curiously, Bulgakov is listed by Mayakovsky in a future "dictionary of obsolete words" along with Surrealism and suicide). In *Bedbug*, Prisypkin is placed into a zoo cage, a gesture that reflects the dehumaniza-tion of that which is "imperfect" from the standpoint of Bolshevik ideology. The play's final scene resounds with clangorous, subversive notes. Breaking drama's fourth wall, Prisypkin appeals to the audience: "Citizens! Brothers! My own people! Darlings! How did you get here? So many of you! When were you unfrozen? Why am I alone in the cage?"[40] Despite the author's intention to humiliate his character as a "class traitor," Prisypkin not only elicits the readers'/viewers' empathy, but also exposes in the design of the Constructivist utopia what now can be clearly recognized as the beginnings of totalitarian violence.

Alongside this rationalist-collectivist modernizing utopia stood an organicist and usually nationalist notion of the peasant community. It was imagined as thriving in intimate contact with forces of nature, as faithful to ancient spiritual traditions, and as defying the destructive forces of Westernization, urbanization and industrialization. This discourse produced such ideologically diverse works as a socialist utopia by the famous economist and sociologist Aleksandr Chaianov (1888–1937), *The Travel of My Brother Aleksei into the Country of the Peasant Utopia* (*Puteshestvie moego brata Alekseiia v stranu krest'iánskoi utopii*, 1920) or a conservative utopia *Beyond the Thistle* (*Za chertopolokhom*, 1921), perfectly fusing monarchism, Orthodoxy, anti-Semitism, and anti-modernism, by the former ataman of the Don Cossacks, General Petr Krasnov (1869–1947), writing in emigration. Both rationalist (Constructivist) and organicist (peasants') cultural programs shared a single conviction about the collectivist subject of his-tory, protecting "us" as the definitive social unit against the unruly "I"; in that sense, they are exploring a single view of post-revolutionary subjectivity. In opposition, a critique of utopian systems developed, featuring a rebellion of the "I" against the dominance of the "we." Zamiatin's novel *We* was a first and influential step in this direction. It was written by an acknowledged master of prose, who had been in the revolutionary movement, for which he was imprisoned and exiled in 1905 and 1911. However, having returned to Petrograd from England in September 1917, Zamiatin had encountered all the horrors of Bolshevik War Communism and was briefly arrested by the Cheka for his article "I Am Afraid" ("Ia boius'," 1921).

The novel appeared first in English translation in 1924, then in Czech (1927) and French (1928). In reverse translation from Czech, a large excerpt in Russian appeared in 1927 in a Prague-based émigré magazine, *Volia Rossii*.[41] In 1928–29, this publication triggered an aggres-sive campaign against Zamiatin in the Soviet press, after which *We* and its author were demonized as the epitome of anti-communism in literature. In the early 1920s the situation had been different: Zamiatin read from the novel during many open events; the publication of *We* was announced by at least two Soviet journals; and several critics, including Voronsky and Tynianov, openly discussed it in print. *We* is often described as the first dystopian representa-tion of totalitarianism, a world in which human individuality is reduced to a mere number. It mocks the early Soviet infatuation with the rationalization of everyday life, as well as Taylor's and Ford's ideas of efficiency as promoted by Bogdanov and Gastev. As a satire of Bolshevism,

We also represents a critique of versions of modernity based on the extreme application of rationality and imposition of coercive control over unconscious and individual desires and personalities. In this respect, *We* clearly resonates with such cinematic dystopias as Fritz Lang's *Metropolis* (1927) and Charlie Chaplin's *Modern Times* (1936).

Arguably, Zamiatin's most acute insight at this formative period of the Soviet political regime was to identify a state-centered religiosity beneath a society organized according to "mathematically calculated happiness." Overemphasized rationality of the OneState does not prevent a blinding religious cult surrounding the state itself, one whose will and rules stand for moral norms and philosophical principles of the "numbers." In this context, the association of the OneState leader with a god appears natural: "It was He. He was descending from the heavens in His aero to be among us, the new Jehovah, as wise and as cruel in his love as the Jehovah of the Ancients."[42]

Zamiatin's favorite thought about the new Middle Ages shines through here: social mores and culture regress, even as modern technological innovation moves forward (fully explained in his essay "Tomorrow" ["Zavtra," 1919]). The unconscious hidden within each "number" can potentially explode the monolith of the OneState. I-330 proclaims: "we [are] anti-Christians." "*We* comes—from God, and *I* comes from the Devil," argues D-503, and the author seems to agree.[43] The Devil also embodies transgressions of societal norms and morals. Such transgressive powers of the unconscious, driving the individual desire for freedom, correspond to the cosmic force of energy as a crucial antagonist to the state of entropy. The revolution fails in *We*: in the novel's finale, D-503 is transformed into a complacent and emotionally dumb human machine, I-330 is tortured to death, and the OneState defeats the rebellion "because reason has to win."[44] This dystopian representation of the "end of history" presupposes rebellion and chaos as the driving forces of the universe, while the human quest for order leads to entropy, stagnation, and a living death. Revolution, which Zamiatin seemed to criticize so harshly, returns as the permanent utopian horizon of any stagnant social order.

This paradoxical transformation of dystopia into a revolutionary utopia testifies to the inseparability of these two seemingly opposite modalities in literature of the 1920s. Not only did utopian striving produce dystopian results, but almost every dystopia also generated a new utopia. Other examples include Mikhail Kozyrev's *Leningrad* (1925) and Mikhail Bulgakov's plays *Adam and Eve* (*Adam i Eva*, 1931) and *Bliss* (*Blazhenstvo*, 1933–34), but the most striking appear in the works of Andrei Platonov.

Andrei Platonov was as multifaceted as the literary legacy he left. He appears as a character in Viktor Shklovsky's *The Third Factory* (*Tret'ia fabrika*, 1926), a highly personal book in which Shklovsky tested the limits of a Soviet writer's freedom. He portrays Platonov as a person who does "real things" and therefore, he argues somewhat disingenuously, is free from the concerns of a professional writer.[45] An authentic proletarian by virtue of his social origin and a veteran of the Civil War, Platonov worked as an irrigation engineer, where attempts to transform nature must have influenced his belief in the revolutionary ideas of utopia. Thomas Seifrid aptly judges that "Platonov has deservedly come to be seen as one of the important early dissenters from Soviet utopianism, whose undermining activities were all the more effective for having been conducted from within that chiliastic world view."[46] By the time he met Shklovsky, Platonov was also working as a writer, and his development involved him in an intense dialogue with utopian discourses. In the works Platonov wrote between 1922 and 1932, one can find a whole spectrum of possibilities: a "positive" utopia in the form of science fiction short stories and novellas; a historical explication in *Epiphany Sluices* (*Epifanskie shliuzy*, 1927); original versions of dystopia in *Chevengur* and *The Foundation Pit*; and an ambivalent fusion of utopia and dystopia in *The Juvenile Sea* (*Iuvenil'noe more*, 1932) and in the unfinished novel *Happy Moscow* (*Schastlivaia Moskva*, 1933).

The loosely connected science-fiction texts *Descendants of the Sun* (*Potomki solntsa*, 1922), *The Lunar Bomb*, and *The Ethereal Tract* read as the strangest narrative in Platonov's legacy: the cycle borders on self-parody yet is also seemingly serious and even visionary. In these texts, several generations of scientists and engineers seek to create "ether channels" to deliver "dead electrons" to living electrons who supposedly consume ether, and by this means radically multiply select material objects. This method, according to the logic of Platonov's heroes, would resolve the problem of food and wealth: a grain of wheat could be instantly enlarged a thousand times and a gram of gold could be transformed into a ton of precious metal. This discovery would change the nature of civilization and forever liberate humanity from dependence on material objects and thus from its materialist values. The connection of this fantastic plan with Nikolai Fedorov's mystical utopia of the resurrection of the dead is not hard to see.[47]

There is also a similarity between this set of ideas and Mikhail Bulgakov's *The Fatal Eggs* (*Rokovye iaitsa*, 1925): Platonov's "ether channels" function in the same way as Bulgakov's "ray of life." In Bulgakov's dystopia, a catastrophe happens, proving that the flow of life cannot be controlled by means of the revolutionary regime. In Platonov's stories, while the invention of the machine leading to the endless multiplication of matter proves successful, the result of the experiment remains ambivalent. First, the final experiment yields some "strange and horrible creature," a monster with enormous mouth and sharp teeth—an artificially enlarged electron. Second, the inventor, after his success, does not stay to elaborate the results, but leaves his home and (following his father's example) starts traveling across the world. His soul, explains Platonov, is not satisfied by his majestic discovery and requires more and more impressions. The parallel between a "hungry electron" and the questing soul suggests a reading of the entire cycle as a metaphor of the search for utopia. Platonov brings to a logical conclusion the vision of communism as the utopian world of material plenty. But this conclusive result fails to satisfy his protagonists, which leads the author to a reconsideration of the communist utopia and, generally speaking, all utopias built upon technological and intellectual progress.

While at work on *The Ethereal Tract*, Platonov wrote *Epiphany Sluices*, depicting the tragic dead-end of any modernization utopia based only on technological progress. He no doubt drew on his own experiences as an engineer, but he set his novella in the Petrine era. The narrative is written in a stylized language including letters to and from British engineer Bertrand Perry, who was commissioned to build channels and sluices connecting the Don and Oka Rivers for new navigation routes. A parallel between the Soviet and Petrine radical modernization projects is a common trope in Russian literature of the 1920–30s.[48] Apart from the sheer terror of his authority, Peter lends his political backing to Perry's engineering work. This proves insufficient to bring about a vision of modernization. Theft, sabotage, and poor planning undermine the project. Resistance to the new navigation routes comes from the Russian people and from nature itself. As a result, the project fails, for which Perry is scapegoated: arrested and sent to Moscow, he finds death at the hands of a homosexual torturer. Bertrand Perry's prototype, John Perry, who served as the channel engineer in Peter the Great's time, did not end this badly: after seventeen years of successful service, he returned to England. It may well be that Platonov wanted to historicize the inevitable failure of a purely rational approach to modernization—as epitomized by Perry—and to justify the need to fuse utopian ideals with emotional involvement, with love, the motif "pedagogically" inverted by Perry's final ordeal.[49]

The fates of the sincerely conceived utopias in *Chevengur* and *The Foundation Pit* look no less catastrophic. In *Chevengur*, communist utopia is created according to an emotional calculus by Kopenkin, the knight of the revolution, and by Chepurny, the head of the local Soviet and local communists. First, they cleanse the entire town of everyone who does not fit their (fantastic) idea of the proletariat (of which they have no experience), then they bring into

Chevengur the poorest of the poor (*prochie*, "the miscellaneous people"), who characterize themselves as "nobody" (*nikto*). Free from labor and exploitation, eating wild herbs and berries, they quickly exhaust the stock of poultry and cattle held from the pre-communist past. Platonov's communists live by the demands of the "poor soul," and thus live out the utopian end of history. Thomas Seifrid detects in the Chevengurians' worldview an "eccentric mix of revolutionary fanaticism with philosophies of Fedorov and Bogdanov," noting "the pessimism with which Platonov had come to regard the prospects for rescue from man's existential lot."[50] In *Chevengur*'s utopia, all living energy fades. This end of history reverses the logic of Zamiatin's theory of energy and entropy. The realization of communist utopia makes for the slow death of the entire town. Symptomatically, communism is associated with Kopenkin's "fair lady," the dead revolutionary Rosa Luxemburg: Kopenkin, the revolutionary knight, "loved the dead, for Rosa Luxemburg was among their number."[51] When a boy dies soon after arrival in Chevengur, the inhabitants claim that he has died from communism, but Kopenkin disagrees: "Maybe it's a plague, but it isn't communism" ("Tut zaraza, a ne kommunizm").[52]

By contrast, *The Foundation Pit* represents an energetic, rather than entropic, version of utopia seen as the practical embodiment of age-old myths, and the essence of human dreams, desires, and aspirations. The first part of the novel depicts the creation of a house for the entire proletariat of the district. Reminiscent of the Tower of Babel, it satirically represents Stalinist industrialization. The second part, narrating collectivization and the elimination of kulaks (wealthy peasants) as a class, broadly employs motifs of Russian fairy tales. In both parts, utopia and death remain inseparably intertwined. The foundation pit for the new Tower of Babel turns into a grave for the girl Nastya (despite the Greek meaning of her full name, Anastasia—resurrection), and the collectivized village stands as a fairy-tale kingdom of the dead: people live in coffins ready to die at any moment. Collectivized peasants admit: "We no longer sense anything, the only thing left within us is ash" ("My teper' nichego ne chuem, v nas odin prakh ostalsia").[53]

In fairy tales, wishes translate into action miraculously, and so, in the world of the peasant we find the laws of fairy tale poetics guarantee the instant transformation of word into deed. Characters perceive words as magic spells. Joseph Brodsky has aptly described the role of language in Platonov's dystopia: "Platonov speaks of a nation which in a sense has become a victim of its own language; or, to put it more accurately, he tells a story about this very language, which turns out to be capable of generating a fictitious world, and then falls into grammatical dependence on it."[54] The material power of the word, which is to say, the ability of an ideologically charged discourse to create monstrous social constructs, demonstrates how the desire for utopia turns against itself by producing total destruction instead of a brave new world.

Neither *Chevengur* nor *The Foundation Pit* could appear in the Soviet press until Perestroika.[55] Perhaps more unexpected was the ban on the novella *The Juvenile Sea*, whose protagonist Nikolai Eduardovich Vermo is depicted with much empathy (his patronymic associated him with Konstantin Eduardovich Tsiolkovsky, the main successor of Fedorov's ideas in Soviet Russia). His utopian projects look unthreatening by comparison with Platonov's other works.[56] After the Stalin-inspired attack on his quasi-documentary chronicle *For the Future Good* (*Vprok*, 1930), the writer was trying to demonstrate his political loyalty in *The Juvenile Sea*, which complied with the norms of official literature.[57] However, the result was a mix of "parodic reaction to the consequences of Stalin's destructive politics" and Platonov's own "farewell" to his ideals of the 1920s.[58]

Platonov's unfinished novel *Happy Moscow* was a different kind of farewell, the story of Moscow Chestnova, a member of Komsomol and an exemplary heroine of the 1930s, first as a parachutist and then as a construction worker on the Moscow subway. Referring both to the

660 PROSE AND DRAMA

heroine's name and the city, the novel's title *Happy Moscow* suggested ambivalence and alle-gory.[59] Depictions of the exquisite pastimes of Soviet youth in combination with the heroine's sexual liberty recall popular pre-revolutionary utopias, such as the nineteenth-century utopian socialist François Marie Charles Fourier's phalanstery or the "fourth dream of Vera Pavlovna" in Chernyshevsky's *What Is to Be Done?* Platonov's heroine appears as a living and breathing promise of happiness inseparable from communism. She has three suitors, and each of them offers his own interpretation of utopian fulfillment: rationalist (engineer Sartorius), sexual/ organicist (Sambikin), and mundane (Komiagin). None of them satisfies Moscow, who real-izes that societal models of happiness are illusory, and she has no personal illusions of her own. Her disappearance from the final part of the book is open to multiple interpretations. But it is clear that the promise of utopian happiness becomes impotent when the weak forces of pity and tenderness, to which Platonov ascribes fundamental importance, and which come forward in the description of Sartorius's new life, play a part.

Platonov's idiosyncratic language strikes the reader as an explosive mix of ideology and phantasmagoria, of official rhetoric and its comical appropriations through colloquial distor-tions. Olga Meerson has shown how his style and language create an effect she calls non-defamiliarization. It deprives the reader of a superior vantage point on the character. The reader sees and understands no more than do Platonov's heroes. This device "lures the reader into a trap of moral responsibility" for the actions of characters who believe in utopia and destroy themselves and life around them.[60] As a result, Platonov's style both glorifies utopia and satirizes it pungently.

The longer prose writings of Platonov remained unknown to the mass reader for nearly the whole Soviet era. By contrast, Aleksandr Belyaev (1884–1942) and Aleksandr Grin (1880–1932) enjoyed enormous popularity. As the respective founders of Soviet science fiction and fantasy, these writers responded to utopian trends in fiction, sometimes critically. Knowledgeable about Fedorov's and Tsiolkovsky's ideas (one of his novellas is called "The Star KETS," an anagram for Tsiolkovsky), Belyaev puts them to the test by creating plots in which the human subject gains immortality and forfeits the body, for example in the novel *The Head of Professor Dowell* (*Golova professora Douelia*, 1925). Alternatively, as in the novel *The Amphibian Man* (*Chelovek-amfibiia*, 1928), Doctor Salvatore acquires power over the natural world and prepares to found a new Eden and new Adam only to be thwarted tragically by the cruelty of social relations. Despite Belyaev's infatuation with scientific ideas, the brightest inventions in his works that promise universal happiness inevitably produce only pain and tragedy. Belyaev's novels and short stories were widely published in the Soviet Union and they may have been more acceptable because his criticism of capitalism camouflaged a more subversive mes-sage.[61] They exhibit a genuine longing for utopia undermined by doubt in rationality as an effective tool for the transformation of society.

Aleksandr Grin, by comparison, fuses utopian narratives with Neo-Romantic poetics. In the majority of his larger-scale, mature works (unlike his early Expressionist stories), Grin creates a virtual reality that is hermetically sealed off from everything Soviet. Akhmatova passed sar-castic judgment on Grin's prose as "translation from the unknown," touching on his stylized vagueness. [62] His invented world is by no means ideal, and it contains inequality and social strife. However, it is also filled with sun and sea and inhabited by heroes who seem to have walked straight out of the books of Edgar Allan Poe, Jules Verne, and Rudyard Kipling. His characters enjoy an inner freedom that empowers them to accomplish miracles and to fly like a bird in *The Glittering World* (*Blistaiushchii mir*, 1923), or to walk on water in *The Waverunner* (*Begushchaia po volnam*, 1928).[63] For Grin, utopia is possible but only as the individual accomplishment of a free spirit able to create imaginary worlds and transcend borders, rather than as a project of social betterment. Yet his utopianism is not escapist, and its meaning verges on the dissident. The popularity of both Grin and Belyaev peaked in the 1960s as their books were republished and became screenplays. It was their versions of utopia that laid the foundation for late Soviet science fiction (including Ivan Efremov and the Strugatsky brothers) and the Neo-Romantic fantasies for young adults by Aleksandr Sharov, Vadim Shefner, Yuri Koval, and Vladislav Krapivin.

Grotesque modernism of the 1920s and 1930s

Literature and especially prose of the 1920s provides a perfect example of what the cultural theorist Geoffrey Galt Harpham, following Thomas Kuhn, calls a paradigm crisis, that is, an interim moment when "anomalies have emerged to discredit an old explanatory paradigm or model, and to make it impossible to continue adhering to it, but before the general acceptance of the new paradigm."[64] The surge of utopian discourses is not the sole proof of the paradigm crisis in literature of the 1920s–30s. A seemingly opposite type of writing, but one that is complementary to the utopian mode, exists in the rich and diverse grotesque literature of the period. By fusing contrasting discourses, modalities, and symbolic systems, the grotesque becomes what Yuri Tynianov called a constructive principle.

Grotesque modernism can render ideas of utopia (Platonov), the rational and the irrational (Zamiatin, Krzhizhanovsky), the ideological and the mundane (Erenburg, Zoshchenko, Erdman, Il´f, and Petrov), lofty and degraded (Vaginov), poetic and vulgar (Olesha, Dobychin), human and animalistic (Bulgakov, Mayakovsky). To a degree, the style builds on earlier works that resisted realist norms. Masters of pre-revolutionary grotesque modernism such as Bely, Sologub, and Remizov embraced the legacies of Gogol and Saltykov-Shchedrin, and grotesque modernism also marks the early works of Mayakovsky and Zamiatin. Zoshchenko's prose and Erdman's comedies endlessly demonstrate how the discourses of power mutate in daily life and how the symbolic power of a representative of the masses builds on the age-old role of a "little person" (malen ´kii chelovek), Russian culture's traditional trope for a subaltern. Power and the powerlessness of the language of the masses is a perennial theme.

Between this style and Bakhtin's theory of carnival, there are certain similarities of type. The scholar's lived experience in the early days of the Soviet Union shaped his work on Rabelais and His World in the 1930s. Although it was written slightly later, Rabelais and His World can sharpen our notion of the grotesque in Russian literature of the 1920s. It distinguishes between two types of grotesque. In the carnivalesque grotesque, the fusion of opposite elements—denigration and vitality, beauty and ugliness, the high and low—"consecrates inventive freedom...liberates from the prevailing point of view of the world, from the conventions and established truths, from clichés, from all that is humdrum and universally accepted."[65] But in the Romantic grotesque, Bakhtin says, motifs of the Doppelgänger, mask, shadow, mannequin, live doll, or body part (as in Gogol's story "The Nose"), signify the dissonance between idealistic aspirations and reality, between dreams and their effects. Grotesque modernism of the 1920s–30s includes both tendencies: Dobychin and Krzhizhanovsky are closest to the Romantic grotesque, while Zoshchenko and Erdman reinvent the tradition of the carnival grotesque.

That dissonance between the real and the ideal resonates powerfully in the work of Dobychin, the author of two small collections of stories and a short novel, The Town of N. After these publications in the 1920s–30s, Dobychin vanished in 1936 in the wake of the prorabotka directed against The Town of N as a "formalist novel." He was largely forgotten until the 1980s, when a volume of his work appeared in New York. During Perestroika, his prose attracted serious critical attention; in the 2000s, it became the subject of a series of annual conferences in Daugavpils, Latvia, Dobychin's hometown, and several collections of articles also appeared.[66] *The Town of N* is narrated from the standpoint of an unnamed boy, from his young years before starting school until his graduation. His favorite personal pronoun throughout the book is "we," which makes his childish perception indistinguishable from the voices and opinions of his mother, his nanny, their acquaintances and friends. However, in the course of the narrative it becomes clear that the boy's voice stands not just for his family circle, but for a large and boundless provincial collective body that unites people of different classes and professions. Frequent references to Gogol's *Dead Souls* begin with the novel's title and underscore the stability of the collective body's life, which is little changed since Gogol's age. Even the Revolution of 1905 cannot shake up provincial life, which through the boy's eyes appears as "a grotesque catalogue of objects, phrases, book titles, echoes of historical, political, social changes—but reduced and redacted.... This list-like narrative lacks any qualitative or thematic hierarchy."[67] The disproportions of perspective are a further effect of the aesthetics of the grotesque in *The Town of N*, where the narrator rarely grasps how significant some object or event might be, and thus can loop back endlessly to try to comprehend a rather trivial detail. Strangely neutral, passing references to the violence of executions or pogroms can also pop up in stunningly short sentences, a brevity that also marks the young narrator's reports on various deaths, including that of his own father. The novel is perhaps equal parts lyric and satire, another point of resemblance to *Dead Souls*. Dobychin describes a provincial town's social intolerance and religious prejudice, with dry quotations of characters' anti-Semitic or anti-Catholic views, but he is not a critic of apolitical "philistines" unable to feel the significance of revolutionary change. For him, "human existence consists of routine, and the revolution, even more than does everyday life, reveals unshakeable clichés beneath human reactions and behavioral motives...."[68] Nevertheless, there is an internal dynamic in this world of static repetition, and it is associated with the narrator's maturation and his steady separation from the collective identity of family and friends; as a radical step in this process (this is also the novel's finale), the narrator gets eyeglasses and realizes that "everything I've seen was wrong."[69]

Like Dobychin, Sigizmund Krzhizhanovsky (1887–1950) was another nearly forgotten writer of the early Soviet period. Many of Krzhizhanovsky's texts fit the Bakhtinian category of Menippean satire, a carnivalesque mode in which grotesque fantasy reveals hidden contradictions in philosophical concepts. Naum Leiderman argues that Krzhizhanovsky's poetics aim at the creation of "thought-images": by "turning abstract terms into things, he extracts from their formal meaning a palpable, thing-like aspect."[70] Krzhizhanovsky experiments with the Enlightenment intellectual tradition by placing its thought-images into fictional conditions where both direct and metaphorical reflections of historical catastrophes unfold before the writer's eyes.

Consider, for example, several texts that refer to Kant's philosophy as the source of grand narratives of the Enlightenment and modernity: "Catastrophe" ("Katastrofa," 1919–20), "The Life-Story of One Thought" ("Zhizneopisanie odnoi mysli," 1920), and "Autobiography of a Corpse" ("Avtobiografiia trupa," 1925).[71] In "Catastrophe," Krzhizhanovsky depicts the imaginary consequences of *The Critique of Pure Reason*. Objects run away, leaving behind pure space and time. Life falls victim to the violence of universalizing thought that deprives things of their individual meaning, although, as the narrator adds, "each thing, no matter how small or frail it may be, is incredibly precious and needs, needs, needs, its own singular meaning" ("nuzhnee nuzhnogo nuzhen ee sobstvennyi nepovtorimyi smysl").[72] Despite the allegorical nature of this narrative, the catastrophe caused by Kant's thought—enlightening and universalizing, abstract and therefore cruel—symptomatically resonates with the effects of Revolution and Civil War, which Krzhizhanovsky witnessed in Kiev, the same violence that was vividly described in Bulgakov's *Days of the Turbins* (*Dni Turbinykh*, 1926). In the relationship between these two catastrophes, textual and contextual, Krzhizhanovsky in effect theorizes the Revolution as the realization of powers hidden within rationalist concepts that shaped modernity. In "The Life-Story of One Thought," written in Kiev in the same year as "Catastrophe," he clarifies a further premise: the destructive potential stems not from the original thoughts of great sages of the Enlightenment, but from oversimplified, flattened, and violated distortions of those ideas. Great philosophy, when turned into ideological dogma, opens the way for historical catastrophe.

Krzhizhanovsky's novella *The Letter Killers Club* (*Klub ubiits bukv*, 1926) consists of several narratives composed by characters who meet weekly to improvise and perform the highly philosophical tales they have composed in their heads; they are "letter killers" in their renunciation of the written word, but their compositions are thickly layered with the debris of culture. Each of their narratives intends to present a stylistic and thematic emblem of an epoch in world culture, from the Renaissance to the present. In the narrative representing modernity, civilization is divided into two classes: those who think and those who act under the control of thinkers, i.e., the bio-robots, or "ex-persons." But this division leads to global catastrophe: bodies of humans turned into robots resist the commanding power of reason. Left alone without the control of the central station, they become dysfunctional and collapse. In Caryl Emerson's words, Krzhizhanovsky is exceptional by his "sensitivity to the integrity of an organism. Interfere beyond a certain point, and humanness disintegrates irreversibly."[73] The result of this triumph of reason is suspiciously similar to the consequences of the First World War or Russia's Civil War: "tens of millions of people crumpled to the ground, their bodies motionless or feebly twitching."[74]

The carnivalesque version of the grotesque found brilliant exponents in Mikhail Zoshchenko and Andrei Platonov. Platonov is mainly known for his tragi-farcical novels about communist construction, but he also wrote such grotesque masterpieces as *The Town of Gradov* (*Gorod Gradov*, 1927), *The Innermost Man* (*Sokrovennyi chelovek*, 1928), "Antiseksus" (1925–26, published 1981), "The State Dweller" ("Gosudarstvennyi zhitel'," 1929), and "Doubtful Makar" ("Usomnivshiisia Makar," 1929). In these novellas and short stories, Platonov frequently uses the perspective of a fool who either literally translates ideological abstractions into everyday life, thus blatantly mocking them, or, driven by revolutionary enthusiasm, creates his own projects for the radical improvement of life in agreement with ideological doctrines. The linguistic experiments of Platonov's simpletons are especially comic: they daringly mix party-speak with everyday colloquialisms, thus creating monstrous hybrids and unintentionally revealing the incompatibility of political abstractions with daily life. This device stems from satirical prose of the seventeenth century, with its mock versions of state directives. But Platonov's fools as if unwittingly ridicule doctrines of the *people*'s state, whose language and logic are supposed to be close to that of simple folk, but are rendered as absurdist phantasms. This effect explains the critical outrage at "Doubtful Makar." Prompted by Stalin's displeasure, the head of the Russian Association of Proletarian Writers, Leopol'd Averbakh, published an angry article simultaneously in two journals and then in *Pravda*, in which he called Platonov a "class enemy" and his story an example of "nihilistic debauchery" (*nigilisticheskaia raspushchennost'*) and hostile ambiguity.[75] In fact, Averbakh provided a stunningly accurate account of the story's carnivalistic grotesque, which undermines every political abstraction and dogma from the standpoint of a quasi-naive simpleton.

Unlike Platonov, who was admired mainly by connoisseurs of literature, Zoshchenko, a member of the Serapion Brothers group, was the most popular writer of the 1920s. Zoshchenko's hilarious short stories appeared in numerous comic magazines and were published as chapbooks; his collected works underwent many reprints (five runs in 1926 alone) and leading actors adored performing his works on stage. Academic scholars were quick to appreciate his virtues, and a book with essays on Zoshchenko by Shklovsky and the eminent philologist Viktor Vinogradov appeared in 1928.[76] A virtuoso practitioner of *skaz*, Zoshchenko significantly expanded its rhetorical possibilities. His early texts represent the voice and worldview of an individual from the Soviet masses, and in the late 1920s he stylistically impersonated an imaginary proletarian writer, as Marietta Chudakova has demonstrated. Zoshchenko satirizes the Soviet "new man," she writes, and stages a performance of the creative mind liberated from supposed superstitions of the past. He literalizes the modernist theme of the "naked man on the naked earth," which, in turn, was deeply resonant with Nietzsche's philosophy.[77]

KEYWORD *Skaz*

Grounded in the writings of nineteenth-century classic writers, *skaz* emerged in Russian criticism of the 1920s as a way to understand contemporary literary experiments (beginning with the work of Zoshchenko and Babel). Boris Eikhenbaum, Yuri Tynianov, and Viktor Vinogradov saw the early genealogy of *skaz* in Gogol and Leskov, defining it as an artistic imitation of oral speech.[78] To use somewhat anachronistic terminology, one could say that they conceptualized *skaz* as performative writing, displaying through verbal means oral speech, gestures, mimicry, and sharp intonations, i.e., orality as a newly discovered form of cultural existence. Shklovsky emphasized the plot function of *skaz*: he observed that in Leskov's story "The Left-Handed Craftsman," *skaz* enables a "secondary ironic perception of the allegedly patriotic tale."[79] *Skaz* was a defining trope in *Russia Washed by Blood (Rossiia, krov'iu umytaia*, 1924) by Artem Veselyi (1899–1938); *The Fall of Dair (Padenie Daira*, 1923) by Aleksandr Malyshkin (1892–1938); *The Guerilla Tales (Partizanskie povesti*, 1923) by Vsevolod Ivanov; *Humus (Peregnoi*, 1923) and *Vireneia* (1924) by Lidia Seifullina (1889–1954); and *Badgers (Barsuki*, 1924) by Leonid Leonov. Zamiatin and Remizov were important practitioners of *skaz* as well. These authors used *skaz* to connect disparate cultural realms, exposing along the way the persistence of age-old feuds, including social, religious, and ethnic antagonisms.

The ornamental version of *skaz* does not typically imply a critical attitude toward the speaking subject. The founding fathers of this kind of *skaz* are again Gogol and Leskov, with important later texts by the creators of ornamental prose in the 1920s, including early Leonid Leonov, Vsevolod Ivanov, and Andrei Sobol (1888–1926). This type of *skaz* receives a new impulse in the "regionalist" stylizations of the 1930s, authors such as Pavel Bazhov (1879–1950), Stepan Pisakhov (1879–1960), and Boris Shergin (1896–1973) and is broadly used much later in Aleksandr Solzhenitsyn's *One Day in the Life of Ivan Denisovich*, in Village Prose, and in a particular form of the intelligentsia's *skaz* developed by Liudmila Petrushevskaya and Vladimir Makanin (1937–2017).

Mikhail Bakhtin in his studies of novelistic heteroglossia arrived at a complementary understanding of *skaz*. He treated it as a form of double-voiced discourse, in which the narrator is distanced from the invisible (and mute) author. Scholars who followed Bakhtin's approach in the 1960s–80s emphasized that a *skaz* narrative does not just imitate oral speech: it creates the image of uneducated, irregular, distorted language, whose deviations both represent and critique the speaking subject.[80] The result can have a political impact. Characters created by means of *skaz* typically tried to express an idiosyncratic understanding of society and life values. They undermined the Soviet doctrine of the class-based cultural superiority of toiling masses and the emergence of a "new Soviet person" by these very idiosyncrasies.

Zoshchenko's immensely successful short story "The Bathhouse" ("Bania," 1925) is emblematic of his entire vision of Soviet society and the "new men" it created. Depicting the comical tortures of a narrator's attempts to wash in a public bathhouse, the story also reads as a metaphor of revolutionary efforts to cleanse society of the vices left over from the imperial past. But this attempt at purgation only redistributes the dirt, producing a constant struggle for the survival of the fittest, and it leaves our poor narrator without his clothes, as if he, like everyone else in the bathhouse, has lost all social and cultural conventions. This anthropological nakedness defines Zoshchenko's characters: exposed, vulnerable, and sadly hilarious. The chronotope of the bathhouse where weaknesses and desires are made visible for all to see is most tangibly represented by the communal apartment, the site for well-known stories like "Nervous People" ("Nervnye liudi," 1924), "Electrification" ("Elektrifikatsiia, 1924"), "A Summer Break" ("Letniaia peredyshka," 1929), and many others. By comparison, there is also the theater or movie house, the space where "The Aristocratic Lady" ("Aristokratka," 1923), "The Actor" ("Akter," 1925), and "The Benefits of Culture" ("Prelesti kul'tury," 1927) take place. Here, a character stripped of identity finds himself in the world of cultural conventions. The lawlessness of the communal apartment or bathhouse invades the space of culture, as when a brawl at the entrance to the movie theater substitutes for the show ("A Cinematic Drama" ["Kinodrama," 1926]), or the actor performing as a victim of theft discovers that his wallet was actually stolen on stage ("The Actor").

In the context of anthropological nakedness everything complex or ideal is reduced to the primitive and crudely materialistic. Ignorance qualifies as a sickness ("The Patient" ["Patsient," 1926]); sickness is explained by the failure of a protagonist to wash for four days ("Four Days" ["Chetyre dnia," 1925]). The magic causing the cattle's suffering happens because the "wizard" simply has stuck a needle into a cow's leg ("The Wizard" ["Koldun," 1924]). A person's character radically improves after vermicide treatment, and in general, "a human being has no character at all, a human being according to the latest scientific data, consists of 180 grams of salt, three pounds of potato flour and a certain amount of liquid. And perhaps your character suffers from an insufficiency of potato flour. That's why you worry" ("Very Simply" ["Ochen' prosto," 1927]).[81]

Zoshchenko reveals the boundless cynicism of the new Soviet person, who emerges as a suspiciously enthusiastic conformist. His characters can reproduce any discourses and serve any ideologies, provided this service sustains their vitality. In fact, they remain indifferent to anything that goes beyond bodily needs; they clumsily disguise their behavior with bits of ideological rhetoric that is barely understood and comically misused. At the same time, they feel constant fear before the complexities of the world around them and strive to simplify it as much as possible. His characters engage in humorous conflicts with elements of modern civilization, using them inappropriately or treating them as more nuisance than source of comfort. For example, in "The Summer Break" and "Electrification," inhabitants of a communal apartment decide to cut off the electricity because it produces too many feuds over payment and reveals too much dirt and destruction.

For Zoshchenko, Revolution and post-revolutionary reality manifest a powerful invasion of the unconscious into everyday life; this invasion burns everything in its wake and leaves behind only grotesque forms of language, culture, and sociality. Zoshchenko's characters and narrators exhibit incoherent speech marked by fragmentation, an inability to distinguish the symbolic from the material, and a mental habit of reductionism. Inarticulate, they communicate with each other by means of violence. The cumulative effect of such speakers is to create a gallery of figures who embody the social unconscious of Soviet society. In his late work and especially in the psychoanalytic diptych *Youth Returned* (*Vozvrashchennaia molodost'*, 1933) and *Before Sunrise* (*Pered voskhodom solntsa*, 1943), he sought a route to the control of reason over "the lower levels" of consciousness and arrived at a method similar to Freud's theory of sublimation.[82] The allegorical meaning of Zoshchenko's "self-therapy" was not missed by the authorities and triggered an infamous attack against him in the 1940s: he became one of the main targets of the so-called *zhdanovshchina* campaign that denounced his satire as a "blackening" of the Soviet people.

A writer similar to Zoshchenko in his treatment of the grotesque, his attention to everyday language, and his life story was Nikolai Erdman (1900–70). He became famous in 1925 when Vsevolod Meyerhold produced Erdman's first full-scale play, *The Mandate* (*Mandat*), in his newly opened theater. By 1928, when Erdman had completed his next and as it turned out last play, *The Suicide* (*Samoubiista*), three of the best Moscow theaters (Meyerhold's, Stanislavsky's MKhAT, and the Vakhtangov Theater) competed for the right to stage the new comedy. Stanislavsky had even received lukewarm approval from Stalin. Yet despite their efforts, in 1931 the play was banned as ideologically questionable. In 1933, during the filming of Grigory Aleksandrov's comedy *Jolly Fellows* (*Veselye rebiata*), for which Erdman had co-written the script, the writer was arrested and exiled to Siberia for the satirical fables he co-authored with Vladimir Mass (1896–1979). After his return from exile, and even before he regained permission to return to Moscow, he wrote a number of scripts for famous films of the 1930s–40s, including Aleksandrov's *Volga-Volga* (although his name did not appear in the credits).[83]

The carnivalesque plot of *The Mandate* includes numerous metamorphoses, mésalliances, and vaudevillian techniques. As a result of comic errors, cross-dressing, eavesdropping, and substitutions, an apolitical Guliachkin is suddenly transformed into a communist, and the Guliachkins' kitchen maid Nast'ka is mistaken for a surviving princess from the Romanov family. The carnivalesque confusion becomes a large-scale metaphor for a society that has lost all stability or predictability; here, anything can happen at any moment. Erdman makes a farce of the post-revolutionary stage of society and of individual minds, what in others' hands is rendered dramatic if not tragic. *The Mandate*'s reversals and transformations suggest instead an inexhaustible optimism and true faith in the human ability to overcome tragedy through laughter.[84]

The tragicomic also marks the grotesque aspects of *The Suicide*, with its mix-ups and substitutions between the living and the dead. In the play, news about the intended suicide of an unemployed Semen Semenovich Podsekal'nikov brings an avalanche of visitors, seeking to use his death as a symbolic statement and elevate him as a sacrificial victim of history on their collective behalf. The monologues and exchanges of Erdman's characters are brilliantly witty but they nonetheless expose the deepest secret of Soviet ethos: its orientation towards death as a value higher than life, its demand for mandatory heroism, its transformation of self-sacrifice into an expected modus vivendi. Zoshchenko had accentuated the primitivism of the anthropologically naked character, but Erdman stresses his humanity: Podsekal'nikov, although self-centered and silly, merits compassion and respect as a human being. Some scenes, while remaining hilariously funny, resonate with *Hamlet*. A monologue about the brief second separating life from death reads as a travesty of "To be or not to be," and Podsekal'nikov's "resurrection," three days and nights after his funeral, echoes Christian mythology. By refusing to kill himself, despite universal pressure, Podsekal'nikov chooses freely for the first time in his life. Ignoring the high ideals for which he is required to die, he affirms his own seemingly insignificant life as meaningful. Podsekal'nikov arrives at this self-realization after the celebrations preceding his suicide, a funeral feast during which he even makes a stupidly brave phone call to the "significant person" in the Kremlin.

Podsekal'nikov is desperately fighting for the "right to whisper" ("You won't hear our whisper behind the noise of socialist construction.... We'll live our entire life whispering"),[85] but he matched up well to the ideological myth of philistinism (*meshchanstvo*). Whereas Soviet writers used the term for the demonization of everyday phenomena resistant to revolutionary enthusiasm and self-sacrificial pathos, Erdman reveals a paradoxical rebirth of Gogol's Akaky Akakievich Bashmachkin, with his immortal plea in the famous lines that Belinsky called the "philanthropic passage": "Let me be. Why do you do this to me?" through which one can hear a hidden claim: "I am your brother." Unlike Gogol and Zoshchenko, Erdman finds in the everyday vitality of philistinism the sole force able to resist the depersonalizing pressure of history. It is this vitality that can generate an ordinary person's ability to survive and to confront the ideology of mandatory self-sacrificial death.

Aligning themselves with a similar vision of vitality and survival, many works of grotesque modernism center on a picaro, rogue, provocateur, thief, imposter, or adventure-seeker—in short, a trickster—who puts his powers of subversive self-creation to the service of cynical survival.[86] The long-lived figure of the trickster was epitomized for the modern reader by such characters as Beaumarchais's Figaro, Gogol's Khlestakov, Mark Twain's Tom Sawyer and Huckleberry Finn, and Jaroslav's Hašek's Švejk. The figure reflects irresolvable contradictions in the lives of ordinary citizens pushed into cynical practices of survival. Soviet tricksters frequently act as ironic supermen able to be free from society, while operating within its bounds. Their behavior demonstrates uncertainty and ambiguity across the full spectrum of new Soviet social truths, making it a form of transgressive self-creation not unlike the practice of zhiznetvorchestvo associated with the Russian Symbolists and their heirs. The trickster's indiscriminate laughter offers a joyful epiphany of cynicism and transforms simple daily gestures into a theatrical show, a ball, a cascade of jokes, puns, and magic tricks.

In Ilya Erenburg's satirical novel *Julio Jurenito* (*Khulio Khurenito*, 1922), the eponymous hero is a philosophical trickster who appropriates and subverts discourses of power and authority, regardless of class origins: sanctimonious values of Western democracy, the old Russian intelligentsia, the new Soviet ideology, Lenin, and the ranks of the Cheka are all excellent targets. In Yuri Olesha's *Envy* (*Zavist'*, 1927), only the trickster-philosopher Ivan Babichev can confront the rationalist utopia of his brother Andrei Babichev. Babel lionizes the trickster-thief Benya Krik in his *Odessa Tales* (1924–26) as the true king of the "plebeian modernity" allegedly abandoned, but in fact extended by the Revolution.[87] Lev Lunts, in his Pirandello-like play *The Apes Are Coming* (*Obez'iany idut*, 1920), places the Jester at the center of a city expecting a catastrophic invasion of apes; only the Jester can mobilize desperate people for the decisive battle. Bulgakov initially depicts the trickster as an embodiment of the Revolution's destructive force in Sharikov in *The Heart of a Dog*, but later reconceptualizes this figure when depicting Satan and his retinue in *The Master and Margarita*.

The most charming Soviet literary trickster of all was Ostap Bender, the protagonist of the novels by Ilya Il'f (1897–1937) and Evgeny Petrov (1903–42), *The Twelve Chairs* (*Dvenadtsat' stul'ev*, 1928) and *The Golden Calf* (*Zolotoi telenok*, journal publication 1931, amended book edition 1934), which became instant classics and an inexhaustible source of witticisms. Bender filled the novels with his own alternative and unorthodox ideology, appearing as the sole free character in the entire Soviet universe. His virtuoso juggling of masks, his glorious disdain for all things Soviet ("Building socialism bores me"),[88] and his principled refusal to engage with the collective utopia or to abandon his individualistic quest all testify to his artistry and intellectual superiority. In Alexander Zholkovsky's adept formulation, Ostap Bender is not "just a charming criminal, but a charming individualist, at his limit—a charming anti-Soviet, though this charm is offered with a heavy pro-Soviet flavor."[89] Although Ostap Bender's capitalist dreams end in failure in both novels, his defeats become insignificant next to his charisma, witticisms, and impeccable elegance. The novels' first critics sensed this immediately, although critics also accused Il'f and Petrov of "thematic pettiness" ("melkotem'e") and "insufficiently profound hatred for the class enemy."[90]

Both novels create a grotesque panorama of social schizophrenia in the Soviet world: a comical disjunction between the personal and social self, between face and mask. All of Il'f and Petrov's characters flaunt radical contradictions in the way they wish to be seen and who they are. The interplay between their social role and identity takes place against the backdrop of the official spectacle of socialism and the unofficial economy of *blat*, a system of non-monetary exchange, social networking, and doublespeak. Ostap Bender's nemesis in *The Golden Calf*, a grand master of the shadow economy, Aleksandr Ivanovich Koreyko, is characteristically undistinguished: at first glance, Ostap does not recognize the underground millionaire among the staff of a typical Soviet office, and then loses him in a crowd of people in gas masks. Unlike Ostap, who can play any social role with equal artistry, Koreyko "could only act two parts, the office worker and the underground millionaire. He didn't know a third."[91]

This social schizophrenia is a symptom of widespread cynicism also found in Zoshchenko's and Erdman's representations of the Soviet world. The fracturing of the self testifies to the disintegration of the desired Soviet subjectivity into autonomous and inadequate social masks—in other words, into cynical consciousness. Modernity and modernization are processed by cynicism and transformed into their opposites. While Ostap artistically exploits this social schizophrenia by openly acting out and multiplying its manifestations, he also turns inadequacy into a carnival: he launches an incalculable parade of social roles and idiolects. His joy-filled language games and theatricalization of life liberate him from the confines of precise social location, and he is artistically absorbed into any momentary role, bending it to his will while never submitting himself. His freedom is at once an example, a temptation, and a provocation, aimed at undermining the unwritten conventions of the Soviet world.

It is unsurprising that the trickster's grotesque mask became an appealing model for many writers' acts of self-creation. Such deft behavior brought a perennial condition of liminality (and thus a certain degree of freedom), and offered a release from fixed notions of identity or social role. Instead, the trickster could playfully juggle many possibilities, privileging none. The literary lore of the 1920s–30s preserved numerous anecdotes about the subversive behavior of Viktor Shklovsky, Aleksei Kruchenykh, and Kornei Chukovsky, among others. In the 1970s, the trickster becomes the manifestation of existential freedom in Grigory Gorin's famed play about the legendary Baron Munchausen, *Most Truthful* (*Samyi pravdivyi*, 1974), and later in the film *That Very Munchausen* (*Tot samyi Miunkhauzen*, 1979, dir. Mark Zakharov). In Fazil Iskander's novel *Sandro of Chegem* (*Sandro iz Chegema*, 1973–79, with new chapters added in 1981), a trickster hero operates as a comical double and counterpart to Stalin. Postmodernist and post-avant-garde artists like Dmitry Prigov, Sergei Kurekhin (1954–96), and members of Mit'ki made trickster behavior the core of their individual performative self-representation as well as an artistic philosophy and practice.

Grotesque modernism was not limited to the Soviet cultural sphere. It acquired equal currency among Russian émigré writers—from Teffi to Poplavsky (in his novel *Apollon Bezobrazov*, 1926–32).[92] However, it was Vladimir Nabokov who transformed it into an influential model of writing connecting Russian modernism with European and American counterparts, as well as opening a pathway to what will later be defined as postmodernism.

CASE STUDY **Vladimir Nabokov**

Born in the same year as Platonov and Olesha, Vladimir Nabokov brought to fruition the project of Russian modernism, yet he stood slightly apart not only from Russian writers remaining in the Soviet Union, but also from his fellow émigré writers. His position in the culture is unique. Nabokov belonged to an aristocratic and wealthy Russian family; he received an excellent education (at home, at the Tenishev school in St. Petersburg, and at

Cambridge University) and spoke with equal fluency Russian, English, and French from early childhood. His father was a prominent liberal politician, one of the founders of the Constitutional Democratic Party (KD/Kadety/Konstitutsionno-demokraticheskaia partiia) and a minister of the Provisional government. After emigrating in 1919, Nabokov found himself in a very different situation, especially after graduation from Cambridge University and the tragic assassination of his father in 1922, when his family's means became quite limited and he had to earn his living in Berlin by giving private lessons. He wrote his magical prose in his spare time. But by the late 1930s, after publishing nine novels in Russian (under the pen-name Vladimir Sirin), Nabokov was recognized as the best Russian writer of the young generation in emigration. In 1940, shortly before his second emigration, this time from war-torn Europe to the United States, he switched from Russian to English, the language that eventually would bring him worldwide fame as the author of *Lolita*, *Pale Fire*, and *Ada*. Amazingly, his English-language prose lost none of the stylistic richness and complexity of his Russian novels. His original style paved the way for a rich idiom that would be eagerly admired and imitated by the following generations of writers in both Russian and English.

Nabokov's easy movement between Russian and English languages and literatures generated paradoxes in the perception of his work and persona by different readerships.[93] After his *Lolita*-inspired fame as an English-language author, he was frequently scorned by admirers who found him cold, arrogant, and not sufficiently Russian. While he called himself an American writer in the 1960s–70s and translated, in collaboration with his son, all his Russian novels into English, Nabokov was very proud of the fact that his books were smuggled into the USSR. He admitted that given the choice he would have written in Russian rather than in English. Despite the official ban on their publication, which lasted until Perestroika, his works reached readers in the Soviet Union and were admired in nonconformist circles: Akhmatova expressed steady curiosity, Nadezhda Mandelstam and Kornei Chukovsky were avid fans, and many underground writers of the generation of the Sixties were under his spell. Andrei Bitov and Sasha Sokolov obviously delight in their affinity with him in their writings, and Nabokov's influence extended even to a very Soviet writer, Valentin Kataev, who engages in a dialogue with Nabokov's poetics of memory in his novels *The Holy Well* (*Sviatoi kolodets*, 1965), *The Grass of Oblivion* (*Trava zabveniia*, 1967), and *My Diamond Wreath* (*Almaznyi moi venets*, 1978).

For many late Soviet writers and readers, Nabokov's oeuvre stood for what Russian modernist literature could have become had it not been interrupted and repressed by the Socialist Realist dictatorship. He epitomized an ideal Russian modernist who saved the legacy of the Silver Age for world literature, when it was taboo in the homeland. It would be fair to say that Nabokov was aware of this mission, although Western critics frequently misread his awareness as a sign of his notorious arrogance and artificiality. His "strong opinions" (a tag that stuck thanks to the title of a collection of his interviews, reviews, and essays) would not necessarily apply to his own literary practice, as many scholars noticed; yet they provided a succinct codex of high modernism which sounded provocative in both Western and Soviet contexts of the 1960s, his heyday as a pundit on literary art. Later, writers of postmodernist inclinations, both in the West (John Barth) and in the Soviet Union as well as among émigrés, lionized Nabokov as the predecessor of postmodernism (along with Borges) and as a model for radical innovation in modernist writing.

No wonder that in Russia of the 1990s–2000s, when modernism and postmodernism were moving into the mainstream, Nabokov became a bestseller. All his novels, lectures, and interviews were translated from English and diligently studied.[94] A veritable Nabokov industry now exists in academic life, and his image was even included in the showcase of Russian culture that opened the Sochi Olympics in 2014, a development which Nabokov himself would undoubtedly have defined as *poshlost'* or, as Nabokov always spelled it in transliteration, *poshlust*.

With this Russian word designating "not only the obviously trashy but also the falsely important, the falsely beautiful, the falsely clever, the falsely attractive,"[95] he named a major societal malaise of modernity. Nabokov tirelessly revealed its presence in Socialist Realism and Nazi culture, in Hollywood and "Freudian voodooism" equal to "generalizations devised by literary mythists and sociologists,"[96] as well as in fashionable intellectualism (Bertrand Russell, "the awful Monsieur Camus and even more awful Monsieur Sartre").[97] Nabokov saw *poshlust* as a worldview in which dangerously grand ideas are dominant. He knew the murderous power of ideas founded on political and moralistic stereotypes, best of all represented by a crowd of cheerful German tourists in "Cloud, Castle, Lake" and Paduk's "Ekwilism" in *Bend Sinister* (1947). The war against *poshlust* constituted one of Nabokov's major aesthetic strategies.

His heroes are a hapless bunch that include the doomed émigré chess-player Aleksandr Ivanovich Luzhin in *The Defense* (*Zashchita Luzhina*, 1930), the young Russian émigré Martyn in *Glory* (*Podvig*, 1931–32), Cincinnatus C., a prisoner penalized for the crime of "gnostical turpitude," or intellectual "opacity" in *The Invitation to a Beheading* (*Priglashenie na kazn'*, 1935–36), and Fedor Godunov-Cherdynstev in *The Gift* (*Dar*, 1937–38), a Russian poet living in Berlin who has more than a little in common with Nabokov himself. Most of his protagonists cultivate their status as members of the Russian intelligentsia and thus try to preserve their unique vision of the world, but *poshlust* takes increasingly aggressive forms, even generating totalitarian violence. One strategy of survival that Nabokov's protagonists sometimes manage to accomplish—if only intellectually—brings escape into their own reality, which proves to be more solid than the world of fictions and simulations created by *poshlust*.

Nabokov's fiction frequently unfolds a conflict between true and false creators, which may seem a variation on Romantic themes. The former, like Luzhin (*The Defense*), Martyn (*Glory*), Godunov-Cherdyntsev (*The Gift*), Cincinnatus C. (*Invitation to a Beheading*), Sebastian Knight and his half-brother V. (*The Real Life of Sebastian Knight*, 1938), Adam Krug (*Bend Sinister*), John Shade (*Pale Fire*, 1962), and Van and Ada (*Ada*, 1969), by force of imagination are able to create the world that rises as more real, estranged (in Shklovsky's sense), and fresh. Nabokov shares with them all the power of his vivid memory, precise vision, and spectacular diction. Their antagonists are false creators like Franz in *King, Queen, Knave* (*Korol', dama, valet*, 1928), Hermann in *Despair* (*Otchaianie*, 1934), Monsieur Pierre (*Invitation to a Beheading*), Chernyshevsky (*The Gift*), the unnamed protagonist of *The Enchanter* (*Volshebnik*, 1938), Clare Quilty (*Lolita*), and Charles Kinbote (*Pale Fire*), who impose their bland and grand ideas onto life, without noticing the violence their impositions produce. Their failures stem from a paradoxical resonance between the power of imagination and life's truth: in Nabokov's world, imagination nourishes loving attention to the intricacies of life, while falsity and stereotypes always ignore these "sunny trifles," preferring generalizations and punishing the living for not fitting their abstract presuppositions.

However, this dichotomy starts to crumble when one considers a parodic streak in Nabokov's false creators who, in many cases, mock and reveal the techniques of their antagonists, the author included. Herman (in *Despair*), probably most famous of Nabokov's fake creators, "allows Nabokov to parody his own sense of art as a step beyond the self and toward a sympathy for others perhaps even richer than life allows."[98] Humbert

Humbert, the protagonist and narrator of *Lolita*, possesses all the characteristics of the true creator;[99] Nabokov generously grants him cultural superiority over American philistines, yet the accomplishment of his poetic project is more destructive for Lolita's life than Quilty's *poshlust*. Even Nikolai Gogol, the Romantic genius of Russian culture, to whom Nabokov dedicated a long essay, is not free of *poshlust* in Nabokov's eyes: "I loathe Gogol's moralistic slant…I deplore his obsession with religion."[100] Nabokov's critique reaches new heights in *The Gift*, where Godunov-Cherdyntsev's biography of Chernyshevsky makes him out to be the epitome of *poshlust*.

By these means, Nabokov converts the intelligentsia's quest for nonconformist resistance to the aggressions of *poshlust*, totalitarian or commercial alike, into the exploration of the place of literature in a modern culture dangerously dependent on big and inevitably false ideas. He explores as well the role that the writer could play before and after large-scale historical catastrophes. His peculiar self-reflective art of prose- and life-creation contains multiple answers to these questions, all of them inseparable from the interplay of images, stylistic devices, and metafictional constructions that characterize his artistic world. Whether some metaphysical ideal lies behind those brilliant surfaces remains a matter for debate and speculation.

What were his artistic principles? Calling reality "one of the few words which mean nothing without quotes," Nabokov held that "the very term 'everyday reality' is utterly static since it presupposes a situation that is permanently observable, essentially objective, and universally known. I suspect that you invented that expert of 'everyday reality.' Neither exists."[101] He declared, "I do not give a damn for morals, in America or elsewhere."[102] Tirelessly making fun of "the Literature of Ideas, which very often is topical trash coming in huge blocks of plaster that are carefully transmitted from age to age until somebody comes along with a hammer and takes a good crack at Balzac, at Gorki, at Mann,"[103] Nabokov methodically attacked Dostoevsky, seeing in his novels the foundation of the twentieth-century "Literature of Ideas." Nabokov defined literature as existing "only insofar as it affords me what I shall bluntly call aesthetic bliss, that is a sense of being somehow, somewhere, connected with other states of being where art (curiosity, tenderness, kindness, ecstasy) is the norm."[104] Dividing novelists into storytellers, teachers, and enchanters, he reserved supremacy among writers for enchanters who not only create in the work of fiction new worlds "having no obvious connection with the worlds we already know," but also enjoy to the fullest the author's right to play cerebral games with the reader.[105] Celebrating the power of the author's individuality as "the perfect dictator,"[106] Nabokov at the same time seeks "a combined sensation of having the whole universe entering you and of yourself wholly dissolving in the universe surrounding you. It is the prison wall of ego suddenly crumbling away with the non-ego rushing in from the outside to save the prisoner—who is already dancing in the open."[107]

These declarations, reminiscent of Oscar Wilde's paradoxes, merged with the decadent and, by Nabokov's lifetime, rather stale impulse to *épater la bourgeoisie*, had a significantly different meaning after the catastrophes of the twentieth century. Despite the aesthetic otherworldliness of his prose, Nabokov experienced his own historical moment unflinchingly. He was a direct victim of the Bolshevik Revolution and Civil War, his father was assassinated by a Russian monarchist, and his family was almost drawn into the abyss of the Holocaust: his wife and son wore yellow stars as Jews when living in Berlin until 1937, and his brother died in a Nazi concentration camp, incarcerated as a homosexual. The writer's cold irony against grand ideas and their promoters tangibly embody his resistance to violence. He identified the sources of violence as the drive toward generalizations and simplifications, and as the fear of true freedom in mass society. These anxieties manifested themselves in ideological dictatorships, nationalist frenzy, and crazed consumerism.

Nabokov's novels constantly return to the story of the invention of the real—probably the central question for both modernism and postmodernism—but his famed self-referentiality complicates this problem and presents the key to his artistic philosophy. As Aleksandr Dolinin astutely writes about *The Gift* (and this characteristic can be applied to Nabokov's entire oeuvre): "Almost every detail of the novel's landscape—a piece of furniture, a building, a street, a square, a forest, a gate, a tram, a fence, a toy—may be reinterpreted, without losing its direct referential meaning, as metonymy of the novel itself, a variation on its central theme: the interrelation between Art and Life."[108] Writing about *Invitation to a Beheading* through the prism of Gnostic mythology, Sergej Davydov argues that in Nabokov's "aesthetic theology," the Demiurge, also known as the author, shares with Cincinnatus his creative powers, since "the partaking of the mystery of creativity is a mortal's only hope—but not a guarantee of immortality," yet he also expects the protagonist to rebel against the author's tyranny.[109] Eric Naiman, in his analysis of *Lolita* as Nabokov's metatext, discloses sexual coding as "a dominant, even detrimental feature of Nabokov's art," affecting first and foremost the relations between the author and the reader:

> Nabokov's literature has a penchant for turning moral questions about life into procedural ones about reading. The intensity of his reader's engagement with his works has much in common with the tortured urgency of the conversations and internal debates that are so compelling in the heroes of Dostoevsky, Tolstoy, and, in some cases Chekhov, but that engagement does not revolve around whether the reader is a good person or whether life is worth living but concerns whether he is a good reader and, implicitly, whether Nabokov is worth reading.[110]

These three examples (and many more are available) suggest a reading of Nabokov's oeuvre as the post-religious questioning of modernity and its promise to manifest one's freedom by playing God and transforming reality according to one's needs and desires. The success or failure of the author, who appears to be doubled or parodied by his characters' (and readers') similar attempts at co-creation, moves to the center of philosophical inquiry. It is the author, "the anthropomorphic deity" and "the perfect dictator," who epitomizes the ultimate freedom and ultimate guilt of the modern subject daring to create reality according to his or her vision, imagination, and talent. It is the author who appears responsible for the ruined lives as well as for the birth of the new worlds "having no obvious connection with the worlds we already know." And it is the reader who faces the challenge of resisting the author's power, trying to imitate his ingenuity, or, at least, identify with the character, who is also an author in his/her own right. This endless perspective of distorting and upturned "mirages in the mirror" constitutes Nabokov's ultimate response to the catastrophes and challenges of modernity: "What I feel to be the real modern world is the world the artist creates, his own mirage, which becomes a new mir ('world' in Russian) by the very act of his shedding, as it were, the age he lives in."[111]

Socialist Realism

Socialist Realism was at the center of all official literary-critical discussions from the early 1930s and generated a new set of vocabularies and image systems. The bylaws of the Union of Soviet Writers featured a definition:

Socialist Realism is the basic method of Soviet literature and literary criticism. It demands of the artist the truthful, historically concrete representation of reality in its revolutionary development. The truthfulness and historical concreteness of the artistic representation of reality must be linked with the task of ideological remaking and education of toiling people in the spirit of socialism. Socialist Realism offers the artist an exceptional opportunity for creative initiative and the choice of diverse forms, styles, and genres.[112]

At first, many writers and critics perceived this formulation as sufficiently broad, believing in the "exceptional opportunity for creative initiative"; however, Socialist Realism's subsequent development proved that its vagueness instead allowed the concept to be deployed as a weapon against any deviations, ideological and formal alike. The practical meaning of Socialist Realism was eventually worked out by ideological campaigns, beginning with the attack on "Formalism and Naturalism" in 1936. The canonical texts that illustrated the method of Socialist Realism were more quickly established: initially, these were texts created in the 1920s by writers close to RAPP (Aleksandr Fadeev, Dmitry Furmanov, Aleksandr Serafimovich, Fedor Gladkov), as well as by Mayakovsky (in the 1920s only). Maxim Gorky's *Mother* was declared to be a model Socialist Realist narrative. Exemplary texts of Socialist Realism were lauded in the critical press and published in large print runs; their authors were decorated with medals and named as heads of the Writers' Union, deputies of the Supreme Soviet, and members of the Central Committee.

Belatedly, one of the first attempts to define its meaning as more than an ideologically charged cliché was the essay "On Socialist Realism" ("Chto takoe sotsialisticheskii realizm" 1957) by Andrei Sinyavsky (writing as Abram Tertz). Initially published in France and clandestinely circulated in Soviet *samizdat* in the 1960s, the essay defined Socialist Realism as a method of ultra-teleological art that illuminated all its subjects with the light of "Supreme Purpose," i.e., communism. It appeared closer to eighteenth-century Russian Neo-Classicism than to any form of Realism: "Socialist Realism starts from an ideal image to which it adapts the living reality. . . . We represent life as we would like it to be and as it is bound to become when it bows to the logic of Marxism. This is why Socialist Realism should really be called 'socialist classicism.'" Sinyavasky characterized Socialist Realist literary production as a "half-classicist half-art, which is none too socialist and not at all realist." He concluded, "a really faithful representation of life cannot be achieved in a language based on teleological concepts." [113]

Indeed, the structure of Stalinist society, with the "party-church" at its core, created a world of pseudo-religiosity.[114] Numerous rituals, symbols, and sacred texts (from Marx and Engels to *The Brief Course of the History of the All-Union Communist Party [Bolshevik]* and Stalin's biography) shaped enormously powerful mythological constructs: the Great Family; the cult of party leaders, war heroes, and labor heroes as new gods and saints; a mythologized version of Soviet and Russian history; and, not least, the constant production of new enemies—class enemies in the 1920s, "enemies of the people" in the 1930s, "rootless cosmopolitans" in the 1940s–50s, and then dissidents in the 1970s, plus ubiquitous agents of imperialism across the entire period. These myths were meant to manage and control social integration, and they justified people's sufferings and troubles by channeling negative emotions towards supposed saboteurs who were blocking socialist progress. Ideological texts alone could not create a modern mythology. This role fell to the arts, primarily literature. How literature came to play a foundational role in propagating all these myths is also the story of Socialist Realism.

However, Socialist Realism was more than the sum total of its ideological ambitions. Created as state-sponsored art oriented towards mass tastes, it inevitably had to revive or create anew the narrative patterns of popular literature. In an ordinary Socialist Realist novel, adventure and spy plots mixed with stories of secular saints and romantic love, all peppered with positive ideological messages and ending on an uplifting note (despite the possible death of a protagonist). The tremendous popularity of *How the Steel Was Tempered* (*Kak zakalialas'* *stal'*, in serial publication in 1934) by Nikolai Ostrovsky (1904–36); *The Virgin Soil Upturned* (*Podniataia tselina*, vol. 1, 1932; vol. 2, 1960) by Mikhail Sholokhov; *The Pedagogical Poem* (*Pedagogicheskaia poema*, 1935) by Anton Makarenko; *Peter I* (*Petr Pervyi*, 1929–34) and *The Road to Calvary* (*Khozhdenie po mukam*, 1941) by Aleksei Tolstoy; and *The Young Guard* by Aleksandr Fadeev cannot be explained away by claims that readers lacked access to other forms of literature or were victims of heavy-handed political promotion. As the literature of the 1960s and Perestroika would demonstrate, the same narrative models could be adapted for anti-Soviet and anti-communist ideology with equal facility (in texts by Yevtushenko, Chingiz Aitmatov [1928–2008], Anatoly Rybakov, Vladimir Dudintsev, Boris Vasil'ev [1924–2013], and Sergei Antonov [1915–95]). Socialist Realism was a peculiar but not unique version of modern aesthetics dominated by mass-oriented ideological messages. From this standpoint, there is not much difference between a Soviet Socialist Realist writer and other forms of ideologically charged art intended for a broader audience: the teleology leads to such formal qualities as the simplification of plot and language, poster-like depiction of protagonists and villains, mandatory happy ending, and clear-cut authorial position.

Many writers otherwise known for their modernist talents attempted to contribute to Socialist Realism. Viktor Shklovsky authored the largest number of chapters in *The Stalin White Sea-Baltic Sea Canal: The History of Construction* (*Belomorsko-Baltiiskii kanal imeni Stalina: Istoriia stroitel'stva*, 1934). Bulgakov flexed his muscles as a Socialist Realist when writing *Batum* (1939), a play about the young Stalin. Olesha wrote the play *A List of Benefits* (*Spisok blagodeianii*, 1931) and the film scenario for *A Strict Youth* (*Strogii iunosha*, 1934). Zoshchenko also contributed a chapter to *The Stalin White Sea-Baltic Sea Canal* and wrote "Stories about Lenin" (1940) for children. Despite their frantic efforts to become successful Socialist Realists, none of these writers achieved the popularity of Ostrovsky or Fadeev: their individual styles did not lend themselves to standardization according to ideology. Some found it impossible to "step on the throat" of their own song, as Mayakovsky had phrased it, and preferred self-destruction to staged radical conversion.

Socialist Realism remained the official method of Soviet literature until the collapse of the USSR, but by the 1960s, its contours became blurred in both literary practice and criticism. An increasing number of officially published works did not promote party doctrines or blunted their ideological thrust. Soviet writers grew increasingly fond of phantasmagoria and the grotesque, and they experimented with metafictional devices and an ambivalent authorial position. These practices poorly suited the dogma of Socialist Realism, producing a new round of discussion, comparable to the debates launched in the early 1930s when the doctrine was first formulated. Still, Soviet critics of the 1970s–80s tried to make it more flexible by introducing the concept of Socialist Realism as an open system, but Western literary critics mainly treated its works as unworthy of literary study.

That changed with the publication of Katerina Clark's pathbreaking study, *The Soviet Novel: History as Ritual* (1981), which inspired a new generation of literary criticism that would draw broadly on anthropology, philosophy, and social theory. For Clark, Socialist Realism represents a peculiar example of Nietzschean narrative art that effectively employed patterns borrowed from myth, fairy tales, and epic.[115] A decade later, Boris Groys published *The Total Art of Stalinism*, also a landmark study. It argued that Socialist Realism emerged from the Russian avant-garde, adopting the avant-garde's striving for the radical transformation of social and political reality and its belief that this could be accomplished by the artists's will and design. In Socialist Realism, however, the role of the demiurge transferred from the artist to the state and its personification, hence the original title (*Gesamtkunstwerk Stalin*) of Groys's monograph.

These two influential approaches made Socialist Realism a continuing and serious object of scholarly study. Subsequent work has affiliated Socialist Realism with the populist tradition in

Russian literature (for example, Tolstoy's books for peasants), and with Gorky's and Lunacharsky's "God-building" project, with their strong Nietzschean influences.[116] Scholars in the 2000s sought to understand Socialist Realism as a form matching the totalitarian version of modernity, uniting the appeal to the masses with utopian efforts at remodeling reality. This new approach was summarized in a monumental volume on the canon of Socialist Realism, created by a large international group led by Hans Günther and Evgeny Dobrenko.[117] Dobrenko in his own scholarship arrived at an understanding of Socialist Realism as the key concept in the cultural semiotics of Soviet society. He argues that it enabled the de-realization of reality, hiding the state capitalist nature of the social world and replacing it with a new, all-encompassing and completely fictional double of reality.[118]

Socialist Realism was created by the joint efforts of state ideology, party officials, writers, and readers (whose presumably undeveloped taste dictated low standards of literary accessibility). It tempered the avant-garde striving for life-creation with folkloric formulae, medieval narrative structures, and popular art of the twentieth century. It recycled various forms of imperial culture, comparable to totalitarian monumental art in Nazi Germany and fascist Italy.[119] Cultural myths created by Socialist Realism presented themselves as both global simulacra of the real and as a pure art form residing in the space of absolute utopia.

While representing in easily digestible form many ideological myths, Socialist Realism aimed to be perceived as the reflection of life rather than as a fictional construct. Inevitably, tropes of the modernist grotesque seemed incompatible with this task, while such seemingly avant-gardist forms as the Futurists' literature of fact were adopted without problem. A vivid if disturbing example of the literature of fact is the volume glorifying a Gulag site: *The Stalin White Sea-Baltic Sea Canal*, which today reads as an exemplary text of Socialist Realism.

Socialist Realist novels could showcase ideological values and achievements, and their fixed formulae delimited most heroes and villains. In *The Soviet Novel*, Katerina Clark demonstrated that the Socialist Realist meta-plot resurrected models from epic tales and medieval hagiographies: "Heroes became larger than life, their feats even more fantastic and epic, and the language of the text ever richer in epithets and imagery transplanted from the folk tradition."[120] Such narratives required a stark division of characters into angelic revolutionaries, demonic counter-revolutionaries, and intelligentsia members who might hesitate, but ultimately choose the Revolution.

The RAPP novels about the Civil War written in the 1920s, such as Dmitry Furmanov's *Chapaev* (1923), Aleksandr Serafimovich's *The Iron Stream* (*Zheleznyi potok*, 1924), Fedor Gladkov's *Cement* (*Tsement*, 1925), and Aleksandr Fadeev's *The Rout* (*Razgrom*, 1927), became classics of Socialist Realism. Along with Gorky's *Mother*, they proved that the Bildungsroman could display the formation of a true communist hero, and the genre became all-important. The Bildungsroman hero would evolve from "spontaneity" (associated with individualism and represented as a failing) towards "consciousness," which is represented positively and which requires complete subjugation to the party and its leaders. Maturation includes a series of temporary death experiences, reminiscent of ancient rites of passage conducted under the guidance of a wise mentor. The final passage signifies symbolic acceptance into the Great Family of the Soviet people. Clark argues that in climactic moments, typically saturated with quasi-religious symbolism (despite the declared atheism of Soviet ideology), the narratives highlight an "extraordinary order of reality": they situate the protagonist in a sphere of ecstatic contact with the specifically Soviet transcendental. The entire journey appears as a spiritual quest for transcendental truth, achieved through larger-than-life deeds and associated with the party and its leadership, or (if the action takes place in an earlier historical period) with the future happiness of the masses, which could be imagined only under the conditions of communism as a substitute for the heavenly kingdom. Conformity to this model explains the wild popularity of such translated works as Raffaello Giovagnoli's *Spartacus* (*Spartaco*, 1874) and Ethel Lilian Voynich's *The Gadfly* (1897).

Some narratives featured an adventure plot and teenage characters: *The Pedagogical Poem* by Anton Makarenko, *A Tale of the Real Man* (*Povest' o nastoiashchem cheloveke*, 1947) by Boris Polevoi, *The Young Guard* by Fadeev, and *The Russian Forest* (*Russkii les*, 1953) by Leonov. Fusing Socialist Realist Bildungsroman, an adventure plot, and elements of Neo-Romanticism was the recipe for literary success invented by Arkady Gaidar (1904–41), author of what became classics for young adults: *The Military Secret* (*Voennaia taina*, 1935), *Fate of the Drummer* (*Sud'ba barabanshchika*, 1939), and *Timur and His Team* (*Timur i ego komanda*, 1940). Valentin Kataev was another strong presence in the young adult version of Socialist Realism: *I, a Son of the Working People* (*Ia, syn trudovogo naroda . . .*, 1937), his tetralogy *Waves of the Black Sea* (*Volny Chernogo moria*, 1936–61), and his wartime novella *The Son of the Regiment* (*Syn polka*, 1945). Also important were *Two Captains* (*Dva kapitana*, 1936–44) and *The Open Book* (*Otkrytaia kniga*, 1946–54) by Kataev's literary foe, Veniamin Kaverin, and Anatoly Rybakov's *The Dagger* (*Kortik*, 1948) and *The Drivers* (*Voditeli*, 1950).

The Bildungsroman model found its most popular embodiment in novels about supposedly real-life experiences of Soviet heroes and martyrs. One spectacular example was *How the Steel Was Tempered* by Nikolai Ostrovsky. A totally unknown author who was dying of bone tuberculosis at the moment of publication, Ostrovsky sent his badly written manuscript to the press where it was edited by literary professionals, and then heavily promoted through *Pravda* and other organs. *How the Steel Was Tempered* and its author became cult phenomena for the entire Soviet period. Ostrovsky modeled his protagonist, Pavel Korchagin, on himself, but he pushed every life situation faced by Korchagin to the extreme: military operations, railroad construction, and even a military training exercise turn into horrific tests of character, invariably exalting Korchagin's suffering and the catastrophic effects on his health. A motionless and blind twenty-four-year old Korchagin in the final part of *How the Steel Was Tempered* emerges as the embodiment of the ultimate ascesis. When he gives everything up, he becomes a revolutionary saint. Korchagin's self-sacrifice confirms the sacred status of the Soviet cause, and his life-story creates in him a Soviet martyr, invoking a religious sublime and beckoning real-life followers (which were, sadly, many).

The pathos of heroic death as the transcendental goal of human existence occupies a central place in Socialist Realist culture. It justified self-sacrifice as the mandatory path for a true Soviet man. Those who refused to sacrifice themselves or were broken by torture were revealed as traitors. The glorification of self-sacrifice and, ultimately, death serves as a powerful ideological tool, and establishes a certain quasi-religious morality: it places heroic death above all of life's values, demeaning individual existence as "philistine." According to this logic, the meaning of an individual life can only emerge posthumously. A life's value in such an ethical system can be established only by institutions of power, which alone have the right to acknowledge or to discredit an individual act of heroism.

The so-called production novel (*proizvodstvennyi roman*) competed with the Soviet Bildungsroman for primacy in the Socialist Realist canon. It depicted a rite of passage undergone in industrial work, and focused less on an individual hero's progress than the fate of a collective. In the course of the narrative, a homogenous group breaks down: some characters emerge as heroes, while others are exposed as hidden or unwitting enemies. The success of the collective maturation depends on the fulfillment of an industrial assignment, be it the construction of a new plant, the establishment of a Stakhanovite record, or the implementation of some daring technological invention. In all cases, these goals require the symbolic or real death of central characters as a sacrificial offering. The frenzied quest for enemies, reminiscent of detective or adventure novels, also plays a part. This genre was best represented in *Hydrocentral* (*Gidrotsentral'*, 1930) by Marietta Shaginian; *The Second Day*, also translated as *Out of Chaos* (*Den' vtoroi*, 1933) by Erenburg; *Time, Forward!* (*Vremia, vpered!*, 1932) by Kataev; *The River Sot* (*Sot'*, 1930) by Leonov; *People from the Back of Beyond* (*Liudi iz zakholust'ia*, 1938) by Aleksandr Malyshkin; Vera Panova's *Kruzhilikha* (1947); and *Far from Moscow* (*Daleko ot Moskvy*, 1948) by Vasily Azhaev (1915–68). Novels about collective farms and the extermination of kulaks, exemplified by Sholokhov's *Virgin Soil Upturned*, scarcely differ in their plot and character structure from the production novels, despite contrasting background (pantheistic and idyllic versus urban).

In the production novel, the hero was typically framed by comrades as contrasting doubles: one comrade was depicted as too empathetic, too inclined to chafe at the cruelties of the regime, the other as merciless and inhuman, insisting on radical measures for the achievement of lofty Soviet goals. The starkest instance of this configuration is Sholokhov's trio of protagonists in *Virgin Soil Upturned*: a former seaman and proletarian, Semen Davydov, runs the collectivization of Cossacks farms (although he is ignorant about their life and traditions), with two Cossacks who assist in this endeavor. They are the kind-hearted chair of the village Soviet, Andrei Razmetnov, devastated by the horrors of collectivization, and the head of the local party unit, Makar Nagul'nov, who rushes toward world revolution and is responsible for the excesses of collectivization (but not for the campaign itself). This configuration lets Sholokhov clear a central character from both "rightist" and "leftist" deviations (similar to party deviations [*uklony*] constantly condemned in smear campaigns in the 1920s–30s) as well as to depict him as the synthesis of mutually exclusive positions: Davydov is both humanistic and party-minded.

The differences among the members of the threesome fade when they are confronted by an enemy figure. In the production/collectivization novel, the role of the enemy was reserved for the concealed representative of the exploitative class. Such anti-heroes typically displayed their evil nature at their very first appearance in the novel even before committing any treachery. However, there were novels in which the author used an enemy figure to express unorthodox or openly critical ideas by conniving to expose the anti-hero and distancing the author from the enemy's worldview. For example, Ilya Erenburg in his production novel *The Second Day* depicts a humanistic and intellectually sophisticated Volodia Safonov, who feels alienated among the builders of Novokuznetsk. Volodia's role in the novel is that of an individualistic anti-hero, i.e., potential enemy, and Erenburg, following the logic of the genre, brings this character to the point of suicide. Despite general praise for Erenburg's depiction of industrialization (including support by Karl Radek in *Izvestia*), the character of Volodia Safonov provoked heated debates and was even likened to a Nazi.[121] What was his sin? Volodia is faithful to the memories of the past and he also is engaged with modernist (i.e., elitist and bourgeois) culture of the present (he loves Babel's prose and Pasternak's poetry). Erenburg gives him an acute sense of justice—as a teenager, for example, he leaves the Young Pioneers organization when it expels a boy for his father's service as a tsarist prosecutor. And despite discrediting Volodia on the level of plot, the author does not try to hide his empathy for an individualistic anti-hero nestled within a narrative that ostensibly seems ideologically correct. Later, Erenburg would admit that he had expressed through Volodia's diary his own most troubling doubts and disappointments about "enthusiastic Soviet youth" and the "heroism of industrialization":

> Volodia Safonov hanged himself. It was me who tried to hang myself. . . . His sensitive conscience was the reason for the suicide. . . . If he had been less conscientious and more practically savvy (*tsepkii*), he wouldn't have hanged himself, but instead become a respected specialist.[122]

Along with Erenburg, Leonid Leonov was also famous for the subversive use of the Socialist Realist anti-hero to critique the ruling ideology. His heroes Protoklitov (*The Road to the Ocean*

[*Doroga na okean*, 1935]) and Gratsiansky (*The Russian Forest*) treat Soviet ideology as a form of social mimicry. The heroes' monologues also expose otherwise hidden logical outcomes of the dominant ideological beliefs, as well as their own profoundly conformist and anti-revolutionary nature. Although Leonov hands his villains spectacular defeat at the respective novels' endings, their stylistically complex voices are in contrast to the cartoonish flatness of the plot.

Erenburg and Leonov, as well as Kataev and Kaverin, managed to assimilate their individual style to the Socialist Realist binary aesthetic. Arguably, their skill was in creating multi-leveled texts that lent themselves to ambiguous readings. They were laying the foundations for the use of Aesopian language in Soviet literature, i.e., the system of codes and signals that could inscribe subversive messages into seemingly loyal texts. However, the possibility for such subversions within official literature was constantly negotiated between the writer and the authorities; the tacit conventions would change with each new political situation. In this respect, Socialist Realism was paradoxically always an open system, despite its unbending rigidity: it was a dangerous game with unpredictable rules.

Women's prose and drama of the 1960s through 1990s

Women characters appeared in Socialist Realist novels, but most of the plots revolved around the heroic actions of men; patriarchal norms were sustained in a variety of ways, perhaps most vividly by the fact that male authors remained so prominent. Women's prose as an independent literary movement began in the Silver Age until breaking off in the 1930s. Despite the official policy of sexual equality, Soviet literature blocked rather than encouraged feminist discourse. The works of officially acknowledged women writers like Lidia Seifullina, Vera Panova (1905–73), Marietta Shaginian (1888–1982), Vanda Vasilevskaia (1906–64), and Galina Nikolaeva (1911–65) scarcely differed stylistically or thematically from writings of Socialist Realism composed by men. But the 1960s saw a rebirth of women's literature in prose that offered new representations of women's lives, followed in the 1970s–80s by a radicalization of feminine discourse in prose and drama.

While women writers of the Thaw years typically knew the poetry of Akhmatova and Tsvetaeva, the artistic innovations of women's prose from the Silver Age were little known, and much of this writing bore the trademark signs of realism. The stimulus for the new women's literature was largely thematic, a reaction against Soviet representations of women in the 1920s to 1950s. In accordance with the official policy of gender equality, women were depicted in literature and film of the Stalin period as heroic participants in building socialism. The indignities of everyday life in a communal apartment, the double burden of family and job duties, the demands of coping with constant economic shortages, inferior medical care, and patriarchal condescension if not sexual harassment, as well as the tragic destinies of women arrested and deported as enemies of the people or as wives or widows of imprisoned men— these dramas of daily life had been absent in official Soviet discourse. Women writers began to fill in the gaps.

Natalia Baranskaya (1908–2004), I. Grekova (pseud. Elena Venttsel, 1907–2002), and Liudmila Petrushevskaya opened out women's perspectives on social problems. They violated established if tacit patriarchal norms with their topical themes, psychological portraiture, and in some cases, radically innovative stylistics. Baranskaya's and Grekova's subversion and direct critique of Soviet patriarchy were mainly expressed at the thematic level, while Petrushevskaya in her prose and drama articulated a new literary idiom, comparable to what Julia Kristeva and Hélène Cixous described as *écriture féminine*. But, for all their differences, Baranskaya, Grekova, and Petrushevskaya were similar in reconceptualizing everyday life as a field of gendered social conflict. They inspired many others, like Inna Varlamova (1923–90), Irina

Velembovskaia (1922–90), Galina Shcherbakova (1932–2010), Viktoria Tokareva (b. 1937), Nina Katerli (b. 1934), Olga Kuchkina (b. 1936), Alla Sokolova (b. 1944), Liudmila Razumovskaia (b. 1946), and Dina Rubina (b. 1953).

Natalia Baranskaya had solid training as a philologist and she was loyal to a pre-Soviet idea of literary modernism. Her political independence was no secret: she was fired from her position as director of the Moscow Pushkin Literary Museum for displaying Gumilev's photograph at an exhibition about Akhmatova and for inviting Brodsky to give a reading at the museum. In 1969, she became nationally famous when her novella *A Week Like Any Other* (*Nedelia kak nedelia*) appeared in *Novyi mir*. Although readers at first thought otherwise, the novella did not reflect Baranskaya's own experience. She was a sixty-one-year old widow whose first husband perished in the Gulag and second died in the Second World War, while the novella's protagonist and narrator, Olga, is a twenty-six-year old Moscow scientist, happily married with two young children. Olga's finely calibrated internal monologue is prompted by a questionnaire at work, asking about "their reproductive behavior and measuring their ability to fulfill both work and domestic responsibilities."[123] The resulting set of reflections is spread over seven days that vividly capture her exhausting efforts to cram a demanding work schedule, care for children and household, mandatory political education, and job-related errands into a typical day. When she ducks into a hair salon for an impulsive haircut, it feels like a remarkable feat of free expression.

Baranskaya portrayed a life that, by Soviet standards, should have been happy, but her heroine instead feels besieged by mounting crises. Critics accused the author of having a narrow-minded point of view (*melkotem'e*). But Baranskaya did not evade social problems—quite the opposite. At the novella's climax, the heroine, Olga, explodes during a political education seminar where she is supposed to speak about "non-antagonistic" contradictions in socialist society. Instead, she unleashes pent-up anger at her daily rat race, displeasing her colleagues, who are also women.[124] The impossible daily circumstances of this woman's life are presented as a fundamental social problem. Baranskaya was the first writer of her era to demonstrate that everyday life (*byt*), while consisting of seemingly trivial problems, is in fact a political issue. Other women writers would build on this perception of *byt* as having political content, as would Yuri Trifonov and Vladimir Makanin in their existentialist prose.

I. Grekova is the pseudonym of a prominent mathematician, Elena Venttsel. Her name is calqued on the French "igrek," a Russian version of "Y" in math formulas (not coincidentally, Baranskaya's characters read Venttsel's math article in *A Week Like Any Other*). Grekova wrote her fictional prose from the perspective of a woman intellectual employed in institutions where pervasive sexism differed only by degree—higher in a military research facility, lower in a university department. Her narrators expose chauvinism with irony and sarcasm, but her heroines behave as if nothing were the matter. Grekova is not focused on women's issues in isolation; she casts them as an integral part of broader social malaise, including the damaging effect of political denunciation in the world of science (*On Maneuver* [*Na ispytaniiakh*, 1967]); remnants of Stalinism that damage family and social relations (*The Hotel Manager* [*Khoziaika gostinitsy*, 1976]); the persecution of true creativity in socialist organized labor (*Ladies Hairdresser* [*Damskii master*, 1963]); and the bureaucratic suffocation of real science in the academy (*The Department* [*Kafedra*, 1978]). Her only work focused on women's experiences is the novel *The Ship of Widows* (*Vdovii parokhod*, 1981). Here she uses a communal apartment to portray five wartime widows of different class origins. In their confined quarters, they become a familial model of the Soviet community. Whereas Socialist Realism promoted the mythology of the Great Family, Grekova creates a deconstructed alternative in which all the roles are played by women.[125]

The 1970s also saw the appearance of a truly feminist Russian literary group, established in Leningrad underground circles. It did not escape official notice or political persecution. The artist and poet Tatiana Mamonova (b. 1943), philosopher Tatiana Goricheva (b. 1947), and writers Natalia Malakhovskaia (b. 1947), Natalia Maltseva, and Iulia Voznesenskaia (1940–2015) compiled the first feminist almanac, *Woman and Russia* (1979), published in translation in Germany, France, and the United States, and then the magazine *Maria* (1980–81). They also organized a feminist club with an articulate religious and anti-Soviet agenda (its first *samizdat*-circulated document was an appeal to Soviet mothers to hide their sons from conscription in the Afghanistan war). These activities won them persecution by the KGB. Some were imprisoned or sent to psychiatric asylums; one participant, the poet Kari Unksova (1941–83), died in a suspicious car accident that was never investigated. Mamonova, Goricheva, and Voznesenskaya eventually emigrated. Their publications denounced as false the officially acclaimed gender equality in the USSR, and they sought to expose the denigrating sexist standards applied to women, not only in official but also in nonconformist spheres. Goricheva, once a brilliant philosophy student at Leningrad University, was an intellectual leader of this group. She corresponded with Heidegger and was forced to emigrate in 1981; however, she returned to the USSR in 1988. She introduced postmodernist theory to the Russian literary scene, even as she argued with its methods and sought to fuse it with Russian Christian philosophy of the early twentieth century.

Her book, *Orthodoxy and Postmodernism* (*Pravoslavie i postmodernizm*, 1991), engaged in direct dialogue with Peter Sloterdijk's influential *Critique of Cynical Reason*, and Goricheva became the first to discuss the phenomenon of Soviet cynicism:

> The Soviet cynic somewhat resembles his Western counterpart, but commands twice the amount of "enlightenment." He is enlightened in the negation of ideology: nowhere in the world is there more contempt toward Marxism than in the Soviet Union.... The Soviet cynic is enlightened because he has no trust in official ideology. His enlightenment goes one step deeper: he has no trust in dissidents, either.[126]

Seeking alternatives to cynicism, Goricheva highlights what she calls "sacred insanity." As a form of hopeless political rebellion and quasi-schizophrenia similar to what Alexei Yurchak would define as "living outside" (*vnye*),[127] the non-cynic shares some of the holy fool's eccentricities: "A holy fool represents the most contemporary, postmodern form of sainthood."[128] Mediated by gestures of life-creation in nonconformist culture and exemplified in such works as Venedikt Erofeev's *Moscow to the End of the Line*, Goricheva found new ways to confront cynicism with words and performances. Her modes of resistance would later be adapted by post-Soviet feminists, including Pussy Riot.

Goricheva's insights unexpectedly resonate with the writings of Liudmila Petrushevskaya, whose prose and drama depict a cynical, obstacle-ridden world in which women battle for survival but do so often in ways that can be self-deluded and morally repugnant. The behavior of a contemporary holy fool is one of the strategies adopted by Petrushevskaya's heroines: they are perceived as fools (not necessarily holy) and eccentrics because they disregard social conventions and norms of propriety. As victims of the fragile, chaotic social order, they and their children remain vulnerable and undefended.

CASE STUDY Liudmila Petrushevskaya

Petrushevskaya started writing in the 1960s, when she was a recent graduate of the school of journalism at Moscow State University and a struggling young mother. At first, she focused on short stories, eliciting an encouraging but firm rejection from the liberal journal *Novyi mir.* One of her very short stories, "Across the Fields" ("Cherez polia") was published in 1972 in the Leningrad journal *Aurora*. About the same time, she joined Aleksei Arbuzov's studio, an incubator for a generation of new dramatists in the early 1980s (participants included Viktor Slavkin [1935–2014], Mark Rozovsky [b. 1937], Nina Sadur [b. 1950], and Aleksei Kazantsev [1945–2007]). In the late 1970s, some of her short plays were staged—usually only for brief runs—in semi-professional theaters. In the 1980s, her plays started to appear at professional Moscow theaters: Sovremennik, MKhAT (Moscow Art Theater), and Lenkom. Only during Perestroika did Petrushevskaya achieve real fame: her fiction and drama appeared in major literary journals and sparked heated critical discussions. The novella "Our Crowd" ("Svoi krug," 1979) scandalized readers when it was published in *Novyi mir* in 1988, at the height of Perestroika, and it became a kind of poster child for the much-disputed dark or cruel writing (*chernukha*) of the era. What horrified readers was that the alcoholism, cruelty, and family dysfunction depicted in the tale was among members of the intelligentsia, and Petrushevskaya heightened the unflinching indictment of her story by choosing that ironic title. No less shocking was her 1992 novel *The Time: Night* (*Vremia noch'*), which made the short list for the first iteration of the Russian Booker Prize. In the 1990s–2000s she published multiple collections of short stories, fairy tales for grown-ups, poetry (*Karamzin*, 2000), memoirs, and a fantasy novel, *Number One, or In the Gardens of Other Possibilities* (*Nomer Odin, ili V sadakh drugikh vozmozhnostei*, 2004). A well-translated volume of her fairy tales for adults attracted fresh attention in the West in 2009.[129]

Petrushevskaya creates an image of the everyday as a war-zone or a sphere of extreme trials. The heroine struggles to endure and often to save her child from dangers like starvation or homelessness, although her actions often put the child in harm's way. Women characters teeter on the brink of constant catastrophe; many are in close proximity to death and infirmity, or themselves gravely ill. Devastated by their unworthy lovers and grownup children, left alone or living with remote relatives, these women live out on a daily basis the catastrophic decay of the social order. The plot settings, similar to the existentialist borderline situation, violate numerous gender conventions. Woman's sexual appetite, family violence, alcoholism, and readiness to betray friends and relations are depicted without moral judgment in scenes and situations that radically transgress the patriarchal rules for women's behavior. These effects were disturbing but also, when seen existentially, meant to be liberating.

Petrushevskaya never formally belonged to any feminist organization, but her representations of women are unashamedly feminist, which explains the scandalizing effect that her works produced on the public and censors alike. She never shies away from representations of the body, often in its least appealing aspects. She unleashed sexuality and, more generally, corporeality in the representation of women. In Helena Goscilo's view, "the poetics of gross externalization was pioneered by Petrushevskaya, universally acknowledged as the patron saint of the 'new physiology'...."[130] At first, critics and censors accused Petrushevskaya of "excessive naturalism," which justified banning her works from publication. Yet even during the Perestroika years, when her work was published more freely, critics and fellow writers also sometimes derogatorily labeled Petrushevskaya's works as a form of "tape-recording," implying a lack of distance from *byt*, and implying the author's unreflective immersion into its linguistic texture. But that immersion in the language of daily life is at the core of Petrushevskaya's aesthetic: her deepest psychological discoveries and aesthetic innovations were grounded in her sensitivity to the new idiom of urban life and its ability to reflect the looming societal crisis.

Her language often makes use of disturbed syntax. Roman Timenchik recognized her creation of a "peculiar hierarchy of values," where the subversion of official life is "embedded in the language itself": in her work, he continues, "we are introduced not to the prose of life, but rather to the poetry of language."[131] This poetry of language fuses with a brutal depiction of women's daily life—with rape, drunken husbands, poverty, sickness, death, and despair at every turn. Taken together, these polar opposites of her discourse stand for what Julia Kristeva defines as "powers of horror"—the fusion of the abject and sacred inscribed into the female subjectivity.[132] This horror is both sociological (relating to late Soviet and post-Soviet social disorder) and anthropological (relating to the human condition in general).

In the 2000s, Petrushevskaya acknowledged the kinship between her drama and prose:

> [A]ll these short stories were drama. They always were designed as monologues. In an ordinary play, the author's voice is hidden behind that of the character. Here, the voice belonged to the collective. And the collective's voice never trusts anybody, exposes everything hidden, it's always right, and always, in a straightforward way, mercilessly inhuman, like a cannibal [po-liudoedski beschelovechen].[133]

This collective voice embodies the shared social discourse in its purest form; adopted as the author's idiom, it reveals societal cruelty, cynicism, and the inhuman behaviors permitted as if they were common sense. It cannot convey any deeper truth and it is as unreliable as all the other voices in Petrushevskaya's fiction. The author has said: "let the reader decide if this voice is right, let him guess and feel pity for those who are being judged by this vox populi. Let him cry. The author would add a few words, genuine words, from which a completely different narrative could be built. Especially important are the words in the finale...."[134] Indeed, the endings of Petrushevskaya's texts often switch the perspective from the account of petty offenses to a vision of universal catastrophe or mythic archetypes. By these means, she reveals in the everyday dramas the logic of timeless tragedies. Readers are called to mourn for ruined lives in these finales.

Petrushevskaya's elevation of the horrid everyday to the level of mythic tragedy is most spectacularly exemplified in her short novel The Time: Night. The narrative perspective belongs to the supposed poet and single mother/grandmother Anna Andrianovna complaining about her meager life and her ungrateful children. Anna Andrianovna's narrative power is so vast that it reaches into her daughter's private diary, which she cites and comments on. She "assumes the tyrannical form of censorship over all narrative" by this act of intrusiveness, providing a powerful metaphor with significance well beyond family relations: "the totalitarian Petrushevskaian mother mirrors the totalitarian Soviet state."[135] But her power is not unlimited: readers recognize, through multiple dramatic ironies and through the slow revelation of just how dysfunctional this family has been, that Anna Andrianovna is not the self-sacrificing or all-seeing figure of enduring female power that she makes herself out to be. Paradoxically, the mask of martyred generosity is shattered most violently when the narrative exposes her similarity to her own demanding and piteously vulnerable elderly mother. Readers see with horror just where she learned her own manipulative machinations toward her adult children.

Anna Andrianovna's story is never just her own, personal narrative, however. The Time: Night is peppered with subtle references to both the ancient Greek goddess Hecate and the Russian fairy-tale witch Baba Yaga.[136] The presence of mythological subtexts transforms the visible plot of the novel into a metaphor with a very broad spectrum of references. Yet this metaphor does not dissolve the hyper-realistic representation of characters; on the contrary, it both channels metaphorical meanings and verifies them. Petrushevskaya uses myth to lampoon her character's deluded megalomania, but also to add depth. We see that this impoverished mother and grandmother, who fancies herself a writer (commenting that her name and patronymic reveals her fated relationship to Anna Andreevna Akhmatova), is also a parody of a totalitarian tyrant, modernist poet, and the mythic Great Mother.

In her plays, Petrushevskaya creates a similar mythological chronotope situated outside of history. Her characters live in a post-catastrophic era and their comically wrong, broken language bears the imprint of cultural degradation. But they have no time to reflect on the historical reasons for every single day of the hell of their existence: this is their only life, and they have to rear children, get food and lodgings, fall in love, and suffer constant disappointments. Historical and existential elements are woven into a seemingly timeless image of the sheer absurdity of daily life. The poverty and hardship of life in the late Soviet era becomes the soil on which various practices of violence grow, almost reflexively reproduced by characters in both words and actions. In her plays, the action progresses by "sorting out" (*vyiasnialovka*), to use Maia Turovskaia's term.[137] With this verbal crossfire, characters blackmail, humiliate, and oppress each other with one single aim: to defend their small living space and their little bit of freedom. The transition from these continuous scenes of sorting out to actual physical violence is almost imperceptible, as when the boxer kills his wife Natasha in *The Uncooked Leg, or a Friends' Meeting* (*Syraia noga, ili Vstrecha druzei*, 1973–78). Although we do not see the murder, we surmise that Natasha is dead, and only this unplanned and unnoticed sacrifice makes possible friendly, non-aggressive communication: "Now we can have a meeting of friends. At last."[138] Petrushevskaya was the first to create an impressive panorama of communicative violence, transforming each conversation into a scandal, and everyday domestic life into military actions between close people.[139]

Petrushevskaya's aesthetic positions and habits of mind were formed in the 1970s, but her publication during Perestroika resonated with a new generation of younger women writers. A number of collections of women's prose appeared at the time, introducing Svetlana Vasilenko (b. 1956), Marina Palei (b. 1955), Elena Makarova (b. 1951), Irina Polianskaia (1952–2004), Valeria Narbikova (b. 1958), and Yulia Kisina (b. 1966), among others.[140] At the same time, plays by Nina Sadur (b. 1950) as well as short stories by Tatyana Tolstaya and Ludmila Ulitskaya were published by prominent journals. Taken together, these writers energized women's literature and Russian literature more generally. Helena Goscilo has suggested that the common feature was their focus on women's corporeal experience: "New women's prose spotlights the grotesque body, the uncensored, disruptive body of apertures and appetites—Bakhtin's lower body stratum."[141] But the future evolution of these writers demonstrated that such a united approach to their work was short-lived. In the 1990s–2000s, they moved in different directions, sometimes geographically as well as professionally: Makarova emigrated to Israel and became involved with pedagogy and the recovery of a post-Terezin legacy of children's art; Tolstaya became the co-host of a popular TV show, *School for Scandal* (*Shkola zlosloviia*, 2002–14); Palei and Kisina settled down in Europe; Vasilenko became the First Secretary of the new (liberal) Writers' Union board.

Tatyana Tolstaya first achieved international fame after the publication of her collection of short stories *On the Golden Porch* (*Na zolotom kryl'tse sideli...*, 1987).[142] Her work epitomized a mainstream version of post-Soviet neo-modernism. Extending the grotesque modernism of the 1920s, and adding a layer of glossy surface that made it seem lovely rather than distorted, Tolstaya's ornate prose playfully conjures up the powers of culture to elevate and justify mundane existence. Cultural legacy ("The Okkervil River" ["Reka Okkervil'"]) and virtuoso falsehood ("The Fakir" ["Fakir"]) turn out to be equally vital forces, serving as fragile shields whose purpose is to defend an individual from the cruel absurdity of the everyday. In most of the early stories, cultural tradition proves to be no defense. Yet Tolstaya's texts nostalgically insist that the charms of these fairy tales of culture retain their potency.

Tolstaya's female characters typically inhabit the gaps between the fairy tales of culture and reality. Cheerful and energetic Verunchik manifests melancholic memories about pre-revolutionary Petersburg culture ("The Okkervil River"); Sonya thinks that she sacrifices herself during the Siege of Leningrad for a starving romantic lover, but in fact she rescues her supposed friend, the serpent-like Ida, who invented the lover as a prank to ridicule Sonya's romanticism ("Sonya," ["Sonia"]); Galia dreams of the world of high culture, emblematized by *Swan Lake*, but she discovers that she has modeled herself on an imposter ("The Fakir"). More than imagination is at stake in these heroines' dialogues with culture: Tolstaya draws in their entire corporeal beings, including their sexuality. The women in her stories do not act as mere receptacles of cultural messages. Rather, they actively embody cultural histories in their individual life stories, thus transforming mundane details of everyday existence into powerful metaphors of large-scale cultural shifts and dramas.

Another type of narrative born within women's prose of the 1990s translates female corporeality into a metaphor of the life force confronting historical catastrophes. Especially notable examples are Vasilenko's novels *Shamara* (1991) and *The Little Fool* (*Durochka*, 2000), as well as Palei's novella *Kabiria from the Bypass Channel* (*Kabiriia s Obvodnogo kanala*, 1991). Along with Petrushevskaya's prose and drama, The New Drama of the 2000s absorbed and transformed this poetics into hypernaturalist discourse to be found in playwrights like the Presniakov brothers (Oleg, b. 1969 and Vladimir, b. 1974) and Ivan Vyrypaev (b. 1974). Some might argue that the net effect of this metaphorization of the female was to sap its feminist component of significance, although representations of women's experiences by women writers continued to be an important cultural presence, also felt in the world of poetry.

Ludmila Ulitskaya has also taken on the themes of historical catastrophe and family life. She interweaves the exploration of female sexuality (and bodily life) with historical narratives of different social groups, above all, the Soviet intelligentsia and Soviet Jews. Particularly her early short stories, collected in the volumes *Girls* (*Devochki*, 2002) and *Poor Relatives* (*Bednye rodstvenniki*, 1994), and the novella *Sonechka* (1992), take up the challenge of surfacing repressed material, both public and private. In her later work, she expands this model into a new type of family novel: in *Medea and Her Children* (*Medeia i ee deti*, 1996), *The Funeral Party* (*Veselye pokhorony*, 1998), *The Kukotsky Enigma* (*Kazus Kukutskogo*, 2000), *Sincerely Yours Shurik* (*Iskrenno Vash Shurik*, 2004), *The Big Green Tent* (*Zelenyi shater*, 2011), and *Jacob's Ladder* (*Lestnitsa Iakova*, 2015). The long list makes palpable how prolific Ulitskaya has been, and her work has also been honored with prizes in and beyond Russia and translated into several languages. She has not shied away from controversy, and has taken strong positions for toleration and openness and, like Tolstaya, been willing to take on the role of public intellectual.[143] To some readers, she has become "a voice of moral authority for differently minded Russians," as was noted by journalist and activist Masha Gessen.[144]

Existentialist prose and drama of the 1960s through 1980s

Taken broadly, even across thematic and stylistic variety, literature of the liberal mainstream of the 1960s–80s features a heretofore unrecognized existentialist discourse. Existentialism was in vogue in the Soviet intelligentsia in the 1960s; the Thaw, which saw the introduction of many significant translations from Western literature, brought works by Sartre (who visited the USSR in 1954 and 1964), Camus, Kafka, and Beckett to Soviet readers. Writings by earlier Russian philosophers who were existentialist in profile, including Nikolai Berdiaev (1874–1948) and Lev Shestov (1866–1938), circulated in the underground. However, these cultural influences are only partly responsible for the emergence of an existentialist current in Soviet literature. A more significant role belongs to the underlying similarity to cultural conditions that gave rise to European existentialism and then aggravated the intellectual crisis of Soviet society. This was a crisis of justifications: on the one hand, lofty ideological goals had proven unattainable or outright dehumanizing; on the other hand, practical needs were closer to being met than in previous decades, yet failed to bring moral satisfaction. In this environment, categories within existentialist aesthetics acquired direct relevance to Soviet life: angst and freedom, existence and essence, borderline situations and the absurd. Due to the domination of restrictive Marxist-Leninist dicta, an existentialist trend emerged not in Soviet philosophy (even underground), but in artistic expression, especially in prose and drama. Here was the language most suitable for the exploration of individual freedom, its potential as well as its dead-ends. Existentialism gave conceptual clarity to profound social and cultural shifts of the post-Stalin era that seemed to enable an individual quest for freedom and yet restrain it with psychological and political shackles.

Vasily Shukshin (1929–74) was one of the first writers of the postwar generation to explore this angst. Born in a remote Altai village and a graduate of the Moscow Institute of Cinematography, he became a popular film actor and director, and a writer associated with Village Prose. His fictional characters are mainly from the countryside or they are first-generation urban dwellers. Sociologically oriented critics tended to explain such characters' distress as an effect of urbanization, which destroyed the peasants' traditional lifestyle. Shukshin's heroes ask questions about the meaning of their lives and find few satisfactory answers. Stranded between a lost peasant culture and a confusing urban modernity, they lack social and cultural direction. Their efforts at making connections with others veer between the comical ("The Oddball" ["Chudik," 1967], "The Microscope" ["Mikroskop," 1969]) and the self-destructive ("The Bastard" ["Suraz," 1970]). Alternatively, Shukshin's unlucky characters channel their existential despair into aggression against those who seem to know what they are living for, or who are just different from the rest of the community ("Put Down" ["Srezal," 1970]). Angst, coupled with humiliated dignity, can also turn into a source of senseless and self-destructive rebellion, as Shukshin shows in his stories and in his novel about the seventeenth-century Cossack uprising led by Stepan Razin, *I Arrived to Bring You Freedom . . . (Ia prishel dat' vam voliu . . .*, 1971).[145]

The intelligentsia characters in the psychological prose of Yuri Trifonov may seem like social antagonists to Shukshin's former peasants, but they are plunged into similar existential crises. Those crises shape the cycle of Trifonov's so-called urban tales: *The Exchange (Obmen,* 1969), *Preliminary Results (Predvaritel'nye itogi*, 1970), *The Long Goodbye (Dolgoe proshchanie*, 1971), and *Another Life (Drugaia zhizn'*, 1975). Critics (among them Vladimir Dudintsev, the author of *Not by Bread Alone*) scolded Trifonov for his fixation on petty everyday commotions. But Trifonov was exploring the existential and emphatically historical meaning of the everyday as the setting where life's most profound conflicts unfold. In an interview with the critic Lev Anninsky published only after Trifonov's death, he memorably exclaimed:

> There is no such thing as everyday literature [*bytovaia literatura*]: the ridiculous concept of the everyday [*byt*] confuses the issue and filters through some bottomless strainer all sides and manifestations of human life. I write about death (in *The Exchange*) and people say that I write about "the everyday." I write about love (in *The Long Good-bye*) and they say the same thing; I write about the disintegration of a family (in *Preliminary Results*), and once again I hear about the everyday; I write about man's battle with bereavement (in *Another Life*) and yet again they talk about the everyday.[146]

In fact, of Trifonov's four urban tales, three are centered around death, which the author consistently interprets as a threshold situation in which his protagonists must make important existential choices.

Over time, Trifonov became more overt in treating his generation's historical experience as an existential matter. His last, posthumously published novel, *The Time and the Place* (*Vremia i mesto*, 1980), while in many ways autobiographical, represents a philosophical culmination. It undermines the distinction between heroic history and the everyday (*byt*) that had been axiomatic in Soviet culture. With a consistency that is nearly didactic, Trifonov exposes "Great History" as a fiction by showing that it actually consists of nothing more than everyday details. Trifonov makes public and private lives complementary and refuses to evaluate their importance according to an expected hierarchy. He presents jarring juxtapositions of seemingly unrelated worlds that cast a shadow on one another, such as the synchronized narration of an abortion and the death of Stalin. The effect of this emphasis on existence as ordinary as well as extraordinary is to deconstruct Soviet grand narratives. In this respect, his approach resonates with that of underground postmodernism of the 1970s and 1980s (Venedikt Erofeev, Moscow Conceptualism).

Vladimir Makanin belongs to the generation after Trifonov's, nicknamed "the generation of forty-year-olds" (*sorokaletnie*).[147] Other notable members include Anatoly Kim (b. 1939), author of deep existentialist novellas and magic realist novels; Ruslan Kireev (b. 1941), author of somewhat sentimental novellas about communal living in the 1950s–60s; and Anatoly Kurchatkin (b. 1944), author of *byt* stories with political subtexts. The critic Igor Dedkov confronted the writers of this generation in his article "When the Lyric Mist Had Dispersed. . . ."[148] He regarded them as conformists typical of the Era of Stagnation (although this term was not used then), and accused them outright of avoiding dangerous social themes in favor of harmless trivialities (criticisms very similar to those directed against Trifonov's urban tales a decade earlier and against Baranskaya before that). But other critics, like Anatoly Bocharov, Aleksandr Ageev, and Irina Rodnianskaia, proved to be highly attuned to the existentialist rather than the social spectrum of this literary trend, and they produced alternative appraisals of its outstanding representatives, above all Vladimir Makanin.

Attempts at existentialist rebellion—whether failed or successful, they are invariably tragic and sometimes tragicomic—dominate Makanin's fiction. Politics is completely excluded from the worldview of his heroes. They rebel against what they call life's inertia (*samotechnost' zhizni*): with this concept, they name their own lack of agency, and the perception of their lives as driven by anonymous and irrational forces, embodied by predetermined stereotypes and tedious routine. These entirely ordinary characters come from various social strata, including office clerks, members of the intelligentsia, and physical laborers. They all discover a lack of autonomy and control in everyday matters. Some channel their existential rebellion into escapism. This is literally the case in the novella "Running away" ("Grazhdanin ubegaiushchii," 1984), or metaphorically, in the novel *The Antecedent* (*Predtecha*, 1982), which depicts an occult "wizard" and the circle of followers around him. Alternatively, existentialist revolt may manifest itself in seemingly senseless aggression against figures of authority. For instance, Tolik Kurenkov, the protagonist of "Anti-leader" ("Antilider," 1983), believes that these petty tyrants embody the irrational and unfair design of life. Makanin avoids one-sided interpretation of his heroes, and critics have regularly written about his "lack of authorial position," meaning his refusal to extract a convenient moral lesson from his ambivalent tales.[149]

Existentialist prose negotiated a boundary between the permissible and impossible in Soviet literature. Its subjects—crises and despair, lack of freedom, tragicomic rebellions—were disguised as non-political events, limited to private life or representative of specific social strata. But some writers took existentialism further and pushed against this barrier separating political and private. Sergei Dovlatov, a leading figure in Leningrad nonconformist circles, left for the United States in 1978, where he became one of the most prominent Russian émigré writers. He took existentialist aesthetics to a new level patently incompatible with the Soviet sense of literary propriety. Dovlatov stands in the line of earlier great practitioners of the absurd, starting with the OBERIU (still virtually banned in the 1970s), and then reintroduced by several Leningrad unofficial writers, such as Boris Vakhtin, Sergei Vol'f (1935–2005), Vladimir Maramzin, Viktor Goliavkin (1929–2002), the poets Vladimir Ufliand, Oleg Grigor'ev, Aleksandr Kondratov, Brodsky's early poetry (*Gorbunov and Gorchakov*, 1965–68), and the poetic groups Verpa and Khelenukty. Dovlatov was the first since OBERIU to flaunt the absurd as a universal factor to be detected everywhere—in the family and in collegial relations, in social rituals, and in emotional experience. Amplified by his taste for hilarious situations and elegant witticisms, Dovlatov's absurdism was dressed up as anecdotes from his life and that of his friends and relatives. His work enjoyed immense popularity, especially in the 1990s when it became available in Russia. His witticisms became an inseparable part of post-Soviet intelligentsia idiom—an impact comparable to that of Griboedov's *Woe from Wit* for earlier generations.

The most original aspect of Dovlatov's prose is his paradoxical combination of the epic and the absurd. Through various narrative devices, such as repetition and ironic distancing, Dovlatov depicts absurdity as a foundation of the epic totality of the world: everything is connected by and through the absurd. His short stories and novellas prove that any single absurd principle can generate a variety of plot situations. In the lives of his characters, absurdity is equivalent to an individual talent (and vice versa): absurdity and talent shatter stereotypes and undermine routine; both produce discomfort and even catastrophe. Although Dovlatov perceives absurdity as a danger, he is secretly attracted to it as an aesthetic phenomenon.[150]

Prose was not the sole preserve of the absurd. Russian playwrights avidly followed the innovations of European theater of the absurd. The works for theater by Sartre and Camus hit Soviet readers just as the public discovered the post-existentialist theater of the absurd in Samuel Beckett, Eugène Ionesco, and Edward Albee. Performed manifestations of existentialist freedom and absurdity, through eccentric acts and gestures, lay the foundation for new theatrical languages explored by such influential directors as Yuri Liubimov (1917–2014), Georgy Tovstonogov (1915–89), and Anatoly Efros (1925–87). Two exponents of existentialist drama are the otherwise quite different playwrights Aleksandr Volodin (1919–2001) and Aleksandr Vampilov (1937–72).

Volodin's plays stand apart from those of his more popular peers—Aleksei Arbuzov (1908–86), famous for his romantic melodramas, and Viktor Rozov (1913–2004), creator of melodramatic social critiques. Volodin belonged to the war generation, but he never wrote about wartime. His fame derives from representations of daily life in the period after the war. A decade before Trifonov's urban tales, Volodin discovered the sphere of the everyday as the source of existentialist conflicts and choices. In his play *Five Evenings* (*Piat' vecherov*, 1959; film version by Nikita Mikhalkov, 1978), the life of the protagonist, Il'in, is in shambles, yet it acquires an unshakeable if elusive value by defying ready-made stereotypes about social success and fulfillment. Volodin's script for Georgy Danelia's popular film *The Autumn Marathon* (*Osennii marafon*, 1979) shows a hero's inability to choose between two women as a failure to exercise existential freedom. The failure eventually destroys the brilliant, kind, and generous hero in what the author called a "sad comedy."

Aleksandr Vampilov, like Shukshin, was a native of Siberia. He radically renewed Russian playwriting, although during his short life (he drowned in Lake Baikal one day before turning thirty-five) only one of his plays was staged, and that in a provincial theater. A whole literary and theatrical generation grew up in the wake of his posthumous success, including Liudmila Petrushevskaya, Vladimir Arro (b. 1932), Alla Sokolova, and Liudmila Razumovskaia; their work was referred to in the late 1970s–early 1980s as "post-Vampilov drama." In Vampilov's tragicomedies, men of the 1960s formed a lost generation deprived of their former ideals and beliefs, left cynical and angry. As in Western existentialist drama of the 1950s–60s, stage actions are predominantly psychological. Often, they test the limits of personal freedom: its possibility, its price, and its conditions. The experiment is facilitated by a threshold situation—death, funeral, suicide attempt, or rape—or its mocking imitation. The protagonists typically find themselves at the crossroads between buried inner potential and the impulses of other characters in the play, each replicating a different aspect of the hero's self-contradictory subjectivity.

Such is the protagonist of Vampilov's most famous play, *The Duck Hunt* (*Utinaia okhota*, published in 1971). Viktor Zilov represents a new hero of our time, "a portrait composed from all the vices of our generation in their full development" (quoting Lermontov). The critic Viktor Toporov was first to detect the features of the superfluous man in Zilov, who has no adequate ambitions for the application of his talents, which, as a result, turn against his intimates and himself.[151] He is a leftover from the Thaw, disappointed in his former aspirations—the "duck hunt" stands for the last remnant of his dreams—and he finds no place in the stifled social climate of the Brezhnev-era Stagnation. Yet he is the freest character in the play, capable of cynical and transgressive acts. Zilov's self-destructive freedom finds its most emblematic embodiment in the play's finale. As noted by Elena Gushanskaia, *The Duck Hunt* has at least three finales.[152] In the first of them, Zilov attempts to kill himself, which completes the arc initiated by his friends' prank in the beginning of the play—they have sent him a funeral wreath with his name on it. The second finale is his quarrel with these very friends, a break with his environment suggesting a new beginning with a clean slate. Yet Zilov rejects both of these actions. Hence, the last and most ambiguous finale: "It is impossible to tell whether he weeps or laughs but his body twitches for a long time, as usually happens with strong laughter or weeping."[153] The character remains incomplete, which testifies to his existential freedom and breaks through the boundaries of simplistic solutions and assessments.

Underground modernisms of the 1960s through 1980s

From the late 1950s, nonconformist writers increasingly sought to generate a discourse that met the post-totalitarian, post-utopian, and post-traumatic conditions of culture, and one that was adequate to the resulting new modes of subjectivity. But in addition to wanting to express the shock of the new, many of these writers also understood the need to reinvent or reimagine nearly lost traditions. They shared a sentiment that would be eloquently expressed by Brodsky in his Nobel Prize lecture in 1987, where he praised cultural continuity and suggested that one path of innovation ran through the taboo language of Russian modernism. He added that "There existed, presumably, another path: the path of further deformation, the poetics of ruins and debris, of minimalism, of choked breath...."[154] Much of the work reviving this "poetics of ruins and debris" was to happen in the literary underground of the late Soviet period.

Some might argue that the campaign against Boris Pasternak's *Doctor Zhivago* marked the birth of underground literature as a cultural institution. By that point, Pasternak had long been a well-established writer. His attempts to publish the novel were rebuffed by *Novyi mir* and the almanac *Literary Moscow*. Only then did he permit the novel's publication abroad.[155] Similarly, Solzhenitsyn's novels *The First Circle* (*V kruge pervom*, 1967–68) and *Cancer Ward* (*Rakovyi korpus*, 1963–66) were sent by the author to *tamizdat* and *samizdat* after the failure of his attempts to publish them in Soviet journals.

The underground prose that snowballed into a powerful phenomenon from the mid-1960s onward had a different genealogy. It was the creation of authors either unknown to the broad public or known in other capacities (as scholars, translators) who, importantly, never intended their texts for Soviet publication and thus never bore in mind any possible reactions from the officialdom (editors, censors). From this perspective, Andrei Sinyavsky and Yuli Daniel, rather than Pasternak and Solzhenitsyn, were the leading lights in the new type of underground literature.

At the time of his arrest, Andrei Sinyavsky was known as a successful literary scholar, author of academic works about Gorky, Mayakovsky, Pasternak, and Picasso; he was a leading critic at *Novyi mir*, a staff researcher at the Moscow Institute of World Literature (IMLI), as well as a part-time professor at Moscow State University and Moscow Art Theater's School. His "criminal" works, including the so-called fantastic tales, the article "On Socialist Realism," and the dystopian novel *Liubimov* (*The Makepeace Experiment*, 1962–63), were published in the West under the pen-name Abram Tertz. Sinyavsky's pseudonym comes from Odessa's urban folklore—the song about a Jewish thief Abrashka Tertz. Once in emigration, Sinyavsky maintained his pen-name because the use of Tertz reflected his understanding of literature as an act of transgression and dissent, criminal by default.[156] In Sinyavsky's own words: "Abram Tertz is a dissident primarily by virtue of his stylistic qualities. But he is an impudent, incorrigible dissident, who provokes indignation and aversion in a conservative and conformist society."[157] This is why Sinyavsky claimed that his disagreements with the Soviet regime were "purely stylistic,"[158] and inseparable from literary creation. His deviation from cultural norms was aesthetic rather than ideological.

Sinyavsky's grotesque prose as well as his essayistic works, such as *Strolls with Pushkin* (*Progulki s Pushkinym*, 1975) and *In Gogol's Shadow* (*V teni Gogolia*, 1975), question first and foremost the stability of the subject and thereby the limits of freedom. In so doing, they ramp up devices familiar from modernism and adopt postmodernist techniques, and one authoritative critic has coined the apt term "archaic postmodernist" for this work, while another sees an existentialist element here.[159] Sinyavsky typically constructs his texts around the voice of an unreliable narrator (or several such narrators, as in *Liubimov*). Readers cannot tell whether the author and characters are trustworthy. In many works, for a good half of the text the reader does not even know *who* the narrator is—a human, alien, of fantastic creature ("Pkhentz" ["Pkhents," 1957]; "Tenants" ["Kvartiranty," 1959]; "You and I" ["Ty i ia," 1959]). While sometimes described as *skaz*, the narrative establishes an unstable relationship between the voices of author and characters, which can seem distinct at times only to merge elsewhere. In "Graphomaniacs" ("Grafomany," 1960), the talentless writer Straustin comically suspects famous writers of plagiarizing his unpublished manuscripts. But his obsession with art as self-expression turns into the opposite compulsion to dissolve the authorial self: "every writer is occupied by one thing alone: self-eli-mi-nation . . . in the hope of stepping aside, overcoming ourselves, and granting access to thoughts from the air."[160]

Sinyavsky finds the highest manifestation of the writer's "self-eli-mi-nation" in Pushkin. In *Strolls with Pushkin*, composed as letters from prison camp to his wife, Maria Rozanova (b. 1929), and published abroad after their emigration, he depicts Pushkin as a paragon of emptiness: "Emptiness was Pushkin's content. Without it he wouldn't have been full, he couldn't have existed, just as there can be no fire without air, no inhalation without exhalation . . . Pushkin was sufficiently empty to see things as they were, without foisting himself off on us as a willful daydreamer, but filling himself up with things to the brim and reacting almost mechanically. . . ."[161] From this emptiness stem all other features assigned by Sinyavsky to Pushkin: "thin erotic legs," "loved to dress up in foreign costumes both on the streets and his verses," "loved no one," "a vampire." Sinyavsky's Pushkin is a lazybones, similar to Gogol's fraudulent government inspector Khlestakov. This characterization infuriated some readers of *Strolls with Pushkin*, particularly Solzhenitsyn and a range of nationalist critics.[162] For Sinyavsky, however, the characterization was not a denigration: all these effects of Pushkin's emptiness signify his unique "freedom of thought and language...that confer a freedom of the world hitherto unprecedented in our literature."[163] This understanding of creativity is also consonant with the theories of "the death of the author," about which Sinyavsky could hardly have known in the isolation of his Mordovia prison camp, where he wrote *Strolls with Pushkin*. Nevertheless, much like Roland Barthes, Sinyavsky sees the writer as a conduit through whom impersonal and mutually contradictory languages pass. It suggests a new interpretation of the subject, who in Sinyavsky's prose appears as the coalescence of numerous dissimilar and even conflicting discursive elements. In the montage-like nature of the subject, Sinyavsky detects the reason for the inevitable doom of the Soviet utopia (most fully explored in *The Makepeace Experiment*), with its dream of social and individual homogenization.

The work of Sinyavsky's co-defendant Yuli Daniel conveys the atmosphere of societal unreality and instability leading to collective vertigo: "everything around, everything that was and is there, is a mirage, phantom, all is elusive and unstable" (*The Atonement* [*Iskuplenie*, 1963]).[164] Abram Tertz interprets such effects philosophically, but Daniel typically tries to embed grotesque motifs in social psychology. In his fiction, everything is unstable, because the Soviet regime has shattered the moral foundations of society. Daniel demonstrates that the totalitarian matrix has penetrated much deeper into individual psychology than optimists from the generation of the Sixties would imagine. For example, in *The Atonement* totalitarian dehumanization reveals itself in the liberal milieu of the Thaw: the novella's protagonist Viktor is attacked by the Gulag survivor Felix for denouncing him and putting Felix in a prison camp. Viktor has not denounced anyone, but just as in the time of the Great Terror, everybody accepts accusations without proof; the mechanism of scapegoating remains, only now at the bidding of the liberal-minded intelligentsia. In Daniel's most famous novella, *This Is Moscow Speaking* (*Govorit Moskva*, 1958), it is enough for the state to announce a "Day of Open Murders" and all the old totalitarian reflexes of fear and conformyi instantly return. State violence acts as a trigger, authorizing the mutual persecution that constituted the core of totalitarianism:

> Complete freedom to kill. Then [in the time of revolution and terror], at least they made more of a show of it. Now they just say: "Go ahead and kill"—and that's that! And another thing, in those days the killers had a whole apparatus at their disposal, an enormous staff, whereas now you have to do it yourself![165]

Daniel almost desperately seeks to preserve an inner sense of dignity and freedom when society rejects these values. In *The Atonement*, Viktor decides to accept the blame for historical crimes—real and imaginary, direct and indirect; however, this Christ-like position lands him in a mental institution. Tolya, the protagonist of *This Is Moscow Speaking*, asks himself: "...what would Don Quixote do on the 10th of August? He'd ride about Moscow on his Rocinante and defend anyone who was attacked."[166] This is exactly what Tolya does on the Day of Open Murders, unlike his friends and his former lover: he resists dehumanization and manifests his freedom. Basically, this decision expresses the birth of dissident ethics as a struggle for dignity without concern for effective action. It is no wonder that Don Quixote, who for classic authors like Turgenev perfectly embodied a mix of idealism and futility, became so popular in the late Soviet period (the poet and dissident Yuri Aikhenval'd composed a two-volume treatise on the theme of Don Quixote in Russian culture, in fact).[167]

There were two versions of the Don Quixote motif in nonconformist literature, exemplified by Georgy Vladimov's (1931–2003) novel *Faithful Ruslan* (*Vernyi Ruslan*, 1975) and Boris Khazanov's *The King's Hour* (*Chas korolia*, 1976). Khazanov creates a legend about the Scandinavian king Cedric who, during the Holocaust in his country, put on a yellow Mogen David on his suit—to display his solidarity with Jews and to protest against Nazism. The result was tragic: he failed to save the Jews, and doomed himself to death. For Khazanov, Cedric's gesture embodies "the testament of an absurd act" as the ultimate, desperate gesture of resistance in impossible circumstances: "The absurd act crosses out reality. Instead of truth, obligatory for all, it offers a truth that is obvious to one person only. Strictly speaking, it means that the one who decided to act in this way has become a living truth himself."[168] This principle is also applicable to the hero of Vladimov's novella—a Gulag guard dog whose name, Ruslan, ironically suggests Pushkin's mock-epic poem *Ruslan and Liudmila* (*Ruslan i Liudmila*, 1820), and its chivalric context. Ruslan defines his freedom and his Quixotic dignity through absurd and dignified action, but his honorable behavior is inseparable from the Gulag norms he has also internalized. Sinyavsky interpreted *Faithful Ruslan* as a parable about the entire Soviet nation, whose most honorable and noble feelings were mobilized for a war against individual freedom, and whose own freedom could only be expressed through the suppression of others.[169]

The genre of parable became a trademark of underground modernist literature about Stalinism and its consequences. Alongside Sinyavsky and Daniel, Vladimov and Khazanov, nonconformist authors such as Yuri Mamleev, Vladimir Maramzin, Aleksandr Zinov'ev, Andrei Amal'rik (1938–80), Mark Kharitonov (b. 1937), and Andrei Romashov (1926–95) also explored its heuristic potential. Among them, a special place belongs to Friedrich Gorenshtein (1932–2002). Better known as the author of film scripts for Andrei Tarkovsky, Andrei Konchalovsky, and Nikita Mikhalkov, Gorenshtein wrote several novels that were unpublished in the USSR, including *The Atonement* (*Iskuplenie*, 1967), *Psalm* (*Psalom*, 1975), and *The Place* (*Mesto*, 1976), and the plays *Berdichev* (1975) and *Debates about Dostoevsky* (*Spory o Dostoevskom*, 1973). Gorenshtein combined the expressiveness of parable with painful naturalism of detail. For example, in *Psalm* he depicts the horror and devastation brought by collectivization, the Second World War and German occupation, and post-war anti-Semitic campaigns—all seen through the eyes of the Anti-Christ, Dan. This mythological character, who arrives on Earth with a mission of Judgment and Retribution, takes pity on the people undergoing the ordeals of the Soviet catastrophe and, ashamed of his assignment, decides to share their tragic destiny.

Many underground writers sought to escape one-dimensional political statements, transforming politically charged material into a set of powerful metaphors. Some sensed the limitations of realist aesthetics and looked for alternatives to convey the traumatic experiences of Soviet history. Not all versions of this new artistic language were heavy or tragic in tone. Literary conventions drawn from the grotesque and the parable shape the most popular genre of late Soviet urban culture, the political joke (*anekdot*). Seth Graham argues that these political jokes created a kind of mass-culture double for official ideology:

> The genre's alternative representations, however, were not merely rebuttals of the progressively less compelling semantic premises of the Party line, but also ironic, stylized rehearsals and exposés of the signifying practices used to communicate those premises.... For much of Soviet history the state treated the entire genre as inherently anti-Soviet.[170]

In fact, each anecdote was a grotesque parable leading up to a comic punchline. The expressivity of the anecdote generated new forms of epic and mock-epic narrative by Yuz Aleshkovsky, Vladimir Voinovich, and Fazil Iskander. These narratives continued a lineage harkening back to grotesque modernism of the 1920s—its poetics and its favorite characters.

Each of these writers built large-scale narratives from chains of anecdotes in which Soviet ideology and officialdom display their fantastic nature, while a protagonist, typically representative of the broad masses, embodies the natural forces of life. This protagonist does battle with the state and eventually triumphs. His power stems from the simple, natural needs of a human organism (first and foremost, sexual), while the realm associated with the regime looks solid but in fact wobbles on a foundation made of words. It takes no more than a misused or mis-heard word to cause its collapse.

All these writers organically rely on principles of carnivalization, sometimes borrowed directly from the world of jokes. Aleshkovsky, however, displays a direct connection to Bakhtin, placing at the center of his prose the "grand people's body"; he surrounds corporeality with signs of carnivalesque excess and virtuoso obscene language—as the only vital counter-weights to the deadening power of totalitarian ideology and politics. Vladimir Voinovich, in his novels about the soldier Ivan Chonkin (1969–79), relies on the traditional motif of the fool who unwittingly exposes ubiquitous idiocy. And Fazil Iskander does something similar in his cycle of short stories *Sandro from Chegem* (*Sandro iz Chegema*—half of it appeared in *Novyi mir* in 1973, the other half circulated in *samizdat*; Ardis published it in full in 1977).

Unlike the writers of Village Prose and unlike Aleshkovsky and Voinovich, Iskander avoids juxtapositions between the world of political power and the realm of ordinary people. *Sandro from Chegem* suggests parallels between the patriarchal Abkhazian village, where Sandro lives, and the new political order established under Stalin; implicitly, Iskander is showing that the Soviet political order was based on archaization rather than modernization. (He also discusses this phenomenon in the story "On a Summer Day" ["Letnim dnem," 1967], in which the Soviet regime is characterized indirectly through parallels with Nazism.[171]) As Iskander sees it, the totalitarian system reorients traditional cultural models toward a deification of the tyrant. These powerful weapons against any manifestations of personal dignity are the inevitable result of politicizing cultural traditionalism. It takes a cunning trickster like Iskander's Sandro to preserve independence under this double pressure. Sandro frequently appears in humiliating or morally questionable situations (like dancing on his knees before Stalin), but against all odds he miraculously remains unhurt, physically as well as psychologically. The regime forces its subjects to don dehumanizing masks, but because Sandro by nature is a master of disguises, none of the assumed identities sticks. Sandro transforms what might otherwise be tragedy into an endless feast, a carnivalesque show in which he possesses the supreme, albeit elusively playful, power. Like any trickster, Sandro is "not immoral, he is a-moral,"[172] and therefore Iskander does not judge his protagonist for conformism. True to type with his zest for life as an endless performance, Sandro preserves his dignity and with it the dignity of the people.

Yuri Mamleev created an idiosyncratic version of the modernist Gothic.[173] In his short sto-ries and novels (e.g., *Shatuny*, 1968), he depicts the Soviet world as literally inhabited by the living dead and generally situated in between the states of life and death. While Aleshkovsky, Voinovich, and Iskander sought in the life of ordinary people healthy forces able to confront simulacra of ideology, Mamleev presented the Soviet condition as the essence of human monstrosity, which he exposed through an aesthetic of the grotesque and the horrifying.[174] Mamleev's version of modernist discourse has been developed by several writers of subse-quent generations—from Viktor Erofeev (*Life with an Idiot* [*Zhizn' s idiotom*, 1980]) to Yulia Kisina (*Dead Artists' Society* [*Obshchestvo mertvykh khudozhnikov*, 2010]) and Pavel Peppershtein (*War Stories* [*Voennye rasskazy*, 2006], *Spring* [*Vesna*, 2010]).[175]

A writer who pursued a somewhat different brand of modernist discourse is Evgeny Kharitonov. He wrote about homosexuality in the absence of any queer discourse and in obvious contrast with Mikhail Kuzmin's ornate style. In Dmitry Prigov's apt description of Kharitonov's prose, "since the time of Rozanov, Russian literature has not known such an example of simultaneously intimate and marginal existence in art, which suggests the resolution of contemporary literary and linguistic problems in the ultimately sincere, riskily sincere level of one's personal life."[176] The "riskily sincere" effect of self-exposure was intensified in Kharitonov's prose by the Soviet criminalization of same-sex love. For Kharitonov, however, the criminal character of the most intimate aspects of his subjectivity facilitates a new degree of self-expression through the literary text. In his manifesto "The Flysheet" ("Listovka," published in 1985), homosexuality, Jewishness, and underground literature appear as synonymous, interchangeable phenomena:

> We are sterile, poisonous blooms, and as such we should be made up into flower arrangements and put in vases for purely decorative purposes. Our Question has points of similarity with The Jewish Question.... Just as Jewish people have to be ridiculed in jokes, and the image of the crafty yid firmly retained in the mind's eye by all non-Jewish humanity to ensure that anti-Semitism should not perish from the earth . . . so too our ethereal flower-like sport with its pollen flying who knows whither must be mocked and transformed by the coarse, direct common sense of common people into a term of abuse, so that immature silly boys should not take it into their heads before their masculine drive has finally become established in them to give in to the weakness of falling in love with themselves.[177]

Kharitonov's vision of literature subverts traditional (Soviet) ideas about its mission and cultural prestige and resonates with Sinyavsky's concept of true literature as transgressive by default. According to Kharitonov, literature is indecent and "sterile" rather than "morally educational"; it is marginalized and ridiculed, rather than honored and celebrated; it is not "for common people" but ultimately offensive to their primitive tastes. Such literature is criminal by default, yet these conditions are vital to the survival of the much-needed transgressive freedom of literature.

Postmodernist literature: From late Soviet underground to post-Soviet mainstream

The cynical character of late socialist culture served as a fertile ground for Soviet postmodernist discourse and cultural practices, which, as in other countries, especially magnified and manifested "incredulity towards metanarratives."[178] Mostly ignorant of Western postmodern theory until the 1990s,[179] Russian underground writers designed their own version of postmodernism without actually knowing the terms in use. In Soviet culture, the metanarratives deconstructed by postmodernists were predominantly those of totalitarian/communist political mythology. In the post-Soviet period, the quasi-sacred metanarratives were recognized in the grand tradition of Russian literature, which envisioned literature as a secular religion and positioned writers as prophets engaged in transcendental quests for timeless (i.e., essentialist) truth and beauty.

While allied with some tendencies already present in Russian modernism and avant-garde (found in writings by Kharms, Nabokov, and Vaginov, for example), the 1970s–80s work by Venedikt Erofeev, Sasha Sokolov, Vladimir Sorokin, Dmitry Prigov, and others displayed signs of a new aesthetics. These include the deconstruction of binary oppositions (especially those held sacred in official or intelligentsia culture) through humor, pastiche, and the verbal highjacking known as *détournements*. Postmodernism fused multiple historical and cultural discourses, stylistics, and temporal realms, to jarring effect. It also scandalized readers with themes of transgression: sexuality, violence, alcoholism, obscenities, and the like. These topics appeared in some women's writings in the 1970s–80s as well, but nonconformist women's prose largely remained unknown to readers until Perestroika, when it was published alongside postmodernist authors. Both sets of writers retained a power to shock their readers.

CASE STUDY *Moscow to the End of the Line* by Venedikt Erofeev

Venedikt Erofeev's *Moscow to the End of the Line* (*Moskva-Petushki*, completed in 1970, first published in 1973; also known in English as *Moscow Circles*) synthesizes key strategies of transgressive self-representation in underground literature. This narrative poem in prose uses a genre reminiscent of Gogol's *Dead Souls*, also subtitled "A Poem" or *poema*. Erofeev wrote it between January and March 1970 and its *samizdat* typescripts and *tamizdat* editions were received ecstatically; some readers memorized it word for word. In the Soviet Union, it was first published only in 1988, in the newly established magazine *Sobriety and Culture* (*Trezvost' i kul'tura*); it is hard to imagine a work of fiction less suited to the anti-alcohol propaganda campaign than this liquor-soaked narrative. It was released in a separate edition in 1990, priced at 3 rubles 62 kopeks—the exact cost of a half-liter bottle of vodka in the 1970s. *Moscow to the End of the Line* attained a unique status: no other text of unofficial culture had greater cultural resonance.[180]

FIGURE V.09. Venedikt Erofeev, 1980s.

The poem and its author became symbols of the Russian underground of the 1970s, symbols that emphatically did not idealize the counterculture, but presented it as both repulsive and charmingly appealing (most extant photographs of Erofeev show him with a glass or a cigarette; for an exception see Figure V.09). Erofeev's protagonist Venichka is marginal by definition: an unemployed alcoholic with no permanent address (at the beginning of the novel he awakens in a building hallway). His route, while geographically determined (the first USSR book edition in 1990 was illustrated with a map of the Vladimir suburban train line, where the station of Petushki is located), expands into a journey from hell to heaven and back. If Petushki is truly heaven, then the Kremlin, in proximity to which Venichka will find his tragic death, is inevitably associated with hell. At the same time, Venichka's journey includes a brief overview of world culture from the perspective of drunkenness, a tale of fantastic wanderings around Europe, and the story of the Revolution in the village of Cherkasovo, to say nothing of the numerous mythological themes and plots that come to life in the hero-narrator's tale. Venichka's train car becomes a genuine liminal zone, at first inhabited by relatively realistic characters ("the woman of a difficult fate," "black-mustache," Mitrich and grandson, the conductor Semenych). Later, on the road back to Moscow, more fantastic characters occupy the train car: Satan, King Mithridates, hordes of Erinyes, Peter, the statue of the Worker and the Kolkhoz Peasant, and the Sphinx. In the final section of the book, time disappears and space is constructed through oxymoronic fusions such as "Petushki. Sadovy Circle," "Petushki. The Kremlin."

Oscillations between high and low, between the bodily carnivalesque and the sublime, characterize the ambivalent positions of Venichka the hero and Venichka the narrator. The high and the low do not negate or annihilate one another, but instead form an ambivalent unity of meaning. In fact, the most stylistically vivid passages are built on the ambivalent juxtaposition of these registers: from the comical comparison between another dose of coriander vodka and St. Teresa's stigmata, to the recipes for cocktails based on dandruff treatment, athlete's foot remedy, and nail polish bearing names like "Balsam of Canaan" or "The Star of Bethlehem" and presented by Venichka as his gifts to God, which it "will be possible to drink in the presence of God and man, in the presence of man and in the name of God."[181]

The gaps in Venichka's being and consciousness confirm Erofeev's attraction to liminal zones. A drunken escapade can acquire a transcendental dimension. In a number of passages related to drinking, as well as in the motifs of blindness and darkness, one finds an intertextual reference to "The Mystical Theology" by the Byzantine theologian Dionysius the Areopagite, whose teachings had a wide circulation in Moscow *samizdat* during the 1960s and 1970s. This tract asserts the apophatic idea that communication with God requires the negation of all intellectual and sensory faculties, since He transcends human experience; communication with the Divine, according to Dionysius, requires plunging "into the Darkness of Unknowing."

While sinking deeper and deeper into drunken darkness, Venichka is killed by four strangers in the poem's finale. The question of who killed Venichka offers a key to the entire poem's meaning. Venichka states that he knows his killers with certainty: "I recognized them at once—I won't tell you who they were."[182] Readers cannot but speculate about their identities, symbolic or otherwise. The four mysterious killers who pursue Venichka in the poem's finale are sometimes associated with Marx, Engels, Stalin, and Lenin, a reading that yields only a rather flat political interpretation out of sync with the poem's intellectual complexity. Alternatively, these mysterious figures remind one of the four evangelists, creators of the Logos, frequently depicted in biblical texts as "living creatures" with heads of Eagle, Lion, Ox, and Man surrounding God's throne. The divine messengers kill Venichka with a blow to the throat—the organ of speech, so this murder might also seem like a subversive paraphrase of Isaiah, the same passage interpreted by Pushkin in his "Prophet" (Isaiah 6:5–8). In these biblical passages, as in Pushkin's poem, man becomes a messenger of God, but Erofeev depicts God's messengers as a murderous force killing the protagonist's individual voice. All these possible prototypes of Venichka's murderers signify the coming of God; His throne, His glory, His voice, and word (Logos). In a sense, Venichka's terrible death embodies the appearance of God: an awl in the throat is Erofeev's theophany.

The striving of divine Logos for absolute supremacy deprives the protagonist/narrator of his own voice—precisely because Venichka's discourse freely, too freely perhaps, dissolves the boundaries between the sacred and the profane, the transcendental and physiological. In a postmodernist manner, it also undermines any sort of power, including the absolute. In *Moscow to the End of the Line*, God and the Logos, the ultimate signifiers of the universal and timeless truth, demand for their presence—and supremacy—the murder of the individual voice and free consciousness. Erofeev's prose poem presupposes that free art can only be created by a subject who inhabits a liminal zone; the understanding of the underground author/artist as a liminal subject, whose quest for the sacred is inseparable from the subversion of all authoritative grand narratives, proved formative and programmatic for postmodernist writings well into the post-Soviet period.

In prose of the 1960s–80s, postmodernism produced two further trends that sometimes overlapped. One focused on the critical subversion of authoritative discourses associated with both ideological formations and the speech patterns of the masses, which were equally alien for nonconformist writers. This tendency found its strongest expression in literary Conceptualism and the Sots-Art movement. The second trend explored languages of selfhood, sometimes radically collapsing the distance between the author's person and the textual narrator, sometimes no less radically mythologizing a biographical author. The latter tendency can be defined as neo-baroque. It produces a fusion of classic baroque tropes (the world as theater, life as a dream) with characteristics of more contemporary culture, like the "society of spectacle" (Guy Debord) and the "hyperreality of simulacra" (Jean Baudrillard).[183] These two trends within Russian underground postmodernism outlived Soviet cultural institutions and persisted in the 1990s–2000s.

Much like poetry, prose texts created by representatives of Moscow Conceptualism thrived on the deconstructions and mockery of symbolic authority—from Soviet official discourse to Russian literary classics. Within postmodernist discourse, works of writers close to the Moscow Conceptualist Circle constituted a specifically Soviet and post-Soviet style that by analogy with the visual art of this period can be defined as Sots-Art.[184] This was a milieu in which artists and writers coexisted in a productive symbiosis. Many members of this circle were both writers and artists, including Dmitry Prigov, Ilya Kabakov, and Vagrich Bakhchanian (1938–2009). Sots-Art exaggerates the hegemonic ambitions of Socialist Realism in order to replace historical and everyday reality with its own symbolic vocabulary, creating a world in which characters manifest signifiers of the ideological language. The result might be a Soviet crest substituting for the sun (as in Eric Bulatov's painting, *Sunrise or Sunset*, Plate 18), or Stalin visited by an ancient muse (in the artists Vitaly Komar's and Aleksandr Melamid's painting from the cycle *Nostalgic Socialist Realism*, 1981–83, shown in Plate 19).

The term Sots-Art was invented by Komar and Melamid in the early 1970s, although this kind of aesthetics had already developed in the visual works of Bakhchanian, Aleksandr Kosolapov (b. 1943), and Leonid Sokov (b. 1941) and in Prigov's poetry of the 1970s. In prose this tendency was best represented by Prigov's "Soviet texts" ("Sovy"), "The Ranks Game" ("Igra v chiny"), and "Descriptions of Objects" ("Opisanie predmetov"); Bakhchanian's short prose and plays, later collected as *The Cherry Hell and Other Plays* (*Vishnevyi ad i drugie p'esy*, 2005); Igor Kholin's cycle of "Kremlin Jokes" ("Kremlevskie shutki," 1993); and short prose by

Arkady Bartov, Evgeny Popov, Yulia Kisina, and Nikolai Baitov. The earliest example of literary Sots-Art came much earlier, and from an unexpected corner: *The Newest Plutarch: An Illustrated Biographical Dictionary of Imaginary Figures of All Countries and Times* (*Noveishii Plutarkh. Illiustrirovannyi biograficheskii slovar' voobrazhaemykh znamenitykh deiatelei vsekh stran i vremen*), completed in 1953 by three inmates of the infamous Vladimir political prison, Daniil Andreev (better known for his mystical treatise *The Rose of the World* [*Roza mira*, 1958, published 1991]), and his cellmates, historian Lev Rakov and physiologist Vasily Parin. One of the latest manifestations of Sots-Art, also of an encyclopedic scope, was the two-volume novel by Pavel Peppershtein and Sergei Anufriev, *The Mythogenous Love of Castes* (*Mifogennaia liubov' kast*, vol. 1, 1999; vol. 2, 2002).

The most provocative version of Sots-Art was created by Vladimir Sorokin. Sorokin explained his literary method as a kind of controlled explosion: "In the 1980s, I used to make little binary literary bombs consisting of two incompatible parts: a Socialist Realist one and the other built on real physiology; as a result, an explosion followed, and it did fill me as a writer with a flash of freedom."[185] At times, the text, even when it has narrative coherence, is reduced to nothing more than meaningless words and chanting. In this respect, Sorokin's Sots-Art resurrects the nonsensical language of *zaum*, with an added helping of obscenities.[186] In accordance with the logic of exposing the hidden violence of all authoritative discourse, Sorokin reveals tangibly abject plots within Socialist Realist discourses, with abundant reference to excrement and gore. He foregrounds physical and sexual power with motifs that invariably elicit a strong emotional reaction, usually revulsion. Along the way, the master tropes of the Socialist Realist worldview are brutally parodied. However, the revelation of the discourse's absurdity coincides with the triumph of the mythological order. Hence the ambivalence of Sots-Art: the disgusting and absurd illustrate mythological harmony, while the harmony elicits only nausea.

Once he began deconstructing Socialist Realist plots and characters, Sorokin soon realized that the same deconstruction was applicable to any other authoritative discourse. He would uncover the unconscious layers of these discourses, the hitherto concealed secret of their sacredness, detecting a source for their symbolic authority in the brutal, bloody violence that harks back to archaic forms of authority. The objects of his artistic analysis came to include Russian literary classics of the nineteenth century (*The Novel* [*Roman*, 1985–89]), twentieth-century modernism (*A Month in Dachau* [*Mesiats v Dakhau*, 1994]), and contemporary dissident discourse (*The Norm* [*Norma*, 1979–83], *The Thirtieth Love of Marina* [*Tridtsataia liubov' Mariny*, 1982–84], and *The Queue* [*Ochered'*, 1983]). Sorokin was frequently accused of vandalizing the cultural heritage, but his method was clearly aimed at exposing the symbolic violence associated with any authoritative rhetoric and discourse.

Dirk Uffelmann defines Sorokin's early aesthetics as "the materialization of metaphors,"[187] or rather their "corporealization," since metaphors are typically translated by Sorokin into bodily functions. In Sorokin's words:

> I work constantly with liminal zones where the body invades the text. For me, this borderline between literature and corporeality was of foremost importance. As a matter of fact, my texts always raise a question of literary corporeality, and I try to decide whether literature is corporeal. I enjoy the moment when literature becomes corporeal and non-literary.[188]

Thus, in his famous novel *Blue Lard* (*Goluboe salo*, 1999), Sorokin translates various narratives of the transcendental into somatic substances. The central motif of the novel is blue lard, "a substance whose entropy equals zero," a materialized harmony, and at the same time, a fat layer that the monstrous bodies of clones of great Russian writers generate in the process of writing. *Blue Lard* incorporates parodic texts written by clones of Tolstoy, Dostoevsky,

Nabokov, and Platonov. Critic and prose writer Mikhail Berg interprets the blue lard as "the essence of sacredness and purity accumulated in Russian literature...the structural element of power in Russian culture—what we might call 'literature-centrism.'"[189] The plot relates the struggle between past-oriented nationalists and characters from the globalized future, and between Stalin and Hitler. The latter are presented as figures in an alternative history (Stalin and Hitler peacefully divide control over the world). The novel ends with a total world collapse triggered by Stalin's injection of blue lard directly into his brain—an ironic metaphor for the merging of literature and dictatorial power.

In the 2000s, Sorokin remained loyal to the principles of Moscow Conceptualism, but became more reader-oriented and eliminated the most extreme elements of gore, violence, and obscenity from his work. He used the arsenal of Conceptualism to target the post-Soviet regime, creating new forms of political satire. As in his earlier works, Sorokin explores the connections between languages of culture and political violence. In his 2006 novel *The Day of the Oprichnik* (*Den' oprichnika*) and its sequel, a collection of short stories, *The Sugar Kremlin* (*Sakharnyi Kreml'*, 2008), he extrapolates neo-traditionalist tendencies to imagine a dystopian Russian state in 2028, with a restored monarchy and medieval societal organization. Political terror is modeled after Ivan the Terrible's *oprichnina* (and depicted with obvious references to Sergei Eisenstein's cinematic treatment in the second part of *Ivan the Terrible*); yet it is combined with futuristic high-tech infrastructure, legalization of drugs, and complete isolation from the West. The neo-traditionalist ideology of national unification around supposedly simple and eternal values manifests itself through the *oprichniks'* deeds, which prove invariably violent—from scenes of a gang rape to a collective heroic song (*bylina*) about a seven-headed dragon that rapes Russia's global foes and sets them on fire. Sorokin's 2010 novella *The Blizzard* (*Metel'*) presents another version of Russia's disastrous de-modernization, this time via a return to nineteenth-century class and cultural distinctions translated by advances in genetic engineering: the novel's Russia is populated by giants and Lilliputians alongside normal-sized people. In *Telluria* (2013), Sorokin depicts post-apocalyptic Eurasia divided into numerous separate realms, each dominated by its own political and cultural discourse: the novel consists of fifty chapters, each one representing "a land" through its idiosyncratic language. As these texts demonstrate, a repressive discourse may emerge from any source, but always functions through the dynamic between the corporeal and the spiritual. Political repression is reinterpreted as the dictatorship of the spiritual—ideological or symbolic (i.e., bodiless)—over discrete human bodies and concrete lives: it is the dictatorship of the discursive over the non-discursive.

The alternative late Soviet trend in postmodernism, the neo-baroque, is best exemplified by the work of Sasha Sokolov (b. 1943). He, too, subverted cultural taboos, but in a different way from the Moscow Conceptualists: he reactivated modernist traditions of transgressive self-creation, and valued modernist sensibilities as a self-sufficient if fruitless quest for "the real" that lies hidden beneath endless layers of cultural simulacra and social spectacles.

A paradoxical synthesis of modernist and postmodernist techniques of self-representation appears in his first novel, *A School for Fools* (*Shkola dlia durakov*, 1973). Written when he was working as a game warden in a hunting preserve for the Soviet elite (an experience he would use for his second novel, *Between Dog and Wolf* [*Mezhdu sobakoi i volkom*, 1980]) and rejected by several Russian émigré publishers as politically vague (official publication was out of the question), the novel was picked up by Carl Proffer, who later translated it into English. *A School for Fools* appeared in Russian in the United States through Proffer's press, Ardis, with Nabokov's blurb calling it an "enchanting, tragic and touching book." In this novel, Sokolov establishes a connection between the subjective world of the creative self and aggressive, traumatic reality littered with the signs of catastrophe. He employs motifs of chaos to create a constant fluctuation between opposite meanings, signifying at once creativity and destruction, beauty and horror, conflicts and endless metamorphoses. An "abnormal" conscience of "pupil so-and-so" transforms the humdrum and meager world of the school for fools and its environs into the scene of eternal myths. The absence of linear order in the protagonist's perception enables endless metamorphoses that form the mythological basis of the novel. Metamorphoses involve words, languages, characters and their voices, and even material objects. The ultimate goal of this process is to regenerate reality, which has been annihilated by historical catastrophes and mundane violence permeating the atmosphere of the school for fools. The protagonist's mythmaking embodies creativity as the principal form of resistance to external chaos. But the greatest accomplishment of "pupil so-and-so" is his horrible cacophonous shout. Filling "the emptiness of empty chambers," the shout elicits "ultramundane terror," generating in response "a monstrous, deafening chorus" of other inmates of the school.[190]

Nevertheless, exuberant word play triumphs over the deadening chaos of social reality in *A School for Fools*: the myth of metamorphoses created by "pupil so-and-so" irreversibly transfigures the station, the river, the girl, the chalk, the freight train, and the school itself with all its inhabitants into an enchanting verbal ballet. But Sokolov's next novel, *Between Dog and Wolf*, displays the opposite scenario: instead of creative metamorphoses triumphing over the chaotic world, the plot depicts the victory of chaos, ensuring the protagonist/narrator's destruction.

With his third novel *Palisandria* (1985, translated into English as *Astrophobia*), Sokolov moved from the tragic to the parodic, from metamorphoses to pastiche and grotesque. In the impossibility of further metamorphoses, the author of *Palisandria* detects symptoms of the post-utopian phase of history. "The day before yesterday at sixteen minutes to nine, timelessness has begun—the time to dare and to create,"[191] declares the novel's protagonist and narrator, Palisandr Dal´berg, a fictional version of Beria's nephew, "the Kremlin orphan," and subsequently supreme ruler of Russia. In Boris Groys's interpretation:

> The world of Stalin's Kremlin in which the hero grows up is described by him as paradise. It is not the prehistorical Paradise, however, but a paradise of history ... Thus, when the hero is banished from paradise, he is driven not into history but from it into a loss of historical memory, into the everyday.[192]

The capricious style and plot of the novel constantly blur, and eventually eliminate, oppositions. The erasure of distinctions between a privileged Soviet aristocrat and a dissident, between an executioner and his victim, youth and old age, male and female, life and death, superman and monster, devalues all imaginable categories; as a result, these transformations do not manifest change, and the world enters into a tedious process of self-replication and self-simulations. Poetic metamorphoses are replaced by déjà vu. *Palisandria* turns out to be a tragic summary of the most daring attempts of European and Russian modernism to unleash the imagination and unconscious. Sokolov's response casts it as a defeat of the creative imagination. As personified by Palisandr Dal´berg, postmodernism becomes a post-historical monster that sucks the life and energy from diverse cultural discourses. After this novel, Sokolov published only short pieces, breaking his silence in 2011 with a book of poetry, *Triptych* (*Triptikh*). Although it confirmed his reputation as a peerless stylist, its critical and popular reception was rather modest.

The neo-baroque version of postmodernism in the post-Soviet period shows up in the highly distinctive poetics of a number of other major figures, among them: Viktor Pelevin, Vladimir Sharov (b. 1952), Mikhail Shishkin (b. 1961), Oleg Iur´ev (b. 1959), Leonid Girshovich (b. 1948), Nikolai Kononov (b. 1958), and Lena Eltang (b. 1964). Just as Sorokin's works are emblematic of Sots-Arts and Conceptualism, the postmodernist neo-baroque is most fully manifested in the works of Viktor Pelevin. Unlike Sorokin, who desacralizes authoritative discourses, Pelevin mythologizes and ironizes the emptiness that follows the deconstruction of grand narratives. He extends the tradition of modernist mythmaking in highly imaginative ways. The characters of Pelevin's phantasmagoric novel *Chapaev and Void* (*Chapaev i Pustota*, 1996; translated into English by Andrew Bromfield as *Buddha's Little Finger* and *Clay Machine-Gun*) are locked away in a mental institution in 1991, the year when the Soviet era came to its end.[193] Each inmate describes a personal myth, based on the realization that life's meaning does not depend on what actually happens, but on fragile illusions that substitute for a vanishing reality. The novel's protagonist Petr Pustota (Void) finds himself in the middle of the Russian Civil War in 1919. Under the command of the legendary Socialist Realist hero and the protagonist of numerous jokes, Vasily Chapaev (here also a possible incarnation of Buddha), Pustota gradually realizes that the question of where illusion ends and reality begins makes no sense, for everything is a void and the product of the void. However, the reverse is also true: the void can become everything and contains the potential for an entire new universe. In grasping his freedom from the power of both simulacra and reality, Pustota acquires the strength to create the world anew, expanding into eternity the limits of his "I," his "inner Mongolia." Pelevin creates a paradoxical Bildungsroman about the transformation of illusions into a reality immutable solely for one individual, a reality that proves a simulation devoid of significance for anyone else. *Chapaev and Void* is also one of the first post-utopian novels in Russian literature: Pelevin's protagonist calls utopia to account (thus, the parallel, more than numerical, between the years 1919 and 1991, suggested by the novel's narrative planes), but soberly recognizes the unrealizability and danger of an attained utopian unity.

Pelevin's 1999 novel bears the title *Generation P* in Russian (*Babylon* in the British edition, *Homo Zapiens* in the American) and demonstrates the transformation of mythmaking in the post-Soviet consumerist and political context.[194] The novel depicts the activities and rituals of post-Soviet copywriters—creators of consumerist media and secular priests of the contemporary hyperreality of simulacra. *Generation P*'s mythological narratives are organized around an empty center as the essence of the media-based mass-production of consumerist illusions in post-Soviet Russia, an ironic metamorphosis of the baroque theme of life as a dream. The empty center of political power in the novel is formed by figures of supreme political and economic authority, who turn out to be computer animations. But every politician, as the novel's characters argue, "is just a television broadcast." In accordance with this logic, the story of the protagonist Tatarsky embodies the path to this empty center. He rises to the summit of mystical (and also economic and political) power for no reason beyond his exotic first name, Vavilen, which echoes Babylon in Russian (*Vavilon*). At the high point of his quest, Tatarsky becomes a virtual mask that basically substitutes for his (non)existence.[195]

Pelevin's subsequent novels revisit earlier themes, such as how to realize oneself in the world of unreality without becoming just another simulacrum. His critique of the society of spectacle manifests itself in a satirical style peppered with politically charged puns and aphorisms; the fantastic plotlines defamiliarize contemporary political situations by means of ironic myth-like motifs. Particularly successful is the novel *The Sacred Book of the Werewolf* (*Sviashchennaia kniga oborotnia*, 2004), which amalgamates mythic and folkloric motifs drawn from Chinese folklore about foxy shapeshifters, Norse mythology of Ragnarök, and Bulgakov's novella *The Heart of a Dog*. Pelevin uses these tongue-in-cheek combinations to allegorize contemporary types: an ancient Chinese fox stands for an underage Moscow prostitute and a postmodernist intellectual; a werewolf represents Russia's political elite, the FSB general responsible for milking the mystical cow producing Russia's oil.[196] The fox embodies the invigorating and restorative component of postmodernist cynicism descended from the long lineage of Soviet tricksters. The wolf reveals the underlying cynical foundations of post-Soviet negative self-identification and the neo-traditionalist politics of the 2000s and 2010s. Each of the protagonists gets what s/he wants: the werewolf-general reaches supreme power, manifested in unlimited destruction, while the werefox-liberal obtains ultimate freedom leading to the subject's disappearance in the nirvana-like Rainbow Stream.

Among other writers gravitating to the neo-baroque, Vladimir Sharov deserves special mention for *The Rehearsals* (*Repetitsii*, 1992), *Before and During* (*Do i vo vremia*, 1993), and *The Resurrection of Lazarus* (*Voskreshenie Lazaria*, 2002). His 2013 novel *The Flight to Egypt* (*Begstvo v Egipet*) won the Russian Booker Prize. Sharov invented a new form of writing about the past. He rejects the categorizations of both historical prose and alternative history, and his tales explicitly deviate from documented facts while remaining within a general historical frame-work. His constant theme is the indivisibility of Russia's spiritual quest, uniting the Schism, the Bolshevik Revolution, and subsequent Terror. Unfailingly, in his novels the Revolution emerges as a striving to attain the Last Judgment and initiate a Second Coming. Readers are left to wonder whether Sharov, rather than denying the reality of the Last Judgment, instead suggests that it has already come and stands unrecognized as the ultimate, monumental event of Russian and Soviet history.

Mikhail Shishkin's writings also absorb various historical registers. He is the master of cen-tos, fusing together multiple quotations and opening an endless skein of cultural references. His works are well suited to critical analysis in terms of Bakhtin's theory of polyphony. Although each of his novels relies on its own semiotic code, the author's description of his 2000 novel *The Seizure of Izmail* (*Vziatie Izmaila*) can be extended to his other works: "Words become heroes, while each one of them defends its own perspective; and phrases stand for styles. It is not the edges of phrases rubbing against each other, but the edges of world-views."[197] Shishkin began his literary career with stylized memoirs of a Russian gentleman living in the first half of the nineteenth century, *Larionov's Notes* (*One Night Awaits Everyone*) (*Zapiski Larionova* [*Vsekh ozhidaet odna noch'*, 1993]), and he follows the lineage of plotless mod-ernist prose (Olesha, Kataev, Pavel Ulitin) that weaves together multiple philosophical, naturalistic, lyrical, historical, and mythical narratives. The result, exemplified by *The Seizure of Izmail*, *Maidenhair* (*Venerin volos*, 2005), and *The Light and the Dark* (*Pis'movnik*, 2010),[198] can be best compared to multi-figure, living and breathing friezes, inscribing Russia's history and the author's personal experience into an endless procession of sufferings and loves, stretching from ancient times to the present. In each of his novels, Shishkin strives for a new language of non-violence and love, and each novel builds a bridge to this imagined utopian space. In his own words:

> Every writer has to create his own non-totalitarian Russian language; he has to design words that didn't exist: "humanity," "falling in love," "civility." The language of the street, television, news-papers, obscenities—this is what I wanted to leave behind when living in Russia, but where can one go? The language into which you want to escape is one that only you can create. This is what I am doing—creating the language of Russian literature.[199]

The non-linear construction of Shishkin's narratives matches his non-linear understanding of history, rejecting any notion of history as progress. This is why his utopian language radically confronts all grand narratives, even as he builds his own verbal edifice out of a vocabulary that is intensely private.

Russian postmodernists did not resemble their Western counterparts who, as of the late Sixties, sought a fusion between experimental and popular literature.[200] Russians long evinced contempt for commercial success and mainstream tastes, partly as a remnant of attitudes in unofficial culture of the Soviet period. But in the 1990s, with the rapid development of popu-lar literature, Russian postmodernists started adopting an agenda similar to that outlined by

Fiedler—bridging gaps between mass and elite literature. One of the first signs of changing attitudes was the publication of *Generation P*, with its playful adaptation of the conspiracy narratives that flooded the Russian book market. It was followed by other Pelevin novels and by the scandalous success of Sorokin's *Blue Lard* (a postmodernist mélange of several popular genres, from sci-fi to alternative history). The effectiveness of this new approach was attested by the public burning of Sorokin's novel and a lawsuit against the author (for "pornography") by the pro-Kremlin youth group Nashi (Ours).

While reaching out to a broader readership, postmodernist literature underwent significant mutations that drew its authors into a dialogue with various texts of identity. These mutations recall Douwe Fokkema's characterizations of the "late phase" in Western culture, which leads to the domination of various forms of "fiction focusing on cultural identity."[201] The examples are multiple. Forms of queer identity are being explored in the experimental prose of Aleksandr Il'ianen (b. 1958), including his novels *And the Finn* (*I Finn . . .*, 1997), *Boutique "Vanity"* (*Butik Vanity*, 2007), and *The Pension* (*Pensiia*, 2015); and of Nikolai Kononov, author of *The Flâneur* (*Flaner*, 2011). Different scripts of Jewishness inform the work of Margarita Khemlin (1960–2015), in her novels *Klotsvog* (2009), *The Last One* (*Krainii*, 2010), and *Investigator* (*Doznavatel'*, 2012). The invention of fantastic ethnocultural identities lies at the center of highly sophisticated mythopoetic novellas by Denis Osokin (b. 1977): *Buntings* (*Ovsianki*, 2008) and *The Celestial Wives of the Meadow Mari* (*Nebesnye zheny lugovykh mari*, 2013), both turned into feature films by Aleksei Fedorchenko. Fluid combinations of gender, culture, and history have produced endless rewritings of personal identity in the prolific work of Linor Goralik across multiple forms, including short prose in *He Said, She Said* (*Govoriat*, 2004)[202] and *In Short* (*Koroche*, 2008), cyberpunk sci-fi in *No* (*Net*, 2005, co-authored with Sergei Kuznetsov), graphic novel in *Bunnypuss* (*Zaiats PTs*, 2007), travelogue in *Biblical Zoo* (*Bibleiskii zoopark*, 2012), and poetry in *So It Was a Horn* (*Tak eto byl gudochek*, 2015). Goralik, who has lived in Israel and Russia, became the leading interviewer of poets for journals and websites in the 2000s, and she has also written about and taught the semiotics of fashion. This crossing of high and middle-brow culture continues trends first seen in the later 1990s.

As part of this extensive process of identity revisions, postmodernist techniques were also employed to aestheticize the Soviet cultural heritage, effecting changes that some identify as a sign of neo-traditionalism. At first, mainly visual genres created a new hyperreality made up of postmodernist simulacra that manipulated Socialist Realist patterns: films and mini-series, television programs, and mass anniversary celebrations marking the victory in the Second World War in 2000, 2005, 2010, and 2015.[203] In literature, a simulative restoration of Socialist Realist aesthetics is also perceptible, but less extensive than in visual culture; symptomatic manifestations of restorative tendencies are also seen in the extremely popular fantasy novels by Sergei Luk'ianenko (b. 1968), *Watches* (*Dozory*, 1998–2012), which includes *Day Watch* and *Night Watch*, both filmed by Timur Bekmambetov; and *The Eurasian Symphony* (*Evraziatskaia simfoniia*, 2000–05), a cycle of quasi-detective-cum-utopian novels written by the sinologist Igor Alimov (b. 1964) and the sci-fi writer Viacheslav Rybakov (under the joint pen-name Holm Van Zaichik). Also significant are the works of Mikhail Elizarov (b. 1973), especially his novels *Pasternak* (2003) and *The Librarian* (*Bibliotekar'*, 2007, winner of the Booker Prize). Elizarov combines nostalgically reproduced Socialist Realist ideology with techniques borrowed from Sorokin and Sharov.

An independent trend of hypernaturalism has developed within the framework of Russian postmodernism. Hans-Thies Lehmann, writing in *Postdramatic Theater*, argues that hypernaturalism as a postmodernist stylistic trend "actually represents a form of *derealization*." He adds that the "heightening of reality" in hypernaturalism "occurs downward: where the toilets are, the scum, that is where we find the figure of the scapegoat, the *pharmakos*. The lowest is not, as in the earlier Naturalism, the truth, the real that has to be revealed because it has been hidden and repressed. Rather, the lowest is now the new 'sacred,' the proper truth, that which explodes norms and rules...."[204] This definition perfectly describes Petrushevskaya's prose and drama, as well as stories by Viktor Erofeev, including *Anna's Body, or The End of Russian Avant-Garde* (*Telo Anny, ili Konets russkogo avangarda*, 1989); Asar Eppel's (1935–2012) *The Grassy Street* (*Travianaia ulitsa*, 1994); and Sergei Kaledin's (b. 1949) *The Placid Cemetery* (*Smirennoe kladbishche*, 1987) and *Stroibat* (1989). Hypernaturalism also marks the novels of Anatoly Korolev (b. 1946), *Eron* (2004), *Man-Tongue* (*Chelovek-iazyk*, 2000), and *To Be Bosch* (*Byt' Boskhom*, 2004), and Dmitry Gorchev's (1963–2010) short stories in *The Wild Life of Gondvana* (*Dikaia zhizn' Gondvany*, 2008). Looking back at the literature of the late Soviet underground, one can recognize incipient hypernaturalism in the poetry of Ian Satunovsky, Leonid Chertkov, Oleg Grigor'ev, Igor Kholin, and Genrikh Sapgir. In their various ways, these writers use the rituals of violence and/or self-destruction—and the motif of the scapegoat is prevalent—to achieve a powerful sense of derealization. Once they have dismantled any sense of the ordinary, they paradoxically heighten reality by rediscovering the lower depths of society and consecrating it.

Critics rarely use the concept of hypernaturalism in the Russian literary context, but the term conveniently encompasses some important trends in post-Soviet literature, especially in prose and theater. Its weak equivalent is the Russian word *chernukha*, a derogatory term that acquired currency in the Perestroika years to designate excessively dark and grim representations of everyday life. Texts labeled as *chernukha* often describe worlds of violence, poverty, prostitution, alcoholism, brutal sexuality, and sickness, including mental illness. These topics were excluded from official Soviet literature, so the writings stood out when they began to appear and the impact also extended to film. In the 2010s, *chernukha* continues to draw attacks from the representatives of the political and cultural establishment for an apparent lack of patriotism. After the surge of hypernaturalism in the prose of the 1990s, the trend was continued mainly within New Drama, a movement of young and middle-aged directors and playwrights who spread their energy and ideas through competitions, festivals, workshops, and theater labs.[205] They used the figure and theme of the scapegoat especially effectively, typically associating it with the lowest societal stratum and using it to expose the ruling rituals of violence.

In 2000, the play *Plasticine* (*Plastilin*) by a young writer from Yekaterinburg, Vasily Sigarev (b. 1977), drew particular attention. It won the Debut and Russian Anti-Booker Prizes and was staged at Moscow's Center for Drama and Directing by Kirill Serebrennikov (b. 1969). This production played a decisive role in the formation of Serebrennikov's theatrical style and became a genuine sensation of the theater season. The success was not limited to Moscow, and the fame emphasized the playwright's significance. In 2002, *Plasticine* was staged by Dominic Cooke at the Royal Court Theater Upstairs, and Sigarev won the *London Evening Standard* award for "Most Promising Playwright." Presenting the award, Tom Stoppard said, "If Dostoyevsky were writing in the 21st century, no doubt he would have written *Plasticine*."[206]

The protagonist of *Plasticine*, a teenager named Maxim, faces threats of unremitting violence. He has no choice but to participate in a constant war since survival is reserved only for aggressors. The alternative is to become a scapegoat, which eventually does become Maxim's fate. Incredibly, Sigarev's provincial world is not gloomy. The spectacles of violence constituting the play's setting and driving its plot are horrible but also saturated with carnivalesque sexuality. *Plasticine*, perhaps more clearly than any other play of the New Drama, captures the moment when carnival disorder—in many respects characteristic of the early 1990s, after the collapse of the Soviet system—stabilizes into a highly problematic and essentially violent norm of everyday life. Freedom in this world of constant carnival turns into a "little terror,"

Tatyana Tolstaya's expression for mundane violence that is its own form of Great Terror, downgraded.[207]

The predominance of violence as a universal form of post-Soviet communication has become the central theme for many playwrights of the late 1990s–2000s, such as Evgeny Grishkovets, the Presniakov brothers, Ivan Vyrypaev, Yuri Klavdiev (b. 1977), and Iaroslava Pulinovich (b. 1987). Through the performative deconstruction of violence, these playwrights reveal contradictions of "negative identity," a form of social and personal self-identification that Lev Gudkov has found to be prevalent in the post-Soviet period.[208] Their plays most often show how intensely such self-identification relies on the creation of an enemy figure—the one who would be humiliated and violated for the immediate, ad hoc production of "us" united against "them." As follows from the plays of the New Drama, post-Soviet culture produces the Other spontaneously and incessantly, making the borders between the Self and the Other flexible; negative identity necessitates violence as a form of social infrastructure, because everyone is a potential Other and therefore a potential enemy.

Hypernaturalism in drama thus acquires a political function: it provides writers with the tools to diagnose the social condition of permanent warfare. In this context, a major role in New Drama was played by Moscow's Teatr.doc, a theater and cultural institution headed by playwrights Elena Gremina (b. 1956) and Mikhail Ugarov (b. 1956). Documentary theater fundamentally undermines popular societal myth with performances based entirely on the words of real people—both the seeming victims of Putin's so-called stabilization and the creators of the new social and political regime of power. These performances dramatize the normalization of the abnormal, and its seeming opposite: the pathology of established social and cultural norms. The personal narratives constituting documentary plays present a tragic mix of compliance, internalization, and resistance to the political rituals of power based on violence. It is a sign of the times and their pathology that plays about alleged marginal groups represent their life as an exotic or sometimes grotesque reflection of commonly accepted norms.

The political message of Teatr.doc became more pointed (and carried more risk for theater employees and performers) during the third term of the Putin presidency (beginning in 2012), an increasingly authoritarian environment. Their documentary plays focused on the most controversial subjects—terrorism, problems of economic migrants, and political persecutions. *One Hour and 18 Minutes* (*Chas Vosemnadtsat'*, 2015) by Gremina investigates the death of the lawyer Sergei Magnitsky; *The Bolotnaia Trial* (*Bolotnyi sud*, 2015) by Polina Borodina tells stories of the relatives of people arrested at a major anti-Putin demonstration on May 6, 2012; *Khamcourt. Continuation* (*Khamsud. Prodolzhenie*, 2012) reenacts the Pussy Riot trial. It is little wonder that after 2014 Teatr.doc became the target of economic and administrative harassment by the authorities, but because it is a rare example of an independent theater (it does not rely on government funding), the theater has persevered.[209]

In-between prose

Late Soviet and post-Soviet literature witnessed a surge of genres combining features of fiction and non-fiction. The roots of this mixed genre harken back to the nineteenth century, but it emerged as an independent form of cultural discourse later and is best described as in-between prose (*promezhutochnaia proza*), a concept especially well developed by Lydia Ginzburg (1902–90) and vividly exemplified in her own work. Ginzburg suggested that the catastrophes and chaos of twentieth-century life required new forms of literary expression, and thus the major literary form from the nineteenth century, the novel, had either to be reimagined for the challenging era of late modernity or to be replaced by a kind of writing yet to be invented. To write between the genre of the novel and any other form of discourse was to write toward a new idea of the person as well: Ginzburg argued, particularly in her late work, that twentieth-century events had shattered the solidity and confidence of the individual person, as exemplified by the heroes of nineteenth-century novels. She was not suggesting, as Roland Barthes and Michel Foucault were to do, that the modern subject was a Romantic fiction ripe for deconstruction, but she did diagnose the problem as a frustrating search for a narrative shape fit to contain that self's evolution and emergence into the social world. The predominance of fragmentary and montaged narratives in her work becomes a formal expression of this ontological and psychological dilemma.[210]

Ginzburg's own writings give excellent examples of the search for suitable form. She planned a massive text that would cross elements of diary and novel, for which her working title was *Home and World* (or *Home and Peace*—her title in Russian, *Dom i mir*, reworks the title *War and Peace* [*Voina i mir*] and her ambitions for the project were as epic as Tolstoy's). But Ginzburg abandoned this idea, and left instead her voluminous notebooks. With their witty aphorisms, brilliant character sketches, and stinging aperçus about the foibles of modern life, the notebooks are built around dated entries, some lengthy and chatty, punctuated by others of startling brevity. The format has its own history, which Ginzburg had studied in her work on the nineteenth-century writer Prince Petr Viazemsky. In her view, he both theorized and practiced in-between prose, quintessentially in his *Old Notebook* (*Staraia zapisnaia knizhka*, 1813–77, edited for publication in 1929 by Ginzburg). As had Viazemsky before her, Ginzburg often noted down conversations in her notebooks; the emphasis on recording oral speech, in all its expressive possibilities and eloquent incompleteness, is a strong feature of in-between prose more generally.[211]

The Russian tradition boasts other examples of in-between prose. Vasily Rozanov's *Fallen Leaves* inspired a similarly free-flowing mix of personal statement with philosophical meditation in Viktor Shklovsky and Andrei Sinyavsky. Both paid direct tribute to Rozanov: Shklovsky authored an important article, "Rozanov" (1921), that he later reworked into a chapter, "Literature beyond the 'plot,'" in *On the Theory of Prose*; Sinyavsky dedicated to *Fallen Leaves* an entire book (*Opavshie list 'ia V. V. Rozanova*, 1982).

Shklovsky also created a highly original version of in-between prose that connects theory and history of literature with self-writing. In his trilogy, *Zoo*, *The Sentimental Journey*, and *The Third Factory*, Shklovsky constructed an analogy between the transformations of life material by literary form (the essence of the Formal method) and the way that Russia's catastrophic history shapes the authorial personality and the social milieu. A powerful example of what later would become a trope of postmodernism (the perception of history as a work of literature that can be written and rewritten), Shklovsky's prose simultaneously presents a groundbreaking theory and a tragic reading of his own life story in the context of the Russian Revolution. Fragmentariness and non-linear connections between fragments became isomorphic reflections of the author's shattered subjectivity.

Sinyavsky's *Voice from the Chorus* (*Golos iz khora*, 1966–71) displays an obvious similarity with Rozanov's *Fallen Leaves*, but in general, his version of in-between prose sat closer to the border zone between literary scholarship and autobiographical writings, in *Strolls with Pushkin* and *In Gogol's Shadow*, or between autobiography and the novel, in *Good Night!* (*Spokoinoi nochi*, 1984). *Good Night!* bore in Russian the subtitle "a novel" (*roman*), but that designation seemed something of a provocation, especially as the text was published under Sinyavsky's hooligan pseudonym Abram Tertz. It had the further distinction of using two colors of ink in its original Russian version, creating two narrative worlds, another jolt to the reader expecting a stable organization of the text.

As important as the prose written at the boundary between autobiography and fiction is prose written between fiction and fact, as exemplified in Osip Mandelstam's writings of the

1920s, particularly his "Fourth Prose" ("Chetvertaia proza," 1930). Even more than the evocative fictional text, *The Egyptian Stamp* (*Egipetskaia marka*, 1928), "Fourth Prose" fractures all narrative and expository elements into such small bits that one senses only the sparsest elements of the scandal that motivates the text's vituperative tone in defense of the Fourth Estate and authorial integrity. Mandelstam's rage at having been targeted in a trumped-up plagiarism scandal is strongly felt.[212] The text, not written for publication and palpably dangerous, is a strange hybrid of historically precise invective, disturbingly suitable literary quotation, and pungent aphorism (and the pithy phrases punctuate the prose dramatically: one of the images most indelibly associated with Mandelstam's poetry, that of stolen air, comes from "Fourth Prose"). Mandelstam used biographical names and nicknames, allusion, and direct assertions of fact in "Fourth Prose." The result is at once hyperbolic and factual.[213]

In later historical moments, in-between prose has served writers hoping to couch political or cultural analysis in experimental narrative frameworks. Ambition of a more formal kind is exemplified by Yuri Olesha's unfinished *Book of Farewell* (*Kniga proshchaniia*, also known as *Not a Day without Writing* [*Ni dnia bez strochki*]) and by Valentin Kataev's novels *The Holy Well* and *My Diamond Wreath*.[214] In seeking to overcome the limitations of Socialist Realism, both writers analyze memories. In-between prose has accommodated dramatic narratives of the Soviet intelligentsia in a form that could be fragmented, self-reflective and self-distancing, free of literary conventions in the depiction of traumas and horrors, historical and personal at the same time. One could argue that Aleksandr Solzhenitsyn's massive *The Gulag Archipelago 1918–1956* (*Arkhipelag GULAG 1918–1956: Opyt khudozhestvennogo issledovaniia*, 1973–75) has many of the hallmarks of in-between prose. By giving his work (in Russian) the subtitle "an experiment in literary investigation," Solzhenitsyn blurs the boundary between fact and art. The author of *The Gulag Archipelago* organized the documentary material by conspicuously literary means. He designed important scenes, such as the 1953 inmates' revolt in Kengir, as self-sufficient narratives with their own dramatic composition. The autobiographical thread about the author's own experience of arrest and incarceration that runs through the vast documentary narrative becomes inseparable from the epic experience of the entire nation devastated by the Gulag.

Pavel Ulitin (1918–86), another significant representative of underground in-between prose, creates a version of the subjective epic radically different from Solzhenitsyn's. In Ilya Kukulin's estimation, Ulitin "appears to be one of the most remarkable innovators in Russian literature comparable by his influence to those writers who have changed European and North-American autobiographical writing."[215] Ulitin builds an autobiographical narrative out of an elaborate montage of quotations, newspaper pictures, and photographs. He leaves in multiple gaps and omissions, thus presenting a story that is both fragmented and intertwined with "foreign" fragments, representing others' selves and discourses.[216] Arrested in 1938 and 1951, Ulitin survived imprisonment in mental institutions, but his writings are not just about his own horrific experience. "The most important part of [Ulitin's hidden] plot is the humiliation and terror undergone by millions of people," notes Kukulin. "Ulitin's montage of fragments replays the trauma and turns it into the aesthetic transfiguration of reality."[217]

The post-Soviet period has seen many varieties of in-between prose, suggesting that the genre remains productive. There were novels combining autobiography and/or essayistic endnotes, such as *The Endless Dead-end* (*Beskonechnyi tupik*, completed in 1987, first full publication in 1997) by Dmitry Galkovsky (b. 1960) and its parody in *The True Story of Green Musicians* (*Podlinnaia istoriia zelenykh muzykantov*, 1999) by Evgeny Popov.[218] Mark Kharitonov wrote a novel about a provincial writer creating in-between prose modeled on Rozanov, *The Lines of Destiny, or Milashevich's Little Trunk* (*Linii sud'by, ili Sunduchok Milashevicha*, 1992); it won the first Russian Booker Prize. Free-flowing prose montage mixes historical observation, anecdotes, semiotic analysis, and self-reflections in texts by prominent literary scholars, including

Mikhail Gasparov (1935–2005), Mikhail Bezrodny (b. 1957), Alexander Zholkovsky, and Mikhail Epshtein (b. 1950), as well as by contemporary artists: Grisha Bruskin (b. 1945), Viktor Pivovarov (b. 1937), and Valentin Vorob´ev (b. 1938). Also notable are the reflections on what might be called self-rewriting in emigration in Zinovy Zinik's (b. 1945) *Emigration as a Literary Device* (*Emigratsiia kak literaturnyi priem*, 2011). Lev Rubinshtein in *Language Cases* (*Sluchai iz iazyka*, 1998), *The Signs of Attention* (*Znaki vnimaniia*, 2012), *Most Likely* (*Skoree vsego*, 2013), and *The Time of Reasons* (*Prichinnoe vremia*, 2016) created his own variation of in-between prose by applying Conceptualist methods of deconstruction to current political and cultural conflicts. Combinations of lyrical prose with cultural criticism include the much-admired volumes of Petr Vail, *Genius Loci* (*Genii mesta*, 1999), and Aleksandr Genis, *Dovlatov and his Environs* (*Dovlatov i okrestnosti*, 1999). What distinguishes the latter from an ordinary critical biography is that Genis tries to write about Dovlatov by following principles from his fiction: an interest in the singular as opposed to typical; a focus on the absurd, disorder, and disorganization; a refusal to assume the position of moral, or any other, authority. The result of Genis's experiment is a critical performance that combines in-between prose with postmodernist meta-fiction.

The in-between prose of the émigré critic and journalist Aleksandr Gol´dshtein (1957–2006) had a significant impact in experimental literary circles. His books *Farewell to Narcissus* (*Proshchanie s Nartsissom*, 1997), *Aspects of the Spiritual Union* (*Aspekty dukhovnogo braka*, 2001), *Remember Famagusta* (*Pomni o Famaguste*, 2004), and *Quiet Fields* (*Spokoinye polia*, 2006) were perceived as an updating of the novel through a free-floating combination of fiction, autobiography, impressionistic travelogues, cultural history, and criticism. Gol´dshtein shows that the challenge Ginzburg identified, namely, what literary prose should be in the aftermath of the Great Russian Novel, continued to spur writers to create new literary forms.[219] Gol´dshtein defines the ambitions he has for his prose in a programmatic essay, "The Literature of Existence" ("Literatura sushchestvovaniia"), that concludes his book *Farewell to Narcissus*. He refers to what has been deemed the "new sincerity," reflecting both the desire for an unmediated expression of individual experience and the postmodernist understanding of sincerity as a complex of rhetorical devices and discursive principles.[220] It is a framework that makes sense for Gol´dshtein's writings. Looking back to Shklovsky and Shalamov, Limonov's *It's Me, Eddie* (*Eto ia Edichka*, 1979), and Kharitonov's queer prose as literary models, Gol´dshtein proclaims an ideal of literature synthesizing genres and media, transcending all barriers, including those separating the biographical author from his/her literary image. "The unification of the word and the talking body" remain as utopian as Antonin Artaud's "theater of cruelty," to which Gol´dshtein also refers.[221] Gol´dshtein's provocations find echoes in innovative work by other writers of his generation, including Arkady Dragomoshchenko, particularly in his novel *Phosphorus* (*Fosfor*, 1994); Bella Ulanovskaia (1943–2005), in *The Journey to Kashgar* (*Puteshestvie v Kashgar*, 1973, published 1993); Leon Bogdanov (1942–87), in *Notes about Tea Parties and Earthquakes* (*Zametki o chaepitiiakh i zemletriaseniiakh*, 1986, published 2002); and Boris Kudriakov (1946–2005).

Some of these instances of in-between prose reached a narrow readership, but they could prove more broadly influential on later generations of writers. Andrei Sergeev's (1933–98) *Stamp Album* (*Al´bom dlia marok*, 1995) collects bits of found language to reconstruct the world of late Soviet underground literary circles to which Sergeev, a prominent translator from English, belonged. Andrei Levkin (b. 1954), in *Vienna, the Operating System* (*Vena, operatsionnaia sistema*, 2012), looks beyond the boundaries of Russian culture to present a different kind of collage, mapping the city of Vienna as if it were a digital device needing explanation to a user. Levkin's work also belongs to a broader trend of "post(non)fiction," a project by Levkin and Kirill Kobrin (b. 1964); without reference to in-between prose, Levkin and Kobrin describe something quite similar, what they call an "unspelled entity," embracing acts of literature that cannot be translated into cinema and cannot be reduced to a story-line.[222] In comparable ways, the poet Polina Barskova has published a book of prose about literary and cultural figures associated with the Leningrad Blockade, *Tableaux Vivants* (*Zhivye kartiny*, 2014). She finds in in-between prose the right vehicle to demonstrate that no coherent, linear narrative about real people in Soviet history can be produced. People's lives consisted of mutually incompatible elements, their biographies and personalities shattered into pieces by the catastrophe that was Soviet history, yet their resistance to degradation and dehumanization is shown to be powerful even if it cannot yield a straightforward narrative.

In-between prose thus remains a compelling and unfinished genre of Russian literature. It has facilitated intense cultural experimentation, a kind of cauldron in which different cultural traditions and discourses swirl around and test each other. Its free format serves as the necessary condition for a narrative performance of subjectivity consisting of multiple, simultaneous textual scenarios, complete with critical reflection; of coexisting conflicting languages; and of the domination of the singular over the universal or the teleological. It has become one of the central literary genres designed to match in its formal shape the fluctuating structure of the self and to reflect upon the self's historical transformations.

Russian literature throughout the twentieth century used both in-between prose and the traditions of recognized genres—novels, short stories, memoirs, narrative poems, drama, and essays—to tell the stories of shared experience. A central experience was necessarily a sequence of violent upheavals and wars that erupted across the decades. We now turn to a broad survey of that material. Afterwards, we conclude our discussion of literature of the twentieth century with narratives that take on the self-conscious task of asking what it means for a generation to try to ask these world-defining questions, if not to provide answers. That task had long fallen to the Russian intelligentsia, and its modern and postmodern narratives of self-definition will be the last rubric of this history.

Catastrophic narratives

Narratives of the Revolution and Civil War

The dream of a purifying revolution penetrated Russian literature deeply starting in the 1860s. The Revolution was imagined as a force able to resolve intractable social and political contradictions, but it also seemed the logical outcome of a perceived cultural crisis, a crisis that thinkers as different as Tolstoy and Blok described. For the Symbolist Andrei Bely, and for others, revolution was an underground, destructive force as well as a creative, fertile act: it could transform human nature in ways clearly influenced by Nietzsche's idea of the superman, if also going beyond his metaphysical and philosophical agenda.[1]

The Revolution of 1905, however, produced a schism in the intelligentsia, vividly seen in the 1909 volume *Landmarks*. Writers attuned to Marxism and populism continued to extol revolution. Gorky depicted revolutionaries as neo-Christians ready to sacrifice themselves in love (in *Mother* and "Summertime" ["Leto," 1909]). Mayakovsky, in a text originally entitled "The Thirteenth Apostle," prophesied:

> Где глаз людей обрывается куцый
> главой голодных орд,
> в терновом венце революций
> грядет шестнадцатый год.[2]

> Where people's gaze breaks off
> at the head of hungry hordes,
> the year 1916 advances
> wearing revolutions' crown of thorns.

The liberal revolution of February 1917 seemed to satisfy the intelligentsia's long-standing dreams and aspirations. Many writers joined with ardor in the work of reforming political institutions, yet some complexities in their views showed through. Quite typical is the example of Aleksandr Blok, who shunned politics before the Revolution. In *Retribution* (*Vozmezdie*, begun 1912, unfinished) he described pre-revolutionary Russia as ready to crush innocent and guilty alike. After the Tsar's abdication and the creation of the Provisional Government, Blok joined the Extraordinary Commission investigating the activities of former ministers and courtiers. Blok's revolutionary enthusiasm embraced even the Bolshevik coup d'état of October 1917: he interpreted their seizure of power as a logical continuation of liberal reforms begun in February. He believed in the necessity of "changing everything," so that, as he put it, "our dishonest, filthy, boring, and ugly life would become fair, pure, joyous, and wonderful in all ways."[3] Blok imagined revolution as a great and sacrificial event, capable of restoring the "spirit of music" and opening the path to a "new eon." In *The Twelve*, a rhapsody of contrasting voices, songs, slogans, and tunes, revolution emerges as a Dionysian whirlwind. Such an interpretation of the Revolution logically followed from the reception of Nietzsche by Russian Symbolists (also exemplified in Viacheslav Ivanov's "Nietzsche and Dionysus," 1904).[4] Blok's Christ appears in the poem's finale as a leader of twelve red patrolmen who are less like apostles than bandits (they kill a woman); Christ signifies a new Dionysus who destroys an old Apollonian order and brings about the "collapse of humanism."[5] However, such enthusiasm faded away under the pressure of the Bolshevik terror, economic collapse, and Civil War. Blok died in 1921, after several failed attempts to leave Russia. Soon many of his friends and colleagues fled, were exiled, or perished. Those who left, along with nearly all of the "old intelligentsia" who remained in Russia, increasingly perceived the Revolution as a tragedy.

In his notes of 1917–18, eloquently titled *The Apocalypse of Our Time* (*Apokalipsis nashego vremeni*), Vasily Rozanov unambiguously defines the revolutionary epoch as the time of Russia's death: "death has come and therefore, the time of death is here."[6] He is in shock: "Rus´ has molted in a matter of two days, maximum three....Amazingly, it completely disintegrated, down to its details, to its tiniest constituent parts."[7] Similarly, Aleksei Remizov, soon after the Bolshevik seizure of power, wrote his "Lay on the Ruin of the Russian Land," echoing in the title the tradition of catastrophic narrative of the medieval and early modern chronicles and stories. But rather than decrying the devastation of Russia by the Mongol invasion, as the medieval original had done, Remizov's "Lay" presents the Bolshevik Revolution as an eschatological event. A profound connoisseur of Russian folklore and traditional culture, Remizov addresses his grief not to political leaders but to the people, the embodiment of traditional culture and the object of almost religious adoration among the intelligentsia.

> Русский народ, что ты сделал?
> Искал свое счастье и все потерял. Одураченный, плюхнулся свиньей в навоз.
> Поверил—
> Кому ты поверил? Ну, пеняй теперь на себя, расплачивайся.
> Землю ты свою забыл колыбельную.
> Где Россия твоя?
> Пусто место.[8]

> O Russian people, what have you done?
> You were searching for happiness but lost everything
> You have been made a fool, fallen into a yard of manure like a pig.
> You believed—
> But whom did you believe? You have only yourself to blame, so try to get even.
> You have forgotten completely your cradle of earth.
> Where is your Russia?
> Barren is that place.

Many others shared the view that Russia was descending into the chaos of prehistory, seeing the people (*narod*) as the antagonists of civilization (and not as the epitome of suffering and genuine spirituality, as had largely been the image of the *narod*). This dismal view of the Revolution united many literary and ideological opponents, such as the former supporter of Bolsheviks Maxim Gorky and the aristocratic, aesthetically conservative Ivan Bunin.[9] Others who held similar views included another former Bolshevik, Evgeny Zamiatin, as expressed in his short stories "The Dragon" ("Drakon," 1918) and "The Cave" ("Peshchera," 1921), and Boris Pasternak, for example in his poem "Russian Revolution" ("Russkaia revoliutsiia," 1918, unpublished in Russia until 1989), which anticipates motifs that appear in *Doctor Zhivago*.

A significant number of writers, however—either wholeheartedly or out of submission to the dictate of the "new Catholicism," as it was called in Zamiatin's passionate essay "I Am Afraid" ("Ia boius'," 1921)—accepted the Revolution and worked towards its cultural and ethical justification. Writers' revolutionary enthusiasm did not always stem from conformism. The project to radically reinvent social and cultural life had considerable appeal. The intelligentsia's traditional understanding of its historical mission to support the masses and their aspirations also played into enthusiasm for the Revolution.

In the 1920s, writers labeled as fellow travelers, despite regular harassment from proletarian and LEF critics alike, produced the most memorable and most complex literary representations of the Revolution and ensuing historical turmoil. Typically born into intelligentsia families and formally independent from the Bolshevik party, they belonged to the generation whose first adult experiences were associated with the Civil War. Some of them served the Reds, like Babel or Pil'niak; some the Whites, like Bulgakov, Kataev, Leonov, Shvarts, a fact that many later hid. Yet they all were scarred by the Revolution: having lived through large-scale catastrophe, they later sought to reenact and conceptualize it in their writing.

A prime example of superb literature created by fellow travelers is the novel *The Naked Year* (*Golyi god*, 1921), written by twenty-eight-year-old Boris Pil'niak, already author of a collection of his prerevolutionary writings (*With the Last Boat* [*S poslednim parokhodom*, 1918]). The publication of *The Naked Year* sparked a heated discussion, and Pil'niak was called both the founder of new Soviet literature and a shameless imitator of Bely and Remizov. In either case, his was the first avant-garde novel about the Revolution, and it shaped a paradigm for representing this dangerous subject. Pil'niak depicts the Revolution as a snowstorm; this metaphor, which is loaded with themes of chaos and cold as well as echoes of Pushkin and Blok, also functions as the novel's swirling structural principle. *The Naked Year* consists of intersecting plotlines loosely connected by symbolic leitmotifs, and the narrative's broken syntax and prosodic patterning create a strong sense of fragmentation. The revolutionary blizzard simultaneously awakens to life the sleepy world of a provincial town, Ordynin, and devastates the oasis of European culture preserved in the daily life of a provincial noble family, the Ordynins, for whom the town is named. The novel's image of revolutionaries as "leather jackets," a new breed of Russian people born from the destruction of the old life, is especially striking:

> . . . leather people in leather jackets (Bolsheviks!),—all the same size, each one a leather beauty, each one strong, with curls in ringlets under the peaked cap pushed back on his head; each had, more than anything else, will power in his protruding cheek-bones, in the lines around his mouth and in his lumbering movements—and audacity. Of Russia's rough, crumbly nationhood—the best slice. . . . Incidentally, none of them has ever read Karl Marx.[10]

One of the most important plotlines inaugurated in *The Naked Year*, and soon established as a self-sufficient narrative, concerns the attempts of the intelligentsia against a backdrop of savage unrest to rationalize the new regime by adducing the age-old liberal ideologies. Thus, in Konstantin Fedin's *Cities and Years* (*Goroda i gody*, 1924), an *intelligent*, Andrei Startsov, despite his sympathy towards revolutionary ideas, accepts neither revolutionary violence nor counter-revolutionary terror. Andrei's death at the hand of his former friend and a fanatic of the Revolution, Kurt Van, frames the narrative, serving as the proof of the Revolution's incompatibility with humanistic values; those who dare to question its truth are doomed to die.

The motif of the New People (Pil'niak's "leather people in leather jackets") resonates with other works of the 1920s. Mainly created by RAPP members, such novels would later, in the 1930s, be glorified as classics of Socialist Realism *avant la lettre* because they pioneered its meta-narrative. According to Katerina Clark, its elements were the transformation of group and individual spontaneity into "consciousness," and the remaking of a striving for freedom and justice into disciplined, voluntary subjugation to the party's will, required to suppress all emotional connections with those now deemed as enemies.[11] The talented Neo-Romantic poet Eduard Bagritsky formulated aphoristically the desirable outcome of the expected forging of humans in the furnace of the Revolution (the citation is from his much longer poem, "TBC," 1929):

> Оглянешься—а вокруг враги;
> Руки протянешь—и нет друзей;
> Но если он скажет: "Солги",—солги.
> Но если он скажет: "Убей",—убей.[12]
>
> You glance around—enemies everywhere;
> You stretch out your hands—friends nowhere;
> Yet if the century says "Lie"—you lie.
> Yet if the century says "Murder"—you murder.[13]

The narrative of heroic "leather jackets" had its negative underside: stories about the horrors of the Civil War and about the tortures and mass killings performed by the Cheka (the infamous Extraordinary Commission, a precursor of the GPU/NKVD/KGB). These tales depict the methodical dehumanization of a sincere Bolshevik hero whose sense of identity is obliterated by the machinery of mass terror. For example, a lengthy episode depicting the Cheka service of an old Bolshevik, Bunchuk, shows him rendered impotent before his beloved in Mikhail Sholokhov's novel *The Quiet Don*. Valentin Kataev drew on first-hand victim's experience in depicting the inquisition machine of the Cheka in his short story "The Father" ("Otets," 1928), which also provided the foundation for his later, much more explicit novella *Werther Has Been Written Already* (*Uzhe napisan Verter*, 1980). Other tales exposing the spiritual and psychological destruction of members of the Cheka included *Chocolate* (*Shokolad*, 1922) by Aleksandr Tarasov-Rodionov (1885–1938) and *Cruelty* (*Zhestokost'*, 1921–22) by Sergei Sergeev-Tsensky (1875–1958). The most profound and dismaying description of the dehumanization produced by the Red Terror on its executioners appears in a lesser-known expressionist novella, *The Sliver* (*Shchepka*, 1923) by a Siberian writer, Vladimir Zazubrin (1895–1938). Rejected by the magazine *Siberian Lights* (*Sibirskie ogni*) in the 1920s, this novella was published only in 1989, and in 1992 Aleksandr Rogozhkin turned it into a feature film, *The Chekist*.

A further influential plotline dating to *The Naked Year* focuses on the quest for a modern synthesis of contrasting cultural traditions that harken back to more ancient times. Many works of the 1920s interpreted Bolshevik enthusiasm coupled with the Civil War's brutality as a consequence of historical processes deeply embedded in Russia's past and especially relevant for provincial areas. In these works, an ornamental stylistics of epic narrative fuses avant-garde fragmentation and a cacophony of voices; educated speech merges with *skaz*, used for the speech of ordinary, frequently illiterate people who are drawn into the cataclysms of revolution and war.

One of the most famous novels about the Revolution and Civil War is *The Quiet Don* (*Tikhii Don*, 1927–40; often translated as *Quiet Flows the Don*) by Mikhail Sholokhov (1905–84).[14] This complex novel explores the possibilities of synthesis within the people's hero Grigory Melekhov, envisaging his life as a range of scenarios balancing the new and the old. Key scenes of the novel are arranged symmetrically. Through parallelism between seemingly disparate episodes, the author reveals the falsity of ideological oppositions while emphasizing the monotony of their practical manifestations—through blood, violence, and the sadistic mutual extermination of Cossacks.

Grigory Melekhov is a true representative of the Cossack masses; through his evolution, the novelist shows how the people, whose life is deeply rooted in nature, seek their equilibrium in a time of historical chaos. Remarkably, the novel reveals that they cannot find any point of stability from which to act or to understand the historical moment. Melekhov is simultaneously an active participant in history and the victim of its forces. His acute sense of personal dignity at first pushes him away from each side of the confrontation—the Reds, the Whites, and the Greens alike. He is not accepted by the new social order, nor can he in turn accept its normalized violence. As a truly novelistic rather than epic character, he always remains, as Mikhail Bakhtin would say, "either greater than his destiny, or lesser than his humanity."[15]

He is "lesser than his humanity" when he tries to subjugate his personal sense of conscience and compassion to ideological dogma. He is "greater than his destiny" when he follows his freedom—the core of his humanity—rejecting terror and humiliation. This earns him the labels of "enemy," "fugitive," and "bandit." His "excess of humanness"[16] constantly undermines situations when Grigory seemingly enjoys power and glory. At these moments, he is drawn away from his military post to the peasants' labor, and filled with tenderness toward his children. He also feels love for Aksinia at such moments—Aksinia, with her sinful beauty, fierce sexuality, and readiness to follow him to the end of the world, who becomes synonymous with both his freedom and his "excess of humanness." Melekhov's torturous oscillation between his wife Natalia and his mistress Aksinia parallels his political choices. He returns to Natalia when he seeks to embrace his destiny, and escapes to Aksinia when he feels the repressive power of the chosen path that is incompatible with his freedom.

Natalia dies a tragic death because of a failed abortion. No less tragic is the death of Aksinia, accidentally killed at the very moment when she and Grigory decide to stay together for good. These losses complete Melekhov's tragedy. Catastrophic history leaves him no way out: "...he raised his hand and saw above him the black sky and the blindingly glittering black disk of the sun."[17] That black sun is what Grigory sees in the novel's finale, after having buried Aksinia, and the image raises his personal tragedy to a philosophical level. It is a picture of the Apocalypse that has already happened. While in the course of the novel nature's life accompanied characters, either resonating or contrasting with their actions and feelings, in the finale, the sun, the symbol of life, and the sky, the symbol of transcendental aspirations, appear dead. The possibility of harmony with nature, essential for the Cossacks' world, is gone forever. Ubiquitous violence has caused social catastrophe and also destroyed the philosophical foundations of the people's life.

Isaac Babel's *Red Cavalry* (*Konarmiia*, completed 1925, published in book form in 1926) draws on similar material about the Cossacks' involvement in the Revolution and Civil War, but its expressionistic and terse short stories are utterly unlike the epic scale of *The Quiet Don*. In Sholokhov's novel, the Cossacks' perspective dominates, but Babel's narrator is an alien among the Cossacks. His hero, Kirill Liutov (Babel himself had used this pseudonym as a journalist in the Red Cossack Army), is not only a Jew but also a member of the intelligentsia; the Cossacks immediately detect his class position and thus they treat him mercilessly. For all the differences from *The Quiet Don*, *The Red Cavalry* is also a book about the failed synthesis between humanism and revolution.

For Babel, this failure devalues the Revolution, as the old Jew Gedali (in the eponymous story) expresses so well:

> The Revolution is a good deed done by good men. But good men do not kill. Hence the Revolution is done by bad men.... Who is going to tell Gedali which is the Revolution and which is the counter-revolution?... We are not simpletons. The International, we know what the International is. And I want the International of good people, I want every soul to be accounted for and given first-class rations. Here, soul, eat, go ahead, go and find happiness in your life.[18]

The violence depicted by Babel in abundance—Jews killed by Cossacks, raped women, torture and murder within the Cossack milieu—proves that Gedali's dream is incompatible with the reality of Revolution and Civil War. Babel was mesmerized by all manifestations of power and violence. His interest in these sensations took him, an Odessa Jew, into the ranks of the Red Cossacks. But he did not simply condone violence. His diary of the Red Army's unfortunate Polish expedition, which served as a basis for *The Red Cavalry*, is full of sarcastic remarks about the "revolutionary Cossacks" and their methods. The critic Abram Lezhnev aptly noted in 1927: "Babel is not a cynic. On the contrary. This is a man wounded by cruelty. He depicts it so frequently because it has stricken him for the rest of his life."[19]

Babel describes the Revolution and its social practices as creating a church of violence in which violence serves as the source, manifestation, and effect of the sacred. His numerous scenes of desecration of sacred objects, synagogues, Catholic churches, and cemeteries show a particularly repugnant side of revolutionary violence. In this context, it is little wonder that violence serves not only as a means of social bonding, but also as a vertical axis that connects the Cossacks—"beasts with principles," as Babel wrote in his diary—with the Soviet sacred personified by Lenin in "My First Goose" ("Moi pervyi gus'") and by Lenin and Trotsky in "Salt" ("Sol'"). This is the sacred of the Revolution itself, mystical rather than rational ("the mysterious curve of Lenin's straight line").[20] The sacred does not just require violence for its existence: it is actually produced by it. The wrenching violence in Babel's tales serves as a perennial reminder of the Revolution's dead ends. Babel assiduously registers the subversive and self-negating inner logic of a new community founded by violence on a mythic scale. Criminal communities like teenage gangs and mafia bands (as noted by Eliot Borenstein) make use of similar methods of coercive social incorporation.[21] However, Babel makes this violent mechanism symbolic and endemic.

CASE STUDY **Isaac Babel**

Isaac Babel's presence in Soviet literature cannot be reduced to his writings. Equally important was his elaborate strategy of self-representation, similar to the Symbolists' life-creation but built on radically different principles. Having begun his literary career before the Revolution, Babel was noticed in 1916 by Maxim Gorky, who published the young writer's stories in the almanac *The Chronicle* (*Letopis'*). Gorky became his greatest fan and lifelong protector. Babel admired Gorky in turn: he developed a legend about himself as a poor Jewish boy who had suffered from discrimination under the tsarist regime, but then met a wise mentor in Gorky who sent him to study life ("the apprentice among the people") in order to become a writer. Later he enthusiastically joined the Revolution as its chronicler and active participant (he even claimed to work briefly for the Cheka as a translator).

However, the actual story was less melodramatic. Babel was born into a middle-class family that lived first in Kishinev, then in Odessa. They witnessed the horrors of the Kishinev pogrom in 1903, but luckily escaped violence. Babel was not accepted to university due to Jewish quotas, but he entered and successfully graduated from the Institute of Commerce in Kiev. From 1916, after moving to Petrograd, he worked toward a degree in law at Bekhterev University. Fluent in French, German, and Yiddish, Babel translated from these languages into Russian. Eventually, he took pains to position himself as a writer situated *between* several languages. Famous for his love of French literature, especially Maupassant and Flaubert (see, for example, his story "Guy de Maupassant"), Babel taunted his critics with the "French trace" in even the Cossack-Jewish brew of *Red Cavalry*. In *The*

Odessa Stories, he preserved Yiddish syntax and idioms while writing in Russian. At the same time, his short story "Salt" is a virtuoso example of Russian *skaz*, and was performed on stage to great acclaim.

Until his arrest in 1939, many observers in the USSR and abroad judged Babel to be one of the most important Soviet writers. This looks like a paradox, since his major works—two books of short stories, *Red Cavalry* and *The Odessa Stories*—all appeared in the first half of the 1920s. In subsequent years, despite sporadic publication of film scripts and two plays, Babel was famed more for his silence than for his new prose. His silence came to be treated as a *literary fact* to be addressed at writers' meetings, including the First Congress of Soviet Writers (1934). His silence provided subject matter even for caricaturists and stand-up comedians.

It also added to numerous legends that surrounded Babel's persona. Not infrequently these were the work of the author himself, who mixed reality with pure fiction. According to his last wife, Antonina Pirozhkova, Babel privately denied the truth of his most ostensibly autobiographical stories about childhood, which include "The Awakening" ("Probuzhdenie"), "In the Basement" ("V podvale"), "Childhood. At Grandmother's" ("Detstvo. U babushki"), "The Story of My Dovecote" ("Istoriia moei golubiatni"), and "First Love" ("Pervaia liubov'"). Other memoirists often note his constant reinvention of himself paired with a passion for mystifications.[22]

Apocryphal stories about Babel's shenanigans over advances on unwritten (or unfinished, or allegedly finished but never submitted) manuscripts circulated alongside accounts that bore witness to his tireless and torturous self-editing. In addition, some of Babel's acquaintances mention new works that he did not show to anyone (although others recall his reading parts of these works to a select public), knowing that they could not be published in contemporary Soviet conditions. Tales of his wisdom and witticisms coexisted with anecdotes about his pranks, jokes, and numerous love affairs. His well-known friendship with Gorky and his alleged conversations with Stalin further inflated Babel's reputation. At the same time, his critical remarks about the regime were duly registered by the OGPU/NKVD and circulated no less broadly than did gossip about his close relations with prominent officers of this dangerous organization, including its creepy bosses—Genrikh Iagoda and Nikolai Ezhov—and about a purported affair with the latter's wife, Evgenia Khaiutina. While Babel's sister's family and his wife lived in emigration (by default a situation that made him politically suspect), he was allowed to visit them and to stay in Europe for extended periods of time, which generated further rumors. Compounding the aura of mystery around Babel's life, even after his execution, were stories about his supposed secret survival; these were lent credibility by some official figures like Konstantin Simonov. Even the date of his tragic death was distorted: it was given as 1942, instead of 1940 by officials. The fate of his archive, confiscated by the NKVD, remains one of the greatest literary mysteries of the Soviet period.

Nor was Babel's path to the Revolution as straight as one might have supposed, considering his active collaboration with Gorky's newspaper *New Life* (*Novaia zhizn'*), a paper well known for its consistent anti-Bolshevik position. As of 1920, Babel lived in Odessa, working for the Soviet press agency of Ukraine; then, unexpectedly, he left the city and, with a journalist's ID under an assumed, non-Jewish name, joined the First Red Cavalry Army to participate in the ill-fated military campaign against independent Poland. The Army consisted mainly of Cossacks, notorious for their anti-Semitism. They had many chances to manifest this sentiment while moving across the former Pale of settlement. Babel served in the Army's newspaper for half a year, recording in his (posthumously published) diary the acts of violence, cruelty, and ideological fanaticism he witnessed. This life experience was transformed into the spectacular style and emotional intensity of Babel's *Red Cavalry* stories, about which Jorge Luis Borges eloquently remarked: "the music of its style contrasts with the almost ineffable brutality of certain scenes."[23]

Babel's *Red Cavalry* brought him universal praise from critics of different aesthetic and ideological positions, both in the USSR (Viktor Shklovsky, Aleksandr Voronsky, Viacheslav Polonsky, Abram Lezhnev, Grigory Gukovsky) and in the emigration (Georgy Adamovich, Mark Slonim).[24] The fact that the legendary commander of the Red Cavalry Semen Budyonny assaulted Babel for the blackening of his army, while Gorky defended the writer but criticized him for the excessive romanticization of the Cossacks, testifies to the elusiveness and ambivalence of the book's meanings. Babel's extravagant expressionist metaphors, powerful lyricism, and brutal plots lent ironic overtones to the epic depiction of the Red Cavalry. These were no ordinary Cossacks: they were Rabelaisian characters playing out Shakespearean conflicts in the recognizable setting of provincial Eastern Europe torn by Civil War disasters.

At this time, Babel was also writing and publishing his *Odessa Stories*. Depicting the world of Jewish gangsters in pre-Revolutionary Odessa, these stories feature loving irony and comic hyperbole. The central character of Benya Krik, the leader of gangsters, emerges as a true man of modernity, refusing to be a victim of his origins and social milieu. With style and bravado, he establishes his transgressive freedom and becomes the unofficial king of Odessa. Although the gangster's elevation to power through violence and transgressions of age-old morals may serve as another subversive metaphor for the Bolshevik Revolution, Benya's freedom proves incompatible with the new regime that the Revolution establishes. This is probably why Babel returned to the image of the Odessa gangster in his later works—notably the play *Sunset* (*Zakat*, 1927), which focused on Benya's father, killed by his sons once he becomes an obstacle to their power. According to Antonina Pirozhkova, in the 1930s Babel was simultaneously writing two novels, one about the Cheka and Chekists, and another (*Kolya Topuz*) about a gangster who tries to adapt to Soviet reality but constantly clashes with its norms.[25]

Babel's published works, as well as film scripts to which he had contributed (including Sergei Eisenstein's unfinished and banned film *The Bezhin Meadow* [*Bezhin lug*, 1937]), testify to his understanding of the Revolution as a phenomenon on a universal scale, invoking epic characters and epic violence. His devotion to the Revolution was motivated both morally (as a response to age-old injustice) and aesthetically. Even in the 1930s his aesthetic justification of the Revolution as a magnificent manifestation of the sublime (beauty mixed with horror) remained intact.[26] At the same time, judging from various memoir accounts, Babel grew increasingly disappointed with the Soviet regime, largely on moral grounds. He realized that one kind of injustice had succeeded another and that it was no less brutal; his pessimism was confirmed by escalating state terror.

Thus, the explanation of Babel's later reluctance to publish most likely lay in the conflict between moral/political and aesthetic attitudes to the Revolution, aggravated by his contradictory desire to investigate its true catastrophe, its conversion into a new repressive regime, and his bitterly clear understanding of the new rules for survival. Babel's elusive ambivalence was not a cunning pose, on this reading, but rather a method of survival without significant moral compromises.

Babel transformed creative ambivalence into a general principle equally applicable to art and life. He was not unique in choosing such a path: a similar strategy (although with different motivations) was exercised by Boris Pil'niak and Ilya Erenburg, Andrei Platonov and Leonid Leonov, Yuri Olesha and Valentin Kataev. Some of them perished in the Great Terror, others outlived Stalin and went on to become Soviet classics. Babel managed to maintain his balancing act until 1939. Ironically, it was his association with Ezhov (by 1939 replaced by Beria as NKVD head) rather than his literary work that triggered his arrest. The NKVD intended to use Babel as the "kingpin" in a show trial of writers, where Erenburg, Olesha, Kataev, and some other writers were to be tried alongside Babel for their anti-Soviet activities. Beaten and tortured, Babel "confessed" to being a French spy and recruiting writers for an anti-Soviet plot. Effectively, he scripted the coming trial. Stalin cancelled the plan, but that did not save Babel. Despite his declaration that his confessions were false and coerced, in February 1940, after a brief and grotesque trial, Babel was executed.[27] His works and his name were banned until his posthumous rehabilitation in 1954.

Beginning in the 1960s, Babel's stories became widely published, well translated, and closely studied in the West, securing for him a well-deserved place among twentieth-century modernist classics and the status of a frequently taught author in Russian and Jewish studies college courses. In the USSR, however, Babel's works were published infrequently, and his *oeuvre* was reluctantly approved as a research topic (his presence in the university curriculum was peripheral at best). In the 1960s and 1970s, state-sponsored anti-Semitism still stood in the way of the writer's posthumous fame. Nonetheless, several scholars enthusiastically laid a foundation for Babel studies in Russia. After the beginning of Perestroika, Babel became the subject of monographs and conferences; his NKVD file was made public, and his books began to appear in millions of copies.[28]

Narratives of the Great Terror I

The Great Terror of 1936–40, with a second, lesser wave in 1947–53, ratcheted up to the point of delirium the single most telling characteristic of the Soviet regime, its reliance on violence. While there were many waves of terror, as Sheila Fitzpatrick has explained, until the Great Terror they were focused mainly on the old privileged classes. But "the Great Terror focused especially on the Communist elite . . . as well as on the intelligentsia and all the 'usual suspects' like kulaks and 'former people.'" Consequently, the category of the class enemy lost its meaning, replaced by the notion of the enemy of the people.[29] Driven neither by class struggle nor the dictatorship of the proletariat, uninhibited violence operated as the Soviet system's primary form of governance, and terror was random.

Russian literature on the Great Terror and Gulag is comparable to Holocaust narratives in its focus on historical and personal trauma, in its sober analysis of the strategies of individual resistance against state terror, and in its exploration of modernity as the "century of camps," in Zygmunt Bauman's phrase.[30] Like the literature of the Holocaust, the literature on the Great Terror and Gulag treats the horror of Soviet experience as an extreme trial for modern culture and its intellectual and symbolic resources. It also exposes the awful truth that the culture found no way to take an effective stand against the assault of systemic violence.

The literary representation of state terror was explicitly banned until 1956. It was increasingly allowed in the early 1960s, and then banned again in the late 1960s, until the greater freedoms of Perestroika (1987–91), but a Socialist Realist text could represent the Gulag as a site of political re-education and molding of the "new Soviet person." Of singular importance was *The Stalin White Sea–Baltic Sea Canal: The History of Construction*, edited by Maxim Gorky, the former leader of the RAPP Leopol'd Averbakh, and one of the Gulag's chief functionaries, Semen Firin. The volume resulted from the expedition of 120 prominent Soviet writers and journalists to the Soviet labor camp whose inmates built the canal. Gorky's introductory first chapter, "The Truth of Socialism," described the canal's construction as the summit of the social experience of re-forging aimed at the former enemies of the Soviet regime, enemies "who had undergone the school of strict discipline, got cured from the rotten intoxication by philistinism—the illness affecting millions of people, which can be treated only by the... honest and proud labor for the construction of the world's first socialist society."[31] Despite its status as an eventual model for the Soviet production novel, this volume was banned in 1937 when the NKVD chiefs glorified in the book were discredited as "hidden enemies." The topic of the Gulag became officially taboo for many years to come. But there are at least three major works of literature created in the Soviet Union of the 1930s–40s that courageously and insightfully analyze the effects of the Great Terror on individual and collective life. They laid foundations for several lasting discursive approaches to the subject.

Anna Akhmatova's cycle of poems *Requiem* has become an iconic text from the Terror. Most of its parts were composed between 1935 and 1940 and preserved in the memory of the poet and a very few close friends. It was published abroad in 1963, and in full in the USSR in 1987. Its composition was a tremendous act of courage on Akhmatova's part, and that awareness of danger amplifies *Requiem*'s emotional force. The emotions are intensified by the cycle's extraordinary mix of rhythms and forms, with haunting ternary meters, terrifyingly simple trochaic couplets, and broken-off musings that open the door on a madness the Terror inevitably created. Akhmatova defined the cycle as "fourteen prayers," and it is a sequence that reverberates with motifs from the Catholic requiem mass, the Bible, Russian folk mourning, Russian history, and the poetry of the Silver Age (represented by references to Akhmatova's own early lyrics).[32] Although comprising poems written in different years, *Requiem* coheres as a mix of lyric and epic, and as the story of the birth of a new historical perspective on catastrophe and terror. In the prose preface to the poem, readers get two images of Akhmatova: a famous poet, and a faceless victim of terror standing in an endless prison line desperate to learn the fate of her arrested son. In the Dedication, this doubling of the lyrical subject is transformed into a juxtaposition of the plural "we" of a shared experience of horrifying incomplete knowledge ("We are in the dark, all of us the same" ["My ne znaem, my povsiudu te zhe"]) and the singular "I," who registers the pain in solitude ("Where are the unwilled girlfriends / Of my two years of madness" ["Gde teper' nevol'nye podrugi / Dvukh moikh osatanelykh let?"]).[33] "We" are victims deformed by suffering, absorbed by the city of death ("Stars of death were above us" ["Zvezdy smerti stoiali nad nami"]); "we" also manifest a tragic connection to earlier victims in Russian history ("I shall howl at the walls of the Kremlin like the Streltsy wives" ["Budu ia, kak streletskie zhenki, / Pod kremlevskimi bashniami vyt'"]).[34] Their suffering is seen in a context larger than any one historical instantiation, even one as horrifying as the Terror; the poem draws its imagery and rhetoric from the Bible as much as from Russian history and Russian poetry.[35] The monument to the poet appearing in the Epilogue is at the same time the monument to the Terror's countless victims: "And if they shut my tormented mouth, / Through which a nation of a hundred million cries" ("I esli zazhmut moi izmuchennyi rot, / Kotorym krichit stomil'onnyi narod").[36] It signifies the resurrection of all who had been absorbed by death—literally and psychologically—in the epicenter of historical catastrophe.

Although born from the same experience of the Terror, the outcome of the collision between an individual self and a collectivist Soviet "we" is reversed in the novella *Sofia Petrovna* by Lydia Chukovskaya, written, as was *Requiem*, during the actual years of the Terror (for *Sofia Petrovna*, 1939–40, first published abroad in 1965, in the USSR in 1988). Chukovskaya (the daughter of the critic and children's writer Kornei Chukovsky) was one of those friends who memorized Akhmatova's *Requiem*, and the author of extensive diary notes about the poet. Her husband, the prominent physicist Matvei Bronshtein, was arrested and killed during the Great Terror. *Sofia Petrovna* represents the Great Terror through the inversion of Socialist Realist tropes and narratives of "reforging human nature" and constructing "a new Soviet woman" by engagement in productive labor, ideological education, and socialist community service.

Chukovskaya places her protagonist Sofia Petrovna, an ordinary intelligentsia woman, at the intersection of two discursive traditions. This heroine descends first from the nineteenth-century types of the state bureaucrat and "little man." Like Gogol's scribe Akaky Akakievich, she is a typist, an unassuming person who gives up her personality for the honor of belonging to the social "we." In the first half of the novella, her life perfectly follows a stereotypical plot sequence about the formation of the new Soviet woman: she joins the workforce after her husband's death and finds activities and personal connections that rise above her own interests. Her work fills her with pride in living harmoniously in Soviet society according to its ideology. But Sofia Petrovna's life is thrown into disarray when her son, a Komsomol member and engineer, is arrested as an enemy of the people. A new life in the prison lines begins. Her faith in the righteousness of the Soviet state and her confidence in her son's innocence come into irresolvable conflict. The more she learns about the utter hopelessness of his situation, the deeper she sinks into insanity. As Chukovskaya explained: "I expressly meant to write a book about society gone mad...."[37] The use of indirect speech allows readers effectively to follow the heroine's disintegrating psyche and, through intense dramatic irony, never lose sight of the social order's mixed messages and cruel manipulation.

Sibelan Forrester noted the similarity between *Sofia Petrovna* and Gorky's *Mother*, an acknowledged prototype of Socialist Realism;[38] here is the second discursive tradition that the novella absorbs seamlessly. Gorky's novel traces the spiritual growth of the mother following her revolutionary son, and Sofia Petrovna similarly looks up to her son as a paragon of the new Soviet man. Yet Chukovskaya turns the logic of the Soviet Bildungsroman inside out by demonstrating that "reforging" leads not to spiritual growth, but, on the contrary, to spiritual suicide. It demands that a subject dehumanize herself, and that a mother betray her child. In the novella's finale, Sofia Petrovna receives a letter from her son, Nikolai, begging her to fight for him, and revealing the tortures he has suffered: "Investigator Ershov beat me and trampled me, and now, I'm deaf in one ear."[39] This is the climax of her internal conflict, and Sofia Petrovna, perhaps in fear, perhaps in incipient insanity, betrays her suffering child by not heeding his cries. She burns the letter, as if it never existed: "Sofia Petrovna threw the flame on the floor and stamped on it."[40]

Like Akhmatova, to whom she read the novella when it was completed, Chukovskaya hid her work until the late 1950s. It first appeared in France, and only in 1962 did she attempt (unsuccessfully) to publish it in the USSR. The destiny of Evgeny Shvarts's play *The Dragon* (*Drakon*, 1943) was no less fraught, although it too eventually reached its audience. Shvarts was a popular author, known for theatrical versions of fairy-tales for children and adults. He ironically and innovatively retold famous plots by Hans-Christian Andersen and other European romantics in *The Naked King* (*Golyi korol'*, 1934); *The Snow Queen* (*Snezhnaia koroleva*, 1939); and *Shadow* (*Ten'*, 1940). *The Dragon* was first produced by the famed theater director Nikolai Akimov, but was cancelled after only a very few performances in 1944. The play remained blacklisted until the 1960s, and even then, there were only short-lived runs (for example, by Akimov at the Leningrad Theater of Comedy in 1962, about the same time that rehearsals of *The Dragon* in Moscow's *Sovremennik* were stopped by the censors). *The Dragon* refers to numerous stories of dragon-slayers, medieval and romantic alike, but reads like a fairy-tale satire of modern totalitarian society. The central artistic discovery of *The Dragon* exposes the unbreakable connection between the tyrant and the people, who are, apparently, his victims. Shvarts's fairy tale demonstrates with clear-sighted sarcasm how the people internalize and then reproduce tyranny; in its fairy-tale logic, this principle suggests the mutual metamorphoses of the Dragon and the people, of the tyrant and his victims. No wonder that, in the first act of the play, the Dragon takes pride in shaping the souls of his subjects according to a tailor's pattern. In the third act, when the Dragon is already dead, these very souls emerge as a collective Dragon. Elsa, who in the first act is selected as a new bride of the Dragon, is forced into marriage with the Burgomaster; she is once again prepared for sacrifice to the tyrant and recognizes the Dragon in her compatriots: "Is it possible that the Dragon hasn't died, but, as it were, turned into a human? Then, this time he's turned into the multiplicity of people, and now they are killing me."[41]

The Dragon was virtually banned, but Shvarts's other plays were produced and filmed. Perhaps he was never arrested because his critique of Stalinist society was disguised as a satire of Nazism, while Soviet associations were left to the conscience of the reader/viewer. Yet a broader anti-totalitarian meaning of Shvarts's *Dragon* was evident even to its first readers. The playwright Leonid Maliugin (1909–68), after reading *The Dragon*, wrote to Shvarts: "Let's agree that this city is located in Germany—and then it will be easier [to talk about the play]."[42] But any acknowledgement that Soviet society was present in Shvarts's allegory would have meant a comparison between Stalinism and Nazism that was so dangerous that even vigilant censors could not bring themselves to mention it as a reason to forbid production. In other words, the double encoding fundamental to the structure of *The Dragon* served as a powerful defense mechanism, even as it constituted the most heretical aspect of the play's content.[43]

Despite the tremendous impediments to putting such thoughts in writing, there were other literary texts written about the Great Terror as it unfolded. Some, mainly poems, were by Gulag inmates (including Anna Barkova, Evgenia Tager, Elena Vladimirova, and Aleksandr Solodovnikov); a number of these were even published within the Gulag, in camp newspapers, or circulated as semi-folk songs. A few other works, such as Nikolai Narokov's novel *Mnimye velichiny* (*False values*, 1952) or Viktor Serge's *Tulaev's Case* (*Delo Tulaeva*, 1938), were created after their authors managed to escape from the USSR. Although discovered much later, as was his poetry, the prose of Pavel Zal'tsman also exemplifies eyewitness writing composed at the time of the Terror. It represents the next entry in the history of Soviet catastrophic narratives, taking the violence of the 1930s and 1940s as material for a powerful new discourse of disrupted mental states. Zal'tsman's novel *The Puppies* (*Shchenki*, written in the 1930s) shows that he absorbed from OBERIU the practice of treating persons, animals, and things in comparable ways. By following the winding paths of two puppies who encounter every manner of person and public event, Zal'tsman is able to retell the traumatic history of the 1930s in an uncannily emotional way. Igor Gulin has said that the novel reads as if Zabolotsky had written *Doctor Zhivago*: "In every sentence of the novel, language seems to invent itself anew."[44] Zal'tsman's Blockade diary is equally expressive and unforgettable.[45] Published only in the 2010s, these writings are belatedly bringing new attention to those who wrote about catastrophe as it unfolded.

With hindsight, one can now see that Akhmatova's poem, Chukovskaya's novella, and Shvarts's play, despite a circulation limited to trusted readers in the 1940s–50s, had an enduring impact on the literary imagination. In the 1960s, *The Dragon* was published in the USSR, and *Requiem* and *Sofia Petrovna* started circulating in *samizdat* and in *tamizdat*. The approaches to the Great Terror their authors pioneered would resonate in the new accounts of the Great Terror that emerged in the post-Stalinist period.

Narratives of the war

In the Soviet Union, what is generally known as the Second World War (1939–45) was effectively replaced by the so-called Great Patriotic War (*Velikaia Otechestvennaia voina*) against Germany from June 22, 1941 to May 9, 1945. The name persists in contemporary Russia. This peculiar socio-cultural construct retains a paradoxically treasured place in the Russian historical memory and cultural imagination. The reasons behind the differentiation between the Great Patriotic War and the Second World War are twofold: first, to obfuscate the Soviet Union's collaboration with Nazi Germany at the outbreak of the Second World War, meant to divide Eastern Europe between two new empires according to the secret protocols of Molotov–Ribbentrop's treaty of 1939; second, to minimize the Allies' contribution to victory and to present the Soviet Union's self-sacrificial struggle for the future of all humanity as the sole cause of Nazism's defeat.

In the history of Russian literature, the war wrought a decisive delineation. It created an opportunity to enhance Socialist Realist aesthetics, whose militant character had finally found a worthy application. In Evgeny Dobrenko's apt formulation, literature of the Great Patriotic War sharpened the "color palette" of Socialist Realism, which did not permit much shading to begin with.[46] Such major themes as the demonization of the enemy and the idealization of self-sacrifice (sometimes referred to in the scholarship as thanatological pathos) resonated with the public's demand for literary expression in a time of war, which explains the genuine popularity of Ilya Erenburg's fiery anti-Nazi journalism, the cult status achieved by the narrative poem *Vasily Terkin* (1942) by Aleksandr Tvardovsky (1910–71), and the huge success of *The Young Guard* by Fadeev.

There was also another side apart from heroism. Suffering and loss on a colossal scale spoke to the need for personal and existential values and not just collectivist and state-centered values. Although this tendency was carefully monitored in wartime literature, publishers could not entirely exclude an appeal that had great potential to mobilize the masses. This focus on one individual explains the great popularity of the poem "Wait for me" ("Zhdi menia . . . ," 1941) by Konstantin Simonov, who worked as a correspondent for the army newspaper and experienced first-hand the trauma of war. Initially published in *Pravda* and then endlessly recopied in soldiers' letters from the front, "Wait for me" is a completely apolitical incantation against death based on quasi-ritualistic repetitions and an appeal to the forces of nature. Addressed to the intensely missed beloved, the poem establishes a mystical connection between the survival of the soldier and the faithful love of the woman who waits for him:

> Жди меня, и я вернусь.
> Только очень жди,
> Жди, когда наводят грусть
> Желтые дожди,
> Жди, когда снега метут,
> Жди, когда жара,
> Жди, когда других не ждут,
> Позабыв вчера.
> Жди, когда из дальних мест
> Писем не придет,
> Жди, когда уж надоест
> Всем, кто вместе ждет.[47]

> Wait for me, and I'll come back!
> Wait with all you've got!

> Wait, when dreary yellow rains
> Tell you, you should not.
> Wait when snow is falling fast,
> Wait when summer's hot,
> Wait when yesterdays are past,
> Others are forgot.
> Wait, when from that far-off place,
> Letters don't arrive.
> Wait, when those with whom you wait
> Doubt if I'm alive.

Simonov's poetry, especially poems from the front included in his collection *With You and Without You* (*S toboi i bez tebia*, 1942), sounded a strong personal note, conferring an intimacy unseen since the 1920s. Rumor had it that Stalin reacted to *With You and Without You*, dedicated to Simonov's wife, the famous actress Valentina Serova, by saying: "This book should have been published in two copies only. One for Simonov, another for Serova." In the event, it reached millions of readers, signifying a new recognition of the value of personal life as a theme in official literature. Simonov created something of a lyrical legend. His poems of the most tragic years, 1941–42, left aside entirely the symbols of Soviet patriotism, red banners, the Kremlin, Stalin, or Lenin. Simonov's lyrical subject cares more about such timeless concepts as honor, friendship, and dignity before death. His version of Neo-Romanticism, as in other texts of this trend, favored the trope of oxymoron, frequently establishing connections between incompatible categories, war and love being the most expressive pairing.

Another and rather different example of a conceptual deviation from the official discourse of the war literature can be found in the short prose of Vasily Grossman. Like Simonov, Grossman served as a frontline correspondent; he spent the entire Stalingrad battle in the ruined city. His journalism and short stories initially remained true to the norms of militant Socialist Realism typical of literature of the Great Patriotic War. However, from around 1943, Russian nationalism was resurgent, epitomized by figures of the imperial past such as Aleksandr Nevsky, the hero of Eisenstein's film released in 1938, and Ivan the Terrible (the first part of Eisenstein's film about Ivan was released in 1944). A strong element of chauvinism and anti-Semitism was felt broadly in the culture.[48] Persecutions of entire ethnic groups for their potential or alleged collaboration with Nazis occurred from the moment the war began. The first victims of this policy were ethnic Germans; in 1943–44, this policy radically expanded to include the Chechens, Kalmyks, Crimean Tatars, the Black Sea Turks, and Greeks, among others. The Jewish Anti-Fascist Committee was exterminated in 1948–49 and the anti-cosmopolitanism campaigns of the late 1940s, culminating in the "doctors' plot," showed the enduring nature of anti-Semitism within the USSR. In this atmosphere, the anti-Semitic core of the Holocaust was a difficult topic to face even after the war.

Nonetheless, and without using the word itself, Grossman in his wartime prose wrote consistently about the Holocaust. His short story "The Old Teacher" ("Staryi uchitel'," 1943), as well as such non-fictional texts as "Ukraine Without Jews" ("Ukraina bez evreev," 1943), "The Murder of the Jews in Berdichev" ("Ubiitstvo evreev v Berdicheve," 1944), and "The Hell of Treblinka" ("Treblinskii ad," 1945), were "the first treatment anywhere, fictional or documentary, in any language, of what was later to be known as the Holocaust."[49] However, the *Black Book* compiled by Grossman and Erenburg about the extermination of Jews on Soviet territories was banned for publication in 1947; Grossman's novel of 1950 *For the Right Cause* (*Za pravoe delo*) about the Stalingrad battle, which includes some motifs of the Holocaust, was attacked. *Life and Fate*, arguably Grossman's masterpiece, made the Holocaust a central theme; its manuscript was confiscated by the KGB. In general, Grossman's publications show that sometimes wartime censorship was more permissive toward issues that would be deemed unacceptable in the postwar years. Some war texts suffered seemingly random treatment.

Consider the different fate of two thematically similar poems: "Before the Attack" ("Pered atakoi," 1942);[50] and "My friend, in a deadly agony" ("Moi tovarishch, v smertel'noi agonii...," 1944).[51] Both poems were written at the front. The first, by Semen Gudzenko (1922–53), was published in a major literary magazine. Although it was later criticized for "excessive natural-ism," it opened the pathway to a literary career for its author. Before his untimely death at the age of thirty-one from war wounds, Gudzenko managed to publish eight books. The second poem, albeit known unofficially to many, appeared in the Soviet press only during Perestroika owing to the efforts of Yevtushenko. It is cited in Grossman's *Life and Fate*, and for a long time it was assumed that the author would never be named. Its author was a former tank soldier, Ion Degen (b. 1925), who never sought acceptance in Soviet literature. He studied medicine, and in 1977 left the Soviet Union for Israel.

Both poems graphically depict the horror of the war and the proximity of death. They undermine any heroic discourse by means of naturalistic detail and a single, striking expres-sionist image: "With a knife I scraped out / someone else's blood from under my nails" ("vykovyrival nozhom / iz-pod nogtei ia krov' chuzhuiu") in Gudzenko's poem; and "Let me warm my hands / Over your steaming blood" ("Dai-ka luchshe sogreiu ladoni ia / Nad dymia-shcheisia krov'iu tvoei") in Degen's. However, there is a striking difference. In Gudzenko's poem, the horror of death and human destruction is overcome first by the spirit of the battle, and then by the final victory over the enemy. He writes: "We are carried across the trenches / by hardened enmity / that punctures necks with bayonets" ("I nas vedet cherez transhei / okochenevshaia vrazhda, / shtykom dyriaviashchaia shei"). Degen offers no such resolution. In his poem, the death of a friend occasions only practical concerns. Far from being cynical, the poem shows its humanity by calibrating the horrors of war to the scale of an ordinary person forced to reconcile himself to his and others' deaths. Degen's poem could not have been accepted as a part of the official Soviet literature about the war. Its lack of transcenden-tal, heroic justifications for war's death and suffering was incompatible with official Soviet discourse. The alternative approach to history represented in his poem persisted in the steadily growing body of work generated by unofficial or underground writers.

Nowhere is this juxtaposition between incompatible representations of the war, one focused on triumphant victory, and the other fundamentally opposed to any such heroic teleology, better seen than in the literature of the Leningrad Siege. A significant eye-witness account was Lydia Ginzburg, *Notes from the Blockade* (*Zapiski blokadnogo cheloveka*, written 1942–1962–1983, first published 1989). It opens with a comment on what it means to read and think about *War and Peace*, as if literary material were as orienting as information about condi-tions of life during the Siege. Within a few paragraphs, the author is explaining that her hero will be referred to as "N," a designation meant as a "fictional composite" ("summarnyi i uslovnyi"); N is "an intellectual in exceptional circumstances" whose story will show what Siege life meant generally but also the "day-to-day existence of one person."[52] Ginzburg fore-grounds the ethical complexities and evasions that defined Blockade life, and she boldly ana-lyzes the notion of personhood that the Blockade created. Her descriptions (of starvation, betrayal, death, dishonesty) take on psychological and philosophical dimensions, as does the very gesture of naming in the work's title (the Russian title literally means *Notes of a Blockade Person*): it is precisely a "blockade person" whom the author wishes to create, not a specific individual, but a composite person whose experiences can expose the assault on individual personhood during the Siege.

Ginzburg's *Notes from the Blockade* were published after decades of delay, but during the war the work of Olga Berggol'ts was known immediately. A widely published Soviet poet, Berggol'ts suffered traumatic losses in the 1930s, including her own arrest and abuse; yet she was able to offer courage and insight to her fellow citizens under siege, both in her writings and in frequent radio broadcasts. In effect, she presents both sides of the war narrative. Her long poem "February Diary" ("Fevral'skii dnevnik," 1942) has a defiantly heroic ending, at times perhaps too resoundingly like the usual iambic pentameter of quite a lot of triumphant Soviet verse. But in its barren opening narrative of people pulling their children's sleds loaded with the scarce food they have managed to find or, worse, with the bodies of those who died in the night, the poem also conveys a stark and dreadful picture of daily life in the city in 1942, as its dateline says at the end; the defiant ending, which predicts victory, seems astonishingly affirmative at a time when surely few could imagine anything other than continued starvation and more death.[53] "February Diary" is typical of Berggol'ts's Siege poetry, with its mix of conflicting discourses and intonations, from the official to the personal, from the stoic to the traumatic. The fortitude required to write such poems during the horrific circumstances of the Blockade is not to be underestimated, but the lasting value of Berggol'ts's poetry may be limited by her unwillingness, even in her later work, to address the guilt of her generation, or to acknowledge how she and other believing communists were sustaining Soviet culture.[54]

Olga Freidenberg (1890–1955), by comparison, was unsparing in her analysis of the Soviet failures that allowed the blockade of Leningrad to happen in the first place; she too wrote as a survivor of the Siege. Freidenberg, the cousin of Boris Pasternak, was a scholar of the classics, folklore, myth, and what we might now call cultural theory.[55] In *Person Besieged* (*Osada cheloveka*, published 1987), Freidenberg emphasizes the grotesque bodily experience of the Blockade in ways downplayed by other authors. The most memorable image in her brief prose account is that of excrement and blocked plumbing, as if the absence of nourishment had created an inversely proportional excess of bodily waste. Her account of the Siege is unflinching, as is her political and ethnographic insight.[56] She writes that, well before the Blockade, daily life was marked by everyday humiliations, fear of arrest, physical hardship, and psychological harm. Stalinist Russia was a huge prison, and in Freidenberg's view, Soviet personhood was fundamentally lived in a state of siege. After one passage in which she describes watching colleagues eat powdered bedbug repellent in desperation and recalls hearing tales of cannibalism, Freidenberg notes that such tales are repeated in horror, but that she found nothing so frightening in them: "how much more terrible was our daily reality, our Russian torment of living persons, our NKVD, Ezhov's terror, the moral scalpels and knives."[57] She finds little to separate psychologically prewar life from the daily experience of bombardment and hunger—an astonishing departure from the pervasive representation of the Blockade as an unforeseen and unprecedented catastrophe. Freidenberg is also unusual among authors of wartime texts in her refusal to write of any sense of collective experience. There is no "we" in her version of the Blockade, only isolated, starving human beings.[58]

Olga Freidenberg's prose works according to a poetic logic, proceeding chronologically, but not always by means of a narrative sequence. She uses numbers repeatedly to measure the intensity of lived experience, reporting how many grams of flour or oil were rationed out each month, how many hours it took to get water, how many people have died, how many hours she was expected to sit at her desk as if at work. Such accounting functions as poetic rhythm, creating the illusion that only the repetitions of adding and subtracting could make sense of a life in which most other forms of social organization were destroyed.

Others occasionally found singular images as expressive as those of Freidenberg. The war poems of Natalia Krandievskaia-Tolstaia (1888–1963) seem simple in their brevity and light touch but the imagery is stark. One poem about the advent of springtime, for example, chooses a grotesque image to represent the strangeness of spring's flourishing after the horrors of the previous winter: the sight of one person after another on the street with a sprig of lilac attached to their gas mask.[59] More significant may be the poetry of a writer who was known for his prose: Gennady Gor (1907–81). His writing shows the lingering influence of OBERIU, whose circles he had frequented (he is comparable to Zal´tsman in this way); their sense of the absurd in representing material reality would have been suitable schooling for what it took to write poetry during the Siege. Gor spent the first winter of 1941 in the blockaded city. Then and over the next two years when he was in evacuation, he wrote ninety-five poems that were found only after his death and published in the 2000s; they are the work of someone living in an extreme psychic state, expecting death at any turn. The poems are more starkly real and more horribly fantastic than nearly any other texts from the period. One poem from June 1942 opens:

> Красная капля в снегу. И мальчик
> С зелёным лицом, как кошка.
> Прохожие идут ему по ногам. По глазам.
> Им некогда. Вывески лезут:
> «Масло», «Булки», «Пиво»,
> Как будто на свете есть булка.[60]

> A red drop in the snow. And a little boy
> With a face turned green, like a cat.
> Pedestrians walk on his legs, his eyes.
> They are in a rush. The sign boards pop out:
> "Butter," "Bread rolls," "Beer,"
> As if anywhere there existed a bread roll.

Like a cinematic establishing shot, the poem's first five lines (of the total of twenty) unfold key motifs of the Siege: cold, injury, a vulnerable child, calloused citizens, the absence of food. The shop signs record the illusion that the daily life of getting and spending might be able to go on under such circumstances, and the signs, which stick out in their absurdity, suggest that language has not caught up with the starvation and daily death of the Blockade. The poem goes on to include motifs that otherwise mark Gor's own work—remembrance of childhood, the fleeting solace of dreams—but the last line brings the poet back to the point at which the poem had begun, for he is one of those who will rush down the horrible sidewalks of the besieged city: "I fear I am late to get water from the Neva" ("Za vodoi na Nevu ia boius´ opozdat´").[61] After the poem's uneven and jagged rhythms, the final line's anapests have their own jolting effect, as if thrusting the poet back into the rhythmic requirements of the daily work required to sustain life.

After the war had ended, its representation became even more codified and ritualized, supplanting war with victory. Heroic teleology and optimistic reconfiguration of the war experience dominated literature and cinema, from triumphal films like *The Fall of Berlin* (*Padenie Berlina*, 1949; dir. Mikhail Chiaureli, script by Petr Pavlenko) to quasi-Tolstoyan panoramic novels like Erenburg's *The Tempest* (*Buria*, 1947) or, on a lower artistic level, *The White Birch* (*Belaia bereza*, 1947, 1952) by the literary apparatchik Mikhail Bubennov. However, even then the literary field was not homogenous.

Several works that did not conform to prevailing cultural tenets were published in the 1940s. Viktor Nekrasov, a recently demobilized sapper in the engineering forces, published *In the Stalingrad Trenches* (*V okopakh Stalingrada*, 1946; an English translation appeared as *Front-line*

Stalingrad in 1962). The editors of *Znamia*, where it was serialized, altered its original title, *Stalingrad*, as too portentous for a mere novella with an understated and ironic tone. Its perspective was unusual: instead of featuring vast battlefields, scenes with Soviet and German generals, Stalin's divine intervention, beast-like Nazis, or an impersonal and omniscient narrator, Nekrasov wrote a nearly anti-heroic work. He is attentive to psychological and historical detail and represents the great battle, which he witnessed, from a narrow and even marginal perspective. Instead of an epic confrontation between armies, Nekrasov evokes the everyday life of a sapper unit, capturing human relations between soldiers and officers, their conversations, and drinking, all without heroic pathos. The narrative perspective belongs to an engineering officer named Kerzhentsev, with whom Nekrasov shared not only his military profession, but also the artistic and literary interests he enjoyed in his youth while growing up in an intelligentsia family in Kiev. Until the very end of the novel, Kerzhentsev does not know what is happening beyond the site to which he is assigned. This is how the war is typically seen from the inside, explains the author. Furthermore, the entire Stalingrad operation is replaced in the novel by a fight for some cisterns, situated in a strategically beneficial position, but one located away from the central events of the battle.

The confrontation between "us" and "them," so typical of wartime literature, plays only a secondary role in the novel's design. German soldiers never enter the plot as characters; rather, they constitute a condition for the action. The main conflict concerns different approaches to fighting: one—heroic, which does not spare human lives; another—prosaic, which tries to achieve the goals with minimal human loss. Nekrasov puts the officer representing the heroic approach, Captain Abrosimov, on trial. After an ill-conceived attack, when Abrosimov forces soldiers into a frontal assault against enemy machine guns that kills three quarters of the regiment, he is stripped of his officer's rank and demoted to a penal battalion. Nekrasov makes vivid use of Socialist Realist conventions in first exposing and then punishing a character deemed the enemy. But he turns this well-worn device against the embodiment of official heroism. These were blatant deviations from genre conventions and from discursive expectations for a novel about the greatest battle of the war. Nonetheless, *In the Stalingrad Trenches* received the Stalin Prize (Second degree) in 1947 and entered the cultural canon. According to the literary lore of the period, the order to honor Nekrasov's novel came directly from Stalin, who just happened to like it.

A completely different representation of the war appeared in novellas by a former Yiddish poet and wartime commander of division reconnaissance, Emmanuil Kazakevich (1913–62). His novellas *The Star* (*Zvezda*, 1947) and *Two in the Steppe* (*Dvoe v stepi*, 1948) abounded in minute detail of everyday life and, like Nekrasov's novel, they avoided bombastic rhetoric. Kazakevich employed an aesthetic more reminiscent of Romanticism or Symbolism than of Socialist Realism to represent the war. In his elegantly and psychologically precise prose, war is a condition in which the boundary between the everyday and the eternal falls away. A distinct sense of the uncanny pervades the text, a category of experience and description most unusual in Soviet literature. In *The Star*, for example, the reconnaissance unit is sent behind the frontlines. It disappears, and yet the radio call-name of the vanished unit continues to resound over the airwaves, reminding other soldiers of their absence. In *Two in the Steppe*, a young lieutenant, Sergei Ogarkov, is caught in the chaos of the summer of 1942, when the German army has broken the front. He fails to deliver in time a message from a surrounded army brigade pleading to retreat; as a result, almost the entire unit perishes in the battle. For this mistake, Ogarkov is tried by a hastily convened military court and sentenced to summary execution, but Headquarters retreats again, and Ogarkov and his guard Dzhurbaev walk for days across the steppe in search of Headquarters in order for him to receive his penalty. This long walk turns into an almost mystical journey across a liminal space between life and death.

During this journey, Ogarkov undergoes a temporary death in order to become his own shade and then be born anew as in ancient rites of passage. When Dzhurbaev is killed in an air raid, Ogarkov carries on, rather than hiding the verdict to avoid his punishment, and eventually he reports to Headquarters. In the end, we learn that Ogarkov is pardoned in his second trial. He returns to the front and finishes the war as a captain in the combat engineering unit. The happy end does not obscure the apocalyptic tenor of the narrative. Together with its existential questioning of the laws of war, the author's compassion toward a supposed coward made *Two in the Steppe* an easy target for critical attack (1948), eventuating in a fourteen-year ban on its republication.

Even more aggressive was the party-sponsored rebuke of Platonov's short story "The Return" published in *Novyi mir*; his stories about war appeared often in book form at the time.[62] While their subject matter might have made them acceptable, their departure from the canon of Socialist Realism in tone and language can be stark and they look surreal alongside more standard writing. Unlike Platonov's other stories about the war, "The Return" is strictly realistic. It depicts the return of an officer, Aleksei Ivanov, to his family, where he discovers that his children have grown up and are now alienated from him; his wife, out of loneliness and despair during his four years of wartime service, has formed an intimate bond with another man. The indignant officer—himself embroiled in an extra-marital liaison—decides to leave his family immediately. But when he sees his children chasing the train on which he is fleeing, he jumps off, and returns to the family.

Moralizing outrage was the response. In "A Slanderous Story" (1947), Vladimir Ermilov asked, "How does Platonov dare to depict Soviet people as morally imperfect?"[63] But Platonov's story was not judgmental, but rather more generous than his critics could tolerate. He feels only compassion for his characters. The story emphasizes the devastation produced by the war in all its survivors, from soldiers and officers to their wives and children. Everyone is traumatized by the war. War survivors, so the story suggests, have yet to find their human essence when the battle ends. Such a message quietly resisted the prevalent message of victory, and Platonov paid a price for writing it. He was effectively blacklisted until his death in 1951, able to publish only his re-worked folk tales.

Aesthetic directions charted by Nekrasov, Kazakevich, and Platonov reflected the complex but unassailable orthodoxy in representations of the war in Soviet literature. However, the late 1950s–60s saw a greater acceptance of features from Nekrasov's novelistic technique. None was more striking than his willingness to explore the inner conflicts when characters resisted Stalinist ideology and presented a challenge to the larger question of what it meant to live in Soviet society. Examples included the so-called "lieutenant" or "trench" prose by young writers who typically served as junior officers during the war: Yuri Bondarev (b. 1924), Grigory Baklanov (1923–2009), Konstantin Vorob'ev (1919–75), Vasil Bykov (1924–2003), and Viktor Astaf'ev (1924–2001). These writers attained astounding, graphic power in their representation of the dehumanizing routine of war, reminiscent of German Expressionism of the 1910s–20s. They all considered Viktor Nekrasov to be their teacher. Each of them faced brutal criticism regarding their use of narrative perspective. A viewpoint from the trenches, typical of these writers (hence the name of the trend) was demonstratively limited in comparison with an omnipresent Tolstoy-like author. However, their perspective was also more democratic and more humane. It implicitly rejected the Socialist Realist logic of mass sacrifice for the sake of victory, which especially irritated the official critics. Under the influence of these writers, Konstantin Simonov radically changed his aesthetic orientation and joined the ranks of proponents and practitioners of trench writing. This about-face is evident in his novelistic trilogy *The Alive and Dead* (*Zhivye i mertvye*, 1959–71) and especially in the cycle of novellas *From Lopatin's Notes* (*Iz zapisok Lopatina*, 1978). Here, he rejects the heroic clichés, instead featuring an ordinary representative of the intelligentsia, the war journalist Lopatin. He is utterly skeptical about the heroic rhetoric, and clearly sees the massive failures in the Soviet military-political system.

These writers reshaped war prose into a dynamic literary trend. Their focus on everyday aspects of life in wartime and on the human price of battlefield victories directly challenged regnant discourses. By drawing attention to the ineffectiveness of the broader social system based on violence and fear, they broke numerous taboos governing the representation of war in Soviet literature. The catastrophic defeats of 1941, the millions of Soviet POWs and their treatment as traitors by Soviet officials, the massive collaboration of Soviet citizens with Germans, the routinization of rape of German women by Soviet soldiers and officers when the Red Army entered Germany, and to some extent even the Holocaust—all these topics were first introduced into public discourse, after long fights with censorship, through the works of the former lieutenants. This process continued well into the 1990s, when Georgy Vladimov, a writer from the generation after the lieutenants, published his novel *The General and His Army* (*General i ego armiia*, 1994). Here, for the first time in Russian literary history, General Andrei Vlasov is sympathetically depicted. His name had long been synonymous with betrayal.

Reliving the experience of war and its traumas in the best works of the lieutenants' prose led to confrontations with the mechanisms of social, and not just military, violence. The trauma could encompass Soviet political terror, which had penetrated every facet of society and which was enhanced by the war. The perennial conflict in these works is between this routine system of repression that belittles human lives and dehumanizes everyone, and the newly found dignity and personal responsibility that young heroes, former schoolboys really, find under fire and refuse to give up. War prose of this kind challenges more triumphalist military writing, and it frequently uses frontline situations to reveal the inhuman disdain of Stalinism for individuals and its mistrust of independent thought and action. Social critique in war prose was accompanied by palpable existentialist motifs in the works of Bykov, who wrote both in Belarusian and Russian and therefore belongs to both literatures; Vorob´ev in his novellas *Killed near Moscow* (*Ubity pod Moskvoi*, 1963) and *The Scream* (*Krik*, 1962); and Astaf´ev in his novella *A Shepherd and Shepherdess* (*Pastukh i pastushka*, written 1967–1971–1989), as well as his post-Soviet novel, *The Damned and the Slain* (*Prokliaty i ubity*, vol. 1 1994; vol. 2 1995). In these fictions, war becomes one extended borderline situation, forcing the protagonist to make a wrenching choice in order to manifest his inner freedom. But as a rule, any possibility of moral choice clashes with the logic of the Soviet system.

Despite the critical potential of war prose, the increasing crisis in Soviet ideology in the cultural history of the 1970s–80s led to the transformation of the painful memory of war into the last tangible foundation of Soviet identity (this process was "restarted" in the 2000s with the "restoration" of Russian imperial identity).[64] This new role for war narratives as foundational in identity construction explains why prose that had seemed initially suspect was embraced by the official discourse. Not only were all these writers showered with official awards and multiple publications, but their poetics even influenced General Secretary Leonid Brezhnev's memoir *The Small Land* (*Malaia zemlia*, 1978), presented by official critics as the supreme achievement of war literature.

The painful experience that did not fit the newly designed identity models and therefore was forced out from official war discourse can be illustrated by two novellas, which follow up the approaches advanced by Platonov and Kazakevich, but with some unusual shifts in perspective. Vsevolod Petrov (1912–78), a war veteran, art historian, and writer from Mikhail Kuzmin's circle, and a friend of Daniil Kharms, wrote *Manon Lescaut of Turdei* in 1946; it appeared only in 2006. Six years later, Boris Ivanov (1928–2015), a veteran of the Leningrad underground, published *Behind the City's Walls: Vedernikov, a Deserter* (*Za stenami goroda: Dezertir Vedernikov*, 2012).

Petrov's *Manon Lescaut of Turdei* has strains of the Neo-Romantic, since its protagonist and narrator projects Abbé Prévost's novel about Manon Lescaut and the Chevalier des Grieux onto a lovely and frivolous nurse, Vera, from a military train-hospital. The narrator falls in love with Vera, knowing in advance that she will soon betray him and even foreseeing her tragic death, or perhaps his own—he does not know which. For him, this love is an opportunity to live life to the fullest, if only briefly; as the narrator believes, life imitates art, rather than the other way around. Oleg Iur'ev argues that Petrov depicts a personal, ahistorical utopia for his own—alienated and mocked—circle of intellectuals, a utopia attainable even in the midst of the war. The openly countercultural meaning of this utopia defying all patriotic pathos permitted Petrov's *Manon* to be read as a polemic with Vera Panova's popular novel *Fellow Travelers* (*Sputniki*, 1946), which also depicted a military hospital-train.[65]

As in Platonov's "Return," Ivanov's novella *Behind the City's Walls: Vedernikov, a Deserter* takes an anti-Romantic and anti-ideological approach to the portrayal of the war. It focuses on the plight of the ordinary human person, trying to survive and to preserve his individuality amidst the irrationality of historical chaos. In Soviet literature, such characters, seen in *Behind the City's Walls* as entirely sane and humane, normally earned condemnation as traitors for their insufficient self-sacrificial heroism. But, as in Petrov's novella, "the [Leningrad] siege in Ivanov's [novella] is an opportunity to escape from the system, from everything Soviet" and "it is a triumph of everything situated outside of the Soviet realm... Vedernikov begins to live as a free person when he becomes a deserter and he dies when he attempts to rejoin the 'common body.'"[66]

In the 2010s, the Great Patriotic War remains a highly charged topic with political implications and therefore one that is increasingly risky. Russian authorities rely heavily on the discourse of war to assert national superiority and to reaffirm a messianic role in the twentieth and twenty-first centuries. It may seem as if the hard work of frontline writers who deconstructed the 1950s–70s heroic narratives was in vain: the old Soviet mythologies have returned in Hollywood-like film productions, where computer-generated imagery revels in blood and gore. Cinema is an influential example of a broader cultural discourse that removes all the contradictions and inner conflicts from war literature as pioneered by Viktor Nekrasov and Vasily Grossman. Will those aesthetic "discoveries" be sustained in future accounts of the Great Patriotic War? Will we witness new mythologizations, followed by inevitable new deconstructions, only this time performed by writers belonging to the generations of grandchildren and great-grandchildren of war veterans? Or will the writers of these generations stay away from this toxic subject, leaving it to the historians and politicians? While this remains an open question, one thing is certain: the literary legacy established by those who fought on the battlefields and then fought to represent war in all its complexities will be felt in the representation of war more generally in Russian literature—be it past, present, or future.

Narratives of the Great Terror II

Although valuable works about the Terror were written as it unfolded, the real beginning of a broad-based literary investigation of the Stalinist Terror and Gulag happened only after Khrushchev's secret speech in 1956 and after the onset of de-Stalinization in the 1960s. In that period, it was Aleksandr Solzhenitsyn who created the dominant discourse of the Great Terror based on the realistic rendering of the life experiences of the Gulag's survivors. *One Day in the Life of Ivan Denisovich* (*Odin den' Ivana Denisovicha*) appeared in *Novyi mir* in November 1962, following a special directive from the Presidium of the Central Committee.

The unprecedented decision to publish proceeded in several stages, directed by the magazine's editor-in-chief Aleksandr Tvardovsky and supported by Khrushchev's aide Vladimir Lebedev. There was a considerable shock value in the novella's direct depiction of ordinary people's suffering in the Gulag, but the secret of its tremendous success lay in its traditional aesthetic. In the hero, Ivan Denisovich Shukhov, readers could easily recognize a character transplanted from nineteenth-century Russian literature: a peasant who suffers from ceaseless state violence wherever he turns. A war prisoner captured by the Germans during the first months of the war, Ivan Denisovich escapes only to be arrested by the Soviets as a presumed German spy—the usual fate of those who survived Nazi capture. Solzhenitsyn depicts him as neither a rebel nor a conformist. Shukhov resists the system by fighting for his life, and by adapting to even the cruelest circumstances as a zek (from the standard acronym ZK, zakliuchennyi, for camp inmates). He carefully preserves his dignity and even finds a measure of freedom in the scene of bricklaying—when, as a true master of his trade, he stands equal to the foreman and mentally rises above his slave-like condition. Ivan Denisovich experiences the joy of inspired labor as he builds a wall to expand the labor camp; the name that Solzhenitsyn chooses for this construction site—Sotsgorodok, a socialist town—intensifies the irony. In general, the work of underfed and frozen inmates in unbearable conditions, almost without hand implements, let alone mechanical tools, reads as a near-parody of Socialist Realist accounts of heroic labor for the construction of socialism. The meaning of Solzhenitsyn's irony is obvious: it is the Shukhovs who are building socialism. The difference between the Gulag and free life thus disappears (as was also true in Freidenberg's much more obscure tale of the Siege): Ivan Denisovich finally admits, "there was no knowing where the living was easier—here or there."[67] Another example of this parallel is found in the earlier work of Vasily Azhaev, also a former Gulag inmate, who published a novel, Far Away from Moscow (Daleko ot Moskvy, 1948), in which he unironically disguises the slave labor of the zeks as free workers' heroic sacrifices for the building of communism.

A decade after One Day, Solzhenitsyn's published The Gulag Archipelago, which generated a powerful cultural and political reaction. It so scared the Soviet authorities that after the publication of the first part of the book in Paris in 1973 they arrested Solzhenitsyn and expelled him from the USSR. It also had a tremendous influence on the European left, triggering a fresh round of revisionism concerning the entire communist legacy. Defined by the author (in the subtitle of The Gulag Archipelago) as "an experiment in literary investigation," this monumental three-volume work mixes many genres and styles. It also encompasses a range of topics, any one of which is fairly substantial: a history of Soviet political terror from 1918 to 1956 (including a detailed comparison of Soviet and tsarist prisons); an ethnography of the prison camp and its types; the autobiographical story of the author's own arrest and imprisonment; invectives and satires directed against Gulag officials; a catalogue of prisoners' ways of talking about their guards; and the stories of many individual prisoners. Each of the narrative's parts focuses on one of the circles of the Gulag's hell (thus indirectly referring to Dante's Inferno, which also provided the guiding metaphor for The First Circle)—arrest, interrogations, first cell, transport, labor camp, exile. The reader follows prisoners along their tragic path, with each step sinking deeper into the realm of lawlessness and universal violence.

The Gulag Archipelago absorbed the life stories of the more than 200 Gulag survivors whom Solzhenitsyn interviewed: "In The Gulag Archipelago the individual and the communal meet on the blurring borderlines between the individual style of the authorial commentary and the voices of the camp inmates, which the author recollects."[68] The stories of famous people fuse with those of ordinary, even nameless, characters: molded by the shared experience of the Gulag, their voices become the chorus in a tragedy. It may well have been the impact of Solzhenitsyn's Gulag Archipelago that led Joseph Brodsky to coin his famous formula: "In a real tragedy, it is not the hero who perishes; it is the chorus."[69] Solzhenitsyn spoke in *The Gulag Archipelago* as the originator of an alternative history written from the standpoint of those silenced in official historiography and propaganda. He transforms a sociology and ethnography of the realm of terror hidden behind the façade of Socialist Realism into an epic presenting the history of Soviet civilization as experienced by its victims. Solzhenitsyn's "we" means the victims of the Gulag (that is, of the Soviet system), who stand as alternative heroes to the Soviet "we" of Socialist Realist narratives (prophetically satirized by Zamiatin in his dystopia *We*). The book thus inverts the discourse of totalitarian power, and it resists a teleology that pits the collective against individual identity.

The publication of *One Day in the Life of Ivan Denisovich* opened the floodgates for the memoirs of Gulag survivors, among which several stand out: Evgenia Ginzburg's *Journey into the Whirlwind* (*Krutoi marshrut*, vol. 1 1967; vol. 2 1979) and Lev Kopelev's *Preserve Forever* (*Khranit' vechno*, 1968); and *samizdat / tamizdat* non-fictional accounts of later prisoners, including Anatoly Marchenko's *My Testimony* (*Moi pokazaniia*, 1967), and Vladimir Bukovsky's *To Build a Castle: My Life as a Dissenter* (*I vozvrashchaetsia veter...*, 1979). *Journey into the Whirlwind* by Evgenia Ginzburg (1904–77) had a special status because it featured the experiences of women, unlike the male experience that dominates *The Gulag Archipelago*. Describing her own eighteen-year Gulag odyssey, Ginzburg incorporates hundreds of life stories of other women in transport and in the camps. Her talent for observation and empathy transformed her memoirs into a large-scale, yet intimate, lyrical narrative about women's suffering at the hands of the Stalinist state. Her memoir was also an important intelligentsia narrative: Ginzburg told the story of a passionate communist woman who eagerly romanticized the 1920s and treated Stalinism as treason to the Revolution, only partially accepting the idea that all communists bore responsibility for the historical tragedy of the Terror.

The poet Anna Barkova also recorded the experiences of women in the camps. She was arrested three times (1934, 1947, and 1957, the last time during the supposedly liberal Thaw; Barkova lived in prison or exile from 1934 to 1965). Leonid Taganov, one of the scholars who brought Barkova's writings to their belated publication, argues that her poetry from the Gulag delivers the theme of senseless yet necessary rebellion, echoing Camus's version of existentialism.[70] Barkova wrote poems and prose in the camps, handing some imagined future reader a grotesque parody of the monstrous representation of imprisoned individuals. Poems like "I would like to see the most terrifying" ("Ia khotela by samogo, samogo strashnogo," 1938) rang out with fiery defiance and a relentless assertion of self-worth; while "The Old Woman" ("Starukha," 1952) mimicked a culture that saw in Barkova and her fellow prisoners nothing but what Shalamov would write about as "goners" (*dokhodiagi*).[71]

Barkova, Ginzburg, Solzhenitsyn, and other like-minded writers of the 1960s debated the Soviet system using its own language and its own principles: they all depicted Stalinist Terror as a negation of ideological boasts about privileges and benefits for ordinary working people. But few of these writers questioned such fundamental ideological tenets as the moral and cultural superiority of the toiling people over the intelligentsia, or the priority of collective values over the individual (Barkova is something of an exception to that last point, however). Symptomatically, in *One Day in the Life of Ivan Denisovich*, the brigade—much celebrated in Soviet literature as a new form of labor-based community—is depicted as a means to collective survival. The Terror in these representations becomes the state's crime against the people (*narod*). These narratives challenge the official line that repressions targeted "enemies of the people," as if defending the *narod* from dangerous conspirators. But neither Solzhenitsyn nor the Gulag writers who came after him addressed such dramatic questions as the *narod*'s own participation in the Terror, or the popular support for the Revolution which had made the Terror possible. Vasily Grossman took up these questions, however, particularly in *Life and*

Fate as well as in his last work, *Forever Flowing* (*Vse techet*, 1963, first published abroad in 1970), which extended the themes of *Life and Fate*.

In *Life and Fate*, Grossman attempted to fulfill the social command of the postwar decade: to create a new *War and Peace* about the Great Patriotic War. Tolstoy's epic novel was heralded during the war as the prime model for Socialist Realist representation of epic events and it generated many imitations. The influence of *War and Peace* on *Life and Fate* can be seen not only in the symmetrical titles, but also in the novels' composition, which follows the lives of several families, mixing battle scenes with everyday dramas, and assigning an enormous role to the authorial voice, which frequently breaks in with passionate generalizing monologues. As Tzvetan Todorov noted, other nineteenth-century models are felt as well: "[Grossman's] characters, like Dostoevsky's, engage in great philosophical debates"; and Todorov finds that ideologically, "the model to which Grossman admitted to feeling closest was Chekhov . . . who brought into Russian literature a new kind of humanism based on the ideas of freedom and loving kindness."[72] Grossman's translator, Robert Chandler, calls *Life and Fate* "a Chekhovian epic about human nature."[73] These associations are only partly convincing: Dostoevsky scarcely belongs among Grossman's favorites (he is directly criticized in the novel for his xenophobia); Chekhov's aesthetics are at odds with epic conclusiveness, which is keenly sought in *Life and Fate*, and Grossman's philosophy of freedom is radically different from that of Chekhov. Still, an orientation towards the classics of Russian literature, which Grossman tries to release from the grip of deadening Socialist Realist interpretations, is foundational in *Life and Fate*.

Despite a plot focus on the Great Patriotic War and, more specifically, on the Stalingrad battle, this novel is about the Great Terror, or more precisely about the "superviolence of totalitarian systems," as Grossman puts it.[74] Unlike Solzhenitsyn, Grossman was spared time in the Gulag, but he lived in its shadow, and he was writing about the Terror with an insider's sorrowful view. His second wife was arrested; he fought for her release and adopted her children (their father perished in 1937). Grossman was twice the target of brutal and direct critical attacks—first for his play *If One Believes Pythagoreans* (*Esli verit' pifagoreitsam*, 1946), and in 1952, for the prequel to *Life and Fate*, the novel *For the Right Cause*. In the electric atmosphere of the time, each of these situations could easily have earned Grossman a sentence in the Gulag.[75]

The author of *Life and Fate* frames the scenes of the Stalingrad battle with the depiction of two concentration camps, Nazi and Soviet. Each reveals a staggering truth in showing that totalitarian violence is not generated only by authorities: it is willfully and at times enthusiastically perpetrated by ordinary people, inmates of the system. The same point about mass collusion in totalitarian violence is prominent in Grossman's representation of the Holocaust in the novel, particularly in the poignant letter that one of the main heroes, Viktor Shtrum, receives from his mother, confined to the ghetto. We know that Grossman's own mother perished in Berdichev. Horrific scenes of the Holocaust, rare in Soviet literature with its tacit ban on the topic, find a terrible complement in the account of an anti-Semitic campaign organized by his scientific institute against Shtrum himself. Even his theoretical discovery (later found to be very useful for the nuclear project) was designated an example of "Jewish science."

On the basis of such similarities, Grossman builds a parallel between Nazism and Communism, which made the publication of *Life and Fate* unimaginable in the USSR (the head of Soviet ideology at the time, Mikhail Suslov, suggested to Grossman that his novel could be published in 200 years). "When we look one another in the face, we're neither of us just looking at a face we hate—no, we're gazing into a mirror," a Gestapo officer, Liss, tells his prisoner, the old Bolshevik Mostovskoy.[76] This parallelism is not limited to the totalitarian methods of governing. According to Grossman's logic, the power and horror of both systems stem from their reliance on the *narod*. He identifies as perpetrators the masses, mass desires and mass instincts, as well as "the hypnotic power of world ideologies"[77] able to mobilize the masses' aggression against individual values and against individual freedom. In this tragic subversion of democratic ideas, Grossman, through his favorite character, Shtrum, sees something reminiscent of the laws of nuclear physics.

In each of the novel's fifteen subplots, Grossman contrived that the central character should experience his or her moment of freedom. Freedom may manifest itself through a fearless conversation (Shtrum, Krymov, Darensky), or in the resistance of a weak individual to the state's pressure (Novikov, Abarchuk, Sofia Levinton, Sokolov), or in a new power obtained outside of the customary (Soviet) system of political restraints (Ershov and Grekov with his unit). In each case, the encounter with freedom proves transformative, most notably when Shtrum makes his breakthrough theoretical discovery after a dangerous political conversation in which "his words and the words of his friends had been determined only by freedom, by bitter freedom."[78] Moments of freedom can exact a terrible penalty, and the novel shows persecution and possible death (Shtrum, Abarchuk, Ershov, Levinton, Grekov) as the price for transgressive freedom.

Solzhenitsyn and Grossman are widely known in the West thanks to excellent translations as well as similarities with classical Russian literature that make their work accessible. Others who wrote about the Great Terror no less powerfully but at some distance from the norms of traditional realism, are typically much less known. Among their number is Varlam Shalamov.[79]

Shalamov spent seventeen years behind barbed wire: he was first arrested in 1929, and released in 1932; in 1937, he was arrested again as a Trotskyite; in five years, in 1943, when his term was coming to an end, he received another ten years for calling the émigré Ivan Bunin a classic of Russian literature. Shalamov was finally released in 1954, but could return to Moscow only in 1956.[80] In the foreword to *Kolyma Tales*, begun shortly after his release from the Gulag, Shalamov explained his attitude to the Gulag as absolutely negative, defying "the fairy tales of literature" and requiring radically new methods of writing. Using the third person, he wrote:

> The author of *Kolyma Tales* considers the labor camp a negative experience for man—from the first to the last hour. Man should not know, should not even hear about it. Not one man becomes better or stronger after the labor camp. The labor camp is a negative experience, a negative school, and the defilement of all—of the staff and the prisoners, of the security guards and the onlookers, the passersby and the readers of belles-lettres.[81]

In his *Kolyma Tales*, Shalamov fuses his life experiences and an account of what he witnessed with the quest for an artistic language adequate to the inhuman absurdity of the Gulag. The experience of the Gulag brings Shalamov to his ultimate insight into the collapse of faith in the humanistic power of reason: "Life does not have a rational basis—that's what our times demonstrate."[82] The required prose, the writer holds, should get rid of all literary conventions and plot-driven teleology; its starting point should be the complete absence of comprehensible meaning or rational justification in the course of human history. The result is an extraordinary revision of modernist style: powerful emotional effect concentrated in minimal expression.

Shalamov defined the aesthetics of *Kolyma Tales* through a series of negative statements:

> *Kolyma Tales* examines people without a biography, without a past or a future. Does their present resemble a savage or humane present?
>
> *Kolyma Tales* is about the fate of martyrs, who were not, could not be, and did not become heroes.
>
> In *Kolyma Tales* . . . there is nothing that could be considered the overcoming of evil or the triumph of good, in terms of the big plan, the artistic plan.
>
> If I had had a different goal, I would have found an entirely different tone, different colors, using the very same artistic principle.[83]

The regime of work and life in the camps in Shalamov's *Kolyma Tales* is not transparent, functional, or rational. Here the disciplinary omnipotence of the authorities yields entirely to chain reactions of unrestrained violence perpetrated by inmates on one another, by professional criminals and against political prisoners. Shalamov shows that the purpose of the Gulag is to kill the prisoner's mind by labor and terror and to transform the human being into a piece of unthinking matter that can be exchanged for pieces of wood, gold, radium, ore, and other natural resources. He mentions several times that the value of raw materials is in direct proportion to the death toll in a given camp: prisoners perished in gold and radium mines much faster than did those in camps that produced coal, timber, or less valuable resources. However, even this equation would be too rational for the world of the *Kolyma Tales*. Focused on the destruction of persons, rather than the production of goods, the Gulag system of violence remains totally inexplicable and arbitrary for its confused and devastated victims.

Shalamov's narrator is a seasoned intellectual who tries to use his reason as a weapon against irrational and impersonal forces. But the author methodically demonstrates how the Gulag's universal violence strips away anything that defines a human being: rationality, language, feelings, and even the survival instinct. The last feeling that remains in the dehumanized human being is anger, and the last instinct is aggression. If Shalamov's heroes manage to survive, they owe it to experience, intuition, and artistic talent, something akin to "magic" (the title of one of the stories), but not to reason or calculation. Consequently, the return to humanity is frequently symbolized in Shalamov's stories as the recollection of a word or a piece of (literary) writing. An eloquent example is the story "Sententious" ("Sententsiia," 1965), with its fathomless first sentence, "People would arise out of nothingness, one after another."[84] In this story, where bare life has become the norm, where the narrator describes himself at first as indifferent to truth and to lies, something like the sensation of being human returns in a mysterious and logic-defying way. The narrator, who totters on the brink of embracing death, observes the poverty of his own language, but even as he feels at a loss for words, one strange, incomprehensible word dawns on him. It has nothing to do with the obscenities and routinized violence of camp life, and it is not a part of the dry, rationed language of the camps.[85] The word is "completely useless in the taiga," thinks the narrator, and it seems to him strangely Roman, a word as if made of stone: "sententious" (in Russian it is "sententsiia").[86] The word is yelled, shrieked into the space of a prisoner's hut, angering the other *zeks*, who call him crazy. It is the first of many revived words, arriving slowly, singly, dangerous and strangely thrilling, uttered as if the narrator were speaking in tongues.[87] These words bear not the semantics of their regular usage but, evacuated of all other meaning, they sound out a measure of dignity and inner freedom.

"Sententious" is dedicated to Nadezhda Mandelstam. In its barren descriptions, the story never strays from the negative poetics of the larger cycle, but it enacts, as all the stories do, an aesthetic that "tests the sheer phatic function of language."[88] It has a counterpart in the story that imagined Osip Mandelstam's death in the camps, "Cherry Brandy" ("Sherri-brendi," 1958), a story of physical immobility and mental courage. The title comes from one of Mandelstam's late poems and is an unmistakable signal that he is the otherwise unnamed poet whose death is foretold in the story's terse, shattering first sentence: "the poet was dying."[89] Shalamov's oneness with Mandelstam and his widow reflects an implacable opposition to Gulag violence and a shared commitment to individual worth even (or especially) when tested to the extreme. There is also a poetic affinity between the starkly crafted sentences of Shalamov's intensely lyric, brutal prose and the unflinching candor of Mandelstam's late Voronezh works.

A less somber conceptualization of the Great Terror marks the unusual prose of Yuri Dombrovsky. His last novel, *The Department of Useless Knowledge* (*Fakul 'tet nenuzhnykh veshchei*, first publication in Paris in 1978), represents the Terror in a manner somewhat reminiscent of

Bulgakov's novel *The Master and Margarita*, although without any devilish interventions. Cosmic forces of evil like the demonic resemble naive amateurs next to the NKVD professionals depicted by Dombrovsky. Like Solzhenitsyn and Shalamov, Dombrovsky knew the Gulag first-hand, having been arrested four times (in 1933, 1936, 1939, and 1947); he spent more than ten years in prisons and the camps. An erudite and charismatic bohemian, Dombrovsky wrote several novels (one of them was confiscated and then returned by the NKVD/KGB) as well as a cycle of novellas about Shakespeare.[90] *The Department of Useless Knowledge* is in many respects autobiographical, based on his short imprisonment in 1936. At the time, Dombrovsky lived in exile in Alma-Ata, worked at the local museum, and had already authored the novel *Derzhavin*. Formally, *The Department of Useless Knowledge* continues the story begun in his 1964 novel *The Keeper of Antiquities (Khranitel' drevnostei)*, published in *Novyi mir*. But Dombrovsky departs from the first-person narrative of *The Keeper of Antiquities*, employing a much broader scope for characters and settings.

The Department of Useless Knowledge creates an expressionist image of the Stalinist Terror. Simultaneously ahistorical and concrete, phantasmal and almost documentary, it blends normally incompatible elements of the rational and the surreal. The rationalist analysis of the logic behind tyrannical regimes, from the reign of Tiberius to that of Stalin, constitutes the central theme of meditations by the protagonist, Georgy Zybin, the keeper of antiquities and a living manifestation of fearlessness in thoughts and actions. His inner conviction that Stalinism is but a link in the chain of tyrannical regimes, all destined to perish, gives him intellectual independence. His position makes him invincible against psychological pressure and corruption, but he is not invulnerable to physical pain.

Among its surreal elements, Dombrovsky's novel presents uncanny motifs of ghosts and vampires projected onto a historically concrete collective portrait of "the regime's faithful"—its NKVD officers, interrogators, and executioners. While spreading death, they all anticipate (but try to ignore) their inevitable doom at the hands of their colleagues: "People disappeared quickly here. They were here, and then vanished. Nobody remembers. There was something mystical in this, something hard to figure out completely or irreversible, like fate."[91] It is Zybin, with his demonstrative refusal to accept the power of surreal monsters, who exposes the fictional nature of power based on terror.

Shortly after the publication of *The Department of Useless Knowledge* in Paris, the sixty-nine-year-old Dombrovsky was beaten by supposedly unknown thugs (presumably, KGB agents) in the lobby of the Writers' Club in Moscow; he died in the hospital from internal bleeding. Dombrovsky had foreseen such a death and described it in what proved to be his last written work: a short story, "Little Arm, Leg, Cucumber" ("Ruchka, nozhka, ogurechik," 1978), published posthumously. Dombrovsky's death is symptomatic of the confusing and hardly liberated cultural atmosphere of the late 1970s when, unlike the earlier Thaw period, references to the Great Terror and Gulag had vanished from the public sphere.

However, this period also witnessed a reevaluation of Stalinist collectivization as a seemingly forgotten form of mass terror; this important work of renaming and reconceiving a past era of terrible violence was accomplished by writers associated with Village Prose. The official narrative of collectivization was embodied in Sholokhov's *The Virgin Land Upturned*, the first volume of which was published in 1932, immediately after collectivization and in the midst of Holodomor, the devastating famine it caused; the second volume of the novel appeared during the Thaw, in 1959. Required reading for graduating classes of every Soviet high school, it was also the basis of a three-part film (1959–61) featuring the stars of Soviet cinema. Both the novel and the film thus spread some key stereotypes about collectivization. Sholokhov depicted a painful, yet necessary campaign leading to the triumph of social justice and the modernization of the countryside. In his portrayal, victims were few and inevitable, while forces of resistance against this sweeping destruction of Russia's villages were demonized as classic villains, remaining isolated among Cossacks who at first reluctantly but then more and more enthusiastically moved toward the collectivized happiness.

Despite the dominance of this Socialist Realist ideological schema, alternative representations of forced collectivization were penned, and by the late Soviet period, they were known to a growing readership. Platonov's *Foundation Pit*, with its surrealist scenes of the collectivized village, was read in *samizdat* as of the 1960s, if not earlier. In 1963, Vasily Grossman completed *Forever Flowing*, which included the bitter monologue of a peasant woman, a former kolkhoz activist, who graphically describes the horrors of collectivization and famine in Ukraine. Smuggled from Europe, this book circulated in *samizdat* in the 1960s and was the first honest literary account of Holodomor. Vladimir Tendriakov (1925–84), a popular author close to the circle of Village Prose writers, wrote autobiographical novellas based on his experience of collectivization: *Bread for the Dog* (*Khleb dlia sobaki*, 1969–70) and *A Couple of Horses* (*Para gnedykh*, 1969–71). These texts remained unpublished until Perestroika, but the writer shared them with his peers.

Accounts of collectivization that contradicted and directly confronted official narratives began to see publication in the USSR around the same time. Among the most prominent publications were Sergei Zalygin's (1913–2000) novella *On the Irtysh* (*Na Irtyshe*, 1964), as well as such epic novels as Vasily Belov's *Eves* (*Kanuny*, vols. 1–3, 1972–84; vol. 4, 1989–91) and Boris Mozhaev's *Peasant Men and Woman* (*Muzhiki i baby*, vol. 1, 1972–73; vol. 2, 1978–80). In these works, Sholokhov's representation of collectivization is turned upside down or mocked as irrelevant. The introduction of kolkhozes is depicted as the brutal destruction of the organic order of peasants' lives that causes justifiable indignation, resistance, and eventually rebellion. Collectivization is shown as having eliminated salutary, responsible forces in village life, while giving power to ineffective, lazy, and rightly despised individuals. Typically (this is especially obvious in Belov's novels), tragic events of collectivization are depicted as the result of invading foreign forces, rather than because of conflicts within the village itself. Whereas in Sholokhov's novel a proletarian Davydov slowly learns to understand and respect the values of the Cossacks' way of life, in Belov's *Eves*, commissars, frequently with Jewish last names, operate in the village as occupiers, hateful to everything national and traditional. These nuances explain why the authorities permitted these publications, with their radical reevaluation of a formidable ideological narrative: exposing the horrors of collectivization was a small price to pay for enhancing the position of the unofficial but influential "Russian Party" among the Soviet elite, which claimed that Communist ideology had disguised the Jewish assault on the Russian people and its national values.[92]

One other writer who managed to break through the ideological roadblock of the 1970s was Yuri Trifonov. The son of a prominent party functionary executed in 1938, Trifonov was scarred for life by the memory of the Great Terror. At the beginning of his career, while still at the Literary Institute, he received the Stalin Prize for the novel *The Students* (*Studenty*, 1950); this account of how to deal with ideologically questionable professors was lauded and then imitated in later actual campaigns. In his best later work, the novella *The House on the Embankment* (*Dom na naberezhnoi*, 1976), Trifonov returns to the events depicted in *The Students*, taking a radically different approach: he relies brilliantly on Aesopian language, saturating the text with hints and allusions.[93] Devoid of any mention of Stalin, the Gulag, or the NKVD, the novella found publication in a Soviet journal (although not without considerable machinations by the editor to get it past the censors).

Trifonov knew that discerning readers would be able to read between the lines. A clever reader would have understood that the first layer of the lyrical protagonist's reminiscences refers to 1937–38, the peak of the Great Terror, while the second part, centered around Vadim

Glebov, refers to 1947–49, the time of an anti-cosmopolitan campaign and a sweeping purge of university humanities departments. Glebov appears as a genuinely new Soviet man, and it is his inner world that the novella recreates. A boy from a communal apartment, he grew up under the shadow of the House on the Embankment—a prestigious apartment building not far from the Moscow Kremlin, designed for the party and government elite. In his teenage years, Glebov visits his classmates' lavish apartments and is filled with secret envy, but then he not-too-secretly enjoys their humiliation when their parents are arrested and the families are ousted from their prized homes. As a university student in the late 1940s, Glebov methodically tries to become someone who could merit such an apartment. When he is announced as the fiancé of his former classmate Sonia Ganchuk, the daughter of a prominent "red professor" of literature, he takes the first step toward that elite status.

Through Glebov's progress, Trifonov offers a subtle analysis of the system of social inequality that organized Soviet power and enabled the Terror. Far from resisting the system, Glebov becomes its compliant servant. Intuitively, he justifies the Terror as a form of social leveraging. Glebov's readiness to engage in betrayal for the sake of social advancement summarizes the entire complex of feelings associated with the House on the Embankment (envy, desire, and resentment at perceived injustice). His ascension to the ranks of the Soviet elite presupposes one more critical condition—an ability (and desire) to forget his betrayals and their motivations: "Whatever one didn't remember ceased to exist. . . . *It had never happened. Or had it?*"[94]

Among Soviet writers, Trifonov was the first to reveal the deeper meaning of the Soviet practice of forgetting about the crimes of the regime. He saw a desire to avoid assigning responsibility for the past in the state and in ordinary people, who did not make political decisions but who also could not be viewed as utterly passive pawns. His novel *The Old Man* (*Starik*, 1978) investigates the forgetting of the catastrophic experience of the Civil War, and takes up the question of responsibility. In effect, he was uncovering the Soviet version of the "banality of evil" as described by Hannah Arendt. But in *House on the Embankment*, forgetting is crucial not only for Glebov but also for the man he betrays, his mentor, the old "red professor" Ganchuk, who in the 1920s–30s had helped create the culture of ideological terror and repression of dissent—in other words, he had created the environment that fostered a generation of Glebovs.

Contemporary historians have noted how viciously the party had recoiled from the implicit challenge to the state mounted by these accounts of the Great Terror. These works of literature seemed to attack the Terror from all angles by questioning the truth-value of its language, its historical rationale, and its intellectual premises. The party met the threat by shutting down the discussion. In the 1980s, a new generation of writers and readers resumed the conversation, staying within the boundaries delineated by the Thaw. Decades after Trifonov's novella, there was still no social consensus about Stalinism or about the consequences and causes of the Terror. The combination of willful obliviousness and late Soviet politics meant that even with the publication of a vast quantity of previously banned material about Stalinism, the culture bore an uncomprehended burden of its traumatic past. That yawning gap in the collective historical experience persisted in the post-Soviet era.

These socio-cultural lapses created the foundation for what Alexander Etkind defines as "warped mourning":

> If the Nazi Holocaust exterminated the Other, the Soviet terror was suicidal. The self-inflicted nature of the Soviet terror has complicated the circulation of three impulses that shape the post-catastrophic world: a cognitive striving to learn about the catastrophe; an emotional desire to mourn for its victims; and an active drive to find justice and take revenge on the perpetrators.[95]

Such "warped mourning" has produced in post-Soviet literature a trend that Etkind called "Magic Historicism" (the resonance with Magic Realism is intentional) and that includes representations of the Stalinist Terror via uncanny and phantasmal imagery (Dombrovsky's *Department of Useless Things* stands as a precursor). Magic Historicism in the representation of Stalinism is found in Leonid Girshovich's *Prais* (1998), an alternative history of Russia after the 1950s, in which Soviet Jews were exiled to the far North, fulfilling Stalin's alleged plan; Vladimir Sorokin's *The Path of Bro* (*Put' Bro*, 2004, part of his *Ice Trilogy*), in which both Gulag and Nazi camps are run by a sect of Gnostics (Brothers of Light), selecting among humans the bearers of the "heavenly light"; and Dmitry Bykov's *Justification* (*Opravdanie*, 2001), where the protagonist-historian explores the idea of the Gulag as a testing lab for the selection, through torture and hardship, of the absolute best among Soviet people, without whom the victory in the Second World War would have been impossible. In Magic Historicism, the memory of the Gulag and the Great Terror functions as a cultural and political unconscious. It is a source of disturbing visions and nightmares, rather than a rationalized and safely distanced chapter of history.

However, the 2010s have seen the publication of narratives nostalgic for terror-based power, like Aleksandr Terekhov's *The Stone Bridge* (*Kamennyi most*, 2009) and Zakhar Prilepin's award-winning *The Abode* (*Obitel'*, 2014). Such novels attempt to normalize the memory of Stalinism by the conventions of romance, adventure, and the Bildungsroman. The reappearance of Stalin's image on billboards for another anniversary of the Victory, his busts in art and antique shops, as well as his monuments on Russian cities' streets, perfectly correspond to this new, disturbing turn of the cultural imagination. Apparently, "warped mourning" facilitates new returns of history.

6

Intelligentsia narratives

I T is fitting that the theme of the intelligentsia, self-consciously thinking about its own mission and history, will be the final topic of our history. Beginning in the nineteenth century, Russian literature has been preoccupied with the question of the intelligentsia's role. Both the intelligentsia and literature were (and still are) perceived in Russian culture as vehicles of social modernization and, at the same time, of moral consciousness. These terms raise the same question, only formulated in a different way. Many intelligentsia narratives address head on the potential conflict between the two: how much advocacy for change must intellectual leaders take on? How, in times of censorship and repression, can that advocacy include honest reflection on the state's behavior? How to balance the state's demand for conformity with the writer's desire to play the role of public intellectual?

Russian Marxists, particularly the Bolshevik wing of the movement, while being a direct offspring of the intelligentsia, came to despise it, seeing its representatives as either not radical enough or as too independent. In his letter to Maxim Gorky of September 15, 1919, Lenin famously called the intelligentsia not the brain, but the excrement of the nation. This attitude explains what happened after the Bolsheviks came to power: during and after the period of War Communism, Lenin's government, on the defensive and fighting for its existence, targeted thinkers and the intelligentsia. Hundreds of university professors, philosophers, economists, writers, and journalists were expelled, most notoriously in 1923, when the so-called Philosophers' Ships set sail. Expulsion and excision of disobedient *intelligenty* anticipated measures that would be taken later, most dramatically during early Stalinization, with its vigorous attempts to impose control and ideological conformity on a class of people educated before 1917. The traditional intelligentsia, descended from their nineteenth-century predecessors who believed in social activism and in individual responsibility on behalf of the whole community, was incompatible with the top-down hegemony of a single-party state in which political goals determined civic and moral values. At the same time, the regime encouraged a properly Soviet intelligentsia coming from previously uneducated classes (mostly industrial workers and craftsmen). Proletarianization and then Cultural Revolution (1928–32) sought to replace the old intelligentsia, and many fell victim to mass political repressions on trumped-up charges. A new class of educated individuals loyal to the government was emerging.

The Soviet cultural condition, however, cannot be reduced to a simplistic opposition within the intelligentsia between those who collaborated with the regime and those who resisted its pressure. The Soviet system, as a state organized around a central political idea, needed an intelligentsia able to produce cultural and ideological proofs of Soviet happiness and superiority. To motivate this work, a broad system of privileges was created, and quite a few people of different generations (including pre-revolutionary generations) joined the ranks of the system's champions: from the "Red Count" Aleksei Tolstoy, the author of the first novel about Stalin and founder of Socialist Realist historical fiction, to Sergei Mikhalkov, the offspring of a venerable aristocratic family who eventually composed two versions of the Soviet anthem and then a post-Soviet anthem as well. Other, much less conformist members of the intelligentsia were also trying to find a compromise with the Soviet system, striving to live, in Pasternak's words "in harmony with all and in accordance with legal order" ("so vsemi soobshcha i naravne s pravoporiadkom").[1] Attempts to be admitted to Soviet officialdom mark even the biographies of writers normally treated as representatives of nonconformist culture, Pil'niak and Bulgakov among them. At the same time, double-think and double-speak, where private discourse radically differed from its public form, were as widespread in the 1920s and 1930s as in the 1960s and 1970s. The numerous intelligentsia diaries from the 1920s to the 1950s published in the post-Soviet period demonstrate that this discrepancy existed even when a private conversation could cost its participants their freedom, let alone during the safer post-Stalin years, when listening to Western radio stations would become the intelligentsia's favorite pastime. However, only a minority poured their disagreement with Soviet ideology into literary texts written for the desk drawer without hope of publication. For the majority, Aesopian language or double-speak permitted an illusion of dissent alongside the possibility of serving the Soviet system.

The Soviet regime, in the expression of the historian Daniel Beer, "instrumentalized" the disciplines of the human sciences to advance a political system.[2] For individuals completely unwilling to serve the state's modernization project, the immediate prospects were dire: public shaming, exclusion from the work place, internal exile, and hard labor. Those who survived these social upheavals became bearers of the old intelligentsia's aesthetic and moral values to a younger generation in the 1960s (among them: Anna Akhmatova, Nadezhda Mandelstam, Lydia Ginzburg, Andrei Egunov, and Yakov Druskin).

The years following the death of Stalin, particularly during the Thaw, allowed a revival of the intelligentsia. The dissident movement that emerged in the 1960s, and its sympathizers, shared the nineteenth-century intelligentsia's sense of personal responsibility, anti-government attitude, and idealism. But they identified with the Decembrists, rather than with the generation of Dobroliubov and Chernyshevsky, whom they saw as paving the way for Leninism and Bolshevism. At the same time, the late 1960s and 1970s witnessed a split reminiscent of the nineteenth-century debate between Slavophiles and Westernizers. Both groups had a clearly anti-Soviet agenda and they operated in the official sphere as well as in the underground. The new generation of Slavophiles (Solzhenitsyn, the Village Prose writers, and the informal Russian Party) blamed the Soviet regime for the departure from national cultural and religious traditions and for the promotion of "alien" (read Jewish and pro-Western) cultural influences. The new Westernizers (former representatives of Youth Prose and other urban writers) believed that the USSR suffered most from its isolation from contemporary Western civilization's main advances, including civil rights, modernist culture, and consumer markets. This ideological conflict unfolded across the late Soviet period until it culminated in irreversible cultural splits between liberals and nationalists in the Perestroika period.

The 1990s witnessed a series of new splits within the intelligentsia. Some revolved around loyalty to a democratically elected post-Soviet government in the 1990s, as reflected in Andrei Sinyavsky's The Russian Intelligentsia (Russkaia intelligentsiia, 1997). After a time of active involvement in politics, the 1990s also brought deep disappointments, as well as a decline in the intelligentsia's welfare and a sense of social and political marginalization. A principle of political non-engagement was adopted by many in the late 1990s and 2000s: "the intelligentsia is the intelligentsia precisely because it keeps its distance from power," as Andrei Bitov said.[3] At the same moment, the literary scholar Mikhail Gasparov suggested that the era of the traditional

Russian intelligentsia was ending.[4] Apparently, a nonconformist political position vis-à-vis power proved to be essential in the intelligentsia's self-identification. Many felt that the intelligentsia's political ineptitude contributed to the failure of nascent democratic institutions, which allowed the Putin regime to emerge. The political developments of the 2010s, marked by growing conservative and neo-traditionalist tendencies, questioned the intelligentsia's time-honored reluctance to engage in Western-type politics and, at the same time, triggered new forms of consolidation, from public rallies to internet-based communities. Time will show whether the stringency of contemporary power structures in Russia will eventually force the intelligentsia to learn how to participate in politics more effectively. Alternatively, the intelligentsia might revert to traditional forms of idealistic and self-sacrificial behavior. With this overview in mind, we turn to the 1900s, to establish the history of the intelligentsia's self-representations across the twentieth century.

Intelligentsia narratives of the 1900s through 1920s

The story of twentieth-century intelligentsia narratives must begin before the Revolution. Casting a backward glance toward the very beginning of the twentieth century, with the knowledge that a revolution would soon change all aspects of cultural life for Russian writers and readers, it is difficult not to focus on the glaring signs of cultural decline, and it is easy to project onto the waning vestiges of imperial culture a doomed will to thrive, against all odds. Understandably, writers are expected to provide a diagnosis and to prognosticate in an era of turmoil. Those living through the period were not blind to the possibilities of a cataclysmic change; and a chain of historical catastrophes, including several wars, filled the imagination of Russians with forebodings of impending doom. Members of the intelligentsia, who had emerged into prominent positions of cultural prestige in the nineteenth century, spoke out about the meanings of events like the social unrest associated with the 1905 Revolution; about philosophical and aesthetic trends from neo-Hegelianism to resurgent Russian spirituality; and about their own significance and position, even as their leadership was challenged from various directions. Their creative self-reinventions and the challenges they faced down were mythologized by succeeding generations of writers.

Fundamental questions of matter and spirit were asked by thinkers as different as Vladimir Solov´ev, whose theories of the divine Sophia had enormous influence on the Symbolists; Petr Struve (1870–1944), for whom a range of social theories was always in play, even as he sought, in his literary essays, to understand the workings of the spirit; and Dmitry Merezhkovsky, who led the way for the Petersburg Religious-Philosophical Meetings in 1901–03, a remarkable site for open, sustained conversation between those within the Orthodox church and their secular counterparts. Conversations and publications about religious matters were a risky activity, given the church's interest in controlling theological conversations. For many of these thinkers, a more fundamental and barely concealed topic was sexuality and the body; they asked whether the body was divine or profane, and whether it was spirit, solid matter, or some combination.

A symbolically powerful event for those who resisted the more materialistic cultural theories was the publication in 1909 of the aptly named collection *Vekhi*, meaning "landmarks," which included essays by Mikhail Gershenzon (1869–1925), Sergei Bulgakov (1871–1944), Nikolai Berdiaev, and others. It went through five editions and elicited powerful public reactions in print and in public gatherings. Those strong reactions were due to several factors: the quality of writing and thinking in *Vekhi*; its arguments for spiritual freedom and religious identity in the face of the seeming rejection of these values as old-fashioned; and the remarkably well-timed emergence of the collection in the years after the 1905 Revolution, such that retrospectively, it seemed as if the volume marked a dramatic moment of historical and cultural transition. The essays ranged widely across topics in ethics, law, spirituality, Russian identity, and the place of the individual in Russian society; scholars now see far greater diversity of viewpoints within the *Vekhi* volume than was noted at the time.[5] But for the most part, and rather self-consciously, contributors foregrounded the intelligentsia's role in forming ideas of law and spirit, of right and wrong, for public consumption, even as they critiqued the intelligentsia's atheism and what many saw as its nihilism. To despise the members of the intelligentsia is a mark of membership; this paradox was in fact reiterated in Gershenzon's contribution to *Vekhi*.[6] The writers of *Vekhi* did not embrace an intelligentsia tradition seen as politically radical and spiritually empty, even if some of them had identified with the political ambitions of radical thinkers, as did Petr Struve, another contributor.[7]

The authors of *Vekhi* undeniably sought to reinvent and reimagine the role of the Russian intelligentsia in a more spiritual, religious direction. They saw a need to collaborate with the government against the danger of a new revolution in order to create a positive and modern culture. Most of them emigrated, taking with them their allegiance to this more spiritual definition of Russian identity; emigration estranged them from Soviet Russia, so their impact seemed to skip over some generations of Russian writers. But it made the delayed impact all the more powerful, for example, after the fall of the Soviet Union in the 1990s, when many of their books and essays were reissued and freshly debated. Emigration also meant that they could continue writing. Berdiaev, for example, left Soviet Russia in 1922 and settled near Paris, where he lived from 1924 until his death in 1948. He completed philosophical works in emigration that he considered among his best.

The Revolution undermined the cultural authority of the intelligentsia. It alienated and persecuted one group of intelligentsia members, and seduced another with unprecedented possibilities. Literature of the 1920s underwent similar perturbations. The most respected and intellectually influential writers variously disappeared from the scene. Many emigrated (such as Merezhkovsky and Gippius, Bunin and Gorky, Kuprin and Bely); others were persecuted, like Gumilev, executed in 1921; some died in the chaos of the Civil War (Rozanov, Khlebnikov) or from disease (Blok). On the other hand, many former Futurists and young writers born in the 1890s and 1900s experienced the post-revolutionary decade as a dramatic time full of aspirations and opportunities. They wrote their way into new forms of self-definition as members of the intellectual vanguard, if not elite.

Narratives about the intelligentsia became one of the most widespread genres in the literature of the 1920s, as a potentially very long list of examples could show. The search for a new place in (or outside of) a rapidly changing country was intertwined with the question of responsibility for the Revolution and ensuing terror. A revision of the intelligentsia's cultural and political agenda and its self-justifications was underway. The resulting texts, many of them novels, gave some account of the transformation of intelligentsia identity: once a driving force of the Revolution, members of the intelligentsia were later its victim. But the treatment of this acute paradox varied. Schematically, the two possibilities can be designated by Gorky's *Klim Samgin* (*Zhizn' Klima Samgina*, begun in 1925) on the one side, and Mandelstam's *Egyptian Stamp* on the other.

Maxim Gorky left *The Life of Klim Samgin* unfinished at his death, after eleven years of work. Its four volumes show us a hero who is distanced from the ideologies and political trends he witnesses over four decades; what looks like his failure to engage may now be read as a perspicacious readiness to regard emerging ideologies as suspect and inherently violent. Richard Freeborn has claimed that the novel "showed up more clearly than any other literary work of the post-revolutionary period the complexities and paradoxes of choice that faced the intelligentsia in pre-1917 Russia."[8] Gorky created a broad and excitingly diverse panorama of the passionate debates that began in the 1880s and continued right up to the Revolution. Klim Samgin is presented as a paradigmatic representative of the intelligentsia and its stereotypical vices. Gorky discredits him by showing that his desire to preserve his individuality from the cacophony of ideological doctrines, like his attempts to stand apart from the turbulent movements of history, drives him to increasingly open conservatism. The result is half-conscious collaboration with the political police. In effect, Gorky argues that the intelligentsia's fixation on individual values leads its representatives away from participation in history; their actions justify their marginalization.

Mandelstam, by comparison, centers his more modernist, fragmented narrative in *The Egyptian Stamp* on the psychological traumas left by the Revolution. The hero is Parnok, mentally crushed as an individual human being. He is shocked when a petty thief is lynched in the summer of 1917 (after the February Revolution, but before the events of October), a scene that stands for the violence of the Revolution as a whole. Parnok is the author's double, creating an estranging shift of perception. Such defamiliarization by historical trauma, according to Mandelstam, stimulates the birth of new literature and a new vision. The trauma pushes the subject away from the mainstream of history, granting in reward the sense of freedom— freedom from a history driven by violent ideologies, and eventually, the freedom of self-invention and self-creation.[9]

Representation of the intelligentsia's victimization reaches its fully mature form in the work of writers who came into their own after the Revolution: Mikhail Bulgakov, Yuri Olesha, and Konstantin Vaginov. A former venereologist and military doctor, Mikhail Bulgakov depicted the intelligentsia's bitter deception by the Revolution in the novel *White Guard* (*Belaia gvardiia*, 1923), later reworked into the play *Days of the Turbins*. For the Turbin family, the Revolution brought humiliation, chaos, and death. Yet despite this bleak and sometimes horrifying background, the general tone of both the novel and the play is surprisingly uplifting and humorous: the author cannot (and does not want to) hide his admiration for the ethics and lifestyle of this intelligentsia family. The Turbins and their friends are depicted as people who preserved their sense of duty toward Russia despite the catastrophic circumstances (as opposed to various governments fighting for domination). In Evgeny Dobrenko's interpretation, the Russian state, represented by "the headquarters scoundrels," betrays its best sons, but they cannot betray Russia, which for the Turbins is at once greater than any form of government and smaller than an abstract Motherland.[10] For the Turbins, a warm family home, filled with love and joy, hidden from catastrophic history behind "cream-colored curtains," is their real motherland. Pictures of the Carpenter of Saardam—the young Peter the Great—decorate their hearth, nicely connecting the ethos of their home with Russian Enlightenment and with Russian Europeanization. These values prove to be more resilient than loyalty to military officials or faith in the pious qualities of the "simple folk." This is why the most heroic act (performed by Colonel Malyshev in the novel and by Colonel Aleksei Turbin in the play) is associated with a decision to defy military duty—a release of cadets who are eager to fight against Petliura's 10,000-bayonet army and undoubtedly would have died in a senseless battle. Saving the lives of these young men from intelligentsia families appears as the sole way to save essential Russian values in this time of national catastrophe.

From this very personal experience of the Revolution, Bulgakov would later arrive at a conviction expressed cogently in his Letter to the Government (1930)—a request to leave the USSR based on the evidence of the incompatibility of his talent and convictions with the Soviet cultural and political mainstream.[11] Bulgakov wrote there of his "deep skepticism towards the revolutionary process which was taking place in my backward country...."[12] This complex representation of the intelligentsia appears in his satirical allegories *The Fatal Eggs* and *The*

Heart of a Dog. Each of these tales focuses on a scientist, Professor Persikov in *The Fatal Eggs* and Doctor Preobrazhensky in *The Heart of a Dog.* Their scientific profession links them to Enlightenment rationalism, and both professors serve science with panache. Their quests for knowledge confront the chaos and ruin of post-revolutionary life, dispelling the supposedly objective character of their science.

In both tales, a great discovery metaphorically associated with the Revolution appears as an accidental byproduct of scientific investigation. In *The Fatal Eggs*, a ray of life is discovered. It speeds up time, accelerating the Darwinian survival of the fittest, and producing a generation of hungry and aggressive monsters:

> In a few instants, these organisms reached their full growth and maturity, merely to produce new generations in their turn. The red strip and then the entire disk quickly became overcrowded, and the inevitable struggle began. The newborn amoebas furiously attacked one another, tearing their victims to shreds and gobbling them. Among the newly born lay the tattered corpses of those which had fallen in the battle for survival. Victory went to the best and the strongest. And these best ones were terrifying.... They were distinguished by extraordinary viciousness and motility.[13]

If the intelligentsia produces revolutionary monsters, is it responsible for them? In *The Fatal Eggs*, Persikov's discovery has disastrous results, but only partially because of his naiveté. It is official support from an incompetent enthusiast that leads to catastrophe. Reptile eggs are delivered instead of the expected chicken eggs, and Persikov's magic rays produce not more chickens but enormous and aggressive snakes, toads, lizards, and other reptiles, and havoc ensues. Persikov dies in the end, sacrificed as a scapegoat:

> Persikov made a step back, barring the door to the study . . . and spread out his arms, as one *crucified.* He wanted to prevent the mob from entering, and he cried out with irritation "This is complete madness, You are utterly *wild beasts.*" . . . A short man with *apelike, crooked* legs, in a torn jacket and a tattered, twisted shirt, dashed out ahead of the others, leaped toward Persikov, and with a frightful blow of a stick opened his skull.[14]

The animalistic motifs are repeated in the description of invading gigantic reptiles created by the misused ray of life: devolution and dehumanization, suggests Bulgakov, directly follow from the Revolution.

In *The Heart of a Dog*, the experiment—another metaphor for the Revolution—also fails. One monster appears as a dog transformed into a man named Sharikov. He takes center stage and starts harassing his creator and all others around him. Bulgakov embodies in Sharikov a distorted version of the Bolshevik utopian concept of the new man, superior due to class origin. Doctor Preobrazhensky tries to improve Sharikov's behavior by pedagogical means, without any success. Preobrazhensky's ideological opponent, the Bolshevik Shvonder, head of the housing committee and the mouth-piece of Soviet ideology, flatters Sharikov and does not urge him to repress his bestial instinct (they prove that he belongs to the "toiling masses"). Preobrazhensky decides to reverse his operation and justifies his decision in a monologue against attempts to speed up evolution. Unlike *The Fatal Eggs*, which was published in the Soviet press, *The Heart of a Dog* was confiscated by the OGPU in 1926 but returned to the author (after Gorky's intervention) three years later. It was first published only in 1968 in a Frankfurt-based Russian magazine; however, it circulated in *samizdat* as of the 1930s.

Bulgakov, a native of Kiev, had arrived in Moscow from Vladikavkaz in 1921. The life story of Yuri Olesha was similar: he came to Moscow from his native Odessa in 1922. For a while, they even worked at the same newspaper, *Gudok (The Whistle).* Olesha continued the investigation of the intelligentsia launched by Bulgakov. But he adopted a different strategy, using several conflicting characters to represent the intelligentsia, thus radically complicating the question of responsibility for the Revolution. His most famous work, the novel *Envy*, clearly revealed something unresolved about the nature of Soviet modernity: debates about this novel began with its first publication in 1927 and have never died down.[15]

On the surface, *Envy* explores an ideological conflict between two intelligentsia parties: one that has chosen unquestionable support for the Revolution and service to its larger goals, and the other whose internal opposition stems from faith in the priority of individual values over those of the collective. The veteran Bolshevik Andrei Babichev, now a Soviet dignitary, the "director of the trust of food industry," has created an innovative industrial giant named The Quarter (*Chetvertak*), which will produce cheap and healthy sausages for the masses. Then there is his adopted son, Volodia Makarov, a football player, and future husband to Andrei's niece Valia. Their critics and "envious" opponents are Nikolai Kavalerov, a homeless poet, and his mentor and symbolic father, Andrei's brother Ivan, a fabulous and mysterious inventor. All these characters convert ideological differences into weapons in their struggle for Valia, Ivan's daughter. She lives in Andrei's home but is intended as a future bride for Makarov, while Kavalerov is secretly in love with her.[16]

Each side of the conflict in *Envy* is equipped with its "machine of desires." Andrei dedicates himself to the Constructivist modernization of the Soviet everyday—and his Quarter emerges as a blueprint for the rationalized future. Makarov (an athlete and new man) confesses to Andrei: "I'm a man-machine.... If I haven't turned into one yet, I want to...."[17] Ivan Babichev also constantly invents fantastic machines, although they are irrational and whimsical, like his childhood invention that may or may not be preprogramming dreams. His creativity reaches its zenith in the invisible machine named Ophelia. In fact, this is an anti-machine: Babichev admits, "I gave the basest of human emotions to the greatest creation of technology! I disgraced the machine."[18]

Another anti-machine contrasted with Volodya's athletic body is Nikolai Kavalerov's optics and imagination, producing an endless stream of extravagant metaphors and similes. These poetic mechanisms of new vision are similar to Shklovsky's defamiliarization. Kavalerov's power of estrangement constitutes real competition to the Quarter. If the latter intends to restructure everyday life, Kavalerov's (and, of course, Olesha's) metaphors restructure the reader's perception of the world, thus reaching far deeper than Andrei Babichev can begin to imagine. Kavalerov's metaphors resonate with modernist and avant-garde art, a parallel suggested by critics in the 1920s, who compared his style to that of Cézanne, Van Gogh, Gauguin, Picasso, and the Cubists.[19] Andrei's and Volodya's positions convey Futurist and Constructivist ideologies; their opponents' joint project is more complex and innovative. Ivan Babichev reproduces the arguments of Dostoevsky's underground man. Freedom, he argues, includes "most trivial human feelings" and presupposes the liberation of the unconscious. In the second part of the novel, Olesha forcefully leads Ivan and Kavalerov to their downfall. But historical defeat will affect the winners as much as the losers. Despite the characters' apparent antagonism, the novel presents all these projects for the future as interconnected and interdependent: the persecution of creative freedom epitomized by Ivan Babichev and Nikolai Kavalerov would be destructive for rationalist utopianism. Mutual hatred dooms both intelligentsia parties to tragic defeat and inevitable victimization.

Konstantin Vaginov, a Petersburg poet and prose writer, is best remembered for two novels. *The Goat's Song* (*Kozlinaia pesn'*, 1928) and *The Works and Days of Svistonov* (*Trudy i dni Svistonova*, 1929) represent young intellectuals as strangely ineffectual, unable either to understand the historical significance of events around them or to incarnate the spiritual values they see as disappearing in the ruins of the present. Vaginov, the son of a tsarist gendarme colonel who was a Red Army soldier during the Civil War, lived out those mixed allegiances and experiences in his own life. He preferred to write with a goose-feather quill by candlelight; he could dance the minuet and the écossaise, was a passionate bibliophile and numismatist; and he joined several quite different Petrograd literary groups, including OBERIU. He surely escaped political repression by an untimely death from tuberculosis. His novels, published in Petrograd along with his two collections of poetry, were almost completely forgotten (and his other works remained unpublished) until the 1970s, when they reappeared in Western publications and then in Russian editions in the late 1980s.[20]

Vaginov's outlook on the victimization of the intelligentsia was radically different from that of Bulgakov or Olesha. His *Goat's Song* has been interpreted both as tragedy and as a comedic, even carnivalesque text. Vaginov does indeed depict a tragedy of the best intelligentsia minds crushed by the new era, the sacrificial goats of the novel's title. Yet he does not just mourn the decline of the Russian intelligentsia under the Soviets, "but with the morose cheerfulness of a coroner captures the disintegration of his characters, who have, unnoticeably to themselves, morphed into the living dead."[21] One of the central characters in *The Goat's Song* is Teptyolkin, an erudite and polyglot philologist, who in the midst of the Civil War gave lectures on Novalis, Homer, and Dante in a southern town, leaving his listeners ecstatic. For good reason, he describes himself and his circle as a final Renaissance island: "In the sea of dogmatism encircling us, we—and only we—have kept the lights of criticism burning. We alone have preserved a respect for scholarship, for the sciences and for man. Acknowledging neither lord nor servant, we have taken our stand on this high tower, against whose granite base the furious waves pound and beat."[22] The Unknown Poet, another protagonist of the novel, compares Teptyolkin's circle with the last pagan poets in the era of early Christianity: "What blasphemy to claim that with the triumph of Christianity the great pagan poets and philosophers of antiquity vanished into thin air! No one understood them; no one had the most rudimentary notion of what they were all about. And so they perished. How lonely these last philosophers must have been, how lonely."[23]

Why, despite these lofty parallels, does Teptyolkin at the end of the novel turn into "a distinguished, albeit obtuse, bureaucrat"?[24] Vaginov questions the concept of culture promoted by Teptyolkin, who venerates it in a truly religious way, isolating its elevated aspects and obfuscating everything else. An idea of culture as a museum of exclusively positive values is the basis for his conversion into a dogmatic Marxist and seems built into the title of the magnum opus he writes, called *The Hierarchy of Meanings*. He dogmatically excludes everything that fails to fit the framework of the eternal, spiritual, and classically beautiful. Vaginov thus links the intelligentsia's quasi-religious attitude towards its cultural legacy and Soviet dogmatism: both ideologies empower their followers by removing contradictions, and by obscuring dark and debased aspects of reality and culture. Teptyolkin-like *intelligenty* fail to be a last bastion of humanist ideals and instead join the chorus of new fanatics. This is indeed the intelligentsia's "goat song" (a literal translation of the Greek "tragedy" and another meaning of the title), in which the highest degree of victimization is achieved through voluntary association with history's victors.

Teptyolkin is not the sole protagonist of *The Goat's Song*. By intertwining his story with those of the Unknown Poet, Kostia Rotikov, and Asfodeliev, Vaginov elaborates a vision of culture that might have become the foundation for dignified resistance to the forces of destruction and dogmatism of "the new Christianity." Paradoxically, he situates this intellectual (and political) position in playfulness, what he calls the "word in a theatrical costume."[25] Such playfulness suggests an ability to see in culture not only luminous ideals, but also abject depravity and chaos, kitsch and comedy—and to absorb these qualities without surrendering to oversimplification, glossing over contradictions, and falling into the sin of a new religiosity, whether preservationist or revolutionary.

Intelligentsia narratives of the 1930s through 1950s

A myriad of Socialist Realist works of the 1930s–50s exposed a conflict between seemingly bad and good representatives of the intelligentsia. The former stubbornly defend their outdated values and suffer moral or physical defeat. The latter gradually attain the understanding necessary to see humanism as a false ideology, and give it up for the "higher humanism" of the proletarian revolution, including the justification and even admiration for state terror against class enemies. For this metamorphosis, the new order rewards the protagonist, despite any non-proletarian origins, with social acceptance and family happiness.

Works of this kind reprise the Bildungsroman to show the moral evolution of intelligentsia heroes as they reconcile their service to the socialist revolutionary cause and its human cost. An exemplary novel featuring this struggle was written by Aleksei Tolstoy, whose political convictions were very far from pro-Bolshevik when he emigrated in 1919 and even when he returned to Petrograd in 1923.[26] However, his novelistic trilogy *The Road to Calvary* laid the foundation for the model Soviet "novel with history." In such a novel, as Maria Litovskaia put it, "one had to fuse 'love,' 'adventure,' and the history of the Bolshevik Communist Party so that fictional characters' life-stories would correspond to the events of the 'grand historical narratives.'"[27] Centered around two young women from the Petersburg intelligentsia at the time of Revolution and Civil War, Tolstoy's novel is full of melodramatic situations, astonishing plot twists, and accidental meetings. In the end, both heroines find happiness, and their beloved men join the Reds and accept communism as the new stabilizing force for the Russian state. In the final scene, all four are listening to a speech about the electrification of Russia, next to Lenin and Stalin in the same audience, and dreaming about their future happiness. The plot has some surface convolutions, but the central characters are entirely stable: they do not give up their values or sacrifice any part of their personalities. And Tolstoy avoids the issue of the intelligentsia's guilt or responsibility for the Revolution: "The pervasive theme of intelligentsia and the revolution in the mid-1920s receives a new, optimistic interpretation: the healthy gravitates to the healthy, and the sick, having undergone suffering, can be restored to health."[28]

Yet there is something fantastic in Tolstoy's version of the intelligentsia narrative. It is symptomatic of Soviet prudishness fashionable in the 1930s that in a context dominated by the turbulence of civil war and more than a few predatory men, these two sisters remain unerringly faithful to an ideal of monogamy. This chaste approach to erotic desire was gladly accepted by the wider readership and eventually laid the foundation for Soviet mass literature. Intelligentsia narratives also mixed melodramatic adventure and official historical narratives, as found in Konstantin Fedin's trilogy *First Joys* (*Pervye radosti*, 1945), *An Extraordinary Summer* (*Neobyknovennoe leto*, 1947–48), and *The Bonfire* (*Koster*, 1961, 1965); and Ilya Erenburg's novels *The Fall of Paris* (*Padenie Parizha*, 1941) and *The Tempest*. These would become the most profitable popular genres among official writers, and their lengthy family sagas became the scripts for the first Soviet TV soap operas. During Perestroika, this genre inspired several huge anti-Stalinist novelistic cycles, including Anatoly Rybakov's continuation of *The Children of Arbat* in *1935 and Other Years* (*Tridtsat' piatyi i drugie gody*, 1988), *Fear* (*Strakh*, 1990), and *Dust and Ash* (*Prakh i pepel*, 1996), and Vasily Aksyonov's trilogy *The Moscow Saga* (*Moskovskaia saga*, 1993–94).

In Boris Pasternak's *Doctor Zhivago*, begun in 1945 and completed in 1955, melodramatic love, adventure, and the history of the Revolution and Civil War appear as expected. Yet in important ways, the novel represents a complete inversion of both the typical Soviet intelligentsia narrative and the Bildungsroman. Centered around two couples, Yuri Zhivago and his wife Tonia, and Lara Gishar and Pasha Antipov, *Doctor Zhivago* (in contradistinction to *The Road to Calvary*) depicts history as a destructive force, ruining human ties, and finally shattering all hope. In

Aleksei Tolstoy's novel, the intelligentsia characters gradually come to fully accept the Revolution, but Pasternak shows the opposite trajectory. Yuri's evolution begins with infatuation with the revolutionary "surgery"; later he grows disappointed with its goals and methods. He finally comes to understand the revolutionary changes as nothing more than brutal violence:

> Reshaping life! People who can say that have never understood a thing about life—they have never felt its breath, its heart—how very much they have seen or done. They look on it as a lump of raw material which needs to be processed by them, to be ennobled by their touch. But life is never a material, a substance to be moulded. If you want to know, life is the principle of self-renewal, it is constantly renewing and remaking and changing and transfiguring itself, it is infinitely beyond your or my theories about it.[29]

Yuri is portrayed as a personification of the intellectual aspects of the life force. His beloved Lara also embodies life, but she is complementary to Yuri, on a more emotional and intuitive plane. Yuri's fate—he is forced to abandon both medicine and literature after the Revolution—has social as well as philosophical meaning. His life story is very different from that of Aleksei Tolstoy's characters, who safely cross the minefield of the Revolution and Civil War without damaging their values or their optimism. Pasternak's novel by comparison pushes forward the perspective of universal degradation—social, cultural, and even anthropological. Lara ends crushed in the Gulag, and their daughter Tania Bezocheredova appears in the Epilogue as a person whose memory and language skills are crippled, an orphan who never knew her parents and who is completely cut off from the traditions of the intelligentsia. Those intelligentsia members who survive historical ordeals typically become sincere conformists. Referring to them, Yuri says, addressing a childhood friend, "I found it painful to listen to you, Nicky, when you told us how you were re-educated and grew up in jail. It was like listening to a circus horse describing how it broke itself in.... Men who are not free, he thought, always idealize their bondage."[30] Such sentences guaranteed that the novel's manuscript would be rejected, as it was, even by *Novyi mir* and *Literary Moscow*, the most liberal publications of the Thaw period.

Pasternak depicts Yuri Zhivago as his alter ego, voicing his most profound thoughts about Russian history, revolution, and culture. Since Yuri is a poet, and the novel ends with a cycle of his poetry, *Doctor Zhivago* can be read as a Künstlerroman, a novel about the growth and evolution of an artist.[31] The assemblage of Yuri's twenty-five poems metaphorically replays the most important scenes of the novel in an emotional, rather than diegetic, summary of Yuri's individual path, which has many parallels to the path of Jesus. The last seven poems also comprise a micro-cycle about Jesus, his death, and expected resurrection. The surname Zhivago derives from the adjective meaning "alive"; this genitive form (*zhivago*) is also an attribute of God in Orthodox prayer. The novel thus has a Christian overlay to the tale of an individual talent desperately fighting the overwhelmingly dehumanizing pressures of history and society. *Doctor Zhivago* portrays the Bolshevik Revolution as a force that destroys the values of an individual life for the sake of abstract ideas and utopian goals; it stampedes the best representatives of the intelligentsia, and smashes human bonds.

This philosophy did not necessarily find an optimal vehicle in the genre of the novel, and many discerning readers, from Akhmatova to Shalamov and Czesław Miłosz, regarded *Doctor Zhivago* as an artistic failure.[32] The reliance on an improbably high number of coincidences and haphazard meetings drew criticism, and was seen to undermine the novel's verisimilitude. The abundance of coincidences might have accurately conveyed the helter-skelter quality of life in a historically tumultuous period, but it achieves the opposite effect. Similarly, the character development has seemed unsuccessful. For instance, Pasternak hardly ever displays the genius of Yuri Zhivago—the poetry is held back until after the epilogue—because in his understanding his protagonist's gift lies in an openness to life expressed, above all, in his attitude to nature. The intended effect backfires: the hero seems remarkable largely by virtue of his confidence in his own greatness, which becomes a gift bestowed on contemporaries privileged to live in his time and know him.

The reception of *Doctor Zhivago* revealed the need for new approaches to the novel, which, in turn, have enriched the understanding of Russian modernism. For example, Boris Gasparov proposed that Pasternak's novel could be read by analogy with a musical text organized by counterpoint. Pasternak unfolds the concept of history, presented in the novel by Yuri's uncle Nikolai Vedeniapin, by means of such a counterpoint. This vision of history suggests that important events emerge in the midst of life's stream, being born from the mundane rather than from something great. Coincidences thus function as counterpoints revealing the meaning of modern history couched in layers of ideology.[33] Igor Smirnov reads *Doctor Zhivago* as a commentary on the entire culture of the twentieth century. In his view, Pasternak's polemical depiction of literary and historical figures or popular philosophical theories is not self-sufficient. These intertexts combine in a unique verbal fresco that critiques utopian thought: "The critique of utopianism in *Doctor Zhivago* reached universal proportions. Pasternak debated not a particular utopia, but utopian thinking taken in a broad perspective: it is a meta-dystopian history of utopias."[34]

Doctor Zhivago resonated deeply with other unofficial narratives of the period. In the same year when Pasternak was completing his novel, the émigré writer Mark Aldanov finished his last novel, *The Suicide (Samoubiistvo)*. It unfolds a broad panorama of Russia and Europe prior to the Revolution of 1917. Very different characters—from the intelligentsia couple, the Lastochkins, to a famous tycoon and supporter of the Revolution, Savva Morozov, from Emperor Franz-Joseph to Lenin—appear in the novel united by the motif of suicide, personal or political. In Aldanov's logic, the Revolution is situated beyond the borders of the narrative, much like the experience of death is situated beyond the limits of human experience; it appears as a colossal gesture of suicide for Russia and its intelligentsia.

A marginalized and Christ-like figure of the artist also appears in a founding text of Soviet underground literature, *The Master and Margarita* by Mikhail Bulgakov. Because the novel, written in 1928–40, was published only in 1966–67, it is doubtful, although not completely impossible, that Pasternak was familiar with it when writing *Doctor Zhivago*. Yet the typological parallelism is more significant in this case than a possible influence. In Marietta Chudakova's interpretation, both novels tell the story of a Second Coming.[35] They represent the post-revolutionary world as post-apocalyptic, challenging their fictional heroes to recognize the advent of that new order.

In Bulgakov's novel, the story of an autobiographical character, the Master, unfolds in parallel to the last stages of the life of Christ, called by his Aramaic name Yeshua Ha-Nozri. In the Jerusalem sequence, Bulgakov recounts Christ's execution and death (without resurrection), a tale that approaches blasphemy. *The Master and Margarita* associates the Second Coming not with Christ but with Satan or Mephistopheles; under the name of Woland, he descends on Soviet Moscow with a band of demonic tricksters. With these parallel tales, Bulgakov crumbles the foundations of sacred narratives, exposing traditional moral values in all their weakness.

Boris Gasparov argues that Bulgakov radically transforms familiar myths to integrate them into his own individual mythology.[36] Gasparov sees in *The Master and Margarita* a culmination of the plots that define Bulgakov's writings about artists: *The Crimson Island (Bagrovyi ostrov,* 1928), *Life of Molière (Zhizn' gospodina de Mol'era,* 1933), *The Last Days of Pushkin (Poslednie dni,* written in 1934–35), and *The Theater Novel (Teatral'nyi roman,* 1937). In *Master and Margarita,*

Bulgakov creates a synthesis of the Gospels, the Book of Revelation, and *Faust*, placing at the center of his myth the writer himself, who has the miraculous ability to create his double through a work of art. Behind the writer must stand a higher power able to sustain the protagonist and protect his word against a hostile world. Out of this basic thematic matrix, numerous plots emerge, lending a mythic character to stories about the survival of the artist. Gasparov's mythopoetic analysis is but one trend in the large body of critical literature dedicated to *The Master and Margarita*. Scholarship focused on deciphering the novel's intertexts and symbols has also flourished. The deciphering often leads to biographical and political contexts; speculations about Woland as a figure for Stalin are especially popular.[37]

Alternatively, the symbols and references are read as a residue of esoteric occult and mythological systems.[38] A number of scholars have established connections between the modernist poetics of the novel and its moral philosophy, which under closer examination is seen to have little in common with Christianity. For example, Justin Weir focuses on meta-fictional poetics in *The Master and Margarita* (the novel within the novel), demonstrating that this device undermines "the tyranny of degraded reason in Soviet society" and triggers "the loss of epistemological certainty."[39] Bulgakov thereby creates a new model of authorship, or more broadly, subjectivity, echoed in the multiple coexisting narratives (which also creates a schizophrenic effect): "The act of claiming responsibility for one's beliefs" becomes "a step in authorship" as much as it is "the constitution of a self"; authorship, as a result, replaces any "profession of faith."[40]

Instead of faithfulness to traditional (Judeo-Christian) moral norms, Bulgakov highlights the fidelity in Yeshua, the Master, and Margarita to themselves, to their individual sense of moral intuition. The theme of staying true to oneself emerges as an imperative and is imprinted with the author's (and presumed readers') experience surviving the years of revolution, war, and growing terror. Villains at Woland's ball are celebrated exactly because they are free of cowardice—ironically, they are also true to themselves, to their distorted identities, which lack "moral intuition."

The Master is similar to Yeshua, true, but more importantly, Yeshua resembles a contemporary *intelligent*. Well-educated and yet deprived of rights and power, Yeshua preserves faith in humanism. Although marginalized, alone, and mocked for his idealism, he insists: "There are no evil people in the world" and "every kind of power is a form of violence against people."[41] To Pilate's famous question, "What is truth?" Yeshua provides an answer emphasizing the provisional and subject-centered nature of all truth: "The truth is, first of all, that your head aches, so badly, in fact, that you're having fainthearted thoughts about death."[42] Bulgakov depicts both Yeshua and the Master as weak and defenseless; their ability to stay true to an inner self impedes survival skills; their nonconformism is not an affirmative, chosen act but something inevitable, out of their control.

Through Pontius Pilate, one of the earliest sympathetically depicted cynics in Russian literature, Bulgakov locates modern cynicism at the foundation point of Judeo-Christian civilization. Although Pilate knows that Yeshua is not guilty, out of fear he betrays himself and his moral instinct when he sends the wandering philosopher to a torturous execution. In this respect, he is not unlike Berlioz, an intellectual sell-out, or the Soviet literary critics who secretly recognize the real value of the Master's novel about Pontius Pilate even as they brutally condemn it: "the authors of these articles weren't saying what they wanted to say, and...that was why they were so furious."[43] Unlike them, Pilate tries to make amends with the secret order to kill Judas and through acts of repentance. His self-betrayal is what Yeshua (or rather Afranius, who could be Woland in disguise)[44] dubs cowardice, "one of the worst of all human vices."[45] Pilate (or is it the author?) echoes the vindication: "No, philosopher, I disagree with you: it is the most terrible vice!"[46]

Pilate overshadows Yeshua as a literary character, just as the Master is eclipsed by the victims of the pranks that Woland and his retinue perform in the Moscow chapters. These characters manifest the negative side of truthfulness to oneself. Bulgakov depicts the Soviet world not as a regime of class hatred, but rather as a realm of unrestrained cynicism and conformism: everyone constantly betrays all that is valuable, including their inner beliefs, for minimal benefit.[47] As tricksters, Woland and his gang relativize all values, which is why good and bad individuals fall victim to them indiscriminately. Woland and his associates flaunt everyday Soviet cynicism in a joyful way, creating a theatrical show, a ball, a cascade of jokes and puns, and a clownish performance, albeit with consequential gunfights and fires. To interpret the performances of Woland and his gang selectively or to see them simply as moral retribution against evildoers would mean failing to recognize the complex ethical texture of the novel. Those characters' place in *The Master and Margarita*, and the help Woland provides to the Master and especially to Margarita, suggest that Bulgakov tries to augment the position of nonconformist intelligentsia by the tricksters' skills and their peculiar philosophy.

Bulgakov's novel attained phenomenal popularity in the 1970s–2000s, when it became something like a secular bible. It also influenced many other writers, from the Strugatsky brothers in *The Lame Fate* (*Khromaia sud 'ba*, 1971–82) and *The Doomed City* (*Grad obrechennyi*, written 1975, published 1988–89) to the more light-hearted Vladimir Orlov in *The Viola Player Danilov* (*Altist Danilov*, 1980). It became an enduring theatrical sensation when staged by Yuri Liubimov in the Moscow Taganka Theater (1977 and for many seasons thereafter).

The novel's extraordinary popularity may also have come from its having wrenched the intelligentsia narrative away from the Bildungsroman, at least for the moment. No longer was the novel bound by a commitment to show the ideological progress of its hero. Debates about the fate of the novel in the twentieth century were also temporarily quieted by Bulgakov's success, although it has to be said that he did not end the crisis in the novel. And the success of his novel on the stage and the integration of poetry into Pasternak's *Doctor Zhivago* both suggest that novelistic fiction did not maintain a monopoly on the tale of the intelligentsia at the middle of the twentieth century. For the most part, that is not a problem taken up by lyric poetry, although we conclude our discussion of this topic by turning to a telling exception.

CASE STUDY Osip Mandelstam's "I lost my way in the sky..."

Osip Mandelstam's relationship to the Revolution and literary politics in the 1920s charts a complex trajectory. Although never an enemy either of the peasantry or the proletariat (he wrote about both with sympathy into the 1930s), he found himself at odds with the increasingly top-down ideological approach to art and also out of sympathy with the personal politics of many colleagues in the Writers' Union. In 1929, a scandal involving a charge of plagiarism, from which Mandelstam was exonerated, would inspire him to lash out at sanctimony and hypocrisy, which he called "literary malice" (*literaturnaia zlost'*) in *The Fourth Prose*, an apologia without apology that is one of the great defenses of creative freedom and the humane values of the intelligentsia.

Circumstances such as the end of NEP, cultural revolution, and state control of the Writers' Union had created a harrowing atmosphere, and while Mandelstam continued to publish as late as 1933, like many other members of the liberal intelligentsia, he felt marginalized. He vented his dismay in a short, savage satire known as the "Stalin Epigram" ("We live, not feeling the land beneath us" ["My zhivem pod soboiu ne chuia strany," 1933]). The poem was leaked to the authorities, Mandelstam was arrested, and he and his wife were exiled, eventually to Voronezh. Although the sentence was open-ended, the

Mandelstams were convinced rightly that he was living on borrowed time. In the course of his years in Voronezh, Mandelstam became *persona non grata* with the literary establishment. Barred in practice from the pages of literary journals, he continued to hope to publish at least "cycles" from the *Voronezh Notebooks* in the *Literary Gazette*. The miracle is that he continued to write, in what was to be his final creative burst in the 1930s.

Although Mandelstam wrote several poems directly addressing Stalinism, his major strategy involved indirect cultural references that placed the tragic experience of the twentieth-century Russian intelligentsia, from which Mandelstam did not separate himself, into a broad historical and cultural context. More in his poetry than in his prose, doubts about the character of the Revolution and its commitment to better goals surfaced. In the *Voronezh Notebooks*, the political terror that emanates from the Kremlin becomes inescapable, however distant. But the search for a greater freedom kept utopia alive and sublimated it into fantasies of escape from the stifling social and political confinement.

Among the late poems, "I lost my way in the sky" (one of a pair with a genetic doublet from the *Third Voronezh Notebook*, the last and shortest grouping of lyrics written between March and April of 1937) conveys through its highly condensed language the despondency and creative disorientation of an *intelligent*.

Заблудился я в небе—что делать?
Тот, кому оно близко,—ответь…
Легче было вам, Дантовых девять
Атлетических дисков, звенеть.

Не разнять меня с жизнью—ей снится
Убивать—и сейчас же ласкать,
Чтобы в уши, в глаза и в глазницы
Флорентийская била тоска.

Не кладите же мне, не кладите
Остролаский лавр на виски,
Лучше сердце мое расколите
Вы на синего звона куски…

И когда я умру, отслуживши,
Всех живущих прижизненный друг,
Чтоб раздался и шире и выше
Отзвук неба во всю мою грудь!

9(?) марта 1937[48]

I lost my way in the sky—what to do?
Answer, you to whom it is close…
It was easier for you, Dante's nine
Athletic spheres, to resound.

I cannot be parted from life: it dreams
Of killing and then straightaway cosseting,
So that Florentine yearning will penetrate
My ears, eyes and eye-sockets.

Do not lay upon me, please do not lay
An angular-caressing laurel on my temples,

> It would be better if you split my heart
> Into pieces of blue sound . . .
>
> And when I perish, having done my service,
> A friend in my lifetime to all the living
> It will be so that, deeper and higher,
> The echo of the sky will fill my chest!

Dante is the master poet invoked here, and his presence invites and warrants the application of allegorical thinking. An interpretation of the poem that proceeds through various levels of meaning (the literal, the moral, the anagogical) follows the hermeneutic method that was part of the interpretative and creative tradition of the exegesis and composition of medieval classics. Two of Mandelstam's favorite works, the *Divine Comedy* and the *Roman de la Rose*, were steeped in the use of allegory to create meaning and to filter experience.

Who is speaking here, under what circumstances, and where? Within a landscape or interior vision that we cannot quite visualize, we perceive that the poem involves a scenario of losing one's way and an appeal for help, the speaker's fear for his life, confusion about whether his life hangs in the balance, yearning for another place, and a prayer not to be awarded poetic laurels lest some murderous sanction follow. Some editions of the poem provide the verb "to sleep" for "to die" in line 5, a clear euphemism for death but a contrasting and gentler posthumous vision. The first and last stanzas provide an arc of movement from anxiety to calm, from dislocation to comfort; the two internal stanzas concentrate feelings of anguish whose origins are not immediately clear, although stanza 2 cites yearning, a retrospective feeling, and stanza 3 anticipates a future torture the speaker hopes to avoid. Readers may also feel that the syntax of the poem creates an occasion for getting lost. Pronouns without clear antecedents, sudden changes of subject, and other syntactic disruptions make the first quatrain alone twisted and enigmatic, a verbal icon of the subject of lost bearings.

Losses of different kinds through parting, forgetting, and misremembering comprise a reflex in Mandelstam's verse. They often occasion concomitant moments of self-awareness and taking stock. Readers already familiar with Mandelstam will recognize the links between the metapoetic discourse in his poetry and his views on the psychology of perception and the nature of poetic inspiration (explored at length in his *Conversation about Dante* [*Razgovor o Dante*, 1933]). This poem too names Dante. Always a keen student of medieval French philology and literature, the subjects he studied at the Sorbonne and Heidelberg, Mandelstam learned Italian in the early 1930s in order to read Dante (and Petrarch) in the original. He took *The Divine Comedy* to Voronezh, and it was a fecund source of images, inspiration, and opportunity to meditate on exile. Mandelstam's intense engagement with Dante culminated in his *Conversation about Dante*, now a classic essay on poetics and the interrelation of the poetic word and science.[49] Within Mandelstam's own late poetry, echoes of the *Divine Comedy* serve different purposes and are often interwoven with other poetic voices.[50] These lines suggest an affinity that is close but problematic. What sort of response to a huge Christian epic can a short poem of sixteen lines present? Is the relation between Mandelstam's speaker and Dante's hero equivalent or ironical? Is the tone of the opening two lines genuinely exasperated, comical, or tragicomic?

If we follow the analogy to Dante, we surmise that the speaker cast in this seemingly surreal predicament has emerged from a hellish underworld—the nine rungs on a steep and therefore athletic trajectory—and is hovering somewhere near the Paradise of the third canticle. Dante's heaven is both spatially and spiritually close ("blizko"). Having been abandoned by Virgil, his guide through hell and purgatory, Dante seems not yet to know that Beatrice will now guide him through the first nine heavens. Mandelstam's speaker might be repeating that liminal uncertainty, or might reflect a later section of *Paradiso* when, having progressed through the nine celestial spheres, Dante and Beatrice approach the Empyrean (and the throne of heaven).

Stanza 3 makes the process of poetic quotation also a question of empathy and emulation. Dante's narrative, we are told, is a dream that occurs some nine hours after he falls asleep; in the course of his journey he will experience further purgatorial dreams, and in the *Vita nuova* (a work to which Mandelstam alluded in his poem "Tristia" [1918] nineteen years earlier), he tells the reader that his encounters with Beatrice were spaced out at intervals of nine years before the dream that leads him back to her. This is a premise that Mandelstam's speaker recalls in recognizing his own state as a dream that extends his life yet threatens both to kill and to caress him. The meaning of life applies to the poet's own biography as well as to the life inscribed in Dante's poem because the latter offers the possibility of survival and transcendence. Whomever the speaker asks for directions on his wandering, whether it is God or Dante (but not the Virgin Mary or Beatrice), he supplicates them not to deprive him of life, understood perhaps primarily as an opportunity to relive the process of spiritual and moral revival that Dante charts.

The degree to which artistic renown or reward and biographies converge is the problem raised in the third stanza. Mandelstam will have seen that not all laureate poets stand the test of time. The *Commedia* contains a large number of false poetic heroes: nine such laureates are relegated to limbo in the course of the poem. Not tempting fate with an unenviable comparison might look the wiser course. From Mandelstam in his position as an imitator, and the author of short lyrics under the spell of a commanding epic, this gesture looks humble. Poetic accolades as depicted by Dante are the gift of secular rulers: while Dante himself never earned the laurel, the Holy Roman Emperor laid the chaplets on Petrarch's head. To bow to a secular rather than artistic authority is suspect and inevitably raises the prospect that the poem works allegorically with reference to Mandelstam's troubled relationship to the state and, indeed, head of state. To wear the wreath would be to accept political rapprochement. Line 9 with its urgent repetition is more than an elegant act of recusal. It is an emphatic denial of presumption, but also an anxious denial of martyrdom, if the oxymoronic "sharp-caressing" ("ostrolaskovyi") refers to a crown of thorns rather than the elongated shape of the laurel wreath in Botticelli's iconic portrait of Dante. Instead of taking that risk of *imitatio Christi*, Mandelstam would prefer to have his heart dismembered. Neither form of self-sacrifice is an enviable fate: reward modeled on the example of Dante would presume permanent exile, and reward modeled on the example of poets laureate would presume capitulation to a government or false fame and limbo. Instead, the images of lines 11–12 offer an alternative by alluding to Orpheus, another poet figure prominent in Mandelstam's earlier poetry. In the myth of Orpheus, physical dismemberment actually preserves his song by dispersing it (and we might think of textual dispersal through quotation as a form of dismemberment and recuperation at which Mandelstam excelled). By contrast, capitulation to the authorities that award the laurel, meaning the acceptance of an official reward, might entail renouncing a state of exile at a cost.

How can the poet assure himself that his star, too, will shine in the poetic firmament? His confession that he has got lost in the sky is also like a confession of error (the root of the verb *zabludit'sia* also suggests *zabluzhdat'sia*). Yet so long as he imagines himself in some unearthly realm, he remains at liberty to contemplate posterity and make mistakes, whereas in other poems in the *Voronezh Notebooks* speech is sometimes furtive, as in the memorable image of lips buried like potsherds murmuring poetic lines.[51] Despite the wish to absorb Dante's yearning—his sense perception totally saturated with Dante's masterpiece as a response to exile—the speaker nonetheless intimates anxiety about whether he can actually compete. The phrase, "It was easier for you . . . to resound," can be glossed as an admission that the great spiritual journey that leads from hell to the throne of God has resounded in posterity with a certainty that the lyric poet might not assume. Will Mandelstam as a lyric poet be lost to posterity if he fails to write an epic? "I've lost my way" finds its way by circling back to a fantasy of return. The conclusion responds to the yearning for survival by fusing images from Lermontov and Pushkin about the fate of the poet.

The year 1937 saw the centennial of Pushkin's death, as well as the escalation of the Terror. The Politburo mobilized the literary establishment to use the occasion to elevate Pushkin definitively to the status of national poet.[52] Everywhere he turned, Mandelstam saw improbable evidence of poetic renown (leading him to wonder blackly in a poem whether there would ever be a "Mandelstam Street," and, if so, then surely as crooked as his name).[53] Was this truly the fulfillment of the prophecy that Pushkin articulated in his imitation of Horace? It looked as though the Soviet state was creating a readership that would make him a companion to all living people, a new model to which the poet-speaker here might aspire.

Yet the survival which Mandelstam's poet envisages for himself is instead a state of living death, borrowed not from Pushkin but from one of Mandelstam's favorite poems by Lermontov, "I walk out onto the road alone" ("Vykhozhu odin ia na dorogu," 1841). Lermontov's Romantic speaker, imbued with the imaginary sympathy of pathetic fallacy, communes with the stars in the sky. As he overhears their conversation, he absorbs their immortal music into his own verse and becomes transported by the fantasy that their inextinguishable energy will become his own. He foresees his own moment of death as a state of suspended consciousness, hoping when he dies "that the force of life will slumber" in his chest and that his chest "will quietly expand" as he breathes.[54] When Mandelstam, whose poem reverberates with echoes of Dante, Pushkin, and Lermontov, hopes that the "echo of the sky" will penetrate more profoundly and with greater exaltation ("shire i vyshe"), his fantasy gives direction to his poetic flights, directing inward to a sensibility (for which the heart is an emblem) that serves as an echo chamber for poetry. In Mandelstam's version of an impossible but wondrous fantasy inspired by Lermontov, the poet continues to breathe even in death. Here the breast of the poet, despite his demise, will be a place of safekeeping (and possibly a sounding board) for the "echo of the sky," including the lines of his predecessors. Like Lermontov, the speaker envisages death as sleep, rest earned after fulfilling his service.

What sort of service does he mean? The idea of service again chimes with a Pushkinian idea of "service to the Muses" ("sluzhen'e muz"), rather than service to the state. If anything earns this poet the reward of posterity, it will have been service to poetry rather than to his political masters. The two questions raised within the poem concern the validity, and dangers, of following an exemplary poet, and self-doubt about the survival of one's poetry and reputation. Is the poet-speaker who follows Dante's example unrepentant and afraid of faltering at the last step just before the ninth celestial sphere? Or is the opening line a confession that the speaker has erred by holding a false opinion (*zabluzhdenie*) and wishes to retract his earlier positions and find a new way? By this date, Mandelstam was the author of poems that seemed to be both diatribe against and panegyric of Stalin, especially the poem known as the "Stalin Ode" ("If I were to take charcoal for the highest praise" ["Kogda b ia ugol' vzial dlia vysshei pokhvaly," 1937]).[55] What is being recanted here, and what the motive for self-criticism is, remains a matter to ponder.

A work that begins with a tortured, tongue-twisting expression ends in a determination to achieve one sort of renown over another. We might finally construe this ending as akin to the anagogical moment in allegory, in which the future event of last judgment is revealed. If the echo of the sky means poetry steeped in the example of Pushkin and Lermontov, and therefore poetry that is deeper in content and also more exalted because uncompromising, then the poem looks like the resolution of a split conscience. On the basis of biographical information and the evidence of other poems, we can suggest that the ambivalence expresses the agonizing dilemma of Mandelstam's predicament and, more broadly, of the *intelligent* of his generation.

Intelligentsia narratives of the 1960s through 1980s

The historical shifts of the 1960s produced a demand for new intelligentsia narratives. Writers and thinkers urgently needed to rethink their relationship to the Soviet regime as part of the larger project of restoring the intelligentsia's authority as a catalyst of cultural innovation and critical thought about power. These new approaches were articulated in specific genres and temporalities: memoirs addressed the past, poetry and youth prose the present, and science fiction looked to the future.

Memoirs offered much-needed alternative conceptualizations of the Soviet past. The period witnessed a virtual explosion of this genre, including Viktor Shklovsky's *Mayakovsky and His Circle* (Zhili-byli, 1962), Konstantin Paustovsky's *Story of a Life* (Povest' o zhizni, 1962), Olga Berggol'ts's *The Daytime Stars* (Dnevnye zvezdy, 1954–75), Veniamin Kaverin's *Hello, Brother! Writing is Very Hard* (Zdravstvui, brat! Pisat' ochen' trudno..., 1965), Valentin Kataev's *The Grass of Oblivion* and *My Diamond Wreath*, and Lydia Chukovskaya's *Notes about Anna Akhmatova* (Zapiski ob Anne Akhmatovoi, published abroad in 1976 and 1980 and circulated in *samizdat*). However, the memoirs of Ilya Erenburg and Nadezhda Mandelstam acquired the greatest importance in the Soviet press and *samizdat* respectively. They exemplify two opposed strategies of self-identification within the intelligentsia, although neither is a classic instance of either type.

The two writers had long been acquainted—Nadezhda Khazina met her future husband Osip Mandelstam through Erenburg—but their lives followed radically different paths. While Nadezhda Mandelstam's biography was associated with unofficial culture and dissidence, Erenburg's seemed to crisscross boundaries between the official and nonconformist spheres of Soviet culture. He enjoyed the reputation of a popular writer and international celebrity beginning in the 1920s; his every book occasioned vigorous debates. Erenburg's political position was unusual: a Soviet citizen, he lived abroad for decades; he was known as a child-hood friend of Bukharin, and was close to many victims of the Great Terror. During the Second World War, he was a popular journalist; he later coedited the banned *Black Book*. Somehow, he escaped the Gulag, survived Stalinism, and became a respected leader of Thaw-era liberalism.[56] His memoirs *People. Years. Life* (Liudi. Gody. Zhizn', 1961–65) were serialized by *Novyi mir* and were at the center of Thaw-era public debates. By comparison, Mandelstam's memoirs *Hope against Hope* (Vospominaniia, published in New York in 1970), *Hope Abandoned* (Vtoraia kniga, published in Paris in 1972), and *The Third Book* (Tret'ia kniga, published in Paris in 1973) were published abroad and circulated in *samizdat*; they too generated fiery debates, but in unofficial circles. Mandelstam did not spare reputations; her portrayals of famous writers were sometimes satirically sharp and not always objective. In both authors' memoirs, the stakes were high—nothing less than historical justifications of the intelligentsia's position vis-à-vis Stalinism and the Soviet regime.

Erenburg formulated a programmatic vision of Soviet culture with the intelligentsia as its main driving force. He presented Russian culture as an integral part of European cultural process. Erenburg's own role as a mediator between the European left intelligentsia and the Soviet avant-garde and modernism made this point tangibly persuasive. As Petr Vail and Aleksandr Genis aptly put it, "Erenburg on principle does not distinguish between Soviet and non-Soviet, between Russian and non-Russian. His characters are mixed up in the most capricious way. Bal´mont, Picasso, Esenin, Modigliani, Lenin, Einstein." Erenburg brought both Western and unknown Russian writers to his readers. Vail and Genis continue, "Voloshin, Tsvetaeva, Mandelstam, Bely, Remizov, Meyerhold, and many others entered the minds of Soviet people through Erenburg's 'encyclopedia,' which was much more inclusive than *The Large Soviet Encyclopedia*."[57]

Erenburg's second point was that the Revolution and its anti-capitalist pathos linked Soviet culture to the Western avant-garde. He thereby redeems Western artists and writers who did not fit into the Socialist Realist paradigm. And he positions the Formalist and avant-garde movements as being the closest to the Revolution and inherently opposed to all forms of repression, including Stalinism. Erenburg presents loyalty to the Revolution and the spirit of the freewheeling 1920s as a path toward anti-Stalinism; in effect, he was salvaging the Soviet project.

Nadezhda Mandelstam, as the widow of the banned poet, had a very different life story. She was not allowed to live in Moscow before the Thaw, and taught English in provincial pedagogical institutes, through it all preserving Mandelstam's poetry. In 1965, already retired, she received a small apartment in a Moscow suburb; her home became an intellectual salon attended by Sinyavsky, Shalamov, Brodsky, Sergei Averintsev, Clarence Brown, and Carl and Ellendea Proffer, among many others.[58] Her memoirs took a radical and unsparing approach to the past. Her narrative remains tightly focused on the Soviet epoch and offers no exit to an alternative history. She shattered lingering illusions about the 1920s as a time of productive cultural freedoms. In her view, the horrors of Stalinism directly followed from the revolutionary destruction of the 1920s:

> It was, after all, these people of the twenties who demolished the old values and invented the formulas which even now come in so handy to justify the unprecedented experiment undertaken by our young State: you can't make an omelet without breaking eggs. Every new killing was excused on the grounds that we were building a remarkable "new" world in which there would be no more violence, and that no sacrifice was too great for it. Nobody noticed that the end had begun to justify the means, and then, as always, gradually been lost sight of.[59]

As she sees it, the 1920s introduced violence against culture as the principle for constructing a new society; the 1930s made this violence the self-perpetuating work of the state machine.

She depicts Osip Mandelstam, the central figure of her memoirs, as a heroic and tragic outcast. Due to his poetic talent, he still possesses symbolic power—an alternative to the power of the state. But that power must end with his inevitable destruction. According to Nadezhda Mandelstam, his faithfulness to his poetic talent forces him into confrontation with the terroristic state. His nonconformism is contrasted with the behavior of a broad panorama of others—enthusiastic henchmen and sycophants, lively cynics, faithful friends, and respected peers. Through this panorama, Mandelstam's memoirs offered a compelling justification of the inner emigration exemplified not only by her husband, but also by Pasternak, Shklovsky,

Akhmatova, Lozinsky, and others. These inner emigrants had given up hope for comfort or wealth, and they lived in the constant expectation of harm at the hands of the state. But they possessed dignity and freedom of thought and speech. Their poetry served as the tangible proof of that freedom.

A political nonconformist in several ways, Nadezhda Mandelstam violated the norms of a great poet's widow: a widow was expected to recount her husband's views and actions, without assuming any positions of her own. She was in no way deferential. In Beth Holmgren's words, "Although she begins writing in the roles of conservator and gatekeeper...she develops into a revisionist cultural critic who begins to acknowledge and explore gender differences." Holmgren set a new agenda for considering Mandelstam's contribution to Russian literature, building on feminist work that looked at women's historical participation in debates about Russia's destiny. She concludes that Nadezhda Mandelstam was "one of the few women writers who transgress the behavioral boundaries for a female *intelligent* and assay a nontraditional critique and reevaluation of their culture and society."[60]

Erenburg and Mandelstam outlined divergent positions for the intelligentsia based in part on how they saw the past: he was more inclined toward revolutionary avant-garde writers, she to the poets of neo-classical modernism. He sought for the intelligentsia positions that facilitated rapprochement with the Soviet regime (minus Stalin). But Mandelstam's three books were powerful precisely because they mustered all available historical and biographical arguments to discredit any such reconciliation. The opposition exemplified by Ilya Erenburg and Nadezhda Mandelstam can be seen in other quasi-memoiristic reflections on the twentieth-century experience of the Russian intelligentsia. Shklovsky's *Mayakovsky and His Circle*, Berggol'ts's *The Daytime Stars*, Ginzburg's *Journey into the Whirlwind*, and Kataev's "mauvistic" novels *The Grass of Oblivion* and especially *My Diamond Wreath* follow the approach of Erenburg's memoirs. Veniamin Kaverin's series *Lighted Windows* (*Osveshchennye okna*, 1970–76), *In the Old House* (*V starom dome*, 1971), *The Evening Day* (*Vechernii den'*, 1977–78), *A Writing Desk* (*Pis'mennyi stol*, 1985), and especially *Epilogue* (*Epilog*, completed in 1979, first published in 1989), and the diary Liubov Shaporina kept from 1898 to 1967 (published in 2012) are nearer to Mandelstam's model. All these texts remain under-studied, but there are several writers of the 1960–70s who have drawn considerable attention for their memoirs or their lightly autobiographical representations of the intelligentsia, and their modifications of the two models set forth by Erenburg and Mandelstam bear a closer look.

Solzhenitsyn was one such writer, and his vision hews close to Nadezhda Mandelstam's paradigm. In his novels, the Stalinist Terror stood as the greatest historical ordeal within which all cultural, moral, social, and political values were tested, not in an abstract way but rather in the harsh conditions of the Gulag. In his semi-autobiographical narratives, *Cancer Ward* and *The First Circle*, Solzhenitsyn created a specific kind of novel where philosophical discussions about the perennial, cursed Russian questions punctuate extensive descriptions of prisoners, their families, guards, and bosses. These descriptions play the role of an existentialist, borderline situation, within which historical catastrophe is converted into an everyday condition. For example, *The First Circle* features a group of men incarcerated in a *sharashka*—a Gulag scientific institute with confined scientists and their free bosses all at risk of more severe incarceration in a concentration camp in the event of scientific failure. The three friends represent three intellectual types: Nerzhin, Solzhenitsyn's alter ego, is focused on Russian history and the intelligentsia's guilt before the simple people; Rubin, a talented writer and thinker, sincerely believes in the righteousness of the communist idea (supposedly distorted by Stalin and his henchmen); and Sologdin, a nationalist and individualist, perceives himself as a rare guardian of Russia's true aristocratic culture. Despite personal friendship, their disagreement grows around a principled question: how to combine hatred of the regime with service to the motherland?

Is it possible to serve Russia by serving the Soviet totalitarian machine, or must these two choices be mutually exclusive? At the same time, the novel's larger plot turns on the betrayal of a state secret by a career diplomat and golden child of the Soviet elite, Innokenty Volodin. His first name, derived from the word for "innocent,"[61] contains the author's answer to the uneasy question about the protagonist's guilt. The novel unfolds as an *agon* of the Soviet intelligentsia and its moral choices. In its final scenes, Rubin's and Sologdin's collaboration with the regime leads to Innokenty's arrest and inevitable death in the Gulag.

In *Cancer Ward*, illness serves as a powerful philosophical metaphor of the Soviet regime. Yet cancer is the means for revealing profound ideological differences among patients made similar by their disease. Although existentialist dread and despair suffuse the plot, *Cancer Ward* interprets Soviet ideological beliefs as a fundamental obstacle standing between a human being and the freedom that would be revealed by the proximity to death. The representative of the intelligentsia, Oleg Kostoglodov, is another autobiographical character, a former Gulag inmate now in permanent internal exile. The ability of Kostoglodov to liberate himself completely from the lies of Soviet ideology gives him the strength to overcome his illness and to live for love and truth.

Much like *One Day in the Life of Ivan Denisovich*, these novels preserve strong discursive connections with Socialist Realism. In *The First Circle*, the entire plot and the system of characters recall narratives organized by a search for the saboteur, the worker whose actions wreck the dreams of socialism. Following that logic, Solzhenitsyn presents a whole panorama of Soviet society, beginning with *zeks* and ending with Stalin (*The First Circle* includes the first ever stream of consciousness monologue attributed to Stalin), all united by crisis and trying to resolve, in different ways, the same social and philosophical problems. But Solzhenitsyn turns this model upside down: because the supposed wrecker, Innokenty Volodin, appears to be the most noble of all characters, his crime looks like an act of dedication to the motherland as opposed to its government.[62] In *Cancer Ward*, the existentialist philosophy of the novel is oversimplified by the authoritative position of the protagonist, who, as in Socialist Realism, arrives at the ultimate truth and wisdom, from the height of which he judges other characters and overcomes death.

The lack of internal freedom, however, is not limited to the circle of diehard Stalinists. *Pushkin House* (*Pushkinskii dom*, completed in 1971) by Andrei Bitov features intellectuals from the generation of the Sixties, so-called children of the Thaw, but its main theme is the struggle against inner non-freedom. In the Soviet Union, Bitov could publish only individual chapters from *Pushkin House*, which was brought out in full in 1978 by Ardis. Although closer stylistically to Nabokov, whom the young writer read in *tamizdat*, than to Nadezhda Mandelstam's memoirs, Bitov produces an intelligentsia narrative not unlike hers in its implicit argument. Bitov had made a name for himself with his subtle psychological novellas about the contemporary intelligentsia, which were at once poetic and caustic. The novel presented the problem of the the intelligentsia from the perspective of Bitov's generation: those born during the Great Terror saw their enthusiasm for Thaw reforms turn to disappointment in the 1970s. *Pushkin House* investigates whether a connection is possible to the kind of intelligentsia and the legacy of Russian culture both Mandelstams valued. In other words, Bitov asks whether the vacuum of symbolic authority created by Stalinism can be filled by his generation's cultural efforts.

The protagonist of *Pushkin House*, the young philologist Leva Odoevtsev, is the son of an exemplary intelligentsia conformist. Bypassing the generation of the fathers, he attempts to connect with his grandfather, a thinker who paid for his independence with decades in the Gulag. His sincere attempt to choose that legacy ends in fiasco, when his grandfather rejects him. The grandfather accuses Leva of having lost the inner freedom that he, as a Gulag survivor, had paradoxically preserved. For Leva's generation, freedom has been replaced by simulation—of values, ideals, and cultures. The form of Bitov's novel also plays on the notion of simulation. What begins as a "remake" of Tolstoy's *Childhood. Boyhood. Youth* changes into mockery of classical texts and citations: the final chapters of *Pushkin House* have titles like "The Bronze People" and "Poor Horseman," conflating *The Bronze Horseman* with *Poor Folk*. The finale turns into open self-parody.

Bitov was uncannily prescient in reformulating the problem of late Soviet intelligentsia in a language close to postmodernist discourse. He converted the anxiety over political conformity into a problem of culture—real, lost, or simulated. Without providing solutions, *Pushkin House* negatively demonstrates the proposition that psychological, intellectual, and political freedom cannot be achieved unless the intelligentsia sheds ideological falsity, hegemonic hierarchies, and ritualistic simulation. Those hegemonic hierarchies are embodied by the literary museum, only apparently destroyed in the novel's climactic scene: the damage turns out to be underwhelming because the majority of exhibits, including Pushkin's death mask, are fake. The cultural past can open for the present only when the museum is truly sacked.

One further example of a text that follows Nadezhda Mandelstam's model bears mention. In his roman à clef about the dissident intelligentsia *The Legacy* (*Nasledstvo*, first published in 1987), Vladimir Kormer (1939–86) reached a conclusion similar to Bitov's, most likely independently. Kormer's characters heroically dedicate their lives to the fight for political freedom, but constantly battle with a lack of internal freedom. He depicts the circle of dissidents (to which he was closely connected) as existentially impoverished, which leads to mutual distrust, individual dramas, and political dead-ends.

Erenburg's strategy of the intelligentsia's self-identification was internalized in the so-called Youth Prose (*molodezhnaia proza*) and poetry, and mainly associated with the journal *Youth*. Among the representatives of this trend were the literary stars of the generation of the Sixties: the poets Evgeny Yevtushenko, Andrei Voznesensky, and Robert Rozhdestvensky; and the prose writers Vasily Aksyonov, Anatoly Gladilin, and Anatoly Kuznetsov. Close to them, although different in important ways, were the poets Bulat Okudzhava and Bella Akhmadulina, the subtle psychological short-story writer Yuri Kazakov (1927–82), the satirists Fazil Iskander and Vladimir Voinovich, and the popular science fiction writers, the brothers Arkady and Boris Strugatsky.

The poets of this generation initially sought to revive fossilized themes of the Revolution and to romanticize the Civil War, which they conceived as a counterweight to the horrors of Stalinism. In Okudzhava's famous song "The Sentimental March" ("Sentimental'nyi marsh," 1957), his lyrical hero dreams of the Red Army's "commissars in dusty helmets" who, instead of angels, would greet him after his death.[63] In "Verses about My Name" ("Stikhi o moem imeni"), Rozhdestvensky proudly wrote about being named after Robert Eikhe, the Civil War commissar and an organizer of the Gulag (the latter fact Rozhdestvensky prefers not to mention, calling his hero "Comrade Revolution"); Eikhe himself perished in the Great Terror.[64] In the narrative poem "Bratsk Station" ("Bratskaia GES," 1965), Yevtushenko inscribes the confrontation with Stalinism into the historical lineage of Russian freedom-fighters, a pantheon that stretches from Stenka Razin and Pugachev to the People's Will and Bolsheviks. Voznesensky, who represented the avant-garde wing of censored poetry, combines symbols of spiritual freedom, epitomized by great artists—Michelangelo, Gauguin, Chagall—with a very different kind of hero, Lenin, in his narrative poem "Longjumeau" (1962–63), a tale set in the 1912 Bolshevik party school in France.

The genuine achievement of such poems lay in prosodic innovations: fresh rhythms, explosive metaphors (Voznesensky was especially famous for these), relaxed intonation, and inexact rhymes (which came to be called "Yevtushenko rhymes"). Readers filled stadiums and concert halls for poetry readings, drawn to the tone of the work as much as to its themes.

The sincerity of this poetry was itself the sign of a new approach to the poetic subject. These poets audaciously placed themselves on the same level as canonized symbols and figures of the official world, and transformed these monumental ideas back into people. Voznesensky in "Longjumeau" claimed: "Russia, I am your capillary vessel. / When I am in pain—you are in pain, Russia" ("Rossiia, ia tvoi kapilliarnyi sosudik. / Mne bol'no kogda—tebe bol'no, Rossiia").[65] The lines, with their obvious echo of Allen Ginsberg's "Howl," caused a scandal in the literary establishment. In each new poem, Yevtushenko flaunted his empathy with diverse types and characters, including a Siberian wedding party, Jews killed in the Holocaust, Great Patriotic War veterans, and Czechs crushed by Soviet tanks in 1968. This enabled him to position himself as articulating nation-wide, if not worldwide, emotions and concerns.

Youth Prose shared many characteristics with poetry: the relaxation of language, the freedom of colloquialisms, ironic intonations, and non-heroic characters.[66] Even more dramatically than did poetry, it reflected the growing disenchantment with the Soviet ideological and political system and any promise of reform. Some leaders of Youth Prose, Aksyonov, Gladilin, and Kuznetsov, ended up emigrating. The case of Vasily Aksyonov is especially telling. The son of Evgenia Ginzburg (the author of *Journey into the Whirlwind*), Aksyonov had no illusions about the nature of Stalinism. A medical doctor by training, he was a true *stilyaga*, something like the Soviet equivalent of 1950s American hipsters: youngsters who protested against the Soviet routine by wearing scandalously bright Western-fashioned clothes, dancing swing and rock-n-roll, and playing jazz. Aksyonov sought the equivalent of this countercultural style in his poetics, which combined influences from the beatniks with an infectious irony and the modernist cult of the artist. In his early prose—the novellas *Colleagues* (*Kollegi*, 1960) and *Ticket to the Stars* (*Zvezdnyi bilet*, 1961), as well as excellent short stories—he created the canon of Youth Prose, in which playful and ironic friends, who from the orthodox point of view should be regarded with suspicion, act in a more noble way than their adult mentors and critics and prove their inner freedom. Aksyonov was soon to outgrow these patterns. In his works of the 1960s, he transformed the idea of friendship into a kind of invisible secret society of free thinkers, including writers, chess grandmasters, jazz musicians, professional athletes, local hooligans, nuclear scientists, and even magi. United by their nonconformism, they feel an ever-increasing alienation and seek various means of escape. If at first these escape attempts looked more or less realistically motivated, by the end of the 1960s they became increasingly fantastic. A radical turning point was the proto-postmodernist novella *Surplussed Barrelware* (*Zatovarennaia bochkotara*, 1968), in which Soviet utopian rhetoric was transformed into an ironic fairytale.

Aksyonov's most mature novel, *Burn* (*Ozhog*, written in 1969–75, first publication by Ardis in 1980), depicts that secret community of geniuses. All five protagonists in this novel survive betrayal by their best friends (whose names are variations on the motif of silver, alluding to Judas's thirty pieces of silver). And all face a devastating defeat of their major creative projects. Vail and Genis aptly characterized this novel as "the historical canvas of collapse and exodus."[67] Although critics find no room for hope in the novel, there is a great deal of festivity amid the declarations of defeat. *Burn* is like an unending orgy, in which drinking, memories, friendship and betrayals, creativity, and sex are all mixed up. Their raucous combination is a powerful form of resistance to the stifling social atmosphere of the Stagnation.

A different, more rationalist aspect of the intelligentsia is featured in the science fiction of Arkady and Boris Strugatsky. They created the figure of the progressor, a representative of an advanced civilization who works in disguise on a remote planet in a repressive, medieval, or totalitarian society that he tries to reform. This motif recurs in their hugely popular novels *Escape Attempt* (*Popytka k begstvu*, 1962), *Hard to Be a God* (*Trudno byt' bogom*, 1964), *Inhabited*

Island (*Obitaemyi ostrov*, 1969; translated by Helen Saltz Jacobson as *Prisoners of Power*), *Snail on the Slope* (*Ulitka na sklone*, 1966–68), *Roadside Picnic* (*Piknik na obochine*, 1972), *Beetle in the Anthill* (*Zhuk v muraveinike*, 1979), and *Waves Put Out the Wind* (*Volny gasiat veter*, 1985; Antonina Bouis translated this novel as *The Time Wanderers*). The figure of the progressor, a contemporary intellectual surrounded by a backward society, served as a powerful trope for the Soviet scientific intelligentsia's alienation from their immediate historical environment and social milieu. The sci-fi conventions essentialized cultural differences by presenting the unenlightened masses as aliens. The Strugatskys usually represented authorities and the masses as symbiotically interconnected, if not indistinguishable from one another. From the standpoint of the progressor, the local authorities on the distant planet are just differently dressed savages. The repressed subalterns elicit no empathy in the progressor (or the reader) due to their enthusiastic collaboration with repressive forces.

The most famous of the Strugatskys' progressors, Rumata in *Hard to Be a God*, is assigned to Arkanar, a remote planet-state. He summarizes the situation there during a quasi-medieval fascist coup d'état: "Wherever grayness triumphs, black robes come to power."[68] Rumata's diagnosis as expressed by this formula is all too translatable: the triumphant grayness suggests mediocrity and the ignorant masses, while the blackness could signify both the black gown of the religious order utilized on Arkanar by Don Reba, making them something like the Black Hundreds, or the similarly black-clad Nazi storm-troopers, the SS.

That clear division of the world into us and them begins to crumble in the Strugatskys' later works. Before, it was obvious who "they" were—medieval Berias and the aggressive masses in *Hard to Be a God* or the Fathers with their propaganda machines in *Inhabited Island*. But in the novels of the 1980s, the clarity becomes obscure. In *Beetle in the Anthill*, an outcast progressor, Abalkin, who is declared to be the alien, is surrounded with an aura of compassion, while Sikorski, the Head of the Bureau of Progressors, who defends "our" independence from the superior alien civilization, is morally repugnant. The binaries that seemed essential are destabilized, and the progressor's focus shifts from transforming the environment to preserving his own identity. In effect, he becomes more concerned about not becoming like *them*, rather than trying to change them or improve their lives. The Strugatskys would go on to write *The Doomed City* and *Burdened by Evil, or Forty Years Later* (*Otiagoshchennye zlom, ili Sorok let spustia*, 1988), where the enlightened progressor (that same representative of the generation of the Sixties) cannot find any means of self-realization other than self-isolation. His mission is inevitably doomed: heroic service to the Enlightenment is replaced by egotistical self-preservation and all-out resistance against the temptations of conformism.

Looking back at twentieth-century intelligentsia narratives, one may read them as the story of high hopes, resistance, and eventual defeat. The defeat is seen through the fusion of initially divergent narrative models set up by Mandelstam and Erenburg, to the point of despair and doubt in the intelligentsia's foundational values. The gap between the intelligentsia and those beyond its realm, the so-called masses, seems unbridgeable. The masses are increasingly perceived as a dangerous source of destruction, little resembling the object of the intelligentsia's enlightenment efforts in earlier decades. All these symptoms can be understood as amplifying the crisis of the Enlightenment paradigm proclaimed by Theodor Adorno and Max Horkheimer in *The Dialectics of Enlightenment*.

However, these same intelligentsia narratives testify to the opposite: their cultural significance and artistic value demonstrate that the intelligentsia remains, despite all the regime's efforts to marginalize and belittle it, the central mover and shaker in society, preserving its mission to be the source of nonconformism and independence. These narratives show that the intelligentsia was not frozen in the posture of the ultimate victim of Soviet historical trauma. By critiquing not only the authorities but the intelligentsia itself, writers (who all belong to the intelligentsia, too) try to exorcise society's most persistent demons, but also manifest the intelligentsia's responsibility for social failures. This responsibility presupposes the rethinking of the intelligentsia's role vis-à-vis society and authorities alike, as well as its historical mission and its moral and cultural principles. To succeed, this reassessment requires a serious process of working through the culture's collective historical trauma. This task is inevitably inherited by writers and thinkers in the post-Soviet period.

Post-Soviet intelligentsia narratives

The 1990s witnessed a dramatic decline in the intelligentsia's social status due to economic hardships and the commercialization of many cultural areas. Internal divisions over attitudes to capitalism, strategies of economic and cultural survival, and the reassessment of the Soviet past sprang up. In the 2000s and especially 2010s, when the economic situation improved dramatically, politics became increasingly authoritarian. For the educated élite, critical issues included Putin and his regime of power, the Russian Orthodox Church, feminism and homophobia, anti-Americanism and Russian nationalism, and as of 2014, the Ukrainian Maidan revolution, the occupation of Crimea, and the "hybrid war" in Eastern Ukraine. These splits revived and aggravated debates of the Perestroika period between liberal and nationalist wings of the intelligentsia. The nationalists, marginalized in the 1990s, began to receive broad support from the government and to establish ideological control over the major media in the 2010s, while liberal discourse virtually vanished from popular media (except for a few newspapers and the TV station *Rain* [*Dozhd '*]). The intelligentsia-driven anti-Putin protests of 2011–12 sealed the liberals' marginality but intensified the sense of urgency to get their viewpoint heard. The protests also proved that some longstanding issues remained unresolved: high symbolic capital and social marginalization; civic awareness and dissociation from the country's majority; confrontation with a powerful state and dependence on it. Such a return of the repressed motivated literary attempts to map post-Soviet transformations of the intelligentsia onto its century-long history.

Especially illuminating in this respect are the narratives of the extremely popular Ludmila Ulitskaya. Her family sagas feature heroines and heroes who display attitudes of freedom in their lifestyle, rather than in their ideological statements or political positions. Their natural liberalism, manifested in free sexuality and dissident activities, pits them against political limits imposed from above. Rather than mere promiscuity, the emancipated sexuality of Ulitskaya's characters stands for freedom from heteronormative sexuality. Political dissent, however, betokens compassion for the offended and the marginalized, as well as for domestic and intimate ties to family and friends—which is especially obvious in *The Green Tent*, which chronicles the history of the Soviet dissident movement through the intertwined love stories of its participants. Ulitskaya's novels generally propose a genealogy that links the contemporary intelligentsia to those who confronted the Soviet regime as a dehumanizing and brutal force. For her, anti-Soviet nonconformism is the fundamental quality of the intelligentsia. One of her most discussed novels in Russia was the bestseller *Daniel Stein, Interpreter* (*Daniel' Shtain, perevodchik*, 2006), which took up the history of the Holocaust and angered both Jewish and Christian members of the intelligentsia. The hero is modeled on the Holocaust survivor Oswald Rufeisen, who fused Christianity and Judaism in his own Church and in his lifelong practices of inclusivity. Elizabeth Skomp and Benjamin Sutcliffe attribute to Ulitskaya a "theology of inclusiveness."[69] In addition to these arguments about religious identity and the intelligentsia, *Daniel Stein, Interpreter* is important in formal, literary terms: Marina Balina argues that this novel, consisting of multiple fictional and real documents, brings together two normally opposing modes: hagiography and decentralized life-writing.[70]

Ulitskaya's prose resonates with other works of the 1990s–2000s, most conspicuously the autobiographical novel by an esteemed Chekhov scholar, Aleksandr Chudakov (1938–2005). In *The Gloom Is Cast on Ancient Steps* (*Lozhitsia mgla na starye stupeni*, 2000), a community of intelligentsia members is exiled by the Soviet regime to a remote town in Kazakhstan; theirs is a story of enlightened Robinson Crusoes thrown into the middle of nowhere. Also notable is Aleksei Ivanov's popular novel about a provincial teacher, *A Geographer Drank Away his Globe* (*Geograf globus propil*, 1995); it depicts an heir to 1970s nonconformism as the only worthy mentor for demoralized post-Soviet generations.

In a dystopian novel, *Slynx* (*Kys'*, 2000), by the star of Perestroika literature, Tatyana Tolstaya, the intelligentsia appear as keepers of the cultural flame in a post-apocalyptic scenario. She goes so far as to end her novel on a scene of public burning and resurrection of the "Oldener"—this is the title of surviving intelligentsia members—by the authorities of the new barbaric Russia. In this grotesque post-apocalyptic fantasy, Tolstaya's favorite themes are vividly clear: the opposition between intelligentsia as Europeanized Russians and the rest of the country allegedly stuck in the middle ages. The novel more broadly explores the tragicomic intellectual quest of its protagonist Benedikt. He fetishizes the book and culture in general, and he suffers an appropriately grotesque penalty: he becomes the Guard responsible for burning "old books" and the co-author of the new draconian law banning the distribution of books. Tolstaya, however, hesitates to question the links between the intelligentsia's strict hierarchization of culture and the terror leading to the post-apocalyptic desert, as suggested by the logic of *Slynx*. The novel's finale reaffirms the intelligentsia's superiority as a social group, while her protagonist, a naive Russian boy seeking the "main book," is humiliated as a fool. Tolstaya holds in contempt changes that threaten the authority of the intelligentsia as a guardian of cherished values.

Vladimir Makanin's novel *Underground, or The Hero of Our Time* (*Andegraund, ili Geroi nashego vremeni*, 1998) exudes a comparable sense of resentment. Petrovich, the protagonist of the novel, is an unpublished underground author and a proclaimed "hero of our time." He represents the cultural underground: he obtains his individual freedom through his reluctance to compete for social advantage, and he reacts violently to any behavior he regards as disrespectful. His penchant for aggression further disqualifies him in the competition for status, but also spares him the communal life-style. The *obshchaga* (dormitory) where he lives and works preserves the distinctive essence of Soviet communality. The erasure of anything individual connects and likens the *obshchaga* to another realm of communality, the mental hospital (*psikhushka*), where people are entirely robbed of selfhood. These sites resonate with Makanin's recurrent images of hive mentality: the village, the generation, the crowd, and a queue of people. Although abstaining from all criticism of his protagonist's choices (including even xenophobic murder), Makanin shows the limits of Petrovich's freedom. Rooted entirely in the social condition of the *obshchaga*, he can have no idea of freedom outside its boundaries. The disintegration of his environment leaves him a true "hero of his time," exposed as a nobody. It is no wonder that eventually he feels nostalgia for the dormitory as a lost paradise.

Makanin sardonically objectifies the intelligentsia's longing for collective identities, but other representatives of post-Soviet realism try to restore the sense of lost collective identity in a straightforward way. The lost sense of belonging to a collective, reinforced by the shared mythologies of history and society, laid the foundation of the identity crisis that became a dominant cultural theme of the 1990s–2000s. One disappointing example of this tendency is Solzhenitsyn, whose cultural influence extended into the post-Soviet period. Lauded in the West and in post-Perestroika Russia as a truth-teller, he disconcertingly espoused controversial positions that fed into nationalist discourses. Although formerly an ardent critic of Soviet ideocracy, from the 1970s he advocated ethnic (Russian) and religious (Orthodox) values as the foundation for proper collective identity, an idea that virtually required the existence of a national Other. Solzhenitsyn predictably finds this Other in the figure of the Russian Jew. This is the subject of his two-volume treatise *Two Hundred Years Together (1795–1995)* (*Dvesti let vmeste [1795–1995]*, 2001–2002), which provoked intense public debate. According to Solzhenitsyn, the Russian state strived to accommodate Jews starting in the eighteenth century, but the Jews responded to Russia's care and concern with ungrateful aggressiveness. The writer depicts Russian Jews as an unproductive stratum committed to the destruction of the Russian state order. He does not hesitate to invest his considerable cultural authority in claims that look indistinguishable from popular anti-Semitic prejudices: the Jews are shown as having organized and benefited from acts committed during the Red Terror, such as the persecution of Christianity and other religions in the 1920s, the collectivization of Russian peasants, and the purges of the 1930s. Solzhenitsyn adds that the Jews flourished even in the Gulag: as prisoners, he writes, they managed to seize administrative positions and thus continue to harm the Russian people.[71]

Solzhenitsyn's stance resonates with that of writers from different generations. Jews in numerous novels of the nationalist Aleksandr Prokhanov (b. 1938) function as synonyms for the liberal intelligentsia in general; anti-Semitic stereotypes are forthrightly used for the demonization of the liberal intelligentsia. Other nationalist or pro-Soviet writers avoid direct anti-Semitic slurs in their attacks on the liberal intelligentsia: one thinks of Eduard Limonov in the self-aggrandizing narratives of the 2000s–10s; his young disciple Zakhar Prilepin in his novel *San'kia* (2006); and Mikhail Elizarov in his novel *Pasternak*. But one senses an internalized anti-Semitism in their routine representations of the intelligentsia as overprivileged, greedy, arrogant, manipulative, self-serving, and demagogic agents of Western cultural imperialism who hate all things Russian. As a healthy alternative to the corrupt liberals, these writers lionize great revolutionaries from Plato to Lenin, and from Hitler to Osama bin Laden. Such figures appear in Limonov's *Sacred Monsters* (*Sviashchennye monstry*, 2004) and *Titans* (*Titany*, 2014); as the semi-fictional character Eikhmanis, an enthusiastic and talented creator of the Gulag in Prilepin's novel *Abode*; as Prokhanov's numerous heroic officers of the KGB/FSB; and as the iron-fisted managers of the Soviet government who dedicated their entire existence to the state in Terekhov's novel *The Stone Bridge*. Abetted by convenient plots, these writers strive to reinscribe intelligentsia members as antiheroes in their newly created grand narratives of state power—a gesture which inevitably revives Socialist Realist tropes and aesthetic models.

In obvious dialogue with Solzhenitsyn and his followers, Dmitry Bykov replicates in his novel *Living Souls* (*ZhD*, 2005) the association between the ideology and ethnic origins of the intelligentsia in order to mock it.[72] An extremely popular media personality, poet, and essayist, Bykov became a true public intellectual during the protest movement of the 2010s. In *Living Souls*, Russia is torn by a civil war between forces whose enduring and cyclical competition Bykov traces through all of Russian history. The two forces are, on the one hand, the Khazars, who stand for liberals, Jews, and Westernizers, and on the other hand, Varangians, who stand for nationalists, statists, and militarists. They endlessly take turns at colonizing Russia. Aleksandr Etkind's theory of internal colonization looks like a compatible historical analysis, but Bykov, as a writer rather than a scholar, uses myth to capture the perception of history as an open wound inflicted on "indigenous" Russians, shown as homeless bums (*vas'ki*) and Russian dervishes. Their religious service unfolds in interminable repetitions, a circularity patterned on physical structures like the Moscow subway's circle line (*kol'tsevaia liniia*).[73] According to Bykov, liberal Khazars offer Russia a dictatorship no less brutal than that of the Varangians. In the words of one character, "If the Varangian colonizations had led to mass death from military drills ... the Khazarian periods of control kept bringing corruption and the rejection of any discipline, which was never in abundance to begin with."[74] Traumatic experience wrought by the Khazarian periods (meaning the experience of liberal internal colonization) sows the seeds of chaos and anarchy in order to propagate new violence and terror.

Bykov makes a case for "indigenous" Russians as an alternative to the colonizers. He contrives a fascinating mythology for this collective unity, and even drafts an outline of their ancient language, echoes of which he claimed to discern in the poetry of Velimir Khlebnikov and the prose of Andrei Platonov. But his depiction of the "indigenous" characters in the novel remains stylized and artificial, a sure sign that the figure is hollow. Their subjectivity is radically limited, as is their power: even the wisest of them, Vasily Ivanovich, is unable to defend a child from a rapist, but can only weep and lament the violence. With the exception of the shaman woman Asha, the *vas'ki* represent an "extended history of an imposed state of angelic subject-lessness and denied agency."[75]

The problem of the intelligentsia vis-à-vis post-imperial nostalgia for grand narratives and ensuing resentment constitutes the focus of the writings of the 2015 winner of the Nobel Prize in literature, Svetlana Alexievich (b. 1948), a Belarusian author writing in Russian. Her books are each dedicated to a specific trauma that has defined USSR history: *The Unwomanly Face of War* (*U voiny ne zhenskoe litso*, 1985) and *The Last Witnesses* (*Poslednie svideteli*, 1985), which treat the Second World War from the perspective of women-soldiers and children, respectively; *Zinky Boys* (*Tsinkovye mal'chiki*, 1991) about the Soviet war in Afghanistan; *Chernobyl Prayer* (*Chernobyl'skaia molitva*, 1997, also translated as *Voices of Chernobyl*) about the effects of the Chernobyl nuclear disaster; *Enchanted with Death* (*Zacharovannye smert'iu*, 1994) and *Second-Hand Time* (*Vremia sekond-khend*, 2013) about the human consequences of Perestroika and the collapse of the Soviet Union.[76]

Each of her books creates a montage of individual narratives of trauma, collecting the residue of Soviet catastrophic history, especially its final stages. There is a sense in which Alexievich creates a chorus of narratives, but connecting the separate voices is a larger tale about the scapegoating of the entire nation. Alexievich shows "Homo Sovieticus" as the ultimate product of the utopian project: "The 'Red Empire' is gone, but the 'Red Man,' Homo Sovieticus, remains. He endures. . . . I'm interested in little people. The little, great people, is how I would put it, because suffering expands people. In my books these people tell their own, little histories, and big history is told along the way."[77] Alexievich preserves the dichotomy between personal ("little") and state-bound ("great") history; she believes that human suffering predicates the historical greatness of a given event.

By calling her cycle of books *The Voices of Utopia*, Alexievich wants to underscore both the traumatic effects of the utopian experiments and nostalgia for the lost utopian ambitions. In her Nobel Lecture, Alexievich said:

> I reconstruct the history of that battle, its victories and its defeats. The history of how people wanted to build the Heavenly Kingdom on earth. Paradise! The City of the Sun! In the end, all that remained was a sea of blood, millions of ruined human lives. There was a time, however, when no political idea of the twentieth century was comparable to communism (or the October Revolution as its symbol), a time when nothing attracted Western intellectuals and people all around the world more powerfully or emotionally.[78]

This utopian idea, despite—or, perhaps, thanks—to its association with "a sea of blood," bears the mark of the sacred for Alexievich's real-life characters and for herself. Her books about the collapse of the USSR can also be read as a lament for the loss of idealism—the utopian justification of human sacrifices—which had been the foundational value for the Russian intelligentsia since the nineteenth century.

Conclusion

Russian literature in the twentieth and twenty-first centuries has witnessed incredible dynamism, marked by a quick pace of literary innovations, transformations in cultural institutions, reinventions of poetics, a re-conceptualization of subjectivity, and constructions and reconstructions of national narratives. It would not be an exaggeration to say that despite the paralyzing influence of Socialist Realism, the evolution of Russian modernism, begun in the Silver Age, has been sustained for the entire period. A seemingly inexhaustible fund of unpublished texts, still arriving as of this writing, proves that artistic discoveries of Russian modernism remain relevant and preserve their power for today's readership. The deferred publications and reception of Sigizmund Krzhizhanovsky, Leonid Dobychin, Pavel Zal'tsman, Pavel Ulitin, and Lydia Ginzburg among others testify to the early, if not premature, emergence of sensibilities and literary discourses that resonated long after their creation. And despite the efforts of Soviet authorities to isolate Russian writers from the supposedly decadent and formalist tendencies of world culture, one can observe a steady synchronicity between Russian and Western literary innovations, affiliating Russian and Italian Futurism, Acmeism and Imagism, Soviet grotesque literature and German Expressionism, OBERIU and DADA, post-Stalinist existentialist prose and drama and French Existentialism. Even the postmodernism of the late Soviet underground emerges simultaneously with its Western counterparts. And the catastrophic history of the Russian twentieth century has injected modernist experimentations with the high intensity of real-life tragedy.

A rereading of twentieth-century Russian literature as a convergence of various modernist tendencies, including Neo-Romantic, avant-gardist, and postmodernist streams, raises a question about the significance of realism as an aesthetic system in the twentieth century. Oddly enough, realism did not completely disappear from the field of literary innovation by moving into the realm of pop literature. If anything, it sustained its groundbreaking role as the most recognizable counterpart and antagonist to Socialist Realism. This peculiar outcome, not at all typical in Western literatures, positions Russian realist writers of the twentieth century between Socialist Realist and modernist influences. Even in Solzhenitsyn's and Grossman's novels, inversions of Socialist Realist plots appear, and their representation of historical catastrophes shares much with the works of modernist writers such as Pasternak, Platonov, Shalamov, and Dombrovsky. As a mediator between the sanctioned and prohibited aesthetics of Socialist Realism and modernism, Realism in the twentieth century enjoyed among the intelligentsia the status of a literary mainstream. At the same time, it sustained the nineteenth-century discourse of the writer as the nation's conscience.

For everyday (non-professional) readers of Russian literature, the great figures of Tolstoy and Dostoevsky, who had solidified the models of the writer as a secular prophet and the conscience of the nation, frequently overshadow the expansive, multidirectional development of Russian literature in the twentieth century. Normally, Western readers and critics lionize those writers who fit aesthetic models set by the nineteenth-century novel (e.g., Solzhenitsyn and Grossman). Such an approach places Russian culture outside of modern history in an imaginary sanctuary of eternal ideas and passions, thus presenting Russian literature as a kind of secular religion, which either highlights Russia's seemingly innate conservatism or justifies the claims for its spiritual superiority—oddly, a favorite mantra of Russian nationalists.

Akhmatova recalled that Gumilev used to tell her, "Anya, please poison me with your own hands, if I begin shepherding the peoples" ("pasti narody").[1] In accordance with this dictum, the majority of Russian modernists and their followers viewed the position of being a national guru ironically. Nonetheless, the entire Soviet sociocultural system treated any non-realist author as a representative of the counterculture. This explains why in periods of political discontent even authors who never sought the role of national conscience reaffirmed their cultural authority as the embodiment of an independent mind and moral judgment. Furthermore, radically experimental authors, to an even greater extent than mainstream realist writers, resisted hegemonic tendencies in culture. In these circumstances, any bold or irreverent poetic gesture became politically meaningful.

Two polar examples well illuminate the new (or rather old) symbolic role of literature in twenty-first century Russia. The closing ceremony of the Winter Olympics in 2014 (shown in Figure v.10) featured a segment hardly imaginable anywhere else. Actors dressed up as Pushkin, Gogol, Tolstoy, Dostoevsky, Chekhov, Mayakovsky, Akhmatova, Bulgakov, Tsvetaeva, Solzhenitsyn, and Brodsky appeared at their desks writing and then mixing with the dancing crowd, while celebrated lines from their writings were recited over the audio system. Portraits of many other Russian writers, from Gumilev to Sholokhov, popped up on the stage's perimeter. The Olympics of 2014 held in Sochi was part and parcel of a burgeoning nationalist and neo-imperialist political turn. Using Russian literature to political ends showed no scruple about including even resistant figures like Solzhenitsyn or Brodsky in order to refurbish an aggressive mythology of Russia's greatness.

As a counterweight to this lavish scene, one may recall a less publicized but no less important episode from the anti-government protests of 2011–12. In May 2012, the Moscow authorities essentially prohibited political rallies after the brutal beating of anti-Putin protesters by the police. Despite this ban, within a week of the fateful rally of May 6, a group of liberal-minded writers—Boris Akunin, Dmitry Bykov, Lev Rubinshtein, Ludmila Ulitskaya, and Sergei Gandlevsky, among others—used social media to invite their readers to participate in "strolls with writers" along Moscow's boulevards.[2] The call was taken up by thousands of followers, who gathered around their favorite authors in Pushkin Square for an unsanctioned "stroll," expressing their protest against the new authoritarianism (see Figure v.11). Unlike the scene with dancing writers at the Olympics closing ceremony, nobody instrumentalized the writers. Rather, they themselves took agency in the organization of the liberal political movement.

FIGURE v.10. The closing ceremony of the 22nd Winter Olympics, Sochi, Russia, 2014.

FIGURE V.11. Dmitry Bykov and the "Stroll with Writers" along the Moscow boulevards, May 13, 2012.

These episodes, despite their obvious dissimilarity, contradict a pervasive impression about the marginalization of literature in the post-Soviet cultural landscape. Beginning with the Perestroika period, Russian critics lamented or lauded, depending on their aesthetic and ideological inclinations, the end of the literature-centrism that supposedly has defined Russian culture since the nineteenth century. In the twenty-first century, that perception has been augmented by the increasingly productive interactions between literature and other art forms, including film and the visual arts; the rise of multilingualism and global Russian literature; and the unpredictable role of technological innovation in possible future changes in what counts as a book or what signifies "literature." Nevertheless, both the Sochi spectacle and the Moscow stroll of writers demonstrate that historical and cultural changes undergone by Russia since the collapse of communism have failed to diminish the symbolic weight of literature and the significance of the writer's role as an intellectual leader or even the conscience of the nation. A new politicization of literature, and the literary debates following the annexation of Crimea and Russian invasion in Ukraine, reinforce the seemingly obliterated idea of the political engagement of writers and the political functions of literature. As most recent phenomena testify, multimedia forms and the use of digital technologies do not diffuse but rather significantly enhance the power (and availability) of literary discourse, which is most tangibly demonstrated by the new surge of Russian poetry disseminated mainly by online channels.

No history, including the history of literature, can ever be complete. Despite the unpredictability of Russia's political future, we leave Russian literature at the threshold of new dramatic changes and transformations, during which its cultural authority will once again be tested by political and economic challenges. They will force writers to make difficult choices and seek new ways to question the unquestionable, to undermine shared beliefs, to destabilize conformity, to test subjectivities, and to record the catastrophes and the forms of endurance of their era. In short, to do what Russian literature has always done.

Guides to Further Reading

Reference Books, Histories, and Companions

Azarova, N. M., et al. (eds.), *Poeziia: uchebnik* (Moscow: OGI, 2016).

Barker, Adele Marie, and Gheith, Jehanne M. (eds.), *A History of Women's Writing in Russia* (Cambridge: Cambridge University Press, 2002).

Berezina, V. G., and Zapadov, A. V. (eds.), *Istoriia russkoi zhurnalistiki XVIII–XIX vekov*, 3rd edn. (Moscow: Vysshaia shkola, 1963).

Berkov, P. N., *Istoriia russkoi zhurnalistiki XVIII veka* (Moscow: Izdatel'stvo AN SSSR, 1952).

Berkov, P. N., *Istoriia russkoi komedii XVIII v.* (Leningrad: Nauka, 1977).

Berkov, P. N., Bykova, T. A., and Gurevich, M. M. (eds.), *Opisanie izdanii grazhdanskoi pechati, 1708–ianvar' 1725 g.* (Moscow: Izdatel'stvo AN SSSR, 1955).

Bethea, David M. (ed.), *The Pushkin Handbook* (Madison: The University of Wisconsin Press, 2005).

Blagoi, D. D., *Istoriia russkoi literatury XVIII veka* (Moscow: Gosudarstvennoe uchebno-pedagogicheskoe izdatel'stvo Ministerstva prosveshcheniia SSSR, 1960).

Bobrova, E. I., Murzanova, M. N., and Petrov, V. A. (eds.), *Istoricheskii ocherk i obzor fondov Rukopisnogo otdela biblioteki Akademii nauk*, vol. 1: *XVIII vek* (Moscow and Leningrad: Izdatel'stvo Akademii nauk SSSR, 1956).

Bogomolov, N. A. (ed.), *Pisateli sovremennoi epokhi: Biobibliograficheskii slovar' russkikh pisatelei XX veka*, vol. 2 (Moscow: Russkoe bibliograficheskoe obshchestvo, EksPrint NV, 1995).

Bykova, T. A., and Kosintsev, P. I., *Opisanie izdanii, napechatannykh pri Petre I: Dopolneniia i prilozheniia* (Leningrad: Izdatel'skii otdel biblioteki AN SSSR, 1972).

Chereiskii, L. A. (ed.), *Pushkin i ego okruzhenie* (Leningrad: Nauka, 1988).

Chuprinin, S. I., *Russkaia literatura segodnia: Bol'shoi putevoditel'* (Moscow: Vremia, 2007).

Čiževskij, D., *History of Russian Literature: From the Eleventh Century to the End of the Baroque*, Slavistic Printings and Reprintings, 12 (The Hague: Mouton, 1960, 3rd printing 1971).

Clark, Katerina, and Dobrenko, Evgeny (eds.), *Soviet Culture and Power: A History in Documents, 1917–1953* (New Haven, CT, and London: Yale University Press, 2007).

Dement'ev, A. G., Zapadov, A. V., and Cherepakhov, M. S. (eds.), *Russkaia periodicheskaia pechat' (1702–1894): Spravochnik* (Moscow: Gosudarstvennoe izdatel'stvo politicheskoi literatury, 1959).

Dobrenko, Evgeny, and Balina, Marina (eds.), *The Cambridge Companion to Twentieth-Century Russian Literature* (Cambridge: Cambridge University Press, 2011).

Dobrenko, Evgeny, and Tihanov, Galin (eds.), *A History of Russian Literary Theory and Criticism: The Soviet Age and Beyond* (Pittsburgh, PA: University of Pittsburgh Press, 2011).

Emerson, Caryl, *The Cambridge Introduction to Russian Literature* (Cambridge: Cambridge University Press, 2008).

Engelstein, Laura, and Sandler, Stephanie (eds.), *Self and Story in Russian History* (Ithaca, NY: Cornell University Press, 2000).

Etkind, Efim, Nivat, Georges, Serman, Ilya, and Strada, Vittorio, *Histoire de la littérature russe*, 7 vols. (Paris: Fayard, 1987–1990).

Filov, V. A., Kopanev, A. I., Savel'eva, E.A., and Shcherbakova, T. P. (eds.), *Svodnyi katalog knig na inostran-nykh iazykakh, izdannykh v Rossii v XVIII veke, 1701–1800*, 4 vols. (Leningrad: Nauka, 1984–2004).

Izdaniia grazhdanskoi pechati vremeni imperatritsy Elizavety Petrovny, 1741–1761, vol. 1: *1741–1755* (Moscow and Leningrad: Izdatel'stvo Akademii nauk SSSR, 1935).

Kameneva, T. N., and Kondakova, T. I. (eds.), *Spisok razyskivaemykh izdanii, ne voshedshikh v Svodnyi katalog russkoi knigi kirillovskoi pechati XVIII veka, 1701–1800* (Moscow: Gosudarstvennaia biblioteka im. V. I. Lenina, 1971).

Kelly, Catriona, *A History of Russian Women's Writing, 1820–1992* (Oxford: Clarendon Press, 1994).

Kliuchevskii, V. O., *A Course in Russian History: The Seventeenth Century*, trans. Natalie Duddington (Chicago: Quandrangle, 1968).

Kochetkova, N. D. (ed.), *Slovar' russkikh pisatelei XVIII veka* (Leningrad: Nauka, 1988–2010).

Kochetkova, N. D. (ed.), *Russkaia literatura. Vek XVIII. Lirika* (Moscow: Khudozhestvennaia literatura, 1990).

Kondakov, I. P. et al. (eds.), *Svodnyi katalog russkoi knigi grazhdanskoi pechati XVIII veka, 1725–1800*, 6 vols. (Moscow: Izdanie Gosudarstvennoi biblioteki imeni V. I. Lenina, Kniga, 1962–1975).

Koshelev, A. D. et al. (eds.), *Iz istorii russkoi kul'tury*, vol. 5: *XIX vek* (Moscow: Iazyki russkoi kul'tury, 1996).

Koz'min, B. P., *Pisateli sovremennoi epokhi: bio-bibliograficheskii slovar' russkikh pisatelei XX veka*, vol. 1 (Moscow: Gosudarstvennaia akademiia khudozhestvennykh nauk, 1928; repr. Moscow: DEM, 1992).

Krusanov, A. V., *Russkii avangard, 1907–1932 (Istoricheskii obzor)*, 3 vols. (Moscow: NLO, 2003–10).

Ledkovsky, Marina, Rosenthal, Charlotte, and Zirin, Mary (eds.), *Dictionary of Russian Women Writers* (Westport, CT: Greenwood Press, 1994).

Leiderman, N. L. (ed.), *Russkaia literatura XX veka: 1917–1920-e gody*, 2 vols. (Moscow: Academia, 2012).

Leiderman, N. L., and Lipovetskii, M. N., *Russkaia literatura XX veka: 1950–1990-e gody*, 2 vols. (Moscow: Academia, 2001).

Leiderman, N. L., Lipovetskii, M. N., and Litovskaia, Maria (eds.), *Russkaia literatura XX veka: 1930-e–seredina 1950-kh godov*, 2 vols. (Moscow: Academia, 2014).

Likhachev, D. S. (ed.), *Istoriia russkoi literatury X–XVII vv.* (Moscow: Prosveshchenie, 1980).

Likhachev, D. S. (ed.), *Slovar' knizhnikov i knizhnosti Drevnei Rusi, X–XIV vv.*, 3 vols. in 7 parts (Leningrad: Nauka, 1987–2004).

Lisovskii, N. M., *Bibliografiia russkoi periodicheskoi pechati, 1703–1900 gg.*, 2 vols. (Moscow: NLO, 1995).

Literaturnaia entsiklopediia russkogo zarubezh'ia, 1918–1940, 4 vols. (Moscow: INION RAN, 1993–2003).

Maiofis, M. L., and Kurilkin, A. R. (eds.), *Kritika pervoi chetverti XIX veka* (Moscow: AST Olimp, 2002).

Manuilov, V. A. (ed.), *Lermontovskaia entsiklopediia* (Moscow: Sovetskaia Entsiklopediia, 1981).

Mel'nikova, N. N., *Izdaniia Moskovskogo universiteta, 1756–1779* (Moscow: Izdatel'stvo Moskovskogo universiteta, 1955).

Mel'nikova, N. N., *Izdaniia, napechatannye v tipografii Moskovskogo Universiteta: XVIII v.* (Moscow: Izdatel'stvo Moskovskogo universiteta, 1966).

Moser, Charles A. (ed.), *The Cambridge History of Russian Literature*, revised edn. (Cambridge: Cambridge University Press, 1992; online 2008).

Muratova, K. D. (ed.), *Istoriia russkoi literatury XIX–nachala XX veka. Bibliograficheskii ukazatel'. Obshchaia chast'* (St. Petersburg: Nauka, 1993).

Nikolaev, P. A. (ed.), *Russkie pisateli, 1800–1917. Biograficheskii slovar'*, 5 vols. (Moscow: Sovetskaia entsiklopediia / Bol'shaia rossiiskaia entsiklopediia, 1989–).

Nikolaev, P. A. (ed.), *Russkie pisateli: biobibliograficheskii slovar'*, 2 vols. (Moscow: Prosveshchenie, 1990).

Nikolaev, P. A. (ed.), *Russkie pisateli 20 veka: Biograficheskii slovar'* (Moscow: Bol'shaia rossiiskaia entsiklopediia, Randevu-AM, 2000).

Nikolaev, S. I. (ed.), *Petr I v russkoi literature XVIII veka. Teksty i kommentarii* (St. Petersburg: Nauka, 2006).

Podskal'skii, Gerkhard, *Khristianstvo i bogoslovskaia literatura v Kievskoi Rusi (988–1237 gg.)*, 2nd edn. (St. Petersburg: Vizantinorossika, 1996).

Polovtsov, A. A. et al. (eds.), *Russkii biograficheskii slovar'*, 25 vols. (St. Petersburg: Izdatel'stvo Imperatorskogo russkogo istoricheskogo obshchestva, 1896–1918).

Raeff, Marc, *Russia Abroad: A Cultural History of the Russian Emigration, 1919–1939* (New York: Oxford University Press, 1990).

Severiukhin, D. Ia. (ed)., *Samizdat Leningrada: 1950-e–1980-e: Literaturnaia entsiklopediia* (Moscow: NLO, 2003).

Shruba, Manfred, *Literaturnye ob"edineniia Moskvy i Peterburga 1890–1917 godov: Slovar'* (Moscow: NLO, 2004).

Skabichevskii, A. M., *Ocherki istorii russkoi tsenzury (1700–1863 g.)* (St. Petersburg: n. p., 1892).

Smirnov, I. P., *Psikhodiakhronologika: psikhoistoriia russkoi literatury ot romantizma do nashikh dnei* (Moscow: NLO, 1994).

Sopikov, V. S., *Biblioteka dlia chteniia, nakhodiashchaiasia v Gostinom dvore pod No. 16 v knizhnoi lavke Vasil'ia Sopikova* (St. Petersburg: n. p., 1800).

Sopikov, V. S., *Opyt rossiiskoi bibliografii*, 5 vols. (St. Petersburg: v Tipografii Imperatorskogo Teatra, 1813–21).

Speranskii, M. N., *Rukopisnye sborniki XVIII veka* (Moscow: Izdatel'stvo Akademii nauk SSSR, 1963).

Stan'ko, A. I., *Russkaia periodicheskaia pechat' XVIII veka* (Rostov-on-Don: Izdatel'stvo Rostovskogo universiteta, 1979).

Stennik, Iu. V. (ed.), *Russkaia literatura. Vek XVIII. Tragediia* (Moscow: Khudozhestvennaia literatura, 1991).

Stepanov, V. P., and Stennik, Iu. V., *Istoriia russkoi literatury XVIII veka: Bibliograficheskii ukazatel'* (Leningrad: Nauka, 1968).

Tarkhova, N. A. (ed.), *Letopis' zhizni i tvorchestva Aleksandra Sergeevicha Griboedova, 1790–1829*, (Moscow: "Minuvshee," 2017).

Terras, Victor (ed.), *Handbook of Russian Literature* (New Haven, CT: Yale University Press, 1985).

Terras, Victor (ed.), *A History of Russian Literature* (New Haven, CT: Yale University Press, 1991).

Topchiev, A. V., Figurovskii, N. A., and Chenakal, V. L. (eds.), *Letopis' zhizni i tvorchestva M. V. Lomonosova* (Moscow and Leningrad: Izdatel'stvo AN SSSR, 1961).

Zaionchkovskii, P. A. (ed.), *Istoriia dorevoliutsionnoi Rossii v dnevnikakh i vospominaniiakh*, 5 vols. in 13 parts (Moscow: Kniga, 1977–89).

Zapadov, A. V., *Russkaia zhurnalistika poslednei chetverti XVIII veka* (Moscow: Izdatel'stvo Moskovskogo gosudarstvennogo universiteta, 1962).

Zapadov, A. V., *Russkaia zhurnalistika XVIII veka* (Moscow: Nauka, 1964).

Zernova, A. S., *Knigi kirillovskoi pechati, izdannye v Mosvke v XVI–XVII vekakh: Svodnyi katalog* (Moscow: Biblioteka SSSR im. V. I. Lenina, 1958).

Zhukov, D. A., and Pushkarev, L. N., *Russkie pisateli XVII veka* (Moscow: Molodaia gvardiia, 1972).

Part I. The Medieval Period

Adrianova-Peretts, V. P., "Siuzhetnoe povestvovanie v zhitiinykh pamiatnikakh XI–XIII vv.," in *Istoki russkoi belletristiki*, ed. Ia. S. Lur'e (Leningrad: Nauka, 1970), 67–107.

Adrianova-Peretts, V. P., "Zadachi izucheniia 'agiograficheskogo stilia' Drevnei Rusi," *TODRL*, 20 (1964), 41–71.

Averintsev, S. S., "Avtorstvo i avtoritet," in *Istoricheskaia poetika. Literaturnye epokhi i tipy khudozhestvennogo soznaniia*, ed. P. A. Grintser (Moscow: Nasledie, 1994), 105–25.

Averintsev, S. S., Andreev, M. L., and Gasparov, M. L., "Kategorii poetiki v smene literaturnykh epokh," in *Istoricheskaia poetika. Literaturnye epokhi i tipy khudozhestvennogo soznaniia*, ed. P. A. Grintser (Moscow: Nasledie, 1994), 3–38.

Birnbaum, Henrik, *Aspects of the Slavic Middle Ages and Slavic Renaissance Culture* (New York: Peter Lang, 1991).

Birnbaum, Henrik, "Fact and Fiction Concerning the Genesis of Literary Russian," *Russian Linguistics*, 3 (1976), 167–80.

Birnbaum, Henrik, *On the Significance of the Second South Slavic Influence for the Evolution of the Russian Literary Language* (Lisse: Peter de Ridder Press, 1976).

Birnbaum, Henrik, "Serbian Models in the Literature and Literary Language of Medieval Russia," *SEEJ*, 23 (1979), 1–13.

Birnbaum, Henrik, and Flier, Michael S. (eds.), *Medieval Russian Culture* (Berkeley: University of California Press, 1984).

Bogatyrev, P. S. (ed.), *Russkoe narodnoe poeticheskoe tvorchestvo* (Moscow: Gosudarstvennoe uchebno-pedagogicheskoe izdatel´stvo, 1954).

Børtnes, Jostein, *Visions of Glory: Studies in Early Russian Hagiography*, trans. Jostein Børtnes and Paul L. Nielsen (Atlantic Highlands, NJ: Humanities Press International, 1988).

Brown, Peter, "The Holy Man in Late Antiquity," in Peter Brown, *Society and the Holy in Late Antiquity* (Berkeley: University of California Press, 1982), 103–52.

Brumfield, William Craft, *A History of Russian Architecture* (Cambridge: Cambridge University Press, 1993).

Bubnov, N. Iu., *Antichnye traditsii v drevnerusskoi literature XI–XVI vv.* (Munich: Verlag Otto Sagner, 1991).

Bubnov, N. Iu., *Knizhnaia kul´tura staroobriadtsev: stat´i raznykh let* (St. Petersburg: BAN, 2007).

Bushkovitch, Paul, "The Formation of a National Consciousness in Early Modern Russia," *Harvard Ukrainian Studies*, 10.3–4 (1986), 355–76.

Cherniavsky, Michael, *Tsar and People: Studies in Russian Myths* (New Haven, CT: Yale University Press, 1961).

Cherniavsky, Michael, "The Old Believers and the New Religion," *Slavic Review*, 25 (1966), 1–39.

Copeland, Rita, *Rhetoric, Hermeneutics and Translation in the Middle Ages: Academic Traditions and Vernacular Texts* (Cambridge: Cambridge University Press, 1991).

Fedotov, G. P., *Sviatye Drevnei Rusi (X–XVII st.)* (Paris: YMCA Press, 1931).

Fedotov, G. P., *The Russian Religious Mind*, 2 vols. (Cambridge, MA: Harvard University Press, 1966).

Fennell, J. L. I., *The Crisis of Medieval Russia, 1200–1304* (London: Longman, 1983).

Fennell, J. L. I., *The Emergence of Moscow, 1304–1359* (London: Secker and Warburg, 1968).

Fennell, J. L. I., and Stokes, Antony D., *Early Russian Literature* (London: Faber and Faber, 1974).

Franklin, Simon, *Byzantium–Rus–Russia: Studies in the Translation of Christian Culture* (Aldershot: Ashgate, 2002).

Franklin, Simon, *Writing, Society and Culture in Early Rus, c.950–1300* (Cambridge: Cambridge University Press, 2002).

Franklin, Simon, and Shepard, Jonathan, *The Emergence of Rus, 750–1200* (London: Longman, 1996).

Gasparov, Boris, *Poetika "Slova o polku Igoreve"* (Vienna: Gesellschaft zur Förderung slawistischer Studien, 1984).

Goldblatt, Harvey, "Formal Structures and Textual Identity: the Case of Prince Andrei M. Kurbskii's First Letter to Tsar Ivan IV Groznyi," *Russian History*, 14 (1987), 155–76.

Goldblatt, Harvey, "Medieval Studies," *SEEJ*, vol. 31 (1987), 12–30.

Halperin, Charles J., *Russia and the Golden Horde: The Mongol Impact on Medieval Russian History* (Bloomington, IN: Indiana University Press, 1985).

Kantorowicz, Ernst, *The King's Two Bodies: A Study in Medieval Political Theology* (Princeton, NJ: Princeton University Press, 1957).

Keenan, Edward, *The Kurbskii-Groznyi Apocrypha: The Seventeenth-Century Genesis of the "Correspondence" attributed to Prince A.M. Kurbskii and Tsar Ivan IV* (Cambridge, MA: Harvard University Press, 1971).

Keenan, Edward, "Muscovite Political Folkways," *Russian Review*, 45 (1986), 115–81.

Kivelson, Valerie, *Cartographies of Tsardom: The Land and Its Meanings in Seventeenth-Century Russia* (Ithaca, NY: Cornell University Press, 2006).

Kliuchevskii, V. O., *Drevnerusskie zhitiia sviatykh kak istoricheskii istochnik* (Moscow: Tipografiia Gracheva, 1871; repr. 1988).

Kloss, B. M., *Nikonovskii svod i russkie letopisi XVI–XVII vekov* (Moscow: Nauka, 1980).

Kloss, B. M., *Pskovskie letopisi* (Moscow: Iazyki slavianskoi kultury, 2003).

Kollmann, Nancy Shields, *By Honor Bound: State and Society in Early Modern Russia* (Ithaca, NY: Cornell University Press, 1999).

Kollmann, Nancy Shields, *Kinship and Politics: The Making of the Muscovite Political System, 1345–1547* (Stanford, CA: Stanford University Press, 1987).

Kollmann, Nancy Shields, "Pilgrimage, Procession, and Symbolic Space in Sixteenth-Century Russian Politics," in *Medieval Russian Culture*, ed. Henrik Birnbaum, Michael S. Flier, and Daniel B. Rowland (Berkeley: University of California Press, 1984), vol. 2, 163–81.

Lenhoff, Gail, *The Martyred Princes Boris and Gleb: A Socio-Cultural Study of the Cult and the Texts* (Columbus, OH: Slavica, 1989).

Lenhoff, Gail, "Toward a Theory of Protogenres in Medieval Russian Letters," *Russian Review*, 43 (1984), 31–54.

Likhachev, D. S., *Chelovek v literature drevnei Rusi* (Moscow: Nauka, 1970).

Likhachev, D. S., *Issledovaniia po drevnerusskoi literature* (Leningrad: Nauka, 1986).

Likhachev, D. S., *Kul'tura Rusi vremeni Andreia Rubleva i Epifaniia Premudrogo (Konets XIV–nachalo XV v.)* (Moscow: Izdatel'stvo AN SSSR, 1962).

Likhachev, D. S., *"Slovo o polku Igoreve" i kul'tura ego vremeni* (Leningrad: Khudozhestvennaia literatura, 1978).

Likhachev, D. S., *Slovo o polku Igoreve* (Leningrad: Khudozhestvennaia literatura, Sovetskii pisatel', 1983).

Likhachev, D. S., and Dmitriev, L. A. (eds.), *Slovo o polku Igoreve i pamiatniki kulikovskogo tsikla: K voprosu o vremeni napisaniia "Slova"* (Moscow and Leningrad: Nauka, 1966).

Madariaga, Isabel de, *Ivan the Terrible: First Tsar of Russia* (New Haven, CT, & London: Yale University Press, 2005).

Martin, Janet, *Medieval Russia, 980–1584* (Cambridge: Cambridge University Press, 1995).

Meyendorff, John, *Rome, Constantinople, Moscow: Historical and Theological Studies* (Crestwood, NY: St. Vladimir's Seminary Press, 1996).

Michels, Georg Bernhard, *At War with the Church: Religious Dissent in Seventeenth-Century Russia* (Stanford, CA: Stanford University Press, 1999).

Minnis, Alistair J., "Late-Medieval Discussions of *Compilatio* and the Role of the *Compilator*," *PBB*, 101 (1979), 385–421.

Minnis, Alistair J., *Medieval Theory of Authorship: Scholastic Literary Attitudes in the Later Middle Ages*, 2nd edn. (Philadelphia: University of Pennsylvania Press, 1988).

Panchenko, A. M., and Uspenskii, B. A., "Ivan Groznyi i Petr Velikii: kontseptsii pervogo monarkha," *TODRL*, 37 (1983), 54–78.

Picchio, Riccardo, "Models and Patterns in the Literary Tradition of Medieval Orthodox Slavdom," in *American Contributions to the Seventh International Congress of Slavists*, ed. Victor Terras (The Hague, Paris: Mouton, 1973), vol. 2, 439–67.

Picchio, Riccardo, "The Impact of Ecclesiastical Culture on Old Russian Literary Techniques," in *Medieval Russian Culture*, ed. Henrik Birnbaum and Michael S. Flier, 2 vols. (Los Angeles: University of California Press, 1984), vol. 1, 247–79.

Priselkov, M. D., *Nestor-letopisets. Opyt istoriko-literaturnoi kharakteristiki* (Petrograd: Brokgaus-Efron, 1923).

Raffensperger, Christian, *Reimagining Europe: Kievan Rus' in the Medieval World* (Cambridge, MA: Harvard University Press, 2012).

Ranchin, A. M., *Stat'i o drevnerusskoi literature* (Moscow: Dialog-MGU, 1999).

Rappoport, P. A., *Building the Churches of Kievan Russia* (Aldershot: Ashgate, 1995).

Ševčenko, Ihor, *Byzantium and the Slavs in Letters and Culture* (Cambridge, MA: Harvard Ukrainian Research Institute, 1991).

Seemann, Klaus-Dieter, "Genres and the Alterity of Old Russian Literature," *SEEJ*, 31.2 (1987), 246–58.

Shaskov, A. T., "Maksim Grek i ideologicheskaia bor′ba v Rossii vo vtoroi polovine XVII–nachale XVIII v.," *TODRL*, 33 (1979), 8–87.

Sobolevskii, A. I., *Perevodnaia literatura Moskovskoi Rusi XIV–XVII vekov. Bibliograficheskie materialy* (St. Petersburg: Tipografiia Imperatorskoi Akademii nauk, 1903).

Sobolevskii, A. I., *Zapadnoe vliianie na literaturu Moskovskoi Rusi XV–XVII vekov* (St. Petersburg: Sinodal′naia tipografiia, 1899; repr. The Hague: Europe Printing, 1966).

Speranskii, M. N., *Istoriia drevnei russkoi literatury. Kievskii period* (Moscow: Izd. M. i S. Sabashnikovykh, 1920; repr. Moscow: "Lan," 2002).

Thomson, Francis J., *The Reception of Byzantine Culture in Mediaeval Russia* (Ashgate: Aldershot, 1999).

Tolochko, A. P., *Kniaz′ v Drevnei Rusi: vlast′, sobstvennost′, ideologiia* (Kiev: Naukova Dumka, 1992).

Toporov, V. N., *Sviatost′ i sviatye v russkoi dukhovnoi kul′ture*, vol. 1: *Pervyi vek khristianstva na Rusi* (Moscow: Gnozis, 1995).

Uspenskii, B. A. *Boris i Gleb: vospriiatie istorii v Drevnei Rusi* (Moscow: Iazyki russkoi kul′tury, 2000).

Uspenskii, B. A. *Kratkii ocherk istorii russkogo literaturnogo iazyka (XI–XIX vv.)* (Moscow: Gnozis, 1994).

Uspenskii, B. A., and Zhivov, V. M., *"Tsar and God" and Other Essays in Russian Cultural Semiotics*, trans. Marcus C. Levitt (Boston: Academic Studies Press, 2012).

Vilkul, T. L., *Liudi i kniaz′ v drevnerusskikh letopisiakh serediny XI–XIII vv.* (Moscow: Kvadriga, 2009).

Vlasto, A. P., *The Entry of the Slavs into Christendom: An Introduction to the Medieval History of the Slavs* (Cambridge: Cambridge University Press, 1970).

Vodoff, V., *Naissance de la chrétienté russe. La conversion du prince Vladimir de Kiev (988) et ses conséquences (XIe–XIIIe siècles)* (Paris: Fayard, 1988).

Wyschogrod, Edith, *Saints and Postmodernism: Revisioning Moral Philosophy* (Chicago, IL: University of Chicago Press, 1990).

Zhivov, V. M., *Sviatost′. Kratkii slovar′ agiograficheskikh terminov* (Moscow: Gnozis, 1994).

Zhivov, V. M., "Religious Reform and the Emergence of the Individual in Russian Seventeenth-Century Literature," in *Religion and Culture in Early Modern Russia and Ukraine*, ed. Samuel H. Baron and Nancy Shields Kollmann (DeKalb, IL: Northern Illinois University Press, 1997), 184–98.

Zhivov, V. M., *Razyskaniia v oblasti istorii i predystorii russkoi kul′tury* (Moscow: Iazyki slavianskoi kul′tury, 2002).

Part II. The Early Modern Period

Alekseeva, T. V. (ed.), *Russkoe iskusstvo barokko: Materialy i issledovaniia* (Moscow: Nauka, 1977).

Avdeev, A. G., *Starorusskaia epigrafika i knizhnost′: Novo-ierusalimskaia shkola epigraficheskoi poezii* (Moscow: Pravoslavnyi Sviato-Tikhonovskii gumanitarnyi universitet, 2006).

Baklanova, N. A., "Evoliutsiia russkoi original′noi bytovoi povesti na rubezhe XVII–XVIII vekov," in *Russkaia literatura na rubezhe dvukh epokh (XVII–nachalo XVIII v.)*, ed. A. N. Robinson (Moscow: Nauka, 1971).

Bercoff, Giovanna Brogi (ed.), *Il Barocco letterario nei paesi slavi* (Rome: NIS, 1996).

Bogdanov, A. P. (ed.), *Pamiatniki obshchestvenno-politicheskoi mysli v Rossii kontsa XVII veka: Literaturnye panegiriki*, 2 vols. (Moscow: Institut istorii SSSR, 1983).

Bushkovitch, Paul, *Religion and Society in Russia: The Sixteenth and Seventeenth Centuries* (New York and Oxford: Oxford University Press, 1992).

Cox, Gary, "Fairy-Tale Plots and Contemporary Heroes in Early Russian Prose Fiction," *Slavic Review*, 39.1 (1980), 85–96.

Demin, A. S., "Russkie staropechatnye predisloviia nachala XVII veka ('Velikaia slabost' v Smutnoe vremia)," in *Tematika i stilistika predislovii i posleslovii*, ed. A. S. Demin (Moscow: Nauka, 1981).

Derzhavina, O. A., *Fatsetsii: Perevodnaia novella v russkoi literature XVII veka* (Moscow: Izd. AN SSSR, 1962).

Derzhavina, O. A., Demin, A. S., and Robinson, A. N., "Poiavlenie teatra i dramaturgii v Rossii v XVII v.," in *Ranniaia russkaia dramaturgiia (XVII–pervoi poloviny XVIII v.)*, vol. 1: *Pervye p'esy russkogo teatra* ed. O. A. Derzhavina, K. N. Lomunov, and A. N. Robinson (Moscow: Nauka, 1972), 7–98.

Dmitriev, L. A., *Zhitiinye povesti russkogo severa kak pamiatniki literatury XIII–XVII vv. Evoliutsiia zhanra legendarno-biograficheskikh skazanii* (Leningrad: Nauka, 1973).

Eleonskaia, A. S., *Russkaia publitsistika vtoroi poloviny XVII veka* (Moscow: Nauka, 1978).

Eremin, I. P., "Poeticheskii stil' Simeona Polotskogo," *TODRL*, 6 (1948), 125–53.

Gasperetti, David, *The Rise of the Russian Novel: Carnival, Stylization, and Mockery of the West* (DeKalb, IL: Northern Illinois University Press, 1998).

Hughes, Lindsey, *Sophia, Regent of Russia 1657–1704* (New Haven, CT: Yale University Press, 1990).

Kivelson, Valerie A., "Through the Prism of Witchcraft: Gender and Social Change in Seventeenth-Century Muscovy," in *Russia's Women: Accommodation, Resistance, Transformation*, ed. Barbara Evans Clements, Barbara Alpern Engel, and Christine D. Worobec (Berkeley and London: University of California Press, 1991), 74–94.

Kotilaine, Jarmo, and Poe, Marshall (eds.), *Modernizing Muscovy: Reform and Social Change in Seventeenth-Century Russia* (London: RoutledgeCurzon: 2004).

Lachmann, Renate, "Aspects of the Russian Language Question in the Seventeenth Century," in *Aspects of the Slavic Language Question*, ed. Riccardo Picchio and Harvey Goldblatt, 2 vols. (New Haven, CT: Yale Concilium on International and Area Studies, 1984), vol. 2, 125–85.

Lachmann, Renate, "Kanon und Gegenkanon in der russischen Kultur des 17. Jahrhunderts," in *Kanon und Zensur: Beiträge zur Archäologie der literarischen Kommunikation II*, ed. Aleida and Jan Assmann, vol. 2, Archäologie der literarischen Kommunikation (Munich: W. Fink, 1987), 124–37.

Lachmann, Renate (ed.), *Slavische Barockliteratur. 2, Gedenkschrift für Dmitrij Tschižewskij (1894–1977)* (Munich: W. Fink, 1983).

Levin, Eve, *Sex and Society in the World of the Orthodox Slavs, 900–1700* (Ithaca, NY: Cornell University Press, 1989).

Markov, N. V., "Russkii stikh XVII veka (materialy k kharakteristike razvitiia)," in *Russkoe stikhoslo-zhenie: Traditsii i problemy razvitiia*, ed. L. I. Timofeev (Moscow: Nauka, 1985), 244–63.

Moiseeva, G. N., *Russkie povesti pervoi treti XVIII veka* (Moscow: Nauka, 1965).

Nikolaev, S. I., *Literaturnaia kul'tura petrovskoi epokhi* (St. Petersburg: Dmitrii Bulanin, 1996).

Nikolaev, S. I., *Pol'skaia poeziia v russkikh perevodakh (Vtoraia polovina XVII–pervaia tret' XVIII veka)* (Leningrad: Nauka, 1989).

Panchenko, A. M., "Dva etapa russkogo barokko," *TODRL*, 32 (1977), 100–6.

Panchenko, A. M., "Literatura 'perekhodnogo veka,'" in *Istoriia russkoi literatury*, vol. 1, *Drevnerusskaia literatura. Literatura XVIII veka*, ed. N. I. Prutskov (Leningrad: Nauka, 1980), 291–407.

Panchenko, A. M., "Neskol'ko zamechanii o genologii knizhnoi poezii XVII veka," *TODRL*, 27 (1972), 236–46.

Panchenko, A. M., "Pridvornye virshi 80-kh godov XVII stoletiia," *TODRL*, 21 (1965), 65–73.

Panchenko, A. M., *Russkaia kul'tura v kanun petrovskikh reform* (Leningrad: Nauka, 1984).

Panchenko, A. M., *Russkaia stikhotvornaia kul'tura XVII veka* (Leningrad: Nauka, 1973).

Panchenko, A. M., "Slovo i Znanie v estetike Simeona Polotskogo (na materiale 'Vertograda mnogotsvetnogo')," *TODRL*, 25 (1970), 232–41.

Pliukhanova, M. B., "O nekotorykh chertakh lichnostnogo soznaniia v Rossii XVII veka," in *Khudozhestvennyi iazyk srednevekov'ia*, ed. V. A. Karpushkin (Moscow: Nauka, 1982), 184–200.

Poliakov, F. B., "Ierarkhiia iazykov i pamiat' kul'tury: pol'skie i neolatinskie elementy v poetike Simeona Polotskogo," in *Traduzione e rielaborazione nelle letterature di Polonia, Ucraina e Russia, XVI–XVIII secolo*, ed. Giovanna Brogi Bercoff, Maria Di Salvo, and Luigi Marinelli (Alessandria: Edizioni dell'Orso, 1999), 249–66.

Robinson, A. N. (ed.), *Simeon Polotskii i ego knigoizdatel'skaia deiatel'nost'* (Moscow: Nauka, 1982).

Romodanovskaia, E. K., *Russkaia literatura na poroge novogo vremeni: Puti formirovaniia russkoi belletristiki perekhodnogo perioda* (Novosibirsk: VO "Nauka," 1994).

Sazonova, L. I., "Printsip ritmicheskoi organizatsii v proizvedeniiakh torzhestvennogo krasnorechiia starshei pory ('Slovo o zakone i blagodati' Ilariona, 'Pokhvala sv. Simeonu i sv. Savve' Domentiana)," *TODRL*, 28 (1974), 30–46.

Sazonova, L. I., *Poeziia russkogo barokko (vtoraia polovina XVII–nachalo XVIII v.)* (Moscow: Nauka, 1991).

Sazonova, L. I., *Literaturnaia kul'tura Rossii: Rannee novoe vremia* (Moscow: Iazyki slavianskikh kul'tur, 2006).

Serman, I. Z., "Bova i russkaia literatura," *Slavica Hierosolymitana*, 7 (1985), 163–70.

Skripil', M. O., "Povest' o Petre i Fevronii muromskikh v ee otnoshenii k russkoi skazke," *TODRL*, 7 (1949), 131–67.

Sofronova, L. A., *Poetika slavianskogo teatra XVII–pervoi poloviny XVIII v.: Pol'sha, Ukraina, Rossiia* (Moscow: Nauka, 1981).

Vroon, Ronald, "From Liturgy to Literature: Prayer and Play in the Early Russian Baroque," in *Culture and Authority in the Baroque*, ed. Massimo Ciavolella and Patrick Coleman (Toronto: Toronto University Press, 2005), 122–37.

Warnke, Frank J., *Versions of Baroque: European Literature in the Seventeenth Century* (New Haven, CT: Yale University Press, 1972).

Zhivov, V. M., *Iz tserkovnoi istorii vremen Petra Velikogo: Issledovaniia i materialy* (Moscow: NLO, 2004).

Part III. The Eighteenth Century

Alekseeva, N. Iu., *Russkaia oda: Razvitie odicheskoi formy v XVII–XVIII vekakh* (St. Petersburg: Nauka, 2005).

Alexander, John T., *Autocratic Politics in a National Crisis: The Imperial Russian Government and Pugachev's Revolt, 1773–1775* (Bloomington: Indiana University Press, 1969).

Alexander, John T., *Catherine the Great: Life and Legend* (New York: Oxford University Press, 1989).

Al'tshuller, Mark, *Predtechi slavianofil'stva v russkoi literature (Obshchestvo "Beseda liubitelei russkogo slova")* (Ann Arbor, MI: Ardis, 1984).

Baehr, Stephen Lessing, *The Paradise Myth in Eighteenth-Century Russia: Utopian Patterns in Early Secular Russian Literature and Culture* (Stanford, CA: Stanford University Press, 1991).

Berkov, P. N., *Lomonosov i literaturnaia polemika ego vremeni* (Leningrad: Izd. AN SSSR, 1936).

Berkov, P. N., *Istoriia russkoi komedii XVIII v.* (Leningrad: Nauka, 1977).

Cracraft, James, *The Petrine Revolution in Russian Imagery* (Chicago, IL: University of Chicago Press, 1997).

Cracraft, James, *The Petrine Revolution in Russian Culture* (Cambridge, MA: Harvard University Press, 2004).

Dixon, Simon, *Catherine the Great* (London: Profile, 2009).

Dixon, Simon, "The Posthumous Reputation of Catherine II in Russia 1797–1837," *SEER*, 77.4 (October 1999), 646–79.

Edelstein, Dan, *The Enlightenment: A Genealogy* (Chicago, IL: University of Chicago Press, 2010).

Golburt, Luba, *The First Epoch: The Eighteenth Century and the Russian Cultural Imagination* (Madison, WI: University of Wisconsin Press, 2014).

Greenleaf, Monika, "Performing Autobiography: The Multiple Memoirs of Catherine the Great (1756–96)," *Russian Review*, 63.3 (July 2004), 407–26.

Grinberg, M. S., and Uspenskii, B. A., *Literaturnaia voina Trediakovskogo i Sumarokova v 1740-kh–nachale 1750-kh godov* (Moscow: RGGU, 2001).

Hammarberg, Gitta, *From the Idyll to the Novel: Karamzin's Sentimentalist Prose* (Cambridge: Cambridge University Press, 1991).

Hughes, Lindsey, *Peter the Great: A Biography* (New Haven, CT: Yale University Press, 2002).

Jones, W. Gareth, *Nikolay Novikov: Enlightener of Russia* (Cambridge: Cambridge University Press, 1984).

Kahn, Andrew, "'Blazhenstvo ne v luchakh Porfira': histoire et fonction de la tranquillité (spokojstvie) dans la pensée et la poésie russes du XVIIIe siècle, de Kantemir au sentimentalisme," *Revue des études slaves*, 74.4 (2002), 669–88.

Kahn, Andrew, "Russian Literature Between Classicism and Romanticism: Poetry, Feeling, Subjectivity," in *The Oxford Handbook of European Romanticism*, ed. Paul Hamilton (Oxford: Oxford University Press, 2016), 493–511.

Kochetkova, N. D., *Literatura russkogo sentimentalizma: Esteticheskie i khudozhestvennye iskaniia* (St. Petersburg: Nauka, 1994).

Lachmann, Renate, "'Pokin', Kupido, strely': Bemerkungen zur Topik der russischen Liebesdichtung des 18. Jahrhunderts," in *Slavistische Studien zum VI. Internationalen Slavistenkongress in Prag 1968*, ed. Erwin Koschmieder and Maximilian Braun (Munich: Trofenik, 1968), 449–74.

Lachmann, Renate, "Introduction," in Feofan Prokopovich, *De Arte Rhetorica Libri X* (Cologne: Böhlau, 1982), xv–cii.

Lauer, Reinhard, *Gedichtform zwischen Schema und Verfall: Sonett, Rondeau, Madrigal, Ballade, Stanze und Triolett in der russischen Literatur des 18. Jahrhunderts* (Munich: W. Fink, 1975).

Levitt, Marcus C., "Catherine the Great," in *Russian Women Writers*, ed. Christine D. Tomei, 2 vols. (New York: Garland, 1999), vol. 1, 3–27.

Levitt, Marcus C., *Early Modern Russian Letters: Texts and Contexts* (Boston, MA: Academic Studies Press, 2009).

Levitt, Marcus C., (ed.), *Early Modern Russian Writers, Late Seventeenth and Eighteenth Centuries* (Detroit, MI: Gale Research, 1995).

Lotman, Iu. M., *Russkaia literatura i kul'tura Prosveshcheniia* (Moscow: Ob"edinennoe gumanitarnoe izdatel'stvo, 1998).

Lotman, Iu. M., and Uspenskii, B. A., "Spory o iazyke v nachale XIX v. kak fakt russkoi kul'tury ('Proisshestvie v tsarstve tenei, ili Sud'bina rossiiskogo iazyka'—neizvestnoe sochinenie Semena Bobrova)," in B. A. Uspenskii, *Izbrannye trudy*, 3 vols. (Moscow: Shkola "Iazyki russkoi kul'tury," 1994–1997), vol. 2, 411–572.

Madariaga, Isabel de, *Russia in the Age of Catherine the Great* (New Haven, CT: Yale University Press, 1981).

Maiofis, M. L., *Vozzvanie k Evrope: Literaturnoe obshchestvo "Arzamas" i rossiiskii modernizatsionnyi proekt 1815–1818 godov* (Moscow: NLO, 2008).

Marker, Gary, *Publishing, Printing, and the Origins of Intellectual Life in Russia, 1700–1800* (Princeton, NJ: Princeton University Press, 1985).

Morozov, A. A., "O vosproizvedenii tekstov russkikh poetov XVIII veka," *Russkaia literatura*, 2 (1966), 175–93.

Proskurina, Vera, *Creating the Empress: Politics and Poetry in the Age of Catherine II* (Boston, MA: Academic Studies Press, 2011).

Pumpianskii, L. V., *Klassicheskaia traditsiia: sobranie trudov po istorii russkoi literatury* (Moscow: Iazyki russkoi kul'tury, 2000).

Raeff, Marc, "Home, School, and Service in the Life of the 18th-Century Russian Nobleman," *SEER*, 40.95 (1962), 295–307.

Raeff, Marc, "Filling the Gap Between Radishchev and the Decembrists," *Slavic Review*, 26.3 (1967), 395–413.

Raeff, Marc, "On the Heterogeneity of the Eighteenth Century in Russia," in *Russia and the World of the Eighteenth Century*, ed. R. P. Bartlett, A. G. Cross, and Karen Rasmussen (Columbus, OH: 1988), 666–80.

Raeff, Marc, *Origins of the Russian Intelligentsia: The Eighteenth-Century Nobility* (New York: Harcourt, Brace and World, 1966).

Raeff, Marc, "The Enlightenment in Russia and Russian Thought in the Enlightenment," in *The Eighteenth Century in Russia*, ed. J. G. Garrard (Oxford: Clarendon, 1973), 25–47.

Reyfman, Irina, *Rank and Style: Russians in State Service, Life, and Literature* (Boston, MA: Academic Studies Press, 2012).

Reyfman, Irina, *Vasilii Trediakovsky: The Fool of the "New" Russian Literature* (Stanford, CA: Stanford University Press, 1990).

Rogger, Hans, *National Consciousness in Eighteenth-Century Russia* (Cambridge, MA: Harvard University Press, 1960).

Rubin-Detlev, Kelsey, "The Letters of Catherine the Great and the Rhetoric of Enlightenment," Ph.D. thesis, University of Oxford, 2015.

Schönle, Andreas, "The Scare of the Self: Sentimentalism, Privacy, and Private Life in Russian Culture, 1780–1820," *Slavic Review*, 57.4 (1998), 723–46.

Serman, I. Z., "A. A. Rzhevskii," in *Poety XVIII veka*, ed. G. P. Makogonenko and I. Z. Serman, 2 vols. (Leningrad: Sovetskii pisatel´, 1972), vol. 1, 189–94.

Serman, I. Z., "Neizdannaia filosoficheskaia poema V. Trediakovskogo," *Russkaia literatura*, 1 (1961), 160–8.

Serman, I. Z., "O poetike Lomonosova (Epitet i metafora)," in *Literaturnoe tvorchestvo M. V. Lomonosova: Issledovaniia i materialy*, ed. P. N. Berkov and I. Z. Serman (Moscow: Izdatel´stvo Akademii Nauk SSSR, 1962), 101–32.

Serman, I. Z., *Poeticheskii stil´ Lomonosova* (Moscow: Nauka, 1966).

Serman, I. Z., "Russkaia poeziia serediny XVIII veka. Sumarokov i ego shkola," in B. P. Gorodetskii (ed.), *Istoriia russkoi poezii v dvukh tomakh*, 2 vols (Leningrad: Nauka, 1968–69), vol. 1 (1968), 90–119.

Serman, I. Z., "V. V. Kapnist i russkaia poeziia nachala XIX veka," *XVIII vek*, 4 (1959), 289–303.

Smoliarova, Tat´iana, *Zrimaia lirika: Derzhavin* (Moscow: NLO, 2011).

Stennik, Iu. V., "O khudozhestvennoi strukture tragedii A. P. Sumarokova," *XVIII vek*, 5 (1962), 273–94.

Stennik, Iu. V., *Zhanr tragedii v russkoi literature: Epokha klassitsizma* (Leningrad: Nauka, 1981).

Uspenskii, B. A., *Iz istorii russkogo literaturnogo iazyka XVIII–nachala XIX veka: Iazykovaia programma Karamzina i ee istoricheskie korni* (Moscow: Izdatel´tvo Moskovskogo universiteta, 1985).

Uspenskii, B. A., and Zhivov, V. M., "Zur Spezifik des Barock in Russland: Das Verfahren der Äquivokation in der russischen Poesie des 18. Jahrhunderts," in *Slavische Barockliteratur. 2, Gedenkschrift für Dmitrij Tschiževskij (1894–1977)*, ed. Renate Lachmann (Munich: W. Fink, 1983), 25–56.

Wirtschafter, Elise Kimerling, *The Play of Ideas in Russian Enlightenment Theater* (DeKalb, IL: Northern Illinois University Press, 2003).

Wolff, Larry, *Inventing Eastern Europe: The Map of Civilization on the Mind of the Enlightenment* (Stanford, CA: Stanford University Press, 1994).

Zaborov, P. R., *Russkaia literatura i Vol´ter, XVIII–pervaia tret´ XIX veka* (Leningrad: Nauka, 1978).

Zapadov, V. A., "Istoriia sozdaniia 'Puteshestviia iz Peterburga v Moskvu' i 'Vol´nosti,'" in A. N. Radishchev, *Puteshestvie iz Peterburga v Moskvu. Vol´nost´*, ed. V. A. Zapadov (St. Petersburg: Nauka, 1992), 475–623.

Zapadov, V. A., "Kratkii ocherk istorii russkoi tsenzury 60–90-kh godov XVIII veka," *Uchenye zapiski Leningradskogo gosudarstvennogo pedagogicheskogo instituta im. A. I. Gertsena*, 414 (1971), 94–135.

Zapadov, V. A., *Literaturnye napravleniia v russkoi literature XVIII veka* (St. Petersburg: IMA Press, 1995).

Zapadov, V. A., *Russkii stikh XVIII—nachala XIX veka (Ritmika)* (Leningrad: LGPI, 1974).

Zhivov, V. M., *Iazyk i kul´tura v Rossii XVIII veka* (Moscow: "Iazyki russkoi kul´tury," 1996).

Zhivov, V. M., *Language and Culture in Eighteenth-Century Russia*, trans. Marcus Levitt (Boston, MA: Academic Studies Press, 2009).

Zhivov, V. M., "The Myth of the State in the Age of Enlightenment and Its Destruction in Late Eighteenth-Century Russia," *Russian Studies in History*, 48.3 (Winter 2009–10), 10–29.

Zhivov, V. M., "'Vsiakaia vsiachina' i sozdanie Ekaterininskogo politicheskogo diskursa," in *Eighteenth-Century Russia: Society, Culture, Economy: Papers from the VII International Conference of the Study Group on Eighteenth-Century Russia, Wittenberg 2004*, ed. Roger Bartlett and Gabriela Lehmann-Carli (Berlin: LIT, 2007), 251–65.

Zhivov, V. M., and Uspenskii, B. A., "Metamorfozy antichnogo iazychestva v istorii russkoi kul'tury XVII–XVIII vv.," *Antichnost' v kul'ture i iskusstve posleduiushchikh vekov* (Moscow: Sovetskii khudozhnik, 1984), 204–85.

Zhivov, V. M., and Uspenskii, B. A., "Tsar' i bog. Semioticheskie aspekty sakralizatsii monarkha v Rossii," in B. A. Uspenskii (ed.), *Iazyki kul'tury i problemy perevodimosti* (Moscow: Nauka, 1987), 47–153.

Zorin, A. L., *Kormia dvuglavogo orla...: Literatura i gosudarstvennaia ideologiia v Rossii v poslednei treti XVIII-pervoi treti XIX veka* (Moscow: NLO, 2001).

Part IV. The Nineteenth Century

Allen, Elizabeth Cheresh (ed.), *Before They Were Titans: Essays on the Early Works of Dostoevsky and Tolstoy* (Boston: Academic Studies Press, 2015).

Al'tshuller, Mark, *Epokha Val'tera Skotta v Rossii: Istoricheskii roman 1830-kh godov* (St. Petersburg: Gumanitarnoe Agentstvo "Akademicheskii proekt," 1996).

Andrew, Joe, *Narrative and Desire in Russian Literature, 1822–49: The Feminine and the Masculine* (London: Macmillan, 1993).

Andrew, Joe, *Narrative Space and Gender in Russian Fiction: 1846–1903* (Amsterdam: Rodopi, 2007).

Bassin, Mark, *Imperial Visions: Nationalist Imagination and Geographical Expansion in the Russian Far East, 1840–1865* (Cambridge: Cambridge University Press, 1999).

Belknap, Robert L., *Plots* (New York: Columbia University Press, 2016).

Bisha, Robin, Gheith, Jehanne M., Holden, Christine, and Wagner, William G. (eds.), *Russian Women, 1698–1917: Experience and Expression, An Anthology of Sources* (Bloomington: Indiana University Press, 2002).

Bowers, Katherine, and Kokobobo, Ani (eds.), *Russian Writers and the Fin de Siècle: The Twilight of Realism* (Cambridge: Cambridge University Press, 2015).

Brintlinger, Angela, and Vinitsky, Ilya (eds.), *Madness and the Mad in Russian Culture* (Toronto: University of Toronto Press, 2007).

Buckler, Julie A., *Mapping St. Petersburg: Imperial Text and Cityshape* (Princeton, NJ: Princeton University Press, 2005).

Cornwell, Neil (ed.), *The Gothic-Fantastic in Nineteenth-Century Russian Literature* (Amsterdam: Rodopi, 1999).

Costlow, Jane T., Sandler, Stephanie, and Vowles, Judith (eds.), *Sexuality and the Body in Russian Culture* (Stanford, CA: Stanford University Press, 1993).

Diment, Galya, *The Autobiographical Novel of Co-Consciousness: Goncharov, Woolf, and Joyce* (Gainesville: University Press of Florida, 1994).

Dinega, Alyssa W. (ed.), *Russian Literature in the Age of Realism*, Dictionary of Literary Biography, 277 (Detroit, MI: Gale, 2003).

Egorov, O. G., *Dnevniki russkikh pisatelei XIX veka: issledovanie* (Moscow: Flinta, Nauka, 2002).

Egorov, O. G., *Russkii literaturnyi dnevnik XIX veka: istoriia i teoriia zhanra: issledovanie* (Moscow: Flinta, Nauka, 2003).

Engel, Barbara Alpern, *Mothers and Daughters: Women of the Intelligentsia in Nineteenth-Century Russia* (Cambridge: Cambridge University Press, 1983).

Etkind, Alexander, *Internal Colonization: Russia's Imperial Experience* (Cambridge: Polity, 2011).

Figes, Orlando, *Natasha's Dance: A Cultural History of Russia* (New York: Metropolitan Books, 2002).

Finke, Michael C., *Metapoesis: The Russian Tradition from Pushkin to Chekhov* (Durham, NC: Duke University Press, 1995).

Geifman, Anna, *Death Orders: The Vanguard of Modern Terrorism in Revolutionary Russia* (Oxford: Praeger, 2010).

Ginzburg, Lydia, *On Psychological Prose*, trans. and ed. Judson Rosengrant, Foreword Edward J. Brown (Princeton, NJ: Princeton University Press, 1991).

Goscilo, Helena, and Holmgren, Beth (eds.), *Russia, Women, Culture* (Bloomington: Indiana University Press, 1996).

Greenleaf, Monika, and Moeller-Sally, Stephen (eds.), *Russian Subjects: Empire, Nation, and the Culture of the Golden Age* (Evanston, IL: Northwestern University Press, 1998).

Hokanson, Katya, *Writing at Russia's Border* (Toronto: University of Toronto Press, 2008).

Holmgren, Beth, *Rewriting Capitalism: Literature and the Market in Late Tsarist Russia and the Kingdom of Poland* (Pittsburgh, PA: University of Pittsburgh Press, 1998).

Holmgren, Beth, (ed.), *The Russian Memoir: History and Literature* (Evanston, IL: Northwestern University Press, 2003).

Hoogenboom, Hilde, *Noble Sentiments and the Rise of Russian Novels* (Toronto: University of Toronto Press, 2016).

Isenberg, Charles, *Telling Silence: Russian Frame Narratives of Renunciation* (Evanston, IL: Northwestern University Press, 1993).

Lalo, Alexei, *Libertinage in Russian Culture and Literature: A Bio-History of Sexualities at the Threshold of Modernity* (Leiden: Brill, 2011).

Layton, Susan, *Russian Literature and Empire: Conquest of the Caucasus from Pushkin to Tolstoy* (Cambridge: Cambridge University Press, 1994).

Liljeström, Marianne, et al. (eds.), *Models of Self: Russian Women's Autobiographical Texts* (Helsinki: Kikimora, 2000).

McLean, Hugh, *Nikolai Leskov: The Man and His Art* (Cambridge, MA: Harvard University Press, 1977).

McReynolds, Louise, *The News under Russia's Old Regime: The Development of a Mass-Circulation Press* (Princeton, NJ: Princeton University Press, 1991).

Maimin, E. A., *Russkaia filosofskaia poeziia: Poety-liubomudry, A. S. Pushkin, F. I. Tiutchev* (Moscow: Nauka, 1976).

Mann, Iu. V., *Dinamika russkogo romantizma* (Moscow: Aspect Press, 1995).

Martinsen, Deborah A. (ed.), *Literary Journals in Imperial Russia* (Cambridge: Cambridge University Press, 1997).

Martinsen, Deborah A., and Maiorova, Olga (eds.), *Dostoevsky in Context* (Cambridge: Cambridge University Press, 2015).

Michelson, Patrick Lally, and Kornblatt, Judith Deutsch (eds.), *Thinking Orthodox in Modern Russia: Culture, History, Context* (Madison: University of Wisconsin Press, 2014).

Morson, Gary Saul, *Prosaics and Other Provocations: Empathy, Open Time, and the Novel* (Brighton, MA: Academic Studies Press, 2013).

Morson, Gary Saul, and Emerson, Caryl, *Mikhail Bakhtin: Creation of a Prosaics* (Stanford, CA: Stanford University Press, 1990).

Nathans, Benjamin, *Beyond the Pale: The Jewish Encounter with Late Imperial Russia* (Berkeley: University of California Press, 2002).

Nepomnyashchy, Catharine Theimer, Svobodny, Nicole, and Trigos, Ludmilla A. (eds.), *"Under the Sky of My Africa": Alexander Pushkin and Blackness* (Evanston, IL: Northwestern University Press, 2006).

Ogden, J. Alexander, and Kalb, Judith E. (eds.), *Russian Novelists in the Age of Tolstoy and Dostoevsky*, Dictionary of Literary Biography, 238 (Detroit, MI: Gale, 2001)

Orwin, Donna Tussing, *Consequences of Consciousness: Turgenev, Dostoevsky, and Tolstoy* (Stanford, CA: Stanford University Press, 2007).

Ram, Harsha, *The Imperial Sublime: A Russian Poetics of Empire* (Madison, WI: University of Wisconsin Press, 2003).

Reyfman, Irina, *How Russia Learned to Write: Literature and the Imperial Table of Ranks* (Madison, WI: University of Wisconsin Press, 2016).

Rosenshield, Gary, *The Ridiculous Jew: The Exploitation and Transformation of a Stereotype in Gogol, Turgenev, and Dostoevsky* (Stanford, CA: Stanford University Press, 2008).

Ruud, Charles A., *Fighting Words: Imperial Censorship and the Russian Press, 1804–1906* (Toronto: University of Toronto Press, 1982).

Rydel, Christine (ed.), *Russian Literature in the Age of Pushkin and Gogol: Poetry and Drama*, Dictionary of Literary Biography, 205 (Detroit, MI: Gale, 1999)

Safran, Gabriella, *Rewriting the Jew: Assimilation Narratives in the Russian Empire* (Stanford, CA: Stanford University Press, 2000).

Safronova, Iuliia, *Russkoe obshchestvo v zerkale revoliutsionnogo terrora, 1879–1881* (Moscow: NLO, 2014).

Sandler, Stephanie, *Commemorating Pushkin: Russia's Myth of a National Poet* (Stanford, CA: Stanford University Press, 2004).

Schrader, Abby M., *Languages of the Lash: Corporal Punishment and Identity in Imperial Russia* (DeKalb, IL: Northern Illinois University Press, 2002).

Scollins, Kathleen, *Acts of Logos in Pushkin and Gogol: Petersburg Texts and Subtexts*, Series Liber Primus (Boston: Academic Studies Press, 2017).

Smith, Alison K., *For the Common Good and Their Own Well-Being: Social Estates in Imperial Russia* (Oxford: Oxford University Press, 2014).

Sobol, Valeria, *Febris Erotica: Lovesickness in the Russian Literary Imagination* (Seattle, WA: University of Washington Press, 2009).

Stroganova, Evgeniia, and Shore, Elizabet (eds.), *Zhenskii vyzov: russkie pisatel'nitsy XIX–nachala XX veka* (Tver': Liliia Print, 2006).

Tartakovskii, A. G., *Russkaia memuaristika i istoricheskoe soznanie XIX veka* (Moscow: Arkheograficheskii tsentr, 1997).

Thompson, Ewa M., *Imperial Knowledge: Russian Literature and Colonialism* (Westport, CT: Greenwood Press, 2000).

Ungurianu, Dan, *Plotting History: The Russian Historical Novel in the Imperial Age* (Madison, WI: University of Wisconsin Press, 2007).

Vassena, Raffaella, and Rebecchini, Damiano (eds.), *Reading in Russia: Practices of Reading and Literary Communication, 1760–1930* (Milan: Ledizioni, 2014).

Vatsuro, V. E., *Goticheskii roman v Rossii* (Moscow: NLO, 2002).

Vatsuro, V. E., and Gillel'son, M. I., *Skvoz' "umstvennye plotiny": Ocherki o knigakh i presse pushkinskoi pory*, 2nd edn. (Moscow: "Kniga," 1986).

Vinitsky, Ilya, *Ghostly Paradoxes: Modern Spiritualism and Russian Culture in the Age of Realism* (Toronto: University of Toronto Press, 2009).

Virolainen, Mariia, *Rech' i molchanie: siuzhety i mify russkoi slovesnosti* (St. Petersburg: Amfora, 2003).

Vostrikov, A. V., *Kniga o russkoi dueli* (St. Petersburg: Izdatel'stvo I. Limbakha, 1998).

Wachtel, Andrew Baruch, *An Obsession with History: Russian Writers Confront the Past* (Stanford, CA: Stanford University Press, 1994).

Part V. The Twentieth and Twenty-First Centuries

Balina, Marina, Condee, Nancy, and Dobrenko, Evgeny (eds.), *Endquote: Sots-Art Literature and Soviet Grand Style* (Evanston, IL: Northwestern University Press, 2000).

Balina, Marina, and Rudova, Larissa (eds.), *Russian Children's Literature and Culture* (New York: Routledge, 2008).

Belaia, G. A., *Literatura v zerkale kritiki: Sovremennye problemy* (Moscow: Sovetskii pisatel', 1986).

Belaia, G. A., *Zakonomernosti stilevogo razvitiia sovetskoi prozy dvadtsatykh godov* (Moscow: Nauka, 1977).

Berg, Mikhail, *Literaturokratiia: Problema prisvoeniia i pereraspredeleniia vlasti v literature* (Moscow: NLO, 2000).

Bethea, David M., *The Shape of Apocalypse in Modern Russian Fiction* (Princeton, NJ: Princeton University Press, 1989).

Bogdanov, K. A., *Vox Populi: Fol'klornye zhanry sovetskoi kul'tury* (Moscow: NLO, 2009).

Borenstein, Eliot, *Men without Women: Masculinity and Revolution in Russian Fiction, 1917–1929* (Durham, NC: Duke University Press, 2000).

Borenstein, Eliot, *Overkill: Sex and Violence in Contemporary Russian Popular Culture* (Ithaca, NY: Cornell University Press, 2008).

Bowlt, John E., and Matich, Olga (eds.), *Laboratories of Dreams: The Russian Avant-Garde and Cultural Experiment* (Stanford, CA: Stanford University Press, 1996).

Boym, Svetlana, *Common Places: Mythologies of Everyday Life in Russia* (Cambridge, MA: Harvard University Press, 1994).

Bykov, D. L., *Sovetskaia literatura: Kratkii kurs* (Moscow: PROZAiK, 2012).

Chernetsky, Vitaly, *Mapping Postcommunist Cultures: Russia and Ukraine in the Context of Globalization* (Montreal: McGill-Queen's University Press, 2007).

Chudakova, M. O., *Izbrannye raboty*, 2 vols. (Moscow: Iazyki russkoi kul'tury, 2001).

Clark, Katerina, *Moscow, the Fourth Rome: Stalinism, Cosmopolitanism, and the Evolution of Soviet Culture, 1931–1941* (Cambridge, MA: Harvard University Press, 2011).

Clark, Katerina, *Petersburg, Crucible of Cultural Revolution* (Cambridge, MA: Harvard University Press, 1995).

Clark, Katerina, *The Soviet Novel: History as Ritual*, 3rd edn (Bloomington and Indianapolis, IN: Indiana University Press, 2000).

Clowes, Edith W., *Russia on the Edge: Imagined Geographies and Post-Soviet Identity* (Ithaca, NY: Cornell University Press, 2011).

Costlow, Jane T., Sandler, Stephanie, and Vowles, Judith (eds.), *Sexuality and the Body in Russian Culture* (Stanford, CA: Stanford University Press, 1993).

Dobrenko, Evgeny, *Political Economy of Socialist Realism*, trans. Jesse M. Savage (New Haven, CT: Yale University Press, 2007).

Dobrenko, Evgeny, *The Making of the State Reader: Social and Aesthetic Contexts of the Reception of Soviet Literature*, trans. Jesse M. Savage (Stanford, CA: Stanford University Press, 1997).

Dobrenko, Evgeny, *The Making of the State Writer: Social and Aesthetic Origins of Soviet Literary Culture*, trans. Jesse M. Savage (Stanford, CA: Stanford University Press, 2001).

Dobrenko, Evgeny, and Lipovetsky, Mark (eds.), *Russian Literature since 1991* (Cambridge: Cambridge University Press, 2015).

Druzhinin, P. A., *Ideologiia i filologiia. Leningrad, 1940-e gody: Dokumental'noe issledovanie*, 2 vols. (Moscow: NLO, 2012).

Dubin, B. V., *Slovo—pis'mo—literatura: Ocherki po sotsiologii sovremennoi kul'tury* (Moscow: NLO, 2001).

Etkind, Alexander, *Warped Mourning: Stories of the Undead in the Land of the Unburied* (Stanford, CA: Stanford University Press, 2013).

Gasparov, B. M., *Literaturnye leitmotivy: Ocherki russkoi literatury XX veka* (Moscow: Nauka, 1994).

Gasparov, B. M., Hughes, Robert P., and Paperno, Irina (eds.), *Cultural Mythologies of Russian Modernism: From the Golden Age to the Silver Age* (Berkeley: University of California Press, 1992).

Gasparov, M. L., *Izbrannye stat'i* (Moscow: NLO, 1995).

Goscilo, Helena, *Dehexing Sex: Russian Womanhood During and After Glasnost* (Ann Arbor: The University of Michigan Press, 1996).

Günther, Hans, and Dobrenko, Evgeny (eds.), *Sotsrealisticheskii kanon* (St. Petersburg: Akademicheskii proekt, 2000).

Gurianova, Nina, *The Aesthetics of Anarchy: Art and Ideology in the Early Russian Avant-Garde* (Berkeley: University of California Press, 2012).

Hellebust, Rolf, *Flesh to Metal: Soviet Literature and the Alchemy of Revolution* (Ithaca, NY: Cornell University Press, 2003).

Heller, Leonid, *Slovo—mera mira: Stat'i o russkoi literature XX veka* (Moscow: MIK, 1994).

Holmgren, Beth, *Women's Works in Stalin's Time: On Lidiia Chukovskaia and Nadezhda Mandelstam* (Bloomington: Indiana University Press, 1993).

Holmgren, Beth (ed.), *The Russian Memoir: History and Literature* (Evanston, IL: Northwestern University Press, 2003).

Iur'ev, O. A., *Zapolnennye ziianiia: Kniga o russkoi poezii* (Moscow: NLO, 2013).

Jaccard, Jean-Philippe, *Literatura kak takovaia: Ot Nabokova k Pushkinu* (Moscow: NLO, 2011).

Janecek, Gerald, *Sight and Sound Entwined: Studies of the New Russian Poetry* (New York: Berghahn Books, 2000).

Janecek, Gerald, *The Look of Russian Literature: Avant-Garde Visual Experiments, 1900–1930* (Princeton, NJ: Princeton University Press, 1984).

Kaspe, Irina, *Iskusstvo otsutstvovat': Nezamechennoe pokolenie russkoi literatury* (Moscow: NLO, 2005).

Kelly, Catriona, and Lovell, Stephen (eds.), *Russian Literature, Modernism and the Visual Arts* (Cambridge: Cambridge University Press, 2000).

Kelly, Catriona, and Shepherd, David (eds.), *Constructing Russian Culture in the Age of Revolution: 1881–1940* (Oxford: Oxford University Press, 1998).

Kelly, Martha M. F., *Unorthodox Beauty: Russian Modernism and Its New Religious Aesthetic* (Evanston, IL: Northwestern University Press, 2016).

Komaromi, Ann, *Uncensored: Samizdat Novels and the Quest for Autonomy in Soviet Dissidence* (Evanston, IL: Northwestern University Press, 2015).

Kozlov, Denis, *The Readers of Novyi Mir: Coming to Terms with the Stalinist Past* (Cambridge, MA: Harvard University Press, 2013).

Krivulin, V. B., *Okhota na Mamonta* (St. Petersburg: Russko-Baltiiskii informatsionnyi tsentr, 1998).

Kukulin, I. V., *Mashiny zashumevshego vremeni: Kak sovetskii montazh stal metodom neofitsial'noi kul'tury* (Moscow: NLO, 2015).

Lahusen, Thomas, and Dobrenko, Evgeny (eds.), *Socialist Realism without Shores* (Durham, NC: Duke University Press, 1997).

Lahusen, Thomas, with Kuperman, Gene (eds.), *Late Soviet Culture: From Perestroika to Novostroika* (Durham, NC: Duke University Press, 1993).

Lavrov, A. V., *Simvolisty i drugie: Stat'i, razyskaniia, publikatsii* (Moscow: NLO, 2015).

Lekmanov, O. A., *Kniga ob akmeizme i drugie raboty* (Tomsk: Vodolei, 2000).

Livak, Leonid, *How It Was Done in Paris: Russian Émigré Literature and French Modernism* (Madison, WI: University of Wisconsin Press, 2003).

Matich, Olga, *Erotic Utopia: The Decadent Imagination in Russia's Fin de Siècle* (Madison, WI: University of Wisconsin Press, 2005).

Naiman, Eric, *Sex in Public: The Incarnation of Early Soviet Ideology* (Princeton, NJ: Princeton University Press, 1997).

Nikol'skaia, T. L., *Avangard i okrestnosti* (St. Petersburg: Izdatel'stvo Ivana Limbakha, 2002).

Platt, Kevin M. F., and Brandenberger, David (eds.), *Epic Revisionism: Russian History and Literature as Stalinist Propaganda* (Madison, WI: University of Wisconsin Press, 2006).

Razuvalova, A. I., *Pisateli-"derevenshchiki": Literatura i konservativnaia ideologiia 1970-kh godov* (Moscow: NLO, 2015).

Sandomirskaia, I. I., *Blokada v slove: Ocherki kriticheskoi teorii i biopolitiki iazyka* (Moscow: NLO, 2013).

Sarnov, B. M., *Stalin i pisateli*, 4 vols. (Moscow: Eksmo, 2008–11).

Savitskii, S. A., *Andegraund: Istoriia i mify leningradskoi neofitsial'noi literatury* (Moscow: NLO, 2002).

Shcheglov, Iu. K., *Proza. Poeziia. Poetika: Izbrannye raboty*, ed. A. K. Zholkovskii and V. A. Shcheglova (Moscow: NLO, 2012).

Skidan, A. V., *Summa poetiki* (Moscow: NLO, 2013).

Stahl, Henrieke, and Rutz, Marion (eds.), *Imidzh, Dialog, Eksperiment: Polia sovremennoi russkoi poezii* (Munich: Kubon and Sagner, 2013).

Steinberg, Mark D., *Proletarian Imagination: Self, Modernity, and the Sacred in Russia, 1910–1925* (Ithaca, NY: Cornell University Press, 2002).

Toker, Leona, *Return from the Archipelago: Narratives of Gulag Survivors* (Bloomington: Indiana University Press, 2000).

Uffelmann, Dirk, *Der erniedrigte Christus: Metaphern und Metonymien in der russischen Kultur und Literatur* (Cologne: Böhlau Verlag, 2010).

Vail', Petr, and Genis, Aleksandr, "60-e: Mir sovetskogo cheloveka, 1947," in Vail' and Genis, *Sobranie sochinenii*, 2 vols. (Ekaterinburg: U-Faktoria, 2003), vol. 1, 507–948.

Vail', Petr, and Genis, Aleksandr, "Sovetskoe barokko," in Vail' and Genis, *Sobranie sochinenii*, 2 vols. (Ekaterinburg: U-Faktoria, 2003), vol. 1, 273–506.

Vatulescu, Cristina, *Police Aesthetics: Literature, Film, and the Secret Police in Soviet Times* (Stanford, CA: Stanford University Press, 2010).

Wachtel, Andrew Baruch, *The Battle for Childhood: Creation of a Russian Myth* (Stanford, CA: Stanford University Press, 1990).

Wachtel, Andrew Baruch, *An Obsession with History: Russian Writers Confront the Past* (Stanford, CA: Stanford University Press, 1994).

Wachtel, Michael, *The Development of Russian Verse: Meter and Its Meanings* (Cambridge: Cambridge University Press, 1998).

Zhitenev, A. A., *Poeziia neomodernizma* (St. Petersburg: Inapress, 2012).

Zholkovskii, A. K., *Bluzhdaiushchie sny i drugie raboty* (Moscow: Nauka, Izdatel'skaia firma "Vostochnaia literatura," 1994).

Zholkovskii, A. K., *Poetika za chainym stolom i drugie razbory* (Moscow: NLO, 2014).

Zholkovskii, A. K., and Shcheglov, Iu. K., *Mir avtora i struktura teksta: Stat'i o russkoi literature* (Tenafly, NJ: Hermitage, 1986).

Zolotonosov, M. N., *Gadiushnik: Leningradskaia pisatel'skaia organizatsiia. Izbrannye stenogrammy s kommentariiami (iz istorii sovetskogo literaturnogo byta 1940–1960-kh godov)* (Moscow: NLO, 2013).

Zubova, L. V., *Iazyki sovremennoi poezii* (Moscow: NLO, 2010).

Notes

Introduction

1. David Damrosch, *How to Read World Literature* (Chichester: Wiley-Blackwell, 2009). See, especially, Chapter 3 ("Reading across Cultures," 46–64) and Chapter 4 ("Reading in Translation," 65–85).

2. A useful account can be found in John Guillory, *Cultural Capital: The Problem of Literary Canon Formation* (Chicago: University of Chicago Press, 1993).

3. See, for example, *Russian Literature Since 1991*, ed. Evgeny Dobrenko and Mark Lipovetsky (Cambridge: Cambridge University Press, 2015).

4. On the contribution of philology to literary history, see James Turner, *Philology: The Forgotten Origins of the Modern Humanities* (Princeton: Princeton University Press, 2015).

5. Alexey Miller, "'Natsiia, Narod, Narodnost'" in Russia in the Nineteenth Century: Some Introductory Remarks to the History of Concepts," *Jahrbücher für Geschichte Osteuropas*, 56 (2008), 379; and David Saunders, "Historians and Concepts of Nationality in Early Nineteenth-Century Russia," *SEER*, 60 (1982), 44–62.

6. See Andy Byford, "S. A. Vengerov: The Identity of Literary Scholarship in Late Imperial Russia," *SEER*, 81 (2003), 1–31; and *Kritiko-bibliograficheskii slovar' russkikh pisatelei i uchenykh*, ed. S. A. Vengerov, 6 vols. (St. Petersburg: Semenovskaia tipo-lit. [I. Efrona], 1889–1904).

7. G. S. Smith, *D. S. Mirsky: A Russian-English Life, 1890–1939* (Oxford: Oxford University Press, 2000).

8. Hans Ulrich Gumbrecht, "Shall We Continue to Write Histories of Literature?," *New Literary History*, 39 (2008), 519–32.

9. Iurii M. Lotman and Boris Uspensky, *Semiotics of Russian Cultural History* (Ithaca, NY: Cornell University Press, 1985).

Part I. The Medieval Period
Introduction

1. Still relevant are the remarks in Georges Florovsky, "The Problem of Old Russian Culture," *Slavic Review*, 21.1 (1962), 1–15.

2. For context, see *Debating the Middle Ages*, ed. Lester K. Little and Barbara H. Rosenwein (Oxford: Blackwell Publishers, 1998), 2–15.

3. For an accessible introduction, see Bernard Comrie and Greville Corbett, *The Slavonic Languages* (London: Routledge, 1993); on the nomenclature for the people who settled in north-eastern Europe in this early period, see Jonathan Shepard, "Rus'," in *Christianization and the Rise of Christian Monarchy: Scandinavia, Central Europe and Rus' c. 900–1200*, ed. N. Berend (Cambridge: Cambridge University Press, 2007), Chapter 9.

4. On the title, see Martin Dimnik, "The Title 'Grand Prince' in Kievan Rus," *Medieval Studies*, 66 (2004), 253–312.

5. For a detailed and clear overview of the history, with considerable attention to the role of the Golden Horde in the game of thrones, see Janet Martin, "North-eastern Russia and the Golden Horde (1246–1359)," in *The Cambridge History of Russia*, 3 vols. (Cambridge: Cambridge University Press, 2008), vol. 1, 127–57.

6. For a succinct account, see A. P. Vlasto, *The Entry of the Slavs into Christendom: An Introduction to the Medieval History of the Slavs* (Cambridge: Cambridge University Press, 1970), 296–307.

Chapter 1

1. A substantial account with analytical bibliographies can be found in Vladimir Vodoff, *Naissance de la chrétienté russe* (Paris: Fayard, 1988).

2. Dimitri Obolensky, *The Byzantine Commonwealth* (London: Weidenfeld and Nicholson, 1971), 184; and for greater detail and a more modern bibliography, see Henrik Birnbaum, "Christianity before Christianization," in *Christianity and the Eastern Slavs: Slavic Cultures in the Middle Ages*, ed. Boris Gasparov and Olga Raevsky-Hughes (Berkeley, CA: University of California Press, 1993), 42–62.

3. See Andrzej Poppe, "How the Conversion of Rus´ was Understood in the Eleventh Century," *Harvard Ukrainian Studies*, 11 (1987), 287–301.

4. See Warren Treadgold, *A History of the Byzantine State and Society* (Stanford: Stanford University Press, 1997), 19.

5. *Povest' vremennykh let*, ed. D. S. Likhachev and B. A. Romanov (Moscow: Izd. AN SSSR, 1950), vol. 1.

6. On these complex issues, an overview can be found in Jonathan Shepard, "Byzantium and Russia in the Eleventh Century: A Study in Political and Ecclesiastical Relations," Ph.D. dissertation, University of Oxford, 1974.

7. References to his paganism can be found in entries for the years 980 and 983 in any edition of the *Primary Chronicle* as part of the foundation narrative of the newly Christian people.

8. See, especially, the chapter "Russia's Byzantine Heritage," in Dimitri Obolensky, *Byzantium and the Slavs* (Crestwood, NY: St. Vladimir's Seminar Press, 1994), 75–109.

9. Riccardo Picchio, "Models and Patterns in the Literary Tradition of Medieval Orthodox Slavdom," in *American Contributions to the Seventh International Congress of Slavists, Kiev, September 1983*, vol. 2: *Literature, Poetics, History*, ed. Paul Debreczeny (Columbus, OH: Slavica, 1983), 439–67.

10. Christian Raffensperger, *Reimagining Europe: Kievan Rus´ in the Medieval World* (Cambridge, MA: Harvard University Press, 2012).

11. Francis J. Thomson, "The Nature of the Reception of Christian Byzantine Culture in the Tenth to Thirteenth Centuries and Its Implications for Russian Culture," *Slavica Gandensia*, 5 (1978), 65–139.

12. Viktor M. Zhivov, *Razyskaniia v oblasti istorii i predystorii russkoi kul'tury* (Moscow: Iazyki slavianskoi kul'tury, 2002), 80.

13. The history of the mission, and the complex debates about its location and the borders of Moravia, is well beyond the limits of our present purpose, although its historical importance for Slavic cultural history is so great that the work of Cyril and Methodius requires mention. For a synthesis of recent archaeological and textual research, see M. Eggers, "The Historical-Geographical Implications of the Cyrillo-Methodian Mission Among the Slavs," in *Thessaloniki Magna Moravia* (Thessaloniki: SS. Cyril and Methodios Center for Cultural Studies, 1999), 65–86. For an accessible non-specialist history, see A. P. Vlasto, *The Entry of the Slavs into Christendom* (Cambridge: Cambridge University Press, 1970). A classic account of the cultural

ambition of the brothers is Francis Dvornik, *Byzantine Missions among the Slavs: SS Constantine-Cyril and Methodius* (New Brunswick, NJ: Rutgers University Press, 1970), who emphasizes their Byzantine learning in arguing that the twin goals of bringing Orthodoxy and Byzantine culture defined their activity.

14. See Horace G. Lunt, "Slavs, Common Slavic, and Old Church Slavonic," in *Litterae Slavicae Medii Aevi: Francisco Venceslao Mareš Sexagenario Oblatae*, ed. František Václav Mareš and Johannes Reinhart (Munich: Verlag Otto Sagner, 1985), 185–209. A summary of literary dialects and the differences between Old Church Slavonic as developed in Bulgaria and the Eastern Slavic dialect can be found in A. P. Vlasto, *A Linguistic History of Russia* (Oxford: Clarendon Press, 1986), 344–65. On the question of whether (and when) Old Church Slavonic was also a vernacular language, see B. A. Uspenskii, *Kratkii ocherk istorii russkogo literaturnogo iazyka (XI–XIX vv.)* (Moscow: Gnozis, 1994), 1–112.

15. Jonathan Shepard and Simon Franklin, *The Emergence of Rus', 750–1200* (London: Longman, 1996).

16. *BLDR*, vol. 1, 193. Horace Lunt has argued that evidence for a school of translators, namely a passage in the *Primary Chronicle* for 1037, does not mean that Iaroslav had books translated from Greek into Slavonic; whatever it means, the phrase is corrupt. See Horace G. Lunt, "On Interpreting the Russian Primary Chronicle: The Year 1037," *SEEJ*, 32 (1988), 251–64.

17. See Alexander Schenker, *The Dawn of Slavic: An Introduction to Slavic Philology* (New Haven, CT: Yale University Press, 1995), 165–238.

18. *BLDR*, vol. 1, 155–66.

19. Simon Franklin, *Writing, Society and Culture in Early Rus, c. 950–1300* (Cambridge: Cambridge University Press, 2002); Ihor Ševčenko, *Byzantium and the Slavs* (Cambridge, MA: Harvard University Press for Ukrainian Research Institute, 1991), 107–51.

20. D. M. Bulanin, *Antichnye traditsii v drevnerusskoi literature XI–XVI vv.* (Munich: Verlag Otto Sagner, 1991).

21. See the readable account in Anthony-Emil N. Tachiaos, *Cyril and Methodius of Thessalonica: The Acculturation of the Slavs* (Crestwood, NY: St. Vladimir's Seminary Press, 2001).

22. For a seminal statement, see D. S. Likhachev, "Drevneslavianskie literatury kak sistema," in *VI Mezhdunarodnyi s"ezd slavistov. Doklady sovetskoi delegatsii* (Moscow: n.p., 1968), 5–48; for a survey of this influential scholar's writings on medieval Russian literature, see D. Obolensky, "Medieval Russian Culture in the Writings of D.S. Likhachev," *Oxford Slavonic Papers*, n.s. 11 (1976), 1–16.

23. On borrowed Greek vocabulary and invention, see Francis J. Thomson, "Old Slavonic Translations: Advantages and Disadvantages of Slavonic as a Literary Language," *Le Langage et l'homme*, 21 (1986), 110–16 (110).

24. See Henry R. Cooper, Jr., *Slavic Scriptures: The Formation of the Church Slavonic Version of the Holy Bible* (Madison, NJ: Fairleigh Dickinson University Press, 2003).

25. See Francis J. Thomson, "The Bulgarian Contribution to the Reception of Byzantine Culture in Kievan Rus': The Myths and the Enigma," *Harvard Ukrainian Studies*, 12–13 (1988–89), 215–61; and Simon Franklin, "Booklearning and Bookmen in Kievan Rus': A Survey of an Idea," *Harvard Ukrainian Studies*, 12–13 (1988–89), 830–48.

26. See Schenker, *The Dawn*, 195.

27. See B. N. Floria, "Skazanie o prelozhenii knig na slavianskii iazyk. Istochniki, vremia i mesto napisaniia," *Byzantinoslavica*, 45 (1985), 121–30; and H. Goldblatt, "On 'rus'skymi pismen' in the *Vita Constantini* and Rus'ian Religious Patriotism," in *Studia Slavica Medievalis et Humanistica Riccardo Picchio Dicata*, ed. Michele Colucci, Giuseppe Dell'Agata, and Harvey Goldblatt, 2 vols. (Rome: Edizione dell'Ateneo, 1986), vol. 1, 311–28.

28. On the form and its origins in Rus´, see E. A. Fet, "O Sofiiskom Prologe kontsa XII–nachala XIII v.," in *Istochnikovedenie i arkheografiia Sibiri*, ed. N. N. Pokrovskii and E. K. Romodanovskaia (Novosibirsk: Nauka, 1977), 78–92; N. D. Bubnov, "Slaviano-russkie prologi," in *Metodicheskoe posobie po opisaniiu slaviano-russkikh rukopisei dlia svodnogo kataloga rukopisei, khraniashchikhsia v SSSR*, ed. Arkheograficheskaia komissiia pri otdelenii istorii AN SSSR (Moscow: n.p., 1973), 274–96; and F. J. Thomson, "'Made in Russia': A Survey of the Translations Allegedly Made in Kievan Russia," in *The Reception of Byzantine Culture in Mediaeval Russia* (Aldershot: Ashgate, 1999), 319–20.

29. Iu. K. Begunov, "Tipologiia oratorskoi prozy Bolgarii i Rusi IX–XII vv.," *Anzeiger für slavische Philologie*, 8 (1975), 133–50.

30. On the legal code of Rus´, see A. A. Zimin, *Pravda Russkaia* (Moscow: Drevnekhranilishche, 1999); and Nancy Shields Kollmann, *Crime and Punishment in Early Modern Russia* (Cambridge: Cambridge University Press, 2012). For an English translation, see *The Laws of Rus´: Tenth to Fifteenth Centuries*, trans. and ed. Daniel H. Kaiser (Salt Lake City: Charles Schlacks Publisher, 1992), 15–19

31. See *Izbornik 1076 goda*, ed. V. S. Golyshenko and S. I. Kotkov (Moscow: Nauka, 1965); and *The Edificatory Prose of Kievan Rus´*, ed. and trans. William R. Veder and A. A. Turilov (Cambridge, MA: Harvard University Press for the Ukrainian Research Institute, 1994).

32. D. Tschižewskij, "On the Question of Genres in Old Russian Literature," *Harvard Slavic Studies*, 2 (1954), 105–15.

33. For a helpful perspective, see Riccardo Picchio and Harvey Goldblatt, "The Formalistic Approach and the Study of Medieval Orthodox Slavic Literature," in *Russian Formalism: A Retrospective Glance: A Festschrift in Honor of Victor Erlich*, ed. Robert L. Jackson and Stephen Rudy (New Haven, CT: Yale Russian and East European Publications, 1985), 272–88.

34. Older discussions rooted in the positivist taxonomies of late nineteenth-century criticism and classification systems assume it will be helpful to apply modern categories and often invent new subcategories to label single works (for example, N. I. Prokof´ev has gone so far as to define as a subgenre the mercantile voyage (*kupecheskoe khozhdenie*): "Khozhdenie: puteshestvie i literaturnyi zhanr," in *Kniga khozhdeniia* (Moscow: 1984), 5–20. The problem with the approach is less one of anachronism than a set of assumptions about form and intentionality and a failure even to ask whether the genres identified existed. For a typical example of the prose tale from the medieval period to the seventeenth century, see N. K. Piksanov, *Starorusskaia povest´. Vvedenie v istoriiu povesti* (Moscow: Gos. Izdatel´stvo, 1923); and D. S. Likhachev, "Sistema literaturnykh zhanrov v drevnei Rusi," in *Slavianskie literatury*, ed. A. N. Robinson (Moscow: Izd. AN SSSR, 1963), 47–70.

35. Advocates of this approach have identified a precedent in the fieldwork of the nineteenth-century historian Vasilii Kliuchevskii, a pioneer in the collection of local hagiographic legends. The observation is made by Gail Lenhoff, "La Littérature de la Russie du nord-est," in *Histoire de la littérature russe*, vol. 1: *Des origines aux Lumières*, ed. Efim Etkind, Georges Nivat, Ilya Serman, and Vittorio Strada (Paris: Fayard, 1987), 134.

36. The work of Wolf-Heinrich Schmidt has been pioneering. See, especially, *Gattungstheoretische Untersuchungen zur altrussischen Kriegserzählung: zur Soziologie mittelalterlicher Gattungen* (Berlin: O. Harrassowitz, 1975), 10–14.

37. English-language readers will find that the best place to start is Gail Lenhoff, "Categories of Early Russian Writing," *SEEJ*, 31 (1987), 259–71.

38. A. N. Robinson, *Literatura drevnei Rusi v literaturnom protsesse srednevekov´ia XI–XIII vv. Ocherki literaturno-istoricheskoi tipologii* (Moscow: Nauka, 1980), 5–45.

39. For an example of liturgical readings composed from longer works, see Boris Uspenskii, *Boris i Gleb: Vospriiatie istorii v Drevnei Rusi* (Moscow: Iazyki russkoi kul´tury, 2000). Of interest on the

problem of recapturing lost voices represented visually, see Elizabeth Sears, "The Iconography of Auditory Perception in the Early Middle Ages: On Psalm Illustration and Psalm Exegesis," in *The Second Sense: Studies in Hearing and Musical Judgement from Antiquity to the Seventeenth Century*, ed. Charles Burnett, Michael Fend, and Penelope Gouk (London: Warburg Institute, 1991), 19–38.

40. See the apparatus in *Izbornik Sviatoslava 1073 goda* (Moscow: Kniga, 1983).

41. On the sources, see Francis J. Thomson, "Chrysostomica Paleoslavica: A Preliminary Study of the Sources of the Chrysorrhoas (*Zlatostruy*) Collection," *Cyrillo-Methodianum*, 6 (1982), 1–65; and E.G. Vodolazkin, "Novoe o paleiakh (nekotorye itogi i perspektivy izucheniia paleinykh tekstov," *Russkaia literatura*, 1 (2007), 3–23.

42. For a survey of this form and its many versions, particularly from the fifteenth century, see A. S. Demin, "Obzor russkikh pis´movnikov XV–XVII vv.," in A. S. Demin, *O drevnerusskom litera-turnom tvorchestve* (Moscow: Iazyki slavianskoi kul´tury, 2003), 178–88.

43. Helpful starting points for further study can be found in V. I. Buganov, *Otechestvennaia istorio-grafiia russkogo letopisaniia. Obzor sovetskoi literatury* (Moscow: Nauka, 1975) and the classic M. D. Priselkov, *Istoriia russkogo letopisaniia XI–XV vekov* (St. Petersburg: Izdatel´stvo Dmitrii Bulanin, 1966); and D. S. Likhachev, *Russkie letopisi i ikh kul´turno-istoricheskoe znachenie* (Leningrad: Izd. AN SSSR, 1947).

44. For a demonstration of complexity surrounding vocabulary, see Horace Lunt, "Lexical variation in the Copies of the Rus´ 'Primary Chronicle': Some Methodological Problems," *Harvard Ukrainian Studies*, 16:1–2 (1994), 10–28.

45. On the complexities of producing a new edition, see Donald Ostrowski, "Striving for Perfection: Transcription of the Laurentian Copy of the *Povest´ Vremennykh Let*," *Russian Linguistics*, 30:3 (2006), 437–51.

46. On the considerable complications in reconstructing versions, see A. A. Shakhmatov, "Kievskii nachal´nyi svod 1095 g.," in *A. A. Shakhmatov, 1864–1920. Sbornik statei i materialov*, ed. S. P. Obnorskii (Moscow: Izd. AN SSSR, 1947), 117–60; Oleg Tvorogov, "Povest´ vremennykh let i Nachal´nyi svod (Tekstologicheskii kommentarii)," *TODRL*, 30 (1975), 3–26; and Donald Ostrowski, "The Načal´nyj Svod Theory and the Povest´ Vremenyx Let," *Russian Linguistics*, 31.3 (2007), 269–308.

47. For a classic account of these annals, see, now in a modern reprint, A. A. Shakhmatov, *Istoriia russkogo letopisaniia* (St. Petersburg: Nauka, 2002).

48. See Edward Keenan, "The Trouble with Muscovy: Some Observations upon Problems of the Comparative Study of Form and Genre in Historical Writing," *Medievalia et Humanistica*, 5 (1974), 103–26.

49. A helpful introduction to this massive topic can be found in Ia. S. Lur´e, "Genealogicheskaia skhema letopisei XI–XVI vv., vkliuchennykh v *Slovar´ knizhnikov i knizhnosti Drevnei Rusi*," *TODRL*, 40 (1985), 190–205.

50. See A. N. Nasonov, *Istoriia russkogo letopisaniia XI–nachala XVIII v.* (Moscow: Izd. AN SSSR, 1969), 305–7, 369–76.

51. See M. D. Priselkov, *Troitskaia letopis´. Rekonstruktsiia teksta* (Moscow: Akademiia nauk, 1950).

52. For an elegant manual, see D. S. Likhachev, *Tekstologiia. Kratkii ocherk* (Leningrad: Nauka, 1964).

53. Likhachev, *Russkie letopisi*, esp. 147–69.

54. On this figure and Byzantine eloquence more generally, a good introduction can be found in J. N. D. Kelly, *Golden Mouth: The Story of John Chrysostom, Ascetic, Preacher, Bishop* (London: Duckworth, 1995).

55. Lynn Staley, "Enclosed Spaces," in *Cultural Reformations: Medieval and Renaissance in Literary History*, ed. Brian Cummings and James Simpson (Oxford: Oxford University Press, 2010), 113–34.

56. See S. Bugoslavskii, "Pouchenie Luki Zhidiati po rukopisiam XV–XVII vv.," *Izvestiia otdela russkogo iazyka i slovestnosti*, 18.2 (1914), 196–237.

57. Cited in K. Neustroev, *Slovo sviatogo Ipolita ob antikhriste v slavianskom perevode po spisku XII veka* (Moscow: 1868), 2.

58. First attested in the *Izbornik velikogo kniazia Sviatoslava Iaroslavicha 1073 goda* (Moscow: Kniga, 1983), 199; for an English translation, see *The Edificatory Prose of Kievan Rus'*, 3–121.

59. Many so-called prefaces were in fact bridge-passages between heterogeneous texts brought together in a chronicle and arranged around the topic of a place or a particular figure such as a saint. In making the transition from one part of an account to another text that had been composed or copied in as interpolation, the scribe might insert such a passage, alerting to a change of mode. For an inventory of several dozen of these moments, see A. S. Demin, "O like chitatelia v knizhnykh predisloviiakh XI–XII vv.," in Demin, *O drevnerusskom literaturnom tvorchestve*, 115–27.

60. See Caryl Emerson, *The Cambridge Introduction to Russian Literature* (Cambridge: Cambridge University Press, 2008), 35–9.

61. On scholarly attempts to reconstruct the contexts and function of the *prolog* and techniques of compilation, see A. S. Demin, "Literaturnye osobennosti izdanii 'Prologa,'" in Demin, *O drevnerusskom literaturnom tvorchestve*, 315–41.

62. Simon Franklin, "Kievan Rus' (1015–1125)," in *The Cambridge History of Russia*, vol. 1: *From Early Rus' to 1689*, ed. Maureen Perrie (Cambridge: Cambridge University Press, 2006), 87.

63. D. M. Bulanin, "Maksim Grek i ideologicheskaia bor'ba v Rossii vo vtoroi polovine XVII–nachale XVIII v.," *TODRL*, 33 (1979), 8–87.

64. See I. U. Budovnits, *Russkaia publitsistika XVI-ogo veka* (Moscow: Izd. AN SSSR, 1947).

65. This account of the author function owes much to the work of Rita Copeland, *Rhetoric, Hermeneutics and Translation in the Middle Ages: Academic Traditions and Vernacular Texts* (Cambridge: Cambridge University Press, 1991).

66. See S. S. Averintsev, "Avtorstvo i avtoritet," in *Istoricheskaia poetika. Literaturnye epokhi i tipy khudozhestvennogo soznaniia*, ed. Pavel Grintser (Moscow: Nasledie, 1994), 105–25.

67. A. J. Minns, "Late-Medieval Discussions of *Compilatio* and the Role of the *Compilator*," *Beiträge zur Geschichte der deutschen Sprache und Literatur*, 101 (1979), 385–421.

68. For a brief gloss on passages of this type, see *Galitsko-Volynskaia letopis'. Tekst. Kommentarii. Issledovanie*, ed. N. F. Kotliar, V. Iu. Franchuk, and A. G. Plakhoni (St. Petersburg: Aleteiia, 2005), 217.

69. For the argument that the Novgorod Chronicle prefers a simpler style to chronicles from Kievan Rus', see M. N. Speranskii, *Iz starinnoi Novgorodskoi literatury XIV v.* (Leningrad: Izd. AN SSSR, 1934).

70. On medieval ethnic groups and situational ethnicity as concepts defining identity, see Florin Curta, *The Making of the Slavs: History and Archaeology of the Lower Danube Region, c. 500–700* (Cambridge: Cambridge University Press, 2001), 6–36.

71. A. J. Minns, *Medieval Theory of Authorship: Scholastic Literary Attitudes in the Later Middle Ages* (Philadelphia: University of Pennsylvania Press, 1988).

72. See Dimitri Obolensky, *Six Byzantine Portraits* (Oxford: Clarendon Press, 1988), 83–114.

73. Riccardo Picchio, "The Function of Biblical Thematic Clues in the Literary Code of Slavia Orthodoxa," *Slavica Hierosolymitana*, 1 (1977), 1–31.

74. Aleksandr Gol'dberg, "K predystorii idei 'Moskva-Tret'ii Rim,'" in *Kul'turnoe nasledie Drevnei Rusi*, ed. V. G. Bazanov (Moscow: Nauka, 1976), 111–16.

75. See V. V. Danilov, "O zhanrovykh osobennostiakh drevnerusskikh khozhdenii," *TODRL*, 18 (1962), 21–37; and O. A. Belobrova, "Cherty zhanra khozhdenii v nekotorykh drevnerusskikh

pis'mennykh pamiatnikakh XVII veka," *TODRL*, 27 (1972), 257–73. Readers might conclude from both of these studies that the hallmarks of the *khozhdenie* are a first-person narrator and a sense of wonder more than any other formal, generic features.

76. Afanasii Nikitin, *Khozhenie za Tri Moria Afanasia Nikitina*, ed. S. Lur'e and L. S. Semenov (Leningrad: Nauka, 1986).

77. B. A. Uspenskii, "Dualisticheskii kharakter russkoi srednevekovoi kul'tury (na materiale 'Khozhdenie za tri moria' Afanasiia Nikitina)," in B. A. Uspenskii, *Izbrannye trudy* (Moscow: Gnozis, 1994), vol. I, 266–72.

78. Among the first to appreciate his literary qualities in the 1930s was the pioneering structuralist and linguist N. S. Trubetskoi. See his brief piece "Khozhdenie Afanasiia Nikitina kak literaturnyi pamiatnik," in *Semiotika*, ed. Iu. S. Stepanov (Moscow: Raduga, 1983), 440–1.

79. Gail Lenhoff and Janet Martin, "The Commercial and Cultural Context of Afanasij Nikitin's *Journey beyond Three Seas*," *Jahrbücher für Geschichte Osteuropas*, 37.3 (1989), 321–44.

80. Valerie Kivelson, *Cartographies of Tsardom: The Land and Its Meaning in Seventeenth-Century Russia* (Ithaca: Cornell University Press, 2006), 57–99.

81. On religion as the most important factor in the medieval description of the Other, see Michael Khodorkovsky, "Constructing Non-Christian Identities in Muscovy," in *Culture and Identity in Muscovy, 1359–1584*, ed. Ann M. Kleimola and Gail D. Lenhoff (Los Angeles: UCLA Slavic Studies, 1997), 248–66; and John W. Slocum, "Who, and When, Were the *Inorodtsy*? The Evolution of the Category of 'Aliens' in Imperial Russia," *Russian Review*, 57 (1998), 173–90.

82. Klaus-Dieter Seemann, *Die altrussische Wallfahrtsliteratur* (Munich: W. Fink Verlag, 1976), 173–204.

83. For the text and commentary, see *PLDR*, vol. 6, 28–41.

Chapter 2

1. For an English translation, see *The Primary Chronicle: Laurentian Text*, trans. and ed. S. Hazard Cross and Olgerd P. Sherbowitz-Wetzor (Cambridge, MA: Harvard University Press, 1973); and *The Povest' vremennykh let: An Interlinear Collation and Paradosis*, ed. Donald Ostrowski, Horace G. Lunt, and David Birnbaum (Cambridge, MA: Harvard Ukrainian Research Institute, 2003). Short of a definitive critical edition of the original, a readable text, modern Russian translation, and critical commentary can be found in *Povest' vremennykh let*, ed. V. P. Adrianova-Perets, D. S. Likhachev, and B. A. Romanov, 2 vols. (Moscow: Izd. AN SSSR, 1950; repr. Nauka, 1996).

2. On the evidence concerning Olga's mission to Constantinople and her conversion, see Mark Whittow, *The Making of Orthodox Byzantium, 600–1025* (Basingstoke: Macmillan, 1996), 253–61.

3. See Cyril Mango, "The Tradition of Byzantine Chronography," *Harvard Ukrainian Studies*, 12–13 (1988–89), 360–72.

4. *PLDR*, vol. I, 265.

5. *PLDR*, vol. I, 257.

6. On narrative and stories as fundamental in hagiography, see V. P. Adrianova-Perets, "Siuzhetnoe povestvovanie v zhitiinykh pamiatnikakh XI–XIII vv.," in *Istoki russkoi belletristiki*, ed. Ia. S. Lur'e (Leningrad: Nauka, 1970), 67–107.

7. *PLDR*, vol. I, 228.

8. *PLDR*, vol. I, 197.

9. For an anthology, see *Byliny*, ed. V. I. Propp and B. N. Putilov, 2 vols. (Moscow: Khudozhestvennaia literatura, 1958).

10. On debates about the origins of the heroic epic songs, see F. J. Oinas, "The Problem of the Aristocratic Origin of Russian *Byliny*," *Slavic Review*, 30:3 (1971), 513–22.

11. For the anthology, see Kirsha Danilov, *Drevnie Rossiiskie stikhotvoreniia, sobrannye Kirsheiiu Danilovym*, ed. Anastasiia Evgen'eva and Boris Putilov (Moscow: Nauka, 1977).

12. Another folklorist, Vsevolod Miller, divided the *byliny* into heroic and non-military, and defined the latter group as either *byliny* novellas or fabliaux. In Soviet studies, this scheme was reworked by Vladimir Propp and Boris Putilov, but the distinctions no longer seem current. See the essays in P. G. Bogatyrev, ed., *Russkoe poeticheskoe tvorchestvo* (Moscow: Gosudarstvennoe uchebno-pedagogicheskoe izdatel´stvo, 1954).

13. For more on the hero and all formal aspects, the seminal discussion remains Vladimir Propp, *Russkii geroicheskii epos* (Moscow: Khudozhestvennaia literatura, 1954), 179–257.

14. M. O. Gabel´, "Formy dialoga v byline," *Naukovi zapiski naukovo-doslidchoi katedri istorii ukrains´koi kul´turi*, 6 (1927), 315–28.

15. *Sermons and Rhetoric of Kievan Rus´*, ed. and trans. Simon Franklin (Cambridge, MA: Harvard University Press for Ukrainian Research Institute, 1991), xvii.

16. A. Avenarius, "Metropolitan Hilarion on the Origin of Christianity in Rus´: The Problem of the Transformation of the Byzantine Influence," in *Proceedings of the International Congress Commemorating the Millennium of Christianity in Rus´-Ukraine*, ed. O. Pritsak and I. Shevchenko (Cambridge, MA: Harvard University Press for Ukrainian Research Institute, 1990), 689–701.

17. On the powerful connections between word and image crafted by Christian homiletics, see Mary J. Carruthers, *The Craft of Thought: Meditation, Rhetoric and the Making of Images, 400–1200* (Cambridge: Cambridge University Press, 1998).

18. See Ellen Hurwitz, "Metropolitan Hilarion's *Sermon on Law and Grace* and Historical Consciousness in Kievan Rus´," *Russian History/Histoire russe*, 7 (1980), 322–33.

19. A. I. Abramov, "Slovo o zakone i blagodati kievskogo mitropolita Ilariona kak russkaia istoriosofskaia reaktsiia na khristiansko-ideologicheskuiu ekspansiiu Vizantii," in *Ideino-filosofskoe nasledie Ilariona Kievskogo*, ed. A. A. Bazhenova (Moscow: Izd. AN SSSR, 1986), Part 2, 82–95.

20. The iconography of the basilica provides some clues as to the early relations of ecclesiastical establishment and ruler. It appears that Iaroslav and his Scandinavian wife (known by her Russianized name, Irene) were pictured in a fresco on the western wall surrounding Christ in his Majesty, with their children represented and named on the adjoining walls. These portraits faced a set of images in the choir of the communion of the Apostles—and seem, in respect of their position, to establish an analogy much like that employed by Ilarion between historical figures and the early Christians. See A. Poppe, "O roli ikonograficheskikh izobrazhenii v izuchenii literaturnykh proizvedenii o Borise i Glebe," *TODRL*, 22 (1966) 24–45.

21. See L. Goppelt, *Typos, the Typological Interpretation of the Old Testament in the New* (Grand Rapids, Michigan: W. B. Eerdmans, 1982); and the essays in *Literary Uses of Typology from the Late Middle Ages to the Present*, ed. Earl Milner (Princeton, NJ: Princeton University Press, 1977).

22. M. Dimnik, "Oleg Svyatoslavovitch and his Patronage of the Cult of SS Boris and Gleb," *Medieval Studies*, 50 (1988), 349–70.

23. Ilarion refers to Vladimir as "khagan," a title used by Steppe groups and an indication of the complex sources of authority and ethnic patchwork. See Peter Golden, "The Question of the Rus´ Quaganate," *Archivum Eurasiae Medii Aevii*, vol. 2 (Wiesbaden: Otto Harrassowitz, 1982), 77–97, quotation on 81; and Jonathan Shepard and Simon Franklin, *The Emergence of Rus´, 750–1200* (London: Longman, 1996), 31 and 38.

24. For essays on all aspects of his work, see the contributions in *Kirill of Turov: Bishop, Preacher, Hymnographer*, ed. Ingunn Lunde (Bergen: University of Bergen, 2000).

25. Iu. K. Begunov, "Tipologiia oratorskoi prozy Bolgarii i Rusi IX–XII vv.," *Anzeiger für slavische Philologie*, 8 (1975), 133–50.

26. I. P. Eremin, "Introduction" to *Literaturnoe nasledie Kirilla Turovskogo*, ed. I. P. Eremin (Berkeley, CA: Berkeley Slavic Specialties, 1989), 7–32; G. Podskalsky, "Das Gebet in der Kiever Rus´: seine Formen, seine Rolle, seine Aussagen," *Orthodoxes Forum*, 2 (1988), 177–91.

27. On his use of typology, see M. N. Speranskii, *Istoriia drevnei russkoi literatury* (Moscow: M. and S. Sabshnikov, 1920), 309.

28. For further description, see V. V. Kolesov, "K kharakteristike poeticheskogo stilia Kirilla Turovskogo," *TODRL*, 36 (1981), 37–49.

29. See I. Lunde, "Kirill of Turov's Rhetoric of Quotation," in *Kirill of Turov*, ed. Lunde, 103–28.

30. N. S. Demkova, "Poetika povtorov v drevnebolgarskoi i drevnerusskoi oratorskoi proze X–XIV vekov," *Vestnik Leningradskogo universiteta: Istoriia iazykoznaniia i literaturovedeniia*, 3 (1988), 25–34.

31. See S. V. Kozlov, "Semanticheskie aspekty 'obraza avtora' v oratorskoi proze Kirilla Turovskogo," *Germenevtika*, 3 (1992), 200–56.

32. Henrik Birnbaum, "Kem byl zagadochnyi Daniil Zatochnik," *TODRL*, 50 (1996), 576–602.

33. For a critical edition with notes, see Daniil Zatočnik, *Slovo e Molenie*, ed. Michele Colucci and Angiolo Danti (Florence: Licosa, 1977).

34. There is no comprehensive study of Biblical allusions in writings of the period. For some helpful specific observations, see T. L. Vikul, "Zaimstvovaniia iz *Vos'miknizhiia* u kievskikh letopistsev XII–nachala XIII vv.," *Ruthenica*, 10 (2012), 102–16.

35. See Jean Blankoff, "Survivances du paganism en vieille Russie," *Problèmes d'histoire du christianisme*, 8 (1979), 29–44; and Francis Conte, *L'Héritage païen de la Russie* (Paris: Albin Michel, 1997). On paganism within a larger cultural pattern of concurrent oppositions, see Iu. M. Lotman and B. U. Uspenskii, "Binary Models in the Dynamics of Russian Culture (to the End of the Eighteenth Century)," in Iurii M. Lotman, Lidiia Ia. Ginsburg, and Boris A. Uspenskii, *The Semiotics of Russian Cultural History*, ed. Alexander D. Nakhimovsky and Alice Nakhimovsky (Ithaca, NY: Cornell University Press, 1985), 30–67.

36. A. N. Pypin, "Drevniaia russkaia literatura. *Skazanie o khozhdenii Bogoroditsy po mukam*," *Otechestvennye zapiski*, 115 (1856), 335–60.

37. On the topic generally, see Giles Constable, "The Imitation of the Body of Christ," in Giles Constable, *Three Studies in Medieval Religion and Social Thought* (Cambridge: Cambridge University Press, 1995), 194–217.

38. Simon Franklin, *Writing, Society and Culture in Early Rus, c. 950–1300* (Cambridge: Cambridge University Press, 2002), 137–45.

39. Generally, see Jostein Børtnes, *Visions of Glory: Studies in Early Russian Hagiography* (Oslo: Solum, 1988).

40. For historical commentary and the document, see I. Iliev, *Byzantine Monastic Foundation Documents: A Complete Translation of the Surviving Founders' Typika and Testaments*, ed. J. Tomas and A. C. Hero (Washginton: Dumbarton Oaks Research Library and Collection, 2000), 125–39.

41. *Polnoe sobranie russkikh letopisei (Rogozhskii letopisets)*, vol. 15.1 (Prague: Arkheograficheskaia kommissiia, 1922), col. 53.

42. For further discussion on the models, see Alexander Kazhdan, "Hermitic, Cenobitic and Secular Ideals in Byzantine Hagiography of the Ninth–Twelfth Centuries," *Greek Orthodox Theological Review*, 30 (1985), 473–87. On time and space in the *Life of St. Stephan*, see Jostein Børtnes, "The Function of Word-Weaving in the Structure of Epiphanius' Life of Saint Stephan, Bishop of Perm'," in *Medieval Russian Culture*, ed. H. Birnbaum and M. S. Flier (Berkeley: University of California Press, 1984), vol. 1, 311–42.

43. For a manual on the topoi and rhetorical modes that define the holy, see Viktor Zhivov, *Sviatost'. Kratkii slovar' agiograficheskikh terminov* (Moscow: Gnosis, 1994). For a work of seminal influence on the notion of the holy from late antiquity, see Peter Brown, *The Cult of the Saints: Its Rise and Function in Latin Christianity* (Chicago: University of Chicago Press, 1981).

44. See A. A. Titov, *Zhitie sv. Leontiia, ep. Rostovskogo* (Iaroslavl', 1892); and for a modern version of the text "Skazanie o Leontii Rostovskom," ed. G. Iu. Filipovskii, in *Drevnerusskie predaniia, XI–XVI vv.*, ed. V. V. Kuskov and V. Noskov (Moscow: Sovetskaia Rossiia, 1982), 125–9.

45. See L. A. Dmitriev, *Zhitiinye povesti russkogo severa kak pamiatniki literatury XIII–XVII vv.* (Leningrad: Nauka, 1973), 185–98.

46. For an accessible collection in English, see *Medieval Slavic Lives of Saints and Princes*, ed. and trans. Marvin Kantor (Ann Arbor, MI: Michigan Slavic Translations, 1983).

47. On the different modes in relation to Kievan saints, see Boris Uspenskii, *Boris i Gleb: vospriatie istorii v Drevnei Rusi* (Moscow: Iazyki russkoi kul'tury, 2000).

48. N. S. Trubetskoi, *Istoriia, kul'tura, iazyk*, ed. V. M. Zhivov (Moscow: Progress, 1995), 603–5.

49. Natalie Challis and Horace W. Dewey, "Divine Folly in Old Kievan Literature: The Tale of Isaac the Cave Dweller," *SEEJ*, 22.3 (1978), 255–64.

50. See Fairy von Lilienfeld, "The Spirituality of the Early Kievan Caves Monastery," in *Christianity and the Eastern Slavs*, ed. B. Gasparov and O. Raevsky-Hughes (Berkeley: University of California Press, 1993), 63–76.

51. For the texts and editions, see *Drevnerusskie pateriki. Kievo-Pecherskii paterik. Volokolamskii paterik*, ed. L. A. Ol'shevskaia and S. N. Travnikov (Moscow: Nauka, 1999).

52. For the history, see *Drevnerusskie pateriki. Kievo-Pecherskii paterik. Volokolamskii paterik*, 7–109; and for a very succinct account, see L. A. Dmitriev, "Kievo-Pecherskii Paterik," in *Izbornik. Sbornik proizvedeniii literatury drevnei Rusi*, ed. L. A. Dmitriev and D. S. Likhachev (Moscow: GIKhL, 1969), 737–77.

53. See Ia. S. Lur'e, "Rol' Tveri v sozdanii russkogo natsional'nogo gosudarstva," *Uchenye zapiski Leningradskogo gos. Universiteta, no. 36. Seriia istoricheskikh nauk*, III (1939), 85–109.

54. For an account, see E. Duchesne, *Le Stoglav, ou les Cent chapitres: recueil des décisions de l'Assemblée ecclésiastique de Moscou, 1551* (Paris: Librairie ancienne Honoré Champion, 1920).

55. For a short account, see V. A. Kuchkin, "O formirovanii Velikikh Minei Chetii mitropolita Makariia," in *Problemy rukopisnoi i pechatnoi knigi* (Moscow: Nauka, 1976), 86–101.

56. A. G. Kuz'min, "O vremeni napisanii Nestorom Zhitia Feodosiia," in *Voprosy literatury i metodiki ee prepodavaniia* (Riazan': Riazanskii gos. Ped. Institut, 1970), 255–63.

57. See Rosemary Morris, *Monks and Laymen in Byzantium, 843–1118* (Cambridge: Cambridge University Press, 1995); and, for examples, see *Three Byzantine Saints*, ed. and trans. Norman H. Baynes and Elizabeth Dawes (London: Mowbrays, 1977).

58. J. Börtnes, "Frame Technique in Nestor's *Life of St. Theodosius*," *Scando-Slavica*, 13 (1967), 5–16.

59. See *PLDR*, vol. 1, 322.

60. On the *Life of St. Antony* as a model of eremitic monasticism, see Aviad Kleinberg, *Histoires des saints. Leur rôle dans la formation de l'Occident* (Paris: Éditions Gallimard, 2005), 134–52.

61. See Gail Lenhoff, "Christian and Pagan Strata in the East Slavic Cult of St. Nicholas," *SEEJ*, 28.2 (1984), 147–63. For an overview of the association of miracles with the Kiev Monastery of the Caves, see Roman Holyk, "The Miracle as Sign and Proof: 'Miraculous Semiotics' in the Medieval and Early Modern Ukrainian Mentality," in *Letters from Heaven: Popular Religion in Russia and Ukraine*, ed. John-Paul Himka and Andriy Zayarnyuk (Toronto: University of Toronto Press, 2006), 76–98.

62. On Byzantine Mariology, see briefly John Meyendroff, *Byzantine Theology: Historical Trends and Doctrinal Themes* (New York: Fordham University Press, 1979), 146–9; and on her role as intercessor, M.-P. Laroche, *Theotokos. Marie Mère de Dieu dans l'expérience spirituelle de l'Église Orthodoxe* (Sisteron: Éditions Présence, 1981), 67–75.

63. See S. A. Ivanov, *Holy Fools in Byzantium and Beyond* (Oxford: Oxford University Press, 2006).

64. For an English translation of this highly readable late sixteenth-century account of Ivan's kingdom, see Heinrich von Staden, *The Land and Government of Muscovy*, ed. and trans. Thomas Esper (Stanford, CA: Stanford University Press, 1967).

65. See G. P. Fedotov, *Sviatye drevnei Rusi, X–XVII stoletii* (Paris: YMCA Press, 1931), 205–19 (on Nikola, 216).

66. Harriet Murav, *Holy Foolishness: Dostoevsky's Novels and the Poetics of Cultural Critique* (Stanford, CA: Stanford University Press, 1992).

67. On the hagiographic sources of this work, and more generally, see Margaret Ziolkowski, *Hagiography and Modern Russian Literature* (Princeton: Princeton University Press, 1988), 136–7.

68. For a definitive survey, see Oliver Ready, *Persisting in Folly: Russian Writers in Search of Wisdom, 1963–2013* (Oxford: Peter Lang, 2017).

69. See Janet Martin, "North-eastern Russia and the Golden Horde (1246–1359)," in *The Cambridge History of Russia*, vol. 1: *From Early Rus' to 1689*, ed. Perrie, 127–57.

70. On attitudes to the steppe peoples, see Donald Ostrowski, *Muscovy and the Mongols: Cross-Cultural Influences on the Steppe Frontier, 1304–1509* (Cambridge: Cambridge University Press, 1998), 14; and Charles Halperin, "The Ideology of Silence: Prejudice and Pragmatism on the Medieval Religious Frontier," *Comparative Studies in Society and History*, 26: 3 (1984), 442–66.

71. For an older view, see, for example, A. E. Presniakov, *The Formation of the Great Russian State: A Study of Russian History in the Thirteenth to Fifteenth Centuries*, trans. A. E. Moorhouse (Chicago: Quadrangle Books, 1970); more nuanced accounts can be found in V. A. Kuchkin, *Formirovanie gosudarstvennoi territorii severo-vostochnoi Rusi v X–XV vv.* (Moscow: Nauka, 1984); and David B. Miller, "Monumental Building as an Indicator of Economic Trends in Northern Rus' in the Late Kievan and Mongol Periods, 1138–1462," *American Historical Review*, 94 (1989), 360–90.

72. Still valuable is A. I. Sobolevskii, *Perevodnaia literatura Moskovskoi Rusi, XIV–XVII vekov: bibliograficheskie materialy* (St. Petersburg: Tipografiia Imperatorskoi Akademii Nauk, 1903); for a more modern account, see D. Bulanin, *Antichnye traditsii v drevnerusskoi literature XI–XVI vv.* (Munich: O. Sagner, 1991).

73. William Veder, "The Slavic *Paterika* on Mount Athos: Features of Text Transmission in Church Slavic," in *Monastic Traditions: Selected Proceeding of the Fourth International Hilandar Conference*, ed. C. E. Gribble (Bloomington, IN: Slavica, 2003), 358–69.

74. See, for a brief example, N. I. Sazonova, "Ob ispravlenii bogosluzhebnykh knig pri patriarkhe Nikone (na materialakh Trebnika)," *Otechestvennaia istoriia*, 4 (2008), 78–83.

75. Dean S. Worth, "The 'Second South Slavic Influence' in the History of the Russian Literary Language," in *American Contributions to the Ninth International Congress of Slavists, Kiev, September 1983*, vol. 1: *Linguistics*, ed. Michael S. Flier (Columbus, OH: Slavica, 1983), 349–72.

76. Micaela S. Iovine, "The History and Historiography of the Second South Slavic Influence," Ph.D. dissertation, Yale University, 1977.

77. For an overview of his life and biographical lacuna, see D. Obolensky, "Kiprian of Kiev and Moscow," in D. Obolensky, *Six Byzantine Portraits* (Oxford: Clarendon Press, 1988), 173–200.

78. For an account of his career and relations with the Grand Prince, see John Meyendorff, *Byzantium and the Rise of Russia* (Crestwood, NY: St. Vladimir's Seminary Press, 1989), 200–26.

79. On literary qualities of *The Life*, see L. A. Dmitriev, "Rol' i znachenie mitropolita Kipriana v istorii drevnerusskoi literatury (k russko-bolgarskim literaturnym sviaziam XIV–XV vv.)," *TODRL*, 19 (1963), 215–64, esp. 241–64.

80. On the wars between the princes and Metropolitan Peter's alliance with Moscow, see Robert Crummey, *The Formation of Muscovy, 1304–1613* (London: Longman, 1987), 37–40. On Peter's life and career, see Meyendorff, *Byzantium and the Rise*, 138–54.

81. A pithy account of his influence can be found in Geoffrey Hosking, *Russia and the Russians: A History from Rus to the Russian Federation* (London: Penguin, 2001), 76–7.

82. David Miller, "The Cult of Saint Sergius of Radonezh and Its Political Uses," *Slavic Review*, 52 (1993), 680–99.

83. For a short life and comprehensive bibliography, see "Epifanii Premudryi," in *Slovar' knizhnikov i knizhnosti Drevnei Rusi*, http://lib.pushkinskijdom.ru/Default.aspx?tabid=3853 (last accessed September 25, 2017).

84. David B. Miller, *Saint Sergius of Radonezh, His Trinity Monastery, and the Formation of the Russian Identity* (DeKalb, IL: Northern Illinois Press, 2010), 70; the same work can be consulted (esp. 42–75) for a lucid attempt to correlate changes in the representation of his anti-Tatar role as characterized in the Kulikovo cycles and its different editions and dynastic and ecclesiastical politics.

85. For an overview with comment on style, see Riccardo Picchio, "Epiphanius the Wise's 'Poetics of Prayer'," *Russica Romana*, 1 (1994), 9–28.

86. For an overview, see D. Obolensky, "Late Byzantine Culture and the Slavs: A Study in Acculturation," in D. Obolensky, *The Byzantine Inheritance of Eastern Europe* (London: Variorum, 1982), 3–26 (Chapter 17).

87. On sources of the style, see L. A. Dmitriev, "Nereshennye voprosy proiskhozhdeniia i istorii ekspressivno-emotsional'nogo stilia XV v.," *TODRL*, 20 (1964), 72–89.

88. This is the observation of Dimitri Obolensky, *Byzantium and the Slavs* (Crestwood, NY: St. Vladimir's Seminary Press, 1994), 235.

89. D. S. Likhachev, *Kul'tura Rusi vremeni Andreia Rubleva i Epifaniia Premudrogo* (Moscow: Izd. AN SSSR, 1962).

90. Henryk Birnbaum has argued that for all its debt to Serbian hagiography, Russian princely lives remain closer to spiritual (and saintly) lives than Serbian lives in which secular virtues come to predominate. See Henryk Birnbaum, "Byzantine Tradition Transformed: The Old Serbian Vita," in *Aspects of the Balkans: Continuity and Change: Contributions to the International Balkan Conference held at UCLA, October 23–28, 1969*, ed. H. Birnbaum and Sperso Vyronis, Jr. (The Hague: Mouton, 1972), 243–84.

91. For a thorough analysis of the tropes, see Faith Kitch, *The Literary Style of Epifanij Premudrij* (Munich: Otto Sagner, 1976).

Chapter 3

1. See, for example, the account of events of 1229 in *The Galician-Volynian Chronicle*, trans. George A. Perfecky (Munich: Wilhelm Fin Verlag, 1973), 33–6.

2. See Giorgetta Revelli, *Boris e Gleb: due protagonisti del medioevo russo (le opere letterarie ad essi dedicate)* (Abano Terme: Piovan, 1987); and Giorgetta Revelli, *Monumenti litterari su Boris e Gleb (Literaturnye pamiatniki o Borise i Glebe)* (Genoa: La Quercia, 1993).

3. L. Müller, "Studien zur altrussischen Legende der Heiligen Boris und Gleb," *Zeitschrift für slawische Philologie*, 23 (1954), 60–77.

4. On parallels between Moravian martyred princes and the Kievans, and more generally on the importance of type rather than genre in the creation of a princely ideal, see Norman Ingham, "The Martyred Prince and the Question of Slavic Cultural Continuity in the Early Middle Ages," in *Medieval Russian Culture*, ed. Henrik Birnbaum and Michael S. Flier (Berkeley: University of California Press, 1984), 31–53.

5. See John Fennell and Antony Stokes, *Early Russian Literature* (London: Faber and Faber, 1974), 11–32; Gail Lenhoff, *The Martyred Princes Boris and Gleb: A Socio-Cultural Study of the Cult and the Texts* (Columbus, Ohio: Slavica, 1989). For a translation, see "The Narrative, Passion, and Encomium of Boris and Gleb," in Marvin Kantor, *Medieval Slavic Lives* (Ann Arbor: University of Michigan, Department of Slavic Languages, 1983), 163–254.

6. See V. Bilenkin, "Chtenie prep. Nestora kak pamiatnik 'gleboborisovskogo kul'ta'," *TODRL*, 47 (1993), 54–65.

7. Cyril Mango, "Saints," in *The Byzantines*, ed. Guglielmo Cavallo (Chicago: University of Chicago Press, 1997), 270.

8. For general remarks and detailed examples of how historical writing whitewashed likely events, see T. L. Vilkul, *Liudi i kniaz' v drevnerusskikh letopisiakh serediny XI–XIII vv.* (Moscow: Kvadriga, 2009), Chapter 2.

9. Comprehensive work on all these aspects and more can be found in the *Entsiklopediia Slova o Polku Igoreve*, ed. L. A. Dmitriev and O. V. Tvorogov, 5 vols. (St. Petersburg: Izdatel'stvo Dmitrii Bulanin, 1995).

10. On intergenerational strife and the historical reality, see V. A. Kuchkin, "'Slovo o polku Igoreve' i mezhdukniazheskie otnosheniia 60-kh godov XI veka," *Voprosy istorii*, 11 (1985), 19–35.

11. On the symbolic language of the dream, see Boris Gasparov, *Poetika Slova o polku Igoreve* (Vienna: Gesellschaft zur Förderung slawistischer Studien, 1984), 60–85.

12. André Mazon, *Le slovo d'Igor* (Paris: Droz, 1940).

13. *La Geste du prince Igor: épopée russe du XIIe siècle*, ed. Henri Grégoire, Roman Jakobson, and Marc Szeftel (New York: Annuaire de l'Institut de philologie et d'histoire orientales et slaves, 1948). Reprinted in Jakobson, *Selected Writings*, vol. 4, 380–410.

14. Dean Worth and Roman Jakobson, *Sofonija's Tale of the Russian-Tatar Battle on the Kulikovo Field* (The Hague: Mouton, 1963).

15. D. S. Mirsky, *A History of Russian Literature: Comprising A History of Russian Literature and Contemporary Russian Literature* (London: Routledge & Kegan Paul, 1949), 15.

16. For a set of historical versions and an anthology of modern adaptations, highly convenient is the Biblioteka Poeta volume *Slovo o Polku Igoreve*, ed. D. S. Likhachev and L. A. Dmitrieva (Leningrad: Sovetskii pisatel', 1985).

17. For the entire chronicle, see *Die Erste Novgoroder Chronik nach ihrer ältesten Redaktion (Synodal-handschrift)*, 1016–333, 1353, ed. and trans. Joachim Dietze (Leipzig and Munich: O. Sagner, 1971).

18. For a compact account of his actions, including fratricide and plundering, see Martin Dimnik, "The Rus' Principalities," in *The Cambridge History of Russia*, vol. 1: *From Early Rus' to 1689*, ed. Maureen Perrie (Cambridge: Cambridge University Press, 2006), 110–12.

19. John Fennell, "The Tale of Baty's Invasion of North-East Rus' and its Reflexion in the Chronicles of the Thirteenth–Fifteenth Centuries," *Russia Mediaevalis*, 3 (1977), 41–78.

20. See R. E. McGrew, "Notes on the Princely Role in Karamzin's *Istorija gosudarstva rossijskago*," *American Slavic and East European Review*, 18.1 (1959), 12–24.

21. *BLDR*, vol. 4, 207.

22. See N. Serebrianskii, *Drevne-russkie kniazheskie zhitiia: obzor redaktsii i teksty* (Moscow: Izdanie Imperatorskogo Obshchestva istorii i drevnostei rossiiskikh pri Moskovskom universitete, 1915), 49–86, 108–21.

23. See L. T. Beletskii, *Literaturnaia istoriia povesti o Merkurii Smolenskom. Issledovanie i teksty* (Petrograd: Rossiiskaia gos. Akademicheskaia tipografiia, 1922).

24. On the history of the text, see the edition by Iu. K. Begunov, *Pamiatnik russkoi literatury XIII veka: "Slovo o pogibeli russkoi zemli"* (Leningrad: Nauka, 1965).

25. V. V. Kuskov, "Retrospektivnaia istoricheskaia analogiia v proizvedeniiakh kulikovskogo tsikla," *Kulikovskaia bitva v literature i iskusstve* (Moscow: Nauka, 1980), 41–56.

26. See V. L. Komarovich, "K literaturnoi istorii Povesti o Nikole Zarazskom," *TODRL*, 5 (1947), 57–72.

27. See Andreas Ebbinghaus, "Quellen und Typen der altrussischen Ikonen-legenden," in *Gattung und Narration in den älteren slawischen Literaturen*, ed. K.-D. Seemann (Wiesbaden: O. Harrassowitz, 1987), 71–84.

28. See I. A. Evseeva, "Povest' o razorenii Riazani Batyem v khronograficheskoi redaktsii XVI v.," in *Drevnerusskaia literatura. Istochnikovedenie*, ed. D. S. Likhachev (Leningrad: Nauka, 1984), 156–71.

29. Henrik Birnbaum, "Serbian Models in the Literature and the Literary Language of Medieval Russia," *SEEJ*, 23 (1979), 1–13. On the cult of military saints as a princely ideal from Boris and Gleb to figures like Bogoliubskii, see Monica White, *Military Saints in Byzantium and Rus, 900–1200* (Cambridge: Cambridge University Press, 2013), 132–81.

30. See the *Povest' o prikhozhenii Stefana Batoriia na grad Pskov*, ed. V. I. Malyshev (Moscow: AN SSSR, 1952), available in *PLDR*, vol. 8, 617–25.

31. On the "Slovo," see A. B. Nikol'skaia, "Slovo mitropolita Kievskogo Ilariona v pozdneishei literaturnoi traditsii," *Slavia*, 7 (1928), 858–60; Vladimir Vodoff, "Le slovo pokhval'noe o velikom kniaze Borise Aleksandroviche: est-il une source historique?," *Essays in Honor of A. A. Zimin*, ed. D. C. Waugh (Columbus, OH: Slavica, 1985), 379–404; on the parallels between chronicle writing and hagiography, see Ia. S. Lur'e, "Nestor XV veka," in Ia. S. Lur'e, *Russkie sovremenniki vozrozhdeniia* (Leningrad: Nauka, 1988), 28–39.

32. On the whole topic of royal charisma, see B. A. Uspenskii, *"Tsar" i Patriarkh: kharizma vlasti v Rossii. Vizantiiskaia model' i ee russkoe pereosmyslenie* (Moscow: Iazyki russkoi kul'tury, 1998).

33. *Skazaniia i povesti o Kulikovskoi bitve*, ed. D. S. Likhachev et al. (Leningrad: Nauka, 1982). Text, modern Russian translations, and commentaries also available in *PLDR*, vol. 4, 96–190.

34. *BLDR*, vol. 6, 45.

35. On the rhetoric of nation formation in these works, see L. V. Cherepnin, *Obrazovanie russkogo tsentralizovannogo gosudarstva v XVI–XVII vekakh* (Moscow: Izdatel'stvo sotsial'noi-ekonomicheskoi literatury, 1960), 636–40; on why the concept is problematic for historiography, see Valerie Kivelson, "Culture and Politics, or the Curious Absence of Muscovite State Building in Current American Historical Writing," *Cahiers du monde russe*, 46.1–2 (2005), 19–28.

36. *BLDR*, vol. 6.

37. E. V. Dushechkina, "Khudozhestvennaia funktsiia chuzhoi rechi v russkom letopisanii," in *Uchenye zapiski Tartuskogo go. Universiteta, vyp. 306. Trudy po russkoi i slavianskoi filologii XXI. Literaturovedenie* (Tartu: Tartuskii gos. universitet, 1973), 65–104.

38. *PLDR*, vol. 4, 138.

39. *Skazaniia i povesti o Kulikovskoi bitve*, ed. Likhachev et al., 46.

40. Robert Crummey, *The Formation of Muscovy, 1304–1613* (London: Longman, 1987), 44–9.

41. Dmitriev, "Rol' i znachenie," 215–55.

42. Donald Ostrowski, "The Growth of Muscovy (1462–1533)," in *The Cambridge History of Russia*, vol. 1: *From Early Rus' to 1689*, ed. Perrie, 213.

43. The fundamental modern studies are by Boris M. Kloss, including "O vremeni sozdaniia Russkogo khronografa," *TODRL*, 26 (1971), 244–55; *Nikonovskii svod i russkie letopisi XVI–XVII vekov* (Moscow: Nauka, 1980).

44. See David B. Miller, "The *Velikie Minei Chetii* and the *Stepennaia kniga* of Metropolitan Makarii and the Origins of Russian National Consciousness," in *Forschungen zur osteuropäischen Geschichte*, vol. 26 (Wiesbaden: Harrassowitz, 1970), 263–382.

45. See Francis Dvornik, "Byzantium, Muscovite Autocracy and the Church," in *Rediscovering Eastern Christendom*, ed. E. L. B. Fry and A. H. Armstrong (London: Darton, Longman, and Todd, 1963), 115; Michael Cherniavsky, "Khan or Basileus: An Aspect of Russian Medieval Political Theory," *Journal of the History of Ideas*, 20 (1959), 459–76.

46. On the guiding myths associated with the Russian coronation, including the legends and regalia of Monomakh, see the account in Richard Wortman, *Scenarios of Power: Myth and Ceremony in Russian Monarchy*, vol. 1: *From Peter the Great to the Death of Nicholas I* (Princeton: Princeton

University Press, 1995), 22–41. See also V. Morozov and A. Chernetsov, "Legenda o Monomakhovykh Regaliiakh v isskustve Moskvy XVI v.," in *Rim. Konstantinopol'. Moskva: Sravnitel'no-istoricheskoe issledovaniie tsentrov ideologii i kul'tury do XVII v.* (Moscow: Institut rosiiskoi istorii, 1986), 367–72.

47. See J. Pelenskii, "The Emergence of the Muscovite Claims to the Byzantine-Kievan 'Imperial Inheritance,'" *Harvard Ukrainian Studies*, 7 (1983), 520–31. For an overview of these parallel models, see Vitalii Petrenko, "The Development of the Concept of Authority within the Russian Orthodox Church," Ph.D. dissertation, University of Durham, 2005, 108–20.

48. See Daniel Rowland, "Moscow—the Third Rome or the New Israel," *Russian Review*, 55 (1994), 591–614.

49. On his life and career, the most helpful source remains E. Denissoff, *Maxime le Grec et l'Occident. Contribution à l'histoire de la pensée religieuse et philosophique de Michel Trivolis* (Paris-Louvain: Desclée, 1942); for a helpful introduction in English, see J. V. Haney, *From Italy to Muscovy: The Life and Works of Maxim the Greek* (Munich: W. Fink, 1973).

50. D. Obolensky, "Maximos the Greek," in D. Obolensky, *Six Byzantine Portraits* (Oxford: Clarendon Press, 1988), 201–19, 218.

51. Obolensky, "Maximos the Greek," 218.

52. For an edition with excellent commentaries, see *Stoglav. Tekst, slovoukazatel'*, ed. G. M. Basile, A. V. Iurasov, and E. B. Emchenko (Moscow: Tsentr gumanitarnykh initsiativ, 2015); on the historical goals, see E. B. Emchenko, *Stoglav: issledovanie i tekst* (Moscow: "Indrik," 2000).

53. The tendency to classify works as a genre has its (tacit) proponents. With respect to this discourse, see V. A. Grikhin, "Drevnerusskie kniazheskie zhitiia," *Russkaia rech'*, 2 (1980), 106–10.

54. L. A. Dmitriev, "Literaturnye sud'by zhanra drevnerusskikh zhitii (tserkovno-sluzhebnyi kanon i siuzhetnoe povestvovanie," *Slavianskie literatury. VII Mezhdunarodnyi s"ezd slavistov*, 400–18.

55. See D. S. Likhachev, "Izobrazhenie liudei v letopisi XII–XIII vekov," *TODRL*, 11 (1954), 12.

56. See Iu. K. Begunov, "Problemy izucheniia torzhestvennogo krasnorechiia iuzhnykh i vostoch-nykh slavian IX–XVI vv. (K postanovke voprosa)," *Slavianskie literatury. VII Mezhdunarodnyi s"ezd slavistov. Varshava, 1973* (Moscow: Nauka, 1973), 392–411.

57. B. Miller, "The Velikije Minej-chetii," 263–382.

58. On the dating and knowledge of the Monomakh legend, see Donald Ostrowski, *Muscovy and the Mongols: Cross-Cultural Influences on the Steppe Frontier, 1304–1509* (Cambridge: Cambridge University Press, 1998), 174–6, and, more generally, Chapter 3 ("Fashioning the khan into a basi-leus") on Church politics and different kingship discourses.

59. V. A. Kuchkin, "'Pouchenie' Vladimira Monomakha i russko-pol'sko-nemetskie otnosheniia 60–70kh godov XV veka," *Sovetskoe slavianovedenie*, 2 (1967), 21–9.

60. Two schools of thought exist on Monomakh's purpose in relation to other historial sources. The question is whether Monomakh's directive is a testament (*riad*) conceived in imitation of "Iaroslav The Wise" aimed at designating his immediate successor in Kiev, or relates to his attempts to arrange succession in the town of Pereiaslavl'. For an overview and interpretation, see Martin Dimnik, *Power Politics in Kievan Rus': Vladimir Monomakkh and his Dynasty, 1054–1246* (Toronto: Pontifical Institute of Mediaeval Studies, 2016), 78–96.

61. See M. P. Alekseev, "Anglosaksonskaia parallel' k *Poucheniiu* Vladimira Monomakha," *TODRL*, 2 (1935), 39–80; there is also helpful information on dating, sources, and models in the com-mentary provided in Aleksei Karpov, *Vladimir Monomakh* (Moscow: Molodaia gvardiia, 2015), 242–69.

62. *PLDR*, vol.1, 392, 396.

63. John Fennell, *The Crisis of Medieval Russia, 1200–1304* (London: Longman, 1983), 101–21.

64. Mari Isoaho, *The Image of Aleksandr Nevskiy in Medieval Russia: Warrior and Saint* (Leiden, Boston: Brill Academic Publishers, 2006).

65. Ia. S. Lur´e, "Vopros o velikokniazheskom titule v nachale feodal´noi voiny XV v.," in *Rossiia na putiakh tsentralizatsii: sbornik statei*, ed. V. T. Pashuto (Moscow: Nauka, 1982), 250–6.

66. V. Malyshev, "Zhizn´ Aleksandra Nevskogo po rukopisi serediny XVII v.," *TODRL*, 5 (1947), 185–94.

67. A. S. Grebeniuk "Priniatie khristianstva i evoliutsiia geroiko-patrioticheskogo soznaniia v russkoi literature XI–XII vv.," *Germenevtika drevnerusskoi literatury*, 8 (Moscow: 1995), 3–15.

68. *PLDR*, vol. 3, 427.

69. *PLDR*, vol. 3, 427.

70. *PLDR*, vol. 3, 435.

71. On the attribution and dating to the 1390s, see A. V. Solov´ev, "Epifanyi Premudryi kak avtor 'Slova o zhitii i prestavlenii Dmitriia Ivanovicha'," *TODRL*, 17 (1961), 85–106; whereas another view holds that the entire work was assembled toward the mid-fifteenth century, on which see M. A. Salmina, "Slovo o zhitii i prestavlenii Dmitriia Ivanovicha," *TODRL*, 25 (1970), 81–104.

72. Harvey J. Goldblatt, "Confessional and National Identity in Early Muscovite Literature," in *Culture and Identity in Muscovy, 1359–1584*, ed. Ann M. Kleimola and Gail D. Lenhoff (Los Angeles: UCLA Slavic Studies, 1997), 84–116.

73. Daniel Rowland, "Did Muscovite Literary Ideology Place Limits on the Power of the Tsar (1540s–1660s)?," *Russian Review*, 49.2 (1990), 125–56.

74. Generally, see Ia. Lurie, "Fifteenth-century Chronicles as a Source for the History of the Formation of the Muscovite State," in *Medieval Russian Culture*, ed. Flier and Rowland, vol. 2, 47–56.

75. See Picchio, "Epiphanius the Wise's 'Poetics of Prayer'," 26–8.

76. *PLDR*, vol. 4, 224.

77. Ernst Kantorowicz, *The King's Two Bodies: A Study in Medieval Political Theology* (Princeton, NJ: Princeton University Press, 1957).

78. Fennell and Stokes, *Early Russian Literature*, 123–26.

79. Hans Robert Jauss, *Aesthetic Experience and Literary Hermeneutics*, trans. Michael Shaw (Minneapolis: University of Minnesota Press, 1982), 270; and Hans Robert Jauss, *Question and Answer: Forms of Dialogic Understanding*, trans. Michael Hays (Minneapolis: University of Minnesota Press, 1989), 197–232 ("Horizon Structure and Dialogicity").

80. A. A. Zimin, "O politicheskikh predposylkakh vozniknoveniia russkogo absoliutizma," in *Absoliutizm v Rossii, XVII–XVIII vv.: Sbornik statei k semidesiatipiatiletiiu so dnia rozhdeniia i sorokapia-tiletiiu nauchnoi i pedagogicheskoi deiatel'nosti B. B. Kafengauza* (Moscow: Izd. AN SSSR, 1964), 18–49.

81. For a modern political biography, see Isabel de Madariaga, *Ivan the Terrible* (New Haven, CT: Yale University Press, 2005).

82. Andrei Pavlov and Maureen Perrie, *Ivan the Terrible* (London: Longman, 2003), 19.

83. N. Belozerskaia, "Tsarskoe venchanie v Rossii," *Russkaia mysl'*, 4.5 (1883), 1–48.

84. See Vladimir Vodoff, "Remarques sur la valeur du terme 'tsar' appliqué aux princes russes avant le milieu du XVᵉ siècle," *Oxford Slavonic Papers*, n.s. 11 (1978), 1–41.

85. See Michael Cherniavsky, "Khan or Basileus: An Aspect of Russian Medieval Political Theory," *Journal of the History of Ideas*, 20 (1959), 459–76.

86. The Harvard historian Edward Keenan suspected that the absence of any sixteenth-century copies of the *Correspondence* and its survival in seventeenth-century versions made its provenance and authenticity dubious. For the forgery claim, which has not commanded assent, see Edward Keenan, *The Kurbskii–Groznyi Apocrypha: The Seventeenth-Century Genesis of the Correspondence between Ivan IV Groznyj and Prince Andrej Kurbsky* (Cambridge, MA: Harvard University Press, 1971), which also contains much remarkable information about the transmission of manuscript

copies; N. E. Andreyev, "The Authenticity of the Correspondence between Ivan IV and Prince Andrey Kurbsky," *SEER*, 53 (1975), 582–8; Niels Rossing and Birgit Rønne, *Apocryphal, Not Apocryphal?: A Critical Analysis of the Discussion Concerning the Correspondence between Tsar Ivan IV Groznyj and Prince Andrej Kurbsij* (Copenhagen: Rosenkilde and Bagger, 1980); and C. J. Halperin, "Edward Keenan and the Kurbskii-Grozny Correspondence in Hindsight," *Jahrbücher für Geschichte Osteuropas*, 46.3 (1998), 376–403.

87. On Ivan's writing as performative, see D. S. Likhachev, "The Histrionics of Ivan the Terrible," *Acta Litteraria Acad. Scientiarum Hungaricae*, 18 (1976), 1–10.

88. For an anthropological perspective, see Clifford Geertz, "Centers, Kings, and Charisma: Reflections on the Symbolics of Power," in *Culture and Its Creators: Essays in Honor of Edward Shils*, ed. Joseph Ben-David and Terry Nichols Clark (Chicago: University of Chicago Press, 1977), 150–71.

89. See S. N. Bogatyrev, "Povedenie Ivana Groznogo i moral'nye normy russkogo obshchestva XVI veka," *Studia Slavica Finlandensia*, 11 (1994), 1–19; and Nancy Shields Kollman, *By Honor Bound: State and Society in Early Modern Russia* (Ithaca, NY: Cornell University Press, 1999).

90. *Perepiska Ivana Groznogo s Andreem Kurbskim*, ed. Ia. S. Lur'e and Iu. D. Rykov (Leningrad: Nauka, 1979), 101.

91. E. V. Petukhov, *Serapion Vladimirskii, russkii propovednik XIII v.* (St. Petersburg: n.p., 1888); and in *PLDR*, vol. 3, 440–55.

92. On exclusion as a model for national definition in the medieval period, there are interesting remarks in Thorlac Turville-Petre, *England the Nation: Language, Literature, and National Identity, 1290–1340* (Oxford: Clarendon Press, 1996), Chapter 1.

93. On the origins of the tale and its link to an account of a battle in which Prine Andrei vanquishes the Volga Bulgars, see *BLDR*, vol. 4, 618.

94. David B. Miller, "The Coronation of Ivan IV of Moscow," *Jahrbücher für Geschichte Osteuropas*, 15 (1967), 559–74.

95. A. A. Zimin, *Peresvetov i ego sovremenniki. Ocherki po istorii russkoi obshchestvennoi mysli serediny XVI veka* (Moscow: Izd. AN SSSR, 1958).

96. *Akty istoricheskie*, no. 159.

97. Nancy Shields Kollman, "Pilgrimage, Procession and Symbolic Space in Sixteenth-Century Russian Politics," in *Medieval Russian Culture*, ed. M. S. Flier and D. Rowland (Berkeley: University of California Press, 1994), vol. 2, 163–81.

98. Michael Flier, "Obraz gosudaria v Moskovskom obriade Verbnogo Voskresen'ia," in *Prostranstvennye ikony. Performativnoe v Vizantii i Drevnei Rusi*, ed. Aleksei Lidov (Moscow: Indrik, 2011), 533–62.

99. B. M. Kloss, *Nikonovskii svod i russkie letopisi XVI–XVII vekov* (Moscow: Nauka, 1980); on the doctrine of the Third Rome, see H. Schaeder, *Moskau das Dritte Rom. Studien zur Geschichte der politischen Theorien in der slawischen Welt* (Darmstadt: n.p., 1957). While the idea of *translatio imperii* has attracted much attention as a statement on Moscow's imperial ideology, Vladimir Vodoff has written on the precise context and the dynastic politics of the principality of Tver'. See Wladimir Vodoff, "L'idée impériale et la vision de Rome à Tver', XIV–XV siècles," in *Atti del I seminario internazionale di studi storici "Da Roma Alla Terza Roma," 21–23 Aprile 1981* (Rome: Ricerca d'Ateneo, 1981), 475–93.

100. *The Domostroi Rules for Russian Households in the Time of Ivan the Terrible*, ed. and trans. C. J. Pouncy (Ithaca, NY: Cornell University Press, 1994).

101. Zimin, *Peresvetov i ego sovremenniki*, 116–20.

102. See Evgenii Golubinskii, *Istoriia kanonizatsii sviatykh v Russkoi tserkvi*, 2nd ed. (Moscow, 1903), 40–109.

103. Pavlov and Perrie, *Ivan the Terrible*, 19.

Part II. The Seventeenth Century
Introduction

1. Despite the title that implies unbroken continuity between the Middle Ages and the seventeenth century, the most recent volumes in the magnificent *Dictionary of Bookmen and the Book of Ancient Russia* cover the period separately. The new seventeenth-century volumes constitute a 3,000-page reference work that contains a vast amount of archival, bibliographic, and prosopographic detail. This resource has the potential to generate much new work. See the *Slovar' knizhnikov i knizhnosti drevnei Rusi*, ed. D. S. Likhachev and D. M. Bulanin, 4 vols., 3rd edn. (St. Petersburg: IRLI, 1992–2004). Throughout Part II, all information about the dating of works uses this source as the most authoritative.

2. For the longevity of the term as a label for popular fiction since the nineteenth century, see *Russkaia demokraticheskaia satira XVII veka*, ed. V. P. Adrianova-Peretts (Moscow: Nauka, 1977).

3. On the nationalist discourse in early scholarship, and the question of a Ukrainian versus Russian party in the seventeenth century, see a summary by Jurij Šerec, "Stefan Yavorsky and the Conflict of Ideologies in the Age of Peter I," *SEER*, 30.74 (1951), 40–62. On the problem of mapping East/West onto the region, a good starting-point is Omeljan Pritsak and John S. Reshtar, "The Ukraine and the Dialectics of Nation-Building," *Slavic Review*, 22.2 (1963), 224–55.

4. A. M. Panchenko, *Russkaia kul'tura v kanun petrovskikh reform* (Leningrad: Nauka, 1984).

5. L. I. Sazonova, *Literaturnaia kul'tura Rossii. Rannee Novoe vremia* (Moscow: Iazyki slavianskikh kul'tur, 2006).

6. See I. Serman, "L'isolationnisme surmonté," in *Histoire de la littérature russe: des origines aux Lumières*, ed. Efim Etkind et al., 7 vols. (Paris: Fayard, 1992), vol. 1, 307–22.

7. See the compilation in *Iz istorii russkoi kul'tury*, ed. A. D. Koshelev, vol. 3: *XVII–nachalo XVIII veka* (Moscow: Shkola "Iazyki russkoi kul'tury," 1996). This is also the thrust of A. N. Robinson, *Bor'ba idei v russkoi literature XVII veka* (Moscow: Nauka, 1974), filtered through a Marxist–Leninist discourse that was still mandatory at the time.

8. James Simpson, "Introduction," *The Oxford English Literary History*, vol. 2: *1350–1547: Reform and Cultural Revolution*, ed. James Simpson (Oxford: Oxford University Press, 2002), 1.

Chapter 1

1. Paul Bushkovitch, *Religion and Society in Russia: The Sixteenth and Seventeenth Centuries* (New York: Oxford University Press, 1992), esp. 111–36; and Maureen Perrie, "Time of Troubles" and "Popular Revolts," in *Cambridge History of Russia*, 3 vols. (Cambridge: Cambridge University Press, 2006), vol. 1, 409–32, 600–17.

2. For a reading of the "Epistle" as a work of "vision" literature, see A. Ia. Gurevich, "Zapadnoevropeiskie videniia potustoronnego mira i 'realizm' srednikh vekov," in *Trudy po znakovym sistemam VIII. K 70-letiiu akad. D. S. Likhacheva*, ed. Z. G. Mints (Tartu: Izadatel'stvo Tartuskogo universiteta, 1977), 3–27.

3. See Boris Unbegaun, *La Langue russe au XVIᵉ siècle (1500–1550)* (Paris: Institut d'études slaves de l'Université de Paris, 1935).

4. Ivan Timofeev, "Iz Vremennika," in *Biblioteka literatury drevnei Rusi*, vol. 14, 287–317, 582, available at http://lib.pushkinskijdom.ru/Default.aspx?tabid=10941 (last accessed November 18, 2017).

5. I. A. Khvorostinin, "Slovesa dnei i tsarei…," in *Russkaia Istoricheskaia Biblioteka* (St. Petersburg: 1909), cols. 536–51; E. P. Semenova, "I. A. Khvorostinin i ego 'Slovesa dnei,'" *TODRL*, 34 (1979), 286–97; and S. F. Platonov, *Drevnerusskie skazaniia i povesti o Smutnom vremeni XVII veka kak istoricheskii istochnik* (St. Petersburg: St. Petersburg University, 1913), 230–4.

6. Ivan Andreev Khvorostinin, "Slovesa dnei, i tsarei, i sviatitelei moskovskikh," available at http://old-ru.ru/08-49.html (last accessed October 3, 2017).

7. *BLDR*, vol. 14, 152–3.

8. Valerie Kivelson, "'The Souls of the Righteous in a Bright Place': Landscape and Orthodoxy in Seventeenth-Century Russian Maps," *Russian Review*, 58 (1999), 1–25.

9. See the biographical entry by Ia. G. Solodkin in the *Slovar' knizhnikov*, vol. 2, 13–20.

10. See Kivelson, "The Souls of the Righteous in a Bright Place," 7.

11. The best edition of the text is *Skazanie Avraamiia Palitsyna*, ed. E. V. Kolosova and O. A. Derzhavina (Moscow: Nauka, 1955).

12. *Skazanie Avraamiia Palitsyna*, 131.

13. *Biblioteka literatury drevnei Rusi*, vol. 14.

14. Visions, widely studied in other literatures, would benefit from further consideration in the Russian field. On works of this kind, see Andrew Galloway, "Visions and Visionaries," in *The Oxford Handbook of Medieval Literature*, ed. Elaine Terharne and Greg Walker (Oxford: Oxford University Press, 2010), 85–106; and Peter Dinzelbacher, *Vision und Visionsliteratur im Mittelalter* (Stuttgart: Anton Hiersemann, 1981).

15. Paul Bushkovitch, "The Era of Miracles," in Bushkovitch, *Religion and Society in Russia*, 100–27 (Chapter 5).

16. Isolde Thyret, "Muscovite Miracle Stories as Sources for Gender-Specific Religious Experience," in *Religion and Culture in Early Modern Russia and Ukraine*, ed. Samuel H. Baron and Nancy Shields Kollmann (DeKalb: Northern Illinois Press, 1997), 115–31.

17. Given the paucity of female characters in Russian medieval and early modern writing, nineteenth-century readings of the tale tended to see her as the embodiment of a native feminine ideal not unlike the heroines of contemporary Realist fiction. See, for example, F. I. Buslaev, "Ideal'nye zhenskie kharaktery Drevnei Rusi," in F. I. Buslaev, *Istoricheskie ocherki russkoi narodnoi slovesnosti i iskusstva*, 2 vols. (St. Petersburg: Tipografiia tovarishchestva "Obshchestvennaia pol'za," 1861), vol. 2, 238–68.

18. See M. B. Pliukhanova, "K probleme genezisa literaturnoi biografii," in *Literatura i publitsistika: problemy vzaimodeistviia*, ed. M. B. Pliukhanova (Tartu: Tartuskii gos. universitet, 1986), 122–32.

19. R. F. Dmitrieva, "Povest' o Tverskom Otroche monastrye i istoricheskie realii," *TODRL*, 24 (1969), 210–13.

20. An excellent edition with modern translation and notes can be found in *Povest' dushepolezna startsa Nikodima Solovetskogo monastyria o nekoem inoke*, ed. A. V. Pigina (St. Petersburg: Dmitrii Bulanin, 2003).

21. See Rufina Dmitrieva, "'Povest' o Petre i Fevronii' v pereskaze A. M. Remizova," *TODRL*, 26 (1971), 155–64.

22. The Law Code of 1649 (Article 11) strictly regulated the commerce and consumption of coffee.

23. E. A. Buchilina, *Dukhovnye stikhi, kanty: sbornik dukhovnykh stikhov Nizhegorodskoi oblasti* (Moscow: Nasledie, 1999), 6.

24. For comparative purposes, see N. I. Prokof'ev, "Videnie kak zhanr v drevnerusskoi literature," *Uchen. zap. MGPI im V. I. Lenina*, 231 (1964), 36–53, and O. V. Chumicheva, "Povest' o videnii inoka Ipatiia i nastroeniia v Solovetskom monastyre nakanune vosstaniia 1667–1676 gg.," *TODRL*, 47 (1993), 551–7.

25. Andreas Ebbinghaus, *Die altrussischen Marienikonen-Legenden* (Berlin: O. Harrassowitz, 1990), 209–19.

26. See Robert Crummey, "Old Belief as Popular Religion: New Approaches," *Slavic Review*, 25.1 (1993), 700–12.

27. Pierre Pascal, *Avvakum et les débuts du Raskol* (Paris: Librarie Ancienne H. Champion, 1938); and Michael Chernyavsky, "Old Believers and the New Religions," *Slavic Review*, 3 (1966), 1–39.

28. A. N. Robinson, *Zhizneopisaniia Avvakuma i Epifaniia: Issledovania i teksty* (Moscow: Izd. AN SSSR, 1963), 146.

29. See George B. Michels, *At War with the Church: Religious Dissent in Seventeenth-Century Russia* (Stanford, CA: Stanford University Press, 1999), 104, 220–4.

30. See N. Iu. Bubnov, "Rukopisnoe nasledie pustozerskikh uznikov," in *Staroobriadcheskaia kniga v Rossii vo vtoroi polovine XVII v.: istochniki, tipy i evoliutsiia* (St. Petersburg: Biblioteka Rossiiskoi Akademii Nauk, 1995), 231–67; and also worth seeing are the facsimile manuscripts reproduced in *Pustozerskii sbornik. Avtografy sochinenii Avvakuma i Epifaniia*, ed. N. S. Demkova, N. F. Droblenkova, and L. I. Sazonova (Leningrad: Nauka, 1975).

31. For the short and long versions of the text with commentary, see N. S. Demkova and A. M. Panchenko, *Povest' o boiaryne Morozovoi* (Moscow: Khudozhestvennaia literatura, 1991).

32. Robinson, *Zhizneopisaniia Avvakuma i Epifaniia*, 143.

33. On rhetoric as culturally marked as "exotic" and "alien" in a world divided conceptually by spiritual boundaries, see the essay by Konstantin Bogdanov, *O krokodilakh v Rossii* (Moscow: NLO, 2006), 68–104.

Chapter 2

1. For theory and a comparative example, see Pierre Bourdieu, *The Rules of Art: Genesis and Structure of the Literary Field*, trans. Susan Emanuel (Stanford, CA: Stanford University Press, 1996); and Alain Viala, *Naissance de l'écrivain: sociologie de la littérature à l'âge classique* (Paris: Minuit, 1985).

2. See R. O. Crummey, "Court Spectacles in Seventeenth-Century Russia: Illusion and Reality," in *Essays in Honor of A. A. Zimin*, ed. Daniel Waugh (Columbus, Ohio: Slavica, 1985), 130–58.

3. For an overview, see Max Okenfuss, *The Rise and Fall of Latin Humanism in Early- Modern Russia: Pagan Authors, Ukrainians, and the Resiliency of Muscovy* (Leiden: E. J. Brill, 1995), 45–63.

4. See V. A. Vodov, "Zarozhdenie kantseliarii moskovskikh velikikh kniazei (seredina XIVv.–1425 g.)," *Istoricheskie zapiski*, 103 (1979), 325–50.

5. See Boris Unbegaun, *La Langue russe au XVIᵉ siècle (1500–1550)* (Paris: Institut d'études slaves de l'Université de Paris, 1935).

6. Cited in *Simeon Polotskii i ego knigoizdatel'skaia deiatel'nost'*, ed. A. N. Robinson (Moscow: Nauka, 1982), 40.

7. Max Okenfuss, *The Discovery of Childhood in Russia: The Evidence of the Slavic Primer* (Newtonville, MA: Oriental Research Partners, 1980).

8. The history of the book in seventeenth-century Moscow has been subjected to thorough revision owing to impressive archival reconstructions of printing, of numerous individual titles, and their distribution and sales to specific parishes and monasteries (a recent estimate gives 140 distribution points all across the land for books emanating from the Pechatnyi dvor). See the material collected in *Moskovskii Pechatnyi dvor—fakt i factor russkoi kul'tury*, ed. I. V. Pozdeeva, V. P. Pushkov, and A. V. Diadkin, 3 vols. (Moscow: Nauka, 2007–11).

9. On the *Prolog* as a representative case in the history of the Muscovite book, see A. V. Dadykin, "O proizvodstve i rasprostranenii pervykh dvukh izdanii *Prologa* na Moskovskom pechatnom dvore," in *Moskovskii Pechatyni*, vol. 1, 49–68.

10. For an example of the activity of one monastery as typical, see N. Iu. Bubnov, "Rabota drevnerusskikh knizhnikov v monastyrskoi biblioteke (Istochniki solovetskogo 'Skazaniia … o novykh knigakh', 1667 g.)," in *Kniga i ee rasprostranenie v Rossii v XVI–XVIII vv. Sbornik trudov*, ed. Sergei Luppov and N. Iu. Bubnov (Leningrad: BAN, 1985), 37–58.

11. The bibliography on the history is large and mainly from the nineteenth century. More recent summaries can be found in L. R. Lewitter, "Poland, the Ukraine and Russia in the 17th Century,"

SEER, 27.68 (1948), 157–71; 28.69 (1949), 414–29; and A. Sydorenko, "Kievan Scholars in Muscovy," *Horizons*, 8.1 (1967), 31–42.

12. On the activities of the Jesuits in Eastern Europe, see Cristina Neagu, "East-Central Europe," in *The Oxford Handbook of Neo-Latin*, ed. Sarah Knight and Stefan Tilg (Oxford: Oxford University Press, 2015), 509–25, with bibliography.

13. On the curriculum, see N. I. Petrov, "O slovesnykh naukakh i literaturnykh zaniatiiakh v Kievskoi Akademii ot nachala ee do preobrazovaniia v 1819 godu," *Trudy Kievskoi Dukhovnoi Akademii*, 7 (1866), 305–30; 11 (1866), 343–88; 12 (1866), 552–69; 1–2 (1867), 82–118; 3 (1867), 465–525; on the influence of Polish classical learning (as one source of the baroque), see Ryszard Łużny, *Pisarze kręgu Akademii Kijowsko-Mohylańskiej a literatura polska; z dziejów związków kulturalnych polsko-wschodniosłowiańskich w XVII–XVIII w.* (Krakow: Nakł. Uniwersytetu Jagiellońskiego, 1966).

14. James Cracraft, "Feofan Prokopovich and the Kiev Academy," in *Russian Orthodoxy under the Old Regime*, ed. Robert L. Nichols and Theofanis George Stavrou (Minneapolis: University of Minnesota Press, 1978), 44–65.

15. Alexander Sydorenko, *The Kievan Academy in the Seventeenth Century* (Ottawa: University of Ottawa Press, 1977), 15.

16. Quoted in S. T. Golubev, *Kievskii mitropolit Petr Mogila i ego spodvizhniki*, 2 vols. (Kiev: Tip. G. T. Korchak-Novitskago, 1883), vol. 1, 18.

17. A. S. Lappo-Danilevskii, *Istoriia russkoi obshchestvennoi mysli i kul'tury XVII–XVIII vv.* (Moscow: Nauka, 1990), 208.

18. For a summary of language usage, see Charles Halperin, "The Russian and Slavonic Languages in Sixteenth-Century Muscovy," *SEER*, 85.1 (2007), 1–24.

19. See A. I. Sobolevskii, *Obrazovannost' Moskovskoi Rusi XV–XVII vekov* (St. Petersburg, 1894).

20. See S. A. Belokurov, *Sil'vestr Medvedev ob ispravlenii bogosluzhebnykh knig pri patriarkakh Nikone i Ioakime* (Moscow: Tipografiia F. Eleonskogo i K°, 1885).

21. On the book culture of the period, see S. P. Luppov, *Kniga v Rossii v XVII veke* (Leningrad: Nauka, 1970), and his *Kniga v Rossii v pervoi chetverti XVIII veka* (Leningrad: Nauka, 1973).

22. *Slovar' knizhnikov i knizhnosti drevnei Rusi*, ed. D. S. Likhachev and D. M. Bulanin, 3rd edn., 4 vols. (St. Petersburg: IRLI, 1992–2004), vol. 3, 12.

23. The biographies and movements of many Kievan churchmen in Russia in the late seventeenth century, the posts that they assumed, and their intellectual profile were last studied extensively by K. V. Kharlampovich, *Malorossiiskoe vliianie na velikorusskuiu tserkovnuiu zhizn'* (Kazan': n.p., 1914; The Hague, 1968). For a modern study of a single important individual, see David Frick, "Introduction," in *Rus' Restored: Selected Writings of Meletij Smotryck'yj, 1610–1630* (Cambridge, MA: Harvard Ukrainian Research Institute, 2005), xv–xlv.

Chapter 3

1. Ivan Zabelin, *Domashnii byt russkikh tsarei v XVI i XVII vv.* (Moscow: Sinodal'naia Tipografiia, 1915; repr. Moscow, 2003); on the connection between authority and image, see Clifford Geertz, "Centers, Kings, and Charisma: Reflections on the Symbolics of Power," in *Culture and Its Creators: Essays in Honor of Edward Shils*, ed. Joseph Ben-David and Terry Nichols (Chicago: University of Chicago Press, 1977), 150–71.

2. See Pierre Pascal, *Avvakum et les débuts du Raskol* (Paris: Librarie Ancienne H. Champion, 1938), 32–49.

3. For the history of composition and the full text, see *Arktakserksovo deistvo. Pervaia p'esa russkogo teatra*, ed. I. M. Kudriavtseva (Moscow: Izd. AN SSSR, 1957).

4. See *Arktakserksovo deistvo*, ed. Kudriavtseva, 34–5.

5. See O. A. Derzhavina, "P'esa o tsare Navukhodonosore na evropeiskoi i russkoi stsene XVII v.," *TODRL*, 24 (1969), 274.

6. While no complete seventeenth-century interludes survive, examples dating from the early eighteenth century seem representative and can be found in "Intermedii" in *PLDR*, vol. 12, 448–62. On the history and performance of these texts, see S. I. Nikolaev, "Russkie intermedii XVII v.: novye materialy," *TODRL*, 55 (2004), 423–6.

7. See Per Bjurström, "Baroque Theatre and the Jesuits," in *Baroque Art: The Jesuit Contribution*, ed. Rudolf Wittkower and Irma B. Jaffe (New York: Fordham University Press, 1972), 99–110.

8. See Kåre Langvik-Johannessen, *Zwischen Himmel und Erde. Eine Studie über Joost von den Vondels biblische Tragödie in gattungsgeschichtlicher Perspektiv* (Oslo: Universitetsforlaget, 1963); and James Parente, *Religious Drama and the Humanist Tradition: Christian Theater in Germany* (Leiden: Brill, 1987), 95–153.

9. See, for example, the conclusion of the "Comedy on the Parable of the Prodigal Son," *PLDR*, vol. 12, 392.

10. For an opposite view and highly tendentious reading of court drama within a Marxist-Leninist reading of the entire century as a class struggle, see A. N. Robinson, *Bor'ba idei v russkoi literature XVII veka* (Moscow: Nauka, 1974), 148–61.

Chapter 4

1. See Gary Marker, "Literacy and Literacy Texts in Muscovy: A Reconsideration," *Slavic Review*, 49.1 (1990), 74–89.

2. Cyrillic printing starts in the late fifteenth century in South Slavic countries and in Venice, and printing in seventeenth-century Muscovy was strictly ecclesiastical. See N. P. Kiselev, "O moskovskom knigopechatanii XVII veka," *Kniga. Issledovaniia i materialy*, 2 (1960), 123–86; and I. V. Pozdeeva, "The Activity of the Moscow Printing House in the First Half of the Seventeenth Century," *Solanus*, 6 (1992), 27–55.

3. Spravshchik Savvaty, "Nastavleniia ucheniku," in Aleksandr Panchenko, *Russkaia stikhotvornaia kul'tura XVII veka* (Leningrad: Nauka, 1973), 254.

4. On the influence of Polish rhetorical treatises on Kievan Humanism, see Paulina Lewin, *Wykłady poetyki w uczelniach rosyjskich XVIII w. (1722–1774) a tradycje polskie* (Wrocław: Zakład Narodowy imienia Ossolińskich, 1972).

5. Simeon Polotskii, *Izbrannoe sochinenie*, ed. I. P. Eremin (Moscow: 1953), 158–9.

6. Cited in *Russkaia staropechatnaia literatura XVI-pervaia chetvert' XVIII veka. Simeon Polotskii i ego knigoizdatel'skaia deiatel'nost'*, ed. V. K. Bylinin et al. (Moscow: "Nauka," 1982); for a list of the sermons that he included in his homily collection by liturgical calendar, see A. S. Eleonskaia, "Rabota Simeona Polotskogo nad podgotovkoi pechati knig 'Obed dushevnyi' i 'Vecheria dushevnaia,'" in *Simeon Polotskii i ego knizoizdatel'skaia deiatel'nost'*, 178–80.

7. See the "Predislovie ko blagochestivomu chitateliu," in Simeon Polockij, *Vertograd mnogocvĕtnyj*, ed. Anthony Hippisley and Lydia I. Sazonova (Cologne: Böhlau, 1996), vol. 1, 3–8.

8. Simeon Polockij, *Vertograd mnogocvĕtnyj*, ed. Anthony Hippisley and Lydia I. Sazonova (Cologne: Böhlau, 2000), vol. 3.

9. A handsome facsimile edition with modern edition of the text and commentary can be found in Simeon Polotsky, *Orel Rossiiskii*, ed. and commentary L. I. Sazonova (Moscow: IMLO, 2015).

10. For a summary, see Peter Rolland, Review of Simeon Polockij, *Vertograd mnogocvĕtnyj, vol. 1, Canadian Slavonic Papers*, 38 (1996), 536–7.

11. Lidiia Sazonova, "'Vertograd mnogotsvetnyi' Simeona Polotskogo kak khristianskii universum: istoriia sozdaniia, poetika, zhanr," in L. I. Sazonova, *Literaturnaia kul'tura Rossii. Rannee Novoe vremia* (Moscow: Iazyki slavianskikh kul'tur, 2006), 558–606.

12. On sources and innovation, see Peter A. Rolland, *"Ut poesia pictura…*: Emblems and Literary Pictorialism in Simon Połacki's Early Verse," *Harvard Ukrainian Studies*, 16.1–2 (1992), 67–86.

13. See L. I. Sazonova, *Poeziia russkogo barokko* (Moscow: Nauka, 1991), 15.

14. *Pis'ma russkikh pisatelei XVIII veka*, ed. G. P. Makogonenko (Leningrad: "Nauka," 1980), 248–9. Letter to Ia. Ia. Shtelin, not later than 1772, with commentary.

15. For a full listing of earlier editions, see the bibliography in *Slovar' knizhnikov i knizhnosti*, 4 vols. (St. Petersburg: Bulanin, 2004), vol. 4, 373.

16. Dmitrii Čiževskij in various publications, following a fashion that extended the baroque as a movement to all the Slavic countries, advocated the view that the first generation of Russian classicist poets came out of the Ukrainian baroque. See, for example, Dmitrii Čiževskij, *Vergleichende Geschichte der slavischen Literatur* (Berlin: De Gruyter, 1968); and Dmitrii Čiževskij, "K problemam literatury barokko u Slavian," in Dmitrii Čiževskij, *Literaturny barok* (Bratislava: Vydv-vo Slovenskej Akademie Vied, 1971). Based on the history of forms and types, his conclusions have not been much adopted within accounts that are more historicized and find a nation-based model of acculturation of Western poetics unconvincing and too narrow. More recent work restricts the use of baroque to the seventeenth century and not beyond, recognizing that its influence was more extensive in architecture and music than in literature. See Giovanna Brogi Bercoff, "La cultura letteraria barocca in Russia," in *Il Barocco letterario nei paesi slavi*, ed. G. B. Bercoff (Rome: NIS, 1996), 223–60; and Olga Dolskaya-Ackerly, "Vasilii Titov and the 'Moscow' Baroque," *Journal of the Royal Musical Association*, 118.2 (1993), 203–22.

17. For a full account of sources, see the extensive apparatus in Simeon Polockij, *Vertograd monogocvĕtnyj*, ed. Anthony Hippisley and Lydia Sazonova (Cologne: Böhlau, 2000), vol. 3.

18. Quoted in Sazonova, *Literaturnaia kul'tura Rossii*, 38.

19. Polockij, *Vertograd mnogocvĕtnyj*, vol. 1, 4.

20. *PLDR*, vol. 12, 213.

21. See Lindsey Hughes, *Sofia, Regent of Russia, 1657–1704* (New Haven, CT, and London: Yale University Press, 1990), 237.

22. On the visual element in his poetry, see Lidiia Sazonova, "Pevets mudrosti," in *Karion Istomin, Kniga liubvi znak* (Moscow: Kniga, 1989), 43–65.

23. See Ivan Fedorov, *Ivan Fedorov's Primer of 1574: Facsimile edition*, comment. by Roman Jakobson (Cambridge, MA: Harvard College Library, 1955); and Karion Istomin, *Bukvar', 1694. Faksimil'noe izdanie* (Leningrad: Avrora, 1981), 1.

24. B. A. Uspenskii, *Pervaia russkaia grammatika na rodnom iazyke. Dolomonosovskii period otechestvennoi rusistiki* (Moscow: Nauka, 1975).

25. Anthony R. Hippisley, *The Poetic Style of Simeon Polotsky* (Birmingham: Department of Russian Language and Literature, University of Birmingham, 1985), 6.

26. On the reception of Polish poetry via translation and imitation in Russia of this period, see S. I. Nikolaev, *Pol'skaia poeziia v russkikh perevodakh, XVII–XVII vv.* (Leningrad: Nauka, 1989).

27. See M. L. Gasparov, "Oppozitsiia 'stikh-proza' i stanovlenie russkogo literaturnogo stikha," in *Russkoe stikhoslozhenie: Traditsii i problemy razvitiia*, ed. Leonid Timofeev (Moscow: Nauka, 1985), 264–76; M. L. Gasparov, *Izbrannye trudy*, 3 vols. (Moscow: Iazyki russkoi kul'tury, 1997), vol. 3, 132–58; and L. I. Timofeev, "Sillabicheskii stikh," *Ars Poetica*, 2 (1928), 37–71.

28. Simeon Polotskii, "Monakh," *PLDR*, vol. 14, 108.

29. Dmitrii Zhukov and Lev Pushkarev, *Russkie pisateli XVII veka* (Moscow: Molodaia gvardiia, 1972), 30.

30. See the anthology and analysis in A. G. Avdeev, *Starorusskaia epigrafika i knizhnost'. Novo-Ierusalimskaia shkola epigraficheskoi poezii* (Moscow: Pravoslavnyi Sviato-Tikhonovskii gumanitarnyi universitet, 2006).

31. Simeon Polotskii, *Izbrannye sochineniia* (Moscow: Izd. AN SSSR, 1953), 115.

32. Polotsky, *Izbrannye sochineniia*, 115.

33. See Dick Higgins, *Pattern Poetry: Guide to an Unknown Literature* (Albany: State University of New York Press, 1987); and Charles L. Drage, *Russian Word-Play Poetry from Simeon Polotskii to Derzhavin: Its Classical and Baroque Context* (London: School of Slavonic and East European Studies, 1993).

34. Hippisley, *The Poetic Style*, 65.

35. On the mixture of classical and Christian, see Hippisley, *The Poetic Style*, 58.

36. Simon Franklin, "Printing Moscow: Significances of the Frontispiece to the 1663 Bible," *SEER*, 88.1–2 (2010), 73–95, quotation on 91.

37. Sazonova, *Literaturnaia kul'tura*, 796–803.

38. The best treatment of her reign can be found in Hughes, *Sophia*. The frontispiece in that study is the original version of this image printed in Amsterdam by Bloteling, most copies of which were destroyed after Sophia was toppled. The Russian version of the image, executed by A. Afanas'ev with the approval of Catherine the Great in 1777, replaced the original Latin text with Slavonic. The authorship of the poem has come under scrutiny and it may be by the Ukrainian writer Ivan Bogdanovsky and not Medvedev (see Hughes, *Sophia*, 168–9).

39. Anthony Hippisley, "The Emblem in the Writings of Simeon Polockij," *SEEJ*, 15.2 (1971), 167–83.

40. Cited in Hippisley, "The Emblem," 11.

41. Simeon Polotskii, "Chelovek," in *Russkaia sillabicheskaia poeziia XVI–XVIII vv.*, ed. A. M. Panchenko (Leningrad: Sovetskii pisatel', 1970), 163.

42. *Russkaia sillabicheskaia poeziia*, ed. Panchenko, 75.

43. *Russkaia sillabicheskaia poeziia*, ed. Panchenko, 78.

44. Mikhail Zlobin, "Proshenie Mikhalka Zlobina," *PLDR*, vol. 10, 29.

45. Karion Istomin, "Domostroi," *PLDR*, vol. 10, 243.

46. *PLDR*, vol. 10, 51.

47. *PLDR*, vol. 12, 217.

48. *Russkaia stikhotvornaia kultura*, ed. Panchenko, 264.

49. *PLDR*, vol. 12, 270.

50. N. Kurganov, *Rossiiskaia universal'naia grammatika* (St. Petersburg: v Tipografii Morskago Shliakhetnogo Kadetskogo Korpusa, 1769), 299.

Chapter 5

1. The pioneer in this form of socio-historical reading of medieval texts is Klaus-Dieter Seemann, especially his *Altrussische Wallfahrtsliteratur: Theorie und Geschichte eines literarischen Genres* (Constance: Habilitationsschrift, 1976).

2. Dmitrij Čiževskij, *History of Russian Literature* (The Hague: Mouton, 1971), 326–31.

3. D. S. Likhachev, *Chelovek v literature drevnei Rusi* (Moscow: Nauka, 1970).

4. See O. A. Derzhavina, *Fatsetsii: perevodnaia novella v russkoi literature XVII veka* (Moscow: Izd. AN SSSR, 1962); and more generally E. Romodanovskaia, "Zapadnye sborniki i original'naia russkaia povest': k voprosu o russifikatsii zaimstvovannykh siuzhetov v literature XVII–nachala XVIII vv.," *TODRL*, 33 (1979), 164–74.

5. *Pamiatniki obshchestvenno-politicheskoi mysli v Rossii kontsa XVII veka: Literaturnye panegiriki*, ed. V. I. Buganov, 2 vols. (Moscow: Izd. AN SSSR, 1983). Also see Viktor Zhivov, "Religious Reform and the Emergence of the Individual in Seventeenth-Century Russian Literature," in *Religion and Culture in Early Modern Russia and Ukraine*, ed. Samuel H. Baron and Nancy Shields Kollmann

(DeKalb: Northern Illinois University Press, 1997), 184; and S. O. Shmidt, "K istorii monastyr-skoi kolonizatsii XVII v. ('Povest' o nachale Oranskogo monastyria')," *Voprosy istorii religii i ateizma*, 12 (1964), 297–309.

6. On a changing economic reality refracted in some tales, see K. V. Bazilevich, *Denezhnaia reforma Alekseia Mikhailovicha i vosstanie v Moskve v 1662 g.* (Moscow: Izd. AN SSSR, 1936).

7. On Bakhtin and laughter as social critique, see, for example, Robert Anchor, "Bakhtin's Truths of Laughter," *Clio*, 14.3 (1985), 235–5; and Mikita Hoy, "Bakhtin and Popular Culture," *New Literary History*, 23.3 (1992), 765–82. Dmitry Likhachev and Aleksandr Panchenko see laughter as a specific reflex of the Russian medieval character as they argue in *Smekh v drevnei Rusi* (Leningrad: Nauka, 1984).

8. For a useful consideration of the relation of make-believe and realism, see Gary Cox, "Fairy-Tale Plots and Contemporary Heroes in Early Russian Prose Fiction," *Slavic Review*, 39 (1980), 85–96.

9. The proximate source was a Polish version, *Wielkie Zwerciadło Przykładow*, probably in the version published in two volumes in 1690–91, derived from the Latin *Speculum exemplorum ex diversis libris in unam laboriose collectum*, dating to 1481–1519. For a short account of transmission from Latin into West Slavic languages, see B. Walczak-Sroczynska, "Wielkie Zwerciadło Przykładow—dzieje tekstologiczne," *Slavia Orientalis*, 4 (1976), 493–508.

10. The text to the entire play can be found in *PLDR*, vol. 12, 371–402.

11. On the source collection, the *Speculum exemplorum ex diversis libris in unam laboriose collectum*, its Polish translations, and amplification into an anthology of approximately 1300 entries, see O. A. Derzhavina, *Velikoe Zertsalo* (Moscow: Nauka, 1965); later copies continue to modify detail, structure, and content.

12. The most comprehensive selection containing 260 novellas can be found, together with an excellent study on sources, in Derzhavina, *Velikoe Zertsalo*.

13. On the popularity of this tale as judged by copies relative to the next ten most widely attested stories, see V. P. Adrianova-Perets, *Russkaia demokraticheskaia satira* (Moscow: Nauka, 1977), 143–67.

14. For a textual history that reconstructs the circulation of different versions, see O. N. Fokina, *"Povest' o brazhnike" v rukopisnykh sbornikakh XVII–XIV v. Tekst i contekst* (Novosibirsk: Novosibirskii gos. universitet, 2008), 340 (with the main redactions printed on 337–49).

15. *PLDR*, vol. 10, 497.

16. See Viktor Zhivov, "Religioznaia reforma i individual'noe nachalo v russkoi literature XVII v.," in *Iz istorii russkoi kul'tury*, ed. A. D. Koshelev, vol. 3: *XVII–nachalo XVIII veka* (Moscow: Iazyki russkoi kul'tury, 1996), 460–86; and Viktor Zhivov, "Handling Sin in Eighteenth-Century Russia," in *Representing Private Lives of the Enlightenment*, ed. Andrew Kahn (Oxford: Voltaire Foundation, 2010), 123–48.

17. On the problem of genre definition, see Marcia Morris, *"The Tale of Savva Grudcyn* and the Poetics of Transition," *SEEJ*, 36.2 (1992), 202–16.

18. On the manuscript tradition and variations, see M. Skripil, "Povest' o Savve Grudtsyne," *TODRL*, 2 (1935), 181–214; *TODRL*, 5 (1947), 225–308.

19. *PLDR*, vol. 10, 44.

20. On folkloric motifs and forms, see A. Iu. Fedorov, "Povest' o Gore i Zlochastii' v ee otnoshenii k volshebnoi skazke," *TODRL*, 44 (1990), 284–99. D. S. Likhachev, who calls "popular versifica-tion" (*narodnoe stikhoslozhenie*) the basis of the work, acknowledges its bookish elements and overall mixture of styles that make genre a moot category. See D. S. Likhachev, "'Povest' o Gore-Zlochastii,'" in D. S. Likhachev, *Izbrannye raboty v trekh tomakh*, 3 vols. (Leningrad: Khudozhestvennaia literatura, 1987), vol. 2, 341.

21. A still helpful bibliography can be found in V. L. Vinogradova, "Povest' o Gore-Zlochastii," *TODRL*, 12 (1956), 622–41. For a version of the text, see "Povest' o Gore-Zlochastii," in

Demokraticheskaia poeziia XVII veka, ed. V. P. Adrianova-Perets (Moscow-Leningrad: Sovetskii pisatel', 1962), 33–44; and *PLDR*, vol. 10, 28–39.

22. See W. S. Harkins, "Russian Folk Ballads and the Tale of Misery and Ill-Fortune," *American Slavic and East European Review*, 13 (1954), 402–13.

23. Likhachev, "Povest' o Gore-Zlochastii," 321–41.

24. *Slovar' knizhnikov i knizhnosti drevnei Rusi*, ed. D. S. Likhachev and D. M. Bulanin, 3rd edn., 4 vols. (St. Petersburg: IRLI, 1992–2004), vol. 2, 132, 209.

25. Much information on the legal activities of the hero and cultural setting can be found in E. V. Dushechkina, *Povest' o Frole Skobeeve: Literaturnyi i istoriko-kul'turnye aspekty izucheniia. Uchebnoe posobie* (St. Petersburg: SPbGU, 2011).

26. For a developmental reading that finds in the seventeenth century a starting point for the emergence of the novel, see, for example, V. Kozhinov, *Proiskhozhdenie romana. Teoretiko-istoricheskii ocherk* (Moscow: Sovetskii pisatel', 1963) or Jurij Streidter, *Der Schelmenroman in Russland: Ein Beitrag zur Geschichte des russischen Romans vor Gogol* (Berlin: Otto Harrassowitz, 1961). For a more subtle account of continuities in the picaresque rather than all fiction, see Marcia Morris, "Russian Variations on the Picaresque: the Narrative Short Form," *Canadian Slavonic Papers*, 34:1–2 (1992), 57–78.

27. See Gitta Hammarberg, "Eighteenth-century Narrative Variations on 'Frol Skobeev,'" *Slavic Review*, 46.3–4 (1987), 529–39.

28. As quoted in Il'ia Serman, "Bova i russkaia literatura," *Slavica Heriosolymitana*, 7 (1985), 163.

29. On the tendency to read fiction for social historical evidence, see Felix J. Oinas, "The Problem of the Aristocratic Origin of Russian Byliny," *Slavic Review*, 30 (1971), 513–22.

30. See V. D. Kuz'mina, "Frantsuzskii rytsarskii roman na Rusi, Ukraine i Belorussii 'Bova' i 'Petr Zlatye Kliuchi,'" *IV Mezhdunarodnyi s"ezd slavistov. Slavianskaia filologiia* (Moscow: Izd. AN SSSR, 1958), vol. 2, 344–96; on the romance in early eighteenth-century book culture, see V. M. Zhivov, *Razyskaniia v oblasti istorii i predystorii russkoi kul'tury* (Moscow: Iazyki slavianskoi kul'tury, 2002), 568–70.

31. For these two different views, see Simon Karlinsky, "Tallemant and the Beginning of the Novel in Russia," *Comparative Literature*, 15 (1963), 226–33; and Iu. M. Lotman, "'Ezda v ostrov liubvi' Trediakovskogo i funktsiia perevodnoi literatury v russkoi kul'ture pervoi poloviny XVIII-ogo veka," in Iu. M. Lotman, *Izbrannye stat'i* (Tallinn: Aleksandra, 1993), 22–9.

Conclusion

1. Dmitrii Aleksandrovich Prigov, "Azbuki," in *Sobranie sochinenii v piati tomakh*, vol. 1: *Moskva. Virshi na kazhdyi den'* (Moscow: NLO, 2016), 645–68.

Part III. The Eighteenth Century

Chapter 1

1. A new synthesis can be found in *The Europeanized Elite in Russia, 1762–1825: Public Role and Subjective Self*, ed. Alexei Evstratov, Andreas Schonle, and Andrei Zorin (DeKalb, IL: Northern Illinois Press, 2016).

2. See Marc Raeff, "On the Heterogeneity of the Eighteenth Century in Russia," in *Russia and the World of the Eighteenth Century*, ed. Roger Bartlett, A. G. Cross, and Karen Rasmussen (Columbus, OH: Slavica, 1986), 666–79.

3. *Choix des meilleurs morceaux de la littérature russe, à dater de sa naissance jusqu'au règne de Catherine II; traduits en français par M. L. Pappa Do Poulo et par le C⁽ᵐ⁾. Gallet* (Paris: Chez Lefort, 1800), vii.

4. See N. A. Kopanev, "O pervykh izdanniakh satir A. Kantemira," *XVIII vek*, 15 (1986), 140–54.

5. An intelligent account of his life and activities remains L. V. Pumpianskii, "Trediakovskii," in *Istoriia russkoi literatury*, ed. G. A. Gukovskii and V. A. Desnitskii, 3 vols. (Moscow and Leningrad, 1941), vol. 3, 215–63.

6. On his early career, see Kirill Ospovat, "Sumarokov—literator v sotsial'nom kontekste 1740–nachala 1760-kh gg.," in *Eighteenth-Century Russia: Society, Culture, Economy: Papers from the VII International Conference of the Study Group on Eighteenth-Century Russia*, ed. Roger Bartlett and Gabriela Lehmann-Carli (Berlin: Lit, 2007), 35–51.

7. Numerous nineteenth-century publications collected information about his life in the context of the history of the Academy of Sciences, where he spent his career. These include works by P. S. Biliarsky, P. P. Pekarsky, and V. V. Sipovsky.

8. Jonathan Israel, *The Radical Enlightenment: Philosophy and the Making of Modernity* (Oxford: Oxford University Press, 2002), 29; on Lomonosov's science and his fame in the popular imagination, see Steven Usitalo, *The Invention of Mikhail Lomonosov: A Russian National Myth* (Brighton, MA: Academic Studies Press, 2013).

9. See, for example, Charles Drage, *Russian Literature in the Eighteenth Century: The Solemn Ode, the Epic, Other Poetic Genres, the Story, the Novel, Drama: An Introduction for University Courses* (London: C. L. Drage, 1978). For a discussion in which meaning is seen as determined by genre, see Iu. V. Stennik, *Zhanr tragedii v russkoi literatury epokhi klassitsizma* (Leningrad: Nauka, 1981).

10. Influential counter-arguments to a monolithic view include E. B. O. Borgerhoff, *The Freedom of French Classicism* (Princeton, NJ: Princeton University Press, 1950); René Wellek, "The Term and Concept of 'Classicism' in Literary History," in *Aspects of the Eighteenth Century*, ed. Earl R. Wasserman (Baltimore, MD: Johns Hopkins Press, 1965), 207–43; Nicholas Cronk, "The Singular Voice: Monologism and French Classical Discourse," *Continuum*, 1 (1989), 175–202; *Histoire de la France littéraire: Classicismes XVIIe–XVIIIe siècle*, ed. Michel Delon and Jean-Charles Darmon (Paris: Presses universitaires de France, 2006).

11. See Marc Fumaroli, *Quand l'Europe parlait français* (Paris: Éditions de Fallois, 2001).

12. For a largely bibliographic account, see *Istoriia russkoi perevodnoi khudozhestvennoi literatury: Drevniaia Rus'. XVIII vek*, ed. Iu. D. Levin (Cologne: Böhlau, 1995–6).

13. John Bucsela, "The Role of Lomonosov in the Development of Russian Literary Style," Ph.D. dissertation, University of Wisconsin, 1963.

14. On these distinctions, see Henri Peyre, "Le classicisme," in *Encyclopédie de la Pléiade. Histoire des littératures*, 3 vols. (Paris: Gallimard, 1956), vol. 2, 110–39.

15. R. A. Budagov, "Iz istorii semantiki prilagatel'nogo 'klassicheskii,'" *Rol' i znachenie literatury XVIII-ogo veka v istorii russkoi kul'tury* (Moscow: Nauka, 1966), 443–8.

16. See G. N. Teplov, "Rassuzhdenie o nachale stikhotvorstva," *Ezhemesiachnye sochineniia*, 1 (1755), 3–14.

17. V. K. Trediakovskii, *Izbrannye proizvedeniia*, ed. L. I. Timofeev (Moscow and Leningrad: Sovetskii pisatel', 1963), 390–7.

18. *Tilemakhida ili stranstvovanie Tilemakha syna Odisseeva, opisannoe v sostave iroicheskoi piimy*, 2 vols. (St. Petersburg, 1766); *Drevniia istoriia ob egiptianakh, o karfagenianakh, ob assiriabakh ... i o grekhakh*, 10 vols. (St. Petersburg, 1749–63); *Rimskaia istoriia ot sozdaniia Rima do Bitvy Aktiiskiia, to est' po okonchanie Respubliki*, 16 vols. (St. Petersburg, 1761–7).

19. See L. V. Pumpianskii, "Lomonosov i nemetskaia shkola razuma," *XVIII vek*, 14 (1983), 3–44; L. V. Pumpianskii, "Trediakovskii i nemetskaia shkola razuma," *Zapadnyi sbornik*, 1 (1937), 157–86.

20. See Umberto Eco, *The Search for the Perfect Language* (London: Fontana, 1997).

21. See V. M. Zhivov, *Iazyk i kul'tura v Rossii XVIII veka* (Moscow: Shkola "Iazyki russkoi kul'tury," 1996), translated into English as *Language and Culture in Eighteenth-Century Russia*, trans. Marcus Levitt (Boston: Academic Studies Press, 2009); and *Dolomonosovskii period russkogo literaturnogo iazyka*, ed. Anders Sjöberg and Ulla Birgegord (Stockholm: Kungl., 1992).

22. Avramii Firsov, *Psaltyr' 1683 goda*, ed. E. A. Tselunova (Munich: O. Sagner, 1989), 6.

23. Bernhard Varenius, *Geografiia general'naia. Nebesnyi i zemnovodnyi krugi kupno s ikh svoistvy i deistvy v trekh knigakh opisuiushcha perevedena s latinska iazyka na rossiiskii . . .* (Moscow: Morskaia akademiia, 1718), a copy of which was held in the library of Peter I.

24. The standard work on this topic is Boris Uspenskii, *Iz istorii russkogo literaturnogo iazyka XVIII–nachala XIX veka: iazykovaia programma Karamzina i ee istoricheskie korni* (Moscow: Izdatel'stvo Moskovskogo universiteta, 1985).

25. See B. A. Uspenskii, "O 'Rossiiskoi grammatike' A. A. Barsova (1783–1788)," in B. A. Uspenskii, *Izbrannye trudy*, 3 vols. (Moscow: Iazyki russkoi kul'tury, 1994), vol. 1, 628–57.

26. Many of Trediakovsky's writings on style and grammar, while rare and available only as first editions through the 1830s, were reprinted by the enterprising publisher Aleksandr Smirdin, whose editions aimed to satisfy a market for the classics at a reasonable price. It is worth comparing V. K. Trediakovskii, *Sochineniia i perevody kak stikhami tak i prozoiu*, 2 vols. (St. Petersburg: pri Imperatorskoi Akademii nauk, 1752) and [V. K. Trediakovskii], *Sochineniia Tred'iakovskogo*, 3 vols, ed. A. S. Smirdin (St. Petersburg: V tipografii Voenno-Uchebnykh Zavedenii, 1849).

27. M. V. Lomonosov, "Predislovie o pol'ze knig tser'kovnykh v rossiiskom iazyke," in M. V. Lomonosov, *Izbrannye sochineniia*, ed. A. A. Morozov (Leningrad: Sovetskii pisatel', 1986), 473. On his language theories, A. I. Sobolevskii, *Lomonosov v istorii russkogo iazyka* (St. Petersburg: Tip. Imp. Akademii nauk, 1911) is still of value.

28. See P. N. Berkov, *Lomonosov i literaturnaia polemika ego vremeni* (Leningrad: Izd. AN SSSR, 1936), 54–63.

29. V. K. Trediakovskii, *Izbrannye*, 390–6. On his rules, see G. A. Gukovskii, "Trediakovskii kak teoretik literatury," *XVIII vek*, 6 (1964), 43–71; Karen Rosenberg, "Between Ancients and Moderns: V. K. Trediakovskij on the Theory of Language and Literature," Ph.D. dissertation, Yale University, 1980. On their relevance and impact at the time, see Irina Reyfman, *Vasilii Trediakovsky: The Fool of the "New" Russian Literature* (Stanford, CA: Stanford University Press, 1991), Chapter 1.

30. Generally on the French debates, see Emmanuel Bury, *Le Classicisme* (Paris: Nathan, 2000); and on Russia, see Rosenberg, "Between Ancients and Moderns," 75–91.

31. A. A. Deriugin, *V. K. Trediakovskii—perevodchik. Stanovlenie klassitsisticheskogo perevoda v Rossii* (Saratov: Izdatel'stvo Saratovskogo universiteta, 1985).

32. For the text and thorough discussion of the philosophy of translation, see Vasilij Kirillovič Trediakovskij, *Psalter 1753*, ed. Reinhold Olesch and Hans Rothe, commentary Alexander Levitsky (Paderborn: Ferdinand Schöningh, 1989), esp. 543–626.

33. The full title is "The Ode to the Blessed Memory of Her Royal Highness the Empress Anna Ioannovna on the Victory over the Turks and Tatars and the Capture of Khotin" ("Oda blazhennyia pamiati gosudaryne imperatritse Anne Ioannovne na pobedu nad Turkami i Tatarami i na vziatie Khotina 1739 goda," 1739), an example of the expansionist tendency of titles to suit occasions. While the Empress Anna is mentioned, she was deceased by 1751 when Lomonosov revised his original version.

34. See Gerda Hüttl-Worth, "Thoughts on the Turning Point in the History of Literary Russian: The Eighteenth Century," *International Journal of Slavic Linguistics and Poetics*, 13 (1970), 125–35.

35. For a survey, see *Istoriia russkoi perevodnoi khudozhestvennoi literatury*, vol. 1, 94–296.

36. Étienne de Condillac, *L'Art d'écrire* (Orléans: Éditions Le Pli, 2002), 61.

37. L. B. Modzalevskii, "Lomonosov i 'O kachestvakh stikhotvortsa rassuzhdenie,'" in *Literaturnoe tvorchestvo M. V. Lomonosova* (Moscow: Akademiia nauk, 1962), 133–62.

38. See D. V. Tiulichev, "Prizhiznennye izdaniia literaturnykh proizvedenii i nekotorykh nauchnykh trudov M. V. Lomonosova," *Lomonosov. Sbornik statei i materialov VIII* (Leningrad, 1983), 49–63; and *Knigoizdatel'skaia deiatel'nost' Peterburgskoi Akademii nauk i M. V. Lomonosov* (Leningrad: Nauka, 1988).

39. See P. N. Berkov, "Problema literaturnogo napravleniia Lomonosova," *XVIII vek*, 5 (1962), 5–32; and N. D. Kochetkova, "M. V. Lomonosov v otsenke russkikh pisatelei-sentimentalistov," *Lomonosov i russkaia literatura*, ed. A. S. Kurilov (Moscow: Nauka, 1987), 267–79.

40. On the impact of English satirical journals in Russia of the period, see Iu. D. Levin, *Vospriiatie angliiskoi literatury v Rossii* (Leningrad: Nauka, 1990), 5–75.

41. Nikolai Koshanskii, *Ruchnaia ritorika* (St. Petersburg: Tip. V. Pavlishchikova, 1816–17), ii.

42. Sumarokov later combined both epistles into a single pamphlet and re-published them separately in 1774 as *Instruction to Those Aspiring to Be Writers* (*Nastavlenie khotiashchim byti pisateliami*).

43. For a highly detailed survey of the context, see N. N. Bulich, *Sumarokov i sovremennaia emu kritika* (St. Petersburg: Tipografiia E. Prats, 1854).

44. A. P. Sumarokov, *Izbrannye proizvedeniia*, ed. P. N. Berkov (Leningrad: Sovetskii pisatel', 1957), 117.

45. See Marcus Levitt, "Was Sumarokov a Lockean Sensualist? On Locke's Reception in Eighteenth-Century Russia," in *A Window on Russia*, ed. Maria di Salvo and Lindsey Hughes (Rome: La Fenice Edizioni, 1996), 219–27.

46. See Simon Karlinsky, *Russian Drama from Its Beginnings to the Age of Pushkin* (Berkeley: University of California Press, 1985), 60–81; there is a wealth of source material and a good bibliography in Amanda Ewington, *A Voltaire for Russia: A. P. Sumarokov's Journey from Poet-Critic to Russian Philosophe* (Evanston, IL: Northwestern University Press, 2010).

47. G. A. Gukovskii, *Russkaia poeziia XVIII v.* (Leningrad: Academiia, 1927), Chapters 7–8.

48. See *Ancients and Moderns in Europe: Comparative Perspectives*, ed. Paddy Bullard and Alexis Tadié (Oxford: Voltaire Foundation, 2016), 1–10.

49. On later literary contests as a form of exchange and gift-giving as well as regulation, see M. L. Maiofis, *Vozzvanie k Evrope: literaturnoe obshchestvo "Arzamas" i rossiiskii modernizatsionnyi proekt 1815–1818 godov* (Moscow: NLO, 2008). See Boris Uspenskii, "K istorii odnoi epigrammy Trediakovskogo (epizod iazykovoi polemiki serediny XVIII veka)," *Russian Linguistics*, 8.2 (1985), 75–127.

50. See B. A. Uspenskii, *Literaturnaia voina Trediakovskogo i Sumarokova v 1740-kh–nach. 1750-kh gg.* (Moscow: RGGU, 2001).

51. Sumarokov, *Izbrannye proizvedeniia*, 125.

52. For much information on the specific points of style disputed and parodied, see Boris Uspenskii, "K istorii odnoi epigrammy Trediakovskogo," in Uspenskii, *Izbrannye trudy*, vol. 2, 343–410 (esp. Appendix II).

53. See Natalia Iu. Alekseeva, "Literaturnaia polemika serediny XVIII v. o perevode stikhov," *XVIII vek*, 24 (2006), 15–34.

54. On French debates about Ancients and Moderns, see Larry Norman, *The Shock of the Ancient: Literature and History in Early Modern France* (Chicago: University of Chicago Press, 2011); on England, see Joseph Levine, *The Battle of the Books: History and Literature in the Augustan Age* (Ithaca, NY: Cornell University Press, 1991).

55. *Poety XVIII veka*, ed. G. P. Makogenenko and I. Z. Serman, 2 vols. (Leningrad: Sovetskii pisatel', 1972), vol. 2, 408.

56. L. M. Arinshtein, "Pope in Russian Translations of the Eighteenth Century," *Studies in Bibliography: Papers of the Bibliographical Society of the University of Virginia*, 24 (1971), 166–75.

57. *Poety XVIII veka*, ed. Makogenenko and Serman, vol. 2, 373.

58. For a fuller account, see Berkov, *Lomonosov i literaturnaia polemika*.

59. L. I. Kulakova, "Neizdannaia poema Ia. B. Kniazhnina: epizod iz istorii literaturnoi polemiki 1765 g. s prilozheniem," in *Russkaia literatura i obshchestvenno-politicheskaia bor'ba XVII–XIX vv.* (Leningrad: Uchen. zap. Gos. Ped. in-ta im. A. I. Gertsena, 1971), 73–93.

60. *Poety XVIII veka*, ed. Makogenenko and Serman, vol. 2, 406.

61. His review can be found in the journal *Plody uedineniia*, 8 (1808), n. p.

62. See Reyfman, *Vasilii Trediakovsky*.

63. M. Altshuller, *Predtechi slavianofil'stva v russkoi literature (Obshchestvo "Beseda liubitelei russkogo slova")* (Ann Arbor, MI: Ardis, 1984).

64. *Essai sur la littérature russe, contenant une liste des gens de lettres Russes qui se sont distingués depuis le Règne de Pierre le Grand. Par un voyageur Russe*, Livorno, 1771. Ms. Harvard University, Houghton Library Collections, v. 42.

65. See Anna Lisa Crone, *The Daring of Derzhavin* (Bloomington, IN: Slavica, 2000).

66. Late in life, around 1809, Derzhavin discussed his own concept of the poetic mind and its visionary flights in "A Consideration of Lyric Poetry, or the Ode" ("Rassuzhdenie o liricheskoi poezii, ili ob ode"); two of the three parts of this essay were published in his lifetime. This work of synthesis shows a highly eclectic set of influences, including Charles Batteux, *Cours de belles lettres ou principes de la littérature*, a staple of classicist pedagogy, as well as drawing on Klopstock, Schlegel, Herder (his essay *Die Lyra. Von der Natur und Wirkung der lyrischen Dichtkunst* [1795–6]). The text and commentary can be found in G. R. Derzhavin, *Sochineniia v 9 tomakh*, ed. I. A. Grot, 9 vols. (St. Petersburg: Izd. Imp. Akademii nauk), vol. 7, 516–627; for a reading of his use of the sublime, see Harsha Ram, *The Imperial Sublime: A Russian Poetics of Empire* (Madison, WI: University of Wisconsin Press, 2003), 93–8.

67. See Andrei Zorin, "Glagol vremen," in A. L. Zorin, A. S. Nemzer, and N. N. Zubkov, *Svoi podvig svershiv* (Moscow: Kniga, 1987), 5–155.

68. Starting with a review of the 1831 edition of his works ("Sochineniia Derzhavina") by N. A. Polevoi in *The Moscow Telegraph* of August 1832, republished in N. A. Polevoi, *Literaturnaia kritika. Stat'i, retsenzii, 1825–1842* (Leningrad: Khudozhestvennaia literatura, 1990), 136–94; for an example of the current dilemmas faced in trying to pin down his genius, see Hans Rothe, "'Izbral on sovsem osobyi put'" (Derzhavin s 1774 po 1785 g.)," *XVIII vek*, 21 (1999), 247–59.

Chapter 2

1. Geoffrey Hosking, *Russia: People and Empire, 1552–1917* (London: Fontana Press, 2000), 311.

2. On the Academy of Fine Arts, see James Cracraft, *The Petrine Revolution in Russian Culture* (Cambridge, MA: Harvard University Press, 2004), 234–56.

3. See Kirill Ospovat, *Terror and Pity: Aleksandr Sumarokov and the Theater of Power in Elizabethan Russia* (Brighton, MA: Academic Studies Press, 2016), 21–32.

4. A. D. Kantemir, *Sobranie stikhotvorenii*, ed. Z. I. Gershkovich (Leningrad: Sovetskii pisatel', 1956), 285.

5. For the history of one episode, see Erin McBurney, "Picturing the Greek Project: Catherine II's Iconography of Conquest and Culture," *Russian Literature*, 75 (2014), 415–43.

6. See T. C. W. Blanning, *The Culture of Power and the Power of Culture: Old Regime Europe 1660–1789* (Oxford: Oxford University Press, 2002).

7. See Vera Proskurina, *Creating the Empress: Politics and Poetry in the Age of Catherine* (Boston: Academic Studies Press, 2011), Chapter 5.

8. There is no comprehensive study of court culture, but much of interest can be found in the following excellent biographies: Isabel de Madariaga, *Russia in the Age of Catherine the Great* (London: Phoenix, 2002); Simon Dixon, *Catherine the Great* (London: Profile, 2009); John T. Alexander, *Catherine the Great: Life and Legend* (New York and Oxford: Oxford University Press, 1989); and in exhibition catalogues about the material culture of her reign, such as the excellent *Treasures of Catherine the Great*, ed. N. R. Guseva, Catherine Phillips, and Aisha Jung (London: Hermitage Development Trust, 2000). Very helpful in this regard is David L. Ranzel, "Character

and Style of Patron–Client Relations in Russia," in *Klientelsysteme im Europea der Frühen Neuzeit*, ed. Antoni Maczak and Elizabeth Mueller-Leuckner (Munich: R. Oldenbourgh, 1988), 211–30.

9. *Correspondance de Catherine Alexéievna, grande-duchesse de Russie, et de Sir Charles H. Williams, ambassadeur d'Angleterre, 1756 et 1757*, ed. Sergei M. Goriainov (Moscow: Société impériale d'histoire et d'antiquités russes, 1909).

10. *Epilog Astsrei. Predstavlennyi na Novgorodskom teatre, pri kontse geroicheskiia komedii Albert Pervyi. Dekabria 6 dnia 1776 goda* (Moscow: Imperatorskii universitet, 1777), i.

11. For a reading of Petrov's odes as an expression of Catherine's imperial ideology, see Andrei Zorin, *Kormia dvuglavogo orla: literatura i gosudarstvennaia ideologiia v Rossii v poslednei treti XVIII–pervoi treti XIX veka* (Moscow: NLO, 2001), Chapter 1. For Petrov's odes, see *Sochineniia V. P. Petrova*, 3 vols. (St. Petersburg: Meditsinskaia tipografiia, 1811). In the absence of a modern edition of Petrov's works, this early nineteenth-century edition remains essential. It is also evidence in the form of book history of how parlous eighteenth-century reputations were in a literary culture defined by amateur interest rather than systematic publication.

12. Ivan Seletskii, *Oda ego siiatel'stvu kniaziu Aleksandru Mikhailovichu Golitsynu na vziatie Khotina podnesena v Kieve ot Toropetskogo kuptsa Ivana Seletskogo, sentiabria 28 dnia, 1769 goda* (St. Petersburg: Imperatorskaia Akademiia nauk, 1769).

13. Raymond Williams, *The Sociology of Culture* (New York: Schocken Books, 1981), 41.

14. *Poety XVIII veka*, ed. G. P. Makogonenko and I. Z. Serman (Leningrad: Sovetskii pisatel', 1972), vol. 1, 483.

15. Few specific studies of clientelism exist, but see the definitive Ulrike Jekutsch, "Vasilii Petrov i Grigorii A. Potemkin. Ob otnosheniiakh poeta i pokrovitelia," *Russian Literature*, 74 (2014), 219–48.

16. *Merkurii*, 11 (1793), as cited in the entry for A. F. Klushin in the *Slovar' russkikh pisatelei XVIII veka*, http://lib.pushkinskijdom.ru/Default.aspx?tabid=1098 (last accessed November 16, 2017).

17. *Oda v zashchitu polosatomu fraku* (St. Petersburg: n.p., 1789).

18. See James von Geldern, "The Ode as a Performative Genre," *Slavic Review*, 50 (1991), 927–39. For an excellent account of the economy of praise, see Luba Golburt, "Vasilii Petrov and the Poetics of Patronage," *Vivliothika: E-Journal of Eighteenth-Century Russian Studies*, 3 (2015), 47–69.

19. Anon., *Oda, kotoruiu Sviateishogo pravitel'stvuiushchego sinoda chlenu... v znak svoego userdiia i vysokopochitaniia prinosit Moskovskaia akademiia 1789 goda iiulia 13 dnia* (Moscow: Tipografiia Komp. Tipografich., 1789).

20. Lomonosov, *Izbrannye proizvedeniia*, 169. On etiquette, see E. N. Marasinova, *Vlast' i lichnost'* (Moscow: Nauka, 2008), 258–63, 300–5.

21. See J. L. Black, *G.-F. Müller and the Imperial Russian Academy* (Kingston: McGill-Queen's University Press, 1986), 102–22.

22. For a comprehensive history, see N. Iu. Alekseeva, *Russkaia oda. Razvitie odicheskoi formy v XVII–XVIII vekakh* (St. Petersburg: Nauka, 2005).

23. R. Vroon, "Sumarokov's Ody torzhestvennye," *Zeitschrift für slavische Philologie*, 55 (1995), 223–63.

24. I. A. Shliapkin, "Vasily Petrovich Petrov, 'karmannyi' stikhotvorets Ekateriny II," *Istoricheskii vestnik*, 11 (1885), 182–206.

25. See, for instance, Karen Rasmussen, "Catherine II and the Image of Peter I," *Slavic Review*, 37 (1978), 57–69.

26. On polish and politeness and the example of the French court culture widely adopted at European courts, see Peter France, *Politeness and Its Discontents: Problems in French Classical Culture* (Cambridge: Cambridge University Press, 1992), 53–74.

27. On the topic broadly, see Michelle Lamarche Marrese, "'The Poetics of Everyday Behavior' Revisited: Lotman, Gender, and the Evolution of Russian Noble Identity," *Kritika*, 11.4 (2010), 701–39.

28. Ospovat, "Sumarokov—literator v sotsial'nom kontekste 1740-nachala 1760-kh gg.," 35–51.

29. Marcus Levitt, "The Illegal Staging of Sumarokov's *Sinav and Truvor* in 1770 and the Problem of Authorial Status in Eighteenth-Century Russia," in *Early Modern Russian Letters: Texts and Contexts* (Boston, MA: Academic Studies Press, 2009), 190–217.

30. *Poety XVIII veka*, vol. 1, 342–5.

31. *Poety XVIII veka*, vol. 1, 108–14.

32. I. S. Barkov, "Ne pol´zu satir ia khvalami voznoshu...," *Poety XVIII veka*, vol. 1, 176.

33. Iu. N. Tynianov, "Oda kak oratorskii zhanr," *Poetika, istoriia, literatura, kino* (Moscow: Nauka, 1977), 227–52.

34. On the trope of geographic extent as an index of fame, see E. V. Dushechkina, "'Ot Moskvy do samykh do okrain...': Formula protiazheniia Rossii," in *Ritoricheskaia traditsiia i russkaia literatura*, ed. P. E. Bukharkin (St. Petersburg: Izd-vo S.-Peterburgskogo universiteta, 2003), 108–25.

35. See Simon Sebag Montefiore, *Prince of Princes: The Life of Potemkin* (London: Weidenfeld and Nicolson, 2000).

36. G. R. Derzhavin, *Stikhotvoreniia*, ed. D. D. Blagoi (Leningrad: Sovetskii pisatel´, 1957), 171–91.

37. See *Teatral´naia zhizn´ Rossii v epokhu Anny Ioanovny: Dokumental´naia khronika 1730–1740*, ed. Liudmila Starikova (Moscow: Radiks, 1995). On Italian theater, especially *commedia*, see Olga Partan, *Vagabonding Masks: The Italian Commedia dell'arte in the Russian Artistic Imagination* (Boston: Academic Studies Press, 2017), Chapters 2 and 3.

38. See I. F. Martynov and I. A. Shankskaia, "Otzvuki literaturno-obshchestvennoi polemiki 1750-kh godov v russkoi rukopisnoi knige (Sbornik A. A. Rzhevskogo)," *XVIII vek*, 11 (1976), 131–48.

39. On the play's critical standing, see Simon Karlinsky, *Russian Drama from Its Beginnings to the Age of Pushkin* (Berkeley: University of California Press, 1985), 71.

40. See Alexei Evstratov, *Les Spectacles francophones à la cour de Russie (1743–1796)* (Oxford: Voltaire Foundation, 2016). See also V. Vsevolod-Gerngross, *Russkii teatr ot istokov do serediny XVIII v.* (Moscow: Izdatel´stvo Akademii nauk, 1957), esp. Chapters 3–7.

41. A. P. Sumarokov, *Izbrannye proizvedeniia*, ed. P. N. Berkov (Leningrad: Sovetskii pisatel´, 1957), 121.

42. The standard history of the comedy remains P. N. Berkov, *Istoriia russkoi komedii XVIII v.* (Leningrad: Nauka, 1977), esp. 59–179.

43. The best overview of his career remains A. N. Pypin in his introduction to *Sochineniia i perevody Vladimira Ignat´evicha Lukina i Bogdana Egorovicha El´chaninova*, ed. P. A. Efremov (St. Petersburg: Glazunov, 1868), i–lxxii.

44. On the link between Plavil´shchikov's views and Fonvizin's writing for the theater, see Peter Hiller, *D. I. Fonvizin und P. A. Plavil´shchikov: Ein Kapitel aus der russischen Theatergeschichte im 18 Jahrhundert* (Munich: Otto Sagner, 1985).

45. P. A. Plavil´shchikov, "Teatr," in *Zritel´*, Parts II and III (1792); the essay was republished in P. A. Plavil´shchikov, *Sochineniia*, 4 vols. (St. Petersburg: 1816), vol. 4, 67–71. For selections, see the anthology *Russkaia literaturnaia kritika XVIII veka*, ed. V. I. Kuleshov (Moscow: Sovetskaia Rossiia, 1978), 216–55.

46. On Fonvizin and the *genre sérieux*, see David Patterson, "Fonvizin's *Nedorosl'* as a Russian Representative of the Genre sérieux," *Comparative Literature Studies*, 14 (1977), 196–204.

47. Ivan Iakovlev, "Perevodchik k chitateliu," in *Pobochnyi syn, ili Ispytaniia dobrodeteli. Drama v piati deistviiakh, perevedena s frantsuzskogo iazyka I. Ia.* (Moscow: Moskovskaia senatskaia tipografiia, 1788), 3.

48. Igor Fedyukin, "Learning to Be Nobles: The Elite and Education in Post-Petrine Russia," Ph.D. Dissertation, University of North Carolina at Chapel Hill, 2009.

49. See M. I. Beliaevskii, "Shkola i sistema obrazovaniia v Rossii v kontse XVIII v.," *Vestnik Moskovskogo universiteta: Seriia istoriko-filologicheskaia*, 21 (1959), 105–20; N. Aristov, *Sostoianie obrazovaniia Rossii v tsarstvovanie Aleksandra I-ogo* (Kiev: Tip. M. P. Fritsa, 1879).

50. N. A. Penchko, *Osnovanie Moskovskogo Universiteta* (Moscow: Izdatel'stvo Moskovskogo univ., 1952), 10–14; and D. A. Tolstoi, *Akademicheskaia gimnaziia v XVIII stoletii* (St. Petersburg: Tip. Imp. Akademii Nauk, 1885), 93–101.

51. A. Iu. Samarin, *Chitatel' v Rossii vo vtoroi polovine XVIII v.* (Moscow: Izdatel'stvo MGUP, 2000).

52. Gary Marker, *Publishing, Printing and the Origins of Intellectual Life in Russia, 1700–1800* (Princeton, NJ: Princeton University Press, 1985), 14; see also the important account of W. G. Jones, *Nikolay Novikov: Enlightener of Russia* (Cambridge: Cambridge University Press, 1984), Chapter 5.

53. Elise Kimerling Wirtschafter, *The Play of Ideas in Russian Enlightenment Theater* (DeKalb, IL: Northern Illinois University Press, 2003).

54. Marc Raeff, "Home, School and Service in the Life of the 18th-Century Russian Nobleman," *SEER*, 40.95 (1962), 295–307.

55. For precise figures, see the articles listed in the bibliography by N. A. Kopanev, *Frantsuzskaia kniga i russkaia kul'tura v seredine XVIII veka (iz istorii mezhdunarodnoi knigotorgovli)* (Leningrad: Nauka, 1988); for overviews, see *Frantsuzskaia kniga v Rossii v XVIII v.*, ed. S. P. Luppov (Leningrad: Nauka, 1986); and his *Kniga v Rossii v seredine XVIII v. Chastnye knizhnye sobraniia* (Leningrad: Nauka, 1989).

56. Kantemir, *Sobranie stikhotvorenii*, 216.

57. Kantemir, *Sobranie stikhotvorenii*, 216.

58. Kantemir, *Sobranie stikhotvorenii*, 59.

59. M. M. Kheraskov, *Izbrannye proizvedeniia*, ed. A. V. Zapadov (Moscow: Sovetskii pisatel', 1961), 79.

60. For an example, see the letter from both the Kheraskovs and the Princess Urusova to Derzhavin of 3 November 1778 complaining of "university chores" ("universitetskie nadobnosti"), in G. R. Derzhavin, *Sochineniia v 9 tomakh*, ed. I. A. Grot, 9 vols. (St. Petersburg: Izd. Imp. Akademii nauk), vol. 5, 308–9, quotation from 308 n.292.

61. See I. Iu. Fomenko, "Avtobiograficheskaia proza G. R. Derzhavina i problema professionalizatsii russkogo pisatelia," *XVIII vek*, 14 (1983), 143–64.

62. N. I. Novikov, *Izbrannye proizvedeniia* (Moscow and Leningrad: Gos. Izdatel'stvo khudozhestvennoi literatury, 1951), 263.

63. *Sobranie luchshikh sochinenii k rasprostraneniiu znanii i k proizvedeniiu udovol'stviia* (Moscow: U Vevera i Skolariia, 1776).

64. Marker, *Publishing, Printing*, 86–7.

65. For an account and the source of these figures, see the studies by V. P. Semennikov, *Knigoizdatel'skaia deiatel'nost' N. I. Novikova i Tipograficheskoi kompanii* (Petrograd: Gosudarstvennoe izdatel'stvo, 1921); and his *Sobranie staraiushcheesia o perevode inostrannykh knig, uchrezhdennoe Ekaterinoi II, 1768–1783* (St. Petersburg: Sirius, 1913).

66. V. Sopikov, *Biblioteka dlia chteniia, nakhodiashchaiasia v Gostinnom dvore pod No. 16 v knizhnoi lavke Vasiliia Sopikova* (St. Petersburg, 1800). A detailed study of St. Petersburg and the book trade, with particular attention to booksellers, can be found in A. A. Zaitseva, *Knizhnaia torgovlia v Sankt-Peterburge vtoroi poloviny XVIII veka* (St. Petersburg: BAN, 2004), 31.

67. Levitt, "The Illegal Staging," 205.

68. On the clash between artistic ambition and social hierarchy, see Irina Reyfman, "Writing, Ranks and the Eighteenth-Century Russian Gentry Experience," in *Representing Private Lives of the Enlightenment*, ed. Andrew Kahn (Oxford: Voltaire Foundation, 2010), 149–66, quotation from 151–8.

69. For a history of the medium, see P. N. Berkov, *Istoriia russkoi zhurnalistiki XVIII v.* (Moscow: Izd. AN SSSR, 1952); supplemented by L. E. Tatarinova, *Russkaia literatura i zhurnalistika XVIII veka* (Moscow: Prospekt, 2001). Also valuable on individual journals are the studies in A. V. Zapadov, *Russkaia zhurnalistika poslednei chetverti XVIII veka* (Moscow: Izdatel'stvo Moskovskogo universiteta, 1962).

70. Much information on obscure individuals who contributed to and edited these often ephemeral journals is to be found in an older study, V. P. Semennikov, *Russkie satiricheskie zhurnaly 1769–1774 gg. Razyskaniia ob izdateliakh ikh i sotrudnikakh* (St. Petersburg: Sirius, 1914).

71. See Andreas Schönle, "The Russian Translation of Voltaire's *Poème sur le désastre de Lisbonne*: I. F. Bogdanovich and the Incipient Cult of Sensibility," *Revue Voltaire*, 9 (2009), 221–39; and Andrew Kahn, "Candide et les problèmes de la réception de l'ouvrage dans la Russie des Lumières," in *Les 250 ans de Candide. Lectures et relectures*, ed. Nicholas Cronk and Nathalie Ferrand (Brussels: Peeters, 2012), 243–69.

72. I. I. Khemnitser, *Polnoe sobranie stikhotvorenii* (Moscow: Sovetskii pisatel', 1963), 143.

73. Much literary material presented for its pedagogical value can be found in the first journal compiled for children by Karamzin and Aleksandr Petrov, *Children's Readings for Heart and Mind* (*Detskoe chtenie dlia serdtsa i razuma*, published between 1785 and 1789). See also G. A. Kosmolinskaia, "Moral'no didakticheskoe chtenie russkogo iunoshestva vtoroi polovine XVIII v.," in *Kniga v Rossii do serediny XIX veka* (Leningrad: Biblioteka Akademii nauk SSSR, 1985), 92–3.

74. G. A. Davydov, "Zhanr druzheskogo poslaniia v poezii M. M. Kheraskova i poetov ego kruga," *Filologicheskie nauki*, 1 (1997), 92–100. On his participation in coteries, see N. D. Kochetkova, "Kheraskov v moskovskom zhurnale Karamzina," *Russkaia literatura*, 4 (2006), 168–82; and N. D. Kochetkova, "Literaturnye posviashcheniia rukovoditeliam uchebnikh zavedenii i nastavnikam," *XVIII vek*, 25 (2008), 39–64.

75. See L. V. Timofeev, *Priiut, liubov'iu muz sogretyi* (St. Petersburg: Nestor-Istoriia, 2007); and Naum Sindalovskii, "Oleninskii kruzhok, ili Peterburg—Priiutino i obratno," *Neva*, 5 (2009), 218–27.

76. *Pis'ma russkikh pisatelei XVIII veka*, ed. G. P. Makogonenko (Leningrad: Nauka, 1980), 348.

77. *Théâtre de l'Hermitage de Catherine II, impératrice de Russie*, 2 vols. (Paris: F. Buisson, 1792).

78. V. P. Semennikov, *Materialy dlia istorii russkoi literatury i dlia slovaria pisatelei epokhi Ekateriny II: na osnovanii dokumentov Arkhiva konferentsii* (St. Petersburg: Sirius, 1914).

79. On sources, a good starting place is W. Gareth Jones, "The Eighteenth-Century View of English Moral Satire: Palliative or Purgative?," in *Great Britain and Russia in the Eighteenth Century: Contacts and Comparisons*, ed. A. G. Cross (Newtonville, MA: Oriental Research Partners, 1979), 75–83.

80. Two excellent general studies on voices and postures are David Nokes, *Raillery and Rage: A Study of Eighteenth-Century Satire* (Brighton: Harvester, 1987); and J. Weisberger, "Satire and Irony as Means of Communication," *Comparative Literature Studies*, 10 (1973), 157–72.

81. A. V. Zapadov, "Zhurnal M. D. Chulkova 'I to i sio' i ego literaturnoe okruzhenie," *XVIII vek*, 2 (1940), 95–141.

82. Isabel de Madariaga, "Catherine and the Philosophes," in *Russia and the West in the Eighteenth Century*, ed. A. G. Cross (Newtonville, MA: Oriental Research Partners, 1983), 30–52; and Franco Venturi, "Beccaria en Russie," in Franco Venturi, *Europe des Lumières. Recherches sur le 18e siècle* (Paris: Mouton, 1971), 45–60.

83. *Novikov i ego sovremenniki*, ed. V. P. Stepanov, *XVIII vek*, 11 (1976).

84. V. D. Rak, "F. A. Emin i Vol'ter," *XVIII vek*, 21 (1999), 151–61.

85. See *Adskaia pochta ili kurier iz ada s pis'mami* (1788), letter 59, http://az.lib.ru/e/emin_f_a/text_1788_adskaya_pochta_olorfo.shtml (last accessed September 23, 2017).

86. N. Novikov, *Satiricheskie zhurnaly N.I. Novikova* (Moscow: Izd-vo Akademii Nauk, 1951), 58; the entire sequence of exchanges from *This and That* can be found in N. I. Novikov, *Izbrannye sochineniia*, 34–65.

87. See Richard S. Wortman, *Scenarios of Power: Myth and Ceremony in Russian Monarchy*, 2 vols. (Princeton, NJ: Princeton University Press, 1995), vol. 1, 122–5.

88. See Nikolai Dobroliubov, "Russkaia satira ekaterinskogo vremeni." http://az.lib.ru/d/dobroljubow_n_a/text_0750.shtml (last accessed April 19 2017).

89. On the debate, see Jones, *Nikolay Novikov*, 40–56.

90. See Franco Venturi, "Nikolaj Ivanovič Novikov," in *Franco Venturi e la Russia*, ed. Antonello Venturi (Milan: Feltrinelli, 2006), 297–329.

91. On problems with publishing Voltaire late in Catherine's reign, see V. D. Rak, *Russkie literaturnye sborniki i periodicheskie izdaniia vtoroi poloviny XVIII veka* (St. Petersburg: Akademicheskii proekt, 1998), 147–95.

92. Nicholas Cronk, "Aristotle, Horace, and Longinus: The Conception of Reader Response," in *The Cambridge History of Literary Criticism*, vol. 3: *The Renaissance*, ed. Glyn P. Norton (Cambridge: Cambridge University Press, 1999), 199–204.

93. See L. Vindt, "Basni sumarokovskoi shkoly," *Poetika*, 1 (1926), 81–92.

94. Kheraskov, *Izbrannye proizvedeniia*, 124.

95. On the idea of civic duty and loyalty to the sovereign, see the discussion in J. L. Black, *Citizens for the Fatherland: Education, Educators, and Pedagogical Ideals in Eighteenth-Century Russia* (Boulder, CO: East European Quarterly, 1979).

96. V. I. Maikov, *Izbrannye proizvedeniia*, ed. A. V. Zapadov (Moscow: Sovetskii pisatel', 1966), 258–9.

97. I. A. Krylov, *Polnoe sobranie sochinenii*, 3 vols. (Moscow: Gos. Izdatel'stvo khudozhestvennoi literatury, 1945–6), vol. 3, 302–5.

98. Krylov, *Polnoe sobranie sochinenii*, vol. 3, 303.

99. Krylov, *Polnoe sobranie sochinenii*, vol. 3, 305.

100. M. N. Murav'ev, "Zabavy voobrazheniia," in M. N. Murav'ev, *Polnoe sobranie sochinenii v 3 tomakh*, 3 vols. (St. Petersburg: Tipografiia Rossiiskoi Akademii, 1819–20), 113–31; and republished in M. N. Murav'ev, *Opyty istorii slovesnosti i nravoucheniia* (Moscow: V Universitetskoi tipografii 1810), vol. 1, 165–80.

101. *Poety XVIII veka*, vol. 1, 187.

102. Novikov, *Izbrannye sochineniia*, 414–17.

103. For a new argument contesting the authorship and originality of the essay, see V. I. Simankov, "O glavnykh prichinakh, ostnosiashchikhsia k prirarshcheniiu khudozhestv i nauk': ob avtorstve stat'i, pripisyvavsheisia N. I. Novikovu, ili tri anoninmykh sochineniia," *Study Group on Eighteenth-Century Russia Newsletter*, 37 (2009), 54–71.

104. *Poety XVIII veka*, vol. 1, 542.

105. I. F. Bogdanovich, *Stikhotvoreniia i poemy*, ed. I. Z. Serman (Leningrad: Sovetskii pisatel', 1957), 45. The poem was published anonymously in 1778 and 1783, and under the author's name only in 1794 when a preface was added. His authorship was well known and rewarded by Catherine; the poem's success allowed him to return to service and make a decent career.

106. M. N. Murav'ev, *Stikhotvoreniia*, ed. L. I. Kulakova (Leningrad: Sovetskii pisatel', 1967), 212.

107. See Andrew Kahn, Introduction to M. N. Murav'ev, *Institutiones rhetoricae: A Treatise of a Russian Sentimentalist* (Oxford: Meeuws, 1995), xxii–xxx; and A. N. Brukhanskii, "M. N. Murav'ev i 'legkoe stikhotvorstvo,'" *XVIII vek*, 4 (1959), 157–71.

108. Murav'ev, *Stikhotvoreniia*, 131–7 (131).

109. Bogdanovich, *Stikhotvoreniia i poemy*, 166.

110. Ia. B. Kniazhnin, *Izbrannye proizvedeniia*, ed. L. I. Kulakova (Leningrad: Sovetskii pisatel', 1961), 643–5 (645).

111. Kniazhnin, *Izbrannye proizvedeniia*, 670.

112. G. R. Derzhavin, *Stikhotvoreniia*, 166.

113. Derzhavin, *Stikhotvoreniia*, 167–8.

114. Derzhavin, *Stikhotvoreniia*, 222.

115. N. M. Karamzin, *Polnoe sobranie stikhotvorenii*, ed. Iu. M. Lotman (Leningrad: Sovetskii pisatel', 1966), 144.

116. See Boris Uspenskii, *Iz istorii russkogo literaturnogo iazyka XVIII–nachala XIX veka: iazykovaia programma Karamzina i ee istoricheskie korni* (Moscow: Izdatel'stvo Moskovskogo universiteta, 1985).

117. On his career and its cultural reputation and authority, see Kirill Ospovat, "Mikhail Lomonosov Writes to His Patron: Professional Ethos, Literary Rhetoric and Social Ambition," *Jahrbücher für Geschichte Osteuropas*, 59.2 (2011), 240–66.

118. For specific texts, see Letters 84 (Bonnet), 41 (Mendelssohn), 123 (Franklin), and 156 (Leibniz) in the *Letters of a Russian Traveler*.

119. *Slovar' russkogo iazyka XVIII veka* (Leningrad: Nauka, 1984), vol. 5, 104.

120. On the character of Derzhavin's boastfulness, see I. Klein, "Poet-samokhval: 'Pamiatnik' Derzhavina i status poeta v Rossii XVIII veka," *NLO*, 65 (2004), 148–70.

121. Murav'ev, *Stikhotvoreniia*, 226–8 (226, 227).

122. G. R. Derzhavin, *Sochineniia Derzhavina*, ed. Ia. Grot, 9 vols. (St. Petersburg: Imp. Akad. Nauk, 1872), vol. 7, 516–628.

123. On ekphrastic representations in poetic works of the period, see Luba Golburt, "Derzhavin's Ruins and the Birth of Historical Elegy," *Slavic Review*, 65.4 (2006), 670–93.

124. Murav'ev, *Stikhotvoreniia*, "Sila geniia," 228.

125. N. M. Karamzin, *Pis'ma russkogo puteshestvennika*, in N. M. Karamzin, *Izbrannye sochineniia v dvukh tomah*, ed. P. Berkov and G. Makogonenko (Moscow: Khudozhestevennaia literatura, 1964), vol. 2, 196.

126. N. M. Karamzin, *Pis'ma russkogo puteshestvennika*, ed. Iu. Lotman, B. A. Uspenskii, and N. Marchenko (Leningrad: Nauka, 1984), 381 (Letter 156).

127. Iu. D. Levin, *Ossian v russkoi literature* (Leningrad: Nauka, Leningradskoe otdelenie, 1980); on Ossianism and the mania for bards, see Fiona Stafford, *The Sublime Savage: A Study of James MacPherson and the Poems of Ossian* (Edinburgh: Edinburgh University Press, 1994).

128. M. N. Murav'ev, "Pokhval'noe slovo Mikhaile Vasil'evichu Lomonosovu," in *O tvorchestve Lomonsova: kritika i issledovaniia*, ed. T. P. Aranzon (Moscow: Fond ekonomicheskogo razvitiia stran, 2008), 19–25.

129. Murav'ev, *Stikhotvoreniia*, 217–23.

130. On the cultural importance of the idea, see Darrin McMahon, *Divine Fury: A History of Genius* (New York: Basic Books, 2013); and Ann Jefferson, *Genius in France: An Idea and Its Uses* (Princeton, NJ: Princeton University Press, 2015).

131. V. K. Trediakovskii, *Sochineniia i perevody kak stikhami, tak i prozoiu*, 2 vols. (St. Petersburg, 1752), vol. 2, 183.

132. A. G. Volkov, "K Solov'iu," in *Poety-radishchevtsy*, ed. V. Orlov and G. A. Likhotin (Leningrad: Sovetskii pisatel', 1979), 263.

133. K. N. Batiushkov, *Optyty v stikakh i proze*, ed. Irina M. Semenko (Moscow: Nauka, 1977), 8–20, 29–35 ("O kharaktere Lomonosova").

134. The indispensable edition can be found in *Spory o iazyke v nachale XIX v. kak fakt russkoi kul'tury. "Proisshestvie v tsarstve tenei, ili Sud'bina rossiiskogo iazyka"—neizvestnoe sochinenie Semena Bobrova*, ed., intro., and commentary, Iu. M. Lotman and B. A. Uspenskii, *Uchenye zapiski Tartuskogo Gos. un-ta*, 358 (*Trudy po russkoi slavianskoi filologii*, vol. 24), 168–322.

Chapter 3

1. See Nicholas V. Riasanovsky, *The Image of Peter the Great in Russian History and Thought* (New York: Oxford University Press, 1985); and Carolyn H. Wilberger, "Peter the Great: An Eighteenth-Century Hero of Our Times?," *Studies on Voltaire and the Eighteenth Century*, 96 (1972), 9–127.

2. On anti-Western undertones, see Hans Rogger, *National Consciousness in Eighteenth-Century Russia* (Cambridge, MA: Harvard University Press, 1960), 32–3.

3. Simon Dixon, *The Modernisation of Russia, 1676–1825* (Cambridge: Cambridge University Press, 1999).

4. The text of the sermon can be found in *Petr I v russkoi literature XVIII veka. Teksty i kommentarii*, ed. S. I. Nikolaev (St. Petersburg: Nauka, 2006), 8–15.

5. For a very useful anthology of eighteenth-century texts on Peter the Great in the period, see *Petr I v russkoi literature XVIII veka*, ed. Nikolaev. On Feofan Prokopovich, see 90–106.

6. *Russkaia literatura. Vek XVIII. Lirika*, ed. N. D. Kochetkova (Moscow: Khudozhestvennaia literatura, 1990), 146–51, quotation from 146 (Andrei Nartov, "Pokhvala Peterburgu").

7. See V. K. Trediakovskii, "Oda IV. Pokhvala Izherskoi zemle i tsarstvuiushchemu gradu Sanktpeterburgu," in V. K. Trediakovskii, *Izbranny proizvedeniia*, ed. L. I. Timofeev (Moscow and Leningrad: Sovetskii pisatel', 1963), 179–81, quotation from 179.

8. For a modern history that sees the entire period in terms of modernization, see Aleksandr Kamenskii, *Rossiiskaia imperiia v XVIII veke. Traditsii i modernizatsii* (Moscow: NLO, 1999).

9. A. D. Kantemir, *Sobranie stikhotvorenii*, ed. Z. I. Gershkovich (Leningrad: Sovetskii pisatel', 1956), 241–51.

10. On Kantemir's knowledge of scientific theory, see I. V. Shkliar, "Formirovanie mirovozzreniia A. Kantemira," *XVIII vek*, 5 (1962), 128–52. The Academy of Sciences followed the state's emphasis on technical education. See Simon Werrett, "An Odd Sort of Exhibition: The St. Petersburg Academy of Sciences in Enlightened Russia," Ph.D. Dissertation, University of Cambridge, 2000.

11. For a survey of debates about the authorship and dating of Satire IX, see L. R. Murav'eva, "Problema tak nazyvaemoi 'deviatoi' satiry A. D. Kantemir," *XVIII vek*, 5 (1962), 153–78.

12. Kantemir, *Sobranie stikhotvorenii*, 180–4.

13. M.V. Lomonosov, *Izbrannye sochineniia*, ed. A. A. Morozov (Leningrad: Sovetskii pisatel', 1986), 115–21.

14. Lomonosov, *Izbrannye sochineniia*, 169–76.

15. Steven Shapin, "The Image of the Man of Science," in *The Cambridge History of Science*, vol. 4: *Eighteenth-Century Science*, ed. Roy Porter et al. (Cambridge: Cambridge University Press, 2003), 159–83.

16. Lomonosov, *Izbrannye sochineniia*, 207–9.

17. *Poety XVIII veka*, ed. G. P. Makogenenko and I. Z. Serman, 2 vols. (Leningrad: Sovetskii pisatel', 1972), vol. 1, 245–8.

18. *Aonidy*, 1 (1796), 78–81; reprinted in *Petr I v russkoi literature XVIII veka*, ed. Nikolaev, 320.

19. See L. V. Pumpianskii, "Lomonosov i nemetskaia shkola razuma," *XVIII vek*, 14 (1983), 23–5; *Poety XVIII veka*, ed. Makogonenko and Serman, vol. 1, 245–50.

20. On Petersburg's location on the right side of the geographic map of Enlightenment, see Larry Wolff, *Inventing Eastern Europe: The Map of Civilization on the Mind of the Enlightenment* (Stanford, CA: Stanford University Press, 1994).

21. Derek Beales, "Philosophical Kingship and Enlightened Despotism," in *The Cambridge History of Eighteenth-Century Political Thought*, ed. Mark Goldie and Robert Wokler (Cambridge: Cambridge University Press, 2006), 495–524, quotation from 518.

22. On the tradition, see Michel Mervaud, "Les *Anecdotes sur le czar Pierre le Grand* de Voltaire: genèse, sources, forme littéraire," *Studies on Voltaire and the Eighteenth Century*, 341 (1996), 89–126; see also Elena Nikanorova and Elena Romodanovskaia, *Istoricheskii anekdot v russkoi literature XVIII veka* (Novosibirsk: Sibirskii khronograf, 2001), 329–417.

23. Evgenii Anisimov, *Petr Velikii. Lichnost' i reformy* (St. Petersburg: Piter, 2009).

24. Friedrich Weber, *Nouveaux Mémoires sur l'état present de la Grande Russie ou Moscovie…* (Paris: Chez Pissot, 1725), xi.

25. The definitive edition and historical commentary is now abbé Chappe d'Auteroche, *Voyage en Sibérie fait par ordre du roi en 1761*, ed. Michel Mervaud and Madeleine Pinault Sørensen, 2 vols. (Oxford: Voltaire Foundation, 2004). On the episode, see Marcus C. Levitt, "An Antidote to Nervous Juice: Catherine the Great's Debate with Chappe d'Auteroche over Russian Culture," *Eighteenth-Century Studies*, 32.1 (1998), 49–63.

26. On the myth of the monument in the nineteenth century, see A. L. Ospovat and R. D. Timenchik, *Pechal'nu povest' sokhranit'*, 2nd revised edn. (Moscow: Kniga, 1987).

27. *Sbornik imperatorskogo russkogo istoricheskogo obshchestva*, vol. 17 (St. Petersburg, 1876), 118, 198–9, available at https://archive.org/details/sbornikimperato005obshgoog (last accessed September 25, 2017); and Denis Diderot and Étienne-Maurice Falconet, *Le Pour et le contre: Correspondance polémique sur le respect de la postérité, Pline et les anciens auteurs qui ont parlé de peinture et de sculpture*, ed. Yves Benot (Paris: Éditeurs français réunis, 1958), 357–64.

28. For the view that social progress is the defining feature of the Enlightenment as a pan-European movement, see John Robertson, *The Enlightenment: A Very Short Introduction* (Oxford: Oxford University Press, 2015).

29. V. I. Maikov, *Izbrannye proizvedeniia*, ed. A. V. Zapadov (Moscow: Sovetskii pisatel', 1966), 284.

30. On Pushkin's attitude to these sources, see Il'ia Feinberg, *Nezavershennye raboty Pushkina* (Moscow: Khudozhestvennaia literatura, 1979), 84–97.

31. Stephen Baehr, *The Paradise Myth in Eighteenth-Century Russia: Utopian Patterns in Early Secular Russian Literature and Culture* (Stanford, CA: Stanford University Press, 1991).

32. *Poety XVIII veka*, ed. Makogonenko and Serman, vol. 1, 395–403.

33. Isabel de Madariaga, "Catherine and the Philosophes," in *Russia and the West in the Eighteenth Century*, ed. A. G. Cross (Newtonville, MA: Oriental Research Partners, 1983), 30–52; and for the exchange in action, "Lettres inédites de Grimm à Catherine II," ed. Sergueï Karp, Nadezhda Plavinskaia, Georges Dulac, and Sergei Iskul, *Recherches sur Diderot et sur l'Encyclopédie*, 10 (1991), 41–55.

34. The best Russian edition with commentary is N. M. Karamzin, *Pis'ma russkogo puteshestvennika*, ed. Iu. M. Lotman, N. A. Marchenko, B. A. Uspenskii (Leningrad: Nauka, 1984); for a complete English translation, see Nikolai Karamzin, *Letters of a Russian Traveller with an Essay on Karamzin's Discourses of Enlightenment*, ed. and trans. Andrew Kahn (Oxford: Voltaire Foundation, 2003).

35. Karamzin, *Letters*, 52 (Letter 13).

36. On the use of persona, see Andreas Schönle, *Authenticity and Fiction in the Russian Literary Journey, 1790–1840* (Cambridge, MA: Harvard University Press, 2000).

37. See Simon Dixon, "Catherine the Great and the Enlightenment," *Leidschrift. Rusland en Europa. Westerse invloeden op Rusland*, 24.2 (2009), 34–43.

38. See D. D. Shamrai, "K istorii tsenzurnogo rezhima Ekateriny II," *XVIII vek*, 3 (1958), 187–207.

39. The anecdote can be found in Louis-Philippe, comte de Ségur, *Œuvres complètes de M. le comte de Ségur*, 3 vols. (Paris: A. Eymery, 1826), vol. 3, 43.

40. The topic has generated a vast scholarly bibliography in Enlightenment studies. For a helpful introduction, see James Van Horn Melton, *The Rise of the Public in Enlightenment Europe* (Cambridge: Cambridge University Press, 2001); there are some helpful remarks on the limita-

tions of the model for Russia in Douglas Smith, *Working the Rough Stone: Freemasonry and Society in Eighteenth-Century Russia* (DeKalb, IL: Northern Illinois University Press, 1999).

41. Cited in Ia. B. Kniazhnin, *Izbrannye proizvedeniia*, ed. L. I. Kulakova (Leningrad: Sovetskii pisatel', 1961), 11.

42. Viktor Zhivov, "'Vsiakaia vsiachina' i sozdanie Ekaterininskogo politicheskogo diskursa," in *Eighteenth-Century Russia: Society, Culture, Economy: Papers from the VII International Conference of the Study Group on Eighteenth-Century Russia, Wittenberg 2004*, ed. Roger Bartlett and Gabriela Lehmann-Carli (Berlin: LIT, 2007), 251–65.

43. Viktor Zhivov, "The Myth of the State in the Age of Enlightenment and Its Destruction in Late Eighteenth-Century Russia," *Russian Studies in History*, 48.3 (2009–10), 10–29.

44. While Fonvizin's two classic plays remained in the repertory, from the 1820s Fonvizin was one of the first eighteenth-century writers to attract research. Prince P. A. Viazemsky's life *Fon-Vizin* (1830) was a pioneering work that related his career as playwright, job as ministerial secretary, and court politics. This is also a work of literary history that periodizes by discussing the "epoch" or "period" of Catherine.

45. See V. A. Zapadov, "Kratkii ocherk istorii russkoi tsenzury 60–90-kh gg. XVIII v.," in *Russkaia literatura i obshchestvenno-politicheskaia bor'ba XVII–XIX vv.* (Leningrad: Uchenye zapiski Leningradskogo universiteta, 1971), 38–60; and M. P. Troianskii, "K stsenicheskoi istorii komedii D. I. Fonvizina 'Brigadir' i 'Nedorosl' v XVIII v.," in *Teatral'noe nasledstvo. Soobshcheniia. Publikatsii* (Moscow: Iskusstvo, 1956), 7–23.

46. Derek Offord, "Denis Fonvizin and the Concept of Nobility: An Eighteenth-Century Russian Echo of a Western Debate," *European History Quarterly*, 35.1 (2005), 9–38. Also worth consulting are Lurana Donnels O'Malley, *The Dramatic Works of Catherine the Great: Theater and Politics in Eighteenth-Century Russia* (Aldershot: Ashgate, 2006); and S. O. Shmidt, "Obshchestvennoe samosoznanie *noblesse russe* v XVI–pervoi treti XIX vv.," *Cahiers du monde russe et soviétique*, 34 (1993), 11–32.

47. Fonvizin's difficulties in getting permission to stage *The Minor* were remembered decades later in the 1820s and noted in print by the minor poet Dmitrii Khvostov (*Nevskii zritel'*, 3.9 [1820], 121). On awareness of the precedent in the nineteenth century, see V. P. Stepanov, "Polemika vokrug D. I. Fonvizina v period sozdaniia *Nedoroslia*", XVIII vek, 15 (1986), 204–29.

48. Catherine's satirical and polemical writings, including the series of "Facts and fictions," can be found in *Sochineniia imperatritsy Ekateriny II na osnovanii podlinnykh rukopisei s ob"iasnitel'nymi primechaniiami A. N. Pypina*, 12 vols. (St. Petersburg: Tip. Akademii nauk, 1850), vol. 3, 1–126.

49. For a detailed reading of the situation, see Vera Proskurina, "Spor o 'svobodoiazychii': Fonvizin i Ekaterina," *NLO*, 105 (2010), 125–44.

50. V. V. Kapnist, *Izbrannye proizvedeniia*, ed. G. V. Ermakova-Bitner and D. S. Babkin (Leningrad: Sovetskii pisatel', 1973), 59–62.

51. Kapnist, *Izbrannye proizvedeniia*, 63–7.

52. See Marc Raeff, "La jeunesse russe à l'aube du XIXᵉ siècle: André Turgenev et ses amis," *Cahiers du monde russe et soviétique*, 8 (1967), 560–86.

53. Isabel de Madariaga, *Russia in the Age of Catherine the Great* (London: Phoenix, 2002), 547; and specifically on Catherine's "repudiation" of Voltaire late in her reign, Christophe Paillard, "Ingérence censoriale et imbroglio éditorial. La censure de la correspondance de Voltaire dans les éditions in-8° et in-12 de Kehl," *Revue Voltaire*, 7 (2007), 275–309. In fact, Catherine was inconsistent in applying censorship and played off Church authorities and the police against one another.

54. Gary Marker, *Publishing, Printing and the Origins of Intellectual Life in Russia, 1700–1800* (Princeton, NJ: Princeton University Press, 1985), 105–9.

55. W. G. Jones, *Nikolay Novikov: Enlightener of Russia* (Cambridge: Cambridge University Press, 1984), 165–6.

56. For a comprehensive account of Radishchev's university years and career with extensive bibliography, see Peter Hoffmann, *Aleksandr Nikolaevič Radiščev (1749–1802). Leben und Werk* (Frankfurt am Main: Peter Lang, 2015).

57. A. N. Radishchev, *Polnoe sobranie sochinenii* (Moscow: Akademiia nauk SSSR, 1938), vol. 1, 177.

58. Radishchev, *Polnoe sobranie sochinenii*, vol. 1, 227.

59. See *Biografiia A. N. Radishcheva, napisannaia ego synoviami* (Leningrad: Izd-vo Akademii Nauk, 1959), 94–5.

60. On the theme in general, see Karen O'Brien, *Narratives of Enlightenment: Cosmopolitan History from Voltaire to Gibbon* (Cambridge: Cambridge University Press, 1997); for Russia, see A. Kamenskii, *Rossiiskaia imperiia v XVIII veke: traditsii i modernizatsiia* (Moscow: NLO, 1999).

61. Simon Dixon, "'Prosveshchenie': Enlightenment in Eighteenth-Century Russia," in *Peripheries of the Enlightenment*, ed. Richard Butterwick, Simon Davies, and Gabriel Sánchez Espinosa (Oxford: Voltaire Foundation, 2008), 229–50.

62. Luba Golburt, *The First Epoch: The Eighteenth Century and the Russian Cultural Imagination* (Madison, WI: University of Wisconsin Press, 2014), 72–113.

63. Modern historians also adopt this view. See, for example, Evgenii Anisimov, *The Reforms of Peter the Great: Progress Through Coercion in Russia*, trans. John T. Alexander (Armonk, NY: M. E. Sharpe, 1993).

64. Much material on sources and argument can be found in T. E. Abramzon, *"Pis'mo o pol'ze stekla" M. V. Lomonosova: opyt kommentarii prosvetitel'skoi entsiklopedii* (Moscow: OGI, 2010). For the poem, see Lomonosov, *Izbrannye sochineniia*, 236–46.

65. Martin Malia, *Russia under Western Eyes: From the Bronze Horseman to the Lenin Mausoleum* (Cambridge, MA: Harvard University Press, 1999).

66. For an overview of the issues as discussed by English and continental thinkers, see Malcolm Jack, *Corruption & Progress: The Eighteenth-Century Debate*, AMS Studies in the Eighteenth Century, no. 11 (New York: AMS Press, 1989).

67. I. F. Bogdanovich, *Stikhotvoreniia i poemy*, ed. I. Z. Serman (Leningrad: Sovetskii pisatel', 1957), 187–95.

68. Maikov, *Izbrannye proizvedeniia*, 257–9.

69. Recent scholarship is coming to see the later period as full of its own tensions in which Enlightenment and Counter-Enlightenment are closely connected rather than opposites (as would be the case with figures who self-identified as enemies of Enlightenment). See, for example, Vincenzo Ferrone, *The Enlightenment: History of an Idea* (Princeton, NJ and Oxford: Princeton University Press, 2015); and Darrin McMahon, *Enemies of the Enlightenment: The French Counter-Enlightenment and the Making of Modernity* (New York and Oxford: Oxford University Press, 2001), esp. Chapters 1 and 3.

70. See Fonvizin, *Sobranie sochinenii v dvukh tomakh*, 2 vols. (Moscow: Khudozhestvennaia literatura, 1959), vol. 1, 209–13.

71. A. P. Sumarokov, *Izbrannye proizvedeniia*, ed. P. N. Berkov (Leningrad: Sovetskii pisatel', 1957), 97.

72. N. I. Novikov, *Satiricheskie zhurnaly N. I. Novikova*, ed. P. N. Berkov (Moscow: Izd-vo Akademii Nauk, 1951), 201–2.

73. Novikov, *Satiricheskie zhurnaly*, 283.

74. For the entire set, see the anthology "Stikhotvornaia polemika," in *Poety XVIII veka*, ed. Makogonenko and Serman, vol. 2, 371–414 (nos. 176–208); for "Zashchishchenie petimetra," see 377–80.

75. Kapnist, *Izbrannye proizvedeniia*, 340.

76. See Wladimir Berelowitch, "Europe ou Asie? Saint-Pétersbourg dans les relations de voyage occidentaux," in *Le Mirage russe au XVIIIᵉ siècle*, ed. Sergei Karp and Larry Wolff (Ferney-Voltaire: Centre international d'étude du XVIIIᵉ siècle, 2001), 57–75.

77. N. I. Novikov, *Izbrannye proizvedeniia*, 373.

78. N. P. Nikolev, "Satira na razvrashchennye nravy nyneshnego veka," in *Poety XVIII veka*, ed. Makogonenko and Serman, vol. 2, 18–20.

79. I. A. Krylov, *Polnoe sobranie sochinenii*, 3 vols. (Moscow: Gos. Izdatel'stvo khudozhestvennoi literatury, 1945–6), vol. 1, 11–282.

80. Krylov, *Polnoe sobranie sochinenii*, vol. 1, 329–37.

81. Nikolai Karamzin, *Izbrannye sochineniia*, ed. P. N. Berkov, 2 vols. (Moscow: Khudozhestvennaia literatura, 1964), vol. 2, 128.

82. Catriona Kelly, *Refining Russia: Advice Literature, Polite Culture, and Gender from Catherine to Yeltsin* (Oxford: Oxford University Press, 2001), Chapter 1.

83. M. M. Shcherbatov, *On the Corruption of Morals in Russia*, trans. Antony Lentin (Cambridge: Cambridge University Press, 1969), 241.

84. On debates in Russia during this period over the influence of the French language as a subject for theater, see G. M. Hammarberg, "Language and Conservative Politics in Alexandrine Russia," in *French and Russian in Imperial Russia*, ed. Derek Offord, Lara Ryazanova-Clarke, Vladislav Rjéoutski, and Gesine Argent, 2 vols. (Edinburgh: Edinburgh University Press), vol. 2, esp. 118–21.

85. See Mark Altshuller, "S. S. Bobrov i russkaia poeziia kontsa XVIII–nachala XIX v.," *Russkaia literatura XVIII v. Epokha klassitsizma* (Moscow: IRLI, 1964), 224–46.

86. For the entire text and commentary, see Iu. M. Lotman and B. A. Uspenskii, "Spory o iazyke v nachale XIX v. kak fakt russkoi kul'tury ('Proisshestvie v tsarstve tenei, ili Sud'bina rossiiskogo iazyka—neizvestnoe sochinenie S. Bobrova')," *Uchenye zapiski Tartuskogo gos.-un-ta*, 358 (1975), 168–322.

87. Radishchev, *Polnoe sobranie sochinenii*, vol. 1, 128.

88. See N. I. Gnedich, "Rassuzhdenie o prichinakh, zamedlivshikh khod nashei slovesnosti," in *Kritika pervoi chetverti XIX-ogo veka* (Moscow: Izdatel'stvo Olimp, 2002), 184–90.

89. For an overview of his reading, note-taking, and interest in cultural philosophy, see I. Iu. Fomenko, "Istoricheskie vzgliady M. N. Murav'eva," *XVIII vek*, 13 (1981), 167–84.

90. M. N. Murav'ev, *Polnoe sobranie sochinenii* (St. Petersburg: Tipografiia Rossiiskoi Akademii, 1819–20), vol. 3, 177–80.

Chapter 4

1. Amanda Ewington, *Russian Women Poets of the Eighteenth and Early Nineteenth Centuries: A Bilingual Edition* (Manchester: Manchester University Press, 2014); and Wendy Rosslyn, *Anna Bunina, 1774–1829, and the Origins of Women's Poetry in Russia* (Lewiston, NY: Edwin Mellen Press, 1997).

2. R. Lauer, *Gedichtform zwischen Schema und Verfall: Sonett, Rondeau, Madrigal, Ballade, Stanze und Triolett in der russischen Literatur des 18. Jahrhunderts* (Munich: W. Fink, 1975).

3. See K. A. Paphmehl, *Freedom of Expression in Eighteenth-Century Russia* (The Hague: Martinus Nijhoff, 1971). For another perspective that sees a more liberal Church, see Robert Nichols, "Orthodoxy and Russia's Enlightenment, 1762–1825," in *Russian Orthodoxy under the Old Regime*, ed. Robert L. Nichols and Theofanis G. Stavrou (Minneapolis: University of Minnesota Press, 1978), 65–89.

4. There is a vast bibliography on the connections between theories of the body and literary representations of sensibility in Western Europe. Good entry points include Jessica Riskin, *Science in the Age of Sensibility: The Sentimental Empiricists of the French Enlightenment* (Chicago: University of Chicago Press, 2002); G. J. Barker-Benfield, *The Culture of Sensibility: Sex and Society in Eighteenth-Century Britain* (Chicago: University of Chicago Press, 1992). There is scope

for equivalent work in Russian literature to integrate a medical humanities approach and the basic work of historical descriptions of Sentimentalism such as N. D. Kochetkova, *Literatura russkogo sentimentalizma: esteticheskie i khudozhestvennye iskannia* (St. Petersburg: Nauka, 1994).

5. The standard work of reference remains S. M. Grombakh, *Russkaia meditsinskaia literatura XVIII veka* (Moscow: Akademiia meditsinskikh nauk, 1953). For an overview of more recent work, see Clare Griffin, "In Search of an Audience: Popular Pharmacies and the Limits of Literate Medicine in Late Seventeenth- and Early Eighteenth-Century Russia," *Bulletin of the History of Medicine*, 89.4 (2015), 705–32.

6. See J. L. Black, *Citizens for the Fatherland: Education, Educators and Pedagogical Ideals in Eighteenth-Century Russia* (Boulder, CO: East European Quarterly, 1979); and Max Okenfuss, "Education and Empire: School Reform in Enlightened Russia," *Jahrbücher für Geschichte Osteuropas*, 27.1 (1979), 41–68.

7. A. D. Kantemir, *Sobranie stikhotvorenii*, ed. Z. I. Gershkovich (Leningrad: Sovetskii pisatel', 1956), 159.

8. See Steven Usitalo, *The Invention of Mikhail Lomonosov: A Russian National Myth* (Brighton, MA: Academic Studies Press, 2013).

9. For the particulars of Catherine's work on her memoirs, see Monika Greenleaf, "Performing Autobiography: The Multiple Memoirs of Catherine the Great (1756–96)," *Russian Review*, 63.3 (2004), 407–26; and Hilde Hoogenboom, "Preface: Catherine the Great and Her Several Memoirs," in *The Memoirs of Catherine the Great*, trans. Mark Cruse and Hilde Hoogenboom (New York: Modern Library, 2005), ix–lxix. See also Alexander Woronzoff-Dashkoff, *Dashkova: A Life of Influence and Exile* (Philadelphia: American Philosophical Society, 2008). For a discussion of Dashkova's memoir, see Marcus C. Levitt, *Early Modern Russian Letters: Texts and Contents: Selected Essays* (Boston: Academic Studies Press, 2009), 379–98. There is no authoritative edition of her memoirs, which exist in two versions. The most recent edition can be found in Princesse Dachkova, *Mon histoire. Mémoires d'une femme de lettres russe à l'époque des Lumières*, ed. Alexander Woronzoff-Dashkoff et al. (Paris: L'Harmattan, 1999).

10. Evgenii Anisimov, "Putniki, proshedshie ran'she nas," in *Bezvremen'e i vremenshchiki: Vospominaniia ob epokhe dvortsovykh perevorotov (1720-e–1760-e gody)* (Leningrad: Khudozhestvennaia literatura, 1991), 20–1.

11. See Anna Maria Summers, "Four Strangers, Life in the Margins," Ph.D. dissertation, Harvard University, 2007, 70.

12. I. M. Dolgorukov, *Kapishche moego serdtsa ili slovar' vsekh tekh lits, s koimi ia byl v raznykh otnosheniiakh v techenii moei zhizni* (Moscow: Nauka, 1997), 14.

13. V. I. Korovin, "Kniaz' Ivan Dolgorukov i 'Kapishche moego serdtsa,'" in Dolgorukov, *Kapishche moego serdtsa*, 283–4.

14. Andrei Zorin, "Eshche raz o 'Dnevnike odnoi nedeli' A. N. Radishcheva: datirovka, zhanr, biograficheskaia problematika (*opyt istoriko-psikhologicheskoi rekonstruktsii*)," *NLO*, 113.1 (2012), 130–56.

15. A. N. Radishchev, "Dnevnik odnoi nedeli," in A. N. Radishchev, *Polnoe sobranie sochinenii*, 3 vols. (Moscow and Leningrad: Izd. AN SSSR, 1938), vol. 1, 141. All subsequent quotations come from pages 139–44 of this edition.

16. For this interpretation, see Andrei Zorin and Andrei Nemzer, "Les paradoxes de la sentimentalité," in *Livre et Lecture en Russie*, ed. Alexandre Stroev (Paris: IMEC, 1996), 100–6.

17. For a reading along class lines, see Joe Andrew, *Women in Russian Literature, 1780–1863* (Basingstoke: Macmillan, 1988), 22–6.

18. Aleksei Rzhevskii, "Portret," *Svobodnye chasy* (June 1763), 358, reprinted as Aleksei Rzhevskii, "Portret," in *Russkaia literatura. Vek XVIII. Lirka*, ed. N. D. Kochetkova (Moscow: Khudozhestvennaia literatura, 1990), 168.

19. Rzhevskii, "Portret," 169.

20. *Pis'ma russkikh pisatelei XVIII veka*, 133–5 (no. 66).

21. A. P. Sumarokov, *Izbrannye proizvedeniia*, ed. P. N. Berkov (Leningrad: Sovetskii pisatel', 1957), 163.

22. N. M. Karamzin, *Polnoe sobranie stikhotvorenii*, ed. Iu. M. Lotman (Leningrad: Sovetskii pisatel', 1966), 192–5. Murav'ev left some notes that suggest that he was thinking about models of consciousness and the workings of imagination. Of particular interest are the pieces collected in his 1820 works, "Interior consciousness" ("Vnutrennee soznanie, vtoroi istochnik poniatii") and "The Linking of Ideas" ("Sovokuplenie idei").

23. Published originally in *Aonidy* I (1796), 135; reprinted in *Russkaia literatura. Vek XVIII. Lirika*, ed. Kochetkova, 565.

24. G. R. Derzhavin, *Stikhotvoreniia*, ed. D. D. Blagoi (Leningrad: Sovetskii pisatel', 1957), 360.

25. Derzhavin, *Stikhotvoreniia*, 206.

26. David Gasperetti, "Matvei Komarov," in *Early Modern Russian Writers: Late Seventeenth and Eighteenth Centuries*, ed. Marcus C. Levitt (Detroit, MI: Gale Research, 1995), 182.

27. Valeria Sobol, *Febris erotica: Lovesickness in the Russian Literary Imagination* (Seattle: University of Washington Press, 2009), Chapter 1.

28. Sumarokov, *Izbrannye proizvedeniia*, 271.

29. Gitta Hammarberg, "The Feminine Chronotope and Sentimentalist Canon Formation," in *Literature, Lives, and Legality in Catherine's Russia*, ed. A. G. Cross and G. S. Smith (Nottingham: Astra Press, 1994), 103–20.

30. I. F. Bogdanovich, *Stikhotvoreniia i poemy*, ed. I. Z. Serman (Leningrad: Sovetskii pisatel', 1957), 155.

31. *Russkaia literature. Vek XVIII. Lirika*, ed. Kochetkova, 555.

32. Marcus Levitt, "Barkoviana and Russian Classicism," in *Eros and Pornography in Russian Culture*, ed. Marcus Levitt and A. Toporkov (Moscow: Ladomir, 1999), 219–36.

33. Imitation of foreign models, both classical and contemporary, were vital to the growth of erotic expression in the Russian lyric. A helpful account of French and German writing, the most important sources for the Russians, can be found in Stéphanie Loubère, *L'Art d'aimer au siècle des Lumières* (Oxford: Voltaire Foundation, 2002); and T. Ziolkowski, *The Classical German Elegy, 1795–1950* (Princeton, NJ: Princeton University Press, 1980).

34. For a detailed history of period interest in and practice of anacreontea, see G. N. Ionin, "Anakreonticheskie stikhi Karamzina i Derzhavina," *XVIII vek*, 8 (1969), 162–78.

35. The point is well made by Anne K. Mellor, "'Anguish no Cessation Knows': Elegy and the British Woman Poet, 1660–1834," in *The Oxford Handbook of the Elegy* (Oxford: Oxford University Press, 2010), 443.

36. V. K. Trediakovskii, *Novyi i kratkii sposob k slozheniiu rossiiskikh stikhov s opredeleniiami do sego nadlezhashchikh zvanii*, in V. K. Trediakovskii, *Izbrannye proizvedeniia*, ed. L. I. Timofeev (Moscow and Leningrad: Sovetskii pisatel', 1963), 396.

37. Bogdanovich, *Stikhotvoreniia i poemy*, 154.

38. *Poety XVIII veka*, ed. G. P. Makogenenko and I. Z. Serman, 2 vols. (Leningrad: Sovetskii pisatel', 1972), vol. 1, 458.

39. On his career and artistic profile, see Irina Reyfman, "Alexey Rzhevsky, Russian Mannerist," in Irina Reyfman, *Rank and Style: Russians in State Service, Life, and Literature* (Boston, MA: Academic Studies Press, 2012), 229–44.

40. Lomonosov, *Izbrannye proizvedeniia*, ed. A. A. Morozov (Leningrad: Sovetskii pisatel', 1986), 255.

41. Derzhavin, *Stikhotvoreniia*, 233.

42. On the ambiguity, see M. P. Alekseev, *Stikhotovrenie Pushkina "Ia pamiatnik sebe vozdvig…": Problemy ego izucheniia* (Leningrad: Nauka, 1967), 58–65.

43. A. S. Pushkin, *Polnoe sobranie sochinenii v desiati tomakh*, 10 vols. (Leningrad: Nauka, 1977–9), vol. 3, 340.

44. See M. G. Al'tshuller, "Krepostnoi poet i perevodchik N. Smirnov," *Frantsuzskii Ezhegodnik* (1967), 261–2.

45. Elizaveta Kheraskova, "Nadezhda," in *Russkaia literatura. Vek XVIII. Lirika*, ed. Kochetkova, 157; and M. N. Kheraskov, *Izbrannye proizvedeniia*, ed. A. V. Zapadov (Moscow: Sovetskii pisatel', 1961), 110.

46. For a survey of Russian knowledge and translation of English lyric poetry, see Iu. D. Levin, *Vospriiatie angliiskoi literatury v Rossii* (Leningrad: Nauka, 1990), 134–230.

47. Ia. B. Kniazhnin, in *Russkaia literatura. Vek XVIII. Lirika*, ed. Kochetkova, 257–74, esp. 270–4.

48. See, for example, *Zapiski Senatora I. V. Lopukhina* in *Rossiia XVIII stoletiia v izdaniiakh Vol'noi russkoi tipografii A. I. Gertsena i N. P. Ogareva, 1859* (Moscow: Nauka, 1990).

49. Derzhavin, *Stikhotvoreniia*, 86.

50. M. V. Milonov, *Satiry, poslaniia i drugie melkie stikhotvoreniia Mikhaila Milonova* (St. Petersburg: Tipografiia Iv. Glazunova, 1819), 24.

51. Andreas Schönle, *Architecture of Oblivion: Ruins and Historical Consciousness in Modern Russia* (DeKalb: Northern Illinois University Press, 2011), 29–46.

52. See John W. Draper, *The Funeral Elegy and the Rise of English Romanticism* (New York: Octagon Books, 1967); on the monument as the locus of patent sensibility in Karamzin, see Andrew Kahn, "Karamzin's Discourses of Enlightenment," *SVEC*, 2003.4 (2003), 527–37.

53. On this practice in the influential English country elegy, see Lorna Clymer, "'Graved in Tropes': The Figural Logic of Epitaphs and Elegies in Blair, Gray, Cowper, and Wordsworth," *ELH*, 62 (1995), 347–86.

54. These poems (and other related lyrics) can be found in the fine anthology *Russkaia literatura: XVIII vek. Lirika*, ed. Kochetkova.

55. Sumarokov, *Izbrannye proizvedeniia*, 140–55.

56. A. D. Kantemir, *Sobranie stikhotvorenii*, ed. Z. I. Gershkovich (Leningrad: Sovetskii pisatel', 1956), 147–57.

57. Trediakovskii, *Izbrannye proizvedeniia*, 192–6.

58. *Russkaia literatura. Vek XVIII. Lirika*, ed. Kochetkova, 154.

59. See Andrew Kahn, "'Blazhenstvo ne v luchakh porphira': histoire et fonction de la tranquillité (*spokojstvie*) dans la pensée et la poésie russes du XVIIIᵉ siècle, de Kantemir au sentimentalisme," *Revue des études slaves*, 4 (2003), 669–88.

60. Derzhavin, *Stikhotvoreniia*, 223.

61. V. V. Kapnist, *Izbrannye proizvedeniia*, ed. G. V. Ermakova-Bitner and D. S. Babkin (Leningrad: Sovetskii pisatel', 1973), 110–14.

62. Stephanie Sandler, *Distant Pleasures: Alexander Pushkin and the Writing of Exile* (Stanford, CA: Stanford University Press, 1989), 23–39.

63. T. G. Smoliarova, *Zrimaia lirika. Derzhavin* (Moscow: NLO, 2011), 403.

64. Derzahvin, *Stikhotvoreniia*, 326–34.

65. Murav'ev, *Stikhotvoreniia*, 158.

66. *Russkaia literatura. Vek XVIII. Lirika*, ed. Kochetkova, 548.

67. See Iu. M. Lotman, *Pushkin. Biografiia pisatelia. Stat'i i zametki, 1960–1990; "Evgenii Onegin." Kommentarii* (St. Petersburg: Iskusstvo-SPB, 1995), 646–67.

Chapter 5

1. On shorter fictions as departures into areas neglected by the novel, see Andrew Kahn, "Russian Literature Between Classicism and Romanticism," in *The Oxford Handbook of European Romanticism*, ed. Paul Hamilton (Oxford: Oxford University Press, 2016), 493–512.

2. On the connection between fictional realities and private lives, see Jean-Marie Goulemot, "Literary Practices: Publicizing the Private," in *A History of Private Life*, trans. Arthur Goldhammer, 5 vols. (Cambridge, MA: Harvard University Press, 1989), vol. 3, 363–95; and Christophe Martin, *Espaces du féminin dans le roman français du dix-huitième siècle* (Oxford: Voltaire Foundation, 2004). On the prevalence of first-person fictions in France, in so many other areas the decisive influence on Russian cultural life, see René Démoris, *Le Roman à la première personne* (Paris: Colin, 1975).

3. N. M. Karamzin, *Izbrannye sochineniia v dvukh tomah*, ed. P. Berkov and G. Makogonenko, 2 vols. (Moscow: Khudozhestevennaia literatura, 1964), vol. 2, 114–15.

4. Karamzin, *Izbrannye proizvedeniia*, vol. 2, 176–9.

5. These figures are based on the bibliographical information in several standard sources: V. V. Sipovskii, *Iz istorii russkogo romana i povesti. Materialy po bibliografii, istorii i teorii russkogo romana* (St. Petersburg: Imp. Akademiia nauk, 1903); *Izdaniia grazhdanskoi pechati vremeni Imperatritsy Elisavety Petrovny, 1741–1761*, ed. V. P. Semennikov (Moscow: Izd. AN SSSR, 1935); *Svodnyi katalog russkoi knigi grazhdanskoi pechati XVIII veka, 1725–1800*, ed. I. P. Kondakov et al., 5 vols. + Suppl. (Moscow, Izd. AN SSSR, 1966); T. N. Kondakova, *Spisok razyskaemykh izdanii, ne voshedshikh v Svodnyi katalog russkoi knigi kirillovskoi pechati XVIII veka, 1701–1800* (Moscow, Izd. AN SSSR, 1971); and *Spisok razyskivaemykh izdanii ne voshedshikh v svodnyi katalog russkoi knigi grazhdanskoi pechati XVIII veka, 1725–1800*, ed. I. M. Polonskaia (Moscow: Gos. biblioteka SSSR im. V. I. Lenina. Otd. Redkikh knig, 1969).

6. For a pan-European perspective on various national traditions, with divergences as much as convergences, see the chapters collected in *Remapping the Rise of the Novel*, ed. Jenny Mander (Oxford: Voltaire Foundation, 2007).

7. Aleksandr Sumarokov, "Pis′mo o chtenii romanov," *Trudoliubivaia pchela* (1759), 374–5; and the article "Nechto o romanakh" ["Something on Novels"], in *Priiatnoe i poleznoe preprovozhdenie vremeni*, Part 6 (1795), 202–9.

8. On European models, see Alexandre Stroev, *Les Aventuriers des Lumières* (Paris: Presses universitaires de France, 1997).

9. On Chulkov's innovations, see Marcia Morris, "Russian Variations on the Picaresque: The Narrative Short Form," *Canadian Slavonic Papers*, 34 (1992), 57–78; and Caryl Emerson, *The Cambridge Introduction to Russian Literature* (Cambridge: Cambridge University Press, 2008), 90–3.

10. For a starting point in an account of the challenges faced by this generation, see Victoria Somoff, *The Imperative of Reliability: Russian Prose on the Eve of the Novel, 1820s–1850s* (Evanston, IL: Northwestern University Press, 2015), 21–42.

Conclusion

1. *Chtenie v torzhestvennom sobranii Imperatorskoi Rossiiskoi Akademii, byvshem v 5-yi den′ Dekabria 1818* (St. Petersburg: Tipografiia V. Plavil′shchikov, 1818).

2. See Iu. M. Lotman and B. A. Uspenskii, "Spory o iazyke v nachale XIX v. kak fakt russkoi kul′tury ('Proisshestvie v tsarstve tenei, ili Sud′bina rossiiskogo iazyka—neizvestnoe sochinenie S. Bobrova')," *Uchenye zapiski Tartuskogo gos.-un-ta*, 358 (1975), 168–322; and Oleg Proskurin, *Literaturnye skandaly Pushkinskoi epokhi* (Moscow: OGI, 2000), 19–46.

3. Classic examples include the essays by N. M. Karamzin, "Why Are There So Few Talented Authors in Russia?" ("Otchego tak malo avtorskikh talantov v Rossii"), in Karamzin, *Izbrannye sochineniia*, 183–8, originally published in his journal *The Herald of Europe* (*Vestnik Evropy*), 14 (1802).

4. Ivan Krylov, *Basni Ivana Krylova* (St. Petersburg: Tipografiia Gubernskogo Pravleniia, 1809).

5. *Tsvetnik izbrannykh stikhotvorenii v pol'zu i udovol'stviia iunosheskogo vozrasta 1816 goda* (Moscow: Universitetskaia Tipografiia, 1816).

6. G. R. Derzhavin, *Lira Derzhavina, ili Izbrannye ego stikhotvoreniia* (Moscow: V Universitetskoi Tipografii, 1817), n.p.

7. On their relationship and the question of influence, see David Bethea, *Realizing Metaphor: Alexander Pushkin and the Life of the Poet* (Madison: University of Wisconsin Press, 1998), 137–99.

Part IV. The Nineteenth Century
Introduction

1. For a discussion of Russians' reaction to the beginning of the new century and their response to the changes of reign, see Irina Reyfman, "Imagery of Time and Eternity in Eighteenth-Century Russian Poetry: Mikhail Murav'ev and Semyon Bobrov," in Irina Reyfman, *Rank and Style: Russians in State Service, Life, and Literature* (Boston: Academic Studies Press, 2012), esp. 249–58.

2. For a discussion of poetry's relative invisibility in the mid-nineteenth century, see Charles A. Moser, "Poets and Poetry in an Antipoetic Age," *Slavic Review*, 1 (1969), 48–62. On Nekrasov's role in reviving the interest in poetry, see Thomas Gaiton Marullo, "Reviving Interest in Verse: The Critical Efforts of Nikolai Nekrasov, 1848–54," *Canadian Slavonic Papers/Revue Canadienne des Slavistes*, 22.2 (1980), 247–59.

Chapter 1

1. See N. D. Kochetkova, "Radishchev i masony," *Russkaia literatura*, 1 (2000), 103–6; E. A. Vil'k, "Chudishche stozevno i Tifon ('Puteshestvie' A. N. Radishcheva v kontekste misticheskoi literatury XVIII v.)," *NLO*, 55 (2002), 151–73.

2. See Nikolai Karamzin, *Pis'ma russkogo puteshestvennika*, ed. Iu. M. Lotman, N. A. Marchenko, B. A. Uspenskii (Leningrad: Nauka, 1984), 62–6. For an English translation, see *Letters of a Russian Traveller*, a translation with an essay by Andrew Kahn (Oxford: Voltaire Foundation, 2003), 90–4.

3. See Iu. M. Lotman and B. A. Uspenskii, eds., "Pis'ma A. A. Petrova k Karamzinu. 1785–1792," in Karamzin, *Pis'ma russkogo puteshestvennika*, 499–512.

4. William Mills Todd III, *The Familiar Letter as a Literary Genre in the Age of Pushkin* (Princeton, NJ: Princeton University Press, 1976), 40–1.

5. For the quotation, see N. M. Karamzin, *Pis'ma N. M. Karamzina k I. I. Dmitrievu* (St. Petersburg, v tip. Imperatorskoi Akademii Nauk, 1866), 35. Karamzin also uses this phrase in his 1794 essay "Filaret k Milodoru," in N. M. Karamzin, *Izbrannye sochineniia v dvukh tomakh*, 2 vols. (Moscow: Khudozhestvennaia literatura, 1964), vol. 2, 252.

6. Boris Eikhenbaum, "Literaturnaia domashnost'," in Boris Eikhenbaum, *Moi vremennik. Slovesnost'. Nauka. Kritika. Smes'* (Leningrad: Izdatel'stvo pisatelei v Leningrade, 1929), 49–86; Joe Peschio, *The Poetics of Impudence and Intimacy in the Age of Pushkin* (Madison: University of Wisconsin Press, 2012), esp. 5, 16–17.

7. David L. Cooper, "*Narodnost'* avant la lettre? Andrei Turgenev, Aleksei Merzliakov, and the National Turn in Russian Criticism," *SEEJ*, 52.3 (2008), 351–69.

8. Ermil Kostrov was the first to translate *The Iliad* in verse. He translated cantos 1–8 and the beginning of 9, using Alexandrines to imitate the Greek hexameter. Gnedich continued Kostrov's unfinished translation. However, Sergei Uvarov (1786–1855), the future minister of education under Nicholas, and at the time a serious scholar of antiquity, wrote "A Letter to

Gnedich about the Greek Hexameter" ("Pis′mo Gnedichu o grecheskom gekzametre," 1813), arguing against Alexandrines and in favor of using the Russian imitation of hexameter first introduced by Trediakovsky. Gnedich accepted Uvarov's arguments and translated *The Iliad* in hexameters, publishing it in 1829. It remains the only translation of Homer's epic into Russian.

9. Its tables of contents are included in Mark Al′tshuller, *Predtechi slavianofil′stva v russkoi literature: Obshchestvo "Beseda liubitelei russkogo slova"* (Ann Arbor, MI: Ardis, 1984), 371–83.

10. O. A. Proskurin, "Kogda zhe Pushkin vstupil v Arzamasskoe obshchestvo? (Iz zametok k teme 'Pushkin i Arzamas')," *Toronto Slavic Quarterly*, 14 (2005), http://sites.utoronto.ca/tsq/14/proskurin14.shtml (last accessed July 7, 2016).

11. Mariia Maiofis, "O chem umalchivaiut protokoly: Politicheskie diskussii v 'Arzamase' v zerkale neosushchestvlennykh reform 1813–1818 godov," in Mariia Maiofis, *Vozzvanie k Evrope: Literaturnoe obshchestvo "Arzamas" i rossiiskii modernizatsionnyi proekt 1815–1818 godov* (Moscow: NLO, 2008), 249–310 (Chapter 5).

12. See *"Arzamas." Sbornik v dvukh knigakh*, ed. V. E. Vatsuro and A. L. Ospovat, 2 vols. (Moscow: Khudozhestvennaia literatura, 1994), esp. vol. 2, 343–445.

13. Joe Peschio, "The Green Lamp," in Peschio, *The Poetics of Impudence*, 60–93 (Chapter 3).

14. For the notion of life-creating, see Irina Paperno, "Introduction" to *Creating Life: The Aesthetic Utopia of Russian Modernism*, ed. Irina Paperno and Joan Delaney Grossman (Stanford, CA: Stanford University Press, 1994), 1–11, quotation on 2.

15. For its discussion as a prank, see Peschio, *The Poetics of Impudence*, 85–7.

16. O. A. Proskurin, *Poeziia Pushkina, ili Podvizhnyi Palimpsest* (Moscow: NLO, 1999), 15; Joe Peschio, "*Ruslan i Liudmila*: Rudeness and Sexual Banter," in Peschio, *The Poetics of Impudence*, 94–114 (Chapter 4).

17. Irina Paperno, "Ob izuchenii poetiki pis′ma," *Uchenye zapiski Tartuskogo gos. Universiteta*, 420 (1977), 148–56; Mikhail Gronas, "Pushkin and the Art of the Letter," in *The Cambridge Companion to Pushkin*, ed. Andrew Kahn (Cambridge: Cambridge University Press, 2006), 130–42.

18. A. S. Pushkin, *Polnoe sobranie sochinenii v desiati tomakh*, ed. B. V. Tomashevskii, 10 vols. (Leningrad: Nauka, 1977–79), vol. 1, 307.

19. Lidiia Ginzburg, *O psikhologicheskoi proze* (Leningrad, Sovetskii pisatel′, 1971), 64. On Stankevich and his circle, see also Edward J. Brown, *Stankevich and His Moscow Circle, 1830–1840* (Stanford, CA: Stanford University Press, 1966).

20. On Stankevich and his relations with Liubov, see John Randolph, *The House in the Garden: The Bakunin Family and the Romance of Russian Idealism* (Ithaca, NY: Cornell University Press, 2007), 174–96; on the dissolution of the engagement, see pp. 223, 261.

21. Randolph, *The House in the Garden*, 226–50.

22. Alexander Herzen, *My Past and Thoughts*, trans. Constance Garnett, intro. Isaiah Berlin (Berkeley, CA: University of California Press, 1982), 62. For the Russian original, see A. I. Gertsen, *Sobranie sochinenii v tridtsati tomakh*, 30 vols. (Moscow: Izd. AN SSSR, 1954–64), vol. 8, 81.

23. Quoted in Irina Paperno, *Chernyshevsky and the Age of Realism: A Study in the Semiotics of Behavior* (Stanford, CA: Stanford University Press, 1988), 146.

24. The literature on Russian women writers is now considerable, and we cite many works below. The pioneering effort of Barbara Heldt, *Terrible Perfection: Women and Russian Literature* (Bloomington: Indiana University Press, 1987) was an inspiration to a generation of scholars in the West. In late Soviet Russia, a number of feminist literary scholars and historians began to do important archival and interpretive work, and collaborations between East and West ensued. Edited collections in the 1990s were one result, for example *Gender Restructuring in Russian Studies*, ed. Marianne Liljeström, Eila Mäntysaari, and Arja Rosenholm (Tampere: University of Tampere, 1993); and now significant monographs have been produced, such as

Irina Savkina, *Razgovory s zerkalom i zazerkal'em: Avtodokumental'nye zhenskie teksty v russkoi literature pervoi poloviny XIX veka* (Moscow: NLO, 2007).

25. Judith Vowles, "The Inexperienced Muse: Russian Women and Poetry in the First Half of the Nineteenth Century," in *A History of Women's Writing in Russia*, ed. Adele Marie Barker and Jehanne M. Gheith (Cambridge: Cambridge University Press, 2002), 62–84. See also Irina Savkina, "Kto i kak pishet istoriiu russkoi zhenskoi literatury," *NLO*, 24 (1997), 359–72.

26. For the poem, see *Tsaritsy muz: Russkie poetessy XIX–nachala XX vv.*, ed. V. V. Uchenova (Moscow: Sovremennik, 1989), 21–4.

27. *Tsaritsy muz*, ed. Uchenova, 51.

28. On Kul'man, see the entry by Bonnie Marshall in *The Dictionary of Russian Women Writers*, ed. Marina Ledkovsky, Charlotte Rosenthal, and Mary Zirin (Westport, CT: Greenwood Press, 1994), 344–6; and M. F. Fainshtein, *Pisatel'nitsy pushkinskoi pory: Istoriko-literaturnye ocherki* (Leningrad: Nauka, 1989), 6–24.

29. See Judith Vowles, "The 'Femininization' of Russian Literature: Women, Language, and Literature in Eighteenth-Century Russia," in *Women Writers in Russian Literature*, ed. Toby Clyman and Diana Greene (Westport, CT: Praeger Publishers, 1994), 35–60; and Gitta Hammarberg, "Gender Ambivalence and Genre Anomalies in Late 18th–Early 19th-Century Russian Literature," *Russian Literature*, 52.1–3, (2002), 299–326.

30. A. S. Pushkin, "Table-talk," in *Polnoe sobranie sochinenii v desiati tomakh*, vol. 8, 67.

31. William Mills Todd III, *Fiction and Society in the Age of Pushkin* (Cambridge, MA: Harvard University Press, 1986), 132.

32. Todd, *Fiction and Society*, 129.

33. Hilde Hoogenboom, "Sentimental Novels and Pushkin: European Literary Markets and Russian Readers," *Slavic Review*, 74.3 (2015), 553–74, quotation on 560, citing A. I. Reitblat, *Ot Bovy k Bal'montu i drugie raboty po istoricheskoi sotsiologii russkoi literatury* (Moscow: NLO, 2009).

34. For extended studies of individual poets, see Diana Greene, *Reinventing Romantic Poetry: Russian Women Poets of the Mid-Nineteenth Century* (Madison, WI: University of Wisconsin Press, 2004). Also useful is Fainshtein, *Pisatel'nitsy pushkinskoi pory*, for its information about publications, cultural and social context, and biography.

35. See Susanne Fusso, "Pavlova's *Quadrille*: The Feminine Variant of (the End of) Romanticism," in *Essays on Karolina Pavlova*, ed. Susanne Fusso and Alexander Lehrman (Evanston, IL: Northwestern University Press, 2001), 118–34.

36. On Pavlova's career, see Catriona Kelly, *A History of Russian Women's Writing 1820–1992* (Oxford: Oxford University Press, 1994), 93–107.

37. For the poems, see Karolina Pavlova, *Polnoe sobranie stikhotvorenii* (Moscow: Sovetskii pisatel', 1964), 89, 135. These comments on the "Duma" poems are highly compressed from Stephanie Sandler and Judith Vowles, "Abandoned Meditation: Karolina Pavlova's Early Poetry," in *Essays on Karolina Pavlova*, ed. Fusso and Lehrman, 32–52. Briusov edited a two-volume set of Pavlova's writings, *Sobranie sochinenii* (Moscow: Izd. K. F. Nekrasova, 1915).

38. See the essay by Vladislav Khodasevich, "Grafinia E. P. Rostopchina: Ee zhizn' i lirika," in Vladislav Khodasevich, *Stati'i o russkoi poezii* (St. Petersburg: Epokha, 1922), 7–42.

39. On her salons in both Petersburg and Moscow, see M. Aronson and S. Reiser, *Literaturnye kruzhki i salony* (St. Petersburg: Akademicheskii proekt, 2001 [1921]), 219–24.

40. See Evdokiia Rostopchina, *Talisman: Izbrannaia lirika. Drama. Dokumenty, pis'ma, vospominaniia* (Moscow: Moskovskii rabochii, 1987), 74–5.

41. For a brief account of Rostopchina's poetry, see Kelly, *History of Russian Women's Writing*, 45–7.

42. See Jehanne Gheith, *Finding the Middle Ground: Krestovskii, Tur, and the Power of Ambivalence in Nineteenth-Century Russian Women's Prose* (Evanston, IL: Northwestern University Press, 2004).

43. Kelly, *History of Russian Women's Writing*, 83.

44. Joe Andrew, *Narrative and Desire in Russian Literature (1822–1849)* (London: Macmillan, 1993), 85. Andrew includes chapters with detailed readings of works by both Gan and Zhukova.

45. See Valeria Sobol, "'Shumom bala utomlennyj': The Physiological Aspect of the Society Ball and the Subversion of Romantic Rhetoric," *Russian Literature*, 69 (2001), 293–314, for a reading of the unnatural settings of balls; on dance more broadly in the first chapter of *Onegin*, including its famous dance performance, see William Mills Todd III, "'The Russian Terpsichore's Soul-Filled Flight': Dance Themes in *Eugene Onegin*," in *Pushkin Today*, ed. David M. Bethea (Bloomington: Indiana University Press, 1993), 13–30.

46. Pushkin's poem to her is "Portret" [1828], in *Polnoe sobranie sochinenii v desiati tomakh*, vol. 3, 66.

47. For a structural analysis of the folkloric and religious origins of images that join the two parts of the story, see A. Zholkovskii, "Morfologiia i istoricheskie korni rasskaza Tolstogo 'Posle bala,'" in A. Zholkovskii, *Bluzhdaiushchie sny: Iz istorii russkogo modernizma* (Moscow: Sovetskii pisatel', 1992), 109–29.

48. For more on the use of French in Russian society, see *French and Russian in Imperial Russia*, ed. Derek Offord, Lara Ryazanova-Clarke, Vladislav Rjéoutski, and Gesine Argent, 2 vols., (Edinburgh: Edinburgh University Press, 2015).

49. These examples as well as the general atmospheres of various salons are featured in Vlada Bunturi, *K priiutu tikhomu besedy prosveshchennoi: Literaturnyi salon v kul'ture Peterburga* (St. Petersburg: Dmitrii Bulanin, 2013), 89–149.

50. Hers is among the especially well-studied salons: see V. E. Vatsuro, *S.D.P: Iz istorii literaturnogo byta pushkinskoi pory* (Moscow: Kniga, 1989).

51. For an exemplary feminist reading of emerging salon culture, see Lina Bernstein, "Women on the Verge of a New Language: Russian Salon Hostesses in the First Half of the Nineteenth Century," in *Russia, Women, Culture*, ed. Helena Goscilo and Beth Holmgren (Bloomington: Indiana University Press, 1996), 209–24.

52. These moments were all recorded by Smirnova about her own salon, excerpted in Aronson and Reiser, *Literaturnye kruzhki i salony*, 203–7.

53. On the emergence of women writers across the century, including observations about early salons, see Arja Rosenholm and Irina Savkina, "How Women Should Write: Russian Women's Writing in the Nineteenth Century," in *Women in Nineteenth-Century Russia: Lives and Culture*, ed. Wendy Rosslyn and Alessandra Tosi (Cambridge: Open Book Publishers, 2012), 161–208.

54. Aronson and Reiser, *Literaturnye kruzhki i salony*, 22–4.

55. Those transitions are well studied in Todd, *Fiction and Society in the Age of Pushkin*, 55–83. For a reading of the rhetorical qualities of albums as well as an account of the social contexts in which they emerged, see also Justyna Beinek, "Making Literature in Albums: Strategies of Authorship in Pushkin's Day," *Toronto Slavic Quarterly* 31 (2010), http://sites.utoronto.ca/tsq/31/Beinek31.shtml (last accessed May 4, 2016); and Larisa Petina, "Strukturnye osobennosti al'boma Pushkinskoi epokhi," *Ruthenia*, http://www.ruthenia.ru/document/529033.html (last accessed July 31, 2016).

56. L. A. Chereiskii, *Pushkin i ego okruzhenie* (Leningrad: Nauka, 1988), 522–3. For the essays on albums, as cited by Lotman and others, see P. L. Iakovlev, "O al'bomakh. (Iz al'boma K. I. I.)," *Blagonamerennyi* 18 (1820), 373–8; and "Al'bomy," *Zapiski moskvicha* (Moscow: S. Selivanovskii, 1828), 122–7.

57. For the poem, see E. A. Baratynskii, *Polnoe sobranie stikhotvorenii* (St. Petersburg: Akademicheskii proekt, 2000), 286, 495. In fairness one should add that multiple versions exist for quite a number of Baratynskii's poems, making him a textologically challenging poet. But it is an intriguing prospect to consider how album poetry, with its potential for intimate forms of address, offered this poet, who was already prone to self-revision, a remarkably suitable forum for quicksilver acts of self-fashioning.

58. Baratynskii, *Polnoe sobranie stikhotvorenii*, 105.

59. Pushkin, *Polnoe sobranie sochinenii v desiati tomakh*, vol. 7, 153.

60. *Al'bom Elizavety Ushakovoi: Faksimil'noe vosproizvedenie*, ed. T. Krasnoborod'ko (St. Petersburg: Logos, 1999), 113.

61. *Al'bom Elizavety Ushakovoi*, 330.

62. Gitta Hammarberg, "Flirting with Words: Domestic Albums 1770–1840," in *Russia, Women, Culture*, ed. Goscilo and Holmgren, 297–320, esp. 298.

63. Lotman observes the coded implications of some pages or positions for album inscribers: Iu. M. Lotman, *Roman A. S. Pushkina "Evgenii Onegin": Kommentarii* (Leningrad: Prosveshchenie, 1980), 243.

64. For a survey of one of the most substantial collections, see V. E. Vatsuro, "Literaturnye al'bomy v sobranii Pushkinskogo doma (1750–1840-e gody)," in *Ezhegodnik Rukopisnogo otdela Pushkinskogo doma na 1977 god*, ed. K. D. Muratova (Leningrad: Nauka, 1979), 3–56. It is followed in that same publication with excerpts selected by Vatsuro: "Iz al'bomnoi liriki i literaturnoi polemiki 1790–1830-kh godov," 61–78.

Chapter 2

1. Mariia Maiofis, "Podzemnye kliuchi: Vokrug arzamasskikh zhurnal'nykh proektov," in Mariia Maiofis, *Vozzvanie k Evrope: Literaturnoe obshchestvo "Arzamas" i rossiiskii modernizatsionnyi proekt 1815–1818 godov* (Moscow: NLO, 2008), 600–76 (Chapter 10).

2. William Mills Todd III, "Periodicals in Literary Life of the Early Nineteenth Century," in *Literary Journals in Imperial Russia*, ed. Deborah A. Martinsen (Cambridge: Cambridge University Press, 1997), 37–63, quotation on 41.

3. Todd, "Periodicals in Literary Life," 42.

4. Todd, "Periodicals in Literary Life," 40.

5. The discussion is based on Chester M. Rzadkiewicz's "N. A. Polevoi's 'Moscow Telegraph' and the Journal Wars of 1825–1834," in *Literary Journals in Imperial Russia*, ed. Martinsen, 64–87.

6. On Senkovsky as journalist, see Melissa Frazier, *Romantic Encounters: Writers, Readers, and the Library for Reading* (Stanford, CA: Stanford University Press, 2007).

7. Robert A. Maguire, "Introduction," in *Literary Journals in Imperial Russia*, ed. Martinsen, 1–8, quotation on 6.

8. See Victor Terras, "Belinsky the Journalist and Russian Literature," in *Literary Journals in Imperial Russia*, ed. Martinsen, 117–28, esp. 120.

9. Catharine Theimer Nepomnyashchy, "Katkov and the Emergence of the 'Russian Messenger,'" *Ulbandus Review*, 1 (1977), 59–89, esp. 63.

10. Robert L. Belknap, "Survey of Russian Journals, 1840–1880," in *Literary Journals in Imperial Russia*, ed. Martinsen, 91–116, esp. 104.

11. Stanley J. Rabinowitz, "*Northern Herald*: From Traditional Thick Journal to Forerunner of the Avant-Garde," in *Literary Journals in Imperial Russia*, ed. Martinsen, 207–27.

12. Deborah Anne Martinsen, "Dostoevsky's *Diary of a Writer*: Journal of the 1870s," in *Literary Journals in Imperial Russia*, ed. Martinsen, 150–68; Kate Holland, "Between Babel and a New Word: *A Writer's Diary* as Monojournal," in Kate Holland, *The Novel in the Age of Disintegration: Dostoevsky and the Problem of Genre in the 1870s* (Evanston, IL: Northwestern University Press, 2013), 131–61 (Chapter 4); Kate Holland, "Dostoevsky's Journalism in the 1870s," in *Dostoevsky in Context*, ed. Deborah A. Martinsen and Olga Maiorova (Cambridge: Cambridge University Press, 2015), 288–94.

13. Sarah Hudspith, "Dostoevsky's Journalism in the 1860s," in *Dostoevsky in Context*, ed. Martinsen and Maiorova, 280–7.

14. See I. P. Foote, *The St. Petersburg Censorship Committee, 1828–1905* (Oxford: W. A. Meeuws, 1992).

15. See Charles Rudd, *Fighting Words: Imperial Censorship and the Russian Press, 1804–1906* (Toronto: University of Toronto Press, 1982), 55–6. For recent work on censorship, see P. S. Reifman, *Tsenzura v dorevoliutsionnoi, sovetskoi i postsovetskoi Rossii*, vol. 1: *Tsenzura v dorevoliutsionnoi Rossii*, issue 1: "Dopetrovskaia Rossiia—pervaia tret' XIX v.," ed. G. G. Superfin (Moscow: Probel-2000, 2015); P. S. Reifman, *Tsenzura v dorevoliutsionnoi, sovetskoi i postsovetskoi Rossii*, vol. 1: *Tsenzura v dorevoliutsionnoi Rossii*, issue 3: "1855–1917 gg.," ed. E. S. Sonina (Moscow: Probel-2000, 2017).

16. The most thorough case history of ecclesiastical censorship remains Aleksandr Kotovich, *Dukhovnaia tsenzura v Rossii (1799–1855)*, (St. Petersburg: Rodnik, 1909).

17. On the careers of censors, see N. G. Patrusheva, *Tsenzor v gosudarstvennoi sisteme dorevoliutsionnoi Rossii* (St. Petersburg: Severnaia zvezda, 2011), 90–169.

18. On Goncharov's service, see Foote, *The St. Petersburg Censorship Committee*, 15, 46; and Rudd, *Fighting Words*, 138–40.

19. The unsystematic nature of censorship in practice during the Imperial period that belies generalizations can be gleaned in much documentary material presented in A. V. Blium, *Russkie pisateli o tsenzure i tsenzorakh: ot Radishcheva do nashikh dnei, 1790–1990, opyty annotirovannoi antologii* (St. Petersburg: Poligraf, 2011); and A. V. Blium, *Ot neolita do Glavlita: dostopamiatnye i zanimatel'nye epizody, sobytiia i anekdoty iz istorii rossiiskoi tsenzury ot Petra Velikogo do nashikh dnei. Sobrany po literaturnym i arkhivnym istochnikam* (St. Petersburg: Iskusstvo Rossii, 2009), 26–68. For a more statistical snapshot, see Benjamin Rigberg, "The Efficacy of Tsarist Censorship Operations, 1894–1917," *Jahrbücher für Geschichte Osteuropas*, n.s. Bd. 14.3 (1966), 327–46.

20. J. M. Coetzee, *Giving Offense: Essays on Censorship* (Chicago: University of Chicago Press, 1996), 42.

21. I. P. Foote, "'In the Belly of the Whale': Russian Authors and Censorship in the Nineteenth Century," *The Slavonic and East European Review*, 68.2 (990), 297.

22. Lev Loseff, *On the Beneficence of Censorship: Aesopian Language in Modern Russian Literature* (Munich: Verlag Otto Sagner, 1984), 114.

23. See Konstantin Sergeevich Aksakov, "Svobodnoe slovo," http://az.lib.ru/a/aksakow_k_s/text_0290.shtml (last accessed November 7, 2017); for the impact of censorship on Nekrasov, see Marullo, "Reviving Interest in Verse," 249.

24. Robert Darnton, *The Forbidden Best-Sellers of Pre-Revolutionary France* (New York: W. W. Norton, 1995).

25. On Pushkin's strategy of publishing *Evgeny Onegin* in installments for gain, see Sergei Gessen, *Knigoizdatel' Aleksandr Pushkin: Literaturnye dokhody Pushkina* (Leningrad: Academia, 1930; facsimile edn. 1987), 95–100. Gessen argues that not only was Pushkin a savvy publisher of his poetic works (Gessen does not discuss his prose), but that he was also the first Russian writer to introduce the idea of copyright by suing August Ol'dekop, who in 1824 reprinted Pushkin's 1821 narrative poem *The Captive of the Caucasus* without Pushkin's permission; see Gessen, *Knigoizdatel' Aleksandr Pushkin*, 42–9.

26. William Mills Todd III, "Dostoevskii as a Professional Writer," in *Cambridge Companion to Dostoevskii*, ed. W. J. Leatherbarrow (Cambridge: Cambridge University Press, 2002), 66–92; also William Mills Todd III, "Dostoevskii kak professional'nyi pisatel': professiia, zaniatiia, etika," *NLO*, 58.6 (2002), 15–43.

27. For a discussion of structural changes in Dostoevsky's novels in connection with his journalistic work, see William Mills Todd III, "The Brothers Karamazov and the Poetics of Serial Publication," *Dostoevsky Studies*, 7 (1986), 88–98; and William Mills Todd III, "'To be Continued': Dostoevsky's Evolving Poetics of Serialized Publication," *Dostoevsky Studies*, 18 (2014), 23–33. Kate Holland observes Dostoevsky's efforts in both the journalistic and novelistic genres to

present *The Adolescent* (a novel written as *Diary of a Writer* was taking shape) as "a work in progress, not merely a narrative *of* transition, but a narrative *in* transition"; she calls it "not so much an object as a process"; see Holland, *The Novel in the Age of Disintegration*, 104 (original emphasis) and 130.

28. William Mills Todd III, "The Birth of a Novel from the Work of Journalism," in *Teaching Nineteenth-Century Russian Literature: Essays in Honor of Robert L. Belknap*, ed. Deborah A. Martinsen, Cathy L. Popkin, and Irina Reyfman (Boston: Academic Studies Press, 2014), 199–217.

29. The argument comes from Sanja Lacan's talk, "Dressing up the Russian Literary Journal: Fashion, Fiction, and Textual Fluidity in 'The Contemporary,'" given at the Association for Slavic, East European, and Eurasian Studies, Annual Convention, San Antonio, TX, November 2014.

30. Todd, "Dostoevskii as a Professional Writer," 87.

31. Sofiia Tolstaia, *Moia zhizn'*, 2 vols. (Moscow: "Kuchkovo pole," 2011) vol. 1, 461, 468, and 485.

32. A. S. Pushkin, *Polnoe sobranie sochinenii v desiati tomakh*, ed. B. V. Tomashevskii, 10 vols. (Leningrad: Nauka, 1977–79), vol. 10, 366.

33. On Nekrasov's contributions to the professionalization of literature, see Mikhail Makeev, *Nikolai Nekrasov: Poet i Predprinimatel' (Ocherki o vzaimodeistvii literatury i ekonomiki)* (Moscow: MAKS Press, 2009).

34. Aleksei Vdovin, "Kritik kak 'organizator' russkoi slovesnosti v 1830–1840-e gg.: V. Belinskii i kontsept 'glava literatury,'" in Aleksei Vdovin, *Kontsept "glava literatury" v russkoi kritike 1830–1860-kh godov* (Tartu: Tartu Ülikooli Kirjastus, 2011), 21–89 (Chapter 1).

35. V. G. Belinskii, "Literaturnye mechtaniia," in V. G. Belinskii, *Polnoe sobranie sochinenii*, 13 vols. (Moscow: Izd. AN SSSR, 1953–59), vol. 1, 21. *Andzhelo*, loosely based on the plot and ethical questions of Shakespeare's *Measure for Measure*, employs rhymed iambic hexameter, a disparity with the original blank verse that Belinsky sees as a fault and therefore proof of Pushkin's decline as a poet.

36. Belinskii, "Literaturnye mechtaniia," 97.

37. V. G. Belinskii, "O russkoi povesti i povestiakh g. Gogolia," in Belinskii, *Polnoe sobranie sochinenii*, vol. 1, 306. Belinsky uses the word "poets" here to signify literature in general, as was often customary at the time.

38. V. G. Belinskii, "Sochineniia Nikolaia Gogolia," in Belinskii, *Polnoe sobranie sochinenii*, vol. 6, 659.

39. V. G. Belinskii, "Vybrannye mesta iz perepiski s druz'iami Nikolaia Gogolia," in Belinskii, *Polnoe sobranie sochinenii*, vol. 10, 60.

40. V. G. Belinskii, [Pis'mo k N. V. Gogoliu], in Belinskii, *Polnoe sobranie sochinenii*, vol. 10, 212.

41. Vdovin, *Kontsept "glavy literatury,"* 76–7.

42. V. G. Belinskii, "Vzgliad na russkuiu literaturu 1847 goda," in Belinskii, *Polnoe sobranie sochinenii*, vol. 10, 296, 313.

43. N. A. Nekrasov, *Kritika. Publitsistika. Pis'ma*, in his *Polnoe sobranie sochinenii i pisem v piatnadtsati tomakh*, 15 vols. (Leningrad: Nauka, 1989), vol. 11, 186.

44. Belinskii, "Vzgliad na russkuiu literaturu 1847 goda," in V. G. Belinskii, *Polnoe sobranie sochinenii*, vol. 10, 385.

45. Apollon Grigor'ev, "Vzgliad na russkuiu literaturu so smerti Pushkina. Stat'ia pervaia," in Apollon Grigor'ev, *Sochineniia v dvukh tomakh*, 2 vols. (Moscow: Khudozhestvennaia literatura, 1990), vol. 2, 66.

46. For a thorough discussion of Gogol's reputation in Russian culture, from the time he entered the literary arena to the end of the twentieth century, see Stephen Moeller-Sally, *Gogol's Afterlife: The Evolution of a Classic in Imperial and Soviet Russia* (Evanston, IL: Northwestern University Press, 2001).

47. The saddest example of this approach is G. A. Gukovsky's book *Realizm Gogolia* (Moscow: Izdatel'stvo khudozhestvennoi literatury, 1959). A brilliant scholar of the Russian eighteenth century, the dazzling lecturer at Leningrad State University, and mentor to the best scholars of the next generation, he was arrested in 1949 and died in prison in 1950. The political pressure under which he had to live and teach affected him as a scholar, and his later works, including the posthumously published book on Gogol, show the influence of vulgar sociological method.

48. See, for example, Igor' Zolotusskii, *Dusha i delo zhizni. Ocherki o Gogole* (Moscow: Pravda, 1981); Igor' Vinogradov, *Gogol'—khudozhnik i myslitel': Khristianskie osnovy mirosozertsaniia* (Moscow: IMLI RAN, Nasledie, 2000); Viktor Guminskii, *Zhizn' i tvorchestvo Gogolia v kontekste pravoslavnoi traditsii. Gogolevskii vestnik*, 1 (Moscow: Nauka, 2007).

49. For the quotation, see V. V. Gippius, *Gogol*, ed. and trans. Robert Maguire (Durham, NC: Duke University Press, 1989), 26.

50. See Roman Koropeckyj and Robert Romanchuk, "Ukraine in Blackface: Performance and Representation in Gogol's *Dikan'ka Tales*, Book I," *Slavic Review*, 62.3 (2003), 525–47; Edyta M. Bojanowska, *Nikolai Gogol: Between Ukrainian and Russian Nationalism* (Cambridge, MA: Harvard University Press, 2007), 37–88.

51. Edyta Bojanowska, "Equivocal Praise and National-Imperial Conundrums: Gogol's 'A Few Words about Pushkin,'" *Canadian Slavonic Papers/Revue canadienne des slavistes*, 51.2–3 (2009), 175–201; Irina Reyfman, "Kammerjunker in 'Notes of a Madman': Gogol's View of Pushkin," in Irina Reyfman, *Rank and Style: Russians in State Service, Life, and Literature* (Boston: Academic Studies Press, 2012), 91–102.

52. For Vengerov's calculations of the number of days Gogol spent in provincial Russia, see S. A. Vengerov, "Gogol' sovershenno ne znal real'noi russkoi zhizni," in S. A. Vengerov, *Sobranie sochinenii*, 5 vols. (St. Petersburg: Prometei, 1913), vol. 2, 124, 127–32, and 135.

53. See, for example, Anne Lounsbery, "'No, This Is Not the Provinces!' Provincialism, Authenticity, and Russianness in Gogol's Day," *Russian Review*, 64.2 (2005), 259–80.

54. Vdovin, *Kontsept "glava literatury,"* 174–8.

55. Aleksei Vdovin, "'Vo glave literatury...': 'radikal'nyi proekt' N. Chernyshevskogo (1855–1862)," in Vdovin, *Kontsept "glava literatury,"* 150–99 (Chapter 3).

56. D. I. Pisarev, "Novyi tip," in D. I. Pisarev, *Polnoe sobranie sochinenii i pisem v dvennadtsati tomakh*, 12 vols. (Moscow: Nauka, 2000–13), vol. 8, 207.

57. D. I. Pisarev, "Staroe barstvo ('Voina i mir,' sochinenie grafa L. N. Tolstogo. Tomy I, II i III. Moskva. 1868)," in Pisarev, *Polnoe sobranie sochinenii i pisem v dvennadtsati tomakh*, vol. 10, 73.

58. A number of claims contained in the material, particularly his view that Dostoevsky's attention to the topic of rape of underage girls had its basis in the writer's own personal conduct, were actively contested by Dostoevsky's widow. See A. G. Dostoevskaia "Otvet Strakhovu," in A. G. Dostoevskaia, *Vospominaniia* (Moscow: Izdatel'stvo "Pravda," 1987), 414–27.

Chapter 3

1. Iurii Lotman, "Russo i russkaia kul'tura XVIII–nachala XIX veka," in Iurii Lotman, *Izbrannye stat'i v trekh tomakh*, 3 vols. (Tallin: Aleksandra, 1992–3), vol. 2, 79.

2. Lidiia Ginzburg, *O psikhologicheskoi proze* (Leningrad: Sovetskii pisatel', 1971), 38.

3. Andrei Zorin, *Poiavlenie geroia: Iz istorii russkoi emotsional'noi kul'tury kontsa XVIII–nachala XIX veka* (Moscow: NLO, 2016), esp. 250–303.

4. Ginzburg, *O psikhologicheskoi proze*, 40–1; A. S. Ianushkevich, "Dnevniki Zhukovskogo kak literaturnyi pamiatnik," in V. A. Zhukovskii, *Polnoe sobranie sochinenii i pisem v 20-ti tt.*, 20 vols. (Moscow: Iazyki russkoi kul'tury, 1999–), vol. 13, 399–405.

5. Gary Marker, "The Enlightenment of Anna Labzina: Gender, Faith, and Public Life in Catherinian and Alexandrian Russia," *Slavic Review*, 59.2 (2000), 371.

6. Marker, "The Enlightenment of Anna Labzina," 273.

7. Marker, "The Enlightenment of Anna Labzina," 372. See also Gary Marker and Rachel May, "Introduction," in Anna Labzina, *Days of a Russian Noblewoman: The Memories of Anna Labzina, 1758–1821*, trans. and ed. Gary Marker and Rachel May (DeKalb, IL: Northern Illinois University Press, 2001), xix–xx.

8. Marker, "The Enlightenment of Anna Labzina," 273; Labzina, *Days of a Russian Noblewoman*, trans. Marker and May, xiv–xv.

9. Iu. M. Lotman, *Besedy o russkoi kul'ture: Byt i traditsii russkogo dvorianstva (XVIII–nachalo XIX veka)* (St. Petersburg: Iskusstvo-SPB, 1994), 302–4.

10. Robin Bisha, Introduction to Varvara Bakunina's "The Persian Campaign of 1796," in *Russian Women, 1698–1917: Experience and Expression, An Anthology of Sources*, ed. Robin Bisha, Jehanne M. Gheith, Christine Holden, and William G. Wagner (Bloomington: Indiana University Press, 2002), 216.

11. "Dvennadtsatyi god v zapiskakh Varvary Ivanovny Bakuninoi," *Russkaia starina*, 47.9 (1885), 391–410.

12. Andrei Zorin, *By Fables Alone: Literature and State Ideology in Late Eighteenth- and Early-Nineteenth-Century Russia* (Brighton, MA: Academic Studies Press, 2014), 223–4, 232–3.

13. See Nadezhda Durova, *Zapiski kavalerist-devitsy*, in Denis Davydov, *Dnevnik partizanskikh deistvii 1812 goda*. Nadezhda Durova, *Zapiski kavalerist-devitsy* (St. Petersburg: Lenizdat, 1985), 325; L. N. Tolstoi, *Sobranie sochinenii v 22 tomakh*, 22 vols. (Moscow, Khudozhestvennaia literatura, 1978–85), vol. 4, 362–3.

14. Mary Zirin, "Durova, Nadezhda Andreevna," in *The Dictionary of Russian Women Writers*, ed. Marina Ledkovsky, Charlotte Rosenthal, and Mary Zirin (Westport, CT: Greenwood Press, 1994), 164–5.

15. Nadezhda Durova, *Izbrannoe* (Moscow: Sovetskaia Rossiia, 1984), 409.

16. Durova, *Izbrannoe*, 410.

17. Ginzburg, *O psikhologicheskoi proze*, 42.

18. Lidiia Ginzburg, "Viazemskii," in P. A. Viazemskii, *Staraia zapisnaia knizhka* (Leningrad: Izd-vo pisateleii "Leningrad," 1929), 11.

19. See Catharine Theimer Nepomnyashchy and Ludmilla A. Trigos, "Introduction: Was Pushkin Black and Does It Matter?," in *Under the Sky of My Africa: Alexander Pushkin and Blackness*, eds. Catharine Theimer Nepomnyashchy, Nicole Svobodny, and Ludmilla A. Trigos, foreword Henry Louis Gates, Jr. (Evanston, IL: Northwestern University Press, 2006), 3–45; N. K. Teletova, "A. P Gannibal: On the Occasion of the Three Hundredth Anniversary of the Birth of Alexander Pushkin's Great-Grandfather," in *Under the Sky of My Africa*, 46–78.

20. Mark Al'tshuller, *Mezhdu dvukh tsarei. Pushkin 1824–1836* (St. Petersburg: Akademicheskii proekt, 2003), 186–98.

21. See T. G. Tsavlovskaia, *Risunki Pushkina* (Moscow: Iskusstvo, 1980), 180. The word "jester" and the beginning of the following unreadable word are crossed out.

22. On Olenina's diary, see Irina Savkina, *Razgovory s zerkalom i zazerkal'em: Avtodokumental'nye zhenskie teksty v russkoi literature pervoi poloviny XIX veka* (Moscow: NLO, 2007), 127–47.

23. A. A. Olenina, *Dnevnik. Vospominaniia* (St. Petersburg: Akademicheskii proekt, 1999), 70.

24. Maria Mörder, "Listki iz dnevnika M. K. Merder (Perevod s frantsuzskogo)," *Russkaia starina*, 53.8 (1900), 385; the English "brutal," in parentheses after "rude," is apparently used by the diary's author.

25. See Hilde Hoogenboom, "Mat´ Gogolia i otets Aksakovykh: Kak Nadezhda Sokhanskaia nashla rodnoi iazyk," in *Fenomen pola v kul´ture/Sex and Gender in Culture*, ed. Natalia Kamenetskaia (Moscow: RGGU, 1998), 149–59.

26. Irina Paperno, *Chernyshevsky and the Age of Realism: A Study in the Semiotics of Behavior* (Stanford, CA: Stanford University Press, 1988), 99.

27. Irina Paperno, "Introduction: Intimacy and History. The Gercen Family Drama Reconsidered," *Russian Literature*, 61.1–2 (2007), 1–65.

28. Ginzburg, *O psikhologicheskoi proze*, 262–3.

29. Paperno, "Introduction," 4.

30. In a footnote to the introduction to her book on Tolstoy's autobiographical narratives, Paperno points out that "fewer than one third of the volumes in the 90-volume edition of his works are occupied by fiction (including manuscript variants)"; see Irina Paperno, *"Who, What Am I?" Tolstoy Struggles to Narrate the Self* (Ithaca, NY: Cornell University Press, 2014), 1 n.1. Our discussion of Tolstoy's autobiographical narratives is indebted to Paperno's study.

31. For the fullest edition of Tolstoy diaries, see L. N. Tolstoi, *Polnoe sobranie sochinenii v 90 tt.*, 90 vols. (Moscow: Gosudarstvennoe izdatel´stvo khudozhestvennoi literatury, 1935–58), vols. 46–58.

32. Tolstoi, *Sobranie sochinenii v 22 tomakh*, vol. 22, 424.

33. On the Tolstoys' difficult marital life, see Alexandra Popoff, *Sophia Tolstoy: A Biography* (New York: Free Press, 2010), esp. Chapters 10, 11, 15, and 17 (in which Leo Tolstoy's separate diaries are discussed).

34. Tolstoi, *Sobranie sochinenii v 22 tomakh*, vol. 22, 411–12.

35. Paperno, *Who, What Am I*, 10.

36. L. N. Tolstoi, "Istoriia vcherashnego dnia," in Tolstoi, *Sobranie sochinenii v 22 tomakh*, vol. 1, 343.

37. Paperno, *Who, What Am I*, 14–17.

38. Tolstoi, *Polnoe sobranie sochinenii v 90 tt.*, vol. 36, 407–15; for commentaries, including the discussion of the first title of *Confession*, see vol. 36, 737–41.

39. Paperno, *Who, What Am I*, 31.

40. The term "autopsychological" is Ginzburg's; see Ginzburg, *O psikhologicheskoi proze*, 258.

41. Andrew Wachtel, *The Battle for Childhood: Creation of a Russian Myth* (Stanford, CA: Stanford University Press, 1990), 7; on "threshold works" in general, see Gary Saul Morson, *The Boundaries of Genre: Dostoevsky's* Diary of a Writer *and the Traditions of Literary Utopia* (Evanston, IL: Northwestern University Press, 1988), esp. Chapter 2, "Threshold Art," 39–68.

42. Tolstoi, *Polnoe sobranie sochinenii v 90 tt.*, vol. 83, 167. It is Gustafson who, using Lydia Gizburg's term, calls the story autopsychological; see Richard Gustafson *Leo Tolstoy: Resident and Stranger* (Princeton, NJ: Princeton University Press, 1986), 192–6.

43. Tolstoi, *Sobranie sochinenii v 22 tomakh*, vol. 12, 47.

44. For a detailed analysis of this story, see Reyfman, "Tolstoy and Gogol: 'Notes of a Madman,'" in Irina Reyfman, *Rank and Style: Russians in State Service, Life, and Literature* (Boston: Academic Studies Press, 2012), 200–11.

45. Scholars of English Romanticism have worked on the interrelated changes in notions of genres. See, for example, Michael G. Cooke, *Acts of Inclusion: Studies Bearing on an Elementary Theory of Romanticism* (New Haven, CT: Yale University Press, 1979); Stuart Curran, *Poetic Form and British Romanticism* (New York: Oxford University Press, 1986); Susan Wolfson, *Formal Changes: The Shaping of Poetry in British Romanticism* (Stanford, CA: Stanford University Press, 1997).

46. V. A. Zhukovskii, *Polnoe sobranie sochinenii i pisem*, 20 vols. (Moscow: Iazyki russkoi kul´tury, 1999–), vol. 1, 56.

47. Zhukovsky also emphasized, as Gray had not, the question of whether that passerby was literate and thus able to read the gravestone's inscription. See Catherine Ciepiela, "Reading Russian Pastoral: Zhukovsky's Translation of Gray's Elegy," in *Rereading Russian Poetry*, ed. Stephanie Sandler (New Haven, CT: Yale University Press, 1999), 31–57.

48. E. A. Baratynskii, *Polnoe sobranie stikhotvorenii* (St. Petersburg: Akademicheskii proekt, 2000), 71. Baratynsky published the poem as "Village Elegy" ("Sel'skaia elegiia") in 1821, and "Native Land" ("Rodina") in 1835; see Baratynskii, *Polnoe sobranie stikhotvorenii*, 453.

49. A. S. Pushkin, *Polnoe sobranie sochinenii v desiati tomakh*, ed. B. V. Tomashevskii, 10 vols. (Leningrad: Nauka, 1977–79), vol. 3, 338.

50. Baratynskii, *Polnoe sobranie stikhotvorenii*, 153.

51. N. N. Gnedich, *Stikhotvoreniia* (Leningrad: Sovetskii pisatel', 1956), 89.

52. A. S. Pushkin, "Elegiia," in Pushkin, *Polnoe sobranie sochinenii v desiati tomakh*, vol. 3, 169.

53. Jerome McGann, *The Romantic Ideology: A Critical Investigation* (Chicago: University of Chicago Press, 1983), 127.

54. Baratynskii, *Polnoe sobranie stikhotvorenii*, 136.

55. M. Iu. Lermontov, *Sochineniia v 6-ti tomakh*, 6 vols. (Moscow: Izd. AN SSSR, 1954–57), vol. 2, 122.

56. A. N. Radishchev, *Polnoe sobranie sochinenii*, 3 vols. (Moscow: Akademiia nauk, 1938–52), vol. 1, 125.

57. Lermontov, *Sochineniia v 6-ti tomakh*, vol. 2, 208.

58. See Luba Golburt, "Alexander Pushkin as a Romantic," in *The Oxford Handbook of European Romanticism*, ed. Paul Hamilton (Oxford: Oxford University Press, 2016), 512–33.

59. Lermontov, *Sochineniia v 6-ti tomakh*, vol. 2, 209.

60. Iakov Polonskii, "Dvoinik," in Iakov Polonskii, *Stikhotvorenniia i poemy* ([Moscow]: Sovetskii pisatel', 1935), 174.

61. N. A. Nekrasov, *Polnoe sobranie stikhotvorenii v trekh tomakh* (Leningrad: Sovetskii pisatel', 1967), vol. 2, 59–65, quotation on 60.

62. N. A. Zabolotskii, *Izbrannye proizvedeniia v dvukh tomakh*, 2 vols. (Moscow: Khudozhestvennaia literatura, 1972), vol. 1, 210.

63. P. A. Viazemskii, *Stikhotvoreniia* (Leningrad: Sovetskii pisatel', 1986), 402.

64. Karolina Pavlova, "Duma," in Karolina Pavlova, *Polnoe sobranie stikhotvorenii* (Moscow: Sovetskii pisatel', 1964), 121.

65. Baratynskii, *Polnoe sobranie stikhotvorenii*, 148.

66. Pushkin, *Polnoe sobranie sochinenii v desiati tomakh*, vol. 3, 130.

67. Pushkin, *Polnoe sobranie sochinenii v desiati tomakh*, vol. 3, 313.

68. For the poem, see *Poety 1790-kh–1810-kh godov*, ed. M. G. Al'tshuller and Iu. M. Lotman (Leningrad: Sovetskii pisatel', 1971), 519.

69. I. M. Semenko, *Poety pushkinskoi pory* (Moscow: Khudozhestvennaia literatura, 1970), 30.

70. Konstantin Batiushkov, *Opyty v stikhakh i proze*, ed. I. M. Semenko (Moscow: Nauka, 1977), 289.

71. Pushkin, *Polnoe sobranie sochinenii v desiati tomakh*, vol. 7, 406.

72. The original was discovered by D'erd' Seke; see D'erd' Seke [György Szőke], "Ob istochnike stikhotvoreniia V. A. Zhukovskogo 'K nei,'" *Russkaia literatura*, 1 (1971), 161–2. The date 1817 is suggested by N. Remorova and A. Ianushkevich in Zhukovskii, *Polnoe sobranie sochinenii i pisem*, vol. 2, 483–4.

73. Zhukovskii, *Polnoe sobranie sochinenii i pisem*, vol. 2, 68.

74. The latest argument is that the correct title should be "March 9, 1823," the date of Zhukovsky's last meeting with Protasova; see I. Poplavskaia, Commentary in V A. Zhukovskii, *Polnoe sobranie sochinenii i pisem*, vol. 2, 619–20.

75. Zhukovskii, *Polnoe sobranie sochinenii i pisem*, vol. 2, 57.

76. Baratynskii, *Polnoe sobranie stikhotvorenii*, 75.

77. Baratynskii, *Polnoe sobranie stikhotvorenii*, 134.

78. V. E. Vatsuro, "E. A. Baratynskii," in *Istoriia russkoi literatury v 4-kh tomakh* (Leningrad: Izd. AN SSSR, 1981), vol. 2, 382.

79. Baratynskii, *Polnoe sobranie stikhotvorenii*, 134.

80. For Pushkin's praise of the poem, see Pushkin, *Sobranie sochinenii v desiati tomakh*, vol. 10, 64 (in a letter to Aleksandr Bestuzhev); for Ginzburg's characterization, see Lidiia Ginzburg, *O lirike* (Moscow: Intrada, 1997), 75.

81. Pushkin, *Polnoe sobranie sochinenii v desiati tomakh*, vol. 1, 280.

82. Pushkin, *Polnoe sobranie sochinenii v desiati tomakh*, vol. 1, 309.

83. See *Taboo Pushkin: Topics, Texts, Interpretations*, ed. Alyssa Dinega Gillespie, Publications of the Wisconsin Center for Pushkin Studies Series, gen. eds. David M. Bethea and Alexander A. Dolinin (Madison: University of Wisconsin Press, 2012).

84. For the quoted poems, see Pushkin, *Polnoe sobranie sochinenii v desiati tomakh*, vol. 1, 280, 297, 301; vol. 2, 146.

85. Pushkin, *Polnoe sobranie sochinenii v desiati tomakh*, vol. 1, 280.

86. Pushkin, *Polnoe sobranie sochinenii v desiati tomakh*, vol. 2, 197.

87. See L. I. Vol′pert, "'Tverskoi Lovelas S.-Peterburgskomu Val′monu zdraviia i uspekhov zhelaet.' (*Opasnye sviazi* Shoderlo de Laklo)," in L. I. Vol′pert, *Pushkin v roli Pushkina. Tvorcheskaia igra po modeliam frantsuzskoi literatury. Pushkin i Stendal′*. Part 1: *Igrovoi mir Pushkina* (Moscow: Iazyki russkoi kul′tury, 1998), 33–59 (Chapter 2).

88. Pushkin, *Polnoe sobranie sochinenii v desiati tomakh*, vol. 3, 128.

89. Michael Wachtel, *A Commentary to Pushkin's Lyric Poetry, 1826–1836* (Madison: University of Wisconsin Press, 2011), 184.

90. Pushkin, *Polnoe sobranie sochinenii v desiati tomakh*, vol. 3, 166.

91. Wachtel, *A Commentary*, 173.

92. Pushkin, *Polnoe sobranie sochinenii v desiati tomakh*, vol. 3, 356.

93. Ginzburg, *O lirike*, 131–2, 148.

94. On Lermontov's Byronism, see David Powelstock, *Becoming Mikhail Lermontov: The Ironies of Romantic Individualism in Nicholas I's Russia* (Evanston, IL: Northwestern University Press, 2005); Elizabeth Cheresh Allen, *A Fallen Idol Is Still a God: Lermontov and the Quandaries of Cultural Transition* (Stanford, CA: Stanford University Press, 2007).

95. Powelstock, *Becoming Mikhail Lermontov*, passim, but esp. 169–71, 174–5; for the quotation see 71.

96. Lermontov, *Sochineniia v 6-ti tomakh*, vol. 1, 299.

97. Lermontov, *Sochineniia v 6-ti tomakh*, vol. 2, 138.

98. Lermontov, *Sochineniia v 6-ti tomakh*, vol. 2, 214.

99. Lermontov, *Sochineniia v 6-ti tomakh*, vol. 2, 109.

100. E. A. Sushkova, "Iz 'Zapisok,'" in M. *Iu Lermontov v vospominaniiakh sovremennikov* (Moscow: Khudozhestvennaia literatura, 1989), 106.

101. Lermontov, *Sochineniia v 6-ti tomakh*, vol. 2, 181.

102. Lermontov, *Sochineniia v 6-ti tomakh*, vol. 2, 190.

103. F. I. Tiutchev, *Polnoe sobranie stikhotvorenii* (Leningrad, Sovetskii pisatel′, 1957), 238.

104. Tiutchev, *Polnoe sobranie stikhotvorenii*, 191.

105. Tiutchev, *Polnoe sobranie stikhotvorenii*, 226.

106. On the connection of the Russian trochaic pentameter with the existential theme of the life path, see Kiril Taranovskii, "O vzaimootnoshenii stikhotvornogo ritma i tematiki," in Kiril Taranovskii, *O poezii i poetike* (Moscow, Iazyki russkoi kul'tury, 2000), 372–403; Mikhail Gasparov, "'Vykhozhu odin ia na dorogu...' (5-st. khorei: detalizatsiia smysla)," in Mikhail Gasparov, *Metr i smysl: ob odnom iz mekhanizmov kul'turnoi pamiati* (Moscow: Rossiiskii gosudarstvennyi gumanitarnyi universitet, 1999), 238–65 (Chapter 10).

107. K. V. Pigarev, Commentary to F. I. Tiutchev, *Sochineniia v dvukh tomakh* (Moscow: Khudozhestvennaia literatura, 1984), vol. 1, 447.

108. Tiutchev, *Polnoe sobranie stikhotvorenii*, 254.

109. Ginzburg, *O lirike*, 227–8.

110. On the role of the third-person narrator in accessing novelistic characters' consciousness, see Victoria Somoff, *The Imperative of Reliability: Russian Prose on the Eve of the Novel, 1820s–1850s* (Evanston, IL: Northwestern University Press, 2015), 9–12.

111. Ginzburg, *O lirike*, 225; I. V. Kozlik, "Romanizatsiia liriki N. A. Nekrasova ('panaevskii' tsikl)," *Russkaia literatura*, 3 (1997), 29–41. In his seminal *Masterstvo Nekrasova*, Kornei Chukovsky points out that some of Nekrasov's contemporaries regarded his deliberately prosaic style as a sign of his degrading poetry; see Kornei Chukovsky, *Masterstvo Nekrasova*, 4th edn. (Moscow, Gosudarstvennoe izdatel'stvo khudozhestvennoi literatury, 1962), 165–8.

112. Nekrasov, *Polnoe sobranie stikhotvorenii v trekh tomakh*, vol. 1, 130.

113. Ol'ga Sedakova, "Nasledstvo Nekrasova v russkoi poezii," http://www.olgasedakova.com/Poetica/221 (last accessed July 8, 2016).

114. Evdokiia Rostopchina, *Talisman: Izbrannaia lirika. Drama. Dokumenty, pis'ma, vospominaniia* (Moscow: Moskovskii rabochii, 1987), 46.

115. Rostopchina, *Talisman*, 72.

116. Pavlova, *Polnoe sobranie stikhotvorenii*, 174.

117. Pavlova, *Polnoe sobranie stikhotvorenii*, 153.

118. See Susan Amert, "Karolina Pavlova's Afterlife in the Poetry of Anna Akhmatova," in *Essays on Karolina Pavlova*, ed. Susanne Fusso and Alexander Lehrman (Evanston, IL: Northwestern University Press, 2001), 164–86, quotation on 175.

119. A. A. Fet, *Polnoe sobranie stikhotvorenii* (Leningrad: Sovetskii pisatel', 1959), 96.

120. For a more psychological approach to these poems, see Patricia Hswe, "Poetry in Perpetuity: Design, Death, and the Beloved in Afanasii Fet's Lyrics to Mariia Lazich," Ph.D. Dissertation, Yale University, 2003.

121. Emily Klenin, *The Poetics of Afanasy Fet* (Cologne: Böhlau, 2002), 8–9.

122. Fet, *Polnoe sobranie stikhotvorenii*, 211. Dmitry Blagoi dates the poem from 1849 and believes it was dedicated to Lazich despite the fact that it is impossible to recognize any concrete woman in this description; for Blagoi's argument, see Dmitrii Blagoi, *Mir kak krasota: o "Vechernikh ogniakh" A. Feta* (Moscow: Khudozhestvennaia literatura, 1975), 13.

123. Fet, *Polnoe sobranie stikhotvorenii*, 215.

124. Fet, *Polnoe sobranie stikhotvorenii*, 269.

125. G. Bialyi, "S. Ia. Nadson," in S. Ia. Nadson, *Polnoe sobranie stikhotvorenii* (St. Petersburg: Gumanitarnoe agentstvo "Akademicheskii proekt," 2001), 34.

Chapter 4

1. See Irina Reyfman, "The Material World of Kievan Rus' as Depicted in the Nicholaevan Era," in *Visualizing Russia: Fedor Solntsev and Crafting a National Past*, ed. Cynthia Hyla Whittaker (Boston: Brill, 2010), 109–26, esp. 121–6.

2. See Victoria Somoff, *The Imperative of Reliability: Russian Prose on the Eve of the Novel, 1820s–1850s* (Evanston, IL: Northwestern University Press, 2015), 42, 45–7.

3. For an excellent sampling of scholarship on Gogol, see Robert A. Maguire, compiler, *Gogol from the Twentieth Century: Eleven Essays* (Princeton, NJ: Princeton University Press, 1974); for an incisive discussion of Gogol's position between the Ukrainian and Russian traditions, see Edyta M. Bojanowska, *Nikolai Gogol: Between Ukrainian and Russian Nationalism* (Cambridge, MA: Harvard University Press, 2007); for illuminative discussions of Gogol's individual stories set in Ukraine, see Iu. M. Lotman, "Problema khudozhestvennogo prostranstva v proze Gogolia," in Iu. M. Lotman, *Izbrannye stat'i v trekh tomakh*, 3 vols. (Tallin, Aleksandra, 1992–3), vol. 1, 413–47; Richard Gregg, "The Curse of Sameness and the Gogolian Esthetic: 'The Tale of the Two Ivans' as Parable," *SEEJ*, 31.1 (1987), 1–9.

4. Griboedov's earlier date of birth, 1790, is suggested by N. A. Tarkhova, in *Letopis' zhizni i tvorchestva Aleksandra Sergeevicha Griboedova, 1790–1829*, compiled N. A. Tarkhova (Moscow: Minuvshee, 2017), 6–10.

5. On the Petersburg tales, see S. G. Bocharov, "Around 'The Nose,'" in *Essays on Gogol: Logos and the Russian Word*, ed. Susanne Fusso and Priscilla Meyer (Evanston, IL: Northwestern University Press, 1992), 19–39; Thomas Seifrid, "Suspicion toward Narrative: The Nose and the Problem of Autonomy in Gogol's 'Nos,'" *Russian Review*, 52.3 (1993), 382–96; R. A. Peace, "The Logic of Madness: Gogol's *Zapiski sumasshedshego*," *Oxford Slavonic Papers*, series 2, 9 (1976), 28–45.

6. On *Inspector General*, see, for example, Iu. M. Lotman, "O Khlestakove," *Uchenye zapiski Tartuskogo gos. universiteta*, 369 (1975), 19–53 (translated as "Concerning Khlestakov," in Iurii Lotman, *The Semiotics of Russian Cultural History*, ed. Alexander D. Nakhimovsky and Alice Stone Nakhimovsky [Ithaca, N.Y.: Cornell University Press, 1985], 150–87); on *Dead Souls*, see Susanne Fusso, *Designing Dead Souls: An Anatomy of Disorder in Gogol* (Stanford, CA: Stanford University Press, 1993).

7. Monika Greenleaf, *Pushkin and Romantic Fashion: Fragment, Elegy, Orient, Irony* (Stanford, CA: Stanford University Press, 1994), 1–18; Paul Debreczeny, *The Other Pushkin: A Study of Alexander Pushkin's Prose Fiction* (Stanford, CA: Stanford University Press, 1983), 25–55.

8. See Somoff, *The Imperative of Reliability*, especially the Introduction.

9. S. P. Shevyrev, "Tri povesti N. Pavlova," *Moskovskii nabliudatel'*, 1.1 (1835), 124.

10. Elizabeth Shepard, "The Society Tale and the Innovative Argument in Russian Prose Fiction in the 1830s," *Russian Literature*, 10.2 (1981), 112–14.

11. For Belinsky's skeptical view of the society tale, see V. G. Belinskii, "O kritike i literaturnykh mneniiakh 'Moskovskogo nabliudatelia,'" in V. G. Belinskii, *Polnoe sobranie sochinenii*, 13 vols. (Moscow: Izd. AN SSSR, 1953–59), vol. 2, 169. On these women writers, see Catriona Kelly, *A History of Russian Women's Writing 1820–1992* (Oxford: Oxford University Press, 1994), Chapters 2–4 and 6 (on Zhukova, Pavlova, Gan, and Olga Shapir); Jehanne Gheith, *Finding the Middle Ground: Krestovskii, Tur, and the Power of Ambivalence in Nineteenth-Century Russian Women's Prose* (Evanston, IL: Northwestern University Press, 2004); Hilde Hoogenboom, "The Society Tale as Pastiche: Mariia Zhukova's Heroines Move to the Country," in *The Society Tale in Russian Literature: From Odoevskii to Tolstoi*, ed. Neil Cornwell (Amsterdam: Rodopi, 1998), 85–97.

12. For a discussion of the society tale as a precursor to the Realist novel, see Somoff, *The Imperative of Reliability*, 63–87, 108–10.

13. Caryl Emerson, "Theory," in *The Cambridge Companion to the Classic Russian Novel*, ed. Malcolm V. Jones and Robin Feuer Miller (Cambridge: Cambridge University Press, 1998), 271–93, quotation on 273.

14. William Mills Todd III, "The Ruse of the Russian Novel," in *The Novel*. Volume 1: *History, Geography, and Culture*, ed. Franco Moretti (Princeton, NJ: Princeton University Press, 2006), 407 (401–23).

15. On the challenges of writing its history, see Jonathan Arac, "What Kind of a History Does a Theory of the Novel Require?," *NOVEL: A Forum on Fiction*, 42.2 (2009), 190–5.

16. Richard Freeborn, *The Rise of the Russian Novel: Studies in the Russian Novel From Eugene Onegin to War and Peace* (Cambridge: Cambridge University Press, 1973), 8.

17. Donna Tussing Orwin, *Consequences of Consciousness: Turgenev, Dostoevsky, and Tolstoy* (Stanford, CA: Stanford University Press, 2007), 11.

18. See Gary Saul Morson and Caryl Emerson, *Mikhail Bakhtin: Creation of a Prosaics* (Stanford, CA: Stanford University Press, 1990).

19. Gary Saul Morson, "Prosaics Evolving," *SEEJ*, 41.1 (1997), 57–73, quotation on 57.

20. For some comparative remarks on the decline of verisimilitude as a criterion in novelistic traditions, see Ilya Kliger, *The Narrative Shape of Truth: Veridiction in Modern European Literature* (Philadelphia: Penn State University Press, 2011), 30–3.

21. V. G. Belinskii, "Rech′ o kritike, proiznesennaia v torzhestvennom sobranii imperatorskogo Sanktpeterburgskogo universiteta, marta 25-go dnia 1842 goda ekstraordin[arnym] profes[sorom] doktorom filosofii, A. Nikitenko," in Belinskii, *Polnoe sobranie sochinenii*, vol. 6, 267–87, quotation on 268; "reality" (*Deistvitel′nost′*) is emphasized in the original.

22. N. G. Chernyshevskii, *Polnoe sobranie sochinenii v 15 tomakh*, 15 vols. (Moscow: Gosudarstvennoe izdatel′stvo khudozhestvennoi literatury, 1939–53), vol. 2, 10.

23. On Leskov's *skaz*, see Boris Eikhenbaum, "'Chrezmernyi' pisatel′ (K 100-letiiu rozhdeniia N. Leskova)," in Boris Eikhenbaum, *O proze. Sbornik statei* (Leningrad: Izdatel′stvo Khudozhestvennaia literatura, 1969), 327–45; Walter Benjamin, "The Storyteller: Reflections on the Work of Nikolai Leskov," in Walter Benjamin, *Illuminations*, ed. Hannah Arendt, trans. Harry Zohn (New York: Schocken Books, 1968), 83–109; Irmhild Christina Sperrle, *The Organic Worldview of Nikolai Leskov* (Evanston, IL: Northwestern University Press, 2002), 159–64.

24. For a seminal study of the anti-nihilist novel, see A. G. Tseitlin, "Siuzhetika antinigilisticheskogo romana," *Literatura i marksizm*, 1 (1929), 33–74; on Pisemsky, see P. G. Pustovoit, *A. F. Pisemskii v istorii russkogo romana* (Moscow: Izdatel′stvo Moskovskogo universiteta, 1969); on the genre of the pamphlet novel, see L. N. Siniakova, *Kontseptsiia cheloveka v romanakh A. F. Pisemskogo 1860–1870-kh gg.: Monografiia* (Novosibirsk: Novosibirskii gosudarstvennyi universitet, 2007).

25. Donald Fanger, *Dostoevsky and Romantic Realism: A Study of Dostoevsky in Relation to Balzac, Dickens, and Gogol* (Chicago: University of Chicago Press, 1967).

26. Roman Iakobson, "O khudozhestvennom realizme," in Roman Iakobson, *Raboty po poetike* (Moscow: Progress, 1987), 387–93.

27. For a historical overview of nineteenth-century practices and modern theory, see Ann Jefferson, "Love and the Wayward Text," in Ann Jefferson, *Reading Realism in Stendhal* (Cambridge: Cambridge University Press, 1988), 45–63 (Chapter 2).

28. Iakobson, "O khudozhestvennom realizme," 388–9.

29. Hayden White, "The Problem of Style in Realistic Representation: Marx and Flaubert," in *The Fiction of Narrative: Essays on History, Literature, and Theory, 1957–2007*, ed. Robert Doran (Baltimore, MD: Johns Hopkins University Press, 2010), 169–87.

Chapter 5

1. See, for example, Elise Kimmerling Wirtschafter, *Social Identity in Imperial Russia* (DeKalb, IL: Northern Illinois University Press, 1997); and Abbot Gleason, "The Terms of Russian Social History," in *Between Tsar and the People: Educated society and the Quest for Public Identity in Late Imperial Russia*, ed. Edith W. Clowes, Samuel D. Kassow, and James L. West (Princeton, NJ: Princeton University Press, 1991), 15–27.

2. According to Nicholas V. Riasanovsky, in 1796, 96.4 percent of the Russian population resided in rural areas; for 1897, the figure was 87.4 percent; the overwhelming majority of them were peasants; see Nicholas V. Riasanovsky, "Afterword: The Problem of the Peasant," in *The Peasant*

in Nineteenth-Century Russia, ed. Wayne S. Vucinich (Stanford, CA: Stanford University Press, 1968), 263–84, quotation on 263; Elise Kimmerling Wirtschafter gives similar figures for rural population in the second half of the nineteenth century: in 1857–58, 49 percent of male peasants were serfs and 46 percent, state peasants; "in 1897, Russia's first-ever empirewide census identified 84 percent of the male population of fifty European provinces as peasants"; see Kimmerling Wirtschafter, *Social Identity in Imperial Russia*, 102, 101.

3. For an overview of settings in nineteenth-century Russian novels, see Robert A. Maguire, "The City," in *The Cambridge Companion to the Classic Russian Novel*, ed. Malcolm V. Jones and Robin Feuer Miller (Cambridge: Cambridge University Press, 1998), 21–40; and Hugh McLean, "The Countryside," in *The Cambridge Companion to the Classic Russian Novel*, 41–60.

4. For a useful general discussion of the Petersburg text, see V. N. Toporov, *Peterburgskii tekst* (Moscow: Nauka, 2009).

5. See Tzvetan Todorov, "Definition of the Fantastic," in Tzvetan Todorov, *The Fantastic: A Structural Approach to a Literary Genre*, trans. Richard Howard (Ithaca, NY: Cornell University Press, 1975), 24–40 (Chapter 2).

6. *Fiziologiia Peterburga*, ed. V. I. Kuleshov (Moscow: Nauka, 1991), 14–37.

7. For a description and thorough analysis of the rich economic, social, and intellectual life in nineteenth-century Nizhnii Novgorod, see Catherine Evtuhov, *Portrait of a Russian Province: Economy, Society, and Civilization in Nineteenth-Century Nizhnii Novgorod* (Pittsburgh, PA: University of Pittsburgh Press, 2011).

8. Jane T. Costlow, *Heart-Pine Russia: Walking and Writing the Nineteenth-century Forest* (Ithaca, NY: Cornell University Press, 2013), 21.

9. For an overview of Russia's imperial conquests, see Andreas Kappeler, *The Russian Empire: A Multiethnic History*, trans. Alfred Clayton (New York: Longman, 2001).

10. See Susan Layton, *Russian Literature and Empire: Conquest of the Caucasus from Pushkin to Tolstoy* (Cambridge: Cambridge University Press, 1994); Katya Hokanson, *Writing at Russia's Border* (Toronto: University of Toronto Press, 2008).

11. Gary Saul Morson, *Anna Karenina in Our Time: Seeing More Wisely* (New Haven, CT: Yale University Press, 2007), 112–13 and 176–7.

12. For an incisive discussion of her decision, see Morson, *Anna Karenina in Our Time*, 113–17.

13. See Liza Knapp, *Anna Karenina and Others: Tolstoy's Labyrinth of Plots* (Madison, WI: Wisconsin University Press, 2016), 25.

14. Marc Raeff, *Origins of the Russian Intelligentsia: The Eighteenth-Century Nobility* (New York: Harcourt Brace Jovanovich, 1966); Michael Confino, "On Intellectuals and Intellectual Traditions in Eighteenth and Nineteenth Century Russia," *Daedalus* (1972), 117–49; D. S. Likhachev, "O russkoi intelligentsii," *Novyi mir*, 2 (1993), 2–9.

15. Lev Tolstoi, *Sobranie sochinenii v 22 tomakh*, 22 vols. (Moscow: Khudozhestvennaia literatura, 1978–85), vol. 8, 418.

16. Confino, "On Intellectuals and Intellectual Traditions in Eighteenth and Nineteenth Century Russia," 117.

17. Nikolai Berdiaev, *Russkaia ideia* (St. Petersburg: Azbuka–klassika, 2008), 55.

18. For a discussion of Dostoevsky's drawings, see B. N. Tikhomirov, "Fedor Mikhailovich Dostoevsky," in *Gogol, Turgenev, Dostoevskii: Kogda izobrazhenie sluzhit slovu* (Moscow: BOSLEN, 2015), 95–185; drawings in the margins of *The Adolescent* are discussed on 163–9.

19. A. P. Chekhov, *Polnoe sobranie sochinenii i pisem v tridtsati tomakh*, 30 vols. (Moscow: Nauka, 1974–83), *Sochineniia*, vol. 9, 311.

20. See, for example, Gregory Freeze, *Parish Clergy in 19th Century Russia* (Princeton, NJ: Princeton University Press, 1983).

21. See Marc Raeff, *Michael Speransky, Statesman of Imperial Russia, 1772–1839*, 2nd edn. (The Hague: Martinus Nijhoff, 1969).

22. F. M. Dostoevskii, *Polnoe sobranie sochinenii v tridtsati tomakh*, 30 vols. (Leningrad: Nauka, 1972–90), vol. 24, 241.

23. Irmhild Christina Sperrle, *The Organic Worldview of Nikolai Leskov* (Evanston, IL: Northwestern University Press, 2002), 114.

24. N. S. Leskov, *Soboriane*, in N. S. Leskov *Sobranie sochinenii v odinnadtsati tomakh*, 11 vols. (Moscow: Gosudarstvennoe izdatel'stvo khudozhestvennoi literatury, 1956–58), vol. 4, 284.

25. Leskov, "Nekreshchennyi pop," in Leskov, *Sobranie sochinenii v odinnadtsati tomakh*, vol. 6, 209.

26. Tolstoi, "Otets Sergii," in Tolstoi, *Sobranie sochinenii v 22 tomakh*, vol. 12, 382.

27. Cathy Popkin, "Zen and the Art of Reading Chekhov ('The Bishop')," in *Anton Chekhov's Selected Stories*, ed. Cathy Popkin (New York: W.W. Norton & Co., 2014), 670–81.

28. Popkin, "Zen and the Art of Reading Chekhov," 676.

29. A. A. Blok, *Sobranie sochinenii* (Moscow: Gosudarstvennoe izdatel'stvo khudozhestvennoi literatury, 1960–63), vol. 3, 347–57, quotation on 348.

30. V. A. Sollogub, *Tarantas*, in V. A. Sollogub, *Tri povesti* (Moscow: Izdatel'stvo Sovetskaia Rossiia, 1978), 142.

31. On how the description of the world of petty bureaucrats encourages the emergence of the fantastic, see Nancy J. Workman, "Unrealism: Bureaucratic Absurdity in Nineteenth-Century Russian Literature," Ph.D. Dissertation, Columbia University, 1998. Her chapters are tellingly titled: "Myopia" (43–104), "Confusion" (105–66), and "Detachment" (167–210).

32. See Carol Apollonio, *Reading against the Grain* (Evanston, IL: Northwestern University Press, 2009).

33. Nancy Workman, "Notes from the Cave: Teaching *Notes from Underground* in a Philosophy Course," in *Teaching Nineteenth-Century Russian Literature: Essays in Honor of Robert L. Belknap*, ed. Deborah A. Martinsen, Cathy L. Popkin, and Irina Reyfman (Boston: Academic Studies Press, 2014), 177–84.

34. Leskov, "Odnodum," in Leskov, *Sobranie sochinenii v odinnadtsati tomakh*, vol. 2, 29.

35. Nikolai Nadezhdin, "Sonmishche nigilistov (Stsena iz literaturnogo balagana)," *Vestnik Evropy*, 1–2 (1829), 3–22.

36. Pisarev wrote frequently about Turgenev's fiction, often with admiration for his affecting and accurate portraiture of a generational type. See, for example, D. S. Pisarev, "Pisemskii, Turgenev i Goncharov" (1861), in D. S. Pisarev, *Polnoe sobranie sochinenii i pisem* (Moscow: Nauka, 2000–), vol. 3, 248–52.

37. See M. E. Saltykov-Shchedrin, *Polnoe sobranie sochinenii* (Moscow: Khudozhestvennaia literatura, 1933–41), vol. 6, 7–380 (Pisarev is specifically ridiculed on 235 and 348).

38. I. S. Turgenev, *Ottsy i deti*, in I. S. Turgenev, *Polnoe sobranie sochinenii i pisem v tridtsati tomakh*, 30 vols. (Moscow: Nauka, 1978–), vol. 7, 50, 113.

39. Leonid Grossman, "Dostoevskii i pravitel'stvennye krugi 1870-kh godov," *Literaturnoe nasledstvo*, 15 (1934), 107. In a note, he names G. E. Blagosvetlov and, particularly, G. Z. Eleseev as possible prototypes.

40. Turgenev, "Smert'," in Turgenev, *Polnoe sobranie sochinenii i pisem v tridtsati tomakh*, vol. 3, 207.

41. N. K. Mikhailovskii, ["Iz polemiki s Dostoevskim"], in N. K. Mikhailovskii, *Literaturnaia kritika i vospominaniia* (Moscow: Iskusstvo, 1995), 190.

42. For an overview of laws and practices of corporal punishment in the imperial period, see Abby M. Schrader, *Languages of the Lash: Corporal Punishment and Identity in Imperial Russia* (DeKalb, IL: Northern Illinois University Press, 2002).

Chapter 6

1. Kate Holland, *The Novel in the Age of Disintegration: Dostoevsky and the Problem of Genre in the 1870s* (Evanston, IL: Northwestern University Press, 2013), esp. 13–22.

2. In many of his writings, Belinsky cites the power of the poet's imagination (of which Shakespeare and Pushkin are his favorite examples) to create universal types based on singular individuals. See, for example, "Literaturnaia khronika" [1838], in V. G. Belinskii, *Polnoe sobranie sochinenii*, 13 vols. (Moscow: Izd. AN SSSR, 1953–59), vol. 2, 346–56. For an overview of Belinsky's interpretation of literary type, see Victor Terras, *Belinskij and Russian Literary Criticism: The Heritage of Organic Aesthetics* (Madison, WI: University of Wisconsin Press, 1974), 117–18, 147–8.

3. For a classic and influential exegesis of the relation between social conditions and character, see Erich Auerbach, "In the Hôtel de la Mole," in Erich Auerbach, *Mimesis: The Representation of Reality in Western Literature*, trans. Willard Trask (Princeton, NJ: Princeton University Press, 1974; first published in German in 1946), 454–92.

4. See Rufus W. Mathewson, *The Positive Hero in Russian Literature* (Stanford, CA: Stanford University Press, 1975); Richard Freeborn, *The Rise of the Russian Novel: Studies in the Russian Novel From* Eugene Onegin *to* War and Peace (Cambridge: Cambridge University Press, 1973).

5. A. S. Pushkin, *Polnoe sobranie sochinenii v desiati tomakh*, ed. B. V. Tomashevskii, 10 vols. (Leningrad: Nauka, 1977–79), vol. 5, 130.

6. On Belinsky's "organic criticism," see Terras, *Belinskij and Russian Literary Criticism*.

7. Jehanne Gheith, "The Superfluous Man and the Necessary Woman: A 'Re-Vision'," *Russian Review*, 55.2 (1996), 226–44, quotation on 230.

8. A. S. Griboedov, *Sochineniia* (Moscow: Khudozhestvennaia literatura, 1988), 129.

9. Rebecca Stanton, "Reading for the Self: Unwrapping the Nested Autobiographies in Lermontov's *A Hero of Our Time*," in *Teaching Nineteenth-Century Russian Literature: Essays in Honor of Robert L. Belknap*, ed. Deborah A. Martinsen, Cathy L. Popkin, and Irina Reyfman (Boston: Academic Studies Press, 2014), 261–73, quotation on 273.

10. See Beth Holmgren, "Questions of Heroism in Goncharov's *Oblomov*," in *Goncharov's* Oblomov: *A Critical Companion*, ed. Galya Diment (Evanston, IL: Northwestern University Press/The American Association of Teachers of Slavic and East European Languages, 1998), 83–4; Anne Lounsbery, "The World on the Back of a Fish: Mobility, Immobility, and Economics in *Oblomov*," *Russian Review*, 70.1 (2011), 43–64; Victoria Somoff, *The Imperative of Reliability: Russian Prose on the Eve of the Novel, 1820s–1850s* (Evanston, IL: Northwestern University Press, 2015), 155.

11. On Olga's unhappiness with Stolz, see Holmgren, "Questions of Heroism in Goncharov's *Oblomov*," 85–6.

12. See V. N. Krivolapov, "Vspomnim o Shtol'tse," *Russkaia literatura*, 3 (1997), 342–66.

13. On Dostoevsky's likely reading of *Princess Ligovskaia* in manuscript, see A. P. Valagin, "Chital li Dostoevskii 'Kniaginiu Kigovskuiu'?," *Dostoevskii: Materialy i issledovaniia*, 3 (1978), 205–9.

14. On the underground man as a failed duelist, see Irina Reyfman, *Ritualized Violence Russian Style: The Duel in Russian Culture and Literature* (Stanford, CA: Stanford University Press, 1999), 214–27.

15. A. P. Chekhov, *Polnoe sobranie sochinenii i pisem v tridtsati tomakh*, 30 vols. (Moscow: Nauka, 1974–83), *Sochineniia*, vol. 7, 453.

16. N. G. Chernyshevskii, *Polnoe sobranie sochinenii v 15 tomakh*, 15 vols. (Moscow: Gosudarstvennoe izdatel'stvo khudozhestvennoi literatury, 1939–53), vol. 5, 156–74, quotation on 160.

17. Chernyshevskii, *Polnoe sobranie sochinenii v 15 tomakh*, vol. 5, 166.

18. P. V. Annenkov, "Literaturnyi tip slabogo cheloveka. Po povodu turgenevskoi 'Asi,'" http://az.lib.ru/a/annenkow_p_w/text_0163.shtml (last accessed October 25, 2016).

19. For an overview of the Romantic debates about genius, see Andrew Kahn, "Invention and Genius," in Andrew Kahn, *Pushkin's Lyric Intelligence* (Oxford: Oxford University Press, 2008), 34–61.

20. See, for example, B. M. Gasparov, "'Ty, Motsart, nedostoin sam sebia,'" *Vremennik Pushkinskoi komissii, 1974* (1977), 115–22.

21. Pushkin, *Polnoe sobranie sochinenii v desiati tomakh*, vol. 5, 306. On Pushkin's modeling Salieri on Jean-Philippe Rameau, see A. A. Dolinin, "Iz kommentariia k 'Motsartu i Sal'eri,'" in *Zapadnyi sbornik. V chest' 80-letiia Petra Romanovicha Zaborova* (St. Petersburg: izd. Pushkinskogo Doma, 2011), 120–34.

22. See David Herman, "A Requiem for Aristocratic Art: Pushkin's 'Egyptian Nights,'" *Russian Review*, 55.4 (1996), 661–80, on Mickiewicz as a possible prototype of Pushkin's character, see 665; Herman quotes Antoni Edward Odyniec (1804–85), a Polish Romantic poet who observed Pushkin's rapturous reaction to Mickiewicz's improvisation and wrote it down.

23. On the genius and the problem of commerce, see Andrew Kahn, "Genius and the Commerce of Poetry," in Kahn, *Pushkin's Lyric Intelligence*, 158–215.

24. V. F. Odoevskii, *Russkie nochi* (Leningrad: Nauka, 1975), 178, 131.

25. Robert A. Maguire, *Exploring Gogol* (Stanford, CA: Stanford University Press, 1994), 143–73.

26. Donald Fanger, *The Creation of Nikolai Gogol* (Cambridge, MA: Belknap Press of Harvard University Press, 1979), 116.

27. N.V. Gogol', *Polnoe sobranie sochinenii v 14-ti tomakh*, 14 vols. (Moscow: Izd. AN SSSR, 1937–52), vol. 3, 214. In this edition, instead of the Day of Algiers the French king is mentioned; the reason for the discrepancy is explained by O. G. Dilaktorskaia in her "Primechaniia" to N. V. Gogol', *Peterburgskie povesti*, ed. O. G. Dilaktorskaia (St. Petersburg: Nauka, 1995), 295n33.

28. Maguire, *Exploring Gogol*, 64–5.

29. Simon Karlinsky, *The Sexual Labyrinth of Nikolai Gogol* (Chicago: University of Chicago Press, 1976), 22.

30. F. M. Dostoevskii, *Zapiski iz podpol'ia*, in F. M. Dostoevskii, *Polnoe sobranie sochinenii v tridtsati tomakh*, 30 vols. (Leningrad: Nauka, 1972–90), vol. 5, 101. Translation comes from Richard Pevear and Larissa Volokhonsky's translation, in Fyodor Dostoevsky, *Notes from Underground* (New York: Vintage Books, 1994), 7.

31. As discussed in Mikhail Bakhtin, *Problems of Dostoevsky's Poetics*, ed. and trans. Caryl Emerson (Minneapolis, MN: University of Minnesota Press, 1984), 137–47.

32. Harriet Murav, *Holy Foolishness: Dostoevsky's Novels and the Poetics of Cultural Critique* (Stanford, CA: Stanford University Press, 1992).

33. Liza Knapp, "The Suffering of Others: Fear and Pity in 'Ward Six,'" in *Anton Chekhov's Selected Stories*, ed. Cathy Popkin (New York: W.W. Norton & Co., 2014), 621–30, quotation on 622.

34. Knapp, "The Suffering of Others," 621; Cathy Popkin, "The Number Devil and the Mermaid of Math: Chekhov's 'Ward Six,'" in *A Convenient Territory: Russian Literature at the Edge of Modernity: Essays in Honor of Barry P. Scherr*, ed. John Kopper and Michael Wachtel (Bloomington, IN: Slavica Publishers, 2015), 1–13.

35. Claire Whitehead, "Anton Chekhov's 'The Black Monk': An Example of the Fantastic?," *SEER*, 85.4 (2007), 619–20, 623–4.

36. Belinsky's understanding of "insignificant men" was far more nuanced than it became later, in Soviet scholarship; see E. M. Sokol, "'Malen'kii chelovek' v tvorchestve russkikh pisatelei 1840-kh godov v svete khristianskoi traditsii: Ot Gogolia k Dostoevskomu," Avtoreferat dissertatsii na stepen' kandidata filologicheskikh nauk, Moscow, 2003, available at http://www.dissercat.

com/content/malenkii-chelovek-v-tvorchestve-russkikh-pisatelei-1840-kh-godov-v-svete-khristianskoi-tradi (last accessed March 30, 2017).

37. Dilaktorskaia, "Primechaniia," 293n22.

38. Carol Apollonio, *Reading Against the Grain* (Evanston, IL: Northwestern University Press, 2009), 14.

39. Cathy Popkin, *The Pragmatics of Insignificance: Chekhov, Zoshchenko, Gogol* (Stanford, CA: Stanford University Press, 1993), 29–31.

40. Pushkin, *Polnoe sobranie sochinenii v desiati tomakh*, vol. 5, 172.

41. M. E. Saltykov-Shchedrin, *Sobranie sochinenii v dvadtsati tomakh*, 20 vols. (Moscow: Khudozhestvennaia literatura, 1965–77), vol. 2, 225.

42. Chekhov, *Polnoe sobranie sochinenii i pisem, Sochineniia*, vol. 8, 332; for the translation, see *Anton Chekhov's Selected Stories*, 315.

43. Irina Savkina, *Provintsialki russkoi literatury (zhenskaia proza 30–40-kh godov XIX veka)* (Wilhelmshorst: F. K Göpfert, 1998), 63 (original emphasis).

44. Savkina, *Provintsialki russkoi literatury*, 67.

45. Catriona Kelly, "Configurations of Authority: Feminism, Modernism, and Mass Culture, 1881–1917," in Catriona Kelly, *A History of Russian Women's Writing 1820–1992* (Oxford: Oxford University Press, 1994), 59–78.

Chapter 7

1. For useful overviews, see Christine Johanson, "Turgenev's Heroines: A Historical Assessment," *Canadian Slavonic Papers/Revue Cannadienne des Slavistes*, 26.1 (1984), 15–23; Sibelan Forrester, "Introduction. Framing the View: Russian Women in the Long Nineteenth Century," in *Women in Nineteenth-Century Russia: Lives and Culture*, ed. Wendy Rosslyn and Alessandra Tosi (Cambridge: Open Book Publishers, 2012), 1–2 (1–18).

2. Nadezda Belyakova and Taisiya Belyakova, "Women's Rights in the Late Russian Empire: The Paradoxes of the Legislative Basis in the Family Sphere," in *Women in Law and Lawmaking in Nineteenth and Twentieth-Century Europe*, ed. Eva Schandevyl (Farnham: Ashgate Publishing, 2014), 199–238, esp. 199; also see Michelle Lamarche Marrese, *A Woman's Kingdom: Noblewomen and the Control of Property in Russia, 1700–1861* (Ithaca, NY: Cornell University Press, 2002). While the lives of noblewomen are better represented in historical accounts, recently historians have begun to pay attention to peasantry and urban dwellers. See, for example, Christine D. Worobec, "Russian Peasant Women's Culture: Three Voices," in *Women in Nineteenth-Century Russia*, ed. Rosslyn and Tosi, 41–62; Barbara Alpern Engel, "Women and Urban Culture," in *Women in Nineteenth-Century Russia*, ed. Rosslyn and Tosi, 19–40.

3. See Mikhail Shishkin, *Russkaia Shveitsariia: literaturno-istoricheskii putevoditel'* (Moscow: Vagrius, 2006), passim.

4. Engel, "Women and Urban Culture," 20–1.

5. Worobec, "Russian Peasant Women's Culture," 46.

6. Iurii Lotman, "Siuzhetnoe prostranstvo russkogo romana XIX stoletiia," in Iurii Lotman, *Izbrannye stat'i v trekh tomakh*, 3 vols. (Tallin, Aleksandra, 1992–3), vol. 3, 91–106, quotations on 98, 104.

7. Ksana Blank, "The Endless Passage: The Making of a Plot in the Russian Novel," Ph.D. Dissertation, Columbia University, 1997.

8. Jehanne Gheith, "The Superfluous Man and the Necessary Woman: A 'Re-Vision'," *Russian Review*, 55.2 (1996), 226–44, esp. 230–2; for a discussion of Odintsova, see Jane T. Costlow, "'Oh-la-la' and 'No-no-no': Odintsova as Woman Alone in *Fathers and Children*," in *A Plot of Her Own: The Female Protagonist in Russian Literature*, ed. Sona Stephan Hoisington (Evanston, IL: Northwestern University Press, 1995), 21–32.

9. For a drastically different take on Tatiana as a "sentimental collage of female attributes" whose "extraordinary vigor and potency" are aesthetic rather than moral and who, in fact, enables the "emergence of a genuinely *novelistic* hero," see Caryl Emerson, "Tatiana," in *A Plot of Her Own*, 6–20, quotations on 6, 7, and 20 (original emphasis).

10. Barbara Heldt, *Terrible Perfection: Women and Russian Literature* (Bloomington: Indiana University Press, 1987), 13; Abram Terts, "Chto takoe sotsialisticheskii realizm?," in Abram Terts, *Fantasticheskii mir Abrama Tertsa* (New York: Inter-Language Literary Associates, 1967), 401–46.

11. Gheith, "The Superfluous Man and the Necessary Woman," 228.

12. M. Iu. Lermontov, *Sochineniia v 6-ti tomakh* (Moscow: Izd. AN SSSR, 1954–57), vol. 6, 233.

13. I. S. Turgenev, "Dnevnik lishnego cheloveka," in I. S. Turgenev, *Polnoe sobranie sochinenii i pisem v tridtsati tomakh*, 30 vols. (Moscow: Nauka, 1978–), vol. 4, 168.

14. On motherhood as a domestic role, see Barbara Engel, "The Petrine Revolution: New Men, New Women," in Barbara Engel, *Women in Russia, 1700–2000* (Cambridge: Cambridge University Press, 2004), 5–26 (Chapter 1); and Richard Stites, "On the Eve," in Richard Stites, *The Women's Liberation Movement in Russia: Feminism, Nihilism, and Bolshevism, 1860–1930* (Princeton, NJ: Princeton University Press, 1990), 3–25.

15. On Olga as *Oblomov's* "true hero," see Beth Holmgren, "Questions of Heroism in Goncharov's *Oblomov*," in *Goncharov's Oblomov: A Critical Companion*, ed. Galya Diment (Evanston, IL: Northwestern University Press/The American Association of Teachers of Slavic and East European Languages, 1998), 77–89, esp. 84–6.

16. F. M. Dostoevskii, *Polnoe sobranie sochinenii v tridtsati tomakh*, 30 vols. (Leningrad: Nauka, 1972–90), vol. 14, 127.

17. Dostoevskii, *Polnoe sobranie sochinenii v tridtsati tomakh*, vol. 14, 18.

18. For an in-depth discussion of Arina Golovlev as a mother who brings devastation to her family, see Jenny Kaminer, *Women with a Thirst for Destruction: The Bad Mother in Russian Culture* (Evanston, IL: Northwestern University Press, 2014), 32–44.

19. A. P. Chekhov, "V ovrage," in A. P. Chekhov, *Polnoe sobranie sochinenii i pisem v tridtsati tomakh*, 30 vols. (Moscow: Nauka, 1974–83), *Sochineniia*, vol. 10, 167; for the translation, see *Anton Chekhov's Selected Stories*, ed. Cathy Popkin (New York: W.W. Norton & Co., 2014), 450.

20. Chekhov, "V ovrage," vol. 10, 172; for the translation, see *Anton Chekhov's Selected Stories*, 453.

21. Robert Louis Jackson, "Three Deaths: A Boy, a Goose, and an Infant," in *Teaching Nineteenth-Century Russian Literature: Essays in Honor of Robert L. Belknap*, ed. Deborah A. Martinsen, Cathy L. Popkin, and Irina Reyfman (Boston: Academic Studies Press, 2014), 115–32, quotation on 127.

22. Jackson, "Three Deaths," 130, 131 (original emphasis).

23. For Jackson's interpretation, see Jackson, "Three Deaths," 131. Both meanings emphasize the importance of Lipa's singing.

24. Svetlana Grenier, "Searching for Freedom in *Eugene Onegin*," in *Teaching Nineteenth-Century Russian Literature*, 274–86, quotation on 282–4.

25. Turgenev, "Dnevnik lishnego cheloveka," 180.

26. A. F. Belousov, "Institutka: sotsial'no-psikhologicheskii tip i kul'turnyi simvol 'peterburgskogo' perioda russkoi istorii," in *Antsiferovskie chteniia. Materialy i tezisy konferentsii (20–22 dekabria 1989 g.)* (Leningrad: Leningradskoe otdelenie Sovetskogo fonda kul'tury, 1989), 180–5.

27. Hugh McLean, "A Woman's Place ... The Young Tolstoy and the 'Woman Question,'" in *Word, Music, History: A Festschrift for Caryl Emerson*, ed. Lazar Fleishman, Gabriella Safran, and Michael Wachtel (Stanford, CA: Stanford University, Department of Slavic Languages and Literatures, 2005), vol. 1, 355–69.

28. B. M. Eikhenbaum, *Lev Tolstoi. Issledovaniia. Sta'ti* (St. Petersburg: Fakul'tet filologii i iskusstv Sankt-Peterburgskogo gos. Universiteta, 2009), 349–59; Marie Sémon, *Les femmes dans l'œuvre de Léon Tolstoï: Romans et nouvelles* (Paris: Institute d'études slaves, 1984), 88.

29. L. N. Tolstoi, *Semeinoe schast'e*, in L. N. Tolstoi, *Sobranie sochinenii v 22 tomakh*, 22 vols. (Moscow: Khudozhestvennaia literatura, 1978–85), vol. 3, 149.

30. See Irina Reyfman, "Female Voice and Male Gaze in Leo Tolstoy's *Family Happiness*," in Irina Reyfman, *Rank and Style: Russians in State Service, Life, and Literature* (Boston, MA: Academic Studies Press, 2012), 172–99. It is noteworthy that, firm as he was in his condemnation of female sexuality, Tolstoy disliked *Family Happiness* as a work of literature and mentioned his dislike more than once.

31. See Donna Tussing Orwin, *Tolstoy's Art and Thought, 1847–1880* (Princeton, NJ: Princeton University Press, 1993), 183–7.

32. Svetlana Grenier, *Representing the Marginal Woman in Nineteenth-Century Russian Literature: Personalism, Feminism, and Polyphony* (Westport, CT: Greenwood Press, 2001), 103–4.

33. Tolstoi, *Sobranie sochinenii v 22 tomakh*, vol. 8, 67.

34. Gary Saul Morson, "Dolly and Stiva: Prosaic Good and Evil," in Gary Saul Morson, *Anna Karenina in Our Time: Seeing More Wisely* (New Haven, CT: Yale University Press, 2007), 33–54 (Chapter 2).

35. Svetlana Slavskaya Grenier, "A Tale of Two Cities: Tolstoy's Gendered Moral Geography in *Anna Karenina*," in *Mapping the Feminine: Russian Women and Cultural Difference*, ed. Hilde Hoogenboom, Catharine Theimer Nepomnyashchy, and Irina Reyfman (Bloomington, IN: Slavica Publishers, 2008), 93–111, quotation 94.

36. Amy Mandelker, *Framing Anna Karenina: Tolstoy, the Woman Question, and the Victorian Novel* (Columbus, OH: Ohio State University Press, 1993), 30–3.

37. Tolstoi, *Sobranie sochinenii v 22 tomakh*, vol. 12, 197–201.

38. Irina Paperno, *Chernyshevsky and the Age of Realism: A Study in the Semiotics of Behavior* (Stanford, CA: Stanford University Press, 1988), 29–36; on Lenin's interpretation of the novel, see Andrew Michael Drozd, *Chernyshevskii's "What Is to Be Done?": A Reevaluation* (Evanston, IL: Northwestern University Press, 2001), 14.

39. Paperno, *Chernyshevsky*, 133–41.

40. Chekhov, *Polnoe sobranie sochinenii i pisem, Pis'ma*, vol. 4, 19, 147.

41. Caryl Emerson, "Chekhov and the Annas," in *Life and Text: Essays in Honour of Geir Kjetsaa on the Occasion of his 60th Birthday*, ed. Erik Egeberg, Audun J. Morch, and Ole Michael Selberg (Oslo: [n.p.], 1997), 121–32; on "Anna around the neck" see 126.

42. A. P. Chekhov, "O liubvi," in Chekhov, *Polnoe sobranie sochinenii i pisem, Sochineniia*, vol. 10, 69; for the translation, see *Anton Chekhov's Selected Stories*, 374.

43. Emerson, "Chekhov and the Annas," 131.

44. Emerson, "Chekhov and the Annas," 128.

45. For a useful overview of the Russian peasant woman in late-nineteenth-century Russian culture, including literature, see Cathy N. Frierzon, "*Baba*: The Peasant Woman—Virago, Eve, or Victim?," in *Peasant Icons: Representations of Rural People in Late Nineteenth Century Russia* (Oxford: Oxford University Press, 1993), 161–80 (Chapter 8).

46. Apollon Grigor'ev, "Posle 'Grozy' Ostrovskogo. Pis'ma k Ivanu Sergeevichu Turgenevu. Pis'mo pervoe; Neizbezhnye voprosy," in Apollon Grigor'ev *Sochineniia v dvukh tomakh* (Moscow: Khudozhestvennaia literatura, 1990), vol. 2, 212–29, quotations on 212, 213.

47. Tolstoi, *Sobranie sochinenii v 22 tomakh*, vol. 11, 100.

48. A. P. Chekhov, "Eger'," in Chekhov, *Polnoe sobranie sochinenii i pisem, Sochineniia*, vol. 4, 81; for the translation, see *Anton Chekhov's Selected Stories*, 40.

49. Chekhov, "Agaf'ia," in his *Polnoe sobranie sochinenii i pisem, Sochineniia*, vol. 5, 28; for the translation see *Anton Chekhov's Selected Stories*, 63.

50. Chekhov, "Agaf'ia," 25; for the translation, see *Anton Chekhov's Selected Stories*, 61.

51. Chekhov, "Agaf'ia," 34; for the translation, see *Anton Chekhov's Selected Stories*, 69.

52. A. S. Dolinin, "Turgenev and Chekhov (Parallel'nyi analiz 'Svidaniia' Turgeneva i 'Egeria' Chekhova)," in A. S. Dolinin, *Dostoevskii i drugie. Stat'i i issledovaniia o russkoi klassicheskoi literature* (Leningrad: Khudozhestvennaia literatura, 1989), 331–73, quotation on 372.

53. Cathy Popkin, "Paying the Price: The Rhetoric of Reckoning in Čekhov's 'Peasant Women,'" *Russian Literature* 35 (1994), 203–22, for the comment on *baby*, see 221n4.

54. A. P. Chekhov, "Baby," in Chekhov, *Polnoe sobranie sochinenii i pisem, Sochineniia*, vol. 7, 342; for the translation, see *Anton Chekhov's Selected Stories*, 215.

55. For Matvei's framing Masha, see Simon Karlinsky, "Chekhov the Gentle Subversive," in *Chekhov: New Perspectives*, ed. René and Nonna D. Wellek (Engelwood Cliffs, NJ: Prentice-Hall, 1984), 46; Popkin, "Paying the Price," 210; Julie W. de Sherbinin, "Chekhov and Russian Religious Culture: Merchants, Martyrs, and 'Peasant Women,'" in *Chekhov's Selected Stories*, 611.

56. Popkin, "Paying the Price," 213, 220.

57. For an overview of this tradition, see Olga Matich, "A Typology of Fallen Women in Nineteenth-Century Russian Literature," in *American Contributions to the Ninth International Congress of Slavists*, ed. Paul Debreczeny (Columbus, OH: Slavica, 1983), vol. 2, 325–43.

58. Alexander Zholkovsky, "A Study in Framing: Pushkin, Bunin, Nabokov," in Alexander Zholkovsky, *Text counter Text: Readings in Russian Literary History* (Stanford, CA: Stanford University Press, 1994), 88–113, esp. 103.

59. V. G. Korolenko, *Izbrannye proizvedeniia* (Leningrad: Leningradskoe gazetno-zhurnal'noe izdatel'stvo, 1947), 45.

60. Paperno, *Chernyshevsky*, 29–30.

61. Lynn Ellen Patyk, "Remembering 'The Terrorism': Sergei Stepniak-Kravchinskii's 'Underground Russia,'" *Slavic Review*, 68.4 (2009), 758–81, quotation on 760; Figner is quoted in this essay.

62. Quoted in Donna Oliver, "Fool or Saint? Writers Reading the Zasulich Case," in *Just Assassins: The Culture of Terrorism in Russia*, ed. and intro. Anthony Anemone (Evanston, IL: Northwestern University Press, 2010), 73–96, quotation on 79.

63. F. M. Dostoevsky, "Zapisi literaturno-kriticheskogo i publitsisticheskogo kharaktera iz zapisnoi tetradi 1880–1881 gg.," in F. M. Dostoevsky, *Polnoe sobranie sochinenii v tridtsati tomakh* (Leningrad: Nauka, 1972–90), vol. 27, 42–87, quotation on 57.

64. For the discussion of Stepniak-Kravchinsky's views on nihilism, see Peter Scotto, "The Terrorist as Novelist: Sergei Stepniak-Kravchinsky," in *Just Assassins*, ed. and intro. Anemone, 97–126, esp. 108.

65. Sergei Stepnyak-Kravchinsky, *Underground Russia: Revolutionary Profiles and Sketches from Life* (New York: C. Scribner's Sons, 1882), 12.

66. Quoted in Oliver, "Fool or Saint?," 75.

67. Oliver, "Fool or Saint?," 75.

68. Stepnyak, *Underground Russia*, 12.

69. Sally A. Boniece, "The Spiridonova Case, 1906: Terror, Myth, and Martyrdom," in *Just Assassins*, ed. and intro. Anemone, 127–62, esp. 129–30.

70. For a treatment of terrorism in Russian literature, see Lynn Ellen Patyk, *Written in Blood: Revolutionary Terrorism and Russian Literary Culture, 1861–1881* (Madison: University of Wisconsin Press, 2017).

71. Lynn Ellen Patyk, "The Byronic Terrorist: Boris Savinkov's Literary Self-mythologization," in *Just Assassins*, ed. and intro. Anemone, 163–90, quotation on 175.

Chapter 8

1. In discussions of national identity and the authenticity of Russian culture, there has been a marked preference from the early 1800s and well into the century for the term *narodnost'* (from

narod, both "nation" and "people") instead of "nationality." See David L. Cooper, *Creating the Nation: Identity and Aesthetics in Early Nineteenth-Century Russia and Bohemia* (DeKalb, IL: Northern Illinois University Press, 2010), esp. Chapters 2, 3, and 8.

2. See E. V. Dushechkina, "Ballada V. A. Zhukovskogo 'Svetlana' v kul'turnom obikhode dorevo-liutsionnoi Rossii," in E. V. Dushechkina, *Svetlana. Kul'turnaia istoriia imeni* (St. Petersburg: Izdatel'stvo Evropeiskogo universiteta, 2007), 12–67 (Chapter 1).

3. On Hume's influence on Karamzin, see Tatiana Artemyeva, "David Hume and the Russian Enlightenment," *The Philosophical Age, Almanac*, 37 ("David Hume and Northern Europe") (2012), 14–16.

4. For a discussion of Russian historical fiction representing tyrants, see Kevin Platt, *Terror and Greatness: Ivan and Peter as Russian Myths* (Ithaca, NY: Cornell University Press, 2011).

5. As studied in Caryl G. Emerson, *Boris Godunov: Transpositions of a Russian Theme* (Bloomington: Indiana University Press, 1986).

6. On the significance of the play in Pushkin's development, see Stephanie Sandler, *Distant Pleasures: Alexander Pushkin and the Writing of Exile* (Stanford, CA: Stanford University Press, 1989), 77–139; and Monika Greenleaf, *Pushkin and Romantic Fashion: Fragment, Elegy, Orient, Irony* (Stanford, CA: Stanford University Press: 1994), 156–204.

7. Greenleaf, *Pushkin and Romantic Fashion*, 204.

8. See Olga Maiorova, "The Varangian Legend: Defining the Nation through the Foundation Myth," in Olga Maiorova, *From the Shadow of Empire: Defining the Russian Nation through Cultural Mythology, 1855–1870* (Madison, WI: University of Wisconsin Press, 2010), 53–93 (Chapter 2); on literature's engagement with the legend, see pp. 73–4.

9. Leo Tolstoy, "Some words on *War and Peace*", in *War and Peace*, trans. Louise and Aylmer Maude, ed. and intro. Amy Mandelker (Oxford: Oxford University Press, 2010), 1309. The translation omits the word "book" (*kniga*) present in the Russian title; see L. N. Tolstoi, *Sobranie sochinenii v 22 tomakh*, 22 vols. (Moscow: Khudozhestvennaia literatura, 1978–85), vol. 4, 356.

10. B. M. Eikhenbaum, *Lev Tolstoi. Issledovaniia. Sta'ti* (St. Petersburg: Fakul'tet filologii i iskusstv Sankt-Peterburgskogo gos. Universiteta, 2009), 474, 486–7.

11. Dominic Lieven, *Russia against Napoleon: The True Story of the Campaigns of* War and Peace (London: Penguin, 2010), 525–6.

12. Lieven, *Russia against Napoleon*, 189–90.

13. Gary Saul Morson, *Hidden in Plain View: Narrative and Creative Potentials in "War and Peace"* (Stanford, CA: Stanford University Press, 1987), 9–36, 42–6.

14. Tolstoy, *War and Peace*, 881.

15. Tolstoy, *War and Peace*, 693.

16. Tolstoy, *War and Peace*, 1199; edited to match the original.

17. Tolstoy, *War and Peace*, 966.

18. Tolstoy, *War and Peace*, 896.

19. Tolstoy, *War and Peace*, 848.

20. Tolstoy, *War and Peace*, 851.

21. Tolstoy, *War and Peace*, 854.

22. Tolstoy, *War and Peace*, 855.

23. Tolstoy, *War and Peace*, 601.

24. Tolstoy, *War and Peace*, 605.

25. Tolstoy, *War and Peace*, 934–8.

26. Maiorova, *From the Shadow of Empire*, 149.

27. Vasily Grossman, *Life and Fate*, trans. Robert Chandler (London: Collins Harvill, 1985), 239.

28. Grossman, *Life and Fate*, 240.

29. Tolstoy, *War and Peace*, 762–3.

30. See Morson, *Hidden in Plain View*, 133–5.

31. See Lieven, *Russia against Napoleon*, 10, 525; Maiorova, *From the Shadow of Empire*, 143–53.

32. Morson, *Hidden in Plain View*, 37.

33. Morson, *Hidden in Plain View*, 271.

34. For a detailed overview of historical novelistic production of the late nineteenth century, see S. M. Liapina, "Russkii istoricheskii roman XIX veka v kontekste kul'turnogo soznaniia," *Istoriia: Fakty i simvoly. Nauchno-teoreticheskii i prikladnoi istoricheskii zhurnal*, 5 (2015), http://historic-journal.ru/2015/russkij-istoricheskij-roman-xix-veka-v-kontekste-kulturnogo-soznaniya/ (last accessed July 19, 2016).

35. Hippolyte Taine, *Histoire de la littérature anglaise*, 5 vols., 2nd edn. (Paris: Librairie de L. Hachette et Cie, 1866-78), vol. 1, xxix, xxxiv. On his theory, see René Wellek, "Hippolyte Taine's Literary Theory and Criticism," *Criticism*, 1.1 (1959), 1–18; for a typical statement of his idea of "national reality" as reflected in literature, see A. N. Pypin, *Istoriia russkoi literatury*, 4 vols., 4th edn. (St. Petersburg: Tipografiia M. M. Stasiulevicha, 1911–13), vol. 1, iii.

36. Laura Engelstein, "Holy Russia in Modern Times: An Essay on Orthodoxy and Cultural Change," *Past and Present*, 173 (2001), 129–56.

37. Alexander Pushkin, *Complete Prose Fiction*, trans. Paul Debreczeny (Stanford, CA: Stanford University Press, 1983), 211; A. S. Pushkin, "Pikovaia dama," in A. S. Pushkin, *Polnoe sobranie sochinenii v desiati tomakh*, 10 vols. (Leningrad: Nauka, 1977–79), vol. 6, 211.

38. See Dominic Lieven, "Russia as Empire and Periphery," in *The Cambridge History of Russia, Volume 2: Imperial Russia, 1689–1917*, ed. Dominic Lieven (Cambridge: Cambridge University Press, 2006), 7–26.

39. For the political dimension and dynamic of the Russian Imperial conversions, see Robert Geraci, *Window on the East: National and Imperial Identities in Late Tsarist Russia* (Ithaca, NY: Cornell University Press, 2001) and Robert Crews, *For Prophet and the Tsar: Islam and Empire in Russia and Central Asia* (Cambridge, MA: Harvard University Press, 2006), 143–292.

40. See, for example, David I. Goldstein, *Dostoyevsky and the Jews* (Austin, TX: University of Texas Press, 1981); Susan McReynolds, *Redemption and the Merchant God: Dostoevsky's Economy of Salvation and Antisemitism* (Evanston, IL: Northwestern University Press, 2008).

41. See, for example, F. M. Dostoevskii, "Mart. Glava vtoraia: I. Evreiskii vopros. II. Pro i contra. III. Status in statu. Sorok vekov bytiia. IV. No da zdravstvuet bratstvo!," in *Dnevnik pisatelia za 1877 g.*, in F. M. Dostoevskii, *Polnoe sobranie sochinenii v tridtsati tomakh*, 30 vols. (Leningrad: Nauka, 1972–90), vol. 25, 74–88.

42. See Gary Saul Morson, "Dostoevsky's Anti-Semitism and the Critics: A Review Article," *SEEJ*, 27.3 (1983), 302–17; Harriet Murav, "Dostoevsky," in Harriet Murav, *Identity Theft: The Jew in Imperial Russia and the Case of Avraam Uri Kovner* (Stanford, CA: Stanford University Press, 2003), 131–55 (Chapter 6); Harriet Murav, "Jews, Race, and Biology," in *Dostoevsky in Context* ed. Deborah A. Martinsen and Olga Maiorova (Cambridge, Cambridge University Press, 2015), 122–30; Eugene M. Avrutin, "Racial Categories and the Politics of (Jewish) Difference in Late Imperial Russia," *Kritika*, 8.1 (2007), 13–40.

43. Elena Tolstaya-Segal has argued that Chekhov let himself create such a complex, but in the end vicious, portrait of an alluring Jewish woman as an outlet for his own rage against Dunia Efros, who had spurned him. See Elena Tolstaya-Segal, "'Tsenzura ne propuskaet': Chekhov i Dunja Efros," *NLO*, 8 (1994), 221–49. For a discussion of stereotypical portrayals of Jews in nineteenth-century literature, see Sander Gilman, *The Jew's Body* (New York, NY: Routledge, 1991).

44. For a persuasive deconstruction of writers' unconscious incorporation of these stereotypes, see Gary Rosenshield, *The Ridiculous Jew: The Exploitation and Transformation of a Stereotype in Gogol, Turgenev, and Dostoevsky* (Stanford, CA: Stanford University Press, 2008).

45. For an excellent discussion of the story, see Robert Louis Jackson, "'If I forget Thee, O Jerusalem': An Essay on Chekhov's 'Rothschild's Fiddle,'" in *Anton Chekhov Rediscovered: A Collection of New Studies with a Comprehensive Bibliography*, ed. Savely Senderovich and Munir Sendich (East Lansing, MI: Russian Language Journal, 1987), 35–49.

46. Andreas Kappeler, *The Russian Empire: A Multiethnic History*, trans. Alfred Clayton (New York: Longman, 2001), 247–8; on Russia's policy to preserve and, sometimes, reproduce local heterogeneity within the empire, see also *Russian Empire: Space, People, Power, 1700–1930*, ed. Jane Burbank, Mark von Hagen, and Anatolyi Remnev (Bloomington: Indiana University Press, 2007).

47. See Valerie A. Kivelson and Ronald Grigor Suny, *Russia's Empires* (New York: Oxford University Press, 2017), 168–73.

48. Pushkin, "Kalmychke," in Pushkin, *Polnoe sobranie sochinenii v desiati tomakh*, vol. 3, 112.

49. I. M. Shapir, "O nerovnosti ravnogo. Poslanie Pushkina 'Kalmychke' na fone makroevoliutsii russkogo poeticheskogo iazyka," in *Kruglyi stol k 75-letiiu Viacheslava Vsevolodovicha Ivanova* (Moscow, Nauka, 2006), 406.

50. Boris Gasparov, "Platonov and Reshetnikov," *Ulbandus Review*, 14 (2011), 111–29, quotation on 115.

51. On the formation of the Russian Empire's self-perception as a multinational and multi-confessional country, see Maiorova, *From the Shadow of Empire*, esp. 3–25 (Introduction).

52. Pushkin, *Polnoe sobranie sochinenii v desiati tomakh*, vol. 5, 180.

53. B. A. Uspenskii, *Filologicheskie razyskaniia v oblasti slavianskikh drevnostei: Relikty iazychestva v vostochnoslavianskom kul'te Nikolaia Marlikiiskogo* (Moscow: Izd. Moskovskogo universiteta, 1982), 199–222.

54. V. A. Zhukovskii, *Polnoe sobranie sochinenii i pisem*, 20 vols. (Moscow: Iazyki russkoi kul'tury, 1999–), vol. 1, 242.

55. S. A. Reiser, "Russkii bog," *Izvestiia otdeleniia literatury i iazyka AN SSSR*, 20.1 (1961), 64–9; on the formula's going out of use, see 65.

56. P. Ia. Chaadaev, "Filosoficheskie pis'ma. Pis'mo pervoe," in P. Ia. Chaadaev, *Stat'i i pis'ma* (Moscow: Sovremennik, 1989), 41.

57. P. Ia. Chaadaev, "Apologiia sumasshedshego," in Chaadaev, *Stat'i i pis'ma*, 157.

58. On the impact of science and Darwinism on Russian thought and social theory from the 1840s, see Aileen Kelly, *The Discovery of Chance: The Life and Thought of Alexander Herzen* (Cambridge, MA: Harvard University Press, 2016), 67–118.

59. Christopher Ely, *This Meager Nature: Landscape and National Identity in Imperial Russia* (DeKalb, IL: Northern Illinois University Press, 2002), 139.

60. F. I. Tiutchev, *Polnoe sobranie stikhotvorenii* (Leningrad: Sovetskii pisatel', 1957), 230 (original emphasis).

61. Dostoevskii, *Polnoe sobranie sochinenii v tridtsati tomakh*, vol. 18, 37.

62. On the cross-generational conversation between the two thinkers, see Marina Kostalevsky, *Dostoevsky and Soloviov: The Art of Integral Vision* (New Haven, CT: Yale University Press, 1997).

63. L. O. Sosnovskii, "Za chto liubil Pushkina V. I. Lenin?," *Pravda*, 127 (1924), n.p.

64. A. Lunacharskii, "Pushkin," *Krasnaia gazeta*, 129 (June 8, 1924), 5.

65. The statistic comes from Stephanie Sandler, *Commemorating Pushkin: Russia's Myth of a National Poet* (Stanford, CA: Stanford University Press, 2004), 109. For a thorough analysis of the 1937 celebration, see Jonathan Platt, *Greetings, Pushkin!: Stalinist Cultural Politics and the Russian National Bard* (Pittsburgh, PA: University of Pittsburgh Press, 2016).

66. As of the writing of this book, there is still no completed full edition of Pushkin's writings, with scholarly commentary. A current ambitious project is *Sochineniia Pushkina* under the general editorship of David Bethea; several volumes have appeared through Moscow's Novoe izdatel´stvo publishing house.

67. The essay can be found in D. S. Pisarev, *Sochineniia v chetyrekh tomakh*, 4 vols. (Moscow: Khudozhestvennaia literatura, 1955–56), vol. 3, 306–417, quotation on 393.

68. Pisarev, *Sochineniia*, vol. 3, 393.

69. Joseph Frank, *Dostoevsky: A Writer in His Time* (Princeton, NJ: Princeton University Press, 2010), 59.

70. Marcus Levitt, *Russian Literary Politics and the Pushkin Celebration of 1880* (Ithaca, NY: Cornell University Press, 1989), 133; see also G. M. Fridlender, "'Rech´ o Pushkine' kak esteticheskoe vyrazhenie samosoznaniia Dostoevskogo," *Russkaia literatura*, 1 (1981), 57–64.

71. F. M. Dostoevskii, "Pushkin, Lermontov i Nekrasov," in *Dnevnik pisatelia za 1877 god*, in Dostoevskii, *Polnoe sobranie sochinenii v tridtsati tomakh*, vol. 26, 114. For Gogol's two characterizations of Pushkin quoted by Dostoevsky, see N. V. Gogol´, *Polnoe sobranie sochinenii v 14-ti tomakh*, 14 vols. (Moscow, Leningrad: Izd. AN SSSR, 1937–52), vol. 8, 50.

72. F. M. Dostoevskii, "Pushkin. (Ocherk)," in Dostoevskii, *Polnoe sobranie sochinenii v tridtsati tomakh*, vol. 26, 136 (Dostoevsky repeats this idea four times), 147 (three times).

73. A. Tseitlin, "Pushkin v istorii russkoi literatury," in *Literaturnaia entsiklopedia v 11 tomakh* (Moscow: OGIZ RSFSR, 1929–39), vol. 9, 413–42, http://feb-web.ru/feb/litenc/encyclop/ (last accessed October 21, 2016).

Conclusion

1. L. N. Tolstoi, *Sobranie sochinenii v 22 tomakh*, 22 vols. (Moscow: Khudozhestvennaia literatura, 1978–85), vol. 15, 78.

2. See Vsevolod Meyerhold, "The Naturalistic Theatre and the Theatre of the Mood," trans. Nora Beeson, *The Tulane Drama Review*, 4.4 (1960), 134–48.

3. *Istoriia russkoi literatury XIX v.*, ed. D. N. Ovsianiko-Kulikovskii, 5 vols. (Moscow: Mir, 1911), vol. 5, 96.

4. D. S. Mirsky, *A History of Russian Literature*, ed. Francis J. Whitfield (New York, NY: Alfred A. Knopf, 1926), 407–8.

Part V.   The Twentieth and Twenty-First Centuries
Chapter 1

1. Omry Ronen, *The Fallacy of the Silver Age in Twentieth-Century Russian Culture* (Amsterdam: Harwood Academic Publishers, 1997).

2. Anna Akhmatova, *Ia—golos vash . . .* (Moscow: Knizhnaia palata, 1989), 243.

3. See the essays collected in *Cultural Mythologies of Russian Modernism: From the Golden Age to the Silver Age*, ed. Boris Gasparov, Robert P. Hughes, and Irina Paperno (Berkeley: University of California Press, 1992).

4. A journal title variously translated, but we follow the convincing argument made in Ronald E. Peterson, "*Vesy*: Its Zodiacal Title," *SEEJ*, 28.1 (1984), 89–92.

5. For a rich discussion of this and other book covers produced by Skorpion, see Jonathan Stone, *The Institutions of Russian Modernism: Conceptualizing, Publishing, and Reading Symbolism* (Evanston, IL: Northwestern University Press, 2017), ch. 5.

6. Olga Matich, *Erotic Utopia: The Decadent Imagination in Russia's Fin de Siècle* (Madison: University of Wisconsin Press, 2005), 213.

7. Clarence Brown, *Mandelstam* (Cambridge: Cambridge University Press, 1973), 38.

8. Avril Pyman, *The Life of Aleksandr Blok*, 2 vols. (Oxford: Oxford University Press, 1979), vol. 1, 228–9.

9. Raymond Cooke, *Velimir Khlebnikov: A Critical Study* (Cambridge: Cambridge University Press, 1987), 6.

10. John E. Malmstad and Nikolay Bogomolov, *Mikhail Kuzmin: A Life in Art* (Cambridge, MA: Harvard University Press, 1999), 20; on Kuzmin's early training in music and his early compositions, see 20–4.

11. For a recreation of the culture and poetry of the café, see *The Stray Dog Cabaret: A Book of Russian Poems*, trans. Paul Schmidt, ed. Catherine Ciepiela and Honor Moore (New York: New York Review of Books, 2007), and see the Introduction by Catherine Ciepiela, vii–xxiii.

12. On OBERIU performances, see A. Dmitrenko and Valerii Sazhin, "Kratkaia istoriia 'chinarei,'" in "*. . . Sborishche druzei, ostavlennykh sud'boiu": "Chinari" v tekstakh, dokumentakh i issledovaniiakh*, ed. Valerii Sazhin, 2 vols. (Moscow: Ladomir, 2000), vol. 1, 5–45, esp. 37–40; Aleksandr Kobrinskii, *Daniil Kharms* (Moscow: Molodaia gvardiia, 2008), 107–15, 145–57; and Valerii Shubinskii, *Daniil Kharms: Zhizn' cheloveka na vetru* (St. Petersburg: Vita Nova, 2008), 249–81.

13. See Barbara Walker, *Max Voloshin and the Russian Literary Circle* (Bloomington: Indiana University Press, 2005).

14. See John E. Bowlt, *Moscow and St. Petersburg 1900–1920: Art, Life, and Culture of the Russian Silver Age* (New York: Vendome Press, 2008).

15. Aleksandr Bogdanov's ideas are well presented in his book *O proletarskoi kul'ture, 1904–1924* (Leningrad and Moscow: Kniga, 1924), esp. 104–41.

16. Evgeny Dobrenko describes the history of "proletarian literature" and the surrounding ideological debates in *The Making of the State Writer: Social and Aesthetic Origins of Soviet Literary Culture* (Stanford, CA: Stanford University Press, 2001), 61–115. He argues that the main reason for Lenin's opposition to Proletkult was that "in Bogdanov's class purism, no role was allotted to a 'socialist state' or a political party" (80).

17. See Edward Brown, *The Proletarian Episode in Russian Literature, 1928–32* (New York: Columbia University Press, 1953); Evgeny Dobrenko, "Literary Criticism and the Transformations of the Literary Field during the Cultural Revolution, 1928–32," in *A History of Russian Literary Theory and Criticism: The Soviet Age and Beyond*, ed. Evgeny Dobrenko and Galin Tihanov (Pittsburgh, PA: University of Pittsburgh Press, 2011), 43–52; Natalia Kornienko, "Literary Criticism and Cultural Policy during the New Economic Policy, 1921–27," in *A History of Russian Literary Theory and Criticism*, ed. Dobrenko and Tihanov, 34–8; and Evgeny Dobrenko, *Aesthetics of Alienation: Reassessment of Early Soviet Cultural Theories* (Evanston, IL: Northwestern University Press, 2005), 10–51.

18. On the LEF aesthetic program, see Mariia Zalambani, *Literatura fakta: Ot avangarda k sotsrealizmu* (St. Petersburg: Akademicheskii proekt, 2006); Kornienko, "Literary Criticism and Cultural Policy," 30–3; and Dobrenko, *Aesthetics of Alienation*, 52–74.

19. On the Pereval Aesthetic program, see Galina Belaia, *Don Kikhoty 20-kh godov: "Pereval" i sud'ba ego idei* (Moscow: Sovetskii pisatel', 1989); and Dobrenko, *Aesthetics of Alienation*, 75–88.

20. See Robert A. Maguire, *Red Virgin Soil and Soviet Literature of the 1920s*, 2nd edn. (Evanston, IL: Northwestern University Press, 2000).

21. *Literaturnye manifesty: Ot simvolizma do "Oktiabria,"* ed. N. L. Brodskii and N. Smirnov (Moscow: Agraf, 2000, reprint of the 1924 edition), 314. For more on the Serapion Brothers, see Boris Frezinskii, *Sud'by Serapionov (portrety i siuzhety)* (St. Petersburg: Akademicheskii proekt, 2003).

22. See Il'ia Kukulin, "Lirika sovetskoi sub"ektivnosti," in *Russkaia literatura XX veka: 1930-e gody–seredina 1950-kh godov*, ed. Naum Leiderman, Mark Lipovetskii, and Mariia Litovskaia, 2 vols. (Moscow: Academia, 2014), vol. 1, 108–18.

23. For further discussion and additional bibliography, see Andrew Kahn, "Poetry of the Revolution," in *Twentieth-Century Russian Literature*, ed. Evgeny Dobrenko and Marina Balina (Cambridge: Cambridge University Press, 2011), 41–58.

24. Both 1884 and 1887 are attested in multiple sources as the year of Kliuev's birth. Michael Makin treats the discrepancies and acts of mythmaking that amplified them in *Nikolai Klyuev: Time and Text, Place and Poet* (Evanston, IL: Northwestern University Press, 2010), 14. We follow Makin and others in giving the birthdate as 1884.

25. See A. I. Mikhailov, *Puti razvitiia novokrest'ianskoi poezii* (Leningrad: Nauka, 1990).

26. See Razumnik Ivanov-Razumnik, "Dve Rossii," *Skify*, 2 (1918), 204–30.

27. On the era's debates and theories, see Kornienko, "Literary Criticism and Cultural Policy"; Caryl Emerson, "Literary Theory in the 1920s: Four Options and a Practicum," in *A History of Russian Literary Theory and Criticism*, ed. Dobrenko and Tihanov, 17–42, 64–89.

28. Among early works on Formalism, most valuable are Victor Erlich, *Russian Formalism: History—Doctrine*, 3rd edn. (New Haven, CT: Yale University Press, 1981); Aage A. Hansen-Löve, *Der russische Formalismus: Methodologische Rekonstruktion seiner Entwicklung aus dem Prinzip der Verfremdung* (Vienna: Verlag der österreichischen Akademie der Wissenschaften, 1978); and Peter Steiner, *Russian Formalism: A Metapoetics* (Ithaca, NY: Cornell University Press, 1984). More recent works include Ian Levchenko, *Drugaia nauka: Russkie formalisty v poiskakh biografii* (Moscow: Izd. dom Vysshei shkoly ekonomiki, 2012); Sergei Ushakin, *Formal'nyi metod: Antologiia russkogo modernizma*, 3 vols. (Ekaterinburg: Kabinetnyi uchenyi, 2015–16); Il'ia Kalinin, "Vernut': veshchi, plat'e, mebel', zhenu i strakh voiny. Viktor Shklovskii mezhdu novym bytom i teoriei ostraneniia," in *Nähe Schaffen, Abstand Halten. Zur Geschichte der Intimität in der Russischen Kultur*, ed. Nadezhda Grigor'eva, Schamma Schahadat, and Igor' Smirnov, special issue of *Wiener Slawistischer Almanach*, 62 (2005), 351–87.

29. See Hilary Fink, *Bergson and Russian Modernism 1910–1930* (Evanston, IL: Northwestern University Press, 1999); and Dragan Kujundzic, *The Returns of History: Russian Nietzscheans after Modernity* (New York: SUNY Press, 1997).

30. Boris Eikhenbaum, "Teoriia 'formal'nogo metoda,'" in Boris Eikhenbaum, *O literature: Raboty raznykh let* (Moscow: Sovetskii pisatel', 1987), 375–408, quotation on 385.

31. See Svetlana Boym, "Poetics and Politics of Estrangement: Viktor Shklovsky and Hannah Arendt," *Poetics Today*, 26.4 (2005), 581–611; Carlo Ginzburg, "Making it Strange: The Prehistory of a Literary Device," in Carlo Ginzburg, *Wooden Eyes: Nine Reflections on Distance*, trans. Martin Ryle and Kate Soper (New York: Columbia University Press, 2001), 1–24; Galin Tihanov, "The Politics of Estrangement: The Case of the Early Shklovsky," *Poetics Today*, 26.4 (2005), 665–96; Cristina Vatulescu, "The Politics of Estrangement: Tracking Shklovsky's Device through Literary and Policing Practices," *Poetics Today*, 27.1 (2006), 35–66; and Evgenii Soshkin, "Priemy ostraneniia: Opyt unifikatsii," *NLO*, 114 (2012), http://www.nlobooks.ru/node/2003 (last accessed February 17, 2017).

32. See Il'ia Kalinin, "Istorichnost' travmaticheskogo opyta: Rutina, revoliutsiia, reprezentatsiia," *NLO*, 124 (2013), http://www.nlobooks.ru/node/4145 (last accessed November 2, 2016).

33. These many dimensions of Bakhtin's thought are addressed in a block of articles entitled "Konteksty Bakhtina," *NLO*, 79 (2006), 7–85.

34. Mikhail Bakhtin, *The Dialogic Imagination: Four Essays*, ed. Michael Holquist, trans. Caryl Emerson and Michael Holquist (Austin: University of Texas Press, 2004), xviii.

35. Michael Holquist, *Dialogism: Bakhtin and His World* (New York: Routledge, 1990), 69.

36. Gary Saul Morson and Caryl Emerson, *Mikhail Bakhtin: Creation of a Prosaics* (Stanford, CA: Stanford University Press, 1990), 139.

37. M. M. Bakhtin, *Sobranie sochinenii v semi tomakh* (Moscow: Russkie slovari, 1996–2012). Despite the title, the collection was completed in six volumes.

38. For an indispensable overview, see Craig Brandist, *The Bakhtin Circle: Philosophy, Culture, Politics* (London: Pluto Press, 2002).

39. See, for example, Ken Hirschkop, *Mikhail Bakhtin: An Aesthetic for Democracy* (Oxford: Oxford University Press, 1999); *Bakhtin and Cultural Theory*, ed. Ken Hirschkop and David Shepherd, 2nd edn. (Manchester: Manchester University Press, 2001).

40. On that darker view of Bakhtin, see Caryl Emerson, "Afterword on the Dark and Radiant Bakhtin," *SEEJ*, 61.2 (2017), 299–310. An exemplary fragmentary text from the war period has appeared in English translation: "Bakhtin on Shakespeare: Excerpts from 'Additions and Changes to *Rabelais*,'" trans. and intro. Sergeiy Sandler, *PMLA*, 129.3 (May, 2014), 522–37; see also Mikhail Bakhtin, "Selections from the Wartime Notebook," trans. Irina Denischenko and Alexander Spektor, *SEEJ*, 61:2 (Summer 2017), 201–32.

41. Marc Raeff, *Russia Abroad: A Cultural History of the Russian Emigration 1919–1939* (New York: Oxford University Press, 1990), 73. Raeff offers a comprehensive account of the history of the several million refugees who fled post-Revolutionary Russia. Compact descriptions of émigré journals and intellectual trends can be found in Boris Lanin, "Experiment and Emigration: Russian Literature 1917–1953," in *The Routledge Companion to Russian Literature*, ed. Neil Cornwell (London and New York: Routledge, 2002), 135–42.

42. See Robert C. Williams, *Culture in Exile: Russian Emigres in Germany, 1881–1941* (Ithaca, NY: Cornell University Press, 1972), 111, 144. See also Oleg Budnitskii and Aleksandr Polian, *Russko-evreiskii Berlin (1920–1941)* (Moscow: NLO, 2013).

43. An attempt to theorize the features of the community is K. Shlegel′, "Russkii Berlin: Popytka podkhoda," in *Russkii Berlin 1920–1945*, ed. M. A. Vasil′eva and L. S. Fleishman (Moscow: Russkii put′, 2006), 9–19.

44. For a description and memoirs by participants, see Iurii Aikhenval′d, "Dom iskusstv v Berline," in *Russkii Berlin*, ed. V. V. Sorokina (Moscow: Izd-vo Moskovskogo universiteta, 2003), 74–97.

45. As observed by Raeff in *Russia Abroad*, 75.

46. As detailed in Simon Karlinsky, *Marina Tsvetaeva: The Woman, Her World, and Her Poetry* (Cambridge: Cambridge University Press, 1985), 117.

47. Reprinted in *Russkii Berlin*, ed. Sorokina, 138.

48. Richard Sheldon, "Shklovsky's *Zoo* and Russian Berlin," *Russian Review*, 29.3 (1970), 262–74; quotation on 270.

49. Valentina Khodasevich (a famous artist and Vladislav's niece) describes with mild irony Shklovsky's ardent courtship and the circumstances of the meeting: see her *Portrety slovami*, excerpted in *Russkii Berlin*, ed. Sorokina, 264.

50. *Zoo* went on to create its own unconventional legacy: in 1998, the American filmmaker Jackie Ochs made a film about the Petersburg poet Arkady Dragomoshchenko and the American LANGUAGE poet Lyn Hejinian, entitled *Letters Not About Love*, recycling not only Shklovsky's subtitle but also his idea of using epistolary exchange as a means to write around the topic of love.

51. Leonid Livak, *How It Was Done in Paris: Russian Émigré Literature and French Modernism* (Madison: University of Wisconsin Press, 2003), 5.

52. As noted in a review of the Ardis volume by Marc Raeff, "The Swan Song of an Émigré Journal," *Russian Review*, 43.3 (1984), 277–83. One might add that another contributor to *Contemporary Notes* was the nationalist Ivan Il′in, who greeted Nazism more enthusiastically.

53. For a concise history of the journal, see Raeff, *Russians Abroad*, 86–90.

54. On his death, see Iurii Terapiano, "Boris Poplavskii," *Literaturnaia zhizn′ russkogo Parizha za polveka* (Jersey City, NJ: Albatross and Third Wave Publishers, 1986), 217–21. Compare Terapiano's apologetic account of Poplavsky as a murder victim to the nuanced reading of self-mythologizing martyrdom and well-planned "Christian" suicide in Livak, *How It Was Done in*

Paris, 82–9. Simon Karlinsky lauded Poplavsky as the outstanding poet of the emigration in "Surrealism in Twentieth-Century Russian Poetry: Churilin, Poplavskii, Zabolotskii," *Slavic Review*, 26.4 (1967), 605–17.

55. Livak, *How It Was Done in Paris*, 45.

56. Sergei Kibal'nik, *Gaito Gazdanov i ekzistentsial'naia traditsiia v russkoi literature* (St. Petersburg: Petropolis, 2012).

57. As a result of Robert Chandler's efforts, translations of Teffi have now appeared in English, including *Subtly Worded*, trans. Robert Chandler and Anne Marie Jackson (London: Pushkin Press, 2014); *Memories: From Moscow to the Black Sea*, trans. Robert Chandler, Elizabeth Chandler, Anne Marie Jackson, and Irina Steinberg (New York: New York Review Books, 2014). See also Robert Chandler, "Stepping across the Ice: Teffi (1872–1952)," *The New Yorker*, September 25, 2014, http://www.newyorker.com/books/page-turner/stepping-across-ice-teffi-1872-1952 (last accessed November 2, 2016).

58. Georgii Adamovich, *Odinochestvo i svoboda*, ed. O. A. Korostelev (St. Petersburg: Aleteia, 2002).

59. Irina Kaspe, *Iskusstvo otsutstvovat': nezamechennoe pokolenie russkoi literatury* (Moscow: NLO, 2005); Vadim Kreid, "Chto takoe 'Parizhskaia nota,'" *Slovo*, 43–44 (2004), http://magazines.russ.ru/slovo/2004/43/kr41.html (last accessed November 2, 2016).

60. On Knorring, Chervinskaia, and other women poets of the Paris emigration, see Catherine Ciepiela, "The Women of Russian Montparnasse," in *A History of Women's Writing in Russia*, ed. Adele Marie Barker and Jehanne M. Gheith (Cambridge: Cambridge University Press, 2002), 117–33. Chinnov's account of his own career can be found in *Conversations in Exile: Russian Writers Abroad*, ed. John Glad (Durham, NC: Duke University Press, 1993), 31–8.

61. On their polemic, see David M. Bethea, *Khodasevich: His Life and Art* (Princeton, NJ: Princeton University Press, 1983), 322–32.

62. On Bunin's writings, see Thomas Gaiton Marullo, *If You See the Buddha: Studies in the Fiction of Ivan Bunin* (Evanston, IL: Northwestern University Press, 1998); and Andrei Shcherbenok, *Dekonstruktsiia i klassicheskaia russkaia literatura: ot ritoriki teksta k ritorike istorii* (Moscow: NLO, 2005), 115–42.

63. In a 1925 inscription to him on her poem *The Swain* (*Molodets*, 1922), as noted in Greta N. Slobin, *Russians Abroad: Literary and Cultural Politics of Diaspora (1919–1939)*, ed. Katerina Clark, Nancy Condee, Dan Slobin, and Mark Slobin (Boston: Academic Studies Press, 2013), 57.

64. The contrast of plain brown paper to decorative border is noted in Greta Nachtailer Slobin, "The Writer as Artist," in *Images of Aleksei Remizov: Drawings and Handwritten and Illustrated Albums from the Thomas P. Whitney Collection* (Amherst, MA: Mead Art Museum, 1985), 13–24, see 17.

65. On the role of Ardis in the history of Russian literature, see the cluster of articles in *NLO*, 125 (2014), www.nlobooks.ru//node/4517 (last accessed November 2, 2016). In 2002, Overlook Press bought Ardis's list and reissued some of its translated titles. Its website includes a capsule history of Ardis: http://www.overlookpress.com/ardis.html (last accessed November 2, 2016).

66. We were unable to secure the rights to reproduce the photograph, taken by Leonid Lubianitsky, but it can be found easily on the web, for example, http://beautifulrus.com/mikhail-baryshnikov-silent-genius/brodsky-baryshnikov-and-rostropovich-performing/ (last accessed April 14, 2017).

67. Some are treated in Adrian Wanner's *Out of Russia: Fictions of a New Translingual Diaspora* (Evanston, IL: Northwestern University Press, 2011). See also Adrian Vanner, "Troinaia identichnost': russkoiazychnye evrei—nemetskie, amerikanskie i izrail'skie pisateli," *NLO*, 127 (2014), http://magazines.russ.ru/nlo/2014/3/11v.html (last accessed November 2, 2016).

68. Some Russian native speakers such as Eugene Hütz and his group Gogol Bordello, and the anti-folk singer Regina Spektor, have also enjoyed success performing their own compositions in English.

69. Robert Maguire charted that process in his study of a single journal, *Red Virgin Soil*.

70. *Soviet Culture and Power: A History in Documents, 1917–1953*, ed. Katerina Clark and Evgeny Dobrenko (New Haven, CT and London: Yale University Press, 2007), 152.

71. *Soviet Culture and Power*, ed. Clark and Dobrenko, 152.

72. *Pervyi Vsesoiuznyi s"ezd sovetskikh pisatelei: Stenograficheskii otchet* (Moscow: Sovetskii pisatel', 1990; reprint of the 1934 edition), 1.

73. *Pervyi Vsesoiuznyi s"ezd sovetskikh pisatelei*, 17.

74. *Pervyi Vsesoiuznyi s"ezd sovetskikh pisatelei*, 11.

75. *Pervyi Vsesoiuznyi s"ezd sovetskikh pisatelei*, 4.

76. All quoted in *Soviet Culture and Power*, ed. Clark and Dobrenko, 169.

77. *Vlast' i khudozhestvennaia intelligentsiia. Dokumenty TsK RKP(b)-VKP(b), VChK-OGPU-NKVD o kul'turnoi politike, 1917–1953*, ed. A. N. Iakovlev, A. N. Artizov, and O. V. Naumov (Moscow: Mezdunarodnyi fond "Demokratiia," 1999), 231.

78. Documented examples of *prorabotka* are analyzed in Oleg Kharkhordin, *Oblichat' i litsemerit': Genealogiia rossiiskoi lichnosti* (St. Petersburg and Moscow: Evropeiskii universitet v Sankt-Peterburge, Letnii sad, 2002), 141–200; Mikhail Zolotonosov, *Okhota na Berggol'ts. Leningrad 1937* (St. Petersburg: Mir, 2015).

79. On the historical role of the 1929 rebuke of Zamiatin and Pil'niak, see Aleksandr Galushkin, "'Delo Pil'niaka i Zamiatina.' Predvaritel'nye itogi rassledovaniia," *Novoe o Zamiatine*, ed. Leonid Geller (Moscow: MIK, 1997), 89–146.

The Shakhty Affair (1928) was one of the precursors of the Great Terror: charges were fabricated against a group of engineers at the Donbass mines. At the Moscow show trial, the engineers were accused of economic counterrevolution and the creation of an underground anti-Soviet organization. Eleven defendants were executed, others incarcerated for decades.

80. Galushkin, "'Delo Pil'niaka,'" 139.

81. Such a campaign at Leningrad State University is described in Petr Druzhinin, *Ideologiia i filologiia. Leningrad, 1940-e gody: Dokumental'noe issledovanie*, 2 vols. (Moscow: NLO, 2012).

82. Boris Iampolskii, "Posledniaia vstrecha s Vasiliem Grossmanom," *Kontinent*, 151 (2012), http://magazines.russ.ru/continent/2012/151/ia12.html (last accessed November 2, 2016).

83. In *Tsena metafory, ili Prestuplenie i nakazanie Siniavskogo i Danielia*, ed. E. M. Velikanova (Moscow: Kniga, 1989), 516.

84. For unofficial histories of the Writers' Union, incorporating rumors and legends, see Benedikt Sarnov, *Perestan'te udivliat'sia!* (Moscow: Agraf, 2006); Benedikt Sarnov, *Stalin i pisateli*, 4 vols. (Moscow: Eksmo, 2008–11); and Benedikt Sarnov, *Esli by Pushkin zhil v nashe vremia* (Moscow: Agraf, 1998).

85. Denis Kozlov and Eleonory Gilburd, "The Thaw as an Event in Russian History," in *The Thaw: Soviet Society and Culture during the 1950s and 1960s*, ed. Denis Kozlov and Eleonory Gilburd (Toronto, Buffalo, NY, and London: University of Toronto Press, 2013), 18–81, quotation on 32.

86. *Russia's Sputnik Generation: Soviet Baby Boomers Talk about Their Lives*, ed. and trans. Donald J. Raleigh (Bloomington: Indiana University Press, 2006), 7. See also Ludmilla Alexeyeva, *The Thaw Generation: Coming of Age in the Post-Stalin Era* (Pittsburgh, PA: University of Pittsburgh Press, 1990); Vladislav Zubok, *Zhivago's Children: The Last Russian Intelligentsia* (Cambridge, MA: Harvard University Press, 2009); and Miriam Dobson, *Khrushchev's Cold Summer: Gulag Returnees, Crime, and the Fate of Reform after Stalin* (Ithaca, NY: Cornell University Press, 2009).

87. *The Thaw*, ed. Kozlov and Gilburd, 36.

864 | NOTES FOR PART V: CHAPTER 1, PP. 525–64

88. The most complex case, that of *Novyi mir*, has been well studied in Denis Kozlov, *The Readers of Novyi Mir: Coming to Terms with the Stalinist Past* (Cambridge, MA: Harvard University Press, 2013).

89. See Evgeny Dobrenko and Ilya Kalinin, "Literary Criticism during the Thaw," in *A History of Russian Literary Theory and Criticism*, ed. Dobrenko and Tihanov, 184–206; and Polly Jones, "The Personal and the Political: Opposition to the Thaw and the Politics of Literary Identity in the 1950s and 1960s," in *The Thaw*, ed. Kozlov and Gilburd, 235–53.

90. See Richard C. Borden, *The Art of Writing Badly: Valentin Kataev's Mauvism and the Rebirth of Russian Modernism* (Evanston, IL: Northwestern University Press, 1999); Mariia Litovskaia, *Feniks poet pered solntsem: Fenomen Valentina Kataeva* (Ekaterinburg: Ural State University Press, 1999); Mariia Litovskaia, "Tvorcheskie vozmozhnosti demonstrativnogo konformizma," *Neprikosnovennyi zapas*, 96.4 (2014), http://magazines.russ.ru/nz/2014/96/13l-pr.html (last accessed November 2, 2016); and M. Kotova and Oleg Lekmanov, *V labirintakh romana-zagadki: Kommentarii k romanu V. Kataeva "Almaznyi moi venets"* (Moscow: Agraf, 2004).

91. See Lev Loseff, *On the Beneficence of Censorship: Aesopian Language in Modern Russian Literature* (Munich: Otto Sagner, 1986), 222–3; and Irina Sandomirskaia, "Bez stali i leni: Aesopian Language and Legitimacy," in *Power and Legitimacy: Challenges from Russia*, ed. Per-Arne Bodin, Stefan Hedlund, and Elena Namli (London: Routledge, 2013), 188–98.

92. For more, see Arkadii Belinkov and Natal'ia Belinkova, *Raspria s vekom* (Moscow: NLO, 2008); Aleksandr Gol'dshtein, "Otshchepenskii 'sots-art' Belinkova," in Gol'dshtein, *Rasstavanie s Nartsissom: Opyty pominal'noi ritoriki* (Moscow: NLO, 1997), 242–59.

93. See Polly Jones, "The Fire Burns On? The *Fiery Revolutionaries* Biographical Series and the Rethinking of Propaganda in the Early Brezhnev Era," *Slavic Review*, 74.1 (2015), 32–56.

94. As argued in Anindita Banerjee, *We Modern People: Science Fiction and the Making of Russian Modernity* (Middletown, CT: Wesleyan University Press, 2012).

95. On science fiction of the 1950s and 1960s, see Matthias Schwartz, *Die Erfindung des Kosmos. Zur sowjetischen Science Fiction und populärwissenschaftlichen Publizistik vom Sputnikflug bis zum Ende der Tauwetterzeit* (Frankfurt: Peter Lang, 2004); and Irina Kaspe, "Taina Temnoi planety, ili Kak uverovat' v budushchee: o 'Tumannosti Andromedy' Ivana Efremova," *Neprikosnovennyi zapas*, 99.1 (2015), http://magazines.russ.ru/nz/2015/99/14k.html (last accessed November 2, 2016).

96. Collections of quasi-nonfictional anecdotes show that the contempt among non-conformists and later émigrés toward the liberal wing of Soviet literature was even more intense than toward officialdom. Sources include Sergei Dovlatov, *Zapisnye knizhki* (St. Petersburg: Iskusstvo, 1992) and Dovlatov, *Ne tol'ko Brodskii: russkaia kul'tura v portretakh i anekdotakh* (Moscow: RIK "Kul'tura," 1992).

97. On the political and ideological institutions of this circle, see Nikolai Mitrokhin, *Russkaia partiia: Dvizhenie russkikh natsionalistov v SSSR, 1953–1985* (Moscow: NLO, 2003).

98. On the nationalist literary criticism in the "long 1970s," see *A History of Russian Literary Theory and Criticism*, ed. Dobrenko and Tikhanov, 209–13.

99. See Galina Belaia, *Literatura v zerkale kritiki: Sovremennye problemy* (Moscow: Sovetskii pisatel', 1988), 31–5; and Kathleen F. Parthé, *Russian Village Prose: The Radiant Past* (Princeton, NJ: Princeton University Press, 1992).

100. Despite his split with nationalist peers in the 1980s, Astaf'ev engaged in a public dispute with Natan Eidel'man that left him open to charges of anti-Semitism. See Konstantin Azadovskii, "Perepiska iz dvukh uglov Imperii," *Voprosy literatury*, 5 (2003), http://magazines.russ.ru/voplit/2003/5/azadov.html (last accessed November 2, 2016).

101. Ann Komaromi, *Uncensored: Samizdat Novels and the Quest for Autonomy in Soviet Dissidence* (Evanston, IL: Northwestern University Press, 2015), 1–25, 129–53; Komaromi, "Samizdat and

Soviet Dissident Publics," *Slavic Review*, 71.1 (2012), 70–90. See also Stanislav Savitskii, *Andegraund: Istoriia i mify leningradskoi neofitsial'noi literatury* (Moscow: NLO, 2002).

102. On the transmediality of *samizdat* see *Samizdat, Tamizdat, and Beyond: Transnational Media during and after Socialism*, ed. Friederike Kind-Kovács and Jesse Labov (Oxford: Berghahn Books, 2013).

103. On the bards' poetry and *magnitizdat*, see Rachel Platonov, *Singing the Self: Guitar Poetry, Community, and Identity in the Post-Stalinist Period* (Evanston, IL: Northwestern University Press, 2012); and Rossen Djagalov, "Avtorskaia pesnia kak zhanrovaia laboratoriia 'sotsializma s chelovecheskim litsom,'" trans. Aleksandr Skidan, *NLO*, 6 (2009), 204–15.

104. For the variety of interpretations of the term "underground," see Savitskii, *Andegraund*, 31–51.

105. An excellent resource is the encyclopedia *Samizdat Leningrada: 1950-e–1980-e*, ed. D. Severiukhin (Moscow: NLO, 2003). See also *Istoriia leningradskoi nepodtsenzurnoi literatury: 1950–1980-e gody*, ed. B. I. Ivanov and B. A. Roginskii (St. Petersburg: Izdatel'stvo DEAN, 2000).

106. Alexei Yurchak, *Everything Was Forever, Until It Was No More: The Last Soviet Generation* (Princeton, NJ: Princeton University Press, 2006), 145.

107. Andrei Sergeev, *Omnibus: Roman, rasskazy, vospominaniia, stikhi* (Moscow: NLO, 2013); the novel-memoir, *Al'bom dlia marok*, included in *Omnibus*, was first published in 1997, and has been translated into English: *Stamp Album: A Collection of People, Things, Relationships, and Words*, trans. Joanne Turnbull (Moscow: Glas, 2002).

108. Joseph Brodsky, "An Appeal for Vladimir Maramzin," *New York Review of Books*, September 19, 1974, http://www.nybooks.com/articles/1974/09/19/an-appeal-for-vladimir-maramzin (last accessed November 2, 2016).

109. Vladimir Shinkarev, "Mit'ki," trans. Rebecca Pyatkevich, in *Late and Post-Soviet Russian Literature: Thaw and Stagnation (1954–1986)*, ed. Mark Lipovetsky and Lisa Ryoko Wakamiya (Boston, MA: Academic Studies Press, 2015), 586–7.

110. Yurchak, *Everything Was Forever*, 242.

111. For key Conceptualist terms, see *Slovar' terminov Moskovskogo kontseptualizma*, ed. Andrei Monastyrskii (Moscow: Ad Marginem, 1999).

112. Irina Balabanova, *Govorit Dmitrii Aleksandrovich Prigov* (Moscow: OGI, 2001), 47.

113. Jean-François Lyotard, "From *The Postmodern Condition: A Report on Knowledge*," in *The Postmodernism Reader: Foundational Texts*, ed. Michael Drolet (London and New York: Routledge, 2004), 123.

114. Dmitrii Prigov, *Raznoobrazie vsego* (Moscow: OGI, 2007), 213.

115. See Marina Grishakova and Silvi Salupere, "A School in the Woods: Tartu–Moscow Semiotics," *Theoretical Schools and Circles in the Twentieth-Century Humanities: Literary Theory, History, Philosophy*, ed. Marina Grishakova and Silvi Salupere (New York: Routledge, 2015), 173–95.

116. An essay that is often regarded as a point of origin for Soviet semiotics, and still a good place to start understanding the Moscow-Tartu School, is V. V. Ivanov, Iu. M. Lotman, A. M. Piatigorskii, V. N. Toporov, and B. A. Uspenskii, "Tezisy k semioticheskomu izucheniiu kul'tur (v primenenii k slavianskim tekstam)," in *Semiotyka i struktura tekstu* (Wrocław: Zakład Narodowy im. Ossolińskich, 1973), 9–32. Translation into English was immediate: "Theses on the Semiotic Study of Cultures (as Applied to Slavic Texts)," in *Structure of Texts and Semiotics of Culture*, ed. J. van der Eng and M. Grygar (The Hague: Mouton, 1973), 1–28.

117. Lotman's landmark book on structuralist poetics was first delivered as lectures in Tartu, by 1962. It appeared as "Lektsii po struktural'noi poetike, vyp. I (Vvedenie, teoriia stikha)," *Uchenye zapiski Tartuskogo gosudarstvennogo universiteta*, 160 (1964), and became available in the West in a reprint from Brown University in 1968.

118. Many of the names and dates are documented in Maxim Waldstein, *The Soviet Empire of Signs: A History of the Tartu School of Semiotics* (Saarbrücken: VDM Verlag Dr. Müller, 2008); see esp. the chart of key figures, 188–90.

119. On *Sotvorenie Karamzina* and for a reappraisal of Lotman's legacy, see Marina Grishakova, "Afterword: Around Culture and Explosion: J. Lotman and the Tartu-Moscow School in the 1980–90s," in Juri Lotman, *Culture and Explosion*, trans. Wilma Clark, ed. Marina Grishakova (Berlin: Mouton de Gruyter, 2009), 177–8. Lotman's Pushkin scholarship made use of similar principles to provide a richer social and cultural context for understanding the emergence of Russia's national poet.

120. First presented in Iu. Lotman, "O semiosfere," *Trudy po znakovym sistemam*, 17 (1984), 5–23; see also Iu. Lotman, *Universe of the Mind: A Semiotic Theory of Culture*, trans. Ann Shukman (Bloomington: Indiana University Press, 1990).

121. A. K. Zholkovskii and Iu. K. Shcheglov, *Mir avtora i struktura teksta: Stat'i o russkoi literature* (Tenafly, NJ: Hermitage Press, 1986).

122. The major theoretical statement is Iurii I. Levin, Dmitrii M. Segal, Roman D. Timenchik, Vladimir N. Toporov, and Tatiana V. Tsiv'ian, "Russkaia semanticheskaia poetika kak potentsial'naia kul'turnaia paradigma," *Russian Literature*, 7–8 (1974), 47–82. A number of other essays appeared in *Russian Literature*, in the *Uchenye zapiski* for the University of Tartu, and in small anthologies of essays published in Tartu, Riga, Moscow, and eventually Jerusalem.

123. B. M. Gasparov, "Tartuskaia shkola 1960-kh godov kak semioticheskii fenomen," in *Iu. M. Lotman i tartusko-moskovskaia semioticheskaia shkola*, ed. A. D. Koshelov (Moscow: Gnozis, 1994 [1989]), 279–94, quotation on 281.

124. That work has of course begun, as several works already cited suggest. See also Il'ia Kalinin, "Tartusko-moskovskaia semioticheskaia shkola: semioticheskaia model' kul'tury / kul'turnaia model' semiotiki," *NLO*, 98 (2009), http://magazines.russ.ru/nlo/2009/98/ka6.html (last accessed November 2, 2016); and Aleksei Semenenko, *The Texture of Culture: An Introduction to Yuri Lotman's Semiotic Theory* (New York: Palgrave Macmillan, 2012).

125. For a comprehensive analysis of Perestroika-period literature about Stalinism, see Margaret Ziolkowski, *Literary Exorcisms of Stalinism: Russian Writers and the Soviet Past* (Rochester, NY: Camden House, 1998); and Rosalind Marsh, *History and Literature in Contemporary Russia* (New York: NYU Press, 1995).

126. Anna Razuvalova, *Pisateli-"derevenshchiki": Literatura i konservativnaia ideologiia 1970-kh godov* (Moscow: NLO, 2015), 420. See also Ol'ga Slavnikova, "Derevenskaia proza lednikovogo perioda," *Novyi mir*, 2 (1999), 198–207; and Maxim Shrayer, "Anti-Semitism and the Decline of Russian Village Prose," *Partisan Review*, 67.3 (2000), 474–85.

127. Boris Dubin, *Slovo—pis'mo—literatura: Ocherki po sotsiologii sovremennoi kul'tury* (Moscow: NLO, 2001), 181.

128. Viktor Erofeev, "Pominki po sovetskoi literature," first published in *Literaturnaia gazeta*, 27, July 4, 1990, 8.

129. See *Reading for Entertainment in Contemporary Russia: Post-Soviet Popular Literature in Historical Perspective*, ed. Stephen Lovell and Birgit Menzel (Munich: Otto Sagner, 2005); Natal'ia Kupina, Mariia Litovskaia, and N. A. Nikolina, *Massovaia literatura segodnia* (Moscow: Flinta/Nauka, 2009); and *Celebrity and Glamour in Contemporary Russia: Shocking Chic*, ed. Helena Goscilo and Vlad Strukov (London: Routledge, 2011).

130. See, for example, Andrei Ranchin, "Romany B. Akunina i klassicheskaia traditsiia," *NLO*, 67 (2004), http://magazines.russ.ru/nlo/2004/67/ran14.html (last accessed November 2, 2016); Elena Baraban, "A Country Resembling Russia: The Use of History in Boris Akunin's Detective Novels," *SEEJ*, 48.3 (2004), 396–420; and G. Tsiplakov, "Zlo, voznikaiushchee v doroge, i dao

Erasta," *Novyi mir*, 11 (2001), http://magazines.russ.ru/novyi_mi/2001/11/ciip.html (last accessed November 2, 2016).

131. See Eliot Borenstein, *Overkill: Sex and Violence in Contemporary Russian Popular Fiction* (Ithaca, NY: Cornell University Press, 2007), 195–239.

132. On socio-cultural processes of the early 2000s, see Lev Gudkov, "Russkii neotraditsionalizm i soprotivlenie peremenam," in Gudkov, *Negativnaia identichnost': Stat'i 1997–2002 godov* (Moscow: NLO; VTsIOM-A, 2004), 552–649.

133. Natal'ia Ivanova, "Svobodnaia i svoenravnaia—ili bessmyslennaia i umiraiushchaia? Zametki ob opredeleniiakh sovremennoi slovesnosti," *Znamia*, 7 (2012), http://magazines.russ.ru/znamia/2012/7/i14.html (last accessed November 2, 2016).

134. Igor' Gulin, "Dva polia," *Openspace.ru*, February 1, 2012, http://os.colta.ru/literature/projects/30291/details/33946/ (last accessed August 15, 2017). In 2009, Ilya Kukulin made a similar observation, arguing that new poetry had become more responsible for cultural innovation than prose; see Il'ia Kukulin, "Obmen roliami," *Openspace.ru*, April 27, 2009, http://os.colta.ru/literature/projects/9533/details/9536/ (last accessed August 15, 2017).

135. See Boris Dubin, *Klassika posle i riadom: Sotsiologicheskie ocherki o literature i kul'ture* (Moscow: NLO, 2010), 280.

136. Many of their publications are linked through http://www.trans-lit.info. See also the work of allied philosophers and theorists, for example Keti Chukhrov, *Byt' i ispolniat': Proekt teatra v filosofskoi kritike iskusstva* (St. Petersburg: Izd. Evropeiskogo universiteta, 2011); and Artem Magun, *Otritsatel'naia revoliutsiia* (St. Petersburg: Izdatel'stvo Evropeiskogo universiteta, 2008).

137. Aleksandr Skidan, "Tezisy k politizatsii iskusstva," *Rastorzhenie* (Moscow: Russkii Gulliver, 2010 [2003]), 214.

138. Kirill Medvedev, "Beyond the Poetics of Privatization," trans. Keith Gessen, *New Left Review*, 82 (2013), 65–83.

139. The web addresses are vavilon.ru, litkarta.ru, postnonfiction.org, and textonly.ru.

140. For a broader historical context, see Henrike Schmidt, K. Teubener, and N. Konradova, *Control + Shift. Public and Private Usages of the Russian Internet* (Norderstedt: BOD-Verlag, 2006); Sergei Kostyrko, "Russkii literaturnyi internet: nachalo," *Novyi zhurnal*, 263 (2011), http://magazines.russ.ru/nj/2011/263/k022.html (last accessed November 2, 2016); and Sergei Kuznetsov, *Oshchupyvaia slona: Zametki po istorii russkogo interneta* (Moscow: NLO, 2004).

141. See also *Digital Russia: The Language, Culture and Politics of New Media Communication*, ed. Michael Gorham, Ingunn Lunde, and Martin Paulsen (London: Routledge, 2014); and *Russkii iazyk i novye tekhnologii*, ed. Gasan Guseinov, M. V. Akhmetova, and V. I. Belikova (Moscow: NLO, 2014).

Chapter 2

1. Michel Foucault, "The Subject and Power," *Critical Inquiry*, 8.4 (Summer 1982), 777–95, quotation on 781.

2. Iurii Tynianov, *Poetika. Istoriia literatury. Kino* (Moscow: Nauka, 1977), 118.

3. Nikolai Bogomolov, "Prose between Symbolism and Realism," in *The Cambridge Companion to Twentieth-Century Russian Literature*, ed. Evgeny Dobrenko and Marina Balina (Cambridge: Cambridge University Press, 2011), 21–40, esp. 22–3.

4. Still valuable as a major study of the poet is Vsevolod Setchkarev, *Studies in the Life and Work of Innokentij Annenskij* (The Hague: Mouton, 1963). Important subsequent work includes Anna Ljundgren, *At the Crossroads of Russian Modernism: Innokentij Annenskij's Poetics* (Stockholm: Almqvist and Wiksell, 1997).

5. See Lars Kleberg, "Vjačeslav Ivanov and the Idea of Theater," in *Theater and Literature in Russia, 1900–1930*, ed. Lars Kleberg and Nils Ake-Nilsson (Stockholm: Almqvist and Wiksell, 1984), 57–70; and Jenny Stelleman, "The Essence of Religion in V. Ivanov's Concept of the Theatre," in *Theatre and Religion*, ed. Günther Ahrens and Hans-Jürgen Diller (Tübingen: Gunther Narr, 1998), 107–22.

6. On this poem, see Olga Soboleva, "On the Sound Structure of *Bacchanalia* by A. Belyi," *Slavonica*, 8.1 (2002), 20–41. For Bely's essay, see Andrei Belyi, "Lirika i eksperiment," in Andrei Belyi, *Kritika. Estetika. Teoriia simvolizma*, ed. A. L. Kazin, 2 vols. (Moscow: Iskusstvo, 1994), vol. 1, 176–226. For the poem, see A. Belyi, *Stikhotvoreniia i poemy* (Moscow-Leningrad: Sovetskii pisatel', 1966), 232.

7. See Simon Karlinsky, "Symphonic Structure in Andrej Belyj's 'Pervoe svidanie,'" *California Slavic Studies*, 6 (1971), 61–70.

8. On the impact of German Romanticism on the Russian Symbolists, see Ada Steinberg, *Word and Music in the Novels of Andrei Bely* (Cambridge: Cambridge University Press, 1982), 12–23; and Michael Wachtel, *Russian Symbolism and Literary Tradition: Goethe, Novalis, and the Poetics of Vyacheslav Ivanov* (Madison: University of Wisconsin Press, 1994).

9. For a study of the first third of the twentieth century as a repetition of and cultural response to many of the literary mechanisms of the first third of the nineteenth, see the essays collected in *Cultural Mythologies of Russian Modernism: From the Golden Age to the Silver Age*, ed. Boris Gasparov, Robert P. Hughes, and Irina Paperno (Berkeley: University of California Press, 1992).

10. Olga Matich, *Erotic Utopia: The Decadent Imagination in Russia's Fin de Siècle* (Madison: University of Wisconsin Press, 2005), 128.

11. See Dennis Ioffe, "The Avant-garde Life-Creation *sub specie* Pragmatics," *Res Philologica*, 23 (2014), 487–507.

12. For essays on specific writers as well as a valuable chronology of translations and studies in the period, see Bernice G. Rosenthal, *New Myth, New World: From Nietzsche to Stalinism* (University Park: Pennsylvania State University Press, 2002), 301–24.

13. On that side of her work, see Sarah Pratt, "Two Dialogues with Chaos: Tiutchev and Gippius," in *Cultural Mythologies of Russian Modernism*, ed. Gasparov et al., 315–26. Matich has provided a broad contextualization of the era in post-Nietzschean terms in *Erotic Utopia*. For "Pauki," see Zinaida Gippius, *Stikhotvoreniia* (St. Petersburg: Akademicheskii proekt, 1999), 139.

14. V. Ivanov, *Freedom and the Tragic Life: A Study in Dostoevsky*, trans. Norman Cameron (New York: Noonday Press, 1952), variously reprinted. On the origins and contexts for Ivanov's treatment of Dostoevsky, see Robert Bird, *The Russian Prospero: The Creative World of Viacheslav Ivanov* (Madison: University of Wisconsin Press, 2006), 28–9, 144–6.

15. V. Ivanov, *Kormchie zvezdy* (St. Petersburg: no pub., 1903); also online at http://rvb.ru/ivanov/2_ lifetime/kz/113.htm (last accessed November 2, 2016).

16. Nikolai S. Gumilev, "Acmeism and the Legacy of Symbolism," in *Selected Works of Nikolai S. Gumilev*, trans. Burton Raffel and Alla Burago (Albany: SUNY Press, 1972), 245–8, quotation on 247. For the Russian original of the essay, see N. S. Gumilev, *Pis'ma o russkoi poezii* (Moscow: Sovremennik, 1990), 55–8.

17. On the Acmeists' attention to detail, see Kirsten Painter, *Flint on a Bright Stone: A Revolution of Precision and Restraint in American, Russian, and German Modernism* (Stanford, CA: Stanford University Press, 2006).

18. Osip Mandel'shtam, "Utro akmeizma," in *Slovo i kul'tura: Stat'i* (Moscow: Sovetskii pisatel', 1987), 169.

19. Foundational works include Kirill Taranovsky, *Essays on Mandel'shtam* (Cambridge, MA: Harvard University Press, 1976), and Omry Ronen, *An Approach to Mandel'shtam* (Jerusalem: The Magnes Press, Hebrew University, 1983).

20. Sof'ia Parnok (Andrei Polianin), "Osip Mandel'shtam. *Kamen. Stikhi*," *Severnye zapiski* (April–May 1916), 242–3, http://www.synnegoria.com/tsvetaeva/WIN/silverage/parnok/mandelstam.html (last accessed November 2, 2016); Maksimilian Voloshin, "Golosa poetov," *Rech'*, 129, June 4, 1917, 3, http://az.lib.ru/w/woloshin_m_a/text_1917_golosa_poetov.shtml (last accessed November 2, 2016).

21. On this manifesto, see Clare Cavanagh, *Osip Mandelstam and the Modernist Creation of Tradition* (Princeton, NJ: Princeton University Press, 1995), 60–4; and Jane Gary Harris, *Osip Mandelstam* (Boston, MA: Twayne, 1988), 18–23.

22. For "Tristia" (1918), see Mandel'shtam, *Polnoe sobranie stikhotvorenii* (St. Petersburg: Gumanitarnoe agentstvo "Akademicheskii proekt," 1995), 146–7.

23. Boris Eikhenbaum, *Anna Akhmatova: Opyt analiza* (Petrograd: Petropechat', 1923); and see V. M. Zhirmunskii, *Tvorchestvo Anny Akhmatovoi* (Leningrad: Sovetskii pisatel', 1973).

24. For the poem, "I wrung my hands under my dark veil..." ("Szhala ruki pod temnoi vual'iu..."), see Anna Akhmatova, *Ia—golos vash...* (Moscow: Knizhnaia palata, 1989), 23. It has been translated in *Poems of Akhmatova*, trans. Stanley Kunitz with Max Hayward (Boston, MA: Little, Brown, 1973), 43.

25. For the poem see Akhmatova, *Ia—golos vash...*, 130–1.

26. A point reiterated in Painter, *Flint on a Bright Stone*, 50–1.

27. See Catriona Kelly, *A History of Russian Women's Writing, 1820–1992* (Oxford: Oxford University Press, 1994), 207–26; and Alexander Zholkovsky, "The Obverse of Stalinism: Akhmatova's Self-Serving Charisma of Selflessness," in *Self and Story in Russian History*, ed. Laura Engelstein and Stephanie Sandler (Ithaca, NY: Cornell University Press, 2000), 46–68.

28. See especially Roman Timenchik, *Anna Akhmatova v 60-e gody* (Moscow: Vodolei, 2005).

29. See Galina Rylkova, *The Archaeology of Anxiety: The Russian Silver Age and Its Legacy* (Pittsburgh, PA: University of Pittsburgh Press, 2007).

30. In *Utopias of One* (Princeton, NJ: Princeton University Press, 2017), Joshua Kotin includes a chapter on Akhmatova's poetics of memory and, in his terms, complicity, based in part on a sustained reading of *Poem Without a Hero*'s dense web of references. It is a topic with a long history within Russian scholarship, and has attracted the attention of poets and poet-scholars as well. See, for example, Inna Lisnianskaia, *Shkatulka s troinym dnom* (Moscow: Izd. Russkii Mir and OSO "Moskovskie uchebniki," 2006 [1995]); Lev Losev, "Geroi 'Poemy bez geroia,'" *Akhmatovskii sbornik*, ed. S. Dediulin and G. Superfin (Paris: Institut slavianovedeniia, 1989), 109–22.

31. For the poem, see Akhmatova, *Ia—golos vash...*, 156–61.

32. For the poem, see Akhmatova, *Ia—golos vash...*, 186–91; the Dido connection is discussed in Susan Amert, *In a Shattered Mirror: The Later Poetry of Anna Akhmatova* (Stanford, CA: Stanford University Press, 1992), 133.

33. Joseph Brodsky, "The Keening Muse," *Less Than One: Selected Essays* (New York: Farrar, Straus & Giroux, 1986), 52, 41.

34. Akhmatova, "Epigramma," in the cycle "Tainy remesla" (1936–1960), in *Ia—golos vash...*, 164.

35. Aleksandr Skidan, writing about later twentieth- and twenty-first-century poetry, has gone so far as to suggest that women's poetry has been more significant than that of men. See "Sil'nee urana: sovremennaia zhenskaia poeziia," *Vozdukh*, 3 (2006), http://www.litkarta.ru/projects/vozdukh/issues/2006-3/skidan-critic/ (last accessed May 29, 2016).

36. On the self-fashioning of women poets in the era, see Jenifer Presto, "Women in Russian Symbolism: Beyond the Algebra of Love," in *A History of Women's Writing in Russia*, ed. Adele Marie Barker and Jehanne M. Gheith (Cambridge: Cambridge University Press, 2002), 134–52.

37. Vladislav Khodasevich, "'Zhenskie' stikhi," *Sobranie sochinenii*, 4 vols. (Moscow: Soglasie, 1996), vol. 2, 208–12.

38. See Matich, *Erotic Utopia*; Jenifer Presto, *Beyond the Flesh: Alexander Blok, Zinaida Gippius, and the Symbolist Sublimation of Sex* (Madison: University of Wisconsin Press, 2008); and Elena Guro, *Selected Writings from the Archives*, ed. Anna Ljunggren and Nina Gourianova (Stockholm: Almqvist and Wiksell, 1995).

39. See Catherine Ciepiela, "The Demanding Woman Poet: On Resisting Marina Tsvetaeva," *PMLA*, 111.3 (1996), 421–34.

40. For Tsvetaeva's biography, see especially Simon Karlinsky, *Marina Tsvetaeva: The Woman, Her World, and Her Poetry* (Cambridge: Cambridge University Press, 1985); Viktoriia Shveitser, *Byt i bytie Mariny Tsvetaevoi* (Moscow: SP Interprint, 1992); and Irina Shevelenko, *Literaturnyi put' Tsvetaevoi: Ideologiia—poetika—identichnost' avtora v kontekste epokhi* (Moscow: NLO, 2002).

41. Kelly, *A History of Russian Women's Writing*, 302.

42. Gerald S. Smith has authored numerous metrical studies of the work, for example: "Compound Meters in the Poetry of Marina Cvetaeva," *Russian Literature*, 8 (1980), 103–23.

43. In *London Review of Books*, 16.17, September 8, 1994, 13–14.

44. Joseph Brodsky, "A Poet and Prose," in *Less Than One* (New York: Farrar, Straus & Giroux, 1986), 176–94, quotation on 178.

45. For the poem, see Marina Tsvetaeva, *Stikhotvoreniia i poemy* (Leningrad: Sovetskii pisatel', 1990), 417.

46. See Diana Lewis Burgin, *Marina Tsvetaeva i transgressivnyi eros: stat'i, issledovaniia*, trans. S. Sivak (St. Petersburg: Inapress, 2000). Tsvetaeva's archive, closed until the year 2000, was catalogued and scrupulously edited for publication by dedicated scholars, including Elena Korkina and Irina Shevelenko. It is a surprise that a writer who moved around as much as Tsvetaeva did, and who lived in such impoverished and chaotic circumstances, was able to leave such an extensive literary legacy of notebooks and letters. See, for example, *Zapisnye knizhki: v dvukh tomakh*, ed. E. V. Korkina and M. G. Krutikova (Moscow: Ellis-Lak, 2000–01).

47. For "Podruga," see Tsvetaeva, *Stikhotvoreniia i poemy*, 65–76. For "Povest' o Sonechke," see Tsvetaeva, *Sobranie sochinenii*, 7 vols. (Moscow: Ellis Lak, 1994), vol. 4, 293–416.

48. Tsvetaeva, *Stikhotvoreniia i poemy*, 66.

49. See Diana Lewis Burgin, "Laid Out in Lavender: Perceptions of Lesbian Love in Russian Literature and Criticism of the Silver Age, 1893–1917," in *Sexuality and the Body in Russian Culture*, ed. Jane T. Costlow, Stephanie Sandler, and Judith Vowles (Stanford, CA: Stanford University Press, 1993), 177–203.

50. Vladislav Khodasevich, "Stikhi Nelli," *Sobranie sochinenii*, ed. John Malmstad and Robert Hughes, 2 vols. (Ann Arbor, MI: Ardis, 1990), vol. 2, 133–5.

51. Valerii Briusov, "Pravo na rabotu," *Sredi stikhov 1894–1924: Manifesty, stat'i, retsenzii*, ed. N. A. Bogomolov and N. V. Kotrelev (Moscow: Sovetskii pisatel', 1990), 414–16.

52. As pointed out in E. A. Kallo's Introduction to *Sub rosa: Adelaida Gertsyk, Sofiia Parnok, Poliksena Solov'eva, Cherubina de Gabriak* (Moscow: Ellis Lak, 1999), 62–74.

53. Anna Barkova, . . . *Vechno ne ta*, ed. L. N. Taganov and O. K. Pereverzev (Moscow: Fond Sergeia Dubova, 2002), 8. In the title poem from that volume, Barkova writes that her style is "stern and sharp" ("Vse moi rechi surovy i rezki"), 25.

54. Barkova, . . . *Vechno ne ta*, 94.

55. Catriona Kelly and Carol Ueland, "Barkova, Anna Aleksandrovna," *Dictionary of Russian Women Writers*, ed. Marina Ledkovsky, Charlotte Rosenthal, and Mary Zirin (Westport, CT: Greenwood Press, 1994), 59.

56. The novel was republished in the first issue of the innovative Petersburg almanac, *Russkaia proza*, Issue A (2011), 13–128. It is included as well in Andrei Nikolev (Andrei N. Egunov), *Sobranie proizvedenii*, ed. Gleb Morev and Valeriia Somsikova, *Wiener Slawistischer Almanach* 53 (1993). On

Egunov see Massimo Maurizio, *"Bespredmetnaia iunost'" A. Egunova: tekst i kontekst* (Moscow: Intrada, 2008).

57. A few poems were prepared by Gennadii Shmakov, *Chast' rechi*, 1 (1980), 102–6. The volume in full appears in Nikolev, *Sobranie proizvedenii*.

58. Tarkovsky's poetry was often published in small-print-run editions in the Soviet period; a three-volume set was after his death. For the two poems mentioned here, see A. Tarkovskii, *Sobranie sochinenii*, 3 vols. (Moscow: Khudozhestvennaia literatura, 1991–93), vol. 1, 242–3, 55, respectively. On Tarkovsky's poetry, see Kitty Hunter-Blair, *Poetry and Film: Artistic Kinship between Arsenii and Andrei Tarkovsky* (London: Tate Publishing, 2014).

59. The insight into containment versus fluidity as Chukhontsev's signature belongs to Gerald S. Smith. For brief appreciations of Chukhontsev, see G. S. Smith, "Sharing the Damage," *Times Literary Supplement*, April 20, 1990, 429; and G. S. Smith, "My High Five," *Rossica*, 20 (2011), 93–6, 104–5. He included several poems by Chukhontsev in *Contemporary Russian Poetry: A Bilingual Anthology*, ed. G. S. Smith (Bloomington: Indiana University Press, 1993), 176–89. Chukhontsev has a good personal website with poems and reviews: http://chuhoncev.poet-premium.ru/index.html (last accessed February 13, 2016).

60. For a comparison of Chukhontsev's Moscow version of the philosophical lyric to Brodsky's orientation to Petersburg, see Igor' Shaitanov, "Effekt tselogo: Poeziia Olega Chukhontseva," *Arion*, 4 (1999), http://magazines.russ.ru/arion/1999/4/shaitan.html (last accessed February 13, 2016).

61. Oleg Chukhontsev, *Probegaiushchii peizazh: Stikhotvoreniia i poemy* (St. Petersburg: Inapress, 1997), 43. Another striking strict-form poem in the same volume contemplates the strains of a wind ensemble playing within hearing distance of Butyrskaia Prison: "Naprotiv Butyrok igraet orkestr dukhovoi" (1972), 123.

62. Lev Losev, *Sobrannoe* (Ekaterinburg: U-Faktoriia, 2000), 187; the poem is also included and translated in *Contemporary Russian Poetry*, ed. Smith, 168–71.

63. A very substantial introduction to the Philological School poets, as well as a republication of the 1977 *samizdat* anthology they published, entitled *40*, is *Filologicheskaia shkola: Teksty. Vospominaniia. Bibliografiia*, ed. Viktor Kulle and Vladimir Ufliand (Moscow: Letnii sad, 2006). They claimed to see themselves as continuing not the neo-classicism of the Petersburg tradition but a line of neo-futurism and the poetics of OBERIU, but, particularly in the case of Losev, this lineage of descent is far from clear-cut. Ufliand, for instance, entitled a statement about one of the poets, "Aleksandr Kondratov, klassicheskii avangardist" (*Filologicheskaia shkola*, ed. Kulle and Ufliand, 400–2). See also Mikhail Pavlovets, "'Otpuzyrites' iz nulia!': Nulevye i pustotnye teksty Aleksandra Kondratova," *Russian Literature*, 78.1–2 (2015), 15–41.

64. A good example that also shows Losev's sense of humor would be the largely untranslatable poem "LEVLOSEV": see L. Losev, *Stikhi* (St. Petersburg: Izdatel'stvo Ivana Limbakha, 2012), http://limbakh.ru/index.php?id=2280 (last accessed July 10, 2016).

65. Losev, *Sobrannoe*, 64. The quotation is from Gerald S. Smith, "Flight of the Angels: The Poetry of Lev Loseff," *Slavic Review*, 47.1 (1988), 76–88, quotation on 77.

66. This observation is repeated and elaborated in the prefatory note Losev attached to the book that contained his long cycle of poems in memory of Brodsky. See Lev Losev, *Posleslovie* (St. Petersburg: Pushkinskii fond, 1998), 5.

67. I. Brodskii. *Stikhotvoreniia; chitaet avtor* (Moscow: Studiia Ardis, 2007). The CD includes the John Donne elegy as well.

68. David M. Bethea, *Joseph Brodsky and the Creation of Exile* (Princeton, NJ: Princeton University Press, 1994), 115. Bethea refers to "Six Years Later" ("Shest' let spustia," 1968), a poem whose title changes are charted in I. Brodskii, *Stikhotvoreniia i poemy*, ed. L. V. Losev, 2 vols. (St. Petersburg: Izd. Pushkinskogo Doma, Izd. "Vita Nova," 2011), vol. 1, 489; for the poem, see vol.

1, 167. For the English translation of "Six Years Later," see Brodsky, *Collected Poems in English*, ed. Ann Kjellberg (New York: Farrar, Straus & Giroux, 2000), 6–7.

69. Lev Loseff, *Joseph Brodsky: A Literary Life*, trans. Jane Ann Miller (New Haven, CT, and London: Yale University Press, 2011), 61. The Russian original is L. Losev, *Iosif Brodskii* (Moscow: Molodaia gvardiia, 2006).

70. Loseff, *Joseph Brodsky*, 63.

71. See Joseph Brodsky, "Flight from Byzantium," in *Less Than One*, 393–446; I. Brodskii, "Meksikanskii divertisment," in Brodskii, *Stikhotvoreniia i poemy*, vol. 1, 355–61. For a translation of the latter, see Brodsky, *Collected Poems in English*, 87–94.

72. These later steps in the evolution of the semantic aureole around Russian blank verse are traced in Michael Wachtel, *The Development of Russian Verse: Meter and Its Meanings* (Cambridge: Cambridge University Press, 1998), 78–118.

73. Brodskii, *Stikhotvoreniia i poemy*, vol. 1, 510.

74. On the latter, see Joseph Brodsky, *"On the Talks in Kabul": A Forum on Politics in Poetry*, ed. Catherine Ciepiela and Stephanie Sandler, *Russian Review*, 61.2 (2002), 186–219.

75. A further turning point is suggested by Losev: Brodsky's first heart surgery, in 1978. Losev observes that Brodsky wrote no new poems in 1979, a rarity in his extremely productive writing life, and then turns to a poetics that is, paradoxically, more life-affirming. See Loseff, *Joseph Brodsky*, 247.

76. Loseff, *Joseph Brodsky*, 182.

77. Brodskii, *Stikhotvoreniia i poemy*, vol. 1, 365. Losev notes in the commentary that Brodsky considered the cycle his major poetic achievement of the 1970s.

78. Brodsky, *Collected Poems in English*, 101.

79. The poem is closely read by G. S. Smith, in " 'Long Growing Dark': Joseph Brodsky's 'August,' " in *Rereading Russian Poetry*, ed. Stephanie Sandler (New Haven, CT: Yale University Press, 1999), 249–55.

80. The poems yielded some virtuoso translations, although, because of the demanding rhyme schemes, some readers find his English poems forced. For the English, see Brodsky, *Collected Poems in English*, 53–4, 67–70, 72–7, and 130–2, respectively. For the Russian, see Brodskii, *Stikhotvoreniia i poemy*, vol. 1, 323–4, 333–6, 338–42, and 378–80.

81. Derek Walcott, "Magic Industry," *New York Review of Books*, 35.18, November 24, 1988, http://www.nybooks.com/articles/1988/11/24/magic-industry/ (last accessed August 21, 2016).

82. Brodsky, "The Keening Muse," in *Less than One*, 52.

83. J. Brodsky, *On Grief and Reason: Essays* (New York: Farrar, Straus & Giroux, 1995), 145–97.

84. Brodsky, *Less Than One*, 457, 460, 461, and 461 respectively.

85. See, for example, Viktor Krivulin, "Leonid Aronzon—sopernik Iosifa Brodskogo," in Viktor Krivulin, *Okhota na mamonta* (St. Peterburg: Russko-Baltiiskii informatsionnyi tsentr, 1998), 152–8. He writes, "compared to the refined aestheticism of his short poems, the wordy and endlessly qualified (*obstoiatel'nyi*) Brodsky in the 1970s seemed heavy and archaic, too earth-bound, too rational" (155).

86. For these poems, see Leonid Aronzon, *Sobranie proizvedenii*, 2 vols. (St. Petersburg: Izdatel'stvo Ivana Limbakha, 2006), vol. 1, 180–3. This volume includes the hand-written version of the "Empty Sonnet," 183, as well as a through-text of all the lines as if in a single verse paragraph, 182. Other poems veer toward Conceptualist verse, for example, "Pauses" ("Pauzy," 1964), which consists entirely of x's filling a nine-line sequence, spaced out in a way that evokes rhythmic remnants of a poem; see Aronzon, *Sobranie proizvedenii*, vol. 1, 69.

87. For the poem, see Aronzon, *Sobranie proizvedenii*, vol. 1, 108. Olga Sedakova singles out this poem for special praise in "Poet kul'minatsii," in *Poetica* (Moscow: Universitet Dmitriia Pozharskogo, 2010), 515–28.

88. Michael Molnar, "Victor Krivulin," *The Independent*, March 28, 2001, http://www.independent.co.uk/news/obituaries/victor-krivulin-5366722.html (last accessed February 14/16).

89. Krivulin, *Okhota na mamonta*, 88–9.

90. For the poem, see Viktor Krivulin, *Stikhi*, 2 vols. (Leningrad and Paris: Beseda, 1988), vol. 1, 80–1.

91. For a compendium of the work, see *Filologicheskaia shkola*, ed. Kulle and Ufliand.

92. There are some brave translations, however: see David MacFadyen, "Where to Find the Russian Language: Mikhail Eremin," *World Literature Today*, 72.1 (1998), 27–32, which has several; see also *In the Grip of Strange Thoughts*, ed. J. Kates (Brookline, MA: Zephyr Press, 1999), 189–202; and Mikhail Eremin, "From *Poems: Book 5*," trans. Alex Cigale, *Asymptote* (July, 2016), http://www.asymptotejournal.com/poetry/mikhail-eremin-poems-5/ (last accessed April 12, 2017).

93. Vladimir Gandel'sman, *Obratnaia lodka* (St. Petersburg: XXI vek, 2005), 240–1.

94. Some locutions have been taken from the translation by Andrey Gritsman in *Crossing Centuries: The New Generation in Russian Poetry*, ed. John High et al. (Jersey City, NJ: Talisman House Publishers, 2000), 428. Gritsman cites the poem as a single eight-line unit. There is a page break between the two quatrains in the Russian publication, which we follow.

95. This is one of three poems closely analyzed, with extensive formal commentary, in Catherine Ciepiela, Christine Dunbar, Susanne Fusso, Katherine Tiernan O'Connor, Sarah Pratt, Stephanie Sandler, G. S. Smith, Michael Wachtel, and Boris Wolfson, "Encounters with Aleksei Tsvetkov: Three Poems with Commentaries and an Interview," *Toronto Slavic Quarterly*, 26 (2008), http://sites.utoronto.ca/tsq/26/index26.shtml (last accessed January 13, 2016).

96. In an interview with Linor Goralik, *Vozdukh*, 3 (2006), 21.

97. Aleksei Tsvetkov, *Edem i drugoe* (Moscow: OGI, 2007), 140.

98. For the poem, see Gandlevskii, *Poriadok slov: stikhi, povest', p'esa, esse* (Ekaterinburg: U-Faktoriia, 2000), 97. It is the subject of several of Zholkovsky's essays about infinitive poetry, including A. K. Zholkovskii, "Gandlevskii, Brodskii, Blok, Tvardovskii: Iz zametok ob infinitivnoi poezii," *Znamia*, 12 (2003), http://magazines.russ.ru/zvezda/2003/12/zholk.html (last accessed April 4, 2016). On images of masculinity in the work of Gandlevsky, see Dunja Popovic, "The Generation That Has Squandered Its Men: The Late Soviet Crisis of Masculinity in the Poetry of Sergei Gandlevskii," *Russian Review*, 70 (2011), 663–76.

99. The former is included in Gandlevskii, *Poriadok slov*, 117–254; and it has appeared in English translation by Susanne Fusso, *Trepanation of the Skull* (DeKalb: Northern Illinois University Press, 2014). The novel *[nrzb]* appeared first in journal form and has been published as a book (Moscow: Izdatel'stvo Inostranka, 2002).

100. Gandlevskii, *Poriadok slov*, 64; the translation is from Gandlevsky, *A Kindred Orphanhood*, trans. Philip Metres (Brookline, MA: Zephyr Press, 2003), 42. The second line of the poem combines in a single word the last names of two early Soviet political figures, Sergo Ordzhonikidze (1886–1937) and Felix Dzerzhinsky (1877–1926), each of whom had plenty of streets named after him.

101. A paradox noted in Dmitrii Bak, *Sto poetov nachala stoletiia* (Moscow: Vremia, 2015), 18.

102. Mikhail Aizenberg, *Drugie i prezhnie veshchi* (Moscow: NLO, 2000), 7.

103. The poem is untitled, beginning "V etom lesu prokhodit granitsa pyli," in Mikhail Aizenberg, *Perekhod na letnee vremia* (Moscow: NLO, 2008), 494.

104. Many have been collected, for example, in *Vzgliad na svobodnogo khudozhnika* (Moscow: Gendal'f, 1997); and *Opravdannoe prisutstvie* (Moscow: Baltrus; Novoe izdatel'stvo, 2008).

105. Some of Dashevsky's reviews (which are not just about poetry) are collected in *Izbrannye stat'i* (Moscow: Novoe izdatel'stvo, 2015). For his 2012 essay "Kak chitat' sovremennuiu poeziiu," see Grigorii Dashevskii, *Stikhotvoreniia i perevody* (Moscow: Novoe izdatel'stvo, 2015), 143–56.

106. "Tai, i bystree, chem snezhnaia griaz'" [1990], in Dashevskii, *Stikhotvoreniia i perevody*, 123.

107. Mikhail Aizenberg, "Grigorii Dashevskii. Genrikh i Semen," *Itogi*, 29 (215) (2000), http://www.litkarta.ru/dossier/aizenberg-o-dashevskom/dossier_993/ (last accessed April 8, 2016).

108. See, for example, Caryl Emerson, "Afterword: On Persons as Open-Ended Ends-In-Themselves (The View from Two Novelists and Two Critics)," in *A History of Russian Philosophy 1830–1930: Faith, Reason, and the Defense of Human Dignity*, ed. G. M. Hamburg and Randall A. Poole (Cambridge: Cambridge University Press, 2010), 381–90.

109. A good resource for studying the extensive heritage of religious verse in Russian is *Molitvy russkikh poetov XI–XIX: Antologiia* (Moscow: Veche, 2009).

110. On the creative use of the liturgical tradition by modernist poets, including Blok, Kuzmin, Pasternak, and Akhmatova, see Martha M. F. Kelly, *Unorthodox Beauty: Russian Modernism and Its Religious Aesthetic* (Evanston, IL: Northwestern University Press, 2016).

111. On the interweaving of these traditions, see Judith Deutsch Kornblatt, *Doubly Chosen: Jewish Identity, the Soviet Intelligentsia, and the Russian Orthodox Church* (Madison: University of Wisconsin Press, 2004).

112. See Andrei Monastyrskii, *Poeticheskii mir* (Moscow: NLO, 2007) for a published version of the 1980s typescripts, with a Foreword by Prigov; especially pertinent is the last section, "Po-drugomu," where the phrase "v tebe net nichego" resounds hundreds of times, creating a vast zone of emptiness (226–327). In an Afterword to the volume, Monastyrsky linked these repetitions to the apophatic tradition (328); this pattern is found in other poets' forays outside Judeo-Christian thought and it circles back to known Orthodox traditions as well. For a recording of Prigov's performance of *Onegin*, see https://www.youtube.com/watch?v=aN51oN6k6Is (last accessed November 23, 2017).

113. See Joseph Brodsky's essay on "Magdalene," a poem from the novel, "A Footnote to a Commentary," trans. Jamey Gambrell and Alexander Sumerkin, in *Rereading Russian Poetry*, ed. Sandler, 183–201; and Ol'ga Sedakova, "Chetyrekhstopnyi amfibrakhii ili 'Chudo' Borisa Pasternaka v russkoi poeticheskoi traditsii," in Ol'ga Sedakova, *Proza* (Moscow: Universitet Dmitriia Pozharskogo, 2010), 206–24.

114. Per-Arne Bodin, *Nine Poems from "Doktor Zhivago": A Study of Christian Motifs in Boris Pasternak's Poetry* (Stockholm: Almqvist and Wiksell, 1976).

115. Martha M. F. Kelly, "Cultural Transformation as Transfiguration in Pasternak's *Doctor Zhivago*," *Russian History*, 40 (2013), 68–89.

116. Mark Steinberg, *Proletarian Imagination: Self, Modernity, and the Sacred in Russia, 1910–1925* (Ithaca, NY: Cornell University Press, 2002), 11. Steinberg's book is a pioneering study of those workers' writings.

117. See K. M. Azadovskii, *Zhizn' Nikolaia Kliueva: dokumental'noe povestvovanie* (St. Petersburg: Izdatel'stvo zhurnala *Zvezda*, 2002); and Michael Makin, "Whose Kliuev, Who Is Kliuev? Polemics of Identity and Poetry," *SEER*, 85.2 (2007), 231–70.

118. M. Gasparov published some poems in *Oktiabr'*, 5 (1989), 149–59; his extensive account of Merkur'eva's life and works appeared in *Litsa*, 5 (1994), 5–97. The fullest collection is Merkur'eva, *Tshcheta: Sobranie stikhotvorenii* (Moscow: Vodolei, 2007). Details about Merkur'eva's life are taken from Gasparov's essay there. Also of note is Catriona Kelly, "Reluctant Sibyls: Gender and Intertextuality in the Works of Adelaida Gertsyk and Vera Merkureva," in *Rereading Russian Poetry*, ed. Sandler, 129–45.

119. For the poetry, see Mariia Shkapskaia, *Chas vechernii* (St. Petersburg: Limbus Press, 2000). On Shkapskaia, see Barbara Heldt, "Motherhood in a Cold Climate: The Poetry and Career of Maria Shkapskaya," in *Rereading Russian Poetry*, ed. Sandler, 237–54.

120. Merkur'eva, *Tshcheta*, 119, 413–26.

121. Merkur′eva, *Tshcheta*, 44–50, 51–3, 199–201.

122. Merkur′eva, *Tshcheta*, 549.

123. Appearing in the same series as Merkur′eva's *Tshcheta* is Zal′tsman, *Signaly Strashnogo suda* (Moscow: Vodolei, 2011). See also the well-curated site http://pavelzaltsman.org (last accessed March 19, 2016). Zal′tsman's work is also now available in English, in translations by Charles Swank and Matvei Yankelevich: *Written in the Dark: Five Poets in the Siege of Leningrad*, ed. Polina Barskova (Brooklyn, NY: Ugly Duckling Presse, 2016), 111–27.

124. Zal′tsman, *Signaly Strashnogo suda*, 113. The scholar and editor Ilya Kukuj and the poet and critic Oleg Iur′ev have led the restoration of Zal′tsman's role in Russian literature.

125. The poem is included in the selection from Shalamov's work in *The Penguin Book of Russian Poetry*, ed. Robert Chandler, Boris Dralyuk, and Irina Mashinski (London: Penguin Books, 2015), 393–8.

126. Varlam Shalamov, *Sobranie sochinenii v shesti tomakh*, 6 vols. plus 1 (Moscow: Knizhnyi Klub Knigovek, 2013), vol. 3, 183–7, quotation on 184; for a published, full translation, see *The Penguin Book of Russian Poetry*, ed. Chandler et al., 394. For "Boiarina Morozova" in Russian, see Shalamov, *Sobranie sochinenii*, vol. 3, 78–9.

127. Zinaida Mirkina (b. 1926) was also of Veniamin Blazhenny's generation, and like him essentially published only after the fall of the Soviet Union. A good example of her poetry is the twelve-line poem "Potustoronnii mir tak pust!" in Z. Mirkina, *Poteria poteri* (Moscow: Evidentis, 2001), 150.

128. His two letters to Chichibabin have now been published: see Svetlana Bunina, "V poezii ia chelovek—lishnii…: Pis′ma Veniamina Blazhennogo Borisu Chichibabinu," *Novyi mir*, 10 (2010), 157–9.

129. Veniamin Blazhennyi, *Moimi ochami* (Moscow: ARGO-Risk, 2005), 58.

130. Veniamin Blazhennyi, *Soraspiat′e* (Moscow: Vremia, 2009), 34. The poem has the long dateline September 1971–January 31, 1989. Those longer datelines, while not a constant, can be found on some poems, including the well-known "V kaloshakh na bosu nogu" (1984–91–92), 72–3.

131. See especially Sergei Magid, *Za gran′iu etogo peizazha. Dnevniki 1997–2001 gg.* (Moscow: Vodolei, 2011). Compare Magid's earnest expression of his own faith: "I don't know God, but I feel Him. I feel Him by means of my sensation that He is. What I feel is not the result of knowledge, it is a fact of my naked skin. The sensation of a gaze. His gaze at my back" (11).

132. Sergei Magid, *V doline Elakh* (Moscow: Vodolei, 2010), 24–5, 184–6.

133. Sergei Magid, *Zona sluzheniia* (Moscow: NLO, 2003), 18–19.

134. Multiple studies of these poets have now appeared, including Josephine von Zitzewitz, *Poetry and the Religious-Philosophical Seminar 1974–1980: Poetry for a Deaf Age* (Oxford: Legenda, 2016). Some focus on only a few poets but offer framing comments that begin to articulate a broader approach, especially Anton Nesterov, "Germenevtika, metafizika, i 'drugaia kritika': O stikhakh Aleksandra Mironova," *NLO*, 61 (2003), http://www.litkarta.ru/dossier/nesterov-o-mironove/dossier_2716/ (last accessed April 2, 2016). One of the participants, however, was the first to begin to claim that the poetry of spirit defined Leningrad unofficial poetry: Viktor Krivulin, "Peterburgskaia spiritual′naia lirika vchera i segodnia (K istorii neofitsial′noi poezii Leningrada 60–80-kh godov)," in *Istoriia leningradskoi nepodtsenzurnoi literatury*, ed. B. I. Ivanov and B. A. Roginskii (St. Petersburg: Izdatel′stvo DEAN, 2000), 99–109.

135. Elena Shvarts, *Sochineniia*, 5 vols. (St. Petersburg: Pushkinskii fond, 2002–08), vol. 5, 20–3; subsequent quotations are from this source.

136. The death of Moses is the concluding vision of Shvarts's "Golosa v pustyne (Po motivam Agady). Mirakl′ o smerti," a cycle dated 1995 that she published only in Shvarts, *Mundus imaginalis* (St. Petersburg: Izdatel′stvo "EZRO"/Literaturnoe obshchestvo "Utkonos," 1996),

99–107, also available online: http://www.vavilon.ru/texts/shvarts1-5.html (last accessed February 25, 2017). The burning bush is mentioned here as well.

137. Aleksandr Mironov, *Izbrannoe: stikhotvoreniia i poemy: 1964–2000* (St. Petersburg: Inapress, 2002).

138. Valerii Shubinskii, "Aleksandr Mironov. *Izbrannoe*," *Novaia kamera khraneniia*, March 20, 2008, http://www.litkarta.ru/dossier/shubinskiy-o-mironove/dossier_2716/ (last accessed April 7, 2016).

139. There are five poems grouped as "Koany" in Aleksandr Mironov, *Bez ognia* (Moscow: Novoe izdatel'stvo, 2009), 45–7, and the spirit of these riddles also informs the short prose opening to his Gnostic cycle, beginning "Ia vkhozhu v etot dom, kak vkhodiat v chisla…" in Mironov, *Izbrannoe*, 27.

140. For example, "Smekh moi, agnche, angele vetrenyi" (1973) in Mironov, *Izbrannoe*, 32.

141. Mironov, *Izbrannoe*, 11, 207–9, 229–33.

142. See for example "…ia zhazhdala stradat' i byt' zabytoi," "Chto obraduet zren'e? Uzor li izvilistykh linii," and "V lesakh, v gorakh, na beregu reki," in Svetlana Kekova, *Na semi khol-makh* (St. Petersburg: Pushkinskii fond, 2001), 39, 53, 59.

143. Inga Kuznetsova, "Interview with Kekova," in *Russian Women Poets*, ed. Valentina Polukhina, *Modern Poetry in Translation*, 20 (2002), 94. This volume also has a small, good selection of Kekova's poetry, trans. Ruth Fainlight, 87–91.

144. Theological and philosophical interrogations are among the central themes in a volume of essays devoted entirely to her work: *Ol'ga Sedakova. Stikhi, smysly, prochteniia*, ed. Stephanie Sandler, Mariia Khotimskaia, Margarita Krimmel', and Oleg Novikov (Moscow: NLO, 2017).

145. See, for example, "Vozvrashchenie bludnogo syna," "Legenda desiataia. Iakov," "Voz-vrashchenie. Stikh ob Aleksee," and "Sant Alessio. Roma," in Ol'ga Sedakova, *Stikhi* (Moscow: Universitet Dmitriia Pozharskogo, 2010), 66–9, 130, 195, 401–2.

146. Sedakova, *Stikhi*, 179–206. The cycle has appeared in English: *In Praise of Poetry*, trans. Caroline Clark, Ksenia Golubovich, and Stephanie Sandler (Rochester, NY: Open Letter Books, 2014), 17–70.

147. Sedakova is the creator of a dictionary of Church Slavonic words whose meanings have changed in modern usage, and her poems often resonate with these layers of meanings. See Ol'ga Sedakova, *Slovar' trudnykh slov. Tserkovnoslaviansko-russkie paronimy*, 2nd edn. (Moscow: Greko-latinskii kabinet Iu. A. Shichalina, 2008). Also significant are Sedakova's many essays on religious and ethical themes. Nearly all are available online, http://www.olgasedakova.com/Moralia (last accessed March 21, 2016).

148. Sergei Averintsev, *Stikhi dukhovnye* (Kiev: Litera, 2001); *Stikhi i perevody* (St. Petersburg: Izdatel'stvo Ivana Limbakha, 2003).

149. A third thinker who should be mentioned, although not a source for Sedakova, is Merab Mamardashvili (1930–90). In general, the interconnections among philosophy, literature, and aesthetic innovation are an emerging field of important scholarly study. To cite only one exemplary book: Thomas Seifrid, *The Word Made Self: Russian Writings on Language 1860–1930* (Ithaca, NY: Cornell University Press, 2005).

150. That side of her work is well explored in Kseniia Golubovich, "Poet i t'ma. Politika khudo-zhestvennoi formy," in *Ol'ga Sedakova: Stikhi, smysly, prochteniia*, ed. Sandler et al., 49–111.

151. Sedakova, *Stikhi*, 415.

152. Joseph Brodsky, *Nativity Poems* (New York: Farrar, Straus & Giroux, 2001), 53. The volume includes the early "Rozhdestvenskii romans," as "Christmas Ballad," in a translation by Glyn Maxwell, 2–5.

153. Boris Khersonskii, *Spirichuels* (Moscow: NLO, 2009), 242–67, 268–81. See also his recreation of the Physiologus, *Novyi Estestvoslov* (Moscow: Art Khaus Media, 2012). In his Foreword to that book, he cites Mandelstam's definition of the genre as a Christianity of beasts and fables as his model.

154. Boris Khersonskii, *Semeinyi arkhiv* (Moscow: NLO, 2006). Khersonsky has followed the threads of Jewish history in other books, including the Hasidic sayings in *Poka ne stemnelo* (Moscow: NLO, 2010), 118–26.

155. See his poems in the aftermath of this war, including *Missa in Tempore Belli/Messa vo vremena voiny* (St. Petersburg: Izdatel´stvo Ivana Limbakha, 2014).

156. Kruglov and Khersonsky also share a loose affiliation with "New Epic writing" (*novyi epos*). On this trend, see Il´ia Kukulin, "Ot Svarovskogo k Zhukovskomu i obratno: O tom, kak metod issledovaniia konstruiruet literaturnyi kanon," *NLO*, 89 (2008), 228–40.

157. As noted in the superb introductory essay to the volume: see Il´ia Kukulin, "Novye Stranstvovaniia po dusham," in Sergei Kruglov, *Natan*; Boris Khersonskii, *V dukhe i istine* (New York: Ailuros, 2012), 5–18.

158. Kruglov, *Natan*; Khersonskii, *V dukhe i istine*, 65.

159. Kruglov, *Natan*; Khersonskii, *V dukhe i istine*, 95.

160. Semen Vengerov used this term broadly for a definition of modernism; Zara Mints narrowed it down to the Lermontov tradition in poetry of the 1910s–1920s. See S. A. Vengerov, "Etapy neoromanticheskogo dvizheniia," in *Russkaia literatura XX veka*, ed. S. A. Vengerov, 3 vols. (Moscow: Izdatel´stvo T-va Mir, 1914), vol. 1, 2–38; Zara Mints, "Futurizm i 'neoromantizm': K probleme genezisa i struktury 'Istorii bednogo rytsaria' Eleny Guro," Mints, *Blok i russkii simvolizm: Izbrannye trudy v 3 kn.*, 3 vols. (St. Petersburg: Iskusstvo-SPb, 2004), vol. 3, 317–26. Kirill Ankudinov writes in several of his works about Neo-Romantism in modern Russian poetry; however, we find his concept essentializing and historically misleading. See, for example, Kirill Ankudinov, *Romantizm bez beregov: Russkaia romanticheskaia poeziia vtoroi poloviny XX–nachala XXI vekov* (Maikop: Adygeiskii gos. universitet, 2015); Kirill Ankudinov, "Sovremennaia neoromanticheskaia poeziia kak 'parallel´naia kul´tura,'" *Vestnik Adygeiskogo gosudarstvennogo universiteta. Seriia 2 "Filologiia i iskusstvovedenie,"* 2 (2007), http://cyberleninka.ru/article/n/sovremennaya-neoromanticheskaya-poeziya-kak-parallelnaya-kultura (Last accessed August 15, 2017).

161. Aleksandr Vertinskii, "Polukrovka," http://www.megalyrics.ru/lyric/alieksandr-viertinskii/polukrovka.htm (last accessed August 11, 2016). A recording of Vertinsky performing this poem is also available: https://www.youtube.com/watch?v=MdudA6VeVi0 (last accessed August 11, 2016).

162. Nikolai Gumilev, *Stikhotvoreniia i poemy* (St. Petersburg: Akademicheskii proekt, 2000), 357. For Gumilev's poems, dates of first publication are given.

163. For an anthology that includes "The Word," see Nikolai Gumilyov, *The Pillar of Fire: Selected Poems*, trans. Richard McKane (London: Anvill Press Poetry, 1999), 166; Gumilev, *Stikhotvoreniia i poemy*, 328.

164. *The Blue Lagoon: Anthology of Modern Russian Poetry*, ed. Konstantin K. Kuzminsky and Gregory L. Kovalev, 5 vols. in 9 (Newtonville, MA: Oriental Research Partners, 1980), vol. 1, 52. On Rivin, see Oleg Iur´ev, "Zapolnennoe ziianie," *Novaia kamera khraneniia* (n.d.) http://www.newkamera.de/lenchr/rivin.html (last accessed August 11, 2016).

165. Eduard Bagritskii, *Stikhotvoreniia i poemy* (Moscow: GIKhL, 1956), 65–7, quotation on 65.

166. A. K. Zholkovskii, "Rai, zamaskirovannyi pod dvor: zametki o poeticheskom mire B. Okudzhavy," in A. K. Zholkovskii i Iu. K. Shcheglov, *Mir avtora i struktura teksta: Stat´i o russkoi literature* (Tenafly, NJ: Hermitage Press, 1986), 279–308.

167. Leonid Dubshan, "O prirode veshchei," in Bulat Okudzhava, *Stikhotvoreniia*, ed. V. N. Sazhin and D. V. Sazhin (St. Petersburg: Akademicheskii proekt, 2001), 51.

168. Gumilev, *Stikhotvoreniia i poemy*, 419.

169. Gumilev, *Stikhotvoreniia i poemy*, 162.

170. On Esenin's performativity, see Oleg Lekmanov and Mikhail Sverdlov, *Sergei Esenin: Biografiia* (Moscow: Astrel', Corpus, 2011), esp. 449–539; and N. L. Leiderman, *Sergei Esenin: Metamorfozy khudozhestvennogo soznaniia* (Ekaterinburg: UGPI, 2007).

171. See Vladimir Novikov, *Pisatel' Vladimir Vysotskii. V Soiuze pisatelei ne sostoial* (Moscow: Interprint, 1991); Andrei Skobelev and Sergei Shaulov, *Vladimir Vysotskii: Mir i slovo*, 2nd edn. (Ufa: BGPU, 2001); and Natal'ia Krymova, *Imena. Vysotskii: Nenapisannaia kniga* (Moscow: GKTSM V. S. Vysotskogo, 2008).

172. Boris Ryzhii, *V kvartalakh dal'nikh i pechal'nykh* (Moscow: Iskusstvo, 2012), 307.

173. Dubshan, "O prirode veshchei," 34.

174. Vladimir Vysotskii, *Pesni*, ed. A. E. Krylov, 2 vols. (Ekaterinburg: U-Faktoriia, 1999), vol. 1, 281.

175. Galich, *Kogda ia vernus'* (Frankfurt am Main: Posev, 1981), 52. In performances of this poem, Galich sometimes recited "and waited for this very line" ("I zhdal etoi samoi stroki"), instead of the final line given here. See http://agalich.free.fr/Ei_strashno_i_dushno.mp3 (last accessed August 21, 2016).

176. Boris Slutskii, *Pokuda nad stikhami plachut...*, ed. Benedikt Sarnov (Moscow: Tekst, 2013), 186–7.

177. Ilya Kukulin, "Narrative Poetry," in *Russian Literature since 1991*, ed. Evgeny Dobrenko and Mark Lipovetsky (Cambridge: Cambridge University Press, 2015), 244–67, quotation on 254.

178. Cited from Svarovskii, *Slava geroiam* (Moscow: NLO, 2015), 51.

179. Published as Feodor Swarovski, "Glory to Heroes," trans. Stephanie Sandler, *World Literature Today*, 85.6 (November–December, 2011), 47.

180. Natal'ia Samutina, "Oni eto my," in Fedor Svarovskii, *Puteshestvenniki vo vremeni* (Moscow: NLO, 2009), 5–25, cited from 11.

181. A memorable example is Svarovsky's poem "Poor Jenny" ("Bednaia Dzhenni"), which is the subject of a close reading and is fully cited in Arkadii Shtypel', "Ob odnom stikhotvorenii Fedora Svarovskogo," *Vozdukh* 3 (2008), http://www.litkarta.ru/projects/vozdukh/issues/2008-3/shtypel-svar/ (last accessed April 14, 2017).

Interlude

1. Zabolotsky's connections to OBERIU are treated elsewhere in this History. For Pasternak's connections to the Futurists, see Christopher J. Barnes, *Boris Pasternak: A Literary Biography*, 2 vols. (Cambridge: Cambridge University Press, 1989–98), vol. 1, 159–73; and Lazar Fleishman, *Boris Pasternak: The Poet and His Politics* (Cambridge, MA: Harvard University Press, 1990), 59–83.

2. John E. Malmstad, "Boris Pasternak—The Painter's Eye," *Russian Review*, 51.3 (July, 1992), 301–18, quotation on 301.

3. The poem is "Fevral'. Dostat' chernil i plakat'!" (1912). For the poem, see Boris Pasternak, *Stikhotvoreniia i poemy*, ed. V. S. Baevskii and E. B. Pasternak, 2 vols. (Leningrad: Sovetskii pisatel', 1990), vol. 1, 75.

4. Andrei Sinyavsky, "Pasternak's Poetry," trans. Rebecca Henderson, in *Pasternak: A Collection of Critical Essays*, ed. Victor Erlich (Englewood Cliffs, NJ: Prentice Hall, 1978), 68–109, quotation on 74, 75. This essay is an expanded and revised translation of the introductory essay Sinyavsky wrote for the Biblioteka poeta edition of Pasternak's poetry.

5. Sinyavsky, "Pasternak's Poetry," 77. Sinyavsky also writes about Pasternak's metaphors, but the influential work was done by Roman Jakobson in "Marginal Notes on the Prose of the Poet Pasternak," trans. Angela Livingstone, in Roman Jakobson, *Language in Literature*, ed. Krystyna Pomorska and Stephen Rudy (Cambridge, MA: Belknap Press at Harvard University Press, 1987), 301–17. The essay was written in German and first appeared in 1935.

6. Pasternak, *Stikhotvoreniia i poemy*, vol. 1, 120.

7. Many of Pasternak's poems have received fine close readings, and this is one of them: see, for example, Anna Ljunggren, "'Sad' i 'Ia sam': Smysl i kompozitsiia stikhotvoreniia 'Zerkalo,'" in *Boris Pasternak and His Times: Selected Papers from the Second International Symposium on Pasternak*, ed. Lazar Fleishman (Berkeley, CA: Berkeley Slavic Specialties, 1989), 224–37; and Greta Matevossian, "Eshche raz o 'Zerkale' Borisa Pasternaka," *Russian Literature* 44 (1998), 433–42.

8. Elena Glazov-Corrigan, *Art After Philosophy: Boris Pasternak's Early Prose* (Columbus, OH: Ohio State University Press, 2013), offers an extensive account of the impact on the poet's aesthetic practice of his sustained study in philosophy in Marburg.

9. Pasternak, *Stikhotvoreniia i poemy*, vol. 1, 183. For a detailed reading of the poem, see Lazar Fleishman, "In Search of the Word: An Analysis of Pasternak's Poem 'Tak nachinaiut...,'" *Zeszyty Naukowe Wyższej Szkoły Pedagogicznej w Bydgoszczy*, Studia Filologiczne; Filologia Rosyjska 31.12 (1989), 65–88.

10. Lidiia Ginzburg, "Zabolotskii dvadtsatykh godov," in Lidiia Ginzburg, *Literatura v poiskakh real'nosti* (Leningrad: Sovetskii pisatel', 1987), 135–46, quotation on 140. That boldness did not leave the poets immune to charting rather complex courses through the political minefields of the era, as is shown sensitively in Fleishman, *Boris Pasternak*, and in Darra Goldstein, *Nikolai Zabolotsky: Play for Mortal Stakes* (Cambridge: Cambridge University Press, 1993).

11. For an extended comparison of the two poems and a reading of "Red Bavaria" in terms of OBERIU poetics, see Sarah Pratt, *Nikolai Zabolotsky: Enigma and Cultural Paradigm* (Evanston, IL: Northwestern University Press, 2000), 118–28.

12. One gets a sense for how Zabolotsky's creative impulse built on lists of implausible topics in a listing of subjects that interested him—the range is astonishing. In part: "...Religious practices. Poems. Various simple phenomena—fights, dinners, dances. Meat and dough. Vodka and beer. Popular astronomy," cited in R. R. Milner-Gulland, "Zabolotsky: Philosopher-Poet," *Soviet Studies* 22.4 (1971), 595–608, quotation on 602.

13. For a reading that emphasizes that aspect, see Simon Karlinsky, "Surrealism in Twentieth-Century Russian Poetry: Churilin, Zabolotskii, Poplavskii," *Slavic Review* 26.4 (1967), 605–17, esp. 614.

14. N. A. Zabolotskii, *Polnoe sobranie stikhotvorenii i poem* (St. Petersburg: Akademicheskii proekt, 2002), 312.

15. Zabolotskii, *Polnoe sobranie stikhotvorenii*, 104; there is a typo in this edition, "slavno" rather than "slovno," here corrected.

16. Zabolotskii, *Polnoe sobranie stikhotvorenii*, 105.

17. Ol'ga Sedakova, "O Zabolotskom," *Krug chteniia* (1995), 83–5, quotation on 83.

18. Pratt, *Nikolai Zabolotsky*, 207. This study also offers a detailed account of Russian Orthodox elements in Zabolotsky's writings.

19. Interesting work has also been published by the poet and scholar Igor' Loshchilov, including an edited collection, *N. A. Zabolotskii: pro et contra: lichnost' i tvorchestvo N. A. Zabolotskogo v otsenke pisatelei, kritikov, issledovatelei: antologiia*, ed. Igor' Loshchilov and Tat'iana Igosheva (St Petersburg: Russkaia khristianskaia gumanitarnaia akademiia, 2010).

20. One aspect of Tsvetaeva's legacy that is similarly idiosyncratic, her prose, has begun to receive fresh scholarly attention. See for example, Monika Greenleaf, "Laughter, Music, and Memory

at the Moment of Danger: Tsvetaeva's 'Mother and Music' in the Light of Modernist Memory Practices," *Slavic Review* 68.4 (2009), 825–47. For an essay that places Tsvetaeva's prose in a tradition of women's writing, see Pamela Chester, "Engaging Sexual Demons in Marina Tsvetaeva's 'Devil': The Body and the Genesis of the Woman Poet," *Slavic Review* 53.4 (1994), 321–38.

21. A volume of Tsvetaeva's lyric *poemy* (thus excluding *Perekop*) was assembled by Elena Korkina, with a short, helpful introduction and full commentary: Tsvetaeva, *Poemy 1920–1927* (St. Petersburg: Abris, 1994).

22. Michael Makin, "Text and Violence in Tsvetaeva's *Molodets*," *Discontinuous Discourses in Modern Russian Literature*, ed. Catriona Kelly, Michael Makin, and David Shepherd (Houndmills, Basingstoke, Hampshire: MacMillan, 1989), 115–35.

23. See, for example, M. S. Smith, "Marina Tsvetaeva's *Perekop*: Recuperation of the Russian Bardic Tradition," *Oxford Slavonic Papers*, n.s., 2.32 (1999), 97–126; and two essays by Catherine Ciepiela: "Leading the Revolution: Tsvetaeva's 'The Pied Piper' and Blok's 'The Twelve,'" in *Marina Tsvetaeva: One Hundred Years*, ed. Viktoria Shweitzer, Jane A. Taubman, Peter Scotto, and Tatyana Babyonyshev (Oakland, CA: Berkeley Slavic Specialties, 1994), 111–30, and "Taking Monologism Seriously: Bakhtin and Tsvetaeva's *The Pied Piper*," *Slavic Review* 53.4 (1994), 1010–24. *The Pied Piper* has now been translated into English as *The Ratcatcher* by Angela Livingstone (Evanston, IL: Northwestern University Press, 1999); Livingstone cites some of the high praise for the poem in her Introduction (see 10–11).

24. On the interconnections between Tsvetaeva's and Pasternak's long poems and their views of epic, lyric, history, and the *poema*, see Ciepiela, *The Same Solitude*, 131–77.

25. Ivanov's work has however been newly translated: Georgy Ivanov, *On the Border of Snow and Melt: Selected Poems*, trans. Jerome Katsell and Stanislav Shvabrin (Santa Monica, CA: Perceval Press, 2011); *Disintegration of the Atom; Petersburg Winters*, trans. Jerome Katsell and Stanislav Shvabrin (Brighton, MA: Academic Studies Press, 2016).

26. A classic 1966 work by Vladimir Markov, in which Ivanov is compared to Prince Viazemsky, was republished in Russia in 1994. See Vladimir Markov, "Russkie tsitatnye poety: zametki o poezii P. A. Viazemskogo i Georgiia Ivanova," Markov, *O svobode i poezii* (St. Petersburg: Izd. Chernysheva, 1994), 214–32. In the 2000s, two biographies of Ivanov appeared: Andrei Ar'ev, *Zhizn' Georgiia Ivanova: dokumental'noe povestvovanie* (St. Petersburg: Zvezda, 2009); and Vadim Kreid, *Georgii Ivanov* (Moscow: Molodaia gvardiia, 2007). See also *Georgii Vladimirovich Ivanov. Issledovaniia i materialy*, ed. Sergei Fediakin (Moscow: Izd. Literaturnogo instituta, 2011).

Chapter 3

1. For her account of the Russian Futurists, see Marjorie Perloff, "The Word Set Free: Text and Image in the Russian Futurist Book," in Marjorie Perloff, *The Futurist Moment: Avant-garde, Avant Guerre, and the Language of Rupture* (Chicago: University of Chicago Press, 1986), 116–61 (Chapter 4).

2. For complete accounts of these and many others, see Vladimir Markov, *Russian Futurism* ([1968] Washington, DC: New Academic Publishing, 2006).

3. See Gerald Janecek, *The Look of Russian Literature: Avant-garde Visual Experiments, 1900–1930* (Princeton, NJ: Princeton University Press, 1984); and Nancy Perloff, *Explodity: Sound, Image, and Word in Russian Futurist Book Art* (Los Angeles: Getty Research Institute, 2016).

4. Cited in Janecek, *The Look of Russian Literature*, 161.

5. On the visual and aural elements of this work, see Nancy Perloff, "*Mirskontsa* (Worldbackwards): Collaborative Book Art and Transrational Sounds," *Getty Research Journal*, 5 (2013), 101–18.

6. For example, in his translation of Velimir Khlebnikov's "Self-Statement," in Khlebnikov, *Collected Works of Velimir Khlebnikov*, trans. Paul Schmidt, 3 vols. (Cambridge, MA: Harvard University Press, 1987), vol. 1, 147.

7. For an account of the enthusiastically received performances, see Markov, *Russian Futurism*, 144–7.

8. Clare Cavanagh, *Lyric Poetry and Modern Politics: Russia, Poland, and the West* (New Haven, CT: Yale University Press, 2009), 89.

9. Roman Jakobson, "On a Generation that Squandered Its Poets," in Jakobson, *Language in Literature*, ed. Krystyna Pomorska and Stephen Rudy (Cambridge, MA: Belknap Press at Harvard University Press, 1987), 273–300, quotation on 274; compare a formulation later in the essay, that Mayakovsky "nurtured in his heart the unparalleled anguish of the present generation" (289).

10. Victor Terras, *A History of Russian Literature* (New Haven, CT: Yale University Press, 1991), 444.

11. Vladimir Maiakovskii, *Sobranie sochinenii*, 6 vols. (Moscow: Biblioteka Ogonek, Izdatel′stvo Pravda, 1973), vol. 1, 69.

12. See Boris Groys, *The Total Art of Stalinism: Avant-garde, Aesthetic Dictatorship, and Beyond*, trans. Charles Rougle (Princeton, NJ: Princeton University Press, 1992).

13. Iurii Karabchievskii, *Voskresenie Maiakovskogo* (Munich: Strana i mir, 1985); A. K. Zholkovskii, "O genii i zlodeistve, o babe i vserossiiskom masshtabe (Progulki po Maiakovskomu)," in A. K. Zholkovskii and Iu. K. Shcheglov, *Mir avtora i struktura teksta: Stat′i o russkoi literature* (Tenafly, NJ: Hermitage Press, 1986), 255–78.

14. Maiakovskii, *Sobranie sochinenii*, vol. 6, 288.

15. Mikhail Vaiskopf, "Vo ves′ logos: religiia Maiakovskogo," in Mikhail Vaiskopf, *Ptitsa-troika i kolesnitsa dushi: Raboty 1978–2003 godov* (Moscow: NLO, 2003), 343–486, quotation on 364.

16. Vaiskopf, "Vo ves′ logos," 427.

17. Iurii Tynianov, "O Khlebnikove," *Literaturnyi fakt* (Moscow: Vysshaia shkola, 1993), 233.

18. See Robin Milner-Gulland, "Khlebnikov's Eye," in *Russian Literature, Modernism and the Visual Arts*, ed. Catriona Kelly and Stephen Lovell (Cambridge: Cambridge University Press, 2000), 197–219. Among V. Grigor′ev's extensive writings on Khlebnikov, see *Velimir Khlebnikov v chetyrekhmernom prostranstve iazyka: Izbrannye raboty. 1958–2000-e gody* (Moscow: Iazyki slavianskikh kul′tur, 2006).

19. Velimir Khlebnikov, *Doski sud′by*, ed. V. V. Babkov (Moscow: Rubezh stoletiia, 2000), with extensive commentary by Babkov.

20. Velimir Khlebnikov, *Sobranie sochinenii*, ed. R. V. Duganov, 6 vols. (Moscow: Nasledie, 2000), in which all cited Khlebnikov texts can be found.

21. The stone women and the broader trend toward archaic culture in the avant-garde are discussed in Michael Kunichika, *"Our Native Antiquity": Archaeology and Aesthetics in the Culture of Russian Modernism* (Boston, MA: Academic Studies Press, 2015).

22. He has also been well translated into French, for example, Velimir Khlebnikov, *Nouvelles du je et du monde*, trans. Jean Claude Lanne (Paris: Imprimerie nationale, 1994); and recently *Œuvres 1919–1922*, trans. Yvan Mignot (Paris: Verdier, 2017).

23. Khlebnikov, *Sobranie sochinenii*, vol. 1, 239.

24. Khlebnikov, *Collected Works*, vol. 3, 39.

25. Sofiia Starkina, *Velimir Khlebnikov. Korol′ vremeni* (St. Petersburg: Vita Nova, 2005), 153.

26. Published in *Pamiat′ teper′ mnogo razvorachivaet: Iz literaturnogo naslediia Kruchenykh*, ed. Nina Gurianova (Berkeley, CA: Berkeley Slavic Specialties, 1999), 162–88.

27. Janecek, *The Look of Russian Literature*, 69.

28. As twice noted by Roman Jakobson, in "On Realism in Art" and "What Is Poetry?," in Jakobson, *Language in Literature*, 19–27, 368–78, see 23 and 370.

29. Aleksei Kruchenykh, *Stikhotvoreniia. Poemy. Romany. Opera*, ed. S. R. Karsitskii (St. Petersburg: Gumanitarnoe agentstvo "Akademicheskii proekt," 2000), 55. One measure of Kruchenykh's

broad influence is the appearance of a volume of his poems translated into English: *Suicide Circus: Selected Poems*, trans. Jack Hirschman, Alexander Kohav, and Venyamin Tseytlin (Los Angeles: Green Integer, 2001).

30. As cited in N. A. Bogomolov, "'Dyr bul shchyl' v kontekste epokhi," *NLO*, 72 (2005), http://magazines.russ.ru/nlo/2005/72/bo8.html (last accessed May 29, 2016). The phrase comes from Pavel Florenskii, *U vodorazdelov mysli* (Moscow: Izdatel'stvo Pravda, 1990), 183–4.

31. Severianin's creation of a persona is the subject of a chapter in Aleksey Berg, "Russian Poetry in the Marketplace: 1800–1917 and Beyond," Ph.D. dissertation, Harvard University, 2013.

32. Markov, *Russian Futurism*, 92–3.

33. Igor' Severianin, "Igor' Severianin beseduet s Igorem Lotarevym o svoem 35-letnem iubilee," in *Igor' Severianin. Tsarstvennyi Paiats. Avtobiograficheskie materialy*, ed. N. Terekhina and N. I. Shubnikova-Guseva (St. Petersburg: Rostok, 2005), 43–5, quotation on 44.

34. Osip Mandel'shtam, "Zametki o poezii," in *Slovo i kul'tura* (Moscow: Sovetskii pisatel', 1987), 71.

35. Influentially by Markov, *Russian Futurism*, 14. But there is *zaum* poetry by Olga Rozanova (1886–1918), who admired Guro's poetry and who was published by Kruchenykh. See *Sto odna poetessa serebrianogo veka*, ed. M. L. Gasparov, O. B. Kushlina, and T. L. Nikol'skaia (St. Petersburg: Izdatel'stvo DEAN, 2000), 183–4.

36. See *Elena Guro. Poet i khudozhnik. 1877–1913. Katalog vystavki. Zhivopis'. Grafika. Rukopisi. Knigi* (St. Petersburg: Mifril, 1994).

37. Elena Guro, *Nebesnye verbliuzhata: Izbrannoe*, ed. Arsen Mirzaev (St. Petersburg: Limbus Press, 2001), 123. Guro reworked and retitled the story as "Arrival in the Village" for her 1909 collection *Hurdy Gurdy*.

38. Guro, *Nebesnye verbliuzhata*, 124.

39. Guro, *Nebesnye verbliuzhata*, 218.

40. See Aleksandr Ulanov, "Vnimatel'naia radost'," a review of E. Guro, *Iz zapisnykh knizhek (1908–1913)*, *Znamia*, 7 (1998), http://magazines.russ.ru/znamia/1998/7/nabl3.html (last accessed December 17, 2015). Ulanov's phrase for her work is "shkola vnimaniia."

41. Milica Banjanin, "Between Symbolism and Futurism: Impressions by Day and by Night in Elena Guro's City Series," *SEEJ*, 37.1 (1993), 67–84, quotations on 69.

42. See Elena Guro, *Zhil na svete rytsar' bednyi*, ed. Evgenii Binevich (St. Petersburg: Fond russkoi poezii, 1999); Elena Guro, *Bednyi rytsar'* (Kolomna: MOK, 2015); and Elena Guro, *Selected Writings from the Archives*, ed. Anna Ljunggren and Nina Gourianova (Stockholm: Almqvist and Wiksell International, 1995).

43. Guro, *Selected Writings from the Archives*, 78 (from Nina Gourianova's introduction to the art criticism).

44. Markov, *Russian Futurism*, 17. See also Vladimir Toporov, "Mif o voploshchenii iunoshi-syna, ego smerti i voskresenii v tvorchestve Eleny Guro," in Vladimir Toporov, *Mif. Ritual. Simvol. Obraz. Issledovaniia v oblasti mifopoeticheskogo* (Moscow: Nauka, 1995), 400–27.

45. Elena Guro, *Sochineniia*, ed. G. K. Perkins (Oakland, CA: Berkeley Slavic Specialties, 1996), 180. This volume includes a well-documented account by Kevin O'Brien of Guro's life and works, and the state of scholarship as of the mid-1990s (375–88).

46. R. Rok, S. Sadikov, O. Erberg et al., "Vozzvanie k Dadaistam: Nichevoki Rossii—Dada Zapada," in *Sobachii iashchik* (Moscow: Khobo, 1923), 13.

47. Igor' Vasil'ev, *Russkii poeticheskii avangard XX veka* (Ekaterinburg: Izdatel'stvo Ural'skogo universiteta, 1999), 27.

48. Ippolit Sokolov, "Bedeker po ekspressionizmu," in *Literaturnye manifesty: Ot simvolizma do "Oktiabria,"* ed. N. L. Brodskii and N. Sidorov ([1924] Moscow: Agraf, 2001), 270.

49. *Russkii ekspressionizm: Teoriia. Praktika. Kritika*, ed. V. N. Terekhina (Moscow: IMLI RAN, 2005), 68.

50. Alexander Vvedensky, "Contracting Syphilis, Amputated Leg, Extracted Tooth," trans. Matvei Yankelevich, in Alexander Vvedensky, *An Invitation for Me to Think*, ed. Eugene Ostashevsky (New York: New York Review Books, 2013), 81. For the Russian original, see A. Vvedenskii, *Vse*, ed. Anna Gerasimova (Moscow: OGI, 2010), 207–8.

51. Branislav Jakovljevic, *Daniil Kharms: Writing and the Event* (Evanston, IL: Northwestern University Press, 2009), 70.

52. Vvedensky, *An Invitation for Me to Think*, xviii and 72; in Russian, "dikoe neponimanie," Vvedenskii, *Vse*, 176.

53. Vvedensky, "The Meaning of the Sea," in *An Invitation for Me to Think*, 16; Vvedenskii, *Vse*, 121.

54. *Oberiu: An Anthology of Russian Absurdism*, ed. Eugene Ostashevsky (Evanston, IL: Northwestern University Press, 2006), 205.

55. *Oberiu*, ed. Ostashevsky, 172; for the Russian original, see N. Zabolotskii, *Polnoe sobranie stikhotvorenii i poem*, 133.

56. *Oberiu*, ed. Ostashevsky, 137; for the Russian, see Daniil Kharms, *Polnoe sobranie sochinenii*, 3 vols. (St. Petersburg: Akademicheskii proekt, 1999), vol. 2, 114.

57. See Jakovljevic, *Daniil Kharms*; M. Iampol'skii, *Bespamiatstvo kak istok (chitaia Kharmsa)* (Moscow: NLO, 1998); Jean-Philippe Jaccard, *Daniil Harms et la fin de l'Avant-garde russe* (Berne: Peter Lang, 1991); Aleksandr Kobrinskii, *Poetika OBERIU v kontekste russkogo literaturnogo avangarda* (St. Petersburg: Izd.-vo russkogo kul'turologicheskogo litseia, 2000); Eugene Ostashevsky, "'Numbers Are Not Bound by Order': The Mathematical Play of Daniil Kharms and His Associates," *SEEJ*, 57.1 (2013), 28–48; Pratt, *Nikolai Zabolotsky*; and Iuliia Valieva, *Igra v bessmyslitsu: Poeticheskii mir Aleksandra Vvedenskogo* (St. Petersburg: Dmitrii Bulanin, 2007).

58. See Sergei E. Biriukov, "Grani neoavangarda: deistvuiushchie litsa, institutsii, gruppy, izdaniia, prezentatsii i t.d.," in *Imidzh, Dialog, Eksperiment: Polia sovremennoi russkoi poezii*, ed. Henrieke Stahl and Marion Rutz (Munich: Kubon & Sagner, 2013), 65–76.

59. See Irina Vinokurova, *"Vsego lish' genii . . .": Sud'ba Nikolaia Glazkova* (Moscow: Vremia, 2008).

60. Cited in Nikolai Glazkov, "Neizvestnye stikhi," *Arion*, 1 (1996), http://magazines.russ.ru/arion/1996/2/arion3.html (last accessed March 15, 2016); the poem with the phrase "vechnyi rab svoei svobody" can also be found here.

61. On his poetry, see Igor' Loshchilov, "Ob odnom stikhotvorenii Vladimira Kazakova," *Poetika iskanii, ili poisk poetiki. Materialy mezhdunarodnoi konferentsii-festivalia "Poeticheskii iazyk rubezha XX–XXI vekov i sovremennye literaturyne strategii" (16–19 maia 2003 goda)*, ed. N. A. Fateeva (Moscow: Institut russkogo iazyka im. V. V. Vinogradova RAN, 2004), 273–80. Kazakov's work was made newly available to readers in a three-volume set by Gileia Publishers in 1995.

62. See for example Elizaveta Mnatsakanova, "Khlebnikov: Klianus' . . .," in Elizaveta Mnatsakanova, *Arcadia: Izbrannye raboty 1972–2002* (Moscow: Izdatel'stvo R. Ellinina, 2006), 117–38. Although published by others, this edition has a sea-blue cover she designed, with her characteristic calligraphic signature.

63. The Requiem first appeared in the special journal created by Mikhail Shemiakin in Paris, *Apollon-77*, and has been multiply reprinted. See "Osen' v lazarete nevinnykh sester: Rekviem v semi chastiakh," *NLO*, 62 (2003), 253–71.

64. See Ry Nikonova, "Uktusskaia shkola," *NLO*, 16 (1995), 221–38.

65. Nikonova as well as other later avant-garde writers (Aygi and Mnatsakanova among them) are treated in Gerald Janecek, *Sight and Sound Entwined: Studies in the New Russian Poetry* (New York: Berghahn Books, 2000). On Nikonova, see also Inna Tigountseva, "Hybrid Forms in Ry Nikonova's Poetry," *SEEJ*, 53.1 (2009), 65–85.

66. Vasilisk Gnedov, *Sobranie sochinenii*, ed. N. Khardzhiev, M. Martsaduri, and S. Sigei, intro. and commentary Sergei Sigei (Trento: Department of the History of European Civilization, University of Trento, 1992).

67. In the first full-length study of Aygi in English, Valentine has emphasized the formative role that Chuvash played in Aygi's poetics. See Sarah Valentine, *Witness and Transformation: The Poetics of Gennady Aygi* (Boston, MA: Academic Studies Press, 2015).

68. Ol′ga Sedakova, "Aigi: Ot″ezd," in Sedakova, *Poetica*, 564.

69. For the poems, see Gennady Aygi, *Field-Russia*, trans. Peter France (New York: New Directions, 2007), 81, 138–40; Gennadii Aigi, *Polia-dvoiniki* (Moscow: OGI, 2006), 150, 175–7.

70. Aigi, *Polia-dvoiniki*, 202.

71. Andrei Ar′ev, "Nichei sovremennik (Viktor Sosnora: sluchai samovoskresheniia)," *Voprosy literatury*, 3 (2001), http://magazines.russ.ru/voplit/2001/3/ar.html (last accessed February 15, 2016).

72. A model for this turn to Russia's medieval history was Zabolotsky, whom Sosnora met in 1958. For a reading of a Sosnora poem that deeply responds to Zabolotsky's poetic world, see Darra Goldstein, "'Moscow in Fences': Viktor Sosnora at the Gate," *Russian Review*, 51.2 (1992), 230–7.

73. A better source for reading the poet, however, is the collection that includes even poems he never thought would be published: Viktor Sosnora, *Stikhotvoreniia* (St. Petersburg: Amfora, 2006, reissued 2011).

74. This side of Sosnora's work is emphasized by Aleksandr Skidan in a review of the 2006 volume of poems for *Kriticheskaia massa*, 3 (2006), http://www.litkarta.ru/dossier/skidan-o-sosnore/dossier_4649/ (last accessed February 15, 2016).

75. Sosnora, *Stikhotvoreniia*, 667.

76. Mnatsakanova has produced CD recordings of a number of her works, and interspersed her readings either with music of her own choosing, for example Richard Strauss's *Alpine Symphony*, or presented the poems with musical accompaniment composed by her friend Wolfgang Musil. See for example *Es kommt die Zeit/Nastanet vremia den′ pridet*, with texts from several of Mnatsakanova's books, undated; in a chronology she created for *Arcadia*, Mnatsakanova lists performances with Musil in 1993 (see 194).

77. Vadim Alekseev, "Khvost, artist complet," *NLO*, 72 (2005), 249.

78. As reported by Tat′iana Nikol′skaia, "Krug Alekseia Khvostenko," in *Istoriia leningradskoi nepodtsenzurnoi literatury: 1950–1980-e gody*, ed. B. I. Ivanov and B. A. Roginskii (St. Petersburg: Izdatel′stvo DEAN, 2000), 92–8; see 92 for the report about the turtle.

79. The best source for reading Khvostenko is the posthumously published volume with some commentary: Aleksei Khvostenko, *Verpa* (Tver: Kolonna Publications; Mitin zhurnal, 2005).

80. For a full listing, see the website http://khvost.indians.ru/ (last accessed September 14, 2017). Expressive, vivid footage of Khvostenko in performance is included in the DVD *Opyt postoronnego tvorcheskogo protsessa* (2004), which also exists as a CD. Khvostenko, in collaboration with Anri Volokhonsky, wrote poems meant for musical performance, collected in A. Kh. V. [Anri Volokhonskii and Aleksei Khvostenko], *Vseobshchee sobranie proizvedenii*, ed. and commentary Il′ia Kukui (Moscow: NLO, 2016) and *Berloga pchel* (Tver: Kolonna Publications; Mitin zhurnal, 2004). These volumes include a discography and extensive accounts of performances.

81. Kirill Medvedev, "Aleksei Khvostenko: Koleso vremeni," *Russkii zhurnal*, August 3, 1999, http://www.litkarta.ru/dossier/medvedev-hvostenko/dossier_2008/ (last accessed March 14, 2016).

82. Closer acquaintance of the Leningrad intelligentsia with the works of OBERIU is often dated to 1967, when Mikhail Meilakh and Anatoly Aleksandrov spoke about them at a student conference in Tartu. Vladimir Erl would go on to work on editions of Kharms and Vvedensky in the 1970s and 1980s. But it was also the case that copies of hard-to-find texts circulated among

members of unofficial circles; some spent considerable time reading pre-revolutionary and rare editions in the Leningrad Public Library, as documented in Stanislav Savitskii, "Khelenukty v teatre povsednevnosti," *NLO*, 30 (1998), 210–59, esp. 218 and 225. Savitsky includes extensive material from his interviews with surviving members and associates of Khelenukty here. See also Stanislav Savitskii, *Andegraund: Istoriia i mify leningradskoi neofitsial'noi literatury* (Moscow: NLO, 2002) for a broader account of unofficial Leningrad literary culture; the book includes extensive listings of groups, individuals, and bibliographical sources.

83. *Samizdat Leningrada 1950-e–1980-e: Literaturnaia entsiklopediia*, ed. D. Severiukhin, V. Dolinin, B. Ivanov, and B. Ostanin (Moscow: NLO, 2003), 359.

84. *Samizdat Leningrada*, ed. Severiukhin et al., 383.

85. A. A. Zhitenev, *Poeziia neomodernizma* (St. Petersburg: Inapress, 2014), 83–5.

86. Khvostenko, *Verpa*, 35. (This annotated volume reprints a number of the earlier collections.)

87. Recorded on Literaturnaia karta, http://www.litkarta.ru/russia/novosibirsk/persons/loshchilov-i/ (last accessed March 14, 2016).

88. Nikolai Kononov, "3000 znakov khoroshikh novostei: O knige V. Ivaniva 'Gorod Vinograd,'" 2010, http://www.litkarta.ru/dossier/3000znakov/dossier_2145/ (last accessed March 14, 2016).

89. Viktor Ivaniv, *Dom gruzchika* (Moscow: NLO, 2015), 72. The English translation is from Viktor Ivaniv, "Rút," trans. Kevin Platt, Bob Perelman, Kit Robinson, and Sarah Dowling, *1913*, 6 (2013), 58, http://www.journal1913.org/1913-journal/1913-a-journal-of-forms-6/ (last accessed March 15, 2016).

90. Nataliia Azarova, *Iazyk filosofii i izayk poezii: Dvizhenie navstrechu* (Moscow: Gnozis, 2010). Azarova is also a co-author and co-editor with Kirill Korchagin, Dmitrii Kuz'min, V. A. Plungian, and others of the massive *Poeziia: uchebnik* (Moscow: OGI, 2016). Among its significant features is a willingness to include contemporary examples in its survey of the formal, historical, social, and aesthetic features of Russian poetry.

91. Azarova has written about and published Aygi's work, for example, "Na grani filosofskogo i poeticheskogo teksta (iz opyta raboty s arkhivom G. Aigi)," *NLO*, 93 (2008), 261–80. She also edited a special journal issue dedicated to his work: *Russian Literature*, Special Issue: Gennadij Ajgi, 79–80 (2016).

92. Azarova's works, particularly in their visual formatting, can be well explored through her website: http://natalia-azarova.com/cgi-bin/index.pl (last accessed March 15, 2016).

93. The significance of visual accompaniment is also observed in Kirill Korchagin, "Vovne i vovnutr'," *OpenSpace*, November 21, 2011, http://www.litkarta.ru/dossier/vovne-i-vovnutr/dossier_808/ (last accessed March 15, 2016).

94. See Studiia A3/Akademiia Zaumi, http://заум.рф/?page_id=5 (last accessed March 15, 2016).

95. His wide-ranging anthology *Roku ukor: poeticheskie nachala* (Moscow: RGGU, 2003) collects texts across decades and includes introductions to visual poetry, anagrams, palindromes, sound poetry, and other topics.

96. An important early publication about Lianozovo poetics is Vladislav Kulakov, "Lianozovo," *Voprosy literatury*, 3 (1991), 3–45.

97. Ian Satunovskii, *Stikhi i proza k stikham*, ed. I. A. Akhmet'ev (Moscow: Virtual'naia galereia, 2012), 621. The quotation comes from an untitled and unfinished prose work, here given the title "[Bol'nichnaia tetrad']," 617–22.

98. For translations of Nekrasov into English, see Vsevolod Nekrasov, *I Live I See*, trans. Ainsley Morse and Bela Shayevich (Brooklyn, NY: Ugly Duckling Presse, 2013).

99. On the minimalism of Lianozovo poetics, see Gerald Janecek, "Vsevolod Nekrasov's Minimalist Poetry," in Janecek, *Sight and Sound Entwined*, 74–90; and Vladislav Kulakov, "Pauza skazhet vam bol'she: minimalizm v sovremennoi russkoi poezii," in Kulakov, *Postfaktum: kniga o stikhakh* (Moscow: NLO, 2007), 199–215.

100. Vladislav Kulakov, "Barachnaia poeziia Igoria Kholina kak klassicheskii epos novoi literatury," Kulakov, *Poeziia kak fakt: Stat'i o stikhakh* (Moscow: NLO, 1999), 157–60, esp. 158.

101. Nekrasov, *I Live I See*, 59. For the Russian, see Vsevolod Nekrasov, *Stikhi 1956–1983*, ed. M.A. Sukhotin, G. B. Zykova, and E. N. Penskaia (Vologda: Biblioteka Moskovskogo kontseptualizma Germana Titova, 2012), 45.

102. Nekrasov, *I Live I See*, 312–13, for both English and Russian.

103. Matthew Jesse Jackson, *The Experimental Group: Ilya Kabakov, Moscow Conceptualism, Soviet Avant-gardes* (Chicago: University of Chicago Press, 2010), 177.

104. Nekrasov, *Stikhi*, 400.

105. For example, Lev Rubinstein, *Thirty-Five New Pages*, trans. Philip Metres and Tatiana Tulchinsky (Brooklyn, NY: Ugly Duckling Presse, 2011); Lev Rubinshtein, *Chetyre teksta iz bol'shoi biblioteki* (Moscow: Vremia, 2011).

106. Lev Rubinshtein, *Bol'shaia kartoteka* (Moscow: NLO, 2015), 450–1.

107. Rubinstein, "Sonnet 66," trans. Michael Molnar, in *Crossing Centuries: The New Generation in Russian Poetry*, ed. John High et al. (Jersey City, NJ: Talisman House Publishers, 2000), 53. The numbers do not align with the Russian, perhaps because the translator was working from a different version; several editions indicate that Rubinshtein made some later changes to the card catalogue poems, of which this is one. In English, the poem has 113 lines; in Russian, 123.

108. This quality of Conceptualism is emphasized in a discussion of Ilya Kabakov's artwork in Jackson, *The Experimental Group*, 45.

109. Dmitrii A. Prigov, *Moskva: Virshi na kazhdyi den'*, ed. Brigitte Obermayr and Georg Witte (Moscow: NLO, 2015), 237.

110. *Slovar' terminov Moskovskoi kontseptual'noi shkoly*, ed. Andrei Monastyrskii (Moscow: Ad Marginem, 1999), 193.

111. Prigov, *Moskva*, 238.

112. Prigov, *Moskva*, 247.

113. Prigov, *Moskva*, 161, 163, 244, 244, respectively.

114. Prigov, *Moskva*, 237.

115. Prigov, *Moskva*, 248.

116. Prigov, *Moskva*, 242.

117. See Jacques Derrida, "Stucture, Sign, and Play in the Discourse of the Human Sciences," in *A Postmodern Reader*, ed. Joseph Natoli and Linda Hutcheon (Albany: SUNY Press, 1993), 223–42, esp. 240–1.

118. Mikhail N. Epstein, "New Currents in Russian Poetry: Conceptualism, Metarealism, and Presentism," in Mikhail N. Epstein, *After the Future: The Paradoxes of Postmodernism and Contemporary Russian Culture*, trans. Anesa Miller-Pogacar (Amherst: University of Massachusetts Press, 1995), 19–50, quotations on 37 and 38.

119. His connection to the LANGUAGE poets has been an especially fruitful site of study. See for example Jacob Edmond, "Arkadii Dragomoshchenko and Poetic Correspondence," in Jacob Edmond, *A Common Strangeness: Contemporary Poetry, Cross-Cultural Encounter, Comparative Literature* (New York: Fordham University Press, 2012), 44–71.

120. See Arkadii Dragomoshchenko, "Sentimental'naia elegiia" and "Nasturtsiia kak real'nost'," in Arkadii Dragomoshchenko, *Opisanie* (St. Petersburg: Izdatel'skii Tsentr "Gumanitarnaia Akademiia," 2000), 254–6, 288–305; and "Ludwig Josef Johann" and "Baudelaire à midi," in Arkadii Dragomoshchenko, *Tavtologiia* (Moscow: NLO, 2011), 15–16, 127. Catherine Ciepiela argues that his "signal accomplishment" was to fuse the strands of Russian modernism with Western postmodernism: Catherine Ciepiela, "The Legacy of the Underground Poets," in

Russian Literature since 1991, ed. Evgeny Dobrenko and Mark Lipovetsky (Cambridge: Cambridge University Press, 2015), 207–25, see 217.

121. Mikhail Iampol′skii, "Poetika kasaniia," in Dragomoshchenko, *Opisanie*, 356–77; and Mikhail Iampol′skii, *Iz khaosa (Dragomoshchenko: poeziia, fotografiia, filosofiia)* (St. Petersburg: Seans, 2015).

122. Ivan Zhdanov, "Portret," in *Poety-metarealisty: Aleksandr Eremenko, Ivan Zhdanov, Aleksei Parshchikov*, ed. Igor′ Klekh (Moscow: MK-Periodika, 2002), 95.

123. See also the translation in Ivan Zhdanov, *The Inconvertible Sky*, trans. John High and Patrick Henry (Jersey City, NJ: Talisman Publishers, 1997), 33.

124. Aleksandr Eremenko, *Stikhi* (Moscow: IMA Press, 1991), 46, quoted in Aleksei Parshchikov, *Rai medlennogo ognia* (Moscow: NLO, 2006), 25.

125. See Aleksei Parshchikov, "SUN Maikla Palmera," in Parshchikov, *Rai medlennogo ognia*, 85–112; the translations are variously available, including a generous selection in *Inostrannaia literatura*, 3 (2013), 223–65; Maikl Palmer, *Sun: Stikhotvoreniia, poema i esse*, trans. Aleksei Parshchikov (Moscow: Kommentarii, 2000); and M. Palmer, *Pod znakom alfavita*, trans. Arkadii Dragomoshchenko and Aleksandr Skidan (St. Petersburg: Poriadok slov, 2015). Several are discussed in "Maikl Palmer: poeziia vsegda est′ nekii vyzov," a conversation with Elena Kostyleva, Michael Palmer, and Aleksandr Skidan, *Colta*, February 3, 2016, http://www.colta.ru/articles/literature/9993 (accessed May 4, 2016).

126. *Poety-metarealisty*, 170. The first publication of the poem is in Aleksei Parshchikov, *Vybrannoe* (Moscow: ITs-Grant, 1996). A recording of Parshchikov reading the poem is included in the memorial website, http://parshchikov.ru/figury-intuitsii/begstvo-2 (last accessed November 11, 2016).

127. For translations of Parshchikov's poetry, see *Third Wave: The New Russian Poetry*, ed. Kent Johnson and Stephen M. Ashby (Ann Arbor: University of Michigan Press, 1992), 16; Parshchikov also co-authored (with Andrew Wachtel) the Introduction to this volume, 1–11.

128. Dragomoshchenko's set of prose fragments by that title appears in *Dust*, trans. Evgeny Pavlov, Thomas Epstein, Shushan Avagyan, and Ana Lučić (Champaign, IL, and London: Dalkey Archive Press, 2008), 91–4, but the image appears in countless other poems as well.

129. Parshchikov's original reads "ia ishchu tebia, soboi ne iavliaias′, / nas, vozmozhno, rassasyvaet zemlia" (*Poety-metarealisty*, 170).

130. Andrew Wachtel, "The Youngest Archaists: Kutik, Sedakova, Kibirov, Parshchikov," in *Rereading Russian Poetry*, ed. Sandler, 270–86, quotation on 283.

131. Tsibulia won the Arkady Dragomoshchenko Prize in 2015. For her poems, see Aleksandra Tsibulia, *Puteshestvie na krai krovi* (Moscow: Russkii Gulliver, 2014).

132. See Dmitrii Kuz′min, "Russkaia poeziia v nachale XXI veka," *Rets*, 48 (2008), http://www.litkarta.ru/dossier/kuzmin-review/ (last accessed May 5, 2016).

133. See Faina Grimberg, "Andrei Ivanovich vozvrashchaetsia domoi," in *Chetyrekhlistnik dlia moego ottsa* (Moscow: NLO, 2012), 17–30; and, to cite two of the Blockade poems, Polina Barskova, "Sdelannost′ (gorodskie kartiny)," in Polina Barskova, *Priamoe upravlenie* (St. Petersburg: Pushkinskii fond, 2005), 66–71; and "Bitva," in Polina Barskova, *Khoziain sada* (St. Petersburg: Knizhnye masterskie, 2016), 113–16.

134. For example, Mariia Stepanova, *Proza Ivana Sidorova* (Moscow: Novoe izdatel′stvo, 2008).

135. For the poems, see Nika Skandiaka, *12/4/2007* (Moscow: NLO, 2007) and poems in *Vozdukh*, nos. 3–4 (2015), http://www.litkarta.ru/projects/vozdukh/issues/2015-3-4/skandiaka/ (last accessed May 17, 2016). For her blogs, see http://pini3.livejournal.com and http://999999.livejournal.com (the latter features translations, which she has also produced extensively).

136. A. A. Zhitenev, *Poeziia neomodernizma* (St. Petersburg: Inapress, 2012), 416.

137. Aleksei Parshchikov, "Vozvrashchenie aury?," *NLO*, 82 (2006), http://www.litkarta.ru/dossier/vozvr-aury/dossier_6135/ (last accessed May 6, 2016).

138. Their work is a subject of Maria Khotimsky, "'A Remedy for Solitude': Translation in the Works of Russian Poets in the Soviet and Post-Soviet Eras," Ph.D. Dissertation, Harvard University, 2011.

139. Examples include Stanislav L'vovskii, *Camera rostrum* (Moscow: NLO, 2008); Mikhail Gronas, *Dorogie siroty* (Moscow: OGI, 2002); and Grigorii Dashevskii, *Neskol'ko stikhotvorenii i perevodov* (Moscow: Kaspar Khauzer, 2014).

Chapter 4

1. Mikhail Bakhtin, "Epic and Novel," in Mikhail Bakhtin, *The Dialogic Imagination: Four Essays*, ed. Michael Holquist, trans. Caryl Emerson and Michael Holquist (Austin: University of Texas Press, 2004), 3–40, esp. 39.

2. Cited from "The End of the Novel," trans. Jane Gary Harris, in Osip Mandelstam, *The Complete Critical Prose and Letters*, ed. Jane Gary Harris (Ann Arbor, MI: Ardis, 1979), 199–200. For the Russian original, see Mandel'shtam, "Konets romana," in Osip Mandel'shtam, *Sobranie sochinenii*, 2 vols. (Moscow: Khudozhestvennaia literatura, 1990), vol. 2, 203. Similarly, Lydia Ginzburg would write that the historical moment itself demanded a search for new narrative forms. For Ginzburg's views, see Chapter 2, "The Poetics of Desk-Drawer Notebooks," in Emily Van Buskirk, *Lydia Ginzburg's Prose: Reality in Search of Literature* (Princeton, NJ: Princeton University Press, 2016), esp. 81–4.

3. See Naum Berkovskii, *Literatura i teatr: Stat'i raznykh let* (Moscow: Iskusstvo, 1969), 148–9.

4. See Aleksandr Chudakov, *Chekhov's Poetics*, trans. Edwina Jannie Cruise and Donald Dragt (Ann Arbor, MI: Ardis, 1983); Aleksandr Chudakov, *Mir Chekhova: Vozniknovenie i utverzhdenie* (Moscow: Sovetskii pisatel', 1986). Chudakov's concept derives from the philosophical approach to Chekhov first developed by Lev Shestov. For the later development of Chekhovian poetics, see Cathy Popkin, *The Pragmatics of Insignificance: Chekhov, Zoshchenko, Gogol* (Stanford, CA: Stanford University Press, 1993).

5. Gary Saul Morson, "*Uncle Vanya* as Prosaic Melodrama," in *Reading Chekhov's Text*, ed. R. L. Jackson (Evanston, IL: Northwestern University Press, 1993), 214–47, quotation on 214. See also G. S. Morson, "Prosaic Chekhov: Metadrama, the Intelligentsia, and *Uncle Vanya*," *Triquarterly*, 80 (1990), 118–59.

6. Morson, "*Uncle Vanya* as Prosaic Melodrama," 225.

7. See Svetlana Evdokimova, "What's So Funny about Losing One's Estate, or Infantilism in *The Cherry Orchard*," *SEEJ*, 44.4 (2000), 623–48.

8. For the story of their relationship, see Pavel Basinskii, *Gor'kii* (Moscow: Molodaia gvardiia, 2005), 252–307.

9. As Dmitry Merezhkovsky wrote in his article "Chekhov and Gorky" (1906): "Sometimes it seems that Gorky's *bosiaki* read the philosopher Nietzsche, although in a cheap and not entirely accurate Russian translation, yet nevertheless they understood him better than members of the Russian intelligentsia"; cited from Dmitrii Merezhkovskii, "Chekhov i Gor'kii," in Dmitrii Merezhkovskii, *Maksim Gor'kii: Pro et contra: antologiia: lichnost' i tvorchestvo Maksima Gor'kogo v otsenke myslitelei i issledovatelei 1890-kh-1910-kh godov*, ed. D. Burlaka (St. Petersburg: Izd. Russkogo Khristianskogo gumanitarnogo instituta, 1997), 643–686, quotation on 658.

10. Dmitrii Bykov, "Sam sebe chelovek: Maksim Gor'kii (1868–1936)," in *Literaturnaia matritsa: Uchebnik, napisannyi pisateliami*, ed. V. Levental', 2 vols. (St. Petersburg: Limbus-Press, 2010), vol. I, 103–30, quotation on 107.

11. Nietzsche's influence on Gorky was discussed starting in the 1900s. The most detailed analysis from that period can be found in the article by M. Gel'rot, "Nitsshe i Gor'kii" initially published in *Russkoe bogatstvo*, 5 (1903), 24–65. However, many other critics, from Nikolai Mikhailovsky to Merezhkovsky, addressed this affinity as well. For recent work, see: Hans Günther, *Der sozialistische Übermensch: Maksim Gor'kij und der sowjetische Heldenmythos* (Stuttgart: J. B. Metzler, 1993); Edith Clowes, "Gorky, Nietzsche, and God-Building," *Fifty Years On: Gorky and His Time*, ed. Nicholas Luker (Nottingham: Astra Press, 1987), 127–44; Bernice Glazer Rosenthal, *New Myth, New World: From Nietzsche to Stalinism* (University Park: Pennsylvania State University Press, 2002), 68–93; Pavel Basinskii, "Maksim Gor'kii," *Russkaia literatura rubezha vekov (1890-e–nachalo 1920-kh godov)*, 2 vols. (Moscow: IMLI RAN, Nauka, 2001), vol. 1, 511–17.

12. Cited from D. S. Mirsky, *Contemporary Russian Literature (1881–1925)* (New York: Alfred Knopf, 1926), 116–17.

13. Mikhail Bakhtin, *Problems of Dostoevsky's Poetics*, ed. and trans. Caryl Emerson (Minneapolis: University of Minnesota Press, 1984), 115.

14. See Naum Leiderman, *Teoriia zhanra: Issledovaniia i razbory* (Ekaterinburg: UO RAN, 2010), 431–60, esp. 453–8.

15. Gorky's "cult of the sacred artistic lie" may stem not only from Nietzsche but also from the Populists' cult of the enlightening intelligentsia as seen in Chernyshevsky's utopian novel *What Is to Be Done?* See Iurii V. Zobnin, "Po tu storonu istiny (sluchai Gor'kogo)," in *Maksim Gor'kii: Pro et contra*, 15–25.

16. Viktor Shklovskii, *Udachi i porazheniia Maksima Gor'kogo* (Tiflis: Zakkniga, 1926), 7.

17. See Richard Stites, *Revolutionary Dreams: Utopian Vision and Experimental Life in the Russian Revolution* (Oxford: Oxford University Press, 1991), 101–23. See also Barry P. Scherr, "God-Building or God-Seeking? Gorky's *Confession* as Confession," *SEEJ*, 44.3 (Autumn 2000), 448–69; Raimund Sesterhenn, *Das Bogostroitel'stvo bei Gor'kij und Lunačarskij bis 1909: Zur ideologischen und literarischen Vorgeschichte der Parteischule von Capri* (Munich: Otto Sagner, 1982).

18. Stephen Hutchings, "Mythic Consciousness, Cultural Shifts, and the Prose of Leonid Andreev," *Modern Language Review* 85.1 (1990), 107–23, cited from 108.

19. Leonid Andreev, *Povesti i rasskazy*, 2 vols. (Moscow: Khudozhestvennaia literatura, 1971), vol. 1, 531.

20. Dmitrii Merezhkovskii, "V obez'iannikh lapakh (O Leonide Andreeve)," *Akropol': Izbrannye literaturno-kriticheskie stat'i* (Moscow: Knizhnaia palata, 1991), 185–208, quotation on 189.

21. The story's problematization of sexual norms is discussed in Fredric H. White, "Peering into the Abyss: Andreev's Rejoinder to Tolstoi's *Kreutzer Sonata*," *Canadian Slavonic Papers/Revue canadienne des slavistes*, 1.3–4 (September–December 2008), 471–86.

22. A. V. Tatarinov, "Leonid Andreev," *Russkaia literatura rubezha vekov*, Book 2, 306.

23. See K. V. Driagin, *Ekspressionizm v Rossii: Dramaturgiia Leonida Andreeva* (Viatka: Izd. Viatskogo pedinstituta imeni Lenina, 1928); Nataliia Bondareva, *Tvorchestvo Leonida Andreeva i nemetskii ekspressionizm* (Orel: Orlovskii gosudarstvennyi universitet, 2005).

24. Mirsky, *Contemporary Russian Literature*, 105.

25. Andreev's reputation in late Soviet scholarship is analyzed in Yuri Leving and Fredrick H. White, *Marketing Literature and Posthumous Legacies: The Symbolic Capital of Leonid Andreev and Vladimir Nabokov* (Lanham: Lexington Books, 2013), 53–68.

26. For later biographies of Gorky, see Tovah Yedlin, *Maxim Gorky: A Political Biography* (Westport, CT: Praeger, 1999); Basinskii, *Gor'kii*; Dmitrii Bykov, *Byl li Gor'kii? Biograficheskii ocherk* (Moscow: AST, 2008); Bykov, *Gor'kii* (Moscow: Molodaia Gvardiia, 2016). For Andreev, see Natal'ia Skorokhod, *Leonid Andreev* (Moscow: Molodaia gvardiia, 2013); Liudmila Ken, *Zhizn' Leonida Andreeva, rasskazannaia im samim i ego sovremennikami* (St. Petersburg: KOSTA, 2010); and see *Leonid Andreev: Materialy i issledovaniia*, ed. V. A. Keldysh and M. V. Koz'menko (Moscow: IMLI, Nasledie, 2000).

27. Vladimir Nabokov, *Speak, Memory: An Autobiography Revisited*, rev. edn. (New York: G. P. Putnam & Sons, 1966), 211.

28. John E. Malmstad and Nikolay Bogomolov, *Mikhail Kuzmin: A Life in Art* (Cambridge, MA: Harvard University Press, 1999), 96.

29. See David M. Bethea, "Sologub, Nabokov, and the Limits of Decadent Aesthetics," *Russian Review*, 63.1 (2004), 48–62.

30. Konstantin Mochul'skii, *Andrei Belyi* (Paris: YMCA Press, 1955), 171.

31. See Leonid Dolgopolov, *Andrei Belyi i ego roman "Peterburg"* (Leningrad: Sovetskii pisatel', 1988), 260–2.

32. Quoted in Mochulskii, *Andrei Belyi*, 171–2.

33. Iu. M. Lotman, "Literatura i mifologiia," in Lotman, *Istoriia i tipologiia russkoi kul'tury* (St. Petersburg: Iskusstvo-SPb, 2002), 727–43, quotation on 743.

34. See Vladimir N. Toporov, "Peterburg i 'peterburgskii tekst russkoi literatury,'" in Toporov, *Mif. Ritual. Simvol. Obraz: Issledovaniia v oblasti mifopoeticheskogo* (Moscow: Progress-Kul'tura, 1995), 259–367.

35. See Stites, *Revolutionary Dreams*; Leonid Heller and Michel Niqueux, *Histoire de l'utopie en Russie* (Paris: Presses universitaires de France, 1995); Boris F. Egorov, *Rossiiskie utopii: Istoricheskii putevoditel'* (St. Petersburg: Iskusstvo-SPb, 2007); and Aleksandr Etkind, *Khlyst: Sekty, literatura i revoliutsiia* (Moscow: NLO, 2013).

36. See George M. Young, *The Russian Cosmists: The Esoteric Futurism of Nikolai Fedorov and His Followers* (Oxford: Oxford University Press, 2012).

37. Evgenii Zamiatin, *Bol'shim detiam skazki* (Berlin and Petrograd: Izdatel'stvo Z. I. Grzhebina, 1922), 46.

38. Mark Steinberg, *Proletarian Imagination: Self, Modernity, and the Sacred in Russia, 1910–1925* (Ithaca, NY: Cornell University Press, 2002), 213.

39. Vladimir Mayakovsky, *The Bedbug and Selected Poetry*, trans. Max Hayward and George Reavey, ed. Patricia Blake (New York: Meridian Books, 1960), 286.

40. Mayakovsky, *The Bedbug and Selected Poetry*, 302.

41. For the full publication history, see J. A. E. Curtis, *The Englishman from Lebedian: A Life of Evgeny Zamiatin* (Brighton, MA: Academic Studies Press, 2013), 164–5.

42. Yevgeny Zamyatin, *We*, trans. Clarence Brown (New York: Penguin Books, 1993), 135.

43. Zamyatin, *We*, 159, 124.

44. Zamyatin, *We*, 225.

45. Viktor Shklovskii, *Tret'ia fabrika* (Moscow: Artel' pisatelei "Krug," 1926), 125–7.

46. Thomas Seifrid, *Andrei Platonov: Uncertainties of Spirit* (Cambridge: Cambridge University Press, 1992), 2.

47. See Young, *The Russian Cosmists*; Irene Masing-Delic, *Abolishing Death: A Salvation Myth of Russian Twentieth-Century Literature* (Stanford, CA: Stanford Univeristy Press, 1992), 76–105.

48. See Kevin Platt, *Terror and Greatness: Ivan and Peter as Russian Myths* (Ithaca, NY: Cornell University Press, 2011), 216–31.

49. See Eric Naiman, "V zhopu prorubit' okno: seksual'naia patologiia kak ideologicheskii kalambur u Andreia Platonova," *NLO*, 32 (1998), http://magazines.russ.ru/nlo/1998/32/naiman.html (last accessed August 12, 2016).

50. Seifrid, *Andrei Platonov*, 123. For commentary on the novel, see Evgeny Iablokov, *Putevoditel' po romanu A. P. Platonova "Chevengur"* (Moscow: Izd. Moskovskogo universiteta, 2012).

51. Andrei Platonov, *Chevengur. Kotlovan* (Moscow: Vremia, 2009), 304.

52. Platonov, *Chevengur. Kotlovan*, 306.

53. Andrei Platonov, *The Foundation Pit*, in Andrei Platonov, *Collected Works*, trans. Thomas Whitney (Ann Arbor, MI: Ardis, 1978), 3–158, quotation on 113. For the Russian, see Platonov, *Chevengur. Kotlovan*, 498.

54. Joseph Brodsky, "Catastrophes in the Air," in Joseph Brodsky, *Less Than One* (New York: Farrar, Straus & Giroux, 1986), 268–303, quotation on 290.

55. Although a few parts of *Chevengur* were published as if separate texts beginning in the 1960s, such as "The Origins of the Master" ("Proiskhozhdenie mastera") and "Kopenkin's Death" ("Smert' Kopenkina"), full publication occurred for *The Foundation Pit* in *Novyi mir*, 6 (1987) and *Chevengur* in *Druzhba narodov*, 3–4 (1988).

56. A notable parallel for Platonov's *Juvenile Sea* appears in Nikolai Zabolotsky's long poems of the 1930s, *A Mad Wolf* (*Bezumnyi volk*, 1931) and *The Triumph of Agriculture* (*Torzhestvo zemledeliia*, 1933). Also an avid follower of Nikolai Fedorov's philosophy, Zabolotsky intended to convey a utopian vision of the forces of nature, especially wild and domestic animals, striving for collectivization. However, critics perceived these poems as a mockery of official politics.

57. See Nina Malygina and I. Matveeva, "Kommentarii," in Platonov, *Efirnyi trakt: Povesti 1920-kh–nachala 1930-kh godov* (Moscow: Vremia, 2009), 552–4.

58. Hans Günther and Il'ia Kukui, "Andrei Platonov," in *Russkaia literatura XX veka: 1930-e gody-seredina 1950-kh godov*, ed. Naum Leiderman, Mark Lipovetskii, and Mariia Litovskaia, 2 vols. (Moscow: Academia, 2014), vol. 2, 245–6.

59. See Hans Günther, "*Schastlivaia Moskva* i arkhetip materi v sovetskoi kul'ture 30-kh godov," in "*Strana filosofov*" *Andreia Platonova. Problemy tvorchestva*, ed. Natal'ia Kornienko (Moscow: Nasledie, Nauka, 1999), vol. 3, 170–5, esp. 172. This volume includes a large cluster of articles and materials on *Happy Moscow* (6–371).

60. Ol'ga Meerson, "*Svobodnaia veshch'*": *poetika neostraneniia u Andreia Platonova* (Berkeley, CA: Berkeley Slavic Specialties, 1997), 19.

61. Belyaev has begun to attract scholarly interest: see Zeev Bar-Sella, *Aleksandr Beliaev* (Moscow: Molodaia gvardiia, 2013); and the site dedicated to Belyaev: http://www.alexandrbelyaev.ru/ (last accessed August 12, 2016).

62. Lidiia Chukovskaia, *Zapiski ob Anne Akhmatovoi*, 3 vols. (Moscow: Soglasie, 1997), vol. 2, 563.

63. See N. G. Medvedeva, "Mifologicheskii neoromantizm Aleksandra Grina," in *Russkaia literatura XX veka: 1917–1920-e gody*, ed. N. L. Leiderman, 2 vols. (Moscow: Academia, 2012), vol. 1, 418–25; Evgenii Iablokov, *Roman Aleksandra Grina "Blistaiushchii mir"* (Moscow: Maks Press, 2005); and Vadim Kovskii, "'Nastoiashchaia vnutrenniaia zhizn'' (Psikhologicheskii romantizm Aleksandra Grina)," in *Realisty i romantiki*, ed. V. E. Kovskii (Moscow: Khudozhestvennaia literatura, 1990), 239–328.

64. Geoffrey G. Harpham, *On the Grotesque: Strategies of Contradiction in Art and Literature* (Princeton, NJ: Princeton University Press, 1982), 17.

65. Mikhail Bakhtin, *Rabelais and His World*, trans. Helene Iswolsky (Cambridge, MA: MIT Press, 1968), 34.

66. For example, *Pisatel' Leonid Dobychin: Vospominaniia. Stat'i. Pis'ma*, ed. Vladimir Bakhtin (St. Petersburg: Zhurnal Zvezda, 1995); and seven issues of *Dobychinskii sbornik* (Daugavpils: Saule, 1998–2011).

67. Dubravka Ugrešić, "O 'Gorode En' Leonida Dobychina," in *Pisatel' Leonid Dobychin*, ed. Bakhtin, 282. For a reading of the novel that successfully defines some of the patterns within this maze of topics, see Richard C. Borden, "The Flogging Angel: Toward a Mapping of Leonid Dobychin's *Gorod En*," *Russian Review*, 60 (April, 2001), 254–74.

68. Andrei Ar'ev, "Dobychin," in *Russkie pisateli XX veka: Biograficheskii slovar'*, ed. P. A. Nikolaev (Moscow: Randevu-AM, Bol'shaia sovetskaia entsiklopediia, 2000), 103.

69. Leonid Dobychin, *Gorod En* (Moscow: Direkt-Media, 2014), 84. The novel has been translated as *The Town of N*, trans. Richard C. Borden with Natasha Belova (Evanston, IL: Northwestern University Press, 1998).

70. Naum Leiderman, "The Intellectual Worlds of Sigizmund Krzhizhanovsky," trans. Caryl Emerson, *SEEJ*, 56.4 (2012), 507–35, quotation on 519.

71. On Krzhizhanovsky's reliance on Kantian material, see Rose Kleiner, "Kantian Zombies in Modernity's Graveyard: Benjaminian Allegory and the Critique of Enlightenment in Sigizmund Krzhizhanovsky," MA thesis, University of Colorado–Boulder, 2014.

72. Sigizmund Krzhizhanovskii, *Sobranie sochinenii v 5-ti tt.*, ed. V. Perel´muter, 5 vols. (St. Petersburg: Symposium, 2001), vol.1, 124; English translation provided by Rose Kleiner.

73. Caryl Emerson, "Introduction," to Sigizmund Krzhizhanovsky, *The Letter Killers Club*, trans. Joanne Turnbull with Nikolai Formozov (New York: New York Review Books Classics, 2011), vii–xviii, quotation on xvi.

74. Krzhizhanovsky, *The Letter Killers Club*, 79.

75. Leopol´d Averbakh, "O tselostnykh masshtabakh i chastnykh Makarakh," *Oktiabr´*, 11 (1929), 165–9, esp. 171; also in *Na literaturnom postu*, 21–2 (1929) and *Pravda*, December 3, 1930.

76. For the essays, see Viktor Shklovskii, "O Zoshchenke i bol´shoi literature"; and Viktor Vinogradov, "Iazyk Zoshchenki," in *Mikhail Zoshchenko: Stat´i i materialy*, ed. Boris Kazanskii and Iurii Tynianov (Moscow: Academia, 1928), 13–25 and 51–92.

77. See Marietta Chudakova, "Poetika Mikhaila Zoshchenko," in Chudakova, *Izbrannye raboty*, 2 vols. Vol 1: *Literatura sovetskogo proshlogo* (Moscow: Iazyki russkoi kul´tury, 2001), 79–244.

78. See Boris Eikhenbaum, "Kak sdelana 'Shinel´' Gogolia," in Eikhenbaum, *O proze* (Leningrad: Khudozhestvennaia literatura, 1969), 306–36; Viktor Vinogradov, "Problema skaza v stilistike," in Vinogradov, *O iazyke khudozhestvennoi prozy* (Moscow: Nauka, 1980), 42–54; and Peter Hodgson, "More on the Matter of Skaz: The Formalist Model," in *From Los Angeles to Kiev*, ed. Vladimir Markov and Dean S. Worth (Columbus, OH: Slavica Publishers, 1983), 119–54.

79. Shklovskii, *Tret´ia fabrika*, 101.

80. See Galina Belaia, *Zakonomernosti stilevogo razvitiia sovetskoi prozy 1920-kh godov* (Moscow: Nauka, 1977); Ekaterina Mushchenko, Vladislav Skobelev, and Lev Kroichik, *Poetika skaza* (Voronezh: Izd. Voronezhskogo universiteta, 1978); and Irwin Titunik, "The Problem of Skaz: Critique and Theory," in *Papers in Slavic Philology*, ed. B. A. Stolz (Ann Arbor, MI: Dept. of Slavic Languages and Literatures, 1977), vol. 1, 276–301.

81. Mikhail Zoshchenko, *Sochineniia. 1920-e gody* (Moscow: Kristall, 2000), 610.

82. On these texts, see Thomas Hodge, "Freudian Elements in Zoshchenko's *Pered voskhodom solntsa* (1943)," *SEER*, 67.1 (1989), 1–28; Rachel May, "Superego as Literary Subtext: Story and Structure in Mikhail Zoshchenko's *Before Sunrise*," *Slavic Review*, 55.1 (1996), 106–24; Aleksandr Etkind, *Eros nevozmozhnogo: Istoriia psikhoanaliza v Rossii* (Moscow: Gnozis-Progress, 1994), 326–31; and A. K. Zholkovskii, *Mikhail Zoshchenko: Poetika nedoveriia* (Moscow: Iazyki russkoi kul´tury, 1999), 13–28.

83. See John Freedman, *Silence's Roar: The Life and Drama of Nikolai Erdman* (Oakville, Ontario: Mosaic Press, 1992).

84. For a comprehensive analysis of *The Mandate*, see Iurii Shcheglov, "Konstruktivistskii balagan Erdmana," *NLO*, 33 (1998), 118–60. See also Kseniia Barinova, *Karnavalizovannaia dramaturgiia Nikolaia Erdmana* (Vladivostok: Izd. Dom Dal´nevostochnogo federal´nogo universiteta, 2012).

85. *The Major Plays of Nikolai Erdman*, trans. and ed. John Freedman (London: Harwood Academic Publishers, 1995), 158.

86. For an extensive account of the significance and genealogy of the Soviet trickster figure, see Mark Lipovetsky, *Charms of the Cynical Reason: The Trickster's Transformations in Soviet and Post-Soviet Culture* (Brighton, MA: Academic Studies Press, 2011).

87. On the concept of "plebeian modernity," see Ilya Gerasimov, "The Subaltern Speaks Out: Urban Plebeian Society in Late Imperial Russia," in *Spaces of the Poor: Perspectives of Cultural Sciences on Urban Slum Areas and Their Inhabitants*, ed. Hans-Christian Petersen (Bielefeld: Transcript, 2013), 47–70; Gerasimov, *Plebeian Modernity: Social Practices, Illegality, and the Urban Poor in Russia, 1906–1916* (Rochester, NY: University of Rochester Press, 2018), esp. 1–54.

88. Ilya Ilf and Evgeny Petrov, *The Little Golden Calf*, trans. Anne O. Fisher (Montpelier, VT: Russian Life Books, 2009), 58.

89. Aleksandr Zholkovskii, *Bluzhdaiushchie sny: Iz istorii russkogo modernizma* (Moscow: Sovetskii pisatel', 1992), 49–50.

90. See A. Zorich, "Kholostoi zalp: Zametki chitatelia," *Prozhektor*, 7–8 (1933), 23–4; and Aleksandr Selivanovskii, "Smekh Il'fa i Petrova," *Literaturnaia gazeta*, August 23, 1932, 3. The criticism of these novels is discussed in Mikhail Odesskii and David Fel'dman, *Miry I.A. Il'fa i E.P. Petrova: Ocherki verbalizovannoi povsednevnosti* (Moscow: RGGU, 2015), 181–203.

91. Ilf and Petrov, *The Little Golden Calf*, 137.

92. Parallel to the reawakened interest in Teffi, Poplavsky's novel has now appeared in English translation: *Apollon Bezobrazov*, trans. John Kopper (Bloomington, IN: Three Strings Press, 2015).

93. See Aleksandr Dolinin, *Istinnaia zhizn' pisatelia Sirina* (St. Petersburg: Akademicheskii proekt, 2004); and Gennadii Barabtarlo, *Sochinenie Nabokova* (St. Petersburg: Izd. Ivana Limbakha, 2011).

94. On the reception of Nabokov in post-Soviet culture, see Leving and White, *Marketing Literature and Posthumous Legacies*, 115–42, 199–222.

95. *The Garland Companion to Vladimir Nabokov*, ed. Vladimir E. Alexandrov (New York and London: Garland Publishers, 1995), 70.

96. Vladimir Nabokov, *Lolita* (New York: Vintage, 1989), 314.

97. Vladimir Nabokov, *Strong Opinions* (New York: McGraw-Hill, 1973), 101.

98. Brian Boyd, *Nabokov: The Russian Years* (Princeton, NJ: Princeton University Press, 1993), 389.

99. For a different approach to Humbert Humbert, see Deborah Martinsen, "*Lolita* as Petersburg Text," *Nabokov Studies*, 13 (2014–15), 39–55.

100. Nabokov, *Strong Opinions*, 156.

101. Nabokov, *Strong Opinions*, 94.

102. Nabokov, *Strong Opinions*, 93.

103. Nabokov, *Lolita*, 315.

104. Nabokov, *Lolita*, 314–15.

105. Nabokov, *Lectures on Literature*, ed. Fredson Bowers (New York: Harcourt Brace Jovanovich/ Bruccoli Clark, 1980), 1.

106. Nabokov, *Strong Opinions*, 69.

107. Nabokov, *Lectures on Literature*, 378.

108. *The Garland Companion to Vladimir Nabokov*, ed. Alexandrov, 162.

109. *The Garland Companion to Vladimir Nabokov*, ed. Alexandrov, 199.

110. Eric Naiman, *Nabokov, Perversely* (Ithaca, NY: Cornell University Press, 2010), 9.

111. Nabokov, *Strong Opinions*, 112.

112. *Pervyi Vsesoiuznyi s"ezd sovetskikh pisatelei: Stenograficheskii otchet* (Moscow: Sovetskii pisatel', 1934, repr. 1990), 712.

113. Abram Tertz, *On Socialist Realism*, trans. George Dennis (New York: Pantheon Books, 1960), 76–7, 91.

114. See Steven Kotkin, *Magnetic Mountain: Stalinism as a Civilization* (Berkeley: University of California Press, 1997), 355–66; and Andrei Sinyavsky, "Stalin: The State-Church," in his *Soviet Civilization: A Cultural History*, trans. Joanne Turnbull with the assistance of Nikolai Formozov (New York: Arcade Publishers, 1990), 81–113.

115. See Katerina Clark, "The Stalinist Myth of the 'Great Family,'" in Katerina Clark, *The Soviet Novel: History as Ritual*, 3rd edn. (Bloomington: Indiana University Press, 2000), 114–35.

116. See Rosenthal, *New Myth, New World*, 293–350.

117. *Sotsrealisticheskii kanon*, ed. Hans Günther and Evgenii Dobrenko (St. Petersburg: Akademicheskii proekt, 2000).

118. Evgeny Dobrenko, *Political Economy of Socialist Realism* (New Haven, CT: Yale University Press, 2007), 45.

119. See Igor Golomshtok, *Totalitarian Art* (London: Harvill Press, 1990).

120. Clark, *The Soviet Novel*, 148.

121. See Boris Frezinskii, "Il'ia Erenburg v 1930-e gody," in *Russkaia literatura XX veka*, ed. Leiderman et al., vol. 2, 173–83.

122. Il'ia Erenburg, *Liudi, gody, zhizn'*, 3 vols. (Moscow: Tekst, 2005), vol. 1, 630.

123. Michele Rivkin-Fish, "From 'Demographic Crisis' to 'Dying Nation': The Politics of Language and Reproduction in Russia," in *Gender and National Identity in Twentieth-Century Russian Culture*, ed. Helena Goscilo and Andrea Lanoux (DeKalb: Northern Illinois University Press, 2006), 151–73, quotation on 151. The importance of the questionnaire as an "imprint of social concerns" is noted in Heldt, *Terrible Perfection: Women and Russian Literature* (Bloomington: Indiana University Press, 1987), 145.

124. As Kelly notes, the scene of the political study group was published in the Soviet Union only in 1989; see Catriona Kelly, *A History of Russian Women's Writing, 1820–1992* (Oxford: Oxford University Press, 1994), 363.

125. On the deconstruction of the Great Family in the novel, see Helena Goscilo, "Foreword," in I. Grekova, *The Ship of Widows*, trans. Cathy Porter (Evanston, IL: Northwestern University Press, 1994), xviii–xix.

126. Tat'iana Goricheva, *Pravoslavie i postmodernizm* (Leningrad: Izd. LGU, 1991), 40–1.

127. Alexei Yurchak, *Everything Was Forever, Until It Was No More: The Last Soviet Generation* (Princeton, NJ: Princeton University Press, 2006), 126–57.

128. Goricheva, *Pravoslavie i postmodernizm*, 57.

129. Ludmilla Petrushevskaya, *There Once Lived a Woman Who Tried to Kill Her Neighbor's Baby: Scary Fairy Tales*, trans. Keith Gessen and Anna Summers (New York: Penguin Books, 2009). It was followed by *There Once Lived a Girl Who Seduced Her Sister's Husband, and He Hanged Himself: Love Stories*, trans. Anna Summers (New York: Penguin Books, 2013); and *There Once Lived a Mother Who Loved Her Children, Until They Moved Back In: Three Novellas about Family*, trans. Anna Summers (New York: Penguin Books, 2014), which includes the two most famous novellas, translated as "The Time Is Night" and "Among Friends."

130. Helena Goscilo, *Dehexing Sex: Russian Womanhood during and after Glasnost* (Ann Arbor: University of Michigan Press, 1996), 95–6.

131. Roman Timenchik, "'Ty—chto?,' ili Vvedenie v teatr Petrushevskoi," in Liudmila Petrushevskaia, *Tri devushki v golubom* (Moscow: Iskusstvo, 1989), 394–8, quotation on 397. See also Petrushevskaya's own observation: "Some of my stories could be reformatted as free verse"; in Liudmila Petrushevskaia, *Deviatyi tom* (Moscow: Eksmo, 2003), 325.

132. See Julia Kristeva, *Powers of Horror: An Essay on Abjection*, trans. Leon S. Roudiez (New York: Columbia University Press, 1982), 54–9.

133. Petrushevskaia, *Deviatyi tom*, 322.

134. Petrushevskaia, *Deviatyi tom*, 322.

135. Helena Goscilo, "Mother as Mothra: Totalizing Narrative and Nurture in Petrushevskaia," in *A Plot of Her Own: The Female Protagonist in Russian Literature*, ed. Sona Hoisington (Evanston, IL: Northwestern University Press, 1995), 112, 105, respectively.

136. See Mark Lipovetsky and Tatiana Mikhailova, " 'How Long Can You Go Crushing Bones, I Ask You?': The 'Bad Mother' In Liudmila Petrushevskaya's *The Time: Night*," in *Transgressive Women in Russian and East European Cultures: From the Bad to the Blasphemous*, ed. Beth Holmgren, Yana Hashamova, and Mark Lipovetsky (London: Routledge, 2016), 112–27.

137. Maiia Turovskaia, *Pamiati tekushchego mgnoveniia* (Moscow: Sovetskii pisatel´, 1987), 131.

138. Petrushevskaia, *Tri devushki v golubom*, 104.

139. For more detailed analysis of Petrushevskaya's drama, see Birgit Beumers and Mark Lipovetsky, *Performing Violence: Literary and Theatrical Experiments of New Russian Drama* (Bristol and Chicago: Intellect, 2008), 75–89; Pavel Rudnev, "Dramaturgiia Petrushevskoi," *Post-Nauka*, June 6, 2015, https://postnauka.ru/video/48112 (last accessed July 29, 2016); and Nataliia Kablukova, "Poetika dramaturgii Petrushevskoi," Ph.D. Dissertation, Tomsk State University, 2003, http://cheloveknauka.com/poetika-dramaturgii-lyudmily-petrushevskoy (last accessed July 29, 2016).

140. On the broader contexts for these emerging figures, see "Introduction," to *Sexuality and the Body in Russian Culture*, ed. Jane T. Costlow, Stephanie Sandler, and Judith Vowles (Stanford, CA: Stanford University Press, 1993), 27–36; and Kelly, *History of Russian Women's Writing*, 357–95.

141. Goscilo, *Dehexing Sex*, 89–90, 105–6.

142. See her books in translations by Jamey Gambrell: *On the Golden Porch* (New York: Knopf, 1990); *Pushkin's Children: Writings on Russia and Russians* (Boston: Houghton Mifflin, 2003); *The Slynx* (Boston: Houghton Mifflin, 2003); *White Walls* (New York: NYRB, 2007). On Tolstaya's literary career, see Helena Goscilo, *The Explosive World of Tatyana N. Tolstaya's Fiction* (Armonk, NJ: M. E. Sharpe, 1996), 3–10.

143. Her political and cultural stance is well analyzed in Elizabeth A. Skomp and Benjamin M. Sutcliffe, *Liudmila Ulitskaya and the Art of Tolerance* (Madison: University of Wisconsin Press, 2015), esp. 130–65.

144. See Masha Gessen, "The Weight of Words," *The New Yorker*, October 6, 2014, http://www.newyorker.com/magazine/2014/10/06/weight-words (last accessed July 16, 2016).

145. On Shukshin's misfit characters, see John Givens, *Prodigal Son: Vasily Shukshin in Soviet Russian Culture* (Evanston, IL: Northwestern University Press, 2000), 57–111.

146. Iurii Trifonov, *Kak slovo nashe otzovetsia . . .*, ed. A. P. Shitov and Ol´ga Trifonova (Moscow: Sovetskaia Rossiia, 1985), 313–14.

147. On his work, see *Routes of Passage: Essays on the Fiction of Vladimir Makanin*, ed. Byron Lindsey and Tatiana Spektor (Bloomington, IN: Slavica, 2008).

148. The article first appeared as "Kogda rasseialsia liricheskii tuman . . .," *Literaturnoe obozrenie*, 8 (1981), 21–32; it is reprinted in Igor´ Dedkov, *Zhivoe litso vremeni* (Moscow: Sovetskii pisatel´, 1986), 220–58.

149. See, for example, Anatolii Bocharov, "Na reke s bystrym techeniem," *Druzhba narodov*, 11 (1984), 231–9; Irina Rodnianskaia, "Neznakomye znakomtsy," in Rodnianskaia, *Khudozhnik v poiskakh istiny* (Moscow: Sovetskii pisatel´, 1989), 108–45; and Aleksandr Ageev, "Istina i svoboda. Vladimir Makanin: Vzgliad iz 1990 goda," *Literaturnoe obozrenie*, 9 (1990), 25–33.

150. A congenial biography of Dovlatov has been written by his friend, the critic Aleksandr Genis, *Dovlatov i okrestnosti: Filologicheskii roman* (Moscow: Vagrius, 1999).

151. Viktor Toporov, "Fenomen ischeznoveniia: 'Lishnie liudi' v proizvedeniiakh sovremennoi prozy," *Literaturnoe obozrenie*, 1 (1988), 22–8. See also Maiia Turovskaia, "Aleksandr Vampilov i ego kritiki," in Turovskaia, *Pamiati tekushchego mgnoveniia*, 128–81; Tat´iana Prokhorova, "Znaki obrashcheniia k lermontovskoi traditsii v p´ese A. Vampilova 'Utinaia okhota,'" *Acta Universitatis Lodziensis, Folia Litteraria Rossica*, 6 (2013), 65–73.

152. See Elena Gushanskaia, *Aleksandr Vampilov: Ocherk tvorchestva* (Leningrad: Sovetskii pisatel´, 1990), 178–260.

153. Alexander Vampilov, *Major Plays*, ed. and trans. Alma Law (New York and London: Routledge, 2006), 72; for the Russian, see Aleksandr Vampilov, "Utinaia okhota," http://www.lib.ru/PXESY/WAMPILOW/vampilov_ohota.txt (last accessed July 29, 2016).

154. Joseph Brodsky, "Uncommon Visage: The Nobel Lecture," in Joseph Brodsky, *On Grief and Reason: Essays* (New York: Farrar, Straus & Giroux, 1995), 56.

155. On the history of the publication of *Doctor Zhivago*, see Ivan Tolstoi, *Otmytyi roman Pasternaka: "Doktor Zhivago" mezhdu KGB i TsRU* (Moscow: Vremia, 2008).

156. Our reading of Sinyavsky mainly reflects the interpretation elaborated by Catharine Theimer Nepomnyashchy in *Abram Tertz and the Poetics of Crime* (New Haven, CT: Yale University Press, 1995). See also *A History of Russian Literary Theory and Criticism: The Soviet Age and Beyond*, ed. Evgeny Dobrenko and Galin Tihanov (Pittsburgh, PA: University of Pittsburgh Press, 2011), 282.

157. Andrey Sinyavsky, "Dissent as Personal Experience," trans. Maria-Regina Kecht, *Yearbook of Comparative and General Literature*, 31 (1982), 21–9, quotation on 27.

158. See Andrei Siniavskii, "Stilisticheskie raznoglasiia," *Iskusstvo kino*, 7 (1989), 34–8.

159. See A. Genis, "Andrei Siniavskii: Estetika arkhaicheskogo postmodernizma," *NLO*, 7 (1994), 277–84; and Mikhail Epshtein, "Mezhdu ekzistentsializmom i postmodernizmom," in Mikhail Epshtein, *Postmodern v Rossii: Literatura i teoriia* (Moscow: Ruslan Elinin, 2000), 206–39.

160. Abram Tertz, *Fantastic Stories* (New York: Grosset & Dunlap, 1967), 195.

161. Andrey Sinyavsky, *Strolls with Pushkin*, trans. Catharine Theimer Nepomnyashchy and Slava I. Yastremski (New Haven, CT: Yale University Press, 1993), 372–3.

162. For the attacks, see Aleksandr Solzhenitsyn, "... Koleblet tvoi trenozhnik," *Vestnik Russkogo Khristianskogo dvizheniia*, 142 (1984), 133–52; and Roman Gul´, "Progulka khama s Pushkinym," *Novyi zhurnal*, 124 (1976), 117–29.

163. Sinyavsky, *Strolls with Pushkin*, 344.

164. Iulii Daniel´, "Iskuplenie," in *Tsena metafory, ili Prestuplenie i nakazanie Siniavskogo i Danielia*, ed. E. M. Velikanova (Moscow: Kniga, 1989), 142.

165. Yulii Daniel (Nikolai Arzhak), "This is Moscow Speaking," trans. Stuart Hood, Harold Shukman, and John Richardson, in *Late and Post-Soviet Literature: Thaw and Stagnation (1954–1986)*, ed. Mark Lipovetsky and Lisa Ryoko Wakamiya (Brighton, MA: Academic Studies Press, 2015), 194–233, quotation on 218.

166. Daniel, "This is Moscow Speaking," 220.

167. See Iurii Aikhenval´d, *Don Kikhot na russkoi pochve* (Moscow: Gendal´f, 1996).

168. Boris Khazanov, *Chas korolia*, E-book (Munich: Im Werden, 2006), 46; http://imwerden.de/pdf/khasanov_chas_korolja.pdf (last accessed July 29, 2016)

169. See Andrei Siniavskii, "Liudi i zveri," in Andrei Siniavskii, *Puteshestvie na Chernuiu rechku i drugie proizvedeniia* (Moscow: Zakharov, 1999), 206–39.

170. Seth Graham, *Resonant Dissonance: The Russian Joke in Cultural Context* (Evanston, IL: Northwestern University Press, 2009), 7, 9. On the culture of the Soviet anecdote, see Abram Terts, "Anekdot v anekdote," in Siniavskii, *Puteshestvie na Chernuiu rechku*, 254–67.

171. For an analysis of "On a Summer Day," see Aleksandr Zholkovskii, "'Letnim dnem': Ezopovskii shedevr Fazilia Iskandera," *Novyi mir* 4 (2015), 166–81.

172. Lewis Hyde, *Trickster Makes the World: Mischief, Myth, and Art* (New York: North Point Press, 1998), 10.

173. Mamleev was a central figure of the so-called Iuzhinsky Alley Circle, an informal occult/ nationalist club. See Birgit Menzel, "Occult and Esoteric Movements in Russia from the 1960s to the 1980s," in *The New Age of Russia: Occult and Esoteric Dimensions*, ed. Birgit Menzel, Michael Hagemeister, and Bernice Glatzer Rosenthal (Munich: Otto Sagner, 2012), 151–85, esp. 162–4.

174. On Mamleev's poetics, see Igor' P. Smirnov, "Evoliutsiia chudovishchnosti," *NLO*, 3 (1993), 303–7.

175. Viktor Erofeev tried to present this lineage as an authoritative paradigm by including Shalamov, Viktor Astaf'ev, Eduard Limonov, Evgeny Kharitonov, Vladimir Sorokin, and many other writers. See his anthology *The Penguin Book of New Russian Writing: Russia's Fleurs Du Mal*, ed. Viktor Erofeev, trans. Andrew Reynolds (New York: Penguin, 1995).

176. Dmitrii Prigov, "Pamiati Evgeniia Kharitonova," in Evgenii Kharitonov, *Slezy na tsvetakh*, ed. Iaroslav Mogutin, 2 vols. (Moscow: Glagol, 1993), vol. 2, 86–92, quotation on 86.

177. Evgeny Kharitonov, "Flysheet," trans. Arch Tait, *Late and Post-Soviet Literature: Thaw and Stagnation*, ed. Lipovetsky and Wakamiya, 537–39, quotation on 538.

178. Jean-François Lyotard, "From *The Postmodern Condition: A Report on Knowledge*," in *The Postmodern Reader: Foundational Texts*, ed. Michael Drolet (London and New York: Routledge, 2004), 123–45, quotation on 123.

179. Tomáš Glanc argues that the alleged isolation of nonconformist writers and artists from Western cultural innovations was a cultivated artistic device, which he defines as the "instrumentalization of closedness." See Tomash Glants, "Avtorstvo i shiroko zakrytye glaza parallel'noi kul'tury," *NLO*, 100 (2009), 405–23.

180. The novel generated multiple literary commentaries, including Irina Paperno and Boris Gasparov, "Vstan' i idi," *Slavica Hierosolymitana*, 5–6 (1981), 389–400; Svetlana Geisser Schnittmann, *Venedikt Erofeev "Moskva-Petushki," ili "The Rest Is Silence"* (Berne: Peter Lang, 1989); *Venedikt Erofeev's Moscow-Petushki: Critical Perspectives*, ed. Karen Ryan-Hayes (Berne: Peter Lang, 1997); Iurii Levin, *Kommentarii k poeme "Moskva-Petushki" Venedikta Erofeeva* (Graz: Grazer Gesellschaft zur Förderung Slawischer Kulturstudien, 1996); and Eduard Vlasov, *Bessmertnaia poema Ven. Erofeeva "Moskva-Petushki": Sputnik pisatelia* (Sapporo: Slavic Research Center, 1998).

181. Venedikt Erofeev, *Moscow to the End of the Line*, trans. H. William Tjalsma (Evanston, IL: Northwestern University Press, 1997), 66.

182. Erofeev, *Moscow to the End of the Line*, 158.

183. Baudrillard develops this idea in many of his works, first and foremost in the essay "Simulacra and Simulations"; see Jean Baudrillard, *Selected Writings*, ed. Mark Poster (Stanford, CA: Stanford University Press, 1988), 166–84.

184. On Sots-Art, see Zinovy Zinik, "Sots-Art (1973)", *Textura: Russian Essays on Visual Culture*, ed. Alla Efimova and Lev Manovich (Chicago: University of Chicago Press, 1993), 70–88 (originally published in *Sintaksis* 3 [1979], 74–102); Boris Groys, *The Total Art of Stalinism: Avant-garde, Aesthetic Dictatorship, and Beyond*, trans. Charles Rougle (Princeton, NJ: Princeton University Press, 1992), 75–102; *EndQuote: Sots-Art Literature and Soviet Grand Style*, ed. Marina Balina, Nancy Condee, and Evgeny Dobrenko (Evanston, IL: Northwestern University Press, 2000).

185. Vladimir Sorokin, "Zakony russkoi metafiziki," interview by Aleksandr Voznesenskii (2006) http://www.srkn.ru/interview/voznesenski.shtml (last accessed August 14, 2016).

186. See Maksim Marusenkov, *Absurdopediia russkoi zhizni Vladimira Sorokina: Zaum', grotesk i absurd* (St. Petersburg: Aleteiia, 2012), 40–71.

187. Dirk Uffelmann, "*Led tronulsia*: The Overlapping Periods in Vladimir Sorokin's Work from the Materialization of Metaphors to Fantastic Substantialism," in *Landslide of the Norm:*

Language Culture in Post-Soviet Russia, ed. Ingunn Lunde and Tine Roesen (Bergen: Slavica Bergensia, 2006), 100–25, quotation on 109. On Sorokin's evolution see also *Vladimir Sorokin's Languages*, ed. Tine Roesen and Dirk Uffelmann (Bergen: Slavic Bergensia, 2013).

188. Vladimir Sorokin, "Literatura ili kladbishche stilisticheskikh nakhodok," in Serafima Roll, *Postmodernisty o postkul'ture* (Moscow: NLO, 1996), 119–30, quotation on 123–4.

189. Mikhail Berg, *Literaturokratiia* (Moscow: NLO, 2000), 113.

190. Sasha Sokolov, *A School for Fools*, trans. Carl Proffer (Ann Arbor, MI: Ardis, 1977), 135–6.

191. Sasha Sokolov, *Astrophobia*, trans. Michael Henry Heim (New York: Grove Weidenfeld, 1989), 68.

192. Groys, *The Total Art of Stalinism*, 102–3.

193. The novel is called *The Clay Machine Gun* in the British publication; the Russian title literally means *Chapaev and Void*.

194. The general trend to change the titles of Pelevin's novels in translation, sometimes, as in this case, differently in the United States and in Britain, sows confusion that Pelevin may himself find rather satisfying.

195. For a comprehensive reading of *Generation P*, see Sofya Khagi, "From *Homo Soveticus* to *Homo sapiens*: Viktor Pelevin's Consumer Dystopia," *Russian Review*, 67 (2008), 559–79.

196. On the symbolism of oil in contemporary Russian literature, see Ilya Kalinin, "Petropoetics," in *Russian Literature since 1991*, ed. Evgeny Dobrenko and Mark Lipovetsky (Cambridge: Cambridge University Press, 2015), 120–44.

197. Nikolai Aleksandrov, "Tot, kto vzial Izmail" (interview with Mikhail Shishkin), *Itogi*, October 12, 2000, http://www.itogi.ru/archive/2000/42/115757.html (last accessed August 14, 2016).

198. Although *Pis'movnik* would translate literally into English as *The Letter Book*, it has appeared in English as *The Light and the Dark*, trans. Andrew Bromfield (London: Quercus, 2013). Also available in English are Shishkin, *Maidenhair*, trans. Marion Schwartz (Rochester, NY: Open Letter, 2012); and Shishkin, *Calligraphy Lesson: The Collected Stories*, trans. Marion Schwartz, Leo Shtulin, Mariya Bashkatova, and Sylvia Maizell (Dallas: Deep Vellum Publishing, 2015).

199. Nataliia Kochetkova, "Mikhail Shishkin: U Boga na Strashnom sude ne budet vremeni chitat' vse knigi" (interview with Mikhail Shishkin), *Izvestiia*, June 22, 2005, http://izvestia.ru/news/303564 (last accessed August 14, 2016).

200. That cross is well described in Leslie Fiedler, "Cross the Border—Close that Gap: Postmodernism," in *American Literature since 1900*, ed. M. Cunliffe (London: Barrie and Jenkins, 1975 [1968]), 344–66.

201. Douwe Fokkema, "The Semiotics of Literary Postmodernism," in *International Postmodernism: Theory and Literary Practice*, ed. H. Bertens and Douwe Fokkema (Amsterdam and Philadelphia: John Benjamins, 1997), 30–3.

202. Excerpts of this text have appeared in English as Linor Goralik, "They Talk," trans. Mikhail Iossel, in *Rasskazy: New Fiction from a New Russia*, ed. Mikhail Iossel and Jeff Parker (Portland, OR: Tin House Books, 2009), 21–32. A complete translation appears in Linor Goralik, *Found Life: Poems, Stories, Comics, a Play, and an Interview*, ed. Ainsley Morse, Maria Vassileva, and Maya Vinokur (New York: Columbia University Press, 2017).

203. See Mark Lipovetsky, "Post-Soc: Transformations of Socialist Realism in the Popular Culture of the Recent Period," in *SEEJ* (Special Issue: *Innovation through Iteration: Russian Popular Culture Today*), 48.3 (2004), 356–77; Serguei Oushakine, "Remembering in Public: On the Affective Management of History," *Ab Imperio*, 1 (2013), 269–302; and Evgeny Dobrenko, "Recycling of the Soviet," in *Russian Literature since 1991*, ed. Dobrenko and Lipovetsky, 20–44.

204. Hans-Thies Lehmann, *Postdramatic Theatre*, trans. Jaren Jürs-Munby (London: Routledge, 2006), 116–17.

205. For more on the history of New Drama as a cultural movement, see Birgit Beumers and Mark Lipovetsky, "Introduction: Contours and Contexts of New Drama," in Beumers and Lipovetsky, *Performing Violence*, 27–43.

206. Hedy Weiss, "A Voice from Mother Russia," *Chicago Sunday Times*, November 20, 2003.

207. See "Great Terror and Little Terror," in Tolstaya, *Pushkin's Children*, 14–26.

208. See Lev Gudkov, *Negativnaia identichnost'*, esp. 262–99.

209. On important trends in post-Soviet Moscow theater, see Monika Greenleaf, "In medias res: Diary of the Moscow Theater Season, 2007–2008," *Slavic Review*, 67.2 (2008), 422–36.

210. On Ginzburg, see Emily Van Buskirk, *Lydia Ginzburg's Prose*; and *Lydia Ginzburg's Alternative Literary Identities*, ed. Emily Van Buskirk and Andrei Zorin (Oxford: Peter Lang, 2012).

211. Pushkin's short *Table-Talk* exemplifies that focus on recording speech, and he in turn knew well the *Specimens of the Table Talk of the late Samuel Taylor Coleridge* (1835), from which he took the English title of his own motley collection.

212. See Clarence Brown, *Mandelstam* (Cambridge: Cambridge University Press, 1973), 124–5, for the basic facts. A reading of the ethics and aesthetics of "Fourth Prose" is found in Michael Eskin, *Ethics and Dialogue in the World of Levinas, Bakhtin, Celan, and Mandelstam* (Oxford: Oxford University Press, 2000).

213. For a reading of "Fourth Prose" in the context of risky post-Revolutionary autobiographies, see Donald Loewen, "Fighting for Breath," in Donald Loewen, *The Most Dangerous Art: Poetry, Politics, and Autobiography after the Russian Revolution* (Lanham: Lexington Books, 2008), 91–120.

214. It was Viktor Shklovsky who gave the title to Olesha's notes for their posthumous publication: *Ni dnia bez strochki: iz zapisnykh knizhek* (Moscow: Sovetskaia Rossiia, 1965). It has appeared in English translation as *No Day without a Line: From Notebooks*, trans. Judson Rosengrandt (Evanston, IL: Northwestern University Press, 1998). In 1999, Violetta Gudkova restored all censorship deletions and republished the text under the title *The Book of Farewell*. See Iurii Olesha, *Kniga proshchaniia* (Moscow: PROZAiK, 2015).

215. Il'ia Kukulin, *Mashiny zashumevshego vremeni: Kak sovetskii montazh stal metodom neofitsial'noi kul'tury* (Moscow: NLO, 2015), 342.

216. Ulitin's method was also used by his friend, the theater critic Aleksandr Asarkan (1930–2004) for the montage-based postcards that he sent to thousands of recipients. On Asarkan, see Vladimir Papernyi's documentary *In Search of Asarkan* (*V posikakh Asarkana*, 2013). See also Zinovii Zinik, "Na puti k 'Artisticheskomu,'" *Teatr*, 9 (1993), 123–42; and Mikhail Aizenberg, "Otkrytki Asarkana," *Znamia*, 11 (2005), http://magazines.russ.ru/znamia/2005/11/ai6.html (last accessed August 14, 2016). Ulitin authored a novel entitled *Anti-Asarkan*, which was confiscated by the KGB: see Zinovii Zinik, "Privetstvuiu Vash neuspekh," in Pavel Ulitin, *Razgovor o rybe* (Moscow: OGI, 2002), http://www.vavilon.ru/texts/zinik1.html (last accessed August 14, 2016).

217. Kukulin, *Mashiny zashumevshego vremeni*, 366–7, 369.

218. See the comparison of these two books in Nadezhda Grigor'eva's review of Popov in *Novaia russkaia kniga*, 3 (2000), http://www.guelman.ru/slava/nrk/nrk3/19.html (last accessed August 14, 2016).

219. On Gol'dshtein's prose as a new form of the novel, see Stanislav L'vovskii, "Bez garantii vozvrashcheniia," *NLO*, 81 (2006), http://magazines.russ.ru/nlo/2006/81/l19.html (last accessed August 14, 2016).

220. On the "new sincerity" in post-Soviet culture, see Ellen Rutten, *Sincerity after Communism: A Cultural History* (New Haven, CT: Yale University Press, 2017).

221. Aleksandr Gol'dshtein, *Proshchanie s Nartsissom: Opyty pominal'noi ritoriki* (Moscow: NLO, 1997), 424.

222. See their description of Post(non)fiction on the site http://postnonfiction.org/about/ (last accessed August 21, 2016).

Chapter 5

1. See Bernice Glatzer Rosenthal, *New Myth, New World: From Nietzsche to Stalinism* (Philadelphia: University of Pennsylvania Press, 2004); and Aleksandr Etkind, "'Odno vremia ia kolebalsia, ne antikhrist li ia': sub"ektivnost', avtobiografiia i goriachaia pamiat' revoliutsii," *NLO*, 73 (2005), http://magazines.russ.ru/nlo/2005/73/etk2.html (last accessed August 14, 2016).

2. Vladimir Maiakovskii, *Sobranie sochinenii*, 6 vols. (Moscow: Biblioteka Ogonek, Izdatel'stvo Pravda, 1973), vol. 1, 70.

3. Aleksandr Blok, "Intelligentsia and Revolution" (1918), in Aleksandr Blok, *Sobranie sochinenii*, 6 vols. (Leningrad: Khudozhestvennaia literatura, Leningradskoe otdelenie, 1982), vol. 4, 229–39, quotation on 232.

4. See Viacheslav Ivanov, "Nitsshe i Dionis," in Viacheslav Ivanov, *Rodnoe i vselenskoe* (Moscow: Respublika, 1994), 26–34, also online at http://www.vehi.net/nitshe/ivanov.html (last accessed August 14, 2016).

5. In support of this interpretation, see Boris Gasparov, "Tema sviatochnogo karnavala v poeme A. Bloka 'Dvenadtsat','" in Boris Gasparov, *Literaturnye leitmotivy: Ocherki po russkoi literature XX veka* (Moscow: Nauka, 1993), 3–27.

6. Vasilii Rozanov, *Sobranie sochinenii*, ed. A. N. Nikoliukin, 12 vols. (Moscow: Respublika, 2000), vol. 12, 8.

7. Rozanov, *Sobranie sochinenii*, vol. 12, 6.

8. Aleksei Remizov, *Sobranie sochinenii*, 10 vols. (Moscow: Russkaia kniga, 2000), vol. 5, 409, also available online at http://rvb.ru/remizov/ss10/01text/vol_5/02text/391.htm (last accessed August 14, 2016).

9. See Gorky's articles for the newspaper *Novaia zhizn'*, collected in the book *Untimely Thoughts: Essays on Revolution, Culture, and the Bolsheviks (1917–1918)*, trans. Herman Ermolaev (New Haven, CT: Yale University Press, 1995); for the Russian, see Maksim Gor'kii, *Nesvoevremnnye mysli: Zametki o revoliutsii i kul'ture* (Moscow: Sovetskii pisatel', 1990). For Ivan Bunin's writings, see his diary of 1918–20, *Okaiannye dni* ([1926] Moscow: Sovetskii pisatel', 1990).

10. Boris Pilnyak, *The Naked Year*, trans. Alexander R. Tulloch (Ann Arbor, MI: Ardis, 1975), 40–1. For the Russian, see Boris Pil'niak, *Sobranie sochinenii*, ed. K. Andronikashvili-Pil'niak, 6 vols. (Moscow: Terra-Knizhnyi klub, 2003), vol. 1, 156.

11. See Katerina Clark, *The Soviet Novel: History as Ritual*, 3rd edn. (Indianapolis: University of Indiana Press, 2000), 82–9.

12. Eduard Bagritskii, "TBC," in Eduard Bagritskii, *Stikhotvoreniia i poemy* (Moscow: GIKhL, 1956), 146–50, quotation on 148.

13. For a discussion of this poem, see Dariusz Tolczyk, *See No Evil: Literary Cover-ups and Discoveries of the Soviet Camp Experience* (New Haven, CT: Yale University Press, 1999), 76.

14. A vast literature discusses whether Mikhail Sholokhov wrote *The Quiet Don*. An important synthesis of the arguments and a case for authorship appears in Herman Ermolaev, *Mikhail Sholokhov and His Art* (Princeton, NJ: Princeton University Press, 1982). The most famous challenger was Aleksandr Solzhenitsyn: see his "Sholokhov and the Riddle of 'The Quiet Don,'" *TLS* (May 24, 2016 [1974]), http://www.the-tls.co.uk/articles/public/sholokhov-and-the-riddle-of-the-quiet-don (last accessed November 13, 2016). The key arguments are these: first, detailed and intimate knowledge of the First World War displayed in the first volume of the novel

suggests an author much older than Sholokhov, who could not have served in the war. Multiple authors might be inferred from the fact that the novel is stylistically heterogeneous and includes lengthy fragments that obviously stand apart from the main narrative (descriptions of Bolsheviks, a diary of someone called Timofei depicting his relationships with Elizaveta Mokhova, chapters about Petrograd in summer 1917 as well as Kornilov's and Kaledin's head-quarters at the Don). But no less questionable are the arguments supporting alternative candi-dates for the authorship of the manuscript allegedly appropriated by Sholokhov. We assume that Sholokhov was *one* of the authors of the novel; no matter its author, the novel itself remains a significant "literary fact" (in Tynianov's term) of twentieth-century Russian culture.

15. Mikhail Bakhtin, *The Dialogic Imagination: Four Essays*, ed. Michael Holquist, trans. Caryl Emerson and Michael Holquist (Austin: University of Texas Press, 2004), 37.

16. Bakhtin, *The Dialogic Imagination*, 37.

17. Mikhail Sholokhov, *The Don Flows Home to the Sea*, trans. Stephen Garry, 2 vols. (New York: Vintage Books, 1966), vol. 2, 772.

18. *The Complete Works of Isaac Babel*, ed. Nathalie Babel, trans. Peter Constantine (New York: W. W. Norton & Company, 2002), 228–9. For the Russian text, see Isaak Babel', *Sochineniia*, ed. Antonina Pirozhkova, 2 vols. (Moscow: Khudozhestvennaia literatura, 1992), vol. 1, 30–1.

19. Abram Lezhnev, *Sovremenniki* (Moscow: Krug, 1927), 121–2.

20. Isaac Babel, "My First Goose," in *Complete Works of Isaac Babel*, 230–3, quotation on 233.

21. See Eliot Borenstein, *Men without Women: Masculinity and Revolution in Russian Fiction, 1917–1929* (Durham, NC: Duke University Press, 2001), 91–104.

22. See Patricia Blake, "Researching Babel's Biography: Adventures and Misadventures," in *The Enigma of Isaac Babel: Biography, History, Context*, ed. Gregory Freidin (Stanford, CA: Stanford University Press, 2009), 3–15; and Val Vinokur, *The Trace of Judaism: Dostoevsky, Babel, Mandelstam, Levinas* (Evanston, IL: Northwestern University Press, 2008), 60–92.

23. Jorge Luis Borges, *Selected Nonfictions*, ed. and trans. Eliot Weinberger (New York: Viking Penguin, 1999), 164.

24. Among 1920s critical publications on Babel, special attention should be paid to the volume *I. Babel: Stat'i i materialy*, ed. Boris Kazanskii and Iurii Tynianov (Leningrad: Academia, 1928), which includes articles by Nikolai Stepanov, Pavel Novitsky, and Grigory Gukovsky. The most representative English-language anthology is *Isaac Babel*, ed. Harold Bloom (New York: Chelsea House Publishers, 1987). See *Isaac Babel's Selected Writings*, ed. Gregory Freidin (New York: W. W. Norton, 2009), 407–517, for essays by Shklovsky, Budyonny, Lionel Trilling, Efraim Sicher, and Gregory Freidin. See also Aleksandr Voronskii, "Literaturnye siluety: Babel'," *Krasnaia Nov'*, 5 (1924), 276–91; Viacheslav Polonskii, "Babel'," in Viacheslav Polonskii, *O literature: Izbrannye raboty* (Moscow: Sovetskii pisatel', 1988), 57–78; Mark Slonim, "Isaak Babel'," in Mark Slonim, *Portrety sovremennykh pisatelei* (Paris: Parabola, 1933), 135–48; Georgii Adamovich, "Rasskazy I. Babelia," in Georgii Adamovich, *Sobranie sochinenii*, 5 vols. (St. Petersburg: Aleteiia, 1998), vol. 1, 233–5.

25. See Antonina Pirozhkova, *At His Side: The Last Years of Isaac Babel*, trans. Anne Frydman and Robert L. Busch (South Royalton, VT: Steerforth, 1996), 107–8.

26. See Gregory Freidin, "Justifying the Revolution as an Aesthetic Phenomenon," *Nietzsche and Soviet Culture: Ally and Adversary*, ed. Bernice Glatzer Rosenthal (Oxford: Oxford University Press, 1994), 149–73; also published as "Babel': Revoliutsiia kak esteticheskii fenomen," *NLO*, 4 (1993), 228–42.

27. On Babel's arrest, investigation, and trial see Sergei Povartsov, *Prichina smerti—rasstrel: Khronika poslednikh dnei Isaaka Babelia* (Moscow: Terra, 1996).

28. See, for example, Vladislav Skobelev, *Massa i lichnost' v russkoi sovetskoi proze 1920-kh godov (k probleme narodnogo kharaktera)* (Voronezh: Voronezhskii gosudarstvennyi universitet, 1975);

Galina Belaia, Evgenii Dobrenko, and Ivan Esaulov, *"Konarmiia" Babelia* (Moscow: RGGU, 1993); Aleksandr Zholkovskii and Mikhail Iampol'skii, *Babel'/Babel* (Moscow: Carte blanche, 1994); and Izrail' Smirin, *Babel' v literaturnom kontekste* (Perm': Permskii gosudarstvennyi pedagogicheskii universitet, 2005).

29. Sheila Fitzpatrick, *Everyday Stalinism: Ordinary Life in Extraordinary Times: Soviet Russia in the 1930s* (Oxford: Oxford University Press, 1999), 190–1.

30. Zygmunt Bauman, "A Century of Camps?," in Zygmunt Bauman, *Life in Fragments: Essays in Postmodern Morality* (Oxford: Blackwell, 1995), 192–205.

31. *Belomorsko-Baltiiskii kanal imeni I. V. Stalina: Istoriia stroitel'stva*, ed. Maksim Gor'kii, Leopol'd Averbakh, and Semen Firin (Moscow: Gosudarstvennoe izdatel'stvo "Istoriia fabrik i zavodov," 1934), 19. For a detailed analysis of this project, see Evgeny Dobrenko, *Political Economy of Socialist Realism* (New Haven, CT: Yale University Press, 2007), 101–44.

32. On the poetics of *Requiem*, see N. Iu. Griakalova, "Fol'klornye traditsii v poezii Anny Akhmatovoi," *Russkaia literatura*, 1 (1982), 47–64; and N. L. Leiderman, "Aktualizatsiia pamiati arkhaicheskikh zhanrov (A. Akhmatova 'Rekviem')," in Naum Leiderman, *Teoriia zhanra: Issledovaniia i razbory* (Ekaterinburg: UO RAN, 2010), 144–57.

33. Akhmatova, *Ia—golos vash...* (Moscow: Knizhnaia palata, 1989), 157.

34. Akhmatova, *Ia—golos vash...*, 157.

35. On the poem's subtexts, with special attention to the framing texts, see Susan Amert, *In a Shattered Mirror: The Later Poetry of Anna Akhmatova* (Stanford, CA: Stanford University Press, 1992), 30–59.

36. Akhmatova, *Ia—golos vash...*, 161.

37. Lidia Chukovskaya, *Sofia Petrovna*, trans. Aline Werth (Evanston, IL: Northwestern University Press, 1996), 112.

38. See S. Forrester, "Mat' Gor'kogo kak literaturnyi istochnik povesti Chukovskoi *Sof'ia Petrovna*," *Voprosy literatury*, 5 (2009), 241–61.

39. Chukovskaya, *Sofia Petrovna*, 109.

40. Chukovskaya, *Sofia Petrovna*, 109.

41. Evgenii Shvarts, *P'esy* (Leningrad: Sovetskii pisatel', 1982), 304.

42. "Iz perepiski Evgeniia Shvartsa," ed. Evgenii Binevich, *Voprosy literatury*, 6 (1977), 228–9.

43. For further discussion, see Lev Loseff, *On the Beneficence of Censorship: Aesopian Language in Modern Russian Literature* (Munich: Otto Sagner, 1986), 125–42.

44. Igor' Gulin, "Roman vospitaniia iazyka," *Kommersant*, June 29, 2012, http://www.kommersant.ru/doc/1963653 (last accessed June 16, 2016). See also Oleg Iur'ev, "Odnoklassniki. Pochti povest' o poslednem pokolenii russkogo literaturnogo modernizma: Vsevolod Petrov i Pavel Zal'tsman," *Novyi mir*, 6 (2013), http://magazines.russ.ru/novyi_mi/2013/6/12ju.html (last accessed August 14, 2016).

45. For the texts, see Pavel Zal'tsman, *Shchenki. Proza 1930–1950-kh godov*, ed. P. Kazarnovskii and I. Kukui (Moscow: Vodolei, 2012).

46. Evgenii Dobrenko, *Metafora vlasti: Literatura stalinskoi epokhi v istoricheskom osveshchenii* (Munich: Otto Sagner, 1993), 249.

47. Konstantin Simonov, *Stikhi i poemy* (Moscow: Molodaia gvardiia, 1952), 48. English translation from *The Poems and Life of Konstantin Simonov*, trans. Mike Manford, http://www.simonov.co.uk/waitforme.htm (last accessed November 13, 2016). The publication and reception of this poem are discussed in Marietta Chudakova, "'Voennoe' stikhotvorenie Simonova 'Zhdi menia...' (iiul' 1941 g.) v literaturnom protsesse sovetskogo vremeni," *NLO*, 58 (2002), 223–59.

48. See David Brandenberger, *National Bolshevism: Stalinist Mass Culture and the Formation of Modern Russian National Identity, 1931–1956* (Cambridge, MA: Harvard University Press, 2002).

49. John Garrard and Carol Garrard, *The Bones of Berdichev: The Life and Fate of Vasily Grossman* (New York: Free Press, 1996), 170.

50. For a full translation, see Semyon Gudzenko, "Before the Attack," trans. Gordon McVay, *20th-Century Russian Poetry: Silver and Steel: An Anthology*, selected by Yevgeny Yevtushenko, ed. Albert G. Todd and Max Hayward (New York: Doubleday, 1993), 711–12. For the Russian, see http://www.world-art.ru/lyric/lyric.php?id=9186 (last accessed August 15, 2016).

51. For a full translation see *20th-Century Russian Poetry*, ed. Todd and Hayward, 768. For the Russian, see http://lib.ru/MEMUARY/1939-1945/DEGEN/ (last accessed August 15, 2016).

52. Lydia Ginzburg, *Notes from the Blockade*, trans. Alan Myers, ed. Emily Van Buskirk (London: Vintage/Penguin Random House, 2016), 1–2. For the Russian original, see *Prokhodiashchie kharaktery. Proza voennykh let. Zapiski blokadnogo cheloveka*, ed. Emili Van Buskirk and Andrei Zorin (Moscow: Novoe izdatel'stvo, 2011), 311.

53. For the poem, see Ol'ga Berggol'ts, *Izbrannye proizvedeniia* (Leningrad: Sovetskii pisatel', 1983), 225–32.

54. The fullest account of Berggol'ts's life and work is Katharine Hodgson, *Voicing the Soviet Experience: The Poetry of Ol'ga Berggol'ts* (Oxford: Oxford University Press, 2003).

55. See Nina Perlina, "Olga Freidenberg on Myth, Folklore, and Literature," *Slavic Review*, 52.2 (1991), 371–84.

56. For an argument that Freidenberg draws on the analytic framework of an anthropologist in writing about the Siege, see Irina Paperno, "'Osada cheloveka': Blokadnye zapiski Ol'gi Freidenberg v antropologicheskoi perspektive," *NLO*, 139 (2016), http://magazines.russ.ru/nlo/2016/3/osada-cheloveka-blokadnye-zapiski-olgi-frejdenberg-v-antropolog.html (last accessed August 15, 2016).

57. O. M. Freidenberg, "Osada cheloveka," *Minuvshee*, 3 (1987), 7–44, quotation on 21.

58. As noted by Nina Perlina, *Olga Freidenberg's Works and Days* (Columbus, OH: Slavica Press, 2002), 189–90.

59. Natal'ia Krandievskaia-Tolstaia, *Grozovyi venok: stikhi i poema* (St. Petersburg: Litsei, 1992), 110.

60. Gennadii Gor, *Stikhotvoreniia 1942–1944* (Moscow: Gileia, 2012), 25. For published translations of Gor's poetry, see *Written in the Dark: Five Poets in the Siege of Leningrad*, ed. Polina Barskova (Brooklyn, NY: Ugly Duckling Presse, 2016), 25–62.

61. Gor, *Stikhotvoreniia*, 25.

62. During the war and soon after, Platonov published several collections of war stories: Andrei Platonov, *Odukhotvorennye liudi* (Moscow: Molodaia gvardiia, 1942; Magadan: Sovetskaia Kolyma, 1943); *Pod nebesami Rodiny* (Ufa: Bashgosizdat, 1942); *Bessmertnyi podvig moriakov* (Moscow: Voenmorizdat, 1943); *Bronia* (Moscow: Voenmorizdat, 1943); *Rasskazy o Rodine* (Moscow: Goslitizdat, 1943); *V storonu zakata solntsa: Rasskazy* (Moscow: Sovetskii pisatel', 1945); *Soldatskoe serdtse* (Moscow: Detgiz, 1946).

63. Vladimir Ermilov, "Klevetnicheskii rasskaz A. Platonova," *Literaturnaia gazeta*, January 4, 1947.

64. See Nina Tumarkin, *The Living and the Dead: The Rise and Fall of the Cult of World War II in Russia* (New York: Basic Books, 1994); Lev Gudkov, "The Fetters of Victory: How the War Provides Russia with Its Identity," *Eurozine*, May 3, 2005, http://www.eurozine.com/the-fetters-of-victory/ (last accessed March 31, 2017); Il'ia Kukulin, "Regulirovanie boli," *Neprikosnovennyi zapas*, 2–3.40–1 (2005), http://magazines.russ.ru/nz/2005/2/ku37.html (last accessed April 7, 2017). For an English translation of this article see: http://www.eurozine.com/the-regulation-of-pain/ (last accessed November 24, 2017).

65. Iur'ev, "Odnoklassniki."

66. Polina Barskova, "Fiktsiia i pravda: chto my uznaem o blokade iz allegorii 'Dezertir Vedernikov' Borisa I. Ivanova," *NLO*, 137 (2016), http://nlobooks.ru/node/7011 (last accessed August 15, 2016).

67. Aleksandr Solzhenitsyn, *One Day in the Life of Ivan Denisovich*, trans. H. T. Willetts (New York: Farrar, Straus, & Giroux, 1991), 178.

68. Leona Toker, *Return from the Archipelago: Narratives of Gulag Survivors* (Bloomington: Indiana University Press, 2000), 107.

69. Brodsky, "Uncommon Visage," in *On Grief and Reason*, 54.

70. See Leonid Taganov, "Zhizn' i tvorchestvo Anny Barkovoi," in Anna Barkova, . . . *Vechno ne ta* (Moscow: Fond Sergeia Dubrova, 2002), 481–2.

71. For the poems, see Barkova, . . . *Vechno ne ta*, 77, 85.

72. Tzvetan Todorov, "The Achievement of Vasily Grossman," in Tzvetan Todorov, *Hope and Memory: Lessons from the Twentieth Century*, trans. David Bellos (Princeton, NJ: Princeton University Press, 2003), 69.

73. Robert Chandler, "Introduction," in Vasily Grossman, *Life and Fate*, trans. Robert Chandler (New York: New York Review Books, 2006), vii–xxvi, quotation on xxiii.

74. Grossman, *Life and Fate*, 215.

75. For Grossman's literary biography until Stalin's death, see Iu. G. Bit-Iunan and D. M. Fel'dman, *Vasilii Grossman v zerkale literaturnykh intrig* (Moscow: Forum, Neolit, 2015).

76. Grossman, *Life and Fate*, 395.

77. Grossman, *Life and Fate*, 215.

78. Grossman, *Life and Fate*, 290.

79. Shalamov's monumental *Kolyma Tales* was long available only piecemeal in English, but a full edition was in press as we were preparing this volume for publication: Varlam Shalamov, *Kolyma Tales*, trans. Donald Rayfield (New York: NYRB Books, 2018).

80. For Shalamov's biography, see Valerii Esipov, *Varlam Shalamov* (Moscow: Molodaia gvardiia, 2012).

81. Varlam Shalamov, "On Prose," trans. Brian R. Johnson, in *Late and Post-Soviet Literature: Thaw and Stagnation (1954–1986)*, ed. Mark Lipovetsky and Lisa Ryoko Wakamiya (Brighton, MA: Academic Studies Press, 2015), 111–26, quotation on 116; Varlam Shalamov, "O proze," in Shalamov, *Sobranie sochinenii v shesti tomakh*, 6 vols. plus 1 (Moscow: Knizhnyi Klub Knigovek, 2013), vol. 5, 144–57, quotation on 148.

82. Varlam Shalamov, Letter to I. P. Sirotinskaia, undated, in Shalamov, *Sobranie sochinenii*, vol. 6, 490. Sirotinskaia also published this letter as an essay, to which she gave the title "Moia proza," as she explains in a prefatory note to their correspondence; in those comments, she dates the letter to 1971. See Shalamov, *Sobranie sochinenii*, vol. 6, 444.

83. Shalamov, "On Prose," 123. For the Russian, see Shalamov, *Sobranie sochinenii*, vol. 5, 148.

84. Shalamov, *Sobranie sochinenii*, vol. 1, 399.

85. The link between rationed food and rationed words is made in a reading of Shalamov's story "Dry Rations" ("Sukhim paikom") in Svetlana Boym, *Another Freedom: The Alternative History of an Idea* (Chicago: University of Chicago Press, 2010), 271.

86. Shalamov, *Sobranie sochinenii*, vol. 1, 404–5.

87. As observed in Nathaniel Golden, *Varlam Shalamov's "Kolyma Tales": A Formalist Analysis* (Amsterdam: Rodopi, 2004), 107.

88. Boym, *Another Freedom*, 274.

89. Shalamov, *Sobranie sochinenii*, vol. 1, 101.

90. For an overview, see Peter Doyle, *Iurii Dombrovskii: Freedom under Totalitarianism* (London: Routledge, 2000).

91. Iurii Dombrovskii, *Sobranie sochinenii*, 6 vols. (Moscow: Terra, 1993), vol. 5, 387.

92. On the role of anti-Semitic discourse in Village Prose, see Anna Razuvalova, *Pisateli-"derevenshchiki": Literatura i konservativnaia ideologiia 1970-kh godov* (Moscow: NLO, 2015), 419–540.

93. There exists a vast scholarly literature on *The House on the Embankment*. See, for example, Thomas Seifrid, "Trifonov's *Dom na naberezhnoi* and the Fortunes of Aesopian Speech," *Slavic Review*, 49.4 (1990), 611–24; and Iurii Leving, "Vlast' i slast' (*Dom na naberezhnoi* Iu V. Trifonova)," *NLO*, 75 (2005), http://magazines.russ.ru/nlo/2005/75/le24.html (last accessed August 15, 2016). On Trifonov's use of Aesopian Language, see Josephine Woll, *Invented Truth: Soviet Reality and the Literary Imagination of Iurii Trifonov* (Durham, NC: Duke University Press, 1991).

94. Yuri Trifonov, *Another Life; The House on the Embankment*, trans. Michael Glenny (Evanston, IL: Northwestern University Press, 1999), 335, 337. Italics in the original.

95. Alexander Etkind, *Warped Mourning: Stories of the Undead in the Land of the Unburied* (Stanford, CA: Stanford University Press, 2013), 8–9.

Chapter 6

1. Boris Pasternak, "Stolet'e s lishnim—ne vchera," in Boris Pasternak, *Stikhotvoreniia i poemy*, ed. V. S. Baevskii and E. B. Pasternak, 2 vols. (Leningrad: Sovetskii pisatel', 1990), vol. 1, 372.

2. See Daniel Beer, *Renovating Russia: The Human Sciences and the Fate of Liberal Modernity, 1880–1930* (Ithaca, NY: Cornell University Press, 2008), 16–17.

3. Lilia Pann, "Andrei Bitov: Est' istoricheskoe vremia, cherez kotoroe ne pereprygnesh'," *Literaturnaia gazeta*, February 28, 1996, 12.

4. Mikhail Gasparov, "Intellektualy, intelligenty, intelligentnost'," in *Rossiiskaia intelligentsiia: istoriia i sud'ba*, ed. T B. Kniazevskaia (Moscow: Nauka, 1999), 5–14, see 8.

5. See *Landmarks Revisited: The Vekhi Symposium 100 Years On*, ed. Robin Aizlewood and Ruth Coates (Boston, MA: Academic Studies Press, 2013).

6. As noted in Gary Saul Morson, "Philosophy in the Nineteenth-Century Novel," in *The Cambridge Companion to the Classic Russian Novel*, ed. Malcolm V. Jones and Robin Feuer Miller (Cambridge: Cambridge University Press, 1998), 150–68, see 150.

7. For an account of trends and thinkers with whom the authors of *Landmarks* were polemicizing, see Marina Mogil'ner, *Mifologiia "podpol'nogo cheloveka": radikal'nyi mikrokozm v Rossii nachala XX veka kak predmet semioticheskogo analiza* (Moscow: NLO, 1999).

8. Richard Freeborn, *The Russian Revolutionary Novel: Turgenev to Pasternak* (Cambridge: Cambridge University Press, 1982), 174.

9. On Mandelstam's novella, see Oleg Lekmanov, M. Kotova, O. Repina, A. Sergeeva-Kliatsis, and S. Sinel'nikov, *Osip Mandel'shtam. "Egipetskaia marka": Poiasneniia dlia chitatelia* (Moscow: OGI, 2012); Charles Isenberg, "The Egyptian Stamp," in Charles Isenberg, *Substantial Proofs of Being: Mandelstam's Literary Prose* (Bloomington, IN: Slavica, 1987), 84–142; and Mark Lipovetsky, "'I pustoe mesto dlia ostal'nykh': Travma i poetika metaprozy v 'Egipetskoi marke' O. Mandel'shtama," in *Travma: Punkty*, ed. Sergei Ushakin and Elena Trubina (Moscow: NLO, 2009), 749–82.

10. Evgeny Dobrenko, "Writing Judgment Day," an introduction to Mikhail Bulgakov, *White Guard*, trans. Marian Schwartz (New Haven, CT: Yale University Press, 2008), xv–xlii, see xxxv.

11. The letter provoked Stalin's famous phone call to the desperate Bulgakov on April 18, 1930, which resulted in the writer's employment at the Moscow Art Theater. This improvement still left his work largely unpublished and banned from the stage. On this episode, see Marietta Chudakova, *Zhizneopisanie Mikhaila Bulgakova* (Moscow: Kniga, 1988), 433–43.

12. Mikhail Bulgakov, *Diaries and Selected Letters*, trans. Roger Cockrell (London: Alma Classics, 2013), 91.

13. Mikhail Bulgakov, *The Fatal Eggs*, in Mikhail Bulgakov, *The Fatal Eggs and Other Soviet Satire, 1918–1963*, ed. and trans. Mirra Ginsburg (New York: Grove Press, 1965), 53–134, quotation on 62–63.

14. Bulgakov, *The Fatal Eggs*, 130; emphasis added.

15. See for example Dmitrii Gorbov, "Opravdanie 'Zavisti,'" *Novyi mir*, 1 (1928); Vladimir Ermilov, "Uchenik gimnazii Shklovskogo (protiv formalisticheskogo epigonstva)," *Na literaturnom postu*, 7 (1929); Viacheslav Polonskii, "Preodolenie 'Zavisti,'" in Viacheslav Polonskii, *Ocherki sovremennoi literatury* (Moscow: Gosizdat, 1930), 5–40; Abram Lezhnev, "Iurii Olesha. 'Zavist','" *Revoliutsiia i kul'tura*, 1 (1929), 98–9; A. Gurvich, "Iurii Olesha," *Krasnaia Nov'*, 3 (1934), 199–222; Osip Brik, "Simuliatsiia nevmeniaemosti," *Novyi Lef*, 7 (1928), 1–3; and Arkadii Belinkov, *Sdacha i gibel' sovetskogo intelligenta. Iurii Olesha*, ed. N. Belinkova (Madrid: Impr. en Ediciones Castilla, 1976), 184–260.

16. Alexander Zholkovsky argues that the system of characters and general meaning of *Envy* has important parallels with *Heart of a Dog*. See Aleksandr Zholkovskii, "Dialog Bulgakova i Oleshi o kolbase, parade chuvstv i Golgofe," *Sintaksis*, 20 (1987), 25–55.

17. Yuri Olesha, *Envy*, trans. Marian Schwartz (New York: New York Review Books, 2004), 63.

18. Olesha, *Envy*, 114.

19. See Marina Kanevskaya, "The Crisis of the Russian Avant-Garde in Iurii Olesha's *Envy*," *Canadian Slavonic Papers*, 43.4 (2001), 475–93.

20. Mikhail Bakhtin was one of Vaginov's friends in the 1920s. He praised Vaginov in the late 1960s, which became a turning point in Vaginov's posthumous reception. See *Besedy V. D. Duvakina s M. M. Bakhtinym* (Moscow: Izd. gruppa "Progress," 1996), 197–8. Bakhtin is depicted as one of the characters, Andrievsky, in *Goat Song*. See Tat'iana Nikol'skaia and Vladimir Erl', "Kommentarii," in Konstantin Vaginov, *Sobranie sochinenii v proze* (St. Petersburg: Akademicheskii proekt, 1999), 522–3.

21. Maria Galina, "Vaginov," in *Russkie pisateli XX veka: Biograficheskii slovar'*, ed. P. A. Nikolaev (Moscow: Bol'shaia sovetskaia entsiklopediia, 2000), 132–3, quotation on 133.

22. Konstantin Vaginov, *The Tower*, trans. Benjamin Sher, http://www.websher.net/srl/twr.html (last accessed August 21, 2016).

23. Vaginov, *The Tower*.

24. Vaginov, *The Tower*. Teptyolkin's rapid transformation resonated with the intellectual evolution of a prominent literary scholar, Lev Pumpiansky (1891–1940), and caused a scandal in the literary milieu after the publication of the novel. See Nikolai Chukovskii, *Literaturnye vospominaniia* (Moscow: Sovetskii pisatel', 1989), 190–1.

25. The title of a poem, "Slovo v teatral'nom kostiume"; see Vaginov, *Stikhotvoreniia i poemy*, ed. Anna Gerasimova (Tomsk: Vodolei, 1999), 147.

26. See Elena Tolstaia, *"Degot' ili med." Aleksei N. Tolstoi kak neizvestnyi pisatel'. 1917–23* (Moscow: Izd. RGGU, 2006).

27. Mariia Litovskaia, "Aristokratiia v demokraticheskie vremena: *Khozhdenie po mukam* A. Tolstogo i *Unesennye vetrom* M. Mitchell kak 'narodnye romany,'" *NLO*, 57 (2002), http://magazines.russ.ru/nlo/2002/57/litov.html (last accessed August 15, 2016).

28. Litovskaia, "Aristokratiia v demokraticheskie vremena."

29. Boris Pasternak, *Doctor Zhivago*, trans. Manya Harari and Max Hayward (New York and London: Everyman's Library, 1991), 358.

30. Pasternak, *Doctor Zhivago*, 519.

31. This sub-genre of the Bildungsroman was widespread in Soviet literature, as epitomized by the novels of Yuri Tynianov, including *Kiukhlia* (1925) and his unfinished *Pushkin* (1935–43).

32. For example: Akhmatova is reported as saying that "the main characters do not come alive, they are made of cardboard, especially cardboard is Zhivago himself. And the author's language is sometimes so carried away that it becomes offensive"; cited from Lidiia Chukovskaia, *Zapiski ob Anne Akhmatovoi*, vol. 2 (Paris: YMCA-Press, 1980), 220. For a survey of critical assessments, mostly negative, see Neil Cornwell, *Pasternak's Novel: Perspectives on "Doctor Zhivago"* (Keele: Essays in Poetics, 1986), 90–103.

33. Boris Gasparov, "Vremennoi kontrapunkt kak formoobrazuiushchii printsip romana Pasternaka *Doktor Zhivago*," in *Boris Pasternak and His Times*, ed. Lazar Fleishman (Berkeley, CA: Berkeley Slavic Specialties, 1989), 315–58.

34. Igor′ Smirnov, *Roman tain "Doktor Zhivago"* (Moscow: NLO, 1996), 89. For a similar approach see Aleksandr Etkind, "Who Wrote *Doctor Zhivago*?," *Russian Studies in Literature*, 39.1 (2002–03), 80–96.

35. See Marietta Chudakova, "Pasternak i Bulgakov: rubezh dvukh literaturnykh tsiklov," *Literaturnoe obozrenie*, 5 (1991), 11–17.

36. See Boris M. Gasparov, "Novyi Zavet v proizvedeniiakh M. A. Bulgakova," and "Iz nabliudenii nad motivnoi strukturoi romana M. A. Bulgakova 'Master i Margarita,'" in Boris Gasparov, *Literaturnye leitmotivy: Ocherki po russkoi literature XX veka* (Moscow: Nauka, 1993), 28–82, 83–123.

37. Examples of the Stalin-centered approach to the novel include Chudakova, *Zhizneopisanie Mikhaila Bulgakova*; Lidiia Ianovskaia, *Treugol′nik Volanda (K istorii romana "Master i Margarita")* (Kiev: Lybid, 1992); Maia Kaganskaia and Zeev Bar-Sella, *Master Gambs i Margarita* (Tel-Aviv: Milev General Systems, 1984); and Abram Vulis, *Roman M. A. Bulgakova "Master i Margarita"* (Moscow: Khudozhestvennaia literatura, 1991).

38. This approach is best represented by Igor′ Belza, "Genealogiia *Mastera i Margarity*," in *Kontekst-1978* (Moscow: Nauka, 1978), 156–248; George Krugovoy, *The Gnostic Novel of Mikhail Bulgakov: Sources and Exegesis* (Lanham, MD: University Press of America, 1991); Mikhail Zolotonosov, *"Master i Margarita" kak putevoditel′ po subkul′ture russkogo antisemitizma* (St. Petersburg: Inapress, 1995); and Svetlana Kul′ius, *"Ezotericheskie" kody romana M. Bulgakova "Master i Margarita" (eksplitsitnoe i implitsitnoe v romane)* (Tartu: Tartu Ülikooli Kirjastus, 1998).

39. Justin Weir, *The Author as Hero: Self and Tradition in Bulgakov, Pasternak, and Nabokov* (Evanston, IL: Northwestern University Press, 2002), 5–6. See also Gary Rosenshield, "*The Master and Margarita* and the Poetics of Aporia: A Polemical Article," *Slavic Review*, 56.2 (1997), 187–211; Susan Amert, "The Dialectics of Closure in Bulgakov's *Master and Margarita*," *Russian Review*, 61.4 (2002), 599–617; Evgenii Iablokov, *Khudozhestvennyi mir Mikhaila Bulgakova* (Moscow: Iazyki slavianskoi kul′tury, 2001); Vera Khimich, *"Strannyi realizm" Mikhaila Bulgakova* (Ekaterinburg: Izd. Ural′skogo Gosudarstvennogo Universiteta, 1996); and Ritta H. Pittman, *The Writer's Divided Self in Bulgakov's "The Master and Margarita"* (New York: St. Martin's Press, 1991).

40. Weir, *The Author as Hero*, 17.

41. Mikhail Bulgakov, *The Master and Margarita*, trans. Diana Burgin and Katherine Tiernan O'Connor (New York: Vintage, 1996), 20, 22.

42. Bulgakov, *Master and Margarita*, 17.

43. Bulgakov, *Master and Margarita*, 121.

44. See Richard W. F. Pope, "Ambiguity and Meaning in *Master and Margarita*: The Role of Afranius," *Slavic Review*, 36.1 (1977), 1–24.

45. Bulgakov, *Master and Margarita*, 272.

46. Bulgakov, *Master and Margarita*, 272.

47. See Jessica E. Merrill, "The Stalinist Subject and Mikhail Bulgakov's *The Master and Margarita*," *Russian Review*, 74.2 (2015), 293–310; Igor′ Reif, "*The Little Golden Calf*, *The Master and Margarita*: A Typology of Mass Thinking in a Totalitarian Society," *Russian Studies in Literature*, 51.1 (2014), 59–79.

48. Osip Mandel′shtam, *Polnoe sobranie sochinenii i pisem v trekh tomakh*, ed. A. G. Mets, 4 vols. (Moscow: Progress-Pleiada, 2009–14), vol. 1, 234.

49. See Alexander Spektor, "The Science of Poetry: Poetic Process as Evolution in Mandel′shtam's 'Conversation about Dante,'" *Slavic Review*, 73.3 (2014), 471–93.

50. For a thorough survey of the Dante theme in Mandelstam with attention to subtextual analysis, see Elena Glazova and Marina Glazova, *Podskazano Dantom. O poetike i poezii Mandel′shtama* (Kyiv: Dukh i litera, 2014).

51. See Clare Cavanagh, *Osip Mandelstam and the Modernist Creation of Tradition* (Princeton, NJ: Princeton University Press, 1995), 246–7.

52. On this cultural and political campaign, see Jonathan Brooks Platt, *Greetings, Pushkin! Stalinist Cultural Politics and the Russian National Bard* (Pittsburgh, PA: University of Pittsburgh Press, 2016). On texts from the Jubilee, see Stephanie Sandler, *Commemorating Pushkin: Russia's Myth of a National Poet* (Stanford, CA: Stanford University Press, 2004), 107–19.

53. Mandel′shtam, *Polnoe sobranie sochinenii*, vol. 1, 198 ("Eto kakaia ulitsa").

54. Citations from Lermontov, *Sobranie sochinenii*, 4 vols. (Moscow: Khudozhestvennaia literatura, 1975), vol. 1, 123. These late echoes of Lermontov are also acts of self-allusion since Lermontov's poem about the Romantic wanderer pervades the lines of "The Ode on a Slate" ("Grifel′naia oda," 1923) and "Concert in a Railway Station" ("Kontsert na vokzale," 1921). On these allusions, see Omry Ronen, *An Approach to Mandel′štam* (Jerusalem: Magnes Press, Hebrew University, 1983), 73–6, *et passim*.

55. Debate has raged on the sincerity of the praise strategies in this poem. For an important reading, see J. M. Coetzee, "Osip Mandelstam and the Stalin Ode," in J. M. Coetzee, *Giving Offense: Essays on Censorship* (Chicago: University of Chicago Press, 1996), 104–17; on the politics of the poem, see Gregory Freidin, *A Coat of Many Colors: Osip Mandelstam and His Mythologies of Self-Presentation* (Berkeley: University of California Press, 1987), 256–60; on the reception of the poem, see Andrew Kahn, "Canonical Mandelstam," in *Canonicity, Twentieth-Century Poetry and Russian National Identity*, ed. Katharine Hodgson and Alexandra Smith (Cambridge: Open Books, 2017), 157–201.

56. For biographies of Erenburg, see Boris Frezinskii, *Il′ia Erenburg (Knigi, liudi, strany)* (Moscow: NLO, 2013); and Joshua Rubenstein, *Tangled Loyalties: The Life and Times of Ilya Ehrenburg* (London: I. B. Tauris, 1996).

57. Petr Vail′ and Aleksandr Genis, *Sobranie sochinenii*, 2 vols. (Ekaterinburg: U-Faktoria, 2003), vol. 1, 551, 553.

58. On Nadezha Mandelstam's life, see *Osip i Nadezhda Mandel'shtamy v rasskazakh sovremennikov*, ed. O. S. Figurnova and M. V. Figurnova (Moscow: Natalis, 2002); and *"Posmotrim, kto kogo pereupriamit . . .": Nadezhda Iakovlevna Mandel′shtam v pis′makh, vospominaniiakh, svidetel′stvakh*, ed. Elena Shubina (Moscow: AST, 2015).

59. Nadezhda Mandelstam, *Hope against Hope*, trans. Max Hayward (London: Penguin Books, 1970), 200.

60. Beth Holmgren, *Women's Works in Stalin's Time: On Lidiia Chukovskaya and Nadezhda Mandelstam* (Bloomington: Indiana University Press, 1993), 172–3.

61. As noted in Lev Loseff, *On the Beneficence of Censorship: Aesopian Language in Modern Russian Literature* (Munich: Otto Sagner, 1986), 149.

62. See the analysis of *The First Circle* in Naum Leiderman, "Po printsipu antiskhemy," *Zvezda*, 8 (2001), 191–205.

63. This song was included in Marlen Khutsiev's film *I Am Twenty (Mne dvadtsat′ let*, 1965). This was the sole poem by a Soviet poet that Nabokov translated into English, as noted in Mikhail

Shishkin's *Russkaia Shveitsariia*, published in *Druzhba narodov*, 4 (2001), http://magazines.russ.ru/druzhba/2001/4/shish.html (last accessed August 16, 2016).

64. Khrushchev dedicated a significant segment of his secret speech at the 20th Party Congress (1956) to the tragic destiny of Eikhe. For the poem, see Robert Rozhdestvenskii, *Luchshie stikhi* (Moscow: AST, 2016), 9–12.

65. Andrei Voznesenskii, *Stikhotvoreniia i poemy*, ed. G. I. Trubnikov, 2 vols. (St. Petersburg: Izd. Pushkinskogo Doma; Vita Nova, 2015), vol. 1, 180.

66. See Galina Belaia, "Rozhdenie novykh stilevykh form kak protsess preodoleniia 'neitral'nogo' stilia," in *Mnogoobrazie stilei sovetskoi literatury: Voprosy tipologii: Revoliutsionnaia deistvitel'nost' i preobrazovanie stilia, stilevye otkrytiia i stilevye tendentsii sovremennoi sovetskoi literatury*, ed. N. K. Gei (Moscow: Nauka, 1978), 460–85; Marietta Chudakova, "Zametki o iazyke sovremennoi prozy," *Novyi mir*, 1 (1972), 212–45, repr. in Marietta Chudakova, *Izbrannye raboty*, 2 vols. *Literatura sovetskogo proshlogo* (Moscow: Iazyki russkoi kul'tury, 2001), vol.1, 245–90.

67. Vail' and Genis, *Sovetskoe barokko*, in Vail' and Genis, *Sobranie sochinenii*, vol. 1, 397.

68. Arkady and Boris Strugatsky, *Hard to Be a God*, trans. Olga Bormashenko (Chicago: Chicago Review Press, 2014), 171.

69. See Elizabeth A. Skomp and Benjamin M. Sutcliffe, *Liudmila Ulitskaya and the Art of Tolerance* (Madison: University of Wisconsin Press, 2015), 130–65. The authors find fault with Ulitskaya for excluding conservatives from her image of the intelligentsia, when (to our mind) Ulitskaya is in fact articulating her own intellectual position and, in the process, providing an important viewpoint on the options open to the intelligentsia in a fraught era of social change.

70. Marina Balina, "(Auto)Biographical Prose," *Russian Literature since 1991*, ed. Evgeny Dobrenko and Mark Lipovetsky (Cambridge: Cambridge University Press, 2015), 200–6.

71. See contrasting points of view on Solzhenitsyn's book in the following reviews: Iokhan Petrovskii-Shtern, "Sud'ba srednei linii," *Neprikosnovennyi zapas*, 4 (2001), http://magazines.russ.ru/nz/2001/4/shtern.html (last accessed August 17, 2016); Andrei Nemzer, "Kak my vmeste mostili dorogu v ad," and "Kak my vmeste zhili v adu," in Andrei Nemzer, *Zamechatel'noe desiatiletie russkoi literatury* (Moscow: Zakharov, 2003), 495–500; and Dmitrii Bykov, "Dvesti let vmeste," *Russkii zhurnal*, http://berkovich-zametki.com/Nomer24/Bykov1.htm (last accessed August 17, 2016).

72. The title of the novel has challenged translators. In Russian, it stands for the written acronym of the railroad (*zheleznaia doroga*) and also the reduced pronounciation of the Russian equivalent for "kike" (*zhid*). An alternative suggested translation for the title is *Jewhad*, not much better.

73. See Aleksandr Etkind, *Internal Colonization: Russia's Imperial Experience* (Cambridge: Polity Press, 2011); Etkind and Mark Lipovetsky, "The Return of a Triton: The Soviet Catastrophe and the Post-Soviet Novel," *Russian Studies in Literature*, 6.4 (2010), 6–48, also in Russian, "Vozvrashchenie tritona: sovetskaia katastrofa i postsovetskii roman," *NLO*, 94 (2008), http://magazines.russ.ru/nlo/2008/94/li17.html (last accessed August 17, 2016).

74. Dmitrii Bykov, *ZhD* (Moscow: Vagrius, 2006), 380–1.

75. S. Oushakine, "(Post)Ideological Novel," in *Russian Literature since 1991*, ed. Dobrenko and Lipovetsky, 45–65, quotation on 63.

76. Alexievich builds on a prior tradition. The genre of documentary "books of memory" was introduced into Russian literature by Sofia Fedorchenko in *The People at War* (*Narod na voine*, 1917), which treats the First World War and the Civil War. In late Soviet culture, this combination of documentary and oral history was revived by Belarusian writers Ales Adamovich, Ianko Bryl, and Vladimir Kolesnik in *I Am from the Fiery Village* (*Ia iz ognennoi derevni*, 1975), about survivors of Nazi terror during the occupation of Belarus. In 1984, *The Blockade Book* (*Blokadnaia*

kniga) by Ales Adamovich and Daniil Granin appeared, based on diaries and survivors' interviews about the Leningrad siege. Alexievich regards Ales Adamovich (1927–94) as her teacher, and she paid tribute to him in her Nobel Lecture. On the continuity between earlier "books of memory" and Alexievich, see Il´ia Kukulin, *Mashiny zashumevshego vremeni: Kak sovetskii montazh stal metodom neofitsial´noi kul´tury* (Moscow: NLO, 2015), 237–60.

77. Svetlana Alexievich, "On the Battle Lost," The Nobel Lecture in Literature (2015), http://www.nobelprize.org/nobel_prizes/literature/laureates/2015/alexievich-lecture_en.html (last accessed November 13, 2016).

78. Alexievich, "On the Battle Lost."

Conclusion

1. Quoted from Mikhail Ardov, Boris Ardov, and Aleksei Batalov, *Legendarnaia Ordynka: sbornik vospominanii* (Moscow: Inapress, 1997), 44–5.

2. See, for example, "Samaia chitaiushchaia strana: Na 'progulku s pisateliami' prishli tysiachi liudei," https://lenta.ru/articles/2012/05/13/reading/ (last accessed November 11, 2016).

Picture Credits

Figures

I.01   Russian State Archives of Ancient Documents (RGADA), Moscow. Photo © 2017
       Fine Art Images/Heritage Images/Scala, Florence
I.02   State Historical Museum, Moscow. Photo © akg-images/Sputnik
I.03   State Tretyakov Gallery, Moscow. Photo © Fine Art Images/age fotostock
I.04   National Museum of Denmark, Copenhagen. Photo © Fine Art Images/age fotostock
I.05   State Historical Museum, Moscow. Photo © akg-images/Bildarchiv Steffens
II.01 Art Museum of Yaroslavl, Russia. Photo © Bridgeman Images
II.02 Institute of Russian Literature, St Petersburg
II.03 State Hermitage Museum, St. Petersburg. Photo © Fine Art Images/Heritage
       Images/age fotostock
II.04 Houghton Library, Harvard University
II.05 Houghton Library, Harvard University
II.06 © State Historical Museum, Moscow
II.07 ART Collection/Alamy Stock Photo
II.08 State Tretyakov Gallery, Moscow. Photo © Sovfoto/Universal Images
       Group/age fotostock
II.09 Лапоть/Wikimedia Commons (CC0 1.0)
II.10 © State Historical Museum, Moscow
II.11 State Russian Museum, St. Petersburg. Photo © Fine Art Images/Heritage
       Images/TopFoto
III.01 State Hermitage Museum, St. Petersburg. Photo © Fine Art Images/age
       fotostock
III.02 State Russian Museum, St. Petersburg. Photo ART Collection/Alamy
       Stock Photo
III.03 State Hermitage Museum, St. Petersburg. Photo © The State Hermitage
       Museum/photo by Vladimir Terebenin
III.04 State Hermitage Museum, St. Petersburg. Photo © The State Hermitage
       Museum/photo by Vladimir Terebenin
III.05 State Hermitage Museum, St. Petersburg. Photo © akg-images/Sputnik
III.06 Reproduced with the permission of the Provost, Fellows and Scholars of The
       Queen's College Oxford
III.07 Houghton Library, Harvard University, RC9.B8648.904z
IV.01 Institute of Russian Literature, St Petersburg
IV.02 Institute of Russian Literature, St Petersburg. Photo © Fine Art Images/age fotostock
IV.03 © De Agostini Picture Library/Bridgeman Images
IV.04 © INTERFOTO/Interfoto Scans/age fotostock
IV.05 Institute of Russian Literature, St Petersburg
IV.06 Institute of Russian Literature, St Petersburg

Plates

Index

Gilman, Charlotte Perkins 652
Ginzburg, Evgenia 731, 758, 761
Ginzburg, Lydia 389, 555, 607, 704–5, 707, 723–4, 767
Giovagnoli, Raffaello 676
Gippius, Vasily 379
Gippius, Zinaida 355, 367, 526, 527, 538, 539, 566, 568, 569, 570, 575, 619, 620, 652, 742
Girshovich, Leonid 699, 738
Gizel, Innokenty 150
Gladilin, Anatoly 550, 552, 760, 761
Gladkov, Fedor 673, 675
Glagolitic alphabet 20
Glasnost 560, 579
Glazkov, Nikolai 624
Glazova, Anna 639, 642, 643
Gleb (Saint) 36, 42, 48, 57, 66, 82, 83, 84, 101, 106
Glinka, Mikhail 411
Glinka, Sergei 366
Gnedich, Nikolai 215, 301, 353, 354, 497
Gnedov, Vasilisk 624, 626
Godunov, Boris 127, 129, 498
Goethe, Johann Wolfgang 350, 406, 517, 544
Gogol, Nikolai 2, 365, 366, 376–83, 434, 450, 451, 481, 517, 838–9
  Arabesques 376
  Dead Souls 359, 377, 381, 427, 472, 662
  Evenings at a Farm near Dikanka 376, 379, 380, 424, 425, 450
  Hanz Kuechelgarten 379, 424
  influence on other writers 378–9, 399, 566, 661, 662, 664, 667, 671
  (The) Inspector General 472
  Mirgorod 376, 379, 424, 425
  "Notes of a Madman" 399, 400, 461, 467–8, 471
  Petersburg Tales 424–5, 468
  "(The) Portrait" 467
  portrayal of bureaucrats 453, 454
  spiritual authority 378–9
Golburt, Luba 292
Goldblatt, Harvey 107
Golden Age 346, 424, 525
(The) Golden Fleece (Zolotoe runo) 526
Golden Horde 72, 73, 93, 95, 96, 99, 105, 106, 107, 109, 114
Goldoni, Carlo 280
Gol'dshtein, Aleksandr 707
Golenishchev-Kutuzov, Pavel 330
Goliavkin, Viktor 687
Golikov, Ivan 270, 272
Golitsyn, Dmitry 288
Golodny, Mikhail 530
Golovkin, M. G. 227
Goncharov, Ivan 194, 365, 366, 367, 371, 383, 427, 428, 456, 463, 464, 478, 492
Goncharova, Natalia 414, 528, 611, 612
Gor, Gennady 725
Goralik, Linor 642, 702
Gorbachev, Mikhail 560
Gorbanevskaya, Natalia 540, 594
Gorbov, Dmitry 530
Gorchev, Dmitry 703
Gorenshtein, Fridrikh 552, 691
Goricheva, Tatiana 556, 593, 680
Gorin, Grigory 551

Gorky, Maxim 447, 518, 526, 531, 536, 537, 543–4, 599, 646–9, 654, 673, 675, 709, 710, 739
  Isaac Babel and 714, 715
  (The) Life of Klim Samgin 742–3
  (The) Lower Depths 648–9
  Soviet scholarship on 651
  (The) Stalin White Sea-Baltic Sea Canal: The History of Construction 717–18
Goscilo, Helena 681, 683
Gottsched, Johann Christoph 208, 212, 216, 232
Gradovsky, G. K. 492
Grass, Günter 549
Gray, Thomas 324, 326, 402, 403
Great Patriotic War 721–9
Great Reforms 346, 367, 371, 428, 458, 491, 496
Great Russian Novel 3, 6, 346, 426–7
Great Terror 530, 543, 550, 574, 623, 624, 717–20
  literary investigation of 729–38
Grech, Nikolai 364, 365, 367, 368, 375
Grecophiles 150, 151, 167, 168, 171
Greek language 17, 21, 211
Green Lamp (Zelenaia Lampa) 351, 353, 539
Greenleaf, Monika 498
Gregori, Johann Gottfried 154, 155
Gregorian Calendar 345
Gregory of Sinai 73
Gregory the Theologian 55
Grekova, I. (Elena Venttsel) 678, 679
Gremina, Elena 704
Greuze, Jean-Baptiste 253
Gribachev, Nikolai 550
Griboedov, Aleksandr 462–3, 551, 687
Grigor'ev, Apollon 368, 378, 383, 484, 514
Grigor'ev, Oleg 687, 703
Grigor'ev, Viktor 615
Grigorovich, Dmitry 435, 444
Grimberg, Faina 642
Grin, Aleksandr 660–1
Grishkovets, Evgeny 536, 704
Gronas, Mikhail 610, 642
Grossheinrich, Karl 356
Grossman, Vasily 501, 547, 722–3, 729, 731–3, 736, 767
grotesque modernism 661–8
Grotius, Hugo 150
Groys, Boris 613, 633, 674
Grushin, Olga 542
Gudkov, Lev 704
Gudzenko, Semen 723
Gukovsky, Grigory 219, 220, 716, 839
Gulag 549, 550, 552, 591, 717, 718, 720, 729, 731–1, 733–4, 738
Gulin, Igor 563, 720
Gumbrecht, Hans Ulrich 4
Gumilev, Lev 574
Gumilev, Nikolai 352, 526, 528, 554, 560, 571, 573, 577, 599, 600, 601, 602, 603, 767
Günther, Hans 889, 891, 894
Gurevich, Liubov 526
Guro, Elena 527, 575, 612, 617–20, 631
Gushanskaia, Elena 688

hagiographies 35–6, 42, 56, 57–62, 84, 106
  characterization 60–1
  compilations 62–5
  female saints 67–8